AMERICAN CONSTITUTIONAL LAW

VOLUME II
THE BILL OF RIGHTS AND SUBSEQUENT AMENDMENTS

Fifth Edition

AMERICAN CONSTITUTIONAL LAW

VOLUME II
THE BILL OF RIGHTS AND
SUBSEQUENT AMENDMENTS

Fifth Edition

Ralph A. Rossum
Claremont McKenna College

G. Alan Tarr
Rutgers University, Camden

BEDFORD / ST. MARTIN'S
Boston ♦ New York

American Constitutional Law, Volume II:
The Bill of Rights and Subsequent Amendments, Fifth Edition

Copyright © 1999 by Worth Publishers, Inc.
All rights reserved.
Manufactured in the United States of America.
Library of Congress Catalog Card Number: 98-84994
ISBN: 0-312-18450-6
Printing: 2   3   4   5
Year: 02 01 00 99

Executive Editor: James R. Headley
Project Director: Scott E. Hitchcock
Editorial Assistant: Brian Nobile
Design Director: Jennie R. Nichols
Production Editor: Douglas Bell
Production Manager: Barbara Anne Seixas
Project Coordination: Ruttle, Shaw & Wetherill, Inc.
Cover Design: Paul Lacy
Cover Photo: U.S. Supreme Court Building (detail):
    Copyright © Tom Wachs/Washington Stock Photo, Inc.
Cover Printer: Phoenix Color Corporation
Composition: Ruttle, Shaw & Wetherill, Inc.
Printing and Binding: R. R. Donnelley & Sons Company

For information, write:

Bedford/St. Martin's
75 Arlington Street
Boston, MA 02116   (617-399-4000)

ABOUT THE
AUTHORS

Ralph A. Rossum received his doctorate from the University of Chicago. He is Henry Salvatori Professor of Political Philosophy and American Constitutionalism at Claremont McKenna College. His other publications include *Congressional Control of the Judiciary: The Article III Option* (1988), *Reverse Discrimination: The Constitutional Debate* (1979) and *The Politics of the Criminal Justice System: An Organizational Analysis* (1978). He is coauthor of *The American Founding: Politics, Statesmanship, and the Constitution* (1981) with Gary McDowell, and of *Police, Criminal Justice, and the Community* (1976), with Alan Bent.

G. Alan Tarr received his doctorate from the University of Chicago. He is professor of political science and director of the Center for State Constitutional Studies at Rutgers University, Camden. Professor Tarr is the author of several books, including *Understanding State Constitutions* (1998), *Judicial Process and Judicial Policymaking*, Second Edition (1998), and *State Supreme Courts in State and Nation* (1987). He has served as a constitutional consultant in Russia, South Africa, and Cyprus. Twice an NEH Fellow, he is currently editor of a fifty-two volume reference series on state constitutions.

To the Memory of Herbert J. Storing

CONTENTS

5. FREEDOM OF SPEECH, PRESS, AND ASSOCIATION   129

6. FREEDOM OF RELIGION   207

CASES

7. CRIMINAL PROCEDURE   267

SEARCH AND SEIZURE **269** • SELF-INCRIMINATION AND COERCED CONFESSIONS **277** • THE RIGHT TO COUNSEL **281** • THE ENTRAPMENT DEFENSE **283** • THE RIGHT TO A SPEEDY TRIAL **284** • THE RIGHT TO CONFRONTATION **285** • PLEA BARGAINING **286** • BAIL AND PRETRIAL DETENTION **287** • CRUEL AND UNUSUAL PUNISHMENTS **288** • PRISONERS' RIGHTS **290** • RETROACTIVE APPLICATION OF CRIMINAL-PROCEDURE GUARANTEES **292** • BASIC THEMES IN THE COURT'S CRIMINAL-PROCEDURE DECISIONS **294** • NOTES **295** • SELECTED READING **297**

CASES

10. VOTING AND REPRESENTATION   537

11. THE RIGHT TO PRIVACY   575

Note to Instructors

If you plan to use both volumes (I and II) of *American Constitutional Law*, Fifth Edition, for a single semester or quarter course, please contact your local SASMP sales representative or call SASMP Faculty Services for information about special packages: 1-800-446-8923.

PREFACE

American Constitutional Law, Fifth Edition, is designed as a basic text for courses in constitutional law and civil liberties. As with the previous editions, its approach to these subjects is based on three major premises.

First, the study of the Constitution and constitutional law is of fundamental importance to a full and coherent understanding of the principles, prospects, and problems of America's democratic republic. Cases should be examined not merely to foster an appreciation of what court majorities have thought of particular issues at certain points in time (although that is obviously important), but also to gain a deeper and fuller understanding of the principles that lie at the very heart of the American constitutional system. To that end, this text emphasizes precedent-setting cases and presents comprehensive expositions of alternative constitutional positions. Substantial excerpts from cases and other constitutionally significant pronouncements have been included so that students can grapple with the arguments and justifications for these alternative positions. To ensure that the best arguments on all sides of a constitutional question are presented, extensive extracts of both concurring and dissenting opinions have been included.

Second, no interpretation of the Constitution can be evaluated properly without an appreciation of what those who initially drafted and ratified the Constitution sought to accomplish. The text incorporates documentary evidence in seeking to identify and explain the original purposes of the Constitution and the means provided for the achievement of those purposes. This inquiry into the Framers' understanding of the Constitution, in turn, furnishes one of the criteria for evaluating judicial decisions and constitutionally significant pronouncements from the executive and legislative branches.

Third, the study of the Constitution involves much more than an examination of its judicial interpretation. The Constitution is not merely what the Supreme Court says it is; its words are not so many empty vessels into which justices can pour meaning. Accordingly, this volume examines the interpretations of a variety of sources. The original understanding of the founding generation is one source. Another, equally indispensable source is, of course, the Supreme Court, whose decisions have influenced so profoundly our understanding of the Constitution and its principles. And because other governmental bodies have contributed significantly to the overall interpretation of the Constitution, this text includes decisions of the lower federal courts and state judiciaries and also extrajudicial materials of constitutional significance such as certain congressional acts and resolutions.

As we approach constitutional questions throughout this text, we begin by turning to the Framers. We do so, however, not so much for specific answers as for general guidance concerning what the Constitution was designed to accomplish. Obviously no interpretation can be expected to conform strictly to the expectations of the Framers. Other legitimate approaches may also contribute to an understanding of the Constitution, relying variously on analysis of the text itself, judicial precedent, constitutional doctrine, logical reasoning, and adaptation of constitutional provisions to changing circumstances. All these approaches are described in Chapter 1.

The structure of the volumes might be seen as a reflection of James Madison's observation in *The Federalist*, No. 51, that "in framing a government which is to be administered by men over men, the great difficulty lies in this: you must first enable the government to control the governed; and in the next place, oblige it to control itself." Chapter 1 explores in general how the Constitution was designed to resolve this difficulty, and Chapter 2 introduces the reader to the actual process of constitutional adjudication. The remainder of this two-volume work systematically examines how the Constitution and its amendments not only grant the national and state governments sufficient power to control the governed, but also oblige these governments to control themselves. Chapters 3 through 6 (Volume I) consider the distribution of power in the national government. As a group, these chapters explore how the constitutional scheme of separation of powers and checks and balances both grants and controls power. Because of the importance of the distribution of power among the branches of the national government, we devote separate chapters to the Judiciary, the Congress, the Presidency, and war and foreign affairs. Chapters 7 through 10 (Volume I) consider the distribution of power between the national government and the states. These chapters focus on federalism, specifically how this institutional means carries out the ends of the Constitution. Chapters 11 and 12 of Volume I, which are repeated as Chapters 3 and 4 in Volume II, consider the division of the protection of rights and economic due process between national and state governments. Finally, Chapters 5 through 11 (Volume II) continue the examination of the distribution of power between the government and the individual. The emphasis in these chapters is not so much on institutional contrivances that oblige the government to control itself as on the Bill of Rights and those subsequent amendments that guarantee specific rights and liberties, an emphasis that illuminates the way in which our most precious rights and liberties increasingly have become dependent for their vindication, not upon constitutional structure but upon what *The Federalist* called mere "parchment barriers."

With the exception of the first two chapters, each chapter opens with an introductory essay which is then followed by cases and, where appropriate, extrajudicial materials. Each essay includes extensive notes which provide valuable explanatory details and references to further materials, and ends with a list of suggested readings including *Federalist* essays, additional cases, and scholarly books and articles. Each case also has its own introductory headnote, which provides historical perspective, indicates where the case stands in relation to current law, and gives the final court vote. Some cases have end notes that elaborate on the short- and long-term consequences of the decision. The text includes four appendices: the Constitution of the United States, a list of Supreme Court justices, a glossary of legal terms, and a table of cases.

One noteworthy innovation that began in 1997 is the creation of a Web site for *American Constitutional Law*, which is found at <www.bedfordstmartins.com/polisci>. We have included three sets of cases at this site. First, we annually post edited versions of the major rulings of the Supreme Court during its just-completed term. Instructors can use these cases to supplement and update the materials presented in the text, and the cases listed at the Web site give a good indication of those cases likely to be included in subsequent editions of *American Constitutional Law*. Second, we have included several cases and other materials that appear in one volume of *American Constitutional Law* but may also be of interest to instructors using the other volume. Cases appearing in Volume I and reproduced at the Web site include *Marbury* v. *Madison, Korematsu* v. *United States, The Civil Rights Cases, Patterson* v. *McLean Credit Union,* and *Jones* v. *Mayer.* Cases and materials appearing in Volume II and reproduced at the Web site include *Scott* v. *Sandford, Rostker* v. *Goldberg, Griswold* v. *Connecticut, Roe* v. *Wade,* and the Civil Rights Act of 1991. Finally, to accommodate the varying needs of instructors while keeping the casebook a manageable length, we have included several cases that appeared in earlier editions of *American Constitutional Law* but do not appear in the fifth edition.

The editorial staff at St. Martin's/Worth, especialy James Headley, executive editor, was cooperative, encouraging, and truly professional. We are also grateful to those scholars who reviewed drafts of the manuscript and contributed valuable comments and suggestions to the five editions. Any errors of fact or interpretation, of course, are solely our responsibility. Finally, we wish to express our gratitude to our wives, Constance and Susan, and to our children, Kristin, Brent, and Pierce Rossum, and Robert and Andrew Tarr, for their patience, understanding, and loving support throughout this project.

Ralph A. Rossum
G. Alan Tarr

★

APPROACHES TO CONSTITUTIONAL INTERPRETATION

THE APPROACHES IN PERSPECTIVE

THE ENDS OF THE CONSTITUTION

THE MEANS TO THE ENDS

NOTES

SELECTED READING

★

1
INTERPRETATION OF
THE CONSTITUTION

"We are under a Constitution, but the Constitution is what the Court says it is."[1] In the more than half-century since Charles Evans Hughes, then governor of New York and later Chief Justice of the Supreme Court, uttered these now-famous words, they have been repeated so often and in so many contexts that they have assumed a prescriptive as well as a descriptive character. But exactly how valid is this prescription for understanding the Constitution?

Hughes's observation certainly contains a degree of truth. Many of the provisions of the Constitution are not self-defining and hence have been the objects of considerable judicial interpretation and construction. Various criminal procedural protections found in Amendments Four through Eight immediately spring to mind. What, after all, makes a particular search or seizure "unreasonable"? What is sufficient to establish "probable cause"? What constitutes "due process of law"? What is a "speedy" trial? What is an "excessive" fine or bail? What is "cruel and unusual punishment"? These constitutional provisions resemble empty vessels into which the United States Supreme Court has had to pour meaning.

Hughes's claim also portrays accurately the perspective taken by lower-court judges and practicing attorneys. However erroneous they may believe the Supreme Court's understanding of a particular constitutional provision to be, they generally shy away from breaking with the previous decisions of the High Bench and offering contrary interpretations. Rather, they usually attempt to accomplish their objectives within the framework of the prevailing Court view.

Although valid to some extent, Hughes's assertion is also misleading (and therefore harmful) in several ways. Above all, it fails to recognize

1

that governmental bodies other than the Supreme Court also contribute to an overall interpretation of the Constitution. By passing the War Powers Resolution of 1973, for example, Congress undertook to define the constitutional limits of the president's powers to initiate and conduct undeclared war, an issue the Supreme Court refused to consider. Likewise, in the Speedy Trial Act of 1984, Congress took upon itself constitutional interpretation in the sphere of criminal procedure, declaring that a defendant not brought to trial within one hundred days of arrest may move for a dismissal of the charges. By so doing, it gave meaning to a constitutional provision that the Supreme Court itself has acknowledged to be more vague than any other procedural right. To cite still another example, in the Voting Rights Act of 1982, Congress held that the Fifteenth Amendment (barring states from denying citizens the right to vote "on account of race, color, or previous condition of servitude") bans not only intentional discrimination against the voting rights of minorities (what the Supreme Court had held) but any electoral scheme that has the effect of preventing minority voters from electing "representatives of their choice." Constitutionally significant pronouncements have also emanated from the executive branch and from the lower federal and state courts. (Statements made by President Abraham Lincoln have had more to do with defining the outer bounds of presidential prerogative than have any statements of the Court, just as actions taken by President Franklin Roosevelt altered the balance of power between the national government and the state far more than any judicial opinion.)

Another problem with Hughes's assertion is that it obscures the extent to which the meaning of the Constitution is agreed on by all concerned parties. Most constitutional provisions are settled; what questions are raised about them pertain not to fundamental meaning, but rather to specific application. Relatively few constitutional provisions have sparked protracted debate and controversy: the Commerce Clause of Article I, Section 8, authorizing Congress to regulate commerce among the several states; the First Amendment guarantees of freedom of speech and of the press; the guarantees of the Fifth and Fourteenth Amendments that no person shall be deprived of life, liberty, or property without due process of law; the Fourteenth Amendment's guarantee that no person shall be denied the equal protection of the laws. Although these provisions are extremely important, the intense debate over them tends to obscure how ably the Constitution has governed our political actions for the past two centuries. By focusing exclusively on them and arguing, implicitly or explicitly, that they are fundamentally without meaning until construed by the Court, some jurists and legal scholars have reinforced the view that the Constitution is deficient in decisive respects and therefore unworthy of vital public support. As a result, the Constitution is deprived of what James Madison in *The Federalist*, No. 49, called "that veneration which time bestows on everything, and without which perhaps the wisest and freest governments would not possess the requisite stability." This is of no minor concern, for, as Madison continues, "the most rational government will not find it a superfluous advantage, to have the prejudices of the community on its side."[2]

Still another problem with the view that the Constitution means only what the Court says it means is that it denies the truth that the Constitution is a public document capable of being understood not only by those who made and ratified it, but also by those who continue to live under it. Justice Joseph Story put the matter succinctly in his *Commentaries on the Constitution of the United States*[3]:

> [E]very word employed in the Constitution is to be expounded in its plain, obvious, and common sense, unless the context provides some ground to control, quality, or enlarge it. Constitutions are not designed for metaphysical or logical subleties, for niceties of expression, for critical propriety, for elaborate shades of meaning, or for the exercise of philosophical acuteness or judicial research. They are instruments of a practical nature, founded on the common business of human life, adapted to common wants, designed for common use, and fitted for common understandings. The people make them; the people adopt them; the people must be supposed to read them, with the help of common sense, and cannot be presumed to admit in them any recondite meaning or extraordinary gloss.

In a popular government, the people should take an active interest in the Constitution that gives form to their politics and protection to their liberties; they should not be discouraged from doing so by talk that the Constitution is some obscure document capable of being understood only by august justices on the Supreme Court.

A related problem: the view that the Constitution is whatever the Court says it is further misleads by suggesting that the Constitution has no meaning in and of itself. If all meaning must be poured into it by the Court, we are unlikely to turn to it for basic instruction on the principles, problems, and prospects of the American regime. The proudest claim of those responsible for framing and ratifying the Constitution was that it provided "a Republican remedy for the diseases most incident to Republican Government."[4] If we strip the Constitution of all independent meaning, we are unlikely to remember the Founders' answers to the basic questions and dilemmas of democratic government—and what is even more regrettable, we are likely to forget the questions themselves.

Yet another negative by-product of presenting the Constitution as devoid of any independent meaning is the encouragement of uncritical public acceptance of Supreme Court decisions. If the Constitution has only that meaning that the Supreme Court gives it, on what basis, other than subjective preference, can anyone object to the Court's interpretations? To illustrate with concrete examples, if the Constitution has no meaning apart from its judicial gloss, on what constitutional basis can anyone object to the Supreme Court's decisions in *Dred Scott* (1857), declaring that blacks could not be citizens, and *Plessy* v. *Ferguson* (1896), upholding racial segregation? Students of the Court implicitly acknowledge this problem by routinely paying lip service to Hughes's assertion and then, as the scholarly journals attest, criticizing at length judicial interpretations that they find wanting infidelity to the language of the Constitution, in scholarship, in craftsmanship, or in deference to the popularly elected branches.

Finally, Hughes's claim ignores the influence that political institutions may have on political behavior. The Court is seen as influencing the Constitution; rarely is the influence the Constitution may have on the Court, or on politics more generally, even considered.

APPROACHES TO CONSTITUTIONAL INTERPRETATION

To avoid the unpalatable ramifications of Hughes's aphorism, we will argue, along with Justice Felix Frankfurter, that the "ultimate touchstone of constitutionality is the Constitution itself and not what the [judges] have said about it."[5] But what, in fact, does the Constitution mean? How are we to understand its provisions and give them effect? In searching for satisfactory answers to these questions, students of the Constitution have come to employ several approaches to constitutional interpretation, each of which has its own strengths and weaknesses.[6]

Textual Analysis

One approach to constitutional interpretation involves explicating the constitutional text simply on the basis of the words found there. The basic claim of this approach seems unarguable: If the Constitution is to control the outcome of a case, and its unadorned text is plain, then constitutional interpretation should stop right there. As Justice Noah Swayne observed in *United States* v. *Hartwell* (1868): "If the language be clear, it is conclusive. There cannot be construction where there is nothing to construe." Justice Scalia applied this approach in *Coy* v. *Iowa* (1988), a case involving the Sixth Amendment's Confrontation Clause. He insisted that its words guaranteed defendants "a right to meet face to face all those who appear and give evidence at trial." He turned to the Latin roots of the word, confront, for guidance: It "ultimately derives from the prefix 'con-' (from 'contra' meaning 'against' or 'opposed') and the noun 'frons' (forehead). Shakespeare was thus describing the root meaning of confrontation when he had Richard the Second say: 'Then call them to our presence—face to face, and frowning brow to brow, ourselves will hear the accuser and the accused freely speak.' "

On the other hand, this approach often is difficult to apply. Although many provisions of the Constitution are perfectly clear, many require extensive construction. Moreover, even if the meanings of all relevant words are perfectly plain, problems of emphasis remain. In many cases, two or more constitutional provisions come into play, and the justices must decide which is to be given priority. To cite just one example of this problem: Does the First Amendment guarantee of freedom of speech and the press supersede the Sixth Amendment guarantee of a trial "by an impartial jury"? As this example indicates, the constitutional text in and of itself cannot resolve all the questions that the Constitution raises.

Precedent

When textual analysis alone is inadequate, many students of the Constitution turn to previously decided cases, searching for answers on the basis of precedent, or *stare decisis* ("to stand by decided matters"). Reliance on precedent, the primary method of legal reasoning in Anglo-American law, adds stability, continuity, and predictability to the entire legal enterprise.

For a variety of reasons, however, reliance on precedent has been applied only sporadically in constitutional law. Many jurists and scholars believe strongly that the Constitution itself, rather than previous decisions of the Court, should supply the standard for decision. Then, too, constitutional cases deal with momentous social and political issues that only temporarily take the form of litigation, and there is wide recognition that these issues cannot be resolved satisfactorily on the same basis as other legal problems. To the minds of some experts in the field, relying on precedent for constitutional interpretation is rather like driving an automobile down a busy street while looking only through the rearview mirror: We get a good notion of where we have been but not where we should be going. As Thomas Hobbes observed in *A Dialogue between a Philosopher and a Student of the Common Laws of England*, "precedents prove only what was done, but not what was well done."[7] If this difficulty confronts the use of precedent in any legal matter, it seems especially troublesome and unnecessary in constitutional law. Most areas of law lack clearly defined ends or purposes and so must evolve via precedent. The common law, for example, is based mainly on longstanding usage or judicial precedent. Constitutional law, on the other hand, has before it (to borrow the language of Judge J. Skelly Wright) certain "directions, goals, and ideals" that are easily discernible in the Constitution. Once discerned, these guideposts make it possible for the Court to decide matters of political and social import not in terms of what previous Courts have held, but in light of what is most conducive to achieving the goals or purposes of the Constitution.[8]

Constitutional Doctrine

When neither the constitutional text nor precedent can provide an adequate account of the meaning of the Constitution, arguments from "constitutional doctrine" may be raised. Constitutional doctrines are formulas—sometimes nothing more than slogans—extracted from a combination of the constitutional text and a series of related cases. The

Equal Protection Clause of the Fourteenth Amendment provides several examples of the development and use of constitutional doctrines. When considered as it applies to questions of race, this clause typically is understood to prohibit discrimination (although the word *discrimination* is nowhere to be found in the amendment); when considered as it applies to questions of legislative apportionment, it typically is understood to require "one person, one vote" (another phrase not found in the text). Similarly, the First Amendment's Establishment Clause, which charges Congress to "make no law respecting an establishment of religion," has been interpreted by many as erecting a "high wall of separatism" between church and state. In these illustrations, the constitutional doctrines enunciated serve as mediating principles that stand between specific controversies and the Constitution, giving meaning and content to ideals embodied in the text.

Although these examples suggest that constitutional doctrines broaden the scope of the constitutional text they reference, this is not invariably the case. The protection against "self-incrimination" provides an excellent illustration. The Fifth Amendment does not use the term, "self-incrimination"; rather, it says: "No person . . . shall be compelled in any criminal case to be a witness against himself." Unlike certain other reformulations of constitutional provisions, such as "separation of church and state" for the Establishment Clause and "freedom of expression" for "the freedom of speech, or of the press," this reformulation is narrower than the constitutional guarantee itself. Individuals can be witnesses against themselves in ways that do not incriminate them; they can, in criminal cases, injure their civil interests or disgrace themselves in the public mind. Thus, unlike the constitutional doctrine limiting the Fifth Amendment to "self-incrimination," the words of the amendment would seem to apply as well to any disclosures that would expose either criminal defendants or witnesses to civil liability or public obloquy.

Over time, many of these doctrines have come to give the constitutional provision in question its only meaning as a guide for decision. This usurpation of the original texts has profound and disturbing implications. As such doctrines become increasingly important, public debate tends to center on the meaning of the doctrines and not on the meaning of the Constitution itself. In reference to the Equal Protection Clause, for example, the contemporary debate over affirmative action/reverse discrimination has focused almost exclusively on such questions as whether this policy is discriminatory against whites and whether the majority should be free to discriminate against itself and on behalf of minority groups if it so wishes; the question of what "equal protection of the law" truly means has been all but forgotten. Equally disturbing is the fact that reducing constitutional provisions to doctrines or slogans often interferes with thoughtful consideration of the constitutional issues. The "one person, one vote" rule provides a case in point. On only the most elemental level does this rule have meaning; when examined outside a very narrow context, it becomes a simplistic and confusing slogan.

After all, the question of permitting certain voters the opportunity to vote two, five, or ten times has never been raised by any of the legislative reapportionment cases. In *Baker* v. *Carr* (1962), for example, the central issue was how much the voter's one vote was to be worth—a question that moved Justice Frankfurter to ask:

> What is this question of legislative apportionment? Appellants invoke the right to vote and have their votes counted. But they are permitted to vote and their votes are counted. They go to the polls, they cast their ballots, they send their representatives to the state councils. Their complaint is simply that the representatives are not sufficiently numerous or powerful—in short, that Tennessee has adopted a basis of representation with which they are not satisfied. Talk of "debasement" or "dilution" is circular talk. One cannot speak of "debasement" or "dilution" of the value of a vote until there is first defined a standard of reference as to what a vote should be worth.

Emphasis on the slogan "one person, one vote" merely obscured these questions and added to doctrinal confusion. Because of this problem, Justice Abe Fortas broke from the Court majority in the legislative reapportionment cases, declaring that such "admittedly complex and subtle" matters must be governed by "substance, not shibboleth." Discussing simplistic formulas such as "one person, one vote," he complained that they "are not surgical instruments"; rather, "they have a tendency to hack deeply—to amputate."[9] Their bluntness often makes them brutally efficient, but such efficiency comes at the price of clarity in constitutional understanding. To a greater or lesser degree, the same criticism can be directed toward many other constitutional doctrines.

Logical Reasoning

Another approach to constitutional interpretation emphasizes the use of logical reasoning as exemplified in the syllogism, a formal argument consisting of a major premise, a minor premise, and a conclusion. The major premise sets forth a proposition, such as "A law repugnant to the Constitution is void." The minor premise contains an assertion related to the major premise: "This particular law is repugnant to the Constitution." From these premises the conclusion logically follows: "This particular law is void." The foregoing example represents the essence of Chief Justice John Marshall's reasoning in *Marbury* v. *Madison* (1803), which formally established the Court's power of judicial review (that is, the power to void legislative or executive acts that it finds to be unconstitutional.)

Marshall himself was well aware, however, that logical analysis is an insufficient method of interpreting the Constitution. Assuming the validity of the major premise, the soundness of the conclusion depends on whether the minor premise is true. However, logic cannot determine whether a particular law is repugnant to the Constitution. Justice

Roberts made things too simple in *United States* v. *Butler* (1936) by arguing that "When an act of Congress is appropriately challenged in the
courts as not conforming to the constitutional mandate the judicial
branch of the Government has only one duty—to lay the article of the
Constitution which is invoked beside the statute which is challenged
and to decide whether the latter squares with the former." Whether an
act in fact squares with the Constitution is a question that must be left
to informed opinion and judgment—informed opinion about the purposes for which the Constitution was established, and judgment of
whether the law in question is consistent with those ends or purposes.
Logical analysis, therefore, must be supplemented with a clear understanding of what *The Federalist*, No. 10, calls the "great objects" of the
Constitution. Even Marshall, the justice most commonly identified with
the use of logical analysis, ultimately based his constitutional interpretations on his understanding of the ends the Constitution was intended to
serve. Marshall believed that the Constitution points beyond itself to the
purposes and policies that it serves, and that in the difficult (and most interesting) cases, constitutional interpretation must turn upon an understanding of the Constitution's proper ends. He confidently observed in
McCulloch v. *Maryland* (1819) that the nature of the Constitution demands "that only its great outlines should be marked, its important objects designated." As for the "minor ingredients" that comprise these objects, he was convinced that they could be "deduced from the nature of
the objects themselves."

The Living Constitution

Based on changing conditions and the lessons of experience, the adaptive, or "living Constitution," approach treats the Constitution more as
a political than as a legal document and holds that constitutional interpretation can and must be influenced by present-day values and the sum
total of the American experience. Although they insist that each generation has the right to adapt the Constitution to its own needs, proponents
of this approach acknowledge that these adaptations must be reconcilable with the language of the Constitution. They would concede, for example, that the provision that each state should have equal representation in the Senate cannot be interpreted to allow for proportional
representation, no matter what the dictates of changing conditions. They
argue, nevertheless, that the meaning of the Commerce Clause, what is
protected by the Fourth Amendment, or the reach of the Eighth Amendment's prohibition of "cruel and unusual punishments" may legitimately change over time.

Defenders of the adaptive approach often cite Marshall's observation
in *McCulloch* that "We must never forget that it is a Constitution we are
expounding," one that is "intended to endure for ages to come, and consequently, to be adapted to the various crises of human affairs."[10] It
should be noted, however, that Marshall was not asserting that the Court

should adapt the Constitution, but was arguing instead that the powers of the Constitution should be understood as broad enough to provide Congress with latitude sufficient to confront various crises in the future. Also cited is the argument Justice Oliver Wendell Holmes put forward in *Missouri* v. *Holland* (1920):

> When we are dealing with words that also are a constituent act, like the Constitution of the United States, we must realize that they have called into life a being the development of which could not have been foreseen completely by the most gifted of its begetters. It was enough for them to realize or to hope that they had created an organism; it has taken a century and cost their successors much sweat and blood to prove that they created a nation. The case before us must be considered in the light of our whole experience and not merely in that of what was said a hundred years ago.[11]

Like the other approaches to constitutional interpretation considered thus far, the adaptive approach has its problems. Most importantly, too much adaptation can render the Constitution and its various provisions so pliant that the original document is no longer able to provide guidance concerning what is to be done. Those who embrace the adaptive approach too often misuse Marshall's statements in *McCulloch* and seek not merely an adaptation *within* the Constitution but rather an adaptation *of* the Constitution; they want not only to devise new means to the ends of the Constitution, but also to adopt entirely new ends as well. Justice White's frustration in *New York* v. *United States* (1992) with the Court's insistence that Congress act in conformity with federalism and the Tenth Amendment is a case in point:

> The Court rejects this . . . argument by resorting to generalities and platitudes about the purpose of federalism being to protect individual rights. Ultimately, I suppose, the entire structure of our federal constitutional government can be traced to an interest in establishing checks and balances to prevent the exercise of tyranny against individuals. But these fears seem extremely far distant to me in a situation such as this. We face a crisis of national proportions in the disposal of low-level radioactive waste . . . For me, the Court's civics lecture has a decidedly hollow ring at a time when action, rather than rhetoric, is needed to solve a national problem.

Justice Brennan's objections to capital punishment also illustrate the problems of the adaptive approach. He continually argued that the objective of the "cruel and unusual punishment" clause of the Eighth Amendment is the promotion of "human dignity" and, by insisting that capital punishment is a denial of human dignity, concluded that capital punishment is unconstitutional,[12] despite the fact that the Constitution permits capital trials when preceded by a "presentment or indictment of a

Grand Jury"; permits a person to be "put in jeopardy of life" provided it is not done twice "for the same offense"; and permits both the national government and the states to deprive persons of their lives provided it is not done "without due process of law." The consequences of such a course of action were recognized by James Madison: "If the sense in which the Constitution was accepted and ratified by the Nation . . . be not the guide in expounding it, there can be no security for a consistent and stable [government], more than for a faithful exercise of its powers."[13]

Original Understanding

This approach is based on the premise that constitutional interpretation must proceed from an understanding of what those who initially drafted and ratified the Constitution intended for it to accomplish. As a consequence, it relies heavily on documentary evidence of the original understanding of the Constitution—especially on the notes taken by James Madison at the Federal Convention of 1787 and on *The Federalist*—to identify what ends the Framers intended the Constitution to achieve, what evils they sought to avoid, and what means they used to achieve these ends and avert these evils. Such reliance on the original understanding of the Framers has often been subjected to harsh criticism, and none harsher than by Justice Brennan who dismissed this approach as "little more than arrogance cloaked as humility. It is arrogant to pretend that from our vantage we can gauge accurately the intent of the Framers on application of principle to specific, contemporary questions."[14] As other critics have pointed out, the Framers' exact intentions are very difficult to determine in many cases. Of the fifty-five delegates present at one or more sessions of the 1787 Convention, for example, some took little or no part in the proceedings. Furthermore, what was said and the reasons given for votes cast are known largely through the remarkable yet necessarily incomplete notes of James Madison.[15] On only a few issues did a majority of the delegates speak, and on no issue did they all speak. Many decisions were compromises that completely satisfied no one, and others carried by the slimmest of majorities. And even if the intentions of the fifty-five delegates could somehow be divined, critics continue, how could we possibly know the intentions of the delegates to the states' ratifying conventions, whose votes put the Constitution into operation, or of the people who elected those delegates? As Justice Robert H. Jackson observed in *Youngstown Sheet & Tube Company* v. *Sawyer* (1952), "Just what our forefathers did envision, or would have envisioned had they foreseen modern conditions, must be divined from materials almost as enigmatic as the dreams Joseph was called to interpret for Pharoah."

Critics also raise a second and more fundamental objection—even if we could know the Framers' intention, why should we be bound by it? As Walton H. Hamilton has noted, "It is a little presumptuous for one generation, through a Constitution, to impose its will on posterity. Posterity has its own problems, and to deal with them adequately, it needs freedom of action, unhampered by the dead hand of the past."[16]

Although these criticisms seem forceful and cogent, they reflect a far too narrow understanding of the approach under discussion. To answer the most fundamental objection first, there should be no question of the founding generation "imposing its will on posterity." This approach seeks to understand the intentions of the Framers not because they were demigods whose judgments must be embraced unreservedly, but because they wrote the very Constitution we are called on to interpret and therefore are and will remain the best possible guides to discovering the ends and means of the constitutional order under which we live. As long as that order remains in force, we need to know as much about the Constitution as possible, including the purposes it was designed to achieve and the evils it was intended to avert. When constitutional questions are raised, therefore, this approach turns to the Founders not for specific answers, but rather for general guidance as to what the Constitution was intended to accomplish and how constitutional questions can be resolved in a manner consistent with these overall intentions. In examining Congress's power under the Commerce Clause to legislate on a particular issue, for example, followers of this approach turn to the founding documents not to ascertain whether the Framers would have favored the specific legislation in question—in all probability, they would never have taken up this question; and even if they had, their specific answers are unlikely to have any contemporary bearing—but to identify the intentions of the Framers to determine whether the objectives of the legislation in question are consistent with the ends for which the Commerce Clause and the Constitution were created. The Framers' intentions are not always clear or definitive, of course. However, protestations that it is very difficult to discover or verify these intentions miss the point. Any evidence pertaining to what the Framers sought to accomplish can only enhance our appreciation of what the Constitution means and what purposes it was designed to achieve, and therefore ought to weigh heavily in our overall understanding of the Constitution.

THE APPROACHES IN PERSPECTIVE

Textual analysis, precedent, constitutional doctrine, logical analysis, adaption, and identification of original understanding have all been used by justices of the Supreme Court as they have engaged in constitutional interpretation and have all therefore contributed to the contemporary understanding of the Constitution. In this book, we are especially guided in our approach to constitutional interpretation by original understanding, following the prudent counsel given by Justice Joseph Story in his *Commentaries on the Constitution of the United States*:

In construing the Constitution of the United States, we are, in the first instance, to consider, what are its nature and objects, its scope and design, as apparent from the structure of the instrument, viewed as a whole and also viewed in its component parts. Where its words are plain, clear and determinate, they require no interpretation . . . Where the words admit of two senses, each of which is conformable to general usage, that sense is to be adopted, which without departing from the literal import of the words, best harmonizes with the nature and objects, the scope and design of the instrument . . . In examining the Constitution, the antecedent situation of the country and its institutions, the existence and operations of the state governments, the powers and operations of the Confederation, in short all the circumstances, which had a tendency to produce, or to obstruct its formation and ratification, deserve careful attention.[17]

The original understanding approach explores what Story calls the Constitution's "nature and objects, its scope and design." It begins by identifying the ends the Framers intended for the Constitution to achieve and the means they used to achieve these ends, and based on that understanding, it proceeds to evaluate the decisions of the Supreme Court and the lower federal and state judiciaries and the constitutionally significant pronouncements of the executive and legislative branches. What are these ends and means? The remainder of this chapter is a brief introduction to this important question.

THE ENDS OF THE CONSTITUTION

Justice Jackson's sentiments notwithstanding, the documentary evidence is far from hopelessly "enigmatic" in spelling out the ends of the Constitution. We can begin with the Preamble and by quoting Justice Joseph Story: "It is an admitted maxim in the ordinary course of the administration of justice, that the preamble of a statute is a key to open the mind of the makers, as to the mischiefs, which are to be remedied, and the objects, which are to be accomplished by the provisions of the statue . . . There does not seem any reason why, in a fundamental law or constitution of government, an equal attention should not be given to the intention of the framers, as stated in the preamble."[18] The Preamble is clear as to the ends of the Constitution: it was ordained and established by "We the People of the United States" in order "to form a more perfect Union, establish Justice, insure domestic Tranquility, provide for the common defense, promote the general Welfare, and secure the Blessings of Liberty to ourselves and our Posterity." The Preamble, when read in conjunction with the rest of the Constitution and the documentary history concerning its drafting and ratification, makes clear that the Founders set out to establish an efficient and powerful guarantor of rights and liberties based on the principle of qualitative majority rule, the principle that the majority not only should rule but should rule well. In *The Federalist*, No. 10, James Madison explicitly stated this goal:

> To secure the public good and private rights against the danger of [an overbearing majority], and at the same time to preserve the spirit and form of popular government is then the great object to which our in-

quiries are directed. Let me add that it is the desideratum by which alone this form of government can be rescued from the opprobrium under which it has so long labored and be recommended to the esteem and adoption of mankind.[19]

As Madison and his colleagues were well aware, the "great object" of their inquiries presented daunting difficulties. They were irrevocably committed to popular or republican government, but historically, popular governments led inevitably to majority tyranny. In such governments, measures were decided "not according to the rules of justice, and the rights of the minor party; but by the superior force of an interested and over-bearing majority." Minority rights were disregarded—as were the "permanent and aggregate interests of the community." Because popular governments too easily allowed for "unjust combinations of the majority as a whole," they typically had proved to be "incompatible with personal security, or the rights of property" and "as short in their lives, as they have been violent in their deaths."[20] Such, according to Madison, was the great "opprobrium" under which "this form of government" had "so long labored."

The most commonly prescribed palliative for the problems of majority tyranny was to render the government powerless. However eager a majority might be to "concert and carry into effect its schemes of oppression," if its governmental vehicle were sufficiently impotent, it would pose no real threat. As William Symmes commented in the Massachusetts State Constitutional Ratifying Convention, "Power was never given . . . but it was exercised, nor ever exercised but it was finally abused."[21] The implication was clear: To prevent abuses, power must be consciously and jealously withheld.

This prescription was not without its shortcomings, however. Carried to an extreme, it rendered government not only powerless but also altogether unworkable. To this view, the leading Framers justifiably and appropriately responded that although the spirit of jealousy was extremely valuable, when carried too far it impinged on another equally important principle of government—that of "strength and stability in the organization of our government, and vigor in its operations."[22] They understood that a strong and stable government was necessary not only to cope with the problems that society faces, but also to render liberty fully secure. In order that popular government "be recommended to the esteem and adoption of mankind," they realized they would have to solve the twofold problem raised by majority rule: to establish a constitution capable of avoiding democratic tyranny on one hand and democratic ineptitude on the other. This problem had overwhelmed the government under the Articles of Confederation and led to the calling of the Federal Convention. Under the Articles, the member states were so powerful and their legislative assemblies so dominant and unchecked that the tyrannical impulses of the majority continually placed in jeopardy the life, liberty, and property of the citizenry; and the central federal government was so infirm and its responsibilities so few and limited that its situation often "bordered on anarchy." The Framers fully appreciated the challenge they faced. As Madison noted, "In framing a government which is to be administered by men over men, the great difficulty lies in this: You must first enable the government to controul the governed; and in the next place, oblige it to controul itself."[23] As we shall see, the Framers rose to this challenge by so arranging the various articles and provisions of the Constitution that they not only granted the federal and state governments sufficient power to control the governed but also obliged them to control themselves through such institutional arrangements and contrivances as the extended republic, separation of powers and checks and balances, and federalism.

THE MEANS TO THE ENDS

The Framers' solution to the problems of republican government was altogether consistent with republican principle. *The Federalist* is replete with references to this matter. Recognizing that "a dependence on the people is no doubt the primary controul on the government," the Framers also understood that experience had "taught mankind the necessity of auxiliary precautions."[24] This understanding was fundamentally shaped by their assessment of human nature. They believed mankind to be driven by self-interest and consumed by the desire for distinction. Men were seen as "ambitious, rapacious, and vindictive" creatures whose passions for "power and advantage" are so powerful and basic that it is folly to expect that they can be controlled adequately by traditional republican reliance on pure patriotism, respect for character, conscience, or religion, or even the not very lofty maxim that "honesty is the best policy." Inevitably, human avarice and lust for power divide men into parties, inflame them with mutual animosity, and render them much more disposed to oppress one another than to cooperate for the common good. Men are predictable in such matters. They will form factions, whether or not there are readily apparent reasons to do so. As their passions lead them in directions contrary to the "dictates of reason and justice," their reason is subverted into providing arguments for self-indulgence rather than incentives to virtue.[25]

Given these sentiments, it is hardly surprising that the Framers placed little faith in improving human nature through moral reformation or in the activities of "enlightened statesmen." The only hope for republican government, they concluded, was the establishment of institutions that would depend on "the ordinary depravity of human nature."[26] Appreciating that human passion and pride were elemental forces that could never be stifled or contained by "parchment barriers,"[27] they sought to harness and direct these forces through the process of mutual checking. Consequently, they included in the Constitution checks and controls that might "make it the interest, even of bad men, to act for the public good."[28] Self-interest, the Framers contended, was one check that nothing could overcome and the principal hope for security and stability in a republican government. The rather ignoble but always reliable inclination of people to follow their own "sober second thoughts of self-interest" would serve to minimize the likelihood of majority tyranny.[29] As the observant Alexis de Tocqueville would later describe it, the Framers relied on institutional mechanisms to check one personal interest with another and to direct the passions with the very same instruments that excite them.

What kinds of institutional mechanisms—what constitutional means—could incorporate and redirect human self-interest in such a way as to enable the federal and state governments to control the governed and, at the same time, oblige those governments to control themselves? The answer to that question can be found in the three principal concepts underpinning the Constitution: the extended republic, separation of powers and checks and balances, and federalism.

The Extended Republic

The multiplicity of interests present in the extended commercial republic established by the Constitution represents one of the principal mechanisms by which the Framers sought to establish an energetic government based on the principle of qualitative majority rule. The advantages of an extended republic can be best seen by examining the defects of a small republic. As Madison noted in *The Federalist*, No. 10, the smaller the republic, "the fewer probably will be the distinct parties and interests composing it; the fewer the distinct parties and interests, the more frequently will a majority be found of the same party; and the smaller the compass within which they are placed, the more easily will they concert and execute their plans of oppression." Thus arises democratic tyranny, which can be prevented only by rendering the government impotent and thereby fostering democratic ineptitude. In contrast, the larger the republic, the greater the variety of interests, parties, and sects present within it and the more moderate and diffused the conflict. In the words of *The Federalist*, No. 10, "Extend the sphere, and you take in a greater variety of parties and interests; you make it less probable that a majority of the whole will have a common motive to invade the rights of other citizens; or if such a common motive exists, it will be more difficult for all who feel it to discover their own strength, and to act in unison with each other."[30]

Because of the "greater variety" of economic, geographic, religious, political, cultural, and ethnic interests that an extended republic takes in, rule by a majority is effectively replaced by rule by ever-changing coalitions of minorities that come together on one particular issue to act as a majority but break up on the next. The coalition of minorities that acts as a majority on the issue of import duties is not likely to remain intact on such issues as national defense or governmental aid to private schools. The very real possibility that allies in one coalition may be opponents in the next encourages a certain moderation in politics, in terms of both the political objectives sought and the political tactics employed.

Political interests become reluctant to raise the political stakes too high: By scoring too decisive a political victory on one issue, an interest may find that it has only weakened itself by devastating a potential ally and thus rendering itself vulnerable to similar treatment in the future. Accordingly, politics is moderated not through idle appeals to conscience and beneficence, but rather through the reliance on the inclination of individuals to look after their own self-interest. As Madison observed in *The Federalist*, No. 51, this diversity of interests assures that "a coalition of a majority of the whole society" will seldom take place "on any other principles than those of justice and the common good."[31] The extended republic thus helped to make it possible for the Framers to give the national government sufficient power to prevent democratic ineptitude without raising the spectre of democratic tyranny.

The Framers' recognition of and reliance on the moderating effects brought about by an extended republic is apparent in such constitutional provisions as the Contract Clause in Article I, Section 10, which prohibits any state from passing laws "impairing the obligation of contracts." Note that only the states are restrained, but the federal government is not—and for good reasons. It was thought that no state, however large, was or would be extensive enough to contain a variety of interests wide enough to prevent majorities from acting oppressively and using their legislative power to nullify contracts for their own advantage. Consequently they had to have their power to do so limited by the Constitution. The federal government, by contrast, was large enough and contained the multiplicity of interests necessary to prevent oppression of this sort and so had no need of constitutional constraint. Thus could majority tyranny be avoided simply by relying on the popular principle to operate naturally in an extended republic. The elegant simplicity of this mechanism was pointed out by Madison: "In the extent and proper structure of the Union, therefore, we behold a Republican remedy for the disease most incident to Republican Government."[32]

Separation of Powers and Checks and Balances

For the Framers, the "great desideratum of politics" was the formation of a "government that will, at the same time, deserve the seemingly opposite epithets—efficient and free."[33] The extended republic was one means by which they sought to realize this objective; a "government of separated institutions sharing powers"[34] was another. They were aware that "the accumulation of all powers legislative, executive, and judiciary in the same hands, whether of one, a few, or many, and whether hereditary, self-appointed, or elective may justly be pronounced the very definition of tyranny," and therefore that "the preservation of liberty requires that the three great departments of power should be separate and distinct."[35] Thus, they sought to construct a government consisting of three coordinate and equal branches, with each performing a blend of functions, thereby balancing governmental powers. Their goal was to structure the government so that the three branches would "by their mutual relations, be the means of keeping each other in their proper places."[36] This the Framers succeeded in doing. They began by giving most legislative power to the Congress, most executive power to the president, and most judicial power to the Supreme Court and to such inferior federal courts as Congress might establish. They then set out to "divide and arrange" the remaining powers in such a manner that each branch could be "a check on the others." Principally, they introduced the principle of bicameralism, under which Congress was divided into the House of Representatives and the Senate, and arranged for the president to exercise certain important legislative powers by requiring yearly addresses on the State of the Union and by providing him with a conditional veto power. They also assumed that the Congress would be restrained by the Supreme Court's power of judicial review and sought to keep the president in check by requiring senatorial confirmation of executive appointees and judicial nominees, mandating that the Senate advise on and consent to treaties, and allowing for impeachment by the Congress. Finally, they supplied the means for keeping the Supreme Court in its "proper place" by giving the Congress budgetary control over the judiciary, the power of impeachment, and the power to regulate the Court's appellate jurisdiction. On top of these specific arrangements, they provided for staggered terms of office (two years for the House, six years for the Senate, four years for the President, and tenure "for good behavior" for the judiciary) to give each branch a further "constitutional check over the others."[37] Knowing that the various branches of the government, even though popularly elected, might from time to time be activated by "an official sentiment opposed to that of the General Government and perhaps to that of the people themselves,"[38] they felt that separation of powers was needed to ensure the fidelity of these popular agents. Separation of powers would provide for a "balance of the parts" that would consist "in the independent exercise of their separate powers and, when their powers are separately exercised, then in their mutual influence and operation on one another. Each part acts and is acted upon, supports and is supported, regulates and is regulated by the rest." This balance would assure that even if these separate parts were to become activated by separate interests, they would nonetheless move "in a line of direction somewhat different from that, which each acting by itself, would have taken; but, at the same time, in a line partaking of the natural direction of each, and formed out of the natural direction of the whole—the true line of publick liberty and happiness."[39]

Not only would such a separation and balancing of powers prevent any branch of government from tyrannizing the people, it would also thwart the majority from tyrannizing the minority. In creating an independent executive and judiciary, the Framers provided a means of temporarily blocking the will of tyrannical majorities as expressed through a compliant or demagogic legislature. Although separation of powers cannot permanently frustrate the wishes of the people, on those occasions when "the interests of the people are at variance with their inclinations" it so structures these institutions that they are able to "withstand the temporary delusions" of people, in order to give them "time and opportunity for more cool and sedate reflection."[40] The prospects for democratic tyranny are dimmed accordingly.

In addition to keeping society free, separation of powers was seen by the Framers as helping to render the government efficient—as minimizing the prospects for democratic ineptitude. Realizing that the democratic process of mutual deliberation and consent can paralyze the government when swift and decisive action is necessary, the Framers reasoned that government would be more efficient if its various functions were performed by separate and distinct agencies. According to James Wilson, a leading member of the Constitutional Convention,

> In planning, forming, and arranging laws, deliberation is always becoming, and always useful. But in the active scenes of government, there are emergencies, in which the man . . . who deliberates is lost. Secrecy may be equally necessary as dispatch. But can either secrecy or dispatch be expected, when, to every enterprise, mutual communication, mutual consultation, and mutual agreement among men, perhaps of discordant views, of discordant tempers, and discordant interests, are indispensably necessary? How much time will be consumed! and when it is consumed, how little business will be done! . . . If, on the other hand, the executive power of government is placed in the hands of one person, who is to direct all the subordinate officers of that department; is there not reason to expect, in his plans and conduct, promptitude, activity, firmness, consistency, and energy.[41]

For the Framers, then, separation of powers not only forestalled democratic tyranny but also provided for an independent and energetic executive able to assure "that prompt and salutory execution of the laws, which enter into the very definition of good Government."[42]

Federalism

The American constitutional system rests on a federal arrangement in which power is shared by the national government and the states. The primary purpose of this arrangement was to provide for a strong central government; however, it has also had the effect of promoting qualitative majority rule. The federalism created by the Framers can best be understood when contrasted to the confederalism that existed under the Articles of Confederation. Confederalism was characterized by three principles:

1. The central government exercised authority only over the individual governments (i.e., states) of which it was composed, never over the individual citizens of whom those governments were composed. Even this authority was limited, the resolutions of the federal authority amounting to little more than recommendations that the states could (and did) disregard.
2. The central government had no authority over the internal affairs of the individual states; its rule was limited mainly to certain external tasks of mutual interest to the member states.

3. Each individual state had an "exact equality of suffrage" derived from the equality of sovereignty shared by all states.[43]

The consequences of these three principles on the operation of the federal government were disastrous. They rendered the Articles of Confederation so weak that it was reduced, in Alexander Hamilton's words, "to the last stage of national humiliation."[44] There was obviously a need for a "more perfect union" and for new arrangements capable of rendering the political structure "adequate to the exigencies of Government and the preservation of the Union."[45]

The new federal structure erected by the Framers corrected each of the difficulties inherent in confederalism. To begin with, the power of the new federal government was enhanced considerably. Not only could it now operate directly on the individual citizen, just as the state governments could, but it could also deal with internal matters: for example, it now could regulate commerce among the several states, establish uniform rules of bankruptcy, coin money, establish a postal system, tax, and borrow money. Moreover, the federal government was made supreme over the states. As Article VI spelled out: "This Constitution, and the laws of the United States which shall be made in pursuance thereof . . . shall be the supreme law of the land."

If the federalism the Framers created strengthened the central government, it also contributed to qualitative majority rule by preserving the presence of powerful states capable of checking and controlling not only the central government but each other as well. Federalism granted the new central government only those powers expressly or implicitly delegated to it in the Constitution and allowed the states to retain all powers not prohibited to them. The states were permitted to regulate intrastate commerce and the health, safety, and welfare of the citizenry (i.e., the police power) and even were authorized to exercise certain powers concurrently with the central government—for example, the power of taxation and the power to regulate interstate commerce—so long as these powers were not exercised in a manner inconsistent with constitutional limitations or federal regulations. Finally, the Framers' federalism also contributed to qualitative majority rule by blending federal elements into the structure and procedures of the central government itself.[46] To take only the most obvious example, it mixed into the Senate the federal principle of equal representation of all states. When joined with bicameralism and separation of powers, this principle directly contributed to qualitative majority rule. For a measure to become law, it would have to pass the Senate, where because of the federal principle of equal representation of all states, the presence of a nationally distributed majority (with the moderating tendencies that provides) virtually would be guaranteed.

This division of power between the federal and state governments also provided another remedy for the ills of democratic ineptitude. As James Wilson emphasized, with two levels of government at their disposal, the people are in a position to assign their sovereign power to whichever level they believed to be more productive in promoting the common good. Moreover, efficiency is gained in still another way. The federal system permits the states to serve as, in the words of Justice John Marshall Harlan, "experimental social laboratories"[47] in which new policies and procedures can be implemented. If these experiments prove to be successful, they can be adopted elsewhere; if they fail, the damage is limited to the particular state in question. Because the risks are lessened, experimentation is encouraged, and the chances of positive reform and better governance are increased accordingly. In a wholly national or unitary system, on the other hand, experimentation can take place only on a national scale, and social inertia and a commitment to the status quo are encouraged.

The enhanced efficiency of the federal system, in turn, dims the prospect of democratic tyranny. As Madison observed in *The Federalist*, No. 20, "Tyranny has perhaps oftener grown out of the assumptions of power, called for, on pressing exigencies, by a defective constitution, than by the full exercise of the largest constitutional authorities."[48]

The Framers saw the multiplicity of interests present in an extended republic, separation of powers and checks and balances, and federalism as contributing to a government that is at once "efficient and free." These institutional mechanisms, operating in conjunction with each other, were designed to prevent the twin evils of democratic ineptitude and democratic tyranny. The Framers' intention was to institute an energetic and efficient government based on the principle of qualitative majority rule, and they systematically and consistently employed these means to achieve that end. This understanding is at the core of the approach to constitutional interpretation utilized in the discussion of the constitutional provisions that follows.

NOTES

1 For Chief Justice Hughes's subsequent qualification of these remarks, see *The Autobiographical Notes of Charles Evans Hughes*, eds. David J. Danielski and J. S. Tulshin (Cambridge, Mass.: Harvard University Press, 1973), p. 143.

2 Alexander Hamilton, James Madison, and John Jay, *The Federalist*, ed. Jacob E. Cooke (New York: World, 1961), p. 340. All subsequent references to *The Federalist* are to this edition.

3 Joseph Story, *Commentaries on the Constitution of the United States*. Vol. I (Boston: Hilliard and Gray, 1833), pp. 436–437.

4 *The Federalist*, No. 10, p. 65.

5 *Graves* v. *O'Keefe* (1939). Justice Frankfurter concurring.

6 See Book III, Chapter V: "Rules of Interpretation," in Story, *Commentaries on the Constitution of the United States*, Vol. I, pp. 382–442. See also Francis Lieber, *Legal and Political Hermeneutics*, 2d ed. (Boston: Charles C. Little & James Brown, 1839), reprinted in *Cardozo Law Review* 16, no. 6 (April 1995): pp. 1879–2105; Christopher Wolfe, *How to Read the Constitution: Originalism, Constitutional Interpretation, and Judicial Power* (Lanham, Md.: Rowman & Littlefield, 1996); and Antonin Scalia, *A Matter of Interpretation* (Princeton, N.J.: Princeton University Press, 1997).

7 Thomas Hobbes, *A Dialogue between a Philosopher and a Student of the Common Laws of England*, ed. Joseph Cropsey (Chicago: University of Chicago Press, 1971), p. 129.

8 See J. Skelly Wright, "Professor Bickel, the Scholarly Tradition, and the Supreme Court," *Harvard Law Review* 84, no. 4 (February 1971):785.

9 *Avery* v. *Midland County* (1968). Mr. Justice Fortas dissenting.

10 See Christopher Wolfe, "A Theory of U.S. Constitutional History," *Journal of Politics* 43, no. 2 (May 1981):301.

11 The same Justice Holmes also wrote, however: "I have not yet adequately expressed the more than anxiety that I feel at the ever increasing scope given to the Fourteenth Amendment. . . . I cannot believe that the Amendment was intended to give us *carte blanche* to embody our economic or moral beliefs in its prohibitions." *Baldwin* v. *Missouri*, 281 U.S. 586, 595 (1930).

12 William J. Brennan, "The Constitution of the United States: Contemporary Ratification," presentation at the Text and Teaching Symposium, Georgetown University, Washington, D.C., October 12, 1985.

13 James Madison, *The Writings of James Madison*, ed. Gaillard Hunt (New York: Putnam, 1900–1910), vol. 9, p. 191.

14 See William J. Brennan, "The Constitution of the United States: Contemporary Ratification," presentation at the Text and Teaching Symposium, Georgetown University Law School, Washington, D.C., October 12, 1985.

15 For a defense of Madison's notes, see his "Preface to the Debates in the Convention of 1787," in *The Records of the Federal Convention of 1787*, ed. Max Farrand (New Haven: Yale University Press, 1937), vol. 3, pp. 539–551.

16 Walton H. Hamilton, "The Constitution—Apropos of Crosskey," *University of Chicago Law Review* 21, no. 1 (Fall 1953): 82. For more contemporary critiques of original intent, see William J. Brennan, "The Constitution of the United States: Contemporary Ratification," Text and Teaching Symposium, Georgetown University, October 12, 1985; Arthur S. Miller, *Toward Increased Judicial Activism: The Political Role of the Supreme Court* (Westport, Conn.: Greenwood Press, 1982); Leonard W. Levy, *Original Intent and the Framers' Constitution* (New York: Macmillan, 1988); and H. Jefferson Powell, "The Original Understanding of Original Intent," *Harvard Law Review* 98 (March 1985): 885–948. For responses to these critiques, see Raoul Berger, "Original Intent and Leonard Levy," *Rutgers Law Review* 42 (Fall 1989): 255–286; Raoul Berger, "The Founders' Views—According to Jefferson Powell," *Texas Law Review* 67 (April 1989): 1033–1096; James H. Hutson, "The Creation of the Constitution: The Integrity of the Documentary Record," *Texas Law Review* 65 (November 1986): 1–39; Charles A. Lofgren, "The Original Understanding of Original Intent?" *Constitutional Commentary* 5 (1988): 77–113; and Gary L. McDowell, *Curbing the Courts: The Constitution and the Limits of Judicial Power* (Baton Rouge: Louisiana State University Press, 1988).

17 Joseph Story, *Commentaries on the Constitution of the United States*, vol. 1, pp. 387–388. See also pp. 322, 404, 412, and 417.

18 Joseph Story, *Commentaries on the Constitution of the United States*, Vol. I, pp. 443–444.

19 *The Federalist*, No. 10, p. 61.

20 *The Federalist*, No. 10, pp. 57–61; No. 51, p. 351.

21 Jonathan Elliot (ed.), *The Debates in the Several State Conventions on the Adoption of the Federal Constitution*, 2d ed. (Philadelphia: Lippincott, 1863), vol. 2, p. 74.

22 Alexander Hamilton in the New York State Ratifying Convention: Elliot, *Debates*, vol. 2, p. 301.

23 *The Federalist*, No. 51, p. 349. See also No. 39, p. 233.

24 Ibid., No. 51, p. 349.

25 See *The Federalist*, No. 6, pp. 28–31; No. 10, pp. 59, 61; No. 15, pp. 96, 97; No. 30, p. 193; No. 42, p. 283; No. 48, p. 334; and No. 63, pp. 426–427. A qualification is necessary at this point. According to *The Federalist:* "As there is a degree of depravity in mankind which requires a certain degree of circumspection and distrust; so there are other qualities in human nature which justify a certain portion of esteem and confidence. Republican government presupposes the existence of these qualities in a higher degree than any other form." *The Federalist*, No. 55, p. 378.

26 *The Federalist*, No. 10, p. 60; No. 78, p. 530.

27 *The Federalist*, No. 25, p. 163; No. 41, pp. 41, 270; No. 48, pp. 333, 338.

28 David Hume, *Political Essays*, ed. Charles W. Handel (Indianapolis: Bobbs-Merrill, 1953), p. 13.

29 The phrase is Frederick Douglass's. See his "The Destiny of Colored Americans," in *The North Star* of November 16, 1849.

30 *The Federalist*, No. 10, pp. 63–64.

31 Ibid., No. 51, p. 353.

32 Ibid., No. 10, p. 65.

33 *The Works of James Wilson*, ed. Robert Green McCloskey (Cambridge, Mass.: Belknap Press of Harvard University Press, 1967), p. 791.

34 Richard E. Neustadt, *Presidential Power* (New York: John Wiley, 1960), p. 33.

35 *The Federalist*, No. 47, p. 324.

36 *The Federalist*, No. 51, pp. 348, 349.

37 Ibid., No. 48, p. 332.

38 James Wilson, in Farrand, *Records*, vol. 1, p. 359.

39 *The Works of James Wilson*, p. 300.

40 *The Federalist*, No. 71, pp. 482–483.

41 *The Works of James Wilson*, pp. 294, 296. See also *The Federalist*, No. 70.

42 *The Federalist*, No. 37, p. 233.

43 See Martin Diamond, "What the Framers Meant by Federalism," in *A Nation of States*, 2d ed., ed. Robert A. Goldwin (Chicago: Rand McNally, 1974), pp. 25–42.

44 See *The Federalist*, No. 9, p. 55; No. 15, p. 73; and No. 22, p. 138.

45 Resolution of the Congress calling for the Federal Convention of 1787, in Farrand, *Records*, vol. 3, p. 14.

46 See Martin Diamond, "*The Federalist* on Federalism: Neither a National Nor a Federal Constitution, But a Composition of Both," *Yale Law Journal* 86, no. 6 (May 1977): 1273–1285.

47 *Roth* v. *United States* (1957).

48 *The Federalist*, No. 20, p. 127.

SELECTED READING

The Federalist, Nos. 1, 6, 9, 10, 15, 37, 39, 47–51, 63, 70–72, 78.

Agresto, John. *The Supreme Court and Constitutional Democracy* (Ithaca, N.Y.: Cornell University Press, 1984).

Anastaplo, George. *The Constitution of 1787: A Commentary* (Baltimore, Md.: Johns Hopkins University Press, 1989).

Baker, Thomas E. *"The Most Wonderful Work . . ." Our Constitution Interpreted* (St. Paul, Minn.: West Publishing Company, 1996).

Black, Charles L. *Decision According to Law* (New York: W. W. Norton, 1981).

Burt, Robert. *The Constitution in Conflict* (Cambridge, Mass.: Belknap Press, 1992).

Diamond, Martin. "Democracy and *The Federalist:* A Reconsideration of the Framers' Intent." *American Political Science Review* 53, no. 1 (March 1959): 52–68.

Douglas, William O. "Stare Decisis." *Columbia Law Review* 49 (1949): 725–758.

Eidelberg, Paul. *The Philosophy of the American Constitution* (New York: Free Press, 1968).

Elliot, Jonathan, ed. *The Debates in the Several State Conventions on the Adoption of the Federal Constitution as Recommended by the General Convention in Philadelphia in 1787.* 5 vols. (Philadelphia: Lippincott, 1963).

Farrand, Max, ed. *The Records of the Federal Convention of 1787.* 4 vols. (New Haven, Conn.: Yale University Press, 1937).

Faulkner, Robert K. *The Jurisprudence of John Marshall* (Princeton, N.J.: Princeton University Press, 1968).

Hickok, Eugene W., ed. *The Bill of Rights: Original Meaning and Current Understanding* (Charlottesville: University Press of Virginia, 1991).

Hickok, Eugene W., McDowell, Gary L., and Costopoulos, Philip J., eds. *Our Peculiar Security: The Written Constitution and Limited Government* (Lanham, Md.: Rowman & Littlefield Publishers, 1993).

Kesler, Charles R., ed. *Saving the Revolution: The Federalist Papers and the American Founding* (New York: Free Press, 1987).

Kurland, Philip B. and Lerner, Ralph, eds. *The Founders' Constitution.* 5 vols. (Chicago: University of Chicago Press, 1987).

Levy, Leonard W. and Mahoney, Dennis J., eds. *The Framing and Ratification of the Constitution* (New York: Macmillan Publishing, 1987).

McClellan, James. *Liberty, Order, and Justice: An Introduction to the Constitutional Principles of American Government,* 2d ed. (Indianapolis, Ind.: Liberty Fund, 1999).

Meese, Edwin. "Toward a Jurisprudence of Original Intention." *Benchmark* 2, no. 1 (1986): 1–10.

Rehnquist, William H. "The Notion of a Living Constitution." *Texas Law Review* 54 (May 1976): 693–707.

Rossum, Ralph A. and McDowell, Gary L., eds. *The American Founding: Politics, Statesmanship, and the Constitution* (Port Washington, N.Y.: Kennikat Press, 1981).

Scalia, Antonin. *A Matter of Interpretation* (Princeton, N.J.: Princeton University Press, 1997).

Storing, Herbert J., ed. *The Complete Anti-Federalist.* 7 vols. (Chicago: University of Chicago Press, 1981).

Wolfe, Christopher. *How to Read the Constitution: Originalism, Constitutional Interpretation, and Judicial Power* (Lantham, Md.: Rowman & Littlefield, 1996).

Wood, Gordon S. *The Creation of the American Republic* (Chapel Hill, N.C.: University of North Carolina Press, 1969).

★

★

2
CONSTITUTIONAL ADJUDICATION

More than 150 years ago, Alexis de Tocqueville observed that "there is hardly a political question in the United States which does not sooner or later turn into a judicial one."[1] Today, as then, Americans tend to transform policy disputes into constitutional issues and to seek resolutions in the courts in general, and in the Supreme Court in particular. The Supreme Court's political and legal roles are inextricably intertwined. By deciding cases that raise important issues concerning the extent, distribution, and uses of governmental power, the Court necessarily participates in governing.

The Supreme Court's dual responsibilities as an interpreter of the Constitution and an agency of government provide the focus for this chapter. Five basic questions will be considered: Who are the justices serving on the U.S. Supreme Court? What is the Supreme Court's position in the American judicial system? How are political questions transformed into legal issues and brought before the justices for resolution? How do the justices go about deciding the cases involving those issues? What happens after the Supreme Court decides? The chapter's final section offers a framework for analyzing judicial decisions and surveys source materials in constitutional law.

THE JUSTICES OF THE SUPREME COURT

Appointment and Tenure

Supreme Court justices are appointed by the president with the advice and consent of the Senate. Once confirmed, a Supreme Court justice— like any other federal judge—serves during "good behavior." Only one justice, Samuel Chase, has ever been impeached by the House of Repre-

sentatives, and the Senate failed to convict him. Usually, appointment to
the Court represents the culmination of a career, and justices tend to remain on the bench until death or retirement. Justice William O. Douglas,
for example, served 36 years on the Court, and Justice Oliver Wendell
Holmes did not retire until he was older than 90. The average tenure for
justices appointed during the twentieth century is more than 14 years.

Choosing Justices

On average, vacancies on the Court occur roughly every two years, so a
president serving two full terms can expect to have a considerable impact on the composition of the Court. President Ronald Reagan named
four justices to the Court during his two terms, and President Bill
Clinton named two justices during his first term. In making these appointments, presidents typically select persons with distinguished careers in public life. Among justices appointed up to 1998, 25 had served
in Congress, and more than 20 had held Cabinet posts. Although prior
judicial experience is not a requirement, all justices appointed since
1975 have served as appellate judges. Presidents also seek appointees
who share their political affiliation (roughly 90 percent of appointees
have been members of the president's party) and their constitutional
views. Thus, President Reagan sought proponents of "judicial restraint,"whereas President Clinton pledged to appoint justices sympathetic to the "right to privacy." Finally, presidents also consider demographic factors in their appointments. President Lyndon Johnson chose
Thurgood Marshall as the first African American on the Supreme Court,
and when Marshall retired, President George Bush replaced him with another African American, Clarence Thomas. President Reagan selected
Sandra Day O'Connor as the first woman on the high court, and in 1993
President Clinton selected Ruth Bader Ginsburg as his first appointee.

The Impact of Appointments

Through their power to appoint Supreme Court justices, presidents frequently can influence the orientation of the Supreme Court. For example, appointments by Presidents Reagan and Bush produced a substantially more conservative Court than existed in preceding decades.
Nevertheless, these presidential efforts do not always succeed. The Senate may refuse to confirm a president's nominees—from 1968–1992, six
nominees were rejected or withdrew when it became apparent they
could not be confirmed. Even when the Senate does confirm nominees,
the process has sometimes been arduous—for example, Justice Clarence
Thomas received Senate approval by a close 52–48 vote after accusations
of sexual harassment were leveled against him during confirmation hearings. Moreover, once on the Court, justices may not behave as the president expected. The president may have misjudged the prospective justice's views, those views may change after the justice is appointed, or

new issues may arise that the president did not anticipate in choosing a justice. When a justice fails to meet the president's expectations, there is nothing the president can do about it.

THE SUPREME COURT IN THE FEDERAL JUDICIAL SYSTEM

Article III of the Constitution established the United States Supreme Court and authorized "such inferior Courts as the Congress may from time to time ordain and establish." Acting under this authority, Congress has created a three-tiered system of federal courts, with the Supreme Court at the apex of the system and the federal courts of appeals and federal district courts below it. During the twentieth century, Congress has added to this system various specialized courts, such as the Court of Military Appeals and the Court of International Trade.

The district courts are the primary trial courts of the federal judicial system, with a single judge presiding over trials in civil or criminal cases. At present, there are ninety-four federal district courts, staffed by 649 judges, serving the fifty states, the District of Columbia, and various U.S. territories. Every state has at least one district court, with more populous states divided into multiple districts. California, New York, and Texas each have four district courts.

The twelve courts of appeals serve as the first-level appellate courts of the federal judicial system, hearing appeals from the district courts, from federal administrative agencies, and from various specialized courts. The courts of appeals typically hear cases as three-judge panels, which are randomly chosen for each case, and decide them by majority vote. Occasionally, however, a court of appeals may hear a case *en banc*, that is, with the court's entire membership participating in the decision of the case. Most courts of appeals are organized into regional "circuits" made up of three or more states. The Seventh Circuit, for example, includes Wisconsin, Illinois, and Indiana. The sole exception is the Court of Appeals for the District of Columbia, which hears large numbers of appeals from federal administrative agencies and serves as a sort of state supreme court for the District of Columbia.

The Supreme Court initially consisted of six justices, and the size of the Court fluctuated until 1869, when Congress established the number of justices at nine. Most cases come to the justices only after they have been tried and reviewed on appeal either by a federal district court and court of appeals or by state trial and appellate courts. The Court's rulings on federal law are binding on all lower courts—in that sense, it is truly a supreme court.

HOW CASES GET TO THE SUPREME COURT

Each year over the past decade, the Supreme Court has received more than 5,000 petitions for review but has decided less than three percent of the cases appealed to it with full opinions. The cases the Court decides must fall within its jurisdiction, that is, it can only decide those cases it is empowered to hear by the Constitution or by statute. Once this requirement is fulfilled, the Court has broad discretion in determining what cases it will decide. The range of discretion available to the Court has increased over time, and with this expanded discretion have come significant shifts in its caseload.

Jurisdiction of the Court

The Supreme Court has both an original jurisdiction (over those cases in which the Court functions as a trial court) and an appellate jurisdiction (over those cases in which the Court may review the decisions of other courts). Article III, Section 2 of the Constitution defines the Court's original jurisdiction but confers its appellate jurisdiction subject to "such Exceptions, and under such Regulations, as Congress shall make."

Original Jurisdiction. The Supreme Court's original jurisdiction extends to cases involving foreign diplomatic personnel and to cases in which a state is a party. Altogether, the Court has decided fewer than two hundred cases under its original jurisdiction. Two developments have minimized the number of cases initiated in the Supreme Court. The Eleventh Amendment, adopted in 1798, withdrew part of the Court's original jurisdiction by prohibiting those who were not citizens of a state from suing it in federal court.[2] More recently, Congress has deflected many potential original-jurisdiction cases to the federal district courts by giving those courts concurrent jurisdiction.

As a result of legislation, the Supreme Court currently retains exclusive original jurisdiction only over legal disputes between two states, which commonly deal with boundaries or with water or mineral rights. Because hearing testimony in even these few cases could prove a major drain on the time and energies of the Court, it typically appoints a Special Master—usually a retired judge—to conduct hearings and report back to it. In deciding these cases, the justices often endorse the findings of the Master.

Appellate Jurisdiction. The Supreme Court hears the vast majority of its cases on appeal from either one of the fifty state court systems or from federal courts, in which instances it operates as the court of last resort. The Court's decisions are final in the sense that there is no court to which one can appeal to reverse them. Its interpretation of statutes can be reversed only by congressional legislation, and its constitutional rulings overturned only by constitutional amendment; in the absence of these remedies, all courts are obliged to follow the Supreme Court's direction in matters of federal law. The Court's decisions also are final in the sense that the Court generally decides cases only after the litigants

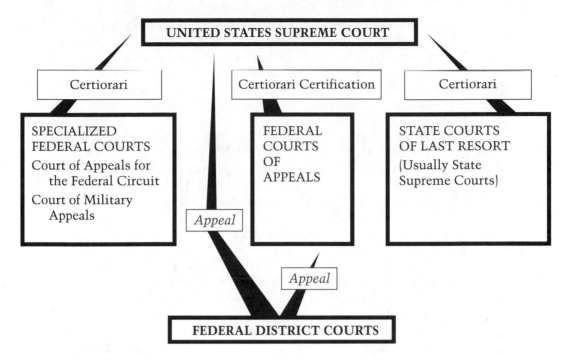

FIGURE 2.1 How Cases Reach the Supreme Court

have exhausted their available appeals to other courts (Figure 2.1). As Justice Robert Jackson put it in *Brown* v. *Allen* (1953): "We are not final because we are infallible, but we are infallible only because we are final."

Cases initiated in state courts usually reach the U.S. Supreme Court on appeal from state supreme courts, although the Court occasionally hears a case on appeal from another state court when no further appeal is available in the state system. In *Thompson* v. *City of Louisville* (1960), for example, the justices accepted a case directly from the police court of Louisville, Kentucky, because under state law the defendant's fine was too low for appeal to any higher state court.[3] Cases initiated in federal district courts normally come to the Court following review by the appropriate court of appeals, but the Court can expedite consideration of cases. In *United States* v. *Nixon* (1974), which involved President Richard Nixon's refusal to surrender tapes of his conversations subpoenaed for use in a criminal prosecution, the importance of the dispute prompted the Court to hear the case immediately after the federal district court ruled.

Over the course of time, the Supreme Court has gained virtually total discretion in determining what cases it hears. Early in the twentieth century, cases on appeal (that is, cases in which the party appealing the case had a right to Supreme Court review) accounted for more than 80 percent of the Court's appellate docket. Because many of these cases raised no significant legal issue, the justices actively lobbied for a reduction in the burden of obligatory review. Congress responded by passing the Judiciary Act of 1925, which drastically reduced the categories of cases in which parties had a right of appeal to the Court. In 1988, again at the urging of the justices, Congress eliminated almost all the Court's remaining mandatory jurisdiction, thereby according the Court nearly total control of its appellate docket.

Even before this legislation, the justices had exercised considerable control over the cases they decided. For one thing, more than 90 percent of the petitions for review came to the Court on writs of certiorari.[4] These petitions ranged from professionally drafted legal presentations in so-called paid cases to lay-drafted petitions submitted *in forma pauperis*.[5] In determining which certiorari petitions to accept, the Court has complete discretion. As the Supreme Court's Rule 10 states, "A review on writ of certiorari is not a matter of right but of judicial discretion, and will be granted only when there are special and important reasons therefor."[6] In recent years, the Court has used its discretion to reduce dramatically the number of cases it hears each term.[7] During the early 1980s, the justices granted review in more than 180 cases per term. In its 1996 term, however, the Court decided only 90 cases with full opinion. Justice David Souter has suggested that this change did not reflect a conscious choice; rather, "it just happened. " Yet whatever the explanation, the Court's increasing selectivity underscores the importance of the process by which the justices select the cases they will hear.

The Decision to Decide

Because the justices receive thousands of petitions for certiorari each year, they must establish criteria for determining which cases warrant review. It may be, as Chief Justice Earl Warren once suggested, that the standards that guide the justices' determinations "cannot be captured in any rule or guidelines that would be meaningful."[8] Nevertheless, this leaves unanswered the basic question of how the Court decides what to decide.

The Case Selection Process. The mechanics of case selection are relatively simple. Each justice has several law clerks (distinguished law school graduates selected annually by the justice after they have already served a year's clerkship), one of whose duties is to screen the petitions for review and prepare memos summarizing the materials. (Since 1972 the influx of cases has prompted several justices to pool their clerks for memo writing, so that the case memos each clerk prepares will be distributed to all participating justices.) Having evaluated the filings with the aid of the clerks' memos, the Chief Justice prepares a "discuss list" of the petitions he believes deserve collective consideration. Other justices can then add cases to the list. Unless a justice requests that a petition be discussed in conference, it is automatically denied. (More than 70 percent of all petitions are disposed of in this manner.)

Collective consideration of the petitions on the discuss list occurs during the three- or four-day conference before the beginning of the Court's term (in October) and at weekly conferences during the term. In the preterm conference, which is devoted exclusively to case selection, the justices dispose of the hundreds of petitions that have accumulated over the summer months. At the outset of its 1996 term, for example, the Court granted review in seven cases, disposed of six more without opinion, and denied review in 1,543 cases.[9] No case is accepted for review, at either the preterm or the regular weekly conference, unless four justices vote to hear it (the so-called rule of four).

Criteria for Case Selection. Because the justices do not publish or explain their votes, it is difficult to determine what factors influenced decisions to grant or deny review in particular cases.[10] The considerations affecting case selection may vary from justice to justice and from case to case. We can identify, however, the general considerations that affect the Court's decisions on petitions for certiorari.

One such consideration is the Court's acknowledged responsibility to promote uniformity and consistency in federal law. Supreme Court Rule 10, "Considerations Governing Review on Certiorari," reflects this responsibility in listing the factors that might prompt the Court to grant certiorari: (1) important questions of federal law on which the Court has not previously ruled; (2) conflicting interpretations of federal law by lower courts; (3) lower-court decisions that conflict with previous Supreme Court decisions; and (4) lower-court departures "from the accepted and usual course of judicial proceedings." This list is neither exhaustive nor binding: Reviews may be granted on the basis of other factors or denied when one or more of the cited factors is present. At times the Court may deny review even when lower courts have reached conflicting decisions on an issue. For example, for several years the justices refused to review challenges to states' use of roadblocks to detect drunk drivers, even though several state courts had disagreed about whether the roadblocks violated the constitutional prohibition on unreasonable searches and seizures. Only in 1990, after rejecting several earlier petitions for certiorari, did the Court address the issue.[11]

In denying certiorari despite disagreement among lower courts, the justices often rely on another case-selection criterion—the intrinsic importance of the issues raised in a case. Although occasionally the Court will reach out to correct gross miscarriages of justice, the justices recognize that they have important responsibilities in the governing of the nation, and they tend to be less concerned with correcting the errors of lower courts than with confronting "questions whose resolution will have immediate importance far beyond the particular facts and parties involved."[12] This criterion, of course, cannot be applied automatically. Some cases, because of the momentous political or legal issues they raise, clearly demand Supreme Court review. *United States* v. *Nixon*, which involved a confrontation over presidential claims of executive privilege, obviously fell into that category. Many other cases, including most *in forma pauperis* petitions, raise relatively minor issues that do not warrant the Court's attention. Whenever the choice is not so clear-cut, further considerations come into play.

Of paramount concern in some decisions to grant review is the effect the case might have on the long-run influence of the Court. Historically, the Court has sought to maintain its influence by avoiding unproductive involvement in political disputes, as when it refused to hear cases challenging the constitutionality of the Vietnam War. The justices also attempt to select cases in which the issues are clear and well-defined enough to facilitate wise and persuasive constitutional decisions.

Finally, the Court usually seeks to avoid unnecessarily inflaming public opinion by limiting the number of controversial issues it addresses at one time and by considering public reaction in choosing cases in which to announce important rulings. Thus, for thirteen years after *Brown* v. *Board of Education* (1954), which outlawed state-mandated school segregation, it refused to consider constitutional challenges to state laws prohibiting interracial marriage.[13] The Court chose *Gideon* v. *Wainright* (1963) to announce that indigent defendants had a right to counsel at trial in part because it involved a relatively minor offense rather than a violent crime.[14]

Perhaps even more important than the maintenance of the Court's influence are the justices' constitutional views—their notions of what constitutional issues are most important and how those issues should be resolved. Specifically, justices may vote to hear a case when they believe that review would further their conception of desirable constitutional policy. In some cases, certain justices might favor review if they believe that a majority of the Court will support their constitutional position, particularly if they disagree with the lower court's decision. Alternatively, if they expect to be in a minority on the Court, they might oppose review rather than risk creation of an unfavorable precedent.

The Changing Agenda. Our discussion of case selection has focused thus far on the factors underlying the selection of particular cases for review. However, the quotation from Tocqueville that opens the chapter suggests a broader perspective. If political questions tend to become judicial questions, then the cases from which the justices select presumably reflect the broad political issues confronting the nation. Put differently, if the Court seeks to decide cases of national concern, then the nation's political concerns necessarily furnish the Court's basic agenda.

The historical record confirms this point. Prior to the Civil War the paramount political issue was the distribution of political power between the national and state governments, and the constitutional cases considered by the Court characteristically required it to define the respective spheres of those governments. Following the Civil War the nation underwent rapid industrial development and the concurrent growth of large-scale economic enterprises, and governmental efforts to deal with these developments played a major role in the Court's constitutional decisions from the 1870s until the late 1930s. In the wake of the New Deal, an expansion in the scope of governmental concerns, facilitated by Court rulings permitting extensive regulation of economic activity, created new conflicts between government and the individual; accordingly, the contemporary Court's constitutional decisions have involved in large measure the delineation of individual rights.

HOW THE COURT DECIDES CASES

In deciding cases, the justices first of all inform themselves about the facts and legal issues in the case and about the more general consequences that can be expected from a ruling. After oral argument, they discuss the case in closed conference and reach a tentative decision. Finally, through the process of opinion writing and continuing discussion, the justices confirm (or in rare instances, reconsider) the decision reached in conference, clarify and develop the basis for the ruling, and attempt to reconcile intracourt differences.

As this summary suggests, the Court's decisions inevitably have a dual aspect. The litigants in a case usually are most concerned with winning or losing: To a convicted felon challenging the constitutionality of a police search that uncovered incriminating evidence, avoiding prison is the primary goal. In announcing decisions, however, the Court justifies its rulings on the basis of principles and standards whose ramifications extend far beyond the confines of the individual case. Indeed, the justices consciously use their discretion to review only cases of broad societal importance. An appreciation of this combination of the specific and the general, of immediate results and broader implications, is crucial to understanding the decision-making of the Supreme Court.

Informing and Persuading the Court

In weighing the merits of a particular case, the Court relies heavily on three sources of information: the briefs of the contending parties, *amicus curiae* (literally, "friend of the court") briefs, and oral argument. In all cases heard by the Court, the lawyers for both parties file legal briefs and then argue the case orally before the justices. In most cases other interested parties submit *amicus* briefs, which increase the range of information available to the justices. Because they resemble each other in basic purpose, the briefs of the parties and *amicus* briefs can be considered together.

Legal Briefs. A legal brief is first and foremost a partisan document—an attempt to persuade a court to rule in favor of one's client or position.

Persuasion takes the form of marshalling and then interpreting favorably the legal materials (precedents, statutes, constitutional provisions) and the facts involved in the case. For *amicus* briefs and for those submitted by the parties, the ultimate goal is to gain a favorable ruling.

Amicus briefs do differ from the briefs filed by the litigants. They ordinarily are filed by parties who are interested primarily in the general constitutional issue the case raises, rather than in the fate of the particular litigants. Some organizations file *amicus* briefs out of concern for the effects the Court's decision might have on them or on their members. In *Regents of the University of California* v. *Bakke* (1978), which involved an affirmative-action program for medical school admissions, several universities with similar programs filed *amicus* briefs, and so did the National Association for the Advancement of Colored People (NAACP) and several Jewish organizations. For other organizations, the principal concern is ideological: They wish to see the Constitution interpreted in a particular way. The American Civil Liberties Union (ACLU), for example, often files *amicus* briefs in First Amendment cases in an effort to gain or preserve a broad interpretation of the amendment's guarantees. Whatever the basis for their interest, those filing *amicus* briefs tend to be concerned largely with the constitutional standards that the Court announces and their implications.

Although legal briefs commonly focus on the interpretation of constitutional provisions, statutes, and precedents relevant to the case, they may also include nonlegal materials. In recent years lawyers have made extensive use of social science research to document conditions within the society, indicate the effects of governmental policies, or forecast the likely effects of a Court ruling. The prototype for such briefs was the famous "Brandeis brief" filed in *Muller* v. *Oregon* (1908). At issue in *Muller* was the constitutionality of an Oregon statute limiting female workers to a ten-hour workday, which the plaintiff challenged as an arbitrary interference with economic liberty. In response, Louis Brandeis, then counsel for the state of Oregon and later a Supreme Court justice, claimed that the law served important public purposes—a claim backed up by over one hundred pages of social and economic data demonstrating that long working hours were dangerous to the health, safety, and morals of working women. Brandeis's success in *Muller* prompted counsel in later cases to adopt a similar approach. In *Brown* v. *Board of Education*, for example, legal arguments for outlawing racial segregation in public education were supplemented by the results of psychological tests showing the adverse effects of segregation on black children. More recently, contending parties in cases involving the constitutionality of the death penalty have included in their briefs extensive data on the deterrent or nondeterrent effect of capital punishment and on the proportion of African Americans among those sentenced to death.

Oral Argument. In oral argument, the attorneys for each party have their last opportunity to influence the Court's decision. In the early nineteenth century, when the Court's docket was less crowded, the greatest lawyers in the country would spend several days arguing a case before the justices. Nowadays, oral presentations usually are limited to a half-hour for each party, although in particularly important cases more time may be allotted. In *Brown* v. *Board of Education II* (1955), which involved the question of how the Court's historic desegregation decision would be implemented, the Court permitted a total of fourteen hours of oral argument.

Despite severe time constraints, oral argument can provide an opportunity for influencing the justices, many of whom view it as vital for clarifying the written arguments presented in the briefs. Through their questions, the justices test the soundness of the opposing legal positions, and in this give-and-take, weaknesses in an argument or lack of preparation by attorneys soon becomes apparent. The justices' questions can also indicate issues on which they are undecided, and effective response to their inquiries can substantially improve a client's chances. As Justice John Marshall Harlan has observed, oral argument "may in many cases make the difference between winning and losing, no matter how good the briefs are."[15]

The Decision-Making Process

On Wednesdays and Fridays during its annual term (October to late June), the Court meets in conference to consider the cases on which it has most recently heard oral argument. Because the confidentiality of these conferences is jealously guarded—only the justices themselves, without law clerks or other Court staff, attend them—our knowledge of them is necessarily fragmentary.

Deliberations begin only after the justices shake hands—a ritual instituted to symbolize that the inevitable disagreements are legal, not personal. The Chief Justice initiates discussion by indicating his views of the case at hand and his vote. The associate justices, in descending order of seniority, similarly present their views and votes, and the tallying of votes produces a tentative decision. Although the discussion at conference can on occasion be quite heated, Chief Justice Rehnquist has noted that, for the most part, justices merely announce their conclusions rather than seeking to persuade their fellow justices. If the Chief Justice has voted with the majority, he determines who will write the opinion of the Court (majority opinion). He may assign the opinion to another member of the majority or retain it for himself. If the Chief Justice finds himself in the minority, the senior justice aligned with the majority assigns the opinion of the Court. The other justices are free to express their views in concurring or dissenting opinions.

How do the justices decide how they will vote? Some scholars maintain that the justices' votes simply reflect their ideological orientations.[16] According to this account, Chief Justice Rehnquist votes as he does because he is a conservative, whereas Justice Thurgood Marshall voted as he did because he was a liberal. Other scholars insist that justices are not free to decide simply on the basis of their preferences, that law constrains the choices that justices make and directs their decisions.[17] Despite these disagreements, some points are clear. Accounts of the justices' deliberations indicate that in conference they rely extensively on legal arguments and precedent to buttress their positions and persuade their colleagues.[18] The emphasis on legal argument suggests that the justices acknowledge their duty to put aside their personal preferences and base their decisions on the Constitution. (Of course, whether they succeed in banishing their personal policy views from their deliberations may well be another matter.) The requirement that decisions be legally justifiable rarely promotes consensus, however. Conscientious justices can and often do disagree about the difficult constitutional issues facing them. In recent terms, dissenting opinions were filed in about two-thirds of the cases the Court decided. Yet although interaction among the justices may have some effect on their votes and a substantial effect on their opinions, the decision-making process is more individual than collective in nature. As Justice Lewis Powell put it, "For the most part, perhaps as much as 90 percent of our total time, we function as nine small, independent law firms."[19] This high degree of individuality, which helps to account for the remarkable consistency of any given justice's voting patterns over time, reflects both the well-developed constitutional views the members of the Court bring to their cases and the limited resources available to them for changing the views of their colleagues.

The vote in conference comprises only the initial phase of decision-making. Even after conference, discussion of cases continues, and during the extended period between the vote and announcement of the decision, the opinion of the Court and any concurring or dissenting opinions are prepared and circulated among the justices for their comments. Reviewing these opinions gives the justices an opportunity to reconsider their initial positions, and a particularly persuasive opinion may lead to a change of vote. On a closely divided Court, defection by a single justice can produce a new majority and, therefore, a different decision.

The likelihood of a postconference vote shift should not be exaggerated. A study of one ten-year period found that the justices' final votes differed from their votes in conference only about 9 percent of the time.[20] Even if no votes are changed, the period between the conference and the announcement of the Court's decision still represents a crucial stage in the decisional process. During this time, the justices who comprise the majority carefully review the opinion of the Court; frequently, they require changes in its language or argument before they will endorse it. Justices Lewis Powell and William Brennan have acknowledged circulating as many as ten drafts of an opinion before one was accepted by the majority.[21] Even after prolonged discussions, deep-seated differences may prevent a Court majority from coalescing behind a single opinion. In *Furman* v. *Georgia* (1971), all five members of the Court majority wrote separate opinions that presented quite disparate grounds for invalidating Georgia's death penalty statute.

Such close scrutiny of the opinion of the Court reflects in part a concern for the soundness of the legal arguments it presents, because public and congressional acceptance of a decision may depend on the persuasiveness of the arguments supporting it. The justices also realize that the justifications for their decision may play a large role in future decisions. The importance of this consideration was highlighted in the decision handed down in *United States* v. *Nixon*, in which the Court unanimously rejected the President's claim of executive privilege and voted to compel him to release the Watergate tapes. Before that decision was announced, several justices refused to join Chief Justice Warren Burger's opinion for the Court, because they felt that it provided too much support for future claims of executive power. Only after the Chief Justice agreed to extensive revisions of the original opinion did all the justices join it.

THE IMPACT OF SUPREME COURT DECISIONS

Most Supreme Court decisions not only resolve disputes between particular litigants, but also have consequences for the nation as a whole. In ruling on the constitutionality of a particular program or practice, the Court also indicates the likely validity of similar programs or practices. In interpreting a constitutional provision, the Court announces standards that may guide future decisions involving that provision. In elaborating constitutional principles, the Court may educate the public about what our basic principles of government require.

Court decisions, like other governmental policies, do not always achieve their intended effects. Decisions may be misunderstood, misrepresented, or ignored; those responsible for carrying out the Court's mandates may seek to evade their responsibilities or may find ways to negate the effectiveness of the mandates; and opposition to Court rulings may lead to attempts to overturn them or to limit their effects. Rather than resolving conflicts, then, Court decisions sometimes merely aggravate them. Only if we understand what happens *after* the Court rules can we fully appreciate the role that the Court plays in governing.

Legal Obligation

A Supreme Court decision invalidating a governmental program imposes legal obligations on three distinct sets of actors. Most immediately, the losing party in the case must either abandon the invalidated program or remedy its constitutional defects. In a case such as *Regents of the University of California* v. *Bakke*, in which it was held that the goal of the affirmative-action plan in question (increased minority-group representation in the medical profession) was within the law but the means employed to achieve this goal were unconstitutional, the university had merely to revise its program such that the goal could be achieved constitutionally. When, however, the aim of an invalidated program is itself unconstitutional, alternative programs designed to accomplish that goal cannot legally be instituted.

In addition, because of the Court's hierarchical position in the American judicial system, its decisions on matters of federal law constitute binding precedent for all other courts, both federal and state. This means that should a litigant challenge a program similar to one invalidated by the Court, lower-court judges are obliged to invalidate it. Moreover, in deciding other cases in which a federal law or constitutional provision comes into play, judges must treat the Court's interpretation as authoritative. As Judge Learned Hand of the Second Circuit Court of Appeals put it, "I have always felt that it was the duty of an inferior court to suppress its own opinions . . . and to try to prophesy what the appellate court would do. God knows, I have often been wrong in that too; but I have at least been obedient, which is as I conceive it a judge's prime duty."[22]

Finally, by striking down a program as unconstitutional, the Court may also oblige other governmental units to discontinue programs similar to the one invalidated. This consequence underlines the crucial importance of the opinion of the Court: The broader the basis for the ruling, the broader the range of affected programs. The progress of school-desegregation decisions illustrates this point. In a series of decisions handed down from 1938 to 1954, the Court ruled that certain segregated school systems had violated the Equal Protection Clause of the Fourteenth Amendment by failing to provide equal educational facilities for black students; but because these rulings were tied to the conditions in specific districts, their effects were not felt outside those districts. Then, in 1954 the Court ruled in *Brown* v. *Board of Education* that separate school systems for blacks and whites were *inherently* unequal and thereby obliged all states operating such systems to dismantle them. By choosing the broader basis for its decision in *Brown*, the Court assured that its ruling would have nationwide effects.

Yet there is considerable controversy over what obligations a Court ruling imposes on government officials. Although they may not legitimately defy the Court's decision in a specific case, they are not obliged in every instance to endorse the Court's interpretation of the Constitution. For such a requirement would imply that the Constitution is what the Court says it is or that the Court can never err in its reading of the Constitution. In the wake of the Court's infamous decision in *Dred Scott* v. *Sandford* (1857), for example, Abraham Lincoln, while professing respect for the Court and acknowledging the authority of its ruling in the case, denied that the Court had correctly interpreted the Constitution and indicated his intention to seek a reversal of the Court's position. More recently, critics of the Supreme Court's ruling in *Roe* v. *Wade* (1973) legalizing abortion adopted various restrictions on abortion that were susceptible to legal challenge, expecting that the resulting litigation would provide an opportunity for the Court to reconsider its position. Eventually, this strategy succeeded, when the Court retreated from *Roe* in *Webster* v. *Reproductive Health Services* (1989) and *Planned Parenthood of Southeastern Pennsylvania* v. *Casey* (1992).

Response to Court Mandates

In invalidating a program or practice, the Supreme Court imposes an obligation to cease the unconstitutional activity or take steps to remedy the constitutional violation. In most cases those affected by the Court's rulings comply with the legal requirements. The mere existence of legal obligations does not guarantee compliance, however, and the cases in which Court mandates have not been carried out have had an importance far greater than their numbers might suggest.

Communication of Court Mandates. If its decisions are to achieve their intended effects, the Court must identify clearly what actions are to be undertaken or what practices eliminated and communicate that mandate to the appropriate officials. Rulings that are unclear or that fail to reach their intended audience are unlikely to have much effect.

Confusion over the exact scope or meaning of Court mandates may stem from disagreement on the Court. Not once during the 1960s, for example, did a majority of the justices agree on standards defining what kinds of sexually explicit materials were protected by the First Amendment. As a result, the Court handed down decisions marked by a multiplicity of opinions, each offering a different standard for determining whether movies or publications were obscene. State and local officials who tried to respect constitutional limitations while enforcing obscenity legislation consequently received little guidance from the Court.

Even when the justices agree among themselves, ambiguities in the opinion of the Court can create uncertainty about the scope of the ruling, as happened in *Escobedo* v. *Illinois* (1964). In *Escobedo,* the Court for the first time recognized that suspects had a right to counsel during police interrogations; but because the opinion of the Court did not clearly define that right, lower courts developed widely divergent interpretations of the ruling. Over an eighteen-month period, 150 cases raising *Escobedo*-type issues were appealed to the Supreme Court. Only after the Court clarified its position in *Miranda* v. *Arizona* (1966) did lower courts consistently enforce the right to counsel.[23]

Finally, the clarity of a Court ruling may disappear as that ruling is transmitted to its intended audience. The transmission to police officers of the Supreme Court's landmark criminal-justice decisions of the 1960s illustrates how confusion can occur at this stage. In determining what the Court required, police officers typically relied for information on nonjudicial sources such as police training sessions, local officials, and the mass media. Often, the Court's message was simplified and distorted in the course of transmission. A study of the initial response to *Miranda* in four Wisconsin police departments, for example, found that despite the clarity of the Court's guidelines, more than half the officers in three departments incorrectly identified what the decision required.[24] However, this is likely to be a problem only in the short run.

Noncompliance.   A more serious concern is noncompliance, the refusal to undertake or refrain from actions as required by Supreme Court rulings. State and federal courts at times have failed to follow or enforce Court decisions, and state supreme courts, in particular, have displayed a penchant for ignoring Court precedents. More frequently, however, noncompliance crops up among state or local officials who resist Court directions to implement unpopular decisions or to observe new and potentially burdensome limitations on the exercise of their powers. Southern school boards, for instance, long sought to evade the Court's school desegregation requirements; in more recent years, Northern school boards did the same. School districts often ignored Court decisions requiring the elimination of prayer and Bible-reading from their schools. When police officers believed that Court decisions hampered their efforts to control crime, they sought to evade limitations on their power to conduct searches and interrogate suspects.

That individuals evade, or seek to evade, their legal responsibilities is nothing new: the very existence of courts testifies to the need to enforce legal norms. Yet noncompliance—particularly if it is widespread—poses a grave threat to the Court's effectiveness, because its capacity to enforce its decisions is limited. As Alexander Hamilton noted in *The Federalist*, No. 78, the judiciary lacks control over "either the sword or the purse" and must "ultimately depend upon the aid of the executive arm even for the efficacy of its judgments." Should the executive prove reluctant to enforce its decisions vigorously, as happened initially after *Brown*, the Court can only depend on the willingness of litigants to initiate cases challenging instances of noncompliance. Even then, as previously noted, it cannot always rely on the lower courts to enforce its rulings. In sum, the Court's effectiveness ultimately depends less on its ability to punish noncompliance than on its ability to persuade the targets of its decisions to comply voluntarily.

Political Impact

In addition to imposing legal obligations, Supreme Court decisions influence public opinion, political activity, and the development of public policies. By upholding a challenged governmental enactment, the justices authoritatively dispose of constitutional objections to its validity and may thereby promote public acceptance of the law's legitimacy. The Court's decision in *Heart of Atlanta Motel* v. *United States* (1964), which upheld a controversial section of the Civil Rights Act of 1964, resolved constitutional questions about the national government's power to ban racial discrimination in public accommodations. Its decisions in

National Labor Relations Board v. *Jones & Laughlin Steel Corporation* (1937) and in subsequent cases validated New Deal efforts to regulate the national economy. As these examples indicate, Supreme Court decisions have played a crucial role in legitimating the federal government's expanding exercise of power.[25] In addition, Court legitimation of one state's law may dispose other states to adopt similar measures. The full development of so-called Jim Crow laws, for example, did not occur until after the Court, in *Plessy* v. *Ferguson* (1896), upheld a Louisiana statute establishing racial segregation in public transportation.[26]

Even when the justices do not invalidate governmental policies, their rulings may still have political repercussions. The justices' interpretation of federal statutes have at times prompted campaigns for congressional action to overturn those interpretations. Thus, after a series of rulings during the late 1980s narrowly construed federal civil-rights statutes, civil-rights groups prevailed on Congress to pass the Civil Rights Act of 1991, reversing several of those decisions. Even rulings upholding governmental action against constitutional challenge may, by focusing attention on the issue, produce a political response. For example, after the Court in *Goldman* v. *Weinberger* (1986) rejected the claim of an Orthodox Jewish psychologist that he had a constitutional right to wear a yarmulke while on active duty in a military hospital, Congress enacted legislation establishing a statutory right to do so.

Decisions invalidating state or federal policies have also produced varied effects. An adverse Court ruling frequently activates the political forces supporting a program to seek alternative means of accomplishing their objectives. Thus five constitutional amendments have been adopted, in whole or in part, to overturn Supreme Court decisions.[27] During recent decades, opponents of Court decisions have sought, unsuccessfully, to strip the Court of its power to hear cases involving school prayer, busing, and abortion.

The response to the Supreme Court's abortion decisions illustrates the potential political consequences of judicial rulings. The Supreme Court's decision in *Roe* v. *Wade* striking down state restrictions on abortion prompted the formation of the pro-life movement, which supported legislation discouraging abortions or making them more difficult to obtain and a constitutional amendment outlawing abortion. More recently, the Court's validation of state laws limiting abortion activated pro-choice forces, which attempted to blunt the effects of the decisions by supporting candidates sympathetic to their cause and by pushing for adoption of state and federal laws protecting abortion rights.

Controversial decisions often generate support and opposition. For example, *Brown* v. *Board of Education* produced not only intransigent resistance by segregationists but also efforts by civil rights groups to solidify and extend the gains they had made. Such decisions have the added effect of subtly changing the political context in which conflicts between such forces occur, by giving proponents of the Court's view the potent political advantage of being able to claim that the Constitution supports their position. Finally, the public support for the Court that promotes voluntary compliance also enables it to influence public opinion. According to public-opinion polls, public attitudes toward desegregation changed markedly after *Brown*.[28] This change may not have resulted solely from the Court's ruling, but it does suggest that the authority of the Court enables it to influence public opinion even on controversial matters.

In sum, Supreme Court decisions establish government policy, just as decisions made by the executive or legislative branches do, and thereby help shape American society. Indeed, if the Court is to fulfill its constitutional functions, it cannot avoid making policy. The important question to ask is whether its policies can be constitutionally justified.

ANALYZING COURT DECISIONS

Because judicial opinions provide justifications for constitutional positions, in reading cases one should bear in mind the modes of constitutional interpretation outlined in Chapter 1. Often it is helpful to "brief," or outline, a case to analyze its major elements (see Box 2.1 for an example). In general, one should look for the following elements that are common to all court cases.

Title and Citation. Case titles usually derive from the names of the parties to the controversy. The party listed first is seeking reversal of an unfavorable lower-court decision, whereas the party listed second typically wants that decision affirmed. If the case comes to the Court on appeal, the parties are referred to as the appellant and the appellee. If the case comes on a writ of certiorari, they are referred to as the petitioner and the respondent.

Facts of the Case. Because all Supreme Court cases arise as disputes between particular litigants, Court decisions represent attempts to apply constitutional principles to unique situations. Full understanding of a Court decision therefore requires an appreciation of the facts underlying the case, which have been established by testimony at trials. Supreme Court justices may differ in interpreting the facts, however; disagreement about the facts, as well as about the proper interpretation of the Constitution, may produce divisions on the Court. Frequently, the opinion of the Court, or majority opinion, summarizes the relevant facts before elaborating the Court's justification for its decision. In other cases, the facts must be pieced together from comments in several opinions. Preceding most cases presented in this volume are summaries of the facts, which indicate the factors one should look for in reading cases.

BOX 2.1 A SAMPLE CASE BRIEF

Texas v. *Johnson*
491 U.S. 397 (1989)

Facts of the Case. Gregory Johnson burned an American flag as a form of political protest. He was arrested and convicted of violating a Texas statute that forbade desecration of the American flag. He appealed his conviction, claiming that his action was protected by the First Amendment. The Texas Court of Criminal Appeals overturned his conviction, and the Supreme Court granted certiorari.

The Law. The Free Speech Clause of the First Amendment, made applicable to states by the Due Process Clause of the Fourteenth Amendment.

Legal Questions.

1. Does Johnson's conduct constitute expressive conduct, thus implicating the 1st Amendment? *Yes.*
2. Did Johnson's burning of the flag disturb the peace? *No.*
3. Is the state's interest in preserving the flag as a national symbol related to the suppression of free expression? *Yes.*
4. Does the Supreme Court's test for expressive conduct enunciated by *United States* v. *O'Brien* apply here? *No.*
5. Does the state have a valid interest in promoting respect for the flag as a symbol of the nation? *Yes.*
6. Can government prohibit flag desecration as a means of promoting that interest? *No.*
7. Is the Texas law constitutional? *No.*

Opinion of the Court (Brennan). Johnson's burning of the American flag was an attempt to convey a political message. When Texas banned flag desecration to promote respect for the flag, it prevented the use of the flag to communicate messages, such as Johnson's, that are critical of the government and of the nation. However, the First Amendment forbids government from prohibiting the expression of ideas and communication of messages merely because they are offensive or disagreeable, and therefore the Texas statute is unconstitutional.

Concurring Opinion (Kennedy). Commitment to the Constitution requires overturning Johnson's conviction, however distasteful it may be to do so.

Dissenting Opinion (Rehnquist). The American flag's unique position as a symbol of the nation justifies special protections against its desecration.

Texas's flag desecration statute does not prevent Johnson from communicating his criticism of the government, because his speech and other actions expressing that criticism were not prohibited or interfered with. The statute only prohibits one means of conveying his message, and it does so in response to the profound regard that Americans have for their flag.

Dissenting Opinion (Stevens). The rules developed for other forms of symbolic expression do not apply here, because of the flag's status as a special symbol of the nation.

Evaluation. The Court's ruling extended the range of expressive actions entitled to First Amendment protection. Forty-eight states and the national government had statutes banning flag desecration, so the effects of the Court's ruling were felt nationwide. Efforts to amend the Constitution to overturn the Court's ruling failed, and a congressional flag-desecration statute passed in the wake of this decision was subsequently invalidated by the Court.

The Law. Supreme Court decisions usually involve the interpretation of three elements of law: constitutional provisions, statutes and/or administrative regulations, and Supreme Court precedents. Large bodies of law have sprung from most constitutional provisions, so it is important to note precisely which provision the Court is interpreting. For example, if a constitutional challenge is raised under the Fourteenth Amendment, the first thing to determine is whether the challenge is based on the Due Process Clause or the Equal Protection Clause.

Legal Questions. A Court decision can be viewed as a response to a particular legal question or series of questions, a clear understanding of which is vital to any proper analysis of the opinions in a case and of the effects of the decision. One way of ensuring such clarity is to frame the questions involved in a yes-or-no format (see Box 2.1 for an example). Usually the Court's answers to the legal questions in a case can be determined from a close reading of the opinion of the Court. However, in cases in which five justices are unable to agree on a single opinion, one must search all opinions in the case for points of majority agreement.

Opinion of the Court. This opinion announces the Court's decision and supplies the justifications for that ruling. Because the decision may serve as a precedent in future cases, close attention should be paid to the chain of reasoning supporting the decision and to its possible implications. Frequently, the best approach is to trace how the Court arrived at its answers to each of the legal questions previously identified.

Concurring Opinions. Members of the Court majority may write concurring opinions either because they agree with the Court's decision but disagree with its justification, in which instance the concurring opinion will offer an alternative justification, or because they agree with both the decision and its justification but wish either to clarify their own view of the case or to respond to arguments made in a dissenting opinion. Determining the basis for the concurrence should be the initial step in analyzing a concurring opinion.

Dissenting Opinions. Dissenting opinions attempt to demonstrate why the Court's decision is wrong. They may point to alleged errors in reasoning, misinterpretation of precedents or constitutional provisions, or misunderstanding of the facts in a case. Analysis of dissenting opinions should focus on the bases of disagreement with the opinion of the Court.

Evaluation. No analysis of a case is complete without an evaluation of the decision. Is the opinion of the Court convincing? Is the decision consistent with previous Court decisions? If not, does the Court provide persuasive reasons for departing from precedent? What are the likely effects of the Court's decision?

SOURCES IN CONSTITUTIONAL LAW

Court Decisions. The official edition of United States Supreme Court decisions, titled *United States Reports,* contains the text of all Supreme Court decisions handed down since 1790. For almost one hundred years, the volumes were issued under the names of individual court reporters. Thus, citations to cases in those volumes generally include the name of the particular reporter: *Marbury* v. *Madison,* 1 Cranch 137 (1803). After Volume 90 (1874), cases are cited only by the volume number of *U.S. Reports.* Thus *Adamson v. California,* 322 U.S. 46, can be found on page 46 of Volume 322.

Two other editions of the Supreme Court's decisions contain supplementary material not found in the official edition. The *Supreme Court Reporter* prefaces the Court's decisions with summaries of the legal issues in the case. Citations are again by volume and page; for example, the citation for *Adamson* is 67 Sup. Ct. 1672. The *Lawyers' Edition of the United States Supreme Court Reports* includes legal analyses of the more important rulings and summarizes the oral arguments of counsel in each case. Citations are by volume and number: for *Adamson,* the citation is 91 L.Ed. 1903.

Prior to publication in bound volumes, Supreme Court decisions are available in loose-leaf format in *U.S. Law Week* and on the Internet. The most accessible online site for Court decisions is the Cornell Law School

Server. This server provides the full text of all Supreme Court decisions since 1990, which can be accessed at <www.law.cornell.edu/supct>, with current decisions posted the same day that they are released by the Court. A number of historic Supreme Court decisions are available as well at <www.law.cornell.edu/supct/cases/historic.html>. For oral arguments from historic Supreme Court cases, the Northwestern University site known as Oyez Oyez Oyez provides recordings digitized from tapes in the National Archives. The site can be accessed at <oyez.at.nwu.edu/oyez.html>. To listen to the arguments, one needs RealAudio software installed on a computer, but Oyez offers a link to another Internet site where this software can be downloaded for free. Finally, edited versions of some Supreme Court cases are available at the website for this text at <www.worthpublishers.com/policenter.html>.

Decisions by lower federal courts and state courts may also be important in studying constitutional law. The *Federal Reporter* series publishes most decisions of the United States Courts of Appeals, and the *Federal Supplement* series publishes selected United States District Court decisions. Important state decisions are published in official versions by the various states. In addition, the privately published *National Reporter* series groups most decisions of state appellate courts in regional reporters. The *Southeastern Reporter*, for example, contains state appellate decisions from West Virginia, Virginia, North Carolina, South Carolina, and Georgia.

Statutes. Statutes (laws) comprise another important source material in constitutional law. The U.S. Government Printing Office initially publishes each federal law separately as so-called slip laws, which are numbered chronologically: The Freedom of Information Act (1974) is cited as Pub. L 93-502, the *93* indicating the Congress and the *502* the numerical order in which the law appears. At the end of each session of Congress, the slip laws are collected and published in chronological order in *Statutes at Large*. Citations to *Statutes at Large* are by volume and page: The Freedom of Information Act is cited as 88 Stat. 1561, the *88* indicating the volume and the *1561* the initial page.

The single most useful official source for researching statutes is the *United States Code*. The *U.S. Code* arranges the law by subject into fifty titles, thus directing the researcher to all the federal laws pertaining to a topic. Each of the fifty titles is subdivided further into chapters, sections, and subsections. Accordingly, the citation for the Freedom of Information Act is 5 U.S.C. §552, the *5* indicating the title and the *552* the section of the code.

Executive-Branch Materials. Among the executive-branch materials that may be of interest in constitutional law are presidential documents, such as executive orders and presidential proclamations, and administrative agency rules and regulations. The most comprehensive source for presidential materials is the *Weekly Compilation of Presidential Documents*, published by the U.S. Government Printing Office. Orders and proclamations of general applicability and legal effect also can be found in the *Federal Register*, the daily official publication of executive branch actions.

The *Federal Register* also contains all rules, regulations, and orders issued by federal administrative agencies. Because the *Register* is published daily, it presents executive-branch materials chronologically. This mass of materials is organized topically in the *Code of Federal Regulations*, which divides the general and permanent rules published in the *Federal Register* into fifty titles representing broad areas subject to federal regulations. Each title is subdivided further into chapters, which usually bear the name of the issuing agency, and into parts, which pertain to specific regulatory areas. For example, the Department of Justice regulations pertaining to production or disclosure of information under the Freedom of Information Act are found at 28 CFR § 16.

NOTES

1   Alexis de Tocqueville, *Democracy in America,* ed. J. P. Mayer (Garden City, N.Y.: Doubleday, 1969), p. 270.

2   Underlying the adoption of the Eleventh Amendment was widespread disenchantment with the Court's decision in *Chisholm* v. *Georgia* (1793), in which it was held that Chisholm, a citizen of South Carolina, could sue the state of Georgia in the federal courts.

3   "Shufflin' Sam" Thompson had been arrested for loitering while waiting in a bar for his bus and shuffling his feet in time to music from a jukebox. When he protested against his arrest, he was also charged with disorderly conduct. He was convicted on both charges and fined $10 for each. Because Kentucky law provided no opportunity to appeal fines of less than $20, Thompson petitioned for Supreme Court review. The Court accepted the case and ruled unanimously that the convictions were not supported by evidence and therefore amounted to a denial of due process of law.

4   Cases may also come to the Supreme Court by *certification*. Under this rarely used procedure, a lower federal court requests instruction from the Supreme Court on a point of law.

5   "Paid" cases are those in which the petitioners have paid the $200 filing fee and supplied the prescribed copies of briefs and other legal materials. An *in forma pauperis* case is one in which an impoverished petitioner requests review of a lower-court decision. These cases generally involve criminal appeals filed by prisoners who cannot afford expert legal assistance. In such cases the Court waives the filing fee and the other requirements it enforces in "paid" cases. For an excellent study of how one *in forma pauperis* petition led to a landmark Supreme Court decision guaranteeing indigent defendants a right to counsel at trial, see Anthony Lewis, *Gideon's Trumpet* (New York: Random House, 1964).

6   The Supreme Court established the procedural rules governing appeals to and the operations of the Court. These rules were revised most recently in 1980.

7   The discussion in this paragraph relies primarily on David M. O'Brien, "The Rehnquist Court's Shrinking Plenary Docket," *Judicature* 81 (1997): 58–65.

8   "Retired Chief Justice Warren Attacks . . . Freund Study Group's Composition and Proposal," *American Bar Association Journal* 59 (July 1973): 728.

9 65 U.S. Law Week 3217 (October 8, 1996).

10 During his tenure on the Supreme Court (1947–58), Justice Harold Burton kept systematic records of the conference votes on whether to hear cases. Studies based on his papers include Doris Marie Provine, *Case Selection in the United States Supreme Court* (Chicago: University of Chicago Press, 1980); S. Sidney Ulmer, "The Decision to Grant Certiorari as an Indicator to Decision 'On the Merits,' " *Polity* 4 (1972); and Ulmer, "Selecting Cases for Supreme Court Review: An Underdog Model," *American Political Science Review* 72 (1978).

11 Lawrence Baum, *The Supreme Court of the United States*, 5th ed. (Washington, D.C.: CQ Press, 1992), p. 116. The case upholding use of such roadblocks is *Michigan Department of State Police* v. *Sitz*, 110 L.Ed.2d 412 (1990).

12 Chief Justice Fred Vinson in "Work of the U.S. Supreme Court," *Texas Bar Journal* 12 (1949): 551.

13 It eventually struck down such laws in the aptly named *Loving* v. *Virginia*, 388 U.S. 1 (1967).

14 Baum, *The Supreme Court*, p. 115.

15 Harlan's statement is reported in Anthony Lewis, *Gideon's Trumpet*, p. 162, n. 23.

16 The leading exposition of this viewpoint is Jeffrey A. Segal and Harold J. Spaeth, *The Supreme Court and the Attitudinal Model* (New York: Cambridge University Press, 1993).

17 See, for example, Lee Epstein and Joseph F. Kobylka, *The Supreme Court and Legal Change: Abortion and the Death Penalty* (Chapel Hill: University of North Carolina Press, 1992).

18 See, for example, Lee Epstein and Jack Knight. *The Choices Justices Make* (Washington, D.C.: CQ Press, 1998); Walter F. Murphy, *Elements of Judicial Strategy* (Chicago: University of Chicago Press, 1964); Alexander M. Bickel, *The Unpublished Opinions of Mr. Justice Brandeis: The Supreme Court at Work* (Cambridge, Mass.: Harvard University Press, 1957); and David O'Brien, *Storm Center: The Supreme Court in American Politics* (New York: W. W. Norton, 1986).

19 Lewis F. Powell, Jr., "What the Justices are Saying . . . ," *American Bar Association Journal* 62 (1976): 1454.

20 Saul Brenner, "Fluidity on the United States Supreme Court: A Reexamination," *American Journal of Political Science* 24 (1980).

21 Henry J. Abraham, *The Judicial Process*, 5th ed. (New York: Oxford University Press, 1986), p. 223.

22 Hand's comment is contained in an intracourt memorandum quoted in Marvin Schick, *Learned Hand's Court* (Baltimore, Md.: Johns Hopkins Press, 1970), p. 167.

23 For a discussion of initial state-court responses to *Escobedo* v. *Illinois* and *Miranda* v. *Arizona*, see Neil T. Romans, "The Role of State Supreme Courts in Judicial Policy Making: *Escobedo, Miranda* and the Use of Impact Analysis," *Western Political Quarterly* 27 (1974): 526–535.

24 Neil A. Milner, *The Court and Local Enforcement: The Impact of Miranda* (Beverly Hills, Cal.: Sage Publications, 1971), p. 225, Table 11-2.

25 For a discussion of the Court's legitimating role, see Charles L. Black, Jr., *The People and the Court* (New York: Macmillan, 1960).

26 See C. Vann Woodward, *The Strange Career of Jim Crow*, rev. ed. (New York: Oxford University Press, 1966).

27 The Eleventh Amendment overruled *Chisholm* v. *Georgia* (1793); the Fourteenth Amendment, *Dred Scott* v. *Sandford* (1857); the Sixteenth Amend-

ment, *Pollock* v. *Farmers' Loan & Trust Co.* (1895); the Twenty-fourth Amendment, which overruled *Breedlove* v. *Suttles* (1937); and the Twenty-sixth Amendment, *Oregon* v. *Mitchell* (1970).

28 Data on changes in attitudes toward descgregation are summarized in Robert Weissberg, *Public Opinion and Popular Government* (Englewood Cliffs, N.J.: Prentice-Hall, 1976), pp. 110–111; and Gerald N. Rosenberg, *The Hollow Hope* (Chicago: University of Chicago Press, 1991), pp. 125–131.

SELECTED READING

Abraham, Henry J. *Justices and Presidents: A Political History of Appointments to the Supreme Court*, 3d ed. (New York: Oxford University Press, 1992).

Baum, Lawrence. *The Supreme Court*, 5th ed. (Washington, D.C.: CQ Press, 1995).

Biskupic, Joan and Elder Witt. *Guide to the U.S. Supreme Court*, 3d ed. (Washington, D.C.: CQ Press, 1997).

Epstein, Lee and Jack Knight. *The Choices Justices Make* (Washington, D.C.: CQ Press, 1998).

———, Jeffery A. Segal, Harold J. Spaeth, and Thomas G. Walker. *The Supreme Court Compendium: Decisions and Developments* (Washington, D.C.: CQ Press, 1993).

Fisher, Louis. *Constitutional Dialogues* (Princeton, N.J.: Princeton University Press, 1988).

Fried, Charles. *Order and Law: Arguing the Reagan Revolution—A Firsthand Account* (New York: Simon & Schuster, 1991).

Gates, John B. and Charles A. Johnson, eds. The *American Courts: A Critical Assessment* (Washington, D.C.: CQ Press, 1991).

Hall, Kermit, ed. *The Oxford Companion to the Supreme Court of the United States* (New York: Oxford University Press, 1992).

Johnson, Charles A. and Bradley C. Canon. *Judicial Policies: Implementation and Impact* (Washington, D.C.: CQ Press, 1984).

Murphy, Walter F. *Elements of Judicial Strategy* (Chicago: University of Chicago Press, 1964).

O'Brien, David M. *Storm Center: The Supreme Court in American Politics*, 3d ed. (New York: W. W. Norton, 1993).

Perry, H. W., Jr. *Deciding to Decide: Agenda Setting in the United States Supreme Court* (Cambridge, Mass.: Harvard University Press, 1991).

Rehnquist, William H. *The Supreme Court: How It Was, How It Is* (New York: William Morrow and Co., 1987).

Rosenberg, Gerald N. *The Hollow Hope: Can Courts Bring About Social Change?* (Chicago: University of Chicago Press, 1991).

Segal, Jeffrey A. and Harold J. Spaeth. *The Supreme Court and the Attitudinal Model.* (Cambridge, Mass.: Cambridge University Press, 1993).

Silverstein, Mark. *Judicious Choices: The New Politics of Supreme Court Confirmations.* (New York: W. W. Norton & Co., 1994).

Stern, Robert L. and Eugene Gressman. *Supreme Court Practice*, 5th ed. (Washington, D.C.: Bureau of National Affairs, 1978).

Tarr, G. Alan. *Judicial Process and Judicial Policymaking*, 2d ed. (Belmont, Calif.: Wadsworth Publishing Co., 1998).

Witt, Elder. *Congressional Quarterly's Guide to the U. S. Supreme Court*, 2d ed. (Washington, D.C.: Congressional Quarterly, 1990).

★

RIGHTS AND THE FOUNDING

Barron v. *Baltimore* (1833)

THE FOURTEENTH AMENDMENT

DUE PROCESS AND THE BILL OF RIGHTS

Palko v. *Connecticut* (1937)
Adamson v. *California* (1947)
Duncan v. *Louisiana* (1968)

NOTES

SELECTED READING

CASES

★

3
RIGHTS UNDER THE CONSTITUTION

The constitutional guarantees for Americans' most fundamental rights—freedom of speech, the free exercise of religion, freedom from unreasonable searches and seizures, and the like—did not appear in the original Constitution. Only with the ratification of the Bill of Rights, amendments added three years after the adoption of the Constitution, were these rights given express constitutional protection. Moreover, the Bill of Rights originally provided protection only against violations of rights by the national government, leaving state governments largely free to deal with rights as they saw fit.[1] Not until the ratification of the Fourteenth Amendment in 1868 did the Constitution include substantial restrictions on state invasions of rights. And not until the second half of the twentieth century did the Supreme Court interpret that amendment as imposing on the states most of the same requirements that had previously been imposed on the national government.

This chapter analyzes these dramatic changes in the protection of rights under the Constitution. Initially, it considers why the original Constitution did not contain express guarantees of rights and how those guarantees became part of the Constitution. Next, it examines the adoption of the Fourteenth Amendment and its effects on the division of responsibility between the national and state governments for the protection of rights. Finally, it traces the U.S. Supreme Court's changing perspectives on extending constitutional protection against state violations of rights.

RIGHTS AND THE FOUNDING

The Creation and Ratification of the Constitution

The Constitution originally did not include a bill of rights because few delegates at the Constitutional Convention believed that one was needed. In fact, neither the Virginia Plan nor the New Jersey Plan, the two major plans of government introduced at the convention, contained a bill of rights. During the latter stages of the convention, the delegates added various rights guarantees to the Constitution on a piecemeal basis. Among these were restrictions on suspending the privilege of the writ of *habeas corpus* (protecting against illegal imprisonment) and bans on *ex post facto* laws (criminalizing conduct after it has already taken place) and on religious tests for federal office. But when George Mason of Virginia proposed, a week before adjournment, that a bill of rights be added to the Constitution, arguing that "[i]t would give great quiet to the people," no state supported his proposal.

This refusal to include a bill of rights in the Constitution did not stem from a hostility to rights. But having witnessed the failure of state declarations of rights to prevent violations of rights, most delegates were skeptical about the efficacy of parchment barriers." Real security for rights, they believed, came not from constitutional prohibitions, but from a well-constructed government that lacked the propensity to violate rights. The creation of such a government was the delegates' primary concern throughout the convention. Thus they believed that the Constitution already protected rights against invasion by the national government by: (1) enumerating and limiting national powers, (2) making governmental officials accountable to the people, (3) promoting the establishment of an extended republic" (see Chapter 1), in which majority factions were unlikely to form, and (4) establishing a system of separation of powers and checks and balances. These features led Alexander Hamilton to conclude in *The Federalist,* No. 84, that "the Constitution is itself, in every rational sense, and to every useful purpose, a bill of rights."[2]

Hamilton argued that the inclusion of a bill of rights was unnecessary: Because the Constitution granted only a limited legislative power to the national government, Congress did not have the power to invade rights. In fact, he suggested, inclusion of a bill of rights could be dangerous. To prohibit Congress from invading the freedom of the press or violating other rights would seem to imply that in the absence of the prohibition, Congress could do just that. So instead of limiting national power, a bill of rights would in effect expand it. In addition, Hamilton noted that no bill of rights could hope to be comprehensive. However, the failure to include a right in the bill of rights would seem to imply that Congress was not prohibited from invading that right. Thus, the inclusion of some rights would in practice make other rights less secure.

Whatever the merits of Hamilton's arguments, they did not persuade the Anti-Federalists, who opposed the ratification of the Constitution. Some Anti-Federalists argued that the Constitution itself undermined

Hamilton's argument: If a non-comprehensive list of rights was dangerous, why did the Constitution already include some rights guarantees? More generally, they emphasized the need to rein in what they viewed as a dangerously powerful national government. "Universal experience," they insisted, demonstrated "that the most express declarations and reservations are necessary to protect the just rights and liberty of mankind from the silent, powerful and ever active conspiracy of those who govern."[3] This argument proved extremely effective.[4] At the Massachusetts ratifying convention, the Federalists were forced to agree to introduce amendments as the price of ratification. Several subsequent ratifying conventions likewise submitted suggestions for amendments along with their instruments of ratification. At least some Anti-Federalists hoped through this process of amendment to undermine the powers of the national government.

The Creation of the Bill of Rights

As a member of the House of Representatives from Virginia, James Madison played the leading role in the creation of the Bill of Rights.[5] Madison prepared an initial list of amendments, largely culled from the proposals submitted by the various states, and pushed vigorously for their consideration in the face of general disinterest on the part of his fellow representatives. Madison's persistence did not stem from a conviction that the absence of a bill of rights was a major defect in the Constitution. Rather, by introducing the amendments, he sought both to quell the fears of citizens sincerely concerned about abuses of governmental power and to forestall the introduction of amendments by opponents of the Constitution that would subvert the new government. As he put it: "it is possible the abuse of the powers of the General Government may be guarded against in a more secure manner than is now done, while no one advantage arising from the exercise of that power shall be damaged or endangered by it."[6]

Madison's strategy succeeded brilliantly. Congress for the most part accepted his amendments and rejected proposals that would have crippled the national government. The states quickly ratified ten of the twelve amendments sent to them, rejecting an amendment affecting representation in the House and belatedly ratifying one regulating congressional pay increases in 1992. Ratification of the ten amendments, the Bill of Rights, reassured the populace that their rights were secure and effectively ended Anti-Federalist efforts to tamper with the Constitution.

Two aspects of the Bill of Rights are particularly noteworthy. First, Madison consciously designed the amendments to avoid the problems raised by Hamilton in *The Federalist*, No. 84. The Ninth Amendment responded to Hamilton's concern that no listing of rights could be comprehensive by noting that "[t]he enumeration in the Constitution, of certain rights, shall not be construed to deny or disparage others retained by the people." The Tenth Amendment responded to the concern that the national government might derive additional powers from the listing of rights by emphasizing that "[t]he powers not delegated to the United States by the Constitution, nor prohibited by it to the States, are reserved to the States respectively, or to the people."

Second, the Bill of Rights only placed restrictions on the national government. Concerned about abuses by factional majorities in the states, Madison had proposed an amendment securing freedom of conscience, freedom of the press, and trial by jury in criminal cases against state violation. The Senate, however, rejected his proposal. In part, the limited reach of the amendments reflected the perceived source of threats to rights—after all, the impetus for the amendments was the creation of a substantially stronger national government. It is also possible that Congress recognized that state declarations of rights already forbade state violations of rights.

When the question of applying the Bill of Rights to the states first arose in *Barron* v. *Baltimore* (1833), the U.S. Supreme Court unanimously confirmed that the Bill of Rights placed restrictions only on the national government. In reaching this conclusion, Chief Justice John Marshall looked to the constitutional text, observing that the First Amendment begins with the phrase "Congress shall make no law" and that no subsequent provision of the Bill of Rights indicates any limitation upon state action. In addition, he reasoned:

> had the framers of these amendments intended them to be limitations on the powers of the state governments, they would have imitated the framers of the original Constitution, and have expressed that intention. Had Congress engaged in the extraordinary occupation of improving the constitutions of the several states by affording the people additional protections from the exercise of power by their own governments in matters which concerned themselves alone, they would have declared this purpose in plain and intelligible language.

The adoption of the Fourteenth Amendment in 1868, however, required a reconsideration of the Court's position in *Barron*. Did that amendment impose on the states the same restrictions that the Bill of Rights had imposed on the national government? If not, what was its effect on the division of responsibility between nation and state for defining and protecting rights? It is to these questions that we now turn.

THE FOURTEENTH AMENDMENT

Constitutional historians disagree vehemently over the meaning of the Fourteenth Amendment. Some scholars argue that the amendment applies the Bill of Rights to the states, guarantees other rights against state infringement as well, and gives the national government broad authority to protect those rights.[7] Reviewing the same evidence, other scholars emphasize the attachment to federalism of the amendment's authors, depict the amendment's aims as specific rather than open-ended, and deny that these aims encompassed the application of the Bill of Rights to the states.[8] Still other scholars take a position between these two extremes.[9] Although we cannot resolve this important scholarly debate, an examination of the history and language of the Fourteenth Amendment is vital to understanding its effects on the protection of rights.

The Creation of the Fourteenth Amendment

The Fourteenth Amendment was the second of three amendments adopted after the Civil War during Reconstruction. Although the Thirteenth Amendment (adopted in 1865) had outlawed slavery, the Southern states sought to perpetuate the economic and social subordination of African Americans through the adoption of the infamous Black Codes. These Black Codes deprived African Americans of basic rights, such as the right to contract and to testify in court, subjected them to heavier penalties for violations of the law, and bound them to employers through harsh vagrancy and apprenticeship provisions. Congress responded to this Southern intransigence with the Civil Rights Act of 1866 and the Fourteenth Amendment. The Civil Rights Act guaranteed to blacks the rights "to make and enforce contracts, to inherit, purchase, lease, sell, hold, and convey real and personal property" and to enjoy the "full and equal benefit of all laws and proceedings for the security of person and property, as is enjoyed by white citizens." The constitutional basis for this enactment, however, remained questionable. Few members of Congress believed that Congress had such power to protect rights against state violation prior to the Civil War. Some concluded that the Thirteenth Amendment, which authorized Congress to enact "appropriate legislation" to enforce its provisions, provided the constitutional basis for the law. They reasoned that the amendment was designed not only to eliminate slavery but also to secure to the emancipated slaves the rights associated with their new status as free men. Others in Congress, however, doubted that the amendment conferred such broad authority, and even after Congress had repassed the law over President Andrew Johnson's veto, doubts lingered about the law's constitutionality.

The Fourteenth Amendment removed those doubts by expanding congressional authority to secure rights against state violation. An initial version of the amendment assigned Congress primary responsibility for protecting rights against state infringement. But in response to objections that such a grant of authority invaded the reserved powers of the states, Section 1 of the amendment was redrafted to ensure that initial responsibility for the protection of rights remained with the states. However, Section 1 also made clear what that responsibility entailed. States were (1) prohibited from abridging the privileges and immunities of citizens of the United States, (2) required to observe due process of law in depriving any person of life, liberty, or property, and (3) prohibited from denying equal protection of the laws to any person. If the states failed to meet their obligations under the amendment, those whose rights had been violated could sue to vindicate their rights. More importantly, Congress, under Section 5 of the amendment, could enforce the provisions of the amendment "'by appropriate legislation."

The Fourteenth Amendment was obviously designed to constitutionalize the Civil Rights Act of 1866. However, the language of the Fourteenth Amendment is considerably broader than the list of rights found in the Civil Rights Act. Did this choice of broader language mean that the amendment's framers intended to do more than merely constitutionalize the Civil Rights Act? If so, what are the privileges and immunities against state abridgement, and what constituted due process of law? Scholars and Supreme Court justices have offered a variety of answers to these questions.

Privileges and Immunities

The Framers of the Fourteenth Amendment expected that its Privileges and Immunities Clause would furnish the primary vehicle for protecting against state infringements on rights. The Privileges and Immunities Clause found in the original Constitution (Article IV, Section 2) forbids discrimination against out-of-staters. More specifically, it prohibits states from distinguishing between their citizens and those of other states in safeguarding "all Privileges and Immunities of Citizens in the several States." The Fourteenth Amendment's Privileges and Immunities Clause extends this protection by prohibiting states from distinguishing among their own citizens with regard to the privileges and immunities of citizens of the United States.

Neither the original Constitution nor the Fourteenth Amendment defines what the privileges and immunities of citizens of the United States are. Some scholars argue that they involve the rights guaranteed to all citizens, including those found in the first ten amendments.[10] In support of this conclusion, they observe first of all that both Representative John Bingham of Ohio, who proposed the amendment, and Senator Jacob Howard of Michigan, who presented the proposal to the Senate, expressly stated that the Fourteenth Amendment made the Bill of Rights applicable to the states. In addition, they note that in *Corfield* v. *Coryell* (1823), a decision quoted approvingly by several congressional proponents of the Fourteenth Amendment, Justice Bushrod Washington offered a broad interpretation of privileges and immunities as including those protections which "belong, of right, to the citizens of all free governments." Finally, they point out that members of Congress frequently complained that the slave states had denied opponents of slavery freedom of speech and other basic rights, and the Framers of the amendment referred directly to such concerns during the debates over the amendment.

Other scholars deny that the Privileges and Immunities Clause made the Bill of Rights applicable to the states.[11] They dismiss Bingham as inconsistent and confused and Howard as unrepresentative of congressional views. Instead, they point to statements by several members of Congress that the clause constitutionalized the Civil Rights Act of 1866. More generally, they stress that the amendment's proponents were strongly committed to federalism and would not have adopted a provision which would have compromised state sovereignty.

In *The Slaughterhouse Cases* (1873), the Supreme Court's first opportunity to interpret the Fourteenth Amendment, the justices gave a very narrow reading to "privileges and immunities," limiting them to such rights as access to the nation's seaports and the privilege of the writ of habeas corpus. This ruling, never overturned, in effect read the Fourteenth Amendment's Privileges and Immunities Clause out of the Constitution. In subsequent cases, therefore, debate shifted from the Privileges and Immunities Clause to the Due Process Clause and its effect on the protection of rights against state violation.

DUE PROCESS AND THE BILL OF RIGHTS

Three separate and distinct views of the the appropriate relationship between the Due Process Clause and the Bill of Rights have been advanced: the "fundamental rights" interpretation, total incorporation, and selective incorporation.

"Fundamental Rights" Interpretation

Advocates of the "fundamental rights" interpretation find no necessary relationship between the Fourteenth Amendment and the guarantees of the Bill of Rights. Rather, they understand the Fourteenth Amendment as protecting "traditional notions" of due process, which were described variously by Justice Henry Brown in *Holden* v. *Hardy* (1898) as those "certain immutable principles of justice which inhere in the very idea of free government which no member of the Union may disregard" and by Justice Benjamin Cardozo in *Palko* v. *Connecticut* (1937) as those principles "implicit in the concept of ordered liberty." As applied to criminal procedure, this interpretation requires that a state grant the defendant "that fundamental fairness essential to the very concept of justice." The Bill of Rights is regarded as a likely, but not necessarily conclusive, indicator of "fundamental fairness." As Justice John Harlan observed in *Griswold* v. *Connecticut* (1965), "The Due Process Clause of the Fourteenth Amendment stands in my opinion on its own bottom." Just as this view of due process does not impose upon the states all the requirements of the Bill of Rights, neither does it restrict the reach of the Fourteenth Amendment to only those rights enumerated in the first eight amendments. Fundamental fairness, not mere compliance with the Bill of Rights, is its touchstone. Consequently, under the "fundamental rights" interpretation a state procedure may violate due process even though its operation is not contrary to any specific guarantee in the first eight amendments.

To its critics, the "fundamental rights" interpretation fosters subjective considerations based on some murky notion of natural justice, and thereby helps to promote an *ad hoc*, personal application of the Fourteenth Amendment. In reply, supporters of this interpretation contend that its application rests on a societal consensus that can be determined quite independently of the justice's personal views, and that various "objective" factors are available to the Court as it determines whether a particular procedural right traditionally has been recognized as an essential ingredient of fairness. Justice Benjamin Curtis cited two such factors in *Murray's Lessee* v. *Hoboken Land and Improvement Company* (1856): the significance attached to the right by the Framers of the Constitution, and the importance of the right as recognized by "those settled usages and modes of proceedings existing in the common and statute law of England, before the immigration of our ancestors, and which are shown not to have been unsuited to their civil and political conditions by having been acted on by them after the settlement of this country." Other often-cited "objective" factors include the subsequent treatment of the right in state courts and legislatures and the significance attached to the right in countries with similar jurisprudential traditions. Although these factors do not provide "a mathematical calculus" for application of the Fourteenth Amendment, the argument continues, they go as far as is possible. After all, as Justice Felix Frankfurter observed,

> "Due Process", unlike some legal rules, is not a technical conception with a fixed content unrelated to time, place, and circumstances. Expressing as it does in its ultimate analysis respect enforced by law for the feeling of just treatment which has been evolved through centuries of Anglo-American constitutional history and civilization, "due process" cannot be imprisoned within the treacherous limits of any formula. Representing a profound attitude of fairness between man and man, and more particularly between the individual and the government, due process is compounded of history, reason, the past course of decisions, and stout confidence in the strength of the democratic faith which we profess. Due process is not a mechanical instrument. It is not a yardstick. It is a process.[12]

To Frankfurter and other proponents of the "fundamental rights" interpretation, judgment as to what due process requires must be made on a case-by-case basis. This interpretation, they continue, should prevail because it is the only interpretation of the Fourteenth Amendment that requires judges to engage in judgment—that activity that uniquely defines the behavior of a judge.

Total Incorporation

According to the total incorporation interpretation, the Fourteenth Amendment was intended simply and exclusively "to extend to all the people of the nation the complete protection of the Bill of Rights." Advocates of total incorporation insist that the legislative history and language of the amendment support total incorporation and that judges are bound by that clear intention of the Founders. In addition, they make the pragmatic argument that, by restricting judges to the specific language of the Bill of Rights, total incorporation avoids much of the subjectivity inherent in a "fundamental rights" approach.

Critics of total incorporation challenge these contentions. They argue that neither the legislative history nor the language of the amendment supports this view. Thus, they point out that the Due Process Clause of the Fourteenth Amendment merely restates a single provision of the Fifth Amendment of the Bill of Rights. Reflecting on this fact in *Hurtado* v. *California*, an 1884 decision in which the Court concluded that the Fourteenth Amendment's Due Process Clause did not require indictment by grand jury in state prosecutions, Justice Stanley Matthews observed:

> According to a recognized canon of interpretation, especially applicable to formal and solemn instruments of constitutional law, we are forbidden to assume, without clear reason to the contrary, that any part of . . . [the Fifth] Amendment is superfluous. The natural and obvious inference is, that in the sense of the Constitution, "due process of law" was not meant or intended to include . . . the institution and procedure of a grand jury in any case. The conclusion is equally irresistible, that when the same phrase was employed in the Fourteenth Amendment to restrain the action of the States, it was used in the same sense and with no greater extent; and that if in the adoption of that amendment it had been part of its purpose to perpetuate the institution of the grand jury in all the States, it would have embodied, as to the Fifth Amendment, express declaration to that effect.

Of course, this argument derives much of its force from the fact that proponents of total incorporation have been forced to base their arguments on the Fourteenth Amendment's Due Process Clause, given the Supreme Court's gutting of the amendment's Privileges and Immunities Clause in *The Slaughterhouse Cases*.

Opponents of total incorporation also reject the notion that it avoids subjectivity. They criticize Justice Black—total incorporation's leading judicial exponent—for merely shifting the focus of judicial inquiry from the flexible concept of fundamental fairness to equally flexible terms in the specific amendments. Such terms as "probable cause," "speedy and public trial," and "cruel and unusual punishments," they observe, are hardly self-defining and must be interpreted in light of the same contemporary notions of fairness considered in applying a "fundamental rights" standard. As Justice Harlan chided Justice Black in *Griswold*, "'Specific' provisions of the Constitution, no less than 'due process' lend themselves readily to 'personal' interpretations by judges whose constitutional outlook is simply to keep the Constitution in supposed 'tune with the times.'" Finally, critics contend that total incorporation imposes an undue burden on the states and deprives them of any opportunity to act as social and legal laboratories—to experiment with reforms designed to enhance the protections and freedom of the people.

Selective Incorporation

Selective incorporation, the third view of the appropriate relationship between the Fourteenth Amendment and the Bill of Rights, combines aspects of both the "fundamental rights" and the total incorporation interpretations. Along with the "fundamental rights" interpretation, it holds that the Fourteenth Amendment encompasses all rights, substantive and procedural, that are "of the very essence of a scheme of ordered liberty." It recognizes that not all rights enumerated in the Bill of Rights are fundamental, and that some rights may be fundamental even if not specifically guaranteed in the Bill of Rights. But in determining whether an enumerated right is fundamental, this interpretation, like the total incorporation view, focuses on the *total* right guaranteed by the individual amendment, not merely on the element of that right before the Court or the application of that right in a particular case. In other words, by deciding that a particular guarantee within the first eight amendments is fundamental, the Supreme Court incorporates that guarantee into the Fourteenth Amendment "whole and intact" and enforces it against the states in every case, according to the same standards applied to the federal government. *Duncan* v. *Louisiana* (1968), which incorporated the right to a jury trial, expressed this understanding: "Because . . . trial by jury in criminal cases is fundamental to the American scheme of justice, we hold that the Fourteenth Amendment guarantees a right of jury trial in all criminal cases which—were they to be tried in a Federal court—would come within the Sixth Amendment's guarantee."

Proponents of selective incorporation maintain that it represents an improvement over both other interpretations. They argue that a fundamental right should not be denied merely because the "totality of circumstances" in a particular case does not disclose "a denial of fundamental fairness," pointing out that judicial evaluation of the factual circumstances surrounding any particular case often is extremely subjective and discretionary. On the other hand, they continue, selective incorporation avoids the rigidity and extremism of total incorporation, under which, for example, the Seventh Amendment right of trial by jury in all suits at common law in excess of twenty dollars logically should be incorporated.

In the view of its detractors, however, selective incorporation is an unacceptable compromise that is inconsistent with the logic and historical support of either of the doctrines it attempts to combine. Those who embrace total incorporation charge that it is merely another example of "natural law due process philosophy." Proponents of "fundamental rights," on the other hand, contend that selective incorporation fails to appreciate the special burdens it imposes on the administration of criminal justice at the state level. They fear that the imposition of a single standard regulating both state and federal practice would either place an unrealistic "constitutional straight-jacket" on the states or result in a relaxing of standards as applied to both state and federal officials, in order to meet the special problems of the states.

Despite these criticisms, selective incorporation during the 1960s replaced the "fundamental rights" interpretation as the dominant view on the Court. Justice William Brennan advanced the doctrine for the first time in his dissent in *Cohen* v. *Hurley* (1961), and just two years later it had the support of at least four justices. It also was accepted by Justice Black, who, although remaining committed to total incorporation, accepted selective incorporation as a lesser evil than the "mysterious and uncertain law concepts" of the "fundamental rights" interpretation.

As Table 3.1 indicates, the Court's endorsement of selective incorporation led to the incorporation of several constitutional guarantees, including eleven dealing with criminal procedure. By 1972, only two criminal procedure guarantees—the Eighth Amendment prohibition of excessive fines and the Fifth Amendment requirement of prosecutions by grand jury indictment—had not been held to apply to the states.

Table 3.1 also reveals that even before the selective-incorporation era, the justices had begun the process of incorporation. Through this process, the Court has in piecemeal fashion achieved almost the same result as if it had endorsed the total incorporation interpretation.

State Constitutional Guarantees

Although the extension of federal protection against states' violations of rights is a relatively recent phenomenon, this does not mean that previously Americans had no protection against state infringements on rights. Rather, as proponents of the "fundamental rights" approach recognized, our federal system rested on the assumption of a rough division of labor in protecting rights. State laws and state constitutions were to serve as the primary guarantees against oppressive state governments, with the federal Constitution securing fundamental rights against state violation only when state judicial processes afforded no redress. Beginning in the mid-twentieth century, however, this balance began to shift. Defendants in state courts began looking primarily to the federal Constitution and federal judicial precedent for vindication of their rights, assuming that state constitutional guarantees either duplicated federal protections or were altogether irrelevant.

During the last 25 years, however, lawyers and scholars have rediscovered state constitutions. Motivated both by rulings of the Burger Court that narrowed rights protections and by its encouragement of reliance on state constitutional guarantees, they have begun to study state

TABLE 3.1 Incorporation of Provisions of the Bill of Rights

Right	Case and Year
First Amendment	
Freedom of speech	*Gitlow* v. *New York* (1925)
Freedom of the press	*Near* v. *Minnesota* (1931)
Freedom of assembly	*De Jonge* v. *Oregon* (1937)
Free exercise of religion	*Cantwell* v. *Connecticut* (1940)
Establishment clause	*Everson* v. *Board of Education* (1947)
Second Amendment	
Right to bear arms	Not incorporated
Third Amendment	
Freedom from quartering of troops in peacetime	Not incorporated
Fourth Amendment	
Unreasonable search and seizure	*Wolf* v. *Colorado* (1949)
Exclusionary rule	*Mapp* v. *Ohio* (1961)
Fifth Amendment	
Grand jury clause	Not incorporated
Self-incrimination clause	*Malloy* v. *Hogan* (1964)
Double jeopardy clause	*Benton* v. *Maryland* (1969)
Sixth Amendment	
Right to a public trial	*In re Oliver* (1948)
Notice clause	*Cole* v. *Arkansas* (1948)
Right to counsel	*Gideon* v. *Wainright* (1963)/ *Argersinger* v. *Hamlin* (1972)
Confrontation clause	*Pointer* v. *Texas* (1965)
Right to impartial jury	*Parker* v. *Gladden* (1966)
Right to a speedy trial	*Klopfer* v. *North Carolina* (1967)
Compulsory process clause	*Washington* v. *Texas* (1967)
Right to jury trial (criminal cases)	*Duncan* v. *Louisiana* (1968)
Seventh Amendment	
Right to jury trial (civil cases)	Not incorporated
Eighth Amendment	
Ban on cruel and unusual punishments	*Robinson* v. *California* (1962)
Ban on excessive bail	*Schilb* v. *Kuebel* (1971)
Ban on excessive fines	Not incorporated
Other	
Right to privacy	*Griswold* v. *Connecticut* (1965)

Source: The United States Department of Justice, 1998.

constitutions more closely and to fashion legal arguments based on the distinctive text and history of those state charters. Although it is unlikely that state constitutions will again become the primary guarantors of rights, this new attention to state constitutions represents a positive step toward reconciling federalism and the protection of rights.

NOTES

1 The original Constitution did impose some restrictions on state violations of rights. For example, Article IV, Section 2 mandates that "[t]he Citizens of each State shall be entitled to all Privileges and Immunities of Citizens in the several States," and Article IV, Section 4 authorizes Congress to "guarantee to every State in this Union a Republican Form of Government." In addition, it should be noted that most state constitutions contained declarations of rights, which also secured rights against state governments.

2 Some modern constitutional authorities have echoed Hamilton. In a speech in 1964, Justice John Marshall Harlan declared: "We are accustomed to speak of the Bill of Rights and the Fourteenth Amendment as the principle guarantees of personal liberty. Yet it would surely be shallow not to recognize that the structure of our political system accounts no less for the free society we have." The Framers, Justice Harlan argued, "staked their faith that liberty would prosper in the new nation not primarily upon declaration of individual rights but upon the kind of government the Union was to have." John M. Harlan, "The Bill of Rights and the Constitution," address at the dedication of the Bill of Rights Room, U.S. Subtreasury Building, New York City, August 9, 1964.

3 Richard Henry Lee to Governor Edmund Randolph, October 16, 1787.

4 Even some proponents of the Constitution—among them, Thomas Jefferson and John Adams—favored the addition of a bill of rights. As Jefferson put it, "a bill of rights is what the people are entitled to against every government on earth, general or particular, and what no government should refuse, or rest on inference." Thomas Jefferson to James Madison, December 20, 1787. Thomas Jefferson, *The Papers of Thomas Jefferson*, Julian P. Boyd, ed. (Princeton, N.J.: Princeton University Press, 1950–), vol. 12, p. 440.

5 Our analysis follows that of Herbert J. Storing, "The Constitution and the Bill of Rights," in Robert A. Goldwin and William A. Schambra, eds., *How Does the Constitution Secure Rights?* (Washington, D.C.: American Enterprise Institute, 1985).

6 *The Debates and Proceedings of the Congress of the United States* (Washington, D.C.: 1834), I, 432.

7 Scholars adopting this expansive interpretation of the Fourteenth Amendment include: Jacobus tenBroek, *The Anti-Slavery Origins of the Fourteenth Amendment* (Berkeley: University of California Press, 1951); Judith A. Baer, *Equality Under the Constitution: Reclaiming the Fourteenth Amendment* (Ithaca, N.Y.: Cornell University Press, 1983); and Michael Kent Curtis, *No State Shall Abridge: The Fourteenth Amendment and the Bill of Rights* (Durham, N.C.: Duke University Press, 1986).

8 This narrower view of the scope of the Fourteenth Amendment is presented in Charles Fairman, "Does the Fourteenth Amendment Incorporate the Bill of

Rights? The Original Understanding," *Stanford Law Review* 2 (1949): 5–138; Raoul Berger, *Government by Judiciary: The Transformation of the Fourteenth Amendment* (Cambridge, Mass.: Harvard University Press, 1977); Berger, *The Fourteenth Amendment and the Bill of Rights* (Norman: University of Oklahoma Press, 1989); and Earl M. Maltz, *Civil Rights, the Constitution, and Congress, 1863–1869* (Lawrence: University Press of Kansas, 1990).

9 See, for example, William E. Nelson, *The Fourteenth Amendment: From Political Principle to Judicial Doctrine* (Cambridge, Mass.: Harvard University Press, 1988); and Michael P. Zuckert, "Completing the Constitution: The Fourteenth Amendment and Constitutional Rights," *Publius: The Journal of Federalism* 22 (1992): 69–91.

10 See, for example, Curtis, *No State Shall Abridge*; and Baer, *Equality Under the Constitution.*

11 See, for example, Berger, *The Fourteenth Amendment and the Bill of Rights*; and Fairman, "Does the Fourteenth Amendment Incorporate the Bill of Rights?"

12 *Joint Anti-Fascist Refugee Committee* v. *McGrath* (1951).

SELECTED READING

The Federalist, No. 84.

Hurtado v. *California*, 110 U.S. 516 (1884).
Rochin v. *California*, 342 U.S. 165 (1952).
The Slaughterhouse Cases, Volume I, Chapter 12.
Williams v. *Florida*, 399 U.S. 78 (1970).

Amar, Akhil Reed. "The Bill of Rights as a Constitution." *Yale Law Journal* 100 (1991): 1131–1210.

Anastaplo, George, *The Amendments to the Constitution: A Commentary* (Baltimore: Johns Hopkins Press, 1995).

Baer, Judith A. *Equality Under the Constitution: Reclaiming the Fourteenth Amendment* (Ithaca, N.Y.: Cornell University Press, 1983).

Barnett, Randy E., ed. *History and Meaning of the Ninth Amendment* (Fairfax, Va.: George Mason University Press, 1989).

Berger, Raoul. *The Fourteenth Amendment and the Bill of Rights* (Norman: University of Oklahoma Press, 1989).

Curtis, Michael Kent. *No State Shall Abridge: The Fourteenth Amendment and the Bill of Rights* (Durham, N.C.: Duke University Press, 1986).

Goldwin, Robert A. *From Parchment to Power: How James Madison Used the Bill of Rights to Save the Constitution* (Washington, D.C.: American Enterprise Institute, 1997).

Goldwin, Robert A. and William A. Schambra, eds. *How Does the Constitution Secure Rights?* (Washington, D.C.: American Enterprise Institute, 1985).

Hickok, Eugene, ed. *The Bill of Rights: Original Meaning and Current Understanding* (Charlottesville: University Press of Virginia, 1991).

Katz, Ellis and G. Alan Tarr, eds. *Federalism and Rights* (Lanham, Md.: Rowman & Littlefield, 1996).

Lutz, Donald S. "The State Constitutional Pedigree of the U.S. Bill of Rights." *Publius: The Journal of Federalism* 22 (1992): 19–45.

Maltz, Earl M. *Civil Rights, the Constitution, and Congress: 1863–1869* (Lawrence: University Press of Kansas, 1990).

Nelson, William E. *The Fourteenth Amendment: From Political Principle to Judicial Doctrine* (Cambridge, Mass.: Harvard University Press, 1988).

Rossum, Ralph A. "*The Federalist's* Understanding of the Constitution as a Bill of Rights," in *Saving the Revolution: The Federalist Papers and the American Founding,* ed. Charles R. Kesler (New York: Free Press, 1987): 219–233.

Schwartz, Bernard. *The Great Rights of Mankind: A History of the American Bill of Rights* (expanded ed.) (Madison, Wisc.: Madison House, 1992).

Veit, Helen E., Kenneth R. Bowling, and Charles Bangs Bickford. *Creating the Bill of Rights: The Documentary Record from the First Federal Congress* (Baltimore: Johns Hopkins University Press, 1991).

Zuckert, Michael P. "Completing the Constitution: The Fourteenth Amendment and Constitutional Rights." *Publius: The Journal of Federalism* 22 (1992): 69–91.

Barron v. Baltimore

32 U.S. (7 Peters) 243; 8 L. Ed. 672 (1833)

In grading and paving its streets, the city of Baltimore redirected the course of several streams flowing into its harbor. As a result, deposits of sand and gravel built up near John Barron's wharf, which was rendered inaccessible to ships. This seriously diminished the wharf's commercial value, and Barron brought suit in county court against the city, alleging a violation of the Fifth Amendment clause that forbids taking private property for public use without just compensation. The county court awarded Barron $4,500 in damages, but the Maryland Court of Appeals for the Western Shore reversed that decision. Barron appealed, and the case was brought before the United States Supreme Court on a writ of error. *Opinion of the Court:* <u>Marshall</u>, *Baldwin, Duvall, Johnson, McLean, Story, Thompson.*

MR. CHIEF JUSTICE MARSHALL delivered the opinion of the Court. . . .

The question thus presented is, we think, of great importance, but not of much difficulty.

The constitution was ordained and established by the people of the United States for themselves, for their own government, and not for the government of the individual states. Each state established a constitution for itself, and, in that constitution, provided such limitations and restrictions on the powers of its particular government as its judgment dictated. The people of the United States framed such a government for the United States as they supposed best adapted to their situation, and best calculated to promote their interests. The powers they conferred on this government were to be exercised by itself; and the limitations on power, if expressed in general terms, are naturally, and, we think, necessarily applicable to the government created by the instrument. They are limitations of power granted in the instrument itself; not of distinct governments, framed by different persons and for different purposes.

If these propositions be correct, the fifth amendment must be understood as restraining the power of the general government, not as applicable to the states. In their several constitutions they have imposed such restrictions on their respective governments as their own wisdom suggested; such as they deemed most proper for themselves. It is a subject on which they judge exclusively, and with which others interfere no farther than they are supposed to have a common interest.

Had the people of the several states, or any of them, required changes in their constitutions; had they required additional safeguards to liberty from the apprehended encroachments of their particular governments: the remedy was in their own hands, and would have been applied by themselves. A convention would have been assembled by the discontented state, and the required improvements would have been made by itself. The unwieldly and cumbrous machinery of procuring a recommendation from two-thirds of congress, and the assent of three-fourths of their sister states, could never have occurred to any human being as a mode of doing that which might be effected by the state itself. Had the framers of these amendments intended them to be limitations on the powers of the state governments, they would have imitated the framers of the original constitution, and have expressed that intention. Had congress engaged in the extraordinary occupation of improving the constitutions of the several states by affording the people additional protection from the exercise of power by their own governments in matters which concerned themselves alone, they would have declared this purpose in plain and intelligible language.

But it is universally understood, it is a part of the history of the day, that the great revolution which established the constitution of the United States, was not effected without immense opposition. Serious fears were extensively entertained that those powers which the patriot statesmen, who then watched over the interests of our country, deemed essential to union, and to the attainment of those invaluable objects for which union was sought, might be exercised in a manner dangerous to liberty. In almost every convention by which the constitution was adopted, amendments to guard against the abuse of power were recommended. These amendments demanded security against the apprehended encroachments of the general government—not against those of the local governments.

In compliance with a sentiment thus generally expressed to quiet fears thus extensively entertained, amendments were proposed by the required majority in congress, and adopted by the states. These amendments contain no expression indicating an intention to apply them to the state governments. This court cannot so apply them.

We are of the opinion that the provision in the fifth amendment to the constitution, declaring that private property shall not be taken for public use without just compensation, is intended solely as a limitation on the exercise of power by the government of the United States, and is not applicable to the legislation of the states. . . .

Palko v. *Connecticut*
302 U.S. 319; 58 S. Ct. 149; 82 L. Ed. 288 (1937)

Frank Palko was indicted for the crime of first-degree murder. A jury found him guilty of second-degree murder, and he was sentenced to life imprisonment. Thereafter, the state of Connecticut, with the permission of the trial judge, appealed to the Connecticut Supreme Court of Errors under a statute that permitted appeals from the rulings and decisions of the trial court "upon all questions of law arising on the trial of criminal cases . . . in the same manner and to the same effect as if made by the accused." The Supreme Court of Errors set aside the trial court's judgment and ordered a new trial, at which Palko was found guilty of first-degree murder and sentenced to death. The conviction was affirmed by the Supreme Court of Errors, and the case was appealed to the United States Supreme Court. Palko contended that the Connecticut statute was unconstitutional in that the Due Process Clause of the Fourteenth Amendment protected individuals from being tried twice for the same offense. *Opinion of the Court: Cardozo, Black, Brandeis, Hughes, McReynolds, Roberts, Stone, Sutherland. Dissent: Butler.*

MR. JUSTICE CARDOZO delivered the opinion of the Court. . . .

The argument for appellant is that whatever is forbidden by the Fifth Amendment is forbidden by the Fourteenth also. The Fifth Amendment, which is not directed to the states, but solely to the federal government, creates immunity from double jeopardy. No person shall be "subject for the same offense to be twice put in jeopardy of life or limb." The Fourteenth Amendment ordains, "nor shall any State deprive any person of life, liberty, or property, without due process of law." To retry a defendant, though under one indictment and only one, subjects him, it is said, to double jeopardy in violation of the Fifth Amendment, if the prosecution is one on behalf of the United States. From this the consequence is said to follow that there is a denial of life or liberty without due process of law, if the prosecution is one on behalf of the People of a State. . . .

We have said that in appellant's view the Fourteenth Amendment is to be taken as embodying the prohibitions of the Fifth. His thesis is even broader. Whatever would be a violation of the original bill of rights (Amendments I to VIII) if done by the federal government is now equally unlawful by force of the Fourteenth Amendment if done by a state. There is no such general rule.

The Fifth Amendment provides, among other things, that no person shall be held to answer for a capital or otherwise infamous crime unless on presentment or indictment of a grand jury. This court has held that, in prosecutions by a state, presentment or indictment by a grand jury may give way to informations at the instance of a public officer. . . . The Fifth Amendment provides also that no person shall be compelled in any criminal case to be a witness against himself. This court has said that, in prosecutions by a state the exemption will fail if the state elects to end it. . . . The Sixth Amendment calls for a jury trial in criminal cases and the Seventh for a jury trial in civil cases at common law where the value in controversy shall exceed twenty dollars. This court has ruled that consistently with those amendments trial by jury may be modified by a state or abolished altogether. . . .

On the other hand, the due process clause of the Fourteenth Amendment may make it unlawful for a state to abridge by its statutes the freedom of speech which the First Amendment safeguards against encroachment by the Congress, . . . or the like freedom of the press, . . . or the free exercise of religion, . . . or the right of peaceable assembly without which speech would be unduly trammeled, . . . or the right of one accused of crime to the benefit of counsel. . . . In these and other situations immunities that are valid as against the federal government by force of the specific pledges of particular amendments have been found to be implicit in the concept of ordered liberty, and thus, through the Fourteenth Amendment, become valid as against the states.

The line of division may seem to be wavering and broken if there is a hasty catalogue of the cases on the one side and the other. Reflection and analysis will induce a different view. There emerges the perception of a rationalizing principle which gives to discrete instances a proper order and coherence. The right to trial by jury and the immunity from prosecution except as the result of an indictment may have value and importance. Even so, they are not of the very essence of a scheme of ordered liberty. To abolish them is

not to violate "a principle of justice so rooted in the traditions and conscience of our people as to be ranked as fundamental." . . . Few would be so narrow or provincial as to maintain that a fair and enlightened system of justice would be impossible without them. What is true of jury trials and indictments is true also, as the cases show, of the immunity from compulsory self-incrimination . . . . This too might be lost, and justice still be done. Indeed, today as in the past there are students of our penal system who look upon the immunity as a mischief rather than a benefit, and who would limit its scope, or destroy it altogether. No doubt there would remain the need to give protection against torture, physical or mental. . . . Justice, however, would not perish if the accused were subject to a duty to respond to orderly inquiry. The exclusion of these immunities and privileges from the privileges and immunities protected against the action of the states has not been arbitrary or casual. It has been dictated by a study and appreciation of the meaning, the essential implications, of liberty itself.

We reach a different plane of social and moral values when we pass to the privileges and immunities that have been taken over from the earlier articles of the federal bill of rights and brought within the Fourteenth Amendment by a process of absorption. These in their origin were effective against the federal government alone. If the Fourteenth Amendment has absorbed them, the process of absorption has had its source in the belief that neither liberty nor justice would exist if they were sacrificed. . . . This is true, for illustration, of freedom of thought, and speech. Of that freedom one may say that it is the matrix, the indispensable condition, of nearly every other form of freedom. With rare aberrations a pervasive recognition of that truth can be traced in our history, political and legal. So it has come about that the domain of liberty, withdrawn by the Fourteenth Amendment from encroachment by the states, has been enlarged by latter-day judgments to include liberty of the mind as well as liberty of action. The extension became, indeed, a logical imperative when once it was recognized, as long ago it was, that liberty is something more than exemption from physical restraint, and that even in the field of substantive rights and duties the legislative judgment, if oppressive and arbitrary, may be overridden by the courts. . . . Fundamental too in the concept of due process, and so in that of liberty, is the thought that condemnation shall be rendered only after trial. . . . The hearing, moreover, must be a real one, not a sham or a pretense. . . . For that reason, ignorant defendants in a capital case were held to have been condemned unlawfully when in truth, though not in form, they were refused the aid of counsel. . . . The decision did not turn upon the fact that the benefit of counsel would have been guaranteed to the defendants by the provisions of the Sixth Amendment if they had been prosecuted in a federal court. The decision turned upon the fact that in the particular situation laid before us in the evidence the benefit of counsel was essential to the substance of a hearing.

. . . On which side of the line the case made out by the appellant has appropriate location must be the next inquiry and the final one. Is that kind of double jeopardy to which the statute has subjected him a hardship so acute and shocking that our polity will not endure it? Does it violate those "fundamental principles of liberty and justice which lie at the base of all our civil and political institutions"? . . . The answer surely must be "no." What the answer would have to be if the state were permitted after a trial free from error to try the accused over again or to bring another case against him, we have no occasion to consider. We deal with the statute before us and no other. The state is not attempting to wear the accused out by a multitude of cases with accumulated trials. It asks no more than this, that the case against him shall go on until there shall be a trial free from the corrosion of substantial legal error. . . . This is not cruelty at all, nor even vexation in any immoderate degree. If the trial had been infected with error adverse to the accused, there might have been review at his instance, and as often as necessary to purge the vicious taint. A reciprocal privilege, subject at all times to the discretion of the presiding judge, . . . has now been granted to the state. There is here no seismic innovation. The edifice of justice stands, its symmetry, to many, greater than before. . . .

Adamson v. *California*
332 U.S. 46; 67 S. Ct. 1672; 91 L. Ed. 1903 (1947)

The Constitution and penal code of California permitted the trial judge and prosecuting attorneys to comment adversely upon, and juries to consider as evidence of guilt, a defendant's failure to testify on his own behalf. Admiral Dewey Adamson had declined to testify at his trial for first-degree murder. In the presentation of the case to the jury, the prosecuting attorneys argued that Adamson's refusal to testify was an indication of his guilt. He was convicted and sentenced to death. His conviction was affirmed by the state supreme court and appealed to the United States Supreme Court. *Opinion of the Court: Reed, Burton, Frankfurter, Jackson, Vinson. Concurring opinion: Frankfurter. Dissenting opinions: Black, Douglas; Murphy, Rutledge.*

MR. JUSTICE REED delivered the opinion of the Court.

. . . Appellant urges that the provision of the Fifth Amendment that no person "shall be compelled in any criminal case to be a witness against himself" is a fundamental national privilege or immunity protected against state abridgment by the Fourteenth Amendment or a privilege or immunity secured, through the Fourteenth Amendment, against deprivation by state action because it is a personal right, enumerated in the federal Bill of Rights. . . .

It is settled law that the clause of the Fifth Amendment, protecting a person against being compelled to be a witness against himself, is not made effective by the Fourteenth Amendment as a protection against state action on the ground that freedom from testimonial compulsion is a right of national citizenship, or because it is a personal privilege or immunity secured by the Federal Constitution as one of the rights of man that are listed in the Bill of Rights.

The reasoning that leads to those conclusions starts with the unquestioned premise that the Bill of Rights, when adopted, was for the protection of the individual against the federal government and its provisions were inapplicable to similar actions done by the states. . . . With the adoption of the Fourteenth Amendment, it was suggested that the dual citizenship recognized by its first sentence secured for citizens federal protection for their elemental privileges and immunities of state citizenship. The *Slaughter-House Cases* decided, contrary to the suggestion, that these rights, as privileges and immunities of state citizenship, remained under the sole protection of the state governments. This Court, without the expression of a contrary view upon that phase of the issues before the Court, has approved this determination. . . . This leaves a state free to abridge, within the limits of the due process clause, the privileges and immunities flowing from state citizenship. This reading of the Federal Constitution has heretofore found favor with the majority of this Court as a natural and logical interpretation. It accords with the constitutional doctrine of federalism by leaving to the states the responsibility of dealing with the privileges and immunities of their citizens except those inherent in national citizenship. It is the construction placed upon the amendment by justices whose own experience had given them contemporaneous knowledge of the purposes that led to the adoption of the Fourteenth Amendment. This construction has become embedded in our federal system as a functioning element in preserving the balance between national and state power. We reaffirm the conclusion . . . that protection against self-incrimination is not a privilege or immunity of national citizenship. . . .

MR. JUSTICE FRANKFURTER, concurring. . . .

The short answer to the suggestion that the provision of the Fourteenth Amendment, which ordains "nor shall any State deprive any person of life, liberty, or property, without due process of law," was a way of saying that every State must thereafter initiate prosecutions through indictment by a grand jury, must have trial by such a jury of twelve in criminal cases, and must have trial by such a jury in common law suits where the amount in controversy exceeds twenty dollars, is that it is a strange way of saying it. It would be extraordinarily strange for a Constitution to convey such specific commands in such a roundabout and inexplicit way. . . . Those reading the English language with the meaning which it ordinarily conveys, those conversant with the political and legal history of the concept of due process, those sensitive to the relations of the States to the central government as well as the relation of some of the provisions of the Bill of Rights to the process of justice, would hardly recognize the Fourteenth Amendment as a cover for the various explicit provisions of the first eight Amendments. Some of these are enduring reflections of experience with human nature, while some express the restricted views of Eighteenth-Century England regarding the best methods for the ascertainment of facts. . . .

It may not be amiss to restate the pervasive function of the Fourteenth Amendment in exacting from the States observance of basic liberties. . . . The Amendment neither comprehends the specific provisions by which the founders deemed it appropriate to restrict the Federal Government nor is it confined to them. The Due Process Clause of the Fourteenth Amendment has an independent potency, precisely as does the Due Process Clause of the Fifth Amendment in relation to the Federal Government. It ought not to require argument to reject the notion that due process of law meant one thing in the Fifth Amendment and another in the Fourteenth. The Fifth Amendment specifically prohibits prosecution of an "infamous crime" except upon indictment; it forbids double jeopardy; it bars compelling a person to be a witness against himself in any criminal case; it precludes deprivation of "life, liberty, or property, without due process of law. . . ." Are Madison and his contemporaries in the framing of the Bill of Rights to be charged with writing into it a meaningless clause? To consider "due process of law" as merely a shorthand statement of other specific clauses in the same amendment is to attribute to the authors and proponents of this Amendment ignorance of, or indifference to, a historic conception which was one of the great instruments in the arsenal of constitutional freedom which the Bill of Rights was to protect and strengthen. . . .

. . . The relevant question is whether the criminal proceedings which resulted in conviction deprived the accused of the due process of law to which the United States Constitution entitled him. Judicial review of that guaranty of the Fourteenth Amendment inescapably imposes upon this Court an exercise of judgment upon the whole course of the proceedings in order to ascertain whether they offend those canons of decency and fairness which express the notions of justice of English-speaking peoples even toward those charged with the most heinous offenses. These standards of justice are not authoritatively formulated anywhere as though as they were prescriptions in a pharmacopoeia. But neither does the application of the Due Process Clause imply that judges are wholly at large. The judicial judgment in applying the Due Process Clause must move within the limits of accepted notions of justice and is not to be based upon the idiosyncrasies of a merely personal judgment. The fact that judges among themselves may differ whether in a particular case a trial offends accepted notions of justice is not disproof that general rather than idiosyncratic standards are applied. An important safeguard against such merely individual judgment is an alert deference to the judgment of the State court under review.

MR. JUSTICE BLACK, dissenting. . . .

This decision reasserts a constitutional theory spelled out in *Twining* v. *New Jersey* [1908], that this Court is endowed by the Constitution with boundless power under "natural law" periodically to expand and contract constitutional standards to conform to the Court's conception of what at a particular time constitutes "civilized decency" and "fundamental liberty and justice." Invoking this *Twining* rule, the Court concludes that although comment upon testimony in a federal court would violate the Fifth Amendment, identical comment in a state court does not violate today's fashion in civilized decency and fundamentals and is therefore not prohibited by the Federal Constitution as amended. . . .

. . . I would not reaffirm the *Twining* decision. I think that decision and the "natural law" the-

ory of the Constitution upon which it relies degrade the constitutional safeguards of the Bill of Rights and simultaneously appropriate for this Court a broad power which we are not authorized by the Constitution to exercise. . . . My reasons for believing that the *Twining* decision should not be revitalized can best be understood by reference to the constitutional, judicial, and general history that preceded and followed the case. That reference must be abbreviated far more than is justified but for the necessary limitations of opinion-writing. . . .

My study of the historical events that culminated in the Fourteenth Amendment, and the expressions of those who sponsored and favored, as well as those who opposed its submission and passage, persuades me that one of the chief objects that the provisions of the Amendment's first section, separately, and as a whole, were intended to accomplish was to make the Bill of Rights, applicable to the states.

. . . I am attaching to this dissent an appendix which contains a résumé, by no means complete, of the Amendment's history. In my judgment that history conclusively demonstrates that the language of the first section of the Fourteenth Amendment, taken as a whole, was thought by those responsible for its submission to the people, and by those who opposed its submission, sufficiently explicit to guarantee that thereafter no state could deprive its citizens of the privileges and protections of the Bill of Rights. . . .

. . . I further contend that the "natural law" formula which the Court uses to reach its conclusion in this case should be abandoned as an incongruous excrescence on our Constitution. I believe that formula to be itself a violation of our Constitution, in that it subtly conveys to courts, at the expense of legislatures, ultimate power over public policies in fields where no specific provision of the Constitution limits legislative power. . . .

It is an illusory apprehension that literal application of some or of all the provisions of the Bill of Rights to the States would unwisely increase the sum total of the powers of this Court to invalidate state legislation. The Federal Government has not been harmfully burdened by the requirement that enforcement of federal laws affecting civil liberty conform literally to the Bill of Rights. Who would advocate its repeal? It must be conceded, of course, that the natural-law-due-process formula, which the Court today reaffirms, has been interpreted to limit substantially this Court's power to prevent state violations of the individual civil liberties guaranteed by the Bill of Rights. But this formula also has been used in the past, and can be used in the future, to license this Court, in considering regulatory legislation, to roam at large in the broad expanses of policy and morals and to trespass, all too freely, on the legislative domain of the states as well as the Federal Government. . . .

MR. JUSTICE MURPHY, with whom MR. JUSTICE RUTLEDGE concurs, dissenting.

While in substantial agreement with the views of MR. JUSTICE BLACK, I have one reservation and one addition to make. . . .

I agree that the specific guarantees of the Bill of Rights should be carried over intact into the first section of the Fourteenth Amendment. But I am not prepared to say that the latter is entirely and necessarily limited by the Bill of Rights. Occasions may arise where a proceeding falls so far short of conforming to fundamental standards of procedure as to warrant constitutional condemnation in terms of a lack of due process despite the absence of a specific provision in the Bill of Rights. . . .

Duncan v. *Louisiana*

391 U.S. 145; 88 S. Ct. 1444; 20 L. Ed. 2d 491 (1968)

Gary Duncan, a black, was convicted in a Louisiana court of simple battery for slapping a white person on the elbow. Under state law, the maximum sentence for this misdemeanor was two years imprisonment and a $300 fine. During his court proceedings, Duncan requested a jury trial, but the judge denied his request, noting that the state constitution permitted jury trials only in instances in which hard labor or capital punishment might be imposed. Sentenced to sixty days in prison and a fine of $150, Duncan unsuccessfully petitioned the Louisiana Supreme Court for review, and then he appealed to the United States Supreme Court. He contended that the Sixth and Fourteenth amendments guaranteed the right to a jury trial in state prosecutions for crimes punishable by two years imprisonment or more. *Opinion of the Court:* <u>White</u>, *Black, Brennan, Douglas, Fortas, White, Marshall. Concurring opinions:* <u>Black</u>, *Douglas;* <u>Fortas</u>. *Dissenting opinion:* <u>Harlan</u>, *Stewart.*

MR. JUSTICE WHITE delivered the opinion of the Court. . . .

The test for determining whether a right extended by the Fifth and Sixth Amendments with respect to federal criminal proceedings is also protected against state action by the Fourteenth Amendment has been phrased in a variety of ways in the opinions of this Court. The question has been asked whether a right is among those "'fundamental principles of liberty and justice which lie at the base of all our civil and political institutions,'" . . . whether it is "basic in our system of jurisprudence," . . . and whether it is "a fundamental right, essential to a fair trial." . . .

The claim before us is that the right to trial by jury guaranteed by the Sixth Amendment meets these tests. The position of Louisiana, on the other hand, is that the Constitution imposes upon the States no duty to give a jury trial in any criminal case, regardless of the seriousness of the crime or the size of the punishment which may be imposed. Because we believe that trial by jury in criminal cases is fundamental to the American scheme of justice, we hold that the Fourteenth Amendment guarantees a right of jury trial in all criminal cases which—were they to be tried in a federal court—would come within the Sixth Amendment's guarantee. Since we consider the appeal before us to be such a case, we hold that the Constitution was violated when appellant's demand for jury trial was refused. . . .

The guarantees of jury trial in the Federal and State Constitutions reflect a profound judgment about the way in which law should be enforced and justice administered. A right to jury trial is granted to criminal defendants in order to prevent oppression by the Government. Those who wrote our constitutions knew from history and experience that it was necessary to protect against unfounded criminal charges brought to eliminate enemies and against judges too responsive to the voice of higher authority. The framers of the constitutions strove to create an independent judiciary but insisted upon further protection against arbitrary action. Providing an accused with the right to be tried by a jury of his peers gave him an inestimable safeguard against the corrupt or overzealous prosecutor and against the compliant, biased, or eccentric judge. If the defendant preferred the common-sense judgment of a jury to the more tutored but perhaps less sympathetic reaction of the single judge, he was to have it. Beyond this, the jury trial provisions in the Federal and State Constitutions reflect a fundamental decision about the exercise of official power—a reluctance to entrust plenary powers over the life and liberty of the citizen to one judge or to a group of judges. Fear of unchecked power, so typical of our State and Federal Governments in other respects, found expression in the criminal law in this insistence upon community participation in the determination of guilt or innocence. The deep commitment of the Nation to the right of jury trial in serious criminal cases as a defense against arbitrary law enforcement qualifies for protection under the Due Process Clause of the Fourteenth Amendment, and must therefore be respected by the States.

Louisiana's final contention is that even if it must grant jury trials in serious criminal cases, the conviction before us is valid and constitutional because here the petitioner was tried for simple battery and was sentenced to only 60 days in the parish prison. We are not persuaded. It is doubtless true that there is a category of petty crimes or offenses which is not subject to the Sixth Amendment jury trial provision and should not be subject to the Fourteenth Amend-

ment jury trial requirement here applied to the States. Crimes carrying possible penalties up to six months do not require a jury trial if they otherwise qualify as petty offenses. . . . But the penalty authorized for a particular crime is of major relevance in determining whether it is serious or not and may in itself, if severe enough, subject the trial to the mandates of the Sixth Amendment. . . . The penalty authorized by the law of the locality may be taken "as a gauge of its social and ethical judgments" . . . of the crime in question. . . . In the case before us the Legislature of Louisiana has made simple battery a criminal offense punishable by imprisonment for up to two years and a fine. The question, then, is whether a crime carrying such a penalty is an offense which Louisiana may insist on trying without a jury.

We think not. . . . Of course the boundaries of the petty offense category have always been ill-defined, if not ambulatory. In the absence of an explicit constitutional provision, the definitional task necessarily falls on the courts, which must either pass upon the validity of legislative attempts to identify those petty offenses which are exempt from jury trial or, where the legislature has not addressed itself to the problem, themselves face the question in the first instance. In either case it is necessary to draw a line in the spectrum of crime, separating petty from serious infractions. This process, although essential, cannot be wholly satisfactory, for it requires attaching different consequences to events which, when they lie near the line, actually differ very little.

. . . In the federal system, petty offenses are defined as those punishable by no more than six months in prison and a $500 fine. In 49 of the 50 States crimes subject to trial without a jury, which occasionally include simple battery, are punishable by not more than one year in jail. Moreover, in the late 18th century in America crimes triable without a jury were for the most part punishable by no more than a six-month prison term, although there appear to have been exceptions to this rule. We need not, however, settle in this case the exact location of the line between petty offenses and serious crimes. It is sufficient for our purposes to hold that a crime punishable by two years in prison is, based on past and contemporary standards in this country, a serious crime and not a petty offense. Consequently, appellant was entitled to a jury trial and it was error to deny it.

MR. JUSTICE BLACK, with whom MR. JUSTICE DOUGLAS joins, concurring. . . .

In closing I want to emphasize that I believe as strongly as ever that the Fourteenth Amendment was intended to make the Bill of Rights applicable to the States. I have been willing to support the selective incorporation doctrine, however, as an alternative, although perhaps less historically supportable than complete incorporation. The selective incorporation process, if used properly, does limit the Supreme Court in the Fourteenth Amendment field to specific Bill of Rights' protections only and keeps judges from roaming at will in their own notions of what policies outside the Bill of Rights are desirable and what are not. And, most importantly for me, the selective incorporation process has the virtue of having already worked to make most of the Bill of Rights' protections applicable to the States.

MR. JUSTICE HARLAN, whom MR. JUSTICE STEWART joins, dissenting.

Every American jurisdiction provides for trial by jury in criminal cases. The question before us is not whether jury trial is an ancient institution, which it is; nor whether it plays a significant role in the administration of criminal justice, which it does; nor whether it will endure, which it shall. The question in this case is whether the State of Louisiana, which provides trial by jury for all felonies, is prohibited by the Constitution from trying charges of simple battery to the court alone. In my view, the answer to that question, mandated alike by our constitutional history and by the longer history of trial by jury, is clearly "no." . . .

The Court's approach to this case is an uneasy and illogical compromise among the views of various Justices on how the Due Process Clause should be interpreted. The Court does not say that those who framed the Fourteenth Amendment intended to make the Sixth Amendment applicable to the States. And the Court concedes that it finds nothing unfair about the procedure by which the present appellant was tried. Nevertheless, the Court reverses his conviction: it holds, for some reason not apparent to me, that the Due Process Clause incorporates the particular clause of the Sixth Amendment that requires trial by jury in federal criminal cases—including, as I read its opinion, the sometimes trivial accompanying baggage of judicial interpretation in federal contexts. . . .

A few members of the Court have taken the position that the intention of those who drafted the first section of the Fourteenth Amendment was simply, and exclusively, to make the provisions of the first eight Amendments applicable to state action. . . . Neither history, nor sense, supports using the Fourteenth Amendment to put the States in a constitutional straitjacket with respect to their own development in the administration of criminal or civil law.

Although I therefore fundamentally disagree with the total incorporation view of the Fourteenth Amendment, it seems to me that such a position does at least have the virtue, lacking in the Court's selective incorporation approach, of internal consistency: we look to the Bill of Rights, word for word, clause for clause, precedent for precedent because, it is said, the men who wrote the Amendment wanted it that way. . . .

Apart from the approach taken by the absolute incorporationists, I can see only one method of analysis that has any internal logic. That is to start with the words "liberty" and "due process of law" and attempt to define them in a way that accords with American traditions and our system of government. This approach, involving a much more discriminating process of adjudication than does "incorporation," is, albeit difficult, the one that was followed throughout the 19th and most of the present century. It entails a "gradual process of judicial inclusion and exclusion," seeking, with due recognition of constitutional tolerance for state experimentation and disparity, to ascertain those "immutable principles . . . of free government which no member of the Union may disregard." . . .

The relationship of the Bill of Rights to this "gradual process" seems to me to be twofold. In the first place it has long been clear that the Due Process Clause imposes some restrictions on state action that parallel Bill of Rights restrictions on federal action. Second, and more important than this accidental overlap, is the fact that the Bill of Rights is evidence, at various points, of the content Americans find in the term "liberty" and of American standards of fundamental fairness. . . .

Today's Court still remains unwilling to accept the total incorporationists' view of the history of the Fourteenth Amendment. This, if accepted, would afford a cogent reason for applying the Sixth Amendment to the States. The Court is also, apparently, unwilling to face the task of determining whether denial of trial by jury in the situation before us, or in other situations, is fundamentally unfair. Consequently, the Court has compromised on the case of the incorporationist position, without its internal logic. It has simply assumed that the question before us is whether the Jury Trial Clause of the Sixth Amendment should be incorporated into the Fourteenth, jot-for-jot and case-for-case, or ignored. Then the Court merely declares that the clause in question is "in" rather than "out." . . .

Since, as I see it, the Court has not even come to grips with the issues in this case, it is necessary to start from the beginning. When a criminal defendant contends that his state conviction lacked "due process of law," the question before this Court, in my view, is whether he was denied any element of fundamental procedural fairness. . . .

The argument that jury trial is not a requisite of due process is quite simple. The central proposition . . . is that "due process of law" requires only that criminal trials be fundamentally fair. As stated above, apart from the theory that it was historically intended as a mere shorthand for the Bill of Rights, I do not see what else "due process of law" can intelligibly be thought to mean. If due process of law requires only fundamental fairness, then the inquiry in each case must be whether a state trial process was a fair one. The Court has held, properly I think, that in an adversary process it is a requisite of fairness, for which there is no adequate substitute, that a criminal defendant be afforded a right to counsel and to cross-examine opposing witnesses. But it simply has not been demonstrated, nor, I think, can it be demonstrated, that trial by jury is the only fair means of resolving issues of fact. . . .

. . . There is a wide range of views on the desirability of trial by jury, and on the ways to make it most effective when it is used; there is also considerable variation from State to State in local conditions such as the size of the criminal caseload, the ease or difficulty of summoning jurors, and other trial conditions bearing on fairness. We have before us, therefore, an almost perfect example of a situation in which the celebrated dictum of Mr. Justice Brandeis should be invoked. It is, he said, "one of the happy incidents of the federal system that a single courageous State may, if its citizens choose, serve as a laboratory. . . ." [*New State Ice Co.* v. *Liebmann* . . . (dissenting opinion). This Court, other courts, and the political process are available to correct any experiments in criminal procedure that prove fundamentally unfair to defendants. That is not what is being done today: instead, and quite without reason, the Court has chosen to impose upon every State one means of trying criminal cases; it is a good means, but it is not the only fair means, and it is not demonstrably better than the alternatives States might devise.

★

THE FOURTEENTH AMENDMENT

THE EVISCERATION OF THE PRIVILEGES OR IMMUNITIES CLAUSE

The Slaughterhouse Cases (1873)

ECONOMIC REGULATION AND THE RISE OF SUBSTANTIVE DUE PROCESS

Munn v. Illinois (1877)
Lochner v. New York (1905)

THE REPUDIATION OF SUBSTANTIVE DUE PROCESS

West Coast Hotel Company v. Parrish (1937)
Williamson v. Lee Optical Company (1955)
BMW of North America, Inc. v. Gore (1996)
United States v. Carolene Products Company (1938)

THE TAKINGS CLAUSE

Hawaii Housing Authority v. Midkiff (1984)
Nollan v. California Coastal Commission (1987)
Lucas v. South Carolina Coastal Council (1992)
Dolan v. City of Tigard (1994)

NOTES

SELECTED READING

CASES

★

4

ECONOMIC DUE
PROCESS AND THE
TAKINGS CLAUSE

$\mathbf{P}$rior to the Civil War, the only constitutional restrictions on the power of the states to regulate economic activity were those found in Article I, Section 10, which prohibits the states from emitting bills of credit, making anything but gold or silver a tender in payment of debts, and passing ex post facto laws or laws impairing obligations of contracts. With the adoption of the Fourteenth Amendment in 1868, this situation changed. As pointed out in Chapter 10, this amendment, especially through its Due Process Clause, supplied the Supreme Court with a potent weapon for invalidating state efforts at economic regulation and for protecting vested property rights. In the early part of the twentieth century, the Due Process Clause was wielded by the Court to strike down state laws that, in its estimation, arbitrarily, unreasonably, and capriciously interfered with the rights of life, liberty, and property.[1] During this period, various justices used the clause to justify substantive reviews of governmental actions, scrutinizing not only how the government acted, but also what the government did.

As with the Contract Clause before it, substantive due process gradually lost its potency, until by the late 1930s it no longer represented a major obstacle to economic regulation by the states. Such obstacles as remain are found in the Takings Clause of the Fifth Amendment as incorporated to apply to the states, in the Court's expanding interpretations of congressional power to regulate commerce among the several states, or in the state constitutions themselves. It was wholly within the realm of civil liberties that substantive due process retained its potency and continued to serve as a constitutional limitation not only on legislative and executive procedure, but also on legislative and executive power to act at all. This chapter traces the rise and decline of substantive due process in the economic realm, as well as its subsequent revival as a strong check on the substance of legislation infringing upon civil liberties. It also explores the emerging significance of the Takings Clause as a check on state regulation of property rights.

THE FOURTEENTH AMENDMENT

The Fourteenth Amendment commands that "no state shall make or enforce any law which shall abridge the privileges or immunities of citizens of the United States; nor shall any State deprive any person of life, liberty, or property, without due process of law; nor deny to any person within its jurisdiction the equal protection of the laws." Out of an acrimonious debate over the specific intentions of the members of the Thirty-ninth Congress who framed this amendment[2] has emerged general agreement as to the overall ends that the amendment was intended to advance and as to how its three major provisions were to serve as means for the advancement of these ends. As a group, the Privileges or Immunities, Due Process, and Equal Protection clauses were intended to place economic and civil liberties on the safe and secure foundation of federal protection. To that end, the Privileges or Immunities Clause was to protect substantive rights (e.g., freedom of speech, religious freedom, the right to engage in lawful occupations, freedom from improper police violence) and the Equal Protection and Due Process clauses were to protect procedural rights, with the former barring legislative discrimination with respect to substantive rights and the latter guaranteeing procedural safeguards and judicial regularity in the enforcement of those rights.

The Fourteenth Amendment can be visualized as a platform erected above the surface of state action for the protection of economic and civil liberties. In this metaphor, the Privileges or Immunities, Due Process, and Equal Protection clauses represent the platform's three legs: Each performs different functions, yet collectively they render the platform stable and secure. The amendment's framers believed that all three legs were essential, but that the Privileges or Immunities Clause would be the most important of the three, because it was designed to be the major load-bearing leg. This design is reflected clearly in Section 5 of the amendment, which provides that "Congress shall have power to enforce, by appropriate legislation, the provisions of this article." Looking at these provisions from the point of view of Congress, the Privileges or Immunities Clause provides the simplest framework for such enforcement legislation. Under that clause, Congress can set out, through a single act or a series of acts, a comprehensive list of the vast number of substantive rights that flow from United States citizenship and make it unlawful for any state, or its agents, to abridge such substantive rights.[3] In contrast, the Due Process and Equal Protection clauses, with their procedural emphases, represent far more elusive reference points for enforcement legislation, because of the formidable technical difficulties involved in avoiding unconstitutional vagueness while framing statutes that protect persons from state deprivation of their lives, liberty, or property "without due process of law" or that guarantee "equal protection of the laws" without interference with essential classificatory schemes.

Just five years after the Fourteenth Amendment was ratified, however, the Supreme Court in *The Slaughterhouse Cases* (1873) effectively kicked out the critical privileges-or-immunities leg and left the protective platform precariously supported by its two spindly procedural legs— due process and equal protection. To keep the platform of protections from collapsing altogether, subsequent Courts have found it imperative to increase substantially the size and strength of these procedural legs. Through judicial interpretation, the justices have added layer upon layer of meaning and coverage to these legs, in an effort to render secure those substantive economic and civil rights that originally were to have been protected by the Privileges or Immunities Clause.

THE EVISCERATION OF THE PRIVILEGES OR IMMUNITIES CLAUSE

In *Butcher's Benevolent Association* v. *Crescent City Livestock Landing and Slaughterhouse Company,* more commonly known as *The Slaughterhouse Cases,* the Court upheld an act of the Louisiana legislature that had conferred upon one firm what was in effect a monopoly of the slaughterhouse business in New Orleans. The plaintiffs had asserted, among other things, that the law in question was in violation of the Fourteenth Amendment. In a 5–4 decision, the Court rejected this claim, principally on the ground of an especially narrow construction of the Privileges or Immunities Clause. Speaking for the majority, Justice Samuel F. Miller drew a distinction between state citizenship and national citizenship and, hence, between those privileges or immunities that accrued to an individual by virtue of state citizenship and those that stemmed from national citizenship. Only the latter, he insisted, were protected by the Fourteenth Amendment.

In distinguishing the privileges or immunities of state citizenship from those of national citizenship, Justice Miller quoted earlier decisions in an effort to demonstrate that the whole body of commonly accepted civil and economic rights—including the right to pursue a lawful employment in a lawful manner, which lay at the heart of *The Slaughterhouse Cases*—fell within the privileges or immunities of state citizenship. Such rights included "protection by the government, with the right to acquire and possess property of every kind, and to pursue and obtain happiness and safety, subject, nevertheless, to such restraints as the [state] government may prescribe for the general good of the whole." Miller contended that the Framers of the Fourteenth Amendment had not intended to transfer this whole body of rights to the protection of the federal government. To interpret the amendment otherwise, he argued, would be to accept consequences "so serious, so far-reaching and pervading" that they would alter radically "the whole theory of the relations of the state and Federal governments to each other." This the Court refused to do, "in the absence of language which expresses such a purpose too clearly to admit of doubt."

Miller and the majority did not argue that national citizenship conferred no privileges or immunities. Although declining to define them precisely, they did suggest that such privileges or immunities included the right of a citizen "to come to the seat of the government to assert any claim he may have upon that government"; the "right of free access to its seaports"; and the right "to demand the care and protection of the Federal government over his life, liberty, and property when on the high seas, or within the jurisdiction of a foreign government." This list left the whole body of traditional economic and civil rights solely under the protection of the states. As far as the federal Constitution was concerned, therefore, the privileges or immunities of the citizens of the separate states remained exactly as they had been before the Fourteenth Amendment was adopted. Justice Miller's argument prompted Justice Stephen B. Field to complain in frustration in his dissent that if that was all the Privileges or Immunities Clause meant, "it was a vain and idle enactment, which accomplished nothing, and most unnecessarily excited Congress and the people on its passage." For Justice Field, the clause was intended to have a "profound significance and consequence." He argued that what the Privileges and Immunities Clause of Article IV, Section 2 "did for the protection of the citizens of one State against hostile and discriminating legislation of other States, the Fourteenth Amendment does for the protection of every citizen of the United States against hostile and discriminating legislation against him in favor of others, whether they reside in the same or in different states."

The *Slaughterhouse* decision knocked out the only substantive (and therefore, the most important) leg supporting the platform of economic and civil liberties erected by the Fourteenth Amendment. It was, in the words of Michael Kent Curtis, "one of the signal disasters of American judicial history."[4] This leg has not been resurrected—with respect to the Privileges and Immunities Clause, the Court's decision in *The Slaughterhouse Cases* is still good law. The Court did announce in *Colgate* v. *Harvey* (1935) that the right of a U.S. citizen to do business and place a loan in a state other than that in which he resided was a privilege of national citizenship, but it expressly overruled that decision and returned to the old interpretation only five years later, holding in *Madden* v. *Kentucky* (1940) that "the right to carry out an incident to a trade, business or calling such as the deposit of money in banks is not a privilege of national citizenship." The *Slaughterhouse* interpretation also was affirmed in *Snowden* v. *Hughes* (1944), in which the Court held that the right to become a candidate for and be elected to a state office was an attribute of state citizenship, not a privilege of national citizenship. Those who had been denied this right, the Court declared, must look to their own state constitutions and laws for redress.[5]

ECONOMIC REGULATION AND THE RISE OF SUBSTANTIVE DUE PROCESS

The permanent emasculation of the Privileges or Immunities Clause left the substantive economic and civil liberties guaranteed by the Fourteenth Amendment wholly dependent for support upon the Due Process and Equal Protection clauses. The *Slaughterhouse* majority, however, also construed these clauses in a narrow, restrictive fashion.[6] In response to the plaintiffs' assertion that the Louisiana statute in question deprived them of their property without due process of law, the Court observed that "under no construction of that provision that we have ever seen, or that we deem admissible, can the restraint imposed by the State of Louisiana . . . be held to be a deprivation of property within the meaning of that provision."[7] And to a plea that the act deprived them of equal protection of the laws, the Court responded that the Equal Protection Clause had been aimed only at laws in the States where the newly emancipated Negroes resided, "which discriminated with gross injustice and hardship against them as a class."

Over time, these narrow interpretations—these spindly legs—have been expanded and enlarged, until today the Due Process and Equal Protection clauses solidly support the protection of a vast array of substantive rights. This chapter and Chapters 5 through 7 of Volume II explore the growth of the Due Process Clause, initially as a means of protecting economic rights and subsequently as a means of protecting civil liberties. Chapters 8 through 10 in Volume II then explore the somewhat later growth of the Equal Protection Clause and the way that this procedural leg, too, has come to protect substantive civil liberties.

The narrow procedural interpretation given the Due Process Clause in *The Slaughterhouse Cases* gave way only gradually to a broader, more substantive understanding. In the significant case of *Munn* v. *Illinois* (1877), the Court reaffirmed the restrictive *Slaughterhouse* interpretation and refused to hold that Illinois legislation setting maximum rates for grain elevators denied the elevator operators use of their property without due process of law. Chief Justice Morrison Waite argued that since the days of the common law, grain elevators and warehouses had been recognized as businesses "clothed with a public interest," and as such were subject to public regulation by the legislature. Although he conceded that this regulatory power might be abused, the Chief Justice insisted that abuse "is no argument against the [law's] existence. For protection against abuses by legislatures the people must resort to the polls, not to the courts." In dissent, Justice Stephen J. Field argued that there was nothing in the character of the grain-elevator business that justified state regulation, and hence Illinois' legislation was "nothing less than a bold assertion of absolute power by the State to control at its discretion the property and business of the citizen, and fix the compensation he shall receive." To Field, this "unrestrained license" to regulate was incompatible with due process of law.

Field's broader conception of due process was articulated further by Justice Joseph Bradley in his concurring opinion in *Davidson* v. *New Orleans* (1878). Justice Miller, writing for the majority in *Davidson*, rejected a New Orleans landowner's claim that he had been deprived of his property without due process of law by being forced to pay a special assessment whose purpose (the draining of swamp lands) allegedly would not benefit him. After confessing that "the Constitutional meaning or value of the phrase 'due process of law' remains today without that satisfactory precision of definition which judicial decisions have given to nearly all the other guarantees of personal rights found in the constitutions of the several States and of the United States," Justice Miller went on to declare that the phrase's meaning, however unclear, must be understood in a procedural sense only:

> It is not possible to hold that a party has, without due process of law, been deprived of his property, when, as regards the issues affecting it, he has, by the laws of the State, a fair trial in a court of justice, according to the modes of proceedings applicable to such a case. . . . This proposition covers the present case. Before the assessment could be collected, or become effective, the statute required that the tableau of assessments should be filed in the proper District Court of the State; that personal service of notice, with reasonable time to object, should be served on all owners who were known and within reach of process, and due advertisement made as to those who were unknown, or could not be found. This was complied with; and the party complaining here appeared, and had a full and fair hearing in the court of first instance, and afterwards in the Supreme Court. If this be not due process of law, then the words can have no definite meaning as used in the Constitution.

Justice Bradley, although agreeing with the decision, insisted that the Due Process Clause had a substantive dimension as well. Making explicit what was implicit in Justice Field's dissent in *Munn*, he argued,

> I think . . . we are entitled under the fourteenth amendment, not only to see that there is some process of law, but "due process of law," provided by the State law when a citizen is deprived of his property; and that, in judging what is "due process of law," respect must be had to the cause and object of the taking, whether under the taxing power, the power of eminent domain, or the power of assessment for local improvements, or none of these: and if found to be suitable or admissible in the special case, it will be adjudged to be "due process of law;" but if found to be arbitrary, oppressive, and unjust, it may be declared to be not "due process of law."

According to this view, the Due Process Clause requires courts to review not only how, procedurally, the government acts (procedural due process)—but also what, substantively, the government does (substantive due process). If the Court discerns that a law is unreasonable—that is, "arbitrary, oppressive, and unjust"—then it is justified in declaring the law to be a denial of due process and, hence, constitutionally infirm.

These substantive due process arguments did not originate with Justices Field and Bradley. As far back as 1856, in *Wynehamer* v. *New York*, the New York Court of Appeals (the state's highest court) had invalidated a Prohibition law on the grounds that such an exercise of the police power infringed on the economic liberty of tavern proprietors to practice their livelihood and therefore denied them due process of law.[8] Justices Field and Bradley, however, were the first to give expression to these sentiments at the level of the United States Supreme Court, and the arguments that they introduced in *Munn* and *Davidson* were to gain ascendency in *Mugler* v. *Kansas* (1887) and *Allgeyer* v. *Louisiana* (1897), and to receive their clearest constitutional expression in *Lochner* v. *New York* (1905).

In *Mugler*, the Court upheld Kansas's Prohibition law but warned that it would begin examining the reasonableness of legislation. Justice John Marshall Harlan stressed that if "a statute purporting to have been enacted to protect the public health, the public morals, or the public safety has no real or substantial relation to those objects, or is a palpable invasion of rights secured by the fundamental law, it is the duty of the Courts to so adjudge." Then, in *Allgeyer*, the Court for the first time relied on substantive due process to invalidate state legislation. Louisiana had enacted legislation designed to regulate out-of-state insurance companies doing business in the state. Justice Rufus Peckham, writing for the majority, argued that the statute in question "is not due process of law, because it prohibits an act which under the federal constitution the defendant has a right to perform." The state's legitimate exercise of its police power, he contended, did not extend to "prohibiting a citizen from making contracts of the nature involved in this case outside of the limits of the jurisdiction of the state, and which are also to be performed outside of such jurisdiction." In the course of his opinion, Justice Peckham forthrightly announced the principle that the right to make contracts was a part of the liberty guaranteed by the Due Process Clause:

> The liberty mentioned in the [Fourteenth] Amendment means not only the right of the citizen to be free from the mere physical restraint of his person, as by incarceration, but the term is deemed to embrace the right of the citizen to be free in the enjoyment of all his faculties; to be free to use them in all lawful ways; to live and work where he will; to earn his livelihood by any lawful calling; to pursue any livelihood or avocation, and for that purpose to enter into all contracts which may be proper, necessary and essential to his carrying out to a successful conclusion the purposes above mentioned.

These substantive due process arguments received their clearest expression in *Lochner* v. *New York,* in which Justice Peckham declared that New York had unreasonably and arbitrarily interfered with the "freedom of master and employee to contract with each other in relation to their employment" by passing a law limiting the number of hours a baker could work in a bakery. Finding no valid health or safety reasons that could justify such a law, Peckham ruled that it amounted to an unreasonable deprivation of liberty (i.e., the liberty to contract) and violated the Due Process Clause. Justices Harlan and Holmes each wrote separate dissents. Justice Harlan charged the majority with "enlarging the scope of the Amendment far beyond its original purpose" and with "bringing under the supervision of this court matters which have been supposed to belong exclusively to the legislative departments of the several States." Justice Holmes penned one of his most memorable passages: "The Fourteenth Amendment does not enact Mr. Spencer's Social Statics. . . . A constitution . . . is made for people of fundamentally differing views."

By embracing the notion of substantive due process, the *Lochner* Court assumed the very role that Justice Miller had warned against in *The Slaughterhouse Cases:* It became a "perpetual censor," reviewing the reasonableness of state efforts at economic regulation. It continued to play this role at least through *Adkins* v. *Children's Hospital* (1923), in which the District of Columbia's minimum wage law for women and children was branded "the product of a naked arbitrary exercise of power" and thus a violation of the Fifth Amendment's Due Process Clause. Prior to *Adkins,* the Court had appeared to moderate its position toward economic legislation. In *Muller* v. *Oregon* (1908) and *Bunting* v. *Oregon* (1917), for example, the justices upheld the constitutionality of state legislation that, respectively, limited the workday for women to ten hours and extended the same maximum-hours limitation to all mill and factory workers. Of decisive importance in both of these decisions, however, was the Court's belief that the regulations in question were a reasonable exercise of the state's police powers—not its subsequent conviction that any judicial inquiry into the substance or reasonableness of economic legislation was inappropriate.

THE REPUDIATION OF SUBSTANTIVE DUE PROCESS

As the Court's subsequent decision in *Adkins* makes apparent, *Muller* and *Bunting* did not represent a repudiation of substantive due process— in these cases the Court merely judged that the economic regulations in question were reasonable; it did not conclude that it was inappropriate for the Court to make such judgments in the first place. The disavowal of substantive due process began somewhat later in *Nebbia* v. *New York* (1934), in which the Court, by a 5–4 vote, upheld the validity of a Depression-era law regulating the price of milk. The New York legislature had sought to prevent ruinous price cutting by establishing a milk control board with power to fix minimum and maximum retail prices, and the appellant claimed that enforcement of the milk price regulations denied him due process of law by preventing him from selling his product at whatever price he desired. In rejecting this claim, Justice Owen Roberts, speaking for the majority, declared,

> So far as the requirement of due process is concerned, and in the absence of other constitutional restrictions, a state is free to adopt whatever economic policy may reasonably be deemed to promote public welfare, and to enforce that policy by legislation adapted to its purpose. The courts are without authority either to declare such policy, or, when it is declared by the legislature, to override it.

What was begun in *Nebbia* was completed in *West Coast Hotel Company* v. *Parrish* (1937). This case arose under a Washington state minimum-wage law that had been passed in 1913 and enforced continuously thereafter, quite irrespective of *Adkins*. In the midst of the intense political controversy generated by President Roosevelt's Court-packing plan, the Court upheld the law. Chief Justice Hughes insisted that the state legislature had the right to use its minimum-wage requirements to help implement its policy of protecting women from exploitive employers. He noted that "the adoption of similar requirements by many States evidences a deepseated conviction both as to the presence of the evil and as to the means adopted to check it. Legislative response to that conviction cannot be regarded as arbitrary or capricious, and that is all we have to decide." The Chief Justice then went even further: "Even if the wisdom of the policy is regarded as debatable and its effects uncertain, still the legislature is entitled to its judgment."

The Court's refusal in *Parrish* to contradict the judgment of the legislature on economic matters and its outright repudiation of substantive due process in the economic realm through the explicit overruling of *Adkins* remain controlling precedents. Subsequent decisions, in fact, suggest a reluctance to subject economic legislation to any constitutional test at all.[9] *Day-Brite Lighting* v. *Missouri* (1952) provides a clear example of this trend. In reviewing a state law that provided that employees could absent themselves from their jobs for four hours on election days and forbade employers from deducting wages for their absence, the Court admitted that the social policy embodied in the law was debatable but pointed out that "our recent decisions make plain that we do not sit as a superlegislature to weigh the wisdom of legislation nor to decide whether the policy it expresses offends the public welfare." This argument was repeated in *Williamson* v. *Lee Optical Company* (1955), which involved a statute that forbade any person but an ophthalmologist or an optometrist from fitting lenses to the face or duplicating or replacing lenses into frames, except on the prescription of an ophthalmologist or optometrist. After acknowledging that the law was "a needless, wasteful requirement in many cases," the Court went on to insist that "the day is gone" when it would strike down "state laws regulatory of business and industrial conditions, because they may be unwise, improvident, or out of harmony with a particular school of thought." Eight years later, in *Ferguson* v. *Skrupa* (1963), the Court applied the same reasoning in upholding a Kansas statute prohibiting anyone except lawyers from engaging in the business of debt adjustment, with Justice Black noting in his majority opinion that "it is up to legislatures, not Courts, to decide on the wisdom and utility of legislation." The *Ferguson* opinion elicited some judicial protests, however. Despite his abiding commitment to judicial self-restraint, Justice John Marshall Harlan felt compelled to protest against what he perceived to be judicial abdication. In his concurrence, he insisted that even economic legislation must bear "a rational relation to a constitutionally permissible objective"—a relationship that he found to exist in the instant case.

Justice Black's words in *Ferguson*, echoing as they do Chief Justice Waite's opinion in *Munn* v. *Illinois*, highlight the full circle traveled by the Court in its consideration of the Due Process Clause and economic rights. The spindly due-process leg in *Munn*, which by *Lochner* had grown enormously in size and strength, had lost its potency by *Parrish* and atrophied to the spindly reed it once again became by *Williamson*. So it has remained, at least until *BMW* v. *Gore* (1996), which raises the interesting question of whether the Court is not once again embracing substantive due process, if not to limit what legislatures can do, at least to limit the size of punitive damage awards that civil juries can impose. In this Alabama case, the Supreme Court held the Due Process Clause of the Fourteenth Amendment prohibits a State from imposing punitive damage awards that are "grossly excessive"—in this instance, a punitive damages award that was 500 times compensatory damages. Justice Stevens for the majority identified three "guideposts" that led the Court to the conclusion that the Alabama courts had entered "the zone of arbitrariness" and deprived the defendant of "elementary notions of fairness": the degree of reprehensibility of the defendant's conduct, the ratio between the punitive award and the plaintiff's actual harm, and the difference between the courts' sanction and legislative sanctions authorized for comparable misconduct. In his dissent, Justice Scalia complained that these guideposts "mark a road to nowhere; they provide no real guidance at all." Justice Ginsburg, in her dissent, likewise objected to the way in which the majority "leads us into territory traditionally within the States' domain" with "only a vague concept of substantive due process, a 'raised eyebrow' test, as its ultimate guide."

It is too early to determine whether *BMW* v. *Gore* is the beginning of a renewed judicial infatuation with substantive due process in the economic realm or whether it will prove to be an isolated, if provocative, exception. What can be said with certainty, however, is that the Court, for whatever reason, has never before embraced substantive due process simultaneously in both the economic and civil liberties realms. When substantive due process was at its height in the economic realm in the early part of the twentieth century, it was nonexistent in the realm of civil liberties, as *Buck* v. *Bell* (1927) makes abundantly clear. In *Buck*, the Court denied a substantive due process objection to a 1924 Virginia statute that, on the grounds of the "health of the patient and the welfare of society," provided for the sexual sterilization of inmates of institutions supported by the State who were found to be afflicted with hereditary forms of insanity or imbecility. The preamble of the Virginia statute declared that the Commonwealth was supporting in various institutions many "defective persons" who, if discharged, would become a menace, but who, if rendered incapable of procreating, might be discharged with safety and become self-supporting, with benefits both to themselves and society; it also declared that experience had shown that "heredity plays an important part in the transmission of insanity, imbecility, etc." Justice Holmes upheld the sterilization of Carrie Buck, whom he described as a "feeble minded white woman," "the daughter of a feeble minded mother," and herself "the mother of an illegitimate feeble minded child." He argued first that the statute met all the requirements of procedural due process: "There can be no doubt that, so far as procedure is concerned, the rights of the patient are most carefully considered, and, as every step in this case was taken in scrupulous compliance with the statute and after months of observation, there is no doubt that, in that respect, the plaintiff in error has had due process of law." But, he noted, Carrie Buck also objected on substantive due process grounds: "The attack is [also] upon the substantive law. It seems to be contended that in no circumstances could such an order be justified." The Court, however, was unpersuaded, and so, just four years after it had found in *Adkins* that a minimum wage law for women and children was "the product of a naked arbitrary exercise of power," it held that Virginia's eugenics-inspired statute passed constitutional muster. Justice Holmes wrote for an eight-member majority (Justice Butler dissented but did not write an opinion) when he declared:

> We have seen more than once that the public welfare may call upon the best citizens for their lives. It would be strange if it could not call upon those who already sap the strength of the State for these lesser sacrifices, often not felt to be such by those concerned, in order to prevent our being swamped with incompetence. It is better for all the world if, instead of waiting to execute degenerate offspring for crime or to let them starve for their imbecility, society can prevent those who are manifestly unfit from continuing their kind. The principle that sustains compulsory vaccination is broad enough to cover cutting the Fallopian tubes. Three generations of imbeciles are enough.[10]

At about the time that the Court was abandoning the protection of economic rights by substantive due process, it was beginning to embrace the concept to protect civil rights. The contemptuous disregard for the civil rights of Carrie Buck was soon replaced by a particular judicial solicitude for the rights of "discrete and insular minorities." In footnote four of the Court's opinion in *United States* v. *Carolene Products Company* (1938), decided just one year after its repudiation of substantive due process in *West Coast Hotel* v. *Parrish*, Justice Harlan Fiske Stone outlined a justification for "more exacting judicial scrutiny" where infringements of civil liberties were involved. The Court's subsequent embrace of substantive due process in the realm of civil liberties will be an underlying concern in the chapters that follow.

THE TAKINGS CLAUSE

Just as the Due Process Clause supplanted the Contract Clause as a means of protecting property rights, so, too, the Takings Clause of the Fifth Amendment as incorporated to apply to the states by the Fourteenth Amendment appears to have supplanted due process. It states that private property shall not "be taken for public use, without just compensation," and is variously referred to as the Takings Clause, the Public Use Clause, or the Just Compensation Clause.

Both the federal and state governments have the power of eminent domain, the power to condemn or expropriate private property for public purposes upon just compensation of the owner. The decision to invoke the power of eminent domain is a legislative one, and the Court has been reluctant to question whether the compensation offered is "just" or whether the confiscated property has been taken for a "public use." In *Hawaii Housing Authority* v. *Midkiff* (1984), for example, the Supreme Court unanimously upheld Hawaii's use of its power of eminent domain to acquire property from large landowners and transfer it to lessees living on single-family residential lots on the land. The purpose of this land condemnation scheme was to reduce the concentration of land ownership, and Justice O'Connor, equating public purpose with public use, declared that "our cases make clear that empirical debates over the wisdom of takings—no less than debates over the wisdom of other kinds of socioeconomic legislation—are not to be carried out in the federal courts."

While the Court has been hesitant to challenge legislative judgments concerning just compensation and public use, it has become increasingly assertive in concluding that various governmental regulations that restrict, diminish, or destroy the value of property can be as much a taking as eminent domain. In *First English Evangelical Lutheran Church* v. *Los Angeles County* (1987), the Court held in a 6–3 decision that a county decision to prohibit a church from constructing buildings on a campground it owned after there had been extensive damage from a flood constituted a taking for which the county must pay compensation. Moreover, the Court continued, once a taking has been determined, the government must compensate the owner for the period during which the taking was in effect. The mere fact that the taking was temporary—either because subsequently invalidated by the courts or repealed by a successor ordinance—does not eliminate the need for compensation. As Chief Justice

Rehnquist noted: "[T]he Los Angeles County ordinances have denied appellant all use of its property for a considerable period of years, and we hold that invalidation of the ordinance without payment of fair value for the use of the property during this period of time would be a constitutionally insufficient remedy."

Nollan v. *California Coastal Commission* (1987) shows the Court's new assertiveness even more clearly. The coastal commission granted a permit to the Nollans to replace a small bungalow on their beachfront lot with a larger house. As a condition, however, the commission insisted that the Nollans grant an easement to the public across their land to the beach. The Nollans claimed that this requirement constituted a taking, and the Supreme Court, with Justice Scalia writing the majority opinion, agreed.

Among the justices on the Court, Justice Scalia appears the most willing to treat the Takings Clause as a successor to the Due Process Clause and use it to strike down governmental regulation of private property. In *Pennell* v. *City of San Jose* (1988), a case involving a rent control ordinance that allowed administrative reductions on rent in case of "tenant hardship," Justice Scalia dissented from Chief Justice Rehnquist's majority decision that the case was not ripe for judicial resolution, reached the merits on the hardship provision, and expanded on the themes he advanced in *Nollan*. He denied the landlords were the cause of the problem at which the hardship provision was aimed. Rather, he insisted that the provision was drafted "to meet a quite different social problem: the existence of some renters who are too poor to afford even reasonably priced housing. But that problem is no more caused or exploited by landlords than it is by the grocers who sell needy renters their food, or the department stores that sell them their clothes, or the employers who pay them their wages, or the citizens of San Jose holding the higher-paying jobs from which they are excluded." Moreover, Scalia continued, "even if the neediness of renters could be regarded as a problem distinctively attributable to landlords in general, it is not remotely attributable to the particular landlords that the ordinance singles out—namely, those who happen to have a 'hardship' tenant at the present time, or who may happen to rent to a 'hardship' tenant in the future, or whose current or future affluent tenants may happen to decline into the 'hardship' category." He then drove home his primary point: "The fact that government acts through the landlord-tenant relationship does not magically transform general public welfare, which must be supported by all the public, into mere 'economic regulation,' which can disproportionately burden particular individuals."

Justice Scalia's insistence in *Pennell* that the government (and hence taxpayer) pay for public welfare and not transfer these costs to particular discrete individuals takes on added significance today, with a public whose appetite for governmental services is greater than its willingness to pay for them, and with his majority opinion for the Court in *Lucas* v. *South Carolina Coastal Council* (1992). In this case, a landowner was deprived of all "economically viable use" of his $1 million property when the state enacted a coastal zone act, designed to prevent beach erosion, that prevented him from building a beachfront home on his property. Justice Scalia held that regulatory takings that deprive land of all economically beneficial use require compensation, regardless of the importance of the public interests served, unless an "inquiry into the nature of the owner's estate shows that the proscribed use interests were not part of his title to begin with."

The Court's takings cases, no less than its substantive due process cases, pose the question of the proper role of the Court. To what extent should the Court be a check on the wishes of the popular branches? To what extent should it protect the few from the wishes of the majority? To what extent should it protect the rights of property with the same dedication it displays for other rights?[11] The 1994 case of *Dolan* v. *City of Tigard* squarely frames these questions. Chief Justice Rehnquist held that "We see no reason why the Takings Clause of the Fifth Amendment, as much a part of the Bill of Rights as the First Amendment or Fourth Amendment, should be relegated to the status of a poor relation" and held that the City of Tigard, Oregon, violated the constitutional rights of Florence Dolan when it held that it would approve her application to expand her plumbing and electric supply store only if she dedicated ten percent of her land to the city.

NOTES

1 For an especially useful essay on this matter, see Edward S. Corwin, "The Supreme Court and the Fourteenth Amendment," *Michigan Law Review* 7 (June 1909): 643.

2 See Raoul Berger, *Government by Judiciary: The Transformation of the Fourteenth Amendment* (Cambridge, Mass.: Harvard University Press, 1977); Jacobus Tenbroek, *Equal under Law* (New York: Macmillan, 1965); Alexander M. Bickel, "The Original Understanding and the Segregation Decision," *Harvard Law Review* 69, no. 1 (November 1955); Charles Fairman, "Does the Fourteenth Amendment Incorporate the Bill of Rights?", *Stanford Law Review* 2, no. 1 (1949); and William W. Van Alstyne, "The Fourteenth Amendment, the 'Right to Vote,' and the Understanding of the Thirty-Ninth Congress," in *Supreme Court Review*, ed. Philip Kurland (Chicago: University of Chicago Press, 1966); and Alford H. Kelly, "Clio and the Court: An Illicit Love Affair," 1965 *Supreme Court Review*.

3 See Corwin, "The Supreme Court and the Fourteenth Amendment"; Tenbroek, *Equal under Law*, pp. 236–238; M. Glenn Abernathy, *Civil Liberties under the Constitution*, 3d ed. (New York: Harper and Row, 1977), pp. 32–33; and Berger, *Government by Judiciary*, pp. 18–19.

4 Michael Kent Curtis, "Resurrecting the Privileges and Immunities Clause and Revising the *Slaughterhouse Cases* without Exhuming *Lochner:* Individual Rights and the Fourteenth Amendment," *Boston College Law Review* 38 (December 1966): 105.

5 Unsuccessful attempts to broaden the scope of privileges and immunities include *Hague* v. *Committee for Industrial Organization* (1939); *Edwards* v. *California* (1941); and *Oyama* v. *California* (1948).

6 It could be said that with respect to the Due Process and Equal Protection clauses, the Court correctly identified the intentions of the Thirty-ninth Con-

gress in drafting these clauses and acted accordingly. But given its concurrent construction of the Privileges or Immunities Clause, the Court's fidelity to the intentions of the Thirty-ninth Congress simply served to exacerbate matters and led directly to the development of substantive due process (discussed below). For an excellent treatment of the development of substantive due process, see Chapter 4: "Doing Justice in the Name of the Law: The Transformation of Due Process of Law," in Eugene W. Hickok and Gary L. McDowell, *Law vs. Justice: Courts and Politics in American Society* (New York: Free Press, 1993), pp. 80–121.

7 The Court accepted without debate the procedural interpretation of due process. For differing views of what due process could have meant, however, see *Scott* v. *Sandford* (1857); *Hepburn* v. *Griswold* (1870); and Edward S. Corwin, "Due Process of Law before the Civil War," *Harvard Law Review* 24 (March 1911): 366*ff.* and (April 1911): 460*ff.*

8 As Justice Comstock put the question: "Do the prohibitions and penalties of the act for the prevention of intemperance, pauperism, and crime pass the utmost boundaries of mere regulation and police, and by their own force, assuming them to be valid and faithfully obeyed and executed, work the essential loss or destruction of the property at which they are aimed? . . . In my judgment, they do plainly work this result."

9 Guy Miller Struve, "The Less-Restrictive-Alternative Principle and Economic Due Process," *Harvard Law Review* 80 (1967): 1463–1488.

10 Carrie Buck also objected on equal protection grounds. Justice Holmes was equally unpersuaded here: "But, it is said . . . this reasoning . . . fails when it is confined to the small number who are in the institutions named and is not applied to the multitudes outside. It is the usual last resort of constitutional arguments to point out shortcomings of this sort. But the answer is that the law does all that is needed when it does all that it can, indicates a policy, applies it to all within the lines, and seeks to bring within the lines all similarly situated so far and so fast as its means allow. Of course, so far as the operations enable whose who otherwise must be kept confined to be returned to the world, and thus open the asylum to others, the equality aimed at will be more nearly reached."

11 See Roger Clegg, "Reclaiming the Takings Clause," *South Carolina Law Review* 46 (Summer 1995): 532–533, 576, who argues that the Court has reduced the Takings Clause to an "ad hoc balancing test" that has "degenerate[d] into a mere mask for judicial predilections." This balancing of (1) the economic impact of the regulation on the claimant, (2) the extent to which the regulation has interfered with the claimant's investment-backed expectations, and (3) the character of the governmental action "results, unsurprisingly, in each justice voting his or her own policy preferences. Clegg concludes: "This balancing has no textual justification, and its lawless result if flatly inconsistent with [the] Constitution's letter and spirit."

SELECTED READING

Adair v. *United States*, 208 U.S. 161 (1908).

Concrete Pipe & Products v. *Construction Laborers Pension Trust*, 508 U.S. 602 (1993).

Coppage v. *Kansas*, 236 U.S. 1 (1915).

Dean v. *Gadsden Times Publishing Company*, 412 U.S. 543 (1973).

Ferguson v. *Skrupa*, 372 U.S. 726 (1963).

First English Evangelical Lutheran Church of Glendale v. *Los Angeles County*, 482 U.S. 304 (1987).

Morehead v. *New York ex rel. Tipaldo*, 298 U.S. 587 (1936).

Pacific Mutual Life Insurance v. *Haslip*, 499 U.S. 1 (1991).

Pennell v. *City of San Jose*, 485 U.S. 1 (1988).

Berger, Raoul. *Government by Judiciary: The Transformation of the Fourteenth Amendment* (Cambridge, Mass.: Harvard University Press, 1977).

Clegg, Roger. "Reclaiming the Takings Clause." *South Carolina Law Review* 46 (Summer 1995): 531–578.

Curtis, Michael Kent. "Resurrecting the Privileges and Immunities Clause and Revising the *Slaughterhouse Cases* without Exhuming *Lochner:* Individual Rights and the Fourteenth Amendment." *Boston College Law Review* 38 (December 1996): 1–106.

Dorn, James A. and Henry G. Manne, eds. *Economic Liberties and the Judiciary* (Fairfax, Va.: George Mason University Press, 1987).

Easterbrook, Frank H. "Substance and Due Process." *1982 Supreme Court Review*, edited by Philip B. Kurland, Gerhard Casper, and Dennis Hutchinson (Chicago: University of Chicago Press, 1983).

Epstein, Richard A. *Takings: Property and the Power of Eminent Domain* (Cambridge, Mass.: Harvard University Press, 1985).

Galie, Peter J. "State Courts and Economic Rights." *Annals* 496 (1988): 76–87.

Kitch, Edmund W. and Clara Ann Bowler. "The Facts of *Munn* v. *Illinois*." *1978 Supreme Court Review*, edited by Philip B. Kurland and Gerhard Casper (Chicago: University of Chicago Press, 1979).

McCloskey, Robert. "Economic Due Process and the Supreme Court: An Exhumation and Reburial." *1962 Supreme Court Review*, edited by Philip B. Kurland (Chicago: University of Chicago Press, 1962).

Nelson, William E. *The Fourteenth Amendment: From Political Principle to Judicial Doctrine* (Cambridge, Mass.: Harvard University Press, 1988).

Porter, Mary Cornelia. "That Commerce Shall Be Free: A New Look at the Old Laissez-Faire Court." *1976 Supreme Court Review*, edited by Philip B. Kurland (Chicago: University of Chicago Press, 1977).

Sallet, Jonathan D. "Regulatory 'Takings' and Just Compensation: The Supreme Court's Search for a Solution Continues." *Urban Lawyer* 18 (1986): 635.

Shapiro, Martin. "The Constitution and Economic Rights." In *Essays on the Constitution of the United States*, edited by M. Judd Harmon (Port Washington, N.Y.: Kennikat Press, 1978).

Siegan, Bernard H. *Economic Liberties and the Constitution* (Chicago: University of Chicago Press, 1981).

Treanor, William Michael. "The Origins and Original Significance of the Just Compensation Clause of the Fifth Amendment." *Yale Law Journal* 94 (1985): 694–717.

Tushnet, Mark. "The Newer Property: Suggestion for the Revival of Substantive Due Process." *1975 Supreme Court Review*, edited by Philip B. Kurland (Chicago: University of Chicago Press, 1976).

Zuckert, Michael P. "Congressional Power Under the Fourteenth Amendment— The Original Understanding of Section Five." *Constitutional Commentary* 3 (1986): 123–147.

The Slaughterhouse Cases

83 U.S. (16 Wallace) 36; 21 L. Ed. 394 (1873)

In 1869, the Louisiana legislature passed an act designed to "protect the health of the City of New Orleans" by granting to the Crescent City Livestock Landing and Slaughterhouse Co. a twenty-five-year monopoly on the sheltering and slaughtering of animals in the city and surrounding parishes. The law required that all other butchers in the New Orleans area come to that company and pay for the use of its abattoir. Although the law was in response to a cholera epidemic and represented an attempt to end contamination of the city's water supply caused by the dumping of refuse into the Mississippi River by small independent slaughterhouses, the state legislature at the time was dominated by carpetbag elements, and charges of corruption were rampant. The Butcher's Benevolent Association, a group of small independent slaughterers who had been deprived of their livelihood by the legislation, challenged the act on the grounds that it violated the Thirteenth Amendment and the Privileges and Immunities, Due Process, and Equal Protection clauses of the Fourteenth Amendment. A state district court and the Louisiana Supreme Court upheld the legislation, at which point this case, along with two others involving the same controversy, was brought to the United States Supreme Court on a writ of error. These three cases have come to be known simply as *The Slaughterhouse Cases. Opinion of the Court: Miller, Clifford, Davis, Hunt, Strong. Dissenting opinions: Bradley; Field, Bradley, Chase, Swayne; Swayne.*

MR. JUSTICE MILLER delivered the opinion of the Court. . . .

The plaintiffs in error . . . allege that the statute is a violation of the Constitution of the United States in these several particulars:

That it creates an involuntary servitude forbidden by the thirteenth article of amendment;

That it abridges the privileges and immunities of citizens of the United States;

That it denies to the plaintiffs the equal protection of the laws; and,

That it deprives them of their property without due process of law; contrary to the provisions of the first section of the fourteenth article of amendment.

This court is thus called upon for the first time to give construction to these articles.

. . . In the light of . . . recent . . . history, . . . and on the most casual examination of the language of these amendments, no one can fail to be impressed with the one pervading purpose found in them all, lying at the foundation of each, and without which none of them would have been even suggested; we mean the freedom of the slave race, the security and firm establishment of that freedom, and the protection of the newly-made freeman and citizen from the oppressions of those who had formerly exercised unlimited dominion over him. . . .

We do not say that no one else but the negro can share in this protection. . . . But what we do say, and what we wish to be understood is, that in any fair and just construction of any section or phrase of these amendments, it is necessary to look to the purpose which we have said was the pervading spirit of them all, the evil which they were designed to remedy, and the process of continued addition to the Constitution, until that purpose was supposed to be accomplished, as far as constitutional law can accomplish it.

The first section of the fourteenth article, to which our attention is more specially invited, opens with a definition of citizenship—not only citizenship of the United States, but citizenship of the States. . . .

"All persons born or naturalized in the United States, and subject to the jurisdiction thereof, are citizens of the United States and of the State wherein they reside." . . .

It declares that persons may be citizens of the United States without regard to their citizenship of a particular State, and it overturns the Dred Scott decision by making *all persons* born within the United States and subject to its jurisdiction citizens of the United States. . . . Not only may a man be a citizen of the United States without being a citizen of a State, but an important element is necessary to convert the former into the latter. He must reside within the State to make him a citizen of it, but it is only necessary that he should be born or naturalized in the United States to be a citizen of the Union.

It is quite clear, then, that there is a citizenship of the United States, and a citizenship of a State, which are distinct from each other, and which depend upon different characteristics or circumstances in the individual.

We think this distinction and its explicit recognition in this amendment of great weight in this argument, because the next paragraph of this same section, which is the one mainly relied on by the plaintiffs in error, speaks only of privileges and immunities of citizens of the United States, and does not speak of those of citizens of the several States. The argument, however, in favor of the plaintiffs rests wholly on the assumption that the citizenship is the same, and the privileges and immunities guaranteed by the clause are the same.

The language is, "No State shall make or enforce any law which shall abridge the privileges or immunities of citizens of the United States." It is a little remarkable, if this clause was intended as a protection to the citizen of a State against the legislative power of his own State, that the word citizen of the State should be left out when it is so carefully used, and used in contradistinction to citizens of the United States, in the very sentence which precedes it. It is too clear for argument that the change in phraseology was adopted understandingly and with a purpose.

Of the privileges and immunities of the citizen of the United States, and of the privileges and immunities of the citizen of the State, and what they respectively are, we will presently consider; but we wish to state here that it is only the former which are placed by this clause under the protection of the Federal Constitution, and that the latter, whatever they may be, are not intended to have any additional protection by this paragraph of the amendment.

If, then, there is a difference between the privileges and immunities belonging to a citizen of the United States as such, and those belonging to the citizen of the State as such, the latter must rest for their security and protection where they have heretofore rested; for they are not embraced by this paragraph of the amendment.

The first occurrence of the words "privileges and immunities" in our constitutional history, is to be found in the fourth of the articles of the old Confederation.

It declares "that . . . the free inhabitants of each of these States . . . shall be entitled to all the privileges and immunities of free citizens in the several States." . . .

In the Constitution of the United States, which superseded the Articles of Confederation, the corresponding provision is found in section two of the fourth article, in the following words: "The citizens of each State shall be entitled to all the privileges and immunities of citizens of the several States." . . .

That constitutional provision . . . did not create those rights, which it called privileges and immunities of citizens of the States. It threw around them in that clause no security for the citizen of the State in which they were claimed or exercised. Nor did it profess to control the power of the State governments over the rights of its own citizens.

Its sole purpose was to declare to the several States, that whatever those rights, as you grant or establish them to your own citizens, or as you limit or qualify, or impose restrictions on their exercise, the same, neither more nor less, shall be the measure of the rights of citizens of other States within your jurisdiction.

It would be the vainest show of learning to attempt to prove by citations of authority, that up to the adoption of the recent amendments, no claim or pretence was set up that those rights depended on the Federal government for their existence or protection, beyond the very few express limitations which the Federal Constitution imposed upon the States—such, for instance, as the prohibition against ex post facto laws, bills of attainder, and laws impairing the obligation of contracts. But with the exception of these and a few other restrictions, the entire domain of the privileges and immunities of citizens of the States, as above defined, lay within the constitutional and legislative power of the States, and without that of the Federal government. Was it the purpose of the fourteenth amendment, by the simple declaration that no State should make or enforce any law which shall abridge the privileges and immunities of *citizens of the United States*, to transfer the security and protection of all the civil rights which we have mentioned, from the States to the Federal government? And where it is declared that Congress shall have the power to enforce that article, was it intended to bring within the power of Congress the entire domain of civil rights heretofore belonging exclusively to the States?

All this and more must follow, if the proposition of the plaintiffs in error be sound. For not only are these rights subject to the control of Congress whenever in its discretion, any of them are supposed to be abridged by State legislation, but that body may also pass laws in advance, limiting and restricting the exercise of legislative power by the States, in their most ordinary and usual functions, as in its judgment it may think proper on all such subjects. And still further, such a construction followed by the reversal of the judgments of the Supreme Court of Louisiana in these cases, would constitute this court a perpetual censor upon all legislation of the States, on the civil rights of their own citizens, with authority to nullify such as it did not approve as consistent with those rights, as they existed at the time of the adoption of this amendment. The argument we admit is not always the most conclusive which is drawn from the consequences urged against the adoption of a particular construction of an instrument. But when, as in the case before us, these consequences are so serious, so far-reaching and pervading, so great a departure from the structure and spirit of our institutions; when the effect is to fetter and degrade the State governments by subjecting them to the control of Congress, in the exercise of powers heretofore universally conceded to them of the most ordinary and fundamental character; when in fact it radically changes the whole theory of the relations of the State and Federal governments to each other and of both these governments to the people; the argument has a force that is irresistible, in the absence of language which expresses such a purpose too clearly to admit of doubt.

We are convinced that no such results were intended by the Congress which proposed these amendments, nor by the legislatures of the States which ratified them.

Having shown that the privileges and immunities relied on in the argument are those which belong to citizens of the States as such, and that they are left to the State governments for security and protection, and not by this article placed under the special care of the Federal government, we may hold ourselves excused from defining the privileges and immunities of citizens of the United States which no State can abridge, until some case involving those privileges may make it necessary to do so.

But lest it should be said that no such privileges and immunities are to be found if those we have been considering are excluded, we venture to suggest some which owe their existence to the Federal government, its National character, its Constitution, or its laws.

One of these is well described in the case of *Crandall* v. *Nevada*. It is said to be the right of the citizen of this great country, protected by implied guarantees of its Constitution, "to come to the seat of government to assert any claim he may have upon that government, to transact any business he may have with it, to seek its protection, to share its offices, to engage in administering its functions. He has the right of free access to its seaports, through which all operations of foreign commerce are conducted, to the subtreasuries, land offices, and courts of justice in the several States." ...

Another privilege of a citizen of the United States is to demand the care and protection of the Federal government over his life, liberty, and property when on the high seas or within the jurisdiction of a foreign government. Of this there can be no doubt, nor that the right depends upon his character as a citizen of the United States. The right to peaceably assemble and petition for redress of grievances, the privilege of the writ of *habeas corpus*, are rights of the citizen guaranteed by the Federal Constitution. The right to use the navigable waters of the United States, however they may penetrate the territory of the several States, all rights secured to our citizens by treaties with foreign nations, are dependent upon citizenship of the United States, and not citizenship of a State. One of these privileges is conferred by the very article under consideration. It is that a citizen of the United States can, of his own volition, become a citizen of any State of the Union by a *bonâ fide* residence therein, with the same rights as other citizens of that State. To these may be added the rights secured by the thirteenth and fifteenth articles of amendment, and by the other clause of the fourteenth, next to be considered.

But it is useless to pursue this branch of the inquiry, since we are of opinion that the rights claimed by these plaintiffs in error, if they have any existence, are not privileges and immunities of citizens of the United States within the meaning of the clause of the fourteenth amendment under consideration. . . .

The argument has not been much pressed in these cases that the defendant's charter deprives the plaintiffs of their property without due process of law. . . .

We are not without judicial interpretation, . . . both State and National, of the meaning of this clause. And it is sufficient to say that under no construction of that provision that we have ever seen, or any that we deem admissible, can the restraint imposed by the State of Louisiana upon the exercise of their trade by the butchers of New Orleans be held to be a deprivation of property within the meaning of that provision.

"Nor shall any State deny to any person within its jurisdiction the equal protection of the laws."

In the light of the history of these amendments, and the pervading purpose of them, which we have already discussed, it is not difficult to give a meaning to this clause. The existence of laws in the States where the newly emancipated negroes resided, which discriminated with gross injustice and hardship against them as a class, was the evil to be remedied by this clause, and by it such laws are forbidden. . . .

The judgments of the Supreme Court of Louisiana in these cases are

Affirmed.

MR. JUSTICE FIELD, dissenting. . . .

The question presented is . . . one of the gravest importance, not merely to the parties here, but to the whole country. It is nothing less than the question whether the recent amendments to the Federal Constitution protect the citizens of the United States against the deprivation of their common rights by State legislation. In my judgment the fourteenth amendment does afford such protection, and was so intended by the Congress which framed and the States which adopted it.

The counsel for the plaintiffs in error have contended, with great force, that the act in question is also inhibited by the thirteenth amendment. . . .

. . . I have been so accustomed to regard it as intended to meet that form of slavery which had previously prevailed in this country, and to which the recent civil war owed its existence, that I was not prepared, nor am I yet, to give to it the extent and force ascribed by counsel. Still it is evident that the language of the amendment is not used in a restrictive sense. It is not confined to African slavery alone. It is general and universal in its application. . . .

It is not necessary, however, . . . to rest my objections to the act in question upon the terms and meaning of the thirteenth amendment. The provisions of the fourteenth amendment, which is properly a supplement to the thirteenth, cover, in my judgment, the case before us, and inhibit any legislation which confers special and exclusive privileges like these under consideration. . . It first declares that "all persons born or naturalized in the United States, and subject to the jurisdiction thereof, are citizens of the United States and of the State wherein they reside." . . .

. . . It recognizes in express terms, if it does not create, citizens of the United States, and it makes their citizenship dependent upon the place of their birth, or the fact of their adoption, and not upon the constitution or laws of any State or the condition of their ancestry. A citizen of a State is now only a citizen of the United States residing in that State. The fundamental rights, privileges, and immunities which belong to him as a free man and a free citizen, now belong to him as a citizen of the United States, and are not dependent upon his citizenship of any State. . . .

The amendment does not attempt to confer any new privileges or immunities upon citizens, or to enumerate or define those already existing. It assumes that there are such privileges and immunities which belong of right to citizens as such, and ordains that they shall not be abridged by State legislation. If this inhibition has no reference to privileges and immunities of this character, but only refers, as held by the majority of the court in their opinion, to such privileges and immunities as were before its adoption specially designated in the Constitution or necessarily implied as belonging to citizens of the United States, it was a vain and idle enactment, which accomplished nothing, and most unnecessarily excited Congress and the people on its passage. With privileges and immunities thus designated or implied no State could ever have interfered by its laws, and no new constitutional provision was required to inhibit such interference. The supremacy of the Constitution and the laws of the United States always controlled any State legislation of that character. But if the amendment refers to the natural and inalienable rights which belong to all citizens, the inhibition has a profound significance and consequence.

What, then, are the privileges and immunities which are secured against abridgment by State legislation? . . .

The terms, privileges and immunities, are not new in the amendment; they were in the Constitution before the amendment was adopted. They are found in the second section of the fourth article, which declares that "the citizens of each State shall be entitled to all privileges and immunities of citizens in the several States," and they have been the subject of frequent consideration in judicial decisions. In *Corfield* v. *Coryell,* Mr. Justice Washington said he had "no hesitation in confining these expressions to those privileges and immunities which were, in their nature, fundamental; which belong of right to citizens of all free governments, and which have at all times been enjoyed by the citizens of the several States which compose the Union, from the time of their becoming free, independent, and sovereign;" and, in considering what those fundamental privileges were, he said that perhaps it would be more tedious than difficult to enumerate them, but that they might be "all comprehended under the following general heads: protection by the government; the enjoyment of life and liberty, with the right to acquire and possess property of every kind, and to pursue and obtain happiness and

safety, subject, nevertheless, to such restraints as the government may justly prescribe for the general good of the whole." This appears to me to be a sound construction of the clause in question. The privileges and immunities designated are those *which of right belong to the citizens of all free governments.* Clearly, among these must be placed the right to pursue a lawful employment in a lawful manner, without other restraint than such as equally affects all persons. . . .

What the clause in question did for the protection of the citizens of one State against hostile and discriminating legislation of other States, the fourteenth amendment does for the protection of every citizen of the United States against hostile and discriminating legislation against him in favor of others, whether they reside in the same or in different States. If under the fourth article of the Constitution equality of privileges and immunities is secured between citizens of different States, under the fourteenth amendment the same equality is secured between citizens of the United States. . . .

This equality of right, with exemption from all disparaging and partial enactments, in the lawful pursuits of life, throughout the whole country, is the distinguishing privilege of citizens of the United States. To them, everywhere, all pursuits, all professions, all avocations are open without other restrictions than such as are imposed equally upon all others of the same age, sex, and condition. The State may prescribe such regulations for every pursuit and calling of life as will promote the public health, secure the good order and advance the general prosperity of society, but when once prescribed, the pursuit or calling must be free to be followed by every citizen who is within the conditions designated, and will conform to the regulations. This is the fundamental idea upon which our institutions rest, and unless adhered to in the legislation of the country our government will be a republic only in name. The fourteenth amendment, in my judgment, makes it essential to the validity of the legislation of every State that this equality of right should be respected. . . .

MR. JUSTICE BRADLEY, dissenting. . . .

In my view, a law which prohibits a large class of citizens from adopting a lawful employment, or from following a lawful employment previously adopted, does deprive them of liberty as well as property, without due process of law. Their right of choice is a portion of their liberty; their occupation is their property. Such a law also deprives those citizens of the equal protection of the laws, contrary to the last clause of the section.

It is futile to argue that none but persons of the African race are intended to be benefited by this amendment. They may have been the primary cause of the amendment, but its language is general, embracing all citizens, and I think it was purposely so expressed.

Munn v. *Illinois*
94 U.S. 113; 24 L. Ed. 77 (1877)

Pursuant to Article XIII of the Illinois Constitution of 1870, which empowered the state legislature to regulate the storage of grain, the Illinois General Assembly enacted a statute in 1871 that required grain warehouses and elevators to obtain operating licenses and that established the maximum rates they could charge for the handling and storage of grain. Ira Y. Munn was convicted in county court of operating a grain warehouse without a license and of charging higher rates than those allowed by the law, and was fined $100. The Illinois Supreme Court affirmed his conviction, and Munn brought the case to the United States Supreme Court on a writ of error. *Opinion of the Court: Waite, Bradley, Clifford, Davis, Hunt, Miller, Swayne. Dissenting opinion: Field, Strong.*

MR. CHIEF JUSTICE WAITE delivered the opinion of the Court.

The question to be determined in this case is whether the general assembly of Illinois can, under the limitations upon the legislative power of the States imposed by the Constitution of the United States, fix by law the maximum of charges for the storage of grain in warehouses at Chicago and other places in the State. . . .

It is claimed that such a law is repugnant—To that part of amendment 14 which ordains that no State shall "deprive any person of life, liberty, or property, without due process of law." . . .

The Constitution contains no definition of the word "deprive," as used in the Fourteenth Amendment. To determine its signification, therefore, it is necessary to ascertain the effect which usage has given it, when employed in the same or a like connection.

While this provision of the amendment is new in the Constitution of the United States, as a limitation upon the powers of the States, it is old as a principle of civilized government. It is found in Magna Charta, and, in substance if not in form, in nearly or quite all the constitutions that have been from time to time adopted by the several States of the Union. By the Fifth Amendment, it was introduced into the Constitution of the United States as a limitation upon the powers of the national government, and by the Fourteenth, as a guaranty against any encroachment upon an acknowledged right of citizenship by the legislatures of the States. . . .

When one becomes a member of society, he necessarily parts with some rights or privileges which, as an individual not affected by his relations to others, he might retain. . . . This does not confer power upon the whole people to control rights which are purely and exclusively private, . . . but it does authorize the establishment of laws requiring each citizen to so conduct himself, and so use his own property, as not unnecessarily to injure another. . . . From this source come the police powers. . . . Under these powers the government regulates the conduct of its citizens one towards another, and the manner in which each shall use his own property, when such regulation becomes necessary for the public good. In their exercise it has been customary in England from time immemorial, and in this country from its first colonization, to regulate ferries, common carriers, hackmen, bakers, millers, wharfingers, innkeepers, &c., and in so doing to fix a maximum of charge to be made for services rendered, accommodations furnished, and articles sold. To this day, statutes are to be found in many of the States upon some or all these subjects; and we think it has never yet been successfully contended that such legislation came within any of the constitutional prohibitions against interference with private property. . . .

This brings us to inquire as to the principles upon which this power of regulation rests, in order that we may determine what is within and what without its operative effect. Looking, then, to the common law, from whence came the right which the Constitution protects, we find that when private property is "affected with a public interest, it ceases to be *juris privati* only." This was said by Lord Chief Justice Hale more than two hundred years ago, in his treatise *De Portibus Maris*, . . . and has been accepted without objection as an essential element in the law of property ever since. Property does become clothed with a public interest when used in a manner to make it of public consequence, and affect the community at large. When, therefore, one devotes his property to a use in which the public has an interest, he, in effect, grants to the public an interest in that use, and must submit to be controlled by the public for the common good, to the extent of the interest he has thus created. He may withdraw his grant by discontinuing the use; but, so long as he maintains the use, he must submit to the control. . . .

. . . When private property is devoted to a public use, it is subject to public regulation. It remains only to ascertain whether the warehouses of these plaintiffs in error, and the business which is carried on there, come within the operation of this principle.

. . . It is difficult to see why, if the common carrier, or the miller, or the ferryman, or the innkeeper, or the wharfinger, or the baker, or the cartman, or the hackney-coachman, pursues a public employment and exercises "a sort of public office," these plaintiffs in error do not. They stand . . . in the very "gateway of commerce," and take toll from all who pass. Their business most certainly "tends to a common charge, and is become a thing of public interest and use." Every bushel of grain for its passage "pays a toll, which is a common charge," and, therefore, according to Lord Hale, every such warehouseman "ought to be under public regulation, viz., that he . . . take but reasonable toll." Certainly, if any business

can be clothed "with a public interest, and cease to be *juris privati* only," this has been. . . .

. . . For our purposes we must assume that, if a state of facts could exist that would justify such legislation, it actually did exist when the statute now under consideration was passed. For us the question is one of power, not of expediency. If no state of circumstances could exist to justify such a statute, then we may declare this one void, because in excess of the legislative power of the State. But if it could, we must presume it did. Of the propriety of legislative interference within the scope of legislative power, the legislature is the exclusive judge. . . .

We know that this is a power which may be abused; but that is no argument against its existence. For protection against abuses by legislatures the people must resort to the polls, not to the courts. . . .

We conclude, therefore, that the statute in question is not repugnant to the Constitution of the United States, and that there is no error in the judgment. . . .

Judgment affirmed.

Mr. Justice Field, with whom Mr. Justice Strong concurs, dissenting. . . .

. . . I am compelled to dissent from the decision of the court in this case, and from the reasons upon which that decision is founded. The principle upon which the opinion of the majority proceeds is, in my judgment, subversive of the rights of private property, heretofore believed to be protected by constitutional guaranties against legislative interference. . . .

The question presented . . . is one of the greatest importance,—whether it is within the competency of a State to fix the compensation which an individual may receive for the use of his own property in his private business, and for his services in connection with it. . . .

. . . The court holds that property loses something of its private character when employed in such a way as to be generally useful. The doctrine declared is that property "becomes clothed with a public interest when used in a manner to make it of public consequence, and affect the community at large;" and from such clothing the right of the legislature is deduced to control the use of the property, and to determine the compensation which the owner may receive for it.

When Sir Matthew Hale, and the sages of the law in his day, spoke of property as affected by a public interest, and ceasing from that cause to be *juris privati* solely, that is, ceasing to be held merely in private right, they referred to property dedicated by the owner to public uses, or to property the use of which was granted by the government, or in connection with which special privileges were conferred. Unless the property was thus dedicated, or some right bestowed by the government was held with the property, either by specific grant or by prescription of so long a time as to imply a grant originally, the property was not affected by any public interest so as to be taken out of the category of property held in private right. But it is not in any such sense that the terms "clothing property with a public interest" are used in this case. From the nature of the business under consideration—the storage of grain—which, in any sense in which the words can be used, is a private business, in which the public are interested only as they are interested in the storage of other products of the soil, or in articles of manufacture, it is clear that the court intended to declare that, whenever one devotes his property to a business which is useful to the public,—"affects the community at large,"—the legislature can regulate the compensation which the owner may receive for its use, and for his own services in connection with it.

If this be sound law, if there be no protection, either in the principles upon which our republican government is founded, or in the prohibitions of the Constitution against such invasion of private rights, all property and all business in the State are held at the mercy of a majority of its legislature. . . .

. . . It is only where some right or privilege is conferred by the government or municipality upon the owner, which he can use in connection with his property, or by means of which the use of his property is rendered more valuable to him, or he thereby enjoys an advantage over others, that the compensation to be received by him becomes a legitimate matter of regulation. Submission to the regulation of compensation in such cases is an implied condition of the grant, and the State, in exercising its power of prescribing the compensation, only determines the conditions upon which its concession shall be enjoyed. When the privilege ends, the power of regulation ceases.

There is nothing in the character of the business of the defendants as warehousemen which called for the interference complained of in this case. Their buildings are not nuisances; their occupation of receiving and storing grain infringes upon no rights of others, disturbs no neighborhood, infects not the air, and in no respect prevents others from using and enjoying their property as to them may seem best. The legislation in question is nothing less than a bold assertion of absolute power by the State to control at its discretion the property and business of the citizen, and fix the compensation he shall receive. The will of the legislature is made the condition upon which the owner shall receive the fruits of his property and the just reward of his labor, industry, and enterprise. . . . The decision of the court in this case gives unrestrained license to legislative will. . . .

I am of opinion that the judgment of the Supreme Court of Illinois should be reversed.

Lochner v. *New York*

198 U.S. 45; 25 S. Ct. 539; 49 L. Ed. 937 (1905)

Joseph Lochner, a Utica, New York, bakery proprietor, was found guilty and fined $50 for violating an 1897 New York law that limited the hours of employment in bakeries and confectionery establishments to ten hours a day and sixty hours a week. When his conviction was sustained by the New York appellate courts, Lochner brought the case to the Supreme Court on a writ of error. *Opinion of the Court:* <u>Peckham</u>, *Brewer, Brown, Fuller, McKenna. Dissenting opinions:* <u>Harlan</u>, *Day, White;* <u>Holmes</u>.

MR. JUSTICE PECKHAM delivered the opinion of the Court. . . .

The statute necessarily interferes with the right of contract between the employer and employés, concerning the number of hours in which the latter may labor in the bakery of the employer. The general right to make a contract in relation to his business is part of the liberty of the individual protected by the Fourteenth Amendment of the Federal Constitution. . . . Under that provision no State can deprive any person of life, liberty or property without due process of law. The right to purchase or to sell labor is part of the liberty protected by this amendment, unless there are circumstances which exclude the right. There are, however, certain powers, existing in the sovereignty of each State in the Union, somewhat vaguely termed police powers, the exact description and limitation of which have not been attempted by the courts. Those powers, broadly stated, . . . relate to the safety, health, morals and general welfare of the public. Both property and liberty are held on such reasonable conditions as may be imposed by the governing power of the State in the exercise of those powers, and with such conditions the Fourteenth Amendment was not designed to interfere. . . .

It must, of course, be conceded that there is a limit to the valid exercise of the police power by the State. There is no dispute concerning this general proposition. Otherwise the Fourteenth Amendment would have no efficacy and the legislatures of the States would have unbounded power, and it would be enough to say that any piece of legislation was enacted to conserve the morals, the health or the safety of the people; such legislation would be valid, no matter how absolutely without foundation the claim might be. The claim of the police power would be a mere pretext—become another and delusive name for the supreme sovereignty of the State to be exercised free from constitutional restraint. This is not contended for. In every case that comes before this court, therefore, where legislation of this character is concerned and where the protection of the Federal Constitution is sought, the question necessarily arises: Is this a fair, reasonable and appropriate exercise of the police power of the State, or is it an unreasonable, unnecessary and arbitrary interference with the right of the individual to his personal liberty or to enter into those contracts in relation to labor which may seem to him appropriate or necessary for the support of himself and his family? Of course the liberty of contract relating to labor includes both parties to it. The one has as much right to purchase as the other to sell labor.

This is not a question of substituting the judgment of the court for that of the legislature. If the act be within the power of the State it is valid, although the judgment of the court might be totally opposed to the enactment of such a law. But the question would still remain: Is it within the police power of the State? and that question must be answered by the court.

The question whether this act is valid as a labor law, pure and simple, may be dismissed in a few words. There is no reasonable ground for interfering with the liberty of person or the right of free contract, by determining the hours of labor, in the occupation of a baker. There is no contention that bakers as a class are not equal in intelligence and capacity to men in other trades or manual occupations, or that they are not able to assert their rights and care for themselves without the protecting arm of the State, interfering with their independence of judgment and of action. They are in no sense wards of the State. Viewed in the light of a purely labor law, with no reference whatever to the question of health, we think that a law like the one before us involves neither the safety, the morals nor the welfare of the public, and that the interest of the public is not in the slightest degree affected by such an act. The law must be upheld, if at all, as a law pertaining to the health of the individual engaged in the occupation of a baker. It does not affect any other portion of the public than those who are engaged in that occupation. Clean and wholesome bread does not depend upon whether the baker works but ten hours per day or only sixty hours a week. . . .

We think the limit of the police power has been reached and passed in this case. There is, in our judgment, no reasonable foundation for holding this to be necessary or appropriate as a health law to safeguard the public health or the health of the individuals who are following the trade of a baker. . . .

We think that there can be no fair doubt that the trade of a baker, in and of itself, is not an unhealthy one to that degree which would authorize the legislature to interfere with the right to labor, and with the right of free contract on the part of the individual, either as employer or employé. In looking through statistics regarding all trades and occupations, it may be true that the trade of a baker does not appear to be as healthy as some other trades, and is also vastly more healthy than still others. . . .

. . . The act is not, within any fair meaning of the term, a health law, but is an illegal interference with the rights of individuals, both employers and employés, to make contracts regarding labor upon such terms as they may think best, or which they may agree upon with the other parties to such contracts. Statutes of the nature of that under review, limiting the hours in which grown and intelligent men may labor to earn their living, are mere meddlesome interferences with the rights of the individual, and they are not saved from condemnation by the claim that they are passed in the exercise of the police power and upon the subject of the health of the individual whose rights are interfered with, unless there be some fair ground, reasonable in and of itself, to say that there is material danger to the public health or to the health of the employés, if the hours of labor are not curtailed. . . .

It was further urged on the argument that restricting the hours of labor in the case of bakers was valid because it tended to cleanliness on the part of the workers, as a man was more apt to be cleanly when not overworked, and if cleanly then his "output" was also more likely to be so. . . . The connection, if any exists, is too shadowy and thin to build any argument for the interference of the legislature. If the man works ten hours a day it is all right, but if ten and a half or eleven his health is in danger and his bread may be unhealthful, and, therefore, he shall not be permitted to do it. This, we think, is unreasonable and entirely arbitrary. . . .

It is manifest to us that the limitation of the hours of labor as provided for in this section of the statute . . . has no such direct relation to and no such substantial effect upon the health of the employé, as to justify us in regarding the section as really a health law. It seems to us that the real object and purpose were simply to regulate the hours of labor between the master and his em-

ployés . . . in a private business, not dangerous in any degree to morals or in any real and substantial degree, to the health of the employés. Under such circumstances the freedom of master and employé to contract with each other in relation to their employment, and in defining the same, cannot be prohibited or interfered with, without violating the Federal Constitution. . . .

Reversed.

MR. JUSTICE HARLAN, with whom MR. JUSTICE WHITE and MR. JUSTICE DAY concur, dissenting. . . .

I take it to be firmly established that what is called the liberty of contract may, within certain limits, be subjected to regulations designed and calculated to promote the general welfare or to guard the public health, the public morals or the public safety. . . .

Granting . . . that there is a liberty of contract which cannot be violated even under the sanction of direct legislative enactment, but assuming, as according to settled law we may assume, that such liberty of contract is subject to such regulations as the State may reasonably prescribe for the common good and the well-being of society, what are the conditions under which the judiciary may declare such regulations to be in excess of legislative authority and void? Upon this point there is no room for dispute; for, the rule is universal that a legislative enactment, Federal or state, is never to be disregarded or held invalid unless it be, beyond question, plainly and palpably in excess of legislative power. . . . If there be doubt as to the validity of the statute, that doubt must therefore be resolved in favor of its validity, and the courts must keep their hands off, leaving the legislature to meet the responsibility for unwise legislation. If the end which the legislature seeks to accomplish be one to which its power extends, and if the means employed to that end, although not the wisest or best, are yet not plainly and palpably unauthorized by law, then the court cannot interfere. In other words, when the validity of a statute is questioned, the burden of proof, so to speak, is upon those who assert it to be unconstitutional. . . .

Let these principles be applied to the present case. . . .

It is plain that this statute was enacted in order to protect the physical well-being of those who work in bakery and confectionery establishments. . . . I find it impossible, in view of common experience, to say that there is here no real or substantial relation between the means employed by the State and the end sought to be accomplished by its legislation. . . . Nor can I say that the statute has no appropriate or direct connection with that protection to health which each State owes to her citizens, . . . or that it is not promotive of the health of the employés in question, . . . or that the regulation prescribed by the State is utterly unreasonable and extravagant or wholly arbitrary. . . . Still less can I say that the statute is, beyond question, a plain, palpable invasion of rights secured by the fundamental law. . . . Therefore I submit that this court will transcend its functions if it assumes to annul the statute of New York. It must be remembered that this statute does not apply to all kinds of business. It applies only to work in bakery and confectionery establishments, in which, as all know, the air constantly breathed by workmen is not as pure and healthful as that to be found in some other establishments or out of doors. . . .

. . . There are many reasons of a weighty, substantial character, based upon the experience of mankind, in support of the theory that, all things considered, more than ten hours' steady work each day, from week to week, in a bakery or confectionery establishment, may endanger the health, and shorten the lives of the workmen, thereby diminishing their physical and mental capacity to serve the State, and to provide for those dependent upon them.

If such reasons exist that ought to be the end of this case, for the State is not amenable to the judiciary, in respect of its legislative enactments, unless such enactments are plainly, palpably, beyond all question, inconsistent with the Constitution of the United States. We are not to presume that the state of New York has acted in bad faith. Nor can we assume that its legislature acted without due deliberation, or that it did not determine this question upon the fullest attainable information, and for the common good. We cannot say that the State has acted without reason nor ought we to proceed upon the theory that its action is a mere sham. Our duty, I submit, is to sustain the statute as not being in conflict with the Federal Constitution, for the reason—

and such is an all-sufficient reason—it is not shown to be plainly and palpably inconsistent with that instrument. . . .

I take leave to say that the New York statute, in the particulars here involved, cannot be held to be in conflict with the Fourteenth Amendment, without enlarging the scope of the Amendment far beyond its original purpose and without bringing under the supervision of this court matters which have been supposed to belong exclusively to the legislative departments of the several States when exerting their conceded power to guard the health and safety of their citizens by such regulations as they in their wisdom deem best. . . .

MR. JUSTICE HOLMES, dissenting. . . .

This case is decided upon an economic theory which a large part of the country does not entertain. If it were a question whether I agreed with that theory, I should desire to study it further and long before making up my mind. But I do not conceive that to be my duty, because I strongly believe that my agreement or disagreement has nothing to do with the right of a majority to embody their opinions in law. It is settled by various decisions of this court that state constitutions and state laws may regulate life in many ways which we as legislators might think as injudicious or if you like as tyrannical as this, and which equally with this interfere with the liberty to contract. Sunday laws and usury laws are ancient examples. A more modern one is the prohibition of lotteries. . . . The Fourteenth Amendment does not enact Mr. Herbert Spencer's Social Statics. . . . A constitution is not intended to embody a particular economic theory, whether of paternalism and the organic relation of the citizen to the State or of *laissez faire*. It is made for people of fundamentally differing views, and the accident of our finding certain opinions natural and familiar or novel and even shocking ought not to conclude our judgment upon the question whether statutes embodying them conflict with the Constitution of the United States.

. . . I think that the word liberty in the Fourteenth Amendment is perverted when it is held to prevent the natural outcome of a dominant opinion, unless it can be said that a rational and fair man necessarily would admit that the statute proposed would infringe fundamental principles as they have been understood by the traditions of our people and our law. It does not need research to show that no such sweeping condemnation can be passed upon the statute be-fore us. A reasonable man might think it a proper measure on the score of health. Men whom I certainly could not pronounce unreasonable would uphold it as a first instalment of a general regulation of the hours of work. . . .

West Coast Hotel Company v. Parrish
300 U.S. 379; 57 S. Ct. 578; 81 L. Ed. 703 (1937)

In 1913 the state legislature of Washington enacted a minimum wage law covering women and minors. The law provided for the establishment of an Individual Welfare Commission, which was authorized "to establish such standards of wages and conditions of labor for women and minors employed within the State of Washington as shall be held hereunder to be reasonable and not detrimental to health and morals, and which shall be sufficient for the decent maintenance of women." Elsie Parrish, employed as a chambermaid by the West Coast Hotel Company, together with her husband brought suit to recover the difference between the wages paid her and the minimum wage fixed pursuant to the state law. The minimum wage for her job was $14.50 for a forty-eight hour week. The trial court decided against Parrish and declared the law to be repugnant to the Due Process Clause of the Fourteenth Amendment. The Washington Supreme Court reversed the trial court and sustained the statute. The hotel company brought the case to the U.S. Supreme Court on appeal. *Opinion of the Court:* Hughes, *Brandeis, Cardozo, Roberts, Stone. Dissenting opinion:* Sutherland, *Butler, McReynolds, Van Devanter.*

MR. CHIEF JUSTICE HUGHES delivered the opinion of the Court.

This case presents the question of the constitutional validity of the minimum wage law of the State of Washington. . . .

The appellant relies upon the decision of this Court in *Adkins* v. *Children's Hospital* . . . , which held invalid the District of Columbia Minimum Wage Act, which was attacked under the due process clause of the Fifth Amendment. . . . The state court has refused to regard the decision in the *Adkins* case as determinative and has pointed to our decisions both before and since that case as justifying its position. We are of the opinion that this ruling of the state court demands on our part a reëxamination of the *Adkins* case. The importance of the question, in which many States having similar laws are concerned, the close division by which the decision in the *Adkins* case was reached, and the economic con-ditions which have supervened, and in the light of which the reasonableness of the exercise of the protective power of the State must be considered, make it not only appropriate, but we think imperative, that in deciding the present case the subject should receive fresh consideration. . . .

. . . The violation alleged by those attacking minimum wage regulation for women is deprivation of freedom of contract. What is this freedom? The Constitution does not speak of freedom of contract. It speaks of liberty and prohibits the deprivation of liberty without due process of law. In prohibiting that deprivation the Constitution does not recognize an absolute and uncontrollable liberty. Liberty in each of its phases has its history and connotation. But the liberty safeguarded is liberty in a social organization which requires the protection of law against the evils which menace the health, safety, morals and welfare of the people. Liberty under the Constitution is thus necessarily subject to the restraints of due process, and regulation which is reasonable in relation to its subject and is adopted in the interests of the community is due process.

. . . What can be closer to the public interest than the health of women and their protection from unscrupulous and overreaching employers? And if the protection of women is a legitimate end of the exercise of state power, how can it be said that the requirement of the payment of a minimum wage fairly fixed in order to meet the very necessities of existence is not an admissible means to that end? The legislature of the State was clearly entitled to consider the situation of women in employment, the fact that they are in the class receiving the least pay, that their bargaining power is relatively weak, and that they are the ready victims of those who would take advantage of their necessitous circumstances. The legislature was entitled to adopt measures to reduce the evils of the "sweating system," the exploiting of workers at wages so low as to be insufficient to meet the bare cost of living, thus making their very helplessness the occasion of a most injurious competition. The legislature had the right to consider that its minimum wage requirements would be an important aid in carrying out its policy of protection. The adoption of similar requirements by many States evidences a deepseated conviction both as to the presence of the evil and as to the means adapted to check it. Legislative response to that conviction cannot be regarded as arbitrary or capricious, and that is all we have to decide. Even if the wisdom of the policy be regarded as debatable and its effects uncertain, still the legislature is entitled to its judgment.

There is an additional and compelling consideration which recent economic experience has brought into a strong light. The exploitation of a class of workers who are in an unequal position with respect to bargaining power and are thus relatively defenceless against the denial of a living wage is not only detrimental to their health and well being but casts a direct burden for their support upon the community. What these workers lose in wages the taxpayers are called upon to pay. The bare cost of living must be met. . . . The community is not bound to provide what is in effect a subsidy for unconscionable employers. The community may direct its law-making power to correct the abuse which springs from their selfish disregard of the public interest. . . .

Our conclusion is that the case of *Adkins* v. *Children's Hospital* . . . should be, and it is, overruled. The judgment of the Supreme Court of the State of Washington is

Affirmed.

MR. JUSTICE SUTHERLAND, dissenting.

It is urged that the question involved should now receive fresh consideration, among other reasons, because of "the economic conditions which have supervened"; but the meaning of the Constitution does not change with the ebb and flow of economic events. We frequently are told in more general words that the Constitution must be construed in the light of the present. If by that it is meant that the Constitution is made up of living words that apply to every new condition which they include, the statement is quite true. But to say, if that be intended, that the words of the Constitution mean today what they did not mean when written—that is, that they do not apply to a situation now to which they would have applied then—is to rob that instrument of the essential element which continues it in force as the people have made it until they, and not their official agents, have made it otherwise. . . .

The judicial function is that of interpretation; it does not include the power of amendment under the guise of interpretation. To miss the point of difference between the two is to miss all that the phrase "supreme law of the land" stands for and to convert what was intended as inescapable and enduring mandates into mere moral reflections. . . .

Coming, then, to a consideration of the Washington statute, it first is to be observed that it is in every substantial respect identical with the statute involved in the *Adkins* case. Such vices as existed in the latter are present in the former. And if the *Adkins* case was properly decided, as we who join in this opinion think it was, it necessarily follows that the Washington statute is invalid. . . .

Neither the statute involved in the *Adkins* case nor the Washington statute, so far as it is involved here, has the slightest relation to the capacity or earning power of the employee, to the number of hours which constitute the day's work, the character of the place where the work is to be done, or the circumstances or surroundings of the employment. The sole basis upon which the question of validity rests is the assumption that the employee is entitled to receive a sum of money sufficient to provide a living for her, keep her in health and preserve her morals. . . .

What we said further, in that case . . . is

equally applicable here . . . : "A statute which prescribes payment without regard to any of these things and solely with relation to circumstances apart from the contract of employment, the business affected by it and the work done under it, is so clearly the product of a naked, arbitrary exercise of power that it cannot be allowed to stand under the Constitution of the United States." . . .

Williamson v. *Lee Optical Company*
348 U.S. 483; 75 S. Ct. 461; 99 L. Ed. 563 (1955)

In 1953 the Oklahoma legislature passed a law that made it unlawful for any person other than a licensed ophthalmologist or optometrist to fit lenses to the face or to duplicate or replace lenses, except upon written prescriptive authority of a licensed ophthalmologist or optometrist. Lee Optical challenged the constitutionality of this law before a federal district court of three judges, alleging in part that it violated the Due Process Clause of the Fourteenth Amendment. The district court agreed, holding portions of the act unconstitutional, and the state of Oklahoma appealed to the Supreme Court. *Opinion of the Court: Douglas, Black, Burton, Clark, Frankfurter, Minton, Reed, Warren. Harlan did not participate.*

MR. JUSTICE DOUGLAS delivered the opinion of the Court. . . .

An ophthalmologist is a duly licensed physician who specializes in the care of the eyes. An optometrist examines eyes for refractive error, recognizes (but does not treat) diseases of the eye, and fills prescriptions for eyeglasses. The optician is an artisan qualified to grind lenses, fill prescriptions, and fit frames.

The effect of § 2 is to forbid the optician from fitting or duplicating lenses without a prescription from an ophthalmologist or optometrist. In practical effect, it means that no optician can fit old glasses into new frames or supply a lens, whether it be a new lens or one to duplicate a lost or broken lens, without a prescription. The District Court . . . rebelled at the notion that a State could require a prescription from an optometrist or ophthalmologist "to take old lenses and place them in new frames and then fit the completed spectacles to the *face* of the eyeglass wearer." . . . It held that such a requirement was

not "reasonably and rationally related to the health and welfare of the people." . . . It was, accordingly, the opinion of the court that this provision of the law violated the Due Process Clause by arbitrarily interfering with the optician's right to do business.

The Oklahoma law may exact a needless, wasteful requirement in many cases. But it is for the legislature, not the courts, to balance the advantages and disadvantages of the new requirement. It appears that in many cases the optician can easily supply the new frames or new lenses without reference to the old written prescription. It also appears that many written prescriptions contain no directive data in regard to fitting spectacles to the face. But in some cases the directions contained in the prescription are essential, if the glasses are to be fitted so as to correct the particular defects of vision or alleviate the eye condition. The legislature might have concluded that the frequency of occasions when a prescription is necessary was sufficient to justify this regulation of the fitting of eyeglasses. Likewise, when it is necessary to duplicate a lens, a written prescription may or may not be necessary. But the legislature might have concluded that one was needed often enough to require one in every case. Or the legislature may have concluded that eye examinations were so critical, not only for correction of vision but also for detection of latent ailments or diseases, that every change in frames and every duplication of a lens should be accompanied by a prescription from a medical expert. To be sure, the present law does not require a new examination of the eyes every time the frames are changed or the lenses duplicated. For if the old prescription is on file with the optician, he can go ahead and make the new fitting or duplicate the lenses. But the law need not be in every respect logically consistent with its aims to be constitutional. It is enough that there is an evil at hand for correction, and that it might be thought that the particular legislative measure was a rational way to correct it.

The day is gone when this Court uses the Due Process Clause of the Fourteenth Amendment to strike down state laws, regulatory of business and industrial conditions, because they may be unwise, improvident, or out of harmony with a particular school of thought. . . . We emphasize again what Chief Justice Waite said in *Munn* v. *Illinois*, . . . "For protection against abuses by legislatures the people must resort to the polls, not to the courts." . . .

BMW of North America, Inc. v. *Gore*
517 U.S. 559, 116 S. Ct. 1589, 134 L. Ed. 2d 809 (1996)

Nine months after Dr. Ira Gore purchased a new black BMW sport sedan for approximately $41,000 from an authorized Alabama dealer, he brought his car to an automobile detailer, who detected evidence that portions of the car had been repainted. Dr. Gore subsequently brought suit in Alabama court for $500,000 in compensatory and punitive damages against the American distributor of BMWs, alleging that the failure to disclose the repainting constituted fraud under Alabama law. At trial, BMW acknowledged that it followed a nationwide policy of not advising its dealer, and hence their customers, of predelivery damage to new cars when the cost of repair did not exceed 3 percent of the car's suggested retail price. The cost of repainting Dr. Gore's vehicle was $601.37 (or about 1.5 percent of its suggested retail price) and therefore fell into that category. The jury returned a verdict finding BMW liable for compensatory damages of $4,000 (its judgment of how much less Dr. Gore's car was worth because it had been repainted) and assessing $4 million in punitive damages (its judgment of the appropriate punishment for BMW for selling approximately 1,000 repainted cars nationally for approximately $4,000 more than each was worth). The trial judge denied BMW's posttrial motion to set aside the punitive damages award, holding, among other things, that the award was not "grossly excessive" and thus did not violate the Due Process Clause of the Fourteenth Amendment as interpreted in two earlier damages cases: *Pacific Mutual Insurance Co.* v. *Haslip*, 499 U.S. 1 (1991), and *TXO Production Corp.* v. *Alliance Resources Corp.*, 509 U.S. 443 (1993). The Alabama Supreme Court agreed, but reduced the award to $2 million on the ground that, in computing the amount, the jury had improperly multiplied Dr. Gore's compensatory damages by the number of similar sales in all States, not just those in Alabama. BMW petitioned the Supreme Court for a writ of certiorari. *Opinion of the Court:* Stevens, *Breyer, Kennedy, O'Connor, Souter. Concurring opinion:* Breyer, *O'Connor, Souter. Dissenting opinions:* Scalia, *Thomas;* Ginsburg, *Rehnquist.*

JUSTICE STEVENS delivered the opinion of the Court.

The Due Process Clause of the Fourteenth Amendment prohibits a State from imposing a "grossly excessive" punishment on a tortfeasor. The wrongdoing involved in this case was the decision by a national distributor of automobiles not to advise its dealers, and hence their customers, of predelivery damage to new cars when the cost of repair amounted to less than 3 percent of the car's suggested retail price. The question presented is whether a $2 million punitive damages award to the purchaser of one of these cars exceeds the constitutional limit. . . .

Punitive damages may properly be imposed to further a State's legitimate interests in punishing unlawful conduct and deterring its repetition. In our federal system, States necessarily have considerable flexibility in determining the level of punitive damages that they will allow in different classes of cases and in any particular case. Most States that authorize exemplary damages afford the jury similar latitude, requiring only that the damages awarded be reasonably necessary to vindicate the State's legitimate interests in punishment and deterrence. Only when an award can fairly be categorized as "grossly excessive" in relation to these interests does it enter the zone of arbitrariness that violates the Due Process Clause of the Fourteenth Amendment. . . .

Elementary notions of fairness enshrined in our constitutional jurisprudence dictate that a person receive fair notice not only of the conduct that will subject him to punishment, but also of the severity of the penalty that a State may impose. Three guideposts, each of which indicates that BMW did not receive adequate notice of the magnitude of the sanction that Alabama might impose for adhering to the nondisclosure policy adopted in 1983, lead us to the conclusion that the $2 million award against BMW is grossly excessive: the degree of reprehensibility of the nondisclosure; the disparity between the harm or potential harm suffered by Dr. Gore and his punitive damages award; and the difference be-

tween this remedy and the civil penalties authorized or imposed in comparable cases. We discuss these considerations in turn.

DEGREE OF REPREHENSIBILITY

Perhaps the most important indicium of the reasonableness of a punitive damages award is the degree of reprehensibility of the defendant's conduct. As the Court stated nearly 150 years ago, exemplary damages imposed on a defendant should reflect "the enormity of his offense." *Day* v. *Woodworth,* 13 How. 363, 371 (1852). This principle reflects the accepted view that some wrongs are more blameworthy than others. Thus, we have said that "nonviolent crimes are less serious than crimes marked by violence or the threat of violence." Similarly, "trickery and deceit" are more reprehensible than negligence.

In this case, none of the aggravating factors associated with particularly reprehensible conduct is present. The harm BMW inflicted on Dr. Gore was purely economic in nature. The presale refinishing of the car had no effect on its performance or safety features, or even its appearance for at least nine months after his purchase. BMW's conduct evinced no indifference to or reckless disregard for the health and safety of others. To be sure, infliction of economic injury, especially when done intentionally through affirmative acts of misconduct, or when the target is financially vulnerable, can warrant a substantial penalty. But this observation does not convert all acts that cause economic harm into torts that are sufficiently reprehensible to justify a significant sanction in addition to compensatory damages. . . .

[T]he record in this case discloses no deliberate false statements, acts of affirmative misconduct, or concealment of evidence of improper motive. We accept, of course, the jury's finding that BMW suppressed a material fact which Alabama law obligated it to communicate to prospective purchasers of repainted cars in that State. But the omission of a material fact may be less reprehensible than a deliberate false statement, particularly when there is a good-faith basis for believing that no duty to disclose exists. That conduct is sufficiently reprehensible to give rise to tort liability, and even a modest award of exemplary damages, does not establish the high degree of culpability that warrants a substantial punitive damages award. Because this case exhibits none of the circumstances ordinarily associated with egregiously improper conduct, we are persuaded that BMW's conduct was not sufficiently reprehensible to warrant imposition of a $2 million exemplary damages award.

RATIO

The second and perhaps most commonly cited indicium of an unreasonable or excessive punitive damages award is its ratio to the actual harm inflicted on the plaintiff. The principle that exemplary damages must bear a "reasonable relationship" to compensatory damages has a long pedigree. Scholars have identified a number of early English statutes authorizing the award of multiple damages for particular wrongs. Some 65 different enactments during the period between 1275 and 1753 provided for double, treble, or quadruple damages. . . .

The $2 million in punitive damages awarded to Dr. Gore by the Alabama Supreme Court is 500 times the amount of his actual harm as determined by the jury. Moreover, there is no suggestion that Dr. Gore or any other BMW purchaser was threatened with any additional potential harm by BMW's nondisclosure policy. . . .

Of course, we have consistently rejected the notion that the constitutional line is marked by a simple mathematical formula, even one that compares actual and potential damages to the punitive award. Indeed, low awards of compensatory damages may properly support a higher ratio than high compensatory awards, if, for example, a particularly egregious act has resulted in only a small amount of economic damages. A higher ratio may also be justified in cases in which the jury is hard to detect or the monetary value of noneconomic harm might have been difficult to determine. It is appropriate, therefore, to reiterate our rejection of a categorical approach. . . . "We need not, and indeed we cannot, draw a mathematical bright line between the constitu-

tionally acceptable and the constitutionally unacceptable that would fit every case. We can say, however, that [a] general concer[n] of reasonableness . . . properly enter[s] into the constitutional calculus." [*Pacific Mutual Life Insurance Co.* v.] *Haslip*, 499 U. S. 1, 18 (1991). In most cases, the ratio will be within a constitutionally acceptable range, and remittitur will not be justified on this basis. When the ratio is a breathtaking 500 to 1, however, the award must surely "raise a suspicious judicial eyebrow."

SANCTIONS FOR COMPARABLE MISCONDUCT

Comparing the punitive damages award and the civil or criminal penalties that could be imposed for comparable misconduct provides a third indicium of excessiveness. . . . In this case the $2 million economic sanction imposed on BMW is substantially greater than the statutory fines available in Alabama and elsewhere for similar malfeasance.

The maximum civil penalty authorized by the Alabama Legislature for a violation of its Deceptive Trade Practices Act is $2,000; other States authorize more severe sanctions, with the maxima ranging from $5,000 to $10,000. Significantly, some statutes draw a distinction between first offenders and recidivists; thus, in New York the penalty is $50 for a first offense and $250 for subsequent offenses. None of these statutes would provide an out-of-state distributor with fair notice that the first violation . . . of its provisions might subject an offender to a multimillion dollar penalty. . . .

[W]e of course accept the Alabama courts' view that the state interest in protecting its citizens from deceptive trade practices justifies a sanction in addition to the recovery of compensatory damages. We cannot, however, accept the conclusion of the Alabama Supreme Court that BMW's conduct was sufficiently egregious to justify a punitive sanction that is tantamount to a severe criminal penalty. . . .

The Judgment is reversed, and the case is remanded for further proceedings not inconsistent with this opinion.

JUSTICE BREYER, with whom JUSTICE O'CONNOR and JUSTICE SOUTER join, concurring.

. . . Members of this Court have generally thought . . . that if "fair procedures were followed, a judgment that is a product of that process is entitled to a strong presumption of validity." And the Court also has found that punitive damages procedures very similar to those followed here were not, by themselves, fundamentally unfair. Thus, I believe it important to explain why this presumption of validity is overcome in this instance.

The reason flows from the Court's emphasis upon the constitutional importance of legal standards that provide "reasonable constraints" within which "discretion is exercised." . . .

This constitutional concern, itself harkening back to the Magna Carta, arises out of the basic unfairness of depriving citizens of life, liberty, or property, through the application, not of law and legal processes, but of arbitrary coercion. Requiring the application of law, rather than a decisionmaker's caprice, does more than simply provide citizens notice of what actions may subject them to punishment; it also helps to assure the uniform general treatment of similarly situated persons that is the essence of law itself. . . .

Legal standards need not be precise in order to satisfy this constitutional concern. But they must offer some kind of constraint upon a jury or court's discretion, and thus protection against purely arbitrary behavior. The standards the Alabama courts applied here are vague and openended to the point where they risk arbitrary results. In my view, although the vagueness of those standards does not, by itself, violate due process, it does invite the kind of scrutiny the Court has given the particular verdict before us.

First, the Alabama statute that permits damages does not itself contain a standard that readily distinguishes between conduct warranting very small, and conduct warranting very large, punitive damages awards. . . .

Second, the Alabama courts, in this case, have applied the "factors" intended to constrain punitive damages awards, in a way that belies that purpose. . . . [A]s the Alabama courts have authoritatively interpreted them, and as their application in this case illustrates, they impose little actual constraint. . . .

Third, the state courts neither referred to, nor made any effort to find, nor enunciated any other standard, that either directly, or indirectly as background, might have supplied the constraining legal force that the statute and [Alabama court] standards lack. . . .

The record before us . . . contains nothing suggesting that the Alabama Supreme Court, when determining the allowable award, applied any "economic" theory that might explain the $2 million recovery. . . . [C]ourts properly tend to judge the rationality of judicial actions in terms of the reasons that were given, and the facts that were before the court, not those that might have been given on the basis of some conceivable set of facts. . . . Therefore, reference to a constraining "economic" theory, which might have counseled more deferential review by this Court, is lacking in this case.

Fourth, I cannot find any community understanding or historic practice that this award might exemplify and which, therefore, would provide background standards constraining arbitrary behavior and excessive awards. . . .

Fifth, there are no other legislative enactments here that classify awards and impose quantitative limits that would significantly cabin the fairly unbounded discretion created by the absence of constraining legal standards. . . .

The upshot is that the rules that purport to channel discretion in this kind of case, here did not do so in fact. That means that the award in this case was both (a) the product of a system of standards that did not significantly constrain a court's, and hence a jury's, discretion in making that award; and (b) was grossly excessive in light of the State's legitimate punitive damages objectives.

The first of these reasons has special importance where courts review a jury-determined punitive damages award. That is because one cannot expect to direct jurors like legislators through the ballot box; nor can one expect those jurors to interpret law like judges, who work within a discipline and hierarchical organization that normally promotes roughly uniform interpretation and application of the law. Yet here Alabama expects jurors to act, at least a little, like legislators or judges, for it permits them, to a certain extent, to create public policy and to apply that policy, not to compensate a victim, but to achieve a policy-related objective outside the confines of the particular case.

To the extent that neither clear legal principles, nor fairly obvious historical or community-based standards (defining, say, especially egregious behavior) significantly constrain punitive damages awards, is there not a substantial risk of outcomes so arbitrary that they become difficult to square with the Constitution's assurance, to every citizen, of the law's protection? The standards here, as authoritatively interpreted, in my view, make this threat real and not theoretical. And, in these unusual circumstances, where legal standards offer virtually no constraint, I believe that this lack of constraining standards warrants this Court's detailed examination of the award.

The second reason—the severe disproportionality between the award and the legitimate punitive damages objectives—reflects a judgment about a matter of degree. I recognize that it is often difficult to determine just when a punitive award exceeds an amount reasonably related to a State's legitimate interests, or when that excess is so great as to amount to a matter of constitutional concern. Yet whatever the difficulties of drawing a precise line, once we examine the award in this case, it is not difficult to say that this award lies on the line's far side. The severe lack of proportionality between the size of the award and the underlying punitive damages objectives shows that the award falls into the category of "gross excessiveness" set forth in this Court's prior cases.

These two reasons taken together overcome what would otherwise amount to a "strong presumption of validity." And, for those two reasons, I conclude that the award in this unusual case violates the basic guarantee of nonarbitrary governmental behavior that the Due Process Clause provides.

JUSTICE SCALIA, with whom JUSTICE THOMAS joins, dissenting.

Today we see that latest manifestation of this Court's recent and increasingly insistent "concern about punitive damages that 'run wild.'" Since the Constitution does not make that concern any of our business, the Court's activities in this area are an unjustified incursion into the province of state governments.

In earlier cases that were the prelude to this decision, I set forth my view that a state trial procedure that commits the decision whether to impose punitive damages, and the amount, to the discretion of the jury, subject to some judicial review for "reasonableness," furnishes a defendant with all the process that is "due." I do not regard the Fourteenth Amendment's Due Process

Clause as a secret repository of substantive guarantees against "unfairness"—neither the unfairness of an excessive civil compensatory award, nor the unfairness of an "unreasonable" punitive award. What the Fourteenth Amendment's procedural guarantee assures is an opportunity to contest the reasonableness of a damages judgment in state court; but there is no federal guarantee a damage award actually be reasonable.

This view, which adheres to the text of the Due Process Clause, has not prevailed in our punitive-damages cases. When, however, a constitutional doctrine adopted by the Court is not only mistaken but also insusceptible of principled application, I do not feel bound to give it stare decisis effect—indeed, I do not feel justified in doing so. Our punitive-damages jurisprudence compels such a response. The Constitution provides no warrant for federalizing yet another aspect of our Nation's legal culture (no matter how much in need of correction it may be), and the application of the Court's new rule of constitutional law is constrained by no principle other than the Justices' subjective assessment of the "reasonableness" of the award in relation to the conduct for which it was assessed.

Because today's judgment represents the first instance of this Court's invalidation of a state-court punitive assessment as simply unreasonably large, I think it a proper occasion to discuss these points at some length.

The most significant aspects of today's decision—the identification of a "substantive due process" right against a "grossly excessive" award, and the concomitant assumption of ultimate authority to decide anew a matter of "reasonableness" resolved in lower court proceedings—are of course not new. *Haslip* and *TXO* revived the notion, moribund since its appearance in the first years of this century, that the measure of civil punishment poses a question of constitutional dimension to be answered by this Court. Neither of those cases, however, nor any of the precedents upon which they relied, actually took the step of declaring a punitive award unconstitutional simply because it was "too big."

At the time of adoption of the Fourteenth Amendment, it was well understood that punitive damages represent the assessment by the jury, as the voice of the community, of the measure of punishment the defendant deserved. Today's decision, though dressed up as a legal opinion, is really no more than a disagreement with the community's sense of indignation or outrage expressed in the punitive award of the Alabama jury, as reduced by the State Supreme Court. It reflects not merely, as the concurrence candidly acknowledges, "a judgment about a matter of degree," but a judgment about the appropriate degree of indignation or outrage, which is hardly an analytical determination. . . .

One might understand the Court's eagerness to enter this field, rather than leave it with the state legislatures, if it had something useful to say. In fact, however, its opinion provides virtually no guidance to legislatures, and to state and federal courts, as to what a "constitutionally proper" level of punitive damages might be. . . .

In . . . its opinion, the Court identifies "[t]hree guideposts" that lead it to the conclusion that the award in this case is excessive: degree of reprehensibility, ratio between punitive award and plaintiff's actual harm, and legislative sanctions provided for comparable misconduct. The legal significance of these "guideposts" is nowhere explored, but their necessary effect is to establish federal standards governing the hitherto exclusively state law of damages. Apparently (though it is by no means clear) all three federal "guideposts" can be overridden if "necessary to deter future misconduct,"—a loophole that will encourage state reviewing courts to uphold awards as necessary for the "adequat[e] protect[ion] of state consumers. By effectively requiring state reviewing courts to concoct rationalizations—whether within the "guideposts" or through the loophole— to justify the intuitive punitive reactions of state juries, the Court accords neither category of institution the respect it deserves.

Of course it will not be easy for the States to comply with this new federal law of damages, no matter how willing they are to do so. In truth, the "guideposts" mark a road to nowhere; they provide no real guidance at all. As to "degree of reprehensibility" of the defendant's conduct, we learn that "nonviolent crimes are less serious than crimes marked by violence or the threat of violence," and that "trickery and deceit" are "more reprehensible than negligence." As to the ratio of punitive to compensatory damages, we are told that a "general concer[n] of reasonableness . . . enter[s] into the constitutional calculus,"—though even "a breathtaking 500 to 1" will not necessarily do anything more than "raise a suspicious judicial eyebrow." And as to legislative sanctions provided for comparable misconduct, they should be accorded "substantial deference." One expects the Court to conclude "To thine own self be true."

These criss-crossing platitudes yield no real answers in no real cases. And it must be noted that the Court nowhere says that these three "guideposts" are the only guideposts; indeed, it makes very clear that they are not—explaining away the earlier opinions that do not really follow these "guideposts" on the basis of additional factors, thereby "reiterat[ing] our rejection of a categorical approach." In other words, even these utter platitudes, if they should ever happen to produce an answer, may be overridden by other unnamed considerations. The Court has constructed a framework that does not genuinely constrain, that does not inform state legislatures and lower courts—that does nothing at all except confer an artificial air of doctrinal analysis upon its essentially ad hoc determination that this particular award of punitive damages was not "fair." . . .

The elevation of "fairness" in punishment to a principle of "substantive due process" means that every punitive award unreasonably imposed is unconstitutional; such an award is by definition excessive, since it attaches a penalty to conduct undeserving of punishment. Indeed, if the Court is correct, it must be that every claim that a state jury's award of compensatory damages is "unreasonable" (because not supported by the evidence) amounts to an assertion of constitutional injury. And the same would be true for determinations of liability. By today's logic, every dispute as to evidentiary sufficiency in a state civil suit poses a question of constitutional moment, subject to review in this Court. That is a stupefying proposition.

For the foregoing reasons, I respectfully dissent.

JUSTICE GINSBURG, with whom THE CHIEF JUSTICE joins, dissenting.

The Court, I am convinced, unnecessarily and unwisely ventures into territory traditionally within the States' domain, and does so in the face of reform measures recently adopted or currently under consideration in legislative arenas. The Alabama Supreme Court, in this case, endeavored to follow this Court's prior instructions; and, more recently, Alabama's highest court has installed further controls on awards of punitive damages. I would therefore leave the state court's judgment undisturbed, and resist unnecessary intrusion into an area dominantly of state concern. . . .

The Court finds Alabama's $2 million award not simply excessive, but grossly so, and therefore unconstitutional. The decision leads us further into territory traditionally within the States' domain, and commits the Court, now and again, to correct "misapplication of a properly stated rule of law." The Court is not well equipped for this mission. Tellingly, the Court repeats that it brings to the task no "mathematical formula," no "categorical approach," no "bright line." It has only a vague concept of sub-stantive due process, a "raised eyebrow" test, as its ultimate guide.

In contrast to habeas corpus review under 28 U. S. C. 2254, the Court will work at this business alone. It will not be aided by the federal district courts and courts of appeals. It will be the only federal court policing the area. The Court's readiness to superintend state court punitive damages awards is all the more puzzling in view of the Court's longstanding reluctance to countenance review, even by courts of appeals, of the size of verdicts returned by juries in federal district court proceedings. And the reexamination prominent in state courts and in legislative arenas serves to underscore why the Court's enterprise is undue.

For the reasons stated, I dissent from this Court's disturbance of the judgment the Alabama Supreme Court has made.

United States v. Carolene Products Company
304 U.S. 144; 58 S. Ct. 778; 82 L. Ed. 1234 (1938)

In what has become a famous footnote in an otherwise unimportant case, Justice Stone developed the justification for "more exact judicial scrutiny" where infringements of civil liberties (as opposed to economic rights) are involved. *Opinion of the Court:* Stone, *Brandeis, Hughes, Roberts. Concurring opinions:* Black; Butler. *Dissenting opinion:* McReynolds. *Cardozo and Reed did not participate.*

MR. JUSTICE STONE delivered the opinion of the Court. . . .

Regulatory legislation affecting ordinary commercial transactions is not to be pronounced unconstitutional unless in the light of the facts made known or generally assumed it is of such a character as to preclude the assumption that it rests upon some rational basis within the knowledge and experience of the legislators.[4]

---

[4] There may be narrower scope for operation of the presumption of constitutionality when legislation appears on its face to be within a specific prohibition of the Constitution, such as those of the first ten amendments, which are deemed equally specific when held to be embraced within the Fourteenth.

It is unnecessary to consider now whether legislation which restricts those political processes which can ordinarily be expected to bring about repeal of undesirable legislation, is to be subjected to more exacting judicial scrutiny under the general prohibitions of the Fourteenth Amendment than are most other types of legislation. . . .

Nor need we enquire whether similar considerations enter into the review of statutes directed at particular religious . . . or national . . . or racial minorities . . . whether prejudice against discrete and insular minorities may be a special condition, which tends seriously to curtail the operation of those political processes ordinarily to be relied upon to protect minorities, and which may call for a correspondingly more searching judicial inquiry.

Hawaii Housing Authority v. *Midkiff*
467 U.S. 229, 104 S. Ct. 2321 81, L. Ed. 2d 186 (1984)

As a result of the feudal land tenure system of the early high chiefs of the Hawaiian Islands, land in Hawaii was concentrated in the hands of a few large landowners. In the mid-1960s, after extensive hearings, the Hawaii Legislature discovered that while the Federal and State Governments owned almost 49 percent of the State's land, another 47 percent was in the hands of only 72 private landowners. To reduce the perceived social and economic problems that resulted from this land concentration, the Hawaii Legislature enacted the Land Reform Act of 1967, which created a land condemnation scheme whereby title in real property could be taken from lessors and transferred to lessees. Under the Act, lessees living on single-family residential lots within tracts at least five acres in size can ask the Hawaii Housing Authority (HHA) to condemn the property on which they live. If the HHA determines that a "public purpose" will be served, it is authorized to designate some or all of the lots in the tract for acquisition. Once it has acquired the "right, title, and interest" in the land, at prices set by a condemnation trial or by negotiation between lessors and lessees, it can sell the land titles to the applicant lessees. After the HHA had held a public hearing on the proposed acquisition of Frank E. Midkiff's lands, he and other trustees of landholding estates filed suit in U.S. District Court for the District of Hawaii, asking that the Act be declared unconstitutional and that its enforcement be enjoined. The District Court held the Act constitutional under the Public Use Clause of the Fifth Amendment, made applicable to the State under the Fourteenth Amendment. The Court of Appeals for the Ninth Circuit reversed, holding that the Act violated the "public use" requirement of the Fifth Amendment, and the HHA appealed to the U.S. Supreme Court. *Unanimous Opinion of the Court: O'Connor, Burger, Blackmun, Brennan, Powell, Rehnquist, Steven, White. Marshall did not participate.*

JUSTICE O'CONNOR delivered the opinion of the Court.

The Fifth Amendment of the United States Constitution provides, in pertinent part, that "private property [shall not] be taken for public use, without just compensation." These cases present the question whether the Public Use Clause of that Amendment, made applicable to the States through the Fourteenth Amendment, prohibits the State of Hawaii from taking, with just compensation, title in real property from lessors and transferring it to lessees in order to reduce the concentration of ownership of fees simple in the State. We conclude that it does not. . . .

The starting point for our analysis of the Act's constitutionality is the Court's decision in

Berman v. *Parker* . . . (1954). In *Berman,* the Court held constitutional the District of Columbia Redevelopment Act of 1945. That Act provided both for the comprehensive use of the eminent domain power to redevelop slum areas and for the possible sale or lease of the condemned lands to private interests. In discussing whether the takings authorized by that Act were for a "public use," . . . the Court stated:

"We deal, in other words, with what traditionally has been known as the police power. An attempt to define its reach or trace its outer limits is fruitless, for each case must turn on its own facts. The definition is essentially the product of legislative determinations addressed to the purposes of government, purposes neither abstractly nor historically capable of complete definition. Subject to specific constitutional limitations, when the legislature has spoken, the public interest has been declared in terms well-nigh conclusive. In such cases the legislature, not the judiciary, is the main guardian of the public needs to be served by social legislation, whether it be Congress legislating concerning the District of Columbia . . . or the States legislating concerning local affairs. . . . This principle admits of no exception merely because the power of eminent domain is involved. " . . .

There is, of course, a role for courts to play in reviewing a legislature's judgment of what constitutes a public use, even when the eminent domain power is equated with the police power. But . . . the Court has made clear that it will not substitute its judgment for a legislature's judgment as to what constitutes a public use "unless the use be palpably without reasonable foundation.". . .

To be sure, the Court's cases have repeatedly stated that "one person's property may not be taken for the benefit of another private person without a justifying public purpose, even though compensation be paid." . . . But where the exercise of the eminent domain power is rationally related to a conceivable public purpose, the Court has never held a compensated taking to be proscribed by the Public Use Clause. . . .

On this basis, we have no trouble concluding that the Hawaii Act is constitutional. The people of Hawaii have attempted, much as the settlers of the original 13 Colonies did, to reduce the perceived social and economic evils of a land oligopoly traceable to their monarchs. The land oligopoly has, according to the Hawaii Legislature, created artificial deterrents to the normal functioning of the State's residential land market and forced thousands of individual homeowners to lease, rather than buy, the land underneath their homes. Regulating oligopoly and the evils associated with it is a classic exercise of a State's police powers. . . . We cannot disapprove of Hawaii's exercise of this power.

Nor can we condemn as irrational the Act's approach to correcting the land oligopoly problem. The Act presumes that when a sufficiently large number of persons declare that they are willing but unable to buy lots at fair prices the land market is malfunctioning. When such a malfunction is signalled, the Act authorizes

HHA to condemn lots in the relevant tract. The Act limits the number of lots any one tenant can purchase and authorizes HHA to use public funds to ensure that the market dilution goals will be achieved. This is a comprehensive and rational approach to identifying and correcting market failure.

Of course, this Act, like any other, may not be successful in achieving its intended goals. But "whether *in fact* the provision will accomplish its objectives is not the question: the [constitutional requirement] is satisfied if . . . the . . . [state] Legislature *rationally could have believed* that the [Act] would promote its objective." . . . When the legislature's purpose is legitimate and its means are not irrational, our cases make clear that empirical debates over the wisdom of takings—no less than debates over the wisdom of other kinds of socioeconomic legislation—are not to be carried out in the federal courts. Redistribution of fees simple to correct deficiencies in the market determined by the state legislature to be attributable to land oligopoly is a rational exercise of the eminent domain power.

The mere fact that property taken outright by eminent domain is transferred in the first instance to private beneficiaries does not condemn that taking as having only a private purpose. The Court long ago rejected any literal requirement that condemned property be put into use for the general public. . . . As the unique way titles were held in Hawaii skewed the land market, exercise of the power of eminent domain was justified. The Act advances its purposes without the State taking actual possession of the land. In such cases, government does not itself have to use property to legitimate the taking; it is only the taking's purpose, and not its mechanics, that must pass scrutiny under the Public Use Clause.

Similarly, the fact that a state legislature, and not the Congress, made the public use determination does not mean that judicial deference is less appropriate. Judicial deference is required because, in our system of government, legislatures are better able to assess what public purposes should be advanced by an exercise of the taking power. State legislatures are as capable as Congress of making such determinations within their respective spheres of authority. . . . Thus, if a legislature, state or federal, determines there are substantial reasons for an exercise of the taking power, courts must defer to its determination that the taking will serve a public use.

The State of Hawaii has never denied that the Constitution forbids even a compensated taking of property when executed for no reason other than to confer a private benefit on a particular private party. A purely private taking could not withstand the scrutiny of the public use requirement; it would serve no legitimate purpose of government and would thus be void. But no purely private taking is involved in this case. The Hawaii Legislature enacted its Land Reform Act not to benefit a particular class of identifiable individuals but to attack certain perceived evils of concentrated property ownership in Hawaii—a legitimate public purpose. Use of the condemnation power to achieve this purpose is not irrational. Since we assume for purposes of this appeal that the weighty demand of just compensation has been met, the requirements of the Fifth and Fourteenth Amendments have been satisfied. Accordingly, we reverse the judgment of the Court of Appeals, and remand these cases for further proceedings in conformity with this opinion.

Nollan v. *California Coastal Commission*
483 U.S. 825, 107 S. Ct. 3141, 97 L. Ed. 2d 677 (1987)

The California Coastal Commission granted a permit to James and Marilyn Nollan to replace a small bungalow on their beachfront lot with a larger house upon the condition that they allow the public an easement to pass across their beach, which was located between two public beaches. The Nollans filed a petition for writ of administrative mandamus asking the Ventura County Superior Court to invalidate the access condition. They argued that the condition could not be imposed absent evidence that their proposed development would have a direct adverse impact on public access to the beach. The Court agreed and remanded the case to the Commission for a full evidentiary hearing on that issue. On remand, the Commission held a public hearing and made further factual findings; it reaffirmed its imposition of the condition, finding that the new house would increase blockage of the view of the ocean, thus contributing to the development of "a 'wall' of residential structures" that would prevent the public "psychologically . . . from realizing a stretch of coastline exists nearby that they have every right to visit." The Nollans filed a supplemental petition for a writ of administrative mandamus with the Superior Court, arguing that imposition of the access condition violated the Takings Clause of the Fifth Amendment, as incorporated against the states by the Fourteenth Amendment. The Superior Court avoided the constitutional question but ruled in their favor on statutory grounds. In its view, the administrative record did not provide an adequate factual basis for concluding that replacement of the bungalow with the house would create a direct or cumulative burden on public access to the sea. The Commission appealed to the California Court of Appeal, which reversed, holding that the access condition violated neither California statutes nor the Takings Clause of the U.S. Constitution. The Nollans appealed to the U.S. Supreme Court. *Opinion of the Court:* <u>Scalia</u>, *Rehnquist, O'Connor, Powell, White. Dissenting opinions:* <u>Brennan</u>, *Marshall;* <u>Blackmun;</u> <u>Stevens;</u> *Blackmun.*

JUSTICE SCALIA delivered the opinion of the Court. . . .

Had California simply required the Nollans to make an easement across their beachfront available to the public on a permanent basis in order to increase public access to the beach, rather than conditioning their permit to rebuild their house on their agreeing to do so, we have no doubt there would have been a taking. To say that the appropriation of a public easement across a landowner's premises does not constitute the taking of a property interest but rather (as Justice Brennan contends) "a mere restriction on its use," is to use words in a manner that deprives them of all their ordinary meaning. Indeed, one of the principal uses of the eminent domain power is to assure that the government be able to require conveyance of just such interests, so long as it pays for them. . . . Perhaps because the point is so obvious, we have never been confronted with a controversy that required us to rule upon it, but our cases' analysis of the effect of other governmental action leads to the same conclusion. We have repeatedly held that, as to property reserved by its owner for private use, "the right to exclude [others is] 'one of the most essential sticks in the bundle of rights that are commonly characterized as property.'" . . .

Given, then, that requiring uncompensated conveyance of the easement outright would violate the Fourteenth Amendment, the question becomes whether requiring it to be conveyed as a condition for issuing a land-use permit alters the outcome. We have long recognized that land-use regulation does not effect a taking if it "substantially advance[s] legitimate state interests" and does not "den[y] an owner economically viable use of his land," *Agins* v. *Tiburon*, 447 U. S. 255, 260 (1980). See also *Penn Central Transportation Co.* v. *New York City*, 438 U. S. 104, 127 (1978) ("[A] use restriction may constitute a 'taking' if not reasonably necessary to the effectuation of a substantial government purpose"). Our cases have not elaborated on the standards for determining what constitutes a "legitimate state interest" or what type of connection between the regulation and the state interest satisfies the requirement that the former "substantially advance" the latter. They have made clear, however, that a broad range of governmental pur-

poses and regulations satisfies these requirements. . . . The Commission argues that among these permissible purposes are protecting the public's ability to see the beach, assisting the public in overcoming the "psychological barrier" to using the beach created by a developed shorefront, and preventing congestion on the public beaches. We assume, without deciding, that this is so—in which case the Commission unquestionably would be able to deny the Nollans their permit outright if their new house (alone, or by reason of the cumulative impact produced in conjunction with other construction,*) would substantially impede these purposes, unless the denial would interfere so drastically with the Nollans' use of their property as to constitute a taking. . . .

The Commission argues that a permit condition that serves the same legitimate police-power purpose as a refusal to issue the permit should not be found to be a taking if the refusal to issue the permit would not constitute a taking. We agree. Thus, if the Commission attached to the permit some condition that would have protected the public's ability to see the beach notwithstanding construction of the new house—for example, a height limitation, a width restriction, or a ban on fences—so long as the Commission could have exercised its police power (as we have assumed it could) to forbid construction of the house altogether, imposition of the condition would also be constitutional. Moreover (and here we come closer to the facts of the present case), the condition would be constitutional even if it consisted of the requirement that the Nollans provide a viewing spot on their property for passersby with whose sighting of the ocean their new house would interfere. Although such a requirement, constituting a permanent grant of continuous access to the property, would have to be considered a taking if it were not attached to a development permit, the Commission's assumed power to forbid construction of the house in order to protect the public's view of

---

*If the Nollans were being singled out to bear the burden of California's attempt to remedy these problems, although they had not contributed to it more than other coastal landowners, the State's action, even if otherwise valid, might violate either the incorporated Takings Clause or the Equal Protection Clause.

the beach must surely include the power to condition construction upon some concession by the owner, even a concession of property rights, that serves the same end. If a prohibition designed to accomplish that purpose would be a legitimate exercise of the police power rather than a taking, it would be strange to conclude that providing the owner an alternative to that prohibition which accomplishes the same purpose is not.

The evident constitutional propriety disappears, however, if the condition substituted for the prohibition utterly fails to further the end advanced as the justification for the prohibition. When that essential nexus is eliminated, the situation becomes the same as if California law forbade shouting fire in a crowded theater, but granted dispensations to those willing to contribute $100 to the state treasury. While a ban on shouting fire can be a core exercise of the State's police power to protect the public safety, and can thus meet even our stringent standards for regulation of speech, adding the unrelated condition alters the purpose to one which, while it may be legitimate, is inadequate to sustain the ban. Therefore, even though, in a sense, requiring a $100 tax contribution in order to shout fire is a lesser restriction on speech than an outright ban, it would not pass constitutional muster. Similarly here, the lack of nexus between the condition and the original purpose of the building restriction converts that purpose to something other than what it was. The purpose then becomes, quite simply, the obtaining of an easement to serve some valid governmental purpose, but without payment of compensation. Whatever may be the outer limits of "legitimate state interests" in the takings and land-use context, this is not one of them. In short, unless the permit condition serves the same governmental purpose as the development ban, the building restriction is not a valid regulation of land use but "an out-and-out plan of extortion.". . .

The Commission claims that it concedes as much, and that we may sustain the condition at issue here by finding that it is reasonably related to the public need or burden that the Nollans' new house creates or to which it contributes. We can accept, for purposes of discussion, the Commission's proposed test as to how close a "fit" between the condition and the burden is re-

quired, because we find that this case does not meet even the most untailored standards. The Commission's principal contention to the contrary essentially turns on a play on the word "access." The Nollans' new house, the Commission found, will interfere with "visual access" to the beach. That in turn (along with other shorefront development) will interfere with the desire of people who drive past the Nollans' house to use the beach, thus creating a "psychological barrier" to "access." The Nollans' new house will also, by a process not altogether clear from the Commission's opinion but presumably potent enough to more than offset the effects of the psychological barrier, increase the use of the public beaches, thus creating the need for more "access." These burdens on "access" would be alleviated by a requirement that the Nollans provide "lateral access" to the beach.

Rewriting the argument to eliminate the play on words makes clear that there is nothing to it. It is quite impossible to understand how a requirement that people already on the public beaches be able to walk across the Nollans' property reduces any obstacles to viewing the beach created by the new house. It is also impossible to understand how it lowers any "psychological barrier" to using the public beaches, or how it helps to remedy any additional congestion on them caused by construction of the Nollans' new house. We therefore find that the Commission's imposition of the permit condition cannot be treated as an exercise of its land-use power for any of these purposes. Our conclusion on this point is consistent with the approach taken by every other court that has considered the question, with the exception of the California state courts.

Justice Brennan argues that imposition of the access requirement is not irrational. In his version of the Commission's argument, the reason for the requirement is that in its absence, a person looking toward the beach from the road will see a street of residential structures including the Nollans' new home and conclude that there is no public beach nearby. If, however, that person sees people passing and repassing along the dry sand behind the Nollans' home, he will realize that there is a public beach somewhere in the vicinity. . . . The Commission's action, however, was based on the opposite factual finding that the wall of houses completely blocked the view of the beach and that a person looking from the road would not be able to see it at all.

Even if the Commission had made the finding that Justice Brennan proposes, however, it is not certain that it would suffice. We do not share Justice Brennan's confidence that the Commission "should have little difficulty in the future in utilizing its expertise to demonstrate a specific connection between provisions for access and burdens on access," . . . that will avoid the effect of today's decision. We view the Fifth Amendment's Property Clause to be more than a pleading requirement, and compliance with it to be more than an exercise in cleverness and imagination. As indicated earlier, our cases describe the condition for abridgment of property rights through the police power as a "*substantial* advanc[ing]" of a legitimate state interest. We are inclined to be particularly careful about the adjective where the actual conveyance of property is made a condition to the lifting of a land-use restriction, since in that context there is heightened risk that the purpose is avoidance of the compensation requirement, rather than the stated police power objective.

We are left, then, with the Commission's justification for the access requirement unrelated to land-use regulation:

> Finally, the Commission notes that there are several existing provisions of pass and repass lateral access benefits already given by past Faria Beach Tract applicants as a result of prior coastal permit decisions. The access required as a condition of this permit is part of a comprehensive program to provide continuous public access along Faria Beach as the lots undergo development or redevelopment. . . .

That is simply an expression of the Commission's belief that the public interest will be served by a continuous strip of publicly accessible beach along the coast. The Commission may well be right that it is a good idea, but that does not establish that the Nollans (and other coastal residents) alone can be compelled to contribute to its realization. Rather, California is free to advance its "comprehensive program," if it wishes, by using its power of eminent domain for this

"public purpose," but if it wants an easement across the Nollans' property, it must pay for it.

Reserved.

JUSTICE BRENNAN, with whom JUSTICE MARSHALL joins, dissenting.

Appellants in this case sought to construct a new dwelling on their beach lot that would both diminish visual access to the beach and move private development closer to the public tidelands. The Commission reasonably concluded that such "buildout," both individually and cumulatively, threatens public access to the shore. It sought to offset this encroachment by obtaining assurance that the public may walk along the shoreline in order to gain access to the ocean. The Court finds this an illegitimate exercise of the police power, because it maintains that there is no reasonable relationship between the effect of the development and the condition imposed.

The first problem with this conclusion is that the Court imposes a standard of precision for the exercise of a State's police power that has been discredited for the better part of this century. Furthermore, even under the Court's cramped standard, the permit condition imposed in this case directly responds to the specific type of burden on access created by appellants' development. Finally, a review of those factors deemed most significant in takings analysis makes clear that the Commission's action implicates none of the concerns underlying the Takings Clause.

Even if we accept the Court's unusual demand for a precise match between the condition imposed and the specific type of burden on access created by the appellants, the State's action easily satisfies this requirement. First, the lateral access condition serves to dissipate the impression that the beach that lies behind the wall of homes along the shore is for private use only. It requires no exceptional imaginative powers to find plausible the Commission's point that the average person passing along the road in front of a phalanx of imposing permanent residences, including the appellants' new home, is likely to conclude that this particular portion of the shore is not open to the public. If, however, that person can see that numerous people are passing and repassing along the dry sand, this conveys the message that the beach is in fact open for use by the public. Furthermore, those persons who go down to the public beach a quarter-mile away will be able to look down the coastline and see that persons have continuous access to the tidelands, and will observe signs that proclaim the public's right of access over the dry sand. The burden produced by the diminution in visual access—the impression that the beach is not open to the public—is thus directly alleviated by the provision for public access over the dry sand. The Court therefore has an unrealistically limited conception of what measures could reasonably be chosen to mitigate the burden produced by a diminution of visual access. . . .

The fact that the Commission's action is a legitimate exercise of the police power does not, of course, insulate it from a takings challenge, for when "regulation goes too far it will be recognized as a taking." *Pennsylvania Coal Co.* v. *Mahon.* Conventional takings analysis underscores the implausibility of the Court's holding, for it demonstrates that this exercise of California's police power implicates none of the concerns that underlie our takings jurisprudence. . . .

. . . The character of the regulation in this case is not unilateral government action, but a condition on approval of a development request submitted by appellants. The state has not sought to interfere with any pre-existing property interest, but has responded to appellants' proposal to intensify development on the coast. Appellants themselves chose to submit a new development application, and could claim no property interest in its approval. They were aware that approval of such development would be conditioned on preservation of adequate public access to the ocean. The State has initiated no action against appellants' property; had the Nollans' not proposed more intensive development in the coastal zone, they would never have been subject to the provision that they challenge.

Examination of the economic impact of the Commission's action reinforces the conclusion that no taking has occurred. Allowing appellants to intensify development along the coast in exchange for ensuring public access to the ocean is a classic instance of government action that produces a "reciprocity of advantage." . . . Appellants have been allowed to replace a one-story 521-square-foot beach home with a two-story 1,674-square-foot residence and an attached two-car garage, resulting in development covering 2,464 square feet of the lot. Such development obviously significantly increases the value of appellants' property; appellants make no contention that this increase is offset by any diminution in value resulting from the deed restriction, much less that the restriction made the property less valuable than it would have been without the new construction. Furthermore, appellants gain an additional benefit from the Commission's permit condition program. They are able to walk along the beach beyond the confines of their own property only because the Commission has required deed restrictions as a condition of approving other new beach developments. Thus appellants benefit both as private landowners and as members of the public from the fact that new development permit requests are conditioned on preservation of public access. . . .

. . . State agencies therefore require considerable flexibility in responding to private desires for development in a way that guarantees the preservation of public access to the coast. They should be encouraged to regulate development in the context of the overall balance of competing uses of the shoreline. The Court today does precisely the opposite, overruling an eminently reasonable exercise of an expert state agency's judgment, substituting its own narrow view of how this balance should be struck. Its reasoning is hardly suited to the complex reality of natural resource protection in the 20th century. I can only hope that today's decision is an aberration, and that a broader vision ultimately prevails.

I dissent.

Lucas v. *South Carolina Coastal Council*

112 S. Ct. 2886, 120 L. Ed. 2d 798 (1992)

In 1986, David Lucas paid $975,000 for two residential lots on the Isle of Palms, a barrier island situated to the east of Charleston, South Carolina. He intended to build single-family houses on them, such as were found on the immediately adjacent lots. At the time, Lucas's lots were not subject to South Carolina's coastal zone building permit requirements. In 1988, however, the South Carolina Legislature enacted the Beachfront Management Act, which had the direct effect of prohibiting Lucas from erecting any permanent habitable structures on his land. He filed suit against the newly created Coastal Council in the South Carolina Court of Common Pleas, contending that the Beachfront Management Act's ban on construction effected a taking of his property under the Fifth and Fourteenth Amendments and therefore required the payment of just compensation. He did not deny the validity of the act as a lawful exercise of South Carolina's police power; he simply contended that the act deprived him of all "economically viable use" of his property and that he was entitled to compensation, regardless of whether the legislature had acted in furtherance of a legitimate police power objective. The state trial court agreed, finding that the ban had rendered Lucas's parcels "valueless," and ordered the Coastal Council to pay Lucas "just compensation" in the amount of $1,232,387.50. The Supreme Court of South Carolina reversed. Since Lucas had not attacked the validity of the statute as such, it found itself bound to accept the uncontested findings of the South Carolina legislature that new construction in the coastal zone of the sort that Lucas intended threatened South Carolina's beaches. It concluded on the basis of *Muglar* v. *Kansas* (1887) and a long line of cases that followed it that when regulation is necessary to prevent "harmful or noxious uses" of property akin to public nuisances, no compensation is owed under the Takings Clause, regardless of the regulation's effect on the property's value. The U.S. Supreme Court granted certiorari. *Opinion of the Court:* Scalia, *O'Connor, Rehnquist, Thomas, White. Concurring in the judgment:* Kennedy. *Dissenting opinions:* Blackmun; Stevens. *Separate statement voting to dismiss the writ of certiorari:* Souter.

JUSTICE SCALIA delivered the opinion of the Court.

Prior to Justice Holmes' exposition in *Pennsylvania Coal Co.* v. *Mahon* (1922), it was generally thought that the Takings Clause reached only a "direct appropriation" of property. *Legal Tender Cases* (1871), or the functional equivalent of a "practical ouster of [the owner's] possession." *Transportation Co.* v. *Chicago* (1879). Justice Holmes recognized in *Mahon*, however, that if the protection against physical appropriations of private property was to be meaningfully enforced, the government's power to redefine the range of interests included in the ownership of property was necessarily constrained by constitutional limits. If, instead, the uses of private property were subject to unbridled, uncompensated qualification under the police power, "the natural tendency of human nature [would be] to extend the qualification more and more until at last private property disappear[ed]." These considerations gave birth in that case to the oft-cited maxim that, "while property may be regulated to a certain extent, if regulation goes too far it will be recognized as a taking." Nevertheless, our decision in *Mahon* offered little insight into when, and under what circumstances, a given regulation would be seen as going "too far" for purposes of the Fifth Amendment. In 70-odd years of succeeding "regulatory takings" jurisprudence, we have generally eschewed any "set formula" for determining how far is too far, preferring to "engag[e] in . . . essentially *ad hoc*, factual inquiries," *Penn Central Transportation Co.* v. *New York City* (1978). We have, however, described at least two discrete categories of regulatory action as compensable without case-specific inquiry into the public interest advanced in support of the restraint. The first encompasses regulations that compel the property owner to suffer a physical "invasion" of his property. In general (at least with regard to permanent invasions), no matter how minute the intrusion, and no matter how weighty the public purpose behind it, we have required compensation. For example, in *Loretto* v. *Teleprompter Manhattan CATV Corp.* (1982), we determined that New York's law requiring landlords to allow television cable companies to emplace cable facilities in their apartment buildings constituted a taking, even though the facilities occupied at most only $1^1/_2$ cubic feet of the landlords' property.

The second situation in which we have found categorical treatment appropriate is where regulation denies all economically beneficial or productive use of land. As we have said on numerous occasions, the Fifth Amendment is violated when land-use regulation "does not substantially advance legitimate state interests or denies an owner economically viable use of his land."

We have never set forth the justification for this rule. Perhaps it is simply, as Justice Brennan suggested, that total deprivation of beneficial use is, from the landowner's point of view, the equivalent of a physical appropriation.

. . . On the other side of the balance, affirmatively supporting a compensation requirement, is the fact that regulations that leave the owner of land without economically beneficial or productive options for its use—typically, as here, by requiring land to be left substantially in its natural state—carry with them a heightened risk that private property is being pressed into some form of public service under the guise of mitigating serious public harm. We think, in short, that there are good reasons for our frequently expressed belief that when the owner of real property has been called upon to sacrifice all economically beneficial uses in the name of the common good, that is, to leave his property economically idle, he has suffered a taking.

The trial court found Lucas's two beachfront lots to have been rendered valueless by respondent's enforcement of the coastal-zone construction ban. Under Lucas's theory of the case, which rested upon our "no economically viable use" statements, that finding entitled him to compensation. Lucas believed it unnecessary to take issue with either the purposes behind the Beachfront Management Act, or the means chosen by the South Carolina Legislature to effectuate those purposes. The South Carolina Supreme Court, however, thought otherwise. In its view, the Beachfront Management Act was no ordinary enactment, but involved an exercise of South Carolina's "police powers" to mitigate the harm to the public interest that petitioner's use of his land might occasion. By neglecting to dispute the findings enumerated in the Act or otherwise to challenge the legislature's purposes, petitioner "concede[d] that the beach/dune area of South Carolina's shores is an extremely valuable public resource; that the erection of new construction, inter alia, contributes to the erosion and destruction of this public resource; and that discouraging new construction in close proximity to the beach/dune area is necessary to prevent a great public harm." In the court's view, these concessions brought petitioner's challenge within a long line of this Court's cases sustaining against Due Process and Takings Clause challenges the State's use of its "policy powers" to enjoin a property owner from activities akin to public nuisances.

It is correct that many of our prior opinions have suggested that "harmful or noxious uses" of property may be proscribed by government regulation without the requirement of compensation. However, we think the South Carolina Supreme Court was too quick to conclude that that principle decides the present case. . . .

A fortiori the legislature's recitation of a noxious-use justification cannot be the basis for departing from our categorical rule that total regulatory takings must be compensated. If it were, departure would virtually always be allowed. The South Carolina Supreme Court's approach would essentially nullify *Mahon's* affirmation of limits to the noncompensable exercise of the police power. . . .

Where the State seeks to sustain regulation that deprives land of all economically beneficial use, we think it may resist compensation only if the logically antecedent inquiry into the nature of the owner's estate shows that the proscribed use interests were not part of his title to begin with. This accords, we think, with our "takings" jurisprudence, which has traditionally been guided by the understandings of our citizens regarding the content of, and the State's power over, the "bundle of rights" that they acquire when they obtain title to property. Confiscatory regulations, i.e., regulations that prohibit all economically beneficial use of land, cannot be newly legislated or decreed (without compensation), but must inhere in the title itself, in the restrictions that background principles of the State's law of property and nuisance already place upon land ownership. . . .

On this analysis, the owner of a lake bed, for example, would not be entitled to compensation when he is denied the requisite permit to engage in a landfilling operation that would have the effect of flooding others' land. Nor the corporate owner of a nuclear generating plant, when it is directed to remove all improvements from its land upon discovery that the plant sits astride an earthquake fault. Such regulatory action may well have the effect of eliminating the land's only economically productive use, but it does not proscribe a productive use that was previously permissible under relevant property and nuisance principles. The use of these properties for what are now expressly prohibited purposes was always unlawful, and (subject to other constitutional limitations) it was open to the State at any point to make the implication of those background principles of nuisance and property law explicit. When, however, a regulation that declares "off-limits" all economically productive or beneficial uses of land goes beyond what the relevant background principles would dictate, compensation must be paid to sustain it. The

"total taking" inquiry we require today will ordinarily entail (as the application of state nuisance law ordinarily entails) analysis of, among other things, the degree of harm to public lands and resources, or adjacent private property, posed by the claimant's proposed activities, the social value of the claimant's activities and their suitability to the locality in question, and the relative ease with which the alleged harm can be avoided through measures taken by the claimant and the government (or adjacent private landowners) alike. The fact that a particular use has long been engaged in by similarly situated owners ordinarily imports a lack of any common-law prohibition. So also does the fact that other landowners, similarly situated, are permitted to continue the use denied to the claimant.

We emphasize that to win its case South Carolina must do more than proffer the legislature's declaration that the uses Lucas desires are inconsistent with the public interest. As we have said, a "State, by ipse dixit, may not transform private property into public property without compensation. . . ." Instead, as it would be required to do if it sought to restrain Lucas in a common-law action for public nuisance, South Carolina must identify background principles of nuisance and property law that prohibit the uses he now intends in the circumstances in which the property is presently found. Only on this showing can the State fairly claim that, in proscribing all such beneficial uses, the Beachfront Management Act is taking nothing. . . .

The judgment is reversed and the cause remanded for proceedings not inconsistent with this opinion.

JUSTICE BLACKMUN, dissenting.

. . . This Court repeatedly has recognized the ability of government, in certain circumstances, to regulate property without compensation no matter how adverse the financial effect on the owner may be. More than a century ago, the Court explicitly upheld the right of States to prohibit uses of property injurious to public health, safety, or welfare without paying compensation: "A prohibition simply upon the use of property for purposes that are declared, by valid legislation, to be injurious to the health, morals, or safety of the community, cannot, in any just sense, be deemed a taking or an appropriation of property." *Mugler* v. *Kansas* (1887). On this basis, the Court upheld an ordinance effectively prohibiting operation of a previously lawful brewery, although the "establishments will become of no value as property."

Mugler was only the beginning in a long line of cases. In none of the cases did the Court sug-

gest that the right of a State to prohibit certain activities without paying compensation turned on the availability of some residual valuable use. Instead, the cases depended on whether the government interest was sufficient to prohibit the activity, given the significant private cost.

Dolan v. City of Tigard
512 U.S. 374, 114 S. Ct. 2309, 129 L. Ed. 2d 304 (1994)

Florence Dolan sought a city permit to expand her plumbing and electric supply store from 9,700 square feet to 17,600 square feet and to pave her 39-space parking lot. The City Planning Commission of Tigard, Oregon, approved her permit application on the condition that she dedicate approximately 10 percent of her 1.67 acre parcel of land to the city for a public greenway along an adjacent creek (to minimize flooding that would be exacerbated by the increases in impervious surfaces associated with her development) and for a pedestrian/bicycle pathway (intended to relieve traffic congestion in the central business district caused by the additional customers visiting her enlarged store). Dolan appealed the Commission's denial of her request for a waiver of this condition to the Land Use Board of Appeals, alleging that the land dedication requirements were unrelated to the proposed development and thus constituted an uncompensated taking of her property in violation of the Fifth Amendment. The Land Use Board of Appeals rejected her appeal, and the State Court of Appeals and the Oregon State Supreme Court both affirmed its decision. The United States Supreme Court granted certiorari. *Opinion of the Court: Rehnquist, Kennedy, O'Connor, Scalia, Thomas. Dissenting opinions: Stevens, Blackmun, Ginsburg; Souter.*

CHIEF JUSTICE REHNQUIST delivered the opinion of the Court.

Petitioner challenges the decision of the Oregon Supreme Court which held that the city of Tigard could condition the approval of her building permit on the dedication of a portion of her property for flood control and traffic improvements. We granted certiorari to resolve a question left open by our decision in *Nollan* v. *California Coastal Commn'n*, 483 U.S. 825 (1987), of what is the required degree of connection between the exactions imposed by the city and the projected impacts of the proposed development. . . .

The Takings Clause of the Fifth Amendment of the United States Constitution, made applicable to the States through the Fourteenth Amendment, *Chicago B. & Q. R. Co.* v. *Chicago*, 166 U.S. 226, 239 (1897), provides: "[N]or shall private property be taken for public use, without just compensation." One of the principal purposes of the Takings Clause is "to bar Government from forcing some people alone to bear public burdens which, in all fairness and justice, should be borne by the public as a whole." *Armstrong* v. *United States*, 364 U.S. 40, 49 (1960). Without question, had the city simply required petitioner to dedicate a strip of land along Fanno

Creek for public use, rather than conditioning the grant of her permit to redevelop her property on such a dedication, a taking would have occurred. Such public access would deprive petitioner of the right to exclude others, "one of the most essential sticks in the bundle of rights that are commonly characterized as property." *Kaiser Aetna* v. *United States*, 444 U.S. 164, 176 (1979).

On the other side of the ledger, the authority of state and local governments to engage in land use planning has been sustained against constitutional challenge as long ago as our decision in *Euclid* v. *Ambler Realty Co.*, 272 U.S. 365 (1926). "Government hardly could go on if to some extent values incident to property could not be diminished without paying for every such change in the general law." *Pennsylvania Coal Co.* v. *Mahon*, 260 U.S. 393, 413 (1922). A land use regulation does not effect a taking if it "substantially advance[s] legitimate state interests" and does not "den[y] an owner economically viable use of his land." *Agins* v. *Tiburon*, 447 U.S. 255, 260 (1980).

The sort of land use regulations discussed in the cases just cited, however, differ in two relevant particulars from the present case. First, they involved essentially legislative determinations classifying entire areas of the city, whereas here the city made an adjudicative decision to condition petitioner's application for a building permit on an individual parcel. Second, the conditions imposed were not simply a limitation on the use petitioner might make of her own parcel, but a requirement that she deed portions of the property to the city. In *Nollan*, we held that governmental authority to exact such a condition was circumscribed by the Fifth and Fourteenth Amendments. Under the well-settled doctrine of "unconstitutional conditions," the government may not require a person to give up a constitutional right—here the right to receive just compensation when property is taken for a public use—in exchange for a discretionary benefit conferred by the government where the property sought has little or no relationship to the benefit.

Petitioner contends that the city has forced her to choose between the building permit and her right under the Fifth Amendment to just compensation for the public easements. Petitioner does not quarrel with the city's authority to exact some forms of dedication as a condition for the granting of a building permit, but challenges the showing made by the city to justify these exactions. She argues that the city has identified "no special benefits" conferred on her, and has not identified any "special quantifiable burdens" created by her new store that would justify the particular dedications required from her which are not required from the public at large.

In evaluating petitioner's claim, we must first determine whether the "essential nexus" exists between the "legitimate state interest" and the permit condition exacted by the city. *Nollan*, 483 U.S., at 837. If we find that a nexus exists, we must then decide the required degree of connection between the exactions and the projected impact of the proposed development. We were not required to reach this question in Nollan, because we concluded that the connection did not meet even the loosest standard. Here, however, we must decide this question. . . .

It seems obvious that a nexus exists between preventing flooding along Fanno Creek and limiting development within the creek's 100-year floodplain. Petitioner proposes to double the size of her retail store and to pave her now-gravel parking lot, thereby expanding the impervious surface on the property and increasing the amount of stormwater runoff into Fanno Creek.

The same may be said for the city's attempt to reduce traffic congestion by providing for alternative means of transportation. . . .

The second part of our analysis requires us to determine whether the degree of the exactions demanded by the city's permit conditions bear the required relationship to the projected impact of petitioner's proposed development. . . .

We think a term such as "rough proportionality" best encapsulates what we hold to be the requirment of the Fifth Amendment. No precise mathematical calculation is required, but the city must make some sort of individualized determination that the required dedication is related both in nature and extent to the impact of the proposed development.

JUSTICE STEVENS' dissent relies upon the proposition that the city's conditional demands for part of petitioner's property are "a species of business regulation that heretofore warranted a strong presumption of constitutional validity." But simply denominating a governmental measure as a "business regulation" does not immunize it from constitutional challenge on the grounds that it violates a provision of the Bill of Rights. In *Marshall v. Barlow's, Inc.*, 436 U.S. 307 (1978), we held that a statute authorizing a warrantless search of business premises in order to detect OSHA violations violated the Fourth Amendment. And in *Central Hudson Gas & Electric Corp. v. Public Service Comm'n. of N.Y.*, 447 U.S. 557 (1980), we held that an order of the New York Public Service Commission, designed to cut down the use of electricity because of a fuel shortage, violated the First Amendment insofar as it prohibited advertising by a utility company to promote the use of electricity. We see no reason why the Takings Clause of the Fifth Amendment, as much a part of the Bill of Rights as the First Amendment or Fourth Amendment, should be relegated to the status of a poor relation in these comparable circumstances. We turn now to analysis of whether the findings relied upon by the city here, first with respect to the floodplain easement, and second with respect to the pedestrian/bicycle path, satisfied these requirements.

It is axiomatic that increasing the amount of impervious surface will increase the quantity and rate of stormwater flow from petitioner's property. Therefore, keeping the floodplain open and free from development would likely confine the pressures on Fanno Creek created by petitioner's development. In fact, because petitioner's property lies within the Central Business District, the Community Development Code already required that petitioner leave 15% of it as open space and the undeveloped floodplain would have nearly satisfied that requirement. But the city demanded more—it not only wanted petitioner not to build in the floodplain, but it also wanted petitioner's property along Fanno Creek for its Greenway system. The city has never said why a public greenway, as opposed to a private one, was required in the interest of flood control.

The difference to petitioner, of course, is the loss of her ability to exclude others. As we have noted, this right to exclude others is "one of the most essential sticks in the bundle of rights that are commonly characterized as property." It is difficult to see why recreational visitors tramping along petitioner's floodplain easement are

sufficiently related to the city's legitimate interest in reducing flooding problems along Fanno Creek, and the city has not attempted to make any individualized determination to support this part of its request. . . .

We conclude that the findings upon which the city relies do not show the required reasonable relationship between the floodplain easement and the petitioner's proposed new building.

With respect to the pedestrian/bicycle pathway, the city has not met its burden of demonstrating that the additional number of vehicle and bicycle trips generated by the petitioner's development reasonably relate to the city's requirement of the pedestrian/bicycle pathway easement. The city simply found that the creation of the pathway "could offset some of the traffic demand . . . and lessen the increase in traffic congestion." . . .

No precise mathematical calculation is required, but the city must make some effort to quantify its findings in support of the dedication for the pedestrian/bicycle pathway beyond the conclusory statement that it could offset some of the traffic demand generated. . . .

The judgment of the Supreme Court of Oregon is reversed, and the case is remanded for further proceedings consistent with this opinion.

JUSTICE STEVENS, with whom JUSTICE BLACKMUN and JUSTICE GINSBURG join, dissenting.

. . . The Court has made a serious error by abandoning the traditional presumption of constitutionality and imposing a novel burden of proof on a city implementing an admittedly valid comprehensive land use plan. Even more consequential than its incorrect disposition of this case, however, is the Court's resurrection of a species of substantive due process analysis that it firmly rejected decades ago. . . .

Dolan has no right to be compensated for a taking unless the city acquires the property interests that she has refused to surrender. Since no taking has yet occurred, there has not been any infringement of her constitutional right to compensation.

Even if Dolan should accept the city's conditions in exchange for the benefit that she seeks, it would not necessarily follow that she had been denied "just compensation" since it would be appropriate to consider the receipt of that benefit in any calculation of "just compensation." . . . The city's conditons are by no means immune from constitutional scrutiny. The level of scrutiny, however, does not approximate the kind of review that would apply if the city had insisted on a surrender of Dolan's First Amendment rights in exchange for a building permit. One can only hope that the Court's reliance today on First Amendment cases, and its candid disavowal of the term "rational basis" to describe its new standard of review, do not signify a reassertion of the kind of superlegislative power the Court exercised during the *Lochner* era.

★

THE MEANING OF THE FIRST AMENDMENT

FIRST AMENDMENT STANDARDS

Gitlow v. New York (1925)
Schenck v. United States (1919)
Dennis v. United States (1951)
Barenblatt v. United States (1959)
Brandenburg v. Ohio (1969)

POLITICAL EXPRESSION

Buckley v. Valeo (1976)

THE REGULATION OF SPEECH

Texas v. Johnson (1989)
R.A.V. v. City of St. Paul (1992)
Tinker v. Des Moines (1969)

RESTRAINTS ON THE PRESS

Near v. Minnesota (1931)
New York Times Company v. United States (1971)
Branzburg v. Hayes (1972)
Red Lion Broadcasting Co. v. Federal Communications Commission (1969)
Memorandum Opinion and Order Federal Communications Commission (1987)

LIBEL AND INVASION OF PRIVACY

New York Times v. Sullivan (1964)

OBSCENITY

Miller v. California (1973)
Paris Adult Theater I v. Slaton (1973)
Reno v. American Civil Liberties Union (1997)
Indianapolis Anti-Pornography Ordinance (1984)

SOME CONCLUSIONS

NOTES

SELECTED READING

CASES

★

5

FREEDOM OF SPEECH, PRESS, AND ASSOCIATION

The First Amendment speaks in strikingly absolute terms: "Congress shall make no law . . . abridging the freedom of speech, or of the press." The Supreme Court's interpretation of these guarantees has been both broader and narrower than a literal reading of the amendment might suggest. The Court has ruled that the amendment protects channels of communication other than speech and press, including those (e.g., television and the Internet) developed since the amendment's adoption. It has also extended some protection to actions undertaken with communicative intent (e.g., demonstrations, picketing, and symbolic acts), even if they do not involve speech. Acknowledging that "effective advocacy of both public and private points of view, particularly controversial ones, is undeniably enhanced by group association," the Court has recognized a First Amendment right to freedom of association.[1] Most importantly, in *Gitlow* v. *New York* (1925) the justices ruled that under the Due Process Clause of the Fourteenth Amendment, the First Amendment's restrictions likewise apply to state regulations of speech and press. Since *Gitlow*, the vast majority of the Court's free speech cases have involved challenges to state or local enactments.

On the other hand, the Court has never held that the First Amendment prohibits all regulation of speech and press.[2] It has upheld restrictions on the time, place, and manner of expression, such as the regulations governing the use of loudspeakers that were challenged in *Kovacs* v. *Cooper* (1949). Constitutional protection has been denied altogether to some categories of expression ("the lewd and the obscene, the profane, the libelous, and the insulting or 'fighting' words") and extended only in a limited way to others, such as commercial advertising.[3] Finally, the Court generally has held that the protection accorded expression depends on the effects it is likely to produce. As Justice Oliver Wendell Holmes noted: "The most stringent protection of free speech would not protect a man in falsely shouting fire in a theater and causing a panic."[4]

General acceptance of these propositions notwithstanding, the Court has not achieved a consensus on First Amendment issues. The justices have at times disagreed sharply on the standards to be applied in evaluating First Amendment claims, on the application of these standards in individual cases, and on the level of deference to be accorded legislative judgments when they impinge on speech and press. In exploring the bases of these differences, this chapter turns first to the debate over the aims of the First Amendment and shows how the differing interpretations of the ends of the First Amendment have found expression in the standards the Court has employed in press and speech cases.

THE MEANING OF THE FIRST AMENDMENT

Because the First Amendment prohibits all laws abridging the freedom of speech and of the press, the meaning of the amendment depends on the scope of those freedoms. In drawing up the Bill of Rights, the Framers were concerned more with protecting existing freedoms than with forging new liberties, and so the understanding of those freedoms which prevailed in English law is relevant to understanding their aims. William Blackstone in *Commentaries on the Law of England* summarized the English law immediately before the American Revolution:

> The liberty of the press . . . consists in laying no previous restraints upon publications, and not in freedom from censure for criminal matter when published.
> . . . [T]o punish (as the law does at present) any dangerous or offensive writings, which when published, shall on a fair and impartial trial be adjudged of a pernicious tendency, is necessary for the preservation of peace and good order, a government and religion, the only solid foundations of civil liberty.[5]

Under English law, then, freedom of the press did not encompass the right to publish whatever one chose without fear of punishment, for that would jeopardize the peace and good order that government was charged with maintaining; it merely encompassed the right to be free from prior censorship. Under this system, the guarantee of a jury trial, which involved judgment by one's peers, presumably ensured that the power to punish press abuses could not be used to suppress legitimate publications.

Clearly, the Framers sought to provide protection as extensive as that existing in England. Many scholars and justices have concluded, however, that the Framers' aims were not so limited.[6] They have observed that because the First Amendment protects not only freedom of the press but also freedom of speech, which cannot be subjected to prior censorship, it must prohibit more than prior restraints on expression. In addition, they have noted that under English law, writers could be punished for seditious libel (criticism of the government)—a position which is inconsistent with the character of the government created by the Constitution. And indeed, when Congress outlawed seditious libel in the Sedition Act of 1798, opponents of the act contended that it violated the First Amendment, and it was repealed within three years.[7]

This focus on the character of the government established by the Constitution leads to a more expansive interpretation of the meaning of the First Amendment. As Justice Harlan Stone noted in his famous *Carolene Products* footnote (see Chapter 3), restrictions on political expression are constitutionally suspect because they cripple the political process and prevent the repeal of undesirable legislation. Only through the unfettered discussion of political alternatives, moreover, can the citizenry reach informed judgments about the policies government should pursue. Justice Louis Brandeis eloquently summarized the political importance of freedom of expression in *Whitney* v. *California* (1927):

> [The Framers] believed that freedom to think as you will and to speak as you think are means indispensable to the discovery of political truth; that without free speech and assembly, discussion would be futile; that with them, discussion affords ordinarily adequate protection against the dissemination of noxious doctrine; that the greatest menace to freedom is an inert people; that public discussion is a political duty; and that this should be a fundamental principle of the American government.[8]

Justice Brandeis' analysis left several important questions unanswered, however. First of all, if the First Amendment protects political speech because it is a prerequisite for self-government, does that protection extend only to speech advocating political alternatives consistent with a system of self-government? More specifically, does the First Amendment protect advocacy of unlawful actions or of the violent overthrow of the government? Then, too, Brandeis referred to free discussion as affording "ordinarily adequate protection against the dissemination of noxious doctrines," which implies that free discussion sometimes will not be adequate. Under what conditions, therefore, may other measures, including the suppression of speech, constitutionally be employed to combat the spread of dangerous views? Finally, in *Whitney* Brandeis dealt solely with political speech and its importance for self-government, thus leaving open the question of whether nonpolitical speech is entitled to First Amendment protection. On the one hand, some of the same arguments used to support political expression can be applied to nonpolitical expression: the suppression of unpopular moral or scientific ideas, like the suppression of political views, can enshrine error and thwart the search for truth. On the other hand, much nonpolitical speech is not concerned with the search for truth. Does the First Amendment extend protection to speech on all subjects? And if so, how broad is the protection it provides?

As these questions suggest, examination of the aims the Framers sought to achieve in adopting the First Amendment has not ended the debate about its meaning. Justices, as well as legal scholars, have arrived at quite different understandings of the ends the First Amendment was designed to serve, and these divergent views have been reflected in the various standards the Court has used in deciding First Amendment cases.

FIRST AMENDMENT STANDARDS

The Bad Tendency Test

The bad tendency test served as the Supreme Court's initial First Amendment standard. During the decade following World War I, in such cases as *Abrams* v. *United States* (1919), *Gitlow* v. *New York* (1925), and *Whitney* v. *California* (1927), the Court employed this standard in upholding the convictions of several political radicals who had advocated violent action. Underlying the bad tendency test is the assumption that the First Amendment, like other constitutional provisions, was designed to promote the public good. It follows that types of speech that have good effects are entitled to constitutional protection, whereas speech that threatens the security, order, or morals of the society may be regulated by the legislature. The decisive consideration, then, is whether the regulated speech is likely to produce bad effects—and this, the Court held, is primarily a legislative question. In defining its own role, the Court declared that "every presumption is to be indulged in favor of the validity of the statute."

In adopting this standard, the Court maintained that the First Amendment was never intended to protect all speech and publications; rather, this amendment, like other provisions of the Bill of Rights, merely embodied guarantees that had existed under English law. Because English law permitted prosecutions for abuses of freedom of the press, so did the First Amendment. And because legislators are popularly elected and are more familiar than judges with societal conditions, legislative judgments about the types of speech that are harmful generally should prevail. Under this standard, therefore, legislation affecting speech and press received no closer judicial scrutiny than did any other legislation.

The Clear-and-Present-Danger Test

Dissatisfaction with the suppression of speech and the press possible under the bad tendency test led to the development of the clear-and-present-danger test, which was first enunciated by Justice Oliver Wendell Holmes in *Schenck* v. *United States* (1919). In Holmes's words, "The question in every case is whether the words are used in such circumstances and are of such a nature as to create a clear and present danger that they will bring about the substantive evils that Congress has a right to prevent." This test resembles the bad tendency test in permitting the punishment of speech that produces harmful effects, but it imposes more exacting criteria for determining harm. The clear-and-present-danger test requires the government to demonstrate that the specific speech, in the context in which it occurred, created a danger to the achievement of permissible governmental objectives, and that the likelihood of harm was both substantial ("clear") and proximate ("present").

Throughout the decade following *Schenck,* Holmes and Justice Louis Brandeis sought to refine the test and clarify its constitutional foundations. Dissenting in *Abrams,* Holmes asserted that the "theory of our Constitution" was that the public interest was best served by fostering a "free trade in ideas." The First Amendment, he argued, reflected the Framers' conviction that "the best test of truth is the power of thought to get itself accepted in the competition of the market."[9] When government intervenes in this marketplace, suppressing harmful speech, it interferes with society's best mechanism for discovering truth. Such intervention, therefore, can be justified only when speech leads to substantial harm so immediately that there is no opportunity for further discussion to exert a corrective effect.

For over a decade the clear-and-present-danger test proved singularly ineffective in protecting speech and press. In no case was the test used to overturn a conviction; and only in *Schenck,* in which Justice Holmes upheld a conviction under the Espionage Act, did a majority of the justices endorse it. In *Herndon* v. *Lowry* (1937), however, the Court relied on it in reversing a conviction for distributing Communist Party literature. From that point until the early 1950s, the clear-and-present-danger test enjoyed broad support as a general standard for deciding First Amendment questions. Frequently alluding to the "preferred position" of First Amendment freedoms and its special responsibility to protect them, the Court generally applied the test to invalidate restrictions on speech and press.

Dennis v. *United States* (1951), in which the Court upheld the convictions of Communist Party leaders for conspiring to advocate the overthrow of the government, marked a fundamental shift away from the clear-and-present-danger test. Chief Justice Fred Vinson asserted that the situation in *Dennis* required a reformulation of Holmes's test: "In each case [courts] must ask whether the gravity of the evil, discounted by its improbability, justifies such invasion of free speech as is necessary to avoid the danger." In dissent, Justices Hugo Black and William Douglas observed that faithful application of Holmes's test meant reversal of the convictions. This in fact explains Vinson's modification of the test. Having determined that the clear-and-present-danger test offered too much protection—"the words cannot mean that before the Government may act, it must wait until the *putsch* is about to be executed, the plans have been laid and the signal is awaited"—Vinson sought to reconcile it with the community's need to deal with perceived threats to its safety. This perception that the clear-and-present-danger test protected too much, together with the dissenters' belief that it protected too little, account for the Court's abandonment of the test. Nevertheless, the Court's opinions in *Brandenburg* v. *Ohio* (1969) and more recent cases have continued to reflect the concerns, if not always the language, of Holmes and Brandeis.

The Balancing Test

In *Kovacs* v. *Cooper* (1949), Justice Felix Frankfurter proposed the balancing test as an alternative to the clear-and-present-danger test and, in particular, to the Court's emphasis on a "preferred position" for First Amendment rights. The balancing test actually is less a standard than an approach. First Amendment cases typically involve conflicts between individual rights and the attainment of other governmental ends. Frankfurter contended that by automatically elevating individual rights to a "preferred position," the Court had oversimplified issues and predetermined outcomes. Such concentration on the single goal of protecting speech, he added, had no constitutional basis because the Constitution was designed to promote a variety of ends. What was necessary, rather, was an impartial balancing of competing claims on a case-by-case basis. Frankfurter urged that in undertaking this task, judges assign great weight to the balancing already undertaken by the legislative branch.

First endorsed by the Court in *American Communications Association* v. *Douds* (1950), balancing was employed during the 1950s and early 1960s in several cases involving persons and groups viewed as subversive. More recently, however, the justices have tended to combine elements of balancing and of "preferred position." When government has sought to achieve legitimate ends by regulating the *mode* of expression, the Court typically has attempted to balance the competing claims of government and of those affected by the regulation, as in its decisions dealing with "symbolic speech" (actions designed to communicate ideas) and with time, place, and manner regulations. But when government has sought to achieve its ends by restricting the *content* or *extent* of expression, the Court usually has adopted a more stringent standard: "balancing of interests with an especially heavy weight given to the claims of speech."[10] Thus the Court in *Gibson* v. *Florida Legislative Investigating Committee* (1963) required that Florida demonstrate an "immediate, substantial and subordinating state interest" to justify a legislative inquiry that intruded on a witness's freedom of association. And in *Elrod* v. *Burns* (1976), it noted that "the interest advanced must be paramount, one of vital importance," in invalidating the patronage dismissal of government workers.[11] Although these requirements conceivably can be met—as *Buckley* v. *Valeo* (1976) demonstrates—the Court's "weighted" balancing affords substantially more protection for expression than did its earlier balancing approach.

Auxiliary Doctrines

The Court does not always decide First Amendment issues on the basis of broad constitutional standards; in some cases, various auxiliary doctrines have provided narrower grounds for the vindication of First Amendment rights. These doctrines focus not on the legitimacy of governmental regulation, but on the means the government has employed to achieve its ends.[12] Among the most important of these standards are the overbreadth and void-for-vagueness doctrines.

A statute is overbroad if it outlaws both unprotected and constitutionally protected speech. The basic defect of such statutes is their excessive deterrent effect. Speakers must guess whether their speech is constitutionally protected despite being proscribed by the statute and may refrain from speaking rather than risk possible punishment for violating it. As a result, the statute achieves its valid purpose only by infringing on First Amendment rights. *Coates* v. *City of Cincinnati* (1971) illustrates how the Court has employed the overbreadth doctrine. In invalidating a city ordinance that made it a criminal offense for "three or more persons to assemble . . . on any of the sidewalks . . . and then conduct themselves in a manner annoying to persons passing by," the Court did not concern itself with the details of Coates's conduct. Even if Coates's actions were not constitutionally protected, it ruled, the ordinance could not be upheld, because it established a standard for restricting the right of assembly that invaded First Amendment rights.

Closely related to the overbreadth standard is the void-for-vagueness doctrine. A statute is void for vagueness when it "either forbids or requires the doing of an act in terms so vague that men of common intelligence must necessarily guess at its meaning and differ as to its application."[13] By failing to provide adequate notice of what constitutes illegal behavior, vague statutes "chill" the exercise of First Amendment rights and delegate inordinate discretionary power to the officials charged with their enforcement.

POLITICAL EXPRESSION

Speaking for the Court in *New York Times* v. *Sullivan* (1964), Justice William Brennan observed that the nation was committed to the "principle that debate on public issues should be uninhibited, robust, and wideopen." Advocacy of radical political change through violence or other nondemocratic means, on the other hand, may threaten the very foundations of government. In addition, restrictions on political expression may be deemed necessary to prevent corruption of the political process or to serve other important societal purposes. This section details how the

Court has dealt with governmental attempts to restrict political expression for national security or other purposes.

National Security

Governmental attempts to limit political expression have been most pronounced during periods of national crisis. The first major conflict over political expression occurred in the late 1790s, when the Sedition Act provoked a bitter controversy (see "Libel and Invasion of Privacy," page 147).

The next significant clash between the perceived requirements of national security and of political expression took place during and immediately after World War I. Following the assassination of President William McKinley by an anarchist in 1902, several states enacted legislation making it unlawful to advocate the violent overthrow of government; and by 1921, two thirds of the states had such laws. In 1917, Congress passed the Espionage Act, which prohibited expression that interfered with the war effort.[14] During the war, almost two thousand prosecutions were brought under the Espionage Act, and many others under state law. Despite the development of the clear-and-present-danger test in *Schenck* v. *United States* (1919) and the incorporation of First Amendment guarantees in *Gitlow* v. *New York* (1925), the Court during this period consistently upheld convictions for political expression in national security cases.

Following World War II, the Cold War between the United States and the Soviet Union intensified concern about the activities of the Communist Party and so-called Communist-front groups. To deal with this perceived threat to national security, the government began to prosecute Communist Party officials under the Smith Act, which forbade advocating or organizing to advocate the overthrow of the government by force or violence. After *Dennis* v. *United States* (1951), in which the Supreme Court sustained the convictions of twelve Communist Party leaders for conspiring to violate the advocacy and organizing provisions of the Act, the government initiated additional prosecutions against Communist Party officials, which resulted in ninety-six convictions.

The Court's interpretation of the Smith Act in *Yates* v. *United States* (1957) and *Scales* v. *United States* (1961), however, severely restricted its usefulness. In *Yates* the Court ruled that the act only proscribed advocacy of participation in overthrowing the government: "Those to whom the advocacy is addressed must be urged to *do* something, now or in the future, rather than merely to *believe in* something."[15] Thus after *Yates*, convictions required proof of participation in a conspiracy to overthrow the government. In *Scales* the Court, although sustaining a conviction under the organizing provision of the act, indicated that mere membership in an organization advocating governmental overthrow was insufficient for conviction. Noting that members might disagree with positions taken by an organization, the Court ruled that the act applied only to "knowing" and "active" members who specifically intended to advance the organization's illegal aims. The importance of this distinction was underlined in *Noto* v. *United States* (1961), in which the justices set aside Noto's conviction because he belonged to an organization that merely engaged in discussions of Communist theory. In the aftermath of *Yates* and *Scales*, Smith Act prosecutions virtually ceased; and the Court's decision in *Brandenburg* v. *Ohio* (1969) has cast serious doubt on the continuing authority of *Dennis*.

During the Cold War era the national and state governments also either instituted or greatly expanded loyalty programs designed to deny public employment or positions of influence to those who might use them for subversive purposes. Initially, the Court endorsed most loyalty requirements. In *Adler* v. *Board of Education* (1952) the justices sustained a New York law that authorized the dismissal of teachers belonging to proscribed organizations, and in *Konigsberg* v. *State Bar of California* (1961) they ruled that persons who refused to answer questions about Communist Party membership could be denied admission to the bar. But gradually the Court imposed significant restrictions on governmental loyalty programs by extending procedural protections to public employees threatened with dismissal on loyalty grounds and by using the overbreadth and void-for-vagueness doctrines to limit the scope of loyalty inquiries. Thus in *United States* v. *Robel* (1967) it struck down as overbroad a federal statute prohibiting members of Communist organizations from working in defense facilities, and in *Keyishian* v. *Board of Regents* (1967) it overruled *Adler*, observing that the New York oath was unconstitutionally vague and penalized mere membership in the Communist Party. Finally, in *Law Students Civil Rights Research Council, Inc.* v. *Wadmond* (1971) the Court limited the *Konigsberg* ruling, restricting inquiries by bar-admission committees to whether prospective lawyers knowingly belonged to organizations committed to overthrowing the government.

Postwar legislative investigations into possible subversive activities also raised First Amendment issues. (See Chapter 4 of Volume I for a discussion of the constitutional questions raised by congressional investigations.) During the 1950s, scores of witnesses were summoned before congressional and state legislative committees to testify about their past and present political associations, and witnesses who refused to testify were cited for contempt. In reviewing contempt convictions, the Supreme Court imposed procedural limitations on the conduct of investigations and announced that it would not tolerate "exposure for the sake of exposure." Not until *Barenblatt* v. *United States* (1959), however, did the Court consider the question of whether witnesses compelled to testify about political associations and beliefs were denied their First Amendment rights. The five-member majority in *Barenblatt* ruled that because the Communist Party was not "an ordinary political party" but an organization committed to the overthrow of the government, Congress's need for information about its activities overrode First Amendment objections.

Yet four years later the Court in *Gibson* v. *Florida Legislative Investigating Committee* (1963) found that the head of the Miami chapter of the National Association for the Advancement of Colored People (NAACP) could not be compelled to furnish membership lists to a state committee investigating possible Communist infiltration.

Other Limitations on Political Expression

The Court has been reluctant to sustain restrictions on political expression that do not serve national security needs. Two decisions involving the freedom of association illustrate this. In *NAACP* v. *Alabama* (1958) the Court ruled that an Alabama law requiring out-of-state organizations to file their membership lists could not be enforced against the NAACP. Although it conceded that Alabama had a legitimate interest in the activities of organizations doing business in the state, the Court noted that disclosure of the NAACP's membership would subject members to reprisals and intimidation, and thereby abridge their right to associate in support of their beliefs. And in *Elrod* v. *Burns* (1976) the justices struck a major blow at the spoils system by invalidating the patronage dismissals of non–policy-making government employees. In the face of claims that patronage was necessary for strong political parties, the Court held that removals based on political affiliation violated government workers' rights of freedom of association and freedom of political belief.

In two areas, however, the Court has sustained limits on political expression. It has recognized, first of all, that the government's special interest in safeguarding the effectiveness and fairness of its operations may justify restrictions on political expression by governmental employees. This position is reflected in *U.S. Civil Service Commission* v. *National Association of Letter Carriers* (1973), in which the justices upheld restrictions on partisan political activity by federal civil servants. Yet public servants do not altogether forfeit their right to express opinions on political matters. In *Rankin* v. *McPherson* (1987), for example, the Court ruled that a clerical worker in a county constable's office could not be discharged for stating, after hearing of an attempt on the President's life, "If they go for him again, I hope they get him."

The Supreme Court has also recognized that government may act to protect the political process from corruption. Thus, laws regulating lobbying and punishing election fraud present no First Amendment difficulty. More problematic, however, are regulations of the electoral process, such as the Federal Election Campaign Act Amendments of 1974. This law, enacted in response to the Watergate scandal and to the spiraling costs of election campaigns, (1) restricted the size of individual and group contributions to political campaigns, (2) limited the amounts that candidates could spend in those campaigns, (3) required disclosure of campaign contributions and expenditures, (4) provided for public financing of presidential campaigns, and (5) established the Federal Election Commission to administer the act. In *Buckley* v. *Valeo* (1976), the Court ruled that the act's limits on campaign contributions did not violate the First Amendment, because they served an important purpose (elimination of corruption) and impinged only minimally on speech interests. The justices did invalidate the limits on campaign expenditures, maintaining that such restrictions limited the communication of political views without contributing significantly to the control of corruption; but they also held that restrictions on expenditures could be imposed as a condition for public financing. Finally, they dismissed as hypothetical the claim that disclosure requirements invaded freedom of association by deterring support for unpopular minor parties.[16]

Perhaps the most important—and controversial—aspect of the *Buckley* decision was the Court's invalidation of limits on spending by candidates to promote their views. Proponents of limits on spending by candidates or groups contend that governmental intervention in the marketplace of ideas is necessary to correct "distortions" resulting from the unequal distribution of wealth in the society. Limiting the participation of wealthy groups and individuals in the marketplace of ideas, they argue, will encourage the dissemination of diverse viewpoints by equalizing opportunities to influence the electorate. While acknowledging that increasing access to the marketplace of ideas is a legitimate goal, the Court in *Buckley* held that the government could not limit the freedom of speech of some groups or individuals in order to achieve it. Moreover, the Court recognized the potential for abuse inherent in permitting government to control the flow of political communication. Thus, in rulings such as *Federal Election Commission* v. *National Conservative Political Action Committee* (1983) and *Colorado Republican Federal Campaign Committee* v. *Federal Election Commission* (1996), the Court has generally adhered to the position it announced in *Buckley*. However, some divisions have developed on the Court. In the *Colorado* case, two justices—John Paul Stevens and Ruth Bader Ginsburg—challenged the Court's greater scrutiny of government limits on campaign spending, contending that regulation of both spending and contributions serves an "important interest in leveling the electoral playing field by constraining the costs of electoral campaigns" and urging deference to Congress. In the same case, Justice Clarence Thomas also attacked the Court's distinction between spending and contributions. He insisted that both are "forms of speech central to the First Amendment" which should be free from regulation, absent a "compelling government interest [in regulation] and legislative means narrowly tailored to serve that interest."

THE REGULATION OF SPEECH

In *Kunz* v. *United States* (1951) Justice Robert Jackson noted that "the vulnerability of various forms of communication to community control must be proportioned to their impact upon other community interests."[17] This observation explains why government may impose more stringent limitations on speech and expressive conduct than on publication. Because a speaker can address larger numbers of people simultaneously, speech is likely to have a more immediate impact than the press will have. And because expressive conduct ("symbolic speech") has an action component, it is more likely to interfere with the attainment of legitimate governmental ends unrelated to the suppression of speech. This section examines to what extent, and for what purposes, government can regulate speech and expressive conduct.

Symbolic Speech

Conduct, as well as speech, can promote the ends of the First Amendment. Demonstrations and picketing, by combining conduct with speech, often can be more effective than speech alone. Even conduct without speech—a refusal to salute a flag, for instance—can be an eloquent form of expression. Accordingly, the Court has long recognized that symbolic speech is entitled to some First Amendment protection. On the other hand, it has never ruled that the mere presence of a communicative element makes conduct immune from regulation. In each case the Court has had to balance the claims of free expression against the pursuit of other governmental objectives.

In *United States* v. *O'Brien* (1968) the Court upheld O'Brien's conviction for burning his draft card in protest against the Vietnam War. Speaking for the Court, Chief Justice Earl Warren proposed a four-part test for determining when a government interest permits the regulation of expressive conduct:

> [A] government regulation is sufficiently justified if it is within the constitutional power of the Government; if it furthers an important or substantial governmental interest; if the governmental interest is unrelated to the suppression of free expression; and if the incidental restriction of alleged First Amendment freedoms is no greater than is essential to the furtherance of that interest.[18]

When expression and conduct are intertwined, in other words, government can regulate the nonspeech element to achieve valid governmental ends. Thus in *O'Brien* the government's interest in the smooth operation of the Selective Service System justified the incidental burden imposed on free expression. In *Clark* v. *Community for Creative Non-Violence* (1984), the Court relied on the *O'Brien* test to uphold the National Park Service's ban on sleeping in national parks. Rejecting the challenge of a group that sought to conduct a "sleep-in" in parks near the nation's Capitol to dramatize the plight of the homeless, the Court observed that the prohibition was not designed to restrict expression and served the valid purpose of maintaining parks "in an attractive and intact condition."

For the governmental regulation to be valid, however, it must be viewpoint-neutral, that is, it must not regulate conduct as a means of restricting the expression of particular ideas. This requirement was decisive in *Texas* v. *Johnson* (1989), in which a sharply divided Court struck down the conviction of a political protestor who had violated Texas's flag-desecration statute by burning the American flag. According to the Court's five-member majority, the flaw in the Texas law was that it permitted the use of the flag to show support for the nation and its institutions but prohibited its use to register dissent. Thus because the ban on flag desecration was not viewpoint-neutral, it violated the First Amendment.

Unprotected Speech

In *Chaplinsky* v. *New Hampshire* (1942), the Supreme Court noted that certain categories of speech were not protected by the First Amendment. Among these were what it termed "fighting words," that is, verbal provocations which amounted to an invitation to fight and thus by their very character posed an immediate threat to public order. In subsequent cases the Court defined "fighting words" narrowly. It was not enough that speech be offensive, or invite dispute, or provoke hostility among listeners: only face-to-face personal insults enjoyed no First Amendment protection. Yet the difficulty of designing a statute confined to such insults has led the Court to overturn several convictions on overbreadth or vagueness grounds, even when the speech at issue clearly constituted "fighting words."

In recent years the issue of what speech is unprotected by the First Amendment has arisen in the context of campus restrictions on racist and sexist expression. Some universities have concluded that the First Amendment does not protect such speech, even if that speech does not involve "fighting words," and have established speech codes on their campuses banning such speech. The University of Michigan, for example, prohibited speech that "stigmatize[d] or victimize[d] an individual on the basis of race, ethnicity, religion, sex, sexual orientation" or several other factors and "create[d] an intimidating, hostile, or demeaning environment for educational pursuits." Other universities have prohibited "fighting words" that vilify individuals on the basis of their membership in various groups. Stanford University, for example, banned "fighting words" that insulted or stigmatized persons "on the basis of their sex, race, color, handicap, religion, sexual orientation, or national and ethnic origin." Advocates of speech codes claim that the speech banned by those codes harms the members of targeted groups. In making this claim, they depart from traditional First Amendment analysis, which views harm as coming not from speech itself but from its close connection to action. They further argue that speech codes, by creating a more congenial environment on campus, encourage minority students to express their ideas, thereby fostering the interchange of ideas.

In *Doe* v. *University of Michigan* (1989), a federal district court rejected such arguments in striking down the University of Michigan's speech code as in violation of the First Amendment. This decision, however, did not affect university speech codes that restricted only speech that met the constitutional standard of "fighting words." Thus far the Supreme Court had not addressed the constitutionality of university speech codes. In *R.A.V.* v. *City of St. Paul* (1992), however, the Court did invalidate a municipal ordinance that outlawed the display of symbols known to "arouse anger, alarm or resentment in others on the basis of race, color, creed, religion, or gender." Speaking for the Court, Justice Antonin Scalia held that St. Paul's ordinance was invalid, even if it merely outlawed "fighting words." For although government can ban "fighting words" altogether, it cannot distinguish among "fighting words" based on hostility toward their ideological content. St. Paul's ordinance was invalid, therefore, because it involved a viewpoint-based distinction: it outlawed "fighting word's" on the basis of race or gender but not, for example, on the basis of political affiliation or sexual preference. Because most speech codes make similar viewpoint-based distinctions, they too are constitutionally suspect under the standard announced in *R.A.V.*

Public Order

Government has a basic responsibility to maintain public order, and all states have statutes punishing actions such as disorderly conduct, breach of the peace, and incitement to riot. When fighting words are not involved, the threat to public order usually arises when proponents of unpopular or controversial views use some form of public assembly—meetings, parades, demonstrations—to reach a broad audience. But that very fact complicates the issue: to penalize speakers merely because their views excite opposition would give unsympathetic listeners a "heckler's veto" over speech. The Supreme Court's decisions have not satisfactorily resolved this issue. In *Feiner* v. *New York* (1951) the Court upheld the conviction for disorderly conduct of a speaker who disobeyed police orders to end a speech that had produced some crowd hostility. In *Edwards* v. *South Carolina* (1963) and *Cox* v. *Louisiana* (1965), on the other hand, it overturned the breach-of-the-peace convictions of civil-rights activists whose demonstrations had also stirred crowd unrest. More recently, the Illinois Supreme Court in *Village of Skokie* v. *National Socialist Party* (1978) upheld the right of the American Nazi Party to demonstrate in Skokie, a predominantly Jewish suburb in which many Holocaust survivors resided. Although the intention of the demonstration's organizers clearly was provocative, the Illinois court concluded that the U.S. Supreme Court's decisions required it to overturn an injunction that would have prevented the demonstration and the displaying of the swastika.

Time, Place, and Manner Regulations

The Court has held that government can impose restrictions on the time, place, and manner of speech on public property in order to promote effective communication or accommodate other legitimate uses of that property, but that in imposing such restrictions it cannot discriminate on the basis of the content of expression. As the Court noted in *Police*

Department of Chicago v. *Mosley* (1972): "Once a forum is opened up to assembly or speaking by some groups, government may not prohibit others from assembling or speaking on the basis of what they intend to say."[19] Thus the Court has struck down permit systems that distinguish on the basis of the content of speech, as in *Carey* v. *Brown* (1980), or that give excessive discretion, and thus the opportunity to discriminate, to local officials, as in *Lakewood* v. *Plain Dealer Publishing Co.* (1988).

Even nondiscriminatory regulations may be constitutionally suspect. Although government can regulate speech on public property in order to accommodate other interests, it may not deny all access to public property for expression. As Justice Owen Roberts emphasized in *Hague* v. *C.I.O.* (1939),

> Wherever the title of streets and parks may rest, they have immemorially been held in trust for the use of the public. . . . The privilege of a citizen of the United States to use the street and parks for communication of views on national questions may be regulated in the interest of all . . . but it must not, in the guise of regulation, be abridged or denied.[20]

On the question of what property must be made available for communicative purposes, the justices have divided. In *Adderley* v. *Florida* (1966), Justice Hugo Black, speaking for the Court, indicated that government could limit expression to that property which traditionally had been used as a public forum. However, in *Tinker* v. *Des Moines* (1969), a case involving the First Amendment rights of students, Justice Abraham Fortas, also speaking for the Court, insisted that the decisive consideration was whether the use of governmental property as a public forum significantly interfered with the purposes to which the property was dedicated. In *Hazelwood School District* v. *Kuhlmeier* (1988) the Court apparently retreated from that position, at least in dealing with the First Amendment rights of students, upholding a principal's censorship of material published in a high school newspaper that he deemed inappropriate.

Government Sponsorship

Government can promote freedom of speech not only by making its property available for communicative purposes but also by providing financial support for speech. The National Endowment for the Arts, for example, underwrites the creation and display of artistic work, and the National Science Foundation awards grants for scientific research. Government also supports speech through its funding of schools and universities and its financing of elections. Even programs not directly concerned with promoting speech, such as the Peace Corps, may promote the communication of ideas.

Yet the power to encourage speech by underwriting it also entails the power to discourage speech by refusing to sponsor it. More specifically, government by its funding decisions can promote some ideas while discouraging others. This raises perplexing First Amendment problems. On the one hand, government obviously has a valid interest in ensuring that its programs achieve their goals, and thus it can limit its support to only that speech that promotes a program's goals. In addition, a governmental failure to fund speech has less dire consequences than a statute outlawing speech: those who are denied funding remain free to communicate their views. On the other hand, government's power to grant or withhold funding may significantly affect the speech of recipients or potential recipients of governmental largesse. Moreover, since government cannot favor particular viewpoints in making its property available for communicative purposes, it might be argued that it also cannot make viewpoint-based decisions in allocating public funds.

Rust v. *Sullivan* (1991), which concerned federal regulations banning abortion counseling at federally funded clinics, afforded the Supreme Court its first opportunity to address the issue. In upholding the regulations, Chief Justice Rehnquist emphasized the power of government to define the limits of programs that it establishes with public funds. The dissenters in *Rust* countered that government cannot require a viewpoint-based suppression of speech as a condition for the acceptance of public funds. During his first week in office, President William Clinton lifted the ban on abortion counseling.

RESTRAINTS ON THE PRESS

Prior Restraints

Prior restraints, which may involve either governmental licensing of publication or bans on publication of particular information, impose a particularly severe burden on communication. To require governmental approval prior to publication brings more materials under official scrutiny and, at minimum, delays even constitutionally protected expression. In addition, the decision to censor typically is reached without the adversarial proceedings and procedural safeguards which accompany criminal prosecutions. For these reasons, English law early on recognized that freedom from prior restraints was essential to freedom of the press. Because the Framers of the First Amendment clearly sought to secure as much press freedom as prevailed in England, the Supreme Court consistently has ruled that prior restraints are constitutionally suspect.

Near v. *Minnesota* (1931) established the Court's basic position on prior restraints. In *Near* the Court struck down a Minnesota law that permitted judges to enjoin publication of "malicious, scandalous and defamatory" newspapers. Speaking for the Court, Chief Justice Charles Evans Hughes recognized that the state had a legitimate interest in curbing such publications and could prosecute those who published them but argued that this interest did not justify prior restraints against publication, as such restraints could be tolerated only in "exceptional cases." To

Hughes, prior restraints were impermissible unless the publication involved jeopardized the country's safety in wartime, threatened public decency (obscenity), incited violence or governmental overthrow, or invaded private rights.

Hughes's analysis in *Near* has governed subsequent decisions on prior restraints, as the Court generally has refused to add to the exceptions Hughes listed. Thus in *Organization for a Better Austin* v. *Keefe* (1971), it struck down prior restraints on the distribution of nonobscene materials. In *Nebraska Press Association* v. *Stuart* (1976), it overturned a judicial "gag order" designed to prevent prejudicial publicity in a murder case. Finally, in *Hazelwood School District* v. *Kuhlmeier* (1988), it permitted censorship of a high school newspaper by school authorities only because its publication was part of the school curriculum rather than independent of it.

The Court has also tended to construe Hughes's exceptions narrowly. In *New York Times* v. *United States* (1971) the justices lifted an injunction restraining publication of the Pentagon Papers, a top-secret account of the nation's involvement in the Vietnam War, despite objections that publication would threaten national security. In *Snepp* v. *United States* (1980), on the other hand, they upheld a contract requiring a former CIA agent to submit his writings for prepublication clearance by the agency.

Governmental Regulation of Newsgathering[21]

Some governmental regulations, even if adopted for legitimate purposes and applicable to all citizens, may restrict reporters' access to information or deter sources from confiding in them. By making newsgathering more difficult, these regulations may deprive the citizenry of information about matters of public concern. In recent decades the Supreme Court has decided several cases involving regulations that impinge on the institutional press's access to information.

In *Richmond Newspapers Inc.* v. *Virginia* (1980) the Supreme Court recognized that, "absent a need to further a state interest of the highest order," the press cannot be prosecuted for publishing truthful information of public interest that is lawfully obtained. This does not mean that reporters have a right to obtain newsworthy information—as the Court noted in *Nixon* v. *Warner Communications* (1978), the First Amendment gives the media no right to information beyond that possessed by the general public. On that basis the justices in *Houchins* v. *KQED* (1978) upheld correctional authorities' refusal to grant reporters special access to prison facilities and to prisoners. Yet this does not mean that government can arbitrarily shield its proceedings from public scrutiny, particularly when those proceedings have historically been open to the public. Thus the Court recognized a right of public access to criminal trials in *Richmond Newspapers* and to certain preliminary hearings in criminal cases in *Press-Enterprise Co.* v. *Superior Court* (1986). Although reporters are accorded no special access, their status as members of the public serves to guarantee their admission.

The Court has also maintained that government may impose the same obligations on the press as on other citizens, even when those requirements may affect newsgathering. In *Branzburg* v. *Hayes* (1972), for example, the Court ruled that reporters must supply relevant information to grand juries, despite the alleged effects of such action on reporters' relationships with confidential sources. Similarly, in *Zurcher* v. *Stanford Daily* (1978) it upheld a warrant under which police searched a newsroom for evidence, despite claims that the search disrupted the newsroom and could lead to the disclosure of confidential sources and information.

In the face of the Court's refusal to provide special protection for the press, other branches have acted to facilitate newsgathering. Passage of the Freedom of Information Act (1966) by Congress and of "sunshine" legislation by state legislatures has expanded the availability of information about governmental activities to the press as well as to the general public. Although Congress has failed to approve legislation shielding reporters from grand jury questioning, fully half of the states currently provide some protection.[22] In the wake of *Zurcher*, finally, Congress enacted the Privacy Protection Act of 1980, which narrowly defined the circumstances under which federal, state, and local law-enforcement officers could conduct unannounced searches of newsrooms.

Governmental Regulation of Broadcast Media

In *Miami Herald Publishing Co.* v. *Tornillo* (1974), the Supreme Court unanimously invalidated a statute requiring newspapers to print replies by political candidates they had attacked. But in *Red Lion Broadcasting Co.* v. *Federal Communications Commission* (1969), it unanimously upheld the Commission's "fairness doctrine," which required broadcasters to provide balanced coverage of controversial issues and to permit victims of personal attacks a right to reply. The contrast between the two cases illustrates the Court's view that the First Amendment permits far greater control by government over the broadcast media than it does over newspapers, magazines, and books.

Federal control over broadcasting began with the Radio Act of 1927, which established a comprehensive licensing scheme under which the federal government determined who could broadcast over the airwaves and, to some extent, what could be broadcast. Subsequent legislation extended federal regulatory authority to cover television and then cable. These enactments authorized the Federal Radio Commission and its successor, the Federal Communications Commission (FCC), to ensure that broadcasting serve the "public interest, convenience or necessity." Acting under this broad authority, the FCC developed various content guidelines, ranging from expectations that stations carry public affairs and children's programs to requirements like the "fairness doctrine." Broadcasters had a strong incentive to adhere to FCC guidelines because failure to do so could jeopardize the renewal of one's broadcasting license. In 1984 Congress enacted the Cable Communications Policy Act, which gave state and local governments control over who would be permitted to erect and operate cable systems. Acting under this authority, local governments have devised licensing (franchise) systems for cable companies, often imposing various content requirements as a condition for receiving a franchise.

The initial rationale for this disparate treatment of the broadcast media was spectrum scarcity. As the Supreme Court put it in *Red Lion Broadcasting Co.* v. *FCC* (1969):

> Broadcast frequencies constituted a scarce resource whose use could be regulated and rationalized only by the Government. Without government control, the medium would be of little use because of the cacaphony of competing voices, none of which could be clearly and predictably heard.

Thus, much like time, place, and manner regulations, government regulation of the airwaves was justified as necessary to promote effective communication. In addition, because government allocation of licenses necessarily excluded other potential licensees, it was argued that government could regulate use of the airwaves to safeguard the public interest and the interests of those without direct access to them.

Technological advances, particularly the development of cable, have largely undermined the argument from spectrum scarcity. Recent arguments for continued government regulation have therefore stressed the need to ensure an appropriate diversity of views over the airwaves and to prevent the owners of radio and television stations from exercising excessive influence through their programming decisions. (This argument for governmental regulation to increase access to the marketplace of ideas and curtail the influence of the wealthy thus resembles the arguments offered for restrictions on campaign spending.) Opponents of governmental regulation, however, have insisted that the multiplicity of broadcasters ensures the availability of diverse perspectives and prevents any broadcaster from exerting excessive influence. More generally, they have argued that the First Amendment places the same restrictions on government in dealing with all communications media, whether broadcast or print. Although the Supreme Court has not had occasion to reconsider its ruling in *Red Lion* in the light of changed technological conditions, in 1987 the Federal Communications Commission repudiated the spectrum-scarcity rationale for regulation and abolished the "fairness doctrine."

LIBEL AND INVASION OF PRIVACY

The Sedition Act of 1798, passed by the Federalist-dominated Congress in an effort to limit criticism of the Adams administration, provoked a serious First Amendment dispute by outlawing "seditious libel"; that is, defamation of government and its officials. The Jeffersonian Republicans challenged the act's constitutionality on the grounds (1) that with the ratification of the First Amendment, only the states had the authority to punish abuses of freedom of the press, and (2) that the crime of seditious libel was inconsistent with republican self-government. Although the Supreme Court never had occasion to rule on the act's constitutionality, President Thomas Jefferson expressed his constitutional judgment by pardoning all persons who had been convicted under the act.

The political nature of the Sedition Act distinguishes it from most libel laws, which seek to protect private individuals from unfair damage to their reputations by authorizing either criminal penalties or civil suits for damages. In *Chaplinsky* v. *New Hampshire* (1942) the Court recognized that libel was one of the categories of expression not protected by the First Amendment. Because libel laws restrict the flow of information, however, the justices have attempted to reconcile the full discussion of public issues with adequate protection for individual reputations.

New York Times v. *Sullivan* (1964) marked the Court's first attempt to distinguish libel from protected expression. Sullivan, a police commissioner in Montgomery, Alabama, had been awarded $500,000 in damages stemming from a newspaper advertisement that contained partially erroneous statements criticizing police mistreatment of blacks. In unanimously overturning the libel judgment, the Court provided broad protection for criticism of public officials. The First Amendment, it asserted, abolished the crime of seditious libel and permits even "vehement, caustic, and unpleasantly sharp attacks on government and public officials." Because erroneous statements are unavoidable in the heat of public debate, "a rule compelling the critic of official conduct to guarantee the truth of all his factual assertions" would unjustifiably inhibit discussion of public affairs. Even false statements about official conduct, therefore, enjoy constitutional protection, unless they are made with "actual malice": that is, "with knowledge that [they were] false or with a reckless disregard of whether or not [they were] false."

Since the *New York Times* decision, the Court has focused on the questions of how "actual malice" can be proved and when this standard of proof is required. The justices declared in *Curtis Publishing Company* v. *Butts* (1967) that serious departures from standard journalistic practice could justify a finding of malice. Mere negligence or errors of judgment are not sufficient, although, as indicated in *Herbert* v. *Lando* (1979), the editorial practices of those responsible for publication may be explored in attempting to prove malice. In the *New York Times* case, this standard of proof was required for articles dealing with the official conduct of an elected official. In order to promote uninhibited discussion of public issues, however, the Court in subsequent cases extended the *New York Times* standard to statements made about candidates for public office, nonelected government employees with authority over the conduct of governmental affairs, and "public figures" in general—that is, individuals who "have thrust themselves to the forefront of particular public controversies in order to influence the resolution of the issues in-volved."[23] However, the Court has continued to distinguish between public figures and private individuals, rejecting the applicability of the *New York Times* standard to publications about private individuals in-voluntarily involved in events of public interest.

A related concern is whether the First Amendment protects publica-tions that violate the privacy of the individual or inflict emotional dis-tress but do not contain malicious falsehoods. *Hustler Magazine* v. *Falwell* (1988) involved a parody of an advertisement depicting Jerry Fal-well, a prominent minister and religious leader, as having had sexual re-lations with his mother. The Supreme Court unanimously ruled that Falwell, as a public figure, could not collect damages for infliction of emotional distress, because the parody did not pretend to be factual and hence did not involve "actual malice" as required by *New York Times* v. *Sullivan*. A second case, *Florida Star* v. *B.J.F.* (1989), involved a suit for invasion of privacy by a rape victim whose name was published in a newspaper, contrary to Florida law. In contrast to *Falwell*, the victim was not a public figure, but the publication contained information that was both accurate and legally obtained. A divided Court held that Florida could prohibit publication of such information only by a law narrowly tailored to achieve "a state interest of the highest order" and that the Florida law failed that demanding test.

OBSCENITY

Obscenity has historically been recognized as a category of expression not entitled to First Amendment protection. But because not all expres-sion dealing with sex is obscene, the Supreme Court has had to devise standards for determining whether sexually oriented materials enjoy First Amendment protection. This has not proved easy. For sixteen years after the Court decided *Roth* v. *United States* (1957), its first major ob-scenity case, never were five justices able to agree on standards for dis-tinguishing obscene from nonobscene materials. Not until *Miller* v. *Cal-ifornia* (1973) did a Court majority unite on a test for identifying obscenity. The standard announced in *Miller* involved three parts:

> (a) Whether "the average person, applying contemporary community standards" would find that the work, taken as a whole, appeals to the prurient interest [that is, arouses lustful thoughts and desires]; (b) whether the work depicts or describes, in a patently offensive way, sexual conduct specifically defined by the applicable state law; and (c) whether the work, taken as a whole, lacks serious literary, artis-tic, political, or scientific value.

This test remains the applicable First Amendment standard in obscenity cases, but—given changes in social norms—prosecutions for the distribu-tion of even hard-core pornography to adults are rare today. Thus, Supreme Court rulings since *Miller* have largely focused on other issues.

First, to what extent can localities regulate nonobscene adult entertainment? In *Erznoznick* v. *City of Jacksonville* (1975) the Court invalidated an ordinance forbidding drive-in theaters from showing films containing nudity when the screen was visible to the general public, and in *Schad* v. *Mount Ephraim* (1981) it struck down on overbreadth grounds a conviction for commercial displays of nude dancing in violation of a community ban on live entertainment. In *Renton* v. *Playtime Theaters* (1986), on the other hand, the justices upheld a zoning ordinance that prohibited adult motion picture theaters from locating within 1,000 feet of any residential zone, church, park, or school. These decisions, taken together, suggest that localities can regulate this type of protected expression, based on its content, as long as the regulation does not altogether suppress the expression and is closely related to a legitimate governmental objective.

Second, what steps can government take to protect children from obscenity and from sexual exploitation? In *New York* v. *Ferber* (1982), the Court unanimously held that government could ban the dissemination of materials that showed children engaged in sexual activity. But the development of new forms of communication, such as cable television and the Internet pose a more difficult problem: How can one simultaneously maintain free speech for adults while protecting children in a medium that is available to both? Federal responses to this problem have not fared well in the Supreme Court. In *Denver Area Educational Tele-Communications Consortium, Inc.* v. *Federal Communications Commission* (1996), the Court invalidated all but one provision of congressional regulations designed to control sexually explicit programming on cable television. One year later, in *Reno* v. *American Civil Liberties Union* (1997), the Court struck down provisions of the Communications Decency Act of 1996 that attempted to regulate "indecent" material on the Internet. In both instances, the Court was concerned to ensure that restrictions designed to protect children did not restrict the availability to adults of materials protected by the First Amendment. The Court's position in these cases suggests the necessity of exploring noncensorial approaches to protecting children from inappropriate material, such as rating systems on television programs, and technological restrictions on access to sexually explicit websites on the Internet.

Third, what penalties can government impose on those who violate obscenity laws? In *Fort Wayne Books* v. *Indiana* (1989) the Court upheld application of a state "racketeering" law to those guilty of multiple obscenity offenses. Under such laws, those convicted not only face stiff fines and jail sentences but also may forfeit all their real and personal property used or acquired in the course of committing the offenses. *Alexander* v. *United States* (1989), in which the Court upheld the application of the Racketeer Influenced and Corrupt Organizations Act (RICO) to the owner of several bookstores and theaters specializing in sexually explicit material, illustrates the effect of these laws. When his conviction on seventeen obscenity counts led to his conviction on three RICO counts, Alexander was ordered to forfeit all his businesses and real estate used to conduct his racketeering enterprise, plus almost $9 million acquired through racketeering activity.

Feminist opponents of pornography have proposed a different approach to its regulation. Pornography is objectionable, they claim, because it degrades and harms women by justifying their treatment as sexual objects. Because it differentially harms women, trafficking in pornography constitutes a form of sexual discrimination, and women should be able to sue those who engage in this type of discrimination. Thus whereas the traditional regulation of obscenity focused on the explicit portrayal of sexual activity, feminist critics are concerned with its implicit endorsement of sexual subordination, and whereas traditional regulation relied on criminal penalties, feminists have sought to control it through the threat of civil suits.

The feminist critique of pornography represents a fundamental challenge to First Amendment jurisprudence, because it asserts that some views are so clearly erroneous and harmful that they should be banished from the marketplace of ideas. In contrast, the Supreme Court has held that the First Amendment does not permit the outlawing of ideas, however loathsome. When the city council of Indianapolis enacted an ordinance incorporating the feminist approach to pornography regulation, lower federal courts quickly invalidated the law, and the Supreme Court affirmed.

SOME CONCLUSIONS

Although the number and variety of the Court's decisions preclude a summary evaluation, some general observations can be made about the Court's interpretation of the First Amendment. To begin with, the Court has over time expanded substantially the range of expression that enjoys First Amendment protection. In large measure, this broadening of the amendment's coverage resulted from the incorporation of the speech and press guarantees. In addition, the Court has ruled that some previously excluded categories of expression are entitled to First Amendment protection. Rulings involving symbolic speech, commercial speech, and freedom of association have been particularly important in extending the scope of the First Amendment.

The Court has also progressively narrowed its definitions of the categories of speech—"the lewd and the obscene, the profane, the libelous, and the insulting or 'fighting' words"—that are not entitled to First Amendment protection. Despite the Court's ruling in *Miller* v. *California* (1973), a broad range of sexually explicit materials enjoy constitutional protection. The Court's ruling in *New York Times* v. *Sullivan* (1964) and succeeding cases have rewritten the law of libel and provided broad protection for criticisms of governmental officials. In addition, its substantive rulings and its use of the void-for-vagueness and overbreadth doctrines virtually have eliminated prosecutions for "fighting words."

Yet as recent controversies over campaign financing, speech codes, and obscenity illustrate, the Court's extension of broad protections for expression has of late come under sustained attack. Rejecting the notion of a self-correcting marketplace of ideas, some commentators have called for intervention by government to ensure what they deem more equitable outcomes. Some critics, fearful that the wealthy can dominate the marketplace of ideas not by the quality of their arguments but by monopolizing communications, propose that government act to reduce their influence. Other critics insist that racist and sexist expression harms members of minority groups and therefore should be regulated or banned. Although these arguments have not received judicial endorsement, they do require proponents of a broad reading of the First Amendment both on and off the Court to clarify the grounds for their position.

Finally, it should be noted that despite the Court's movement toward broader protection for expression, the justices have not developed a general standard for resolving First Amendment cases. Rather, the contemporary Court appears to be avoiding broad doctrine in favor of a case-by-case approach, with standards limited to particular areas of First Amendment law (e.g., obscenity, libel). Whether this approach can ensure the principled development of First Amendment law remains to be seen.

NOTES

1 *NAACP* v. *Alabama*, 357 U.S. 449, 460 (1958). Since freedom of association is tied to expression, however, it does not require the invalidation of legislation which impinges on groups but has only a marginal effect on their expression. Thus in *Roberts* v. *United States Jaycees*, 468 U.S. 609 (1984), the Court upheld a state law which prohibited private associations from discriminating on the basis of sex.

2 Justice Hugo Black argued, albeit unsuccessfully, that the First Amendment imposed an absolute ban. His views are summarized in *Smith* v. *California* (1959) and in Edmund Cahn, "Mr. Justice Black and First Amendment Absolutes: A Public Interview," *New York University Law Review* 37 (1962). See also Justice William Douglas's opinion in *Brandenburg* v. *Ohio* (1969).

3 *Chaplinsky* v. *New Hampshire*, 315 U.S. 568, 572 (1942). For a discussion of the protection accorded commercial speech, see *Central Hudson Gas Company* v. *Public Service Commission* (1980).

4 *Schenck* v. *United States*, 249 U.S. 47, 52 (1919).

5 William Blackstone, *Commentaries on the Laws of England* (1765–1769), 2d rev. ed., ed. Thomas Cooley (Chicago: 1872), Book 4, pp. 151-152. For an analysis of the English and colonial background of the First Amendment, see Leonard Levy, *Legacy of Suppression: Freedom of Speech and Press in Early American History* (Cambridge, Mass.: Harvard University Press, 1960).

6 For contrasting views about the scope of First Amendment protection, see Thomas I. Emerson, *Toward a General Theory of the First Amendment* (New York: Random House, 1967); Alexander Meiklejohn, *Political Freedom: The Constitutional Powers of the People* (New York: Oxford University Press, 1960); and Robert Bork, "Neutral Principles and Some First Amendment Problems," *Indiana Law Journal* 47 (1971).

7 Those who opposed the Sedition Act on First Amendment grounds did not necessarily believe that prosecution for seditious libel was inconsistent with

democratic government: the First Amendment imposed limitations only on Congress, and state legislatures remained free to punish the crime. See Walter Berns, *The First Amendment and the Future of American Democracy* (New York: Basic Books, 1977), Chapter 3.

8 *Whitney* v. *California,* 274 U.S. 357, 375 (1927).

9 *Abrams* v. *United States,* 250 U.S. 616, 630 (1919).

10 Martin Shapiro, *Freedom of Speech: The Supreme Court and Judicial Review* (Englewood Cliffs, N.J.: Prentice-Hall, 1966), p. 152.

11 *Gibson* v. *Florida Legislative Investigating Committee,* 372 U.S. 539, 551 (1963) and *Elrod* v. *Burns,* 427 U.S. 347, 362 (1976).

12 From this it follows that the government can replace a law invalidated as overbroad or void for vagueness with a more narrowly or precisely drawn statute that meets constitutional requirements.

13 *Connally* v. *General Construction Co.,* 269 U.S. 385, 391 (1926).

14 As Zechariah Chaffee observed, "It became criminal to advocate heavier taxation instead of bond issues, to state that conscription was unconstitutional though the Supreme Court had not yet held it valid, to say that the sinking of merchant ships was legal, to urge that a referendum should have preceded our declaration of war, to say that the war was contrary to the teachings of Christ. Men have been punished for criticizing the Red Cross and the Y.M.C.A., while under the Minnesota Espionage Act it has been held a crime to discourage women from knitting by the remark, 'No soldier ever sees those socks.'" *Free Speech in the United States* (Cambridge, Mass.: Harvard University Press, 1941), pp. 51–52, note 12.

15 *Yates* v. *United States,* 354 U.S. 298, 325 (1957).

16 The Court in *Buckley* also upheld the constitutionality of the campaign finance program, which had been challenged as an invalid exercise of the spending power, and struck down congressional appointment of some members of the Federal Election Commission. After the latter ruling, Congress vested the appointment power in the president, as constitutionally required (see Chapter 5 of Volume 1).

17 *Kunz* v. *United States,* 340 U.S. 290, 307–08 (1951).

18 *United States* v. *O'Brien,* 391 U.S. 367, 377 (1968).

19 *Police Department of Chicago* v. *Mosley,* 408 U.S. 92, 96 (1972).

20 *Hague* v. *C.I.O.,* 307 U.S. 496, 515–516 (1939).

21 Government may also restrict the flow of information to the public by classifying sensitive information over which it has control by restricting access to it. That government has a valid interest in maintaining the confidentiality of some information has long been recognized, and the inevitable complaints over excessive governmental secrecy have been dealt with largely through executive-branch actions and legislation such as the Freedom of Information Act.

22 See Maurice Van Gerpen, *Privileged Communication and the Press* (Westport, Conn.: Greenwood Press, 1979), Chapter 6.

23 This definition of a "public figure" is from *Gertz* v. *Robert Welch, Inc.,* 418 U.S. 323, 345 (1974).

SELECTED READING

Alexander v. *United States,* 509 U.S. 544 (1993).
American Booksellers Association v. *Hudnut,* 771 F.2d 323 (1985).
Branti v. *Finkel,* 445 U.S. 507 (1980).

Central Hudson Gas Company v. *Public Service Commission,* 447 U.S. 557 (1980).
Hazelwood School District v. *Kuhlmeier,* 484 U.S. 260 (1988).
Hustler Magazine v. *Falwell,* 485 U.S. 46 (1988).
Richmond Newspapers, Inc. v. *Virginia,* 448 U.S. 555 (1980).
*United State*s v. *O'Brien,* 391 U.S. 367 (1968).
Village of Skokie v. *National Socialist Party of America,* 373 N.E.2d 21 (1978).
Whitney v. *California,* 274 U.S. 357 (1927).

Baker, C. Edwin. *Human Liberty and Freedom of Speech* (New York: Oxford University Press, 1989).
Berns, Walter. *The First Amendment and the Future of American Democracy* (New York: Basic Books, 1976).
Bollinger, Lee C. *The Tolerant Society; Freedom of Speech and Extremist Speech in America* (New York: Oxford University Press, 1986).
Bork, Robert H. "Neutral Principles and Some First Amendment Problems." *Indiana Law Journal* 47 (1971): 1–35.
Collins, Ronald K. L., and David Stover. *The Death of Discourse* (Boulder, Colo.: Westview Press, 1996).
Downs, Donald A. *Nazis in Skokie: Freedom, Community, and the First Amendment* (Notre Dame, Ind.: Notre Dame University Press, 1985).
Downs, Donald A. *The New Politics of Pornography* (Chicago: University of Chicago Press, 1989).
Emerson, Thomas I. *The System of Freedom of Expression* (New York: Random House, 1970).
Fish, Stanley. *There's No Such Thing as Free Speech* (New York: Oxford University Press, 1994).
Graber, Mark A. *Transforming Free Speech: The Ambiguous Legacy of Civil Libertarianism* (Berkeley: University of California Press, 1991).
Levy, Leonard W. *Emergence of a Free Press* (New York: Oxford University Press, 1985).
MacKinnon, Catherine. *Only Words* (Cambridge, Mass.: Harvard University Press, 1993).
Meiklejohn, Alexander. *Political Freedom: The Constitutional Powers of the People* (New York: Harper & Row, 1960).
Pool, Ithiel de Sola. *Technologies of Freedom* (Cambridge, Mass.: Harvard University Press, 1983).
Powe, Lucas A., Jr. *American Broadcasting and the First Amendment* (Berkeley: University of California Press, 1987).
Sunstein, Cass R. *Democracy and the Problem of Free Speech* (New York: Free Press, 1993).

Gitlow v. *New York*
268 U.S. 652, 45 S. Ct. 625, 69 L. Ed. 1138 (1925)

Benjamin Gitlow, a member of the Left Wing Section of the Socialist Party, was convicted of violating the New York criminal anarchy law by advocating the forceful overthrow of the government and circulating a paper advocating governmental overthrow. The specific basis for the indictment was Gitlow's publication of *The Left Wing Manifesto*, which proclaimed that the goal of so-called revolutionary socialism was to destroy the "bourgeois state" through "revolutionary mass action" and that depicted capitalism as "in the process of disintegration and collapse." No evidence of any effects following from circulation of Gitlow's publication was introduced at trial. When the New York Court of Appeals affirmed his conviction, Gitlow appealed his case to the Supreme Court. *Opinion of the Court:* <u>Sanford</u>, *Taft, Van Devanter, McReynolds, Sutherland, Butler, Stone. Dissenting opinion:* <u>Holmes</u>, *Brandeis.*

MR. JUSTICE SANFORD delivered the opinion of the Court. . . .

. . . The sole contention here is, essentially, that <u>as there was no evidence of any concrete result flowing from the publication of the Manifesto or of circumstances showing the likelihood of such result</u>, the statute as construed and applied by the trial court penalizes the mere utterance, as such, of "doctrine" having no quality of incitement, without regard either to the circumstances of its utterance or to the likelihood of unlawful sequences; and that, as the exercise of the right of free expression with relation to government is only punishable "in circumstances involving likelihood of substantive evil," the statute contravenes the due process clause of the Fourteenth Amendment. The argument in support of this contention rests primarily upon the following propositions: 1st, That the "liberty" protected by the Fourteenth Amendment includes the liberty of speech and of the press; and 2nd, That while liberty of expression "is not absolute," it may be restrained "only in circumstances where its exercise bears a causal relation with some substantive evil, consummated, attempted or likely," and as the statute "takes no account of circumstances," it unduly restrains this liberty and is therefore unconstitutional. . . .

The statute does not penalize the utterance or publication of abstract "doctrine" or academic discussion having no quality of incitement to any concrete action. It is not aimed against mere historical or philosophical essays. It does not restrain the advocacy of changes in the form of government by constitutional and lawful means. What it prohibits is language advocating, advising or teaching the overthrow of organized government by unlawful means. These words imply urging to action. . . .

The Manifesto, plainly, is neither the statement of abstract doctrine nor, as suggested by counsel, mere prediction that industrial disturbances and revolutionary mass strikes will result spontaneously in an inevitable process of evolution in the economic system. It advocates and urges in fervent language mass action which shall progressively foment industrial disturbances and through political mass strikes and revolutionary mass action overthrow and destroy organized parliamentary government. . . .

The means advocated for bringing about the destruction of organized parliamentary government, namely, mass industrial revolts usurping the functions of municipal government, political mass strikes directed against the parliamentary state, and revolutionary mass action for its final destruction, necessarily imply the use of force and violence, and in their essential nature are inherently unlawful in a constitutional government of law and order. That the jury were warranted in finding that the Manifesto advocated not merely the abstract doctrine of overthrowing organized government by force, violence and unlawful means, but action to that end, is clear.

For present purposes we may and do assume that freedom of speech and of the press—which are protected by the First Amendment from abridgment by Congress—are among the fundamental personal rights and "liberties" protected by the due process clause of the Fourteenth Amendment from impairment by the States. . . .

It is a fundamental principle, long established, that the freedom of speech and of the press which is secured by the Constitution, does not confer an absolute right to speak or publish, without responsibility, whatever one may choose, or an unrestricted and unbridled license that gives immunity for every possible use of language and prevents the punishment of those who abuse this freedom. . . .

That a State in the exercise of its police power may punish those who abuse this freedom by utterances inimical to the public welfare, tending to corrupt public morals, incite to crime, or disturb the public peace, is not open to question. . . .

By enacting the present statute the State has determined, through its legislative body, that utterances advocating the overthrow of organized government by force, violence and unlawful means, are so inimical to the general welfare and involve such danger of substantive evil that they may be penalized in the exercise of its police power. That determination must be given great weight. Every presumption is to be indulged in favor of the validity of the statute. . . . The State cannot reasonably be required to measure the danger from every such utterance in the nice balance of a jeweler's scale. A single revolutionary spark may kindle a fire that, smouldering for a time, may burst into a sweeping and destructive conflagration. It cannot be said that the State is acting arbitrarily or unreasonably when in the exercise of its judgment as to the measures necessary to protect the public peace and safety, it seeks to extinguish the spark without waiting until it has enkindled the flame or blazed into the conflagration. It cannot reasonably be required to defer the adoption of measures for its own peace and safety until the revolutionary utterances lead to actual disturbances of the public peace or imminent and immediate danger of its own destruction; but it may, in the exercise of its judgment, suppress the threatened danger in its incipiency. . . .

We cannot hold that the present statute is an arbitrary or unreasonable exercise of the police power of the State unwarrantably infringing the freedom of speech or press; and we must and do sustain its constitutionality.

This being so it may be applied to every utterance—not too trivial to be beneath the notice of the law—which is of such a character and used with such intent and purpose as to bring it within the prohibition of the statute. . . . In other words, when the legislative body has determined generally, in the constitutional exercise of its discretion, that utterances of a certain kind involve such danger of substantive evil that they may be punished, the question whether any specific utterance coming within the prohibited class is likely, in and of itself, to bring about the substantive evil, is not open to consideration. It is sufficient that the statute itself be constitutional and that the use of the language comes within its prohibition. . . .

MR. JUSTICE HOLMES, dissenting.

MR. JUSTICE BRANDEIS and I are of opinion that this judgment should be reversed. . . . If what I think the correct test is applied, it is manifest that there was no present danger of an attempt to overthrow the government by force on the part of the admittedly small minority who shared the defendant's views. It is said that this manifesto was more than a theory, that it was an incitement. Every idea is an incitement. It offers itself for belief and if believed it is acted on unless some other belief outweighs it or some failure of energy stifles the movement at its birth. The only difference between the expression of an opinion and an incitement in the narrower sense is the speaker's enthusiasm for the result. Eloquence may set fire to reason. But whatever may be thought of the redundant discourse before us it had no chance of starting a present conflagration. If in the long run the beliefs expressed in proletarian dictatorship are destined to be accepted by the dominant forces of the community, the only meaning of free speech is that they should be given their chance and have their way.

Schenck v. United States
249 U.S. 47, 39 S. Ct. 247, 63 L. Ed. 470 (1919)

Charles Schenck, general secretary of the Socialist Party, was convicted of violating the various provisions of the Espionage Act of 1917 by conspiring to obstruct military recruitment and cause insubordination in the armed forces. The charges stemmed from the fact that Schenck had mailed to fifteen thousand men who were eligible for military service leaflets that claimed that the draft was unconstitutional and urged the potential draftees to "assert your rights." *Opinion of the Court: Holmes, White, McKenna, Day, Van Devanter, Pitney, McReynolds, Brandeis, Clarke.*

MR. JUSTICE HOLMES delivered the opinion of the Court. . . .

The document in question upon its first printed side recited the first section of the Thirteenth Amendment, said that the idea embodied in it was violated by the Conscription Act and that a conscript is little better than a convict. In impassioned language it intimated that conscription was despotism in its worst form and a monstrous wrong against humanity in the interest of Wall Street's chosen few. It said "Do not submit to intimidation," but in form at least confined itself to peaceful measures such as a petition for the repeal of the act. The other and later printed side of the sheet was headed "Assert Your Rights." It stated reasons for alleging that any one violated the Constitution when he refused to recognize "your right to assert your opposition to the draft," and went on "If you do not assert and support your rights, you are helping to deny or disparage rights which it is the solemn duty of all citizens and residents of the United States to retain." It described the arguments on the other side as coming from cunning politicians and a mercenary capitalist press, and even silent consent to the conscription law as helping to support an infamous conspiracy. It denied the power to send our citizens away to foreign shores to shoot up the people of other lands, and added that words could not express the condemnation such cold-blooded ruthlessness deserves, &c., &c., winding up "You must do your share to maintain, support and uphold the rights of the people of this country." Of course the document would not have been sent unless it had been intended to have some effect, and we do not see what effect it could be expected to have upon persons subject to the draft except to influence them to obstruct the carrying of it out. The defendants do not deny that the jury might find against them on this point.

But it is said, suppose that that was the tendency of this circular, it is protected by the First Amendment to the Constitution. Two of the strongest expressions are said to be quoted respectively from well-known public men. It well may be that the prohibition of laws abridging the freedom of speech is not confined to previous restraints, although to prevent them may have been the main purpose. . . . We admit that in many places and in ordinary times the defendants in saying all that was said in the circular would have been within their constitutional rights. But the character of every act depends upon the circumstances in which it is done. . . . The most stringent protection of free speech would not protect a man in falsely shouting fire in a theatre and causing a panic. It does not even protect a man from an injunction against uttering words that may have all the effect of force. . . . The question in every case is whether the words used are used in such circumstances and are of such a nature as to create a clear and present danger that they will bring about the substantive evils that Congress has a right to prevent. It is a question of proximity and degree. When a nation is at war many things that might be said in time of peace are such a hindrance to its effort that their utterance will not be endured so long as men fight and that no Court could regard them as protected by any constitutional right. It seems to be admitted that if an actual obstruction of the recruiting service were proved, liability for words that produced that effect might be enforced. The statute of 1917 in § 4 punishes conspiracies to obstruct as well as actual obstruction. If the act, (speaking, or circulating a paper,) its tendency and the intent with which it is done are the same, we perceive no ground for saying that success alone warrants making the act a crime.

Judgments affirmed.

Dennis v. United States

341 U.S. 494, 71 S. Ct. 857 95 L. Ed. 1137 (1951)

In 1940, Congress passed the Smith Act, under which persons could be punished for advocating the overthrow of the government by force or violence or for organizing a group that advocated such action. In 1948, Eugene Dennis and ten other leaders of the Communist Party were indicted under the Smith Act for willfully and knowingly conspiring "(1) to organize as the Communist Party of the United States a society, group and assembly of persons who teach and advocate the overthrow and destruction of the Government of the United States by force and violence, and (2) knowingly and willfully to advocate and teach the duty and necessity of overthrowing and destroying the Government of the United States by force and violence." After a long and spectacular trial marked by conflict between the judge and the defense attorneys, all the defendants were convicted. When the convictions were upheld on appeal, the Supreme Court granted certiorari but limited its review to whether the relevant provisions of the Smith Act violated the First Amendment or were void for vagueness. *Plurality opinion:* _Vinson_, _Reed_, _Burton_, _Minton_. *Concurring opinions:* _Frankfurter_; _Jackson_. *Dissenting opinions:* _Black_; _Douglas_. *Not participating: Clark.*

MR. CHIEF JUSTICE VINSON announced the judgment of the Court and an opinion in which MR. JUSTICE REED, MR. JUSTICE BURTON and MR. JUSTICE MINTON join. . . .

The obvious purpose of the statute is to protect existing Government, not from change by peaceable, lawful and constitutional means, but from change by violence, revolution and terrorism. That it is within the *power* of the Congress to protect the Government of the United States from armed rebellion is a proposition which requires little discussion. The question with which we are concerned here is whether the *means* which it has employed conflict with the First and Fifth Amendments to the Constitution.

One of the bases for the contention that the means which Congress has employed are invalid takes the form of an attack on the face of the statute on the grounds that by its terms it prohibits academic discussion of the merits of Marxism-Leninism, that it stifles ideas and is contrary to all concepts of a free speech and a free press. . . .

The very language of the Smith Act negates the interpretation which petitioners would have us impose on that Act. It is directed at advocacy, not discussion. Thus, the trial judge properly charged the jury that they could not convict if they found that petitioners did "no more than pursue peaceful studies and discussions or teaching and advocacy in the realm of ideas." . . . Congress did not intend to eradicate the free discussion of political theories, to destroy the traditional rights of Americans to discuss and evaluate ideas without fear of governmental sanction. . . .

Speech is not an absolute, above and beyond control by the legislature when its judgment, subject to review here, is that certain kinds of speech are so undesirable as to warrant criminal sanction. Nothing is more certain in modern society than the principle that there are no absolutes, that a name, a phrase, a standard has meaning only when associated with the considerations which gave birth to the nomenclature. . . . To those who would paralyze our Government in the face of impending threat by encasing it in a semantic straitjacket we must reply that all concepts are relative.

In this case we are squarely presented with the application of the "clear and present danger" test, and must decide what that phrase imports. . . . Overthrow of the Government by force and violence is certainly a substantial enough interest for the Government to limit speech. Indeed, this is the ultimate value of any society, for if a society cannot protect its very structure from armed internal attack, it must follow that no subordinate value can be protected. If, then, this interest may be protected, the literal problem which is presented is what has been meant by the use of the phrase "clear and present danger" of the utterances bringing about the evil within the power of Congress to punish.

Obviously, the words cannot mean that before the Government may act, it must wait until the *putsch* is about to be executed, the plans have been laid and the signal is awaited. If Government is aware that a group aiming at its overthrow is attempting to indoctrinate its members and to commit them to a course whereby they will strike when the leaders feel the circumstances permit, action by the Government is required. The argument that there is no need for Government to concern itself, for Government is strong, it possesses ample powers to put down a rebellion, it may defeat the revolution with ease needs no answer. For that is not the question. Certainly an attempt to overthrow the Government by force, even though doomed from the outset because of inadequate numbers or power of the revolutionists, is a sufficient evil for Congress to prevent. The damage which such attempts create both physically and politically to a nation makes it impossible to measure the validity in terms of the probability of success, or the immediacy of a successful attempt. In the instant case the trial judge charged the jury that they could not convict unless they found that petitioners intended to overthrow the Government "as speedily as circumstances would permit." This does not mean, and could not properly mean, that they would not strike until there was certainty of success. What was meant was that the revolutionists would strike when they thought the time was ripe. We must therefore reject the contention that success or probability of success is the criterion. . . .

Chief Judge Learned Hand, writing for the majority below, interpreted the phrase as follows: "In each case [courts] must ask whether the gravity of the 'evil,' discounted by its improbability, justifies such invasion of free speech as is necessary to avoid the danger." . . . We adopt this statement of the rule. As articulated by Chief Judge Hand, it is as succinct and inclusive as any other we might devise at this time. It takes into consideration those factors which we deem relevant, and relates their significances. More we cannot expect from words.

Likewise, we are in accord with the court below, which affirmed the trial court's finding that the requisite danger existed. The mere fact that from the period 1945 to 1948 petitioners' activities did not result in an attempt to overthrow the Government by force and violence is of course no answer to the fact that there was a group that was ready to make the attempt. The formation by petitioners of such a highly organized conspiracy, with rigidly disciplined members subject to call when the leaders, these petitioners, felt that the time had come for action, coupled with the inflammable nature of world conditions, similar uprisings in other countries, and the touch-and-go nature of our relations with countries with whom petitioners were in the very least ideologically attuned, convince us that their convictions were justified on this score. And this analysis disposes of the contention that a conspiracy to advocate, as distinguished from the advocacy itself, cannot be constitutionally restrained, because it comprises only the preparation. It is the existence of the conspiracy which creates the danger. . . . If the ingredients of the reaction are present, we cannot bind the Government to wait until the catalyst is added. . . .

We hold that §§ 2 (a) (1), 2 (a) (3) and 3 of the Smith Act do not inherently, or as construed or applied in the instant case, violate the First Amendment and other provisions of the Bill of Rights, or the First and Fifth Amendments because of indefiniteness. Petitioners intended to overthrow the Government of the United States as speedily as the circumstances would permit. Their conspiracy to organize the Communist Party and to teach and advocate the overthrow of the Government of the United States by force and violence created a "clear and present danger" of an attempt to overthrow the Government by force and violence. They were properly and constitutionally convicted for violation of the Smith Act. The judgments of conviction are

Affirmed.

MR. JUSTICE FRANKFURTER, concurring in affirmance of the judgment.

Few questions of comparable import have come before this Court in recent years. The appellants maintain that they have a right to advocate a political theory, so long, at least, as their advocacy does not create an immediate danger of obvious magnitude to the very existence of our present scheme of society. On the other hand, the Government asserts the right to safeguard the security of the Nation by such a measure as the Smith Act. Our judgment is thus solicited on a conflict of interests of the utmost concern to the well-being of the country. This conflict of interests cannot be resolved by a dogmatic preference for one or the other, nor by a sonorous formula which is in fact only a euphemistic disguise for an unresolved conflict. If adjudication is to be a rational process, we cannot escape a candid examination of the conflicting claims with full recognition that both are supported by weighty title-deeds. . . .

But how are competing interests to be assessed? Since they are not subject to quantitative ascertainment, the issue necessarily resolves itself into asking, who is to make the adjustment?—who is to balance the relevant factors and ascertain which interest is in the circumstances to prevail? Full responsibility for the choice cannot be given to the courts. Courts are not representative bodies. They are not designed to be a good reflex of a democratic society. Their judgment is best informed, and therefore most dependable, within narrow limits. . . .

Primary responsibility for adjusting the interests which compete in the situation before us of necessity belongs to the Congress. . . . We are to set aside the judgment of those whose duty it is to legislate only if there is no reasonable basis for it. . . .

It is not for us to decide how we would adjust the clash of interests which this case presents were the primary responsibility for reconciling it ours. Congress has determined that the danger created by advocacy of overthrow justifies the ensuing restriction on freedom of speech. The determination was made after due deliberation, and the seriousness of the congressional purpose is attested by the volume of legislation passed to effectuate the same ends.

Can we then say that the judgment Congress exercised was denied it by the Constitution? Can we establish a constitutional doctrine which forbids the elected representatives of the people to make this choice? Can we hold that the First Amendment deprives Congress of what it deemed necessary for the Government's protection?

To make validity of legislation depend on judicial reading of events still in the womb of time—a forecast, that is, of the outcome of forces at best appreciated only with knowledge of the topmost secrets of nations—is to charge the judiciary with duties beyond its equipment. . . .

The wisdom of the assumptions underlying the legislation and prosecution is another matter. . . .

Civil liberties draw at best only limited strength from legal guaranties. Preoccupation by our people with the constitutionality, instead of with the wisdom, of legislation or of executive action is preoccupation with a false value. . . . Focusing attention on constitutionality tends to make constitutionality synonymous with wisdom. When legislation touches freedom of thought and freedom of speech, such a tendency is a formidable enemy of the free spirit. Much that should be rejected as illiberal, because repressive and envenoming, may well be not unconstitutional. The ultimate reliance for the deepest needs of civilization must be found outside their vindication in courts of law. . . .

MR. JUSTICE JACKSON, concurring. . . .

The "clear and present danger" test was an innovation by Mr. Justice Holmes in the *Schenck* [v. *United States* (1919)] case, reiterated and refined by him and Mr. Justice Brandeis in later cases, all arising before the era of World War II that revealed the subtlety and efficacy of modernized revolutionary techniques used by totalitarian parties. In those cases, they were faced with convictions under so-called criminal syndicalism statutes aimed at anarchists but which, loosely construed, had been applied to punish socialism, pacifism, and left-wing ideologies, the charges often resting on farfetched inferences which, if true, would establish only technical or trivial violations. They proposed "clear and present danger" as a test for the sufficiency of evidence in particular cases.

I would save it, unmodified, for application as a "rule of reason" in the kind of case for which it was devised. . . . But its recent expansion has extended, in particular to Communists, unprecedented immunities. Unless we are to hold our Government captive in a judge-made verbal trap, we must approach the problem of a well-organized, nation-wide conspiracy, such as I have described, as realistically as our predecessors faced the trivialities that were being prosecuted until they were checked with a rule of reason.

I think reason is lacking for applying that test to this case.

MR. JUSTICE BLACK, dissenting. . . .

. . . The opinions for affirmance indicate that the chief reason for jettisoning the rule is the expressed fear that advocacy of Communist doctrine endangers the safety of the Republic. Undoubtedly, a governmental policy of unfettered communication of ideas does entail dangers. To the Founders of this Nation, however, the benefits derived from free expression were worth the risk. They embodied this philosophy in the First Amendment's command that "Congress shall make no law . . . abridging the freedom of speech, or of the press. . . ." I have always believed that the First Amendment is the keystone of our Government, that the freedoms it guarantees provide the best insurance against destruction of all freedom. At least as to speech in the realm of public matters, I believe that the "clear and present danger" test does not "mark the furthermost constitutional boundaries of protected expression" but docs "no more than recognize a minimum compulsion of the Bill of Rights." *Bridges* v. *California*. . . .

So long as this Court exercises the power of judicial review of legislation, I cannot agree that the First Amendment permits us to sustain laws suppressing freedom of speech and press on the basis of Congress' or our own notions of mere "reasonableness." Such a doctrine waters down the First Amendment so that it amounts to little more than an admonition to Congress. The Amendment as so construed is not likely to protect any but those "safe" or orthodox views which rarely need its protection. . . .

Public opinion being what it now is, few will protest the conviction of these Communist petitioners. There is hope, however, that in calmer times, when present pressures, passions and fears subside, this or some later Court will restore the First Amendment liberties to the high preferred place where they belong in a free society.

MR. JUSTICE DOUGLAS, dissenting.

If this were a case where those who claimed protection under the First Amendment were teaching the techniques of sabotage, the assassination of the President, the filching of documents from public files, the planting of bombs, the art of street warfare, and the like, I would have no doubts. The freedom to speak is not absolute; the teaching of methods of terror and other seditious conduct should be beyond the pale along with obscenity and immorality. This case was argued as if those were the facts. The argument imported much seditious conduct into the record. That is easy and it has popular appeal, for the activities of Communists in plotting and scheming against the free world are common knowledge. But the fact is that no such evidence was introduced at the trial. There is a statute which makes a seditious conspiracy unlawful. Petitioners, however, were not charged with a "conspiracy to overthrow" the Government. They were charged with a conspiracy to form a party and groups and assemblies of people who teach and advocate the overthrow of our Government by force or violence and with a conspiracy to advocate and teach its overthrow by force and violence. It may well be that indoctrination in the techniques of terror to destroy the Government would be indictable under either statute. But the teaching which is condemned here is of a different character. . . .

There comes a time when even speech loses its constitutional immunity. . . . Yet free speech is the rule, not the exception. The restraint to be constitutional must be based on more than fear, on more than passionate opposition against the speech, on more than a revolted dislike for its contents. There must be some immediate injury to society that is likely if speech is allowed. . . .

The nature of Communism as a force on the world scene would, of course, be relevant to the issue of clear and present danger of petitioners' advocacy within the United States. But the primary consideration is the strength and tactical position of petitioners and their converts in this country. On that there is no evidence in the record. If we are to take judicial notice of the threat of Communists within the nation, it should not be difficult to conclude that *as a political party* they are of little consequence. . . . In America they are miserable merchants of unwanted ideas; their wares remain unsold. The fact that their ideas are abhorrent does not make them powerful.

The political impotence of the Communists in this country does not, of course, dispose of the problem. Their numbers; their positions in industry and government; the extent to which they have in fact infiltrated the police, the armed services, transportation, stevedoring, power plants, munitions works, and other critical places—these facts all bear on the likelihood that their advocacy of the Soviet theory of revolution will endanger the Republic. But the record is silent on these facts. If we are to proceed on the basis of judicial notice, it is impossible for me to say that the Communists in this country are so potent or so strategically deployed that they must be suppressed for their speech. . . .

. . . Free speech—the glory of our system of government—should not be sacrificed on anything less than plain and objective proof of danger that the evil advocated is imminent. On this record no one can say that petitioners and their converts are in such a strategic position as to have even the slightest chance of achieving their aims.

Barenblatt v. *United States*
360 U.S. 109, 79 S. Ct. 1081, 3 L. Ed. 2d 1115 (1959)

Lloyd Barenblatt, who had previously served as a psychology instructor at the University of Michigan and at Vassar College, was subpoenaed to testify by a subcommittee of the House Un-American Activities Committee, which was conducting hearings dealing with alleged Communist infiltration into the field of education. He refused to answer subcommittee questions pertaining to his past or present membership in the Communist Party and other groups, asserting that the First Amendment barred a legislative inquiry into his political beliefs and associations. After being convicted of contempt of Congress, he appealed the conviction primarily on First Amendment grounds. *Opinion of the Court:* Harlan, *Frankfurter, Clark, Whittaker, Stewart. Dissenting opinions:* Black, *Warren, Douglas;* Brennan.

MR. JUSTICE HARLAN delivered the opinion of the Court.

. . . The power of inquiry has been employed by Congress throughout our history, over the whole range of the national interests concerning which Congress might legislate or decide upon due investigation not to legislate; it has similarly been utilized in determining what to appropriate from the national purse, or whether to appropriate. The scope of the power of inquiry, in short, is as penetrating and far-reaching as the potential power to enact and appropriate under the Constitution.

Broad as it is, the power is not, however, without limitations. Since Congress may only investigate into those areas in which it may potentially legislate or appropriate, it cannot inquire into matters which are within the exclusive province of one of the other branches of the Government. . . . And the Congress, in common with all branches of the Government, must exercise its powers subject to the limitations placed by the Constitution on governmental action, more particularly in the context of this case the relevant limitations of the Bill of Rights. . . .

Petitioner's various contentions resolve themselves into three propositions: First, the compelling of testimony by the Subcommittee was neither legislatively authorized nor constitutionally permissible because of the vagueness of Rule XI of the House of Representatives, Eighty-third Congress, the charter of authority of the parent Committee. Second, petitioner was not adequately apprised of the pertinency of the Subcommittee's questions to the subject matter of the inquiry. Third, the questions petitioner refused to answer infringed rights protected by the First Amendment. . . .

. . . Rule XI authorized this Subcommittee to compel testimony within the framework of the investigative authority conferred on the Un-American Activities Committee. Petitioner contends that *Watkins* v. *United States* [1957] nevertheless held the grant of this power in all circumstances ineffective because of the vagueness of Rule XI in delineating the Committee jurisdiction to which its exercise was to be appurtenant. . . .

Petitioner also contends, independently of *Watkins*, that the vagueness of Rule XI deprived the Subcommittee of the right to compel testimony in this investigation into Communist activity. . . . Granting the vagueness of the Rule, we may not read it in isolation from its long history in the House of Representatives. Just as legislation is often given meaning by the gloss of legislative reports, administrative interpretation, and long usage, so the proper meaning of an authorization to a congressional committee is not to be derived alone from its abstract terms unrelated to the definite content furnished them by the course of congressional actions. The Rule comes to us with a "persuasive gloss of legislative history," . . . which shows beyond doubt that in pursuance of its legislative concerns in the domain of "national security" the House has clothed the Un-American Activities Committee with pervasive authority to investigate Communist activities in this country. . . .

. . . From the beginning, without interruption to the present time, and with the undoubted knowledge and approval of the House, the Committee has devoted a major part of its energies to the investigation of Communist activities. . . .

In the context of these unremitting pursuits, the House has steadily continued the life of the Committee at the commencement of each new Congress; it has never narrowed the powers of the Committee, whose authority has remained throughout identical with that contained in Rule XI; and it has continuingly supported the Committee's activities with substantial appropriations. Beyond this, the Committee was raised to the level of a standing committee of the House in 1945, it having been but a special committee prior to that time.

In light of this long and illuminating history it can hardly be seriously argued that the investigation of Communist activities generally, and the attendant use of compulsory process, was beyond the purview of the Committee's intended authority under Rule XI. . . .

Undeniably a conviction for contempt . . . cannot stand unless the questions asked are pertinent to the subject matter of the investigation. . . .

. . . What we deal with here is whether petitioner was sufficiently apprised of "the topic under inquiry" thus authorized "and the connective reasoning whereby the precise questions asked related to it." *Watkins*. . . . In light of his prepared memorandum of constitutional objections there can be no doubt that this petitioner was well aware of the Subcommittee's authority and purpose to question him as it did. . . . The subject matter of the inquiry had been identified at the commencement of the investigation as Communist infiltration into the field of education. . . . Further, petitioner had stood mute in the face of the Chairman's statement as to why he had been called as a witness by the Subcommittee. And, lastly, . . . petitioner refused to answer questions as to his own Communist Party affiliations, whose pertinency of course was clear beyond doubt. . . .

The precise constitutional issue confronting us is whether the Subcommittee's inquiry into petitioner's past or present membership in the Communist Party transgressed the provisions of the First Amendment, which of course reach and limit congressional investigations. . . .

. . . Undeniably, the First Amendment in some circumstances protects an individual from being compelled to disclose his associational relationships. However, the protections of the First Amendment, unlike a proper claim of the privilege against self-incrimination under the Fifth Amendment, do not afford a witness the right to resist inquiry in all circumstances. Where First Amendment rights are asserted to bar governmental interrogation resolution of the issue always involves a balancing by the courts of the competing private and public interests at stake in the particular circumstances shown. . . .

The first question is whether this investigation was related to a valid legislative purpose, for Congress may not constitutionally require an individual to disclose his political relationships or other private affairs except in relation to such a purpose. . . .

That Congress has wide power to legislate in the field of Communist activity in this Country, and to conduct appropriate investigations in aid thereof, is hardly debatable. The existence of such power has never been questioned by this Court, and it is sufficient to say, without particularization, that Congress has enacted or considered in this field a wide range of legislative measures, not a few of which have stemmed from recommendations of the very Committee whose actions have been drawn in question here. In the last analysis this power rests on the right of self-preservation, "the ultimate value of any society." *Dennis* v. *United States* [1951]. . . . Justification for its exercise in turn rests on the long and widely accepted view that the tenets of the Communist Party include the ultimate overthrow of the Government of the United States by force and violence, a view which has been given formal expression by the Congress.

. . . To suggest that because the Communist Party may also sponsor peaceable political reforms the constitutional issues before us should now be judged as if that Party were just an ordinary political party from the standpoint of national security, is to ask this Court to blind itself to world affairs which have determined the whole course of our national policy since the close of World War II. . . .

Nor can we accept the further contention that this investigation should not be deemed to have been in furtherance of a legislative purpose because the true objective of the Committee and of the Congress was purely "exposure." So long as Congress acts in pursuance of its constitutional power, the Judiciary lacks authority to intervene on the basis of the motives which spurred the exercise of that power. . . . Having scrutinized this record we cannot say that the unanimous panel of the Court of Appeals which first considered this case was wrong in concluding that "the primary purposes of the inquiry were in aid of legislative processes." . . .

We conclude that the balance between the individual and the governmental interests here at stake must be struck in favor of the latter, and that therefore the provisions of the First Amendment have not been offended.

We hold that petitioner's conviction for contempt of Congress discloses no infirmity, and that the judgment of the Court of Appeals must be

Affirmed.

MR. JUSTICE BLACK, with whom The CHIEF JUSTICE and MR. JUSTICE DOUGLAS concur, dissenting. . . .

It goes without saying that a law to be valid must be clear enough to make its commands understandable. For obvious reasons, the standard of certainty required in criminal statutes is more exacting than in noncriminal statutes. This is simply because it would be unthinkable to convict a man for violating a law he could not understand. This Court has recognized that the stricter standard is as much required in criminal contempt cases as in all other criminal cases, and has emphasized that the "vice of vagueness" is especially pernicious where legislative power over an area involving speech, press, petition and assembly is involved. . . .

Measured by the foregoing standards, Rule XI cannot support any conviction for refusal to testify. . . .

. . . On the Court's own test, the issue is whether Barenblatt can know with sufficient certainty, at the time of his interrogation, that there is so compelling a need for his replies that infringement of his rights of free association is justified. The record does not disclose where Barenblatt can find what that need is. There is certainly no clear congressional statement of it in Rule XI. Perhaps if Barenblatt had had time to read all the reports of the Committee to the House, and in addition had examined the appropriations made to the Committee he, like the Court, could have discerned an intent by Congress to allow an investigation of communism in education. Even so he would be hard put to decide what the need for this investigation is since Congress expressed it neither when it enacted Rule XI nor when it acquiesced in the Committee's assertions of power. Yet it is knowledge of this need—what is wanted from him and why it is wanted—that a witness must have if he is to be in a position to comply with the Court's rule that he balance individual rights against the requirements of the State. I cannot see how that knowledge can exist under Rule XI. . . . I would hold that Rule XI is too broad to be meaningful and cannot support petitioner's conviction. . . .

The First Amendment says in no equivocal language that Congress shall pass no law abridging freedom of speech, press, assembly or petition. The activities of this Committee, authorized by Congress, do precisely that, through exposure, obloquy and public scorn. . . .

To apply the Court's balancing test under [present] circumstances is to read the First Amendment to say "Congress shall pass no law abridging freedom of speech, press, assembly and petition, unless Congress and the Supreme Court reach the joint conclusion that on balance the interest of the Government in stifling these freedoms is greater than the interest of the people in having them exercised." This is closely akin to the notion that neither the First Amendment nor any other provision of the Bill of Rights should be enforced unless the Court believes it is *reasonable* to do so. . . . This violates the genius of our *written* Constitution. . . .

But even assuming what I cannot assume, that some balancing is proper in this case, I feel that the Court after stating the test ignores it completely. At most it balances the right of the Government to preserve itself, against Barenblatt's right to refrain from revealing Communist affiliations. Such a balance, however, mistakes the factors to be weighed. In the first place, it completely leaves out the real interest in Barenblatt's silence, the interest of the people as a whole in being able to join organizations, advocate causes and make political "mistakes" without later being subjected to governmental penalties for having dared to think for themselves. It is this right, the right to err politically, which keeps us strong as a Nation. For no number of laws against communism can have as much effect as the personal conviction which comes from having heard its arguments and rejected them, or from having once accepted its tenets and later recognized their worthlessness. Instead, the obloquy which results from investigations such as this not only stifles "mistakes" but prevents all but the most courageous from hazarding any views which might at some later time become disfavored. This result, whose importance cannot be overestimated, is doubly crucial when it affects the universities, on which we must largely rely for the experimentation and development of new ideas essential to our country's welfare. It is these interests of society, rather than Barenblatt's own right to silence, which I think the Court should put on the balance against the demands of the Government, if any balancing process is to be tolerated. Instead they are not mentioned, while on the other side the demands of the Government are vastly overstated and called "self preservation." It is admitted that this Committee can only seek information for the purpose of suggesting laws, and that Congress' power to make laws in the realm of speech and association is quite limited, even on the Court's test. Its interest in making such laws in the field of education, primarily a state function, is clearly narrower still. Yet the Court styles this attenuated interest self-preservation and allows it to overcome the need our country has to let us all think, speak, and associate politically as we like and without fear of reprisal. Such a result reduces "balancing" to a mere play on words. . . .

Finally, I think Barenblatt's conviction violates the Constitution because the chief aim, purpose and practice of the House Un-American Activities Committee, as disclosed by its many reports, is to try witnesses and punish them because they are or have been Communists or because they refuse to admit or deny Communist affiliations. The punishment imposed is generally punishment by humiliation and public shame. . . .

The same intent to expose and punish is manifest in the Committee's investigation which led to Barenblatt's conviction. The declared purpose of the investigation was to identify to the people of Michigan the individuals responsible for the, alleged, Communist success there. . . . As a result of its Michigan investigation, the Committee called upon American labor unions to amend their constitutions, if necessary, in order to deny membership to any Communist Party member. This would, of course, prevent many workers from getting or holding the only kind of jobs their particular skills qualified them for. The Court, today, barely mentions these statements, which, especially when read in the context of past reports by the Committee, show unmistakably what the Committee was doing. . . .

I do not question the Committee's patriotism and sincerity in doing all this. I merely feel that it cannot be done by Congress under our Constitution. . . .

Brandenburg v. *Ohio*
395 U.S. 444, 89 S. Ct. 1827, 23 L. Ed. 2d 430 (1969)
Charles Brandenburg, a local Ku Klux Klan leader, was convicted under Ohio's Criminal Syndicalism Act, which prohibited "advocating . . . the

duty, necessity, or propriety of crime, sabotage, violence, or unlawful methods of terrorism as a means of accomplishing industrial or political reform." The evidence in the case included two television films that showed Brandenburg addressing two Klan meetings. The most provocative element in his speeches was the statement that "if our President, our Congress, our Supreme Court, continues to suppress the white, Caucasian race, it's possible that there might have to be some revengence taken." *Opinion of the Court* per curiam: *Warren, Black, Douglas, Harlan, Brennan, Stewart, White, Fortas, Marshall. Concurring opinions:* Black; Douglas, *Black.*

PER CURIAM. . . .

The Ohio Criminal Syndicalism Statute was enacted in 1919. From 1917 to 1920, identical or quite similar laws were adopted by 20 States and two territories. . . . In 1927, this Court sustained the constitutionality of California's Criminal Syndicalism Act, the text of which is quite similar to that of the laws of Ohio. *Whitney* v. *California* [1927]. The Court upheld the statute on the ground that, without more, "advocating" violent means to effect political and economic change involves such danger to the security of the State that the State may outlaw it. . . . But *Whitney* has been thoroughly discredited by later decisions. . . . These later decisions have fashioned the principle that the constitutional guarantees of free speech and free press do not permit a State to forbid or proscribe advocacy of the use of force or of law violation except where such advocacy is directed to inciting or producing imminent lawless action and is likely to incite or produce such action. . . .

Measured by this test, Ohio's Criminal Syndicalism Act cannot be sustained. The Act punishes persons who "advocate or teach the duty, necessity, or propriety" of violence "as a means of accomplishing industrial or political reform"; or who publish or circulate or display any book or paper containing such advocacy; or who "justify" the commission of violent acts "with intent to exemplify, spread or advocate the propriety of the doctrines of criminal syndicalism"; or who "voluntarily assemble" with a group formed "to teach or advocate the doctrines of criminal syndicalism." Neither the indictment nor the trial judge's instructions to the jury in any way refined the statute's bald definition of the crime in terms of mere advocacy not distinguished from incitement to imminent lawless action.

Accordingly, we are here confronted with a statute which, by its own words and as applied, purports to punish mere advocacy and to forbid, on pain of criminal punishment, assembly with others merely to advocate the described type of action. Such a statute falls within the condemnation of the First and Fourteenth Amendments. The contrary teaching of *Whitney* v. *California* . . . cannot be supported, and that decision is therefore overruled.

Reversed.

MR. JUSTICE DOUGLAS, concurring.

While I join the opinion of the Court, I desire to enter a *caveat.* . . .

. . . I see no place in the regime of the First Amendment for any "clear and present danger" test, whether strict and tight as some would make it, or free-wheeling as the Court in *Dennis* rephrased it.

When one reads the opinions closely and sees when and how the "clear and present danger" test has been applied, great misgivings are aroused. First, the threats were often loud but always puny and made serious only by judges so wedded to the *status quo* that critical analysis made them nervous. Second, the test was so twisted and perverted in *Dennis* [v. *United States* (1951)] as to make the trial of those teachers of Marxism an all-out political trial which was part and parcel of the cold war that has eroded substantial parts of the First Amendment.

One's beliefs have long been thought to be sanctuaries which government could not invade. *Barenblatt* [v. *United States* (1959)] is one example of the ease with which that sanctuary can be violated. The lines drawn by the Court between the criminal act of being an "active" Communist and the innocent act of being a nominal or inactive Communist mark the difference only between deep and abiding belief and casual or uncertain belief. But I think that all matters of belief are beyond the reach of subpoenas or the probings of investigators. That is why the invasions of privacy made by investigating committees were notoriously unconstitutional. That is the deep-seated fault in the infamous loyalty-security hearings which, since 1947 when President Truman launched them, have processed 20,000,000 men and women. Those hearings were primarily concerned with one's thoughts, ideas, beliefs, and convictions. They were the most blatant violations of the First Amendment we have ever known.

The line between what is permissible and not subject to control and what may be made impermissible and subject to regulation is the line between ideas and overt acts.

The example usually given by those who would punish speech is the case of one who falsely shouts fire in a crowded theatre.

This is, however, a classic case where speech is brigaded with action. . . . They are indeed inseparable and a prosecution can be launched for the overt acts actually caused. Apart from rare instances of that kind, speech is, I think, immune from prosecution. Certainly there is no constitutional line between advocacy of abstract ideas as in *Yates* [v. *United States* (1957)] and advocacy of political action as in *Scales* [v. *United States* (1961)]. The quality of advocacy turns on the depth of the conviction; and government has no power to invade that sanctuary of belief and conscience.

Buckley v. *Valeo*
424 U.S. 1, 96 S. Ct. 612, 46 L. Ed. 2d 659 (1976)

Distressed by the campaign abuses documented during the Watergate investigations, Congress in 1974 amended the Federal Election Campaign Act of 1971, introducing a comprehensive set of electoral reforms. The Court of Appeals for the District of Columbia in large measure sustained the act, and the Supreme Court considered its constitutionality on appeal. The following excerpts deal primarily with the act's limits on contributions to candidates for federal office, its limits on expenditures in support of such candidates, and its provisions compelling disclosure of campaign contributions. In addition, the Court upheld the constitutionality of a system of federal financing of presidential campaigns and invalidated provisions for appointment of some members of the Federal Election Commission by the president *pro tem* of the Senate and the Speaker of the House. *Opinion of the Court per curiam: Burger, Brennan, Stewart, White, Marshall, Blackmun, Powell, Rehnquist. Concurring in part and dissenting in part: Burger; White; Marshall; Blackmun; Powell; Rehnquist. Not participating: Stevens.*

PER CURIAM.

. . . The statutes at issue summarized in broad terms, contain the following provisions: (a) individual political contributions are limited to $1,000 to any single candidate per election, with an overall annual limitation of $25,000 by any contributor; independent expenditures by individuals and groups "relative to a clearly identified candidate" are limited to $1,000 a year; campaign spending by candidates for various federal offices and spending for national conventions by political parties are subject to prescribed limits; (b) contributions and expenditures above certain threshold levels must be reported and publicly disclosed; (c) a system for public funding of Presidential campaign activities is established by Subtitle H of the Internal Revenue Code; and (d) a Federal Election Commission is established to administer and enforce the legislation.

I. CONTRIBUTION AND EXPENDITURE LIMITATIONS

A. General Principles

The Act's contribution and expenditure limitations operate in an area of the most fundamental First Amendment activities. Discussion of public issues and debate on the qualifications of candidates are integral to the operation of the system of government established by our Constitution. The First Amendment affords the broadest protection to such political expression. . . . Appellees contend that what the Act regulates is conduct, and that its effect on speech and association is incidental at most. Appellants respond that contributions and expenditures are at the very core of political speech, and that the Act's limitations thus constitute restraints on First Amendment liberty that are both gross and direct.

We cannot share the view that the present Act's contribution and expenditure limitations are comparable to the restrictions on conduct upheld in [*United States* v. *O'Brien* (1968)]. The expenditure of money simply cannot be equated with such conduct as destruction of a draft card. Some forms of communication made possible by the giving and spending of money involve speech alone, some involve conduct primarily, and some involve a combination of the two. Yet this Court has never suggested that the dependence of a communication on the expenditure of money operates itself to introduce a nonspeech element or to reduce the exacting scrutiny required by the First Amendment. . . .

Even if the categorization of the expenditure of money as conduct were accepted, the limitations challenged here would not meet the *O'Brien* test because the governmental interests advanced in support of the Act involve "suppressing communication." . . . Nor can the Act's contribution and expenditure limitations be sustained . . . by reference to the constitutional principles reflected in [the Court's time, place, and manner cases]. . . . The critical difference between this case and those . . . cases is that the present Act's contribution and expenditure limitations impose direct quantity restrictions on political communication and association by persons, groups, candidates, and political parties in addition to any reasonable time, place, and manner regulations otherwise imposed.

A restriction on the amount of money a person or group can spend on political communication during a campaign necessarily reduces the quantity of expression by restricting the number of issues discussed, the depth of their exploration, and the size of the audience reached. This is because virtually every means of communicating ideas in today's mass society requires the expenditure of money. . . .

The expenditure limitations contained in the Act represent substantial rather than merely theoretical restraints on the quantity and diversity of political speech. The $1,000 ceiling on spending "relative to a clearly identified candidate," . . . would appear to exclude all citizens and groups except candidates, political parties, and the institutional press from any significant use of the most effective modes of communication.

By contrast, . . . a limitation upon the amount that any one person or group may contribute to a candidate or political committee entails only a marginal restriction upon the contributor's ability to engage in free communication. A contribution serves as a general expression of support for the candidate and his views, but does not communicate the underlying basis for the support. . . . A limitation on the amount of money a person may give to a candidate or campaign organization thus involves little direct restraint on his political communication, for it permits the symbolic expression of support evidenced by a contribution but does not in any way infringe the contributor's freedom to discuss candidates and issues. While contributions may result in political expression if spent by a candidate or an association to present views to the voters, the transformation of contributions into political debate involves speech by someone other than the contributor.

. . . The overall effect of the Act's contribution ceilings is merely to require candidates and political committees to raise funds from a greater number of persons and to compel people who would otherwise contribute amounts greater than the statutory limits to expend such funds on direct political expression, rather than to reduce the total amount of money potentially available to promote political expression. . . .

B. Contribution Limitations

It is unnecessary to look beyond the Act's primary purpose—to limit the actuality and appearance of corruption resulting from large individual financial contributions—in order to find a constitutionally sufficient justification for the $1,000 contribution limitation. . . . To the extent that large contributions are given to secure a political *quid pro quo* from current and potential office holders, the integrity of our system of representative democracy is undermined. Although the scope of such pernicious practices can never be reliably ascertained, the deeply disturbing examples surfacing after the 1972 election demonstrate that the problem is not an illusory one.

Of almost equal concern . . . is the impact of the appearance of corruption stemming from public awareness of the opportunities for abuse inherent in a regime of large individual financial contributions. . . .

Appellants contend that the contribution limitations must be invalidated because bribery laws and narrowly drawn disclosure requirements constitute a less restrictive means of dealing with "proven and suspected *quid pro quo* arrangements." But . . . Congress was surely entitled to conclude that disclosure was only a partial measure, and that contribution ceilings were a necessary legislative concomitant. . . .

We find that, under the rigorous standard of review established by our prior decisions, the weighty interests served by restricting the size of financial contributions to political candidates are sufficient to justify the limited effect upon First Amendment freedoms caused by the $1,000 contribution ceiling. . . .

C. Expenditure Limitations . . .

We find that the governmental interest in preventing corruption and the appearance of corruption is inadequate to justify § 608 (e)(1)'s ceiling on independent expenditures. First, assuming, *arguendo*, that large independent expenditures pose the same dangers of actual or apparent *quid pro quo* arrangements as do large contributions, § 608 (e)(1) does not provide an answer that sufficiently relates to the elimination of those dangers. Unlike the contribution limitations' total ban on the giving of large amounts of money to

candidates, § 608 (e)(1) prevents only some large expenditures. So long as persons and groups eschew expenditures that in express terms advocate the election or defeat of a clearly identified candidate, they are free to spend as much as they want to promote the candidate and his views. . . . It would naively underestimate the ingenuity and resourcefulness of persons and groups desiring to buy influence to believe that they would have much difficulty devising expenditures that skirted the restriction on express advocacy of election or defeat but nevertheless benefited the candidate's campaign. . . . Second, . . . the independent advocacy restricted by the provision does not presently appear to pose dangers of real or apparent corruption comparable to those identified with large campaign contributions. . . . Section 608 (b)'s contribution ceilings rather than § 608 (e)(1)'s independent expenditure limitation prevent attempts to circumvent the Act through prearranged or coordinated expenditures amounting to disguised contributions. . . .

It is argued, however, that the ancillary governmental interest in equalizing the relative ability of individuals and groups to influence the outcome of elections serves to justify the limitation on express advocacy of the election or defeat of candidates imposed by § 608 (e)(1)'s expenditure ceiling. But the concept that government may restrict the speech of some elements of our society in order to enhance the relative voice of others is wholly foreign to the First Amendment. . . .

Limitation on Expenditures by Candidates from Personal or Family Resources.

The primary governmental interest served by the Act—the prevention of actual and apparent corruption of the political process—does not support the limitation on the candidate's expenditure of his own personal funds. . . . Indeed, the use of personal funds reduces the candidate's dependence on outside contributions and thereby counteracts the coercive pressures and attendant risks of abuse to which the Act's contribution limitations are directed.

The ancillary interest in equalizing the relative financial resources of candidates competing for elective office, therefore, provides the sole relevant rationale for 608 (a)'s expenditure ceiling. That interest is clearly not sufficient to justify the provision's infringement of fundamental First Amendment rights. . . .

Limitations on Campaign Expenditures.

The campaign expenditure ceilings appear to be designed primarily to serve the governmental interests in reducing the allegedly skyrocketing costs of political campaigns, . . . [But] the mere growth in the cost of federal election campaigns in and of itself provides no basis for governmental restrictions on the quantity of campaign spending and the resulting limitation on the scope of federal campaigns. The First Amendment denies government the power to determine that spending to promote one's political views is wasteful, excessive, or unwise. In the free society ordained by our Constitution it is not the government, but the people—individually as citizens and candidates and collectively as associations and political committees—who must retain control over the quantity and range of debate on public issues in a political campaign. . . .

II. REPORTING AND DISCLOSURE REQUIREMENTS

A. General Principles

. . . Unlike the overall limitations on contributions and expenditures, the disclosure requirements impose no ceiling on campaign-related activities. But we have repeatedly found that compelled disclosure, in itself, can seriously infringe on privacy of association and belief guaranteed by the First Amendment. . . . Since *NAACP* v. *Alabama* [1958] we have required that the subordinating interests of the State must survive exacting scrutiny. We also have insisted that there be a "relevant correlation" or "substantial relation" between the governmental interest and the information required to be disclosed. . . . But we have acknowledged that there are governmental interests sufficiently important to outweigh the possibility of infringement, particularly when the "free functioning of our national institutions" is involved. *Communist Party* v. *Subversive Activities Control Bd.* (1961). . . .

The governmental interests sought to be vindicated by the disclosure requirements are of this magnitude. They fall into three categories. First, disclosure provides the electorate with information "as to where political campaign money comes from and how it is spent by the candidate" in order to aid the voters in evaluating those who seek federal office. It allows voters to place each candidate in the political spectrum more precisely than is often possible solely on the basis of party labels and campaign speeches. The sources of a candidate's financial support also alert the voter to the interests to which a candidate is most likely to be responsive and thus facilitate predictions of future performance in office.

Second, disclosure requirements deter actual corruption and avoid the appearance of corruption by exposing large contributions and expenditures to the light of publicity. . . .

Third, and not least significant, recordkeeping, reporting, and disclosure requirements are an essential means of gathering the data necessary to detect violations of the contribution limitations described above.

B. Application to Minor Parties and Independents

Appellants contend that the Act's requirements are overbroad insofar as they apply to contributions to minor parties and independent candidates because the governmental interest in this information is minimal and the danger of significant infringement on First Amendment rights is greatly increased.

In *NAACP* v. *Alabama* the organization had "made an uncontroverted showing that on past occasions revelation of the identity of its rank-and-file members [had] exposed these members to economic reprisal, loss of employment, threat of physical coercion, and other manifestations of public hostility," . . . and the State was unable to show that the disclosure it sought had a "substantial bearing" on the issues it sought to clarify. . . . No record of harassment on a similar scale was found in this case. We agree with the Court of Appeals' conclusion that *NAACP* v. *Alabama* is inapposite where, as here, any serious infringement on First Amendment rights brought about by the compelled disclosure of contributors is highly speculative. . . .

MR. CHIEF JUSTICE BURGER, concurring in part and dissenting in part. . . .

. . . no legitimate public interest has been shown in forcing the disclosure of modest contributions that are the prime support of new, unpopular, or unfashionable political causes. There is no realistic possibility that such modest donations will have a corrupting influence especially on parties that enjoy only "minor" status. . . . In any event, the dangers to First Amendment rights here are too great. Flushing out the names of supporters of minority parties will plainly have a deterrent effect on potential contributors. . . .

I agree fully with that part of the Court's opinion that holds unconstitutional the limitations the Act puts on campaign expenditures which "place substantial and direct restrictions on the ability of candidates, citizens, and associations to engage in protected political expression, restrictions that the First Amendment cannot tolerate.". . . Yet when it approves similarly stringent limitations on contributions, the Court ignores the reasons it finds so persuasive in the context of expenditures. For me contributions and expenditures are two sides of the same First Amendment coin.

By limiting campaign contributions, the Act restricts the amount of money that will be spent on political activity—and does so directly.

The Court's attempt to distinguish the communication inherent in political *contributions* from the speech aspects of political *expenditures* simply "will not wash." We do little but engage in word games unless we recognize that people—candidates and contributors—spend money on political activity because they wish to communicate ideas, and their constitutional interest in doing so is precisely the same whether they or someone else utters the words.

The Court attempts to make the Act seem less restrictive by casting the problem as one that goes to freedom of association rather than freedom of speech. I have long thought freedom of association and freedom of expression were two peas from the same pod. The contribution limitations of the Act impose a restriction on certain forms of associational activity that are for the most part, as the Court recognizes, . . . harmless in fact. And the restrictions are hardly incidental in their effect upon particular campaigns. . . .

At any rate, the contribution limits are a far more severe restriction on First Amendment activity than the sort of "chilling" legislation for which the Court has shown such extraordinary concern in the past. . . .

MR. JUSTICE WHITE, concurring in part and dissenting in part.

. . . I dissent . . . from the Court's view that the expenditure limitations of 18 U.S.C. §§ 608 (c) and (e) . . . violate the First Amendment. . . .

Since the contribution and expenditure limitations are neutral as to the content of speech and are not motivated by fear of the consequences of the political speech of particular candidates or of political speech in general, this case depends on whether the nonspeech interests of the Federal Government in regulating the use of money in political campaigns are sufficiently urgent to justify the incidental effects that the limitations visit upon the First Amendment interests of candidates and their supporters.

. . . The Court . . . accepts the congressional judgment that the evils of unlimited contributions are sufficiently threatening to warrant restriction regardless of the impact of the limits on the contributor's opportunity for effective speech and in turn on the total volume of the candidate's political communications by reason of his inability to accept large sums from those willing to give.

. . . Congress was plainly of the view that these expenditures also have corruptive potential; but the Court strikes down the provision, strangely enough claiming more insight as to what may improperly influence candidates than is possessed by the majority of Congress that passed this bill and the President who signed it. Those supporting the bill undeniably included many seasoned professionals who have been deeply involved in elective processes and who have viewed them at close range over many years. . . .

Texas v. *Johnson*

491 U.S. 397, 109 S. Ct. 2533, 105 L. Ed. 2d 342 (1989)

During the Republican National Convention in Dallas in 1984. Gregory Johnson participated in a demonstration, dubbed the "Republican War Chest Tour," to protest the policies of the Reagan administration and of certain Dallas-based corporations. The demonstrators marched through the Dallas streets, chanting slogans, and staged "die-ins" outside various corporate locations to dramatize the consequences of nuclear war. The demonstration ended in front of Dallas City Hall, where Johnson unfurled an American flag given to him by a fellow demonstrator (who had taken it from outside a building along the route), doused it with kerosene, and set it on fire. While the flag burned, the protestors chanted: "America, the red, white, and blue, we spit on you." Johnson was subsequently arrested and convicted of violating a Texas law prohibiting the "desecration of venerated objects," including the national flag. The law defined "desecrate" as "deface, damage, or otherwise physically mistreat in a way that the actor knows will seriously offend one or more persons likely to observe or discover his action."

The opinion of the Court applies the *"O'Brien* test," derived from *United States* v. *O'Brien* (1968), for determining the constitutionality of governmental regulations of expressive conduct. Under that test, "a governmental regulation is sufficiently justified if it is within the constitutional power of the government; if it furthers an important or substantial governmental interest; if the governmental interest is unrelated to the suppression of free expression; and if the incidental restriction of alleged First Amendment freedoms is no greater than is essential to the furtherance of that interest." *Opinion of the Court:* Brennan, *Marshall,* Blackmun, Scalia, Kennedy. *Concurring opinion:* Kennedy. *Dissenting opinions:* Rehnquist, *White, O'Connor:* Stevens.

JUSTICE BRENNAN delivered the opinion of the Court.

. . . After publicly burning an American flag as a means of political protest, Gregory Lee Johnson was convicted of desecrating a flag in violation of Texas law. This case presents the question whether his conviction is consistent with the First Amendment. We hold that it is not.

. . . Johnson was convicted of flag desecration for burning the flag rather than for uttering insulting words. This fact somewhat complicates our consideration of his conviction under the First Amendment. We must first determine whether Johnson's burning of the flag constituted expressive conduct, permitting him to invoke the First Amendment in challenging his conviction. . . . If his conduct was expressive, we next decide whether the State's regulation is related to the suppression of free expression. . . . If the State's regulation is not related to expression, then the less stringent standard we announced in *United States* v. *O'Brien* for regulations of noncommunicative conduct controls. . . . If it is, then we are outside of *O'Brien*'s test, and we must ask whether this interest justifies Johnson's conviction under a more demanding standard. . . .

In deciding whether particular conduct possesses sufficient communicative elements to bring the First Amendment into play, we have asked whether "[a]n intent to convey a particularized message was present, and [whether] the likelihood was great that the message would be understood by those who viewed it." . . .

. . . The State of Texas conceded for purposes of its oral argument in this case that Johnson's conduct was expressive conduct, . . . Johnson burned an American flag as part—indeed, as the culmination—of a political demonstration that coincided with the convening of the Republican Party and its renomination of Ronald Reagan for President. The expressive, overtly political nature of this conduct was both intentional and overwhelmingly apparent. . . . In these circumstances, Johnson's burning of the flag was conduct "sufficiently imbued with elements of communication," . . . to implicate the First Amendment. . . .

In order to decide whether *O'Brien*'s test applies here, therefore, we must decide whether Texas has asserted an interest in support of Johnson's conviction that is unrelated to the suppression of expression. . . . The State offers two separate interests to justify this conviction: preventing breaches of the peace, and preserving the flag as a symbol of nationhood and national unity. We hold that the first interest is not implicated on this record and that the second is related to the suppression of expression.

. . . Texas claims that its interest in preventing breaches of the peace justifies Johnson's conviction for flag desecration. However, no disturbance of the peace actually occurred or threatened to occur because of Johnson's burning of the flag. . . . The only evidence offered by the State at trial to show the reaction to Johnson's actions was the testimony of several persons who had been seriously offended by the flag-burning. . . .

The State's position, therefore, amounts to a claim that an audience that takes serious offense at particular expression is necessarily likely to disturb the peace and that the expression may be prohibited on this basis. Our precedents do not countenance such a presumption. . . .

Thus, we have not permitted the Government to assume that every expression of a provocative idea will incite a riot, but have instead required careful consideration of the actual circumstances surrounding such expression, asking whether the expression "is directed to inciting or producing imminent lawless action and is likely to incite or produce such action." *Brandenburg* v. *Ohio*, . . . (1969). . . .

We . . . conclude that the State's interest in maintaining order is not implicated on these facts. . . .

The State also asserts an interest in preserving the flag as a symbol of nationhood and national unity. . . . The State, apparently, is concerned that such conduct will lead people to believe either that the flag does not stand for nationhood and national unity, but instead reflects other, less positive concepts, or that the concepts reflected in the flag do not in fact, exist, that is, we do not enjoy unity as a Nation. These concerns blossom only when a person's treatment of the flag communicates some message, and thus are related "to the suppression of free expression" within the meaning of *O'Brien*. We are thus outside of *O'Brien*'s test altogether.

It remains to consider whether the State's interest in preserving the flag as a symbol of nationhood and national unity justifies Johnson's con-

viction. . . . According to Texas, if one physically treats the flag in a way that would tend to cast doubt on either the idea that nationhood and national unity are the flag's referents or that national unity actually exists, the message conveyed thereby is a harmful one and therefore may be prohibited.

. . . If there is a bedrock principle underlying the First Amendment, it is that the Government may not prohibit the expression of an idea simply because society finds the idea itself offensive or disagreeable. . . .

We have not recognized an exception to this principle even where our flag has been involved. In *Street* v. *New York* . . . (1969), we held that a State may not criminally punish a person for uttering words critical of the flag. . . . Nor may the Government, we have held in *West Virginia State Board of Education* v. *Barnette* (1943), in which the Court invalidated a compulsory flag salute law, compel conduct that would evince respect for the flag. . . .

. . . In short, nothing in our precedents suggests that a State may foster its own view of the flag by prohibiting expressive conduct relating to it. . . . To conclude that the Government may permit designated symbols to be used to communicate only a limited set of messages would be to enter territory having no discernible or defensible boundaries. Could the Government, on this theory, prohibit the burning of state flags? Of copies of the Presidential seal? Of the Constitution? In evaluating these choices under the First Amendment, how would we decide which symbols were sufficiently special to warrant this unique status? To do so, we would be forced to consult our own political preferences, and impose them on the citizenry, in the very way that the First Amendment forbids us to do. . . .

. . . It is not the State's ends, but its means, to which we object. It cannot be gainsaid that there is a special place reserved for the flag in this Nation, and thus we do not doubt that the Government has a legitimate interest in making efforts to "preserv[e] the national flag as an unalloyed symbol of our country." . . . We reject the suggestion, urged at oral argument by counsel for Johnson, that the Government lacks "any state interest whatsoever" in regulating the manner in which the flag may be displayed. . . . Congress has, for example, enacted precatory regulations describing the proper treatment of the flag, . . .

and we cast no doubt on the legitimacy of its interest in making such recommendations. To say that the Government has an interest in encouraging proper treatment of the flag, however, is not to say that it may criminally punish a person for burning a flag as a means of political protest. "National unity as an end which officials may foster by persuasion and example is not in question. The problem is whether under our Constitution compulsion as here employed is a permissible means for its achievement." Barnette. . . .

CHIEF JUSTICE REHNQUIST, with whom JUSTICE WHITE and Justice O'CONNOR join, dissenting.

In holding this Texas statute unconstitutional, the Court ignores Justice Holmes' familiar aphorism that "a page of history is worth a volume of logic." *New York Trust Co.* v. *Eisner* . . . (1921). For more than 200 years, the American flag has occupied a unique position as the symbol of our Nation, a uniqueness that justifies a governmental prohibition against flag burning in the way respondent Johnson did here. . . .

The American flag . . . does not represent the views of any particular political party, and it does not represent any particular political philosophy. The flag is not simply another "idea" or "point of view" competing for recognition in the marketplace of ideas. Millions and millions of Americans regard it with an almost mystical reverence regardless of what sort of social, political, or philosophical beliefs they may have. I cannot agree that the First Amendment invalidates the Act of Congress, and the laws of 48 of the 50 States, which make criminal the public burning of the flag. . . .

. . . the Court insists that the Texas statute prohibiting the public burning of the American flag infringes on respondent Johnson's freedom of expression. . . . Johnson was free to make any verbal denunciation of the flag that he wished; indeed, he was free to burn the flag in private. He could publicly burn other symbols of the Government or effigies of political leaders. He did lead a march through the streets of Dallas, and conducted a rally in front of the Dallas City Hall. He engaged in a "die-in" to protest nuclear weapons. He shouted out various slogans during the march, including: "Reagan, Mondale which will it be? Either one means World War III"; "Ronald Reagan, killer of the hour, Perfect example of US power"; and "red, white and blue, we spit on you, you stand for plunder, you will go under." . . . For none of these acts was he arrested or prosecuted; it was only when he proceeded to burn publicly an American flag stolen from its rightful owner that he violated the Texas statute. . . . The Texas statute deprived Johnson of only one rather inarticulate symbolic form of protest—a form of protest that was profoundly offensive to many—and left him with a full panoply of other symbols and every conceivable form of verbal expression to express his deep disapproval of national policy. Thus, in no way can it be said that Texas is punishing him because his hearers—or any other group of people—were profoundly opposed to the message that he sought to convey. Such opposition is no proper basis for restricting speech or expression under the First Amendment. It was Johnson's use of this particular symbol, and not the idea that he sought to convey by it or by his many other expressions, for which he was punished. . . . But the Court today will have none of this. The uniquely deep awe and respect for our flag felt by virtually all of us are bundled off under the rubric of "designated symbols," . . . that the First Amendment prohibits the government from "establishing." But the government has not "established" this feeling; 200 years of history have done that. The government is simply recognizing as a fact the profound regard for the American flag created by that history when it enacts statutes prohibiting the disrespectful public burning of the flag.

R.A.V. v. *City of St. Paul*
505 U.S., 112 S. Ct. 2538, 120 L. Ed. 2d 305 (1992)

R.A.V., together with several other teenagers, constructed a crude cross out of broken chair legs and burned the cross in the yard of a black family. He was arrested and charged with, among other things, violating St. Paul's Bias-Motivated Crime Ordinance, which forbade the display of a symbol "including, but not limited to, a burning cross or Nazi swastika, which one knows or has reasonable grounds to know arouses anger, alarm or resentment in others on the basis of race, color, creed, religion, or gender." The trial court dismissed this charge, ruling that the St. Paul ordinance violated the First Amendment because it was substantially overbroad and impermissibly restricted expression based on its content. The Minnesota Supreme Court reversed this ruling, contending that the ordinance only restricted "fighting words," which the United States Supreme Court in *Chaplinsky* v. *New Hampshire* (1942) had ruled were not entitled to First Amendment protection. The U.S. Supreme Court then granted certiorari. *Opinion of the Court:* Scalia, *Rehnquist, Kennedy, Souter, Thomas. Concurring opinions:* White, *Blackmun, O'Connor, Stevens (in part);* Blackmun; Stevens; *White (in part), Blackmun (in part).*

Justice Scalia delivered the opinion of the Court.

I

Assuming, arguendo, that all of the expression reached by the ordinance is proscribable under the "fighting words" doctrine, we nonetheless conclude that the ordinance is facially unconstitutional in that it prohibits otherwise permitted speech solely on the basis of the subjects the speech addresses.

The First Amendment generally prevents government from proscribing speech, see, e.g., *Cantwell* v. *Connecticut* (1940), or even expressive conduct, see, e.g., *Texas* v. *Johnson* (1989), because of disapproval of the ideas expressed. Content-based regulations are presumptively invalid. From 1791 to the present, however, our society, like other free but civilized societies, has permitted restrictions upon the content of speech in a few limited areas, which are "of such slight social value as a step to truth that any benefit that may be derived from them is clearly outweighed by the social interest in order and morality." *Chaplinsky* [v. *New Hampshire* (1942)]. . . .

. . . [T]hese areas of speech can, consistently with the First Amendment, be regulated because of their constitutionally proscribable contents (obscenity, defamation, etc.), not that they are categories of speech entirely invisible to the Constitution, so that they may be made the vehicles for content discrimination unrelated to their distinctively proscribable content. Thus, the government may proscribe libel; but it may not

make the further content discrimination of proscribing only libel critical of the government. . . .

The proposition that a particular instance of speech can be proscribable on the basis of one feature (e.g., obscenity) but not on the basis of another (e.g., opposition to the city government) is commonplace, and has found application in many contexts. We have long held, for example, that nonverbal expressive activity can be banned because of the action it entails, but not because of the ideas it expresses—so that burning a flag in violation of an ordinance against outdoor fires could be punishable, whereas burning a flag in violation of an ordinance against dishonoring the flag is not. Similarly, we have upheld reasonable "time, place, or manner" restrictions, but only if they are "justified without reference to the content of the regulated speech." *Ward* v. *Rock Against Racism* (1989).

. . . Even the prohibition against content discrimination that we assert the First Amendment requires is not absolute. It applies differently in the context of proscribable speech than in the area of fully protected speech. . . . When the basis for the content discrimination consists entirely of the very reason the entire class of speech at issue is proscribable, no significant danger of idea or viewpoint discrimination exists. Such a reason, having been adjudged neutral enough to support exclusion of the entire class of speech from First Amendment protection, is also neutral enough to form the basis of distinction within the class. To illustrate: A State might choose to prohibit only that obscenity which is the most patently offensive in its prurience—i.e., that which involves the most lascivious displays of sexual activity. But it may not prohibit, for example, only that obscenity which includes offensive political messages. . . .

II

Applying these principles to the St. Paul ordinance, we conclude that, even as narrowly construed by the Minnesota Supreme Court, the ordinance is facially unconstitutional. Although the phrase in the ordinance, "arouses anger, alarm or resentment in others," has been limited by the Minnesota Supreme Court's construction to reach only those symbols or displays that amount to "fighting words," the remaining, unmodified terms make clear that the ordinance applies only to "fighting words" that insult, or provoke violence, "on the basis of race, color, creed, religion or gender." Displays containing abusive invective, no matter how vicious or severe, are permissible unless they are addressed to one of the specified disfavored topics. Those who wish to use "fighting words" in connection with other ideas—to express hostility, for example, on the basis of political affiliation, union membership, or homosexuality—are not covered. The First Amendment does not permit St. Paul to impose special prohibitions on those speakers who express views on disfavored subjects.

In its practical operation, moreover, the ordinance goes even beyond mere content discrimination, to actual viewpoint discrimination. Displays containing some words—odious racial epithets, for example—would be prohibited to proponents of all views. But "fighting words" that do not themselves invoke race, color, creed, religion, or gender—aspersions upon a person's mother, for example—would seemingly be usable ad libitum in the placards of those arguing in favor of racial, color, etc. tolerance and equality, but could not be used by that speaker's opponents.

One could hold up a sign saying, for example, that all "anti-Catholic bigots" are misbegotten; but not that all "papists" are, for that would insult and provoke violence "on the basis of religion." St. Paul has no such authority to license one side of a debate to fight freestyle, while re-

quiring the other to follow Marquis of Queensbury Rules.

. . . Finally, St. Paul and its amici defend the conclusion of the Minnesota Supreme Court that, even if the ordinance regulates expression based on hostility towards its protected ideological content, this discrimination is nonetheless justified because it is narrowly tailored to serve compelling state interests. Specifically, they assert that the ordinance helps to ensure the basic human rights of members of groups that have historically been subjected to discrimination, including the right of such group members to live in peace where they wish. We do not doubt that these interests are compelling, and that the ordinance can be said to promote them. But the "danger of censorship" presented by a facially content-based statute requires that that weapon be employed only where it is "necessary to serve the asserted [compelling] interest." *Burson* v. *Freeman* (1992). The existence of adequate content-neutral alternatives thus "undercut[s] significantly" any defense of such a statute, casting considerable doubt on the government's protestations that "the asserted justification is in fact an accurate description of the purpose and effect of the law." The dispositive question in this case, therefore, is whether content discrimination is reasonably necessary to achieve St. Paul's compelling interests; it plainly is not. An ordinance not limited to the favored topics, for example, would have precisely the same beneficial effect. In fact the only interest distinctively served by the content limitation is that of displaying the city council's special hostility toward the particular biases thus singled out. That is precisely what the First Amendment forbids. The politicians of St. Paul are entitled to express that hostility—but not through the means of imposing unique limitations upon speakers who (however benightedly) disagree.

*　*　*

Let there be no mistake about our belief that burning a cross in someone's front yard is reprehensible. But St. Paul has sufficient means at its disposal to prevent such behavior without adding the First Amendment to the fire. The judgment of the Minnesota Supreme Court is reversed, and the case is remanded for proceedings not inconsistent with this opinion.

JUSTICE WHITE, with whom JUSTICE BLACKMUN and JUSTICE O'CONNOR join, and with whom Justice Stevens joins [in part], concurring in the judgment.

I agree with the majority that the judgment of the Minnesota Supreme Court should be reversed. However, our agreement ends there.

. . . This Court's decisions have plainly stated that expression falling within certain limited categories so lacks the values the First Amendment was designed to protect that the Constitution affords no protection to that expression. *Chaplinsky* v. *New Hampshire* (1942), made the point in the clearest possible terms:

> There are certain well-defined and narrowly limited classes of speech, the prevention and punishment of which have never been thought to raise any Constitutional problem. . . . It has been well observed that such utterances are no essential part of any exposition of ideas, and are of such slight social value as a step to truth that any benefit that may be derived from them is clearly outweighed by the social interest in order and morality.

. . . This categorical approach has provided a principled and narrowly focused means for distinguishing between expression that the government may regulate freely and that which it may regulate on the basis of content only upon a showing of compelling need.

. . . In its decision today, the majority holds that the First Amendment protects those narrow categories of expression long held to be undeserving of First Amendment protection—at least to the extent that lawmakers may not regulate some fighting words more strictly than others because of their content. The Court announces that such content-based distinctions violate the First Amendment because "the government may not regulate use based on hostility—or favoritism, towards the underlying message expressed." Should the government want to criminalize certain fighting words, the Court now requires it to criminalize all fighting words. . . .

. . . Fighting words are not a means of exchanging views, rallying supporters, or registering a protest; they are directed against individuals to provoke violence or to inflict injury. Therefore, a ban on all fighting words or on a subset of the fighting words category would restrict only the social evil of hate speech, without creating the danger of driving viewpoints from the marketplace.

. . . As I see it, the Court's theory does not work and will do nothing more than confuse the law. Its selection of this case to rewrite First Amendment law is particularly inexplicable, because the whole problem could have been avoided by deciding this case under settled First Amendment principles. I would decide the case on overbreadth grounds. We have emphasized time and again that overbreadth doctrine is an exception to the established principle that "a person to whom a statute may constitutionally be applied will not be heard to challenge that statute on the ground that it may conceivably be applied unconstitutionally to others, in other situations not before the Court." *Broadrick* v. *Oklahoma* [1973]. A defendant being prosecuted for speech or expressive conduct may challenge the law on its face if it reaches protected expression, even when that person's activities are not protected by the First Amendment. This is because "the possible harm to society in permitting some unprotected speech to go unpunished is outweighed by the possibility that protected speech of others may be muted."

. . . I agree with petitioner that the ordinance is invalid on its face. Although the ordinance as construed reaches categories of speech that are constitutionally unprotected, it also criminalizes a substantial amount of expression that—however repugnant—is shielded by the First Amendment.

In attempting to narrow the scope of the St. Paul antibias ordinance, the Minnesota Supreme Court relied upon two of the categories of speech and expressive conduct that fall outside the First Amendment's protective sphere: words that incite "imminent lawless action," *Brandenburg* v. *Ohio* (1969), and "fighting" words, *Chaplinsky* v. *New Hampshire*. [T]he Minnesota Supreme Court drew upon the definition of fighting words that appears in *Chaplinsky*—words "which by their very utterance inflict injury or tend to incite an immediate breach of the peace." However, the Minnesota court emphasized (tracking the language of the ordinance) that "the ordinance censors only those displays that one knows or should know will create anger, alarm or resentment based on racial, ethnic, gender or religious bias."

. . . Our fighting words cases have made clear, however, that such generalized reactions are not sufficient to strip expression of its constitutional protection. The mere fact that expressive activity causes hurt feelings, offense, or resentment does not render the expression unprotected. . . . The ordinance is therefore fatally overbroad and invalid on its face.

Tinker v. *Des Moines*
393 U.S. 503, 89 S. Ct. 733, 21 L. Ed. 2d 731 (1969)

The petitioners in this case—two high school students and a junior high student—were suspended from school for wearing black armbands to class as a protest against the Vietnam War and for failing to remove the armbands when requested to do so. They sought a Federal injunction against enforcement of the school regulation prohibiting students from wearing armbands to school, which had been adopted two days before, in anticipation of the protest. After the Court of Appeals divided evenly on the issue, the Supreme Court granted certiorari. *Opinion of the Court: Fortas, Warren, Douglas, Brennan, Stewart, White, Marshall. Concurring opinions: Stewart; White. Dissenting opinions: Black; Harlan.*

MR. JUSTICE FORTAS delivered the opinion of the Court. . . .

First Amendment rights, applied in light of the special characteristics of the school environment, are available to teachers and students. It can hardly be argued that either students or teachers shed their constitutional rights to freedom of speech or expression at the schoolhouse gate. This has been the unmistakable holding of this Court for almost 50 years. . . . On the other hand, the Court has repeatedly emphasized the need for affirming the comprehensive authority of the States and of school officials, consistent with fundamental constitutional safeguards, to prescribe and control conduct in the schools. . . . Our problem lies in the area where students in the exercise of First Amendment rights collide with the rules of the school authorities.

. . . Our problem involves direct, primary First Amendment rights akin to "pure speech." The school officials banned and sought to punish petitioners for a silent, passive expression of opinion, unaccompanied by any disorder or disturbance on the part of petitioners. There is here no evidence whatever of petitioners' interference, actual or nascent, with the schools' work or of collision with the rights of other students to be secure and to be let alone. Accordingly, this case does not concern speech or action that intrudes upon the work of the schools or the rights of other students. . . .

The District Court concluded that the action of the school authorities was reasonable because it was based upon their fear of a disturbance from the wearing of the armbands. But, in our system, undifferentiated fear or apprehension of disturbance is not enough to overcome the right to freedom of expression. . . .

In order for the State in the person of school officials to justify prohibition of a particular expression of opinion, it must be able to show that its action was caused by something more than a mere desire to avoid the discomfort and unpleasantness that always accompany an unpopular viewpoint. . . .

In the present case, the District Court made no such finding, and our independent examination of the record fails to yield evidence that the school authorities had reason to anticipate that the wearing of the armbands would substantially interfere with the work of the school or impinge upon the rights of other students. . . .

On the contrary, the action of the school authorities appears to have been based upon an urgent wish to avoid the controversy which might result from the expression, even by the silent symbol of armbands, of opposition to this Nation's part in the conflagration in Vietnam. . . .

It is also relevant that the school authorities did not purport to prohibit the wearing of all symbols of political or controversial significance. The record shows that students in some of the schools wore buttons relating to national political campaigns, and some even wore the Iron Cross, traditionally a symbol of Nazism. The order prohibiting the wearing of armbands did not extend to these. Instead, a particular symbol— black armbands worn to exhibit opposition to this Nation's involvement in Vietnam—was singled out for prohibition. Clearly, the prohibition of expression of one particular opinion, at least without evidence that it is necessary to avoid material and substantial interference with schoolwork or discipline, is not constitutionally permissible. . . .

The principle of these cases is not confined to the supervised and ordained discussion which takes place in the classroom. The principal use to which the schools are dedicated is to accommodate students during prescribed hours for the purpose of certain types of activities. Among those activities is personal intercommunication among the students. This is not only an inevitable part of the process of attending school; it is also an important part of the educational process. A student's rights, therefore, do not embrace merely the classroom hours. When he is in the cafeteria, or on the playing field, or on the campus during the authorized hours, he may express his opinions, even on controversial subjects like the conflict in Vietnam, if he does so without "materially and substantially interfering with the requirements of appropriate discipline in the operation of the school" and without colliding with the rights of others. . . . But conduct by the student, in class or out of it, which for any reason— whether it stems from time, place, or type of behavior—materially disrupts classwork or involves substantial disorder or invasion of the rights of others is, of course, not immunized by the constitutional guarantee of freedom of speech. . . .

Reversed and remanded.

MR. JUSTICE BLACK, dissenting.

Assuming that the Court is correct in holding that the conduct of wearing armbands for the purpose of conveying political ideas is protected by the First Amendment, . . . the crucial remaining questions are whether students and teachers may use the schools at their whim as a platform for the exercise of free speech—"symbolic" or "pure"—and whether the courts will allocate to themselves the function of deciding how the pupils' school day will be spent. While I have always believed that under the First and Fourteenth Amendments neither the State nor the Federal Government has any authority to regulate or censor the content of speech, I have never believed that any person has a right to give speeches or engage in demonstrations where he pleases and when he pleases. . . .

While the record does not show that any of these armband students shouted, used profane language, or were violent in any manner, detailed testimony by some of them shows their armbands caused comments, warnings by other students, the poking of fun at them, and a warning by an older football player that other, nonprotesting students had better let them alone. There is also evidence that a teacher of mathematics had his lesson period practically "wrecked" chiefly by disputes with Mary Beth Tinker, who wore her armband for her "demonstration." Even a casual reading of the record shows that this armband did divert students' minds from their regular lessons, and that talk, comments, etc., made John Tinker "self-conscious" in attending school with his armband. While the absence of obscene remarks or boisterous and loud disorder perhaps justifies the Court's statement that the few armband students did not actually "disrupt" the classwork, I think the record overwhelmingly shows that the armbands did exactly what the elected school officials and principals foresaw they would, that is, took the students' minds off their classwork and diverted them to thoughts about the highly emotional subject of the Vietnam war. . . .

In my view, teachers in state-controlled public schools are hired to teach there. . . . Certainly a teacher is not paid to go into school and teach subjects the State does not hire him to teach as a part of its selected curriculum. Nor are public school students sent to the schools at public expense to broadcast political or any other views to educate and inform the public. The original idea of schools, which I do not believe is yet abandoned as worthless or out of date, was that children had not yet reached the point of experience and wisdom which enabled them to teach all of their elders. It may be that the Nation has outworn the old-fashioned slogan that "children are to be seen not heard," but one may, I hope, be permitted to harbor the thought that taxpayers send children to school on the premise that at their age they need to learn, not teach. . . .

Near v. *Minnesota*
283 U.S. 697, 51 S. Ct. 625, 75 L. Ed. 1357 (1931)

The Saturday Press published a series of articles charging that various Minneapolis public officials were dishonest and incompetent and that they were responsible for the racketeering and bootlegging in the city. The publication also called for a special grand jury to investigate the situation. Under a state law that authorized abatement of a "malicious, scandalous and defamatory newspaper," the state secured a court order that required *The Saturday Press* to cease publication. When the state supreme court affirmed the court order, the case was appealed to the United States Supreme Court. *Opinion of the Court:* Hughes, *Holmes, Brandeis, Stone, Roberts. Dissenting opinion:* Butler, *Van Devanter, McReynolds, Sutherland.*

MR. CHIEF JUSTICE HUGHES delivered the opinion of the Court. . . .

Without attempting to summarize the contents of the voluminous exhibits attached to the complaint, we deem it sufficient to say that the articles charged in substance that a Jewish gangster was in control of gambling, bootlegging and racketeering in Minneapolis, and that law enforcing officers and agencies were not energetically performing their duties. Most of the charges were directed against the Chief of Police; he was charged with gross neglect of duty, illicit relations with gangsters, and with participation in graft. The County Attorney was charged with knowing the existing conditions and with failure to take adequate measures to remedy them. The Mayor was accused of inefficiency and dereliction. One member of the grand jury was stated to be in sympathy with the gangsters. A special grand jury and a special prosecutor were demanded to deal with the situation in general, and, in particular, to investigate an attempt to assassinate one Guilford, one of the original defendants, who, it appears from the articles, was shot by gangsters after the first issue of the periodical had been published. There is no question but that the articles made serious accusations against the public officers named and others in connection with the prevalence of crimes and the failure to expose and punish them. . . .

This statute, for the suppression as a public nuisance of a newspaper or periodical, is unusual, if not unique, and raises questions of grave importance transcending the local interests involved in the particular action. It is no longer open to doubt that the liberty of the press, and of speech, is within the liberty safeguarded by the due process clause of the Fourteenth Amendment from invasion by state action. . . . In maintaining this guaranty, the authority of the State to enact laws to promote the health, safety, morals and general welfare of its people is necessarily admitted. The limits of this sovereign power must always be determined with appropriate regard to the particular subject of its exercise. . . . It is . . . important to note precisely the purpose and effect of the statute as the state court has construed it.

First. The statute is not aimed at the redress of individual or private wrongs. Remedies for libel remain available and unaffected. The statute, said the state court, "is not directed at threatened libel but at an existing business which, generally speaking, involves more than libel." It is aimed at the distribution of scandalous matter as "detrimental to public morals and to the general welfare," tending "to disturb the peace of the community" and "to provoke assaults and the commission of crime." . . .

Second. The statute is directed not simply at the circulation of scandalous and defamatory statements with regard to private citizens, but at the continued publication by newspapers and periodicals of charges against public officers of corruption, malfeasance in office, or serious neglect of duty. Such charges by their very nature create a public scandal. They are scandalous and defamatory within the meaning of the statute, which has its normal operation in relation to publications dealing prominently and chiefly with the alleged derelictions of public officers. . . .

Third. The object of the statute is not punishment, in the ordinary sense, but suppression of the offending newspaper or periodical. . . . Under this statute, a publisher of a newspaper or periodical, undertaking to conduct a campaign to expose and to censure official derelictions, and devoting his publication principally to that purpose, must face not simply the possibility of a verdict against him in a suit or prosecution for libel, but a determination that his newspaper or periodical is a public nuisance to be abated, and that this abatement and suppression will follow unless he is prepared with legal evidence to prove the truth of the charges and also to satisfy the court that, in addition to being true, the matter was published with good motives and for justifiable ends. This suppression is accomplished by enjoining publication and that restraint is the object and effect of the statute. . . .

Fourth. The statute not only operates to suppress the offending newspaper or periodical but to put the publisher under an effective censorship. When a newspaper or periodical is found to be "malicious, scandalous and defamatory," and is suppressed as such, resumption of publication is punishable as a contempt of court by fine or imprisonment. . . .

The question is whether a statute authorizing such proceedings in restraint of publication is consistent with the conception of the liberty of the press as historically conceived and guaranteed. In determining the extent of the constitutional protection, it has been generally, if not universally, considered that it is the chief purpose of the guaranty to prevent previous restraints upon publication. The struggle in England, directed against the legislative power of the licenser, resulted in renunciation of the censorship of the press. The liberty deemed to be established was thus described by Blackstone: "The liberty of the press is indeed essential to the nature of a free state; but this consists in laying no *previous* restraints upon publications, and not in freedom from censure for criminal matter when published. Every freeman has an undoubted right to lay what sentiments he pleases before the public; to forbid this, is to destroy the freedom of the press; but if he publishes what is improper, mischievous or illegal, he must take the consequence of his own temerity." . . .

The criticism upon Blackstone's statement has not been because immunity from previous restraint upon publication has not been regarded as deserving of special emphasis, but chiefly because that immunity cannot be deemed to exhaust the conception of the liberty guaranteed by state and federal constitutions. . . .

The objection has also been made that the principle as to immunity from previous restraint is stated too broadly, if every such restraint is deemed to be prohibited. That is undoubtedly true; the protection even as to previous restraint is not absolutely unlimited. But the limitation has been recognized only in exceptional cases. . . . No one would question but that a government might prevent actual obstruction to its recruiting service or the publication of the sailing dates of transports or the number and location of troops. On similar grounds, the primary requirements of decency may be enforced against obscene publications. The security of the community life may be protected against incitements to acts of violence and the overthrow by force of orderly government. The constitutional guaranty of free speech does not "protect a man from an injunction against uttering words that may have all the effect of force. . . . These limitations are not applicable here. Nor are we now concerned with questions as to the extent of authority to prevent publications in order to protect private rights according to the principles governing the exercise of the jurisdiction of courts of equity. . . .

The exceptional nature of its limitations places in a strong light the general conception that liberty of the press, historically considered and taken up by the Federal Constitution, has meant, principally although not exclusively, immunity from previous restraints or censorship. The conception of the liberty of the press in this country had broadened with the exigencies of the colonial period and with the efforts to secure freedom from oppressive administration. That liberty was especially cherished for the immunity it afforded from previous restraint of the publication of censure of public officers and charges of official misconduct. . . .

For these reasons we hold the statute, so far as it authorized the proceedings in this action under clause (b) of section one, to be an infringement of the liberty of the press guaranteed by the Fourteenth Amendment. . . .

Judgment reversed.

New York Times Company v. United States
403 U.S. 713; 91 S. Ct. 2140; 29 L. Ed. 2d 822 (1971)

In late March 1971, *The New York Times* obtained from Daniel Ellsberg, who was associated with the Pentagon, a copy of the Pentagon Papers (a classified Defense Department study of United States involvement in Indochina). On June 12, 1971, after prolonged editorial consideration of the material, the *Times* began publication of excerpts from the multivolume study. When the *Times* ignored a Justice Department request to halt further publication, the attorney general obtained an injunction in federal district court—the first federal injunction ever sought against newspaper publication. From this point the case proceeded with extraordinary speed through the federal courts. By June 19, both the *Times* and the *Washington Post*, which had also begun publication of the materials, were under restraining orders imposed by federal courts of appeal. The Supreme Court agreed to hear the cases on June 25, heard oral argument a day later, and on June 29 announced its decision. (For a related case, see *Gravel* v. *United States,* in Chapter 4 of Volume I.) *Opinion of the Court per curiam:* Black, Douglas, Brennan, Stewart, White, Marshall. *Separate opinions:* Black, Douglas; Douglas, Black; Brennan; Stewart, White; White, Stewart; Marshall. *Dissenting opinions:* Burger; Harlan, Burger, Blackmun; Blackmun.

PER CURIAM. . . .

"Any system of prior restraints of expression comes to this Court bearing a heavy presumption against its constitutional validity." *Bantam Books, Inc.* v. *Sullivan* [1963]. . .The Government "thus carries a heavy burden of showing justification for the imposition of such a restraint." *Organization for a Better Austin* v. *Keefe* [1971]. . . . The District Court for the Southern District of New York in the *New York Times* case and the District Court for the District of Columbia and the Court of Appeals for the District of Columbia Circuit in the *Washington Post* case held that the Government had not met that burden. We agree.

MR. JUSTICE BLACK, with whom MR. JUSTICE DOUGLAS joins, concurring.

I adhere to the view that the Government's case against the *Washington Post* should have been dismissed and that the injunction against the *New York Times* should have been vacated without oral argument when the cases were first presented to this Court. I believe that every moment's continuance of the injunctions against these newspapers amounts to a flagrant, indefensible, and continuing violation of the First Amendment. . . .

In the First Amendment the Founding Fathers gave the free press the protection it must have to fulfill its essential role in our democracy. The press was to serve the governed, not the governors. The Government's power to censor the press was abolished so that the press would remain forever free to censure the Government. The press was protected so that it could bare the secrets of government and inform the people. Only a free and unrestrained press can effectively expose deception in government. And paramount among the responsibilities of a free press is the duty to prevent any part of the government from deceiving the people and sending them off to distant lands to die of foreign fevers and foreign shot and shell. In my view, far from deserving condemnation for their courageous reporting, the *New York Times*, the *Washington Post*, and other newspapers should be commended for serving the purpose that the Founding Fathers saw so clearly. In revealing the workings of government that led to the Vietnam war, the newspapers nobly did precisely that which the Founders hoped and trusted they would do. . . .

. . . We are asked to hold that despite the First Amendment's emphatic command, the Executive Branch, the Congress, and the Judiciary can make laws enjoining publication of current news and abridging freedom of the press in the name of "national security."

The word "security" is a broad, vague generality whose contours should not be invoked to abrogate the fundamental law embodied in the First Amendment. The guarding of military and diplomatic secrets at the expense of informed representative government provides no real security for our Republic. The Framers of the First Amendment, fully aware of both the need to defend a new nation and the abuses of the English and Colonial governments, sought to give this new society strength and security by providing that freedom of speech, press, religion, and assembly should not be abridged. . . .

MR. JUSTICE BRENNAN, concurring.

The error that has pervaded these cases from the outset was the granting of any injunctive relief whatsoever, interim or otherwise. The entire thrust of the Government's claim throughout these cases has been that publication of the material sought to be enjoined "could," or "might," or "may" prejudice the national interest in various ways. But the First Amendment tolerates absolutely no prior judicial restraints of the press predicated upon surmise or conjecture that untoward consequences may result. . . . Our cases have thus far indicated that such cases may arise only when the Nation "is at war," . . . during which times "no one would question but that a government might prevent actual obstruction to its recruiting service or the publication of the sailing dates of transports or the number and location of troops." *Near* v. *Minnesota* [1931]. . . . Even if the present world situation were assumed to be tantamount to a time of war, or if the power of presently available armaments would justify even in peacetime the suppression of information that would set in motion a nuclear holocaust, in neither of these actions has the Government presented or even alleged that publication of items from or based upon the material at issue would cause the happening of an event of that nature. . . .

MR. JUSTICE STEWART, with whom MR. JUSTICE WHITE joins, concurring. . . .

In the absence of the governmental checks and balances present in other areas of our national life, the only effective restraint upon executive policy and power in the areas of national defense and international affairs may lie in an enlightened citizenry—in an informed and critical public opinion which alone can here protect the values of democratic government. For this reason, it is perhaps here that a press that is alert, aware, and free most vitally serves the basic purpose of the First Amendment. For without an informed and free press there cannot be an enlightened people.

Yet it is elementary that the successful conduct of international diplomacy and the maintenance of an effective national defense require both confidentiality and secrecy. Other nations can hardly deal with this Nation in an atmosphere of mutual trust unless they can be assured that their confidences will be kept. And within our own executive departments, the development of considered and intelligent international policies would be impossible if those charged with their formulation could not communicate with each other freely, frankly, and in confidence. In the area of basic national defense the frequent need for absolute secrecy is, of course, self-evident.

I think there can be but one answer to this dilemma, if dilemma it be. The responsibility must be where the power is. If the Constitution gives the Executive a large degree of unshared power in the conduct of foreign affairs and the maintenance of our national defense, then under the Constitution the Executive must have the largely unshared duty to determine and preserve the degree of internal security necessary to exercise that power successfully. It is an awesome responsibility, requiring judgment and wisdom of a high order. I should suppose that moral, political, and practical considerations would dictate that a very first principle of that wisdom would be an insistence upon avoiding secrecy for its own sake. . . . But be that as it may, it is clear to me that it is the constitutional duty of the Executive—as a matter of sovereign prerogative and not as a matter of law as the courts know law—through the promulgation and enforcement of executive regulations, to protect the confidentiality necessary to carry out its responsibilities in the fields of international relations and national defense.

This is not to say that Congress and the courts have no role to play. Undoubtedly Congress has the power to enact specific and appropriate criminal laws to protect government property and preserve government secrets. . . . And if a criminal prosecution is instituted, it will be the responsibility of the courts to decide the applicability of the criminal law under which the charge is brought. . . .

But in the cases before us we are asked neither to construe specific regulations nor to apply specific laws. We are asked, instead, to perform a function that the Constitution gave to the Executive, not the Judiciary. We are asked, quite simply, to prevent the publication by two newspapers of material that the Executive Branch insists should not, in the national interest, be published. I am convinced that the Executive is correct with respect to some of the documents involved. But I cannot say that disclosure of any of them will surely result in direct, immediate, and irreparable damage to our Nation or its people. That being so, there can under the First Amendment be but one judicial resolution of the issues before us. I join the judgments of the Court.

MR. JUSTICE WHITE, with whom MR. JUSTICE STEWART joins, concurring. . . .

The Government's position is simply stated: The responsibility of the Executive for the conduct of the foreign affairs and for the security of the Nation is so basic that the President is entitled to an injunction against publication of a newspaper story whenever he can convince a court that the information to be revealed threatens "grave and irreparable" injury to the public interest; and the injunction should issue whether or not the material to be published is classified, whether or not publication would be lawful under relevant criminal statutes enacted by Congress, and regardless of the circumstances by which the newspaper came into possession of the information.

At least in the absence of legislation by Congress, based on its own investigations and findings, I am quite unable to agree that the inherent powers of the Executive and the courts reach so far as to authorize remedies having such sweeping potential for inhibiting publications by the press. . . .

. . . Terminating the ban on publication of the relatively few sensitive documents the Government now seeks to suppress does not mean that the law either requires or invites newspapers or others to publish them or that they will be immune from criminal action if they do. . . .

. . . Congress has addressed itself to the problems of protecting the security of the country and the national defense from unauthorized disclosure of potentially damaging information. . . . It has not, however, authorized the injunctive remedy against threatened publication. It has apparently been satisfied to rely on criminal sanctions and their deterrent effect on the responsible as well as the irresponsible press.

Mr. Chief Justice Burger, dissenting. . . .

. . . In these cases, the imperative of a free and unfettered press comes into collision with another imperative, the effective functioning of a complex modern government and specifically the effective exercise of certain constitutional powers of the Executive. Only those who view the First Amendment as an absolute in all circumstances—a view I respect, but reject—can find such cases as these to be simple or easy. . . .

It is not disputed that the *Times* has had unauthorized possession of the documents for three to four months, during which it has had its expert analysts studying them, presumably digesting them and preparing the material for publication. . . . No doubt this was for a good reason; the analysis of 7,000 pages of complex material drawn from a vastly greater volume of material would inevitably take time and the writing of good news stories takes time. But why should the United States Government, from whom this information was illegally acquired by someone, along with all the counsel, trial judges, and appellate judges be placed under needless pressure? After these months of deferral, the alleged "right to know" has somehow and suddenly become a right that must be vindicated instanter.

. . . As I see it, we have been forced to deal with litigation concerning rights of great magnitude without an adequate record, and surely without time for adequate treatment either in the prior proceedings or in this Court. . . . I am not prepared to reach the merits [of the case].

I would affirm the Court of Appeals for the Second Circuit and allow the District Court to complete the trial aborted by our grant of certiorari, meanwhile preserving the status quo in the *Post* case.

MR. JUSTICE HARLAN, with whom THE CHIEF JUSTICE and Mr. Justice BLACKMUN join, dissenting.

. . . The scope of the judicial function in passing upon the activities of the Executive Branch of the Government in the field of foreign affairs is very narrowly restricted. This view is, I think, dictated by the concept of separation of powers upon which our constitutional system rests.

In a speech on the floor of the House of Representatives, Chief Justice John Marshall, then a member of that body, stated: "The President is the sole organ of the nation in its external relations, and its sole representative with foreign nations." . . . From that time, shortly after the founding of the Nation, to this, there has been no substantial challenge to this description of the scope of executive power. . . .

From this constitutional primacy in the field of foreign affairs, it seems to me that certain conclusions necessarily follow. Some of these were stated concisely by President Washington, de-

clining the request of the House of Representatives for the papers leading up to the negotiation of the Jay Treaty:

"The nature of foreign negotiations requires caution, and their success must often depend on secrecy; and even when brought to a conclusion a full disclosure of all the measures, demands, or eventual concessions which may have been proposed or contemplated would be extremely impolitic; for this might have a pernicious influence on future negotiations, or produce immediate inconveniences, perhaps danger and mischief, in relation to other powers." . . .

The power to evaluate the "pernicious influence" of premature disclosure is not, however, lodged in the Executive alone. I agree that, in performance of its duty to protect the values of the First Amendment against political pressures, the judiciary must review the initial Executive determination to the point of satisfying itself that the subject matter of the dispute does lie within the proper compass of the President's foreign relations power. Constitutional considerations forbid "a complete abandonment of judicial control." Cf. *United States* v. *Reynolds*, [1953]. Moreover, the judiciary may properly insist that the determination that disclosure of the subject matter would irreparably impair the national security be made by the head of the Executive Department concerned—here the Secretary of State or the Secretary of Defense—after actual personal consideration by that officer. This safeguard is required in the analogous area of executive claims of privilege for secrets of state. . . .

But in my judgment the judiciary may not properly go beyond these two inquiries and redetermine for itself the probable impact of disclosure on the national security. . . .

Even if there is some room for the judiciary to override the executive determination, it is plain that the scope of review must be exceedingly narrow. I can see no indication in the opinions of either the District Court or the Court of Appeals in the *Post* litigation that the conclusions of the Executive were given even the deference owing to an administrative agency, much less that owing to a co-equal branch of the Government operating within the field of its constitutional prerogative.

Accordingly, I would vacate the judgment of the Court of Appeals for the District of Columbia Circuit on this ground and remand the case for further proceedings in the District Court. Before the commencement of such further proceedings, due opportunity should be afforded the Government for procuring from the Secretary of State or the Secretary of Defense or both an ex-

pression of their views on the issue of national security. The ensuing review by the District Court should be in accordance with the views expressed in this opinion. And for the reasons stated above I would affirm the judgment of the Court of Appeals for the Second Circuit.

Branzburg v. Hayes

408 U.S. 665, 92 S. Ct. 2646, 33 L. Ed. 2d 626 (1972)

In *Branzburg* the Court considered together three cases involving reporters' refusal to testify before grand juries. In one case, Paul Branzburg, a reporter for the Louisville *Courier-Journal,* refused to answer grand jury questions about the identity of persons he had observed processing hashish from marijuana. In the other two cases, Paul Pappas and Earl Caldwell refused to testify before grand juries investigating the activities of the Black Panthers, a radical group. *Opinion of the Court: White, Burger, Blackmun, Powell, Rehnquist. Concurring opinion: Powell. Dissenting opinions: Douglas; Stewart, Brennan, Marshall.*

MR. JUSTICE WHITE delivered the opinion of the Court. . . .

The issue in these cases is whether requiring newsmen to appear and testify before State or federal grand juries abridges the freedom of speech and press guaranteed by the First Amendment. We hold that it does not . . .

Petitioners Branzburg and Pappas and respondent Caldwell press First Amendment claims that may be simply put: that to gather news it is often necessary to agree either not to identify the source of information published or to publish only part of the facts revealed, or both; that if the reporter is nevertheless forced to reveal these confidences to a grand jury, the source so identified and other confidential sources of other reporters will be measurably deterred from furnishing publishable information, all to the detriment of the free flow of information protected by the First Amendment. . . . The heart of the claim is that the burden on news gathering resulting from compelling reporters to disclose confidential information outweighs any public interest in obtaining the information. . . .

It is clear that the First Amendment does not invalidate every incidental burdening of the press that may result from the enforcement of civil or criminal statutes of general applicability. . . . It has generally been held that the First Amendment does not guarantee the press a con-

stitutional right of special access to information not available to the public generally. . . .

Despite the fact that news gathering may be hampered, the press is regularly excluded from grand jury proceedings, our own conferences, the meetings of other official bodies gathered in executive session, and the meetings of private organizations. Newsmen have no constitutional right of access to the scenes of crime or disaster when the general public is excluded, and they may be prohibited from attending or publishing information about trials if such restrictions are necessary to assure a defendant a fair trial before an impartial tribunal. . . .

It is thus not surprising that the great weight of authority is that newsmen are not exempt from the normal duty of appearing before a grand jury and answering questions relevant to a criminal investigation. . . .

A number of States have provided newsmen a statutory privilege of varying breadth, but the majority have not done so, and none has been provided by federal statute. Until now the only testimonial privilege for unofficial witnesses that is rooted in the Federal Constitution is the Fifth Amendment privilege against compelled self-incrimination. We are asked to create another by interpreting the First Amendment to grant newsmen a testimonial privilege that other citizens do not enjoy. This we decline to do. Fair and effective law enforcement aimed at providing security for the person and property of the individual is a fundamental function of government, and the grand jury plays an important, constitutionally mandated role in this process. On the records now before us, we perceive no basis for holding that the public interest in law enforcement and in ensuring effective grand jury proceedings is insufficient to override the consequential, but uncertain, burden on news gathering that is said to result from insisting that reporters, like other citizens, respond to relevant questions put to them in the course of a valid grand jury investigation or criminal trial. . . .

. . . The administration of a constitutional newsman's privilege would present practical and conceptual difficulties of a high order. Sooner or later, it would be necessary to define those categories of newsmen who qualified for the privilege, a questionable procedure in light of the traditional doctrine that liberty of the press is the right of the lonely pamphleteer who uses carbon paper or a mimeograph just as much as of the large metropolitan publisher who utilizes the latest photocomposition methods. . . . Freedom of the press is a "fundamental personal right" which "is not confined to newspapers and periodicals. It necessarily embraces pamphlets and leaflets. . . . "The press in its historic connotation comprehends every sort of publication which affords a vehicle of information and opinion." *Lovell* v. *Griffin* [1938]. . . . The informative function asserted by representatives of the organized press in the present cases is also performed by lecturers, political pollsters, novelists, academic researchers, and dramatists. Almost any author may quite accurately assert that he is contributing to the flow of information to the public, that he relies on confidential sources of information, and that these sources will be silenced if he is forced to make disclosures before a grand jury. . . .

Finally, . . . news gathering is not without its First Amendment protections, and grand jury investigations if instituted or conducted other than in good faith, would pose wholly different issues for resolution under the First Amendment. Official harassment of the press undertaken not for purposes of law enforcement but to disrupt a reporter's relationship with his news sources would have no justification. Grand juries are subject to judicial control and subpoenas to motions to quash. We do not expect courts will forget that grand juries must operate within the limits of the First Amendment as well as the Fifth.

MR. JUSTICE STEWART, with whom MR. JUSTICE BRENNAN and MR. JUSTICE MARSHALL join, dissenting.

The Court's crabbed view of the First Amendment reflects a disturbing insensitivity to the critical role of an independent press in our society. . . . The Court in these cases holds that a newsman has no First Amendment right to protect his sources when called before a grand jury. The Court thus invites state and federal authorities to undermine the historic independence of the press by attempting to annex the journalistic profession as an investigative arm of government. Not only will this decision impair performance of the press' constitutionally protected functions, but it will, I am convinced, in the long run harm rather than help the administration of justice. . . .

The reporter's constitutional right to a confidential relationship with his source stems from the broad societal interest in a full and free flow of information to the public. It is this basic concern that underlies the Constitution's protection of a free press. . . .

Enlightened choice by an informed citizenry is the basic ideal upon which an open society is premised, and a free press is thus indispensable to a free society. Not only does the press enhance personal self-fulfillment by providing the people with the widest possible range of fact and opinion, but it also is an incontestable precondition of self-government. . . . As private and public aggregations of power burgeon in size and the pressures for conformity necessarily mount, there is obviously a continuing need for an independent press to disseminate a robust variety of information and opinion through reportage, investigation, and criticism, if we are to preserve our constitutional tradition of maximizing freedom of choice by encouraging diversity of expression. . . .

In keeping with this tradition, we have held that the right to publish is central to the First Amendment and basic to the existence of constitutional democracy. . . .

No less important to the news dissemination process is the gathering of information. News must not be unnecessarily cut off at its source, for without freedom to acquire information the right to publish would be impermissibly compromised. Accordingly, a right to gather news, of some dimensions, must exist. . . .

The right to gather news implies, in turn, a right to a confidential relationship between a reporter and his source. This proposition follows as a matter of simple logic once three factual predicates are recognized: (1) newsmen require informants to gather news; (2) confidentiality—the promise or understanding that names or certain aspects of communications will be kept off the record—is essential to the creation and maintenance of a news-gathering relationship with informants; and (3) an unbridled subpoena power—the absence of a constitutional right protecting, in *any* way, a confidential relationship from compulsory process—will either deter sources from divulging information or deter reporters from gathering and publishing information.

Posed against the First Amendment's protection of the newsman's confidential relationships in these cases is society's interest in the use of the grand jury to administer justice fairly and effectively. . . . Yet the longstanding rule making

every person's evidence available to the grand jury is not absolute. The rule has been limited by the Fifth Amendment, the Fourth Amendment, and the evidentiary privileges of the common law. . . .

In striking the proper balance between the public interest in the efficient administration of justice and the First Amendment guarantee of the fullest flow of information, we must begin with the basic proposition that because of their "delicate and vulnerable" nature . . . and their transcendent importance for the just functioning of our society, First Amendment rights require special safeguards. . . .

Accordingly, when a reporter is asked to appear before a grand jury and reveal confidences, I would hold that the government must (1) show that there is probable cause to believe that the newsman has information which is clearly relevant to a specific probable violation of law; (2) demonstrate that the information sought cannot be obtained by alternative means less destructive of First Amendment rights; and (3) demonstrate a compelling and overriding interest in the information. . . .

Red Lion Broadcasting Co. v. *Federal Communications Commission*
395 U.S. 367, 89 S. Ct. 1794, 23 L. Ed. 2d 371 (1969)

The Federal Communications Commission for many years imposed on television and radio broadcasters a "fairness doctrine," requiring that broadcasters present discussion of public issues and that each side of those issues be given fair coverage. In this case it ruled that the Red Lion Broadcasting Company had failed to meet its obligation under the doctrine by broadcasting a personal attack on Fred Cook, a left-wing author, and ordered it to send a transcript of the program to Cook and provide him with reply time, whether or not he could pay for it. On appeal, the Court of Appeals for the District of Columbia Circuit upheld the FCC position. After the commencement of the Red Lion litigation, the FCC adopted regulations designed to make the personal-attack aspect of the fairness doctrine more precise and more readily enforceable. The Court of Appeals for the Seventh Circuit, however, held that these regulations violated the First Amendment in *Radio Television News Directors Association* v. *United States* (referred to as *RTNDA* by the Supreme Court). The Supreme Court granted certiorari in both *Red Lion* and *RTNDA* and decided them jointly. *Opinion of the Court:* <u>White</u>, *Warren, Black, Harlan, Brennan, Stewart, Fortas, Marshall. Not participating: Douglas.*

MR. JUSTICE WHITE delivered the opinion of the Court.

The broadcasters challenge the fairness doctrine and its specific manifestations in the personal attack and political editorial rules on conventional First Amendment grounds, alleging that the rules abridge their freedom of speech and press. Their contention is that the First Amendment protects their desire to use their allotted frequencies continuously to broadcast whatever they choose, and to exclude whomever they choose from ever using that frequency. No man may be prevented from saying or publishing what he thinks, or from refusing in his speech or other utterances to give equal weight to the views of his opponents. This right, they say, applies equally to broadcasters.

A

Although broadcasting is clearly a medium affected by a First Amendment interest, differences in the characteristics of news media justify differences in the First Amendment standards applied to them. For example, the ability of new technology to produce sounds more raucous than those of the human voice justifies restrictions on the sound level, and on the hours and places of use, of sound trucks so long as the restrictions are reasonable and applied without discrimination. *Kovacs* v. *Cooper* (1949). . . .

When two people converse face to face, both should not speak at once if either is to be clearly understood. But the range of the human voice is so limited that there could be meaningful communications if half the people in the United States were talking and the other half listening. Just as clearly, half the people might publish and the other half read. But the reach of radio signals is incomparably greater than the range of the human voice and the problem of interference is a massive reality. The lack of know-how and equipment may keep many from the air, but only a tiny fraction of those with resources and intelligence can hope to communicate by radio at the same time if intelligible communication is to be had, even if the entire radio spectrum is utilized in the present state of commercially acceptable technology.

It was this fact, and the chaos which ensued from permitting anyone to use any frequency at whatever power level he wished, which made necessary the enactment of the Radio Act of 1927 and the Communications Act of 1934. It would be strange if the First Amendment, aimed at protecting and furthering communications, prevented the Government from making radio communication possible by requiring licenses to broadcast and by limiting the number of licenses so as not to overcrowd the spectrum.

This has been the consistent view of the Court. Congress unquestionably has the power to grant and deny licenses and to eliminate existing stations. No one has a First Amendment right to a license or to monopolize a radio frequency; to deny a station license because "the public interest" requires it "is not a denial of free speech."

By the same token, as far as the First Amendment is concerned those who are licensed stand no better than those to whom licenses are refused. A license permits broadcasting, but the licensee has no constitutional right to be the one who holds the license or to monopolize a radio frequency to the exclusion of his fellow citizens. There is nothing in the First Amendment which prevents the Government from requiring a licensee to share his frequency with others and to conduct himself as a proxy or fiduciary with obligations to present those views and voices which are representative of his community and which would otherwise, by necessity, be barred from the airwaves.

This is not to say that the First Amendment is irrelevant to public broadcasting. The people as a whole retain their interest in free speech by radio and their collective right to have the medium function consistently with the ends and purposes of the First Amendment. It is the right of the viewers and listeners, not the right of the broadcasters, which is paramount. It is the purpose of the First Amendment to preserve an uninhibited marketplace of ideas in which truth will ultimately prevail, rather than to countenance monopolization of that market, whether it be by the Government itself or a private licensee. It is the right of the public to receive suitable access to social, political, esthetic, moral, and other ideas and experiences which is crucial here. That right may not constitutionally be abridged either by Congress or by the FCC.

B

Rather than confer frequency monopolies on a relatively small number of licensees, in a Nation of 200,000,000, the Government could surely have decreed that each frequency should be shared among all or some of those who wish to use it, each being assigned a portion of the broadcast day or the broadcast week. The ruling and regulations at issue here do not go quite so far. They assert that under specified circumstances, a licensee must offer to make available a reasonable amount of broadcast time to those who have a view different from that which has already been expressed on his station. The expression of a political endorsement, or of a personal attack while dealing with a controversial public issue, simply triggers this time sharing. As we have said, the First Amendment confers no right on licensees to prevent others from broadcasting on "their" frequencies and no right to an unconditional monopoly of a scarce resource which the Government has denied others the right to use.

Nor can we say that it is inconsistent with the First Amendment goal of producing an informed public capable of conducting its own affairs to require a broadcaster to permit answers to personal attacks occurring in the course of discussing controversial issues, or to require that the political opponents of those endorsed by the station be given a chance to communicate with the public. Otherwise, station owners and a few networks would have unfettered power to make time available only to the highest bidders, to communicate only their own views on public issues, people and candidates, and to permit on the air only those with whom they agreed. There is no sanctuary in the First Amendment for unlimited private censorship operating in a medium not open to all. "Freedom of the press from governmental interference under the First Amendment does not sanction repression of that freedom by private interests." *Associated Press* v. *United States* (1945).

C

It is strenuously argued, however, that if political editorials or personal attacks will trigger an obligation in broadcasters to afford the opportunity for expression to speakers who need not pay for time and whose views are unpalatable to the licensees, then broadcasters will be irresistibly forced to self-censorship and their coverage of controversial public issues will be eliminated or at least rendered totally ineffective. Such a result would indeed be a serious matter, for should licensees actually eliminate their coverage of controversial issues, the purposes of the doctrine would be stifled. . . .

That this will occur now seems unlikely, however, since if present licensees should suddenly prove timorous, the Commission is not powerless to insist that they give adequate and fair attention to public issues. It does not violate the First Amendment to treat licensees given the privilege of using scarce radio frequencies as proxies for the entire community, obligated to give suitable time and attention to matters of great public concern. To condition the granting or renewal of licenses on a willingness to present representative community views on controversial issues is consistent with the ends and purposes of those constitutional provisions forbidding the abridgment of freedom of speech and freedom of the press.

In view of the scarcity of broadcast frequencies, the Government's role in allocating those frequencies, and the legitimate claims of those unable without governmental assistance to gain access to those frequencies for expression of their views, we hold the regulations and ruling at issue here are both authorized by statute and constitutional. The judgment of the Court of Appeals in *Red Lion* is affirmed and that in *RTNDA* reversed and the causes remanded for proceedings consistent with this opinion.

Memorandum Opinion and Order
Federal Communications Commission
2 FCC Rec'd. Vol. 17 (August 4, 1987)

The Federal Communications Commission's "fairness doctrine" had long required broadcasters who presented views on controversial issues of public importance to grant access to those who held opposing views. The Commission ruled that television station WTVH had violated the "fairness doctrine" when it broadcast a series of editorial advertisements advocating the construction of a nuclear plant but failed to broadcast any contrasting viewpoints on the issue. On appeal, the Court of Appeals for the District of Columbia Circuit held that the FCC had acted improperly in not responding to station's argument that the fairness doctrine violated the First Amendment and remanded the case to the Commission for reconsideration. In its *1985 Fairness Report*, the Commission had already raised questions about the doctrine, concluding that it discouraged broadcasting on controversial issues of public importance and encouraged excessive governmental intrusion into the operations of the electronic press. In light of the importance of the issue, the Commission invited comments from the interested members of the public and, based on not only those comments but also its earlier report and its experience in administering the doctrine, issued its opinion.

CONSTITUTIONAL CONSIDERATIONS UNDER *RED LION*

37. Eighteen years ago, the Supreme Court, in *Red Lion Broadcasting Co.* v. *FCC*, clearly articulated a First Amendment standard for evaluating broadcast regulation which provided less protection to the speech of broadcast journalists than that accorded to journalists in other media. The Court held that, "[i]n view of the scarcity of broadcast frequencies, the Government's role in allocating those frequencies, and the legitimate claims of those unable without government assistance to gain access to those frequencies for expression of their views," the government could require persons who were granted a license to operate "as a proxy or fiduciary with obligations to present those views and voices which are representative of his community."

The Court in *Red Lion* expressly stated that it would reconsider its holding "if experience with the administration of [the fairness doctrine] indicates that [it] ha[s] the net effect of reducing rather than enhancing the volume and quality of coverage [of controversial issues of public importance]."

2. Application of the *Red Lion* Standard

39. Under the standard enunciated by the Supreme Court for assessing the constitutionality of broadcast regulation, "it is the right of the viewers and listeners and not the broadcasters which are paramount." This standard permits the government to regulate the speech of broadcasters in order to promote the interest of the public in obtaining access to diverse viewpoints.

(a) Chilling Effect of the Doctrine

42. In the *1985 Fairness Report*, the Commission evaluated the efficacy of the fairness doctrine in achieving its regulatory objective. Based upon the compelling evidence of record, the Commission determined that the fairness doctrine, in operation, thwarts the purpose that it is designed to promote. Instead of enhancing the discussion of controversial issues of public importance, the Commission found that the fairness doctrine, in operation, "chills" speech.

43. The Commission documented that the fairness doctrine provides broadcasters with a powerful incentive not to air controversial issue programming above that minimal amount required by the first part of the doctrine. Each time a broadcaster presents what may be construed as a controversial issue of public importance, it runs the risk of a complaint being filed, resulting in litigation and penalties, including loss of license. This risk still exists even if a broadcaster has met its obligations by airing contrasting viewpoints, because the process necessarily involves a vague standard, the application and meaning of which is hard to predict. Therefore, by limiting the amount of controversial issue programming to that required by the first prong

(i.e., its obligation to cover controversial issues of vital importance to the community), a licensee is able to lessen the substantial burdens associated with the second prong of the doctrine (i.e., its obligation to present contrasting viewpoints) while conforming to the strict letter of its regulatory obligations. The licensee, consistent with its fairness doctrine obligations, may forego coverage of other issues that, although important, do not rise to the level of being vital.

45. Furthermore, the Commission determined that the doctrine inherently provides incentives that are more favorable to the expression of orthodox and well-established opinion with respect to controversial issues than to less established viewpoints. The Commission pointed out that a number of broadcasters who were denied or threatened with the denial of renewal of their licenses on fairness grounds had provided controversial issue programming far in excess of the typical broadcaster. Yet these broadcasters espoused provocative opinions that many found to be abhorrent and extreme, thereby increasing the probability that these broadcasters would be subject to fairness doctrine challenges. The Commission consequently expressed concern that the doctrine, in operation, may have penalized or impeded the expression of unorthodox or unpopular opinion, depriving the public of debates on issues of public opinion that are "uninhibited, robust, and wide-open." The doctrine's encouragement to cover only major or significant viewpoints, with which much of the public will be familiar, inhibits First Amendment goals of ensuring that the public has access to innovative and less popular viewpoints.

46. As noted above, these various incentives are not merely speculative. The record compiled in the fairness inquiry revealed over 60 reported instances in which the fairness doctrine inhibited broadcasters' coverage of controversial issues.

(b) The Extent and Necessity of Government Intervention into Editorial Discretion

53. In this regard, the Commission noted that, under the fairness doctrine, a broadcaster is only required to air "*major* viewpoints and shades of opinion" to fulfill its balanced programming obligation under the second part of the doctrine. In administering the fairness doctrine, therefore,

the Commission is obliged to differentiate between "significant" viewpoints which warrant presentation to fulfill the balanced programming obligation and those viewpoints that are not deemed "major" and thus need not be presented. The doctrine forces the government to make subjective and vague value judgments among various opinions on controversial issues to determine whether a licensee has complied with its regulatory obligations.

54. In addition, the Commission expressed concern that the fairness doctrine provides a dangerous vehicle—which had been exercised in the past by unscrupulous officials—for the intimidation of broadcasters who criticize governmental policy. It concluded that the inherently subjective evaluation of program content by the Commission in administering the doctrine contravenes fundamental First Amendment principles. We reaffirm these determinations and find that enforcement of the fairness doctrine necessarily injects the government into the editorial process of broadcast journalists.

61. In sum, the fairness doctrine in operation disserves both the public's right to diverse sources of information and the broadcaster's interest in free expression. Its chilling effect thwarts its intended purpose, and it results in excessive and unnecessary government intervention into the editorial processes of broadcast journalists. We hold, therefore, that under the constitutional standard established by *Red Lion* and its progeny, the fairness doctrine contravenes the First Amendment and its enforcement is no longer in the public interest.

65. We believe that the *1985 Fairness Report*, as reaffirmed and further elaborated on in today's action, provides the Supreme Court with the basis on which to reconsider its application of constitutional principles that were developed for a telecommunications market that is markedly different from today's market. We further believe that the scarcity rationale developed in the *Red Lion* decision and successive cases no longer justifies a different standard of First Amendment review for the electronic press.

72. Today's telecommunications market offers individuals a plethora of information outlets to which they have access on a daily basis. Indeed, this market is strikingly different from even that offered by the daily print media. While there are

11,443 broadcast stations nationwide, recent evidence indicates that there are only 1657 daily newspapers overall. On a local level, 96% of the public has access to five or more television stations, while only 125 cities have two or more local newspapers. The one-newspaper town is becoming an increasing phenomenon. Our review of the Supreme Court's statements on the relationship between constitutional principles and technological developments leads us to conclude that it would now be appropriate for the Supreme Court to reassess its *Red Lion* decision.

78. Nevertheless, we recognize that technological advancements and the transformation of the telecommunications market described above have not eliminated spectrum scarcity. All goods, however, are ultimately scarce, and there must be a system through which to allocate their use. Although a free enterprise system relies heavily on a system of property rights and voluntary exchange to allocate most of these goods, other methods of allocation, including first-come-first-served, administrative hearings, lotteries, and auctions, are or have been relied on for certain other goods. Whatever the method of allocation, there is not any logical connection between the method of allocation for a particular

good and the level of constitutional protection afforded to the uses of that good.

97. We believe that the role of the electronic press in our society is the same as that of the printed press. Both are sources of information and viewpoint. Accordingly, the reasons for proscribing government intrusion into the editorial discretion of print journalists provide the same basis for proscribing such interference into the editorial discretion of broadcast journalists. The First Amendment was adopted to protect the people *not from journalists, but from government.* It gives the people the right to receive ideas that are unfettered by government interference. We fail to see how that right changes when individuals choose to receive ideas from the electronic media instead of the print media. There is no doubt that the electronic media is powerful and that broadcasters can abuse their freedom of speech. But the framers of the Constitution believed that the potential for abuse of private freedoms posed far less a threat to democracy than the potential for abuse by a government given the power to control the press. We concur. We therefore believe that full First Amendment protections against content regulation should apply equally to the electronic and the printed press.

New York Times v. *Sullivan*
376 U.S. 254, 84 S. Ct. 710, 11 L. Ed. 2d 686 (1964)

L. B. Sullivan, commissioner of public affairs in Montgomery, Alabama, brought suit charging that he had been libeled by an advertisement that a civil rights group published in *The New York Times.* The ad, which criticized the treatment of blacks by the Montgomery police, contained several minor factual errors. A jury in Alabama awarded Sullivan $500,000 in damages, and the state supreme court affirmed the trial judgment. Meanwhile, similar suits were filed by other plaintiffs in Alabama against the *Times* and the Columbia Broadcasting Company for combined damages of $7 million. *Opinion of the Court:* <u>Brennan</u>, *Warren, Clark, Harlan, Stewart, White. Concurring opinions:* <u>Black</u>, *Douglas;* <u>Goldberg</u>, *Douglas.*

MR. JUSTICE BRENNAN delivered the opinion of the Court.

We are required in this case to determine for the first time the extent to which the constitutional protections for speech and press limit a State's power to award damages in a libel action

brought by a public official against critics of his official conduct. . . .

Under Alabama law as applied in this case, a publication is "libelous per se" if the words "tend to injure a person . . . in his reputation" or to "bring [him] into public contempt"; the trial court stated that the standard was met if the words are such as to "injure him in his public office, or impute misconduct to him in his office, or want of official integrity, or want of fidelity to a public trust. . . . "The jury must find that the words were published "of and concerning" the plaintiff, but where the plaintiff is a public official his place in the governmental hierarchy is sufficient evidence to support a finding that his reputation has been affected by statements that reflect upon the agency of which he is in charge. Once "libel per se" has been established, the defendant has no defense as to stated facts unless he can persuade the jury that they were true in all their particulars. . . . Unless he can discharge the burden of proving truth, general damages are presumed, and may be awarded without proof of pecuniary injury. . . .

The question before us is whether this rule of liability, as applied to an action brought by a public official against critics of his official conduct, abridges the freedom of speech and of the press that is guaranteed by the First and Fourteenth Amendments. . . .

. . . We consider this case against the background of a profound national commitment to the principle that debate on public issues should be uninhibited, robust, and wide-open, and that it may well include vehement, caustic, and sometimes unpleasantly sharp attacks on government and public officials. . . .

Authoritative interpretations of the First Amendment guarantees have consistently refused to recognize an exception for any test of truth—whether administered by judges, juries, or administrative officials—and especially one that puts the burden of proving truth on the speaker. . . . Erroneous statement is inevitable in free debate, and . . . it must be protected if the freedoms of expression are to have the "breathing space" that they "need . . . to survive," *N.A.A.C.P.* v. *Button*, 1963. . . .

Injury to official reputation affords no more warrant for repressing speech that would otherwise be free than does factual error. . . . Criticism of . . . official conduct does not lose its constitutional protection merely because it is effective criticism and hence diminishes . . . official reputations.

If neither factual error nor defamatory content suffices to remove the constitutional shield from criticism of official conduct, the combination of the two elements is no less inadequate. This is the lesson to be drawn from the great controversy over the Sedition Act of 1798, . . . which first crystallized a national awareness of the central meaning of the First Amendment. . . .

Although the Sedition Act was never tested in this Court, the attack upon its validity has carried the day in the court of history. Fines levied in its prosecution were repaid by Act of Congress on the ground that it was unconstitutional. . . . A broad consensus has developed that the Act, because of the restraint it imposed upon criticism of government and public officials, was inconsistent with the First Amendment.

What a State may not constitutionally bring about by means of a criminal statute is likewise beyond the reach of its civil law of libel. The fear of damage awards under a rule such as that invoked by the Alabama courts here may be markedly more inhibiting than the fear of prosecution under a criminal statute. . . . The judgment awarded in this case—without the need for any proof of actual pecuniary loss—was one thousand times greater than the maximum fine provided by the Alabama criminal statute, and one hundred times greater than that provided by the Sedition Act. . . .

The state rule of law is not saved by its allowance of the defense of truth. . . . A rule compelling the critic of official conduct to guarantee the truth of all his factual assertions—and to do so on pain of libel judgments virtually unlimited in amount—leads to . . . "self-censorship." Allowance of the defense of truth, with the burden of proving it on the defendant, does not mean that only false speech will be deterred. . . . Under such a rule, would-be critics of official conduct may be deterred from voicing their criticism, even though it is believed to be true and even though it is in fact true, because of doubt whether it can be proved in court or fear of the expense of having to do so. They tend to make only statements which "steer far wider of the unlawful zone." *Speiser* v. *Randall* 1958. . . . The rule thus dampens the vigor and limits the variety of public debate. It is inconsistent with the First and Fourteenth Amendments.

The constitutional guarantees require, we think, a federal rule that prohibits a public official from recovering damages for a defamatory falsehood relating to his official conduct unless he proves that the statement was made with "actual malice"—that is, with knowledge that it was false or with reckless disregard of whether it was false or not. . . .

Since respondent may seek a new trial, we deem that considerations of effective judicial administration require us to review the evidence in the present record to determine whether it could constitutionally support a judgment for respondent. . . .

Applying these standards, we consider that the proof presented to show actual malice lacks the convincing clarity which the constitutional standard demands, and hence that it would not constitutionally sustain the judgment for respondent under the proper rule of law. . . .

Reversed and remanded.

MR. JUSTICE BLACK, with whom MR. JUSTICE DOUGLAS joins, concurring.

I concur in reversing this half-million-dollar judgment against the New York Times Company and the four individual defendants. . . . I vote to reverse exclusively on the ground that the Times

and the individual defendants had an absolute, unconditional constitutional right to publish in the Times advertisement their criticisms of the Montgomery agencies and officials. . . .

The half-million-dollar verdict . . . give[s] dramatic proof . . . that state libel laws threaten the very existence of an American press virile enough to publish unpopular views on public affairs and bold enough to criticize the conduct of public officials. . . .

In my opinion the Federal Constitution has dealt with this deadly danger to the press in the only way possible without leaving the free press open to destruction—by granting the press an absolute immunity for criticism of the way public officials do their public duty. . . . To punish the exercise of this right to discuss public affairs or to penalize it through libel judgments is to abridge or shut off discussion of the very kind most needed. This Nation, I suspect, can live in peace without libel suits based on public discussions of public affairs and public officials. But I doubt that a country can live in freedom where its people can be made to suffer physically or financially for criticizing their government, its actions, or its officials.

Miller v. *California*
413 U.S. 15, 93 S. Ct. 2607, 37 L. Ed. 2d 419 (1973)

Paris Adult Theater I v. *Slaton*
413 U.S. 49, 93 S. Ct. 2628, 37 L. Ed. 2d 446 (1973)

In these companion cases, the Burger Court sought to develop more adequate obscenity standards. In *Miller* the appellant had been convicted of violating a California law that prohibited the mailing of unsolicited obscene materials. The trial court in this case had instructed the jury to evaluate the materials' obscenity in light of the contemporary community standards in California. In *Slaton*, state officials had sued under Georgia civil law to enjoin the showing of two allegedly obscene films. The trial court ruled that the display of these films to consenting adults was constitutionally protected. The Georgia Supreme Court reversed, and the United States Supreme Court granted certiorari.

The Court divided identically on the two cases. Chief Justice Burger's opinion of the Court is taken from *Miller;* Justice Brennan's dissent, from *Slaton. Opinion of the Court: Burger, White, Powell, Blackmun, Rehnquist. Dissenting opinions: Douglas; Brennan, Stewart, Marshall.*

Mr. Chief Justice Burger delivered the opinion of the Court. . . .

This much has been categorically settled by the Court, that obscene material is unprotected by the First Amendment. . . . We acknowledge, however, the inherent dangers of undertaking to regulate any form of expression. State statutes designed to regulate obscene materials must be carefully limited. . . .

The basic guidelines for the trier of fact must be: *(a)* whether "the average person, applying contemporary community standards" would find that the work, taken as a whole, appeals to the prurient interest . . . *(b)* whether the work depicts or describes, in a patently offensive way, sexual conduct specifically defined by the applicable state law; and *(c)* whether the work, taken as a whole, lacks serious literary, artistic, political, or scientific value. . . .

We emphasize that it is not our function to propose regulatory schemes for the States. That must await their concrete legislative efforts. It is possible, however, to give a few plain examples of what a state statute could define for regulation under the second part *(b)* of the standard announced in this opinion. . . .

(a) Patently offensive representations or descriptions of ultimate sexual acts, normal or perverted, actual or simulated.

(b) Patently offensive representations or descriptions of masturbation, excretory functions, and lewd exhibition of the genitals.

Sex and nudity may not be exploited without limit by films or pictures exhibited or sold in places of public accommodation any more than live sex and nudity can be exhibited or sold without limit in such public places. At a minimum, prurient, patently offensive depiction or description of sexual conduct must have serious literary, artistic, political, or scientific value to merit First Amendment protection. . . . For example, medical books for the education of physicians and related personnel necessarily use graphic illustrations and descriptions of human anatomy. In resolving the inevitably sensitive questions of fact and law, we must continue to rely on the jury system, accompanied by the safeguards that judges, rules of evidence, presumption of innocence and other protective features provide, as we do with rape, murder, and a host of other offenses against society and its individual members.

Mr. Justice Brennan, author of the opinions of the Court, or the plurality opinions in *Roth* v. *United States* [1957], *Jacobellis* v. *Ohio* [1964], *Ginzburg* v. *United States* [1966], *Mishkin* v. *New York* [1966], and *Memoirs* v. *Massachusetts* [1966], has abandoned his former position and now maintains that no formulation of this Court, the Congress, or the States can adequately distinguish obscene material unprotected by the First Amendment from protected expression. . . . Paradoxically, Mr. Justice Brennan indicates that suppression of unprotected obscene material is permissible to avoid exposure to unconsenting adults, as in this case, and to juveniles, although he gives no indication of how the division between protected and nonprotected materials may be drawn with greater precision for these purposes than for regulation of commercial exposure to consenting adults only. . . . If the inability to define regulated materials with ultimate, godlike precision altogether removes the power of the States or the Congress to regulate, then "hard core" pornography may be exposed without limit to the juvenile, the passerby, and the consenting adult alike, as, indeed, Mr. Justice Douglas contends. . . .

It is certainly true that the absence, since *Roth* [v. *United States* (1957)], of a single majority view of this Court as to proper standards for testing obscenity has placed a strain on both state and federal courts. But today, for the first time since *Roth* was decided in 1957, a majority of this Court has agreed on concrete guidelines to isolate "hard core" pornography from expression protected by the First Amendment. . . . No amount of "fatigue" should lead us to adopt a convenient "institutional" rationale—an absolutist, "anything goes" view of the First Amendment—because it will lighten our burdens. . . .

Under a national Constitution, fundamental First Amendment limitations on the powers of the States do not vary from community to community, but this does not mean that there are, or should or can be, fixed, uniform national standards of precisely what appeals to the "prurient interest" or is "patently offensive." These are essentially questions of fact, and our nation is simply too big and too diverse for this Court to reasonably expect that such standards could be articulated for all 50 States in a single formulation, even assuming the prerequisite consensus exists. . . .

It is neither realistic nor constitutionally sound to read the First Amendment as requiring that the people of Maine or Mississippi accept public depiction of conduct found tolerable in Las Vegas, or New York City. . . . The primary concern with requiring a jury to apply the standard of "the average person, applying contemporary community standards" is to be certain that, so far as material is not aimed at a deviant group, it will be judged by its impact on an average person, rather than a particularly susceptible or sensitive person—or indeed a totally insensitive one. . . . We hold the requirement that the jury evaluate the materials with reference to "contemporary standards of the State of California" serves this protective purpose and is constitutionally adequate.

Vacated and remanded for further proceedings.

MR. JUSTICE BRENNAN, with whom MR. JUSTICE STEWART and MR. JUSTICE MARSHALL join, dissenting.

This case requires the Court to confront once again the vexing problem of reconciling state efforts to suppress sexually oriented expression with the protections of the First Amendment, as applied to the States through the Fourteenth Amendment. No other aspect of the First Amendment has, in recent years, demanded so substantial a commitment of our time, generated such disharmony of views, and remained so resistant to the formulation of stable and manageable standards. I am convinced that the approach initiated 15 years ago in *Roth* v. *United States* . . . and culminating in the Court's decision today, cannot bring stability to this area of the law without jeopardizing fundamental First Amendment values, and I have concluded that the time has come to make a significant departure from that approach. . . .

. . . We have failed to formulate a standard that sharply distinguishes protected from unprotected speech, and out of necessity, we have resorted to the *Redrup* [v. *New York* (1967)] approach, which resolves cases as between the parties, but offers only the most obscure guidance to legislation, adjudication by other courts, and primary conduct. . . .

Of course, the vagueness problem would be largely of our own creation if it stemmed primarily from our failure to reach a consensus on any one standard. But after 16 years of experimentation and debate I am reluctantly forced to the conclusion that none of the available formulas, including the one announced today, can reduce the vagueness to a tolerable level while at the same time striking an acceptable balance between the protections of the First and Fourteenth Amendments, on the one hand, and on the other the asserted state interest in regulating the dissemination of certain sexually oriented materials. Any effort to draw a constitutionally acceptable boundary on state power must resort to such indefinite concepts as "prurient interest," "patent offensiveness," "serious literary value," and the like. The meaning of these concepts necessarily varies with the experience outlook, and even idiosyncrasies of the person defining them. . . .

The vagueness of the standards in the obscenity area produces a number of separate problems, and any improvement must rest on an understanding that the problems are to some extent distinct. First, a vague statute fails to provide adequate notice to persons who are engaged in the type of conduct that the statute could be thought to proscribe. . . .

In addition to problems that arise when any criminal statute fails to afford fair notice of what it forbids, a vague statute in the areas of speech and press creates a second level of difficulty. We have indicated that "stricter standards of permissible statutory vagueness may be applied to a statute having a potentially inhibiting effect on speech; a man may the less be required to act at his peril here, because the free dissemination of ideas may be the loser." *Smith* v. *California* [1959]. . . . To implement this general principle, and recognizing the inherent vagueness of any definition of obscenity, we have held that the definition of obscenity must be drawn as narrowly as possible so as to minimize the interference with protected expression. . . . A vague statute in this area creates a third, although admittedly more subtle, set of problems. These problems concern the institutional stress that inevitably results where the line separating protected from unprotected speech is excessively vague. . . .

As a result of our failure to define standards with predictable application to any given piece of material, there is no probability of regularity in obscenity decisions by state and lower federal courts. That is not to say that these courts have performed badly in this area or paid insufficient attention to the principles we have established. The problem is, rather, that one cannot say with certainty that material is obscene until at least five members of this Court, applying inevitably obscure standards, have pronounced it so. The number of obscenity cases on our docket gives ample testimony to the burden that has been placed upon this Court.

But the sheer number of the cases does not define the full extent of the institutional problem. For, quite apart from the number of cases involved and the need to make a fresh constitutional determination in each case, we are tied to the "absurd business of perusing and viewing the miserable stuff that pours into the Court. . . ." *Interstate Circuit, Inc.* v. *Dallas*, [1959]. . . . In addition, the uncertainty of the standards creates a continuing source of tension between state and federal courts, since the need for an independent determination by this Court seems to render superfluous even the most conscientious analysis by state tribunals. And our inability to justify our decisions with a persuasive rationale—or indeed, any rationale at all—necessarily creates the impression that we are merely second-guessing state court judges.

. . . Given these inevitable side-effects of state efforts to suppress what is assumed to be *unprotected* speech, we must scrutinize with care the state interest that is asserted to justify the suppression. For in the absence of some very substantial interest in suppressing such speech, we can hardly condone the ill-effects that seem to flow inevitably from the effort. . . .

. . . While I cannot say that the interests of the State—apart from the question of juveniles and unconsenting adults—are trivial or nonexistent, I am compelled to conclude that these interests cannot justify the substantial damage to constitutional rights and to this Nation's judicial machinery that inevitably results from state efforts to bar the distribution even of unprotected material to consenting adults. . . . I would hold, therefore, that at least in the absence of distribution to juveniles or obtrusive exposure to unconsenting adults, the First and Fourteenth Amendments prohibit the state and federal governments from attempting wholly to suppress sexually oriented materials on the basis of their allegedly "obscene" contents. Nothing in this approach precludes those governments from taking action to serve what may be strong and legitimate interests through regulation of the manner of distribution of sexually oriented material. . . .

Reno v. *American Civil Liberties Union*
521 U.S. S. Ct. 2329, 138 L. Ed. 2d 874 117 (1997)

Congress enacted the Telecommunications Act of 1996 to encourage the rapid deployment of new telecommunications technologies. After committee hearings on the act, amendments were added in executive committee and on the floor of Congress with the purpose of protecting minors from harmful materials on the Internet. These amendments came to be known as the Communications Decency Act of 1996 (CDA). Section 223(a)(1) of CDA criminalized the "knowing" transmission of "obscene or indecent" messages to any recipient under eighteen years of age. Section 223(d) prohibited the "knowing," sending, or displaying to minors of any message "that, in context, depicts or describes, in terms patently offensive as measured by contemporary community standards, sexual or excretory activities or organs." CDA also established defenses against prosecution under the act for those who took "good faith, effective actions" to restrict access to minors and for those who restricted access by requiring designated forms of age proof, such as a verified credit card or an adult identification number.

Immediately after enactment of CDA, several plaintiffs filed suit, challenging sections 223(a)(1) and 223(d) as in violation of the First Amendment. A three-judge District Court convened pursuant to the act entered a preliminary injunction against enforcement of both challenged provisions, and the Government appealed this ruling to the Supreme Court under the act's special review provisions. *Opinion of the Court: Stevens, Scalia, Kennedy, Souter, Thomas, Ginsburg, Breyer. Opinion concurring in the judgment in part and dissenting in part: O'Connor, Rehnquist.*

JUSTICE STEVENS delivered the opinion of the Court.

At issue is the constitutionality of two statutory provisions enacted to protect minors from "indecent" and "patently offensive" communications on the Internet. Notwithstanding the legitimacy and importance of the congressional goal of protecting children from harmful materials, we agree with the three-judge District Court that the statute abridges "the freedom of speech" protected by the First Amendment.

The District Court made extensive findings of fact, most of which were based on a detailed stipulation prepared by the parties. The findings describe the character and the dimensions of the Internet, the availability of sexually explicit material in that medium, and the problems confronting age verification for recipients of Internet communications. Because those findings provide the underpinnings for the legal issues, we begin with a summary of the undisputed facts.

Sexually explicit material on the Internet includes text, pictures, and chat and "extends from the modestly titillating to the hardest-core." Though such material is widely available, users seldom encounter such content accidentally. "A document's title or a description of the document will usually appear before the document itself . . . and in many cases the user will receive detailed information about a site's content before he or she need take the step to access the document. Almost all sexually explicit images are preceded by warnings as to the content." For that reason, the "odds are slim" that a user would enter a sexually explicit site by accident. Unlike communications received by radio or television, "the receipt of information on the Internet requires a series of affirmative steps more deliberate and directed than merely turning a dial. A child requires some sophistication and some ability to read to retrieve material and thereby to use the Internet unattended."

Systems have been developed to help parents control the material that may be available on a home computer with Internet access. "Although parental control software currently can screen for certain suggestive words or for known sexually explicit sites, it cannot now screen for sexually explicit images." Nevertheless, the evidence indicates that "a reasonably effective method by which parents can prevent their children from accessing sexually explicit and other material which parents may believe is inappropriate for their children will soon be available."

The problem of age verification differs for different uses of the Internet. The District Court categorically determined that there "is no effective way to determine the identify or the age of a user who is accessing material through e-mail, mail exploders, newsgroups or chat rooms." The Government offered no evidence that there was a reliable way to screen recipients and participants in such fora for age. Moreover, even if it were technologically feasible to block minors' access to newsgroups and chat rooms containing discussions of art, politics or other subjects that potentially elicit "indecent" or "patently offensive" contributions, it would not be possible to block their access to that material and "still allow them access to the remaining content, even if the overwhelming majority of that content was not indecent."

Technology exists by which an operator of a Web site may condition access on the verification of requested information such as a credit card number or an adult password. Credit card verification is only feasible, however, either in connection with a commercial transaction in which the card is used, or by payment to a verification agency. Using credit card possession as a surrogate for proof of age would impose costs on noncommercial Web sites that would require many of them to shut down. For that reason, at the time of the trial, credit card verification was "effectively unavailable to a substantial number of Internet content providers." Moreover, the imposition of such a requirement "would completely bar adults who do not have a credit card and lack the resources to obtain one from accessing any blocked material."

Commercial pornographic sites that charge their users for access have assigned them passwords as a method of age verification. The record does not contain any evidence concerning the reliability of these technologies. Even if passwords are effective for commercial purveyors of indecent material, the District Court found that an adult password requirement would impose significant burdens on noncommercial sites, both because they would discourage users from accessing their sites and because the cost of creating and maintaining such screening systems would be "beyond their reach."

In sum, the District Court found: "Even if credit card verification or adult password verification were implemented, the Government presented no testimony as to how such systems could ensure that the user of the password or credit card is in fact over 18. The burdens imposed by credit card verification and adult password verification systems make them effectively unavailable to a substantial number of Internet content providers."

In arguing for reversal, the Government contends that the CDA is plainly constitutional under three of our prior decisions: (1) *Ginsberg* v. *New York* (1968); (2) *FCC* v. *Pacifica Foundation* (1978); and (3) *Renton* v. *Playtime Theatres, Inc.* (1986). A close look at these cases, however, raises—rather than relieves—doubts concerning the constitutionality of the CDA.

In *Ginsberg*, we upheld the constitutionality of a New York statute that prohibited selling to minors under 17 years of age material that was considered obscene as to them even if not obscene as to adults. In four important respects, the statute upheld in *Ginsberg* was narrower than the CDA. First, we noted in *Ginsberg* that "the prohibition against sales to minors does not bar parents who so desire from purchasing the magazines for their children." Under the CDA, by contrast, neither the parents' consent—nor even their participation—in the communication would avoid the application of the statute. Sec-

ond, the New York statute applied only to commercial transactions, whereas the CDA contains no such limitation. Third, the New York statute cabined its definition of material that is harmful to minors with the requirement that it be "utterly without redeeming social importance for minors." The CDA fails to provide us with any definition of the term "indecent" as used in 223(a)(1) and, importantly, omits any requirement that the "patently offensive" material covered by 223(d) lack serious literary, artistic, political, or scientific value. Fourth, the New York statute defined a minor as a person under the age of 17, whereas the CDA, in applying to all those under 18 years, includes an additional year of those nearest majority.

In *Pacifica*, we upheld a declaratory order of the Federal Communications Commission, holding that the broadcast of a recording of a 12-minute monologue entitled "Filthy Words" that had previously been delivered to a live audience "could have been the subject of administrative sanctions." . . . [T]here are significant differences between the order upheld in *Pacifica* and the CDA. First, the order in *Pacifica*, issued by an agency that had been regulating ratio stations for decades, targeted a specific broadcast that represented a rather dramatic departure from traditional program content in order to designate when—rather than whether—it would be permissible to air such a program in that particular medium. The CDA's broad categorical prohibitions are not limited to particular times and are not dependent on any evaluation by an agency familiar with the unique characteristics of the Internet. Second, unlike the CDA, the Commission's declaratory order was not punitive; we expressly refused to decide whether the indecent broadcast "would justify a criminal prosecution." Finally, the Commission's order applied to a medium which as a matter of history had "received the most limited First Amendment protection," in large part because warnings could not adequately protect the listener from unexpected program content. The Internet, however, has no comparable history. Moreover, the District Court found that the risk of encountering indecent material by accident is remote because a series of affirmative steps is required to access specific material.

In *Renton*, we upheld a zoning ordinance that kept adult movie theaters out of residential neighborhoods. The ordinance was aimed, not at the content of the films shown in the theaters, but rather at the "secondary effects"—such as crime and deteriorating property values—that these theaters fostered. According to the Government, the CDA is constitutional because it constitutes a sort of "cyberzoning" on the Internet. But the CDA applies broadly to the entire universe of cyberspace. And the purpose of the CDA is to protect children from the primary effects of "indecent" and "patently offensive" speech, rather than any "secondary" effect of such speech. These precedents, then, surely do not require us to uphold the CDA and are fully consistent with the application of the most stringent review of its provisions.

Regardless of whether the CDA is so vague that it violates the Fifth Amendment, the many ambiguities concerning the scope of its coverage render it problematic for purposes of the First Amendment. For instance, each of the two parts of the CDA uses a different linguistic form. The first uses the word "indecent," while the second speaks of material that "in context, depicts or describes, in terms patently offensive as measured by contemporary community standards, sexual or excretory activities or organs." Given the absence of a definition of either term, this difference in language will provoke uncertainty among speakers about how the two standards relate to each other and just what they mean.

The vagueness of the CDA is a matter of special concern for two reasons. First, the CDA is a content-based regulation of speech. The vagueness of such a regulation raises special First Amendment concerns because of its obvious chilling effect on free speech. Second, the CDA is a criminal statute. In addition to the opprobrium and stigma of a criminal conviction, the CDA threatens violators with penalties including up to two years in prison for each act of violation. The severity of criminal sanctions may well cause speakers to remain silent rather than communicate even arguably unlawful words, ideas, and images.

The Government argues that the statute is no more vague than the obscenity standard this Court established in *Miller* v. *California* (1973). But that is not so. Just because a definition including three limitations is not vague, it does not follow that one of those limitations, standing by

itself, is not vague. Each of *Miller's* additional two prongs—(1) that, taken as a whole, the material appeal to the "prurient" interest, and (2) that it "lac[k] serious literary, artistic, political, or scientific value"—critically limits the uncertain sweep of the obscenity definition. The second requirement is particularly important because, unlike the "patently offensive" and "prurient interest" criteria, it is not judged by contemporary community standards. This "societal value" requirement, absent in the CDA, allows appellate courts to impose some limitations and regularity on the definition by setting, as a matter of law, a national floor for socially redeeming value.

We are persuaded that the CDA lacks the precision that the First Amendment requires when a statute regulates the content of speech. In order to deny minors access to potentially harmful speech, the CDA effectively suppresses a large amount of speech that adults have a constitutional right to receive and to address to one another. That burden on adult speech is unacceptable if less restrictive alternatives would be at least as effective in achieving the legitimate purpose that the statute was enacted to serve. It is true that we have repeatedly recognized the governmental interest in protecting children from harmful materials. But that interest does not justify an unnecessarily broad suppression of speech addressed to adults. "[R]egardless of the strength of the government's interest" in protecting children, "[t]he level of discourse reaching a mailbox simply cannot be limited to that which would be suitable for a sandbox."

In arguing that the CDA does not so diminish adult communication, the Government relies on the incorrect factual premise that prohibiting a transmission whenever it is known that one of its recipients is a minor would not interfere with adult-to-adult communication. The findings of the District Court make clear that this premise is untenable. Given the size of the potential audience for most messages, in the absence of a viable age verification process, the sender must be charged with knowing that one or more minors will likely view it. Knowledge that, for instance, one or more members of a 100-person chat group will be minor—and therefore that it would be a crime to send the group an indecent message—would surely burden communication among adults.

The District Court found that at the time of

trial existing technology did not include any effective method for a sender to prevent minors from obtaining access to its communications on the Internet without also denying access to adults. The Court found no effective way to determine the age of a user who is accessing material through e-mail, mail exploders, newsgroups, or chat rooms. As a practical matter, the Court also found that it would be prohibitively expensive for noncommercial—as well as some commercial—speakers who have Web sites to verify that their users are adults. These limitations must inevitably curtail a significant amount of adult communication on the Internet. By contrast, the District Court found that "[d]espite its limitations, currently *available user-based* software suggests that a reasonably effective method by which *parents* can prevent their children from accessing sexually explicit and other material which *parents* may believe is inappropriate for their children will soon be widely available."

The breadth of this content-based restriction of speech imposes an especially heavy burden on the Government to explain why a less restrictive provision would not be as effective as the CDA. It has not done so. Particularly in the light of the absence of any detailed findings by the Congress, or even hearings, addressing the special problems of the CDA, we are persuaded that the CDA is not narrowly tailored if that requirement has any meaning at all. We agree with the District Court's conclusion that the CDA places an unacceptably heavy burden on protected speech, and that the defenses do not constitute the sort of "narrow tailoring" that will save an otherwise patently invalid unconstitutional provision. For the foregoing reasons, the judgment of the district court is affirmed.

It is so ordered.

JUSTICE O'CONNOR, with whom THE CHIEF JUSTICE joins, concurring in the judgment in part and dissenting in part.

I write separately to explain why I view the Communications Decency Act of 1996 (CDA) as little more than an attempt by Congress to create "adult zones" on the Internet. The creation of "adult zones" is by no means a novel concept. States have long denied minors access to certain establishments frequented by adults. The Court has previously sustained such zoning laws, but

only if they respect the First Amendment rights of adults and minors. That is to say, a zoning law is valid if (i) it does not unduly restrict adult access to the material; and (ii) minors have no First Amendment right to read or view the banned material. As applied to the Internet as it exists in 1997, the "display" provision and some applications of the "indecency transmission" and "specific person" provisions fail to adhere to the first of these limiting principles by restricting adults' access to protected materials in certain circumstances. Unlike the Court, however, I would invalidate the provisions only in those circumstances.

Our cases make clear that a "zoning" law is valid only if adults are still able to obtain the regulated speech. If the law does not unduly restrict adults' access to constitutionally protected speech, however, it may be valid. In *Ginsberg* v. *New York* (1968), for example, the Court sustained a New York law that barred store owners from selling pornographic magazines to minors in part because adults could still buy those magazines. The Court in *Ginsberg* concluded that the New York law created a constitutionally adequate adult zone simply because, on its face, it denied access only to minors. The Court did not question—and therefore necessarily assumed—that an adult zone, once created, would succeed in preserving adults' access while denying minors' access to the regulated speech. Before today, there was no reason to question this assumption, for the Court has previously only considered laws that operated in the physical world, a world that with . . . the twin characteristics of geography and identity [that] enable the establishment's proprietor to prevent children from entering the establishment, but to let adults inside.

The electronic world is fundamentally different. Since users can transmit and receive messages on the Internet without revealing anything about their identities or ages, it is not currently possible to exclude persons from accessing certain messages on the basis of their identity. Cyberspace differs from the physical world in another basic way: Cyberspace is malleable. Thus, it is possible to construct barriers in cyberspace and use them to screen for identity, making cyberspace more like the physical world and, consequently, more amenable to zoning laws. This transformation of cyberspace is already underway. Internet speakers (users who post material on the Internet) have begun to zone cyberspace itself through the use of "gateway" technology. Such technology requires Internet users to enter information about themselves—perhaps an adult identification number or a credit card number—before they can access certain areas of cyberspace, much like a bouncer checks a person's driver's license before admitting him to a nightclub.

Despite this progress, the transformation of cyberspace is not complete. Although gateway technology has been available on the World Wide Web for some time now, it is not . . . ubiquitous in cyberspace, and because without it "there is no means of age verification," cyberspace still remains largely unzoned—and unzoneable. User-based zoning is also in its infancy. Although the prospects for the eventual zoning of the Internet appear promising, I agree with the Court that we must evaluate the constitutionality of the CDA as it applies to the Internet as it exists today.

Given the present state of cyberspace, I agree with the Court that the "display" provision cannot pass muster. Until gateway technology is available throughout cyberspace, and it is not in 1997, a speaker cannot be reasonably assured that the speech he displays will reach only adults because it is impossible to confine speech to an "adult zone." Thus, the only way for a speaker to avoid liability under the CDA is to refrain completely from using indecent speech. But this forced silence impinges on the First Amendment right of adults to make and obtain this speech and, for all intents and purposes, "reduce[s] the adult population [on the Internet] to reading only what is fit for children." As a result, the "display" provision cannot withstand scrutiny.

The "indecency transmission" and "specific person" provisions present a closer issue, for they are not unconstitutional in all of their applications. [B]oth provisions are constitutional as applied to a conversation involving only an adult and one or more minors, e.g., when an adult speaker sends an e-mail knowing the addressee is a minor, or when an adult and minor converse by themselves or with other minors in a chat room. In this context, these provisions are no different from the law we sustained in *Ginsberg*. The analogy to *Ginsberg* breaks down, however, when more than one adult is a party to the con-

versation. If a minor enters a chat room otherwise occupied by adults, the CDA effectively requires the adults in the room to stop using indecent speech. If they did not, they could be prosecuted under the "indecency transmission" and "specific person" provisions for any indecent statements they make to the group, since they would be transmitting an indecent message to specific persons, one of whom is a minor. The CDA is therefore akin to a law that makes it a crime for a bookstore owner to sell pornographic magazines to anyone once a minor enters his store. Even assuming such a law might be constitutional in the physical world as a reasonable alternative to excluding minors completely from the store, the absence of any means of excluding minors from chat rooms in cyberspace restricts the rights of adults to engage in indecent speech in those rooms.

There is no question that Congress intended to prohibit certain communications between one adult and one or more minors. There is also no question that Congress would have enacted a narrower version of these provisions had it known a broader version would be declared unconstitutional. I would therefore sustain the "indecency transmission" and "specific person" provisions to the extent they apply to the transmission of Internet communications where the party initiating the communication knows that all of the recipients are minors.

Whether the CDA substantially interferes with the First Amendment rights of minors, and thereby runs afoul of the second characteristic of valid zoning laws, presents a closer question. Because the CDA denies minors the right to obtain material that is "patently offensive"—even if it has some redeeming value for minors and even if it does not appeal to their prurient interests—Congress' rejection of the *Ginsberg* "harmful to minors" standard means that the CDA could ban some speech that is "indecent" (i.e., "patently offensive") but that is not obscene as to minors. I do not deny this possibility, but to prevail in a facial challenge, it is not enough for a plaintiff to show "some" overbreadth. Our cases require a proof of "real" and "substantial" overbreadth, *Broadrick* v. *Oklahoma* (1973), and appellees have not carried their burden in this case. In my view, the universe of speech constitutionally protected as to minors but banned by the CDA—

i.e., the universe of materials that is "patently offensive," but which nonetheless has some redeeming value for minors or does not appeal to their prurient interest—is a very small one. Appellees cite no examples of speech falling within this universe and do not attempt to explain why that universe is substantial "in relation to the statute's plainly legitimate sweep." Accordingly, in my view, the CDA does not burden a substantial amount of minors' constitutionally protected speech.

Thus, the constitutionality of the CDA as a zoning law hinges on the extent to which it substantially interferes with the First Amendment rights of adults. Because the rights of adults are infringed only by the "display" provision and by the "indecency transmission" and "specific person" provisions as applied to communications involving more than one adult, I would invalidate the CDA only to that extent. Insofar as the "indecency transmission" and "specific person" provisions prohibit the use of indecent speech in communications between an adult and one or more minors, however, they can and should be sustained. The Court reaches a contrary conclusion, and from that holding I respectfully dissent.

Indianapolis Anti-Pornography Ordinance (1984)

In 1984 the City-County Council of Indianapolis and Marion County, Indiana, pioneered a new approach to regulating pornography. The council concluded that pornography's implicit endorsement of the sexual subordination of women constitutes a form of sex discrimination which degrades and harms all women. It therefore authorized any woman to sue those trafficking in pornography for violating her civil rights.

The ordinance was struck down in *American Booksellers Association, Inc.* v. *Hudnut*, and the Supreme Court summarily affirmed that ruling.

Be it ordered by the City-County Council of the City of Indianapolis and of Marion County, Indiana:

(a) Findings. The City-County Council hereby makes the following findings: . . .

(2) Pornography is a discriminatory practice based on sex because its effect is to deny women equal opportunities in society. Pornography is central in creating and maintaining sex as a basis of discrimination. Pornography is a systematic practice of exploitation and subordination based on sex which differentially harms women. The bigotry and contempt it promotes, with the acts of aggression it fosters, harm women's opportunities for equality of rights in employment, education, access to and use of public accommodations, and acquisition of real property, and contribute significantly to restricting women in particular from full exercise of citizenship and participation in public life, including in neighborhoods.

(b) It is the purpose of this ordinance . . .

(8) To prevent and prohibit all discriminatory practices of sexual subordination or inequality through pornography.

(g) Discriminatory practice shall mean and include the following: . . .

(4) Trafficking in pornography: The production, sale, exhibition, or distribution of pornography.

(A) City, state and federally funded public libraries or private and public university and college libraries in which pornography is available for study, including on open shelves, shall not be construed to be trafficking in pornography, but special display presentations of pornography in said places is sex discrimination.

(B) The formation of private clubs or associations for purposes of trafficking in pornography is illegal and shall be considered a conspiracy to violate the civil rights of women.

(C) Any woman has a cause of action hereunder as a woman acting against the subordination of women. Any man, child or transsexual who alleges injury by pornography in the way women are injured by it shall also have a cause of action under this chapter.

(5) Coercion into pornographic performance. . . .

(6) Forcing pornography on a person: The forcing of pornography on any woman, man, child or transsexual in any place of employment, in education, in a home, or in any public place, except that a man, child or transsexual must allege and prove injury in the same way that a woman is injured in order to have a cause of action.

(7) Assault or physical attack due to pornography: The assault, physical attack, or injury of any woman, man, child, or transsexual in a way that is directly caused by specific pornography. The injured party shall have a claim for damages against the perpetrator(s), maker(s), distributor(s), seller(s), and exhibitor(s), and for an injunction against the specific pornography's further exhibition, distribution, or sale. . . .

(8) Defenses. Where the materials which are the subject matter of a cause of action under (4), (5), (6), or (7) of this section are pornography, it shall not be a defense that the defendant did not know or intend that the materials were pornography or sex discrimination. . . .

(v) Pornography shall mean the sexually explicit subordination of women, graphically depicted, whether in pictures or words, that includes one or more of the following:

(1) Women are presented as sexual objects who enjoy pain or humiliation; or

(2) Women are presented as sexual objects who experience sexual pleasure in being raped; or

(3) Women are presented as sexual objects tied up or cut up or mutilated or bruised or physically hurt, or as dismembered or truncated or fragmented or severed into body parts; or

(4) Women are presented being penetrated by objects or animals; or

(5) Women are presented in scenarios of degradation, injury, abasement, torture, shown as filthy or inferior, bleeding, bruised, or hurt in a context that makes these conditions sexual. . . .

(bb) Sexually explicit shall mean actual or simulated:

(1) Sexual intercourse, including genital-genital, oral-genital, anal-genital or oral-anal, whether between persons of the same or opposite sex or between women and animals; or

(2) Uncovered exhibition of the genitals, pubic region, buttocks or anus of any person.

Struck down
too close to p.c.
traditional obsenity

★

ESTABLISHMENT OF RELIGION

Everson v. Board of Education (1947)
School District of Abington Township v. Schempp (1963)
Lemon v. Kurtzman (1971)
Wallace v. Jaffree (1985)
Lee v. Weisman (1992)
Board of Education of Kiryas Joel Village School District v. Grumet (1994)
Rosenberger v. University of Virginia (1995)

FREE EXERCISE OF RELIGION

West Virginia Board of Education v. Barnette (1943)
Sherbert v. Verner (1963)
Lyng v. Northwest Indian Cemetery Protective Association (1988)
Employment Division, Department of Human Resources of Oregon v. Smith (1990)
City of Boerne v. Flores, Archbishop of San Antonio (1997)

RECONCILING THE RELIGION CLAUSES

TRENDS AND PROSPECTS

NOTES

SELECTED READING

CASES

★

6
FREEDOM OF RELIGION

"**C**ongress shall make no law respecting an establishment of religion, or prohibiting the free exercise thereof." The religion clauses of the First Amendment impose two restrictions: the Establishment Clause requires a degree of separation between church and state, and the Free Exercise Clause recognizes a sphere of religious liberty that Congress cannot invade. For almost 150 years the Supreme Court had little occasion to construe these constitutional provisions. Since 1940, however, the Court has decided over 80 religion cases. This proliferation of cases has resulted in large part from the incorporation of the religion clauses in *Cantwell* v. *Connecticut* (1940) and *Everson* v. *Board of Education* (1947), which brought state and local accommodations of religion under constitutional scrutiny for the first time.[1] The expansion of governmental activity impinging on religious practices and religiously motivated action has also contributed to the rise in litigation, as has increasing religious diversity in the United States. And along with the Court's greater involvement in disputes over religion has come intense controversy. This chapter describes how the Court has interpreted the Establishment and Free Exercise Clauses and analyzes the ongoing debate over the meaning of those provisions.

ESTABLISHMENT OF RELIGION

Everson and the Purposes of the Establishment Clause

In *Everson* v. *Board of Education* (1947) the Supreme Court outlined the interpretation of the Establishment Clause that guided its decisions through the early 1980s. Although the justices split, 5–4, in upholding New Jersey's program of providing free bus transportation to both public and nonpublic school children, both the majority and dissenters in *Everson* agreed that the Establishment Clause was meant to erect a "wall of separation" between church and state. Justice Hugo Black summarized the Court's position:

> The "establishment of religion" clause of the First Amendment means at least this: Neither a state nor the Federal Government can set up a church. Neither can pass laws which aid one religion, aid all religions, or prefer one religion over another. Neither can force nor influence a person to go to or to remain away from church against his will or force him to profess a belief or disbelief in any religion. No person can be punished for entertaining or professing religious beliefs or disbeliefs, for church attendance or non-attendance. No tax in any amount, large or small, can be levied to support any religious activities or institutions, whatever they may be called, or whatever form they may adopt to teach or practice religion. Neither a state nor the Federal Government can, openly or secretly, participate in the affairs of any religious organizations or groups and vice versa.

Three aspects of Black's statement deserve particular emphasis. First, the Court held that the Establishment Clause imposes restrictions on state activity as stringent as those imposed on the national government. Second, it ruled that the Establishment Clause prohibits any aid to religion and requires a strict neutrality not only among religions but also between religion and irreligion. Finally, as the divisions on the Court in *Everson* indicated, Black's standard did not lend itself to automatic application, and thus its endorsement by the Court did not foreclose disagreement in future Establishment Clause cases.

To support its interpretation of the Establishment Clause, the Court looked to the Framers' aims in adopting this provision. And in seeking those aims, the justices focused not on the debates in the First Congress, but on the struggle for religious liberty in Virginia, which had culminated in the disestablishment of the Episcopal Church. The history of this struggle, the Court maintained, supplied the key to understanding the Establishment Clause. To begin with, the long dispute in Virginia had engaged the attention of the other states, several of which were influenced by its outcome to eliminate their own religious establishments. Thus, the Court reasoned, the victory for religious liberty in Virginia created a national climate of opinion favorable to the separation of church and state. Even more important, the leaders of the anti-establishment forces in Virginia, James Madison and Thomas Jefferson, also played a major role in the development and adoption of the Bill of Rights. The Court therefore concluded that the views they expressed during the Virginia campaign in favor of a strict separation of church and state were incorporated into the First Amendment.

Although the Court subsequently devised various standards for detecting violations of the Establishment Clause, the decisions handed down until the 1980s for the most part reflected the view of the clause's purposes outlined in *Everson*. Thus the Court consistently ruled against government attempts to promote particular religious views. Examples include *School District of Abington Township* v. *Schempp* (1963), in which the Court invalidated requirements for Bible reading and the recitation of the Lord's Prayer in the public schools; and *Epperson* v. *Arkansas* (1968), in which it overturned an Arkansas law that prohibited teaching about evolution. It also has struck down enactments penalizing individuals for their religious beliefs or disbelief: in *Torasco* v. *Watkins* (1961), it unanimously invalidated a Maryland constitutional provision that established a religious test for public office; and in *McDaniel* v. *Paty* (1978), it struck down a Tennessee law that disqualified clergy from serving as state legislators. Finally, the justices invalidated more evenhanded efforts to aid religion on the ground that they violated governmental neutrality between religion and irreligion. New York's establishment of a nondenominational prayer for public school children, struck down in *Engel* v. *Vitale* (1962), fell into this category, as did a Champaign, Illinois, program of releasing students from classes for religious instruction on school premises, invalidated in *McCollum* v. *Board of Education* (1948).

Alternatives to *Everson*

Ever since *Everson*, some scholars have insisted that the justices, through excessive reliance on the Virginia struggle for religious liberty, had misinterpreted the religion clauses of the First Amendment.[2] Drawing upon this research in his dissent in *Wallace* v. *Jaffree* (1985), Justice William Rehnquist presented a substantially different account of the Establishment Clause. According to Rehnquist, the debate in the First Congress indicated that the Founders did not contemplate a "wall of separation" between church and state. Because most members of the founding generation believed that political liberty was more secure where religion flourished, they did not oppose using religious means, including nondiscriminatory aid to religion, to achieve valid governmental ends. Nor did they object to governmental support for religion and accommodation of the religious character of the American people. And both governmental practice and scholarly commentary for over a century after the ratification of the First Amendment reflected this view. As long as the national government neither established a national church nor gave preference to a particular religion, its actions supporting or accommodating religion were viewed as consistent with the Establishment Clause.

Acceptance of this interpretation of the Establishment Clause does not require repudiation of all the Court's decisions. If laws mandating prayer and Bible reading in public schools entail governmental support for particular religious views, then their invalidation by the Court was correct. Equally unexceptionable were the Court's decisions in *McGowan* v. *Maryland* (1961), upholding Sunday closing laws, and in *Walz* v. *Tax Commission* (1970), upholding tax exemptions for churches, in that the challenged programs served legitimate governmental purposes. And recent rulings which are difficult to square with *Everson*— such as *Lynch* v. *Donnelly* (1984), permitting inclusion of a crèche in a Christmas display on public property, and *Marsh* v. *Chambers* (1985), upholding government payment of a chaplain to conduct prayers at the beginning of state legislative sessions—might be upheld as accommodations of the populace's religious beliefs.

On the other hand, some Court rulings cannot be reconciled with Chief Justice Rehnquist's interpretation of the Establishment Clause. The Court's invalidation of Alabama's silent prayer statute in *Jaffree* is a prime example, since government merely accommodated students' religious beliefs without favoring any particular creed. The same could be said of *Lee* v. *Weisman* (1992), in which the Court struck down the practice of having clergy offer prayers at public school graduations. Even more important deviations are the Court's rulings on aid to nonpublic schools, to which we shall turn shortly.

Other justices have also sought an alternative to the strict separation of church and state endorsed in *Everson*. Several have suggested that the basic concern underlying the Establishment Clause is not separation but governmental neutrality both among religions and between religion and nonreligion. According to this view, governmental endorsement of particular religions or religion in general violates the Establishment Clause. This explains the Court's ruling in *Board of Education of Kiryas Joel Village School District* v. *Grumet* (1994), in which it invalidated New York's creation of a special school district to serve the residents of a religiously homogeneous village. Yet not every governmental action that benefits religion or religious groups violates neutrality. Indeed, a concern for governmental neutrality explains recent Court rulings invalidating state policies that discriminated against religion, even though the states argued that failure to discriminate would violate the separation of church and state. In *Zobrest* v. *Catalina Foothills School District* (1993), for example, the Court rejected the state's claim that its provision of a sign-language interpreter to a deaf child attending a parochial school would violate the Establishment Clause because it would aid in the transmission of religious teaching to the student. According to the Court, governmental neutrality required that the state provide this service even-handedly to all deaf students, regardless of whether they chose a secular or a religious education. Similarly, in *Rosenberger* v. *University of Virginia* (1995), the Court upheld a challenge to the University's refusal to subsidize publication of a religious magazine published by a student group. If the university funded secular publications by student groups, the Court held, its failure to fund the religious publications based on their content discriminated against religious expression and thus violated neutrality.

Aid to Education

Perhaps the most difficult Establishment Clause question faced by the justices has been the validity of governmental aid to programs that benefit both sectarian and nonsectarian institutions. The aid program at issue in *Everson* v. *Board of Education* illustrates the difficulties posed by this question. On the one hand, state reimbursement for the cost of transporting children to sectarian schools clearly facilitates attendance at those schools and thus seems inconsistent with the no-aid requirement announced in *Everson*. On the other hand, for the state to deny transportation to students merely because they attend religious schools would appear to reflect governmental hostility to, rather than neutrality toward, religion. And as the expansion of governmental aid programs has made the consequences of exclusion from them more severe, conflicts over aid programs have increased in both intensity and frequency.

Initially, even while endorsing the view of the Establishment Clause announced in *Everson*, the Court concluded that some aid programs were constitutionally permissible. In *Everson* itself, the Court upheld New Jersey's transportation program, and in *Board of Education* v. *Allen* (1968) it rejected a challenge to a New York law requiring local school boards to lend textbooks to students in private and parochial schools. Even though these programs arguably facilitated attendance at sectarian schools, the Court noted that the aid served legitimate secular purposes, went to the students rather than to religious institutions, and did not directly assist those institutions in accomplishing their religious objectives. Dissenters in these cases, however, insisted that the programs violated the Establishment Clause's no-aid requirement and that the textbooks at issue in *Allen*, whatever their content, could be used to promote religious belief.[3] Apparently these arguments had some effect, for the Court in subsequent cases struck down various programs providing instructional materials and auxiliary services to parochial schools.

The Court first reviewed major aid programs to private (including sectarian) schools in *Lemon* v. *Kurtzman* (1971). At issue were two state programs: Pennsylvania's program directly reimbursed nonpublic elementary and secondary schools for the costs of teachers' salaries, textbooks, and instructional materials in specific secular subjects; and Rhode Island's provided a 15 percent salary supplement to teachers of secular subjects in nonpublic elementary and secondary schools. With only a single dissent, the Court invalidated both programs. Speaking for the Court, Chief Justice Warren Burger announced a three-pronged test, culled from previous Court decisions, for programs challenged under the Establishment Clause: "First, the statute must have a secular legislative purpose; second, its principal or primary effect must be one that neither advances nor inhibits religion; finally, the statute must not foster an excessive entanglement with religion." Applying this test to the programs in *Lemon*, Burger concluded that although both had secular legislative purposes, both involved excessive governmental entanglement with the sectarian schools. A prime purpose of sectarian elementary and secondary education, he noted, is to inculcate religious belief, not only through religious instruction but also by creating a pervasively religious atmosphere in the schools. And because all aspects of sectarian elementary and secondary education promote the schools' religious goals, aid to such schools unconstitutionally involves government in fostering religious belief. Moreover, Burger continued, even if a school sought to compartmentalize its religious and secular instruction, excessive governmental policing of the school's operations would be required to ensure that the aid served only secular purposes. Finally, the Chief Justice pointed out that such aid programs had the effect of promoting political divisions along religious lines, "one of the principal evils against which the First Amendment was intended to protect."

Nevertheless, in *Tilton* v. *Richardson* (1971) the Court sustained the constitutionality of the Higher Education Facilities Act of 1963, under which private colleges received federal grants and loans to construct buildings to be used solely for secular purposes.[4] Over the protests of three justices who had joined the *Lemon* majority, Chief Justice Burger distinguished the program in *Tilton* from those invalidated in *Lemon* on two bases: (1) the colleges receiving funds did not inject religious teaching into their secular courses nor view religious indoctrination as one of their primary functions; (2) that the character of the aid—one-time, single-purpose, and nonideological—precluded both political divisions along sectarian lines and excessive administrative entanglements.

In cases involving aid to nonpublic elementary and secondary education decided by the Court since 1971, the *Lemon* decision's emphasis on the educational mission of the schools receiving aid has played a crucial role. When states attempt to ensure that aid is not used to advance religion by policing its use, their programs run the risk of invalidation on entanglement grounds. However, state aid without policing may have a primary effect of advancing religion, since the Court has held that religious and secular education are inextricably mixed in sectarian elementary and secondary schools. Although this appears to suggest that any aid to sectarian schools violates the Constitution, the Court has not taken this position. Instead, it has attempted to distinguish between aid which advances the schools' religious mission and aid which does not.

However, the Court has splintered badly in considering specific aid programs. Its rulings are difficult to reconcile, and insofar as they are reconcilable, they seem to rest on rather tenuous distinctions. For example, in *Board of Education* v. *Allen* (1968), the Court upheld lending textbooks to students in nonpublic schools; but in *Meek* v. *Pittenger* (1975) and *Wolman* v. *Walter* (1977), it invalidated lending other instructional materials, such as maps, films, and laboratory equipment. In *Levitt* v.

Committee for Public Education (1973), it struck down reimbursement for state-mandated testing when the tests were prepared by parochial school personnel; but in *Committee for Public Education* v. *Regan* (1980), it upheld reimbursement when the tests were prepared by the state. Finally, in *Zobrest* v. *Catalina Foothills School District* (1993), it upheld state provision of a sign language interpreter to a deaf student attending a sectarian school; but in *School District of Grand Rapids* v. *Ball* (1985) and *Aguilar* v. *Felton* (1985), it struck down state provision of remedial and enrichment programs by public school personnel in sectarian schools. Thus, as Justice Byron White wryly noted, the Court's rulings have "sacrifice[d] clarity and predictability for flexibility."[5] This, of course, has created problems for states attempting to provide aid to students in sectarian schools without running afoul of constitutional limitations. Indeed, the number of school-aid cases coming before the Court testifies to the difficulties that states have had in discerning the line between permissible and impermissible programs.

The problem is not merely that the three-pronged test developed in *Lemon* is difficult to apply or that its requirement of monitoring aid without entanglement creates, in Chief Justice Rehnquist's words, an "insoluble paradox." According to critics both on and off the Court, the problem goes much deeper. The Court's approach prevents government from pursuing legitimate secular ends, such as provision of education, through programs that benefit religious institutions but are neutral between religion and nonreligion. As dissatisfaction with the approach pioneered in *Lemon* has grown, the justices have upheld several neutral programs that aided students pursuing education in religious schools. In *Witters* v. *Washington Department of Services for the Blind* (1986), the Court ruled that the Establishment Clause did not bar a vocational tuition grant to a blind person who wished to use it to attend a Christian college and become a minister or missionary. In *Zobrest* v. *Catalina Foothills School District* (1993), the Court upheld the provision of a sign-language interpreter to a deaf student attending a sectarian school. And in *Agostini* v. *Felton* (1997), it overruled *Aguilar* v. *Felton* (1985), which had prohibited the provision of remedial instruction to disadvantaged children if that instruction took place on the premises of sectarian schools.

Whether the justices will undertake a more fundamental reassessment of their rulings on aid to nonpublic schools remains to be seen. The occasion for such a reassessment may be provided by constitutional challenges to the "school choice" programs now being initiated in some states. Under these programs, students receive financial vouchers from the government, which they can use to attend the school of their choice (including sectarian schools). The Supreme Court has already invalidated grants and tax benefits specifically geared to parents of children attending nonpublic schools (*Committee for Public Education* v. *Nyquist* [1973]). However, it has upheld tax credits made available to all parents for tuition and other educational expenses (*Mueller* v. *Allen* [1983]). A constitutional challenge would require the justices to determine whether "school choice" more closely resembles the program struck down in *Nyquist* or the one upheld in *Mueller*. But it might also prompt the justices to reconsider altogether their approach to governmental aid to nonpublic education.

FREE EXERCISE OF RELIGION

In a sense, the basic aims of the Free Exercise Clause have been achieved without judicial intervention. One reason the clause was inserted in the Constitution was to ensure that individuals could pursue their religious convictions without impediment, and the multiplicity of denominations in the United States today indicates that religious liberty is flourishing. On occasion, the Supreme Court has confronted discrimination against a religious group—in *Church of Lukumi Babalu Aye* v. *Hialeah* (1993), for example, it struck down an ordinance directed against the Santeria religion, which employed animal sacrifice as one of its rites. However, perhaps because no single denomination is predominant, overt governmental hostility toward religions seldom has posed a serious problem.[6] The free-exercise cases coming to the Court typically have involved a more delicate issue: how to resolve conflicts between governmental regulations serving secular ends and the demands of individuals' religious beliefs.

Governmental regulations can burden or conflict with the claims of conscience in a variety of ways. Some regulations may place an indirect burden on particular groups of believers. For example, by establishing a uniform day of rest, the Pennsylvania Sunday closing law, which was upheld in *Braunfeld* v. *Brown* (1961), placed Orthodox Jews and other Sabbatarians at a competitive disadvantage by in effect requiring them to close their businesses two days a week. Other regulations may establish eligibility requirements for governmental benefits which force believers to choose between their religious convictions and those benefits. A prime example was South Carolina's denial of unemployment compensation to a Seventh-day Adventist who refused jobs that required her to work on Saturday (her Sabbath)—an action the state based on an enactment requiring potential recipients to accept "available suitable work." (The Court in *Sherbert* v. *Verner* [1963] ruled that this denial of benefits violated the free exercise of religion.) Still other governmental regulations may oblige individuals to perform or refrain from actions in violation of their religious convictions. Among the cases raising such issues are *Jacobson* v. *Massachusetts* (1905), in which the Court upheld compulsory vaccination for smallpox despite resistance on religious grounds, and *Goldman* v. *Weinberger* (1986), in which the Court rejected the claim of an Orthodox Jewish psychologist that he be permitted to wear a yarmulke while on duty in uniform at a military hospital. Finally, as *Lyng* v. *Northwest Indian Cemetery Protective Association* (1988) reveals, governmental actions may make it difficult for adherents of site-specific religions to practice their faith. In that case the Court refused to block development of portions of national forest, even though Native American groups viewed the land as sacred.

Braunfeld and *Sherbert* marked a major shift in the Court's interpretation of the Free Exercise Clause. Before 1960 the Court relied on the secular regulation rule in evaluating free-exercise claims. Under this rule, legislation was held to be invalid if it did not serve legitimate, nonreligious governmental ends or if it was directed against particular sects; if those requirements were met, however, the fact that the legislation conflicted with some persons' perceived religious obligations did not invalidate it or qualify them for exemptions. According to this interpretation, the Constitution does not require government to accord special recognition to religious beliefs or religiously motivated behavior. To hold that religious claims should prevail over the accomplishment of government's legitimate aims, the Court maintained, would be to admit their superior validity—a position that conflicts with the neutrality toward religion enjoined by the First Amendment. By granting religious exemptions from general legislation, moreover, government in effect could be providing an inducement for individuals to profess particular religious beliefs. Thus even when striking down enactments challenged on religious grounds, as in *West Virginia Board of Education* v. *Barnette* (1943), the Court emphasized that believers and nonbelievers alike were exempt from their requirements.

In *Braunfeld*, Chief Justice Earl Warren enunciated a more exacting standard for evaluating legislation challenged on free-exercise grounds. In upholding Pennsylvania's Sunday closing law, he noted that the state could not achieve its important secular goal of a uniform day of rest through any alternative means that was less burdensome on religious practice. Presumably, then, legislation that imposed a substantial burden on religious practices would be upheld only if (1) it served an important state aim and (2) that aim could not be advanced by a less restrictive means. The latter criterion provided the basis of the *Sherbert* ruling, in which Justice William Brennan, speaking for the Court, observed that even if South Carolina's aim of deterring fraudulent claims were a compelling one, it had not demonstrated that less restrictive means of preventing fraud were ineffective. In *Wisconsin* v. *Yoder* (1972) the Court emphasized the first aspect of Warren's test, ruling that requiring Amish children to attend school beyond the eighth grade did not serve an important state purpose.

This new and more stringent free-exercise standard thus sought to reduce conflicts between legal and religious obligations by extending greater protection to religiously motivated conduct. Proponents hailed the standard's emphasis on accommodation as consistent with the solicitude for religious commitments and respect for the autonomy of religious organizations mandated by the First Amendment. They also noted that such accommodations were particularly important as the scope of governmental regulation expanded, increasing the frequency of collisions between secular and religious requirements. And adoption of this standard in fact had an immediate beneficial effect on legislation, stimulating governmental efforts to accommodate religious convictions in designing programs.[7]

Nevertheless, not all the results of the Court's new approach were positive. For one thing, this approach required the justices to balance the claims of government against those of religious adherents. Thus, it suffered from the difficulty common to balancing tests: the outcome of the balancing often depended on who was doing it. As the conflict between Justices Sandra Day O'Connor and William Brennan in *Lyng* v. *Northwest Indian Cemetery Protective Association* (1988) illustrates, even those justices who accepted this approach to free-exercise issues have disagreed over how the balance should be struck in particular cases.

In addition, if religious beliefs qualify an individual for otherwise unavailable benefits or exemptions, then there may be an inducement to profess such beliefs, and government must judge the validity of individual claims. This situation raises two problems. In the first place, officials must judge the sincerity of an individual's beliefs, since religious beliefs may be professed solely in order to escape obligations or prohibitions. And as the problems encountered in administering the conscientious objector exemption to military service reveal, such determinations can be difficult. Secondly, even if an individual's beliefs are sincere, officials must determine whether the beliefs are religious in nature: nonreligious beliefs, however strongly held, do not create an exemption from legal obligations. This judgment has been complicated by the broad definition of religion given by the Court in interpreting the conscientious objector exemption, under which nontheistic and purely personal beliefs may qualify as religious.[8] Paradoxically, then, the Court's aim of freeing religious belief from the burden of government regulation can be accomplished only by a much deeper governmental involvement in the religious realm: defining what constitutes a religion and judging the sincerity of individuals' beliefs.

Such considerations led the Court to re-embrace the secular regulation rule in *Employment Division, Department of Human Resources of Oregon* v. *Smith* (1990). At issue in *Smith* was Oregon's refusal to grant unemployment benefits to two employees who had been fired from their jobs for using peyote, an illegal hallucinogenic drug, as part of the ritual of the Native American Church. Speaking for the Court, Justice Antonin Scalia denied that the Free Exercise Clause required government to grant exemptions from neutral, generally applicable laws. Such a requirement, he insisted, would make "each conscience . . . a law unto itself." However, Justice Scalia's position drew intense criticism. In her concurring opinion in *Smith*, Justice O'Connor charged that the opinion of the Court diverged from "well-settled First Amendment jurisprudence." Other critics charged that the Court had embraced an unduly narrow conception of religious liberty. In addition, they argued that although on its face the Court's position seemed neutral among religions, in fact it worked to the disadvantage of minority religions. Mainstream religions would be able to protect themselves in the political process, either by blocking legislation that impinged on their religious practices or by obtaining statutory exemptions. But government would enact laws that inadvertently burdened the practice of minority religions, because their adherents lack the numbers and influence necessary to prevail in the political process.[9]

At the urging of a wide spectrum of religious groups, Congress in 1993 responded to the Court's position in *Smith* by enacting the Religious Freedom Restoration Act (RFRA), which was designed to restore the free-exercise standard enunciated in *Sherbert*. More specifically, the act forbade actions by either the Federal government or state governments that burdened a person's exercise of religion, unless it could be demonstrated that imposing the burden "(1) is in furtherance of a compelling governmental interest; and (2) is the least restrictive means of furthering that compelling governmental interest." As its constitutional basis for enacting RFRA, Congress relied on section 5 of the Fourteenth Amendment, which gave it the "power to enforce, by appropriate legislation" the rights protected by the Fourteenth Amendment (including the free exercise of religion). However, in *City of Boerne* v. *Flores, Archbishop of San Antonio* (1997), the Supreme Court rejected this claim. The power to enforce the obligations of the Fourteenth Amendment, the Court reasoned, does not include the power to alter the meaning of those obligations. Otherwise, Congress would be able to change the meaning of the Constitution by statute, thus undermining the Constitution's status as "superior paramount law, unchangeable by ordinary means." If *Smith* is to be overturned, the mechanism will have to be constitutional amendment rather than congressional legislation.

RECONCILING THE RELIGION CLAUSES

In interpreting the Establishment Clause, the Supreme Court has held that government may neither favor not disfavor religion. Yet in free-exercise cases before *Smith*, it insisted that government must exempt believers from some general legal requirements, in effect using religion as a criterion for distributing benefits. Thus the aims of the religion clauses, at least under these interpretations, seem inconsistent. How can one reconcile the Establishment Clause's mandate of neutrality between religion and irreligion with the Free Exercise Clause's demand for accommodation of religiously motivated actions?

Four answers to this question have been suggested. One is to admit that the Court's interpretations are inconsistent but to insist that this inconsistency is constitutionally warranted, since it reflects a natural antagonism between the Establishment and Free Exercise Clauses. Thus in striking down aid to religion while requiring the accommodation of religious beliefs in the application of general legislation, the Court is merely fulfilling the somewhat opposed purposes of the two provisions. Although this view prevailed on the Court before *Smith*, it is subject to two telling objections. First, it depreciates the Constitution by assuming that it incorporates an incoherent understanding of the proper relation between government and religion. Second, it offers no guidance for determining whether one should opt for neutrality or accommodation in resolving specific disputes.

These problems have led some justices and constitutional scholars to locate the problem not in the Constitution but in the Court's interpretations. According to one view, the Court has interpreted the Establishment Clause in an overly rigid fashion that unduly restricts governmental efforts to promote the free exercise of religion. Justice Potter Stewart, dissenting in the school prayer cases, voiced this criticism when he insisted that in providing opportunities for voluntary religious observances in the public schools, government merely accommodates the religious convictions of the populace. Justice Byron White dissented from the Court's aid-to-education cases on similar grounds, asserting that governmental programs that make it possible for individuals to pursue a religious education constitute an accommodation consistent with—and indeed, appropriate to—the First Amendment's primary concern, which is religious liberty.

Other observers have concluded that the Court has improperly interpreted the Free Exercise Clause before *Smith*. According to this view, best expressed in Justice John Marshall Harlan's dissent in *Sherbert*, a requirement that states accommodate religious convictions in their legislation violates that neutrality between religion and irreligion which was a prime purpose of the First Amendment. Only by reinstitution of the secular regulation rule, this argument goes, can the Court properly reconcile its establishment and free-exercise positions.

Finally, Chief Justice Rehnquist and Justices Scalia and Thomas have proposed a reconsideration of the Court's approach to both the Establishment and Free Exercise Clauses. Agreeing with Justice Harlan that the secular regulation rule is the appropriate standard in free-exercise cases, they have insisted that government is not constitutionally required to accommodate believers in designing legislation. Yet because their interpretation of the Establishment Clause does not require governmental neutrality between religion and irreligion, there is no constitutional bar to governmental efforts to accommodate religion. Their position thus permits government wide discretion in determining whether and when to grant exemptions from general statutory requirements.

TRENDS AND PROSPECTS

Although its rulings on school prayer and other publicly supported religious practices excited considerable controversy, for many years the Supreme Court continued to reaffirm its decisions and the understanding of the Establishment Clause underlying them. However, rulings since 1983 suggest that the Court is rethinking its separationist posture.

In upholding Pawtucket's crèche display in *Lynch* v. *Donnelly* (1984) and the prayer beginning sessions of the Nebraska legislature in *Marsh* v. *Chambers* (1983), the Court indicated that the Establishment Clause does not bar some governmental efforts to recognize the nation's religious heritage. Even while invalidating Alabama's moment-of-silence law in *Wallace* v. *Jaffree,* several justices noted that more carefully drawn statutes would survive constitutional scrutiny.

A similar ferment is evident in the Court's recent aid-to-nonpublic-education cases. The Court has abandoned the three-pronged test announced in *Lemon* v. *Kurtzman.* The implications of this move are apparent in *Zobrest* v. *Catalina Foothills School District* (1993) and *Agostini* v. *Felton* (1997), in which the Court rejected establishment challenges to programs providing aid in an evenhanded fashion to students attending public schools and those attending religious schools. Nevertheless, the abandonment of the *Lemon* test did not resolve the deep divisions on the Court. These divisions are likely to spur further litigation, affording an opportunity to develop a new approach that can unite the Court.

Finally, the Court's reinstitution of the secular-regulation rule in *Smith* and the criticism it engendered reveal a fundamental disagreement about the meaning of the Free Exercise Clause. Congress attempted to prescribe a free-exercise standard in the Religious Freedom Restoration Act of 1993, but the Court ruled in *City of Boerne* v. *Flores, Archbishop of San Antonio* (1997) that this exceeded congressional power. In the aftermath of *Boerne,* it may be that the focus will change from whether religious exemptions are constitutionally required to whether they are warranted as a matter of public policy. Congress and state legislatures will have to consider whether accommodations to religious scruples can be instituted without compromising important statutory objectives.

NOTES

1 Some authorities assert that the Free Exercise Clause was incorporated in *Hamilton* v. *Board of Regents of the University of California* (1934).
2 Early works criticizing the Court's historical scholarship include James M. O'Neill, *Religion and Education Under the Constitution* (New York: Harper, 1949), and Mark DeWolfe Howe, *The Garden and the Wilderness* (Chicago: University of Chicago Press, 1965). More recent critical studies include Michael J. Malbin, *Religion and Politics* (Washington, D.C.: American Enterprise Institute, 1978), and Robert L. Cord, *Separation of Church and State: Historical Fact and Current Fiction* (New York: Lambeth Press, 1982).
3 It should be noted that Justice Hugo Black, who wrote the opinion of the Court in *Everson,* dissented in *Allen*—as did Justice William Douglas, the only other member of the *Everson* majority still on the Court at the time *Allen* was decided.
4 The Court did invalidate a provision of the law that permitted colleges to use the buildings for religious purposes twenty years after receiving the funds.

5 *Committee for Public Education* v. *Regan* (1980).

6 On the importance of religious diversity for religious liberty, see *The Federalist*, Nos. 10 and 51.

7 For parallel statutory developments, see Title VII of the Civil Rights Act of 1964, 42 U.S.C. secs. 200e *et seq.*, and the Equal Employment Opportunity Commission regulations on accommodating religious beliefs, 29 C.F.R. sec. 1605.1(a) (3).

8 See *United States* v. *Seeger* (1965) and *Welsh* v. *United States* (1970).

9 Critical assessments of the Court's approach in *Smith* include Michael W. McConnell, "Free Exercise Revisionism and the *Smith* Decision," *University of Chicago Law Review* 57 (1990), 1609–1654; and Douglas Laycock, "Formal, Substantive, and Disaggregated Neutrality Toward Religion," *DePaul Law Review* 39 (1990), 993–1018.

SELECTED READING

Cantwell v. *Connecticut*, 310 U.S. 296 (1940).
Lynch v. *Donnelly*, 465 U.S. 668 (1984).
Mueller v. *Allen*, 463 U.S. 388 (1983).
Reynolds v. *United States*, 98 U.S. 145 (1878).
United States v. *Ballard*, 322 U.S. 78 (1948).

Adams, Arlin M. and Charles J. Emmerich. *A Nation Dedicated to Religious Liberty: The Constitutional Heritage of the Religion Clauses* (Philadelphia: University of Pennsylvania Press, 1990).

Carter, Stephen L. *The Culture of Disbelief: How American Law and Politics Trivialize Religious Devotion* (New York: Basic Books, 1993).

Choper, Jesse H. "The Religion Clauses of the First Amendment: Reconciling the Conflict." *University of Pittsburgh Law Review* 41 (1980): 673–701.

Cord, Robert L. *Separation of Church and State: Historical Fact and Current Fiction* (New York: Lambeth Press, 1982).

Curry, Thomas J. *The First Freedoms: Church and State in America to the Passage of the First Amendment* (New York: Oxford University Press, 1986).

Graglia, Lino A. "*Church of Lu Kumi Babalu Aye:* of Animal Sacrifice and Religious Persecution," *Georgetown Law Journal*, 85 (1996): 1–69.

Howe, Mark DeWolfe. *The Garden and the Wilderness* (Chicago: University of Chicago Press, 1965).

Levy, Leonard W. *The Establishment Clause: Religion and the First Amendment* (New York: Macmillan, 1986).

McConnell, Michael W. "Accommodation of Religion." In Philip B. Kurland, Gerhard Casper, and Dennis J. Hutchinson. *The Supreme Court Review* 1985 (Chicago: University of Chicago Press, 1986).

McConnell, Michael W. "The Origins and Historical Understanding of Free Exercise of Religion." *Harvard Law Review* 103 (1990): 1409–1517.

Miller, William Lee. *The First Liberty: Religion and the American Republic* (New York: Alfred A. Knopf, 1985).

"Religion Symposium." *Journal of Contemporary Legal Issues* 7 (1996): 275–516.

Tarr, G. Alan. "Church and State in the States." *Washington Law Review* 64 (1989): 73–110.

Everson v. *Board of Education*

330 U.S. 1; 67 S. Ct. 504; 91 L. Ed. 711 (1947)

A New Jersey statute authorized local school boards to make rules and contracts for the transportation of students to and from schools. Acting under this statute, the Ewing Township Board of Education authorized reimbursement to parents of money spent for transportation to Catholic parochial schools as well as to public schools. Arch Everson, a taxpayer in the school district, challenged the transportation program as a violation of the state constitution (a claim rejected by the state supreme court) and the Federal Constitution. *Opinion of the Court:* _Black_, Vinson, Reed, Douglas, Murphy. *Dissenting opinions:* _Jackson_, Frankfurter; _Rutledge_, Frankfurter, Jackson, Burton.

MR. JUSTICE BLACK delivered the opinion of the Court. . . .

This Court has previously recognized that the provisions of the First Amendment, in the drafting and adoption of which Madison and Jefferson played such leading roles, had the same objective and were intended to provide the same protection against governmental intrusion on religious liberty as the Virginia [Bill for Religious Liberty]. . . .

The "establishment of religion" clause of the First Amendment means at least this: Neither a state nor the Federal Government can set up a church. Neither can pass laws which aid one religion, aid all religions, or prefer one religion over another. Neither can force nor influence a person to go to or to remain away from church against his will or force him to profess a belief or disbelief in any religion. No person can be punished for entertaining or professing religious beliefs or disbeliefs, for church attendance or non-attendance. No tax in any amount, large or small, can be levied to support any religious activities or institutions, whatever they may be called, or whatever form they may adopt to teach or practice religion. Neither a state nor the Federal Government can, openly or secretly, participate in the affairs of any religious organizations or groups and *vice versa*. In the words of Jefferson, the clause against establishment of religion by law was intended to erect "a wall of separation between church and State." . . .

. . . New Jersey cannot consistently with the "establishment of religion" clause of the First Amendment contribute tax-raised funds to the support of an institution which teaches the tenets and faith of any church. On the other hand, other language of the amendment commands that New Jersey cannot hamper its citizens in the free exercise of their own religion. Consequently, it cannot exclude individual Catholics, Lutherans, Mohammedans, Baptists, Jews, Methodists, Non-believers, Presbyterians, or the members of any other faith, *because of their faith, or lack of it*, from receiving the benefits of public welfare legislation. While we do not mean to intimate that a state could not provide transportation only to children attending public schools, we must be careful, in protecting the citizens of New Jersey against state-established churches, to be sure that we do not inadvertently prohibit New Jersey from extending its general state law benefits to all its citizens without regard to their religious belief.

Measured by these standards, we cannot say that the First Amendment prohibits New Jersey from spending tax-raised funds to pay the bus fares of parochial school pupils as a part of a general program under which it pays the fares of pupils attending public and other schools. It is undoubtedly true that children are helped to get to church schools. There is even a possibility that some of the children might not be sent to the church schools if the parents were compelled to pay their children's bus fares out of their own pockets when transportation to a public school would have been paid for by the State. The same possibility exists where the state requires a local transit company to provide reduced fares to school children including those attending parochial schools, or where a municipally owned transportation system undertakes to carry all school children free of charge. Moreover, state-paid policemen, detailed to protect children going to and from church schools from the very real hazards of traffic, would serve much the same purpose and accomplish much the same result as state provisions intended to guarantee free transportation of a kind which the state deems to be best for the school children's welfare. And parents might refuse to risk their children to the serious danger of traffic accidents going to and from parochial schools, the approaches to which were not protected by policemen. Similarly, parents might be reluctant to permit their children to attend schools which the state had cut off from such general government services as ordinary police and fire protection, connections for sewage disposal, public highways and sidewalks. Of course, cutting off church schools from these services, so separate and so indisputably marked off from the religious function, would make it far more difficult for the schools to operate. But such is obviously not the purpose of the First Amendment. That Amendment requires the state to be a neutral in its relations with groups of religious believers and non-believers; it does not require the state to be their adversary. State power is no more to be used so as to handicap religions than it is to favor them. . . .

The First Amendment has erected a wall between church and state. That wall must be kept high and impregnable. We could not approve the slightest breach. New Jersey has not breached it here.

Affirmed.

MR. JUSTICE JACKSON, dissenting.

. . . The Court's opinion marshals every argument in favor of state aid and puts the case in its most favorable light, but much of its reasoning confirms my conclusions that there are no good grounds upon which to support the present legislation. In fact, the undertones of the opinion, advocating complete and uncompromising separation of Church from State, seem utterly discordant with its conclusion yielding support to their commingling in educational matters. The case which irresistibly comes to mind as the most fitting precedent is that of Julia who, according to Byron's reports, "whispering 'I will ne'er consent,'—consented." . . .

The Court sustains this legislation by assuming two deviations from the facts of this particular case. . . .

The Court concludes that this "legislation, as applied, does no more than provide a general program to help parents get their children, regardless of their religion, safely and expeditiously to and from accredited schools," and it draws a comparison between "state provisions intended to guarantee free transportation" for school children with services such as police and fire protection, and implies that we are here dealing with "laws authorizing new types of public services . . ." This hypothesis permeates the opinion. The facts will not bear that construction.

The Township of Ewing is not furnishing transportation to the children in any form; it is not operating school buses itself or contracting for their operation; and it is not performing any public service of any kind with this taxpayer's money. All school children are left to ride as ordinary paying passengers on the regular buses operated by the public transportation system. What the Township does, and what the taxpayer complains of, is at stated intervals to reimburse parents for the fares paid, provided the children attend either public schools or Catholic Church schools. This expenditure of tax funds has no possible effect on the child's safety or expedition in transit. As passengers on the public buses they travel as fast and no faster, and are as safe and no safer, since their parents are reimbursed as before.

In addition to thus assuming a type of service that does not exist, the Court also insists that we must close our eyes to a discrimination which does exist. The resolution which authorizes disbursement of this taxpayer's money limits reimbursement to those who attend public schools and Catholic schools. That is the way the Act is applied to this taxpayer.

The New Jersey Act in question makes the character of the school, not the needs of the children, determine the eligibility of parents to reimbursement. The Act permits payment for transportation to parochial schools or public schools but prohibits it to private schools operated in whole or in part for profit. . . .

MR. JUSTICE RUTLEDGE with whom MR. JUSTICE FRANKFURTER, MR. JUSTICE JACKSON and MR. JUSTICE BURTON agree, dissenting. . . .

The Amendment's purpose was not to strike merely at the official establishment of a single sect, creed or religion, outlawing only a formal relation such as had prevailed in England and some of the colonies. Necessarily it was to uproot all such relationships. But the object was broader than separating church and state in this narrow sense. It was to create a complete and permanent separation of the spheres of religious activity and civil authority by comprehensively forbidding every form of public aid or support for religion. . . .

No provision of the Constitution is more closely tied to or given content by its generating history than the religious clause of the First Amendment. It is at once the refined product and the terse summation of that history. The history includes not only Madison's authorship and the proceedings before the First Congress, but also the long and intensive struggle for religious freedom in America, more especially in Virginia, of which the Amendment was the direct culmination. . . .

All the great instruments of the Virginia struggle for religious liberty thus became warp and woof of our constitutional tradition, not simply by the course of history, but by the common unifying force of Madison's life, thought and sponsorship. He epitomized the whole of that tradition in the Amendment's compact, but nonetheless comprehensive, phrasing.

. . . Madison opposed every form and degree of official relation between religion and civil authority. For him religion was a wholly private matter beyond the scope of civil power either to restrain or to support. . . . In no phase was he more unrelentingly absolute than in opposing state support or aid by taxation. Not even "three pence" contribution was thus to be exacted from any citizen for such a purpose. . . .

In view of this history no further proof is needed that the Amendment forbids any appropriation, large or small, from public funds to aid or support any and all religious exercises. . . .

New Jersey's action . . . exactly fits the type of exaction and the kind of evil at which Madison and Jefferson struck. Under the test they framed it cannot be said that the cost of transportation is no part of the cost of education or of the religious instruction given. That it is a substantial and a necessary element is shown most plainly by the continuing and increasing demand for the state to assume it. Nor is there pretense that it relates only to the secular instruction given in religious schools or that any attempt is or could be made toward allocating proportional shares as between the secular and the religious instruction. It is precisely because the instruction is religious and relates to a particular faith, whether one or another, that parents send their children to religious schools. . . . And the very purpose of the state's contribution to defray the cost of conveying the pupil to the place where he will receive not simply secular, but also and primarily religious, teaching and guidance. . . .

. . . The matter is not one of quantity, to be measured by the amount of money expended. Now as in Madison's day it is one of principle, to keep separate the separate spheres as the First Amendment drew them; to prevent the first experiment upon our liberties; and to keep the question from becoming entangled in corrosive precedents. . . .

School District of Abington Township v. Schempp
374 U.S. 203; 83 S. Ct. 1560; 10 L. Ed. 2d 844 (1963)

One year after the Court in *Engel* v. *Vitale* invalidated the use of a government-composed prayer for voluntary recitation in New York public schools, it considered the more widespread practice of Bible reading in the public schools. A Pennsylvania law required daily Bible reading, and a Baltimore school board regulation required both Bible reading and daily recitation of the Lord's Prayer. Both programs permitted students to absent themselves from the religious exercises on parental request.

Perhaps to allay the intense criticism that greeted the *Engel* decision, the opinion of the Court was assigned to Justice Clark, an elder in the Presbyterian Church, and concurring opinions were filed by Justice Brennan, a Catholic, and Justice Goldberg, a Jew. *Opinion of the Court: Clark, Warren, Black, Douglas, Harlan, Brennan, White, Goldberg. Concurring opinions: Douglas; Brennan; Goldberg, Harlan. Dissenting opinion: Stewart.*

Mr. JUSTICE CLARK delivered the opinion of the Court. . . .

The wholesome "neutrality" of which this Court's cases speak . . . stems from a recognition of the teachings of history that powerful sects or groups might bring about a fusion of governmental and religious functions or a concert or dependency of one upon the other to the end that official support of the State or Federal Government would be placed behind the tenets of one or of all orthodoxies. This the Establishment Clause prohibits. And a further reason for neutrality is found in the Free Exercise Clause, which recognizes the value of religious training, teaching and observance and, more particularly, the right of every person to freely choose his own course with reference thereto, free of any compulsion from the state. This the Free Exercise Clause guarantees. Thus, as we have seen, the two clauses may overlap. . . . [T]he Establishment Clause has been directly considered by this Court eight times in the past score of years and, with only one Justice dissenting on the point, it has consistently held that the clause withdrew all legislative power respecting religious belief or the expression thereof. The test may be stated as follows: what are the purpose and the primary effect of the enactment? If either is the advancement or inhibition of religion then the enactment exceeds the scope of legislative power as circumscribed by the Constitution. That is to say that to withstand the strictures of the Establishment Clause there must be a secular legislative purpose and a primary effect that neither advances nor inhibits religion. . . . The distinction between the two clauses is apparent—a violation of the Free Exercise Clause is predicated on coercion while the Establishment Clause violation need not be so attended.

Applying the Establishment Clause principles to the cases at bar we find that the States are requiring the selection and reading at the opening of the school day of verses from the Holy Bible and the recitation of the Lord's Prayer by the students in unison. These exercises are prescribed as part of the curricular activities of students who are required by law to attend school. . . .

. . . Surely the place of the Bible as an instrument of religion cannot be gainsaid, and the State's recognition of the pervading religious character of the ceremony is evident from the rule's specific permission of the alternative use of the Catholic Douay version as well as the recent amendment permitting nonattendance at the exercises. None of these factors is consistent with the contention that the Bible is here used either as an instrument for nonreligious moral inspiration or as a reference for the teaching of secular subjects.

The conclusion follows that in both cases the laws require religious exercises and such exercises are being conducted in direct violation of the rights of the appellees and petitioners. . . .

It is insisted that unless these religious exercises are permitted a "religion of secularism" is established in the schools. We agree of course that the State may not establish a "religion of secularism" in the sense of affirmatively opposing or showing hostility to religion, thus "preferring those who believe in no religion over those who do believe" *Zorach* v. *Clauson* [1952]. We do not agree, however, that this decision in any sense has that effect. In addition, it might well be said that one's education is not complete without a study of comparative religion or the history of religion and its relationship to the advancement of civilization. It certainly may be said that the Bible is worthy of study for its literary and historic qualities. Nothing we have said here indicates that such study of the Bible or of religion, when presented objectively as part of a secular program of education, may not be effected consistently with the First Amendment. But the exercises here . . . are religious exercises, required by the States in violation of the command of the First Amendment that the Government maintain strict neutrality, neither aiding nor opposing religion.

Finally, we cannot accept that the concept of neutrality, which does not permit a State to require a religious exercise even with the consent of the majority of those affected, collides with the majority's right to free exercise of religion. While the Free Exercise Clause clearly prohibits the use of state action to deny the rights of free exercise to *anyone*, it has never meant that a majority could use the machinery of the State to practice its beliefs. . . .

MR. JUSTICE BRENNAN, concurring. . . .

. . . The specific question before us has aroused vigorous dispute whether the architects of the First Amendment—James Madison and Thomas Jefferson particularly—understood the prohibition against any "law respecting an establishment of religion" to reach devotional exercises in the public schools. . . . But I doubt that their view, even if perfectly clear one way or the other, would supply a dispositive answer to the question presented by these cases. A more fruitful inquiry, it seems to me, is whether the practices here challenged threaten those consequences which the Framers deeply feared; whether, in short, they tend to promote that type of interdependence between religion and state which the First Amendment was designed to prevent. . . .

A too literal quest for the advice of the Founding Fathers upon the issues of these cases seems to me futile and misdirected for several reasons: First, on our precise problem the historical record is at best ambiguous, and statements can readily be found to support either side of the proposition. The ambiguity of history is understandable if we recall the nature of the problems uppermost in the thinking of the statesmen who fashioned the religious guarantees; they were concerned with far more flagrant intrusions of government into the realm of religion than any that our century has witnessed. . . .

Second, the structure of American education has greatly changed since the First Amendment was adopted. In the context of our modern emphasis upon public education available to all citizens, any views of the eighteenth century as to

whether the exercises at bar are an "establishment" offer little aid to decision. . . .

Third, our religious composition makes us a vastly more diverse people than were our forefathers. They knew differences chiefly among Protestant sects. Today the Nation is far more heterogeneous religiously, including as it does substantial minorities not only of Catholics and Jews but as well of those who worship according to no version of the Bible and those who worship no God at all. . . . In the face of such profound changes, practices which may have been objectionable to no one in the time of Jefferson and Madison may today be highly offensive to many persons, the deeply devout and the nonbelievers alike. . . .

Fourth, the American experiment in free public education available to all children has been guided in large measure by the dramatic evolution of the religious diversity among the population which our public schools serve . . . . It is implicit in the history and character of American public education that the public schools serve a uniquely *public* function: the training of American citizens in an atmosphere free of parochial, divisive, or separatist influences of any sort—an atmosphere in which children may assimilate a heritage common to all American groups and religions. . . . This is a heritage neither theistic nor atheistic, but simply civic and patriotic. . . .

MR. JUSTICE STEWART, dissenting.

I think the records in the two cases before us are so fundamentally deficient as to make impossible an informed or responsible determination of the constitutional issues presented. Specifically, I cannot agree that on these records we can say that the Establishment Clause has necessarily been violated. . . .

. . . While in many contexts the Establishment Clause and the Free Exercise Clause fully complement each other, there are areas in which a doctrinaire reading of the Establishment Clause leads to irreconcilable conflict with the Free Exercise Clause.

A single obvious example should suffice to make the point. Spending federal funds to employ chaplains for the armed forces might be said to violate the Establishment Clause. Yet a lonely soldier stationed at some faraway outpost could surely complain that a government which did *not* provide him the opportunity for pastoral guidance was affirmatively prohibiting the free exercise of his religion. And such examples could readily be multiplied. The short of the matter is simply that the two relevant clauses of the First Amendment cannot accurately be reflected in a sterile metaphor which by its very nature may distort rather than illumine the problems involved in a particular case. . . .

That the central value embodied in the First Amendment—and, more particularly, in the guarantee of "liberty" contained in the Fourteenth—is the safeguarding of an individual's right to free exercise of his religion has been consistently recognized. . . . It is this concept of constitutional protection . . . which makes the cases before us such difficult ones for me. For there is involved in these cases a substantial free exercise claim on the part of those who affirmatively desire to have their children's school day open with the reading of passages from the Bible. . . .

It might . . . be argued that parents who want their children exposed to religious influences can adequately fulfill that wish off school property and outside school time. With all its surface persuasiveness, however, this argument seriously misconceives the basic constitutional justification for permitting the exercises at issue in these cases. For a compulsory state educational system so structures a child's life that if religious exercises are held to be an impermissible activity in schools, religion is placed at an artificial and state-created disadvantage. Viewed in this light, permission of such exercises for those who want them is necessary if the schools are truly to be neutral in the matter of religion. And a refusal to permit religious exercises thus is seen, not as the realization of state neutrality, but rather as the establishment of a religion of secularism, or at the least, as government support of the beliefs of those who think that religious exercises should be conducted only in private. . . .

What our Constitution indispensibly protects is the freedom of each of us, be he Jew or Agnostic, Atheist, Buddhist or Freethinker, to believe or disbelieve, to worship or not worship, to pray or keep silent, according to his own conscience, uncoerced and unrestrained by government. It is conceivable that these school boards, or even all school boards, might eventually find it impossible to administer a system of religious exercises during school hours in such a way as to meet this constitutional standard—in such a way as completely to free from any kind of official coercion those who do not affirmatively want to participate. But I think we must not assume that school boards so lack the qualities of inventiveness and good will as to make impossible the achievement of that goal. . . .

Lemon v. *Kurtzman*
403 U.S. 602; 91 S. Ct. 2105; 29 L. Ed. 745 (1971)

Lemon marked the Supreme Court's first consideration of the constitutionality of state programs providing aid to church-affiliated elementary and secondary schools. Under the Pennsylvania Nonpublic Elementary and Secondary Education Act, Pennsylvania purchased specified secular educational services from nonpublic schools by reimbursing them for the cost of teachers' salaries, textbooks, and instructional materials in various secular subjects. A three-judge federal district court dismissed the complaint regarding the program in *Lemon* v. *Kurtzman.* Under the Rhode Island Salary Supplement Act, Rhode Island paid teachers of secular subjects in nonpublic elementary schools a supplement of 15 percent of their annual salary. In *Early* v. *DiCenso* (1970) a three-judge federal district court struck down the act as a violation of the Establishment Clause. The Court consolidated these cases for argument with *Tilton* v. *Richardson. Opinion of the Court:* Burger, *Black, Douglas, Harlan, Stewart, Blackmun. Concurring opinions:* Douglas, *Black;* Brennan. *Dissenting opinion:* White. *Not participating: Marshall.*

MR. CHIEF JUSTICE BURGER delivered the opinion of the Court. . . .

Every analysis in this area must begin with consideration of the cumulative criteria developed by the Court over many years. Three such tests may be gleaned from our cases. First, the statute must have a secular legislative purpose; second, its principal or primary effect must be one that neither advances nor inhibits religion. . . ; finally, the statute must not foster "an excessive government entanglement with religion." . . .

Inquiry into the legislative purposes of the Pennsylvania and Rhode Island statutes affords no basis for a conclusion that the legislative intent was to advance religion. On the contrary, the statutes themselves clearly state that they are intended to enhance the quality of the secular education in all schools covered by the compulsory attendance laws. There is no reason to believe the legislatures meant anything else. A State always has a legitimate concern for maintaining minimum standards in all schools it allows to operate. . . .

The two legislatures, however, have . . . recognized that church-related elementary and secondary schools have a significant religious mission and that a substantial portion of their activities is religiously oriented. They have therefore sought to create statutory restrictions designed to guarantee the separation between secular and religious educational functions and to ensure that State financial aid supports only the former. . . . We need not decide whether these legislative precautions restrict the principal or primary effect of the programs to the point where they do not offend the Religion Clauses, for we conclude that the cumulative impact of the entire relationship arising under the statutes in each State involves excessive entanglement between government and religion. . . .

In order to determine whether the government entanglement with religion is excessive, we must examine the character and purposes of the institutions that are benefited, the nature of the aid that the State provides, and the resulting relationship between the government and the religious authority. . . .

Rhode Island Program

The District Court made extensive findings on the grave potential for excessive entanglement that inheres in the religious character and purpose of the Roman Catholic elementary schools of Rhode Island, to date the sole beneficiaries of the Rhode Island Salary Supplement Act.

The church schools involved in the program are located close to parish churches. This understandably permits convenient access for religious exercises since instruction in faith and morals is part of the total educational process. The school buildings contain identifying religious symbols such as crosses on the exterior and crucifixes, and religious paintings and statues either in the classrooms or hallways. Although only approximately 30 minutes a day are devoted to direct religious instruction, there are religiously oriented extracurricular activities. Approximately two-thirds of the teachers in these schools are nuns of various religious orders. Their dedicated efforts provide an atmosphere in which religious instruction and religious vocations are natural and proper parts of life in such schools.

On the basis of these findings the District Court concluded that the parochial schools constituted "an integral part of the religious mission of the Catholic Church."

The dangers and corresponding entanglements are enhanced by the particular form of aid that the Rhode Island Act provides. . . .

In [Board of Education v.] Allen [1968], the Court refused to make assumptions, on a meager record, about the religious content of the textbooks that the State would be asked to provide. We cannot, however, refuse here to recognize that teachers have a substantially different ideological character from books. In terms of potential for involving some aspect of faith or morals in secular subjects, a textbook's content is ascertainable, but a teacher's handling of a subject is not.

We need not and do not assume that teachers in parochial schools will be guilty of bad faith or any conscious design to evade the limitations imposed by the statute and the First Amendment. We simply recognize that a dedicated religious person, teaching in a school affiliated with his or her faith and operated to inculcate its tenets, will inevitably experience great difficulty in remaining religiously neutral. . . .

To ensure that no trespass occurs, the State has therefore carefully conditioned its aid with pervasive restrictions. An eligible recipient must teach only those courses that are offered in the public schools and use only those texts and materials that are found in the public schools. In addition the teacher must not engage in teaching any course in religion.

A comprehensive, discriminating, and continuing state surveillance will inevitably be required to ensure that these restrictions are obeyed and the First Amendment otherwise respected. Unlike a book, a teacher cannot be inspected once so as to determine the extent and intent of his or her personal beliefs and subjective acceptance of the limitations imposed by the First Amendment. These prophylactic contacts will involve excessive and enduring entanglement between state and church. . . .

There is another area of entanglement in the Rhode Island program that gives concern. The statute excludes teachers employed by nonpublic schools whose average per-pupil expenditures on secular education equal or exceed the comparable figures for public schools. In the event that the total expenditures of an otherwise eligible school exceed this norm, the program requires the government to examine the schools records in order to determine how much of the total expenditures is attributable to secular education and how much to religious activity. This kind of state inspection and evaluation of the religious content of a religious organization is fraught with the sort of entanglement that the Constitution forbids. It is a relationship pregnant with dangers of excessive government direction of church schools and hence of churches. . . .

Pennsylvania Program

. . . The very restrictions and surveillance necessary to ensure that teachers play a strictly non-ideological role give rise to entanglements between church and state. The Pennsylvania statute, like that of Rhode Island, fosters this kind of relationship. . . .

The Pennsylvania statute, moreover, has the further defect of providing state financial aid directly to the church-related school. . . . The history of government grants of a continuing cash subsidy indicates that such programs have almost always been accompanied by varying measures of control and surveillance. The government cash grants before us now provide no basis for predicting that comprehensive measures of

surveillance and controls will not follow. In particular the government's post-audit power to inspect and evaluate a church-related school's financial records and to determine which expenditures are religious and which are secular creates an intimate and continuing relationship between church and state. . . .

A broader base of entanglement of yet a different character is presented by the divisive political potential of these state programs. In a community where such a large number of pupils are served by church-related schools, it can be assumed that state assistance will entail considerable political activity. Partisans of parochial schools, understandably concerned with rising costs and sincerely dedicated to both the religious and secular educational mission of their schools, will inevitably champion this cause and promote political action to achieve their goals. Those who oppose state aid, whether for constitutional, religious, or fiscal reasons, will inevitably respond and employ all of the usual political campaign techniques to prevail. Candidates will be forced to declare and voters to choose. It would be unrealistic to ignore the fact that many people confronted with issues of this kind will find their votes aligned with their faith.

Ordinarily political debate and division, however vigorous or even partisan, are normal and healthy manifestations of our democratic system of government, but political division along religious lines was one of the principal evils against which the First Amendment was intended to protect. . . . The potential divisiveness of such conflict is a threat to the normal political process. . . .

The potential for political divisiveness related to religious belief and practice is aggravated in these two statutory programs by the need for continuing annual appropriations and the likelihood of larger and larger demands as costs and populations grow. . . .

MR. JUSTICE WHITE, dissenting.

Our prior cases have recognized the dual role of parochial schools in American society: they perform both religious and secular functions. It is enough for me that the States and the Federal Government are financing a separable secular function of overriding importance in order to sustain the legislation here challenged. That religion and private interests other than education may substantially benefit does not convert these laws into impermissible establishments of religion.

. . . Where a state program seeks to ensure the proper education of its young, in private as well as public schools, free exercise considerations at least counsel against refusing support for students attending parochial schools simply because in that setting they are also being instructed in the tenets of the faith they are constitutionally free to practice. . . .

The Court strikes down the Rhode Island statute on its face. No fault is found with the secular purpose of the program; there is no suggestion that the purpose of the program was aid to religion disguised in secular attire. Nor does the Court find that the primary effect of the program is to aid religion rather than to implement secular goals. The Court nevertheless finds that impermissible "entanglement" will result from administration of the program.

The Court thus creates an insoluble paradox for the State and the parochial schools. The State cannot finance secular instruction if it permits religion to be taught in the same classroom; but if it exacts a promise that religion not be so taught—a promise the school and its teachers are quite willing and on this record able to give—and enforces it, it is then entangled in the "no entanglement" aspect of the Court's Establishment Clause jurisprudence. . . .

With respect to Pennsylvania, the Court, accepting as true the factual allegations of the complaint, as it must for purpose of a motion to dismiss, would reverse the dismissal of the complaint and invalidate the legislation. The critical allegations, as paraphrased by the Court, are that "the church-related elementary and secondary schools are controlled by religious organizations, have the purpose of propagating and promoting a particular religious faith, and conduct their operations to fulfill that purpose." . . . From these allegations the Court concludes that forbidden entanglements would follow from enforcing compliance with the secular purpose for which the state money is being paid.

I disagree. There is no specific allegation in the complaint that sectarian teaching does or would invade secular classes supported by state funds. That the schools are operated to promote a particular religion is quite consistent with the view that secular teaching devoid of religious instruction can successfully be maintained. . . . I would no more here than in the Rhode Island case substitute presumption for proof that religion is or would be taught in state-financed secular courses or assume that enforcement measures would be so extensive as to border on a free exercise violation. . . .

I do agree, however, that the complaint should not have been dismissed for failure to state a cause of action. . . . Hence, I would reverse the judgment of the District Court and remand the case for trial, thereby holding the Pennsylvania legislation valid on its face but leaving open the question of its validity as applied to the particular facts of this case. . . .

Wallace v. *Jaffree*
472 U.S. 38; 105 S. Ct. 2479; 86 L. Ed. 2d 29 (1985)

Beginning in the late 1970s, roughly half the states passed legislation authorizing a "moment of silence" at the outset of classes in public schools. This case provided the Supreme Court its first opportunity to consider the constitutionality of such laws. At issue was a 1981 Alabama law, under which "a period of silence not to exceed one minute in duration shall be observed for meditation or voluntary prayer." (This law superseded a 1978 Alabama enactment which authorized a moment of silence but did not mention prayer.) Ishmael Jaffree, who had three children in Alabama public schools, challenged the 1981 law, claiming that it violated the First Amendment, made applicable to the states by the Fourteenth Amendment. The district court, in an unusual opinion, ruled against Jaffree, claiming that the Establishment Clause did not bar states from establishing a religion. The court of appeals reversed, ruling that the statute did not serve a secular purpose, and the state appealed to the Supreme Court. *Opinion of the Court: Stevens, Brennan, Marshall, Blackmun, Powell. Concurring opinions: Powell; O'Connor. Dissenting opinions: Burger; White; Rehnquist.*

JUSTICE STEVENS delivered the opinion of the Court.

When the Court has been called upon to construe the breadth of the Establishment Clause, it has examined the criteria developed over a period of many years. Thus, in *Lemon* v. *Kurtzman* (1971), we wrote:

"Every analysis in this area must begin with consideration of the cumulative criteria developed by the Court over many years. Three such tests may be gleaned from our cases. First, the statute must have a secular legislative purpose; second, its principal or primary effect must be one that neither advances nor inhibits religion; finally, the statute must not foster 'an excessive government entanglement with religion.'" It is the first of these three criteria that is most plainly implicated by this case. As the District Court correctly recognized, no consideration of the second or third criteria is necessary if a statute does not have a clearly secular purpose. . . .

In applying the purpose test, it is appropriate to ask "whether government's actual purpose is to endorse or disapprove of religion." In this case, the answer to that question is dispositive. For the record not only provides us with an unambiguous affirmative answer, but it also reveals that the enactment of § 16-1-20.1 was not motivated by any clearly secular purpose—indeed, the statute had *no* secular purpose.

The sponsor of the bill that became § 16-1-20.1, Senator Donald Holmes, inserted into the legislative record—apparently without dissent—a statement indicating that the legislation was an "effort to return voluntary prayer" to the public schools. Later Senator Holmes confirmed this purpose before the District Court. In response to the question whether he had any purpose for the legislation other than returning voluntary prayer to public schools, he stated, "No, I did not have no other purpose in mind." The State did not present evidence of *any* secular purpose. . . .

The legislative intent to return prayer to the public schools is, of course, quite different from merely protecting every student's right to engage in voluntary prayer during an appropriate moment of silence during the school day. The 1978 statute already protected that right, containing nothing that prevented any student from engaging in voluntary prayer during a silent minute of meditation. Appellants have not identified any secular purpose that was not fully served by § 16-1-20 before the enactment of § 16-1-20.1. Thus, only two conclusions are consistent with the text of § 16-1-20.1: (1) the statute was enacted to convey a message of State endorsement and promotion of prayer; or (2) the statute was enacted for no purpose. No one suggests that the statute was nothing but a meaningless or irrational act.

. . . The Legislature enacted § 16-1-20.1 despite the existence of § 16-1-20 for the sole purpose of expressing the State's endorsement of prayer activities for one minute at the beginning of each school day. The addition of "or voluntary prayer" indicates that the State intended to characterize prayer as a favored practice. Such an endorsement is not consistent with the established principle that the government must pursue a course of complete neutrality toward religion.

JUSTICE O'CONNOR, concurring in the judgment.

A state sponsored moment of silence in the public schools is different from state sponsored vocal prayer or Bible reading. First, a moment of silence is not inherently religious. Silence, unlike prayer or Bible reading, need not be associated with a religious exercise. Second, a pupil who participates in a moment of silence need not compromise his or her beliefs. During a moment of silence, a student who objects to prayer is left to his or her own thoughts, and is not compelled to listen to the prayers or thoughts of others. For these simple reasons, a moment of silence statute does not stand or fall under the Establishment Clause according to how the Court regards vocal prayer or Bible reading. . . .

The analysis above suggests that moment of silence laws in many States should pass Establishment Clause scrutiny because they do not favor the child who chooses to pray during a moment of silence over the child who chooses to meditate or reflect. Alabama Code § 16-1-20.1 does not stand on the same footing. However deferentially one examines its text and legislative history, however objectively one views the message attempted to be conveyed to the public, the conclusion is unavoidable that the purpose of the statute is to endorse prayer in public schools. I accordingly agree with the Court of Appeals that the Alabama statute has a purpose which is in violation of the Establishment Clause, and cannot be upheld.

JUSTICE REHNQUIST, dissenting.

Thirty-eight years ago this Court, in *Everson* v. *Board of Education* summarized its exegesis of Establishment Clause doctrine thus:

"In the words of Jefferson, the clause against establishment of religion by law was intended to erect 'a wall of separation between church and State.'"

It is impossible to build sound constitutional doctrine upon a mistaken understanding of constitutional history, but unfortunately the Establishment Clause has been expressly freighted with Jefferson's misleading metaphor for nearly forty years. When we turn to the record of the proceedings in the First Congress leading up to the adoption of the Establishment Clause of the Constitution, including Madison's significant contributions thereto, we see a far different picture of its purpose than the highly simplified "wall of separation between church and State." . . .

On the basis of record of these proceedings in the House of Representatives, James Madison was undoubtedly the most important architect among the members of the House of the amendments which became the Bill of Rights, but it was James Madison speaking as an advocate of sensible legislative compromise, not as an advocate of incorporating the Virginia Statute of Religious Liberty into the United States Constitution. . . . His original language "nor shall any national religion be established" obviously does not conform to the "wall of separation" between church and State idea which latter day commentators have ascribed to him. His explanation on

the floor of the meaning of his language—"that Congress should not establish a religion, and enforce the legal observation of it by law" is of the same ilk. When he replied to Huntington in the debate over the proposal which came from the Select Committee of the House, he urged that the language "no religion shall be established by law" should be amended by inserting the word "national" in front of the word "religion."

It seems indisputable from these glimpses of Madison's thinking, as reflected by actions on the floor of the House in 1789, that he saw the amendment as designed to prohibit the establishment of a national religion, and perhaps to prevent discrimination among sects. He did not see it as requiring neutrality on the part of government between religion and irreligion. Thus the Court's opinion in *Everson*—while correct in bracketing Madison and Jefferson together in their exertions in their home state leading to the enactment of the Virginia Statute of Religious Liberty—is totally incorrect in suggesting that Madison carried these views onto the floor of the United States House of Representatives when he proposed the language which would ultimately become the Bill of Rights. . . .

None of the other Members of Congress who spoke during the August 15th debate expressed the slightest indication that they thought the language before them from the Select Committee, or the evil to be aimed at, would require that the Government be absolutely neutral as between religion and irreligion. The evil to be aimed at, so far as those who spoke were concerned, appears to have been the establishment of a national church, and perhaps the preference of one religious sect over another; but it was definitely not concern about whether the Government might aid all religions evenhandedly. . . .

The actions of the First Congress, which re-enacted the Northwest Ordinance for the governance of the Northwest Territory in 1789, confirm the view that Congress did not mean that the Government should be neutral between religion and irreligion. . . . [This Ordinance] provided that "[r]eligion, morality, and knowledge, being necessary to good government and the happiness of mankind, schools and the means of education shall forever be encouraged." Land grants for schools in the Northwest Territory were not limited to public schools. It was not until 1845 that

Congress limited land grants in the new States and Territories to nonsectarian schools. . . .

As the United States moved from the 18th into the 19th century, Congress appropriated time and again public moneys in support of sectarian Indian education carried on by religious organizations. Typical of these was Jefferson's treaty with the Kaskaskia Indians, which provided annual cash support for the Tribe's Roman Catholic priest and church. It was not until 1897, when aid to sectarian education for Indians had reached $500,000 annually, that Congress decided thereafter to cease appropriating money for education in sectarian schools. This history shows the fallacy of the notion found in *Everson* that "no tax in any amount" may be levied for religious activities in any form.

Joseph Story, a member of this Court from 1822 to 1845, and during much of that time a professor at the Harvard Law School, published by far the most comprehensive treatise on the United States Constitution that had then appeared. Volume 2 of Story's Commentaries on the Constitution of the United States discussed the meaning of the Establishment Clause of the First Amendment this way:

"Probably at the time of the adoption of the Constitution, and of the amendment to it now under consideration [First Amendment], the general if not the universal sentiment in America was, that Christianity ought to receive encouragement from the State so far as was not incompatible with the private rights of conscience and the freedom of religious worship. An attempt to level all religions, and to make it a matter of state policy to hold all in utter indifference, would have created universal disapprobation, if not universal indignation." . . .

It would seem from this evidence that the Establishment Clause of the First Amendment had acquired a well-accepted meaning: it forbade establishment of a national religion, and forbade preference among religious sects or denominations. . . . There is simply no historical foundation for the proposition that the Framers intended to build the "wall of separation" that was constitutionalized in *Everson*.

Notwithstanding the absence of an historical basis for this theory of rigid separation, the wall idea might well have served as a useful albeit misguided analytical concept, had it led this Court to unified and principled results in Establishment Clause cases. The opposite, unfortunately, has been true; in the 38 years since *Everson* our Establishment Clause cases have been neither principled nor unified. . . . Whether due to its lack of historical support or its practical unworkability, the *Everson* "wall" has proven all but useless as a guide to sound constitutional adjudication. . . . It should be frankly and explicitly abandoned. . . .

The Framers intended the Establishment Clause to prohibit the designation of any church as a "national" one. The Clause was also designed to stop the Federal Government from asserting a preference for one religious denomination or sect over others. Given the "incorporation" of the Establishment Clause as against the States via the Fourteenth Amendment in *Everson*, States are prohibited as well from establishing a religion or discriminating between sects. As its history abundantly shows, however, nothing in the Establishment Clause requires government to be strictly neutral between religion and irreligion, nor does that Clause prohibit Congress or the States from pursuing legitimate secular ends through nondiscriminatory sectarian means.

Lee v. *Weisman*

505 U.S.; 112 S. Ct. 2649; 120 L. Ed. 2d 467 (1992)

For many years the public middle schools and high schools in Providence, Rhode Island, invited members of the clergy to offer prayers at graduation ceremonies. In line with that practice, Robert E. Lee, principal of the Bishop Middle School, invited Rabbi Leslie Gutterman to offer an invocation and benediction as part of the school's graduation ceremony. When Rabbi Gutterman accepted, the principal sent him a pamphlet entitled "Guidelines for Civic Occasions," prepared by the National Conference of Christians and Jews, which recommended that public prayers at non-sectarian civic events be composed with "inclusiveness and sensitivity."

Four days before the ceremony, Daniel Weisman, the father of Deborah Weisman, who was graduating, sought a temporary restraining order in the United States District Court for the District of Rhode Island to prohibit school officials from including an invocation and benediction in the graduation ceremony. The court denied the motion for lack of adequate time to consider it. Although attendance was not mandatory, Deborah and her family attended the graduation, where the prayers were recited.

After the graduation, Daniel Weisman sought a permanent injunction barring school officials from inviting the clergy to deliver prayers at future graduations. He noted that his daughter was enrolled in high school in the district and argued that prayers would likely be offered at her high school graduation. The District Court ruled that the practice of including invocations and benedictions in public school graduations violated the Establishment Clause. The Court of Appeals affirmed, and the Supreme Court granted certiorari. *Opinion of the Court: Kennedy, Blackmun, Stevens, O'Connor, Souter. Concurring opinions: Blackmun, Stevens, O'Connor; Souter, Stevens, O'Connor. Dissenting opinion: Scalia, Rehnquist, White, Thomas.*

JUSTICE KENNEDY delivered the opinion of the Court.

The government involvement with religious activity in this case is pervasive, to the point of creating a state-sponsored and state-directed religious exercise in a public school. Conducting this formal religious observance conflicts with settled rules pertaining to prayer exercises for students, and that suffices to determine the question before us. The principle that government may accommodate the free exercise of religion does not supersede the fundamental limitations imposed by the Establishment Clause. It is beyond dispute that, at a minimum, the Constitution guarantees that government may not coerce anyone to support or participate in religion or its exercise, or otherwise act in a way which "establishes a [state] religion or religious faith, or tends to do so." *Everson* v. *Board of Education of Ewing* (1947). The State's involvement in the school prayers challenged today violates these central principles.

That involvement is as troubling as it is undenied. A school official, the principal, decided that an invocation and a benediction should be given; this is a choice attributable to the State, and from a constitutional perspective it is as if a state statute decreed that prayers should occur. The

principal chose the religious participant, here a rabbi, and that choice is also attributable to the State. . . . The State's role did not end with the decision to include a prayer and with the choice of clergyman. Principal Lee provided Rabbi Gutterman with a copy of the "Guidelines for Civic Occasions," and advised him that his prayers should be nonsectarian. Through these means the principal directed and controlled the content of the prayer. . . . Though the efforts of the schools officials in this case to find common ground appear to have been a good-faith attempt to recognize the common aspects of religions and not the divisive ones, our precedents do not permit school officials to assist in composing prayers as an incident to a formal exercise for their students. *Engel* v. *Vitale* (1962). And these same precedents caution us to measure the idea of a civic religion against the central meaning of the Religion Clauses of the First Amendment, which is that all creeds must be tolerated and none favored. The suggestion that government may establish an official or civic religion as a means of avoiding the establishment of a religion with more specific creeds strikes us as a contradiction that cannot be accepted.

The degree of school involvement here made it clear that the graduation prayers bore the imprint of the State and thus put school-age children who objected in an untenable position. We turn our attention now to consider the position of the students, both those who desired the prayer and she who did not.

To endure the speech of false ideas or offensive content and then to counter it is part of learning how to live in a pluralistic society, a society which insists upon open discourse towards the end of a tolerant citizenry. And tolerance presupposes some mutuality of obligation. It is argued that our constitutional vision of a free society requires confidence in our own ability to accept or reject ideas of which we do not approve, and that prayer at a high school graduation does nothing more than offer a choice. By the time they are seniors, high school students no doubt have been required to attend classes and assemblies and to complete assignments exposing them to ideas they find distasteful or immoral or absurd or all of these. Against this background, students may consider it an odd measure of justice to be subjected during the course of their education to ideas deemed offensive and irreligious, but to be denied a brief, formal prayer ceremony that the school offers in return. This argument cannot prevail, however. It overlooks a fundamental dynamic of the Constitution.

The First Amendment protects speech and religion by quite different mechanisms. Speech is protected by insuring its full expression even when the government participates, for the very object of some of our most important speech is to persuade the government to adopt an idea as its own. The method for protecting freedom of worship and freedom of conscience in religious matters is quite the reverse. In religious debate or expression the government is not a prime participant, for the Framers deemed religious establishment antithetical to the freedom of all. The Free Exercise Clause embraces a freedom of conscience and worship that has close parallels in the speech provisions of the First Amendment, but the Establishment Clause is a specific prohibition on forms of state intervention in religious affairs with no precise counterpart in the speech provisions. The explanation lies in the lesson of history that was and is the inspiration for the Establishment Clause, the lesson that in the hands of government what might begin as a tolerant expression of religious views may end in

a policy to indoctrinate and coerce. A state-created orthodoxy puts at grave risk that freedom of belief and conscience which are the sole assurance that religious faith is real, not imposed.

As we have observed before, there are heightened concerns with protecting freedom of conscience from subtle coercive pressure in the elementary and secondary public schools. Our decisions in *Engel* v. *Vitale* (1962) and *Abington Township School District* [v. *Schempp* (1963)] recognize, among other things, that prayer exercises in public schools carry a particular risk of indirect coercion. . . . What to most believers may seem nothing more than a reasonable request that the nonbeliever respect their religious practices, in a school context may appear to the nonbeliever or dissenter to be an attempt to employ the machinery of the State to enforce a religious orthodoxy.

We need not look beyond the circumstances of this case to see the phenomenon at work. The undeniable fact is that the school district's supervision and control of a high school graduation ceremony places public pressure, as well as peer pressure, on attending students to stand as a group or, at least, maintain a respectful silence during the Invocation and Benediction. This pressure, though subtle and indirect, can be as real as any overt compulsion. Of course, in our culture standing or remaining silent can signify adherence to a view or simple respect for the views of others. And no doubt some persons who have no desire to join a prayer have little objection to standing as a sign of respect for those who do. But for the dissenter of high school age, who has a reasonable perception that she is being forced by the State to pray in a manner her conscience will not allow, the injury is no less real. There can be no doubt that for many, if not most, of the students at the graduation, the act of standing or remaining silent was an expression of participation in the Rabbi's prayer. That was the very point of the religious exercise. It is of little comfort to a dissenter, then, to be told that for her the act of standing or remaining in silence signifies mere respect, rather than participation. What matters is that, given our social conventions, a reasonable dissenter in this milieu could believe that the group exercise signified her own participation or approval of it.

Finding no violation under these circumstances would place objectors in the dilemma of participating, with all that implies, or protesting. We do not address whether that choice is acceptable if the affected citizens are mature adults, but we think the State may not, consistent with the Establishment Clause, place primary and secondary school children in this position. Research in psychology supports the common assumption that adolescents are often susceptible to pressure from their peers toward conformity, and that the influence is strongest in matters of social convention. . . . To recognize that the choice imposed by the State constitutes an unacceptable constraint only acknowledges that the government may no more use social pressure to enforce orthodoxy than it may use more direct means.

The injury caused by the government's action, and the reason why Daniel and Deborah Weisman object to it, is that the State, in a school setting, in effect required participation in a religious exercise. It is, we concede, a brief exercise during which the individual can concentrate on joining its message, meditate on her own religion, or let her mind wander. But the embarrassment and the intrusion of the religious exercise cannot be refuted by arguing that these prayers, and similar ones to be said in the future, are of a de minimis character. To do so would be an affront to the Rabbi who offered them and to all those for whom the prayers were an essential and profound recognition of divine authority.

. . . There was a stipulation in the District Court that attendance at graduation and promotional ceremonies is voluntary. Petitioners and the United States, as amicus, made this a center point of the case, arguing that the option of not attending the graduation excuses any inducement or coercion in the ceremony itself. The argument lacks all persuasion. . . . Everyone knows that in our society and in our culture high school graduation is one of life's most significant occasions. A school rule which excuses attendance is beside the point. Attendance may not be required by official decree, yet it is apparent that a student is not free to absent herself from the graduation exercise in any real sense of the term "voluntary," for absence would require forfeiture of those intangible benefits which have motivated the student through youth and all her high school years. Graduation is a time for family and those closest to the student to celebrate success and express mutual wishes of gratitude and re-

spect, all to the end of impressing upon the young person the role that it is his or her right and duty to assume in the community and all of its diverse parts. . . .

. . . The Government's argument gives insufficient recognition to the real conflict of conscience faced by the young student. The essence of the Government's position is that with regard to a civic, social occasion of this importance it is the objector, not the majority, who must take unilateral and private action to avoid compromising religious scruples, here by electing to miss the graduation exercise. This turns conventional First Amendment analysis on its head. It is a tenet of the First amendment that the State cannot require one of its citizens to forfeit his or her rights and benefits as the price of resisting conformance to state-sponsored religious practice. To say that a student must remain apart from the ceremony at the opening invocation and closing benediction is to risk compelling conformity in an environment analogous to a classroom setting, where we have said that the risk of compulsion is especially high.

. . . Inherent differences between the public school system and a session of a State Legislature distinguish this case from *Marsh* v. *Chambers* (1983). . . . The atmosphere at the opening of a session of a state legislature where adults are free to enter and leave with little comment and for any number of reasons cannot compare with the constraining potential of the one school event most important for the student to attend. The influence and force of a formal exercise in a school graduation are far greater than the prayer exercise condoned in *Marsh*. The *Marsh* majority in fact gave specific recognition to this distinction and placed particular reliance on it in upholding the prayers at issue there. For the reasons we have stated, the judgment of the Court of Appeals is

Affirmed.

JUSTICE SOUTER, with whom JUSTICE STEVENS and JUSTICE O'CONNOR join, concurring.

. . . Whatever else may define the scope of accommodation permissible under the Establishment Clause, one requirement is clear: accommodation must lift a discernible burden on the free exercise of religion. Concern for the position of religious individuals in the modern regulatory state cannot justify official solicitude for a religious practice unburdened by general rules; such gratuitous largesse would effectively favor religion over disbelief. By these lights one easily sees that, in sponsoring the graduation prayers at issue here, the State has crossed the line from permissible accommodation to unconstitutional establishment.

Religious students cannot complain that omitting prayers from their graduation ceremony would, in any realistic sense, "burden" their spiritual callings. To be sure, many of them invest this rite of passage with spiritual significance, but they may express their religious feelings about it before and after the ceremony. They may even organize a privately sponsored baccalaureate if they desire the company of like-minded students. Because they accordingly have no need for the machinery of the State to affirm their beliefs, the government's sponsorship of prayer at the graduation ceremony is most reasonably understood as an official endorsement of religion and, in this instance, of theistic religion.

Petitioners would deflect this conclusion by arguing that graduation prayers are no different from presidential religious proclamations and similar official "acknowledgments" of religion in public life. But religious invocations in Thanksgiving Day addresses and the like, rarely noticed, ignored without effort, conveyed over an impersonal medium, and directed at no one in particular, inhabit a pallid zone worlds apart from official prayers delivered to a captive audience of public school students and their families. Madison himself respected the difference between the trivial and the serious in constitutional practice. Realizing that his contemporaries were unlikely to take the Establishment Clause seriously enough to forgo a legislative chaplainship, he suggested that "[r]ather than let this step beyond the landmarks of power have the effect of a legitimate precedent, it will be better to apply to it the legal aphorism de minimis non curat lex. . . ." But that logic permits no winking at the practice in question here. When public school officials, armed with the State's authority, convey an endorsement of religion to their students, they strike near the core of the Establishment Clause. However "ceremonial" their messages may be, they are flatly unconstitutional.

JUSTICE SCALIA, with whom the CHIEF JUSTICE, JUSTICE WHITE, and JUSTICE THOMAS join, dissenting.

. . . In holding that the Establishment Clause prohibits invocations and benedictions at public-school graduation ceremonies, the Court—with nary a mention that it is doing so—lays waste a tradition as old as public-school graduation ceremonies themselves, and that is a component of an even more longstanding American tradition of nonsectarian prayer to God at public celebrations generally. As its instrument of destruction, the bulldozer of its social engineering, the Court invents a boundless, and boundlessly manipulable, test of psychological coercion. . . . Today's opinion shows more forcefully than volumes of argumentation why our Nation's protection, that fortress which is our Constitution, cannot possibly rest upon the changeable philosophical predilections of the Justices of this Court, but must have deep foundations in the historic practices of our people.

. . . The Court presumably would separate graduation invocations and benedictions from other instances of public "preservation and transmission of religious beliefs" on the ground that they involve "psychological coercion." . . . A few citations of "[r]esearch in psychology" that have no particular bearing upon the precise issue here cannot disguise the fact that the Court has gone beyond the realm that judges know what they are doing. The Court's argument that state officials have "coerced" students to take part in the invocation and benediction at graduation ceremonies is, not to put too fine a point on it, incoherent.

. . . The Court declares that students' "attendance and participation in the [invocation and benediction] are in a fair and real sense obligatory." But what exactly is this "fair and real sense"? According to the Court, students at graduation who want "to avoid the fact or appearance of participation" in the invocation and benediction are psychologically obligated by "public pressure, as well as peer pressure, . . . to stand as a group or, at least, maintain respectful silence" during those prayers.

. . . The Court's notion that a student who simply sits in "respectful silence" during the invocation and benediction (when all others are standing) has somehow joined—or would somehow be perceived as having joined—in the prayers is nothing short of ludicrous. We indeed live in a vulgar age. But surely "our social conventions" have not coarsened to the point that anyone who does not stand on his chair and shout obscenities can reasonably be deemed to have assented to everything said in his presence. Since the Court does not dispute that students exposed to prayers at graduation ceremonies retain (despite "subtle coercive pressures") the free will to sit, there is absolutely no basis for the Court's decision. It is fanciful enough to say that "a reasonable dissenter," standing head erect in a class of bowed heads, "could believe that the group exercise signified her own participation or approval of it." It is beyond the absurd to say that she could entertain such a belief while pointedly declining to rise.

But let us assume the very worst, that the nonparticipating graduate is "subtly coerced" . . . to stand! . . . The Court acknowledges that "in our culture standing . . . can signify adherence to a view or simple respect for the views of others." . . . But if it is a permissible inference that one who is standing is doing so simply out of respect for the prayers of others that are in progress, then how can it possibly be said that a "reasonable dissenter . . . could believe that the group exercise signified her own participation or approval"? Quite obviously, it cannot. I may add, moreover, that maintaining respect for the religious observances of others is a fundamental civic virtue that government (including the public schools) can and should cultivate—so that even if it were the case that the displaying of such respect might be mistaken for taking part in the prayer, I would deny the dissenter's interest in avoiding even the false appearance of participation constitutionally trumps the government's interest in fostering respect for religion generally.

The opinion manifests that the Court itself has not given careful consideration to its test of psychological coercion. For if it had, how could it observe, with no hint of concern or disapproval, that students stood for the Pledge of Allegiance, which immediately preceded Rabbi Gutterman's invocation? The government can, of course, no more coerce political orthodoxy than religious orthodoxy. Moreover, since the Pledge of Allegiance has been revised since [*West Virginia Board of Education* v.] *Barnette* to include the phrase "under God," recital of the Pledge would appear to raise the same Establishment Clause issue as the invocation and benediction. If students were psychologically coerced to remain standing during invocation, they must also have

been psychologically coerced, moments before, to stand for (and thereby, in the Court's view, take part in or appear to take part in) the Pledge. Must the Pledge therefore be barred from the public schools (both from graduation ceremonies and from the classroom)? In *Barnette* we held that a public-school student could not be compelled to recite the Pledge; we did not even hint that she could not be compelled to observe respectful silence—indeed, even to stand in respectful silence—when those who wished to recite it did so. Logically, this ought to be the next project for the Court's bulldozer.

. . . The other "dominant fac[t]" identified by the Court is that "[s]tate officials direct the performance of a formal religious exercise at school graduation ceremonies. . . . All the record shows is that principals of the Providence public schools, acting within their delegated authority, have invited clergy to deliver invocations and benedictions at graduations; and that Principal Lee invited Rabbi Gutterman, provided him a two-page flyer, prepared by the National Conference of Christians and Jews, giving general advice on inclusive prayer for civic occasions, and advised him that his prayers at graduation should be nonsectarian. . . . The Court identifies nothing in the record remotely suggesting that school officials have ever drafted, edited, screened, or censored graduation prayers, or that Rabbi Gutterman was a mouthpiece of the school officials.

. . . The deeper flaw in the Court's opinion does not lie in its wrong answer to the question whether there was state-induced "peer-pressure" coercion; it lies, rather, in the Court's making violation of the Establishment Clause hinge on such a precious question. The coercion that was a hallmark of historical establishments of religion was coercion of religious orthodoxy and of financial support *by force of law and threat of penalty*. . . . The Establishment Clause was adopted to prohibit such an establishment of religion at the federal level (and to protect state establishments of religion from federal interference). I will further acknowledge for the sake of argument that, as some scholars have argued, by 1790 the term "establishment" had acquired an additional meaning—financial support of religion generally, by public taxation—that reflected the development of "general or multiple" establishments, not limited to a single church. But that would still be an establishment coerced by force of law. . . . But there is simply no support for the proposition that the officially sponsored nondenominational invocation read by Rabbi Gutterman—with no one legally coerced to recite them—violated the Constitution of the United States. To the contrary, they are so characteristically American they could have come from the pen of George Washington or Abraham Lincoln himself.

Thus, while I have no quarrel with the Court's general proposition that the Establishment Clause "guarantees that government may not coerce anyone to support or participate in religion or its exercise," I see no warrant for expanding the concept of coercion beyond acts backed by threat of penalty—a brand of coercion that, happily, is readily discernible to those of us who have made a career of reading the disciples of Blackstone rather than of Freud. The Framers were indeed opposed to coercion of religious worship by the National Government; but, as their own sponsorship of nonsectarian prayer in public events demonstrates, they understand that "[s]peech is not coercive; the listener may do as he likes."

This historical discussion places in revealing perspective the Court's extravagant claim that the State has "for all practical purposes" and "in every practical sense" compelled students to participate in prayers at graduation. Beyond the fact, stipulated to by the parties, that attendance at graduation is voluntary, there is nothing in the record to indicate that failure of attending students to take part in the invocation or benediction was subject to any penalty or discipline.

. . . The reader has been told much in this case about the personal interest of Mr. Weisman and his daughter, and very little about the personal interests on the other side. They are not inconsequential. Church and state would not be such a difficult subject if religion were, as the Court apparently thinks it to be, some purely personal avocation that can be indulged entirely in secret, like pornography, in the privacy of one's room. For most believers it is not that, and has never been. Religious men and women of almost all denominations have felt it necessary to acknowledge and beseech the blessing of God as a people, and not just as individuals, because they believe in the "protection of divine Providence," as the Declaration of Independence put it, not just for individuals but for societies; because they believe God to be, as Washington's first Thanksgiving Proclamation put it, the "Great Lord and Ruler of Nations." One can believe in the effectiveness of such public worship, or one can deprecate and deride it. But the longstanding American tradition of prayer at official ceremonies displays with unmistakable clarity that the Establishment Clause does not forbid the government to accommodate it.

Board of Education of Kiryas Joel Village School District v. *Grumet*
512 U.S. 687; 114 S. Ct. 248; 129 L. Ed. 2d 546 (1994)

The Village of Kiryas Joel in New York is a religious enclave of Satmar Hasidim, practitioners of a strict form of Judaism. It was incorporated in 1977 under New York's general village incorporation law, with its boundaries intentionally drawn to exclude all but Satmars. The residents of Kiryas Joel established parochial schools, segregated by gender, at which their children receive a religiously based education. These schools, however, did not offer special education services for handicapped children, who were entitled under federal law to receive such services even if enrolled in private schools. Initially, the Monroe-Woodbury Central School District, which included the Village of Kiryas Joel, provided the services at an annex to one of the village's private schools. The District ended that arrangement in 1985 after the Supreme Court's rulings in *Aguilar* v. *Felton* (1985) and *School District of Grand Rapids* v. *Ball* (1985), which invalidated state provision of supplemental educational services in sectarian schools. Children from Kiryas Joel needing special education services then attended public schools outside the village, but most of their parents withdrew them from these schools, citing "the panic, fear and trauma [the children] suffered in leaving their own community and being with people whose ways were so different." To deal with this situation, the New York Legislature in 1989 established a separate school district that followed village lines. (This enactment is referred to in the Court's opinions as Chapter 748.) This new district operated only a special education program for handicapped children, with other children continuing to attend their parochial schools. Several neighboring districts also enrolled their handicapped Hasidic students in the district's special education program on a tuition basis.

[handwritten margin note: get up public school for the region which obtained children from certain Orthodox Jews]

Chapter 748 was challenged in state court as a violation of the Establishment Clause. The trial court agreed, and both the intermediate appellate court and the New York Court of Appeals, the state's supreme court, affirmed the trial court's decision. The U.S. Supreme Court then granted certiorari. *Opinion of the Court:* Souter, *Blackmun, Stevens, Ginsburg, O'Connor (in part). Concurring opinions:* Blackmun; Stevens, *Blackmun, Ginsburg;* O'Connor, Kennedy. *Dissenting opinion:* Scalia, *Rehnquist, Thomas.*

JUSTICE SOUTER delivered the opinion of the Court.

"A proper respect for both the Free Exercise and the Establishment Clauses compels the State to pursue a course of 'neutrality' toward religion," *Committee for Public Education and Religious Liberty* v. *Nyquist* (1973), favoring neither one religion over others nor religious adherents collectively over nonadherents. Chapter 748, the statute creating the Kiryas Joel Village School District, departs from this constitutional command by delegating the State's discretionary authority over public schools to a group defined by its character as a religious community, in a legal and historical context that gives no assurance that governmental power has been or will be exercised neutrally.

Larkin v. *Grendel's Den, Inc.* (1982) provides an instructive comparison with the litigation before us. There, the Court was requested to strike down a Massachusetts statute granting religious bodies veto power over applications for liquor licenses. Under the statute, the governing body of any church, synagogue, or school located within 500 feet of an applicant's premises could, simply by submitting written objection, prevent the Alcohol Beverage Control Commission from issuing a license. [T]he Court found that in two respects the statute violated "the wholesome 'neutrality' of which this Court's cases speak," *School District of Abington Township* v. *Schempp* (1963). The Act brought about a "fusion of governmental and religious functions" by delegating "important, discretionary governmental powers" to religious bodies, thus impermissibly entangling government and religion. And it lacked "any 'effective means of guaranteeing' that the delegated power '[would] be used exclusively for secular, neutral, and nonideological purposes'"; this, along with the "significant symbolic benefit to religion" associated with "the mere appearance of a joint exercise of legislative authority by Church and State," led the Court to conclude that the statute had a " 'primary' and 'principal' effect of advancing religion." Comparable constitutional problems inhere in the statute before us. . . .

The Establishment Clause problem presented by Chapter 748 is more subtle, but it resembles the issue raised in *Larkin* to the extent that the earlier case teaches that a State may not delegate its civic authority to a group chosen according to a religious criterion. Authority over public schools belongs to the State, and cannot be delegated to a local school district defined by the State in order to grant political control to a religious group. What makes this litigation different from *Larkin* is the delegation here of civic power to the "qualified voters of the village of Kiryas Joel," as distinct from a religious leader such as the village rov, or an institution of religious government like the formally constituted parish council in *Larkin*. In light of the circumstances of this case, however, this distinction turns out to lack constitutional significance.

It is, first, not dispositive that the recipients of state power in this case are a group of religious individuals united by common doctrine, not the group's leaders or officers. Although some school district franchise is common to all voters, the State's manipulation of the franchise for this district limited it to Satmars, giving the sect exclusive control of the political subdivision. In the circumstances of this case, the difference between thus vesting state power in the members of a religious group as such instead of the officers of its sectarian organization is one of form, not substance.

Of course, Chapter 748 delegates power not by express reference to the religious belief of the Satmar community, but to residents of the "territory of the village of Kiryas Joel." Thus the second (and arguably more important) distinction between this case and *Larkin* is the identification here of the group to exercise civil authority in terms not expressly religious. But our analysis does not end with the text of the statute at issue, and the context here persuades us that Chapter 748 effectively identifies these recipients of governmental authority by reference to doctrinal adherence, even though it does not do so expressly. We find this to be the better view of the facts because of the way the boundary lines of the school district divide residents according to religious affiliation, under the terms of an unusual and special legislative act.

It is undisputed that those who negotiated the village boundaries when applying the general village incorporation statute drew them so as to exclude all but Satmars, and that the New York Legislature was well aware that the village remained exclusively Satmar in 1989 when it adopted Chapter 748. The significance of this fact to the state legislature is indicated by the further fact that carving out the village school district ran counter to customary districting practices in the State. Indeed, the trend in New York is not toward dividing school districts but toward consolidating them. . . .

The origin of the district in a special act of the legislature, rather than the State's general laws governing school district reorganization, is likewise anomalous. Although the legislature has established some 20 existing school districts by special act, all but one of these are districts in name only, having been designed to be run by private organizations serving institutionalized children.

The one school district petitioners point to that was formed by special act of the legislature to serve a whole community, as this one was, is a district formed for a new town, much larger and more heterogeneous than this village, being built on land that straddled two existing districts.

Thus the Kiryas Joel Village School District is exceptional to the point of singularity, as the only district coming to our notice that the legislature carved from a single existing district to serve local residents.

Because the district's creation ran uniquely counter to state practice, following the lines of a religious community where the customary and neutral principles would not have dictated the same result, we have good reasons to treat this district as the reflection of a religious criterion for identifying the recipients of civil authority. Not even the special needs of the children in this community can explain the legislature's unusual Act, for the State could have responded to the concerns of the Satmar parents without implicating the Establishment Clause, as we explain in some detail further on. We therefore find the legislature's Act to be substantially equivalent to defining a political subdivision and hence the qualification for its franchise by a religious test, resulting in a purposeful and forbidden "fusion of governmental and religious functions." *Larkin* v. *Grendel's Den*, 459 U.S., at 126. . . .

The fact that this school district was created by a special and unusual Act of the legislature also gives reason for concern whether the benefit received by the Satmar community is one that the legislature will provide equally to other religious (and nonreligious) groups. This is the second malady the *Larkin* Court identified in the law before it, the absence of an "effective means of guaranteeing" that governmental power will be and has been neutrally employed.

The anomalously case-specific nature of the legislature's exercise of state authority in creating this district for a religious community leaves the Court without any direct way to review such state action for the purpose of safeguarding a principal at the heart of the Establishment Clause, that government should not prefer one religion to another, or religion to irreligion.

Because the religious community of Kiryas Joel did not receive its new governmental authority simply as one of many communities eligible for equal treatment under a general law, we have no assurance that the next similarly situated group seeking a school district of its own will receive one; unlike an administrative agency's denial of an exemption from a generally applicable law, which "would be entitled to a judicial audience." . . .

In finding that Chapter 748 violates the requirement of governmental neutrality by extending the benefit of a special franchise, we do not deny that the Constitution allows the state to accommodate religious needs by alleviating special burdens. But accommodation is not a principle without limits, and what petitioners seek is an adjustment to the Satmars' religiously grounded preferences that our cases do not countenance. Prior decisions have allowed religious communities and institutions to pursue their own interests free from governmental interference, but we have never hinted that an otherwise unconstitutional delegation of political power to a religious group could be saved as a religious accommodation. Petitioners' proposed accommodation singles out a particular religious sect for special treatment, and whatever the limits of permissible legislative accommodations may be, it is clear that neutrality as among religions must be honored.

JUSTICE STEVENS, with whom JUSTICE BLACKMUN and JUSTICE GINSBURG join, concurring.

New York created a special school district for the members of the Satmar religious sect in response to parental concern that children suffered "panic, fear and trauma" when "leaving their own community and being with people whose ways were so different." To meet those concerns, the State could have taken steps to alleviate the children's fear by teaching their schoolmates to be tolerant and respectful of Satmar customs. Action of that kind would raise no constitutional concerns and would further the strong public interest in promoting diversity and understanding in the public schools.

Instead, the State responded with a solution that affirmatively supports a religious sect's interest in segregating itself and preventing its children from associating with their neighbors. The isolation of these children, while it may protect them from "panic, fear and trauma," also unquestionably increased the likelihood that they would remain within the fold, faithful adherents of their parents' religious faith. By creating a school district that is specifically intended to shield children from contact with others who have "different ways," the State provided official support to cement the attachment of young adherents to a particular faith. It is telling, in this regard, that two thirds of the school's full-time students are Hasidic handicapped children from *outside* the village; the Kiryas Joel school thus serves a population far wider than the village—one defined less by geography than by religion.

Affirmative state action in aid of segregation of this character is, I believe, fairly characterized as establishing, rather than merely accommodating, religion. For this reason, as well as the reasons set out in JUSTICE SOUTER's opinion, I am persuaded that the New York law at issue in these cases violates the Establishment Clause of the First Amendment.

JUSTICE O'CONNOR, concurring in part and concurring in the judgment.

I think there is one other accommodation that would be entirely permissible: the 1984 scheme, which was discontinued because of our decision in *Aguilar*. The Religion Clauses prohibit the government from favoring religion, but they provide no warrant for discriminating *against* religion. All handicapped children are entitled by law to government-funded special education. If the government provides this education on-site at public schools and at nonsectarian private schools, it is only fair that it provide it on-site at sectarian schools as well.

I thought this to be true in *Aguilar*, and I still believe it today. The Establishment Clause does not demand hostility to religion, religious ideas, religious people, or religious schools. It is the Court's insistence on disfavoring religion in *Aguilar* that led New York to favor it here. The court should, in a proper case, be prepared to reconsider *Aguilar*, in order to bring our Establishment Clause jurisprudence back to what I think is the proper track—government impartiality, not animosity, towards religion.

JUSTICE SCALIA, with whom the CHIEF JUSTICE and JUSTICE THOMAS join, dissenting.

Unlike most of our Establishment Clause cases involving education, these cases involve no public funding, however slight or indirect, to private religious schools. They do not involve private schools at all. The school under scrutiny is a public school specifically designed to provide a public secular education to handicapped students. The superintendent of the school, who is not Hasidic, is a 20-year veteran of the New York City public school system, with expertise in the area of bilingual, bicultural, special education. The teachers and therapists at the school all live outside the village of Kiryas Joel. While the village's private schools are profoundly religious and strictly segregated by sex, classes at the public school are co-ed and the curriculum secular. The school building has the bland appearance of a public school, unadorned by religious symbols or markings; and the school complies with the laws and regulations governing all other New York State public schools. There is no suggestion, moreover, that this public school has gone too far in making special adjustments to the religious needs of its students. In sum, these cases involve only public aid to a school that is public as can be. The only thing distinctive about the school is that all the students share the same religion.

None of our cases has ever suggested that there is anything wrong with that. In fact, the Court has specifically *approved* the education of students of a single religion on a neutral site adjacent to a private religious school. For these very good reasons, JUSTICE SOUTER's opinion does not focus upon the school, but rather upon the school district and the New York Legislature that created it. His arguments, though sometimes intermingled, at two: that reposing governmental power in the Kiryas Joel School District is the same as reposing governmental power in a religious group; and that in enacting the statute creating the district, the New York State Legislature was discriminating on the basis of religion, *i.e.*, favoring the Satmar Hasidim over others.

For his thesis that New York has unconstitutionally conferred governmental authority upon the Satmar sect, JUSTICE SOUTER relies extensively, and virtually exclusively, upon *Larkin* v. *Grendel's Den, Inc.* (1982). JUSTICE SOUTER believes that the present case "resembles" *Grendel's Den* because that case "teaches that a state may not delegate its civic authority *to a group chosen according to a religious criterion.*" That misdescribes both what that case taught (which is that a state may not delegate its civil authority *to a church*), and what this case involves (which is a group chosen according to cultural characteristics). . . .

JUSTICE SOUTER's position boils down to the quite novel proposition that any group of citizens (say, the residents of Kiryas Joel) can be invested with political power, but not if they all belong to the same religion. Of course such *disfavoring* of religion is positively antagonistic to the purposes of the Religion Clauses, and we have rejected it before.

III

In turn, next, to JUSTICE SOUTER's second justification for finding an establishment of religion: his facile conclusion that the New York Legislature's creation of the Kiryas Joel School District was religiously motivated. But in the Land of the Free, democratically adopted laws are not so easily impeached by unelected judges. To establish the unconstitutionality of a facially neutral law on the mere basis of its asserted religiously preferential (or discriminatory) effects—or at least to establish it in conformity with our precedents—JUSTICE SOUTER "must be able to show the absence of a neutral, secular basis" for the law. *Gillette* v. *United States.*

There is of course no possible doubt of a secular basis here. The New York Legislature faced a unique problem in Kiryas Joel: a community in which all the non-handicapped children attend private schools, and the physically and mentally disabled children who attend public school suffer the additional handicap of cultural distinctiveness. It would be troublesome enough if these peculiarly dressed, handicapped students were sent to the next town, accompanied by their similarly clad but unimpaired classmates. But all the unimpaired children of Kiryas Joel attend private school. The handicapped children suffered sufficient emotional trauma from their predicament that their parents kept them home from school. Surely the legislature could target this problem, and provide a public education for these students, in the same way it addressed, *by a similar law*, the unique needs of children institutionalized in a hospital.

Since the obvious presence of a neutral, secular basis renders the asserted preferential effect of this law inadequate to invalidate it, JUSTICE SOUTER is required to come forward with direct evidence that religious preference was the objective. His case could scarcely be weaker. It consists, briefly, of this: The People of New York created the Kiryas Joel Village School District in order to further the Satmar religion, rather than for any proper secular purpose, because (1) they created the district in an extraordinary manner—by special Act of the legislature, rather than under the State's general laws governing school-district reorganization; (2) the creation of the district ran counter to a State trend toward consolidation of school districts; and (3) the District includes only adherents of the Satmar religion. On this indictment, no jury would convict.

One difficulty with the first point is that it is not true. There was really nothing so "special" about the formation of a school district by an Act of the New York Legislature. The State has created both large school districts and small specialized school districts for institutionalized children, through these special Acts. But in any event all that the first point proves, and the second point as well (countering the trend toward consolidation), is that New York regarded Kiryas Joel as a special case, requiring special measures. I should think it *obvious* that it did, and obvious that it *should have*. But even if the New York Legislature had never before created a school district by special statute (which is not true), and even if it had done nothing but consolidate school districts for over a century (which is not true), how could the departure from those past practices possibly demonstrate that the legislature had religious favoritism in mind? It could not. To be sure, when there is no special treatment there is no possibility of religious favoritism; but it is not logical to suggest that when there *is* special treatment there is *proof* of religious favoritism.

JUSTICE SOUTER's case against the statute comes down to nothing more, therefore, than his third point: the fact that all the residents of the Kiryas Joel Village School District are Satmars. But all its residents also wear unusual dress, have unusual civic customs, and have not much to do with people who are culturally different from them. . . .

On what basis does JUSTICE SOUTER conclude that it is the theological distinctiveness rather than the cultural distinctiveness that was the basis for New York State's decision? The normal assumption would be that it was the latter, since it was not theology but dress, language, and cultural alienation that posed the educational problem for the children. JUSTICE SOUTER not only does not adopt the logical assumption, he does not even give the New York Legislature the benefit of the doubt.

IV

But even if Chapter 748 were intended to create a special arrangement for the Satmars *because of* their religion (not including, as I have shown in Part I, any conferral of governmental power upon a religious entity), it would be a permissible accommodation. . . .

In today's opinion, the Court seems uncomfortable with this aspect of our constitutional tradition. Although it acknowledges the concept of accommodation, it quickly points out that it is "not a principle without limits," and then gives reasons why the present case exceeds those limits, reasons which simply do not hold water. "[W]e have never hinted," the Court says, "that an otherwise unconstitutional delegation of political power to a religious group could be saved as a religious accommodation." Putting aside the circularity inherent in referring to a delegation as "otherwise unconstitutional" when its constitutionality turns on whether there is an accommodation, if this statement is true, it is only because we have never hinted that delegation of political power to citizens who share a particular religion could be unconstitutional.

The second and last reason the Court finds accommodation impermissible is, astoundingly, the mere risk that the State will not offer accommodation to a similar group in the future, and that neutrality will therefore not be preserved. . . .

At bottom, the Court's "no guarantee of neutrality" argument is an assertion of *this Court's* inability to control the New York Legislature's future denial of comparable accommodation.

The Court's demand for "up front" assurances of a neutral system is at war with both traditional accommodation doctrine and the judicial role. . . . Most efforts at accommodation seek to solve a problem that applies to members of only one or a few religions. Not every religion uses wine in its sacraments, but that does not make an exemption from Prohibition for sacramental wine-use impermissible, nor does it require the State granting such an exemption to explain in advance how it will treat every other claim for dispensation from its controlled-substances laws. . . . The record is clear that the necessary guarantee can and will be provided, after the fact, *by the courts.*

V

A few words in response to the separate concurrences: JUSTICE STEVENS adopts, for these cases, a rationale that is almost without limit. The separate Kiryas Joel school district is problematic in his view because "[t]he isolation of these children, while it may protect them from 'panic, fear and trauma,' also unquestionably increased the likelihood that they would remain within the fold, faithful adherents of their parents' religious faith."

JUSTICE STEVENS' statement is less a legal analysis than a manifesto of secularism. It surpasses mere rejection of accommodation, and announces a positive hostility to religion—which, unlike all other noncriminal values, the state must not assist parents in transmitting to their offspring.

Rosenberger v. *University of Virginia*
515 U.S. 819; 115 S. Ct. 2510; 132 L. Ed. 2d 700 (1995)

The Student Activity Fund (SAF) at the University of Virginia receives its money from mandatory student fees and supports extracurricular student activities related to the University's educational purposes. In order to qualify for SAF support, a student organization must be recognized as a "Contracted Independent Organization" (CIO) by the University. CIOs are required by University regulation to include in their dealings with third parties and in all written materials a disclaimer, stating that the CIO is independent of the University and that the University is not responsible for the CIO.

The University of Virginia authorizes payment from the SAF to outside contractors for the printing costs of student publications. The University's Guidelines recognize various categories of CIOs that can receive such payment, including "student news, information, opinion, entertainment, or academic communications media groups." The Guidelines, however, specify that the costs of certain activities of CIOs that are otherwise eligible for funding, including religious activities, cannot be reimbursed by the SAF.

Wide Awake Productions (WAP), which was formed by Ronald Rosenberger and other undergraduates in 1990, qualified as a CIO. The organization published a newspaper, *Wide Awake: A Christian Perspective at the University of Virginia*, whose mission was "to challenge Christians to live, in word and deed, according to the faith they proclaim and to encourage students to consider what a personal relationship with Jesus Christ means." When WAP requested the SAF to pay the costs of printing the newspaper, the SAF denied the request on the grounds that *Wide*

Awake was a "religious activity." After appeals of the decision within the University proved unavailing, WAP, *Wide Awake,* and three of its editors filed suit in federal court, charging that the refusal to authorize payment of the printing costs solely on the basis of *Wide Awake's* religious orientation violated their rights to freedom of speech and press, to the free exercise of religion, and to equal protection of the laws. In response, the University of Virginia contended that underwriting the printing costs of a religious publication would violate the Establishment Clause. After the District Court and the Court of Appeals ruled for the University, the United States Supreme Court granted certiorari. *Opinion of the Court: Kennedy, Rehnquist, O'Connor, Scalia, Thomas. Concurring opinions: O'Connor, Thomas. Dissenting opinion: Souter, Stevens, Ginsburg, Breyer.*

JUSTICE KENNEDY delivered the opinion of the Court.

It is axiomatic that the government may not regulate speech based on its substantive content or the message it conveys. *Police Department of Chicago* v. *Mosley* (1972). Other principles follow from this precept. In the realm of private speech or expression, government regulation may not favor one speaker over another. *City Council of Los Angeles* v. *Taxpayers for Vincent* (1984). Discrimination against speech because of its message is presumed to be unconstitutional. These rules informed our determination that the government offends the First Amendment when it imposes financial burdens on certain speakers based on the content of their expression.

These principles provide the framework forbidding the State from exercising viewpoint discrimination, even when the limited public forum is one of its own creation. In a case involving a school district's provision of school facilities for private uses, we declared that "[t]here is no question that the District, like the private owner of property, may legally preserve the property under its control for the use to which it is dedicated." *Lamb's Chapel* v. *Center Moriches Union Free School District* (1993). The necessities of confining a forum to the limited and legitimate purposes for which it was created may justify the State in reserving it for certain groups or for the discussion of certain topics. Once it has opened a limited forum, however, the State must respect the lawful boundaries it has itself set. The State may not exclude speech where its distinction is not "reasonable in light of the purpose served by the forum," nor may it discriminate against speech on the basis of its viewpoint. Thus, in determining whether the State is acting to preserve the limits of the forum it has created so that the exclusion of a class of speech is legitimate, we have observed a distinction between, on the one hand, content discrimination, which may be permissible if it preserves the purposes of that limited forum, and, on the other hand, viewpoint discrimination, which is presumed impermissible when directed against speech otherwise within the forum's limitations.

The most recent and most apposite case is our decision in *Lamb's Chapel.* There, a school district had opened school facilities for use after school hours by community groups for a wide variety of social, civic, and recreational purposes. The district, however, had enacted a formal policy against opening facilities to groups for religious purposes. Invoking its policy, the district rejected a request from a group desiring to show a film series addressing various child-rearing questions from a "Christian perspective."

Our conclusion was unanimous: "[I]t discriminates on the basis of viewpoint to permit school property to be used for the presentation of all views about family issues and child-rearing except those dealing with the subject matter from a religious standpoint."

The University tries to escape the consequences of our holding in *Lamb's Chapel* by urging that this case involves the provision of funds rather than access to facilities. To this end the University relies on our assurance in *Widmar* v. *Vincent.* There, in the course of striking down a public university's exclusion of religious groups from use of school facilities made available to all other student groups, we stated: "Nor do we question the right of the University to make academic judgments as to how best to allocate scarce resources."

The quoted language in *Widmar* was but a proper recognition of the principle that when the State is the speaker, it may make content-based choices. The distinction between the University's own favored message and the private speech of students is evident in the case before us. The University itself has taken steps to ensure the distinction in the agreement each CIO must sign. The University declares that the student groups eligible for SAF support are not the University's agents, are not subject to its control, and are not its responsibility. Having offered to pay the third-party contractors on behalf of private speakers who convey their own messages, the University may not silence the expression of selected viewpoints.

Vital First Amendment speech principles are at stake here. The first danger to liberty lies in granting the State the power to examine publications to determine whether or not they are based on some ultimate idea and if so for the State to classify them. The second, and corollary, danger is to speak from the chilling of individual thought and expression. That danger is especially real in the University setting, where the State acts against a background and tradition of thought and experiment that is at the center of our intellectual and philosophic tradition. For the University, by regulation, to cast disapproval on particular viewpoints of its students risks the suppression of free speech and creative inquiry in one of the vital centers for the nation's intellectual life, its college and university campuses.

Based on the principles we have discussed, we hold that the regulation invoked to deny SAF support, both in its terms and in its application to these petitioners, is a denial of their right of free speech guaranteed by the First Amendment. It remains to be considered whether the violation following from the University's action is excused by the necessity of complying with the Constitution's prohibition against state establishment of religion. We turn to that question.

A central lesson of our decisions is that a significant factor in upholding governmental programs in the face of Establishment Clause attack is their neutrality towards religion. The governmental program here is neutral toward religion.

There is no suggestion that the University created it to advance religion or adopted some ingenious device with the purpose of aiding a religious cause. The object of the SAF is to open a forum for speech and to support various student enterprises, including the publication of newspapers, in recognition of the diversity and creativity of student life.

The neutrality of the program distinguishes the student fees from a tax levied for the direct support of a church or group of churches. A tax of that sort, of course, would run contrary to Establishment Clause concerns dating from the earliest days of the Republic. . . .

It does not violate the Establishment Clause for a public university to grant access to its facilities on a religion-neutral basis to a wide spectrum of student groups, including groups which use meeting rooms for sectarian activities, accompanied by some devotional exercises. There is no difference in logic or principle, and no difference of constitutional significance, between a school using its funds to operate a facility to which students have access, and a school paying a third-party contractor to operate the facility on its behalf. The latter occurs here. The University provides printing services to a broad spectrum of student newspapers qualified as CIOs by reason of their officers and membership. Any benefit to religion is incidental to the government's provision of secular services for secular purposes on a religion-neutral basis.

To obey the Establishment Clause, it was not necessary for the University to deny eligibility to student publications because of their viewpoint. The neutrality commanded of the State by the separate Clauses of the First Amendment was compromised by the University's course of action. The viewpoint discrimination inherent in the University's regulation required public officials to scan and interpret student publications to discern their underlying philosophic assumptions respecting religious theory and belief. That course of action was a denial of the right of free speech and would risk fostering a pervasive bias or hostility to religion, which could undermine the very neutrality the Establishment Clause requires. There is no Establishment Clause violation in the University's honoring its duties under the Free Speech Clause.

The judgment of the Court of Appeals must be, and is, reversed.

It is so ordered.

JUSTICE O'CONNOR, concurring.

"We have time and again held that the government generally may not treat people differently based on the God or gods they worship, or don't worship." *Board of Education of Kiryas Joel Village School District* v. *Grumet* (1994). As JUSTICE SOUTER demonstrates, however, there exists another axiom in the history and precedent of the Establishment Clause. "Public funds may not be used to endorse the religious message." *Bowen* v. *Kendrick* (1988).

This case lies at the intersection of the principle of government neutrality and the prohibition on state funding of religious activities. It is clear that the University has established a generally applicable program to encourage the free exchange of ideas by its students, an expressive marketplace that includes some 15 student publications with predictably divergent viewpoints. It is equally clear that petitioners' viewpoint is religious and that publication of *Wide Awake* is a religious activity, under both the University's regulation and a fair reading of our precedents. Not to finance *Wide Awake,* according to petitioners, violates the principle of neutrality by sending a message of hostility toward religion. To finance *Wide Awake,* argues the University, violates the prohibition on direct state funding of religious activities.

When bedrock principles collide, they test the limits of categorical obstinacy and expose the flaws and dangers of a Grand Unified Theory that may turn out to be neither grand nor unified. The Court today does only what courts must do in many Establishment Clause cases—focus on specific features of a particular government action to ensure that it does not violate the Constitution. By withholding from *Wide Awake* assistance that the University provides generally to all other student publications, the University has discriminated on the basis of the magazine's religious viewpoint in violation of the Free Speech Clause. And particular features of the University's program—such as the explicit disclaimer, the disbursement of funds directly to third-party vendors, the vigorous nature of the forum at issue, and the possibility for objecting students to opt out—convince me that providing such assistance in this case would not carry the danger of impermissible use of public funds to endorse *Wide Awake's* religious message.

JUSTICE SOUTER, with whom JUSTICE STEVENS, JUSTICE GINSBURG and JUSTICE BREYER join, dissenting.

The Court today, for the first time, approves direct funding of core religious activities by an arm of the State. It does so, however, only after erroneous treatment of some familiar principles of law implementing the First Amendment's Establishment and Speech Clauses, and by viewing the very funds in question as beyond the reach of the Establishment Clause's funding restrictions as such. Because there is no warrant for distinguishing among public funding sources for purposes of applying the First Amendment's prohibition of religious establishment, I would hold that the University's refusal to support petitioners' religious activities is compelled by the Establishment Clause. I would therefore affirm.

This writing is no merely descriptive examination of religious doctrine or even of ideal Christian practice in confronting life's social and personal problems. Nor is it merely the expression of editorial opinion that incidentally coincides with Christian ethics and reflects a Christian view of human obligation. It is straightforward exhortation to enter into a relationship with God as revealed in Jesus Christ, and to satisfy a series of moral obligations derived from the teachings of Jesus Christ. These are not the words of "student news, information, opinion, entertainment, or academic communicatio[n] . . ." (in the language of the University's funding criterion), but the words of "challenge [to] Christians to live, in word and deed, according to the faith they proclaim and . . . to consider what a personal relationship with Jesus Christ means" (in the language of *Wide Awake's* founder). The subject is not the discourse of the scholar's study or the seminar room, but of the evangelist's mission station and the pulpit. It is nothing other than the preaching of the word, which (along with the sacraments) is what most branches of Christianity offer those called to the religious life.

Using public funds for the direct subsidization of preaching the word is categorically forbidden under the Establishment Clause, and if the Clause was meant to accomplish nothing else, it was meant to bar this use of public money. Evidence on the subject antedates even the Bill of Rights itself, as may be seen in the writings of Madison, whose authority on questions about the meaning of the Establishment Clause is well settled.

Four years before the First Congress proposed the First Amendment, Madison gave his opinion on the legitimacy of using public funds for religious purposes, in the Memorial and Remonstrance Against Religious Assessments, which played the central role in ensuring the defeat of the Virginia tax assessment bill in 1786 and framed the debate upon which the Religion Clauses stand:

> Who does not see that . . . the same authority which can force a citizen to contribute three pence only of his property for the support of any one establishment, may force him to conform to any other establishment in all cases whatsoever?

Madison wrote against a background in which nearly every Colony had exacted a tax for church support, the practice having become "so commonplace as to shock the freedom-loving colonials into a feeling of abhorrence."

Madison's Remonstrance captured the colonists' "conviction that individual religious liberty could be achieved best under a government which was stripped of all power to tax, to support, or otherwise to assist any or all religions, or to interfere with the beliefs of any religious individual or group." Their sentiment as expressed by Madison in Virginia, led not only to the defeat of Virginia's tax assessment bill but also directly to passage of the Virginia Bill for Establishing Religious Freedom, written by Thomas Jefferson. That bill's preamble declared that "to compel a man to furnish contributions of money for the propagation of opinions which he disbelieves, is sinful and tyrannical," and its text provided "[t]hat no man shall be compelled to frequent or support any religious worship, place, or ministry whatsoever. . . ." We have "previously recognized that the provisions of the First Amendment, in the drafting and adoption of which Madison and Jefferson played such leading roles, had the same objective and were intended to provide the same protection against governmental intrusion on religious liberty as the Virginia statute."

The principle against direct funding with public money is patently violated by the contested use of today's student activity fee. Like today's taxes generally, the fee is Madison's threepence. The University exercises the power of the State to compel a student to pay it, and the use of any part of it for the direct support of religious activity thus strikes at what we have repeatedly held to be the heart of the prohibition on establishment. The Court, accordingly, has never before upheld direct state funding of the sort of proselytizing published in *Wide Awake* and, in fact, has categorically condemned state programs directly aiding religious activity. Even when the Court has upheld aid to an institution performing both secular and sectarian functions, it has always made a searching enquiry to ensure that the institution kept the secular activities separate from its sectarian ones, with any direct aid flowing only to the former and never the latter.

Why does the Court not apply this clear law to these clear facts and conclude, as I do, that the funding scheme here is a clear constitutional violation? The answer is that the Court focuses on a subsidiary body of law, which it correctly states but ultimately misapplies. . . .

[T]he relationship between the prohibition on direct aid and the requirement of evenhandedness when affirmative government aid does result in some benefit to religion reflects the relationship between basic rule and marginal criterion. At the heart of the Establishment Clause stands the prohibition against direct public funding, but that prohibition does not answer the questions that occur at the margins of the Clause's application. Is any government activity that provides any incidental benefit to religion likewise unconstitutional? Would it be wrong to put out fires in burning churches, wrong to pay the bus fares of students on the way to parochial schools, wrong to allow a grantee of special education funds to spend them at a religious college? These are the questions that call for drawing lines, and it is in drawing them that evenhandedness becomes important.

Evenhandedness as one element of a permissibly attenuated benefit is, of course, a far cry from evenhandedness as a sufficient condition of constitutionality for direct financial support of religious proselytization, and our cases have unsurprisingly repudiated any such attempt to cut the Establishment Clause down to a mere prohibition against unequal direct aid.

Since I cannot see the future I cannot tell whether today's decision portends much more than making a shambles out of student activity fees in public colleges. Still, my apprehension is whetted by Chief Justice Burger's warning in *Lemon* v. *Kurtzman* (1971): "in constitutional adjudication some steps, which when taken were thought to approach 'the verge,' have become the platform for yet further steps. A certain momentum develops in constitutional theory and it can be a 'downhill thrust' easily set in motion but difficult to retard or stop."

I respectfully dissent.

West Virginia Board of Education v. *Barnette*

319 U.S. 624; 63 S. Ct. 1178; 87 L. Ed. 1628 (1943)

In 1942 the West Virginia Board of Education adopted a regulation requiring the flag salute and Pledge of Allegiance as a part of regular public school activities. Students who refused to participate were deemed insubordinate and expelled, with readmission denied until compliance. During their expulsion, such students were considered "unlawfully absent," and both they and their parents were subject to prosecution. Walter Barnette, a Jehovah's Witness, brought suit to enjoin the compulsory flag salute, contending that it required his children to violate the religious commandment not to worship graven images.

The Supreme Court had considered the flag-salute issue only three years previously, in *Minersville School District* v. *Gobitis*. In that case Justice Felix Frankfurter, speaking for an 8–1 majority, held that the compulsory flag salute did not violate the Free Exercise Clause of the First Amendment. Since *Gobitis*, however, Justices Robert Jackson and Wiley Rutledge had replaced two members of the Court majority. In addition, two other members of the *Gobitis* majority, Justices Hugo Black and William Douglas, had repudiated their *Gobitis* votes in *Jones* v. *Opelika* (1942). When a three-judge district court enjoined enforcement of the regulation, the Court agreed to hear the case on appeal. *Opinion of the Court: Jackson, Stone, Black, Douglas, Murphy, Rutledge. Concurring opinion: Black, Douglas. Dissenting opinions: Roberts, Reed; Frankfurter.*

MR. JUSTICE JACKSON delivered the opinion of the Court.

The freedom asserted by these appellees does not bring them into collision with rights asserted by any other individual. The sole conflict is between authority and rights of the individual. The State asserts power to condition access to public education on making a prescribed sign and profession and at the same time to coerce attendance by punishing both parent and child. The latter stand on a right of self-determination in matters that touch individual opinion and personal attitude.

As the present CHIEF JUSTICE said in dissent in the *Gobitis* case, the State may "require teaching by instruction and study of all in our history and in the structure and organization of our government, including the guaranties of civil liberty, which tend to inspire patriotism and love of country." . . . Here, however, we are dealing with a compulsion of students to declare a belief. They are not merely made acquainted with the flag salute so that they may be informed as to what it is or even what it means. The issue here is whether this slow and easily neglected route to aroused loyalties constitutionally may be shortcut by substituting a compulsory salute and slogan. . . .

There is no doubt that, in connection with the pledges, the flag salute is a form of utterance. Symbolism is a primitive but effective way of communicating ideas. The use of an emblem or flag to symbolize some system, idea, institution, or personality, is a short cut from mind to mind. . . .

It is also to be noted that the compulsory flag salute and pledge requires affirmation of a belief and an attitude of mind. It is not clear whether the regulation contemplates that pupils forego any contrary convictions of their own and become unwilling converts to the prescribed ceremony or whether it will be acceptable if they simulate assent by words without belief and by a gesture barren of meaning. It is now a commonplace that censorship or suppression of expression of opinion is tolerated by our Constitution only when the expression presents a clear and present danger of action of a kind the State is empowered to prevent and punish. It would seem that involuntary affirmation could be commanded only on even more immediate and urgent grounds than silence. But here the power of compulsion is invoked without any allegation that remaining passive during a flag salute ritual creates a clear and present danger that would justify an effort even to muffle expression. To sustain the compulsory flag salute we are required to say that a Bill of Rights which guards the individual's right to speak his own mind, left it open to public authorities to compel him to utter what is not in his mind. . . .

Nor does the issue as we see it turn on one's possession of particular religious views or the sincerity with which they are held. While religion supplies appellees' motive for enduring the discomforts of making the issue in this case, many citizens who do not share these religious views hold such a compulsory rite to infringe constitutional liberty of the individual. It is not necessary to inquire whether non-conformist beliefs will exempt from the duty to salute unless we first find power to make the salute a legal duty. . . .

. . . It was said that the flag-salute controversy confronted the Court with "the problem which Lincoln cast in memorable dilemma: 'Must a government of necessity be too *strong* for the lib-

erties of its people, or too *weak* to maintain its own existence?' " and that the answer must be in favor of strength. . . . If validly applied to this problem, the utterance cited would resolve every issue of power in favor of those in authority and would require us to override every liberty thought to weaken or delay execution of their policies. . . . To enforce those rights today is not to choose weak government over strong government. It is only to adhere as a means of strength to individual freedom of mind in preference to officially disciplined uniformity for which history indicates a disappointing and disastrous end.

. . . It was also considered in the *Gobitis* case that functions of educational officers in States, counties and school districts were such that to interfere with their authority "would in effect make us the school board for the country." . . . The Fourteenth Amendment, as now applied to the States, protects the citizen against the State itself and all of its creatures—Boards of Education not excepted. These have, of course, important, delicate, and highly discretionary functions, but none that they may not perform within the limits of the Bill of Rights. . . .

Such Boards are numerous and their territorial jurisdiction often small. But small and local authority may feel less sense of responsibility to the Constitution, and agencies of publicity may be less vigilant in calling it to account. The action of Congress in making flag observance voluntary and respecting the conscience of the objector in a matter so vital as raising the Army contrasts sharply with these local regulations in matters relatively trivial to the welfare of the nation. . . .

. . . The *Gobitis* opinion reasoned that this is a field "where courts possess no marked and certainly no controlling competence," that it is committed to the legislatures as well as the courts to guard cherished liberties and that it is constitutionally appropriate to "fight out the wise use of legislative authority in the forum of public opinion and before legislative assemblies rather than to transfer such a contest to the judicial arena," since all the "effective means of inducing political changes are left free." . . .

The very purpose of a Bill of Rights was to withdraw certain subjects from the vicissitudes of political controversy, to place them beyond the reach of majorities and officials and to establish them as legal principles to be applied by the courts. One's right to life, liberty, and property, to free speech, a free press, freedom of worship and assembly, and other fundamental rights may not be submitted to vote; they depend on the outcome of no elections. . . . They are susceptible of restriction only to prevent grave and immediate danger to interests which the State may lawfully protect. . . .

. . . Lastly, and this is the very heart of the *Gobitis* opinion, it reasons that "National unity is the basis of national security," that the authorities have "the right to select appropriate means for its attainment," and hence reaches the conclusion that such compulsory measures toward "national unity" are constitutional. . . .

If there is any fixed star in our constitutional constellation, it is that no official, high or petty, can prescribe what shall be orthodox in politics, nationalism, religion, or other matters of opinion or force citizens to confess by word or act their faith therein. If there are any circumstances which permit an exception, they do not now occur to us. . . .

The decision of this Court in *Minersville School District* v. *Gobitis* . . . [is] overruled, and the judgment enjoining enforcement of the West Virginia regulation is

Affirmed.

MR. JUSTICE FRANKFURTER, dissenting.

One who belongs to the most vilified and persecuted minority in history is not likely to be insensible to the freedoms guaranteed by our Constitution. Were my purely personal attitude relevant I should wholeheartedly associate myself with the general libertarian views in the Court's opinion, representing as they do the thought and action of a lifetime. But as judges we are neither Jew nor Gentile, neither Catholic nor agnostic. We owe equal attachment to the Constitution and are equally bound by our judicial obligations whether we derive our citizenship from the earliest or the latest immigrants to these shores. As a member of this Court I am not justified in writing my private notions of policy into the Constitution, no matter how deeply I may cherish them or how mischievous I may deem their disregard. The duty of a judge who must decide which of two claims before the Court shall prevail, that of a State to enact and

enforce laws within its general competence or that of an individual to refuse obedience because of the demands of his conscience, is not that of the ordinary person. It can never be emphasized too much that one's own opinion about the wisdom or evil of a law should be excluded altogether when one is doing one's duty on the bench. The only opinion of our own even looking in that direction that is material is our opinion whether legislators could in reason have enacted such a law. In the light of all the circumstances, including the history of this question in this Court, it would require more daring than I possess to deny that reasonable legislators could have taken the action which is before us for review. Most unwillingly, therefore, I must differ from my brethren with regard to legislation like this. I cannot bring my mind to believe that the "liberty" secured by the Due Process Clause gives this Court authority to deny to the State of West Virginia the attainment of that which we all recognize as a legitimate legislative end, namely, the promotion of good citizenship, by employment of the means here chosen. . . .

Under our constitutional system the legislature is charged solely with civil concerns of society. If the avowed or intrinsic legislative purpose is either to promote or to discourage some religious community or creed, it is clearly within the constitutional restrictions imposed on legislatures and cannot stand. But it by no means follows that legislative power is wanting whenever a general non-discriminatory civil regulation in fact touches conscientious scruples or religious beliefs of an individual or a group. . . Were this so, instead of the separation of church and state, there would be the subordination of the state on any matter deemed within the sovereignty of the religious conscience. . . .

We are told that a flag salute is a doubtful substitute for adequate understanding of our institutions. The states that require such a school exercise do not have to justify it as the only means for promoting good citizenship in children, but merely as one of diverse means for accomplishing a worthy end. We may deem it a foolish measure, but the point is that this Court is not the organ of government to resolve doubts as to whether it will fulfill its purpose. Only if there be no doubt that any reasonable mind could entertain can we deny to the states the right to resolve doubts their way and not ours. . . .

Of course patriotism can not be enforced by the flag salute. But neither can the liberal spirit be enforced by judicial invalidation of illiberal legislation. Our constant preoccupation with the constitutionality of legislation rather than with its wisdom tends to preoccupation of the American mind with a false value. The tendency of focussing attention on constitutionality is to make constitutionality synonymous with wisdom, to regard a law as all right if it is constitutional.

Such an attitude is a great enemy of liberalism. Particularly in legislation affecting freedom of thought and freedom of speech much which should offend a free-spirited society is constitutional. Reliance for the most precious interests of civilization, therefore, must be found outside of their vindication in courts of law. Only a persistent positive translation of the faith of a free society into the convictions and habits and actions of a community is the ultimate reliance against unabated temptations to fetter the human spirit.

Sherbert v. Verner

374 U.S. 398, 83 S. Ct. 1790, 10 L. Ed. 2d 965 (1963)

Under South Carolina's unemployment compensation act, a worker was considered ineligible for benefits if although able to work and available for work, he "failed, without good cause . . . to accept available suitable work when offered him by the employment office or the employer." Adell Sherbert, a Seventh-Day Adventist, was fired from her job and then refused other jobs because those jobs required her to work on Saturday, her Sabbath. Her application for unemployment compensation was denied because she had refused "available suitable work." She then sued the South Carolina Unemployment Security Commission, contending that the denial of benefits infringed upon the free exercise of her religion. *Opinion of the Court: Brennan, Warren, Black, Clark, Goldberg. Concurring opinions: Douglas; Stewart. Dissenting opinion: Harlan, White.*

MR. JUSTICE BRENNAN delivered the opinion of the Court.

We turn first to the question whether the disqualification for benefits imposes any burden on the free exercise of appellant's religion. We think it is clear that it does. . . . Here not only is it apparent that appellant's declared ineligibility for benefits derives solely from the practice of her religion, but the pressure upon her to forego that practice is unmistakable. The ruling forces her to choose between following the precepts of her religion and forfeiting benefits, on the one hand, and abandoning one of the precepts of her religion in order to accept work, on the other hand. Governmental imposition of such a choice puts the same kind of burden upon the free exercise of religion as would a fine imposed against appellant for her Saturday worship.

Nor may the South Carolina court's construction of the statute be saved from constitutional

infirmity on the ground that unemployment compensation benefits are not appellant's "right" but merely a "privilege." It is too late in the day to doubt that the liberties of religion and expression may be infringed by the denial of or placing of conditions upon a benefit or privilege. . . . Conditions upon public benefits cannot be sustained if they so operate, whatever their purpose, as to inhibit or deter the exercise of First Amendment freedoms. . . .

We must next consider whether some compelling state interest enforced in the eligibility provisions of the South Carolina statute justifies the substantial infringement of appellant's First Amendment right. It is basic that no showing merely of a rational relationship to some colorable state interest would suffice; in this highly sensitive constitutional area."[o]nly the gravest abuses, endangering paramount interests, give occasion for permissible limitation," *Thomas* v.

Collins 1945. . . . No such abuse or danger has been advanced in the present case. The appellees suggest no more than a possibility that the filing of fraudulent claims by unscrupulous claimants feigning religious objections to Saturday work might not only dilute the unemployment compensation fund but also hinder the scheduling by employers of necessary Saturday work. . . . There is no proof whatever to warrant such fears of malingering or deceit as those which the respondents now advance. . . . It is highly doubtful whether such evidence would be sufficient to warrant a substantial infringement of religious liberties. For even if the possibility of spurious claims did threaten to dilute the fund and disrupt the scheduling of work, it would plainly be incumbent upon the appellees to demonstrate that no alternative forms of regulation would combat such abuses without infringing First Amendment rights. . . .

In holding as we do, plainly we are not fostering the "establishment" of the Seventh-day Adventist religion in South Carolina, for the extension of unemployment benefits to Sabbatarians in common with Sunday worshippers reflects nothing more than the governmental obligation of neutrality in the face of religious differences . . . . Our holding today is only that South Carolina may not constitutionally apply the eligibility provisions so as to constrain a worker to abandon his religious convictions respecting the day of rest. This holding but reaffirms a principle that we announced a decade and a half ago, namely that no State may "exclude individual Catholics, Lutherans, Mohammedans, Baptists, Jews, Methodists, Non-believers, Presbyterians, or the members of any other faith, *because of their faith,* or *lack of it,* from receiving the benefits of public welfare legislation." *Everson* v. *Board of Education* [1947]. . . .

The judgment of the South Carolina Supreme Court is reversed and the case is remanded for further proceeding not inconsistent with this opinion.

It is so ordered.

MR. JUSTICE STEWART, concurring in the result.

Although fully agreeing with the result which the Court reaches in this case, I cannot join the Court's opinion. This case presents a double-barreled dilemma, which in all candor I think the Court's opinion has not succeeded in papering over. The dilemma ought to be resolved. . . .

I am convinced that no liberty is more essential to the continued vitality of the free society which our Constitution guarantees than is the religious liberty protected by the Free Exercise Clause explicit in the First Amendment and imbedded in the Fourteenth. . . . There are many situations where legitimate claims under the Free Exercise Clause will run into head-on collision with the Court's insensitive and sterile construction of the Establishment Clause. The controversy now before us is clearly such a case. . . .

. . . If the appellant's refusal to work on Saturdays were based on indolence, or on a compulsive desire to watch the Saturday television programs, no one would say that South Carolina could not hold that she was not "available for work" within the meaning of its statute. That being so, the Establishment Clause as construed by this Court not only *permits* but affirmatively *requires* South Carolina equally to deny the appellant's claim for unemployment compensation when her refusal to work on Saturdays is based upon her religious creed. . . .

. . . This poses no problem for me, because I think the Court's mechanistic concept of the Establishment Clause is historically unsound and constitutionally wrong. . . . I think that the guarantee of religious liberty embodied in the Free Exercise Clause affirmatively requires government to create an atmosphere of hospitality and accommodation to individual belief or disbelief. In short, I think our Constitution commands the positive protection by government of religious freedom—not only for a minority, however small—not only for the majority, however large—but for each of us. . . .

MR. JUSTICE HARLAN, whom MR. JUSTICE WHITE joins, dissenting.

. . . What the Court is holding is that if the State chooses to condition unemployment compensation on the applicant's availability for work, it is constitutionally compelled to *carve out an exception*—and to provide benefits—for those whose unavailability is due to their religious convictions. Such a holding has particular significance in two respects.

First, despite the Court's protestations to the contrary the decision necessarily overrules

Braunfeld v. *Brown.* . . . The secular purpose of the statute before us today is even clearer than that involved in *Braunfeld.* And just as in *Braunfeld*—where exceptions to the Sunday closing laws for Sabbatarians would have been inconsistent with the purpose to achieve a uniform day of rest and would have required case-by-case inquiry into religious beliefs—so here, an exception to the rules of eligibility based on religious convictions would necessitate judicial examination of those convictions and would be at odds with the limited purpose of the statute to smooth out the economy during periods of industrial instability. . . .

Second . . . The State . . . must *single out* for financial assistance those whose behavior is religiously motivated, even though it denies such as-

sistance to others whose identical behavior (in this case, inability to work on Saturdays) is not religiously motivated. . . .

. . . I cannot subscribe to the conclusion that the State is constitutionally *compelled* to carve out an exception to its general rule of eligibility in the present case. Those situations in which the Constitution may require special treatment on account of religion are, in my view, few and far between. . . . Such compulsion in the present case is particularly inappropriate in light of the indirect, remote, and insubstantial effect of the decision below on the exercise of appellant's religion and in light of the direct financial assistance to religion that today's decision requires. . . .

Lyng v. *Northwest Indian Cemetery Protective Association*

485 U.S. 439; 108 S. Ct. 1319; 99 L. Ed. 2d 534 (1988)

In 1982 the United States Forest Service decided to build a six-mile paved road (the G-O road) through federal land, including the Chimney Rock area of the Six Rivers National Forest, to link two preexisting roads. In doing so, the Service rejected the recommendation of a study it had commissioned, which argued that the road not be built or that a route outside the Chimney Rock area be selected. Because this area had historically been used by certain Native Americans for religious rituals that depended on privacy, silence, and an undisturbed natural setting, the study concluded that building the road would irreparably harm the religious areas.

Although the Forest Service rejected the study's recommendations, the route it selected avoided archeological sites and was removed as far as possible from the sites used for spiritual activities. At about the same time, the Service approved a management plan permitting limited timber harvesting in the area, with protective zones around all religious sites.

The respondents in this case filed suit in District Court, claiming that the road proposal and the decision to permit timber harvesting violated their rights under the Free Exercise Clause. The District Court issued a permanent injunction against the road construction and timber harvesting, and the Court of Appeals affirmed. *Opinion of the Court: O'Connor, Rehnquist, White, Stevens, Scalia. Dissenting opinion: Brennan, Marshall, Blackmun.*

JUSTICE O'CONNOR delivered the opinion of the Court.

This case requires us to consider whether the First Amendment's Free Exercise Clause forbids the Government from permitting timber har-

vesting in, or constructing a road through, a portion of a National Forest that has traditionally been used for religious purposes by members of three American Indian tribes in northwestern California. We conclude that it does not. . . . It is undisputed that the Indian respondents' beliefs are sincere and that the Government's purposed actions will have severe adverse effects on the practice of their religion. Respondents contend that the burden on their religious practices is heavy enough to violate the Free Exercise Clause unless the Government can demonstrate a compelling need to complete the G-O road or to engage in timber harvesting in the Chimney Rock area. We disagree. . . .

In *Bowen* v. *Roy* . . . (1986), we considered a challenge to a federal statute that required the States to use Social Security numbers in administering certain welfare programs. Two applicants for benefits under these programs contended that their religious beliefs prevented them from acceding to the use of a Social Security number for their two-year-old daughter because the use of a numerical identifier would " 'rob the spirit' of [their] daughter and prevent her from attaining greater spiritual power." . . . The Court rejected this kind of challenge in *Roy:*

> The Free Exercise Clause simply cannot be understood to require the Government to conduct its own internal affairs in ways that comport with the religious beliefs of particular citizens. Just as the Government may not insist that [the Roys] engage in any set form of religious observance, so [they] may not demand that the Government join in their chosen religious practices by refraining from using a number to identify their daughter. . . .
>
> . . . The Free Exercise Clause affords an individual protection from certain forms of governmental compulsion; it does not afford an individual a right to dictate the conduct of the Government's internal procedures. . . .

The building of a road or the harvesting of timber on publicly owned land cannot meaningfully be distinguished from the use of a Social Security number in *Roy*. In both cases, the challenged government action would interfere significantly with private persons' ability to pursue spiritual fulfillment according to their own religious beliefs. In neither case, however, would the affected individuals be coerced by the Government's action into violating their religious beliefs; nor would either governmental action pe-

nalize religious activity by denying any person an equal share of the rights, benefits, and privileges enjoyed by other citizens.

We are asked to distinguish this case from *Roy* on the ground that the infringement on religious liberty here is "significantly greater," or on the ground that the government practice in *Roy* was "purely mechanical" whereas this case involves "a case-by-case substantive determination as to how a particular unit of land will be managed." . . .

These efforts to distinguish *Roy* are unavailing. This Court cannot determine the truth of the underlying beliefs that led to the religious objections here or in *Roy*, . . . and accordingly cannot weigh the adverse effects on the Roys and compare them with the adverse effects on respondents. Without the ability to make such comparisons, we cannot say that the one form of incidental interference with an individual's spiritual activities should be subjected to a different constitutional analysis than the other. . . .

. . . Whatever may be the exact line between unconstitutional prohibitions on the free exercise of religion and the legitimate conduct by government of its own affairs, the location of the line cannot depend on measuring the effects of a governmental action on a religious objector's spiritual development. . . .

Even if we assume that we should accept the Ninth Circuit's prediction, according to which the G-O road will "virtually destroy the Indians ability to practice their religion," . . . the Constitution simply does not provide a principle that could justify upholding respondents' legal claims. However much we might wish that it were otherwise government simply could not operate if it were required to satisfy every citizen's religious needs and desires. A broad range of government activities—from social welfare programs to foreign aid to conservation projects—will always be considered essential to the spiritual well-being of some citizens, often on the basis of sincerely held religious beliefs. Others will find the very same activities deeply offensive, and perhaps incompatible with their own search for spiritual fulfillment and with the tenets of their religion. The First Amendment must apply to all citizens alike, and it can give to none of them a veto over public programs that do not prohibit the free exercise of religion. The Constitution does not, and courts cannot, offer to reconcile the various competing demands on government, many of them rooted in sincere religious belief, that inevitably arise in so diverse a society as ours. That task, to the extent that it is feasible, is for the legislatures and other institutions. Cf. The Federalist No. 10 (suggesting that the effects of religious factionalism are best restrained through competition among a multiplicity of religious sects). . . .

Perceiving a "stress point in the long-standing conflict between two disparate cultures," the dissent attacks us for declining to "balanc[e] these competing and potentially irreconcilable interests, choosing instead to turn this difficult task over to the federal legislature." . . . Seeing the Court as the arbiter, the dissent proposes a legal test under which it would decide which public lands are "central" or "indispensable" to which religions, and by implication which are "dispensable" or "peripheral," and would then decide which government programs are "compelling" enough to justify "infringement of those practices." . . . We would accordingly be required to weigh the value of every religious belief and practice that is said to be threatened by any government program. Unless a "showing of 'centrality,'" . . . is nothing but an assertion of centrality, . . . the dissent thus offers us the prospect of this Court holding that some sincerely held religious beliefs and practices are not "central" to certain religions, despite protestations to the contrary from the religious objectors who brought the lawsuit. In other words, the dissent's approach would require us to rule that some religious adherents misunderstand their own religious beliefs. We think such an approach cannot be squared with the Constitution or with our precedents, and that it would cast the judiciary in a role that we were never intended to play.

JUSTICE BRENNAN, with whom JUSTICE MARSHALL and JUSTICE BLACKMUN join, dissenting.

"'[T]he Free Exercise Clause,'" the Court explains today, "'is written in terms of what the government cannot do to the individual, not in terms of what the individual can exact from the government.'" . . . Pledging fidelity to this unremarkable constitutional principle, the Court nevertheless concludes that even where the Government uses federal land in a manner that

threatens the very existence of a Native American religion, the Government is simply not "*doing*" anything to the practitioners of that faith. Instead, the Court believes that Native Americans who request that the Government refrain from destroying their religion effectively seek to exact from the Government *de facto* beneficial ownership of federal property. These two astonishing conclusions follow naturally from the Court's determination that federal land-use decisions that render the practice of a given religion impossible do not burden that religion in a manner cognizable under the Free Exercise Clause, because such decisions neither coerce conduct inconsistent with religious belief nor penalize religious activity. The constitutional guarantee we interpret today, however, draws no such fine distinctions between types of restraints on religious exercise, but rather is directed against any form of governmental action that frustrates or inhibits religious practice. Because the Court today refuses even to acknowledge the constitutional injury respondents will suffer, and because this refusal essentially leaves Native Americans with absolutely no constitutional protection against perhaps the gravest threat to their religious practices, I dissent. . . .

The Court does not for a moment suggest that the interests served by the G-O road are in any way compelling, or that they outweigh the destructive effect construction of the road will have on respondents' religious practices. . . . Respondents here have demonstrated that construction of the G-O road will completely frustrate the practice of their religion, for as the lower courts found, the proposed logging and construction activities will virtually destroy respondents' religion, and will therefore necessarily force them into abandoning those practices altogether. Indeed, the Government's proposed activities will restrain religious practice to a far greater degree here than in any of the cases cited by the Court today. . . . The Court attempts to explain the line it draws by arguing that the protections of the Free Exercise Clause "cannot depend on measuring the effects of a governmental action on a religious objector's spiritual development," . . . for in a society as diverse as ours, the Government cannot help but offend the "religious needs and desires" of some citizens. . . . While I agree that governmental action that simply offends religious sensibilities may not be challenged under the Clause, we have recognized that laws that affect spiritual development by impeding the integration of children into the religious community or by increasing the expense of adherence to religious principles—in short, laws that frustrate or inhibit religious *practice*—trigger the protections of the constitutional guarantee. Both common sense and our prior cases teach us, therefore, that governmental action that makes the practice of a given faith more difficult necessarily penalizes that practice and thereby tends to prevent adherence to religious belief. The harm to the practitioners is the same regardless of the manner in which the Government restrains their religious expression, and the Court's fear that an "effects" test will permit religious adherents to challenge governmental actions they merely find "offensive" in no way justifies its refusal to recognize the constitutional injury citizens suffer when governmental action not only offends but actually restrains their religious practices. Here, respondents have demonstrated that the Government's proposed activities will completely prevent them from practicing their religion, and such a showing . . . entitles them to the protections of the Free Exercise Clause. . . .

I believe it appropriate, therefore, to require some showing of "centrality" before the Government can be required either to come forward with a compelling justification for its proposed use of federal land or to forego that use altogether. . . .

The Court today suggests that such an approach would place courts in the untenable position of deciding which practices and beliefs are "central" to a given faith and which are not, and invites the prospect of judges advising some religious adherents that they "misunderstand their own religious beliefs." In fact, however, courts need not undertake any such inquiries: like all other religious adherents, Native Americans would be the arbiters of which practices are central to their faith, subject only to the normal requirement that their claims be genuine and sincere. The question for the courts, then, is not whether the Native American claimants understand their own religion, but rather, whether they have discharged their burden of demonstrating, as the Amish did with respect to the compulsory school law in *Yoder*, that the land-use decision poses a substantial and realistic threat of undermining or frustrating their religious practices. Ironically, the Court's apparent solicitude for the integrity of religious belief and its desire to forestall the possibility that courts might second-guess the claims of religious adherents leads to far greater inequities than those the Court postulates: today's ruling sacrifices a religion at least as old as the Nation itself, along with the spiritual well-being of its approximately 5,000 adherents, so that the Forest Service can build a 6-mile segment of road that two lower courts found had only the most marginal and speculative utility, both to the Government itself and to the private lumber interests that might conceivably use it.

Employment Division, Department of Human Resources of Oregon v. *Smith*

494 U.S. 872; 110 S. Ct. 1595; 108 L. Ed. 2d 876 (1990)

Alfred Smith and Galen Black, members of the Native American Church, were fired from their jobs with a private drug-rehabilitation organization when it became known that they ingested peyote, an illegal hallucinogenic drug, for sacramental purposes at the church's religious ceremonies. Their application for unemployment compensation was denied under a state law disqualifying employees discharged for work-related misconduct. After the Oregon Court of Appeals and the Oregon Supreme Court ruled that the denials violated Smith's and Black's free-exercise rights, the United States Supreme Court vacated the judgment, remanding the case for a determination of whether the sacramental use of peyote violated Oregon's controlled substance law. The Oregon Supreme Court concluded that it did but ruled that such an application of the law violated the Free Exercise Clause. The U.S. Supreme Court then granted certiorari. *Opinion of the Court: Scalia, Rehnquist, White, Stevens, Kennedy. Concurring in the judgment: O'Connor, joined in part by Brennan, Marshall, Blackmun. Dissenting opinion: Blackmun, Brennan, Marshall.*

JUSTICE SCALIA delivered the opinion of the Court.

This case requires us to decide whether the Free Exercise Clause of the First Amendment permits the State of Oregon to include religiously inspired peyote use within the reach of its general criminal prohibition on use of that drug, and thus permits the State to deny unemployment benefits to persons dismissed from their jobs because of such religiously inspired use.

The Free Exercise Clause of the First Amendment, which has been made applicable to the States by incorporation into the Fourteenth Amendment, provides that "Congress shall make no law respecting an establishment of religion, or *prohibiting the free exercise thereof* . . ." The free exercise of religion means, first and foremost, the right to believe and profess whatever religious doctrine one desires. Thus, the First Amendment obviously excludes all "governmental regulation of religious *beliefs* as such." . . .

. . . But the "exercise of religion" often involves not only belief and profession but the performance of (or abstention from) physical acts: assembling with others for a worship service, participating in sacramental use of bread and wine, proselytizing, abstaining from certain foods or certain modes of transportation. It would be true, we think (though no case of ours has involved the point), that a state would be "prohibiting the free exercise [of religion]" if it sought to ban such acts or abstentions only when they are engaged in for religious reasons, or only because of the religious belief that they display. It would doubtless be unconstitutional, for example, to ban the casting of "statues that are to be used for worship purposes" or to prohibit bowing down before a golden calf.

Respondents in the present case, however, seek to carry the meaning of "prohibiting the free exercise [of religion]" one large step further. They contend that their religious motivation for using peyote places them beyond the reach of a criminal law that is not specifically directed at their religious practice, and that is concededly constitutional as applied to those who use the drug for other reasons. They assert, in other words, that "prohibiting the free exercise [of religion]" includes requiring any individual to observe a generally applicable law that requires (or forbids) the performance of an act that his religious belief forbids (or requires). As a textual matter, we do not think the words must be given that meaning. It is no more necessary to regard the collection of a general tax, for example, as "prohibiting the free exercise [of religion]" by those citizens who believe support of organized government to be sinful, than it is to regard the same tax as "abridging the freedom . . . of the press" of those publishing companies that must pay the tax as a condition of staying in business. It is a permissible reading of the text, in one case as in the other, to say that if prohibiting the exercise of religion (or burdening the activity of printing) is not the object of the tax but merely the incidental effect of a generally applicable and otherwise valid provision, the First Amendment has not been offended.

Our decisions reveal that the latter reading is the correct one. We have never held that an individual's religious beliefs excuse him from compliance with an otherwise valid law prohibiting conduct that the State is free to regulate. On the contrary, the record of more than a century of our free exercise jurisprudence contradicts that proposition. . . . The only decisions in which we have held that the First Amendment bars application of a neutral, generally applicable law to religiously motivated action have involved not the Free Exercise Clause alone, but the Free Exercise Clause in conjunction with other constitutional protections, such as freedom of speech and of the press, or the right of parents to direct the education of their children. The present case does not present such a hybrid situation, but a free-exercise claim unconnected with any communicative activity or parental right. Respondents urge us to hold, quite simply, that when otherwise prohibitable conduct is accompanied by religious convictions, not only the convictions but the conduct itself must be free from governmental regulation. We have never held that, and decline to do so now. There being no contention that Oregon's drug law represents an attempt to regulate religious beliefs, the communication of religious beliefs, or the raising of one's children in those beliefs, the rule to which we have adhered ever since *Reynolds* [v. *U.S.* (1878)] plainly controls.

Respondents argue that even though exemption from generally applicable criminal laws need not automatically be extended to religiously motivated actors, at least the claim for a religious exemption must be evaluated under the balancing test set forth in *Sherbert* v. *Verner* (1963). Under the *Sherbert* test, governmental actions that substantially burden a religious practice must be justified by a compelling governmental interest. Applying that test we have, on three occasions, invalidated state unemployment compensation rules that conditioned the availability of benefits upon an applicant's willingness to work under conditions forbidden by his religion. We have never invalidated any governmental action on the basis of the *Sherbert* test except the denial of unemployment compensation. Although we have sometimes purported to apply the *Sherbert* test in contexts other than that, we have always found the test satisfied. In recent years we have abstained from applying the *Sherbert* test (outside the unemployment compensation field) at all. . . .

We conclude today that the sounder approach, the approach in accord with the vast majority of our precedents, is to hold the test inapplicable to such challenges. The government's ability to enforce generally applicable prohibitions of socially harmful conduct, like its ability to carry out other aspects of public policy, "cannot depend on measuring the effects of a governmental action on a religious objector's spiritual development." To make an individual's obligation to obey such a law contingent upon the law's coincidence with his religious beliefs, except where the State's interest is "compelling"—permitting him, by

virtue of his beliefs, "to become a law unto himself," *Reynolds* v. *United States*—contradicts both constitutional tradition and common sense.

The "compelling government interest" requirement seems benign, because it is familiar from other fields. But using it as the standard that must be met before the government may accord different treatment on the basis of race, or before the government may regulate the content of speech, is not remotely comparable to using it for the purpose asserted here. What it produces in those other fields—equality of treatment, and an unrestricted flow of contending speech—are constitutional norms; what it would produce here—a private right to ignore generally applicable laws—is a constitutional anomaly.

Values that are protected against government interference through enshrinement in the Bill of Rights are not thereby banished from the political process. Just as a society that believes in the negative protection accorded to the press by the First Amendment is likely to enact laws that affirmatively foster the dissemination of the printed word, so also a society that believes in the negative protection accorded to religious belief can be expected to be solicitous of that value in its legislation as well. It is therefore not surprising that a number of States have made an exception to their drug laws for sacramental peyote use. But to say that a nondiscriminatory religious-practice exemption is permitted, or even that it is desirable, is not to say that it is constitutionally required, and that the appropriate occasions for its creation can be discerned by the courts. It may fairly be said that leaving accommodation to the political process will place at a relative disadvantage those religious practices that are not widely engaged in; but that unavoidable consequence of democratic government must be preferred to a system in which each conscience is a law unto itself or in which judges weigh the social importance of all laws against the centrality of all religious beliefs.

Because respondents' ingestion of peyote was prohibited under Oregon law, and because that prohibition is constitutional, Oregon may, consistent with the Free Exercise Clause, deny respondents unemployment compensation when their dismissal results from use of the drug. The decision of the Oregon Supreme Court is accordingly reversed.

JUSTICE O'CONNOR, with whom JUSTICE BRENNAN, JUSTICE MARSHALL, and JUSTICE BLACKMUN join as to Parts I and II, concurring in the judgment.*

Although I agree with the result the Court reaches in this case, I cannot join its opinion. In my view, today's holding dramatically departs from well-settled First Amendment jurisprudence, appears unnecessary to resolve the question presented, and is incompatible with our Nation's fundamental commitment to individual religious liberty.

The Court today interprets the [Free Exercise] Clause to permit the government to prohibit, without justification, conduct mandated by an individual's religious beliefs, so long as that prohibition is generally applicable. But a law that prohibits certain conduct—conduct that happens to be an act of worship for someone—manifestly does prohibit that person's free exercise of his religion. A person who is barred from engaging in religiously motivated conduct is barred from freely exercising his religion regardless of whether the law prohibits the conduct only when engaged in for religious reasons, only by members of that religion, or by all persons. It is difficult to deny that a law that prohibits religiously motivated conduct, even if the law is generally applicable, does not at least implicate First Amendment concerns.

The Court responds that generally applicable laws are "one large step" removed from laws aimed at specific religious practices. The First Amendment, however, does not distinguish between laws that are generally applicable and laws that target particular religious practices. Indeed, few States would be so naive as to enact a law directly prohibiting or burdening a religious practice as such. Our free exercise cases have all concerned generally applicable laws that had the effect of significantly burdening a religious practice. If the First Amendment is to have any vitality, it ought not be construed to cover only the extreme and hypothetical situation in which a State directly targets a religious practice. . . .

To say that a person's right to free exercise has been burdened, of course, does not mean that he has an absolute right to engage in the conduct.

Under our established First Amendment jurisprudence, we have recognized that the freedom to act, unlike the freedom to believe, cannot be absolute. Instead, we have respected both the First Amendment's express textual mandate and the governmental interest in regulation of conduct by requiring the Government to justify any substantial burden on religiously motivated conduct by a compelling state interest and by means narrowly tailored to achieve that interest. The compelling interest test effectuates the First Amendment's command that religious liberty is an independent liberty, that it occupies a preferred position, and that the Court will not permit encroachments upon this liberty, whether direct or indirect, unless required by clear and compelling governmental interests "of the highest order."

The Court attempts to support its narrow reading of the Clause by claiming that "[w]e have never held that an individual's religious beliefs excuse him from compliance with an otherwise valid law prohibiting conduct that the State is free to regulate." But as the Court later notes, as it must, in cases such as *Cantwell* [v. *Connecticut* (1940)] and [*Wisconsin* v.] *Yoder* we have in fact interpreted the Free Exercise Clause to forbid application of a generally applicable prohibition to religiously motivated conduct. The Court endeavors to escape from our decisions in *Cantwell* and *Yoder* by labeling them "hybrid" decisions, but there is no denying that both cases expressly relied on the Free Exercise Clause, and that we have consistently regarded those cases as part of the mainstream of our free exercise jurisprudence. Moreover, in each of the other cases cited by the Court to support its categorical rule, we rejected the particular constitutional claims before us only after carefully weighing the competing interests. That we rejected the free exercise claims in those cases hardly calls into question the applicability of First Amendment doctrine in the first place. Indeed, it is surely unusual to judge the vitality of a constitutional doctrine by looking to the win–loss record of the plaintiffs who happen to come before us. . . .

The Court today gives no convincing reason to depart from settled First Amendment jurisprudence. There is nothing talismanic about neutral laws of general applicability or general criminal prohibitions, for laws neutral toward religion can coerce a person to violate his religious conscience or intrude upon his religious duties just

---

*Although Justice Brennan, Justice Marshall, and Justice Blackmun join Parts I and II of this opinion, they do not concur in the judgment.

as effectively as laws aimed at religion. Although the Court suggests that the compelling interest test, as applied to generally applicable laws, would result in a "constitutional anomaly," the First Amendment unequivocally makes freedom of religion, like freedom from race discrimination and freedom of speech, a "constitutional nor[m]," not an "anomaly." As the language of the Clause itself makes clear, an individual's free exercise of religion is a preferred constitutional activity.

JUSTICE BLACKMUN, with whom JUSTICE BRENNAN and JUSTICE MARSHALL join, dissenting.

I agree with JUSTICE O'CONNOR's analysis of the applicable free exercise doctrine, and I join parts I and II of her opinion. As she points out, "the critical question in this case is whether exempting respondents from the State's general criminal prohibition 'will unduly interfere with fulfillment of the governmental interest.'" I do disagree, however, with her specific answer to that question.

In weighing respondents' clear interest in the free exercise of their religion against Oregon's asserted interest in enforcing its drug laws, it is important to articulate in precise terms the state interest involved. It is not the State's broad interest in fighting the critical "war on drugs" that must be weighed against respondents' claim, but the State's narrow interest in refusing to make an exception for the religious, ceremonial use of peyote.

The State's interest in enforcing its prohibition, in order to be sufficiently compelling to outweigh a free exercise claim, cannot be merely abstract or symbolic. The State cannot plausibly assert that unbending application of a criminal prohibition is essential to fulfill any compelling interest, if it does not, in fact, attempt to enforce that prohibition. In this case, the State actually has not evinced any concrete interest in enforcing its drug laws against religious users of peyote. Oregon has never sought to prosecute respondents, and does not claim that it has made significant enforcement efforts against other religious users of peyote. The State's asserted interest thus amounts only to the symbolic preservation of an unenforced prohibition. But a government interest in "symbolism, even symbolism for so worthy a cause as the abolition of unlawful drugs," *Treasury Employees* v. *Von Raab* (1989) Scalia, J., dissenting, cannot suffice to abrogate the constitutional rights of individuals.

Similarly, this Court's prior decisions have not allowed a government to rely on mere speculation about potential harms, but have demanded evidentiary support for a refusal to allow a religious exception. The State proclaims an interest in protecting the health and safety of its citizens from the dangers of unlawful drugs. It offers, however, no evidence that the religious use of peyote has ever harmed anyone. The actual findings of other courts cast doubt on the State's assumption that religious use of peyote is harmful.

The fact that peyote is classified as a Schedule I controlled substance does not, by itself, show that any and all uses of peyote, in any circumstance, are inherently harmful and dangerous. The Federal Government, which created the classifications of unlawful drugs from which Oregon's drug laws are derived, apparently does not find peyote so dangerous as to preclude an exemption for religious use. . . .

The carefully circumscribed ritual context in which respondents used peyote is far removed from the irresponsible and unrestricted recreational use of unlawful drugs. The Native American Church's internal restrictions on, and supervision of, its members' use of peyote substantially obviate the State's health and safety concerns. Moreover, just as in *Yoder*, the values and interests of those seeking a religious exemption in this case are congruent to a great degree, with those the State seeks to promote through its drug laws. Not only does the Church's doctrine forbid nonreligious use of peyote; it also generally advocates self-reliance, familial responsibility, and abstinence from alcohol. There is considerable evidence that the spiritual and social support provided by the Church has been effective in combatting the tragic effects of alcoholism of the Native American population. Far from promoting the lawless and irresponsible use of drugs, Native American Church members' spiritual code exemplifies values that Oregon's drug laws are presumably intended to foster.

The State also seeks to support its refusal to make an exception for religious use of peyote by invoking its interest in abolishing drug trafficking. There is, however, practically no illegal traffic in peyote. Peyote simply is not a popular drug; its distribution for use in religious rituals has nothing to do with the vast and violent traffic in illegal narcotics that plagues this country.

Finally, the State argues that granting an exception for religious peyote use would erode its interest in the uniform, fair, and certain enforcement of its drug laws. The State fears that, if it grants an exemption for religious peyote use, a flood of other claims to religious exemptions will follow. It would then be placed in a dilemma, it says, between allowing a patchwork of exemptions that would hinder its law enforcement efforts, and risking a violation of the Establishment Clause by arbitrarily limiting its religious exemptions. The State's apprehension of a flood of other religious claims is purely speculative. Almost half the States, and the Federal Government, have maintained an exemption for religious peyote use for many years, and apparently have not found themselves overwhelmed by claims to other religious exemptions. Allowing an exemption for religious peyote use would not necessarily oblige the State to grant a similar exemption to other religious groups. The unusual circumstances that make the religious use of peyote compatible with the State's interests in health and safety and in preventing drug trafficking would not apply to other religious claims. That the State might grant an exemption for religious peyote use, but deny other religious claims arising in different circumstances, would not violate the Establishment Clause. Though the State must treat all religions equally, and not favor one over another, this obligation is fulfilled by the uniform application of the "compelling interest" *test* to all free exercise claims, not by reaching uniform *results* as to all claims. . . .

For these reasons, I conclude that Oregon's interest in enforcing its drug laws against religious use of peyote is not sufficiently compelling to outweigh respondents' right to the free exercise of their religion. Since the State could not constitutionally enforce its criminal prohibition against respondents, the interests underlying the State's drug laws cannot justify its denial of unemployment benefits.

City of Boerne v. *Flores, Archbishop of San Antonio*
521 U.S. ____; 117 S. Ct. 2157; 138 L. Ed. 2d 624 (1997)

In *Sherbert* v. *Verner* (1963), the Court ruled that the Free Exercise Clause required government to exempt religious believers from generally applicable laws that burdened their religious practices, unless the laws were justified by a compelling governmental interest and were narrowly tailored to achieve that interest. However, in *Department of Human Resources of Oregon* v. *Smith*, the Supreme Court abandoned that position. In 1993, Congress responded to *Smith* by enacting the Religious Freedom Restoration Act (RFRA), which was "to restore the compelling interest test set forth in *Sherbert* v. *Verner* . . . and to guarantee its application in all cases where free exercise of religion is substantially burdened."

St. Peter Catholic Church, located in Boerne, Texas, was built in 1923 to seat about 230 worshippers and was too small to accommodate the parish's growing congregation. The Archbishop of San Antonio thus applied for a building permit to enlarge the church. A few months previous, however, the Boerne City Council had authorized the city's Historic Landmark Commission to prepare a preservation plan with proposed historic landmarks and districts. Under the plan, the Commission had to preapprove construction affecting historic landmarks or buildings in historic districts. Relying on the ordinance and the designation of a historic district that included the church, the Commission denied the application to enlarge the church. The Archbishop filed suit in federal district court, relying primarily on RFRA in challenging the permit denial. The

District Court concluded that RFRA exceeded Congress's enforcement power under Section 5 of the Fourteenth Amendment. The Fifth Circuit reversed, finding RFRA to be constitutional, and the Supreme Court granted certiorari. *Opinion of the Court: Kennedy, Rehnquist, Stevens, Thomas, Ginsburg, and (in part) Scalia. Concurring opinion: Stevens. Concurring in part: Scalia, Stevens. Dissenting opinions: O'Connor, Breyer (in part); Souter, Breyer.*

JUSTICE KENNEDY delivered the opinion of the Court.

[*Employment Division*] v. *Smith* held that neutral, generally applicable laws may be applied to religious practices even when not supported by a compelling governmental interest. Members of Congress in hearings and floor debates . . . criticized the Court's reasoning, and this disagreement resulted in the passage of RFRA. The Act's mandate applies to any "branch, department, agency, instrumentality, and official (or other person acting under color of law) of the United States," as well as to any "State, or . . . subdivision of a State." The Act's universal coverage is confirmed in section 2000bb-3(a), under which RFRA "applies to all Federal and State law, and the implementation of that law, whether statutory or otherwise, and whether adopted before or after [RFRA's enactment]."

Congress relied on its Fourteenth Amendment enforcement power in enacting the most far reaching and substantial of RFRA's provisions, those which impose its requirements on the States. The parties disagree over whether RFRA is a proper exercise of Congress' section 5 power "to enforce" by "appropriate legislation" the constitutional guarantee that no State shall deprive any person of "life, liberty, or property, without due process of law" nor deny any person "equal protection of the laws."

In defense of the Act respondent contends that RFRA is permissible enforcement legislation. Congress, it is said, is only protecting by legislation one of the liberties guaranteed by the Fourteenth Amendment's Due Process Clause, the free exercise of religion, beyond what is necessary under *Smith*. It is said the congressional decision to dispense with proof of deliberate or overt discrimination and instead concentrate on a law's effects accords with the settled understanding that section 5 includes the power to enact legislation designed to prevent as well as remedy constitutional violations. It is further contended that Congress' section 5 power is not limited to remedial or preventive legislation. All must acknowledge that section 5 is "a positive grant of legislative power" to Congress, *Katzenbach* v. *Morgan* (1966). Legislation which deters or remedies constitutional violations can fall within the sweep of Congress' enforcement power even if in the process it prohibits conduct which is not itself unconstitutional and intrudes into "legislative spheres of autonomy previously reversed to the States." *Fitpatrick* v. *Bitzer* (1976). For example, the Court upheld a suspension of literacy tests and similar voting requirements under Congress' parallel power to enforce the provisions of the Fifteenth Amendment, as a measure to combat racial discrimination in voting, *South Carolina* v. *Katzenbach* (1966), despite the facial constitutionality of the tests under *Lassiter* v. *Northampton County Bd. of Elections* (1959). We have also concluded that other measures protecting voting rights are within Congress' power to enforce the Fourteenth and Fifteenth Amendments, despite the burdens those measures placed on the State. It is also true, however, that "as broad as the congressional enforcement power is, it is not unlimited." *Oregon* v. *Mitchell* (1970) (opinion of Black, J.). In assessing the breadth of section 5's enforcement power, we begin with its text. Congress' power under section 5 extends only to "enforc[ing]" the provisions of the Fourteenth Amendment. The design of the Amendment and the text of section 5 are inconsistent with the suggestion that Congress has the power to decree the substance of the Fourteenth Amendment's restrictions on the States. Legislation which alters the meaning of the Free Exercise Clause cannot be said to be enforcing the Clause. Congress does not enforce a constitutional right by changing what the right is. It has been given the power "to enforce," not the power to determine what constitutes violation. Were it not so, what Congress would be enforcing would no longer be, in any meaningful sense, the "provisions of [the Fourteenth Amendment]."

The Fourteenth Amendment's history confirms the remedial, rather than substantive, nature of the Enforcement Clause. In February, Republican Representative John Bingham of Ohio reported the following draft amendment to the House of Representatives on behalf of the Joint Committee [on Reconstruction]: "The Congress shall have power to make all laws which shall be necessary and proper to secure to the citizens of each State all privileges and immunities of citizens in the several States, and to all persons in the several States equal protection in the rights of life, liberty, and property." The proposal encountered immediate opposition [because] the proposed Amendment gave Congress too much legislative power at the expense of the existing constitutional structure. [T]he House voted to table the proposal until April . . . making the defeat of the proposal. [T]he Joint Committee began drafting a new article of Amendment, which it reported to Congress on April 30, 1866. Under the revised Amendment, Congress' power was no longer plenary but remedial. Congress was granted the power to make the substantive constitutional prohibitions against the States effective. After revisions not relevant here, the new measure passed both Houses and was ratified in July 1868 as the Fourteenth Amendment.

The remedial and preventive nature of Congress' enforcement power, and the limitation inherent in the power, were confirmed in our earliest cases on the Fourteenth Amendment. In the *Civil Rights Cases* (1883), the Court invalidated sections of the Civil Rights Act of 1875 which prescribed criminal penalties for denying to any person "the full enjoyment of" public accommodations and conveyances, on the grounds that it exceeded Congress' power by seeking to regulate private conduct. The Enforcement Clause, the Court said, did not authorize Congress to pass "general legislation upon the rights of the citizen, but corrective legislation; that is, such as may be necessary and proper for counteracting such laws as the State may adopt or enforce, and which, by the amendment, they are prohibited from making or enforcing." Although the specific holdings of these early cases might have

been superseded or modified, their treatment of Congress' section 5 power as corrective or preventive, not definitional, has not been questioned. Recent cases have continued to revolve around the question of whether section 5 legislation can be considered remedial.

If Congress could define its own powers by altering the Fourteenth Amendment's meaning, no longer would the Constitution be "superior paramount law, unchangeable by ordinary means." It would be "on a level with ordinary legislative acts, and, like other acts, . . . alterable when the legislature shall please to alter it." *Marbury* v. *Madison* [1803]. Under this approach, it is difficult to conceive of a principle that would limit congressional power. Shifting legislative majorities could change the Constitution and effectively circumvent the difficult and detailed amendment process contained in Article V.

Respondent contends that RFRA is a proper exercise of Congress' remedial or preventive power. The Act, it is said, is a reasonable means of protecting the free exercise of religion as defined by *Smith*. It prevents and remedies laws, which are enacted with the unconstitutional object of targeting religious beliefs and practices. RFRA is so out of proportion to a supposed remedial or preventive object that it cannot be understood as responsive to, or designed to prevent, unconstitutional behavior. It appears, instead, to attempt a substantive change in constitutional protections. Preventive measures prohibiting certain types of laws may be appropriate when there is reason to believe that many of the laws affected by the congressional enactment have a significant likelihood of being unconstitutional. RFRA is not so confined. Sweeping coverage ensures its intrusion at every level of government, displacing laws and prohibiting official actions of almost every description and regardless of subject matter. RFRA's restrictions apply to every agency and official of the Federal, State, and local Governments. RFRA applies to all federal and state law, statutory or otherwise, whether adopted before or after its enactment. RFRA has no termination date or termination mechanism. Any law is subject to challenge at any time by any individual who alleges a substantial burden on his or her free exercise of religion.

The reach and scope of RFRA distinguish it from other measures passed under Congress' enforcement power, even in the area of voting rights. The stringent test RFRA demands of state laws reflects a lack of proportionality or congruence between the means adopted and the legitimate end to be achieved. The substantial costs RFRA exacts, both in practical terms of imposing a heavy litigation burden on the States and in terms of curtailing their traditional general regulatory power, far exceed any pattern or practice of unconstitutional conduct under the Free Exercise Clause as interpreted in *Smith*. Simply put, RFRA is not designed to identify and counteract state laws likely to be unconstitutional because of their treatment of religion. When Congress acts within its sphere of power and responsibilities, it has not just the right but the duty to make its own informed judgment on the meaning and force of the Constitution. Were it otherwise, we could not afford Congress the presumption of validity its enactments now enjoy. [B]ut as the provisions of the federal statute here invoked are beyond congressional authority, it is this Court's precedent, not RFRA, which must control. It is for Congress in the first instance to "determin[e] whether and what legislation is needed to secure the guarantees of the Fourteenth Amendment," and its conclusions are entitled to much deference. Congress' discretion is not unlimited, however, and the courts retain the power, as they have since *Marbury* v. *Madison*, to determine if Congress has exceeded its authority under the Constitution. Broad as the power of Congress is under the Enforcement Clause of the Fourteenth Amendment, RFRA contradicts vital principles necessary to maintain separation of powers and the federal balance. The judgment of the Court of Appeals sustaining the Act's constitutionality is reversed.

It is so ordered.

JUSTICE STEVENS, concurring.

In my opinion, the Religious Freedom Restoration Act of 1993 (RFRA) is a "law respecting an establishment of religion" that violates the First Amendment to the Constitution. If the historic landmark on the hill in Boerne happened to be a museum or an art gallery owned by an atheist, it would not be eligible for an exemption from the city ordinances that forbid an enlargement of the structure. Because the landmark is owned by the Catholic Church, it is claimed that RFRA gives its owner a federal statutory entitlement to an exemption from a generally applicable, neutral civil law. Whether the Church would actually prevail under the statute or not, the statute has provided the Church with a legal weapon that no atheist or agnostic can obtain. This government preference for religion, as opposed to irreligion, is forbidden by the First Amendment. *Wallace* v. *Jaffree* (1985).

JUSTICE O'CONNOR, with whom JUSTICE BREYER [joins in part], dissenting.

I dissent from the Court's disposition of this case. I agree with the Court that the issue before us is whether the Religious Freedom Restoration Act (RFRA) is a proper exercise of Congress' power to enforce § 5 of the Fourteenth Amendment. But as a yardstick for measuring the constitutionality of RFRA, the Court uses its holding in *Employment Division, Department of Human Resources of Oregon* v. *Smith* (1990), the decision that prompted Congress to enact RFRA as a means of more rigorously enforcing the Free Exercise Clause. I remain of the view that *Smith* was wrongly decided, and I would use this case to reexamine the Court's holding there. Therefore, I would direct the parties to brief the question whether *Smith* represents the correct understanding of the Free Exercise Clause and set the case for reargument. If the Court were to correct the misinterpretation of the Free Exercise Clause set forth in *Smith*, it would simultaneously put our First Amendment jurisprudence back on course and allay the legitimate concerns of a majority in Congress who believe that *Smith* improperly restricted religious liberty. We would then be in a position to review RFRA in light of a proper interpretation of the Free Exercise Clause.

7
CRIMINAL
PROCEDURE

The Constitution strongly emphasizes the protection of the rights of defendants in the criminal process. The original document contains no fewer than seven provisions specifically addressed to this matter—these are in keeping with the Founders' concern to protect minorities (in this case, unpopular criminal defendants) from the tyrannical excesses of an oppressive outraged majority. Article I, Section 9, restricts suspension of the privilege of the writ of habeas corpus "unless when in cases of rebellion or invasion the public safety may require it" and prohibits the passage of bills of attainder or ex post facto laws. Article II, Section 2, provides the president with the power to grant reprieves and pardons. Article III, Section 2, provides for trial by jury for "all crimes except in cases of impeachment" and further directs that the trial "shall be held in the state where the said crimes shall have been committed." Article III, Section 3, narrowly and precisely defines what constitutes treason against the United States. Finally, Article IV, Section 2, specifies the procedure for the extradition of criminal defendants.

The Bill of Rights places an even greater stress on criminal procedure. Of the twenty-three separate rights enumerated in the first eight amendments, thirteen relate to the treatment of criminal defendants. The Fourth Amendment guarantees the right of the people to be secure "in their persons, houses, papers, and effects" against unreasonable searches and seizures and prohibits the issuance of warrants without probable cause. The Fifth Amendment requires prosecution by grand jury indictment for all "capital, or otherwise infamous" crimes (excepting certain military cases) and prohibits placing a person "twice in jeopardy of life or limb" for the same offense or compelling him to be "a witness against himself." The Sixth Amendment lists several rights that the accused shall enjoy "in all criminal prosecutions": a speedy and public trial by an impartial jury of the state and district in which the crime has been committed, notice of the "nature and cause of the accusation," confrontation of hostile witnesses; compulsory process for obtaining favorable witnesses; and assistance of counsel. The Eighth Amendment adds prohibitions against the imposition of excessive bails and fines and the infliction of cruel and unusual punishments. And in addition to these specific guarantees, the Fifth Amendment adds a general prohibition against deprivation of life, liberty, or property without due process of law.

Those provisions spelled out in the original constitution obviously were understood to apply only to the federal government; and initially, so were the criminal procedural protections spelled out in the Bill of Rights. When the question of applying the Bill of Rights to the states first arose, Chief Justice John Marshall declared in *Barron* v. *Baltimore* (1833) that the first ten amendments were enacted as limitations upon the national government alone. Marshall observed that the opening sentence of the First Amendment begins with the phrase "Congress shall make no law . . . " and that nowhere in the subsequent provisions of the Bill of Rights can be found any limitations upon state action. Further, he reasoned,

> had the framers of these amendments intended them to be limitations on the powers of the state governments, they would have imitated the framers of the original Constitution, and have expressed that intention. Had Congress engaged in the extraordinary occupation of improving the constitutions of the several states by affording the people additional protection from the exercise of power by their own governments in matters which concerned themselves alone, they would have declared this purpose in plain and intelligible language.

Since the adoption of the Fourteenth Amendment in 1868, however, all of this has changed. Through a series of decisions, the Supreme Court has held that the Fourteenth Amendment incorporates most of the criminal procedural guarantees of the Bill of Rights and has applied them equally to the states as to the federal government. (See Chapter 3 for a full discussion of the incorporation doctrine.) The only two Bill of Rights guarantees directly related to criminal procedure that have not been held to apply to the states are the Eighth Amendment prohibition against excessive fines and the Fifth Amendment requirement of prosecution by grand jury indictment. Remarkably, the Supreme Court has never been presented with an opportunity to rule on the prohibition against excessive fines, but it is generally assumed that this guarantee will be incorporated if the issue is squarely presented. The Fifth Amendment requirement of grand jury indictment, on the other hand, was specifically held not to be guaranteed by the Fourteenth Amendment in

Hurtado v. *California* (1884), which continues to be followed as valid precedent. The following sections outline the development and current legal status of the major criminal procedural protections of Amendments Four through Eight.

SEARCH AND SEIZURE

Legal Parameters

The Fourth Amendment forbids "unreasonable searches and seizures"—not all searches and seizures, only those that are "unreasonable." In general, the Supreme Court has followed the rule that searches are reasonable if they are based on a warrant obtained from a magistrate, who may issue the warrant only if law enforcement officials have demonstrated, through introduction of evidence, that there is probable cause to believe that the search will uncover evidence of criminal activity.[1] (In *Aguilar* v. *Texas* [1964] the Court ruled that probable-cause standards are the same for state and federal magistrates.)

Failure to obtain a warrant does not automatically render a search or seizure unreasonable. The Supreme Court has provided a number of exceptions to the requirement that a warrant be obtained, the most important of which is a search incident to a lawful arrest.[2] The rationale for this exception is that an arresting officer needs to be free to search a defendant in order to remove weapons (to protect the officer's safety) and evidence (to prevent its destruction). Officers are not permitted, however, to search just anybody and then use the evidence thereby obtained to justify the original arrest. Generally speaking, officers cannot use the fruits of a search as justification for the arrest; grounds for arrest must exist for the search incident to the arrest to be valid. And as *Chimel* v. *California* (1968) made clear, neither do the officers have much latitude in searching premises under the control of validly arrested defendants. The officers in *Chimel* arrested the defendant in his house and, over his objections and without a search warrant, proceeded to search his entire three-bedroom house, including attic, garage, and workshop. Items obtained from this search subsequently were admitted in evidence against the defendant during his trial for burglary, and he was convicted. The Supreme Court, in a 7–2 decision, declared that such a widespread search was unreasonable and overturned his conviction. Justice Potter Stewart, speaking for the Court, noted that although there is solid justification for a search of the arrestee's person and of "the area 'within his immediate control'—construing that phrase to mean the area within which he might gain possession of a weapon or destructable evidence," there is no comparable justification for "routinely searching any room other than that in which an arrest occurs—or, for that matter, for searching through all the desk drawers or other closed or concealed areas in that room itself. Such searches, in the absence of well-organized exceptions, may be made only under the authority of a search warrant."

A second exception to the warrant requirement is the "plain view" doctrine. As the Court held in *Harris* v. *United States* (1968), "It has long been settled that objects falling in the plain view of an officer who has a right to be in the position to have that view are subject to seizure and may be introduced in evidence." This doctrine covers observations made by officers standing on public property and peering into car windows or the windows of dwellings, as well as observations made by officers who are on a defendant's property in the pursuit of legitimate business.[3] It also appears to cover aerial surveillance. In *California* v. *Ciraolo* (1985), the Supreme Court, in a 5–4 decision upheld the use of an airplane flying at 1,000 feet to confirm an anonymous tip that marijuana was being grown in the petitioner's backyard. Chief Justice Burger noted that the police observations took place within public nagivable airspace in a physically nonintrusive manner. He argued that "in an age where private and commercial flight in the public airways is routine, it is unreasonable for respondent to expect that his marijuana plants were constitutionally protected from being observed with the naked eye from an altitude of 1,000 feet." Stressing that any member of the flying public in this airspace who cared to glance down could have seen everything that the officer observed, he concluded that "the Fourth Amendment simply does not require the police traveling in the public airways at this altitude to obtain a warrant in order to observe what is visible to the naked eye." Justice Powell dissented; he argued that the petitioner did have a reasonable expectation of privacy as "the actual risk to privacy from commercial or pleasure aircraft is virtually nonexistent. Travelers on commercial flights, as well as private planes used for business or personal reasons, normally obtain at most a fleeting, anonymous, and nondiscriminating glimpse of the landscape and buildings over which they pass. The risk that a passenger on such a plane might observe private activities, and might connect those activities with particular people, is simply too trivial to protect against." And, in *Florida* v. *Riley* (1989), it upheld as reasonable the use of a helicopter that at 400 feet circled twice over a greenhouse, allowing a deputy sheriff to make naked-eye observations through the openings of the greenhouse's roof and through its open sides of marijuana plants. Justice White acknowledged that the helicopter was flying below the lower limits of nagivable airspace allowed for fixed-wing aircraft but insisted that "any member of the public could legally have been flying over Riley's property in a helicopter at the altitude of 400 feet and could have observed Riley's greenhouse." Justice O'Connor supplied the critical fifth vote but only by concurring in the judgment; she observed that "public use of altitudes lower than that—particularly public observations from helicopters circling over the curtilage of a home—may be sufficiently rare that police surveillance from such altitudes would violate reasonable expectations of privacy."[4]

Law officers also are permitted to search a vehicle on probable cause without a warrant. The Court first recognized this right during the Prohibition era, in *Carroll* v. *United States* (1925), citing as its justification the fact that a vehicle can be moved quickly out of the locality or jurisdiction in which the warrant must be sought. The so-called automobile exception has spawned considerable litigation, and the Court repeatedly has been obliged to clarify this area of the law and to determine whether particular warrantless searches have been justified. Unfortunately, its efforts at clarification often have been unsatisfactory, providing inadequate or even contradictory advice to police, prosecutors, and courts attempting to discharge their responsibilities in a manner consistent with the Fourth Amendment. Nowhere is this failure to provide specific guidance more apparent than in the cases of *Robbins* v. *California* (1981) and *New York* v. *Belton* (1981), both decided on the same day. In Robbins the justices held that a warrantless search of a package wrapped in opaque plastic and stored in the luggage area of a station wagon violated the Fourth Amendment; but in *Belton*, they ruled that a warrantless search of a zippered pocket of a jacket found in an automobile's passenger compartment did not violate the amendment. Following a public outcry over such vacillation, the Court addressed this matter again in *United States* v. *Ross* (1982). This time, a six-member majority set forth the ground rules for the "automobile exception." To begin with, the *Ross* majority announced, the exception applies to vehicle searches that are supported by probable cause to believe that the vehicle contains contraband or other evidence of criminality. In these cases, a search is reasonable if it is based on objective facts that would justify the issuance of a warrant by a magistrate. When police officers have probable cause to search an entire vehicle, the justices continued, they may conduct a warrantless search of every part of the vehicle and its contents, including all containers and packages, that may conceal the object of the search. In such cases, the scope of the search is not defined by the nature of the container in which the contraband or evidence of criminality is secreted, but rather by the object of the search and the places in which there is probable cause to believe that it may be found. As Justice Stevens noted for the majority, "Probable cause to believe that undocumented aliens are being transported in a van will not justify a warrantless search of a suitcase."[5]

Obtaining consent to search constitutes a fourth exception to the warrant requirement: Fourth Amendment rights, like other criminal-procedure rights, can be waived by the individual. (State courts generally have been more willing to assume consent than have the federal courts, which have gone on record as declaring that consent to search "is not lightly to be inferred."[6])

The Court's 1985 decision in *New Jersey* v. *T.L.O.* identified still another exception, permitting school officials to search students who are under their authority without a warrant. Justice White held for the Court majority that the legality of a search of a student should depend not on a showing of probable cause but simply on the reasonableness, under all the circumstances, of the search. Determining the reasonableness of any search involves a determination of whether the search was justified at its inception and whether, as conducted, it was reasonably related in scope to the circumstances that justified the school official's intervention in the first place. *Vernonia School District* v. *Acton* (1995) built on *T.L.O.* and upheld a school drug policy that authorized random urinalysis drug testing of student athletes. The Court held that "Fourth Amendment rights, no less than First and Fourteenth Amendment rights, are different in public schools than elsewhere" and that the "reasonableness" of a search "cannot disregard the schools' custodial and tutelary responsibility for children." It noted that, "For their own good and that of their classmates, public school children are routinely required to submit to various physical examinations, and to be vaccinated against various diseases. . . . Particularly with regard to medical examinations and procedures, therefore, students within the school environment have a lesser expectation of privacy than members of the population generally."

Yet another exception, established in *Warden* v. *Hayden* (1967), allows the police to enter premises without an arrest or search warrant when in "hot pursuit" of a fleeing suspect, and having entered, to seize evidence uncovered in the search for the suspect.

The seventh exception to the warrant requirement is the investigative technique known as stop and frisk, the long-established police practice of stopping suspicious persons on the street or in other public places for purposes of questioning them or conducting some other form of investigation and, incident to the stoppings, of searching ("frisking") the suspects for dangerous weapons. Because such searches commonly were employed when there were no grounds to arrest the suspect and to search him incident to arrest, their constitutionality was challenged in the courts. In *Terry* v. *Ohio* (1968), Chief Justice Earl Warren provided a clear answer to this question. Speaking for an eight-member majority (only Justice William Douglas dissented), he declared,

> When an officer is justified in believing that the individual whose suspicious behavior he is investigating at close range is armed and presently dangerous to the officer or to others, it would appear completely unreasonable to deny the officer the power to take necessary measures to determine whether the person is in fact carrying a weapon and to neutralize the threat of physical harm. . . . There must be a narrowly drawn authority to permit a reasonable search for weapons for the protection of the police officer, where he has reason to believe that he is dealing with an armed and dangerous individual, regardless of whether he has probable cause to arrest the individual for a crime. The officer need not be absolutely certain that the individual is armed; the issue is whether a reasonably prudent man in the circumstances would be warranted in the belief that his safety or that of others was in danger.

The court's recognition of the reasonableness of protecting the officer's safety is also apparent in *Pennsylvania* v. *Mimms* (1977) and *Maryland* v. *Wilson* (1997). In *Mimms*, the Court held that a police officer may as a matter of course order the driver of a lawfully stopped car to exit the vehicle. It declared that "[t]he touchstone of our analysis under the Fourth Amendment is always 'the reasonableness in all the circumstances of the particular governmental invasion of a citizen's personal security'" and held that reasonableness "depends 'on a balance between the public interest and the individual's right to personal security free from arbitrary interference by law officers.'" On the public interest side of the balance, the Court found the officer's "practice to order all drivers [stopped in traffic stops] out of their vehicles as a matter of course" as a "precautionary measure" to protect his safety to be "both legitimate and weighty." On the other side of the balance, it noted that the driver's car was already validly stopped for a traffic infraction and it deemed the additional intrusion of asking him to step outside his car *de minimis.*"Accordingly, it concluded that "once a motor vehicle has been lawfully detained for a traffic violation, the police officers may order the driver to get out of the vehicle without violating the Fourth Amendment's proscription of unreasonable seizures." In *Wilson,* it extended the same rule to passengers as well. After stopping a passenger car for speeding, a Maryland state trooper observed Wilson, "very nervous" and sitting in the front seat, and ordered him from the car. As Wilson exited the car, a quantity of crack cocaine fell to the ground, whereupon he was arrested and charged with possession of cocaine with intent to distribute. Wilson sought to suppress the evidence, arguing that the trooper's order to step out of the car was an unreasonable seizure under the Fourth Amendment. Rejecting Wilson's contention, Chief Justice Rehnquist noted for a seven-member majority that "danger to an officer from a traffic stop is likely to be greater when there are passengers in addition to the driver in the stopped car." And, "[w]hile there is not the same basis for ordering the passengers out of the car as there is for ordering the driver out, the additional intrusion on the passenger is minimal." "[A]s a practical matter, the passengers are already stopped by virtue of the stop of the vehicle. The only change in their circumstances which will result from ordering them out of the car is that they will be outside of, rather than inside of, the stopped car. Outside the car, the passengers will be denied access to any possible weapon that might be concealed in the interior of the passenger compartment."

The 1973 decisions in *United States* v. *Robinson* and *Gustafson* v. *Florida* had previously modified the general rule that a warrantless search is valid only if it is incident to a lawful arrest. Both cases involved arrests for motor vehicle violations; and in both, subsequent searches of the offenders uncovered narcotics, and the evidence so obtained later was used to obtain convictions. In affirming both convictions, Justice William Rehnquist, writing for the majority in *Robinson* and a plurality in *Gustafson,* expanded the permissible limits of *Terry's* stop-and-frisk doctrine. Under the circumstances of these cases, he held, a search incident to a valid arrest was not limited to a pat-down of the outer garments for weapons. These searches were not unreasonable, he continued, even though the arresting officers did not suspect either that the offenders were armed or that they might destroy evidence of the crime for which the arrests had been made. As Rehnquist declared in *Robinson,*

> As custodial arrest of a suspect based on probable cause is a reasonable intrusion under the Fourth Amendment, that intrusion being lawful, a search incident to the arrest requires no additional justification.

An eighth and final exception to the warrant requirement has recently been introduced by the Court: drug testing. In *Skinner* v. *Railway Labor Executives Association* (1989), the Court sustained drug testing of railroad employees involved in train accidents and held that, in certain circumstances, reasonableness does not require a warrant, probable cause, or even any measure of individualized suspicion. The Court concluded that the demonstrated frequency of drug and alcohol use by railroad employees and the demonstrated connection between such use and grave harm rendered the drug testing a reasonable means of protecting society. In *National Treasury Employees Union* v. *Von Raab*, decided the same day, the Court went even further and sustained the constitutionality of urine testing for those U.S. Customs Service employees involved directly in drug interdiction or whose positions required them to carry firearms. Justice Kennedy concluded for a five-member majority that the government had a "compelling interest" in "safeguarding our borders" and that public safety outweighs the privacy expectations of the Customs Service employees. Justice Scalia, who concurred in *Skinner,* filed a sharp dissent, describing the drug-testing rules of the Customs Service as "a kind of immolation of privacy and human dignity." In *Michigan Department of State Police* v. *Sitz* (1990), the Supreme Court addressed a variation on the drug-testing theme; six of its members Court held that Michigan's highway sobriety checkpoint program was "consistent with the Fourth Amendment." In his majority opinion, Chief Justice Rehnquist relied heavily on *United States* v. *Martinez-Fuerte* (1976), which used a balancing test in upholding checkpoints for detecting illegal aliens, and on *Von Raab* to argue that, while a Fourth Amendment "seizure" occurs when a vehicle is stopped at a checkpoint, on balance the seizure is reasonable. "[T]he balance of the State's interest in preventing drunken driving, the extent to which this system can reasonably be said to advance that interest, and the degree of intrusion upon individual motorists who are briefly stopped, weighs in favor of the state program."

As *Chandler* v. *Miller* (1997) makes clear, not all drug-testing schemes pass constitutional muster. In an 8–1 decision, the Court held unconstitutional a Georgia statute that required candidates for state office to certify that they have taken a urinalysis drug test within 30 days prior to qualifying for nomination or election and that the test result was negative. Georgia relied heavily on *Von Raab*, but Justice Ginsburg's majority opinion denied that it was "a decision opening broad vistas for suspicionless searches" and insisted that it "must be read in its unique context." She then proceeded to note "a telling difference between *Von Raab* and Georgia's candidate drug-testing program." In *Von Raab*, the Court concluded that it was "not feasible to subject employees [required to carry firearms or concerned with interdiction of controlled substances] and their work product to the kind of day-to-day scrutiny that is the norm in more traditional office environments." In contrast, candidates for public office "are subject to relentless scrutiny—by their peers, the public, and the press. Their day-to-day conduct attracts attention notably beyond the norm in ordinary work environments." She concluded that while "the candidate drug test Georgia has devised" was "well-meant," it nevertheless diminished "personal privacy for a symbol's sake. The Fourth Amendment shields society against that state action."

Electronic Surveillance

The Supreme Court first confronted the issue of electronic surveillance in *Olmstead* v. *United States* (1928), which involved the wiretapping of a gang of rumrunners. Here the justices concluded that the Fourth Amendment was not applicable, because there had been no trespass of a constitutionally protected area and no seizure of a physical object. The *Olmstead* doctrine was not repudiated until *Katz* v. *United States* (1967), in which the Court declared that the Fourth Amendment "protects people, not places" and held that electronic surveillance conducted outside the judicial process, whether or not it involves trespass, is *per se* unreasonable. In an attempt to limit *Katz* and to clarify exactly what was expected of law enforcement personnel, Congress included in the Omnibus Crime Control and Safe Streets Act of 1968 a title on the interception and disclosure of wire or oral communication, which provided for a system of judicially approved interceptions at the request of the attorney-general.

Remedies for Violations

Although the Fourth Amendment forbids unreasonable searches and seizures, it does not prescribe a remedy for those whose rights have been violated. Addressing this issue for the first time in *Weeks* v. *United States* (1914), the Supreme Court declared that the appropriate remedy was exclusion of the illegally obtained evidence. The justices did not hold that the Fourth Amendment of its own force barred from criminal prosecutions the use of illegally seized, or "tainted," items: that is, they did not consider the Fourth Amendment to constitute a rule of evidence. But without such an exclusionary rule, they argued, the Fourth Amendment would present no effective deterrent to improper searches and seizures. This holding meant that as a federal rule of evidence—which in its supervisory function the Court could impose on the entire federal judiciary— illegally obtained evidence could not be used in federal prosecutions.

The *Weeks* decision, however, dealt only with federal prosecutions. Because the Fourth Amendment had not yet been incorporated through the Fourteenth Amendment to apply to the states, most states continued to follow the old common-law rule that relevant evidence obtained under any circumstances was admissible. Not until *Wolf* v. *Colorado* (1949) did the Supreme Court have occasion to rule on these state practices. In that decision the Court concluded, in an opinion written by Justice Frankfurter, that "the security of one's privacy against arbitrary intrusion by the police—which is at the core of the Fourth Amendment—is basic to a free society. It is therefore implicit in 'the concept of ordered liberty' and as such enforceable against the States through the Due Process Clause." Although holding that the Fourth Amendment guarantee against unreasonable searches and seizures was enforceable against the states through the Fourteenth Amendment, the *Wolf* majority did not consider the exclusionary rule announced in *Weeks* to be an "essential ingredient" of that guarantee. The Court denied that the exclusionary rule had any constitutional status, asserting instead that it was merely a pragmatic remedy developed under the Court's powers to supervise the federal judicial system. Not until *Mapp* v. *Ohio* (1961) did the Court finally abandon the *Wolf* doctrine and impose the exclusionary rule on state proceedings as well. In *Mapp*, it concluded that the exclusionary rule, by removing the incentive to disregard the Fourth Amendment, constituted "the only effectively available way . . . to compel respect for the constitutional guarantee."

Ever since *Mapp*, the exclusionary rule has been under heavy attack.[7] In his dissent in *Bivens* v. *Six Unknown Named Agents* (1971), Chief Justice Burger proposed its elimination and an end to what he called the "universal capital punishment we inflict on all evidence when police error is shown in its acquisition." He urged Congress to enact a statute that would waive sovereign immunity as to the illegal acts of law enforcement officials committed in the performance of assigned tasks; create a cause of action for damages sustained by any persons aggrieved by the conduct of governmental agents in violation of the Fourth Amendment or statutes regulating official conduct; create a quasijudicial tribunal, patterned after the then-existing U.S. Court of Claims, to adjudicate all claims under the statute; substitute this remedy for the exclusionary rule; and direct that no evidence, otherwise admissible, would be excluded from any criminal proceeding because of a violation of the Fourth Amendment. He believed this would provide a more "meaningful and effective remedy against unlawful conduct by governmental officials" and that it would afford "some remedy to completely innocent persons who are sometimes the victims of illegal police conduct."

While a majority of the Court has never accepted Chief Justice Burger's argument for the complete elimination of the exclusionary rule, it has come to recognize a "good faith" exception to it. In *United States* v. *Leon* (1984), *Massachusetts* v. *Sheppard* (1984), and *Arizona* v. *Evans* (1995), the Court has held that the exclusionary rule should not be applied so as to suppress the introduction of evidence at a criminal trial obtained in the reasonable belief that the search and seizure at issue was consistent with the Fourth Amendment. As Justice White wrote for a six-member majority in *Leon*, a case in which the defendant claimed that the police had obtained a warrant on the basis of an affidavit that was insufficient to establish probable cause: The exclusionary rule "cannot be expected, and should not be applied, to deter objectively reasonable law enforcement activity."

> This is particularly true, we believe, when an officer acting in objective good faith has obtained a search warrant from a judge or magistrate and acted within its scope. In most such cases, there is no police illegality and thus nothing to deter. It is the magistrate's responsibility to determine whether the officer's allegations establish probable cause and if so, to issue a warrant comporting in form with the requirements of the Fourth Amendment. In the ordinary case, an officer cannot be expected to question the magistrate's probable cause determination or his judgment that the form of the warrant is technically sufficient. "[O]nce the warrant issues, there is literally nothing more the policeman can do in seeking to comply with the law. . . ." Penalizing the officer for the magistrate's error, rather than his own, cannot logically contribute to the deterrence of Fourth Amendment violations.

Leon dealt with a violation of Fourth Amendment rights not by the police but the courts. So, too, did *Evans*, which dealt with the question of whether evidence seized in violation of the Fourth Amendment by a police officer who acted in reliance on a police computer record indicating the existence of an outstanding arrest warrant—a record that was subsequently determined to be erroneous—must be suppressed by virtue of the exclusionary rule regardless of the source of error. As it turned out, the arrest warrant had previously been quashed, but court personnel had failed to notify the police of this fact so that they could correct their computer records. In a 7–2 opinion, Chief Justice Rehnquist held that the evidence need not be excluded. He made three principal points: First, the exclusionary rule exists to deter "police misconduct, not mistakes by court employees"; second, there was no evidence that "court employees are included to ignore or subvert the Fourth Amendment or that lawlessness among these actors requires application of the extreme sanction of exclusion"; and third, there was no reason to believe applying the exclusionary rule "will have a significant effect on court employees responsible for informing the police that a warrant has been quashed." As he continued, "court clerks are not adjuncts to the law enforcement team engaged in the often competitive enterprise of ferreting out crime" and therefore "have no stake in the outcome of particular criminal prosecutions."

SELF-INCRIMINATION AND COERCED CONFESSIONS

The Fifth Amendment provides that no person "shall be compelled in any criminal case to be a witness against himself." Along with other provisions of the Bill of Rights, this privilege originally was restricted to federal prosecutions. And in both *Twining* v. *New Jersey* (1908) and *Adamson* v. *California* (1947), the Supreme Court rejected the argument that the exception to compulsory self-incrimination was a "fundamental right" and hence necessary to a system of "ordered liberty." In the 1964 case of *Malloy* v. *Hogan*, however, it overruled those precedents and, through the Fourteenth Amendment, extended this protection to the states as well. As Justice William Brennan stated for the Court, "The Fourteenth Amendment secures against state invasion the same privilege that the Fifth Amendment guarantees against federal infringement—the right of a person to remain silent unless he chooses to speak in the unfettered exercise of his own will, and to suffer no penalty—for such silence."

Long before *Malloy*, the Court had placed limitations upon police interrogation techniques and the admissibility of confessions thereby obtained. In *Brown* v. *Mississippi* (1936) the Court overturned the conviction of three defendants whom police had physically tortured in order to extort confessions. Chief Justice Charles Evans Hughes made abundantly clear in *Brown* the Court's belief that the use of such confessions violated the Due Process Clause of the Fourteenth Amendment: "The freedom of the state in establishing its policy is the freedom of constitutional government and is limited by the requirement of due process of law. Because a state may dispense with a jury trial,[8] it does not follow that it may substitute a trial by ordeal. The rack and torture chamber may not be substituted for the witness stand." *Brown* was extended in *Chambers* v. *Florida* (1940), in which the Court again overturned a state conviction—this time because the defendant had been arrested on suspicion, without a warrant; denied contact with friends or attorneys; and questioned for long periods of time by different squads of police officers.

Brown and *Chambers* were followed by a long line of cases in which the Court addressed questions concerning the admissibility of confession on an *ad hoc* basis, employing the "totality of circumstances" rule: Under this guideline, the Court sought to determine whether the specific circumstances surrounding the obtaining of a particular confession (the nature of the charge; the age, maturity, and educational achievements of the defendant; the degree of pressure put upon him or her; the length of interrogation; etc.) constituted coercion and thereby rendered the confession inadmissible. This guideline suffered from one major drawback: it provided the police and the prosecution with little guidance as to what practices did or did not pass constitutional muster. As a consequence, the Court found itself confronted with a barrage of "coerced confessions" cases dealing with such police practices as attempts to gain the sympathy of the defendant through a childhood friend on the police force,[9] threats to bring a defendant's wife into custody for questioning,[10] threats to place the defendant's children in the custody of welfare officials,[11] and interrogations of wounded defendants under the influence of so-called truth serums.[12] To free itself from this perpetual stream of litigation, the Warren Court in *Miranda* v. *Arizona* (1966) broke completely with past cases and, rejecting the *ad hoc* "totality of circumstances" rule, announced specific procedures that the police would have to follow during interrogations, and declared that any statements elicited in violation of these procedures would be inadmissible.

Miranda was a highly controversial decision. The Democratic-controlled Congress responded swiftly and directly, declaring in Section 3501 of the Omnibus Safe Streets and Crime Control Act of 1968 that a voluntary confession was admissible, irrespective of his conformity to *Miranda*. That provision proclaimed: "[A] confession . . . shall be admissible in evidence if it is voluntarily given" and that voluntariness shall be determined on the basis "of all the circumstances surrounding the giving of the confession, including . . . whether or not [the] defendant was advised or knew that he was not required to make any statement . . . ; whether or not [the] defendant had been advised prior to questioning of his right to the assistance of counsel; and . . . whether or not [the] defendant was without the assistance of counsel when questioned." To remove all doubt, it continued: "The presence or absence of any of the above-mentioned factors . . . need not be conclusive on the issue of voluntariness of the confession." Interestingly, however, as Justice Scalia pointed out in *Davis* v. *United States* (1994), Section 3501 "has been studiously avoided by every Administration, not only in this Court but in the lower courts, since its enactment more than 25 years ago." Scalia noted that "The United States' repeated refusal to invoke Section 3501, combined with the courts' traditional (albeit merely prudential) refusal to consider arguments not raised, has caused the federal judiciary to confront a host of *Miranda* issues that might be entirely irrelevant under federal law. Worse still, it may have produced—during an era of intense national concern about the problem of runaway crime—the acquittal and the nonprosecution of many dangerous felons, enabling them to continue their depredations upon our citizens. There is no excuse for this." He therefore announced that "I will no longer be open to the argument that this Court should continue to ignore the commands of Section 3501 simply because the Executive declines to insist that we observe them."

The Burger and Rehnquist Courts have refused to overturn the *Miranda* decision, but they have modified it in such decisions as *Harris* v. *New York* (1971), *Oregon* v. *Hass* (1975), *Nix* v. *Williams* (1984), *New York* v. *Quarles* (1984), and *Duckworth* v. *Eagan* (1989). The six-member majority in *Harris* held that although statements made to the police by defendants who have not been advised of their *Miranda* rights cannot be introduced as evidence for the prosecution's case-in-chief, they can be employed to impeach the credibility of defendants who testify in their own behalf and, in so doing, contradict earlier statements. In so ruling, the Court refused to construe the privilege against self-incrimination to include the right to commit perjury.[13] At issue in *Hass* were the rights of a suspect in police custody who, having received and accepted the full warnings prescribed by *Miranda*, later stated that he would like to telephone a lawyer; after being told he could not do so before reaching the station, he then provided inculpatory information. Such information, the Court ruled, was admissible in evidence at the suspect's trial solely for impeachment purposes after he had taken the stand and testified to the contrary, knowing that such information has been ruled inadmissible for the prosecution's case-in-chief.

In *Williams*, the Court held in a 7–2 vote that evidence obtained in violation of the *Miranda* decision need not be suppressed if it would have been inevitably discovered by lawful means. And, in *Quarles*, the Court recognized a "public safety exception" to the requirement that *Miranda* warnings be given before a suspect's answers may be admitted into evidence. As Justice Rehnquist reasoned:

> The police, in this case, in the very act of apprehending a suspect, were confronted with the immediate necessity of ascertaining the whereabouts of a gun which they had every reason to believe the suspect had just removed from his empty holster and discarded in the supermarket. So long as the gun was concealed somewhere in the supermarket, with its actual whereabouts unknown, it obviously posed more than one danger to the public safety: an accomplice might make use of it, a customer or employee might later come upon it.

To ensure that further danger to the public did not result from the concealment of the gun in a public area, the Court held that the police did not have to advise the suspect of his *Miranda* rights before questioning him about the whereabouts of the gun and that the suspect's response, in which he pointed out the gun's location, did not have to be excluded.

Finally, in *Duckworth*, the Court held that informing a suspect that an attorney would be appointed for him "if and when you go to court" does not render *Miranda* warnings inadequate. Chief Justice Rehnquist argued for a five-member majority that *Miranda* warnings need not be given in the exact form described in *Miranda* but simply must reasonably convey to suspects their rights.

It should be noted that not all self-incrimination cases are concerned with trial court procedures or pretrial police interrogation techniques. A case in point is *South Dakota* v. *Neville* (1983), in which Justice O'Connor held for a seven-member majority that admission into evidence of a defendant's refusal to submit to a blood-alcohol test does not offend his privilege against self-incrimination and that it is not fundamentally unfair in violation of due process to use a defendant's refusal to take the blood-alcohol test as evidence of guilt, even though the police failed to warn him that refusal could be used against him at trial. Another example is *Selective Service System* v. *Minnesota Public Interest Research Group* (1984), in which the Court held, 6–2, that a statute denying federal financial aid to male students who failed to register for the draft did not violate the privilege against self-incrimination of nonregistrants.

THE RIGHT TO COUNSEL

The Sixth Amendment declares that "in all criminal prosecutions, the accused shall enjoy the right . . . to have Assistance of Counsel for his defense." Until well into the twentieth century, this language was construed to guarantee only that the accused could employ and bring to trial a lawyer of his own choosing. No provision was made for the indigent defendant who might want and even badly need assistance of counsel, but was unable to afford an attorney. The language was permissive only; it imposed no duty on the government to provide free counsel.

In 1932 the Court began to expand this interpretation, holding in *Powell* v. *Alabama* that in capital felony cases, right to counsel is secured by the Due Process Clause of the Fourteenth Amendment. Six years later, in *Johnson* v. *Zerbst,* the Court further broadened the right to counsel to include appointment of counsel for indigent defendants in all federal criminal proceedings, capital or noncapital: "The Sixth Amendment," the Court declared, "withholds from federal courts, in all criminal proceedings, the power and authority to deprive an accused of his life or liberty unless he has or waives the assistance of counsel."

Although the Court held that the Sixth Amendment required appointment of counsel for indigent criminal defendants in federal prosecutions, it was reluctant to interpret the Fourteenth Amendment's Due Process Clause in such a way as to impose the same requirements on the states. When presented with the opportunity to do so in *Betts* v. *Brady* (1942), Justice Owen Roberts examined the constitutional, judicial, and legislative history of the states from colonial days and concluded for a six-member majority that "this material demonstrates that, in the great majority of States, it has been the considered judgment of the people, their representatives and their courts that appointment of counsel is not a fundamental right essential to a fair trial. On the contrary, the matter has generally been deemed one of legislative policy. In the light of this evidence, we are unable to say that the concept of due process incorporated in the Fourteenth Amendment obligates the States, whatever may be their own views, to furnish counsel in every such case." In dissent, Justice Black stressed that "whether a man is innocent cannot be determined from a trial in which, as here, denial of counsel has made it impossible to conclude, with any satisfactory degree of certainty, that the defendant's case was adequately presented."

Justice Black's dissent eventually was vindicated in the celebrated case of *Gideon* v. *Wainwright* (1963), in which the Court overruled *Betts* and unanimously concluded that an indigent defendant's right to court-appointed counsel is fundamental and essential to a fair trial in state as well as federal felony prosecutions. Justice Black declared for the Court that precedent, reason, and reflection "require us to recognize that in our adversary system of criminal justice, any person hauled into court, who is too poor to hire a lawyer, cannot be assured a fair trial unless counsel is provided for him." Observing that the government hires lawyers to prosecute and defendants with money hire lawyers to defend, he concluded that "lawyers in criminal courts are necessities, not luxuries." The *Gideon* ruling did not extend the right to assistance of counsel to all criminal prosecutions, however. Misdemeanor offenses were excluded from coverage until *Argersinger* v. *Hamlin* (1972), in which the Court unanimously held that "absent a knowing and intelligent waiver, no person may be imprisoned for any offense, whether classified as petty, misdemeanor, or felony, unless he was represented by counsel at his trial."[14]

The Court has not only held that the right to assistance of counsel must be guaranteed in all trials where defendants can be sentenced to a term of imprisonment but has also held that this constitutional principle is not limited simply to the presence of counsel at trial. As it declared in *United States* v. *Wade* (1967),

> it is central to that principle that in addition to counsel's presence at trial, the accused is guaranteed that he need not stand alone against the state at any stage of the prosecution, formal or informal, in court or out, where counsel's absence might derogate from the accused's right to a fair trial.

On the basis of this principle, the Court has ruled that the accused has the right to counsel at such "critical stages" as in-custody police interrogation following arrest, *Escobedo* v. *Illinois* and *Miranda* v. *Arizona*; the police lineup held for eyewitness identification, *United States* v. *Wade* and *Gilbert* v. *California*; the preliminary hearing, *Coleman* v. *Alabama*; the arraignment, *Hamilton* v. *Alabama*; at his appeal, *Douglas* v. *California*, and even at a posttrial proceeding for the revocation of probation and parole, *Mempa* v. *Rhay*.[15]

The Court's decisions from *Powell* to *Argersinger* raised a serious question: Does a defendant in a criminal trial have a constitutional right to proceed without counsel when he voluntarily and intelligently elects to do so? Stated another way, can a state constitutionally haul a person into its criminal courts and there force a lawyer upon him, even when he insists that he wants to conduct his own defense? The Court gave a negative answer to this question in *Faretta* v. *California* (1975). Justice Stewart, speaking for a six-member majority, stressed that the language of the provision provides for "assistance" of counsel and that "an assistant, however expert, is still an assistant." Developing this argument further, he concluded that to thrust counsel upon an unwilling defendant would violate the logic of the amendment: "In such a case, counsel is not an assistant, but a master; and the right to make a defense is stripped of the personal character upon which the Amendment insists."

Justice Harry Blackmun challenged this conclusion in his dissent: "The Court seems to suggest that so long as the accused is willing to pay the consequences of his folly, there is no reason for not allowing a defendant the right to self-representation. . . . That view ignores the established principle that the interest of the State in a criminal prosecution 'is not that it shall win a case, but that justice shall be done.' "

Chaplin & Drysdale, Chartered v. *United States* (1989) posed for the Court an interesting right-to-counsel question arising out of the federal government's ongoing war against drugs: Can the federal government constitutionally enforce a statute authorizing forfeiture to the government of assets acquired as a result of drug law violations if the criminal defendant intends to use these assets to pay legal fees for his defense? In a 5–4 decision, Justice White concluded for the Court that the government can; he observed, among other things, that a defendant in a drug case has no more Sixth Amendment right to use funds obtained from an illegal drug enterprise to pay for his defense than a robbery suspect has "to use funds he has stolen from a bank." Justice Blackmun's dissent called into question the adequacy of the very guarantee of right to court-appointed counsel secured by the Court in *Gideon* v. *Wainwright*:

> The main effect of forfeitures under the [Continuing Criminal Enterprise] Act, of course, will be to deny the defendant the right to retain counsel, and therefore the right to have his defense designed and presented by an attorney he has chosen and trusts. If the Government restrains the defendant's assets before trial, private counsel will be unwilling to continue to take on the defense. . . . The resulting relationship between the defendant and his court-appointed counsel will likely begin in distrust, and be exacerbated to the extent that the defendant perceives his new-found "indigency" as a form of punishment imposed by the Government in order to weaken his defense. If the defendant had been represented by private counsel earlier in the proceedings, the defendant's sense that the Government has stripped him of his defenses will be sharpened by the concreteness of his loss. Appointed counsel may be inexperienced and undercompensated and, for that reason, may not have adequate opportunity or resources to deal with the special problems presented by what is likely to be a complex trial. The already scarce resources of the public defender's office will be stretched to the limit. Facing a lengthy trial against a better-armed adversary, the temptation to recommend a guilty plea will be great. The result, if the defendant is convicted, will be a sense, often well grounded, that justice was not done.

THE ENTRAPMENT DEFENSE

Entrapment may be defined as "the conception and planning of an offense by an officer, and his procurement of its commission by one who would not have perpetrated it except for the trickery, persuasion, or fraud of the officer."[16] Two opposing versions of the entrapment defense have been formulated and defended by various members of the Court. The first may be referred to as the federal approach, since it has been adopted by a majority of the Court in each of the major entrapment decisions[17] and is generally followed by the lower federal courts. The federal approach focuses on the conduct and propensities of the particular defendant in each individual case. If defendants are not predisposed to commit crimes of the nature charged, they may avail themselves of the defense. If they are ready and willing to commit such an offense at any favorable opportunity, however, then the entrapment defense will fail, regardless of the nature and extent of the government's participation. Because of the focus on the defendant's predisposition, this approach is frequently referred to as the "subjective" test.

The other version of the entrapment defense may be labeled the "hypothetical-person" approach. Expressed in the concurring and dissenting opinions of the same Supreme Court cases that employ the federal approach, this approach concentrates on the quality of police or government conduct rather than on the predisposition of the accused. It subscribes to the view that governmental conduct that falls below certain minimum standards will not be tolerated, thus relieving from criminal responsibility a defendant who commits a crime as a result of such conduct. This approach will not condone conduct by law enforcement officials that presents too great a risk that a hypothetical, law-abiding person will be induced to commit a crime that he or she would not otherwise have committed. Thus, the individual who commits the criminal offense, although technically guilty, will be relieved of criminal responsibility, and further prosecution will be barred. Proponents of this approach hope to deter unlawful governmental activity in the instigation of crime and to preserve the purity of the criminal justice system. As with all questions involving the legality of law enforcement methods, the "hypothetical-person" defense submits the issue of entrapment to the judge, while the jury decides the issue under the federal defense. Because of its exclusive concentration on the conduct of the police and its disregard of the defendant's predisposition, this approach is often referred to as the "objective" test.

In *Jacobson* v. *United States* (1992), the Supreme Court's latest consideration of the entrapment defense, all of the justices employed the federal approach, but split over whether or not the defendant was predisposed to purchase child pornography when he was induced to do so by an undercover police sting operation. Five justices concluded that the police had implanted in Jacobson the disposition to purchase illegal child pornography; four insisted that he was already predisposed to make such a purchase and all the government did was induce him to act on that predisposition—that is, provide him the opportunity to do so.

THE RIGHT TO A SPEEDY TRIAL

The Sixth Amendment assures the accused the right to a speedy trial. However, as Justice Powell remarked in *Barker* v. *Wingo* (1972), this right "is a more vague concept than other procedural rights. It is, for example, impossible to determine with precision when the right has been denied. We cannot definitely say how long is too long in a system where justice is supposed to be swift but deliberate." The vague quality of the right to a speedy trial led the Court in *Barker* to embrace a "balancing test" to determine whether the right had been violated. Four factors were to be weighed in the balance: length of delay, the reason for the delay, the defendant's assertion of his right, and prejudice to the defendant.

Conceding that this "difficult and sensitive balancing process" necessarily would compel the courts to approach speedy trial cases on an *ad hoc* basis, the Court insisted that this way of proceeding comported with the requirements of the judicial process. The Court was reluctant to go so far as to hold that the Constitution required a criminal defendant to be offered a trial within a specified time period. Against the undoubted clarity and definiteness of a time limit, the Court observed, must be weighed the fact that it would "require this Court to engage in legislative or rulemaking activity, rather than in the adjudicative process to which we should confine our efforts." It went on to note that although legislatures were free to prescribe reasonable periods of time, consistent with constitutional standards, within which criminal trials must begin, its own approach had to be less precise. Seeking such precision, Congress passed with the Speedy Trial Act of 1974, which ordered that criminal defendants be brought to trial within 100 days.

Doggett v. *United States* (1992) represents the Court's most recent consideration of the "speedy trial" provision. In it, the Court reversed the defendant's conviction for conspiracy to import and distribute cocaine on the grounds that an eight-and-a-half-year period between indictment and trial denied him of his constitutional right to a speedy trial; it condemned the "Government's egregious persistence in failing to prosecute" the defendant, even though the defendant was not held in detention during that period and claimed to be unaware he was under indictment, and despite the fact that the government was unaware of his whereabouts. (It was believed he was in prison in Panama.) Justice Thomas was prompted to observe in dissent that "so engrossed is the Court in applying the multifactor balancing test set forth in *Barker* that it loses sight of the nature and purpose of the speedy trial guarantee set forth in the Sixth Amendment."

THE RIGHT TO CONFRONTATION

The Confrontation Clause of the Sixth Amendment guarantees an accused person the right "to be confronted with witnesses against him." It is one of two clauses in the Bill of Rights (the other being the Compulsory Process Clause) that explicitly address the right of criminal defendants to elicit evidence in their defense from witnesses at trial. As Justice Stewart said in *Faretta* v. *California* (1975), "[W]hen taken together, [they] guarantee that a criminal charge may be answered in a manner now considered fundamental to the fair administration of American justice—through the calling and interrogation of favorable witnesses, the cross-examination of adverse witnesses, and the orderly introduction of evidence. In short, the[y] . . . constitutionalize the right in an adversary criminal trial to make a defense as we know it." In *Pointer* v. *Texas* (1965), the Court incorporated the Confrontation Clause to apply to the states.

The Supreme Court has held that the right to confrontation (1) includes the accused's right to cross-examine those witnesses who are produced by the state; (2) severely limits the use of "hearsay" evidence (although the Court has allowed for such exceptions as the introduction of prior testimony of former witnesses who die before trial); and (3) limits the admissibility, at a trial of two or more defendants, of a confession that implicates a defendant other than the confessor. In *Coy* v. *Iowa* (1988), Justice Scalia for the majority held that the Confrontation Clause also literally guarantees "the defendant a face-to-face meeting with witnesses appearing before the trier of fact"; consequently, it overturned the conviction of a criminal defendant (in this case, a man convicted of two counts of engaging in lascivious acts with a child) because an Iowa statute allowed the two thirteen-year-old girls he was charged with sexually assaulting to testify behind a large screen that shielded them from the defendant. While Justice O'Connor joined the majority opinion in *Coy*, she made clear in her concurrence that she believed that certain exceptions existed to Scalia's literalist interpretation; she had in mind "use of one- or two-way closed circuit television," which for her raised no Confrontation Clause problems. Scalia finessed this issue by announcing that "we leave for another day . . . the question whether any exceptions exist." That day came two years later in *Maryland* v. *Craig* (1990), when Justice O'Connor declared for a six-member majority that the right to "a face-to-face meeting" is not absolute; that the central concern of the Confrontation Clause is to ensure the reliability of the evidence against a criminal defendant by subjecting it to rigorous testing in the context of an adversary proceeding; and that use of one-way closed circuit television testimony for child victims in sexual abuse cases is consistent with the central concern of the right to confrontation. Justice Scalia dissented, complaining that "Seldom has this Court failed so conspicuously to sustain a categorical guarantee of the Constitution against the tide of prevailing current opinions."

PLEA BARGAINING

Plea bargaining, in which a defendant agrees to plead guilty in return for a reduced charge or sentence, has become such a central feature of the criminal justice system that it currently occurs in approximately 90 percent of all criminal cases in the United States. In *Brady* v. *United States* (1970) the Supreme Court gave its approval to most forms of plea bargaining. Speaking for the Court majority, Justice Byron White announced the Court's refusal to hold that "a guilty plea is compelled and invalid under the Fifth Amendment whenever motivated by the defendant's desire to accept the certainty or probability of a lesser penalty rather than face a wider range of possibilities extending from acquittal to conviction and a higher penalty authorized by law for the crime charged. . . . We cannot hold that it is unconstitutional for the State to extend a benefit to a defendant who in turn extends a substantial benefit to the State. . . ."

Since *Brady*, the Court has sought to formalize the procedures for plea bargaining. In *Santo Bello* v. *New York* (1971), for example, it held that if a defendant, relying on a prosecutor's promise, enters a guilty plea, due process of law requires that the prosecutor's promise be kept or that the defendant be given some form of relief—typically, an opportunity to withdraw the guilty plea. Later, in its most comprehensive effort to define plea-bargaining procedures, the Court issued and sent to the Congress for approval a set of amendments to Rule 11 of the Federal Rules of Criminal Procedure. These amendments were approved, with several changes, by Congress and became effective in 1975.

BAIL AND PRETRIAL DETENTION

Bail and pretrial detention have perhaps raised fewer constitutional questions than any other practices in the criminal justice system. This is in part because the "excessive fines and bails" clause of the Eighth Amendment has never been incorporated to apply to the states and in part because the Supreme Court has never established an absolute right to bail. In determining whether bail will be granted, and the conditions under which it will be granted, courts have traditionally asked just one question: Will the accused abscond or appear as required at his trial? Increasingly, however, a second question is also being asked: Will the accused constitute a danger to the community and the safety of others by committing additional crimes while free on bail? Both the Supreme Court and the Congress have recently given their endorsement to the asking of this second question and to the use of preventive detention when the answer to this second question mandates it.

In *Schall* v. *Martin* (1984), the Supreme Court upheld by a vote of 7–2 the preventive detention provision of the New York Family Court Act that authorized pretrial detention of juveniles accused of acts of delinquency based on the finding that there was "serious risk" that the juvenile "may before the return date commit an act which if committed by an adult would constitute a crime." Justice Rehnquist held for the majority that preventive detention under the statute served the legitimate state objective of protecting both the juvenile and the society from the hazards of pretrial crime and that it was therefore "compatible with the 'fundamental fairness' demanded by the Due Process Clause." And, in the Comprehensive Crime Control Act of 1984, passed later that same year, Congress provided that, if, after a hearing pursuant to the provisions of that act, a "judicial officer finds that no condition or combination of conditions will reasonably assure the appearance of the person as required and the safety of any other person and the community, he shall order the detention of the person prior to trial." Interestingly, given this

chapter's previous discussion of the exclusionary rule, Congress specifically declared that "the rules concerning admissibility of evidence in
criminal trials do not apply to the presentation and consideration of information" at the preventive detention hearing. These preventive detention provisions were upheld by the Supreme Court in *United States* v.
Salerno (1987).

CRUEL AND UNUSUAL PUNISHMENTS

The Eighth Amendment protects against the infliction of "cruel and unusual punishments." This phraseology, derived from the English Bill of
Rights of 1689, originally was understood to refer to such ancient practices as branding, drawing and quartering, burning alive, and crucifixion.
But as Chief Justice Warren noted in *Trop* v. *Dulles* (1958), the Court
must determine the meaning of the Eighth Amendment from the
"evolving standards of decency that mark the progress of a maturing society." Put simply, whatever the amendment was originally intended to
mean must be of less importance to the Court than what "evolving standards of decency" require. How the Court views these standards is of as
much interest to the states as to the federal government, because *Robinson* v. *California* (1962), which invalidated a California statute that
made it a misdemeanor to be "addicted to the use of narcotics," made
this particular provision applicable to the states through the Fourteenth
Amendment.

Perhaps the most dramatic issue arising out of *Robinson* and its incorporation of the protection against cruel and unusual punishment has
been that of capital punishment. In *Furman* v. *Georgia* (1972), a badly
split Court rendered invalid every state death-penalty statute then in existence. In a brief *per curiam* order, the five members of the majority
were able to agree that "the imposition and the carrying out of the death
penalty in these cases constitute cruel and unusual punishment in violation of the Eighth and Fourteenth Amendments." They could agree on
little more however—as attested by the fact that each member of the majority wrote a separate opinion.

Although *Furman* foreclosed executions under state statutes then in
existence, it did not declare that capital punishment inevitably was unconstitutional. Encouraged by the fact that only Justices William Brennan and Thurgood Marshall regarded all death penalty statutes as *per se*
unconstitutional, state legislatures were quick to adopt new capital punishment statutes designed to meet the objections of the other members
of the *Furman* majority. Ultimately, new death penalty schemes were
adopted by at least 37 states. With the enactment of these new laws, the
Court was forced once again to confront the question of the constitutionality of the death penalty. And in 1976, by a 7–2 vote in *Gregg* v. *Georgia*,
it held the death penalty is a constitutionally permissible punishment,
at least for carefully defined categories of murder.[18] The same plurality
that spoke for the Court on this basic issue, however, went on to say that

the Eighth Amendment requires that the sentencing authority be provided with carefully controlled discretion; a bifurcated trial was seen as the ideal procedure. Mandatory death penalty statutes were regarded as unconstitutional.

Since *Gregg* v. *Georgia*, a solid majority of the Supreme Court has refused to reconsider the general constitutionality of capital punishment. In fact, in *Barefoot* v. *Estelle* (1983), it upheld expedited procedures to review habeas corpus petitions filed by death row inmates, displaying an increasing impatience with the endless stays of execution that defense attorneys were securing in the lower courts.[19] In *Pulley* v. *Harris* (1984), it rejected the contention that the Eighth Amendment requires that, before a state appellate court affirms a death sentence, it must engage in a comparative proportionality review, in which it compares the sentence in the case before it with the penalties imposed in similar cases to determine whether they are proportional. To inquire whether a penalty in a particular case is unacceptable because disproportionate to the punishment imposed on others convicted of the same crime would, Justice White wrote for a seven-member majority, depart from *Gregg* and the provisions for the exercise of controlled discretion approved there. In *McCleskey* v. *Kemp* (1987), the Court found no merit in the contention that Georgia's capital punishment process violated the Eighth and Fourteenth Amendments because a statistical study purported to show a disparity in Georgia's imposition of the death sentence based on the race of the murder victim. In *Stanford* v. *Kentucky* (1989), it sustained the constitutionality of imposing capital punishment on individuals for crimes they had committed at 16 or 17 years of age.[20] In *Penry* v. *Lynaugh* (1989), it rejected the contention that it was cruel and unusual punishment under the Eighth Amendment to execute Johnny Penry because he was mildly to moderately retarded and had the reasoning capacity of a 7-year-old. As Justice O'Connor held for the Court:

> Mental retardation is a factor that may well lessen a defendant's culpability for a capital offense. But we cannot conclude today that the Eighth Amendment precludes the execution of any mentally retarded person of Penry's ability convicted of a capital offense simply by virtue of their mental retardation alone. So long as sentencers can consider and give effect to mitigating evidence of mental retardation in imposing sentence, an individualized determination of whether "death is the appropriate punishment" can be made in each particular case. While a national consensus against execution of the mentally retarded may someday emerge reflecting "the evolving standards of decency that mark the progress of a maturing society," there is insufficient evidence of such a consensus today.

Finally, in *Payne* v. *Tennessee* (1991), the Court voted 6–3 to overturn its recent decisions of *Booth* v. *Maryland* (1988) and *South Carolina* v. *Gathers* (1989) and declared that the Eighth Amendment does not prohibit a capital sentencing jury from considering "victim impact" evidence relating to the personal characteristics of the victim and the emotional impact of the crimes on the victim's family.

In recent years, the Court has reviewed other issues that also have raised questions concerning cruel and unusual punishment. In *Ingraham* v. *Wright* (1977), it held that the Cruel and Unusual Punishments Clause did not apply to "traditional practices in public schools" such as paddling. In *Hudson* v. *McMillian* (1992), it held that use of "excessive physical force" by prison guards subjected a prisoner to "cruel and unusual punishment" even though no serious physical injury resulted. In dissent, Justice Thomas noted that "for generations, judges and commentators regarded the Eighth Amendment as applying only to tortious punishments meted out by statutes or sentencing judges, and not generally to any hardship that might befall a prisoner during incarceration"; he dismissed the majority opinion as an unfortunate consequence of the Court having "cut the Eighth Amendment loose from its historical moorings" and argued instead that the prisoner should have sought, and the Court should have provided, relief under the Due Process Clause of the Fourteenth Amendment. In *Solem* v. *Helm* (1983), the Court held that the Eighth Amendment prohibits sentences that are disproportionate to the crime committed and ruled that a sentence of life imprisonment without possibility of parole imposed under a South Dakota recidivist statute upon a defendant who was convicted of uttering a "no account" check for $100 and who had three prior convictions for third-degree burglary, one prior conviction for obtaining money under false pretenses, one prior conviction for larceny, and one prior conviction for third-offense driving while intoxicated, was significantly disproportionate to his crime and prohibited by the Cruel and Unusual Punishments Clause. However, in *Harmelin* v. *Michigan* (1991), a five-member majority held that the Eighth Amendment does not prohibit the imposition of a mandatory term of life in prison without possibility of parole for possessing more than 650 grams of cocaine. The majority divided on whether *Solem* v. *Helm*, which had concluded that the Eighth Amendment contains a proportionality principle, should be overturned. Justice Scalia, making a textualist argument, said that it should; Justice Kennedy, wishing to adhere to precedent and therefore arguing implausibly that the Michigan law somehow passed *Solem's* proportionality test, said it should not.

PRISONERS' RIGHTS

On conviction and imprisonment, a profound change occurs in a person's legal status. Duly convicted prisoners lose entirely many freedoms enjoyed by free persons; however, they do not relinquish all rights. As the Supreme Court noted in *Wolf* v. *McDonell* (1974), "though his rights may be diminished by the needs and exigencies of the institutional environment, a prisoner is not wholly stripped of constitutional protections when he is imprisoned for crime. There is no iron curtain drawn between the Constitution and the prisons of this country."

There is no question that prisoners always retain the right to the minimal conditions necessary for human survival (i.e., the right to food, clothing, shelter, and medical care). The right of prisoners to a non-life-threatening environment goes beyond the provision of life's necessities; it includes their right to be protected from one another and from themselves. On this last point, lower courts have been more responsive to prisoners' claims than the Supreme Court and have found that prison crowding is unconstitutional. As a federal district court in Florida asserted in *Costello* v. *Wainwright* (1975), prison crowding "endangers the very lives of the inmates" and therefore violates the Eighth Amendment's guarantee against cruel and unusual punishments. The Supreme Court's reluctance to follow the lower courts is understandable, for empirical studies flatly contradict the assertion that crowding is life-threatening. Not only are the overall death rates, accidental death rates, and homicide and suicide rates of inmates two to three times lower than for comparable groups of parolees (controlling for age, race, and sex), but no statistically significant correlations exist between measures of crowding (density and occupancy) and inmate death rates.[21]

Beyond agreement that inmates have the minimal right to a non-life-threatening environment, legal debate rages. Some courts and legal scholars have taken their cues from the Sixth Circuit Court of Appeals in *Coffin* v. *Reichard* (1944) and have declared that prisoners retain all the rights of ordinary citizens except those expressly or by necessary implication taken by law. The Supreme Court's decision in *Procunier* v. *Martinez* (1974) followed this line of reasoning when it held that it would employ a strict scrutiny standard of review to evaluate claims that the rights of prisoners were being denied. It declared that it would sustain limitations of prisoners' rights only if they furthered an important or substantial governmental interest and if they were no greater than necessary to protect that interest.

Fundamentally opposed to *Coffin* and *Procunier* is the view, now dominant on the Supreme Court, that inmates are without rights except for those conferred by law or necessarily implied and that, as a consequence, courts should employ the reasonableness test to assess the legitimacy of restrictions on what prisoners assert to be their rights. In *Turner* v. *Safley* (1987), the Supreme Court articulated this position and rejected the use of strict scrutiny in prisoners' rights cases. Writing for a five-member majority, Justice O'Connor declared that "when a prison regulation impinges on inmates' constitutional rights, the regulation is valid if it is reasonably related to legitimate penological interests." O'Connor announced a four-prong test for measuring reasonableness: (1) Is there "a 'valid, rational connection' between the prison regulation and the legitimate government interest put forward to justify it"? (2) "Are alternative means of exercising the right . . . open to prison inmates"? (3) What is "the impact [that] accommodation of the asserted constitutional right will have on guards and other inmates, and on the allocation of prison resources generally"?, and (4) Is "the absence of ready alternatives . . . evidence of the reasonableness of the prison regulation"? Employing this four-prong test, Justice O'Connor rejected a First Amendment challenge to a Missouri ban on inmate-to-inmate correspondence because the prohibition on correspondence was "logically connected" to legitimate security concerns. In *O'Lone* v. *Shabazz* (1987), the Court applied the same reasonableness test to sustain New Jersey prison policies that resulted in Muslim inmates' inability to attend weekly congregational services.

Security concerns generally trump the claims of prisoners' rights; the Court is hesitant to recognize inmate claims that have the potential of putting at risk the prison itself, the guards, other inmates, or the petitioner. Justice Rehnquist in *Jones* v. *North Carolina Prisoners' Union* (1977) summarized well the Court's deferential approach to these issues: "It is enough to say that they [prison officials] have not been conclusively shown to be wrong in this view. The interest in preserving order and authority in prisons is self-evident."

Applying this reasoning, the Court has denied inmates' claims to a First Amendment right to organize as a prisoners' labor union; rejected the contention that an inmate's right to privacy protects against routine strip and body-cavity searches; and has refused to recognize any inmate legal rights in the ordinary classification process or interprison transfer. As the Court said in *Moody* v. *Daggett* (1976), no due process issues are implicated by "the discretionary transfer of state prisoners to a substantially less agreeable prison, even where the transfer visit[s] a 'grievous loss' upon the inmate. The same is true of prisoner classification and eligibility for rehabilitative programs."

Beyond assuring life's necessities for inmates, the Court has consistently recognized inmates' claims in only two areas: their due process right of access to the courts and their liberty interest in retaining "good time" and avoiding solitary confinement. Concerning the former, the Court has repeatedly insisted that inmates have the right to access to legal redress and that this right of access to the courts requires either an adequate law library or assistance from persons trained in the law (although not necessarily lawyers). Concerning the latter, the Court has held in *Wolf* v. *McDonnell* that inmates have a liberty interest in the good-time credit they have acquired and that they may not be stripped of these credits without a hearing before an impartial tribunal. The Court has not considered either of these rights to jeopardize prison security. Access to the courts poses no problems at all, and as the Court has made explicit in *Hewitt* v. *Helms* (1978) and *Superintendent* v. *Hill* (1985), prison disciplinary proceedings can follow (and need not precede) solitary confinement and can impose sanctions based on the lax evidentiary standard of "some evidence."

RETROACTIVE APPLICATION
OF CRIMINAL-PROCEDURE GUARANTEES

In interpreting the provisions of the Bill of Rights in such a manner as to expand the procedural protections of criminal defendants and incorporating those provisions through the Fourteenth Amendment to apply to the states, the Court was forced to consider whether its interpretations and incorporations should be given retroactive effect: that is, whether they should be made available to criminal defendants whose cases had already been litigated under rules deemed constitutionally permissible at the time. Until 1965, this question was always answered in the affirmative, for reasons cited by Professor Herman Schwartz: "New constitutional doctrines are not conceptions but rather reflections of principles of 'ordered liberty' fundamental to our legal system. Such principles are equally applicable to past and present trials, for an ethical society cannot seek to retain the fruits of past defaults."[22]

Nevertheless, this commitment to unlimited retroactivity was abandoned in *Linkletter* v. *Walker* (1965), in which Justice Tom Clark concluded for a seven-member majority that the "Constitution neither prohibits nor requires retrospective effect." Instead, he argued, "We must . . . weigh the merits and demerits in each case by looking to the prior history of the rule in question, its purpose, effect, and whether retrospective operation will further or retard its operation."

Several factors contributed to the Court's shift in this matter. The most important, perhaps, was the essentially activist character of the Warren Court. Ineluctable retroactivity was an automatic check, an "inherent restraint," on judicial innovations, because it required that the new rule be applied to all relevant previous cases and that judicial hearings be granted to all those convicted under the old rule to determine whether their rights had been violated and whether, as a consequence, they were eligible for a new trial, outright release, return of all fines, or even damages. It compelled the Court to confront in a most direct manner the possible undesirable consequences of adopting a new rule.

A second factor for the Court's departure from unlimited retroactivity was its desire to forestall hostile public reaction to its more controversial decisions. A case in point was *Johnson* v. *New Jersey* (1966), which limited the retroactive effect of *Escobedo* v. *Illinois* and *Miranda* v. *Arizona* to those cases in which the trial actually had begun after the dates on which *Escobedo* and *Miranda* were decided. *Johnson* was an intensely practical decision by a Court attempting to minimize the hostility that *Escobedo* and *Miranda* had generated. A third, and closely related factor behind the Court's shift was the volatile and provocative problem of federalism. The need to sustain and, indeed, encourage viable and healthy federal-state relationships often intruded on the Court's considerations of retroactivity. Each time the Court incorporated another Bill of Rights guarantee to apply to the states, it imposed new responsibilities on the states in the realm of criminal procedure. The inevitable consequence was hostility to federal-court intervention. Aware of this exacerbating influence on already strained federal-state relations, the Court frequently sought to mitigate the tension by limiting the impact of its decisions through prospective application. Such Court awareness was apparent in *Linkletter* v. *Walker*, in which Justice Clark announced that retroactive application of *Mapp* would not "add harmony to the delicate state-federal relationship."

With virtually all the provisions of the Bill of Rights eventually incorporated to apply to the states, and with the advent of the more judicially restrained Burger and Rehnquist Courts, the problems posed by full retroactive application of criminal procedural guarantees largely disappeared. So, too, has the Court's adherence to *Linkletter*. In *Teague* v. *Lane* (1989), a majority of the Court rejected the *Linkletter* approach to retroactivity and agreed to apply the approach set forth by Justice Harlan in his opinions in *Desist* v. *United States* (1969) and *Mackey* v. *United States* (1971), pursuant to which new constitutional rules are to be applied to all cases on direct review that are not yet final but are not to be applied to previous final judgments attacked on collateral review, except in extraordinary cases in which "fundamental fairness" would be denied by not applying the new rule.

BASIC THEMES IN THE COURT'S
CRIMINAL-PROCEDURE DECISIONS

Four basic themes emerge from our review of what the Supreme Court has done in the realm of criminal procedure. In the first place, the Court has been required to pour meaning into the many ambiguous provisions of the Bill of Rights—a task it has accomplished through its power of judgment.

A second theme is the emphasis the Court has placed on protecting minority interests from the potentially tyrannical tendencies of the majority. Recognizing the unequal impact that criminal procedure has had on the poor and on racial minorities the Court has undertaken to eliminate the official aspects of this inequality.

A third basic theme is the Court's growing insistence on uniform constitutional standards applicable in both state and federal systems. In so insisting, the justices have all but repudiated the traditional view that states are to serve as laboratories, experimenting with novel social and legal schemes and thereby sparing the nation as a whole of the need to suffer the consequences of failure. Although the Court's approach has ensured a certain uniformity of criminal procedure throughout the land, it has also stifled creativity, checked innovation, and jeopardized federalism—an important means to the overall ends of the Constitution.

The final basic theme emerging from our review of the Court's decisions in criminal procedure is a movement toward broadly stated rulings. In recent years the Court has gone far beyond the proscription of particular unconstitutional practices to prescribe affirmative standards of conduct that it regards as essential to safeguard against such practices. In *Miranda,* for example, to avoid the potential violation of a defendant's privilege against self-incrimination during pretrial police interrogations, the Court required that the defendant be advised of his rights and given the right to consult with counsel before and during any interrogation. The use of such prescriptive rulings has certain obvious advantages. They reduce uncertainty and provide police, prosecutors, and lower-court personnel with specific instruction as to which procedures do or do not pass constitutional muster. And they spare the Court the need to pass individual judgment on each and every criminal prosecution, thereby enabling it to devote its time and attention to the further development and refinement of fundamental constitutional protections.

But the movement toward broadly stated rulings is not an unmixed blessing, for it represents a substantial departure from the "judicial" function. Instead of judging the merits of a particular "case or controversy," as charged by Article III of the Constitution, the Court increasingly has become involved in general lawmaking. The consequences of this shift are rather far-reaching. Lawmaking typically emphasizes the formulation and general administration of societywide policies; it is not concerned with the fates of particular individuals or the alleviation of specific instances of injustice. Traditionally, the latter concerns have been left to the judiciary, which understood its function to be the dispensation of justice and equity on an individual, case-by-case level. As the Court abandons this traditional role, there appears to be no other institution ready to step in and take its place.

NOTES

1 In *Richards* v. *Wisconsin*, the Supreme Court held that police officers executing search warrants are not always required to knock and announce their presence. It declared that "[i]n order to justify a 'no-knock' entry, the police must have a reasonable suspicion that knocking and announcing their presence, under the particular circumstances, would be dangerous or futile, or that it would inhibit the effective investigation of the crime by, for example, allowing the destruction of evidence."

2 *California* v. *Hodari D.*, 499 U.S. 621 (1991), dealt with the question of when an arrest actually takes place. Hodari D., a juvenile, fled when a police car approached him. An officer gave chase on foot, whereupon the juvenile tossed away what appeared to be a small rock. The officer tackled and handcuffed the juvenile, recovered the discarded rock which was found to be crack cocaine, and charged him with drug possession. The juvenile's attorneys sought to suppress the evidence of cocaine, claiming that it was the fruit of an illegal search. They claimed that the juvenile was "seized" or placed under arrest at the moment the officer made a "show of authority" by beginning to run toward him; that at that time, the police officer did not have reasonable grounds to suspect that the juvenile had crack cocaine in his possession; and that therefore the discarded cocaine could not be introduced as evidence because the grounds for the arrest must exist for the search incident to the arrest to be valid. The prosecution contended that the juvenile, by fleeing, ignored the police officer's "show of authority" and was not "seized" or arrested until he was tackled; that the crack cocaine was discarded prior to the arrest; and that therefore the recovered drug could be used as a valid basis for the arrest. The Supreme Court, in a 7–2 opinion, overturned a California court of appeals decision and agreed with the prosecution. Justice Scalia declared: "An arrest requires either physical force or, where that is absent, submission to the assertion of authority."

3 *Chimel* did not qualify the "plain view" exception: incident to arrest, instrumentalities of crime can be seized if they are in plain view, even if they are not within the immediate control of the person arrested. *Arizona* v. *Hicks*, 480 U.S. 321 (1987), makes clear, however, that there is a "distinction between 'looking' at a suspicious object in plain view and 'moving' it even a few inches." In a 6–3 decision, the Court overturned the conviction of the defendant for armed robbery because, while the police officer had a right to be in the room where a turntable was in plain view, his suspicion that the turntable was stolen and his movement of the turntable several inches so that he could read the serial number on its back constituted an unreasonable search in the absence of a search warrant.

4 A related issue is whether the Fourth Amendment prohibits a warrantless search and seizure of garbage left for collection on the street curb. In *California* v. *Greenwood*, 486 U.S. 35 (1988), the Court held in a 7–2 decision that the respondents, who were convicted of narcotic trafficking based on evidence found in garbage they had placed at their curb, had no "objectively reasonable" expectation of privacy in their garbage, as "it is common knowledge that plastic garbage bags left on or at the side of a public street are readily accessible to animals, children, scavengers, snoops, and other members of the public. . . . Moreover, respondents placed their refuse at the curb for the express purpose of conveying it to a third party, the trash collector, who might himself have sorted through respondents' trash or permitted others, such as the police, to do so."

5. See *California* v. *Acevedo*, 500 U.S. 565, 580 (1991): "Until today, this Court has drawn a curious line between the search of an automobile that coincidentally turns up a container and the search of a container that coincidentally turns up in an automobile. The protections of the Fourth Amendment must not turn on such coincidences. We therefore interpret *Carroll* as providing one rule to govern all automobile searches. The police may search an automobile and the containers within it where they have probable cause to believe contraband or evidence is contained."

6 See *Schneckloth* v. *Bustamonte* (1973).

7 See Dallin H. Oaks, "Studying the Exclusionary Rule in Search and Seizure," *University of Chicago Law Review* 37 (1970): 665–753; John Kaplan, "The Limits of the Exclusionary Rule," *Stanford Law Review* 26 (1974): 1027–1055; and Steven Schlesinger, *Exclusionary Injustice* (New York: Marcel Dekker, 1977).

8 This, of course, was to change in *Duncan* v. *Louisiana*, 391 U.S. 145 (1968). See Chapter 3.

9 *Spano* v. *New York* (1959).

10 *Rodgers* v. *Richmond* (1961).

11 *Lynumn* v. *Illinois* (1963).

12 Townsend v. Sain (1963).

13 *Harris* raises serious questions: Will not juries who hear statements, introduced as evidence, that the defendant is lying in the witness stand simply treat these statements as evidence of guilt? Will they be able to govern their thoughts by this subtle distinction?

14 Because the defendant in *Argersinger* had been convicted of carrying a concealed weapon and sentenced to ninety days in jail, the Court left unconsidered the question of whether counsel was required even in cases in which there was no prospect of imprisonment (i.e., in which only a fine was im-

posed). That issue was resolved in *Scott* v. *Illinois* (1979), in which the Court limited the *Argersinger* holding to instances in which the defendant is in fact sentenced to a term of imprisonment.

15 See *McNeil* v. *Wisconsin*, 501 U.S. 171 (1991), in which the Court held that individuals have two separate and distinct rights to counsel. They have a Sixth Amendment right, which is offense-specific and does not attach until the initiation of adversary judicial proceedings, and a *Miranda*, or Fifth Amendment right, which is not offense-specific and which is intended to protect a suspect's "desire to deal with the police only through counsel."

16 *Sorrells* v. *United States* (1932).

17 *Hampton* v. *United States* (1976); *United States* v. *Russell* (1973); *Sherman* v. *United States* (1958); and *Sorrells* v. *United States* (1932).

18 In *Coker* v. *Georgia* (1977) the Court held that the death penalty for rape constituted cruel and unusual punishment.

19 See *Felker* v. *Turpins*, 518 U.S. 651 (1996), in which the Supreme Court upheld the Antiterrorism and Effective Death Penalty Act of 1996 which required dismissal of a claim presented in a state prisoner's second or successive federal habeas application if the claim was also presented in a prior application, compelled dismissal of a claim that was not presented in a prior federal application, and created a "gatekeeping" mechanism in the federal courts of appeal to requiring prospective applicants to establish a *prima facie* showing that their applications satisfy the act's other requirements.

20 In *Thompson* v. *Oklahoma* (1988), the Court held that the Eighth and Fourteenth Amendments prohibited the execution of a defendant convicted of first-degree murder for an offense committed when the defendant was 15 years old.

21 Ralph A. Rossum, "The Problem of Prison Crowding: On the Limits of Prison Capacity and Judicial Capacity," *Benchmark* I, no. 6: 22–30.

22 Herman Schwartz, "Retroactivity, Reliability, and Due Process," *University of Chicago Law Review* 33 (1966): 753.

SELECTED READING

Argersinger v. *Hamlin*, 407 U.S. 25 (1972).

Arizona v. *Hicks*, 480 U.S. 321 (1987).

Caplin & Drysdale v. *United States*, 491 U.S. 617 (1989).

Davis v. *United States*, 512 U.S. 452 (1994)

Doggett v. *United States*, 505 U.S. 647 (1992).

Faretta v. *California*, 422 U.S. 806 (1975).

Florida v. *Riley*, 488 U.S. 445 (1989)

Furman v. *Georgia*, 408 U.S. 238 (1972).

Leon v. *United States*, 468 U.S. 897 (1984).

Michigan Department of State Police v. *Sitz*, 496 U.S. 455 (1990)

Pennsylvania v. *Mimms*, 434 U.S. 106 (1977)

Pulley v. *Harris*, 456 U.S. 37 (1984).

Stone v. *Powell*, 428 U.S. 465 (1976).

Twining v. *New Jersey*, 211 U.S. 78 (1908).

Amar, Akhil Reed. *The Constitution and Criminal Procedure* (New Haven, Conn.: Yale University Press, 1997).

Berger, Raoul. *Death Penalties: The Supreme Court's Obstacle Course* (Cambridge, Mass.: Harvard University Press, 1982).

Berkson, Larry. *The Concept of Cruel and Unusual Punishment* (Lexington, Mass.: Lexington Books, 1975).

Berns, Walter F. *For Capital Punishment: Crime and the Morality of the Death Penalty* (New York: Basic Books, 1979).

Black, Charles L. *Capital Punishment: The Inevitability of Caprice and Mistake* (New York: Norton, 1974).

Bodenhamer, David J. *Fair Trial: Rights of the Accused in American History* (New York: Oxford University Press, 1992).

Brennan, William J. "Constitutional Adjudication and the Death Penalty: A View from the Court." *Harvard Law Review* 100 (December 1986): 313–331.

Cohen, Fred. "The Law of Prisoners' Rights: An Overview." *Criminal Law Bulletin* 24 (1988): 331–349.

Fallon, Richard H., Jr. and Daniel J. Meltzer. "New Law, Non-Retroactivity, and Constitutional Remedies." *Harvard Law Review* 104 (June 1991): 1731–1833.

Hickok, Eugene W. *The Bill of Rights: Original Meaning and Current Understanding* (Charlottesville: University Press of Virginia, 1991).

Kamisar, Yale. "Is the Exclusionary Rule an 'Illogical' or 'Unnatural' Interpretation of the Fourth Amendment?" *Judicature* 62 (April 1978): 66–84.

Kennedy, Randall, *Race, Crime, and the Law* (New York: Pantheon Books, 1997).

Lewis, Anthony. *Gideon's Trumpet* (New York: Vintage, 1964).

Miller, Kent S. and Michael L. Radelet. *Executing the Mentally Ill: The Criminal Justice System and the Case of Alvin Ford* (Newbury Park, Calif.: Sage Publications, 1993).

Oaks, Dallin H. "Studying the Exclusionary Rule in Search and Seizure." *University of Chicago Law Review* 37 (1970): 665–753.

Pizzi, William T. "*Batson* v. *Kentucky:* Curing the Disease but Killing the Patient." *1987 Supreme Court Review*, edited by Philip B. Kurland, Gerhard Casper, and Dennis J. Hutchinson (Chicago: University of Chicago Press, 1988).

Rossum, Ralph A. "The Entrapment Defense and the Teaching of Political Responsibility: The Supreme Court as Republican Schoolmaster." *American Journal of Criminal Law*, VI (1978): 287–306.

Rossum, Ralph A. *The Politics of the Criminal Justice System: An Organizational Analysis* (New York: Marcel Dekker, 1978).

Schlesinger, Steven R. *Exclusionary Injustice* (New York: Marcel Dekker, 1977).

Schulhofer, Stephen J. "On the Fourth Amendment Rights of the Law-Abiding Public." *1989 Supreme Court Review*, edited by Gerhard Casper and Dennis J. Hutchinson (Chicago: University of Chicago Press, 1990).

Sigler, Jay A. *Double Jeopardy: The Development of a Legal and Social Policy* (Ithaca, N.Y.: Cornell University Press, 1969).

Tarr, G. Alan and Mary Cornelia Porter. *State Supreme Courts in State and Nation* (New Haven, Conn.: Yale University Press, 1988).

Wilbanks, William. *The Myth of a Racist Criminal Justice System* (Monterey, Calif.: Brooks/Cole Publishing, 1987).

Wilson, James Q., ed. *Crime and Public Policy*. 2d ed. (San Francisco: Institute for Contemporary Studies, 1994).

Vernonia School District v. *Acton*
515 U.S. 646; 115 S. Ct. 2386; 132 L. Ed. 2d 564 (1995)

Movtivated by the discovery that athletes were leaders in the student drug culture and the concern that drug use increases the risk of sports-related injury, School District 47J in the logging town of Vernonia, Oregon, adopted in the fall of 1989 the Student Athlete Drug Policy, which authorized random urinalysis drug testing of students who participated in its athletic programs. In the fall of 1991, Wayne Acton, a seventh-grade student, was denied participation in the school's football program when he and his parents refused to consent to the drug testing. They filed suit, seeking declaratory and injunctive relief on the grounds that the school district's policy violated the Fourth and Fourteenth Amendments and the Oregon Constitution. The U.S. District Court denied their claims, but the Court of Appeal for the Ninth Circuit reversed, holding that the school district's policy violated both the Federal and State Constitutions. The Supreme Court granted certiorari. *Opinion of the Court: Scalia, Breyer, Ginsburg, Kennedy, Rehnquist, Thomas. Concurring opinion: Ginsburg. Dissenting opinion: O'Connor, Souter, Stevens.*

JUSTICE SCALIA delivered the opinion of the Court.

The Student Athlete Drug Policy adopted by School District 47J in the town of Vernonia, Oregon, authorizes random urinalysis drug testing of students who participate in the District's school athletics programs. We granted certiorari to decide whether this violates the Fourth and Fourteenth Amendments to the United States Constitution.

The Policy applies to all students participating in interscholastic athletics. Students wishing to play sports must sign a form consenting to the testing and must obtain the written consent of their parents. Athletes are tested at the beginning of the season for their sport. In addition, once each week of the season the names of the athletes are placed in a "pool" from which a student, with the supervision of two adults, blindly draws the names of 10 percent of the athletes for random testing. Those selected are notified and tested that same day, if possible.

The student to be tested completes a specimen control form which bears an assigned number. Prescription medications that the student is taking must be identified by providing a copy of the prescription or a doctor's authorization. The student then enters an empty locker room accompanied by an adult monitor of the same sex. Each boy selected produces a sample at a urinal, remaining fully clothed with his back to the monitor, who stands approximately 12 to 15 feet behind the student. Monitors may (though do not always) watch the student while he produces the sample, and they listen for normal sounds of urination. Girls produce samples in an enclosed bathroom stall, so that they can be heard but not observed. After the sample is produced, it is given to the monitor, who checks it for temperature and tampering and then transfers it to a vial.

The samples are sent to an independent laboratory, which routinely tests them for amphetamines, cocaine, and marijuana. Other drugs, such as LSD, may be screened at the request of the District, but the identity of a particular student does not determine which drugs will be tested. The laboratory's procedure are 99.94 percent accurate. The District follows strict procedures regarding the chain of custody and access to test results. The laboratory does not know the identity of the students whose samples it tests. It is authorized to mail written test reports only to the superintendent and to provide test results to District personnel by telephone only after the requesting official recites a code confirming his authority. Only the superintendent, principals, vice-principals, and athletic directors have access to test results, and the results are not kept for more than one year.

If a sample tests positive, a second test is administered as soon as possible to confirm the result. If the second test is negative, no further action is taken. If the second test is positive, the athlete's parents are notified, and the school principal convenes a meeting with the student and his parents, at which the student is given the option of (1) participating for six weeks in an assistance program that includes weekly urinalysis, or (2) suffering suspension from athletics for the remainder of the current season and the next athletic season. The student is then retested prior to the start of the next athletic season for which he or she is eligible. The Policy states that a second offense results in automatic imposition of option (2); a third offense in suspension for the remainder of the current season and the next two athletic seasons. . . .

The Fourth Amendment to the United States Constitution provides that the Federal Government shall not violate "[t]he right of the people to be secure in their persons, houses, papers, and effects, against unreasonable searches and seizures, . . ." We have held that the Fourteenth Amendment extends this constitutional guarantee to searches and seizures by state officers, *Elkins* v. *United States*, 364 U.S. 206, 213 (1960), including public school officials, *New Jersey* v. *T. L. O.*, 469 U.S. 325, 336–337 (1985). In *Skinner* v. *Railway Labor Executives' Assn.*, 489 U.S. 602, 617 (1989), we held that state-compelled collection and testing of urine, such as that required by the Student Athlete Drug Policy, constitutes a "search" subject to the demands of the Fourth Amendment. See also *Treasury Employees* v. *Von Raab*, 489 U.S. 656, 665 (1989).

As the text of the Fourth Amendment indicates, the ultimate measure of the constitutionality of a governmental search is "reasonableness." At least in a case such as this, where there was no clear practice, either approving or disapproving the type of search at issue, at the time the constitutional provision was enacted, whether a particular search meets the reasonableness standard "'is judged by balancing its intrusion on the individual's Fourth Amendment interests against its promotion of legitimate governmental interests.'" Where a search is undertaken by law enforcement officials to discover evidence of criminal wrongdoing, this Court has said that reasonableness generally requires the obtaining of a judicial warrant. Warrants cannot be issued, of course, without the showing of probable cause required by the Warrant Clause. But a warrant is not required to establish the reasonableness of *all* government searches; and when a warrant is not required (and the Warrant Clause therefore not applicable), probable cause is not invariably required either. A search unsupported by probable cause can be constitutional, we have said, "when special needs, beyond the normal need for law enforcement, make the warrant and probable-cause requirement impracticable." *Griffin* v. *Wisconsin*, 483 U.S. 868, 873 (1987).

We have found such "special needs" to exist in the public-school context. There, the warrant requirement "would unduly interfere with the maintenance of the swift and informal disciplinary procedures [that are] needed," and "strict adherence to the requirement that searches be based upon probable cause" would undercut "the substantial need of teachers and administrators for freedom to maintain order in the schools." The school search we approved in *T. L. O.*, while not based on probable cause, *was* based on individualized *suspicion* of wrongdoing. As we explicitly acknowledged, however, "'the Fourth Amendment imposes no irreducible requirement of such suspicion.'" We have upheld suspicionless searches and seizures to conduct drug testing of railroad personnel involved in train accidents; to conduct random drug testing of federal customs officers who carry arms or are involved in drug interdiction; and to maintain automobile checkpoints looking for illegal immigrants and contraband and drunk drivers.

The first factor to be considered is the nature of the privacy interest upon which the search here at issue intrudes. The Fourth Amendment does not protect all subjective expectations of privacy, but only those that society recognizes as "legitimate." What expectations are legitimate varies, of course, with context, depending, for example, upon whether the individual asserting the privacy interest is at home, at work, in a car, or in a public park. In addition, the legitimacy of certain privacy expectations vis-à-vis the State may depend upon the individual's legal relationship with the State. For example, . . . although a "probationer's home, like anyone else's, is protected by the Fourth Amendmen[t]," the supervisory relationship between probationer and State justifies "a degree of impingement upon [a probationer's] privacy that would not be constitutional if applied to the public at large." Central, in our view, to the present case is the fact that the subjects of the Policy are (1) children, who (2) have been committed to the temporary custody of the State as schoolmaster. . . .

Fourth Amendment rights, no less than First and Fourteenth Amendment rights, are different in public schools than elsewhere; the "reasonableness" inquiry cannot disregard the school's custodial and tutelary responsibility for children. For their own good and that of their classmates, public school children are routinely required to submit to various physical examinations, and to be vaccinated against various diseases. . . . In the 1991–1992 school year, all 50 States required public-school students to be vaccinated against diphtheria, measles, rubella, and polio. Particularly with regard to medical examinations and procedures, therefore, "students within the school environment have a lesser expectation of privacy than members of the population generally."

Legitimate privacy expectations are even less with regard to student athletes. School sports are not for the bashful. They require "suiting up" before each practice or event, and showering and changing afterwards. Public-school locker rooms, the usual sites for these activities, are not notable for the privacy they afford. The locker rooms in Vernonia are typical: no individual dressing rooms are provided; shower heads are lined up along a wall, unseparated by any sort of partition or curtain; not even all the toilet stalls have doors. . . .

There is an additional respect in which school athletes have a reduced expectation of privacy. By choosing to "go out for the team," they voluntarily subject themselves to a degree of regulation even higher than that imposed on students generally. In Vernonia's public schools, they must submit to a preseason physical exam (James testified that his included the giving of a urine sample, App. 17), they must acquire adequate insurance coverage or sign an insurance waiver, maintain minimum grade point average, and comply with any "rules of conduct, dress, training hours and related matters as may be established for each sport by the head coach and athletic director with the principal's approval." Somewhat like adults who choose to participate in a "closely regulated industry," students who voluntarily participate in school athletics have reason to expect intrusions upon normal rights and privileges, including privacy.

Having considered the scope of the legitimate expectation of privacy at issue here, we turn next to the character of the intrusion that is complained of. We recognized in *Skinner* that collecting the samples for urinalysis intrudes upon "an excretory function traditionally shielded by great privacy." We noted, however, that the degree of intrusion depends upon the manner in which production of the urine sample is monitored. Under the District's Policy, male students produce samples at a urinal along a wall. They remain fully clothed and are only observed from behind, it at all. Female students produce samples in an enclosed stall, with a female monitor standing outside listening only for sounds of tampering. These conditions are nearly identical to those typically encountered in public restrooms, which men, women, and especially school children use daily. Under such conditions, the privacy interests compromise by the process of obtaining the urine sample are in our view negligible.

The other privacy-invasive aspect of urinalysis is, of course, the information it discloses concerning the state of the subject's body, and the materials he has ingested. In this regard it is significant that the tests at issue here look only for drugs, and not for whether the student is, for example, epileptic, pregnant, or diabetic. Moreover, the drugs for which the samples are screened are standard, and do not vary according to the identity of the student. And finally, the results of the tests are disclosed only to a limited class of school personnel who have a need to know; and they are not turned over to law enforcement authorities or used for any internal disciplinary function. . . .

Finally, we turn to consider the nature and immediacy of the governmental concern at issue here, and the efficacy of this means for meeting it. . . . That the nature of the concern is important—indeed, perhaps compelling—can hardly be doubted. Deterring drug use by our Nation's schoolchildren is at least as important as enhancing efficient enforcement of the Nation's laws against the importation of drugs . . . or deterring drug use by engineers and trainmen. . . . School years are the time when the physical, psychological, and addictive effects of drugs are most severe. "Maturing nervous systems are more critically impaired by intoxicants than mature ones are; childhood losses in learning are lifelong and profound"; "children grow chemically dependent more quickly than adults, and their record of recovery is depressingly poor." And of course the effects of a drug-infested school are visited not just upon the users, but upon the entire student body and faculty, as the educational process is disrupted. In the present case, moreover, the necessity for the State to act is magnified by the fact that this evil is being visited not just upon individuals at large, but upon children for whom it has undertaken a special responsibility of care and direction. Finally, it must not be lost sight of that this program is directed more narrowly to drug use by school athletes, where the risk of immediate physical harm to the drug user or those with whom he is playing his sport is particularly high. Apart from psychological effects, which include impairment of judgment, slow reaction time, and a lessening of the perception of pain, the particular drugs screened by the District's Policy have been demonstrated to pose substantial physical risks to athletes. . . .

As to the efficacy of this means for addressing the problem: It seems to us self-evident that a drug problem largely fueled by the "role model" effect of athletes' drug use, and of particular danger to athletes, is effectively addressed by making sure that athletes do not use drugs. Respondents argue that a "less intrusive means to the same end" was available, namely, "drug testing on suspicion of drug use." We have repeatedly refused to declare that only the "least intrusive" search practicable can be reasonable under the Fourth Amendment. Respondents' alternative entails substantial difficulties—if it is indeed practicable at all. It may be impracticable, for one thing, simply because the parents who are willing to accept random drug testing for athletes are not willing to accept accusatory drug testing for all students, which transforms the process into a badge of shame. Respondents' proposal brings the risk that teachers will impose testing arbitrarily upon troublesome but not drug-likely students. It generates the expense of defending lawsuits that charge such arbitrary imposition, or that simply demand greater process before accusatory drug testing is imposed. And not least of all, it adds to the ever-expanding diversionary duties of schoolteachers the new function of spotting and bringing to account drug abuse, a task for which they are ill prepared, and which is not readily compat-

ible with their vocation. . . . In many respects, we think, testing based on "suspicion" of drug use would not be better, but worse.

Taking into account all the factors we have considered above—the decreased expectation of privacy, the relative unobtrusiveness of the search, and the severity of the need met by the search—we conclude Vernonia's Policy is reasonable and hence constitutional.

We caution against the assumption that suspicionless drug testing will readily pass constitutional muster in other contexts. The most significant element in this case is the first we discussed: that the Policy was undertaken in furtherance of the government's responsibilities, under a public-school system, as guardian and tutor of children entrusted to its care. . . .

The Ninth Circuit held that Vernonia's Policy not only violated the Fourth Amendment, but also, by reason of that violation, contravened Article I, ¶9 of the Oregon Constitution. Our conclusion that the former holding was in error means that the latter holding rested on a flawed premise. We therefore vacate the judgment, and remand the case to the Court of Appeals for further proceedings consistent with this opinion.

JUSTICE O'CONNOR, with whom JUSTICE STEVENS and JUSTICE SOUTER join, dissenting.

. . . For most of our constitutional history, mass, suspicionless searches have been generally considered *per se* unreasonable within the meaning of the Fourth Amendment. And we have allowed exceptions in recent years only where it has been clear that a suspicion-based regime would be ineffectual. Because that is not the case here, I dissent. . . .

. . . [H]aving misconstrued the fundamental role of the individualized suspicion requirement in Fourth Amendment analysis, the Court never seriously engages the practicality of such a requirement in the instant case. And that failure is crucial because nowhere is it *less* clear that an individualized suspicion requirement would be ineffectual than in the school context. In most schools, the entire pool of potential search targets—is under constant supervision by teachers and administrators and coaches, be it in classrooms, hallways, or locker rooms.

The record here indicates that the Vernonia schools are no exception. The great irony of this case is that most (though not all) of the evidence the District introduced to justify its suspicion-less drug-testing program consisted of first- or second-hand stories of particular, indentifiable students acting in ways that plainly gave rise to reasonable suspicion of in-school drug use—and thus that would have justified a drug-related search under our *T. L. O.* decision. . . .

In light of all this evidence of drug use by particular students, there is a substantial basis for concluding that a vigorous regime of suspicion-based testing (for which the District appears already to have rules in place) would have gone a long way toward solving Vernonia's school drug problem while preserving the Fourth Amendment rights of James Acton and other like him. And were there any doubt about such a conclusion, it is removed by indications in the record that suspicion-based testing could have been supplemented by an equally vigorous campaign to have Vernonia's parents encourage their children to submit to the District's *voluntary* drug testing program. In these circumstances, the Fourth Amendment dictates that a mass, suspicionless search regime is categorically unreasonable.

I recognize that a suspicion-based scheme, even where reasonably effective in controlling in-school drug use, may not be *as* effective as a mass, suspicionless testing regime. In one sense, that is obviously true—just as it is obviously true that suspicion-based law enforcement is not as effective as mass, suspicionless enforcement might be. "But there is nothing new in the realization" that Fourth Amendment protections come with a price. *Arizona* v. *Hicks,* 480 U.S. 321, 329 (1987). Indeed, the price we pay is higher in the criminal context, given that police do not closely observe the entire class of potential search targets (all citizens in the area) and must ordinarily adhere to the rigid requirements of a warrant and probable cause. . . .

On this record, then, it seems to me that the far more reasonable choice would have been to focus on the class of students found to have violated published school rules against severe disruption in class and around campus—disruption that had a strong nexus to drug use, as the District established at trial. Such a choice would have two of the virtues of a suspicion-based regime: testing dramatically fewer students, tens as against hundreds, and giving students control, through their behavior, over the likelihood that they would be tested.

National Treasury Employees Union v. *Von Raab*
489 U.S. 656; 109 S. Ct. 1384; 103 L. Ed. 2d 685 (1989)

The United States Customs Service has as a primary enforcement mission the interdiction and seizure of illegal drugs smuggled into the country. It implemented a drug-screening program requiring urinalysis tests from Service employees seeking transfer or promotion to positions having a direct involvement in drug interdiction or whose positions required them to carry firearms or handle classified material. Among other things, the program required that applicants be notified that their selection depends on successful completion of drug screening, sets forth procedures for collection and analysis of the requisite samples and procedures designed both to ensure against adulteration or substitution of specimens and to limit the intrusion on employee privacy, and provides that test results may not be turned over to any other agency, including criminal prosecutors, without the employees' written consent. The National Treasury Employees Union filed suit against the Commissioner of the U.S. Customs Service on behalf of Customs employees seeking covered positions, alleging that the drug-testing program violated the Fourth Amendment. The District Court for the Eastern District of Louisiana agreed and enjoined the program. The Court of Appeals for the Fifth Circuit vacated the injunction, holding that, while the program amounts to a search within the meaning of the Fourth Amendment, such searches are reasonable in light of their limited scope and the Customs Services's strong interest in detecting drug use among employees in covered positions. The Supreme Court granted certiorari. *Opinion of the Court: Kennedy, Blackmun, O'Connor, Rehnquist, White. Dissenting opinions: Marshall, Brennan; Scalia, Stevens.*

JUSTICE KENNEDY delivered the opinion of the Court.

We granted certiorari to decide whether it violates the Fourth Amendment for the United States Customs Service to require a urinalysis test from employees who seek transfer or promotion to certain positions. . . . We now affirm so much of the judgment of the court of appeals as upheld the testing of employees directly involved in drug interdiction or required to carry firearms. We vacate the judgment to the extent it upheld the testing of applicants for positions requiring the incumbent to handle classified materials, and remand for further proceedings.

In *Skinner* v. *Railway Labor Executives Association* . . . decided today, we hold that federal regulations requiring employees of private railroads to produce urine samples for chemical testing implicate the Fourth Amendment, as those tests invade reasonable expectations of privacy. . . . In view of our holding in *Railway Labor Executives* that urine tests are searches, it follows that the Customs Service's drug testing program must meet the reasonableness requirement of the Fourth Amendment.

While we have often emphasized, and reiterate today, that a search must be supported, as a general matter, by a warrant issued upon probable cause, . . . our decision in *Railway Labor Executives* reaffirms the longstanding principle that neither a warrant nor probable cause, nor, indeed, any measure of individualized suspicion, is an indispensable component of reasonableness in every circumstance. . . . *New Jersey v. T. L. O.* . . . As we note in *Railway Labor Executives*, our cases establish that where a Fourth Amendment intrusion serves special governmental needs, beyond the normal need for law enforcement, it is necessary to balance the individual's privacy expectations against the Government's interests to determine whether it is impractical to require a warrant or some level of individualized suspicion in the particular context. . . .

It is clear that the Customs Service's drug testing program is not designed to serve the ordinary needs of law enforcement. Test results may not be used in a criminal prosecution of the employee without the employee's consent. The purposes of the program are to deter drug use among those eligible for promotion to sensitive positions within the Service and to prevent the promotion of drug users to those positions. These substantial interests, no less than the Government's concern for safe rail transportation at issue in *Railway Labor Executives*, present a special need that may justify departure from the ordinary warrant and probable cause requirements. . . .

Petitioners do not contend that a warrant is required by the balance of privacy and governmental interests in this context, nor could any such contention withstand scrutiny. We have recognized before that requiring the Government to procure a warrant for every work-related intrusion "would conflict with 'the common-sense realization that government offices could not function if every employment decision became a constitutional matter.'" . . . The Customs Service has been entrusted with pressing responsibilities, and its mission would be compromised if it were required to seek search warrants in connection with routine, yet sensitive, employment decisions.

Furthermore, a warrant would provide little or nothing in the way of additional protection of personal privacy. A warrant serves primarily to advise the citizen that an intrusion is authorized by law and limited in its permissible scope and to interpose a neutral magistrate between the citizen and the law enforcement officer "engaged in the often competitive enterprise of ferreting out crime." . . . Under the Customs program, every employee who seeks a transfer to a covered position knows that he must take a drug test, and is likewise aware of the procedures the Service must follow in administering the test. A covered employee is simply not subject "to the discretion of the official in the field." . . . The process becomes automatic when the employee elects to apply for, and thereafter pursue, a covered position. Because the Service does not make a discretionary determination to search based on a judgment that certain conditions are present, there are simply "no special facts for a neutral magistrate to evaluate." . . .

Even where it is reasonable to dispense with the warrant requirement in the particular circumstances, a search ordinarily must be based on probable cause. . . . Our cases teach, however, that the probable-cause standard " 'is peculiarly related to criminal investigations.' " . . . In particular, the traditional probable-cause standard may be unhelpful in analyzing the reasonableness of routine administrative functions, . . . especially where the Government seeks to *prevent* the development of hazardous conditions or to detect violations that rarely generate articulable grounds for searching any particular place or person. . . . Our precedents have settled that, in certain limited circumstances, the Government's need to discover such latent or hidden conditions, or to prevent their development, is sufficiently compelling to justify the intrusion on privacy entailed by conducting such searches without any measure of individualized suspicion. . . . We think the Government's need to conduct the suspicionless searches required by the Customs program outweighs the privacy interests of employees engaged directly in drug interdiction, and of those who otherwise are required to carry firearms. . . . The Government has a compelling interest in ensuring that front-line interdiction personnel are physically fit, and have unimpeachable integrity and judgment. Indeed, the Government's interest here is at least as important as its interest in searching travelers entering the country. We have long held that travelers seeking to enter the country may be stopped and required to submit to a routine search without probable cause, or even founded suspicion, "because of national self protection reasonably requiring one entering the country to identify himself as entitled to come in, and his belongings as effects which may be lawfully brought in." . . . This national interest in self protection could be irreparably damaged if those charged with safeguarding it were, because of

their own drug use, unsympathetic to their mission of interdicting narcotics. A drug user's indifference to the Service's basic mission or, even worse, his active complicity with the malefactors, can facilitate importation of sizable drug shipments or block apprehension of dangerous criminals. The public interest demands effective measures to bar drug users from positions directly involving the interdiction of illegal drugs.

The public interest likewise demands effective measures to prevent the promotion of drug users to positions that require the incumbent to carry a firearm, even if the incumbent is not engaged directly in the interdiction of drugs. Customs employees who may use deadly force plainly "discharge duties fraught with such risks of injury to others that even a momentary lapse of attention can have disastrous consequences." . . . We agree with the Government that the public should not bear the risk that employees who may suffer from impaired perception and judgment will be promoted to positions where they may need to employ deadly force. Indeed, ensuring against the creation of this dangerous risk will itself further Fourth Amendment values, as the use of deadly force may violate the Fourth Amendment in certain circumstances. . . .

Against these valid public interests we must weigh the interference with individual liberty that results from requiring these classes of employees to undergo a urine test. The interference with individual privacy that results from the collection of a urine sample for subsequent chemical analysis could be substantial in some circumstances. . . .

. . . It is plain that certain forms of public employment may diminish privacy expectations even with respect to such personal searches. Employees of the United States Mint, for example, should expect to be subject to certain routine personal searches when they leave the workplace every day. Similarly, those who join our military or intelligence services may not only be required to give what in other contexts might be viewed as extraordinary assurances of trustworthiness and probity, but also may expect intrusive inquiries into their physical fitness for those special positions. . . .

We think Customs employees who are directly involved in the interdiction of illegal drugs or who are required to carry firearms in the line of duty . . . have a diminished expectation of privacy in respect to the intrusions occasioned by a urine test. Unlike most private citizens or government employees in general, employees involved in drug interdiction reasonably should expect effective inquiry into their fitness and probity. Much the same is true of employees who are required to carry firearms. Because successful performance of their duties depends uniquely on their judgment and dexterity, these employees cannot reasonably expect to keep from the Service personal information that bears directly on their fitness. . . . While reasonable tests designed to elicit this information doubtless infringe some privacy expectations, we do not believe these expectations outweigh the Government's compelling interests in safety and in the integrity of our borders.

Without disparaging the importance of the governmental interests that support the suspicionless searches of these employees, petitioners nevertheless contend that the Service's drug testing program is unreasonable in two particulars. First, petitioners argue that the program is unjustified because it is not based on a belief that testing will reveal any drug use by covered employees. In pressing this argument, petitioners point out that the Service's testing scheme was not implemented in response to any perceived drug problem among Customs employees, and that the program actually has not led to the discovery of a significant number of drug users. . . . Counsel for petitioners informed us at oral argument that no more than 5 employees out of 3,600 have tested positive for drugs. . . . Second, petitioners contend that the Service's scheme is not a "sufficiently productive mechanism to justify [its] intrusion upon Fourth Amendment interests," . . . because illegal drug users can avoid detection with ease by temporary abstinence or by surreptitious adulteration of their urine specimens. . . . These contentions are unpersuasive.

Petitioners' first contention evinces an unduly narrow view of the context in which the Service's testing program was implemented. . . .

The mere circumstance that all but a few of the employees tested are entirely innocent of wrongdoing does not impugn the program's validity. . . . The Service's program is designed to prevent the promotion of drug users to sensitive positions as much as it is designed to detect these employees who use drugs. Where, as here, the possible harm against which the Government seeks to guard is substantial, the need to prevent its occurrence furnishes an ample justification for reasonable searches calculated to advance the Government's goal.

We think petitioners' second argument—that the Service's testing program is ineffective because employees may attempt to deceive the test by a brief abstention before the test date, or by adulterating their urine specimens—overstates the case. As the Court of Appeals noted, addicts may be unable to abstain even for a limited period of time, or may be unaware of the "fadeaway effect" of certain drugs. . . . More importantly, the avoidance techniques suggested by petitioners are fraught with uncertainty and risks for those employees who venture to attempt them. A particular employee's pattern of elimination for a given drug cannot be predicted with perfect accuracy, and, in any event, this information is not likely to be known or available to the employee. . . . Thus, contrary to petitioners' suggestion, no employee reasonably can expect to deceive the test by the simple expedient of abstaining after the test date is assigned. Nor can he expect attempts at adulteration to succeed, in view of the precautions taken by the sample collector to ensure the integrity of the sample. . . .

In sum, we believe that Government has demonstrated that its compelling interests in safeguarding our borders and the public safety outweigh the privacy expectations of employees who seek to be promoted to positions that directly involve the interdiction of illegal drugs or that require the incumbent to carry a firearm. We hold that the testing of these employees is reasonable under the Fourth Amendment.

We are unable, on the present record, to assess the reasonableness of the Government's testing program insofar as it covers employees who are required "to handle classified material." . . .

It is not clear, however, whether the category defined by the Service's testing directive encompasses only those Customs employees likely to gain access to sensitive information. Employees who are tested under the Service's scheme include those holding such diverse positions as "Accountant," "Accounting Technician," "Animal Caretaker," "Attorney (All)," "Baggage

Clerk," "Co-op Student (All)," "Electric Equipment Repairer," "Mail Clerk/Assistant," and "Messenger." . . . Yet it is not evident that those occupying these positions are likely to gain access to sensitive information, and this apparent discrepancy raises in our minds the question whether the Service has defined this category of employees more broadly than necessary to meet the purpose of the Commissioner's directive.

We cannot resolve this ambiguity on the basis of the record before us, and we think it is appropriate to remand the case to the court of appeals for such proceedings as may be necessary to clarify the scope of this category of employees subject to testing. . . .

The judgment of the Court of Appeals for the Fifth Circuit is affirmed in part and vacated in part, and the case is remanded for further proceedings consistent with this opinion.

JUSTICE MARSHALL, with whom JUSTICE BRENNAN joins, dissenting.

For the reasons stated in my dissenting opinion in *Skinner* v. *Railway Labor Executives Association*, . . . I also dissent from the Court's decision in this case. Here, as in *Skinner*, the Court's abandonment of the Fourth Amendment's express requirement that searches of the person rest on probable cause is unprincipled and unjustifiable. But even if I believed that balancing analysis was appropriate under the Fourth Amendment, I would still dissent from today's judgment, for the reasons stated by Justice Scalia in his dissenting opinion.

JUSTICE SCALIA, with whom JUSTICE STEVENS joins, dissenting. . . .

Until today this Court had upheld a bodily search separate from arrest and without individualized suspicion of wrongdoing only with respect to prison inmates, relying upon the uniquely dangerous nature of that environment. . . . Today, in *Skinner*, we allow a less intrusive bodily search of railroad employees involved in train accidents. I joined the Court's opinion there because the demonstrated frequency of drug and alcohol use by the targeted class of employees, and the demonstrated connection between such use and grave harm, rendered the search a reasonable means of protecting society. I decline to join the Court's opinion in the present case be-

cause neither frequency of use nor connection to harm is demonstrated or even likely. In my view the Customs Service rules are a kind of immolation of privacy and human dignity in symbolic opposition to drug use.

The Fourth Amendment protects the "right of the people to be secure in their persons, houses, papers, and effects, against unreasonable searches and seizures." While there are some absolutes in Fourth Amendment law, as soon as those have been left behind and the question comes down to whether a particular search has been "reasonable," the answer depends largely upon the social necessity that prompts the search. . . .

The Court's opinion in the present case, however, will be searched in vain for real evidence of a real problem that will be solved by urine testing of Customs Service employees. . . . It is not apparent to me that a Customs Service employee who uses drugs is significantly more likely to be bribed by a drug smuggler, any more than a Customs Service employee who wears diamonds is significantly more likely to be bribed by a diamond smuggler—unless, perhaps, the addiction to drugs is so severe, and requires so much money to maintain, that it would be detectable even without benefit of a urine test. Nor is it apparent to me that Customs officers who use drugs will be appreciably less "sympathetic" to their drug-interdiction mission, any more than police officers who exceed the speed limit in their private cars are appreciably less sympathetic to their mission of enforcing the traffic laws. (The only difference is that the Customs officer's individual efforts, if they are irreplaceable, can theoretically affect the availability of his own drug supply—a prospect so remote as to be an absurd basis of motivation.) Nor, finally, is it apparent to me that urine tests will be even marginally more effective in preventing gun-carrying agents from risking "impaired perception and judgment" than is their current knowledge that, if impaired, they may be shot dead in unequal combat with unimpaired smugglers—unless, again, their addiction is so severe that no urine test is needed for detection.

What is absent in the Government's justifications—notably absent, revealingly absent, and as far as I am concerned dispositively absent—is the recitation of *even a single instance* in which any of the speculated horribles actually occurred: an instance, that is, in which the cause of bribe-taking, or of poor aim, or of unsympathetic law enforcement, or of compromise of classified information, was drug use.

. . . In *Skinner*, . . . we pointed to a long history of alcohol abuse in the railroad industry, and noted that in an 8-year period 45 train accidents and incidents had occurred because of alcohol- and drug-impaired railroad employees, killing 34 people, injuring 66, and causing more than $28 million in property damage. . . . In the present case, by contrast, not only is the Customs Service thought to be "largely drug-free," but the connection between whatever drug use may exist and serious social harm is entirely speculative. . . .

Today's decision would be wrong, but at least of more limited effect, if its approval of drug testing were confined to that category of employees assigned specifically to drug interdiction duties. Relatively few public employees fit that description. But in extending approval of drug testing to that category consisting of employees who carry firearms, the Court exposes vast numbers of public employees to this needless indignity. . . .

There is only one apparent basis that sets the testing at issue here apart from all these other situations—but it is not a basis upon which the Court is willing to rely. I do not believe for a minute that the driving force behind these drug-testing rules was any of the feeble justifications put forward by counsel here and accepted by the Court. The only plausible explanation, in my view, is what the Commissioner himself offered in the concluding sentence of his memorandum to Customs Service employees announcing the program: "Implementation of the drug screening program would set an important example in our country's struggle with this most serious threat to our national health and security." . . . Or as respondent's brief to this Court asserted: "if a law enforcement agency and its employees do not take the law seriously, neither will the public on which the agency's effectiveness depends." . . . What better way to show that the Government is serious about its "war on drugs" than to subject its employees on the front line of that war to this invasion of their privacy and affront to their dignity? To be sure, there is only a slight chance that it will prevent some serious public harm resulting from Service employee drug use, but it will show to the world that the Service is "clean," and—most important of all—will demonstrate the determination of the Government to eliminate this scourge of our society! I think it obvious that this justification is unacceptable; that the impairment of individual liberties cannot be the means of making a point; that symbolism, even symbolism for so worthy a cause as the abolition of unlawful drugs, cannot validate an otherwise unreasonable search.

Mapp v. *Ohio*

367 U.S. 643; 81 S. Ct. 1684; 6 L. Ed. 2d 1081 (1961)

On May 23, 1957, Cleveland police officers came to Dollree Mapp's residence, acting on information that a bombing-case suspect and betting equipment might be found there. They requested entrance, but Mapp refused to admit them without a search warrant. When she refused a second time, the police forced their way into her duplex apartment and subdued and handcuffed her when she grabbed and placed in her bosom a paper that they informed her was a valid search warrant. The officers subjected her entire residence and its contents to a thorough search and in a basement trunk found materials that provided the basis for her conviction of possessing obscene materials. The Ohio Supreme Court affirmed her conviction, and the United States Supreme Court granted certiorari. *Opinion of the Court: Clark, Black, Brennan, Douglas, Warren. Concurring opinions: Black; Douglas. Dissenting opinion: Harlan, Frankfurter, Whittaker. Separate memorandum: Stewart.*

MR. JUSTICE CLARK delivered the opinion of the Court.

Appellant stands convicted of knowingly having had in her possession and under her control certain lewd and lascivious books, pictures, and photographs in violation [of Ohio law]. . . . The Supreme Court of Ohio found that her conviction was valid though "based primarily upon the introduction in evidence of lewd and lascivious books and pictures unlawfully seized during an unlawful search of defendant's home." . . .

The State says that even if the search were made without authority, or otherwise unreasonably, it is not prevented from using the unconstitutionally seized evidence at trial, citing *Wolf* v. *Colorado*, . . . (1949), in which this Court did indeed hold "that in a prosecution in a State court for a State crime the Fourteenth Amendment does not forbid the admission of evidence obtained by an unreasonable search and seizure." . . .

. . . In the year 1914, in *Weeks* [v. *United States*,] this Court "for the first time" held that "in a federal prosecution the Fourth Amendment barred the use of evidence secured through an illegal search and seizure." . . . This Court has ever since required of federal law officers a strict adherence to that command which this Court has held to be a clear, specific, and constitutionally required—even if judicially implied—deterrent safeguard without insistence upon which the Fourth Amendment would have been reduced to "a form of words." . . .

In 1949, 35 years after Weeks was announced, this Court, in *Wolf* v. *Colorado, supra,* again for the first time, discussed the effect of the Fourth Amendment upon the States through the operation of the Due Process Clause of the Fourteenth Amendment. Nevertheless, after declaring that the "security of one's privacy against arbitrary intrusion by the police" is "implicit in 'the concept of ordered liberty' and as such enforceable against the States through the Due Process Clause." . . . and announcing that it "stoutly adhere[d]" to the *Weeks* decision, the Court decided that the *Weeks* exclusionary rule would not then be imposed upon the States as "an essential ingredient of the right." . . .

Today we once again examine *Wolf's* constitutional documentation of the right to privacy free from unreasonable state intrusion, and after its dozen years on our books, are led by it to close the only courtroom door remaining open to evidence secured by official lawlessness in flagrant abuse of that basic right, reserved to all persons as a specific guarantee against that very same unlawful conduct. We hold that all evidence obtained by searches and seizures in violation of the Constitution is, by that same authority, inadmissible in a state court. . . .

Since the Fourth Amendment's right of privacy has been declared enforceable against the States through the Due Process Clause of the Fourteenth, it is enforceable against them by the same sanction of exclusion as is used against the Federal Government. Were it otherwise, then just as without the *Weeks* rule the assurance against unreasonable federal searches and seizures would be "a form of words," valueless and undeserving of mention in a perpetual charter of inestimable human liberties, so too, without that rule the freedom from state invasions of privacy would be so ephemeral and so neatly severed from its conceptual nexus with the freedom from all brutish means of coercing evidence as not to merit this Court's high regard as a freedom "implicit in the concept of ordered liberty."

. . . This Court has not hesitated to enforce as strictly against the States as it does against the Federal Government the rights of free speech and of a free press, the rights to notice and to a fair, public trial, including, as it does, the right not to be convicted by use of a coerced confession, however logically relevant it be, and without regard to its reliability. . . . Why should not the same rule apply to what is tantamount to coerced testimony by way of unconstitutional seizure of goods, papers, effects, documents, etc.? We find that as to the Federal Government, the Fourth and Fifth Amendments and, as to the States, the freedom from unconscionable invasions of privacy and the freedom from convictions based upon coerced confessions do enjoy an "intimate relation" in their perpetuation of "principles of humanity and civil liberty [secured] . . . only after years of struggle." . . . The very least that together they assure in either sphere is that no man is to be convicted on unconstitutional evidence. . . .

Moreover, our holding that the exclusionary rule is an essential part of both the Fourth and

Fourteenth Amendments is not only the logical dictate of prior cases, but it also makes very good sense. There is no war between the Constitution and common sense. Presently, a federal prosecutor may make no use of evidence illegally seized, but a State's attorney across the street may, although he supposedly is operating under the enforceable prohibitions of the same Amendment. Thus the State, by admitting evidence unlawfully seized, serves to encourage disobedience to the Federal Constitution which it is bound to uphold. . . . In nonexclusionary States, federal officers, being human, were by it invited to and did, as our cases indicate, step across the street to the State's attorney with their unconstitutionally seized evidence. Prosecution on the basis of that evidence was then had in a state court in utter disregard of the enforceable Fourth Amendment. If the fruits of an unconstitutional search had been inadmissible in both state and federal courts, this inducement to evasion would have been sooner eliminated. . . .

There are those who say as did Justice (then Judge) Cardozo, that under our constitutional exclusionary doctrine "[t]he criminal is to go free because the constable has blundered." . . . In some cases this will undoubtedly be the result. But . . . "there is another consideration—the imperative of judicial integrity." . . . The criminal goes free, if he must, but it is the law that sets him free. Nothing can destroy a government more quickly than its failure to observe its own laws, or worse, its disregard of the charter of its own existence. . . .

The ignoble shortcut to conviction left open to the State tends to destroy the entire system of constitutional restraints on which the liberties of the people rest. Having once recognized that the right to privacy embodied in the Fourth Amendment is enforceable against the States, and that the right to be secure against rude invasions of privacy by state officers is, therefore, constitutional in origin, we can no longer permit that right to remain an empty promise. Because it is enforceable in the same manner and to like effect as other basic rights secured by the Due Process Clause, we can no longer permit it to be revocable at the whim of any police officer who, in the name of law enforcement itself, chooses to suspend its enjoyment. Our decision, founded on reason and truth, gives to the individual no more than that which the Constitution guarantees him, to the police officer no less than that to which honest law enforcement is entitled, and, to the courts, that judicial integrity so necessary in the true administration of justice. . . .

MR. JUSTICE BLACK, concurring . . .

I am still not persuaded that the Fourth Amendment, standing alone, would be enough to bar the introduction into evidence against an accused of papers and effects seized from him in violation of its commands. For the Fourth Amendment does not itself contain any provision expressly precluding the use of such evidence, and I am extremely doubtful that such a provision could properly be inferred from nothing more than the basic command against unreasonable searches and seizures. Reflection on the problem, however, in the light of cases coming before the Court since *Wolf*, has led me to conclude that when the Fourth Amendment's ban against unreasonable searches and seizures is considered together with the Fifth Amendment's ban against compelled self-incrimination, a constitutional basis emerges which not only justifies but actually requires the exclusionary rule. . . .

Memorandum of MR. JUSTICE STEWART. . . .

. . . I would . . . reverse the judgment in this case because I am persuaded that the provision of . . . the Ohio [obscenity law], upon which the petitioner's conviction was based, is, in the words of Mr. Justice Harlan, not "consistent with the rights of free thought and expression assured against state action by the Fourteenth Amendment."

MR. JUSTICE HARLAN, whom MR. JUSTICE FRANKFURTER and MR. JUSTICE WHITTAKER join, dissenting.

In overruling the *Wolf* case the Court, in my opinion, has forgotten the sense of judicial restraint which, with due regard for *stare decisis*, is one element that should enter into deciding whether a past decision of this Court should be overruled. Apart from that I also believe that the *Wolf* rule represents sounder Constitutional doctrine than the new rule which now replaces it. . . .

From the Court's statement of the case one would gather that the central, if not controlling, issue on this appeal is whether illegally state-seized evidence is Constitutionally admissible in a state prosecution, an issue which would of course face us with the need for re-examining *Wolf*. However, such is not the situation. For, although that question was indeed raised here and below among appellant's subordinate points, the new and pivotal issue brought to the Court by this appeal is whether § 2905.34 of the Ohio Revised Code making criminal the *mere* knowing possession or control of obscene material, and under which appellant has been convicted, is consistent with the rights of free thought and expression assured against state action by the Fourteenth Amendment. That was the principal issue which was decided by the Ohio Supreme Court, which was tendered by appellant's Jurisdictional Statement, and which was briefed and argued in this Court. . . .

In this posture of things, I think it fair to say that five members of this Court have simply "reached out" to overrule *Wolf*. With all respect for the views of the majority, and recognizing that *stare decisis* carries different weight in Constitutional adjudication than it does in nonconstitutional decision, I can perceive no justification for regarding this case as an appropriate occasion for re-examining *Wolf*. . . .

The occasion which the Court has taken here is in the context of a case where the question was briefed not at all and argued only extremely tangentially. The unwisdom of overruling *Wolf* without full-dress argument is aggravated by the circumstance that that decision is a comparatively recent one (1949) to which three members of the present majority have at one time or other expressly subscribed, one to be sure with explicit misgivings. I would think that our obligation to the States, on whom we impose this new rule, as well as the obligation of orderly adherence to our own processes would demand that we seek that aid which adequate briefing and argument lends to the determination of an important issue. It certainly has never been a postulate of judicial power that mere altered disposition, or subsequent membership on the Court, is sufficient warrant for overturning a deliberately decided rule of Constitutional law. . . .

I am bound to say that what has been done is not likely to promote respect either for the Court's adjudicatory process or for the stability of its decisions. Having been unable, however, to persuade any of the majority to a different procedural course, I now turn to the merits of the present decision. . . .

I would not impose upon the States this federal exclusionary remedy. The reasons given by the majority for now suddenly turning its back on *Wolf* seem to me notably unconvincing.

First, it is said that "the factual grounds upon which *Wolf* was based" have since changed, in that more States now follow the *Weeks* exclusionary rule than was so at the time *Wolf* was decided. While that is true, a recent survey indicates that at present one-half of the States still adhere to the common-law non-exclusionary rule . . . But in any case surely all this is beside the point, as the majority itself indeed seems to recognize. Our concern here, as it was in *Wolf*, is not with the desirability of that rule but only with the question whether the States are Constitutionally free to follow it or not as they may themselves determine, and the relevance of the disparity of views among the States on this point lies simply in the fact that the judgment involved is a debatable one. . . .

The preservation of a proper balance between state and federal responsibility in the administration of criminal justice demands patience on the part of those who might like to see things move faster among the States in this respect. Problems of criminal law enforcement vary widely from State to State. One State, in considering the totality of its legal picture, may conclude that the need for embracing the *Weeks* rule is pressing because other remedies are unavailable or inadequate to secure compliance with the substantive Constitutional principle involved. Another, though equally solicitous of Constitutional rights, may choose to pursue one purpose at a time, allowing all evidence relevant to guilt to be brought into a criminal trial, and dealing with Constitutional infractions by other means. Still another may consider the exclusionary rule too rough-and-ready a remedy, in that it reaches only unconstitutional intrusions which eventuate in criminal prosecution of the victims. Further, a State after experimenting with the *Weeks* rule for a time may, because of unsatisfactory experience with it, decide to revert to a non-exclusionary rule. And so on. From the standpoint of Constitutional permissibility in pointing a State in one direction or another, I do not see at all why "time has set its face against" the considerations which led Mr. Justice Cardozo, then chief judge of the New York Court of Appeals, to reject for New York in *People* v. *Defore*, . . . the *Weeks* exclusionary rule. For us the question remains, as it has always been, one of state power, not one of passing judgment on the wisdom of one state course or another. . . .

Further, we are told that imposition of the *Weeks* rule on the States makes "very good sense," in that it will promote recognition by state and federal officials of their "mutual obligation to respect the same fundamental criteria" in their approach to law enforcement, and will avoid " 'needless conflict between state and federal courts.' " . . .

An approach which regards the issue as one of achieving procedural symmetry or of serving administrative convenience surely disfigures the boundaries of this Court's functions in relation to the state and federal courts. Our role in promulgating the *Weeks* rule and its extensions . . . was quite a different one than it is here. There, in implementing the Fourth Amendment, we occupied the position of a tribunal having the ultimate responsibility for developing the standards and procedures of judicial administration within the judicial system over which it presides. Here we review state procedures whose measure is to be taken not against the specific substantive commands of the Fourth Amendment but under the flexible contours of the Due Process Clause. . . .

I regret that I find so unwise in principle and so inexpedient in policy a decision motivated by the high purpose of increasing respect for Constitutional rights. But in the last analysis I think this Court can increase respect for the Constitution only if it rigidly respects the limitations which the Constitution places upon it, and respects as well the principles inherent in its own processes. In the present case I think we exceed both, and that our voice becomes only a voice of power, not of reason.

Olmstead v. *United States*
277 U.S. 438; 48 S. Ct. 564; 72 L. Ed. 944 (1928)

Roy Olmstead and several accomplices were convicted in federal district court of conspiring to violate the National Prohibition Act by unlawfully possessing, transporting, and importing intoxicating liquors. At trial, the government presented incriminating evidence obtained by federal agents who wiretapped telephone lines at points between the defendants' homes and their offices. The Court of Appeals for the Ninth Circuit affirmed the convictions over objections that this wiretap evidence was inadmissible under the Fourth Amendment protection from unreasonable searches and seizures and the Fifth Amendment guarantee against self-incrimination. The Supreme Court granted certiorari. *Opinion of the Court: Taft, McReynolds, Sanford, Sutherland, Van Devanter. Dissenting opinions: Brandeis; Butler; Holmes; Stone.*

MR. CHIEF JUSTICE TAFT delivered the opinion of the Court. . . .

There is no room in the present case for applying the Fifth Amendment unless the Fourth Amendment was first violated. There was no evidence of compulsion to induce the defendants to talk over their many telephones. They were continually and voluntarily transacting business without knowledge of the interception. Our consideration must be confined to the Fourth Amendment. . . .

The well known historical purpose of the Fourth Amendment, directed against general warrants and writs of assistance, was to prevent the use of governmental force to search a man's house, his person, his papers and his effects; and to prevent their seizure against his will. . . .

The Amendment itself shows that the search is to be of material things—the person, the house, his papers or his effects. The description of the warrant necessary to make the proceeding lawful, is that it must specify the place to be searched and the person or *things* to be seized. . . .

. . . The Amendment does not forbid what was done here. There was no searching. There was no seizure. The evidence was secured by the use of the sense of hearing and that only. There was no entry of the houses or offices of the defendants.

By the invention of the telephone, fifty years ago, and its application for the purpose of extending communications, one can talk with another at a far distant place. The language of the Amendment cannot be extended and expanded to include telephone wires reaching to the whole world from the defendant's house or office. The intervening wires are not part of his house or office any more than are the highways along which they are stretched. . . .

Congress may of course protect the secrecy of telephone messages by making them, when intercepted, inadmissible in evidence in federal criminal trials, by direct legislation, and thus depart from the common law of evidence. But the courts may not adopt such a policy by attributing an enlarged and unusual meaning to the Fourth Amendment. The reasonable view is that one who installs in his house a telephone instrument with connecting wires intends to project his voice to those quite outside, and that the wires beyond his house and messages while passing over them are not within protection of the Fourth Amendment. Here those who intercepted the projected voices were not in the house of either party to the conversation.

Neither the cases we have cited nor any of the many federal decisions brought to our attention hold the Fourth Amendment to have been violated as against a defendant unless there has been an official search and seizure of his person, or such a seizure of his papers or his tangible material effects, or an actual physical invasion of his house "or curtilage" for the purpose of making a seizure.

We think, therefore, that the wire tapping here disclosed did not amount to a search or seizure within the meaning of the Fourth Amendment.

What has been said disposes of the only question that comes within the terms of our order granting certiorari in these cases. But some of our number, departing from that order, have concluded that there is merit in the two-fold objection overruled in both courts below that evidence obtained through intercepting of telephone messages by government agents was inadmissible because the mode of obtaining it was unethical and a misdemeanor under the law of Washington. To avoid any misrepresentation of our views of that objection we shall deal with it in both of its phases.

While a Territory, the English common law prevailed in Washington and thus continued after her admission in 1889. The rules of evidence in criminal cases in courts of the United States sitting there, consequently are those of the common law. . . .

The common law rule is that the admissibility of evidence is not affected by the illegality of the means by which it was obtained. . . .

Nor can we, without the sanction of congressional enactment, subscribe to the suggestion that the courts have a discretion to exclude evidence, the admission of which is not unconstitutional, because unethically secured. This would be at variance with the common law doctrine generally supported by authority. There is no case that sustains, nor any recognized text book that gives color to such a view. Our general experience shows that much evidence has always been receivable although not obtained by conformity to the highest ethics. The history of criminal trials shows numerous cases of prosecutions of oath-bound conspiracies for murder, robbery, and other crimes, where officers of the law have disguised themselves and joined the organizations, taken the oaths and given themselves every appearance of active members engaged in the promotion of crime, for the purpose of securing evidence. Evidence secured by such means has always been received.

A standard which would forbid the reception of evidence if obtained by other than nice ethical conduct by government officials would make society suffer and give criminals greater immunity than has been known heretofore. In the absence of controlling legislation by Congress, those who realize the difficulties in bringing offenders to justice may well deem it wise that the exclusion of evidence should be confined to cases where rights under the Constitution would be violated by admitting it.

MR. JUSTICE HOLMES, dissenting.

. . . It is desirable that criminals should be detected, and to that end that all available evidence should be used. It also is desirable that the Government should not itself foster and pay for other crimes, when they are the means by which the evidence is to be obtained. We have to choose, and for my part I think it a less evil that some criminals should escape than that the Government should play an ignoble part. . . .

MR. JUSTICE BRANDEIS, dissenting. . . .

The Government makes no attempt to defend the methods employed by its officers. Indeed, it concedes that if wire-tapping can be deemed a search and seizure within the Fourth Amendment, such wire-tapping as was practiced in the case at bar was an unreasonable search and seizure, and that the evidence thus obtained was inadmissible. But it relies on the language of the Amendment; and it claims that the protection given thereby cannot properly be held to include a telephone conversation.

"We must never forget," said Mr. Chief Justice Marshall in *McCulloch* v. *Maryland*, . . . "that it is a constitution we are expounding." Since then, this Court has repeatedly sustained the exercise of power by Congress, under various clauses of that instrument, over objects of which the Fathers could not have dreamed. . . . We have likewise held the general limitations on the powers of Government, like those embodied in the due process clauses of the Fifth and Fourteenth Amendments, do not forbid the United States or the States from meeting modern conditions by regulations which "a century ago, or even half a century ago, probably would have been rejected as arbitrary and oppressive." . . . Clauses guaranteeing to the individual protection against specific abuses of power, must have similar capacity of adaptation to a changing world.

When the Fourth and Fifth Amendments were adopted, "the form that evil had theretofore taken," had been necessarily simple. Force and violence were then the only means known to man by which a Government could directly effect self-incrimination. It could compel the individual to testify—a compulsion effected, if need be, by torture. It could secure possession of his papers and other articles incident to his private life—a seizure effected, if need be, by breaking and entry. Protection against such invasion of "the sanctities of a man's home and the privacies of life" was provided in the Fourth and Fifth Amendments by specific language. . . . But "time works changes, brings into existence new conditions and purposes." Subtler and more far-reaching means of invading privacy have become available to the Government. Discovery and invention have made it possible for the Government, by means far more effective than stretching upon the rack, to obtain disclosure in court of what is whispered in the closet.

Moreover, "in the application of a constitution, our contemplation cannot be only of what has been but of what may be." The progress of science in furnishing the Government with means of espionage is not likely to stop with wire-tapping. Ways may some day be developed by which the Government, without removing papers from secret drawers, can reproduce them in court, and by which it will be enabled to expose to a jury the most intimate occurrences of the home. Advances in the psychic and related sciences may bring means of exploring unexpressed beliefs, thoughts and emotions. . . . Can it be that the Constitution affords no protection against such invasions of individual security?

. . . The makers of our Constitution undertook to secure conditions favorable to the pursuit of happiness. They recognized the significance of man's spiritual nature, of his feelings and of his intellect. They knew that only a part of the pain, pleasure and satisfactions of life are to be found in material things. They sought to protect Americans in their beliefs, their thoughts, their emotions and their sensations. They conferred, as against the Government, the right to be let alone—the most comprehensive of rights and the right most valued by civilized men. To protect that right, every unjustifiable intrusion by the Government upon the privacy of the individual, whatever the means employed, must be deemed a violation of the Fourth Amendment. And the use, as evidence in a criminal proceeding, of facts ascertained by such intrusion must be deemed a violation of the Fifth.

Applying to the Fourth and Fifth Amendments the established rule of construction, the defendants' objections to the evidence obtained by wire-tapping must, in my opinion, be sustained. It is, of course, immaterial where the physical connection with the telephone wires leading into the defendants' premises was made. And it is also immaterial that the intrusion was in aid of law enforcement. Experience should teach us to be most on our guard to protect liberty when the Government's purposes are beneficent. Men born to freedom are naturally alert to repel invasion of their liberty by evil-minded rulers. The greatest dangers to liberty lurk in insidious encroachment by men of zeal, well-meaning but without understanding.

Independently of the constitutional question, I am of opinion that the judgment should be reversed. By the laws of Washington, wire-tapping

is a crime. . . . To prove its case, the Government was obliged to lay bare the crimes committed by its officers on its behalf. A federal court should not permit such a prosecution to continue. . . .

Decency, security and liberty alike demand that government officials shall be subjected to the same rules of conduct that are commands to the citizen. In a government of laws, existence of the government will be imperilled if it fails to observe the law scrupulously. Our Government is the potent, the omnipresent teacher. For good or for ill, it teaches the whole people by its example. Crime is contagious. If the Government becomes a lawbreaker, it breeds contempt for law; it invites every man to become a law unto himself; it invites anarchy. To declare that in the administration of the criminal law the end justifies the means—to declare that the Government may commit crimes in order to secure the conviction of a private criminal—would bring terrible retribution. Against that pernicious doctrine this Court should resolutely set its face.

Katz v. *United States*
389 U.S. 342; 88 S. Ct. 507; 19 L. Ed. 2d 576 (1967)

Charles Katz was convicted in federal district court of violating a federal statute by transmitting wagering information to Miami and Boston from a telephone booth in Los Angeles. At trial, the government introduced a recording of his phone conversations made by FBI agents using an electronic listening device attached to the outside of the booth. The court of appeals, in affirming Katz's conviction, rejected his contention that the recording had been obtained in violation of the Fourth Amendment, on the grounds that there was no physical entrance into the area occupied by the defendant. The Supreme Court granted certiorari. *Opinion of the Court: Stewart, Brennan, Douglas, Fortas, Harlan, Warren, White. Concurring opinions: Douglas, Brennan; Harlan; White. Dissenting opinion: Black. Marshall did not participate.*

MR. JUSTICE STEWART delivered the opinion of the Court.

. . . The petitioner has strenuously argued that the booth was a "constitutionally protected area." The Government has maintained with equal vigor that it was not. But this effort to decide whether or not a given "area," viewed in the abstract, is "constitutionally protected" deflects attention from the problem presented by this

case. For the Fourth Amendment protects people, not places. What a person knowingly exposes to the public, even in his own home or office, is not a subject of Fourth Amendment protection. . . . But what he seeks to preserve as private, even in an area accessible to the public, may be constitutionally protected. . . .

The Government stresses the fact that the telephone booth from which the petitioner made his calls was constructed partly of glass, so that he was as visible after he entered it as he would have been if he had remained outside. But what he sought to exclude when he entered the booth was not the intruding eye—it was the uninvited ear. He did not shed his right to do so simply because he made his calls from a place where he might be seen. No less than an individual in a business office, in a friend's apartment, or in a taxicab, a person in a telephone booth may rely upon the protection of the Fourth Amendment. One who occupies it, shuts the door behind him, and pays the toll that permits him to place a call is surely entitled to assume that the words he utters into the mouthpiece will not be broadcast to the world. To read the Constitution more narrowly is to ignore the vital role that the public telephone has come to play in private communication.

The Government contends, however, that the activities of its agents in this case should not be tested by Fourth Amendment requirements, for the surveillance technique they employed involved no physical penetration of the telephone booth from which the petitioner placed his calls. It is true that the absence of such penetration was at one time thought to foreclose further Fourth Amendment inquiry, *Olmstead* v. *United States* . . .

. . . The underpinnings of *Olmstead* [v. *United States* (1928)] and *Goldman* [v. *United States* (1942)] have been so eroded by our subsequent decisions that the "trespass" doctrine there enunciated can no longer be regarded as controlling. The Government's activities in electronically listening to and recording the petitioner's words violated the privacy upon which he justifiably relied while using the telephone booth and thus constituted a "search and seizure" within the meaning of the Fourth Amendment. The fact that the electronic device employed to achieve that end did not happen to penetrate the wall of the booth can have no constitutional significance.

The question remaining for decision, then, is whether the search and seizure conducted in this case complied with constitutional standards. In that regard, the Government's position is that its agents acted in an entirely defensible manner: They did not begin their electronic surveillance until investigation of the petitioner's activities had established a strong probability that he was using the telephone in question to transmit gam-

bling information to persons in other States, in violation of federal law. Moreover, the surveillance was limited, both in scope and in duration, to the specific purpose of establishing the contents of the petitioner's unlawful telephonic communications. The agents confined their surveillance to the brief periods during which he used the telephone booth, and they took great care to overhear only the conversations of the petitioner himself. . . .

The Government urges that, because its agents relied upon the decisions in *Olmstead* and *Goldman*, and because they did no more here than they might properly have done with prior judicial sanction, we should retroactively validate their conduct. That we cannot do. It is apparent that the agents in this case acted with restraint. Yet the inescapable fact is that this restraint was imposed by the agents themselves, not by a judicial officer. They were not required, before commencing the search, to present their estimate of probable cause for detached scrutiny by a neutral magistrate. They were not compelled, during the conduct of the search itself, to observe precise limits established in advance by a specific court order. Nor were they directed, after the search had been completed, to notify the authorizing magistrate in detail of all that had been seized. In the absence of such safeguards, this Court has never sustained a search upon the sole ground that officers reasonably expected to find evidence of a particular crime and voluntarily confined their activities to the least intrusive means consistent with that end. . . . "Over and again this Court has emphasized that the mandate of the [Fourth] Amendment requires adherence to judicial processes," . . . and that searches conducted outside the judicial process, without prior approval by judge or magistrate, are *per se* unreasonable under the Fourth Amendment—subject only to a few specifically established and well-delineated exceptions. . . .

MR. JUSTICE BLACK, dissenting. . . .

While I realize that an argument based on the meaning of words lacks the scope, and no doubt the appeal, of broad policy discussions and philosophical discourses on such nebulous subjects as privacy, for me the language of the Amendment is the crucial place to look in construing a written document such as our Constitution. The

Fourth Amendment. . . . protects "persons, houses, papers, and effects, against unreasonable searches and seizures. . . ." These words connote the idea of tangible things with size, form, and weight, things capable of being searched, seized, or both. . . . The Amendment further establishes its Framers' purpose to limit its protection to tangible things by providing that no warrants shall issue but those "particularly describing the place to be searched, and the persons or things to be seized." A conversation overheard by eavesdropping whether by plain snooping or wiretapping, is not tangible and, under the normally accepted meanings of the words, can neither be searched nor seized. In addition the language of the second clause indicates that the Amendment refers not only to something tangible so it can be seized but to something already in existence so it can be described. Yet the Court's interpretation would have the Amendment apply to overhearing future conversations which by their own nature are nonexistent until they take place. How can one "describe" a future conversation, and, if one cannot, how can a magistrate issue a warrant to eavesdrop one in the future? It is argued that information showing what is expected to be said is sufficient to limit the boundaries of what later can be admitted into evidence; but does such general information really meet the specific language of the Amendment which says "particularly describing"? Rather than using language in a completely artificial way, I must conclude that the Fourth Amendment simply does not apply to eavesdropping. . . .

Powell v. *Alabama*
287 U.S. 45; 53 S. Ct. 55; 77 L. Ed. 158 (1932)

In 1931, Ozie Powell and six other black defendants were convicted in Scottsboro, Alabama, for the rape of two white girls. Their trial lasted one day, and they were all sentenced to death. They had been arrested, tried, and sentenced in what Justice Sutherland was to call "an atmosphere of tense, hostile, and excited public sentiment." The defendants were too poor to retain counsel, and the trial judge vaguely appointed all members of the Alabama bar to represent them. The Alabama Supreme Court affirmed their conviction, with the chief justice writing a strong dissent on the grounds that the defendents had not been given a fair trial. The United States Supreme Court granted certiorari. The *Powell* case is the first of a series referred to as the Scottsboro cases, so termed because of the location of the trial. *Opinion of the Court: Sutherland, Brandeis, Cardozo, Hughes, Roberts, Stone, Van Devanter. Dissenting opinion: Butler, McReynolds.*

MR. JUSTICE SUTHERLAND delivered the opinion of the Court. . . .

The record shows that immediately upon the return of the indictment defendants were arraigned and pleaded not guilty. Apparently they were not asked whether they had, or were able to employ, counsel, or wished to have counsel appointed; or whether they had friends or relatives who might assist in that regard if communicated with. That it would not have been an idle ceremony to have given the defendants reasonable opportunity to communicate with their families and endeavor to obtain counsel is demonstrated by the fact that, very soon after conviction, able counsel appeared in their behalf. This was pointed out by Chief Justice Anderson in the course of his dissenting opinion. "They were nonresidents," he said, "and had little time or opportunity to get in touch with their families and friends who were scattered throughout two other states, and time has demonstrated that they could or would have been represented by able counsel had a better opportunity been given by a reasonable delay in the trial of the cases, judging from the number and activity of counsel that appeared immediately or shortly after their conviction." . . .

It is hardly necessary to say that, the right to counsel being conceded, a defendant should be afforded a fair opportunity to secure counsel of his own choice. Not only was that not done here, but such designation of counsel as was attempted was either so indefinite or so close upon the trial as to amount to a denial of effective and substantial aid in that regard.

. . . Until the very morning of the trial no lawyer had been named or definitely designated to represent the defendants. Prior to that time, the trial judge had "appointed all the members of the bar" for the limited "purpose of arraigning the defendants." Whether they would represent the defendants thereafter if no counsel appeared in their behalf, was a matter of speculation only, or, as the judge indicated, of mere anticipation on the part of the court. Such a designation, even if made for all purposes, would, in our opinion, have fallen short of meeting, in any proper sense, a requirement for the appointment of counsel. How many lawyers were members of the bar does not appear; but, in the very nature of things, whether many or few, they would not, thus collectively named, have been given that clear appreciation of responsibility or impressed with that individual sense of duty which should and naturally would accompany the appointment of a selected member of the bar, specifically named and assigned. . . .

. . . The Constitution of Alabama provides that in all criminal prosecutions the accused shall enjoy the right to have the assistance of counsel; and a state statute requires the court in a capital case, where the defendant is unable to employ counsel, to appoint counsel for him. The state supreme court held that these provisions had not been infringed, and with that holding we are powerless to interfere. The question, however, which it is our duty, and within our power, to decide, is whether the denial of the assistance of counsel contravenes the due process clause of the Fourteenth Amendment to the federal Constitution. . . .

One test which has been applied to determine whether due process of law has been accorded in given instances is to ascertain what were the settled usages and modes of proceeding under the common and statute law of England before the Declaration of Independence, subject, however, to the qualification that they be shown not to

have been unsuited to the civil and political conditions of our ancestors by having been followed in this country after it became a nation. . . . Plainly, . . . this test, as thus qualified, has not been met in the present case. . . .

It never has been doubted by this court, or any other so far as we know, that notice and hearing are preliminary steps essential to the passing of an enforceable judgment, and that they, together with a legally competent tribunal having jurisdiction of the case, constitute basic elements of the constitutional requirement of due process of law. . . .

What, then, does a hearing include? Historically and in practice, in our country as least, it has always included the right to the aid of counsel when desired and provided by the party asserting the right. The right to be heard would be, in many cases, of little avail if it did not comprehend the right to be heard by counsel. Even the intelligent and educated layman has small and sometimes no skill in the science of law. If charged with crime, he is incapable, generally, of determining for himself whether the indictment is good or bad. He is unfamiliar with the rules of evidence. Left without the aid of counsel he may be put on trial without a proper charge, and convicted upon incompetent evidence, or evidence irrelevant to the issue or otherwise inadmissible. He lacks both the skill and knowledge adequately to prepare his defense, even though he have a perfect one. He requires the guiding hand of counsel at every step in the proceedings against him. Without it, though he be not guilty, he faces the danger of conviction because he does not know how to establish his innocence. If that be true of men of intelligence, how much more true is it of the ignorant and illiterate, or those of feeble intelligence. If in any case, civil or criminal, a state or federal court were arbitrarily to refuse to hear a party by counsel, employed by and appearing for him, it reasonably may not be doubted that such a refusal would be a denial of a hearing, and, therefore, of due process in the constitutional sense. . . .

In the light of the facts . . . —the ignorance and illiteracy of the defendants, their youth, the circumstances of public hostility, the imprisonment and the close surveillance of the defendants by the military forces, the fact that their friends and families were all in other states and communication with them necessarily difficult, and above all that they stood in deadly peril of their lives—we think the failure of the trial court to give them reasonable time and opportunity to secure counsel was a clear denial of due process.

But passing that, and assuming their inability, even if opportunity had been given, to employ counsel, as the trial court evidently did assume, we are of opinion that, under the circumstances just stated, the necessity of counsel was so vital and imperative that the failure of the trial court to make an effective appointment of counsel was likewise a denial of due process within the meaning of the Fourteenth Amendment. Whether this would be so in other criminal prosecutions, or under other circumstances, we need not determine. All that it is necessary now to decide, as we do decide, is that in a capital case, where the defendant is unable to employ counsel, and is incapable adequately of making his own defense

because of ignorance, feeble mindedness, illiteracy, or the like, it is the duty of the court, whether requested or not, to assign counsel for him as a necessary requisite of due process of law; and that duty is not discharged by an assignment at such a time or under such circumstances as to preclude the giving of effective aid in the preparation and trial of the case. To hold otherwise would be to ignore the fundamental postulate, already adverted to, "that there are certain immutable principles of justice which inhere in the very idea of free government which no member of the Union may disregard." . . . In a case such as this, whatever may be the rule in other cases, the right to have counsel appointed, when necessary, is a logical corollary from the constitutional right to be heard by counsel. . . .

The judgments must be reversed and the causes remanded for further proceedings not inconsistent with this opinion.

Gideon v. Wainwright
372 U.S. 335; 83 S. Ct. 792; 9 L. Ed. 2d 799 (1963)

Clarence Gideon was charged in Florida state court with breaking into a pool hall with the intent to commit a misdemeanor—a felony under Florida law. Gideon appeared at his trial without a lawyer and without the funds necessary to retain one, and he requested the trial judge to appoint a lawyer for him. The trial judge refused, citing a Florida statute that permitted the appointment of counsel only in capital cases. Gideon then proceeded to conduct his own defense, and he was found guilty by the jury and sentenced to five years in prison by the judge. Once in prison, Gideon sought release by suing out a writ of habeas corpus against Wainwright, the state director of corrections. The Florida Supreme Court denied relief and Gideon presented an *in forma pauperis* petition to the United States Supreme Court, asserting that the trial judge's refusal to appoint counsel for him was a denial of rights guaranteed by the Sixth and Fourteenth Amendments. The Supreme Court granted certiorari and appointed Abe Fortas, later to serve as an associate justice of the Supreme Court, to represent him in this proceeding. *Opinion of the Court: Black, Brennan, Douglas, Goldberg, Stewart, Warren, White. Concurring opinion: Douglas, Concurring in result: Clark; Harlan.*

MR. JUSTICE BLACK delivered the opinion of the Court. . . .

. . . Since 1942, when *Betts* v. *Brady*, was decided by a divided Court, the problem of a defendant's federal constitutional right to counsel in a state court has been a continuing source of con-

troversy and litigation in both state and federal courts. To give this problem another review here, we granted certiorari. . . . [We] requested both sides to discuss in their briefs and oral arguments the following: "Should this Court's holding in *Betts* v. *Brady* be reconsidered?" . . .

The Sixth Amendment provides, "In all criminal prosecutions, the accused shall enjoy the right . . . to have the Assistance of Counsel for his defence." We have construed this to mean that in federal courts counsel must be provided for defendants unable to employ counsel unless the right is competently and intelligently waived. Betts argued that this right is extended to indigent defendants in state courts by the Fourteenth Amendment. . . . The Court concluded that "appointment of counsel is not a fundamental right, essential to a fair trial.". . . It was for this reason the *Betts* Court refused to accept the contention that the Sixth Amendment's guarantee of counsel for indigent federal defendants was extended to or, in the words of that Court, "made obligatory upon the States by the Fourteenth Amendment.". . .

We think the Court in *Betts* was wrong . . . in concluding that the Sixth Amendment's guarantee of counsel is not one of these fundamental rights. Ten years before *Betts* v. *Brady*, this Court, after full consideration of all the historical data examined in *Betts*, had unequivocally declared that "the right to the aid of counsel is of this fundamental character." *Powell* v. *Alabama* . . . (1932). While the Court at the close of its *Powell* opinion did by its language, as this Court frequently does, limit its holding to the particular facts and circumstances of that case, its conclusions about the fundamental nature of the right to counsel are unmistakable. Several years later, in 1936, the Court reemphasized what it had said about the fundamental nature of the right to counsel in this language:

"We concluded that certain fundamental rights, safeguarded by the first eight amendments against federal action, were also safeguarded against state action by the due process of law clause of the Fourteenth Amendment, and among them the fundamental right of the accused to the aid of counsel in a criminal prosecution." *Grosjean* v. *American Press Co.* (1936).

And again in 1938 this Court said:

"[The assistance of counsel] is one of the safeguards of the Sixth Amendment deemed necessary to insure fundamental human rights of life and liberty." . . . *Johnson* v. *Zerbst* . . . (1938). . . .

. . . In deciding as it did—that "appointment of counsel is not a fundamental right, essential to a fair trial"—the Court in *Betts* v. *Brady* made an abrupt break with its own well-considered precedents. In returning to these old precedents, sounder we believe than the new, we but restore constitutional principles established to achieve a fair system of justice. Not only these precedents but also reason and reflection require us to recognize that in our adversary system of criminal justice, any person haled into court, who is too poor to hire a lawyer, cannot be assured a fair trial unless counsel is provided for him. This seems to us to be an obvious truth. Governments, both state and federal, quite properly spend vast sums of money to establish machinery to try defendants accused of crime. Lawyers to prosecute are everywhere deemed essential to protect the public's interest in an orderly society. Similarly, there are few defendants charged with crime, few indeed, who fail to hire the best lawyers they can get to prepare and present their defenses. That government hires lawyers to prosecute and defendants who have the money hire lawyers to defend are the strongest indications of the widespread belief that lawyers in criminal courts are necessities, not luxuries. The right of one charged with crime to counsel may not be deemed fundamental and essential to fair trials in some countries, but it is in ours. From the very beginning, our state and national constitutions and laws have laid great emphasis on procedural and substantive safeguards designed to assure fair trials before impartial tribunals in which every defendant stands equal before the law. This noble ideal cannot be realized if the poor man charged with crime has to face his accusers without a lawyer to assist him. . . .

The judgment is reversed and the cause is remanded to the Supreme Court of Florida for further action not inconsistent with this opinion.

Miranda v. *Arizona*
384 U.S. 436; 86 S. Ct. 1602; L. Ed. 2d 694 (1966)

Miranda consolidates for decision four cases, all of which raised the issue of the admissibility into evidence of statements obtained from defen-

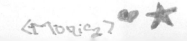

dants during pretrial custodial police interrogation. In each of these cases, the defendants were convicted on the basis of confessions made after periods of police questioning during which they were not informed of their rights to counsel and to remain silent. The crimes for which they were convicted included murder, kidnapping, rape, and robbery. *Opinion of the Court: Warren, Black, Brennan, Douglas, Fortas. Dissenting opinions: Clark; Harlan, Stewart, White; White, Harlan, Stewart.*

Mr. Chief Justice Warren delivered the opinion of the Court.

The cases before us raise questions which go to the roots of our concepts of American criminal jurisprudence: the restraints society must observe consistent with the Federal Constitution in prosecuting individuals for crime. More specifically, we deal with the admissibility of statements obtained from an individual who is subjected to custodial police interrogation and the necessity for procedures which assure that the individual is accorded his privilege under the Fifth Amendment to the Constitution not to be compelled to incriminate himself. . . .

Our holding will be spelled out with some specificity in the pages which follow but briefly stated it is this: the prosecution may not use statements, whether exculpatory or inculpatory, stemming from custodial interrogation of the defendant unless it demonstrates the use of procedural safeguards effective to secure the privilege against self-incrimination. By custodial interrogation, we mean questioning initiated by law enforcement officers after a person has been taken into custody or otherwise deprived of his freedom of action in any significant way. As for the procedural safeguards to be employed, unless other fully effective means are devised to inform accused persons of their right of silence and to assure a continuous opportunity to exercise it, the following measures are required. Prior to any questioning, the person must be warned that he has a right to remain silent, that any statement he does make may be used as evidence against him, and that he has a right to the presence of an attorney, either retained or appointed. The defendant may waive effectuation of these rights, provided the waiver is made voluntarily, knowingly and intelligently. If, however, he indicates in any manner and at any stage of the process that he wishes to consult with an attorney before speaking there can be no questioning. Like-

wise, if the individual is alone and indicates in any manner that he does not wish to be interrogated, the police may not question him. The mere fact that he may have answered some questions or volunteered some statements on his own does not deprive him of the right to refrain from answering any further inquiries until he has consulted with an attorney and thereafter consents to be questioned.

The constitutional issue we decide in each of these cases is the admissibility of statements obtained from a defendant questioned while in custody or otherwise deprived of his freedom of action in any significant way. In each, the defendant was questioned by police officers, detectives, or a prosecuting attorney in a room in which he was cut off from the outside world. In none of these cases was the defendant given a full and effective warning of his rights at the outset of the interrogation process. In all the cases, the questioning elicited oral admissions, and in three of them, signed statements as well which were admitted at their trials. They all thus share salient features—incommunicado interrogation of individuals in a police-dominated atmosphere, resulting in self-incriminating statements without full warnings of constitutional rights. . . .

An understanding of the nature and setting of this in-custody interrogation is essential to our decisions today. The difficulty in depicting what transpires at such interrogations stems from the fact that in this country they have largely taken place incommunicado. . . .

. . . Interrogation still takes place in privacy. Privacy results in secrecy and this in turn results in a gap in our knowledge as to what in fact goes on in the interrogation rooms. A valuable source of information about present police practices, however, may be found in various police manuals and texts, which document procedures employed with success in the past, and which recommend various other effective tactics. These texts are used by law enforcement agencies themselves as guides. It should be noted that these texts professedly present the most enlightened and effective means presently used to obtain statements through custodial interrogation. By considering these texts and other data, it is possible to describe procedures observed and noted around the country. . . .

From these representative samples of interrogation techniques, the setting prescribed by the manuals and observed in practice becomes clear. In essence, it is this: To be alone with the subject is essential to prevent distraction and to deprive him of any outside support. The aura of confidence in his guilt undermines his will to resist. He merely confirms the preconceived story the police seek to have him describe. Patience and persistence, at times relentless questioning, are employed. To obtain a confession, the interrogator must "patiently maneuver himself or his quarry into a position from which the desired objective may be attained." When normal procedures fail to produce the needed result, the police may resort to deceptive stratagems such as giving false legal advice. It is important to keep the subject off balance, for example, by trading on his insecurity about himself or his surroundings. The police then persuade, trick or cajole him out of exercising his constitutional rights. . . .

In the cases before us today, given this background, we concern ourselves primarily with this interrogation atmosphere and the evils it can bring. In No. 759, *Miranda* v. *Arizona*, the police arrested the defendant and took him to a special interrogation room where they secured a confession. In No. 760, *Vignera* v. *New York*, the defendant made oral admissions to the police after interrogation in the afternoon, and then signed an inculpatory statement upon being questioned by an assistant district attorney later the same evening. In No. 761, *Westover* v. *United States*, the defendant was handed over to the Federal Bureau of Investigation by local authorities after they had detained and interrogated him for a lengthy period, both at night and the following morning. After some two hours of questioning, the federal officers had obtained signed statements from the defendant. Lastly, in No. 584, *California* v. *Stewart*, the local police held the defendant five days in the station and interrogated him on nine separate occasions before they secured his inculpatory statement.

In these cases, we might not find the defendants' statements to have been involuntary in traditional terms. Our concern for adequate safeguards to protect precious Fifth Amendment rights is, of course, not lessened in the slightest. In each of the cases, the defendant was thrust into an unfamiliar atmosphere and run through menacing police interrogation procedures. The potentiality for compulsion is forcefully apparent, for example, in *Miranda*, where the indigent Mexican defendant was a seriously disturbed individual with pronounced sexual fantasies, and in *Stewart*, in which the defendant was an indigent Los Angeles Negro who had dropped out of school in the sixth grade. To be sure, the records do not evince overt physical coercion or patent psychological ploys. The fact remains that in none of these cases did the officers undertake to afford appropriate safeguards at the outset of the interrogation to insure that the statements were truly the product of free choice.

It is obvious that such an interrogation environment is created for no purpose other than to subjugate the individual to the will of his examiner. This atmosphere carries its own badge of intimidation. To be sure, this is not physical intimidation, but it is equally destructive of human dignity. The current practice of incommunicado interrogation is at odds with one of our Nation's most cherished principles—that the individual may not be compelled to incriminate himself. Unless adequate protective devices are employed to dispel the compulsion inherent in custodial surroundings, no statement obtained from the defendant can truly be the product of his free choice. . . .

From the foregoing, we can readily perceive an intimate connection between the privilege against self-incrimination and police custodial questioning. . . . We have recently noted that the privilege against self-incrimination—the essential mainstay of our adversary system—is founded on a complex of values. . . . All these policies point to one overriding thought: the constitutional foundation underlying the privilege is the respect a government—state or federal—must accord to the dignity and integrity of its citizens. To maintain a "fair state-individual balance," to require the government "to shoulder the entire load," . . . to respect the inviolability of human personality, our accusatory system of criminal justice demands that the government seeking to punish an individual produce the evidence against him by its own independent labors, rather than by the cruel, simple expedient of compelling it from his own mouth. . . . In sum, the privilege is fulfilled only when the person is guaranteed the right "to remain silent unless he chooses to speak in the unfettered exercise of his own will."

The question in these cases is whether the privilege is fully applicable during a period of custodial interrogation. In this Court, the privilege has consistently been accorded a liberal construction. . . . We are satisfied that all the principles embodied in the privilege apply to informal compulsion exerted by law-enforcement officers during in-custody questioning. An individual swept from familiar surroundings into police custody, surrounded by antagonistic forces, and subjected to the techniques of persuasion described above cannot be otherwise than under compulsion to speak. As a practical matter, the compulsion to speak in the isolated setting of the police station may well be greater than in courts or other official investigations, where there are often impartial observers to guard against intimidation or trickery. . . .

Today, then, there can be no doubt that the Fifth Amendment privilege is available outside of criminal court proceedings and serves to protect persons in all settings in which their freedom of action is curtailed in any significant way from being compelled to incriminate themselves. We have concluded that without proper safeguards the process of in-custody interrogation of persons suspected or accused of crime contains inherently compelling pressures which work to undermine the individual's will to resist and to compel him to speak where he would not otherwise do so freely. In order to combat these pressures and to permit a full opportunity to exercise the privilege against self-incrimination, the accused must be adequately and effectively apprised of his rights and the exercise of those rights must be fully honored.

It is impossible for us to foresee the potential alternatives for protecting the privilege which might be devised by Congress or the States in the exercise of their creative rule-making capacities. Therefore we cannot say that the Constitution necessarily requires adherence to any particular solution for the inherent compulsions of the interrogation process as it is presently conducted.

Our decision in no way creates a constitutional straitjacket which will handicap sound efforts at reform, nor is it intended to have this effect. We encourage Congress and the States to continue their laudable search for increasingly effective ways of protecting the rights of the individual while promoting efficient enforcement of our criminal laws. However, unless we are shown other procedures which are at least as effective in apprising accused persons of their right of silence and in assuring a continuous opportunity to exercise it, the following safeguards must be observed.

At the outset, if a person in custody is to be subjected to interrogation, he must first be informed in clear and unequivocal terms that he has the right to remain silent. For those unaware of the privilege, the warning is needed simply to make them aware of it—the threshold requirement for an intelligent decision as to its exercise. More important, such a warning is an absolute prerequisite in overcoming the inherent pressures of the interrogation atmosphere. It is not just the subnormal or woefully ignorant who succumb to an interrogator's imprecations, whether implied or expressly stated, that the interrogation will continue until a confession is obtained or that silence in the face of accusation is itself damning and will bode ill when presented to a jury. Further, the warning will show the individual that his interrogators are prepared to recognize his privilege should he choose to exercise it.

The Fifth Amendment privilege is so fundamental to our system of constitutional rule and the expedient of giving an adequate warning as to the availability of the privilege so simple, we will not pause to inquire in individual cases whether the defendant was aware of his rights without a warning being given. Assessments of the knowledge the defendant possessed, based on information as to his age, education, intelligence, or prior contact with authorities, can never be more than speculation; a warning is a clearcut fact. More important, whatever the background of the person interrogated, a warning at the time of the interrogation is indispensable to overcome its pressures and to insure that the individual knows he is free to exercise the privilege at that point in time.

The warning of the right to remain silent must be accompanied by the explanation that anything said can and will be used against the individual in court. This warning is needed in order to make him aware not only of the privilege, but also of the consequences of forgoing it. It is only through an awareness of these consequences that there can be any assurance of real understanding and intelligent exercise of the privilege. Moreover, this warning may serve to make the individual more acutely aware that he is faced with a phase of the adversary system—that he is not in the presence of persons acting solely in his interest.

The circumstances surrounding in-custody interrogation can operate very quickly to overbear the will of one merely made aware of his privilege by his interrogators. Therefore, the right to have counsel present at the interrogation is indispensable to the protection of the Fifth Amendment privilege under the system we delineate today. Our aim is to assure that the individual's right to choose between silence and speech remains unfettered throughout the interrogation process. A once-stated warning, delivered by those who will conduct the interrogation, cannot itself suffice to that end among those who most require knowledge of their rights. A mere warning given by the interrogators is not alone sufficient to accomplish that end. . . . Thus, the need for counsel to protect the Fifth Amendment privilege comprehends not merely a right to consult with counsel prior to questioning, but also to have counsel present during any questioning if the defendant so desires. . . .

In order fully to apprise a person interrogated of the extent of his rights under this system then, it is necessary to warn him not only that he has the right to consult with an attorney, but also that if he is indigent a lawyer will be appointed to represent him. Without this additional warning, the admonition of the right to consult with counsel would often be understood as meaning only that he can consult with a lawyer if he has one or has the funds to obtain one. The warning of a right to counsel would be hollow if not couched in terms that would convey to the indigent—the person most often subjected to interrogation—the knowledge that he too has a right to have counsel present. As with the warnings of the right to remain silent and of the general right to counsel, only by effective and express explanation to the indigent of this right can there be as-

surance that he was truly in a position to exercise it. . . .

If the interrogation continues without the presence of an attorney and a statement is taken, a heavy burden rests on the government to demonstrate that the defendant knowingly and intelligently waived his privilege against self-incrimination and his right to retained or appointed counsel. This Court has always set high standards of proof for the waiver of constitutional rights, and we re-assert these standards as applied to in-custody interrogation. Since the State is responsible for establishing the isolated circumstances under which the interrogation takes place and has the only means of making available corroborated evidence of warnings given during incommunicado interrogation, the burden is rightly on its shoulders.

Whatever the testimony of the authorities as to waiver of rights by an accused, the fact of lengthy interrogation or incommunicado incarceration before a statement is made is strong evidence that the accused did not validly waive his rights. . . .

The warnings required and the waiver necessary in accordance with our opinion today are, in the absence of a fully effective equivalent, prerequisites to the admissibility of any statement made by a defendant. . . .

Our decision is not intended to hamper the traditional function of police officers in investigating crime. . . . When an individual is in custody on probable cause, the police may, of course, seek out evidence in the field to be used at trial against him. Such investigation may include inquiry of persons not under restraint. General on-the-scene questioning as to facts surrounding a crime or other general questioning of citizens in the fact-finding process is not affected by our holding. It is an act of responsible citizenship for individuals to give whatever information they may have to aid in law enforcement. In such situations the compelling atmosphere inherent in the process of in-custody interrogation is not necessarily present. . . .

Over the years the Federal Bureau of Investigation has compiled an exemplary record of effective law enforcement while advising any suspect or arrested person, at the outset of an interview, that he is not required to make a statement, that any statement may be used against him in court, that the individual may obtain the services of an attorney of his own choice and, more recently, that he has a right to free counsel if he is unable to pay. . . .

The practice of the FBI can readily be emulated by state and local enforcement agencies. The argument that the FBI deals with different crimes than are dealt with by state authorities does not mitigate the significance of the FBI experience.

The experience in some other countries also suggests that the danger to law enforcement in curbs on interrogation is overplayed. . . .

Because of the nature of the problem and because of its recurrent significance in numerous cases, we have to this point discussed the relationship of the Fifth Amendment privilege to police interrogation without specific concentration on the facts of the cases before us. We turn now to these facts to consider the application to these cases of the constitutional principles discussed above. In each instance, we have concluded that statements were obtained from the defendant under circumstances that did not meet constitutional standards for protection of privilege. . . .

MR. JUSTICE WHITE, with whom MR. JUSTICE HARLAN and MR. JUSTICE STEWART join, dissenting. . . .

. . . The Court's duty to assess the consequences of its action is not satisfied by the utterance of the truth that a value of our system of criminal justice is "to respect the inviolability of the human personality" and to require government to produce the evidence against the accused by its own independent labors. . . . More than the human dignity of the accused is involved; the human personality of others in the society must also be preserved. Thus the values reflected by the privilege are not the sole desideratum; society's interest in the general security is of equal weight.

The obvious underpinning of the Court's decision is a deep-seated distrust of all confessions. As the Court declares that the accused may not be interrogated without counsel present, absent a waiver of the right to counsel, and as the Court all but admonishes the lawyer to advise the accused to remain silent, the result adds up to a judicial judgment that evidence from the accused should not be used against him in any way, whether compelled or not. This is the not so subtle overtone of the opinion—that it is inherently

wrong for the police to gather evidence from the accused himself. And this is precisely the nub of this dissent. I see nothing wrong or immoral, and certainly nothing unconstitutional, in the police's asking a suspect whom they have reasonable cause to arrest whether or not he killed his wife or in confronting him with the evidence on which the arrest was based, at least where he has been plainly advised that he may remain completely silent. . . . Until today, "the admissions or confessions of the prisoner, when voluntarily and freely made, have always ranked high in the scale of incriminating evidence." . . . Particularly when corroborated, as where the police have confirmed the accused's disclosure of the hiding place of implements or fruits of the crime, such confessions have the highest reliability and significantly contribute to the certitude with which we may believe the accused is guilty. Moreover, it is by no means certain that the process of confessing is injurious to the accused. To the contrary it may provide psychological relief and enhance the prospects for rehabilitation. . . .

The most basic function of any government is to provide for the security of the individual and of his property. . . . These ends of society are served by the criminal laws which for the most part are aimed at the prevention of crime. Without the reasonably effective performance of the task of preventing private violence and retaliation, it is idle to talk about human dignity and civilized values. . . . There is, in my view, every reason to believe that a good many criminal defendants who otherwise would have been convicted on what this Court has previously thought to be the most satisfactory kind of evidence will now, under this new version of the Fifth Amendment, either not be tried at all or will be acquitted if the State's evidence, minus the confession, is put to the test of litigation.

I have no desire whatsoever to share the responsibility for any such impact on the present criminal process.

In some unknown number of cases the Court's rule will return a killer, a rapist or other criminal to the streets and to the environment which produced him, to repeat his crime whenever it pleases him. As a consequence, there will not be a gain, but a loss, in human dignity. The real concern is not the unfortunate consequences of this new decision on the criminal law as an abstract, disembodied series of authoritative pro-scriptions, but the impact on those who rely on the public authority for protection and who without it can only engage in violent self-help with guns, knives and the help of their neighbors similarly inclined. There is, of course, a saving factor: the next victims are uncertain, unnamed and unrepresented in this case. . . .

Much of the trouble with the Court's new rule is that it will operate indiscriminately in all criminal cases, regardless of the severity of the crime or the circumstances involved. It applies to every defendant, whether the professional criminal or one committing a crime of momentary passion who is not part and parcel of organized crime. It will slow down the investigation and the apprehension of confederates in those cases where time is of the essence, such as kidnapping, . . . and some of those involving organized crime. In the latter context the lawyer who arrives may also be the lawyer for the defendant's colleagues and can be relied upon to insure that no breach of the organization's security takes place even though the accused may feel that the best thing he can do is to cooperate.

At the same time, the Court's *per se* approach may not be justified on the ground that it provides a "bright line" permitting the authorities to judge in advance whether interrogation may safely be pursued without jeopardizing the admissibility of any information obtained as a consequence. Nor can it be claimed that judicial time and effort, assuming that is a relevant consideration, will be conserved because of the case of application of the new rule. Today's decision leaves open such questions as whether the accused was in custody, whether his statements were spontaneous or the product of interrogation, whether the accused has effectively waived his rights, and whether nontestimonial evidence introduced at trial is the fruit of statements made during a prohibited interrogation, all of which are certain to prove productive of uncertainty during investigation and litigation during prosecution. For all these reasons, if further restrictions on police interrogation are desirable at this time, a more flexible approach makes much more sense than the Court's constitutional straitjacket which forecloses more discriminating treatment by legislative or rule-making pronouncements.

MR. JUSTICE HARLAN with whom MR. JUSTICE STEWART and MR. JUSTICE WHITE join, dissenting.

I believe the decision of the Court represents poor constitutional law and entails harmful consequences for the country at large. How serious these consequences may prove to be only time can tell. But the basic flaws in the Court's justification seem to me readily apparent now once all sides of the problem are considered. . . .

While the fine points of this scheme are far less clear than the Court admits, the tenor is quite apparent. The new rules are not designed to guard against police brutality or other unmistakably banned forms of coercion. Those who use third-degree tactics and deny them in court are equally able and destined to lie as skillfully about warnings and waivers. Rather, the thrust of the new rules is to negate all pressures, to reinforce the nervous or ignorant suspect, and ultimately to discourage any confession at all. The aim in short is toward "voluntariness" in a utopian sense, or to view it from a different angle, voluntariness with a vengeance.

Without at all subscribing to the generally black picture of police conduct painted by the Court, I think it must be frankly recognized at the outset that police questioning allowable under due process precedents may inherently entail some pressure on the suspect and may seek advantage in his ignorance or weaknesses. The atmosphere and questioning techniques, proper and fair though they be, can in themselves exert a tug on the suspect to confess, and in this light "[t]o speak of any confessions of crime made after arrest as being 'voluntary' or 'uncoerced' is somewhat inaccurate, although traditional. A confession is wholly and incontestably voluntary only if a guilty person gives himself up to the law and becomes his own accuser." . . . Until today, the role of the Constitution has been only to sift out *undue* pressure, not to assure spontaneous confessions.

The Court's new rules aim to offset these minor pressures and disadvantages intrinsic to any kind of police interrogation. The rules do not serve due process interests in preventing blatant coercion since, as I noted earlier, they do nothing to contain the policeman who is prepared to lie from the start. The rules work for reliability in confessions almost only in the Pickwickian sense that they can prevent some from being given at all. . . .

How much harm this decision will inflict on law enforcement cannot fairly be predicted with accuracy. Evidence on the role of confessions is notoriously incomplete . . . and little is added by the Court's reference to the FBI experience and the resources believed wasted in interrogation. . . . We do know that some crimes cannot be solved without confessions, that ample expert testimony attests to their importance in crime control, and that the Court is taking a real risk with society's welfare in imposing its new regime on the country. The social costs of crime are too great to call the new rules anything but a hazardous experimentation. . . .

The Court in closing its general discussion invokes the practice in federal and foreign jurisdictions as lending weight to its new curbs on confessions for all the States. A brief résumé will suffice to show that none of these jurisdictions

has struck so one-sided a balance as the Court does today. Heaviest reliance is placed on the FBI practice. Differing circumstances may make this comparison quite untrustworthy, but in any event the FBI falls sensibly short of the Court's formalistic rules. For example, there is no indication that FBI agents must obtain an affirmative "waiver" before they pursue their questioning. Nor is it clear that one invoking his right to silence may not be prevailed upon to change his mind. And the warning as to appointed counsel apparently indicates only that one will be assigned by the judge when the suspect appears before him; the thrust of the Court's rules is to induce the suspect to obtain appointed counsel before continuing the interview. . . .

In conclusion: Nothing in the letter or the spirit of the Constitution or in the precedents squares with the heavy-handed and one-sided action that is so precipitously taken by the court in the name of fulfilling its constitutional responsibilities. . . .

Nix v. Williams

inevitable discovery exception

467 U.S. 431, 104 S. Ct. 2501, 81 L. Ed. 2d (1984)

The facts of this criminal case and its lengthy and intricate appellate history are summarized in the opinion below. *Opinion of the Court: Burger, Blackmun, O'Connor, Powell, Rehnquist, White. Concurring opinion: White. Concurring in the judgment: Stevens. Dissenting opinion: Brennan, Marshall.*

CHIEF JUSTICE BURGER delivered the opinion of the Court.

We granted certiorari to consider whether, at respondent Williams' second murder trial in state court, evidence pertaining to the discovery and condition of the victim's body was properly admitted on the ground that it would ultimately or inevitably have been discovered even if no violation of any constitutional or statutory provision had taken place.

On December 24, 1968, 10-year-old Pamela Powers disappeared from a YMCA building in Des Moines, Iowa, where she had accompanied her parents to watch an athletic contest. Shortly after she disappeared, Williams was seen leaving the YMCA carrying a large bundle wrapped in a blanket; a 14-year-old boy who had helped Williams

open his car door reported that he had seen "two legs in it and they were skinny and white."

Williams' car was found the next day 160 miles east of Des Moines in Davenport, Iowa. Later several items of clothing belonging to the child, some of Williams' clothing, and an army blanket like the one used to wrap the bundle that Williams carried out of the YMCA were found at a rest stop on Interstate 80 near Grinnell, between Des Moines and Davenport. A warrant was issued for Williams' arrest.

Police surmised that Williams had left Pamela Powers or her body somewhere between Des Moines and the Grinnell rest stop where some of the young girl's clothing had been found. On December 26, the Iowa Bureau of Criminal Investigation initiated a large-scale search. Two hundred volunteers divided into teams began the search 21 miles east of Grinnell, covering an area several miles to the north and south of Interstate 80. They moved westward from Poweshiek County, in which Grinnell was located, into Jasper County. Scarchers were instructed to check all roads, abandoned farm buildings, ditches, "culverts, and any other place in which the body of a small child could be hidden.

Meanwhile, Williams surrendered to local police in Davenport, where he was promptly arraigned. Williams contacted a Des Moines attorney who arranged for an attorney in Davenport to meet Williams at the Davenport police station. Des Moines police informed counsel they would pick Williams up in Davenport and return him to Des Moines without questioning him. Two Des Moines detectives then drove to Davenport, took Williams into custody, and proceeded to drive him back to Des Moines.

During the return trip, one of the policemen, Detective Leaming, began a conversation with Williams, saying:

"I want to give you something to think about while we're traveling down the road. . .They are predicting several inches of snow for tonight, and I feel that you yourself are the only person that knows where this little girl's body is . . . and if you get a snow on top of it you yourself may be unable to find it. And since we will be going right past the area [where the body is] on the way into Des Moines, I feel that we could stop and locate the body, that the parents of this little girl should be entitled to a Christian burial for the little girl who was snatched away from them on Christmas [E]ve and murdered. . . . [A]fter a snow storm [we may not be] able to find it at all."

Leaming told Williams he knew the body was in the area of Mitchellville—a town they would be passing on the way to Des Moines. He concluded the conversation by saying, "I do not want you to answer me. . . . Just think about it. . . ."

Later, as the police car approached Grinnell, Williams asked Leaming whether the police had found the young girl's shoes. After Leaming replied that he was unsure, Williams directed the police to a point near a service station where he said he had left the shoes; they were not found. As they continued to drive to Des Moines, Williams asked whether the blanket had been found and then directed the officers to a rest area

in Grinnell where he said he had disposed of the blanket; they did not find the blanket. At this point Leaming and his party were joined by the officers in charge of the search. As they approached Mitchellville, Williams, without any further conversation, agreed to direct the officers to the child's body.

The officers directing the search had called off the search at 3 P.M., when they left the Grinnell Police Department to join Leaming at the rest area. At that time, one search team near the Jasper County-Polk County line was only two and one-half miles from where Williams soon guided Leaming and his party to the body. The child's body was found next to a culvert in a ditch beside a gravel road in Polk County, about two miles south of Interstate 80, and essentially within the area to be searched.

First Trial

In February 1969 Williams was indicted for first-degree murder. Before trial in the Iowa court, his counsel moved to suppress evidence of the body and all related evidence including the condition of the body as shown by the autopsy. The ground for the motion was that such evidence was the "fruit" or product of Williams' statements made during the automobile ride from Davenport to Des Moines and prompted by Leaming's statements. The motion to suppress was denied.

The jury found Williams guilty of first-degree murder; the judgment of conviction was affirmed by the Iowa Supreme Court. . . . Williams then sought release on habeas corpus in the United States District Court for the Southern District of Iowa. That court concluded that the evidence in question had been wrongly admitted at Williams' trial; . . . a divided panel of the Court of Appeals for the Eighth Circuit agreed. . . .

We granted certiorari . . . and a divided Court affirmed, holding that Detective Leaming had obtained incriminating statements from Williams by what was viewed as interrogation in violation of his right to counsel. *Brewer* v. *Williams*. . . . (1977). . . .

Second Trial

At Williams' second trial in 1977 in the Iowa court, the prosecution did not offer Williams' statements into evidence, nor did it seek to show that Williams had directed the police to the child's body. However, evidence of the condition of her body as it was found, articles and photographs of her clothing, and the results of post mortem medical and chemical tests on the body were admitted. The trial court concluded that the State had proved by a preponderance of the evidence that, if the search had not been suspended and Williams had not led the police to the victim, her body would have been discovered *"within a short time"* in essentially the same condition as it was actually found. The trial court also ruled that if the police had not located the body, "the search would clearly have been taken up again where it left off, given the extreme circumstances of this case and the body would [have] been found *in short order."* . . .

In finding that the body would have been discovered in essentially the same condition as it was actually found, the court noted that freezing temperatures had prevailed and tissue deterioration would have been suspended. . . . The challenged evidence was admitted and the jury again found Williams guilty of first-degree murder; he was sentenced to life in prison.

On appeal, the Supreme Court of Iowa again affirmed . . . . That court held that there was in fact a "hypothetical independent source" exception to the Exclusionary Rule.

. . . The Iowa court then reviewed the evidence *de novo* and concluded that the State had shown by a preponderance of the evidence that, even if Williams had not guided police to the child's body, it would inevitably have been found by lawful activity of the search party before its condition had materially changed.

In 1980 Williams renewed his attack on the state-court conviction by seeking a writ of habeas corpus in the United States District Court for the Southern District of Iowa. The District Court conducted its own independent review of the evidence and concluded, as had the state courts, that the body would inevitably have been found by the searchers in essentially the same condition it was in when Williams led police to its discovery. The District Court denied Williams' petition. . . .

The Court of Appeals for the Eighth Circuit reversed. . . .

We granted the State's petition for certiorari, . . . and we reverse.

The Iowa Supreme Court correctly stated that the "vast majority" of all courts, both state and federal, recognize an inevitable discovery exception to the Exclusionary Rule. We are now urged to adopt and apply the so-called ultimate or inevitable discovery exception to the Exclusionary Rule.

. . . The Exclusionary Rule applies not only to the illegally obtained evidence itself, but also to other incriminating evidence derived from the primary evidence. . . .

The core rationale consistently advanced by this Court for extending the Exclusionary Rule to evidence that is the fruit of unlawful police conduct has been that this admittedly drastic and socially costly course is needed to deter police from violations of constitutional and statutory protections. This Court has accepted the argument that the way to ensure such protections is to exclude evidence seized as a result of such violations notwithstanding the high social cost of letting persons obviously guilty go unpunished for their crimes. On this rationale, the prosecution is not to be put in a better position than it would have been in if no illegality had transpired.

By contrast, the derivative evidence analysis ensures that the prosecution is not put in a *worse* position simply because of some earlier police error or misconduct. The independent source doctrine allows admission of evidence that has been discovered by means wholly independent of any constitutional violation. That doctrine, although closely related to the inevitable discovery doctrine, does not apply here; Williams' statements to Leaming indeed led police to the child's body, but that is not the whole story. The independent source doctrine teaches us that the interest of society in deterring unlawful police conduct and the public interest in having juries receive all probative evidence of a crime are properly balanced by putting the police in the same, not a *worse*, position than they would have been in if no police error or misconduct had occurred. . . . When the challenged evidence has an independent source, exclusion of such evidence would put the police in a worse position than they would have been in absent any error or violation. There is a functional similarity between these two doctrines in that exclusion of evidence that would inevitably have been discovered would also put the government in a worse position, because the police would have obtained that evidence if no misconduct had taken place. Thus, while the independent source exception would not justify admission of evidence in this case, its rationale is wholly consistent with and justifies our adoption of the ultimate or inevitable discovery exception to the Exclusionary Rule.

It is clear that the cases implementing the Exclusionary Rule "begin with the premise that the challenged evidence is *in some sense* the product of illegal governmental activity." . . . Of course, this does not end the inquiry. If the prosecution can establish by a preponderance of the evidence that the information ultimately or inevitably would have been discovered by lawful means—here the volunteers' search—then the deterrence rationale has so little basis that the evidence should be received. Anything less would reject logic, experience, and common sense.

Williams contends that because he did not waive his right to the assistance of counsel, the Court may not balance competing values in deciding whether the challenged evidence was properly admitted. He argues that, unlike the Exclusionary Rule in the Fourth Amendment context, the essential purpose of which is to deter police misconduct, the Sixth Amendment Exclusionary Rule is designed to protect the right to a fair trial and the integrity of the factfinding process. Williams contends that, when those interests are at stake, the societal costs of excluding evidence obtained from responses presumed involuntary are irrelevant in determining whether such evidence should be excluded. We disagree.

Exclusion of physical evidence that would inevitably have been discovered adds nothing to either the integrity or fairness of a criminal trial. The Sixth Amendment right to counsel protects against unfairness by preserving the adversary process in which the reliability of proffered evidence may be tested in cross-examination. . . . Here, however, Detective Leaming's conduct did nothing to impugn the reliability of the evidence in question—the body of the child and its condition as it was found, articles of clothing found on the body, and the autopsy. No one would seriously contend that the presence of counsel in the police car when Leaming appealed to Williams' decent human instincts would have had any

bearing on the reliability of the body as evidence. Suppression, in these circumstances, would do nothing whatever to promote the integrity of the trial process, but would inflict a wholly unacceptable burden on the administration of criminal justice.

Nor would suppression ensure fairness on the theory that it tends to safeguard the adversary system of justice. To assure the fairness of trial proceedings, this Court has held that assistance of counsel must be available at pretrial confrontations where "the subsequent trial [cannot] cure a[n otherwise] one-sided confrontation between prosecuting authorities and the uncounseled defendant." . . . Fairness can be assured by placing the State and the accused in the same positions they would have been in had the impermissible conduct not taken place. However, if the government can prove that the evidence would have been obtained inevitably and, therefore, would have been admitted regardless of any overreaching by the police, there is no rational basis to keep that evidence from the jury in order to ensure the fairness of the trial proceedings. In that situation, the State has gained no advantage at trial and the defendant has suffered no prejudice. Indeed, suppression of the evidence would operate to undermine the adversary system by putting the State in a *worse* position than it would have occupied without any police misconduct. Williams' argument that inevitable discovery constitutes impermissible balancing of values is without merit.

. . . Three courts independently reviewing the evidence have found that the body of the child inevitably would have been found by the searchers. Williams challenges these findings, asserting that the record contains only the "*post hoc* rationalization" that the search efforts would have proceeded two and one-half miles into Polk County where Williams had led police to the body.

When that challenge was made at the suppression hearing preceding Williams' second trial, the prosecution offered the testimony of Agent Ruxlow of the Iowa Bureau of Criminal Investigation. Ruxlow had organized and directed some 200 volunteers who were searching for the child's body. . . . The searchers were instructed "to check all the roads, the ditches, any culverts. . . . If they came upon any abandoned farm build-

consumer research company, "Midlands Data Research," seeking a response from those who "believe in the joys of sex and the complete awareness of those lusty and youthful lads and lasses of the neophite [sic] age." The letter never explained whether "neophite" referred to minors or young adults. Petitioner responded: "Please feel free to send me more information, I am interested in teenage sexuality. Please keep my name confidential."

Petitioner then heard from another Government creation, "Heartland Institute for a New Tomorrow" (HINT), which proclaimed that it was "an organization founded to protect and promote sexual freedom and freedom of choice. We believe that arbitrarily imposed legislative sanctions restricting *your* sexual freedom should be rescinded through the legislative process."

By March 1987, 34 months had passed since the Government obtained petitioner's name from the mailing list of the California bookstore, and 26 months had passed since the Postal Service had commenced its mailings to petitioner. Although petitioner had responded to surveys and letters, the Government had no evidence that petitioner had ever intentionally possessed or been exposed to child pornography. The Postal Service had not checked petitioner's mail to determine whether he was receiving questionable mailings from persons—other than the Government—involved in the child pornography industry.

At this point, a second Government agency, the Customs Service, included petitioner in its own child pornography sting, "Operation Borderline," after receiving his name on lists submitted by the Postal Service. Using the name of a fictitious Canadian company called "Produit Outaouais," the Customs Service mailed petitioner a brochure advertising photographs of young boys engaged in sex. Petitioner placed an order that was never filled.

The Postal Service also continued its efforts in the Jacobson case, writing to petitioner as the "Far Eastern Trading Company Ltd." The letter began:

> As many of you know, much hysterical nonsense has appeared in the American media concerning "pornography" and what must be done to stop it from coming across your borders. This brief letter does not allow us to give much comments; however, why is your

government spending millions of dollars to exercise international censorship while tons of drugs, which makes yours the world's most crime ridden country are passed through easily.

The letter went on to say:

> [W]e have devised a method of getting these to you without prying eyes of U.S. Customs seizing your mail. . . . After consultations with American solicitors, we have been advised that once we have posted our material through your system, it cannot be opened for any inspection without authorization of a judge.

The letter invited petitioner to send for more information. It also asked petitioner to sign an affirmation that he was "not a law enforcement officer or agent of the U.S. Government acting in an undercover capacity for the purpose of entrapping Far Eastern Trading Company, its agents or customers." Petitioner responded. A catalogue was sent, and petitioner ordered *Boys Who Love Boys*, a pornographic magazine depicting young boys engaged in various sexual activities. Petitioner was arrested after a controlled delivery of a photocopy of the magazine.

When petitioner was asked at trial why he placed such an order, he explained that the Government had succeeded in piquing his curiosity.

> Well, the statement was made of all the trouble and the hysteria over pornography and I wanted to see what the material was. It didn't describe the—I didn't know for sure what kind of sexual action they were referring to in the Canadian letter. . . .

In petitioner's home, the Government found the *Bare Boys* magazines and materials that the Government had sent to him in the course of its protracted investigation, but no other materials that would indicate that petitioner collected or was actively interested in child pornography.

There can be no dispute about the evils of child pornography or the difficulties that laws and law enforcement have encountered in eliminating it. Likewise, there can be no dispute that the Government may use undercover agents to enforce the law. "It is well settled that the fact that offiers or employees of the Government merely afford opportunities or facilities for the commission of the offense does not defeat the prosecution. Artifice and strategem may be employed to catch those engaged in criminal enterprises." *Sorrells* v. *United States*, 287 U.S. 435, 441 (1932); *Sherman* v. *United States*, 356 U.S., at 372; *United States* v. *Russell*, 411 U.S. 423 (1973).

In their zeal to enforce the law, however, Government agents may not originate a criminal design, implant in an innocent person's mind the disposition to commit a criminal act, and then induce commission of the crime so that the Government may prosecute. Where the Government has induced an individual to break the law and the defense of entrapment is at issue, as it was in this case, the prosecution must prove beyond reasonable doubt that the defendant was disposed to commit the criminal act prior to first being approached by Government agents.

That is not what happened here. By the time petitioner finally placed his order, he had already been the target of 26 months of repeated mailings and communications from Government agents and fictitious organizations. Therefore, although he had become predisposed to break the law by May 1987, it is our view that the Government did not prove that this predisposition was independent and not the product of the attention that the Government had directed at petitioner since January 1985.

The prosecution's evidence of predisposition falls into two categories: evidence developed prior to the Postal Service's mail campaign, and that developed during the course of the investigation. The sole piece of preinvestigation evidence is petitioner's 1984 order and receipt of the *Bare Boys* magazines. But this is scant if any proof of petitioner's predisposition to commit an illegal act, the criminal character of which a defendant is presumed to know. It may indicate a predisposition to view sexually oriented photographs that are responsive to his sexual tastes; but evidence that merely indicates a generic inclination to act within a broad range, not all of which is criminal, is of little probative value in establishing predisposition.

Furthermore, petitioner was acting within the law at the time he received these magazines. Receipt through the mails of sexually explicit depictions of children for noncommercial use did not become illegal under federal law until May 1984, and Nebraska had no law that forbade petitioner's possession of such material until 1988. Evidence of predisposition to do what once was lawful is not, by itself, sufficient to show predisposition to do what is now illegal, for there is a common understanding that most people obey the law even when they disapprove of it. This obedience may reflect a generalized respect for legality or the fear of prosecution, but for whatever reason, the law's prohibitions are matters of consequence. Hence, the fact that petitioner legally ordered and received the *Bare Boys* magazine does little to further the Government's burden of proving that petitioner was predisposed to commit a criminal act. This is particularly true given petitioner's unchallenged testimony was that he did not know until they arrived that the magazines would depict minors.

The prosecution's evidence gathered during the investigation also fails to carry the Government's burden.

The strong arguable inference is that, by waving the banner of individual rights and disparaging the legitimacy and constitutionality of efforts to restrict the availability of sexually explicit materials, the Government not only excited petitioner's interest in sexually explicit materials banned by law but also exerted substantial pressure on petitioner to obtain and read such material as part of a fight against censorship and the infringement of individual rights. . . .

Petitioner's ready response to these solicitations cannot be enough to establish beyond reasonable doubt that he was predisposed, prior to the Government acts intended to create predisposition, to commit the crime of receiving child pornography through the mails. The evidence that petitioner was ready and willing to commit the offense came only after the Government had devoted 2½ years to convincing him that he had or should have the right to engage in the very behavior proscribed by law. Rational jurors could not say beyond a reasonable doubt that petitioner possessed the requisite predisposition prior to the Government's investigation and that it existed independent of the Government's many and varied approaches to petitioner. As was explained in *Sherman*, where entrapment was found as a matter of law, "the Government [may not] pla[y] on the weaknesses of an innocent party and beguil[e] him into committing crimes which he otherwise would not have attempted."

JUSTICE O'CONNOR, with whom the CHIEF JUSTICE and JUSTICE KENNEDY join, and with whom JUSTICE SCALIA joins except as to Part II, dissenting.

Keith Jacobson was offered only two opportunities to buy child pornography through the mail. Both times, he ordered. Both times, he asked for opportunities to buy more. He needed no Government agent to coax, threaten, or persuade him; no one played on his sympathies, friendship, or suggested that his committing the crime would further a greater good. In fact, no Government agent ever contacted him face-to-face. The Government contends that from the enthusiasm with which Mr. Jacobson responded to the chance to commit a crime, a reasonable jury could permissibly infer beyond a reasonable doubt that he was predisposed to commit the crime. I agree.

The first time the Government sent Mr. Jacobson a catalog of illegal materials, he ordered a set of photographs advertised as picturing "young boys in sex action fun." He enclosed the following note with his order: "I received your brochure and decided to place an order. If I like your product, I will order more later." For reasons undisclosed in the record, Mr. Jacobson's order was never delivered.

The second time the Government sent a catalog of illegal materials, Mr. Jacobson ordered a magazine called *Boys Who Love Boys*, described as "11 year old and 14 year old boys get it on in every way possible. Oral, anal sex and heavy masturbation. If you love boys, you will be delighted with this." Along with his order, Mr. Jacobson sent the following note: "Will order other items later. I want to be discreet in order to protect you and me." The Government, the Court holds, failed to provide evidence that Mr. Jacobson's obvious predisposition at the time of the crime was "independent and not the product of the attention that the Government had directed at petitioner." In so holding, I believe the Court fails to acknowledge the reasonableness of the jury's inference from the evidence, redefines "predisposition," and introduces a new requirement that Government sting operations have a reasonable suspicion of illegal activity before contacting a suspect.

This Court has held previously that a defendant's predisposition is to be assessed as of the time the Government agent first suggested the crime, not when the Government agent first became involved. Until the Government actually makes a suggestion of criminal conduct, it could not be said to have "implant[ed] in the mind of an innocent person the disposition to commit the alleged offense and induce its commission. . . ." *Sorrells* v. *United States*, 287 U.S. 435 (1932).

Today, the Court holds that Government conduct may be considered to create a predisposition to commit a crime, even before any Government action to induce the commission of the crime. In my view, this holding changes entrapment doctrine. Generally, the inquiry is whether a suspect is predisposed before the Government induces the commission of the crime, not before the Government makes initial contact with him.

The rule that preliminary Government contact can create a predisposition has the potential to be misread by lower courts as well as criminal investigators as requiring that the Government must have sufficient evidence of a defendant's predisposition *before it ever seeks to contact him.* Surely the Court cannot intend to impose such a requirement, for it would mean that the Government must have a reasonable suspicion of criminal activity before it begins an investigation, a condition that we have never before imposed. The Court denies that its new rule will affect run-of-the-mill sting operations, and one hopes that it means what it says. Nonetheless, after this case, every defendant will claim that something the Government agent did before soliciting the crime "created" a predisposition that was not there before. For example, a bribe taker will claim that the description of the amount of money available was so enticing that it implanted a disposition to accept the bribe later offered. A drug buyer will claim that the description of the drug's purity and effects was so tempting that it created the urge to try it for the first time. In short, the Court's opinion could be read to prohibit the Government from advertising the seductions of criminal activity as part of its sting operation, for fear of creating a predisposition in its suspects. That limitation would be especially likely to hamper sting operations such as this one, which mimic the advertising done by genuine purveyors of pornography. No doubt the Court would protest that its opinion does not stand for so broad a proposition, but the apparent lack of a principled basis for distinguishing these scenarios exposes a flaw in the more limited rule the Court today adopts.

ale is all the more troubling be-
ot distinguish between Govern-
that merely highlights the tempta-
rime itself, and Government conduct
atens, coerces, or leads a suspect to
a crime in order to fulfill some other
obligation. For example, in *Sorrells*, the Government agent repeatedly asked for illegal liquor,
coaxing the defendant to accede on the ground
that "one former war buddy would get liquor for
another." In *Sherman*, the Government agent
played on the defendant's sympathies, pretending
to be going through drug withdrawal and begging
the defendant to relieve his distress by helping
him buy drugs.

The Government conduct in this case is not
comparable. While the Court states that the
Government "exerted substantial pressure on petitioner to obtain and read such material as part
of a fight against censorship and the infringement of individual rights," one looks at the
record in vain for evidence of such "substantial
pressure." The most one finds is letters advocating legislative action to liberalize obscenity laws,
letters which could easily be ignored or thrown
away. Much later, the Government sent separate
mailings of catalogs of illegal materials. No-

where did the Government suggest that the proceeds of the sale of the illegal materials would be
used to support legislative reforms.

The crux of the Court's concern in this case is
that the Government went too far and "abused"
the "processes of detection and enforcement" by
luring an innocent person to violate the law.
Consequently, the Court holds that the Government failed to prove beyond a reasonable doubt
that Mr. Jacobson was predisposed to commit
the crime. It was, however, the jury's task, as the
conscience of the community, to decide whether
or not Mr. Jacobson was a willing participant in
the criminal activity here or an innocent dupe.
The jury is the traditional "defense against arbitrary law enforcement." *Duncan* v. *Louisiana*,
391 U.S. 145, 156 (1968). Indeed, in *Sorrells*, in
which the Court was also concerned about
overzealous law enforcement, the Court did not
decide itself that the Government conduct constituted entrapment, but left the issue to the
jury. There is no dispute that the jury in this
case was fully and accurately instructed on the
law of entrapment, and nonetheless found Mr.
Jacobson guilty. Because I believe there was sufficient evidence to uphold the jury's verdict, I respectfully dissent.

Coy v. Iowa
487 U.S. 1012; 108 S. Ct. 2798; 101 L. Ed. 2d 857 (1988)

John Avery Coy was charged with sexually assaulting two 13-year-old
girls as they camped out in the back yard of the house next to his. At his
trial, pursuant to a 1985 Iowa statute intended to protect child victims of
sexual abuse, a screen was placed between him and the girls during their
testimony. The screen blocked him from their sight but allowed him to
see them dimly and to hear them. The trial court rejected his contention
that the use of the screen violated the Confrontation Clause of the Sixth
Amendment. Coy was convicted, and the Iowa Supreme Court affirmed.
The U.S. Supreme Court granted certiorari. *Opinion of the Court: Scalia,
Brennan, Marshall, O'Connor, Stevens, White. Concurring opinion:
O'Connor, White. Dissenting opinion: Blackmun, Rehnquist. Not participating: Kennedy.*

JUSTICE SCALIA delivered the opinion of the Court.

Appellant was convicted of two counts of lascivious acts with a child after a jury trial in
which a screen placed between him and the two
complaining witnesses blocked him from their
sight. Appellant contends that this procedure,

authorized by state statute, violated his Sixth
Amendment right to confront the witnesses
against him.

Appellant objected strenuously to use of the
screen, based first of all on his Sixth Amendment
confrontation right. He argued that, although the

device might succeed in its apparent aim of making the complaining witnesses feel less uneasy in giving their testimony, the Confrontation Clause directly addressed this issue by giving criminal defendants a right to face-to-face confrontation. He also argued that his right to due process was violated, since the procedure would make him appear guilty and thus erode the presumption of innocence. The trial court rejected both constitutional claims, though it instructed the jury to draw no inference of guilty from the screen.

The Sixth Amendment gives a criminal defendant the right "to be confronted with the witnesses against him." This language "comes to us on faded parchment," with a lineage that traces back to the beginnings of Western legal culture. There are indications that a right of confrontation existed under Roman law. The Roman Governor Festus, discussing the proper treatment of his prisoner, Paul, stated: "It is not the manner of the Romans to deliver any man up to die before the accused has met his accusers face to face, and has been given a chance to defend himself against the charges." Acts 25:16. It has been argued that a form of the right of confrontation was recognized in England well before the right to jury trial.

Most of this Court's encounters with the Confrontation Clause have involved either the admissibility of out-of-court statements or restrictions on the scope of cross-examination. The reason for that is not, as the State suggests, that these elements are the essence of the Clause's protection—but rather, quite to the contrary, that there is at least some room for doubt (and hence litigation) as to the extent to which the Clause includes those elements, whereas, as Justice Harlan put it, "[s]imply as a matter of English" it confers at least "a right to meet face to face all those who appear and give evidence at trial." *California* v. *Green*, 399 U.S. 149 (1970). Simply as a matter of Latin as well, since the word "confront" ultimately derives from the prefix "con-" (from "contra" meaning "against" or "opposed") and the noun "frons" (forehead). Shakespeare was thus describing the root meaning of confrontation when he had Richard the Second say: "Then call them to our presence—face to face, and frowning brow to brow, ourselves will hear the accuser and the accused freely speak. . . ." *Richard II*, act 1, sc. 1.

We have never doubted, therefore, that the Confrontation Clause guarantees the defendant a face-to-face meeting with witnesses appearing before the trier of fact. . . .

More recently, we have described the "literal right to 'confront' the witness at the time of trial" as forming "the core of the values furthered by the Confrontation Clause." *California* v. *Green*.

The Sixth Amendment's guarantee of face-to-face encounter between witness and accused serves ends related both to appearances and to reality. This opinion is embellished with references to and quotations from antiquity in part to convey that there is something deep in human nature that regards face-to-face confrontation between accused and accuser as "essential to a fair trial in a criminal prosecution." What was true of old is no less true in modern times. President Eisenhower once described face-to-face confrontation as part of the code of his home town of Abilene, Kansas. In Abilene, he said, it was necessary to "[m]eet anyone face to face with whom you disagree. You could not sneak up on him from behind, or do any damage to him, without suffering the penalty of an outraged citizenry. . . . In this country, if someone dislikes you, or accuses you, he must come up in front. He cannot hide behind the shadow." The phrase still persists, "Look me in the eye and say that." Given these human feelings of what is necessary for fairness, the right of confrontation "contributes to the establishment of a system of criminal justice in which the perception as well as the reality of fairness prevails."

The perception that confrontation is essential to fairness has persisted over the centuries because there is much truth to it. A witness "may feel quite differently when he has to repeat his story looking at the man whom he will harm greatly by distorting or mistaking the facts. It is always more difficult to tell a lie about a person 'to his face' than 'behind his back.'" In the former context, even if the lie is told, it will often be told less convincingly. The Confrontation Clause does not, of course, compel the witness to fix his eyes upon the defendant; he may studiously look elsewhere, but the trier of fact will draw its own conclusions. The State can hardly gainsay the profound effect upon a witness of standing in the presence of the person the witness accuses, since that is the very phenomenon it relies upon to establish the potential "trauma" that allegedly justified the extraordinary procedure in the present case. That face-to-face presence may, unfortunately, upset the truthful rape victim or abused child; but by the same token it may confound and undo the false accuser, or reveal the child coached by a malevolent adult. It is a truism that constitutional protections have costs.

The remaining question is whether the right to confrontation was in fact violated in this case. The screen at issue was specifically designed to enable the complaining witnesses to avoid viewing appellant as they gave their testimony, and the record indicates that it was successful in this objective. It is difficult to imagine a more obvious or damaging violation of the defendant's right to a face-to-face encounter.

The State suggests that the confrontation interest at stake here was outweighed by the necessity of protecting victims of sexual abuse. It is true that we have in the past indicated that rights conferred by the Confrontation Clause are not absolute, and may give way to other important interests. The rights referred to in those cases, however, were not the right narrowly and explicitly set forth in the Clause, but rather rights that are, or were asserted to be, reasonably implicit—namely, the right to cross-examine, the right to exclude out-of-court statements, and the asserted right to face-to-face confrontation at some point in the proceedings other than the trial itself. To hold that our determination of what implications are reasonable must take into account other important interests is not the same as holding that we can identify exceptions, in light of other important interests, to the irreducible literal meaning of the clause: "a right to *meet face to face* all those who appear and give evidence *at trial.*" We leave for another day, however, the question whether any exceptions exist. Whatever they may be, they would surely be allowed only when necessary to further an important public policy. The State maintains that such necessity is established here by the statute, which creates a legislatively imposed presumption of trauma. Our cases suggest, however, that even as to exceptions from the normal implications of the Confrontation Clause, as opposed to its most literal application, something more than the type of generalized finding underlying such a statute is needed when the exception is not "firmly . . . rooted in our jurisprudence." The exception created by the Iowa statute, which was passed in 1985, could hardly be viewed as firmly rooted. Since there have been no individualized findings that these particular witnesses needed special protection, the judgment here could not be sustained by any conceivable exception.

The State also briefly suggests that any Confrontation Clause error was harmless beyond a reasonable doubt under the standard of *Chapman* v. *California*, 386 U.S. 18 (1967). We have recognized that other types of violations of the Confrontation Clause are subject to that harmless error analysis, and see no reason why denial of face-to-face confrontation should not be treated the same. An assessment of harmlessness cannot include consideration of whether the witness's testimony would have been unchanged, or the jury's assessment unaltered, had there been confrontation; such an inquiry would obviously involve pure speculation, and harmlessness must therefore be determined on the basis of the remaining evidence. The Iowa Supreme Court had no occasion to address the harmlessness issue, since it found no constitutional violation. In the circumstances of this case, rather than decide whether the error was harmless beyond a reasonable doubt, we leave the issue for the court below.

JUSTICE O'CONNOR, with whom JUSTICE WHITE joins, concurring.

I agree with the Court that appellant's rights under the Confrontation Clause were violated in this case. I write separately only to note my view that those rights are not absolute but rather may give way in an appropriate case to other competing interests so as to permit the use of certain procedural devices designed to shield a child witness from the trauma of courtroom testimony.

Child abuse is a problem of disturbing proportions in today's society.

Many States have determined that a child victim may suffer trauma from exposure to the harsh atmosphere of the typical courtroom and have undertaken to shield the child through a variety of ameliorative measures. We deal today with the constitutional ramifications of only one such measure, but we do so against a broader backdrop. Iowa appears to be the only State authorizing the type of screen used in this case. A full half of the States, however, have authorized the use of one- or two-way closed-circuit television. Statutes sanctioning one-way systems generally permit the child to testify in a separate room in which only the judge, counsel, technicians, and in some cases the defendant, are present. The child's testimony is broadcast into the courtroom for viewing by the jury. Two-way systems permit the child witness to see the courtroom and the defendant over a video monitor. In addition to such closed-circuit television procedures, 33 States (including 19 of the 25 authorizing closed-circuit television) permit the use of video-taped testimony, which typically is taken in the defendant's presence.

While I agree with the Court that the Confrontation Clause was violated in this case, I wish to make clear that nothing in today's decision necessarily dooms such efforts by state legislatures to protect child witnesses.

Thus, I would permit use of a particular trial procedure that called for something other than face-to-face confrontation if that procedure was necessary to further an important public policy. The protection of child witnesses is, in my view and in the view of a substantial majority of the States, just such a policy. The primary focus therefore likely will be on the necessity prong. I agree with the Court that more than the type of generalized legislative finding of necessity present here is required. But if a court makes a case-specific finding of necessity, as is required by a number of State statutes, our cases suggest that the strictures of the Confrontation Clause may give way to the compelling state interest of protecting child witnesses. Because nothing in the Court's opinion conflicts with this approach and this conclusion, I join it.

JUSTICE BLACKMUN, with whom the CHIEF JUSTICE joins, dissenting.

I find it necessary to discuss my disagreement with the Court for two reasons. First, the minimal extent of the infringement on appellant's Confrontation Clause interests is relevant in considering whether competing public policies justify the procedures employed in this case. Second, I fear that the Court's apparent fascination with the witness' ability to see the defendant will lead the States that are attempting to adopt innovations to facilitate the testimony of child-victims of sex abuse to sacrifice other, more central, confrontation interests,

such as the right to cross-examination or to have the trier of fact observe the testifying witness. . . .

Whether or not "there is something deep in human nature" that considers critical the ability of a witness to see the defendant while the witness is testifying, that was not a part of the common law's view of the confrontation requirement. "There never was at common law any recognized right to an indispensable thing called confrontation *as distinguished from cross-examination.*" (emphasis in original). 5 J. Wigmore, Evidence § 1397, p. 158 (J. Chadbourn rev. 1974). I find Dean Wigmore's statement infinitely more persuasive than President Eisenhower's recollection of Kansas justice, or the words Shakespeare placed in the mouth of his Richard II concerning the best means of ascertaining the truth. . . . In fact, Wigmore considered it clear that the right of confrontation is provided "not for the idle purpose of gazing upon the witness, or *of being gazed upon by him,*" but, rather, to allow for cross-examination (emphasis added). . . .

Indisputably, the state interests behind the Iowa statute are of considerable importance. Between 1976 and 1985, the number of reported incidents of child maltreatment in the United States rose from .67 million to over 1.9 million, with an estimated 11.7 percent of those cases in 1985 involving allegations of sexual abuse. The prosecution of these child sex-abuse cases poses substantial difficulties because of the emotional trauma frequently suffered by child witnesses who must testify about the sexual assaults they have suffered.

The fear and trauma associated with a child's testimony in front of the defendant has two serious identifiable consequences: It may cause psychological injury to the child, and it may so overwhelm the child as to prevent the possibility of effective testimony, thereby undermining the truth-finding function of the trial itself. Because of these effects, a State properly may consider the protection of child witnesses to be an important public policy. In my view, this important public policy, embodied in the Iowa statute that authorized the use of the screening device, outweighs the narrow Confrontation Clause right at issue here—the "preference" for having the defendant within the witness' sight while the witness testifies.

Comprehensive Crime Control Act of 1984
P.L. 98-473

Among the more controversial chapters of the Comprehensive Crime Control Act of 1984 was the Bail Reform Act of 1984, in which Congress, which had previously authorized preventive detention in the District of Columbia Court Reform and Criminal Procedures Act of 1970, increased its availability to the entire federal court system.

§3142. Release or Detention of a Defendant Pending Trial

(a) IN GENERAL.—Upon the appearance before a judicial officer of a person charged with an offense, the judicial officer shall issue an order that, pending trial, the person be—

(1) released on his personal recognizance or upon execution of an unsecured appearance bond, pursuant to the provisions of subsection (b);

(2) released on a condition or combination of conditions pursuant to the provisions of subsection (c);

(3) temporarily detained to permit revocation of conditional release, deportation, or exclusion pursuant to the provisions of subsection (d); or

(4) detained pursuant to the provisions of subsection (e).

(e) DETENTION.—If, after a hearing pursuant to the provisions of subsection (f), the judicial officer finds that no condition or combination of conditions will reasonably assure the appearance of the person as required and the safety of any other person and the community, he shall order the detention of the person prior to trial. In a case described in (f)(1), a rebuttable presumption arises that no condition or combination of conditions will reasonably assure the safety of any other person and the community if the judge finds that—

(1) the person has been convicted of a Federal offense that is described in subsection (f)(1), or of a State or local offense that would have been an offense described in subsection (f)(1) if a circumstance giving rise to Federal jurisdiction had existed;

(2) the offense described in paragraph (1) was committed while the person was on release pending trial for a Federal, State, or local offense; and

(3) a period of not more than five years has elapsed since the date of conviction, or the release of the person from imprisonment, for the offense described in paragraph (1), whichever is later.

(f) DETENTION HEARING.—The judicial officer shall hold a hearing to determine whether any condition or combination of conditions set forth in subsection (c) will reasonably assure the appearance of the person as required and the safety of any other person and the community in a case—

(1) upon motion of the attorney for the Government, that involves—

(A) a crime of violence;

(B) an offense for which the maximum sentence is life imprisonment or death;

(C) an offense for which a maximum term of imprisonment of ten years or more is prescribed in the Controlled Substances Act . . . , the Controlled Substances Import and Export Act . . . , or section 1 of the Act of September 15, 1980 . . . ; or

(D) any felony committed after the person had been convicted of two or more prior offenses described in sub-paragraphs (A) through (C), or two or more State or local offenses that would have been offenses described in sub-paragraphs (A) through (C) if a circumstance giving rise to Federal jurisdiction had existed; or

(2) upon motion of the attorney for the Government or upon the judicial officer's own motion, that involves—

(A) a serious risk that the person will flee;

(B) a serious risk that the person will obstruct or attempt to obstruct justice, or threaten, injure, or intimidate, or attempt to threaten, injure, or intimidate, a prospective witness or juror.

The hearing shall be held immediately upon the person's first appearance before the judicial officer unless that person, or the attorney for the Government, seeks a continuance. Except for good cause, a continuance on motion of the person may not exceed five days, and a continuance on motion of the attorney for the Government may not exceed three days. During a continuance, the person shall be detained, and the judicial officer, on motion of the attorney for the Government or on his own motion, may order that, while in custody, a person who appears to be a narcotics addict receive a medical examination to determine whether he is an addict. At the hearing, the person has the right to be represented by counsel, and, if he is financially unable to obtain adequate representation, to have counsel appointed for him. The person shall be afforded an opportunity to testify, to present witnesses on his own behalf, to cross-examine witnesses who appear at the hearing, and to present information by proffer or otherwise. The rules concerning admissibility of evidence in criminal trials do not apply to the presentation and consideration of information at the hearing. The facts the judicial officer uses to support a finding pursuant to subsection (e) that no condition or combination of conditions will reasonably assure the safety of any other person and the community shall be supported by clear and convincing evidence. The person may be detained pending completion of the hearing.

(g) FACTORS TO BE CONSIDERED.—The judicial officer shall, in determining whether there are conditions of release that will reasonably assure the appearance of the person as required and the safety of any other person and the community, take into account the available information concerning—

(1) the nature and circumstances of the offense charged, including whether the offense is a crime of violence or involves a narcotic drug;

(2) the weight of the evidence against the person;

(3) the history and characteristics of the person, including—

(A) his character, physical and mental condition, family ties, employment, financial resources, length of residence in the community, community ties, past conduct, history relating to drug or alcohol abuse, criminal history, and record concerning appearance at court proceedings; and

(B) whether, at the time of the current offense or arrest, he was on probation, on parole, or on other release pending trial, sentencing, appeal, or completion of sentence for an offense under Federal, State, or local law; and

(4) the nature and seriousness of the danger to any person or the community that would be posed by the person's release. In considering the conditions of release . . . the judicial officer may upon his own motion, or shall upon the motion of the Government, conduct an inquiry into the source of the property to be designated for potential forfeiture or offered as collateral to secure a bond, and shall decline to accept the designation, or the use as collateral, of property that, because of its source, will not reasonably assure the appearance of the person as required.

§3147. Penalty for an Offense Committed While on Release

A person convicted of an offense committed while released pursuant to this chapter shall be sentenced, in addition to the sentence prescribed for the offense to—

(1) a term of imprisonment of not less than two years and not more than ten years if the offense is a felony; or

(2) a term of imprisonment of not less than ninety days and not more than one year if the offense is a misdemeanor.

A term of imprisonment imposed pursuant to this section shall be consecutive to any other sentence of imprisonment.

Gregg v. *Georgia*
428 U.S. 153; 96 S. Ct. 2909; 49 L. Ed. 2d 859 (1976)

In *Furman* v. *Georgia* (1972), the Supreme Court in effect struck down all capital punishment laws as they then existed in the states. The reasons for the Court's action are summarized in the following opinion. In an effort to conform to what it understood to be the requirements of *Furman*, the Georgia legislature immediately revised its death penalty statute. Under the provisions of this revised statute, Troy Leon Gregg was charged with two counts of armed robbery and two counts of murder. At the trial stage of the bifurcated proceeding now required by the statute, the jury found Gregg guilty of all the charges against him. At the penalty stage, the judge instructed the jury that it could recommend either a sentence of death or a sentence of life in prison on each count, that it was free to consider mitigating or aggravating circumstances, if any, as presented by the parties; and that it would not be authorized to consider imposing the death sentence unless it first found beyond a reasonable doubt (1) that the murders were committed while Gregg was engaged in the commission of other capital felonies, *viz.*, the armed robberies of the victims; (2) that he committed the murders for the purpose of receiving the victims' money and automobile; or (3) that the murders were "outrageously and wantonly vile, horrible, and inhuman" in that they "involved the depravity of the mind of the defendant." The jury found the first and second of these aggravating circumstances and returned a sentence of death. Under Georgia's revised statute, the Georgia Supreme Court was required to review Gregg's conviction. After reviewing the trial transcript and record and considering the evidence and sentence in similar cases, the court upheld the death sentence for the murders, concluding that they had not resulted from prejudice or any other arbitrary factor and were not excessive or disproportionate to the penalty applied in similar cases. It vacated the armed robbery sentences, however, on the ground that the death penalty had rarely been imposed in Georgia for that offense. Gregg petitioned the Supreme Court for a writ of certiorari, charging that imposition of the death sentence under the Georgia statute was "cruel and unusual" punishment under the Eighth and Fourteenth amendments. *Judgment of the Court: Stewart, Powell, Stevens. Concurring in the judgment: White, Burger, Rehnquist; Blackmun. Dissenting opinions: Brennan; Marshall.*

MR. JUSTICE STEWART, MR. JUSTICE POWELL, and MR. JUSTICE STEVENS announced the judgment of the Court and filed an opinion delivered by MR. JUSTICE STEWART. . . .

We address initially the basic contention that the punishment of death for the crime of murder is, under all circumstances, "cruel and unusual" in violation of the Eighth and Fourteenth Amendments of the Constitution. . . . Until *Furman* v. *Georgia* (1972), the Court never confronted squarely the fundamental claim that the punishment of death always, regardless of the enormity of the offense or the procedure followed in imposing the sentence, is cruel and unusual punishment in violation of the Constitution. Although this issue was presented and addressed in *Furman*, it was not resolved by the Court. Four Justices would have held that capital punishment is not unconstitutional *per se*[*]; two Justices would have reached the opposite conclusion[†]; and three Justices, while agreeing that the statutes then before the Court were invalid as ap-

---

[*]Blackmun, Burger, Powell, Rehnquist.
[†]Brennan, Marshall.

plied, left open the question whether such punishment may ever be imposed.‡ We now hold that the punishment of death does not invariably violate the Constitution.

. . . The Eighth Amendment has not been regarded as a static concept. As Chief Justice Warren said, in an oft-quoted phrase, "[t]he Amendment must draw its meaning from the evolving standards of decency that mark the progress of a maturing society." . . . Thus, an assessment of contemporary values concerning the infliction of a challenged sanction is relevant to the application of the Eighth Amendment. As we develop below more fully, . . . this assessment does not call for a subjective judgment. It requires, rather, that we look to objective indicia that reflect the public attitude toward a given sanction.

But our cases also make clear that public perceptions of standards of decency with respect to criminal sanctions are not conclusive. A penalty also must accord with "the dignity of man," which is the "basic concept underlying the Eighth Amendment." . . . This means, at least, that the punishment not be "excessive." When a form of punishment in the abstract (in this case, whether capital punishment may ever be imposed as a sanction for murder) rather than in the particular (the propriety of death as a penalty to be applied to a specific defendant for a specific crime) is under consideration, the inquiry into "excessiveness" has two aspects. First, the punishment must not involve the unnecessary and wanton infliction of pain. . . . Second, the punishment must not be grossly out of proportion to the severity of the crime. . . .

Of course, the requirements of the Eighth Amendment must be applied with an awareness of the limited role to be played by the courts. . . .

. . . In assessing a punishment selected by a democratically elected legislature against the constitutional measure, we presume its validity. We may not require the legislature to select the least severe penalty possible so long as the penalty selected is not cruelly inhumane or disproportionate to the crime involved. And a heavy burden rests on those who would attack the judgment of the representatives of the people.

. . . We now consider specifically whether the sentence of death for the crime of murder is a *per se* violation of the Eighth and Fourteenth Amendments to the Constitution. We note first that history and precedent strongly support a negative answer to this question. . . .

The imposition of the death penalty for the crime of murder has a long history of acceptance both in the United States and in England. The common-law rule imposed a mandatory death sentence on all convicted murderers. . . . And the penalty continued to be used into the 20th century by most American States, although the breadth of the common-law rule was diminished, initially by narrowing the class of murders to be punished by death and subsequently by widespread adoption of laws expressly granting juries the discretion to recommend mercy. . . .

It is apparent from the text of the Constitution itself that the existence of capital punishment was accepted by the Framers. At the time the Eighth Amendment was ratified, capital punishment was a common sanction in every State. Indeed, the First Congress of the United States enacted legislation providing death as the penalty for specified crimes. . . . The Fifth Amendment, adopted at the same time as the Eighth, contemplated the continued existence of the capital sanction by imposing certain limits on the prosecution of capital cases: "No person shall be held to answer for a capital, or otherwise infamous crime, unless on a presentment or indictment of a Grand Jury . . . ; nor shall any person be subject for the same offense to be twice put in jeopardy of life or limb; . . . nor be deprived of life, liberty, or property, without due process of law. . . ." And the Fourteenth Amendment, adopted over three-quarters of a century later, similarly contemplates the existence of the capital sanction in providing that no State shall deprive any person of "life, liberty, or property" without due process of law.

For nearly two centuries, this Court, repeatedly and often expressly, has recognized that capital punishment is not invalid *per se*. . . .

Four years ago, the petitioners in *Furman* and its companion cases predicated their argument primarily upon the asserted proposition that standards of decency had evolved to the point where capital punishment no longer could be tol-

---

‡Douglas, Stewart, White.

erated. The petitioners in those cases said, in effect, that the evolutionary process had come to an end, and that standards of decency required that the Eighth Amendment be construed finally as prohibiting capital punishment for any crime regardless of its depravity and impact on society. This view was accepted by two Justices. Three other Justices were unwilling to go so far; focusing on the procedures by which convicted defendants were selected for the death penalty rather than on the actual punishment inflicted, they joined in the conclusion that the statutes before the Court were constitutionally invalid.

The petitioners in the capital cases before the Court today renew the "standards of decency" argument, but developments during the four years since *Furman* have undercut substantially the assumptions upon which their argument rested. Despite the continuing debate, dating back to the 19th century, over the morality and utility of capital punishment, it is now evident that a large proportion of American society continues to regard it as an appropriate and necessary criminal sanction.

The most marked indication of society's endorsement of the death penalty for murder is the legislative response to *Furman*. The legislatures of at least 35 States have enacted new statutes that provide for the death penalty for at least some crimes that result in the death of another person. And the Congress of the United States, in 1974, enacted a statute providing the death penalty for aircraft piracy that results in death. . . . All of the post-*Furman* statutes make clear that capital punishment itself has not been rejected by the elected representatives of the people.

The jury also is a significant and reliable objective index of contemporary values because it is so directly involved. . . . The action of juries in many States since *Furman* is fully compatible with the legislative judgments, reflected in the new statutes, as to the continued utility and necessity of capital punishment in appropriate cases. At the close of 1974 at least 254 persons had been sentenced to death since *Furman*, and by the end of March 1976, more than 460 persons were subject to death sentences.

As we have seen, however, the Eighth Amendment demands more than that a challenged punishment be acceptable to contemporary society. The Court also must ask whether it comports with the basic concept of human dignity at the core of the Amendment . . . . The sanction imposed cannot be so totally without penological justification that it results in the gratuitous infliction of suffering. . . .

The death penalty is said to serve two principal social purposes: retribution and deterrence of capital crimes by prospective offenders.

In part, capital punishment is an expression of society's moral outrage at particularly offensive conduct. This function may be unappealing to many, but it is essential in an ordered society that asks its citizens to rely on legal processes rather than self-help to vindicate their wrongs.

. . . "Retribution is no longer the dominant objective of the criminal law," . . . but neither is it a forbidden objective nor one inconsistent with our respect for the dignity of men. . . . Indeed, the decision that capital punishment may be the appropriate sanction in extreme cases is an expression of the community's belief that certain crimes are themselves so grievous an affront to humanity that the only adequate response may be the penalty of death.

Statistical attempts to evaluate the worth of the death penalty as a deterrent to crimes by potential offenders have occasioned a great deal of debate. The results simply have been inconclusive. . . .

Although some of the studies suggest that the death penalty may not function as a significantly greater deterrent than lesser penalties, there is no convincing empirical evidence either supporting or refuting this view. We may nevertheless assume safely that there are murderers, such as those who act in passion, for whom the threat of death has little or no deterrent effect. But for many others, the death penalty undoubtedly is a significant deterrent. There are carefully contemplated murders, such as murder for hire, where the possible penalty of death may well enter into the cold calculus that precedes the decision to act. And there are some categories of murder, such as murder by a life prisoner, where other sanctions may not be adequate.

The value of capital punishment as a deterrent of crime is a complex factual issue the resolution of which properly rests with the legislatures, which can evaluate the results of statistical studies in terms of their own local conditions and with a flexibility of approach that is not available to the courts . . . . Indeed, many of the post-*Furman* statutes reflect just such a responsible effort to define those crimes and those criminals for which capital punishment is most probably an effective deterrent. . . . Considerations of federalism, as well as respect for the ability of a legislature to evaluate, in terms of its particular state, the moral consensus concerning the death penalty and its social utility as a sanction, require us to conclude, in the absence of more convincing evidence, that the infliction of death as a punishment for murder is not without justification and thus is not unconstitutionally severe.

Finally, we must consider whether the punishment of death is disproportionate in relation to the crime for which it is imposed. There is no question that death as a punishment is unique in its severity and irrevocability. . . . When a defendant's life is at stake, the Court has been particularly sensitive to insure that every safeguard is observed. . . . But we are concerned here only with the imposition of capital punishment for the crime of murder, and when a life has been taken deliberately by the offender, we cannot say that the punishment is invariably disproportionate to the crime. It is an extreme sanction, suitable to the most extreme of crimes.

We hold that the death penalty is not a form of punishment that may never be imposed, regardless of the circumstances of the offense, regardless of the character of the offender, and regardless of the procedure followed in reaching the decision to impose it. . . .

While *Furman* did not hold that the infliction of the death penalty *per se* violates the Constitution's ban on cruel and unusual punishments, it did recognize that the penalty of death is different in kind from any other punishment imposed under our system of criminal justice. Because of the uniqueness of the death penalty, *Furman* held that it could not be imposed under sentencing procedures that created a substantial risk that it would be inflicted in an arbitrary and capricious manner.

. . . The concerns expressed in *Furman* that the penalty of death not be imposed in an arbitrary or capricious manner can be met by a carefully drafted statute that ensures that the sentencing authority is given adequate information and guidance. As a general proposition these concerns are best met by a system that provides for a bifurcated proceeding at which the sentencing authority is apprised of the information relevant to the imposition of sentence and provided with standards to guide its use of the information.

. . . Georgia's new sentencing procedures require as a prerequisite to the imposition of the death penalty, specific jury findings as to the circumstances of the crime or the character of the defendant. Moreover to guard further against a situation comparable to that presented in *Furman*, the Supreme Court of Georgia compares each death sentence with the sentences imposed on similarly situated defendants to ensure that the sentence of death in a particular case is not disproportionate. On their face these procedures seem to satisfy the concerns of *Furman*. No longer should there be "no meaningful basis for distinguishing the few cases in which [the death penalty] is imposed from the many cases in which it is not." . . .

The basic concern of *Furman* centered on those defendants who were being condemned to death capriciously and arbitrarily. Under the procedures before the Court in that case, sentencing authorities were not directed to give attention to the nature or circumstances of crime committed or to the character or record of the defendant. Left unguided, juries imposed the death sentence in a way that could only be called freakish. The new Georgia sentencing procedures, by contrast, focus the jury's attention on the particularized nature of the crime and the particularized characteristics of the individual defendant. While the jury is permitted to consider any aggravating or mitigating circumstances, it must find and identify at least one statutory aggravating factor before it may impose a penalty of death. In this way the jury's discretion is channeled. No longer can a jury wantonly and freakishly impose the death sentence; it is always circumscribed by the legislative guidelines. In addition, the review function of the Supreme Court of Georgia affords additional assurance that the concerns that prompted our decision in *Furman* are not present to any significant degree in the Georgia procedure applied here.

For the reasons expressed in this opinion, we hold that the statutory system under which Gregg was sentenced to death does not violate the Constitution. Accordingly, the judgment of the Georgia Supreme Court is affirmed.

MR. JUSTICE BRENNAN, dissenting.

... Death for whatever crime and under all circumstances "is truly an awesome punishment. The calculated killing of a human being by the State involves, by its very nature, a denial of the executed person's humanity.... An executed person has indeed 'lost the right to have rights.'" Death is not only an unusually severe punishment, unusual in its pain, in its finality, and in its enormity, but it serves no penal purpose more effectively than a less severe punishment; therefore the principle inherent in the Clause that prohibits pointless infliction of excessive punishment when less severe punishment can adequately achieve the same purposes invalidates the punishment....

The fatal constitutional infirmity in the punishment of death is that it treats "members of the human race as nonhumans, as objects to be toyed with and discarded. [It is] thus inconsistent with the fundamental premise of the Clause that even the vilest criminal remains a human being possessed of common human dignity." ... As such it is a penalty that "subjects the individual to a fate forbidden by the principle of civilized treatment guaranteed by the [Clause]." I therefore would hold, on that ground alone, that death is today a cruel and unusual punishment prohibited by the Clause. "Justice of this kind is obviously no less shocking than the crime itself, and the new 'official' murder, far from offering redress for the offense committed against society, adds instead a second defilement to the first." ...

MR. JUSTICE MARSHALL, dissenting. . . .

In *Furman* I concluded that the death penalty is constitutionally invalid for two reasons. First, the death penalty is excessive.... And second, the American people, fully informed as to the purposes of the death penalty and its liabilities would in my view reject it as morally unacceptable....

Since the decision in *Furman*, the legislatures of 35 States have enacted new statutes authorizing the imposition of the death sentence for certain crimes, and Congress has enacted a law providing the death penalty for air piracy resulting in death.... I would be less than candid if I did not acknowledge that these developments have a significant bearing on a realistic

assessment of the moral acceptability of the death penalty to the American people. But if the constitutionality of the death penalty turns, as I have urged, on the opinion of an *informed* citizenry, then even the enactment of new death statutes cannot be viewed as conclusive. In *Furman*, I observed that the American people are largely unaware of the information critical to a judgment on the morality of the death penalty, and concluded that if they were better informed they would consider it shocking, unjust, and unacceptable.... A recent study, conducted after the enactment of the post-*Furman* statutes, has confirmed that the American people know little about the death penalty, and that the opinions of an informed public would differ significantly from those of a public unaware of the consequences and effects of the death penalty.

Even assuming, however, that the post-*Furman* enactment of statutes authorizing the death penalty renders the prediction of the views of an informed citizenry an uncertain basis for a constitutional decision, the enactment of those statutes has no bearing whatsoever on the conclusion that the death penalty is unconstitutional because it is excessive. An excessive penalty is invalid under the Cruel and Unusual Punishments Clause "even though popular sentiment may favor" it. . . . The inquiry here, then, is simply whether the death penalty is necessary to accomplish the legitimate legislative purposes in punishment, or whether a less severe penalty—life imprisonment—would do as well. . . .

The two purposes that sustain the death penalty as nonexcessive in the Court's view are general deterrence and retribution. . . . The evidence I reviewed in *Furman* remains convincing, in my view, that "capital punishment is not necessary as a deterrent to crime in our society." The justification for the death penalty must be found elsewhere.

The other principal purpose said to be served by the death penalty is retribution. The notion that retribution can serve as a moral justification for the sanction of death finds credence in the opinion of my Brothers Stewart, Powell, and Stevens. . . . It is this notion that I find to be the most disturbing aspect of today's unfortunate decision. . . . To be sustained under the Eighth Amendment, the death penalty must "[comport] with the basic concept of human dignity at the core of the Amendment." . . . The objective in imposing it must be "[consistent] with our re-spect for the dignity of other men." . . . Under these standards, the taking of life "because the wrong-doer deserves it" surely must fall, for such a punishment has as its very basis the total de-nial of the wrong-doer's dignity and worth. . . .

Woodson v. North Carolina
428 U.S. 280; 96 S. Ct. 2978; 49 L. Ed. 2d 944 (1976)

In *Gregg* v. *Georgia,* the Supreme Court rejected the argument that the imposition of the death penalty under any circumstances is cruel and un-usual punishment in violation of the Eighth and Fourteenth Amend-ments and upheld the constitutionality of Georgia's capital punishment statute, in which the legislature channeled the jury's discretionary power to impose the death penalty through a bifurcated proceeding and manda-tory appellate review. Not every state, however, responded in a like man-ner to the problem of unbridled jury discretion as raised by *Furman* v. *Georgia.* In North Carolina, for example, the legislature revised its capi-tal punishment statute so as to make the death penalty mandatory for first-degree murder. In this companion case to *Gregg,* James Woodson was convicted of first-degree murder and, as required by the statute, was sentenced to death. The Supreme Court of North Carolina affirmed, and the United States Supreme Court granted certiorari. *Judgment of the Court:* Stewart, *Powell, Stevens. Concurring in the judgment:* Brennan; Marshall. *Dissenting opinions:* Blackmun; Rehnquist; White, *Burger,* Rehnquist.

MR. JUSTICE STEWART, MR. JUSTICE POWELL, and MR. JUSTICE STEVENS announced the judgment of the Court and filed an opinion delivered by Mr. JUSTICE STEWART. . . .

. . . In ruling on the constitutionality of the sentences imposed on the petitioners under this North Carolina statute, the Court now ad-dresses for the first time the question whether a death sentence returned pursuant to a law im-posing a mandatory death penalty for a broad category of homicidal offenses constitutes cruel and unusual punishment within the meaning of the Eighth and Fourteenth Amendments. The issue, like that explored in *Furman,* involves the procedure employed by the State to select per-sons for the unique and irreversible penalty of death. . . .

. . . The history of mandatory death penalty statutes in the United States reveals that the practice of sentencing to death all persons con-victed of a particular offense has been rejected as unduly harsh and unworkably rigid. The two cru-cial indicators of evolving standards of decency respecting the imposition of punishment in our society—jury determinations and legislative en-actments—both point conclusively to the repudi-ation of automatic death sentences. At least since the Revolution, American jurors have, with some regularity, disregarded their oaths and re-fused to convict defendants where a death sen-tence was the automatic consequence of a guilty verdict. As we have seen, the initial movement to reduce the number of capital offenses and to separate murder into degrees was prompted in part by the reaction of jurors as well as by re-formers who objected to the imposition of death as the penalty for any crime. Nineteenth century journalists, statesmen, and jurists repeatedly observed that jurors were often deterred from convicting palpably guilty men of first-degree murder under mandatory statutes. Thereafter, continuing evidence of jury reluctance to convict persons of capital offenses in mandatory death penalty jurisdictions resulted in legislative authorization of discretionary jury sentencing . . . . The consistent course charted by the state legislatures and by Congress since the middle of the past century demonstrates that the aversion of jurors to mandatory death penalty statutes is shared by society at large. . . .

It is now well established that the Eighth Amendment draws much of its meaning from "the evolving standards of decency that mark the progress of a maturing society." . . . As the above discussion makes clear, one of the most significant developments in our society's treatment of capital punishment has been the rejection of the common-law practice of inexorably imposing a death sentence upon every person convicted of a specified offense. North Carolina's mandatory death penalty statute for first-degree murder departs markedly from contemporary standards respecting the imposition of the punishment of death and thus cannot be applied consistently with the Eighth and Fourteenth Amendments' requirement that the State's power to punish "be exercised within the limits of civilized standards." . . .

A separate deficiency of North Carolina's mandatory death sentence statute is its failure to provide a constitutionally tolerable response to *Furman's* rejection of unbridled jury discretion in the imposition of capital sentences. Central to the limited holding in *Furman* was the conviction that the vesting of standardless sentencing power in the jury violated the Eighth and Fourteenth Amendments. . . . American juries have persistently refused to convict a significant portion of persons charged with first-degree murder of that offense under mandatory death penalty statutes. . . . In view of the historic record, it is only reasonable to assume that many juries under mandatory statutes will continue to consider the grave consequences of a conviction in reaching a verdict. North Carolina's mandatory death penalty statute provides no standards to guide the jury in its inevitable exercise of the power to determine which first-degree murderers shall live and which shall die. And there is no way under the North Carolina law for the judiciary to check arbitrary and capricious exercise of that power through a review of death sentences. . . .

A third constitutional shortcoming of the North Carolina statute is its failure to allow the particularized consideration of relevant aspects of the character and record of each convicted defendant before the imposition upon him of a sentence of death. . . . A process that accords no significance to relevant facets of the character and record of the individual offender or the circumstances of the particular offense excludes from consideration in fixing the ultimate punishment of death the possibility of compassionate or mitigating factors stemming from the diverse frailties of humankind. It treats all persons convicted of a designated offense not as uniquely individual human beings, but as members of a faceless, undifferentiated mass to be subject to the blind infliction of the penalty of death.

. . . Consideration of both the offender and the offense in order to arrive at a just and appropriate sentence has been viewed as a progressive and humanizing development. . . . While the prevailing practice of individualizing sentencing determinations generally reflects simply enlightened policy rather than a constitutional imperative, we believe that in capital cases the fundamental respect for humanity underlying the Eighth Amendment . . . requires consideration of the character and record of the individual offender and the circumstances of the particular offense as a constitutionally indispensable part of the process of inflicting the penalty of death. . . .

For the reasons stated, we conclude that the death sentences imposed upon the petitioners under North Carolina's mandatory death sentence statute violated the Eighth and Fourteenth Amendments and therefore must be set aside.

Roberts v. *Louisiana*
428 U.S. 325; 96 S. Ct. 3001; 49 L. Ed. 2d 974 (1976)

Stanislaus Roberts was found guilty of first-degree murder and was sentenced to death under Louisiana's capital punishment statute, which had been amended after *Furman* v. *Georgia* to make the death penalty mandatory for those convicted of first-degree murder. The Louisiana Supreme Court affirmed, and the United States Supreme Court granted certiorari. For the reasons stated in Justice Stewart's opinion in the companion case of *Woodson* v. *North Carolina*, Justice Stevens, speaking for himself and for Justices Stewart and Powell, announced the judgment of the court and invalidated Louisiana's mandatory death penalty statute. Justice White, dissenting, wrote an opinion that responds to the judgments of the Court in both *Roberts* and *Woodson*. *Judgment of the Court: Stewart, Powell, Stevens. Concurring in the judgment: Brennan; Marshall. Dissenting opinions: Blackmun; Burger; White, Blackmun, Burger, Rehnquist.*

MR. JUSTICE WHITE, with whom THE CHIEF JUSTICE, MR. JUSTICE BLACKMUN, and MR. JUSTICE REHNQUIST join, dissenting. . . .

I cannot conclude that the current Louisiana first-degree murder statute is insufficiently different from the statutes invalidated in *Furman's* wake to avoid invalidation under that case. . . .

The difference between a jury having and not having the lawful discretion to spare the life of the defendant is apparent and fundamental. It is undeniable that the unfettered discretion of the jury to save the defendant from death was a major contributing factor in the developments which led us to invalidate the death penalty in *Furman* v. *Georgia*. This factor Louisiana has now sought to eliminate by making the death penalty compulsory upon a verdict of guilty in first-degree murder cases. As I see it, we are now in no position to rule that the State's present law, having eliminated the overt discretionary power of juries, suffers from the same constitutional infirmities which led this Court to invalidate the Georgia death penalty statute in *Furman* v. *Georgia*. . . .

Nor am I convinced that the Louisiana death penalty for first-degree murder is . . . vulnerable because the prosecutor is vested with discretion as to the selection and filing of charges, by the practice of plea bargaining or by the power of executive clemency. . . . The Louisiana statutes . . . define the elements of first-degree murder, and I cannot accept the assertion that state prosecutors will systematically fail to file first-degree murder charges when the evidence warrants it or to seek convictions for first-degree murder on less than adequate evidence. Of course, someone *must* exercise discretion and judgment as to what charges are to be filed and against whom; but this essential process is nothing more than the rational enforcement of the State's criminal law and the sensible operation of the criminal justice system. The discretion with which Louisiana's prosecutors are invested and which appears to be no more than normal, furnishes no basis for inferring that capital crimes will be prosecuted so arbitrarily and frequently that the present death penalty statute is invalid under *Furman* v. *Georgia*. . . .

The plurality offers two additional reasons for invalidating the Louisiana statute. . . .

The plurality holds the Louisiana statute unconstitutional for want of a separate sentencing proceeding in which the sentencing authority may focus on the sentence and consider some or all of the aggravating and mitigating circumstances. Implicit in the plurality's holding that a separate proceeding might be held at which the sentencer may consider the character and record of the accused is the proposition that States are constitutionally prohibited from considering any crime no matter how defined so serious that every person who commits it should be put to death regardless of extraneous factors related to his character. . . . I cannot agree. It is axiomatic that the major justification for concluding that a given defendant deserves to be punished is that he committed a crime. Even if the character of the accused *must* be considered under the Eighth Amendment, surely a State is not constitutionally forbidden to provide that the commission of certain crimes conclusively establishes that the criminal's character is such that he deserves death. Moreover, quite apart from the character of a criminal, a State should constitutionally be able to conclude that the need to deter some crimes and that the likelihood that the death penalty will succeed in deterring these crimes is such that the death penalty may be made mandatory for all people who commit them. Nothing resembling a reasoned basis for the rejection of these propositions is to be found in the plurality opinion. The fact that juries at times refused to convict despite the evidence [does not] prove that the mandatory nature of the sentence was the burr under the jury's saddle rather than that one or more persons on those juries were opposed in principle to the death penalty under whatever system it might be authorized or imposed. Surely if every nullifying jury had been interrogated at the time and had it been proved to everyone's satisfaction that all or a large part of the nullifying verdicts occurred because certain members of these juries had been opposed to the death penalty in any form, rather than because the juries involved were reluctant to impose the death penalty on the particular defendants before them, it could not be concluded that either those juries or the country had condemned mandatory punishments as distinguished from the death penalty itself. The plurality nevertheless draws

such an inference even though there is no more reason to infer that jury nullification occurred because of opposition to the death penalty in particular cases than because one or more of the 12 jurors on the critical juries were opposed to the death penalty in any form and stubbornly refused to participate in a guilty verdict. . . .

. . . The more fundamental objection than the plurality's muddled reasoning is that in *Gregg* v. *Georgia* . . . it lectures us at length about the role and place of the judiciary and then proceeds to ignore its own advice, the net effect being to suggest that observers of this institution should pay more attention to what we do than what we say. The plurality claims that it has not forgotten what the past has taught about the limits of judicial review; but I fear that it has again surrendered to the temptation to make policy for and to attempt to govern the country through a misuse of the powers given this Court under the Constitution.

McCleskey v. *Kemp*
481 U.S. 279, 107 S. Ct. 1756, 95 L. Ed. 2d 262 (1987)

Warren McCleskey was convicted in a Georgia trial court of two counts of armed robbery and the murder of a white police officer and was sentenced to death. The Georgia Supreme Court affirmed. McCleskey then petitioned the U.S. District Court for the Northern District of Georgia for habeas corpus relief, claiming that the Georgia capital sentencing process was administered in a racially discriminatory manner in violation of the Eighth and Fourteenth Amendments. To support his claim, he introduced a statistical study (prepared by Professor David Baldus and described in Justice Powell's opinion of the Court) that showed a disparity in the imposition of the death sentence in Georgia based on the murder victim's race and, to a lesser extent, on the defendant's race. The District Court rejected his claims and dismissed his petition; the Court of Appeals for the Eleventh Circuit affirmed; and the U.S. Supreme Court granted certiorari. *Opinion of the Court:* <u>Powell</u>, *O'Connor, Rehnquist, Scalia, White. Dissenting opinions:* <u>Brennan</u>, *Blackmun, Marshall, Stevens;* <u>Blackmun</u>, *Marshall, Stevens;* <u>Stevens</u>, *Blackmun.*

JUSTICE POWELL delivered the opinion of the Court.

This case presents the question whether a complex statistical study that indicates a risk that racial considerations enter into capital sentencing determinations proves that petitioner McCleskey's capital sentence is unconstitutional under the Eighth or Fourteenth Amendment.

McCleskey, a black man, was convicted of two counts of armed robbery and one count of murder. . . .

On appeal, the Supreme Court of Georgia affirmed the convictions and sentences. . . .

McCleskey next filed a petition for a writ of habeas corpus in the federal District Court for the Northern District of Georgia. His petition raised 18 claims, one of which was that the Georgia capital sentencing process is administered in a racially discriminatory manner in violation of the Eighth and Fourteenth Amendments to the United States Constitution. In support of his claim, McCleskey proffered a statistical study performed by Professors David C. Baldus, George Woodworth, and Charles Pulaski (the Baldus study) that purports to show a disparity in the imposition of the death sentence in Georgia based on the race of the murder victim and, to a lesser extent, the race of the defendant. The Baldus study is actually two sophisticated statistical studies that examine over 2,000 murder cases that occurred in Georgia during the 1970s. The raw numbers collected by Professor Baldus indicate that defendants charged with killing white persons received the death penalty in 11% of the cases, but defendants charged with killing blacks received the death penalty in only 1% of the cases. The raw numbers also indicate a reverse racial disparity according to the race of the defendant: 4% of the black defendants received the death penalty, as opposed to 7% of the white defendants.

Baldus also divided the cases according to the combination of the race of the defendant and the race of the victim. He found that the death penalty was assessed in 22% of the cases involving black defendants and white victims; 8% of the cases involving white defendants and white victims; 1% of the cases involving black defendants and black victims; and 3% of the cases involving white defendants and black victims. Similarly, Baldus found that prosecutors sought the death penalty in 70% of the cases involving black defendants and white victims; 32% of the cases involving white defendants and white victims; 15% of the cases involving black defendants and black victims; and 19% of the cases involving white defendants and black victims.

Baldus subjected his data to an extensive analysis, taking account of 230 variables that could have explained the disparities on nonracial grounds. One of his models concludes that, even after taking account of 39 nonracial variables, defendants charged with killing white victims were 4.3 times as likely to receive a death sentence as defendants charged with killing blacks. According to this model, black defendants were 1.1 times as likely to receive a death sentence as other defendants. Thus, the Baldus study indicates that black defendants, such as McCleskey, who kill white victims have the greatest likelihood of receiving the death penalty. . . .

McCleskey's first claim is that the Georgia capital punishment statute violates the Equal Protection Clause of the Fourteenth Amendment. He argues that race has infected the administration of Georgia's statute in two ways: persons who murder whites are more likely to be sentenced to death than persons who murder blacks, and black murderers are more likely to be sentenced to death than white murderers. As a black defendant who killed a white victim, McCleskey claims that the Baldus study demonstrates that he was discriminated against because of his race and because of the race of his victim. . . .

We agree with the Court of Appeals, and every other court that has considered such a challenge, that this claim must fail.

Our analysis begins with the basic principle that a defendant who alleges an equal protection violation has the burden of proving "the existence of purposeful discrimination." A corollary to this principle is that a criminal defendant must prove that the purposeful discrimination "had a discriminatory effect" on him. Thus, to prevail under the Equal Protection Clause, McCleskey must prove that the decisionmakers in *his* case acted with discriminatory purpose. He offers no evidence specific to his own case that would support an inference that racial considerations played a part in his sentence. Instead, he relies solely on the Baldus study. . . .

Each particular decision to impose the death penalty is made by a petit jury selected from a properly constituted venire. Each jury is unique in its composition, and the Constitution requires that its decision rest on consideration of innumerable factors that vary according to the characteristics of the individual defendant and the facts of the particular capital offense. . . .

McCleskey's statistical proffer must be viewed in the context of his challenge. McCleskey challenges decisions at the heart of the State's criminal justice system. . . .

Implementation of these laws necessarily requires discretionary judgments. Because discretion is essential to the criminal justice process, we would demand exceptionally clear proof before we would infer that the discretion has been abused. The unique nature of the decisions at issue in this case also counsel against adopting such an inference from the disparities indicated by the Baldus study. Accordingly, we hold that the Baldus study is clearly insufficient to support an inference that any of the decisionmakers in McCleskey's case acted with discriminatory purpose.

McCleskey also suggests that the Baldus study proves that the State as a whole has acted with a discriminatory purpose. He appears to argue that the State has violated the Equal Protection Clause by adopting the capital punishment statute and allowing it to remain in force despite its allegedly discriminatory application. But " '[d]iscriminatory purpose' . . . implies more than intent as volition or intent as awareness of consequences. It implies that the decisionmaker, in this case a state legislature, selected or reaffirmed a particular course of action at least in part 'because of,' not merely 'in spite of,' its adverse effects upon an identifiable group." . . .

For this claim to prevail, McCleskey would have to prove that the Georgia Legislature enacted or maintained the death penalty statute *because of* an anticipated racially discriminatory effect. In *Gregg* v. *Georgia*, 428 U.S. 153 (1976), this Court found that the Georgia capital sentencing system could operate in a fair and neutral manner. There was no evidence then, and there is none now, that the Georgia Legislature enacted the capital punishment statute to further a racially discriminatory purpose. . . .

McCleskey also argues that the Georgia capital punishment system is arbitrary and capricious in *application,* and therefore his sentence is excessive, because racial considerations may influence capital sentencing decisions in Georgia. We now address this claim.

To evaluate McCleskey's challenge, we must examine exactly what the Baldus study may show. Even Professor Baldus does not contend that his statistics *prove* that race enters into any capital sentencing decisions or that race was a factor in McCleskey's particular case. Statistics at most may show only a likelihood that a particular factor entered into some decisions. There is, of course, some risk of racial prejudice influencing a jury's decision in a criminal case. There are similar risks that other kinds of prejudice will influence other criminal trials. . . .

McCleskey asks us to accept the likelihood allegedly shown by the Baldus study as the constitutional measure of an unacceptable risk of racial prejudice influencing capital sentencing decisions. This we decline to do. . . .

Where the discretion that is fundamental to our criminal process is involved, we decline to assume that what is unexplained is invidious. In light of the safeguards designed to minimize racial bias in the process, the fundamental value of jury trial in our criminal justice system, and the benefits that discretion provides to criminal defendants, we hold that the Baldus study does not demonstrate a constitutionally significant risk of racial bias affecting the Georgia capital sentencing process.

Two additional concerns inform our decision in this case. First, McCleskey's claim, taken to its logical conclusion, throws into serious question the principles that underlie our entire criminal justice system. The Eighth Amendment is not limited in application to capital punishment, but applies to all penalties. Thus, if we accepted McCleskey's claim that racial bias has impermissibly tainted the capital sentencing decision, we could soon be faced with similar claims as to other types of penalty. Moreover, the claim that his sentence rests on the irrelevant factor of race easily could be extended to apply to claims based on unexplained discrepancies that correlate to membership in other minority groups, and even to gender. . . . Also, there is no logical reason that such a claim need be limited to racial or sexual bias. If arbitrary and capricious punishment is the touchstone under the Eighth Amendment, such a claim could—at least in theory—be based upon any arbitrary variable, such as the defendant's facial characteristics, or the physical attractiveness of the defendant or the victim, that some statistical study indicates may be influential in jury decisionmaking. As these examples illustrate, there is no limiting principle to the type of challenge brought by McCleskey. . . .

Second, McCleskey's arguments are best presented to the legislative bodies. It is not the responsibility—or indeed even the right—of this Court to determine the appropriate punishment for particular crimes. It is the legislatures, the elected representatives of the people, that are "constituted to respond to the will and consequently the moral values of the people." Legislatures also are better qualified to weigh and "evaluate the results of statistical studies in terms of their own local conditions and with a flexibility of approach that is not available to the courts." Capital punishment is now the law in more than two thirds of our States. It is the ultimate duty of courts to determine on a case-by-case basis whether these laws are applied consistently with the Constitution. Despite McCleskey's wide ranging arguments that basically challenge the validity of capital punishment in our multi-racial society, the only question before us is whether in his case, the law of Georgia was properly applied. We agree with the District Court and the Court of Appeals for the Eleventh Circuit that this was carefully and correctly done in this case.

JUSTICE BRENNAN, with whom JUSTICE MARSHALL joins, and with whom JUSTICE BLACKMUN and JUSTICE STEVENS join in part, dissenting.

Adhering to my view that the death penalty is in all circumstances cruel and unusual punishment forbidden by the Eighth and Fourteenth Amendments, I would vacate the decision below insofar as it left undisturbed the death sentence imposed in this case. . . .

The Court today holds that Warren McCleskey's sentence was constitutionally imposed. It finds no fault in a system in which lawyers must tell their clients that race casts a large shadow on the capital sentencing process. The Court arrives at this conclusion by stating that the Baldus study cannot "*prove* that race enters into any capital sentencing decisions or that race was a factor in McCleskey's particular case." Since, according to Professor Baldus, we cannot say "to a moral certainty" that race influenced a decision, we can identify only "a likelihood that a particular factor entered into some decisions," and "a discrepancy that appears to correlate with race." This "likelihood" and "discrepancy," holds the Court, is insufficient to establish a constitutional violation. The Court reaches this conclusion by placing four factors on the scales opposite McCleskey's evidence: the desire to encourage sentencing discretion, the existence of "statutory safeguards" in the Georgia scheme, the fear of encouraging widespread challenges to other sentencing decisions, and the limits of the judicial

role. The Court's evaluation of the significance of petitioner's evidence is fundamentally at odds with our consistent concern for rationality in capital sentencing, and the considerations that the majority invokes to discount that evidence cannot justify ignoring its force. . . .

Defendants challenging their death sentences thus never have had to prove that impermissible considerations have actually infected sentencing decisions. We have required instead that they establish that the system under which they were sentenced posed a significant risk of such an occurrence. McCleskey's claim does differ, however, in one respect from these earlier cases: it is the first to base a challenge not on speculation about how a system *might* operate, but on empirical documentation of how it *does* operate.

The Court assumes the statistical validity of the Baldus study and acknowledges that McCleskey has demonstrated a risk that racial prejudice plays a role in capital sentencing in Georgia. Nonetheless, it finds the probability of prejudice insufficient to create constitutional concern. Close analysis of the Baldus study, however, in light of both statistical principles and human experience, reveals that the risk that race influenced McCleskey's sentence is intolerable by any imaginable standard.

The Baldus study indicates that, after taking into account 230 nonracial factors that might legitimately influence a sentencer, the jury *more likely than not* would have spared McCleskey's life had his victim been black. The study distinguishes between those cases in which (1) the jury exercises virtually no discretion because the strength or weakness of aggravating factors usually suggests that only one outcome is appropriate; and (2) cases reflecting an "intermediate" level of aggravation, in which the jury has considerable discretion in choosing a sentence. McCleskey's case falls into the intermediate range. In such cases, death is imposed in 34% of white-victim crimes and 14% of black-victim crimes, a difference of 139% in the rate of imposition of the death penalty. In other words, just under 59%—almost 6 in 10—defendants comparable to McCleskey would not have received the death penalty if their victims had been black.

Furthermore, even examination of the sentencing system as a whole, factoring in those cases in which the jury exercises little discretion, indicates the influence of race on capital sentencing. For the Georgia system as a whole, race accounts for a six percentage point difference in the rate at which capital punishment is imposed. Since death is imposed in 11% of all white-victim cases, the rate in comparably aggravated black-victim cases is 5%. The rate of capital sentencing in a white-victim case is thus 120% greater than the rate in a black-victim case. Put another way, over half—55%—of defendants in white-victim crimes in Georgia would not have been sentenced to die if their victims had been black. Of the more than 200 variables potentially relevant to a sentencing decision, race of the victim is a powerful explanation for variation in death sentence rates—as powerful as nonracial aggravating factors such as a prior murder conviction or acting as the principal planner of the homicide.

These adjusted figures are only the most conservative indication of the risk that race will influence the death sentences of defendants in Georgia. Data unadjusted for the mitigating or aggravating effect of other factors show an even more pronounced disparity by race. The capital sentencing rate for all white-victim cases was almost *11 times* greater than the rate for black-victim cases. Furthermore, blacks who kill whites are sentenced to death nearly *22 times* the rate of blacks who kill blacks, and more than *7 times* the rate of whites who kill blacks. In addition,

prosecutors seek the death penalty for 70% of black defendants with white victims, but for only 15% of black defendants with black victims, and only 19% of white defendants with black victims. Since our decision upholding the Georgia capital sentencing system in *Gregg*, the State has executed 7 persons. All of the 7 were convicted of killing whites, and 6 of the 7 executed were black. Such execution figures are especially striking in light of the fact that, during the period encompassed by the Baldus study, only 9.2% of Georgia homicides involved black defendants and white victims, while 60.7% involved black victims.

The majority thus misreads our Eighth Amend-ment jurisprudence in concluding that McCleskey has not demonstrated a degree of risk sufficient to raise constitutional concern. The determination of the significance of his evidence is at its core an exercise in human moral judgment, not a mechanical statistical analysis. It must first and foremost be informed by awareness of the fact that death is irrevocable, and that as a result "the qualitative difference of death from all other punishments requires a greater degree of scrutiny of the capital sentencing determination." For this reason, we have demanded a uniquely high degree of rationality in imposing the death penalty. A capital sentencing system in which race more likely than not plays a role does not meet this standard.

Stanford v. *Kentucky*
492 U.S. 361, 109 S. Ct. 2969, 105 L. Ed. 2d 306 (1989)

The Supreme Court granted certiorari in two consolidated cases, *Stanford* v. *Kentucky* and *Wilkins* v. *Missouri*, to decide whether the Eighth Amendment precludes the death penalty for individuals who commit crimes at 16 or 17 years of age. The facts are presented in Justice Scalia's opinion below. *Opinion of the Court: <u>Scalia</u>, Kennedy, O'Connor, Rehnquist, White. Concurring opinion: <u>O'Connor</u>. Dissenting opinion: <u>Brennan</u>, Blackmun, Marshall, Stevens.*

JUSTICE SCALIA . . . delivered the opinion of the Court. . . .

These two consolidated cases require us to decide whether the imposition of capital punishment on an individual for a crime committed at 16 or 17 years of age constitutes cruel and unusual punishment under the Eighth Amendment.

The first case . . . involves the shooting death of 20-year-old Baerbel Poore in Jefferson County, Kentucky. Petitioner Kevin Stanford committed the murder on January 7, 1981, when he was approximately 17 years and 4 months of age. Stanford and his accomplice repeatedly raped and sodomized Poore during and after their commission of a robbery at a gas station where she worked as an attendant. They then drove her to a secluded area near the station, where Stanford shot her point-blank in the face and then in the back of her head. The proceeds from the robbery were roughly 300 cartons of cigarettes, two gallons of fuel and a small amount of cash. A corrections officer testified that petitioner explained the murder as follows: " '[H]e said, I had to shoot her, [she] lived next door to me and she would recognize me. . . . I guess we could have tied her up or something or beat [her up] . . . and tell her if she tells, we would kill her. . . . Then after he said that he started laughing.' " . . .

After Stanford's arrest, a Kentucky juvenile court conducted hearings to determine whether he should be transferred for trial as an adult under Ky. Rev. Stat. § 208.170. . . . The statute provided that juvenile court jurisdiction could be waived and an offender tried as an adult if he was either charged with a Class A felony or capital crime, or was over 16 years of age and charged with a felony. Stressing the seriousness of petitioner's offenses and the unsuccessful attempts of the juvenile system to treat him for numerous instances of past delinquency, the juvenile court found certification for trial as an adult to be in the best interest of petitioner and the community.

Stanford was convicted of murder, first-degree sodomy, first-degree robbery, and receiving stolen property, and was sentenced to death and 45 years in prison. The Kentucky Supreme Court affirmed the death sentence, rejecting Stanford's "deman[d] that he has a constitutional right to treatment" . . . Finding that the record clearly demonstrated that "there was no program or treatment appropriate for the appellant in the juvenile justice system," the court held that the juvenile court did not err in certifying petitioner for trial as an adult. The court also stated that petitioner's "age and the possibility that he might be rehabilitated were mitigating factors appropriately left to the consideration of the jury that tried him." . . .

The second case before us today . . . involves the stabbing death of Nancy Allen, a 26-year-old mother of two who was working behind the sales counter of the convenience store she and David Allen owned and operated in Avondale, Missouri. Petitioner Heath Wilkins committed the murder on July 27, 1985, when he was approximately 16 years and 6 months of age. The record reflects that Wilkins' plan was to rob the store and murder "whoever was behind the counter" because "a dead person can't talk." While Wilkins' accomplice, Patrick Stevens, held Allen, Wilkins stabbed her, causing her to fall to the floor. When Stevens had trouble operating the cash register, Allen spoke up to assist him, leading Wilkins to stab her three more times in her chest. Two of these wounds penetrated the victim's heart. When Allen began to beg for her life, Wilkins stabbed her four more times in the neck, opening her carotid artery. After helping themselves to liquor, cigarettes, rolling papers, and approximately $450 in cash and checks, Wilkins and Stevens left Allen to die on the floor.

Because he was roughly six months short of the age of majority for purposes of criminal prosecution, . . . Wilkins could not automatically be tried as an adult under Missouri law. Before that could happen, the juvenile court was required to terminate juvenile court jurisdiction and certify Wilkins for trial as an adult under § 211.071, which permits individuals between 14 and 17 years of age who have committed felonies to be tried as adults. Relying on the "viciousness, force and violence" of the alleged crime, petitioner's maturity, and the failure of the juvenile justice system to rehabilitate him after previous delinquent acts, the juvenile court made the necessary certification.

Wilkins was charged with first-degree murder, armed criminal action, and carrying a concealed weapon. After the court found him competent, petitioner entered guilty pleas to all charges. A punishment hearing was held, at which both the State and petitioner himself urged imposition of the death sentence. Evidence at the hearing revealed that petitioner had been in and out of juvenile facilities since the age of eight for various acts of burglary, theft, and arson, had attempted to kill his mother by putting insecticide into Tylenol capsules, and had killed several animals in his neighborhood. Although psychiatric testimony indicated that Wilkins had "personality disorders," the witnesses agreed that Wilkins was aware of his actions and could distinguish right from wrong. . . . On mandatory review of Wilkins' death sentence, the Supreme Court of Missouri affirmed, rejecting the argument that the punishment violated the Eighth Amendment. . . .

The thrust of both Wilkins' and Stanford's arguments is that imposition of the death penalty on those who were juveniles when they committed their crimes falls within the Eighth Amendment's prohibition against "cruel and unusual punishments." Wilkins would have us define juveniles as individuals 16 years of age and under; Stanford would draw the line at 17.

Neither petitioner asserts that his sentence constitutes one of "those modes or acts of punishment that had been considered cruel and unusual at the time that the Bill of Rights was adopted." . . . At that time, the common law set the rebuttable presumption of incapacity to commit any felony at the age of 14, and theoretically permitted capital punishment to be imposed on anyone over the age of 7. . . .

Thus petitioners are left to argue that their punishment is contrary to the "evolving standards of decency that mark the progress of a maturing society," *Trop* v. *Dulles*, . . . (1958). . . . They are correct in asserting that this Court has "not confined the prohibition embodied in the Eighth Amendment to 'barbarous' methods that were generally outlawed in the 18th century," but instead has interpreted the Amendment "in a flexible and dynamic manner." . . . In determining what standards have "evolved," however, we have looked not to our own conceptions of decency, but to those of modern American society as a whole. . . .

"[F]irst" among the "objective indicia that reflect the public attitude toward a given sanction'" are statutes passed by society's elected representatives. . . . Of the 37 States whose laws permit capital punishment, 15 decline to impose it upon 16-year-old offenders and 12 decline to impose it on 17-year-old offenders. This does not establish the degree of national consensus this Court has previously thought sufficient to label a particular punishment cruel and unusual. . . .

Petitioners make much of the recently enacted federal statute providing capital punishment for certain drug-related offenses, but limiting that punishment to offenders 18 and over. . . . That reliance is entirely misplaced. To begin with, the statute in question does not embody a judgment by the Federal Legislature that *no* murder is heinous enough to warrant the execution of such a youthful offender, but merely that the narrow class of offense it defines is not. The congressional judgment on the broader question, if apparent at all, is to be found in the law that permits 16- and 17-year-olds (after appropriate findings) to be tried and punished as adults for *all* federal offenses, including those bearing a capital penalty that is not limited to 18-year-olds. . . . Moreover, even if it were true that no federal statute permitted the execution of persons under 18, that would not remotely establish—in the face of a substantial number of state statutes to the contrary—a national consensus that such punishment is inhumane, any more than the absence of a federal lottery establishes a national consensus that lotteries are socially harmful. To be sure, the absence of a federal death penalty for 16- or 17-year-olds (if it existed) might be evidence that there is no national consensus *in favor of* such punishment. It is not the burden of Kentucky and Missouri, however, to establish a national consensus approving what their citizens have voted to do; rather, it is the "heavy burden" of petitioners . . . to establish a national consensus *against* it. . . .

Having failed to establish a consensus against capital punishment for 16- and 17-year-old offenders through state and federal statutes, . . . petitioners seek to demonstrate it through other indicia, including public opinion polls, the views of interest groups and the positions adopted by various professional associations. We decline the invitation to rest constitutional law upon such uncertain foundations. A revised national consensus so broad, so clear and so enduring as to justify a permanent prohibition upon all units of democratic government must appear in the operative acts (laws and the application of laws) that the people have approved.

We also reject petitioners' argument that we should invalidate capital punishment of 16- and 17-year-old offenders on the ground that it fails to serve the legitimate goals of penology. According to petitioners, it fails to deter because juveniles, possessing less developed cognitive skills than adults, are less likely to fear death; and it fails to exact just retribution because juveniles, being less mature and responsible, are also less morally blameworthy. In support of these claims, petitioners . . . marshall an array of socioscientific evidence concerning the psychological and emotional development of 16- and 17-year-olds.

If such evidence could conclusively establish the entire lack of deterrent effect and moral responsibility, resort to the Cruel and Unusual Punishments Clause would be unnecessary; the Equal Protection Clause of the Fourteenth Amendment would invalidate these laws for lack of rational basis. . . . But as the adjective "socioscientific" suggests (and insofar as evaluation of moral responsibility is concerned perhaps the adjective "ethicoscientific" would be more apt), it is not demonstrable that no 16-year-old is "adequately responsible" or significantly deterred. It is rational, even if mistaken, to think the contrary. The battle must be fought, then, on the field of the Eighth Amendment; and in that struggle socioscientific, ethicoscientific, or even purely scientific evidence is not an available weapon. The punishment is either "cruel *and* unusual" (*i.e.*, society has set its face against it) or it is not. The audience for these arguments, in other words, is not this Court but the citizenry of the United States. It is they, not we, who must be persuaded. For as we stated earlier, our job is to *identify* the "evolving standards of decency"; to determine, not what they *should* be, but what they *are.* We have no power under the Eighth Amendment to substitute our belief in the scientific evidence for the society's apparent skepticism. In short, we emphatically reject petitioner's suggestion that the issues in this case permit us to apply our "own informed judgment," . . . regarding the desirability of permitting the death penalty for crimes by 16- and 17-year-olds.

We reject the dissent's contention that our approach, by "largely return[ing] the task of defining the contours of Eighth Amendment protection to political majorities," leaves "'[c]onstitutional doctrine [to] be formulated by the acts of those institutions which the Constitution is supposed to limit'" . . . When this Court cast loose from the historical moorings consisting of the original application of the Eighth Amendment, it did not embark rudderless upon a wide-open sea. Rather, it limited the Amendment's extension to those practices contrary to the "evolving *standards* of decency that mark the progress of a maturing *society.*" . . . It has never been thought that this was a shorthand reference to the preferences of a majority of this Court. By reaching a decision supported neither by constitutional text nor by the demonstrable current standards of our citizens, the dissent displays a failure to appreciate that "those institutions which the Constitution is supposed to limit" include the Court itself. To say, as the dissent says, that "it is for *us* ultimately to judge whether the Eighth Amendment permits imposition of the death penalty," . . . — and to mean that as the dissent means it, *i.e.*, that it is for *us* to judge, not on the basis of what we perceive the Eighth Amendment originally prohibited, or on the basis of what we perceive the society through its democratic processes now overwhelmingly disapproves, but on the basis of what we think "proportionate" and "measurably contributory to acceptable goals of punishment"—to say and mean that, is to replace judges of the law with a committee of philosopher-kings. . . .

We discern neither a historical nor a modern societal consensus forbidding the imposition of capital punishment on any person who murders at 16 or 17 years of age. Accordingly, we conclude that such punishment does not offend the Eighth Amendment's prohibition against cruel and unusual punishment.

JUSTICE BRENNAN, with whom JUSTICE MARSHALL, JUSTICE BLACKMUN, and JUSTICE STEVENS join, dissenting.

I believe that to take the life of a person as punishment for a crime committed when below the age of 18 is cruel and unusual and hence is prohibited by the Eighth Amendment. . . . The rejection of the death penalty for juveniles by a majority of the States, the rarity of the sentence for juveniles, both as an absolute and a comparative matter, the decisions of respected organizations in relevant fields that this punishment is unacceptable, and its rejection generally throughout the world, provide to my mind a strong grounding for the view that it is not constitutionally tolerable that certain States persist in authorizing the execution of adolescent offenders. It is unnecessary, however, to rest a view that the Eighth Amendment prohibits the execution of minors solely upon a judgment as to the meaning to be attached to the evidence of contemporary values outlined above, for the execution of juveniles fails to satisfy two well-established and independent Eighth Amendment requirements—that a punishment not be disproportionate, and that it make a contribution to acceptable goals of punishment. . . .

Justice Scalia forthrightly states in his . . . opinion that Eighth Amendment analysis is at an end once legislation and jury verdicts relating to the punishment in question are analyzed as indicators of contemporary values. . . .

Justice Scalia's approach would largely return the task of defining the contours of Eighth Amendment protection to political majorities. . . . The promise of the Bill of Rights goes unfulfilled when we leave "[c]onstitutional doctrine [to] be formulated by the acts of those institutions which the Constitution is supposed to limit," . . . as is the case under Justice Scalia's positivist approach to the definition of citizens' rights. This Court abandons its proven and proper role in our constitutional system when it hands back to the very majorities the Framers distrusted the power to define the precise scope of protection afforded by the Bill of Rights, rather than bringing its own judgment to bear on that question, after complete analysis. . . .

Proportionality analysis requires that we compare "the gravity of the offense," understood to include not only the injury caused, but also the defendant's culpability, with "the harshness of the penalty." . . . In my view, juveniles so generally lack the degree of responsibility for their crimes that is a predicate for the constitutional imposition of the death penalty that the Eighth Amendment forbids that they receive that punishment. . . .

Under a second strand of Eighth Amendment inquiry into whether a particular sentence is excessive and hence unconstitutional we ask whether the sentence makes a measurable contribution to acceptable goals of punishment. . . . The two "principal social purposes" of capital punishment are said to be "retribution and the deterrence of capital crimes by prospective offenders." . . . Unless the death penalty applied to persons for offenses committed under 18 measur-

ably contributes to one of these goals, the Eighth Amendment prohibits it. . . .

"[R]etribution as a justification for executing [offenders] very much depends on the degree of [their] culpability." . . . I have explained . . . why I believe juveniles lack the culpability that makes a crime so extreme that it may warrant, according to this Court's cases, the death penalty; and why we should treat juveniles as a class as exempt from the ultimate penalty. These same considerations persuade me that executing juveniles "does not measurably contribute to the retributive end of ensuring that the criminal gets his just deserts." . . . A punishment that fails the Eighth Amendment test of proportionality because disproportionate to the offender's blameworthiness by definition is not justly deserved.

Nor does the execution of juvenile offenders measurably contribute to the goal of deterrence. Excluding juveniles from the class of persons eligible to receive the death penalty will have little effect on any deterrent value capital punishment may have for potential offenders who are over 18: these adult offenders may of course remain eligible for a death sentence. The potential deterrent effect of juvenile executions on adolescent offenders is also insignificant. The deterrent value of capital punishment rests "on the assumption that we are rational beings who always think before we act, and then base our actions on a careful calculation of the gains and losses involved." . . . As noted, "[t]he likelihood that the teenage offender has made the kind of cost-benefit analysis that attaches any weight to the possibility of execution is so remote as to be virtually nonexistent." . . . Because imposition of the death penalty on persons for offenses committed under the age of 18 makes no measurable contribution to the goals of either retribution or deterrence, it is "nothing more than the purposeless and needless imposition of pain and suffering," . . . and is thus excessive and unconstitutional.

Payne v. *Tennessee*
111 S. Ct. 2597, 115 L. Ed. 2d 720 (1991)

Pervis Tyrone Payne was convicted by a Tennessee jury of the first-degree murders of Charisse Christopher and her two-year-old daughter. During the sentencing phase of the trial, victim impact evidence was introduced, and in arguing for the death penalty, the prosecutor commented on the effects of the crimes upon the victims' family. The jury sentenced Payne to death on each of the murder counts. The Tennessee Supreme Court affirmed, rejecting the contention that the admission of the victim impact evidence and the prosecutor's closing arguments violated Payne's Eighth Amendment rights under *Booth* v. *Maryland* (1987) and South *Carolina* v. *Gathers* (1989), which held that evidence and argument relating to the victim and the impact of the victim's death on the victim's family are *per se* inadmissible at a capital sentencing hearing. The Supreme Court granted certiorari. *Opinion of the Court: Rehnquist, Kennedy, O'Connor, Scalia, Souter, White. Concurring opinions: O'Connor, Kennedy, White; Scalia, Kennedy, O'Connor; Souter, Kennedy. Dissenting opinions: Marshall, Blackmun; Stevens, Blackmun.*

CHIEF JUSTICE REHNQUIST delivered the opinion of the Court.

In this case we reconsider our holdings in *Booth* v. *Maryland*, 482 U.S. 496 (1987), and *South Carolina* v. *Gathers*, 490 U.S. 805 (1989), that the Eighth Amendment bars the admission of victim impact evidence during the penalty phase of a capital trial.

The petitioner, Pervis Tyrone Payne, was convicted by a jury on two counts of first-degree murder and one count of assault with intent to commit murder in the first degree. He was sentenced to death for each of the murders, and to 30 years in prison for the assault.

The victims of Payne's offenses were 28-year-old Charisse Christopher, her 2-year-old daughter Lacie, and her 3-year-old son Nicholas. The three lived together in an apartment in Millington, Tennessee, across the hall from Payne's girlfriend, Bobbie Thomas. On Saturday, June 27, 1987, Payne visited Thomas' apartment several times in expectation of her return from her mother's house in Arkansas, but found no one at home. On one visit, he left his overnight bag, containing clothes and other items for his weekend stay, in the hallway outside Thomas' apartment. With the bag were three cans of malt liquor.

Payne passed the morning and early afternoon injecting cocaine and drinking beer. Later, he drove around the town with a friend in the friend's car, each of them taking turns reading a pornographic magazine. Sometime around 3 p.m., Payne returned to the apartment complex, entered the Christophers' apartment, and began making sexual advances towards Charisse. Charisse resisted and Payne became violent. A neighbor who resided in the apartment directly beneath the Christophers, heard Charisse screaming, "'Get out, get out,' as if she were telling the children to leave." The noise briefly subsided and then began, "'horribly loud.'" The neighbor called the police after she heard a "blood-curdling scream" from the Christopher apartment.

When the first police officer arrived at the scene, he immediately encountered Payne who was leaving the apartment building so covered with blood that he appeared to be "'sweating blood.'" The officer confronted Payne, who responded "'I'm the complainant'." When the officer asked, "'What's going on up there?'" Payne struck the officer with the overnight bag, dropped his tennis shoes, and fled.

Inside the apartment, the police encountered a horrifying scene. Blood covered the walls and floor throughout the unit. Charisse and her children were lying on the floor in the kitchen. Nicholas, despite several wounds inflicted by a butcher knife that completely penetrated through his body from front to back, was still breathing. Miraculously, he survived, but not until after undergoing seven hours of surgery and a transfusion of 1700 cc's of blood—400 to 500 cc's more than his estimated normal blood volume. Charisse and Lacie were dead.

Charisse's body was found on the kitchen floor on her back, her legs fully extended. She had sustained 42 direct knife wounds and 42 defensive wounds on her arms and hands. The wounds were caused by 41 separate thrusts of a butcher knife. None of the 84 wounds inflicted by Payne were individually fatal; rather, the cause of death was most likely bleeding from all of the wounds.

Lacie's body was on the kitchen floor near her mother. She had suffered stab wounds to the chest, abdomen, back, and head. The murder weapon, a butcher knife, was found at her feet. Payne's baseball cap was snapped on her arm near her elbow. Three cans of malt liquor bearing Payne's fingerprints were found on a table near her body, and a fourth empty one was on the landing outside the apartment door.

Payne was apprehended later that day hiding in the attic of the home of a former girlfriend. As he descended the stairs of the attic, he stated to the arresting officers, "Man, I aint killed no woman." According to one of the officers, Payne had "a wild look about him. His pupils were contracted. He was foaming at the mouth, saliva. He appeared to be very nervous. He was breathing real rapid." He had blood on his body and clothes and several scratches across his chest. It was later determined that the blood stains matched the victims' blood types. A search of his pockets revealed a packet containing cocaine residue, a hypodermic syringe wrapper, and a cap from a hypodermic syringe. His overnight bag, containing a bloody white shirt, was found in a nearby dumpster.

At trial, Payne took the stand and, despite the overwhelming and relatively uncontroverted evidence against him, testified that he had not harmed any of the Christophers. Rather he asserted that another man had raced by him as he was walking up the stairs to the floor where the Christophers lived. He stated that he had gotten blood on himself when, after hearing moans from the Christophers' apartment, he had tried to help the victims. According to his testimony, he panicked and fled when he heard police sirens and noticed the blood on his clothes. The jury returned guilty verdicts against Payne on all counts.

During the sentencing phase of the trial, Payne presented the testimony of four witnesses: his mother and father, Bobbie Thomas, and Dr. John T. Huston, a clinical psychologist specializing in criminal court evaluation work. Bobbie Thomas testified that she met Payne at church, during a time when she was being abused by her husband. She stated that Payne was a very caring person, and that he devoted much time and attention to her three children, who were being affected by

her marital difficulties. She said that the children had come to love him very much and would miss him, and that he "behaved just like a father that loved his kids." She asserted that he did not drink, nor did he use drugs, and that it was generally inconsistent with Payne's character to have committed these crimes.

Dr. Huston testified that based on Payne's low score on an IQ test, Payne was "mentally handicapped." Huston also said that Payne was neither psychotic nor schizophrenic, and that Payne was the most polite prisoner he had ever met. Payne's parents testified that their son had no prior criminal record and had never been arrested. They also stated that Payne had no history of alcohol or drug abuse, he worked with his father as a painter, he was good with children, and that he was a good son.

The State presented the testimony of Charisse's mother, Mary Zvolanek. When asked how Nicholas had been affected by the murders of his mother and sister, she responded:

> He cries for his mom. He doesn't seem to understand why she doesn't come home. And he cries for his sister Lacie. He comes to me many times during the week and asks me, Grandmama, do you miss my Lacie. And I tell him yes. He says, I'm worried about my Lacie.

In arguing for the death penalty during closing argument, the prosecutor commented on the continuing effects of Nicholas' experience, stating:

> But we do know that Nicholas was alive. And Nicholas was in the same room. Nicholas was still conscious. His eyes were open. He responded to the paramedics. He was able to follow their directions. He was able to hold his intestines in as he was carried to the ambulance. So he knew what happened to his mother and baby sister.
>
> There is nothing you can do to ease the pain of any of the families involved in this case. There is nothing you can do to ease the pain of Bernice or Carl Payne, and that's a tragedy. There is nothing you can do basically to ease the pain of Mr. and Mrs. Zvolanek, and that's a tragedy. They will have to live with it the rest of their lives. There is obviously nothing you can do for

Charisse and Lacie Jo. But there is something that you can do for Nicholas.

Somewhere down the road Nicholas is going to grow up, hopefully. He's going to want to know what happened. And he is going to know what happened to his baby sister and his mother. He is going to want to know what type of justice was done. He is going to want to know what happened. With your verdict, you will provide the answer.

In the rebuttal to Payne's closing argument, the prosecutor stated:

You saw the videotape this morning. You saw what Nicholas Christopher will carry in his mind forever. When you talk about cruel, when you talk about atrocious, and when you talk about heinous, that picture will always come into your mind, probably throughout the rest of your lives.

. . . No one will ever know about Lacie Jo because she never had the chance to grow up. Her life was taken from her at the age of two years old. So, no, there won't be a high school principal to talk about Lacie Jo Christopher, and there won't be anybody to take her to her high school prom. And there won't be anybody there—there won't be her mother there or Nicholas' mother there to kiss him at night. His mother will never kiss him good night or pat him as he goes off to bed, or hold him and sing him a lullaby.

[Petitioner's attorney] wants you to think about a good reputation, people who love the defendant and things about him. He doesn't want you to think about the people who love Charisse Christopher, her mother and daddy who loved her. The people who loved little Lacie Jo, the grandparents who are still here. The brother who mourns for her every single day and wants to know where his best little playmate is. He doesn't have anybody to watch cartoons with him, a little one. These are the things that go into why it is especially cruel, heinous, and atrocious, the burden that that child will carry forever.

The jury sentenced Payne to death on each of the murder counts.

The Supreme Court of Tennessee affirmed the conviction and sentence. The court rejected Payne's contention that the admission of the grandmother's testimony and the State's closing argument constituted prejudicial violations of his rights under the Eighth Amendment as applied in *Booth* v. *Maryland* and *South Carolina* v. *Gathers.* The court characterized the grandmother's testimony as "technically irrelevant," but concluded that it "did not create a constitutionally unacceptable risk of an arbitrary imposition of the death penalty and was harmless beyond a reasonable doubt."

The court determined that the prosecutor's comments during closing argument were "relevant to [Payne's] personal responsibility and moral guilt." The court explained that "[w]hen a person deliberately picks a butcher knife out of a kitchen drawer and proceeds to stab to death a twenty-eight-year-old mother, her two and one-half year old daughter and her three and one-half year old son, in the same room, the physical and mental condition of the boy he left for dead is surely relevant in determining his 'blameworthiness.'" The court concluded that any violation of Payne's rights under *Booth* and *Gathers* "was harmless beyond a reasonable doubt."

We granted certiorari to reconsider our holdings in *Booth* and *Gathers* that the Eighth Amendment prohibits a capital sentencing jury from considering "victim impact" evidence relating to the personal characteristics of the victim and the emotional impact of the crimes on the victim's family.

In *Booth,* the defendant robbed and murdered an elderly couple. As required by a state statute, a victim impact statement was prepared based on interviews with the victims' son, daughter, son-in-law, and granddaughter. The statement, which described the personal characteristics of the victims, the emotional impact of the crimes on the family, and set forth the family members' opinions and characterizations of the crimes and the defendant, was submitted to the jury at sentencing. The jury imposed the death penalty. The conviction and sentence were affirmed on appeal by the State's highest court.

The Court held by a 5-to-4 vote that the Eighth Amendment prohibits a jury from considering a victim impact statement at the sentencing phase of a capital trial. The Court made clear that the admissibility of victim impact evidence was not to be determined on a case-by-case basis, but that such evidence was *per se* inadmissible in the sentencing phase of a capital case except to the extent that it "relate[d] directly to the circumstances of the crime." In *Gathers*, decided two years later, the Court extended the rule announced in *Booth* to statements made by a prosecutor to the sentencing jury regarding the personal qualities of the victim.

The *Booth* Court began its analysis with the observation that the capital defendant must be treated as a "'uniquely individual human being[g],'" and therefore the Constitution requires the jury to make an individual determination as to whether the defendant should be executed based on the "'character of the individual and the circumstances of the crime.'" The Court concluded that while no prior decision of this Court had mandated that only the defendant's character and immediate characteristics of the crime may constitutionally be considered, other factors are irrelevant to the capital sentencing decision unless they have "some bearing on the defendant's 'personal responsibility and moral guilt.'" To the extent that victim impact evidence presents "factors about which the defendant was unaware, and that were irrelevant to the decision to kill," the Court concluded, it has nothing to do with the "blameworthiness of a particular defendant." Evidence of the victim's character, the Court observed, "could well distract the sentencing jury from its constitutionally required task [of] determining whether the death penalty is appropriate in light of the background and record of the accused and the particular circumstances of the crime." The Court concluded that, except to the extent that victim impact evidence relates "directly to the circumstances of the crime," the prosecution may not introduce such evidence at a capital sentencing hearing because "it creates an impermissible risk that the capital sentencing decision will be made in an arbitrary manner."

Booth and *Gathers* were based on two premises: that evidence relating to a particular victim or to the harm that a capital defendant causes a victim's family do not in general reflect on the defendant's "blameworthiness," and that only evidence relating to "blameworthiness" is relevant to the capital sentencing decision. However, the assessment of harm caused by the defendant as a result of the crime charged has understandably been an important concern of the criminal law, both in determining the elements of the offense and in determining the appropriate punishment. Thus, two equally blameworthy criminal defendants may be guilty of different offenses solely because their acts cause differing amounts of harm. "If a bank robber aims his gun at a guard, pulls the trigger, and kills his target, he may be put to death. If the gun unexpectedly misfires, he may not. His moral guilt in both cases is identical, but his responsibility in the former is greater."

"We have held that the State cannot preclude the sentencer from considering 'any relevant mitigating evidence' that the defendant proffers in support of a sentence less than death." *Eddings* v. *Oklahoma*, 455 U.S. 104, 114 (1982). Thus we have, as the Court observed in *Booth*, required that the capital defendant be treated as a "'uniquely individual human bein[g].'" But it was never held or even suggested in any of our cases preceding *Booth* that the defendant, entitled as he was to individualized consideration, was to receive that consideration wholly apart from the crime which he had committed. The language quoted from *Woodson* in the *Booth* opinion was not intended to describe a class of evidence that *could not* be received, but a class of evidence which *must* be received. Any doubt on the matter is dispelled by comparing the language in *Woodson* with the language from *Gregg* v. *Georgia*, quoted above, which was handed down the same day as *Woodson*. This misreading of precedent in *Booth* has, we think, unfairly weighted the scales in a capital trial; while virtually no limits are placed on the relevant mitigating evidence a capital defendant may introduce concerning his own circumstances, the State is barred from either offering "a glimpse of the life" which a defendant "chose to extinguish," or demonstrating the loss to the victim's family and to society which have resulted from the defendant's homicide.

Payne echoes the concern voiced in the *Booth* case that the admission of victim impact evidence permits a jury to find that defendants whose victims were assets to their community are more deserving of punishment than those whose victims are perceived to be less worthy. As a general matter, however, victim impact evidence is not offered to encourage comparative judgments of this kind—for instance, that the killer of a hardworking, devoted parent deserves the death penalty, but that the murderer of a reprobate does not. It is designed to show instead *each* victim's "uniqueness as an individual human being," whatever the jury might think the loss to the community resulting from his death might be. The facts of *Gathers* are an excellent illustration of this: the evidence showed that the victim was an out of work, mentally handicapped individual, perhaps not, in the eyes of most, a significant contributor to society, but nonetheless a murdered human being.

Under our constitutional system, the primary responsibility for defining crimes against state law, fixing punishments for the commission of these crimes, and establishing procedures for criminal trials rests with the States.

"Within the constitutional limitations defined by our cases, the States enjoy their traditional latitude to prescribe the method by which those who commit murder should be punished." *Blystone* v. *Pennsylvania*, 494 U.S. 299, 309 (1990). The States remain free, in capital cases, as well as others, to devise new procedures and new remedies to meet felt needs. Victim impact evidence is simply another form or method of informing the sentencing authority about the specific harm caused by the crime in question, evidence of a general type long considered by sentencing authorities. We think the *Booth* Court was wrong in stating that this kind of evidence leads to the arbitrary imposition of the death penalty. In the majority of cases, and in this case, victim impact evidence serves entirely legitimate purposes. In the event that evidence is introduced that is so unduly prejudicial that it renders the trial fundamentally unfair, the Due Process Clause of the Fourteenth Amendment provides a mechanism for relief. Courts have always taken into consideration the harm done by the defendant in imposing sentence, and the evidence adduced in this case was illustrative of the harm caused by Payne's double murder.

We are now of the view that a State may properly conclude that for the jury to assess meaningfully the defendant's moral culpability and blameworthiness, it should have before it at the sentencing phase evidence of the specific harm caused by the defendant. "[T]he State has a legitimate interest in counteracting the mitigating evidence which the defendant is entitled to put in, by reminding the sentencer that just as the murderer should be considered as an individual, so too the victim is an individual whose death represents a unique loss to society and in particular to his family." *Booth*, 482 U.S., at 517 (Justice White, dissenting). By turning the victim into a "faceless stranger at the penalty phase of a capital trial," *Gathers*, 490 U.S., at 821 (Justice O'-Connor, dissenting), *Booth* deprives the State of the full moral force of its evidence and may prevent the jury from having before it all the information necessary to determine the proper punishment for a first-degree murder.

The present case is an example of the potential for such unfairness. The capital sentencing jury heard testimony from Payne's girlfriend that they met at church, that he was affectionate, caring, kind to her children, that he was not an abuser of drugs or alcohol, and that it was inconsistent with his character to have committed the murders. Payne's parents testified that he was a good son, and a clinical psychologist testified that Payne was an extremely polite prisoner and suffered from a low IQ. None of this testimony was related to the circumstances of Payne's brutal crimes. In contrast, the only evidence of the impact of Payne's offenses during the sentencing phase was Nicholas's grandmother's description—in response to a single question—that the child misses his mother and baby sister. Payne argues that the Eighth Amendment commands that the jury's death sentence must be set aside because the jury heard this testimony. But the testimony illustrated quite poignantly some of the harm that Payne's killing had caused; there is nothing unfair about allowing the jury to bear in mind that harm at the same time as it considers the mitigating evidence introduced by the defendant. The Supreme Court of Tennessee in this case obviously felt the unfairness of the rule pronounced by *Booth* when it said "[i]t is an affront to the civilized members of the human race to say that at sentencing in a capital case, a parade of witnesses may praise the background, character and good deeds of Defendant (as was done in this case), without limitation as to relevancy, but nothing may be said that bears upon the character of, or the harm imposed, upon the victims."

In *Gathers*, as indicated above, we extended the holding of *Booth* barring victim impact evidence to the prosecutor's argument to the jury. Human nature being what it is, capable lawyers trying cases to juries try to convey to the jurors that the people involved in the underlying events are, or were, living human beings, with something to be gained or lost from the jury's verdict. Under the aegis of the Eighth Amendment, we have given the broadest latitude to the defendant to introduce relevant mitigating evidence reflecting on his individual personality, and the defendant's attorney may argue that evidence to the jury. Petitioner's attorney in this case did just that. For the reasons discussed above, we now reject the view—expressed in *Gathers*—that a State may not permit the prosecutor to similarly argue to the jury the human cost of the crime of which the defendant stands convicted. We reaffirm the view expressed by Justice Cardozo in *Snyder* v. *Massachusetts*, 291 U.S. 97 (1934): "justice, though due to the accused, is due to the accuser also. The concept of fairness must not be strained till it is narrowed to a filament. We are to keep the balance true."

We thus hold that if the State chooses to permit the admission of victim impact evidence and prosecutorial argument on that subject, the Eighth Amendment erects no *per se* bar. A State may legitimately conclude that evidence about the victim and about the impact of the murder on the victim's family is relevant to the jury's decision as to whether or not the death penalty should be imposed. There is no reason to treat such evidence differently than other relevant evidence is treated.

Payne and his *amicus* argue that despite these numerous infirmities in the rule created by *Booth* and Gathers, we should adhere to the doctrine of *stare decisis* and stop short of overruling those cases. *Stare decisis* is the preferred course because it promotes the evenhanded, predictable, and consistent development of legal principles, fosters reliance on judicial decisions, and contributes to the actual and perceived integrity of the judicial process. Adhering to precedent "is usually the wise policy, because in most matters it is more important that the applicable rule of law be settled than it be settled right." *Burnet* v. *Coronado Oil & Gas Co.*, 285 U.S. 393, 406 (1932) (Justice Brandeis, dissenting). Nevertheless, when governing decisions are unworkable or are badly reasoned, "this Court has never felt constrained to follow precedent." *Smith* v. *Allwright*, 321 U.S.

649, 665 (1944). *Stare decisis* is not an inexorable command; rather, it "is a principle of policy and not a mechanical formula of adherence to the latest decision." *Helvering* v. *Hallock*, 309 U.S. 106, 119 (1940). This is particularly true in constitutional cases, because in such cases "correction through legislative action is practically impossible." *Burnet* v. *Coronado Oil & Gas Co.*, 285 U.S., at 407 (Justice Brandeis, dissenting). Considerations in favor of *stare decisis* are at their acme in cases involving property and contract rights, where reliance interests are involved. The opposite is true in cases such as the present one involving procedural and evidentiary rules.

Applying these general principles, the Court has during the past 20 Terms overruled in whole or in part 33 of its previous constitutional decisions. *Booth* and *Gathers* were decided by the narrowest of margins, over spirited dissents challenging the basic underpinnings of those decisions. They have been questioned by members of the court in later decisions, and have defied consistent application by the lower courts. Reconsidering these decisions now, we conclude for the reasons heretofore stated, that they were wrongly decided and should be, and now are, overruled. We accordingly affirm the judgment of the Supreme Court of Tennessee.

Affirmed.

JUSTICE O'CONNOR, with whom JUSTICE WHITE and JUSTICE KENNEDY join, concurring.

We do not hold today that victim impact evidence must be admitted, or even that it should be admitted. We hold merely that if a State decides to permit consideration of this evidence, "the Eighth Amendment erects no *per se* bar." If, in a particular case, a witness' testimony or a prosecutor's remark so infects the sentencing proceeding as to render it fundamentally unfair, the defendant may seek appropriate relief under the Due Process Clause of the Fourteenth Amendment. . . .

"Murder is the ultimate act of depersonalization." It transforms a living person with hopes, dreams, and fears, into a corpse, thereby taking away all that is special and unique about the person. The Constitution does not preclude a State from deciding to give some of that back.

JUSTICE SCALIA, with whom JUSTICE O'CONNOR and JUSTICE KENNEDY join as to Part II, concurring.

The response to Justice Marshall's strenuous defense of the virtues of *stare decisis* can be found in the writings of Justice Marshall himself. That doctrine, he has reminded us, "is not 'an imprisonment of reason.'" *Guardians Assn.* v. *Civil Service Comm'n of New York City*, 463 U.S. 582, 618 (1983) (Justice Marshall, dissenting). If there was ever a case that defied reason, it was *Booth* v. *Maryland*, imposing a constitutional rule that had absolutely no basis in constitutional text, in historical practice, or in logic. Justice Marshall has also explained that "'[t]he jurist concerned with public confidence in, and acceptance of the judicial system might well consider that, however admirable its resolute adherence to the law as it was, a decision contrary to the public sense of justice as it is, operates, so far as it is known, to diminish respect for the courts and for law itself.'"

Booth's stunning *ipse dixit*, that a crime's unanticipated consequences must be deemed "irrelevant" to the sentence, conflicts with a public sense of justice keen enough that it has found voice in a nationwide "victim's rights" movement.

Today, however, Justice Marshall demands of us some "special justification"—*beyond* the mere conviction that the rule of *Booth* significantly harms our criminal justice system and is egregiously wrong—before we can be absolved of exercising "[p]ower, not reason." I do not think that is fair. In fact, quite to the contrary, what would enshrine power as the governing principle of this Court is the notion that an important constitutional decision with plainly inadequate rational support *must* be left in place for the sole reason that it once attracted five votes.

JUSTICE SOUTER, with whom JUSTICE KENNEDY joins, concurring.

To hold, however, that in setting the appropriate sentence a defendant must be considered in his uniqueness is not to require that only unique qualities be considered. While a defendant's anticipation of specific consequences to the victims of his intended act is relevant to sentencing, such detailed foreknowledge does not exhaust the category of morally relevant fact. One such fact that is known to all murderers and relevant to the blameworthiness of each one was identified by the *Booth* majority itself when it barred the sentencing authority in capital cases from considering "the full range of foreseeable consequences of a defendant's actions." Murder has foreseeable consequences. When it happens, it is always to distinct individuals, and after it happens other victims are left behind. Every defendant knows, if endowed with the mental competence for criminal responsibility, that the life he will take by his homicidal behavior is that of a unique person, like himself, and that the person to be killed probably has close associates, "survivors," who will suffer harms and deprivations from the victim's death. Just as defendants know that they are not faceless human ciphers, they know that their victims are not valueless fungibles, and just as defendants appreciate the web of relationships and dependencies in which they live, they know that their victims are not human islands, but individuals with parents or children, spouses or friends or dependents. Thus, when a defendant chooses to kill, or to raise the risk of a victim's death, this choice necessarily relates to a whole human being and threatens an association of others, who may be distinctly hurt. The fact that the defendant may not know the details of a victim's life and characteristics, or the exact identities and needs of those who may survive, should not in any way obscure the further facts that death is always to a "unique" individual, and harm to some group of survivors is a consequence of a successful homicidal act so foreseeable as to be virtually inevitable.

That foreseeability of the killing's consequences imbues them with direct moral relevance and evidence of the specific harm caused when a homicidal risk is realized is nothing more than evidence of the risk that the defendant originally chose to run despite the kinds of consequences that were obviously foreseeable. It is morally both defensible and appropriate to consider such evidence when penalizing a murderer, like other criminals, in light of common knowledge and the moral responsibility that such knowledge entails. Any failure to take account of a victim's individuality and the effects of his death upon close survivors would thus more appropriately be called an act of lenity than their consideration an invitation to arbitrary sentencing. Indeed, given a defendant's option to introduce relevant evidence in mitigation, sentencing without such evidence of victim impact may be seen as a significantly imbalanced process.

JUSTICE MARSHALL, with whom JUSTICE BLACKMUN joins, dissenting.

Power, not reason, is the new currency of this Court's decisionmaking. Four Terms ago, a five–Justice majority of this Court held that "victim impact" evidence of the type at issue in this case could not constitutionally be introduced during the penalty phase of a capital trial. By another 5–4 vote, a majority of this Court rebuffed an attack upon this ruling just two Terms ago. Nevertheless, having expressly invited respondent to renew the attack, today's majority overrules *Booth* and *Gathers* and credits the dissenting views expressed in those cases. Neither the law nor the facts supporting *Booth* and *Gathers* underwent any change in the last four years. Only the personnel of this Court did.

In dispatching *Booth* and *Gathers* to their graves, today's majority ominously suggests that an even more extensive upheaval of this Court's precedents may be in store. Renouncing this Court's historical commitment to a conception of "the judiciary as a source of impersonal and reasoned judgments," *Moragne* v. *States Marine Lines*, 398 U.S. 375 (1970), the majority declares itself free to discard any principle of constitutional liberty which was recognized or reaffirmed over the dissenting votes of four Justices and with which five or more Justices *now* disagree. The implications of this radical new exception to the doctrine of *stare decisis* are staggering. The majority today sends a clear signal that scores of established constitutional liberties are now ripe for reconsideration, thereby inviting the very type of open defiance of our precedents that the majority rewards in this case. Because I believe that this Court owes more to its constitutional precedents in general and to *Booth* and *Gathers* in particular, I dissent.

Carried to its logical conclusion, the majority's debilitated conception of *stare decisis* would destroy the Court's very capacity to resolve authoritatively the abiding conflicts between those with power and those without. If this Court shows so little respect for its own precedents, it can hardly expect them to be treated more respectfully by the state actors whom these decisions are supposed to bind. By signaling its willingness to give fresh consideration to any constitutional liberty recognized by a 5–4 vote "over spirited dissen[t]," the majority invites

state actors to renew the very policies deemed unconstitutional in the hope that this Court may now reverse course, even if it has only recently reaffirmed the constitutional liberty in question.

Indeed, the majority's disposition of this case nicely illustrates the rewards of such a strategy of defiance. The Tennessee Supreme Court did nothing in this case to disguise its contempt for this Court's decisions in *Booth* and *Gathers*. Summing up its reaction to those cases, it concluded:

> It is an affront to the civilized members of the human race to say that at sentencing in a capital case, a parade of witnesses may praise the background, character and good deeds of Defendant (as was done in this case), without limitation as to relevancy, but nothing may be said that bears upon the character of, or harm imposed, upon the victims.

Offering no explanation for how this case could possibly be distinguished from *Booth* and *Gathers*—for obviously, there is none to offer—the court perfunctorily declared that the victim-impact evidence and the prosecutor's argument based on this evidence "did not violate either [of those decisions]." It cannot be clearer that the court simply declined to be bound by this Court's precedents. . . .

Far from condemning this blatant disregard for the rule of law, the majority applauds it. In the Tennessee Supreme Court's denigration of *Booth* and *Gathers* as "an affront to the civilized members of the human race," the majority finds only confirmation of "the unfairness of the rule pronounced by" the majorities in those cases. It is hard to imagine a more complete abdication of this Court's historic commitment to defending the supremacy of its own pronouncements on issues of constitutional liberty.

In light of the cost that such abdication exacts on the authoritativeness of *all* of this Court's pronouncements, it is also hard to imagine a more short-sighted strategy for effecting change in our constitutional order.

Today's decision charts an unmistakable course. If the majority's radical reconstruction of the rules for overturning this Court's decisions is to be taken at face value—and the majority offers us no reason why it should not—then the overruling of *Booth* and *Gathers* is but a preview of an even broader and more far-reaching assault upon this Court's precedents. Cast aside today are those condemned to face society's ultimate penalty. Tomorrow's victims may be minoritics, women, or the indigent. Inevitably, this campaign to resurrect yesterday's "spirited dissents" will squander the authority and the legitimacy of this Court as a protector of the powerless.

I dissent.

JUSTICE STEVENS, with whom JUSTICE BLACKMUN joins, dissenting.

Until today our capital punishment jurisprudence has required that any decision to impose the death penalty be based solely on evidence that tends to inform the jury about the character of the offense and the character of the defendant. Evidence that serves no purpose other than to appeal to the sympathies or emotions of the jurors has never been considered admissible. Thus, if a defendant, who murdered a convenience store clerk in cold blood in the course of an armed robbery, offered evidence unknown to him at the time of the crime about the immoral character of his victim, all would recognize immediately that the evidence was irrelevant and inadmissible. Evenhanded justice requires that the same constraint be imposed on the advocate of the death penalty.

The majority thus does far more than validate a State's judgment that "the jury should see 'a quick glimpse of the life the petitioner chose to extinguish.' " Instead, it allows a jury to hold a defendant responsible for a whole array of harms that he could not foresee and for which he is therefore not blameworthy. Justice Souter argues that these harms are sufficiently foreseeable to hold the defendant accountable because "[e]very defendant knows, if endowed with the mental competence for criminal responsibility, that the life he will take by his homicidal behavior is that of a unique person, like himself, and that the person who will be killed probably has close associates, 'survivors,' who will suffer harms and deprivations from the victim's death." But every juror and trial judge knows this much as well. Evidence about who those survivors are and what harms and deprivations they have suffered is therefore not necessary to apprise the sentencer of any information that was actually foreseeable to the defendant. Its only function can be to "divert the jury's attention away from the defendant's background and record, and the circumstances of the crime."

Given the current popularity of capital punishment in a crime-ridden society, the political appeal of arguments that assume that increasing the severity of sentences is the best cure for the cancer of crime, and the political strength of the "victims' rights" movement, I recognize that today's decision will be greeted with enthusiasm by a large number of concerned and thoughtful citizens. The great tragedy of the decision, however, is the danger that the "hydraulic pressure" of public opinion that Justice Holmes once described—and that properly influences the deliberations of democratic legislatures—has played a role not only in the Court's decision to hear this case, and in its decision to reach the constitutional question without pausing to consider affirming on the basis of the Tennessee Supreme Court's rationale, but even in its resolution of the constitutional issue involved. Today is a sad day for a great institution.

Harmelin v. *Michigan*
111 S. Ct. 2680, 115 L. Ed. 2d 836 (1991)

Ronald Allen Harmelin was convicted under Michigan law of possessing more than 650 grams of cocaine and was sentenced to a mandatory term of life in prison without possibility of parole. The Michigan Court of Appeals rejected his contention that the sentence violated the "cruel and unusual punishments" clause of the Eighth Amendment and affirmed his conviction. The U.S. Supreme Court granted certiorari. *Judgment of the Court: Scalia, Rehnquist. Concurring in part and concurring in the judgment: Kennedy, O'Connor, Souter. Dissenting opinions: White, Blackmun, Stevens; Marshall; Stevens, Blackmun.*

JUSTICE SCALIA delivered the opinion of the Court.

Petitioner claims that his sentence is unconstitutionally "cruel and unusual" for two reasons. First, because it is "significantly disproportionate" to the crime he committed. Second, because the sentencing judge was statutorily required to impose it, without taking into account the particularized circumstances of the crime and of the criminal.

The Eighth Amendment, which applies against the States by virtue of the Fourteenth Amendment, see *Robinson* v. *California*, 370 U.S. 660 (1962), provides: "Excessive bail shall not be required, nor excessive fines imposed, nor cruel and unusual punishments inflicted."

In *Solem* v. *Helm*, 463 U.S. 277 (1983), [we] set aside under the Eighth Amendment, because it was disproportionate, a sentence of life imprisonment without possibility of parole, imposed under a South Dakota recidivist statute for successive offenses that included three convictions of third-degree burglary, one of obtaining money by false pretenses, one of grand larceny, one of third-offense driving while intoxicated, and one of writing a "no account" check with intent to defraud.

Solem based its conclusion principally upon the proposition that a right to be free from disproportionate punishments was embodied within the "cruell and unusuall Punishments" provision of the English Declaration of Rights of 1689, and was incorporated, with that language, in the Eighth Amendment. As a textual matter, of course, it does not: a disproportionate punishment can perhaps always be considered "cruel," but it will not always be (as the text also requires) "unusual." The error of *Solem's* assumption is confirmed by the historical context and contemporaneous understanding of the English guarantee.

We think it most unlikely that the English Cruel and Unusual Punishments Clause was meant to forbid "disproportionate" punishments. There is even less likelihood that the proportionality of punishment was one of the traditional "rights and privileges of Englishmen" apart from the Declaration of Rights, which happened to be included in the Eighth Amendment. Indeed, even those scholars who believe the principle to have been included within the Declaration of Rights do not contend that such a prohibition was reflected in English practice—nor could they. For in 1791, England punished over 200 crimes with death (until 1826, all felonies, except mayhem and petty larceny, were punishable by death). By 1830 the class of offenses punishable by death was narrowed to include "only" murder, attempts to murder by poisoning, stabbing, shooting etc.; administering poison to procure abortion, sodomy, rape, statutory rape, and certain classes of forgery.

Unless one accepts the notion of a blind incorporation, however, the ultimate question is not what "cruell and unusuall punishments" meant in the Declaration of Rights, but what its meaning was to the Americans who adopted the Eighth Amendment. Even if one assumes that the Founders knew the precise meaning of that English antecedent, a direct transplant of the English meaning to the soil of American constitutionalism would in any case have been impossible. There were no common-law punishments in the federal system, so that the provision must have been meant as a check not upon judges but upon the Legislature

Wrenched out of its common-law context, and applied to the actions of a legislature, the word "unusual" could hardly mean "contrary to law." But it continued to mean (as it continues to mean today) "such as [does not] occu[r] in ordinary practice," Webster's 1828 edition, "[s]uch as is [not] in common use," Webster's 2d International. According to its terms, then, by forbidding "cruel *and unusual* punishments," the Clause disables the Legislature from authorizing particular forms or "modes" of punishment—specifically, cruel methods of punishment that are not regularly or customarily employed.

The language bears the construction, however—and here we come to the point crucial to resolution of the present case—that "cruelty and unusualness" are to be determined not solely with reference to the punishment at issue ("Is life imprisonment a cruel and unusual punishment?") but with reference to the crime for which it is imposed as well ("Is life imprisonment cruel and unusual punishment for possession of unlawful drugs?"). The latter interpretation would make the provision a form of proportionality guarantee. The arguments against it, however, seem to us conclusive.

First of all, to use the phrase "cruel and unusual punishment" to describe a requirement of proportionality would have been an exceedingly vague and oblique way of saying what Americans were well accustomed to saying more directly. The notion of "proportionality" was not a novelty (though then as now there was little agreement over what it entailed). In 1778, for example, the Virginia Legislature narrowly rejected a comprehensive "Bill for Proportioning Punishments" introduced by Thomas Jefferson. Proportionality provisions had been included in several state constitutions. See, *e.g.,* Pa. Const., § 38 (1776) (punishments should be "in general more proportionate to the crimes"); S.C. Const., Art. XL (1778) (same); N.H. Bill of Rights, Pt. 1, Art. XVIII (1784) ("all penalties ought to be proportioned to the nature of the offence"). There is little doubt that those who framed, proposed, and ratified the Bill of Rights were aware of such provisions, yet chose not to replicate them. Both the New Hampshire Constitution, adopted 8 years before ratification of the Eighth Amendment, and the Ohio Constitution, adopted 12 years after, contain, in separate provisions, a prohibition of "cruel and unusual punishments" ("cruel or unusual," in New Hampshire's case) and a requirement that "all penalties ought to be proportioned to the nature of the offence." N.H. Bill of Rights, Arts. XVIII, XXXIII (1784). Ohio Const., Art. VIII, §§ 13, 14 (1802).

Secondly, it would seem quite peculiar to refer to cruelty and unusualness *for the offense in question,* in a provision having application only to a new government that had never before defined offenses, and that would be defining new and peculiarly national ones. Finally and most conclusively, as we proceed to discuss, the fact that what was "cruel and unusual" under the Eighth Amendment was to be determined without reference to the particular offense is confirmed by all available evidence of contemporary understanding.

The Eighth Amendment received little attention during the proposal and adoption of the Federal Bill of Rights. However, what evidence exists from debates at the state ratifying conventions that prompted the Bill of Rights as well as the Floor debates in the First Congress which proposed it "confirm[s] the view that the cruel and unusual punishments clause was directed at prohibiting certain *methods* of punishment."

The early commentary on the Clause contains no reference to disproportionate or excessive sentences, and again indicates that it was designed to outlaw particular *modes* of punishment. One commentator wrote:

> Under the [Eighth] amendment the infliction of cruel and unusual punishments, is also prohibited. The various barbarous and cruel punishments inflicted under the laws of some other countries, and which profess not to be behind the most enlightened nations on earth in civilization and refinement, furnish sufficient reasons for this express prohibition. Breaking on the wheel, flaying alive, rending assunder with horses, various species of horrible tortures inflicted in the inquisition, maiming, mutilating and scourging to death, are wholly alien to the spirit of our humane general constitution. B. Oliver, The Rights of an American Citizen 186 (1832).

We think it enough that t*hose who framed and approved the Federal Constitution* chose, for whatever reason, not to include within it the guarantee against disproportionate sentences that some State Constitutions contained. It is worth noting, however, that there was good reason for that choice—a reason that reinforces the necessity of overruling *Solem.* While there are relatively clear historical guidelines and accepted practices that enable judges to determine which *modes* of punishment are "cruel and unusual," *proportionality* does not lend itself to such analysis. Neither Congress nor any state legislature has ever set out with the objective of crafting a penalty that is "disproportionate," yet as some of the examples mentioned above indicate, many enacted dispositions seem to be so—because they were made for other times or other places, with different social attitudes, different criminal epidemics, different public fears, and different prevailing theories of penology. This is not to say that there are no absolutes; one can imagine extreme examples that no rational person, in no time or place, could accept. But for the same reason these examples are easy to decide, they are certain never to occur.* The real function of a constitutional proportionality principle, if it exists, is to enable judges to evaluate a penalty that *some* assemblage of men and women *has* considered proportionate—and to say that it is not. For that real-world enterprise, the standards seem so inadequate that the proportionality principle becomes an invitation to imposition of subjective values.

Our 20th-century jurisprudence has not remained entirely in accord with the proposition that there is no proportionality requirement in the Eighth Amendment, but neither has it departed to the extent that *Solem* suggests. In *Weems* v. *United States,* 217 U.S. 349 (1910), a government disbursing officer convicted of making false entries of small sums in his account book was sentenced by Philippine courts to 15 years of *cadena temporal.* That punishment, based upon the Spanish Penal Code, called for incarceration at " 'hard and painful labor' " with chains fastened to the wrists and ankles at all times. Several "accessor[ies]" were superadded, including permanent disqualification from holding any position of public trust, subjection to "[government] surveillance" for life, and "civil interdiction," which consisted of deprivation of " 'the rights of parental authority, guardianship of person or property, participation in the family council [, etc.]'."

---

*Justice White argues that the Eighth Amendment must contain a proportionality principle because otherwise legislatures could "mak[e] overtime parking a felony punishable by life imprisonment." We do not in principle oppose the "parade of horribles" form of argumentation, see Scalia, Assorted Canards of Contemporary Legal Analysis, *40 Case W.Res.L.Rev.* 581, 590–593 (1989–1990). Justice White's argument has force only for those who believe that the Constitution prohibited everything that is intensely undesirable. As Justice Frankfurter reminded us, "[t]he process of Constitutional adjudication does not thrive on conjuring up horrible possibilities that never happen in the real world and devising doctrines sufficiently comprehensive in detail to cover the remotest contingency." *New York* v. *United States,* 326 U.S. 572, 583 (1946). It seems to us no more reasonable to hold that the Eighth Amendment forbids "disproportionate punishment" because otherwise the State could impose life imprisonment for a parking offense, than it would be to hold that the Takings Clause forbids "disproportionate taxation" because otherwise the State could tax away all income above the subsistence level.

Justice McKenna, writing for himself and three others, held that the imposition of *cadena temporal* was "Cruel and Unusual Punishment." (Justice White, joined by Justice Holmes, dissented.) That holding, and some of the reasoning upon which it was based, was not at all out of accord with the traditional understanding of the provision we have described above. The punishment was both (1) severe *and* (2) unknown to Anglo-American tradition. . . .

Other portions of the opinion, however, suggest that mere disproportionality, by itself, might make a punishment cruel and unusual. . . .

Since it contains language that will support either theory, our later opinions have used *Weems,* as the occasion required, to represent either the principle that "the Eighth Amendment bars not only those punishments that are "barbaric' but also those that are 'excessive' in relation to the crime committed," or the principle that only a "unique . . . punishmen[t]," a form of imprisonment different from the "more traditional forms . . . imposed under the Anglo-Saxon system," can violate the Eighth Amendment.

Petitioner claims that his sentence violates the Eighth Amendment for a reason in addition to its disproportionality. He argues that it is "cruel and unusual" to impose a mandatory sentence of such severity, without any consideration of so-called mitigating factors such as, in his case, the fact that he had no prior felony convictions. He apparently contends that the Eighth Amendment requires Michigan to create a sentencing scheme whereby life in prison without possibility of parole is simply the most severe of a range of available penalties that the sentencer may impose after hearing evidence in mitigation and aggravation.

As our earlier discussion should make clear, this claim has no support in the text and history of the Eighth Amendment. Severe, mandatory penalties may be cruel, but they are not unusual in the constitutional sense, having been employed in various forms throughout our Nation's history. As noted earlier, mandatory death sentences abounded in our first Penal Code. They were also common in the several States—both at the time of the founding and throughout the 19th century. See *Woodson* v. *North Carolina.* There can be no serious contention, then, that a sentence which is not otherwise cruel and unusual becomes so simply because it is "mandatory."

Petitioner's "required mitigation" claim, like his proportionality claim, does find support in our death-penalty jurisprudence. We have held that a capital sentence is cruel and unusual under the Eighth Amendment if it is imposed without an individual determination that that punishment is "appropriate"—whether or not the sentence is "grossly disproportionate." Petitioner asks us to extend this so-called "individualized capital sentencing doctrine" to an "individualized mandatory life in prison without parole sentencing doctrine." We refuse to do so.

Our cases creating and clarifying the "individualized capital sentencing doctrine" have repeatedly suggested that there is no comparable requirement outside the capital context, because of the qualitative difference between death and all other penalties. We have drawn the line of required individualized sentencing at capital cases, and see no basis for extending it further.

The judgment of the Michigan Court of Appeals is

Affirmed.

JUSTICE KENNEDY, with whom JUSTICE O'CONNOR and JUSTICE SOUTER join, concurring in part and concurring in the judgment.

I write this separate opinion because my approach to the Eighth Amendment proportionality analysis differs from Justice Scalia's. Regardless of whether Justice Scalia or the dissent has the best of the historical argument, *stare decisis* counsels our adherence to the narrow proportionality principle that has existed in our Eighth Amendment jurisprudence for 80 years. Although our proportionality decisions have not been clear or consistent in all respects, they can be reconciled, and they require us to uphold petitioner's sentence.

Our decisions recognize that the Cruel and Unusual Punishments Clause encompasses a narrow proportionality principle.

The Eighth Amendment proportionality principle also applies to noncapital sentences. Close analysis of our decisions yields some common principles that give content to the uses and limits of proportionality review.

The first of these principles is that the fixing of prison terms for specific crimes involves a substantive penological judgment that, as a general matter, is "properly within the province of legislatures, not courts."

The second principle is that the Eighth Amendment does not mandate adoption of any one penological theory.

Third, marked divergences both in underlying theories of sentencing and in the length of prescribed prison terms are the inevitable, often beneficial, result of the federal structure. . . .

The fourth principle at work in our cases is that proportionality review by federal courts should be informed by "'objective factors to the maximum possible extent.'" The most prominent objective factor is the type of punishment imposed.

All of these principles—the primacy of the legislature, the variety of legitimate penological schemes, the nature of our federal system, and the requirement that proportionality review be guided by objective factors—inform the final one: the Eighth Amendment does not require strict proportionality between crime and sentence. Rather, it forbids only extreme sentences that are "grossly disproportionate" to the crime.

With these considerations stated, it is necessary to examine the challenged aspects of petitioner's sentence: its severe length and its mandatory operation.

In light of the gravity of petitioner's offense, a comparison of his crime with his sentence does not give rise to an inference of gross disproportionality. To set aside petitioner's mandatory sentence would require rejection of the collective wisdom of the Michigan Legislature and, as a consequence, the Michigan citizenry. We have never invalidated a penalty mandated by a legislature based only on the length of sentence, and, especially with a crime as severe as this one, we should do so only in the most extreme circumstance.

For the foregoing reasons, I conclude that petitioner's sentence of life imprisonment without parole for his crime of possession of more than 650 grams of cocaine does not violate the Eighth Amendment.

JUSTICE WHITE, with whom JUSTICE BLACKMUN and JUSTICE STEVENS join, dissenting.

The Eighth Amendment provides that "[e]xcessive bail shall not be required, nor excessive fines imposed, nor cruel and unusual punishments inflicted."

The language of the Amendment does not refer to proportionality in so many words, but it does forbid "excessive" fines, a restraint that suggests that a determination of excessiveness should be based at least in part on whether the fine imposed is disproportionate to the crime committed.

Justice Scalia argues that all of the available evidence of the day indicated that those *who drafted and approved the Amendment* "chose . . . not to include within it the guarantee against disproportionate sentences that some State Constitutions contained." Even if one were to accept the argument that the First Congress did not have in mind the proportionality issue, the evidence would hardly be strong enough to come close to proving an affirmative decision against the proportionality component. Had there been an intention to exclude it from the reach of the words that otherwise could reasonably be construed to include it, perhaps as plain-speaking Americans, the Members of the First Congress would have said so.

Two dangers lurk in Justice Scalia's analysis. First, he provides no mechanism for addressing a situation in which a legislature makes overtime parking a felony punishable by life imprisonment. He concedes that "one can imagine extreme examples that no rational person, in no time or place, could accept," but attempts to offer reassurance by claiming that "for the same reason these examples are easy to decide, they are certain never to occur." This is cold comfort indeed, for absent a proportionality guarantee, there would be no basis for deciding such cases should they arise.

Second, as I have indicated, Justice Scalia's position that the Eighth Amendment addresses only modes or methods of punishment is quite inconsistent with our capital punishment cases, which do not outlaw death as a mode or method of punishment, but instead put limits on its application. If the concept of proportionality is downgraded in the Eighth Amendment calculus, much of this Court's capital penalty jurisprudence will rest on quicksand.

Petitioner, a first-time offender, was convicted of possession of 672 grams of cocaine.

The statute under which he was convicted provides that a person who knowingly or intentionally possesses any of various narcotics, including cocaine, "[w]hich is in an amount of 650 grams or more of any mixture containing that substance is guilty of a felony and shall be imprisoned for life." No particular degree of drug purity is required for a conviction. There is no room for judicial discretion in the imposition of the life sentence upon conviction. The asserted purpose of the legislative enactment of these statutes was to "'stem drug traffic'" and reach "'drug dealers.'"

Application of *Solem*'s proportionality analysis leaves no doubt that the Michigan statute at issue fails constitutional muster. The statutorily mandated penalty of life without possibility of parole for possession of narcotics is unconstitutionally disproportionate in that it violates the Eighth Amendment's prohibition against cruel and unusual punishment. Consequently, I would reverse the decision of the Michigan Court of Appeals.

JUSTICE MARSHALL, dissenting.

I agree with Justice White's dissenting opinion, except insofar as it asserts that the Eighth Amendment's Cruel and Unusual Punishments Clause does not proscribe the death penalty. I adhere to my view that capital punishment is in all instances unconstitutional. See *Gregg* v. *Georgia*, 428 U.S. 153, 231 (1976) (Justice Marshall, dissenting).

JUSTICE STEVENS, with whom JUSTICE BLACKMUN joins, dissenting.

A mandatory sentence of life imprisonment without the possibility of parole must rest on a rational determination that the punished "criminal conduct is so atrocious that society's interest in deterrence and retribution wholly outweighs any considerations of reform or rehabilitation of the perpetrator." Serious as this defendant's crime was, I believe it is irrational to conclude that every similar offender is wholly incorrigible.

Turner v. Safley

482 U.S. 78, 107 S. Ct. 2254, 95 L. Ed. 2d 64 (1987)

Leonard Safley and other inmates brought a class action suit challenging two regulations of the Missouri Division of Corrections relating to inmate-to-inmate correspondence and inmate marriages. The U.S. District Court for the Western District of Missouri relied on *Procunier* v. *Martinez*, 416 U.S. 396 (1974), and, applying a strict scrutiny standard of review, found both regulations unconstitutional. The Court of Appeals for the Eighth Circuit affirmed, and the Supreme Court granted certiorari. *Opinion of the Court: O'Connor, Powell, Rehnquist, Scalia, White. Concurring in part and dissenting in part: Stevens, Blackmun, Brennan, Marshall.*

JUSTICE O'CONNOR delivered the opinion of the Court.

This case requires us to determine the constitutionality of regulations promulgated by the Missouri Division of Corrections relating to inmate marriages and inmate-to-inmate correspondence. The Court of Appeals for the Eighth Circuit, applying a strict scrutiny analysis, concluded that the regulations violate respondents' constitutional rights. We hold that a lesser standard of scrutiny is appropriate in determining the constitutionality of the prison rules. Applying that standard, we uphold the validity of the correspondence regulation, but we conclude that the marriage restriction cannot be sustained. . . .

Two regulations are at issue here. The first of the challenged regulations relates to correspondence between inmates at different institutions. It permits such correspondence "with immediate family members who are inmates in other correctional institutions," and it permits correspondence between inmates "concerning legal matters." Other correspondence between inmates, however, is permitted only if "the classification/treatment team of each inmate deems it in the best interest of the parties involved." . . . The District Court found that the rule "as practiced is that inmates may not write non-family inmates." . . .

The challenged marriage regulation, . . . permits an inmate to marry only with the permission of the superintendent of the prison, and provides that such approval should be given only "when there are compelling reasons to do so." . . .

The term "compelling" is not defined, but prison officials testified at trial that generally only a pregnancy or the birth of an illegitimate child would be considered a compelling reason. . . . The District Court issued a memorandum opinion and order finding both the correspondence and marriage regulations unconstitutional. The court, relying on *Procunier* v. *Martinez*, . . . applied a strict scrutiny standard. . . .

The Court of Appeals for the Eighth Circuit affirmed. . . . The Court of Appeals held that the District Court properly used strict scrutiny in evaluating the constitutionality of the Missouri correspondence and marriage regulations. Under *Procunier* v. *Martinez*, the correspondence regulation could be justified "only if it furthers an important or substantial governmental interest unrelated to the suppression of expression, and the limitation is no greater than necessary or essential to protect that interest." . . . The correspondence regulation did not satisfy this standard because it was not the least restrictive means of achieving the security goals of the regulation. In the Court of Appeals' view, prison officials could meet the problem of inmate conspiracies by exercising their authority to open and read all prisoner mail. . . . The Court of Appeals also concluded that the marriage rule was not the least restrictive means of achieving the asserted goals of rehabilitation and security. . . .

We begin, as did the courts below, with our decision in *Procunier* v. *Martinez*, . . . which described the principles that necessarily frame our analysis of prisoners' constitutional claims. The first of these principles is that federal courts must take cognizance of the valid constitutional claims of prison inmates. . . . Prison walls do not form a barrier separating prison inmates from the protections of the Constitution. Hence, for example, prisoners retain the constitutional right to petition the Government for the redress of grievances; . . . they are protected against invidious racial discrimination by the Equal Protection Clause of the Fourteenth Amendment; . . . and they enjoy the protections of due process. . . . Because prisoners retain these rights, "[w]hen a prison regulation or practice offends a fundamental constitutional guarantee, federal courts will discharge their duty to protect constitutional rights." . . .

. . . A second principle identified in *Martinez*, however, is the recognition that "courts are ill equipped to deal with the increasingly urgent problems of prison administration and reform." . . . As the *Martinez* Court acknowledged, "the problems of prisons in America are complex and intractable, and, more to the point, they are not readily susceptible of resolution by decree." . . . Running a prison is an inordinately difficult undertaking that requires expertise, planning, and the commitment of resources, all of which are peculiarly within the province of the Legislative and Executive Branches of Government. Prison administration is, moreover, a task that has been committed to the responsibility of those branches, and separation of powers concerns counsel a policy of judicial restraint. Where a state penal system is involved, federal courts have . . . additional reason to accord deference to the appropriate prison authorities. . . .

Our task, then, as we stated in *Martinez*, is to formulate a standard of review for prisoners' constitutional claims that is responsive both to the "policy of judicial restraint regarding prisoner complaints and [to] the need to protect constitutional rights." . . . As the Court of Appeals acknowledged, *Martinez* did not itself resolve the question that it framed. . . . We resolve it now: when a prison regulation impinges on inmates' constitutional rights, the regulation is valid if it is reasonably related to legitimate penological interests. In our view, such a standard is necessary if "prison administrators . . . , and not the courts, [are] to make the difficult judgments concerning institutional operations." . . . Subjecting the day-to-day judgments of prison officials to an inflexi-

ble strict scrutiny analysis would seriously hamper their ability to anticipate security problems and to adopt innovative solutions to the intractable problems of prison administration. The rule would also distort the decisionmaking process, for every administrative judgment would be subject to the possibility that some court somewhere would conclude that it had a less restrictive way of solving the problem at hand. Courts inevitably would become the primary arbiters of what constitutes the best solution to every administrative problem, thereby "unnecessarily perpetuat[ing] the involvement of the federal courts in affairs of prison administration." . . .

. . . Several factors are relevant in determining the reasonableness of the regulation at issue. First, there must be a "valid, rational connection" between the prison regulation and the legitimate governmental interest put forward to justify it. . . . Thus, a regulation cannot be sustained where the logical connection between the regulation and the asserted goal is so remote as to render the policy arbitrary or irrational. Moreover, the governmental objective must be a legitimate and neutral one. . . .

A second factor relevant in determining the reasonableness of a prison restriction, . . . is whether there are alternative means of exercising the right that remain open to prison inmates. Where "other avenues" remain available for the exercise of the asserted right, . . . courts should be particularly conscious of the "measure of judicial deference owed to corrections officials . . . in gauging the validity of the regulation."

A third consideration is the impact accommodation of the asserted constitutional right will have on guards and other inmates, and on the allocation of prison resources generally. . . .

. . . Finally, the absence of ready alternatives is evidence of the reasonableness of a prison regulation. . . . By the same token, the existence of obvious, easy alternatives may be evidence that the regulation is not reasonable, but is an "exaggerated response" to prison concerns. This is not a "least restrictive alternative" test: prison officials do not have to set up and then shoot down every conceivable alternative method of accommodating the claimant's constitutional complaint. . . . But if an inmate claimant can point to an alternative that fully accommodates the prisoner's rights at *de minimis* cost to valid penological interests, a court may consider that as evidence that the regulation does not satisfy the reasonable relationship standard. . . .

Applying our analysis to the Missouri rule barring inmate-to-inmate correspondence, we conclude that the record clearly demonstrates that the regulation was reasonably related to legitimate security interests. We find that the marriage restriction, however, does not satisfy the reasonable relationship standard, but rather constitutes an exaggerated response to petitioners' rehabilitation and security concerns. . . .

. . . According to the testimony at trial, the Missouri correspondence provision was promulgated primarily for security reasons. Prison officials testfied that mail between institutions can be used to communicate escape plans and to arrange assaults and other violent acts. . . .

The prohibition on correspondence between institutions is logically connected to these legitimate security concerns. . . . Moreover, the correspondence regulation does not deprive prisoners of all means of expression. Rather, it bars communication only with a limited class of other people with whom prison officials have particular cause to be concerned—inmates at other institutions within the Missouri prison system.

. . . The Missouri marriage regulation prohibits inmates from marrying unless the prison superintendent has approved the marriage after finding that there are compelling reasons for doing so. . . . Generally only pregnancy or birth of a child is considered a "compelling reason" to approve a marriage. . . . Even under the reasonable relationship test, the marriage regulation does not withstand scrutiny. . . . No doubt legitimate security concerns may require placing reasonable restrictions upon an inmate's right to marry, and may justify requiring approval of the superintendent. The Missouri regulation, however, represents an exaggerated response to such security objectives. There are obvious, easy alternatives to the Missouri regulation that accommodate the right to marry while imposing a *de minimis* burden on the pursuit of security objectives. . . .

JUSTICE STEVENS, with whom JUSTICE BRENNAN, JUSTICE MARSHALL, and JUSTICE BLACKMUN join, concurring in part and dissenting in part. . . .

To the extent that this Court affirms the judgment of the Court of Appeals, I concur in its opinion. I respectfully dissent from the Court's partial reversal of that judgment on the basis of its own selective forays into the record. When all the language about deference and security is set to one side, the Court's erratic use of the record to affirm the Court of Appeals only partially may rest on an unarticulated assumption that the marital state is fundamentally different from the exchange of mail in the satisfaction, solace, and support it affords to a confined inmate. Even if such a difference is recognized in literature, history or anthropology, the text of the Constitution more clearly protects the right to communicate than the right to marry. In this case, both of these rights should receive constitutional recognition and protection.

★

RACE AND THE FOUNDING

RACIAL DESEGREGATION

Plessy v. *Ferguson* (1896)
Brown v. *Board of Education* (1954)
Bolling v. *Sharpe* (1954)
Brown v. *Board of Education* (1955)
Swann v. *Charlotte-Mecklenburg Board of Education* (1971)
Milliken v. *Bradley* (1974)
Missouri v. *Jenkins* (1995)
United States v. *Fordice* (1992)

PRIVATE DISCRIMINATION AND THE CONCEPT OF STATE ACTION

Shelley v. *Kraemer* (1948)
Moose Lodge No. 107 v. *Irvis* (1972)
Palmore v. *Sidoti* (1984)

RACIAL DISCRIMINATION IN JURY TRIALS

Georgia v. *McCollum* (1992)

PROOF OF DISCRIMINATION: IMPACT VERSUS INTENT

Wards Cove Packing Co. v. *Atonio* (1989)
The Civil Rights Act of 1991

NOTES

SELECTED READING

CASES

★

8

THE EQUAL PROTECTION CLAUSE AND RACIAL DISCRIMINATION

The Fourteenth Amendment declares that "No state . . . shall deny any person within its jurisdiction the equal protection of the laws." As noted in Chapter 4, the meaning of this clause was first explored by the Supreme Court in the *Slaughterhouse Cases* (1873), in which case, Justice Samuel Miller construed its words narrowly and argued that it prohibited only racial discrimination. At that time, the Court refused to entertain the notion that the Equal Protection Clause could be used to protect the rights of other classes of citizens.

The exact words of the clause, however, guarantee equal protection to all "persons," not simply to ex-slaves or black persons, and over time, the narrow and spindly equal-protection leg of *Slaughterhouse* has grown into a substantial pillar upholding the protection of civil rights. Today, it is viewed as prohibiting all state action that invidiously discriminates against "suspect classifications" or that impinges on "fundamental rights." As a result, the Court is now called on to invoke its protections in cases in which discrimination against blacks is altogether absent, as in litigation challenging ameliorative racial preference (i.e., affirmative action/reverse discrimination), gender-based classifications, economic inequality, and restrictions on the exercise of the franchise. Chapter 9 takes up these "newer" equal-protection issues and reviews the various analytical frameworks the justices have employed in ruling on these controversial matters. In this chapter, we concentrate exclusively on the race-discrimination issues raised by the Constitution and the Equal Protection Clause.

RACE AND THE FOUNDING

Although the post–Civil War amendments in general, and the Fourteenth Amendment in particular, have figured prominently in most analyses of race and the Constitution, the original Constitution also contains three provisions germane to this issue. The Founders have been subjected to considerable obloquy because of these provisions, which set forth the Three-fifths Compromise, allow for the importation of slaves for twenty years, and mandate the return of fugitive slaves to their masters. As Herbert Storing put it, the Founders' response to slavery and the problems of race usually is perceived to be "one to be lived down rather than lived up to."[1] The prominent black historian John Hope Franklin articulated a commonly held view when he charged the Founders with "betraying the ideals to which they gave lip service" by speaking "eloquently at one moment for the brotherhood of man" while denying it "in the next moment . . . to their black brothers." Particularly repugnant to Franklin and others was the Framers' apparent willingness to "degrade the human spirit by equating five black men [or more accurately, five black slaves] with three white men." Summarizing this moral legacy, Franklin declared: "Having created a tragically flawed revolutionary doctrine and a Constitution that did not bestow the blessings of liberty on its posterity, the Founding Fathers set the stage for every succeeding generation of Americans to apologize, compromise, and temporize on those principles of liberty that were supposed to be the very foundation of our system of government and way of life."[2] Citing as further evidence Chief Justice Roger Taney's pronouncement in *Dred Scott* v. *Sandford* (1857) that "the right of property in a slave is distinctly and expressly affirmed in the Constitution," advocates of this point of view assert confidently that the Founders first denied blacks the rights of man listed in the Declaration of Independence and then sanctioned slavery and black inferiority in the Constitution.

The historical record reads quite differently, however. To begin with, the Founders clearly understood that blacks, like all humans everywhere, were created equal and endowed with unalienable rights. As Professor Storing points out, "They did not say that all men were actually secured in the exercise of their rights or that they had the power to provide such security; but there was no doubt about the rights."[3] Powerful support for this point of view can be adduced from the nineteenth and final indictment against the British Crown included in Thomas Jefferson's initial draft of the Declaration of Independence:

> He [the King] has waged cruel war against human nature itself, violating its most sacred rights of life and liberty in the persons of a distant people who never offended him, captivating and carrying them into slavery in another hemisphere, or to incure miserable death in their transportation thither. This piratical warfare, the opprobrium of infidel powers, is the warfare of the Christian king of Great

Britain. Determined to keep open a market where MEN should be bought and sold, he has prostituted his negative [used his veto power] for suppressing every legislative attempt to prohibit or to restrain this execrable commerce; and that this assemblage of horrors might want no fact of distinguished die, he is now exciting these very people to rise in arms among us, and to purchase that liberty of which he deprived them, by murdering the people upon whom he also obtruded them; thus paying off former crimes committed against the liberties of one people with crimes which he urges them to commit against the lives of another.[4]

This "vehement philippic against negro slavery," as John Adams termed it, eventually was dropped from the Declaration by the Continental Congress. First of all, it simply was not true that the British Crown was solely responsible for the evils of slavery: the colonists themselves were willing and active participants in the slave trade. Also, the Southern states would not have joined in a unanimous Declaration of Independence that contained language they deemed offensive to them and their "peculiar institution." Those outraged by slavery were willing to concede on this point, for they recognized that refusal to do so would not free a single slave and would in all likelihood destroy the possibility of political independence and union. Moreover, they comforted themselves in the knowledge that the Declaration's self-evident truth that all men are created equal had in no way been diluted and that the full force of its claims could be asserted and advanced under more propitious circumstances. Abraham Lincoln understood this perfectly. In a June 26, 1857, speech responding to the *Dred Scott* decision that he delivered in Springfield, Illinois, Lincoln declared:

> I think the authors of that notable instrument intended to include *all* men, but they did not intend to declare that all men were equal *in all respects*. They did not mean to say all were equal in color, size, intellect, moral developments, or social capacity. They defined with tolerable distinctness, in what respects they did consider all men created equal—equal in "certain inalienable rights, among which are life, liberty, and the pursuit of happiness." This they said, and this they meant. They did not mean to assert the obvious untruth, that they were then actually enjoying that equality, not yet, that they were about to confer it immediately upon them. In fact, they had no power to confer such a boon. They meant simply to declare the *right*, so that the *enforcement* of it might follow as fast as circumstances should permit. They meant to set up a standard maxim for free society, which should be familiar to all, and revered by all; constantly looked to, constantly labored for, and even though never perfectly attained, constantly approximated, and thereby constantly spreading and deepening its influence, and augmenting the happiness and value of life to all people of all colors everywhere.[5]

The Framers of the Constitution conceded no more to slavery than did the signers of the Declaration of Independence. No form of the word *slave* appears in the Constitution, and the text alone gives no clue that it concerns slavery at all. The Framers believed that some concessions to slavery were necessary in order to secure the Union, with its promise of a broad and long-lasting foundation of freedom. Their problem was to make the minimum concessions consistent with that end, to express those concessions in language that would not sanction slavery, and to avoid blotting the Constitution with the stain of slavery. How well they succeeded was revealed in the words of the former slave Frederick Douglass:

> I hold that the Federal Government was never, in its essence, anything but an anti-slavery government. Abolish slavery tomorrow, and not a sentence or syllable of the Constitution need be altered. It was purposely so framed as to give no claim, no sanction to the claim, of property in man. If in its origin slavery had relation to the government, it was only as the scaffolding to the magnificent structure, to be removed as soon as the building was completed.[6]

Douglass's reference to "scaffolding" is illuminating: the Framers' support of slavery was strong enough to allow the structure of the new Union to be built but unobstrusive enough to fade from view when the job was done. A detailed look at the three slave provisions reveals this point clearly.

Article 1, Section 2 of the Constitution provides that "Representatives and direct Taxes shall be apportioned among the several States . . . according to their respective Numbers, which shall be determined by adding to the whole Number of free Persons, including those bound to Service for a Term of Years, and excluding Indians not taxed, three fifths of all other Persons." The origins of the phrase "three-fifths of all other Persons" (referring to slaves) lay in a dispute over whether legislative representation should be based on numbers of people or on wealth. During the Constitutional Convention, James Madison sought to sidestep that issue by suggesting that numbers were a good index, or proxy indicator, of wealth. The productivity of slaves, however, was generally understood to be lower than that of free men, and because wealth could claim inclusion in the basis for apportioning representation and was the sole basis for apportioning direct taxes, some discount for slaves seemed appropriate. In fact, the "three-fifths" figure had been used under the Articles of Confederation as a guide to apportioning population for purposes of laying requisitions on the states. So in actual fact, the Founders employed the Three-fifths Clause more as a guideline for measuring wealth than as a method of counting human beings represented in government.

The three-fifths rule was offensive to many of the Founders, as it suggested that slaves lacked full humanity. The antislavery Founders appreciated, however, that the South would not yield to a stronger national government unless its property interests were represented at least to the extent of the three-fifths standard. As Martin Diamond noted, "The Convention was faced with the same kind of problem that faced Lincoln later: Not striking the bargain would have freed not a single slave while it would have destroyed the possibility of union. And only a strong union, which would engender a national commercial economy, held out the hope that slavery would gradually be eliminated."[7] To most of the Founders, only the expectation that slavery would become unprofitable in a commercial republic and ultimately wither away rendered the three-fifths compromise palatable as a temporary expedient.

The second slave provision in the Constitution, found in Article 1, Section 9, reads: "The Migration or Importation of such Persons as any of the States now existing shall think proper to admit shall not be prohibited by the Congress prior to the year one thousand eight hundred and eight, but a tax or duty may be imposed on such Importation, not exceeding ten dollars for each Person." In *Dred Scott*, Chief Justice Taney relied on this provision to support his claim that the Constitution "distinctly and expressly" affirmed the right of property in a slave. And it was, in fact, a major concession to slavery: it protected not merely the existing slave population, but also the importation of new slaves, and thereby guaranteed a substantial increase in the slave population and an equally substantial augmentation of the slave problem. Yet this concession was carefully limited. To begin with, the provision did not guarantee a right, but, rather, postponed a power to prohibit. Further, it limited Congress's power to prohibit only to those states "now existing": in other words, the convention viewed slavery as a traditional or vested interest that was to be preserved for a time but that Congress did not have to allow to spread to new states. Fairly interpreted, then, the second slave provision gave only temporary respite to an illicit trade. The presumption was that after twenty years, Congress would forbid this trade—and in fact, Congress did so.

Article 4, Section 2, contains the third slave provision in the Constitution, which addresses the issue of fugitive slaves in the following terms: "No person held to Service or Labour in one State, under the Laws thereof, escaping into another, shall, in Consequence of any Law or Regulation thereof, be discharged from such Service or Labour, but shall be delivered up on Claim of the Party to whom such Service or Labour may be due." Another major concession to slavery, this provision amounted to a form of nationalization of slave property, in the sense that every resident of a free state was obliged to assist in the enforcement of the institution of slavery, at least insofar as fugitive slaves were involved. Like its model in the Northwest Ordinance, which outlawed slavery in the Northwest Territory, the fugitive-slave provision represented the price that had to be paid for a broader freedom. The Founders were willing to pay this price, although they were intent on defining it narrowly. An early version of this provision, agreed to by the convention, read: "If any person bound to service or labour in any of the U——— States shall escape into another State, he or she shall not be discharged from such service or labour, in consequence of any regulations subsisting in the State to which they escape, but shall be delivered up to the person justly claiming their service or labour." The Committee on Style subsequently revised it to read: "No person legally held to service or labour in one state, escaping into another, shall in consequence of regulations subsisting therein be discharged from such service or labour, but shall be delivered up on claim of the party to whom such service or labour may be due." The Committee on Style thus withdrew from the master the claim that he "justly claimed" the services of his slave and acknowledged only that the slave's labor "may be due" to the master. This was further revised so that a slave was no longer defined as one "legally held to service or labour," but rather as one "bound to service or labour." The Founders' motivation in these revisions is apparent. Knowing that a provision for the return of fugitive slaves had to be made to win ratification of the Constitution, they carefully chose language that would give as little sanction as possible to the idea that property in slaves had the same moral status as other kinds of property. Overall, the Founders' viewed slavery, in the words of Professor Storing, as "an evil to be tolerated, allowed to enter the Constitution only by the back door, grudgingly, unacknowledged, on the presumption that the house would be truly fit to live in only when it was gone, and that it would ultimately be gone."[8]

And ultimately, slavery was gone. It lasted longer than the Founders had anticipated, largely because the invention of the cotton gin made the growing of cotton profitable and the plantation slavery system that could grow cotton on a large scale economically viable. Only with the Civil War, the Emancipation Proclamation, and the ratification of the Thirteenth Amendment was slavery finally brought to an end. The former slaves then were made the political equals of their former masters via the Fourteenth Amendment's reversal of *Dred Scott* and its declaration that blacks are citizens of the United States and the states in which they reside, and the Fifteenth Amendment's conferral upon them of the franchise. Finally, the Privileges or Immunities, Due Process, and Equal Protection clauses of the Fourteenth Amendment provided the ex-slaves, and all others, with additional means to achieve the original ends of the Constitution and to check the tyrannical and discriminatory tendencies of the majority.

Of the three branches of government, the judiciary has been the most active and influential in interpreting and enforcing the momentous clauses of the Fourteenth Amendment. The Court's emasculation of the Privileges or Immunities Clause was discussed in Chapter 4, and its extensive and varied applications of the Due Process Clause were considered in Chapters 4 through 7. Here, we will examine the ways in which the Equal Protection Clause has been used as a means to protect against racial discriminations.

RACIAL DESEGREGATION

In interpreting the words of the Equal Protection Clause in the *Slaughterhouse Cases* (1873), the Court declared that "the existence of laws in the States where the newly emancipated Negroes resided, which discriminated with gross injustice and hardship against them as a class, was the evil to be remedied by this clause, and by it such laws are forbidden." Thus, it argued that the Equal Protection Clause applied only to blacks. But, what protection did the clause provide them? As a result of the private and public discriminations perpetrated against the "newly emancipated Negroes," the Court was soon forced to define specifically what it understood the Equal Protection Clause to mean. Its response came in the *Civil Rights Cases* (1883) and in *Plessy* v. *Ferguson* (1896).

In the landmark *Civil Rights Cases* (see Chapter 7 of Volume I), the Court limited the protection of the Equal Protection Clause to "state action" only. It held that only discrimination by the states was prohibited and that Congress could not penalize private persons for discriminating against blacks. Absent state action (i.e., in the presence of private discrimination alone), the Court held, the Equal Protection Clause could not be invoked for protection. The concept of state action is in and of itself a complex issue that is discussed separately below. For the moment, the point to be stressed is that the *Civil Rights Cases* limited the concept of equal protection to a narrow class of cases and left entirely to the states the task of prohibiting private racial discrimination. (Justice Harlan's argument in his dissent in the *Civil Rights Cases* that Congress has power under Section 1 and 5 of the Fourteenth Amendment to protect the civil rights of citizens and therefore to prohibit private discrimination was unavailing.)

At this juncture came the *Plessy* decision, which limited the protections offered by the Equal Protection Clause even in cases in which state action was present. In upholding a Louisiana statute that ordered railroads to provide "equal but separate accommodations for the white and colored races," Justice Henry Brown, speaking for the *Plessy* majority, declared that the clause guaranteed to blacks political and civil equality but that it could not put them "on the same plane" socially with whites. Social equality could not be legislated, Brown argued, for it stemmed from "natural affinities, a mutual appreciation of each other's merits, and a voluntary consent of individuals." What the plaintiff Plessy sought, the Court believed, was social equality. To Plessy's contention that the enforced separation of the races stamped him with the badge of inferiority, the Court responded that nothing in the Louisiana statute pronounced him to be inferior, and if he and others of his race felt inferior, that was because they had chosen to put that construction upon the statute. At play here, the Court suggested, was a psychological problem, not a legal one:

[Plessy's] argument necessarily assumes that if, as has been more than once the case, and is not unlikely to be so again, the colored race should become the dominant power in the state legislature, and should enact a law in precisely similar terms, it would thereby relegate the white race to an inferior position. We imagine that the white race, at least, would not acquiesce in this assumption.

Part of this psychological understanding of racial discrimination was subsequently "rejected" in *Brown* v. *Board of Education* (1954) in which the Court held that the "separate but equal" formula is inherently unequal because it generates feelings of inferiority in members of minority groups. It must be emphasized, however, that not all of the psychological understanding of discrimination present in *Plessy* has been repudiated. Justice Brown's belief that whites cannot be discriminated against because they will not feel stigmatized or inferior has never been overruled and, in fact, has been of decisive importance in sustaining the constitutional validity of, among other things, ameliorative racial preference. In *Regents of the University of California* v. *Bakke* (1978), for instance, Justice William Brennan offered the following observations in seeking to justify the use of racial quotas* by the medical school of the University of California at Davis:

> Nor was Bakke in any sense stamped as inferior by the Medical School's rejection of him. . . . [T]here is absolutely no basis for concluding that Bakke's rejection as a result of Davis's use of racial preference will affect him throughout his life in the same way as the segregation of the Negro school children in *Brown I* would have affected them. Unlike discrimination against racial minorities, the use of race preferences for remedial purposes does not inflict a pervasive injury upon individual whites in the sense that wherever they go or whatever they do there is a significant likelihood that they will be treated as second-class citizens because of their color.

Justice John Marshall Harlan, as the lone dissenter in *Plessy*, rebutted the majority's contention that if blacks felt that Louisiana's "equal but separate" statute branded them as inferior, it was simply because they had put that construction upon it: "Every one knows that the statute in question had its origin in the purpose, not so much to exclude white persons from railroad cars occupied by blacks, as to exclude colored people from coaches occupied by or assigned to white persons. . . . No one would be so wanting in candor to assert the contrary." More central to his dissent, however, was his eloquent and now-famous declaration that "our Constitution is color blind, and neither knows nor tolerates classes among citizens." It has become commonplace to assert that these words finally were vindicated by the Court's unanimous decision in *Brown*.[9] But here too, the Court's post-*Brown* decisions concerning

---

*This issue is dealt with at greater length in Chapter 9.

ameliorative racial preference give pause. The principle that the Constitution is color blind is considered by many to be unduly simplistic and inappropriate for today's complexities; some observers have argued that although color blindness may be an appropriate long-term goal, "our society cannot be completely color blind in the short term if we are to have a color blind society in the long term."[10]

In sum, *Plessy* limited the protections of the Equal Protection Clause by legitimating the concept of "equal but separate" (or "separate but equal," as it soon came to be known). Once the principle of racial segregation was in place and constitutionally recognized, it proved difficult to remove. Despite decades of noble effort spearheaded in large part by the National Association for the Advancement of Colored People (NAACP),[11] not until the celebrated *Brown* decision, handed down fifty-eight years later, was "separate but equal" finally rooted out. Efforts to overturn *Plessy* largely were confined to, and ultimately prevailed in, the field of education. Although this focus on segregation in education unquestionably was a wise litigation strategy, as the fraudulent character of the protection afforded by "separate but equal" was nowhere more obvious, it did present a certain irony. In *Plessy*, Justice Brown relied heavily on the fact there was racial segregation in the schools of Boston and the District of Columbia to sustain racial segregation in railroad coaches in Louisiana: "The establishment of separate schools for white and colored children . . . has been held to be a valid exercise of the legislative power even by courts of States where the political rights of the colored race have been longest and most earnestly enforced."

The initial attempts to overturn *Plessy* and the "separate but equal" doctrine in education were inauspicious. In *Cumming* v. *Richmond County Board of Education* (1899), in fact, the plaintiffs found that the Court was willing to tolerate even "separate and unequal." This case arose out of a Georgia school board's decision to discontinue the existing black high school in order to use the building and facilities for black elementary education. Whereas no new black high school was established, the white high schools were continued, and black taxpayers and parents brought suit to restrain the school board from using money to support the white high school until equal facilities for black students had been provided. A unanimous Supreme Court sidestepped the question of segregation; denied that the discontinuance of the black school violated the Equal Protection Clause; and stressed that an injunction to close the white schools was not the proper legal remedy, as it would not help the black children.

The problems of reconciling *Cumming* and its progeny with the demands of equal protection finally prompted the Court in the 1930s to emphasize the need for equality in segregation. "Separate but equal" facilities were to be just that; "separate and unequal" treatment, at least in higher education, would no longer be tolerated. *Missouri Ex Rel Gaines* v. *Canada* (1938) is significant in this regard. Missouri had refused to admit blacks to the University of Missouri School of Law, providing instead state reimbursement of tuition fees for any of its black citizens who could gain admission to law schools in neighboring states in which segregation was not enforced. Missouri argued that this provision satisfied the "separate but equal" requirement, but the Supreme Court ruled that if facilities within the state were provided for the legal education of white students, equal facilities for black students also had to be made available in the state.

In subsequent cases the Court continued to insist on equal educational facilities for blacks pursuing postbaccalaureate studies. The most important of these was *Sweatt* v. *Painter* (1950), which held, in effect, that if educational facilities were segregated, they had to be equal not only quantitatively but also qualitatively. At issue was a law school for blacks that Texas had hastily established as a means of avoiding the desegregation of the University of Texas Law School. In the view of the Court, even if the black school were equal to the all-white law school "in terms of number of the faculty, variety of courses and opportunity for specialization, size of the student body, scope of the library, and availability of law review and other activities"—which it most assuredly was not—it clearly was unequal with respect to those "qualities which are incapable of objective measurement but which make for greatness in a law school. Such qualities, to name but a few, include reputation of the faculty, experience of the administration, position and influence of the alumni, standing in the community, traditions and prestige." The Court's message in *Sweatt* was plain and blunt: segregation *per se* was not yet unconstitutional, but the requirements of "separate but equal" henceforth would be all but impossible to meet.

The NAACP prudently had begun its assault on segregated education at the postgraduate and professional level, where the inequalities that black students suffered could be documented most easily. Because only a few blacks were seeking admission to these programs, moreover, the public's reaction to the Court's decisions would be uneventful. The *Missouri* and *Sweatt* decisions, however, paved the way for the NAACP's assault on segregation at all levels of public education, which bore fruit in *Brown*. In that landmark decision, handed down on May 17, 1954, by a unanimous Court, Chief Justice Earl Warren held that "in the field of public education the doctrine of "separate but equal' has no place." Soon after the decision was rendered, the *New York Times* editorialized that "it is fifty-eight years since the supreme Court, with Justice Harlan dissenting, established the doctrine of 'separate but equal' provision for the white and Negro races on interstate carriers. It is forty-three years since John Marshall Harlan passed from this earth. Now the words he used in his lonely dissent in an 8-to-1 decision in the case of *Plessy* v. *Ferguson* in 1896 have become a part of the law of the land." Although noting that *Brown* "dealt solely with segregation in the public schools," the *Times* insisted that "there was not one word in Chief Justice Warren's opinion that was inconsistent with the earlier views of Justice Harlan."[12]

The *Times*'s statement expresses the conventional wisdom that *Brown* realized Justice Harlan's famous dissenting dictum. A closer look at the *Brown* opinion, however, belies this claim. Chief Justice Warren did not invalidate "separate but equal" because it departed from the principle that the Constitution is color blind; he invalidated it because of the psychological damage it caused blacks. "Separate but equal" is inherently unequal, he insisted, because it "generates feelings of inferiority [in blacks] as to their status in the community that may affect their hearts and minds in a way unlikely ever to be undone"—a conclusion he supported by citations to the literature of social psychology. Accordingly, it can be argued that Chief Justice Warren's opinion had more in common with Justice Brown's majority opinion in *Plessy* than with Justice Harlan's dissent. Central to both Chief Justice Warren and Justice Brown was the question of the psychological damage caused by segregation; they differed only in the answers they gave, not in the questions they asked. Neither understood the Equal Protection Clause in the way that Justice Harlan did—as a flat prohibition against the use of race as the basis for classifying or categorizing individuals. Contrary to commonly held opinion, then, Justice Harlan's dissenting words have never been vindicated. This point must be understood if confusion is to be avoided, for the Supreme Court has continued to regard the Equal Protection Clause as a means for preventing or mitigating the psychological damage caused by racial discrimination, not as a barrier to race-conscious classifications.

In *Bolling* v. *Sharpe* (1954), a companion case to *Brown*, the Court also invalidated racial segregation in the public schools of the District of Columbia. Because the Equal Protection Clause of the Fourteenth Amendment applies only to the states, and not to the federal government, the justices based this decision on the Due Process Clause of the Fifth Amendment. In finding it "unthinkable" that the Constitution could impose a lesser duty on the federal government than on the states, they employed a substantive due-process argument to end this practice. Chief Justice Warren reasoned as follows: "Liberty . . . cannot be restricted except for a proper governmental objective. Segregation in public education is not reasonably related to any proper governmental objective, and thus imposes on Negro children of the District of Columbia a burden that constitutes an arbitrary deprivation of their liberty. . . ." The Court has relied on this same line of argument in subsequent cases to impose the standards of the Equal Protection Clause on national legislation—even though, to repeat, the Fourteenth Amendment is not directed toward the national government.

Brown and its companion cases established the fundamental principle that "racial discrimination in public education is unconstitutional"; they did not, however, address the question of how this fundamental principle was to be implemented. Instead, the Court postponed a decision on the application of *Brown*, restored the case to its docket for argument during the next term, and invited all interested parties to present their views on how its decision could be carried out. These hearings were held in April 1955, and on May 31 of that year the Court ruled in what is commonly called *Brown II* that the cases would be remanded to the courts in which they had originated, which were ordered to fashion decrees of enforcement on equitable principles and with regard to "varied local school problems."[13] The Supreme Court directed the lower courts to determine whether the actions or proposals of the various school authorities constituted "good faith implementation of the governing constitutional principles" and charged them with requiring a "prompt and reasonable start toward full compliance" with *Brown I* and with ensuring that the parties to these cases be admitted to public schools "on a racially non-discriminatory basis with all deliberate speed."[14]

Brown I and *Brown II* were met with stiff resistance throughout the South. The resisters redoubled their efforts after the Court, through a series of *per curiam* orders, extended the desegregation requirement, which originally had been confined to public education, to public recreational facilities, golf courses, bus transportation, public parks, athletic contests, airport restaurants, courtroom seating, public auditoriums, and jails.[15] Resistance took a number of forms, including threatened or actual violence. Major incidents involving violence occurred in Clinton, Tennessee, in 1956; in Little Rock, Arkansas, in 1957; in New Orleans in 1960; and at the University of Mississippi in 1962. On these occasions, the Court was quick to act and unequivocal in its condemnation. In the especially significant case of *Cooper* v. *Aaron* (1958), the Court unanimously held that the violent resistance to the desegregation plan of the schools of Little Rock was "directly traceable" to Arkansas's governor and legislature and warned that the constitutional prohibition of racial discrimination in school admissions "can neither be nullified openly and directly by state legislators or state executive or judicial officers, nor nullified indirectly by them through evasive schemes for segregation." Then, in extraordinary language, the Court explicitly asserted its supreme authority as constitutional expositor. Declaring that *Marbury* v. *Madison* established "the basic principle that the federal judiciary is supreme in the exposition of the law of the Constitution, and that [this] principle has ever since been respected by this Court and the Country as a permanent and indispensable feature of our Constitutional system," it held that "it follows that the interpretation of the Fourteenth Amendment enunciated by this Court in the *Brown* case is the Supreme Law of the Land, and Art. VI of the Constitution makes it of binding effect on the States."

More often, resistance took the form of delaying tactics by local school boards that, either on their own initiative or under the compulsion of a federal district court order, were charged with preparing desegregation plans. Even those boards willing to act usually preferred to await a court decision mandating such action, in order to justify their actions to those in the community opposed to *Brown* and to desegregation.

When ordered to act, moreover, the boards often instituted measures that stopped short of actual desegregation. "Freedom of choice" plans, under which each pupil supposedly was free to choose the school to be attended but which in fact resulted in very few transfers out of black schools, represented one such measure. For some time, this foot-dragging proved successful—after all, the Supreme Court seemingly had sanctioned these measures in *Brown II*, as it had not required either the school authorities or the lower courts to take immediate steps to "admit pupils to public schools on a racially nondiscriminatory basis" but had only imposed on them the duty to realize this goal "with all deliberate speed." By 1968, however, the Court's patience had run out, and in *Green* v. *County School Board of New Kent County* it announced that school boards had a positive duty to eliminate, "root and branch," the historic and pervasive effects of racial discrimination. This required the formulation of plans that promised prompt conversion to a desegregated system. The goal, the Court underlined, was the achievement of a "unitary, nonracial system of public education." The following year, in *Alexander* v. *Holmes County Board of Education*, the Court more pointedly declared that the "continued operation of segregated schools under a standard of allowing 'all deliberate speed' for desegregation is no longer constitutionally permissible" and demanded that every district immediately end dual school systems and begin to operate unitary schools alone.

The question of exactly what the Court expected when it ordered the operation of unitary school systems has not yet been resolved definitively, but a review of its subsequent decisions yields some indications. In *Swann* v. *Charlotte-Mecklenburg Board of Eduation* (1971), it held that where *de jure* segregation existed in the past, school authorities must dismantle the dual school system by taking positive action to create an integrated school system. Among the measures deemed appropriate for eliminating "all vestiges of state-imposed segregation" were remedial altering of attendance zones, clustering, and busing. The Court acknowledged that these measures "may be administratively awkward, inconvenient, and even bizarre in some situations and may impose burdens on some," but it insisted that during this remedial period such inconveniences were necessary evils. In defending this extraordinary use of the judiciary's equity power, the Court emphasized that "absent a constitutional violation there would be no basis for judicially ordering assignment of students on a racial basis. All things being equal, with no history of discrimination, it might well be desirable to assign pupils to schools nearest their homes. But all things are not equal in a system that has been deliberately constructed and maintained to enforce racial segregation."

Soon thereafter, the Court in *Keyes* v. *School District No. 1, Denver, Colorado* (1973) brought school desegregation and busing to the northern states. Although *de facto* segregation—or, to use Nathan Glazer's phrase, racial concentration[16]—undeniably existed in the Denver schools, neither the city nor the state had ever required racial segregation by law.

Keyes thus provided the Court with the opportunity to rule on whether such *de facto* segregation was unconstitutional, but the justices avoided this question. Noting that the Denver school authorities in drawing attendance boundaries, assigning teachers, and locating new schools, had acted and were continuing to support *de facto* segregation in a few of the district's schools, the Court argued that the school district had engaged in *de jure* segregation even in the absence of school segregation laws. In separate concurring opinions, however, Justices William Douglas and Lewis Powell argued that the *de jure/de facto* distinction should be abandoned and that segregation, for whatever reason, should be declared unconstitutional.

The Court continued to sidestep the question of whether *de facto* segregation is constitutionally proscribed in *Columbus Board of Education* v. *Penick* (1979) and *Dayton Board of Education* v. *Brinkman* (1979). In these companion cases, a badly split Supreme Court affirmed lower federal-court rulings ordering wide-scale busing to achieve racial balance in the public school systems of Columbus and Dayton, Ohio. However, the justices did not hold that *de facto* segregation resulting from housing patterns was unconstitutional; they merely accepted lower-court determinations that at the time that *Brown I* was decided, the public school systems of both cities were officially segregated on the basis of race, not by state law but as consequence of policies pursued by the cities' boards of education.

The breadth of what the Court majority in *Columbus* and *Dayton* was prepared to recognize as *de jure* segregation effectively obviated any need to clarify the constitutional status of *de facto* segregation. It also raised problems, however. As Justice Potter Stewart objected in his dissent, the Court appeared to reason that "if such an officially authorized segregated school system can be found to have existed in 1954, then any current racial separation in the schools will be presumed to have been caused by acts in violation of the Constitution." However, he continued,

> much has changed in 25 years, in the Nation at large and in Dayton and Columbus in particular. Minds have changed with respect to racial relationships. Perhaps more importantly, generations have changed. The prejudices of these School Boards of 1954 (and earlier) cannot realistically be assumed to haunt the school boards of today. Similarly . . . , school systems have changed. Dayton and Columbus are both examples of the dramatic growth and change in urban school districts. It is unrealistic to assume that the hand of 1954 plays any major part in shaping the current school systems in either city.

Continuing on this same theme, Justice William Rehnquist criticized the Court's finding of *de jure* segregation as running counter to the expectations "that the existence of violations of constitutional rights be carefully and clearly defined before a federal court invades the ambit of local control, and that the subsequent displacement of local authority be limited to that necessary to correct the identified violations." Given the majority's encompassing understanding of *de jure* segregation and the sweep of the remedies it was willing to sustain in the *Columbus* and *Dayton* cases, he speculated "that a school system's only hope of avoiding a judicial receivership might be a voluntary dismantling of its neighborhood school program."

In *Milliken* v. *Bradley* (1974) the Court addressed the question of whether increasingly black city school districts and largely white suburban school districts should be required, in the words of *Green* v. *New Kent County* (1968), to consolidate into a "single unitary nonracial system of public education." In *Milliken*, however, a five-member majority rejected massive interdistrict busing as a remedy for the *de jure* segregation found in the Detroit school system. Chief Justice Warren Burger, speaking for the majority, ruled that the federal district court's decree bringing fifty-three suburban school districts into Detroit's desegregation plan was unjustified, because the Court had been shown no evidence of significant violations by these outlying school districts or any interdistrict violations. *Milliken* v. *Bradley* returned to the Supreme Court again in 1977, and at that time the Court upheld a district court order requiring remedial educational programs as part of its desegregation decrees. *Milliken II* marked the Court's first approval of desegregation remedies that not only involved assignment of students to schools on the basis of race but also pierced the core of educational programs; it involved the federal courts more than ever before in educational policy-making. How much more involved the courts were subsequently to become is apparent in *Missouri* v. *Jenkins* (1990) and *United States* v. *Fordice* (1992). In *Jenkins*, Federal District Court Judge Russell Clark found that the Kansas City school district and the State of Missouri were guilty of operating a segregated school system and issued an order detailing a desegregation remedy and the financing necessary to implement it. His remedy was comprehensive and extraordinarily expensive. Among other things, he mandated that every high school, every middle school, and half of the elementary schools in the school district become magnet schools; costs for implementing his remedial plan were placed between $500,000,000 and $700,000,000. Justice Kennedy was later to describe Judge Clark's capital improvement plan as follows:

> [H]igh school in which every classroom will have air conditioning, an alarm system, and 15 microcomputers; a 2,000-square-foot planetarium; greenhouses and vivariums; a 25-acre farm with an air-conditioned meeting room for 104 people; a Model United Nations wired for language translation; broadcast capable radio and television studios with an editing and animation lab; a temperature controlled art gallery; movie editing and screening rooms; a 3,500-square-foot dust-free diesel mechanics room; 1,875-square-foot elementary school an-

imal rooms for use in a Zoo Project; swimming pools; and numerous other facilities.

To pay for this remedy, Judge Clark ordered the State of Missouri to cover 75 percent of the costs, with the school district contributing the rest. When it became clear that state tax limitation laws prohibited the school district from raising property tax rates sufficiently to meet its 25 percent obligation, he enjoined the operation of these state laws and ordered that the district property tax levy be increased from $2.05 to $4.00 per $100 of assessed valuation. When his decree reached the Supreme Court, it unanimously concluded that Judge Clark had abused his discretion; however, a majority held that he abused it only by specifying the tax levy, not by demanding of the school district that it fully fund his remedy. In *United States* v. *Fordice,* the Court addressed the efforts of the State of Mississippi to dismantle the dual university system that its laws once mandated. It overturned the conclusion of both the District Court and the Court of Appeals that the adoption and implementation of race-neutral admission policies were sufficient to demonstrate that Mississippi had completely abandoned its prior dual system. In so doing, it placed in potential jeopardy the continued existence of state-supported "historically black institutions." Justice Thomas, in his concurring opinion, attempted to rule out that prospect: "Although I agree that a State is not constitutionally required to maintain its historically black institutions as such, I do not understand our opinion to hold that a State is forbidden from doing so. It would be ironic, to say the least, if the institutions that sustained blacks during segregation were themselves destroyed in an effort to combat its vestiges."

Three additional cases must also be mentioned in this review of the Court's efforts to clarify what *Alexander* v. *Holmes* requires, for they reveal the Court's ever-increasing commitment to extricate school districts from ongoing judicial supervision and remedial decrees and to restore to state and local authorities control of their systems. The first is *Pasadena City Board of Education* v. *Spangler* (1976). In it, the Court held in a 6–2 decision that once the affirmative duty to desegregate has been accomplished (i.e., once a unitary school system has been achieved), school authorities are under no compulsion to readjust attendance zones each year to keep up with population shifts. Reaffirming what it had said in *Swann,* the Court declared that once dual school systems have been dismantled, subsequent changes in the racial composition of particular schools within these systems that are caused solely by shifts in population and in no way by segregatory actions by school officials do not justify further district-court reassignment and busing orders.

The second case is *Freeman* v. *Pitts* (1992), in which the Court unanimously concluded that federal district courts have the authority to relinquish supervision and control over school districts in incremental stages before full compliance with its desegregation order has been achieved in every area of school operations. It therefore allowed the U.S. District Court for the Northern District of Georgia to return to the DeKalb County School System (suburban Atlanta) control over student assignment, transportation, physical facilities, and extracurricular activities, areas in which the school system had demonstrated full compliance, while retaining court supervision over the areas of faculty and administrative assignments and the quality of education, where compliance had not been fully achieved.

The third is *Missouri* v. *Jenkins* (1995), a follow-up case to the 1990 litigation described above. When minority student achievement levels in the Kansas City school district continued to remain below "national norms," despite court-ordered spending of over $940 million to eliminate the past effects of racial segregation, Judge Clark ordered Missouri to fund salary increases for virtually all instructional and noninstructional staff with the school district and to continue to fund remedial "quality education" programs. He reasoned that these increases would eliminate the vestiges of state-imposed segregation by improving the "desegregative attractiveness" of the city's schools and by reversing "white flight" to the suburbs. The Supreme Court granted certiorari and reversed, holding that Judge Clark's order was "simply too far removed from an acceptable implementation of a permissible means to remedy previous legally-mandated segregation." Chief Justice Rehnquist declared that "[j]ust as demographic changes independent of *de jure* segregation will affect the racial composition of student assignments, so too will numerous external factors beyond the control of the . . . school district and the State affect minority student achievement. So long as these external factors are not the result of segregation, they do not figure in the remedial calculus. Insistence upon academic goals unrelated to the effects of legal segregation unwarrantably postpones the day when the . . . school district will be able to operate on its own." In a lengthy and powerful concurring opinion, Justice Thomas harshly criticized Judge Clark for assuming that if "a school district today is black, it must be educationally inferior" and for exercising his "virtually unlimited equitable powers" to "trample upon principles of federalism and separation of powers" as he pursued "other agendas unrelated to the narrow purpose of precisely remedying a constitutional harm."

PRIVATE DISCRIMINATION AND THE
CONCEPT OF STATE ACTION

As noted above, the prohibitions of the Equal Protection Clause are limited to "state action" only. Since the *Civil Rights Cases* the Court consistently has held that private discriminations are not prohibited by the Fourteenth Amendment; only applicable state laws, it has ruled, can address this problem.[17] In hewing to this principle, the justices have had to address the question of what exactly constitutes "state action." The term obviously comprehends statutes enacted by national, state, or local legislative bodies and official actions of all governmental officers, but difficult problems arise when the conduct of private individuals or groups is challenged as racially discriminatory. In such cases the Court has had to determine whether these private actors are performing a government function or are sufficiently involved with or encouraged by the state so that they, too, should be held to the same constitutional obligations as the states themselves.

The "white primary" cases, which involved a series of ploys by the southern states to bar blacks from participating in primary elections, reflect how the Court has dealt with cases of governmental function. In *Newberry* v. *United States* (1921), the justices held that primary elections were "in no real sense part of the manner of holding elections" and thus were not subject to constitutional or congressional control. Many states in the "one-party South," aware that winning the Democratic primary was tantamount to winning the general election, thereupon openly set out to discriminate against black voters in primaries. For example, the Texas legislature in 1923 passed a law flatly prohibiting blacks from voting in that state's Democratic primaries. When the Supreme Court invalidated this statute in *Nixon* v. *Herndon* (1927), on the grounds that it was "a direct and obvious infringement" of the Equal Protection Clause, segregationist politicians sought to keep blacks from voting in ways that did not involve state action.[18] Again in Texas, the Democratic Party convention, on its own authority and without any state legislation on the subject, adopted a resolution confining party membership to white citizens. The Court unanimously concluded in *Grovey* v. *Townsend* (1935) that this action did not violate the Fourteenth Amendment, because it had been taken by the party and not by the state; the justices thus endorsed the view that political parties were private clubs, uncontrolled by constitutional limitations on official action, and that the primaries they held constitutionally were not part of the election process. This position was abandoned in *United States* v. *Classic* (1941), a Louisiana ballot-tampering case in which the Court held that the state's election laws made the primary an "integral part" of the process of electing congressmen and that the Democratic primary was actually "the only stage of the election procedure" in which a voter's choice was of any significance. *Classic* did not directly address the issue of the "white primary," but its implications were clear. After acknowledging that primaries performed a governmental function, the Court no longer could persist in the view that the parties conducting them were unaffected with public responsibilities. When the occasion to rule on "white primaries" presented itself in *Smith* v. *Allwright* (1944), the Court directly reversed the *Grovey* decision, announced that the Democratic Party was "an agency of the State," and declared that the party's use of the "white primary" constituted state action in violation of the Constitution.

State action can also result from state involvement in or encouragement of private discrimination. *Burton* v. *Wilmington Parking Authority*

(1961) involved a parking facility owned and operated by an agency of the state of Delaware. To help finance the building, the agency leased some of its space to commercial operations, one of which was a segregated restaurant. A majority of the Court held that because of its location in and relationship to the parking facility, the restaurant had lost its "purely private" character. The relationship between the restaurant and parking facility was mutually beneficial—the former provided the latter with revenue and the latter provided the former with customers. By failing to require the restaurant to serve all customers, the state, in the words of the Court, had "made itself a party to the refusal of service" and had "elected to place its power, property and prestige behind the admitted discrimination."

The sit-in cases present even more dramatic evidence of how state encouragement of private discrimination can become state action. During the 1960s, civil-rights advocates frequently staged sit-ins at variety and drug stores that maintained segregated lunch counters. To protest such discrimination, blacks would take seats at lunch counters and, when refused service, continue to sit there until arrested, typically for breach of the peace or trespass. In a series of sit-in cases, the Court consistently reversed the convictions that resulted from these arrests, often on the ground that the policy of segregation that had led to the sit-ins was governmentally inspired and thus amounted to "state action" in violation of the Equal Protection Clause. In *Peterson* v. *Greenville* (1963), for example, a city ordinance actually required separation of the races in restaurants. *Lombard* v. *Louisiana* (1963) featured no such ordinance, but the Court ruled that city officials had coerced the restaurant manager to operate a segregated facility. In *Griffin* v. *Maryland* (1964) the Court held that an amusement park's exclusion of blacks constituted state action because, to enforce this private policy, the park had employed a deputy sheriff who, although off-duty, wore his badge and purported to exercise his official powers.

A more difficult state action question, which the Court has never answered fully, is whether state action is entirely a negative concept that prohibits states and their agents from practicing racial discrimination, or whether it is also a positive concept that imposes on the states an affirmative obligation to prevent private racial discrimination. Initially, the Court was content to define equal protection negatively and to view the state action doctrine as simply prohibiting the states from acting in a discriminatory manner against blacks. Since *Shelley* v. *Kraemer* (1948), however, the Court increasingly has come to hold that the state must take positive steps to prevent racial discrimination by private parties or to overcome the effects of past discrimination.[19]

In *Shelley* the Court held that judicial enforcement of racially restrictive covenants (i.e., agreements entered into by property owners, binding them not to sell or lease their properties to blacks or other minorities) constituted governmental involvement in racial discrimination and thus amounted to state action. The Court reasoned as follows:

> We have no doubt that there has been state action in these cases in the full and complete sense of the phrase. The undisputed facts disclosed that petitioners were willing purchasers of properties upon which they desired to establish homes. The owners of the properties were willing sellers; and contracts of sale were accordingly consummated. It is clear that but for the active intervention of the state courts, supported by the full panoply of state power, petitioners would have been free to occupy the properties in question without restraint.

The Court thus reached the curious conclusion that a contract might be legally valid but unenforceable in court. It appeared to hold that courts would not enforce private property rights, however legal, that had been exercised in a discriminatory manner, on the ground that court enforcement would constitute discriminatory state action.[20] Because private rights count for little unless they can be legally enforced, the Court here came close to destroying the distinction between private action and state action. As a consequence, *Shelley* provoked the following line of inquiry: Could a police officer remove a black trespasser from the private residence of a white if the white concedes that the reason he wants the black removed is personal prejudice against blacks?

The Court continued to expand the concept of state action in *Reitman* v. *Mulkey* (1967). Voting 5–4, the Court, concluded in *Reitman* that California was guilty of violating the Equal Protection Clause because its citizens had ratified an amendment to the California state constitution that repealed a law prohibiting racial discrimination in the sale and rental of private dwellings. In his opinion for the Court, Justice Byron White acknowledged that California itself was not guilty of discrimination. He contended, however, that when the voters of California approved the amendment in question, which nullified existing open-housing laws and provided that property owners had "absolute discretion" to sell or rent to persons of their choice, "the right to discriminate, including the right to discriminate on racial grounds, was embodied in the state's basic charter, immune from legislative, executive or judicial regulation at any level of the state government. Those practicing racial discriminations need no longer rely on their personal choice. They could now evoke express constitutional authority."

According to the *Reitman* ruling, discriminatory private action becomes discriminatory state action if the state takes any action allowing such discrimination. Logically, the next step in this chain of reasoning would be the conclusion that discriminatory private action becomes discriminatory state action if the state fails to prohibit such discrimination. As *Moose Lodge No. 107* v. *Irvis* (1972) indicated, however, the Court was not willing to take such a step. In this 6–3 decision, the Court held that discrimination by a private club did not constitute state action simply because the club held a state liquor license. In so doing, the Court reaffirmed Justice Arthur Goldberg's statement in *Bell* v. *Maryland*

(1964) that "rights pertaining to privacy and private association are themselves constitutionally protected liberties," and that included among those rights is the right of a person "to close his home or club to any person . . . on the basis of personal prejudices including race."

As *Palmore* v. *Sidoti* (1984) makes clear, however, this private racial prejudice cannot be invoked by any instrumentality of government to justify racial classifications. In unanimously holding that the reality of private biases and the possible injury they might inflict are not permissible considerations for removal of an infant child from the custody of its natural mother in racially mixed household custody cases, the Court offered one of its clearest statements on the constitutional test it employs in racial discrimination cases: Racial "classifications are subject to the most exacting scrutiny; to pass constitutional muster, they must be justified by a compelling governmental interest and must be 'necessary to the accomplishment of its legitimate purpose.'"

RACIAL DISCRIMINATION IN JURY TRIALS

Since *Strauder* v. *West Virginia* (1880), the Supreme Court has held that racial discrimination by the state in jury selection violates the Equal Protection Clause. In *Strauder*, the Court invalidated a state law that allowed only white men to serve as jurors. In *Swain* v. *Alabama* (1965), it held that black defendants could challenge on equal protection grounds a state's exercise of peremptory challenges (the rejection of potential jurors without cause, i.e., without providing a reason) to exclude members of their race from their petit juries. To do so, however, they could not rely simply on the pattern of jury strikes in their own particular cases; rather, they would have to introduce evidence of a systematic exclusion of blacks through the use of peremptories over a period of time. In *Batson* v. *Kentucky* (1986), the Court relaxed the evidentiary requirements of *Swain* and held that a black defendant could establish a *prima facie* case of purposeful discrimination in the selection of jurors based solely on the prosecutor's exercise of peremptory challenges at the defendant's trial. Justice Powell declared for the *Batson* majority that "[t]he harm from discriminatory jury selection extends beyond that inflicted on the defendant and the excluded juror to touch the entire community. Selection procedures that purposefully exclude black persons from juries undermine public confidence in the fairness of our system of justice." In dissent, Justice Rehnquist argued:

> In my view, there is simply nothing "unequal" about the State using its peremptory challenges to strike blacks from the jury in cases involving black defendants, so long as such challenges are also used to exclude whites in cases involving white defendants, Hispanics in cases involving Hispanic defendants, Asians in cases involving Asian defendants, and so on. This case-specific use of peremptory challenges by the State does not single out blacks, or members of any other race for that matter, for discriminatory treatment. Such use of

peremptories is at best based upon seat-of-the-pants instincts, which are undoubtedly crudely stereotypical and may in many cases be hopelessly mistaken. But as long as they are applied across the board to jurors of all races and nationalities, I do not see—and the Court most certainly has not explained—how their use violates the Equal Protection Clause.

In 1991, the Court carried *Batson* to new heights. In *Powers* v. *Ohio*, it held that a prosecutor in a trial of a white criminal defendant is prohibited from excluding black jurors on the basis of race; in his dissent, Justice Scalia declared himself "unmoved" by "this white defendant's complaint that he sought to be tried by an all-white jury." And, in *Edmonson* v. *Leesville Concrete Company*, the Court held that even private litigants in civil actions cannot exercise their peremptory challenges in a racially discriminatory manner. Justice Kennedy held for a six-member majority that "[W]hen private litigants participate in the selection of jurors, they serve an important function within the government and act with its substantial assistance. If peremptory challenges based on race were permitted, persons could be required by summons to be put at risk of open and public discrimination as a condition of their participation in the justice system. The injury to excluded jurors would be the direct result of governmental delegation and participation." Justice O'Connor objected: "Not everything that happens in a courtroom is state action. A trial, particularly a civil trial, is by design largely a stage on which private parties may act; it is a forum through which they can resolve their disputes in a peaceful and ordered manner. The government erects the platform; it does not thereby become responsible for all that occurs upon it. . . . I believe that a peremptory strike by a private litigant is fundamentally a matter of private choice and not state action."

Once *Batson* and *Edmonson* had established that neither prosecutors nor private litigants in civil cases could use their peremptory challenges in a racially discriminatory manner, the next and only remaining question for the Court concerning peremptory strikes came in *Georgia* v. *McCollum* (1992). In *McCollum,* the Court had to decide whether defendants in criminal cases were likewise prohibited from engaging in racial discrimination in their use of peremptories. Justice Blackmun held for a seven-member majority that they were.[21] In dissent, Justice Scalia commented on the "sheer inanity" of the proposition that "a criminal defendant, in the process of defending himself against the state, is held to be acting on behalf of the state."[22]

PROOF OF DISCRIMINATION: IMPACT VERSUS INTENT

By blurring the distinction between discriminatory private action and discriminatory state action, the Court expanded considerably the concept of state action. This approach to state action would have rendered the states much more vulnerable to charges of discrimination had the Court subsequently not sharpened the distinction between discriminatory impact and discriminatory intent or purpose. It did so by holding in *Washington* v. *Davis* (1976), *Village of Arlington Heights* v. *Metropolitan Housing Development Corporation* (1977), and *Mount Healthy City Board of Education* v. *Doyle* (1977) that the constitutionality of state action hinged not on a racially disproportionate impact, but only on the ground that the challenged action would not have been undertaken "but for" the presence of an invidious discriminatory purpose.

Washington and *Arlington Heights* represented substantial departures from the prevailing judicial belief, as stated by the Fifth Circuit Court of Appeals in *United States Ex Rel. Seals* v. *Wiman* (1962), that it should not be necessary for either the plaintiff or the judiciary "to go so far as to establish ill will, evil motive, or absence of good faith. . . . Objective results are largely to be relied on in the application of the Constitutional text." *Washington* upheld the recruiting procedures (including a written personnel test) of the District of Columbia police department, even though those procedures excluded a disproportionately large number of black applicants. The *Arlington Heights* case held that the Chicago suburb in question had not practiced racial discrimination by refusing to rezone a tract of land from single-family to multifamily usage so that a racially integrated low- and moderate-income housing project could be built. Together, these cases explicitly set forth the Court's position that in and of itself, the racially discriminatory effect of an official action is not sufficient to render that action unconstitutional. As the Court said in *Washington*, "Disproportionate impact is not irrelevant, but it is not the sole touchstone [of racial discrimination]." Henceforth, proof of racially discriminatory intent or purpose would be required to show a violation of the Equal Protection Clause. *Arlington Heights* not only reaffirmed this view but also offered the lower courts guidance on how to conduct a "proper and sensitive" inquiry into whether racially discriminatory intent exists. In addition to "the impact of the official action," which was viewed simply as one evidentiary source, Justice Powell's majority opinion directed a consideration of such other evidence as the historical background of the challenged action, the specific sequence of events leading up to the challenged action, departures from normal procedures, and contemporary statements of the decision-making body.

Mount Healthy and footnote 21 of *Arlington Heights* added the important "but for" qualification. In *Mount Healthy* the Court acknowledged that the petitioner school board's decision not to rehire a nontenured teacher had been motivated in part by conduct on the part of the teacher that was protected by the First Amendment. But that fact alone, the Court went on, did not necessarily amount to a constitutional violation justifying remedial action; rather, the trial court should have attempted to determine whether the school board had shown by a preponderance of the evidence that it would have dismissed the teacher even in the absence of the protected conduct. As a result of this decision, the courts will accept as constitutional an action that bears a rational relation to a legitimate state interest, even if an illegitimate purpose also motivated that action. Although *Mount Healthy* dealt only with freedom of speech, footnote 21 of *Arlington Heights* left no doubt that the principle it enunciated applied with no less force to cases involving racial discrimination. The footnote cited *Mount Healthy* and declared, "Proof that the decision by the Village was motivated in part by a racially discriminatory purpose would not necessarily have required invalidation of the challenged decision. Such proof would, however, have shifted to the Village the burden of establishing that the same decision would have resulted even had the impermissible purpose not been considered." This requirement that invidious discriminatory purpose be a "but for" cause of the challenged state action shows that what the Court may give with one hand (enhanced opportunity to bring discrimination suits based on an expanded concept of state action), it may take away with the other (increased difficulty in winning these suits because of the need to prove discriminatory intent or purpose). The Court's 1990 decision in *Wards Cove Packing Co.* v. *Atonio* is a case in point. Although the Court was dealing with Title VII of the Civil Rights Act of 1964 and not the Equal Protection Clause, its language left no doubt that it was implicitly overturning *Griggs* v. *Duke Power Co.* (1971) and that a majority of the Court did not consider the showing of disparate impact to be the same as the establishment of racial discrimination. In turn, of course, what the Court takes away, the Congress can restore—at least in matters where the Court is engaged in statutory construction. In the Civil Rights Act of 1991, Congress expressly rejected the Court's interpretation in *Wards Cover* and made it clear that the test for the federal judiciary to apply in cases in which the plaintiffs allege discriminatory employment practices is impact, not intent.

NOTES

1 Herbert J. Storing, "Slavery and the Moral Foundations of the American Republic," *The Moral Foundations of the American Republic*, ed. Robert H. Horwitz (Charlottesville, Va.: University Press of Virginia, 1977), p. 214. The discussion that follows relies heavily on this source.

2 John Hope Franklin, "The Moral Legacy of the Founding Fathers," *University of Chicago Magazine*, Summer 1975: 10–13.

3 Storing, "Slavery and the Moral Foundations of the American Republic," p. 214.

4 Quoted in Carl Becker, *The Declaration of Independence* (New York: Vintage, 1942), p. 212.

5 Richard N. Current (ed.), *The Political Thought of Abraham Lincoln* (New York: Bobbs-Merrill Company, Inc., 1967), pp. 88–89. Emphasis in the original.

6 Frederick Douglass, "Address for the Promotion of Colored Enlistments," July 6, 1863, in *The Life and Writings of Frederick Douglass*, ed. Philip S. Foner (New York: International Publishers, 1950), vol. 3, p. 365.

7 Martin Diamond, *The Founding of the Democratic Republic* (Itasca, Ill.: F.E. Peacock, 1981), p. 39.

8 Storing, "Slavery and the Moral Foundations of the American Republic," p. 225.

9 See, for example, Alfred H. Kelly and Winfred A. Harbison, *The American Constitution: Its Origins and Development*, 4th ed. (New York: W. W. Norton, 1970), p. 916.

10 *Associated General Contractors* v. *Altshuler* (First Cir., 1973).

11 On the critical role played by the NAACP throughout the entire desegregation process, see Daniel M. Berman, *It Is So Ordered: The Supreme Court Rules on School Segregation* (New York: W. W. Norton, 1966); Clement E. Vose, "Litigation as a Form of Pressure Group Activity," *Annals of the American Academy of Political and Social Science* 319 (September 1958); and Richard Kluger, *Simple Justice: The History of Brown* v. *Board of Education and Black America's Struggle for Equality* (New York: Knopf, 1976).

12 *New York Times*, May 23, 1954, p. 10E.

13 The primary responsibility for implementing *Brown* thus fell on the forty-eight federal district-court judges serving in the eleven southern states. Nearly all were southern and shared the views of the white southern establishment, and all were subject to the social pressures of their communities. In addition, many were personally unsympathetic to *Brown*. Not surprisingly, in many cases they moved very slowly in implementing school desegregation plans. The ten judges constituting the Federal Courts of Appeal for the Fourth and Fifth Circuits, who were responsible for reviewing the district judges' decisions, were somewhat further removed from the pressures of local situations and hence were able to take a more conscientious view of their obligations to enforce the Supreme Court's rulings. As a consequence, they overturned many district-court decisions. See Jack W. Peltason, *Fifty-Eight Lonely Men* (New York: Harcourt, Brace & World, 1961).

14 The Court's implementation decision in *Brown II* has been subjected to harsh criticism. See Lino A. Graglia, *Disaster by Decree: The Supreme Court Decisions on Race and the Schools* (Ithaca, N.Y.: Cornell University Press, 1976), pp. 31–45. The Court's use of the phrase "all deliberate speed" has been particularly criticized. See Louis Lusky, "Racial Discrimination and the Federal Law," *Columbia Law Review* 63 (1963): 1172, n. 37: "Conceptually, the 'deliberate speed' formula is impossible to justify. . . . Judicial review has been founded in the judicial duty to give a litigant his rights under the Constitution. But the apparently successful plaintiff in the *Brown* case got no more than a promise that, some time in the indefinite future, other people would be given the rights which the Court said he had." In short, *Brown II* permitted the black plaintiffs in *Brown I* to be denied any relief from the legal wrongs that they were found to have suffered, provided that steps were taken to protect other blacks, at some later date, from similar wrongs.

15 *Mayor of Baltimore* v. *Dawson* (1955); *Holmes* v. *City of Atlanta* (1955); *Gayle* v. *Browder* (1956); *New Orleans City Park Improvement Association* v. *Detiege* (1958); *State Athletic Cmsn.* v. *Dorsey* (1959); *Turner* v. *Memphis* (1962); *Johnson* v. *Virginia* (1963); and Lee v. *Washington* (1968). These cases simply cited *Brown* as the controlling precedent. Because *Brown* addressed only segregation in public education, the Court opened itself up for a barrage of criticism—and not just from those who mourned the passing of segregation—when it failed to spell out constitutional principles and neglected to provide a reasoned argument against segregation in these other areas of public

activity. See Herbert Wechsler, "Toward Neutral Principles of Constitutional Law," *Harvard Law Review* 73 (1959): 1, 22.

16 Nathan Glazer, *Affirmative Discrimination* (New York: Basic Books, 1975), p. 96.

17 However, recall the discussion in Chapter 7 of Volume I concerning *Jones* v. *Alfred H. Mayer Company* (1968), *Runyon* v. *McCrary* (1976), *Patterson* v. *McLean Credit Union* (1989), and Congress's enforcement powers under Section 2 of the Thirteenth Amendment.

18 See also *Nixon* v. *Condon* (1932).

19 This transformation of the concept of state action is akin to the transformation of the Sixth Amendment's right to counsel, discussed in Chapter 7. Originally, the Court had understood the guarantee of right to counsel in a negative sense (i.e., as prohibiting the federal government from denying to a defendant the right to employ counsel); only quite recently has the Court come to understand this right in a more positive or affirmative sense (i.e., as imposing on the government the duty to provide counsel for those who cannot afford private representation).

20 As Professor Lino Graglia has noted: "*Shelley* has been rightly described as constitutional law's *Finnegan's Wake:* no one has ever claimed to understand the Court's reasoning or to think that it made sense. The Court purported to find unconstitutional state action in state court enforcement of a racially restrictive covenant between private parties, even though the Court would not find and has not found state action in state court enforcement of other private acts of discrimination. A state may, for example, enforce a will making a bequest contingent upon the beneficiary's marrying a person of a particular religious faith." Graglia, "Judicial Review on the Basis of 'Regime Principles': A Prescription for Government by Judiciary," *South Texas Law Journal* 26 (Fall 1985): 450.

21 See *J.E.B.* v. *Alabama ex rel. T. B.*, 511 U.S. 127 (1994), in which the Court held that intentional discrimination on the basis of gender by state actors in the use of peremptory strikes violates the Equal Protection Clause.

22 See, however, *Purkett* v. *Elem*, 514 U.S. 765 (1995), in which the Court severely limited *Batson* and its progeny by holding, in a *per curiam* opinion, that a challenge to the use of a peremptory strike as racially motivated can be rebutted by an explanation that is neither persuasive nor even plausible, so long as it is race-neutral. "What it means to be a 'legitimate reason' is not a reason that makes sense, but a reason that does not deny equal protection."

SELECTED READING

The Federalist, Nos. 42, 54.

Barrows v. *Jackson*, 346 U.S. 249 (1953).
Bazemore v. *Friday*, 478 U.S. 385 (1986).
Cooper v. *Aaron*, 358 U.S. 1 (1958).
Dayton Board of Education v. *Brinkman*, 443 U.S. 526 (1979).
Freeman v. *Pitts*, 503 U.S. 465 (1992)
Griffin v. *County School Board of Prince Edward County*, 337 U.S. 218 (1964).
Griggs v. *Duke Power Co.*, 401 U.S. 424 (1971).

Reitman v. *Mulkey*, 387 U.S. 369 (1967).
Sweatt v. *Painter*, 339 U.S. 629 (1950).
Wright v. *Emporia City Council*, 407 U.S. 451 (1972).
Yick Wo v. Hopkins, 118 U.S. 356 (1886).

Berger, Raoul. *Government by Judiciary: The Transformation of the Fourteenth Amendment* (Cambridge, Mass.: Harvard University Press, 1977).

Bickel, Alexander M. "The Original Understanding and the Segregation Decision." *Harvard Law Review* 69 (1955): 1–65.

Graglia, Lino A. *Disaster by Decree: The Supreme Court Decisions on Race and the Schools* (Ithaca, N.Y.: Cornell University Press, 1976).

Kennedy, Randall. *Race, Crime, and the Law* (New York: Pantheon Books, 1997).

Kluger, Richard. *Simple Justice* (New York: Knopf, 1976).

Lofgren, Charles A. *The Plessy Case: A Legal-Historical Interpretation* (New York: Oxford University Press, 1986).

McDowell, Gary L. *Equity and the Constitution: The Supreme Court, Equitable Relief, and Public Policy* (Chicago: University of Chicago Press, 1982).

Peltason, Jack. *Fifty-Eight Lonely Men: Southern Federal Judges and School Desegregation* (New York: Harcourt, 1961).

Pizzi, William T. "*Batson* v. *Kentucky:* Curing the Disease but Killing the Patient." *1987 Supreme Court Review*, edited by Philip B. Kurland, Gerhard Casper, and Dennis J. Hutchinson (Chicago: University of Chicago Press, 1988).

Rosenberg, Gerald N. *The Hollow Hope: Can Courts Bring About Social Change?* (Chicago: University of Chicago Press, 1991.)

Rossum, Ralph A. "*Plessy, Brown,* and the Reverse Discrimination Cases: Consistency and Continuity in Judicial Approach." *American Behavioral Scientist 28 (*1985): 785–806.

Strauss, David A. "The Myth of Colorblindness." In *1986 Supreme Court Review,* edited by Philip B. Kurland, Gerhard Casper, and Dennis J. Hutchinson (Chicago: University of Chicago Press, 1987).

TenBroek, Jacobus. *Equal under Law* (Berkeley: University of California Press, 1965).

Thernstrom, Stephan, and Thernstrom, Abigail. *America in Black and White: One Nation, Indivisible* (New York: Simon & Schuster, 1997).

Vose, Clement E. *Caucasians Only: The Supreme Court, the NAACP, and the Restrictive Covenant Cases* (Berkeley: University of California Press, 1959).

Wiecek, William M. "The Witch at the Christening: Slavery and the Constitution's Origins." In *The Framing and Ratification of the Constitution*, edited by Leonard W. Levy and Dennis J. Mahoney (New York: Macmillan, 1987).

Wolf, Eleanor P. *Trial and Error: The Detroit School Segregation Case* (Detroit: Wayne State University Press, 1981).

Wolters, Raymond. *The Burden of Brown* (Knoxville: University of Tennessee Press, 1984).

Woodward, C. Vann. *The Strange Career of Jim Crow* (New York: Oxford University Press, 1966).

Plessy v. *Ferguson*

163 U.S. 537; 16 S. Ct. 1138; 41 L. Ed. 256 (1896)

An 1890 Louisiana statute required railroads to "provide equal but separate accommodations for the white and colored races." The law made it a criminal offense for any passenger to occupy a "coach or compartment to which by race he does not belong." Plessy, who was seven-eighths white and one-eighth black, refused to relinquish a seat assigned to white passengers. He was imprisoned in the parish jail in New Orleans and charged with violating the statute. During the course of his trial, Plessy petitioned the Louisiana Supreme Court to enjoin the trial judge, John Ferguson, from continuing the proceedings against him. After the court rejected his petition, Plessy brought the case to the United States Supreme Court on a writ of error. He claimed that Louisiana's statute violated the guarantees of the Thirteenth and Fourteenth amendments. *Opinion of the Court:* <u>Brown</u>, *Field, Fuller, Gray, Peckham, Shiras, White. Dissenting opinion:* <u>Harlan</u>. *Not participating: Brewer.*

MR. JUSTICE BROWN delivered the opinion of the Court. . . .

The constitutionality of this act is attacked upon the ground that it conflicts both with the Thirteenth Amendment of the Constitution, abolishing slavery, and the Fourteenth Amendment, which prohibits certain restrictive legislation on the part of the States.

1. That it does not conflict with the Thirteenth Amendment, which abolished slavery and involuntary servitude, except as a punishment for crime, is too clear for argument. Slavery implies involuntary servitude—a state of bondage; the ownership of mankind as a chattel, or at least the control of the labor and services of one man for the benefit of another, and the absence of a legal right to the disposal of his own person, property and services. . . .

A statute which implies merely a legal distinction between the white and colored races—a distinction which is founded in the color of the two races, and which must always exist so long as white men are distinguished from the other race by color—has no tendency to destroy the legal equality of the two races, or reestablish a state of involuntary servitude. Indeed, we do not understand that the Thirteenth Amendment is strenuously relied upon by the plaintiff in error in this connection.

2. By the Fourteenth Amendment, all persons born or naturalized in the United States, and subject to the jurisdiction thereof, are made citizens of the United States and of the State wherein they reside; and the States are forbidden from making or enforcing any law which shall abridge the privileges or immunities of citizens of the United States, or shall deprive any person of life, liberty or property without due process of law, or deny to any person within their jurisdiction the equal protection of the laws.

The proper construction of this amendment was first called to the attention of this court in the *Slaughterhouse Cases*, . . . which . . . said generally that its main purpose was to establish the citizenship of the negro; to give definitions of citizenship of the United States and of the States, and to protect from the hostile legislation of the States the privileges and immunities of citizens of the United States, as distinguished from those of citizens of the States.

The object of the amendment was undoubtedly to enforce the absolute equality of the two races before the law, but in the nature of things it could not have been intended to abolish distinctions based upon color, or to enforce social, as distinguished from political equality, or a commingling of the two races upon terms unsatisfactory to either. Laws permitting, and even requiring, their separation in places where they are liable to be brought into contact do not necessarily imply the inferiority of either race to the other, and have been generally, if not universally, recognized as within the competency of the state legislatures in the exercise of their police power.

The most common instance of this is connected with the establishment of separate schools for white and colored children, which has been held to be a valid exercise of the legislative power even by courts of States where the political rights of the colored race have been longest and most earnestly enforced.

One of the earliest of these cases is that of *Roberts* v. *City of Boston* 1849, . . . in which the Supreme Judicial Court of Massachusetts held that the general schools committee of Boston had power to make provision for the instruction of colored children in separate schools established exclusively for them, and to prohibit their attendance upon the other schools. . . . Similar laws have been enacted by Congress under its general power of legislation over the District of Columbia, . . . as well as by the legislatures of many of the States, and have been generally, if not uniformly, sustained by the courts. . . .

So far, then, as a conflict with the Fourteenth Amendment is concerned, the case reduces itself to the question whether the statute of Louisiana is a reasonable regulation, and with respect to this there must necessarily be a large discretion on the part of the legislature. In determining the question of reasonableness it is at liberty to act with reference to the established usages, customs and traditions of the people, and with a view to the promotion of their comfort, and the preservation of the public peace and good order. Gauged by this standard, we cannot say that a law which authorizes or even requires the separation of the two races in public conveyances is unreasonable, or more obnoxious to the Fourteenth Amendment than the acts of Congress requiring separate schools for colored children in the District of Columbia, the constitutionality of which does not seem to have been questioned, or the corresponding acts of state legislatures.

We consider the underlying fallacy of the plaintiff's argument to consist in the assumption that the enforced separation of the two races stamps the colored race with a badge of inferiority. If this be so, it is not by reason of anything found in the act, but solely because the colored race chooses to put that construction upon it. The argument necessarily assumes that if, as has been more than once the case, and is not unlikely to be so again, the colored race should become the dominant power in the state legisla-

ture, and should enact a law in precisely similar terms, it would thereby relegate the white race to an inferior position. We imagine that the white race at least would not acquiesce in this assumption. The argument also assumes that social prejudices may be overcome by legislation, and that equal rights cannot be secured to the negro except by an enforced commingling of the two races. We cannot accept this proposition. If the two races are to meet upon terms of social equality, it must be the result of natural affinities, a mutual appreciation of each other's merits and a voluntary consent of individuals. . . . Legislation is powerless to eradicate racial instincts or to abolish distinctions based upon physical differences, and the attempt to do so can only result in accentuating the difficulties of the present situation. If the civil and political rights of both races be equal one cannot be inferior to the other civilly or politically. If one race be inferior to the other socially, the Constitution of the United States cannot put them upon the same plane. . . .

The judgment of the court below is, therefore,
Affirmed.

Mr. Justice Harlan, dissenting.

The Thirteenth Amendment does not permit the withholding or the deprivation of any right necessarily inhering in freedom. It not only struck down the institution of slavery as previously existing in the United States, but it prevents the imposition of any burdens or disabilities that constitute badges of slavery or servitude. It decreed universal civil freedom in this country. The court has so adjudged. But that amendment having been found inadequate to the protection of the right of those who had been in slavery, it was followed by the Fourteenth Amendment, which added greatly to the dignity and glory of American citizenship and to the security of personal liberty. . . .

It was said in argument that the statute of Louisiana does not discriminate against either race, but prescribes a rule applicable alike to white and colored citizens. But this argument does not meet the difficulty. Every one knows that the statute in question had its origin in the purpose not so much to exclude white persons from railroad cars occupied by blacks, as to exclude colored people from coaches occupied by or assigned to white persons. Railroad corporations of Louisiana did not make discrimination among whites in the matter of accommodation for travellers. The thing to accomplish was, under the guise of giving equal accommodation for whites and blacks, to compel the latter to keep to themselves while travelling in railroad passenger coaches. No one would be so wanting in candor as to assert the contrary. The fundamental objection, therefore, to the statute is that it interferes with the personal freedom of citizens. "Personal liberty," it has been well said, "consists in the power of locomotion, of changing situation, or removing one's person to whatsoever places one's own inclination may direct, without imprisonment or restraint, unless by due course of law." . . . If a white man and a black man choose to occupy the same public conveyance on a public highway, it is their right to do so, and no government, proceeding alone on grounds of race, can prevent it without infringing the personal liberty of each. . . .

The white race deems itself to be the dominant race in this country. And so it is, in prestige, in achievements, in education, in wealth and in power. So, I doubt not, it will continue to be for all time, if it remains true to its great heritage and holds fast to the principles of constitutional liberty. But in view of the Constitution, in the eye of the law, there is in this country no superior dominant ruling class of citizens. There is no caste here. Our Constitution is color-blind, and neither knows nor tolerates classes among citizens. In respect of civil rights, all citizens are equal before the law. The humblest is the peer of the most powerful. The law regards man as man, and takes no account of his surroundings or of his color when his civil rights as guaranteed by the supreme law of the land are involved. It is, therefore, to be regretted that this high tribunal, the final expositor of the fundamental law of the land, has reached the conclusion that it is competent for a State to regulate the enjoyment by citizens of their civil rights solely upon the basis of race.

In my opinion, the judgment this day rendered will, in time, prove to be quite as pernicious as the decision made by this tribunal in the *Dred Scott* case. . . . The destinies of the two races, in this country, are indissolubly linked together, and the interests of both require that the common government of all shall not permit the seeds of race hate to be planted under the sanction of law. What can more certainly arouse race hate, what more certainly create and perpetuate a feeling of distrust between these races, than state enactments, which, in fact, proceed on the ground that colored citizens are so inferior and degraded that they cannot be allowed to sit in public coaches occupied by white citizens? That, as all will admit, is the real meaning of such legislation as was enacted in Louisiana. . .

The arbitrary separation of citizens, on the basis of race, while they are on a public highway, is a badge of servitude wholly inconsistent with the civil freedom and the equality before the law established by the Constitution. It cannot be justified upon any legal grounds. . . .

Brown v. *Board of Education*
347 U.S. 483; 74 S. Ct. 693; 98 L. Ed. 591 (1954)

The facts in this landmark case are set out in the opinion. *Unanimous opinion:* <u>Warren</u>, *Black, Burton, Clark, Douglas, Frankfurter, Jackson, Minton, Reed.*

MR. CHIEF JUSTICE WARREN delivered the opinion of the Court.

These cases come to us from the States of Kansas, South Carolina, Virginia, and Delaware. They are premised on different facts and different local conditions, but a common legal question justifies their consideration together in this consolidated opinion.

In each of the cases, minors of the Negro race, through their legal representatives, seek the aid of the courts in obtaining admission to the public schools of their community on a nonsegregated basis. In each instance, they have been denied admission to schools attended by white children under laws requiring or permitting segregation according to race. This segregation was alleged to deprive the plaintiffs of the equal protection of the laws under the Fourteenth Amendment. In each of the cases other than the Delaware case, a three-judge federal district court denied relief to the plaintiffs on the so-called "separate but equal" doctrine announced by this Court in *Plessy* v. *Ferguson.* . . . Under that doctrine, equality of treatment is accorded when the races are provided substantially equal facilities, even though these facilities be separate. In the Delaware case, the Supreme Court of Delaware adhered to that doctrine, but ordered that the plaintiffs be admitted to the white schools because of their superiority to the Negro schools.

The plaintiffs contend that segregated public schools are not "equal" and cannot be made "equal," and that hence they are deprived of the equal protection of the laws. Because of the obvious importance of the question presented, the Court took jurisdiction. Argument was heard in the 1952 Term, and reargument was heard this Term on certain questions propounded by the Court.

Reargument was largely devoted to the circumstances surrounding the adoption of the Fourteenth Amendment in 1868. It covered exhaustively consideration of the Amendment in Congress, ratification by the states, then existing practices in racial segregation, and the views of proponents and opponents of the Amendment. This discussion and our own investigation convince us that, although these sources cast some light, it is not enough to resolve the problem with which we are faced. At best, they are inconclusive. The most avid proponents of the post-War Amendments undoubtedly intended them to remove all legal distinctions among "all persons born or naturalized in the United States." Their opponents, just as certainly, were antagonistic to both the letter and the spirit of the Amendments and wished them to have the most limited effect. What others in Congress and the state legislatures had in mind cannot be determined with any degree of certainty.

An additional reason for the inconclusive nature of the Amendment's history, with respect to segregated schools, is the status of public education at that time. In the South, the movement toward free common schools, supported by general taxation, had not yet taken hold. Education of white children was largely in the hands of private groups. Education of Negroes was almost nonexistent, and practically all of the race were illiterate. In fact, any education of Negroes was forbidden by law in some states. Today, in contrast, many Negroes have achieved outstanding success in the arts and sciences as well as in the business and professional world. It is true that public school education at the time of the Amendment had advanced further in the North, but the effect of the Amendment on Northern States was generally ignored in the congressional debates. Even in the North, the conditions of public education did not approximate those existing today. The curriculum was usually rudimentary; ungraded schools were common in rural areas; the school term was but three months a year in many states; and compulsory school attendance was virtually unknown. As a consequence, it is not surprising that there should be so little in the history of the Fourteenth Amendment relating to its intended effect on public education.

In the first cases in this Court construing the Fourteenth Amendment, decided shortly after its adoption, the Court interpreted it as proscribing all state-imposed discriminations against the Negro race.* The doctrine of "separate but equal" did not make its appearance in this Court until 1896 in the case of *Plessy* v. *Ferguson,* . . . involving not education but transportation. American courts have since labored with the doctrine for over half a century. In this Court, there have been six cases involving the "separate but equal" doctrine in the field of public education. In *Cumming* v. *Board of Education of Richmond County* [1899] . . . and *Gong Lum* v. *Rice* . . . , the validity of the doctrine itself was not challenged. In more recent cases, all on the graduate school level, inequality was found in that specific benefits enjoyed by white students were denied to Negro students of the same educational qualifications. . . . In none of these cases was it necessary to reexamine the doctrine to grant relief to the Negro plaintiff. And in *Sweatt* v. *Painter,* . . . the Court expressly reserved decision on the question whether *Plessy* v. *Ferguson* should be held inapplicable to public education.

---

*In Re *Slaughterhouse Cases,* 1873, . . . *Strauder* v. *West Virginia,* 1880. . . .

In the instant cases, that question is directly presented. Here, unlike *Sweatt* v. *Painter*, there are findings below that the Negro and white schools involved have been equalized, or are being equalized, with respect to buildings, curricula, qualifications and salaries of teachers, and other "tangible" factors. Our decision, therefore, cannot turn on merely a comparison of these tangible factors in the Negro and white schools involved in each of the cases. We must look instead to the effect of segregation itself on public education.

In approaching this problem, we cannot turn the clock back to 1868 when the Amendment was adopted, or even to 1896 when *Plessy* v. *Ferguson* was written. We must consider public education in the light of its full development and its present place in American life throughout the Nation. Only in this way can it be determined if segregation in public schools deprives these plaintiffs of the equal protection of the laws.

Today, education is perhaps the most important function of state and local governments. Compulsory school attendance laws and the great expenditures for education both demonstrate our recognition of the importance of education to our democratic society. It is required in the performance of our most basic public responsibilities, even service in the armed forces. It is the very foundation of good citizenship. Today it is a principal instrument in awakening the child to cultural values, in preparing him for later professional training, and in helping him to adjust normally to his environment. In these days, it is doubtful that any child may reasonably be expected to succeed in life if he is denied the opportunity of an education. Such an opportunity, where the state has undertaken to provide it, is a right which must be made available to all on equal terms.

We come then to the question presented: Does segregation of children in public schools solely on the basis of race, even though the physical facilities and other "tangible" factors may be equal, deprive the children of the minority group of equal educational opportunities? We believe that it does.

In *Sweatt* v. *Painter* [1950], . . . , in finding that a segregated law school for Negroes could not provide them equal educational opportunities, this Court relied in large part on "those qualities which are incapable of objective measurement but which make for greatness in a law school." In *McLaurin* v. *Oklahoma State Regents* [1950], . . . the Court, in requiring that a Negro admitted to a white graduate school be treated like all other students, again resorted to intangible considerations: " . . . his ability to study, to engage in discussions and exchange views with other students, and, in general, to learn his profession." Such considerations apply with added force to children in grade and high schools. To separate them from others of similar age and qualifications solely because of their race generates a feeling of inferiority as to their status in the community that may affect their hearts and minds in a way unlikely ever to be undone. The effect of this separation on their educational opportunities was well stated by a finding in the Kansas case by a court which nevertheless felt compelled to rule against the Negro plaintiffs:

"Segregation of white and colored children in public schools has a detrimental effect upon the colored children. The impact is greater when it has the sanction of the law; for the policy of separating the races is usually interpreted as denoting the inferiority of the negro group. A sense of inferiority affects motivation of a child to learn. Segregation with the sanction of law, therefore, has a tendency to retard the education and mental development of negro children and to deprive them of some of the benefits they would receive in a racially integrated school system." Whatever may have been the extent of psychological knowledge at the time of *Plessy* v. *Ferguson*, this finding is amply supported by modern authority.** Any language in *Plessy* v. *Ferguson* contrary to this finding is rejected.

**K.B. Clark, Effect of Prejudice and Discrimination on Personality Development (Midcentury White House Conference on Children and Youth, 1950); Witmer and Kotinsky, Personality in the Making (1952), c. VI; Deutscher and Chein, The Psychological Effects of Enforced Segregation: A Survey of Social Science Opinion, 26 J. Psychol. 259 (1948); Chein, What are the Psychological Effects of Segregation Under Conditions of Equal Facilities?, 3 Int. J. Opinion and Attitude Res. 229(1949); Brameld, Educational Costs, in Discrimination and National Welfare (McIver, ed., 1949), 44–48; Frazier, The Negro in the United States (1949), 674–681. And see generally Myrdal, An American Dilemma (1944).

We conclude that in the field of public education the doctrine of "separate but equal" has no place. Separate educational facilities are inherently unequal. Therefore, we hold that the plaintiffs and others similarly situated for whom the actions have been brought are, by reason of the segregation complained of, deprived of the equal protection of the laws guaranteed by the Fourteenth Amendment. This disposition makes unnecessary any discussion whether such segregation also violates the Due Process Clause of the Fourteenth Amendment.

Because these are class actions, because of the wide applicability of this decision, and because of the great variety of local conditions, the formulation of decrees in these cases presents problems of considerable complexity. On reargument, the consideration of appropriate relief was necessarily subordinated to the primary question—the constitutionality of segregation in public education. We have now announced that such segregation is a denial of the equal protection of the laws. In order that we may have the full assistance of the parties in formulating decrees, the cases will be restored to the docket, and the parties are requested to present further argument on Questions 4 and 5 previously propounded by the Court for the reargument this Term.*** The Attorney General of the United States is invited to participate. The Attorneys General of the States requiring or permitting segregation in public education will also be permitted to appear as *amici curiae* upon request to do so by September 15, 1954, and submission of briefs by October 1, 1954. . . .

***4. Assuming it is decided that segregation in public schools violates the Fourteenth Amendment.

"(a) would a decree necessarily follow providing that, within the limits set by normal geographic school districting, Negro children should forthwith be admitted to schools of their choice, or

"(b) may this Court, in the exercise of its equity powers, permit an effective gradual adjustment to be brought about from existing segregated systems to a system not based on color distinctions?

"5. On the assumption on which questions 4(a) and (b) are based, and assuming further that this Court will exercise its equity powers to the end described in question 4(b),

"(a) should this Court formulate detailed decrees in these cases;

"(b) if so, what specific issues should decrees reach;

"(c) should this Court appoint a special master to hear evidence with a view to recommending specific terms for such decrees;

"(d) should this Court remand to the courts of first instance with directions to frame decrees in these cases, and if so, what general directions should the decrees of this Court include and what procedures should the courts of first instance follow in arriving at the specific terms of more detailed decrees?"

Bolling v. *Sharpe*

segregated schools in DC was unconstitutional

347 U.S. 497; 74 S. Ct. 686; 98 L. Ed. 583 (1954)

In this companion case to Brown v. *Board of Education*, the Supreme Court reviewed the validity of segregation in the public schools of the District of Columbia. *Unanimous opinion:* <u>Warren</u>, *Black, Burton, Clark, Douglas, Frankfurter, Jackson, Minton, Reed.*

MR. CHIEF JUSTICE WARREN delivered the opinion of the Court.

This case challenges the validity of segregation in the public schools of the District of Columbia. The petitioners, minors of the Negro race, allege that such segregation deprives them of due process of law under the Fifth Amendment. They were refused admission to a public school attended by white children solely because of their race. They sought the aid of the District Court for the District of Columbia in obtaining admission. That court dismissed their complaint. We granted a writ of certiorari before judgment in the Court of Appeals because of the importance of the constitutional question presented. . . .

We have this day held that the Equal Protection Clause of the Fourteenth Amendment prohibits the states from maintaining racially segregated public schools. The legal problem in the District of Columbia is somewhat different, however. The Fifth Amendment, which is applicable in the District of Columbia, does not contain an equal protection clause as does the Fourteenth Amendment, which applies only to the states. But the concepts of equal protection and due process, both stemming from our American ideal of fairness, are not mutually exclusive. The "equal protection of the laws" is a more implicit safeguard of prohibited unfairness than "due process of law," and, therefore, we do not imply that the two are always interchangeable phrases. But, as this Court has recognized, discrimination may be so unjustifiable as to be violative of due process.

Classifications based solely upon race must be scrutinized with particular care, since they are contrary to our traditions and hence constitutionally suspect. As long ago as 1896, this Court declared the principle "that the Constitution of the United States, in its present form, forbids, so far as civil and political rights are concerned, discrimination by the General Government, or by the States, against any citizen because of his race." And in *Buchanan* v. *Warley* 1917, . . . the Court held that a statute which limited the right of a property owner to convey his property to a person of another race was, as an unreasonable discrimination, a denial of due process of law.

Although the Court has not assumed to define "liberty" with any great precision, that term is not confined to mere freedom from bodily restraint. Liberty under law extends to the full range of conduct which the individual is free to pursue, and it cannot be restricted except for a proper governmental objective. Segregation in public education is not reasonably related to any proper governmental objective, and thus it imposes on Negro children of the District of Columbia a burden that constitutes an arbitrary deprivation of their liberty in violation of the Due Process Clause.

In view of our decision that the Constitution prohibits the states from maintaining racially segregated public schools, it would be unthinkable that the same constitution would impose a lesser duty on the Federal Government. We hold that racial segregation in the public schools of the District of Columbia is a denial of the due process of law guaranteed by the Fifth Amendment to the Constitution.

For the reasons set out in *Brown* v. *Board of Education*, this case will be restored to the docket for reargument on Questions 4 and 5 previously propounded by the Court. . . .

It is so ordered.

Brown v. *Board of Education*

349 U.S. 294; 75 S. Ct. 753; 99 L. Ed. 1083 (1955)

In this 1955 decision, often referred to as *Brown II*, the Supreme Court dealt with the question of how its decision in *Brown I* was to be implemented. *Unanimous opinion:* <u>Warren</u>, *Black, Burton, Clark, Douglas, Frankfurter, Harlan, Minton, Reed*

MR. CHIEF JUSTICE WARREN delivered the opinion of the Court.

These cases were decided on May 17, 1954. The opinions of that date, declaring the fundamental principle that racial discrimination in public education is unconstitutional, are incorporated herein by reference. All provisions of federal, state, or local law requiring or permitting such discrimination must yield to this principle. There remains for consideration the manner in which relief is to be accorded. . . .

Full implementation of these constitutional principles may require solution of varied local school problems. School authorities have the pri-

mary responsibility for elucidating, assessing, and solving these problems; courts will have to consider whether the action of school authorities constitutes good faith implementation of the governing constitutional principles. Because of their proximity to local conditions and the possible need for further hearing, the courts which originally heard these cases can best perform this judicial appraisal. Accordingly, we believe it appropriate to remand the cases to those courts.

In fashioning and effectuating the decrees, the courts will be guided by equitable principles. Traditionally, equity has been characterized by a practical flexibility in shaping its remedies and by a facility for adjusting and reconciling public and private needs. These cases call for the exercise of these traditional attributes of equity power. At stake is the personal interest of the plaintiffs in admission to public schools as soon as practicable on a nondiscriminatory basis. To effectuate this interest may call for elimination of a variety of obstacles in making the transition to school systems operated in accordance with the constitutional principles set forth in our May 17, 1954, decision. Courts of equity may properly take into account the public interest in the elimination of such obstacles in a systematic and effective manner. But it should go without saying that the vitality of these constitutional principles cannot be allowed to yield simply because of disagreement with them.

While giving weight to these public and private considerations, the courts will require that the defendants make a prompt and reasonable start toward full compliance with our May 17, 1954, ruling. Once such a start has been made, the courts may find that additional time is necessary to carry out the ruling in an effective manner. The burden rests upon the defendants to establish that such time is necessary in the public interest and is consistent with good faith compliance at the earliest practicable date. To that end, the courts may consider problems related to administration, arising from the physical condition of the school plant, the school transportation system, personnel, revision of school districts and attendance areas into compact units to achieve a system of determining admission to the public schools on a nonracial basis, and revision of local laws and regulations which may be necessary in solving the foregoing problems. They will also consider the adequacy of any plans the defendants may propose to meet these problems and to effectuate a transition to a racially nondiscriminatory school system. During this period of transition, the courts will retain jurisdication of these cases. . . .

. . . The cases . . . are remanded to the district courts to take such proceedings and enter such orders and decrees consistent with this opinion as are necessary and proper to admit to public schools on a racially nondiscriminatory basis with all deliberate speed the parties to these cases.

It is so ordered.

Swann v. *Charlotte-Mecklenburg Board of Education*
402 U.S. 1; 91 S. Ct. 1267; 28 L. Ed. 2d 554 (1971)

Under a school desegregation plan approved by a federal district court in 1965 for the Charlotte-Mecklenburg County school system (the student population of which was 71 percent white and 29 percent black), nearly two-thirds of the system's black students attended schools that were at least 99 percent black. Following the Supreme Court's decision in *Green* v. *School District of New Kent County* (1968), which charged school districts with an "affirmative duty" to take whatever steps might be necessary to eliminate all vestiges of a dual school system and establish in its place "a unitary system in which racial discrimination would be eliminated root and branch," John Swann and other petitioners entered federal district court and sought further desegregation of the Charlotte-Mecklenburg system. As a result, the district court ordered the school board in 1969 to provide a plan for faculty and student desegregation. Finding the board's submission unsatisfactory, the court appointed a desegregation expert, Dr. John Finger, to submit a desegregation plan. In 1970 the court adopted a modified version of the board's plan for the faculty and for the junior and senior high schools, and the Finger plan for the elementary schools. The school board appealed to the Court of Appeals for the Fourth Circuit, where that part of the district court's orders relating to the faculty and secondary schools was affirmed but that part relating to the elementary schools was vacated. In the estimation of the Fourth Circuit, the Finger plan would have unreasonably burdened elementary school pupils and the board. After further court proceedings and consideration of additional desegregation plans, the district court again ordered that the Finger plan be put into effect. Both parties petitioned the Supreme Court for a writ of certiorari. *Unanimous opinion: Burger, Black, Blackmun, Brennan, Douglas, Harlan, Marshall, Stewart, White.*

MR. CHIEF JUSTICE BURGER delivered the opinion of the Court.

We granted certiorari in this case to review important issues as to the duties of school authorities and the scope of powers of federal courts under this Court's mandates to eliminate racially separate public schools established and maintained by state action. . . .

This case and those argued with it arose in states having a long history of maintaining two sets of schools in a single school system deliberately operated to carry out a governmental policy to separate pupils in schools solely on the basis of race. That was what *Brown* v. *Board of Education* was all about. These cases present us with the problem of defining in more precise terms than heretofore the scope of the duty of school authori- ties and district courts in implementing *Brown I* and the mandate to eliminate dual systems and establish unitary systems at once. . . .

The problems encountered by the district courts and courts of appeal make plain that we should now try to amplify guidelines, however incomplete and imperfect, for the assistance of school authorities and courts. . . .

The objective today remains to eliminate from the public schools all vestiges of state-imposed segregation. . . . If school authorities fail in their affirmative obligations under [our earlier] holdings, judicial authority may be invoked. Once a right and a violation have been shown, the scope of a district court's equitable powers to remedy past wrongs is broad, for breadth and flexibility are inherent in equitable remedies. . . . In seeking to define even in broad and general terms how far this remedial power extends it is important to remember that judicial powers may be exercised only on the basis of a constitutional violation. . . . Judicial authority enters only when local authority defaults.

The central issue in this case is that of student assignment, and there are essentially four problem areas. . . .

(1) Racial Balances or Racial Quotas

We do not reach in this case the question whether a showing that school segregation is a consequence of other types of state action, without any discriminatory action by the school authorities, is a constitutional violation requiring remedial action by a school desegregation decree. This case does not present that question and we therefore do not decide it. . . .

In this case it is urged that the District Court has imposed a racial balance requirement of 71–29% on individual schools. The fact that no such objective was actually achieved—and would appear to be impossible—tends to blunt that claim, yet in the opinion and order of the District Court . . . we find that court directing: "that efforts should be made to reach 71–29 ratio in the various schools so that there will be no basis for contending that one school is racially different from the others. . . ."

The District Judge went on to acknowledge that variation "from that norm may be unavoidable." This contains intimations that the "norm" is a fixed mathematical racial balance reflecting the pupil constituency of the system. If we were to read the holding of the District Court to require, as a matter of substantive constitutional right, any particular degree of racial balance or mixing, that approach would be disapproved and we would be obliged to reverse. The constitutional command to desegregate schools does not mean that every school in every community must always reflect the racial composition of the school system as a whole. . . .

Awareness of the racial composition of the whole school system is likely to be a useful starting point in shaping a remedy to correct past constitutional violations. In sum, the very limited use made of mathematical ratios was within the equitable remedial discretion of the District Court.

(2) One-Race Schools

The record in this case reveals that familiar phenomenon that in metropolitan areas minority groups are often found concentrated in one part of the city. . . . Schools all or predominately of one race in a district of mixed population will require close scrutiny to determine that school assignments are not part of state-enforced segregation.

In light of the above, it should be clear that the existence of some small number of one-race, or virtually one-race, schools within a district is not in and of itself the mark of a system which still practices segregation by law. . . .

The court should scrutinize such schools, and the burden upon the school authorities will be to satisfy the court that their racial composition is not the result of present or past discriminatory action on their part. . . .

(3) Remedial Altering of Attendance Zones

The maps submitted in these cases graphically demonstrate that one of the principal tools employed by school planners and by courts to break up the dual school system has been a frank—and sometimes drastic—gerrymandering of school districts and attendance zones. An additional step was pairing, "clustering," or "grouping" of schools with attendance assignments made deliberately to accomplish the transfer of Negro students out of formerly segregated Negro schools and transfer of white students to formerly all-Negro schools. More often than not, these zones are neither compact nor contiguous; indeed they may be on opposite ends of the city. As an interim corrective measure, this cannot be said to be beyond the broad remedial powers of a court.

Absent a constitutional violation there would be no basis for judicially ordering assignment of students on a racial basis. All things being equal, with no history of discrimination, it might well be desirable to assign pupils to schools nearest their homes. But all things are not equal in a system that has been deliberately constructed and maintained to enforce racial segregation. The remedy for such segregation may be administratively awkward, inconvenient and even bizarre in some situations and may impose burdens on some; but all awkwardness and inconvenience cannot be avoided in the interim period when remedial adjustments are being made to eliminate the dual school systems.

No fixed or even substantially fixed guidelines can be established as to how far a court can go, but it must be recognized that there are limits. The objective is to dismantle the dual school system. "Racially neutral" assignment plans proposed by school authorities to a district court may be inadequate; such plans may fail to counteract the continuing effects of past school segregation resulting from discriminatory location of school sites or distortion of school size in order to achieve or maintain an artificial racial separation. When school authorities present a district court with a "loaded game board," affirmative action in the form of remedial altering of attendance zones is proper to achieve truly nondiscriminatory assignments. . . . We hold that the pairing and grouping of noncontiguous school zones is a permissible tool and such action is to be considered in light of the objectives sought. . . .

(4) Transportation of Students

The scope of permissible transportation of students as an implement of a remedial decree has never been defined by this Court and by the very nature of the problem it cannot be defined with precision. No rigid guidelines as to student transportation can be given for application to the infinite variety of problems presented in thousands of situations. . . . The District Court's conclusion that assignment of children to the school nearest their home serving their grade would not produce an effective dismantling of the dual system is supported by the record.

Thus the remedial techniques used in the District Court's order were within that court's power to provide equitable relief; implementation of the decree is well within the capacity of the school authority.

The decree provided that the buses used to implement the plan would operate on direct routes. . . . The trips for elementary school pupils average about seven miles and the District Court found that they would take "not over 35 minutes at the most." This system compares favorably with the transportation plan previously operated in Charlotte under which each day 23,600 students on all grade levels were transported an average of 15 miles one way for an average trip requiring over an hour. In these circumstances, we find no basis for holding that the local school authorities may not be required to employ bus transportation as one tool of school desegregation. Desegregation plans cannot be limited to the walk-in school.

An objection to transportation of students may have validity when the time or distance of travel is so great as to risk either the health of the children or significantly impinge on the educational process. District courts must weigh the soundness of any transportation plan in light of what is said in subdivisions (1), (2), and (3) above. . . .

On the facts of this case, we are unable to conclude that the order of the District Court is not reasonable, feasible and workable. . . .

It does not follow that the communities served by such systems will remain demographically stable, for in a growing, mobile society, few will do so. Neither school authorities nor district courts are constitutionally required to make year-by-year adjustments of the racial composition of student bodies once the affirmative duty to desegregate has been accomplished and racial discrimination through official action is eliminated from the system. This does not mean that federal courts are without power to deal with future problems, but in the absence of a showing that either the school authorities or some other agency of the State has deliberately attempted to fix or alter demographic patterns to affect the racial composition of the schools, further intervention by a district court should not be necessary.

Milliken v. *Bradley*
418 U.S. 717; 94 S. Ct. 3112; 41 L. Ed. 2d 1069 (1974)

Ronald Bradley and other black students, together with the Detroit branch of the NAACP, brought a class action suit charging Michigan governor William Milliken, the state board of education, the state superintendent of public instruction, and the city school board and superintendent with racial segregation and seeking implementation of a plan to establish a unitary nonracial school system. The federal district court upheld the respondent's charges, found violations of constitutional rights by both city and state officials, and ordered the Detroit School Board to formulate a desegregation plan for the city; in addition, state officials were ordered to submit desegregation plans encompassing the three-county metropolitan area, despite the fact that the eighty-five school districts in these three counties were not parties to the action and there was no claim that they had committed constitutional violations. The district court subsequently permitted some of these surrounding school districts to appear and present arguments relevant to the formulation of a regional plan for racial balance in the schools, but prohibited them from asserting any claim or defense on issues previously adjudicated or from reopening any issue previously decided. Contending that "school districts are simply matters of political convenience and may not be used to deny constitutional rights," without citing any evidence that the suburban school districts had committed acts of *de jure* segregation, the district court appointed a panel to submit a desegregation plan encompassing a designated area consisting of 53 of the 85 suburban school districts plus Detroit. The court also ordered the Detroit school board to acquire at least 295 school buses for the purpose of transporting students to and from outlying districts. The Court of Appeals for the Sixth Circuit affirmed the substance of the district court's decision but remanded the case, in order to provide the affected suburban school districts with the opportunity to be heard as to the scope and implementation of such a remedy, and vacated the order as to the bus acquisitions, subject to its reimposition at an appropriate time. The governor and other state officials petitioned the Supreme Court for a writ of certiorari. *Opinion of the Court: Burger, Blackmun, Powell, Rehnquist, Stewart. Concurring opinion: Stewart. Dissenting opinions: Douglas; Marshall, Brennan, Douglas, White; White, Brennan, Douglas, Marshall.*

MR. CHIEF JUSTICE BURGER delivered the opinion of the Court.

We granted certiorari in these consolidated cases to determine whether a federal court may impose a multidistrict, areawide remedy to a single district *de jure* segregation problem absent any finding that the other included school districts have failed to operate unitary school systems within their districts, absent any claim or finding that the boundary lines of any affected school district were established with the purpose of fostering racial segregation in public schools, absent any finding that the included districts committed acts which effected segregation within the other districts, and absent a meaningful opportunity for the included neighboring school districts to present evidence or be heard on the propriety of a multidistrict remedy or on the question of constitutional violations by those neighboring districts. . . .

Viewing the record as a whole, it seems clear that the District Court and the Court of Appeals shifted the primary focus from a Detroit remedy to the metropolitan area only because of their conclusion that total desegregation of Detroit would not produce the racial balance which they perceived as desirable. Both courts proceeded on an assumption that the Detroit schools could not be truly desegregated—in their view of what constituted desegregation—unless the racial composition of the student body of each school substantially reflected the racial composition of the population of the metropolitan area as a whole. The metropolitan area was then defined as Detroit plus 53 of the outlying school districts. . . .

Here the District Court's approach to what constituted "actual desegregation" raises the fundamental question . . . as to the circumstances in which a federal court may order desegregation relief that embraces more than a single school district. The court's analytical starting point was its conclusion that school district lines are no more than arbitrary lines on a map "drawn for political convenience." Boundary lines may be bridged where there has been a constitutional violation calling for inter-district relief, but, the notion that school district lines may be casually ignored or treated as a mere administrative convenience is contrary to the history of public education in our country. No single tradition in public education is more deeply rooted than local control over the operation of schools; local autonomy has long been thought essential both to the maintenance of community concern and support for public schools and to quality of the educational process. . . .

The Michigan educational structure involved in this case, in common with most States, provides for a large measure of local control and a review of the scope and character of these local powers indicates the extent to which the interdistrict remedy approved by the two courts could disrupt and alter the structure of public education in Michigan. The metropolitan remedy would require, in effect, consolidation of 54 independent school districts historically administered as separate units into a vast new super school district. . . . Entirely apart from the logistical and other serious problems attending large-scale transportation of students, the consolidation would give rise to an array of other problems in financing and operating this new school system. Some of the more obvious questions would be: What would be the status and authority of the present popularly elected school boards? Would the children of Detroit be within the jurisdiction and operating control of a school board elected by the parents and residents of other districts? What board or boards would levy taxes for school operations in these 54 districts constituting the consolidated metropolitan area? What provisions could be made for assuring substantial equality in tax levies among the 54 districts, if this were deemed requisite? What provisions would be made for financing? Would the validity of long-term bonds be jeopardized unless approved by all of the component districts as well as the State? What body would determine that portion of the curricula now left to the discretion of local school boards? Who would establish attendance zones, purchase school equipment, locate and construct new schools, and indeed attend to all the myriad day-to-day decisions that are necessary to school operations affecting potentially more than three quarters of a million pupils? . . .

It may be suggested that all of these vital operational problems are yet to be resolved by the District Court, and that this is the purpose of the Court of Appeals' proposed remand. But it is obvious from the scope of the inter-district remedy itself that absent a complete restructuring of the laws of Michigan relating to school districts the District Court will become first, a de facto "legislative authority" to resolve these complex questions, and then the "school superintendent" for the entire area. This is a task which few, if any, judges are qualified to perform and one which would deprive the people of control of schools through their elected representatives.

Of course, no state law is above the Constitution. School district lines and the present laws with respect to local control, are not sacrosanct and if they conflict with the Fourteenth Amendment federal courts have a duty to prescribe appropriate remedies. . . . But our prior holdings have been confined to violations and remedies within a single school district. We therefore turn to address, for the first time, the validity of a remedy mandating cross-district or inter-district consolidation to remedy a condition of segregation found to exist in only one district.

The controlling principle consistently expounded in our holdings is that the scope of the remedy is determined by the nature and extent of the constitutional violation. . . . Before the boundaries of separate and autonomous school districts may be set aside by consolidating the separate units for remedial purposes or by imposing a cross-district remedy, it must first be shown that there has been a constitutional viola-

tion within one district that produces a significant segregative effect in another district. Specifically it must be shown that racially discriminatory acts of the state or local school districts, or of a single school district have been a substantial cause of inter-district segregation. Thus an inter-district remedy might be in order where the racially discriminatory acts of one or more school districts caused racial segregation in an adjacent district, or where district lines have been deliberately drawn on the basis of race. In such circumstances an inter-district remedy would be appropriate to eliminate the inter-district segregation directly caused by the constitutional violation. Conversely, without an inter-district violation and inter-district effect, there is no constitutional wrong calling for an inter-district remedy.

The record before us, voluminous as it is, contains evidence of de jure segregated conditions only in the Detroit schools; indeed, that was the theory on which the litigation was initially based and on which the District Court took evidence. . . . With no showing of significant violation by the 53 outlying school districts and no evidence of any inter-district violation or effect, the court went beyond the original theory of the case as framed by the pleadings and mandated a metropolitan area remedy. To approve the remedy ordered by the court would impose on the outlying districts, not shown to have committed any constitutional violation, a wholly impermissible remedy based on a standard not hinted at in Brown I and II or any holding of this Court.

In dissent Mr. Justice White and Mr. Justice Marshall undertake to demonstrate that agencies having statewide authority participated in maintaining the dual school system found to exist in Detroit. They are apparently of the view that once such participation is shown, the District Court should have a relatively free hand to reconstruct school districts outside of Detroit in fashioning relief. . . . The difference between us arises instead from established doctrine laid down by our cases. . . . Terms such as "unitary" and "dual" systems, and "racially identifiable schools," have meaning, and the necessary federal authority to remedy the constitutional wrong is firmly established. But the remedy is necessarily designed, as all remedies are, to restore the victims of discriminatory conduct to the position they would have occupied in the absence of such conduct. Disparate treatment of White and Negro students occurred within the Detroit school system, and not elsewhere, and on this record the remedy must be limited to that system.

The constitutional right of the Negro respondents residing in Detroit is to attend a unitary school system in that district. Unless petitioners drew the district lines in a discriminatory fashion, or arranged for White students residing in the Detroit district to attend schools in Oakland and Macomb Counties, they were under no constitutional duty to make provisions for Negro students to do so. The view of the dissenters, that the existence of a dual system in *Detroit* can be made the basis for a decree requiring cross-district transportation of pupils cannot be supported on the grounds that it represents merely the devising of a suitable flexible remedy for the violation of rights already established by our prior decisions. It can be supported only by drastic expansion of the constitutional right itself, an expansion without any support in either constitutional principle or precedent.

Accepting, *arguendo*, the correctness of [the lower courts'] finding of State responsibility for the segregated conditions within the city of Detroit, it does not follow that an inter-district remedy is constitutionally justified or required. With a single exception, . . . there has been no showing that either the State or any of the 85 outlying districts engaged in activity that had a cross-district effect. The boundaries of the Detroit School District, which are coterminous with the boundaries of the city of Detroit, were established over a century ago by neutral legislation when the city was incorporated; there is no evidence in the record, nor is there any suggestion by the respondents, that either the original boundaries of the Detroit School District, or any other school district in Michigan, were established for the purpose of creating, maintaining or perpetuating segregation of races. There is no claim and there is no evidence hinting that petitioners and their predecessors, or the 40-odd other school districts in the tricounty area—but outside the District Court's "desegregation area"—have ever maintained or operated anything but unitary school systems. Unitary school systems have been required for more than a century by the Michigan

Constitution as implemented by state law. Where the schools of only one district have been affected, there is no constitutional power in the courts to decree relief balancing the racial composition of that district's schools with those of the surrounding districts. . . .

We conclude that the relief ordered by the District Court and affirmed by the Court of Appeals was based upon an erroneous standard and was unsupported by record evidence that acts of the outlying districts affected the discrimination found to exist in the schools of Detroit. Accordingly, the judgment of the Court of Appeals is reversed and the case is remanded for further proceedings consistent with this opinion leading to prompt formulation of a decree directed to eliminating the segregation found to exist in Detroit city schools, a remedy which has been delayed since 1970.

Reversed and remanded.

MR. JUSTICE DOUGLAS, dissenting.

So far as equal protection is concerned we are now in a dramatic retreat from the 8-to-1 decision in 1896 that Blacks could be segregated in public facilities provided they received equal treatment. . . .

. . . There is so far as the school cases go no constitutional difference between *de facto* and *de jure* segregation. Each school board performs state action for Fourteenth Amendment purposes when it draws the lines that confine it to a given area, when it builds schools at particular sites, or when it allocates students. The creation of the school districts in Metropolitan Detroit either maintained existing segregation or caused additional segregation. Restrictive covenants maintained by state action or inaction build black ghettos. It is state action when public funds are dispensed by housing agencies to build racial ghettos. Where a community is racially mixed and school authorities segregate schools, or assign black teachers to black schools or close schools in fringe areas and build new schools in black areas and in more distant white areas, the State creates and nurtures a segregated school system, just as surely as did those States involved in *Brown* v. *Board of Education,* . . . when they maintained dual school systems.

. . . It is conceivable that ghettos develop on their own without any hint of state action. But since Michigan by one device or another has over the years created black school districts and white school districts, the task of equity is to provide a unitary system for the affected area where, as here, the State washes its hands of its own creations.

MR. JUSTICE WHITE, with whom MR. JUSTICE DOUGLAS, MR. JUSTICE BRENNAN, and MR. JUSTICE MARSHALL join, dissenting. . . .

Regretfully, and for several reasons, I can join neither the Court's judgment nor its opinion. The core of my disagreement is that deliberate acts of segregation and their consequences will go unremedied, not because a remedy would be infeasible or unreasonable in terms of the usual criteria governing school desegregation cases, but because an effective remedy would cause what the Court considers to be undue administrative inconvenience to the State. The result is that the State of Michigan, the entity at which the Fourteenth Amendment is directed, has successfully insulated itself from its duty to provide effective desegregation remedies by vesting sufficient power over its public schools in its local school districts. If this is the case in Michigan, it will be the case in most States. . . .

The Detroit school district is both large and heavily populated. It covers 139.6 square miles, encircles two entirely separate cities and school districts, and surrounds a third city on three sides. Also, whites and Negroes live in identifiable areas in the city. The 1970 public school enrollment in the city school district totalled 289,763 and was 63.6% Negro and 34.8% white. If "racial balance" were achieved in every school in the district, each school would be approximately 64% Negro. A remedy confined to the district could achieve no more desegregation. Furthermore, the proposed intracity remedies were beset with practical problems. None of the plans limited to the school district was satisfactory to the District Court. The most promising proposal, submitted by respondents, who were the plaintiffs in the District Court, would "leave many of its schools 75 to 90 percent Black." . . . Transportation on a "vast scale" would be required; 900 buses would have to be purchased for the transportation of pupils who are not now bussed. . . . The District Court also found that the plan "would change a school system which is now Black and white to one that would be perceived as Black, thereby increasing the flight of whites from the city and the system, thereby increasing the Black student population," . . . For the District Court, "[t]he conclusion, under the evidence in this case, is inescapable that relief of segregation in the public schools of the City of Detroit cannot be accomplished within the corporate geographical limits of the city." . . .

Despite the fact that a metropolitan remedy, if the findings of the District Court accepted by the Court of Appeals are to be credited, would more effectively desegregate the Detroit schools, would prevent resegregation, and would be easier and more feasible from many standpoints, the Court fashions out of whole cloth an arbitrary rule that remedies for constitutional violations occurring in a single Michigan school district must stop at the school district line. . . .

I am surprised that the Court, sitting at this distance from the State of Michigan, claims better insight than the Court of Appeals and the District Court as to whether an interdistrict remedy for equal protection violations practiced by the State of Michigan would involve undue difficulties for the State in the management of its public schools.

I am even more mystified how the Court can ignore the legal reality that the constitutional violations, even if occurring locally, were committed by governmental entities for which the State is responsible and that it is the State that must respond to the command of the Fourteenth Amendment. An interdistrict remedy for the infringements that occurred in this case is well within the confines and powers of the State, which is the governmental entity ultimately responsible for desegregating its schools. . . . I cannot understand, nor does the majority satisfactorily explain, why a federal court may not order an appropriate interdistrict remedy, if this is necessary or more effective to accomplish this constitutionally mandated task. In this case, both the right and the States' Fourteenth Amendment violation have concededly been fully established, and there is no acceptable reason for permitting the party responsible for the constitutional violation to contain the remedial powers of the federal court within administrative boundaries over which the transgressor itself has plenary power. . . .

Until today, the permissible contours of the equitable authority of the district courts to remedy the unlawful establishment of a dual school system have been extensive, adaptable, and fully responsive to the ultimate goal of achieving "the greatest possible degree of actual desegregation." There are indeed limitations on the equity powers of the federal judiciary, but until now the Court had not accepted the proposition that effective enforcement of the Fourteenth Amendment could be limited by political or administrative boundary lines demarcated by the very State responsible for the constitutional violation and for the disestablishment of the dual system. . . .

Finally, I remain wholly unpersuaded by the Court's assertion that "the remedy is necessarily designed, as all remedies are, to restore the victims of discriminatory conduct to the position they would have occupied in the absence of such conduct." . . . In the first place, under this premise the Court's judgment is itself infirm; for had the Detroit school system not followed an official policy of segregation throughout the 1950's and 1960's, Negroes and whites would have been going to school together. There would have been no, or at least not as many, recognizable Negro schools and no, or at least not as many, white schools, but "just schools," and neither Negroes nor whites would have suffered from the effects of segregated education, with all its shortcomings. Surely the Court's remedy will not restore to the Negro community, stigmatized as it was by the dual school system, what it would have enjoyed over all or most of this period if the remedy is confined to present-day Detroit; for the maximum remedy available within that area will leave many of the schools almost totally black, and the system itself will be predominantly black and will become increasingly so. . . .

MR. JUSTICE MARSHALL, with whom MR. JUSTICE DOUGLAS, MR. JUSTICE BRENNAN, and MR. JUSTICE WHITE join, dissenting. . . .

I cannot subscribe to this emasculation of our constitutional guarantee of equal protection of the laws and must respectfully dissent. Our precedents, in my view, firmly establish that where, as here, state-imposed segregation has been demonstrated, it becomes the duty of the State to eliminate root and branch all vestiges of racial discrimination and to achieve the greatest possible degree of actual desegregation.

. . . The District Court's decision to expand its desegregation decree beyond the geographical limits of the city of Detroit rested in large part on its conclusions that the State of Michigan was ultimately responsible for curing the condition of segregation within the Detroit city schools, and that a Detroit-only remedy would not accomplish this task. In my view, both of these conclusions are well supported by the facts of this case and by this Court's precedents. . . .

We held in *Swann* that where *de jure* segregation is shown, school authorities must make "every effort to achieve the greatest possible degree of actual desegregation." . . . If these words have any meaning at all, surely it is that school authorities must, to the extent possible, take all practicable steps to ensure that Negro and white children in fact go to school together. This is, in the final analysis, what desegregation of the public schools is all about.

Because of the already high and rapidly increasing percentage of Negro students in the Detroit system, as well as the prospect of white flight, a Detroit-only plan simply has no hope of achieving actual desegregation. Under such a plan white and Negro students will not go to school together. Instead, Negro children will continue to attend all-Negro schools. The very event that *Brown I* was aimed at will not be cured, but will be perpetuated for the future. . . .

. . . The flaw of a Detroit-only decree is not that it does not reach some ideal degree of racial balance or mixing. It simply does not promise to achieve actual desegregation at all. It is one thing to have a system where a small number of students remain in racially identifiable schools. It is something else entirely to have a system where all students continue to attend such schools. . . .

Under a Detroit-only decree, Detroit schools will clearly remain racially identifiable in comparison with neighboring schools in the metropolitan community. Schools with 65% and more Negro students will stand in sharp and obvious contrast to schools in neighboring districts with less than 2% Negro enrollment. Negro students will continue to perceive their schools as segregated educational facilities and this perception will only be increased when whites react to a Detroit-only decree by fleeing to the suburbs to avoid integration. School district lines, however innocently drawn, will surely be perceived as fences to separate the races when, under a Detroit-only decree, white parents withdraw their children from the Detroit city schools and move to the suburbs in order to continue them in all-white schools. The message of this action will not escape the Negro children in the city of Detroit. . . . It will be of scant significance to Negro children who have for years been confined by *de jure* acts of segregation to a growing core of all-Negro schools surrounded by a ring of all-white schools that the new dividing line between the races is the school district boundary. . . .

The State must also bear part of the blame for the white flight to the suburbs which would be forthcoming from a Detroit-only decree and would render such a remedy ineffective. Having created a system where whites and Negroes were intentionally kept apart so that they could not become accustomed to learning together, the State is responsible for the fact that many whites will react to the dismantling of the segregated system by attempting to flee to the suburbs. Indeed, by limiting the District Court to a Detroit-only remedy and allowing that flight to the suburbs to succeed, the Court today allows the State to profit from its own wrong and to perpetuate for years to come the separation of the races it achieved in the past by purposeful state action. . . .

Desegregation is not and was never expected to be an easy task. Racial attitudes ingrained in our Nation's childhood and adolescence are not quickly thrown aside in its middle years. But just as the inconvenience of some cannot be allowed to stand in the way of the rights of others, so public opposition, no matter how strident, cannot be permitted to divert this Court from the enforcement of the constitutional principles at issue in this case. Today's holding, I fear, is more a reflection of a perceived public mood that we have gone far enough in enforcing the Constitution's guarantee of equal justice than it is the product of neutral principles of law. In the short run, it may seem to be the easier course to allow our great metropolitan areas to be divided up each into two cities—one white, the other black—but it is a course, I predict, our people will ultimately regret. I dissent.

Missouri v. *Jenkins*
515 U.S. 70; 115 S. Ct. 2038; 132 L. Ed. 2d 63 (1995)

In this 18-year-old school desegregation litigation, on the orders of the U.S. District Court for the Western District of Missouri, the State of Missouri had already spent over $940 million to eliminate the past effects of racial segregation in the Kansas City, Missouri, School District (KCMSD)—See *Missouri* v. *Jenkins*, 495 U.S. 33 (1990). Because of the district court's orders, annual per-pupil costs (excluding capital costs) in the KCMSD were $9,412—two to three times higher than for any other school district in the State. In this particular dispute, the State of Missouri challenged a 1993 order by the district court requiring the State to fund salary increases for virtually all instructional and noninstructional staff with the KCMSD and to continue to fund remedial "quality education" programs because student achievement levels were still "at or below national norms at many grade levels." The Court of Appeals for the Eighth Circuit rejected the State's challenge, observing that these increases were designed to eliminate the vestiges of state-imposed segregation by improving the "desegregative attractiveness" of the KCMSD and by reversing "white flight" to the suburbs. It also rejected the State's request for a determination of partial unitary status under *Freeman* v. *Pitts*, 503 U.S. 467 (1992). The Supreme Court granted certiorari. *Opinion of the Court:* Rehnquist, *Kennedy, O'Connor, Scalia, Thomas. Concurring opinions: O'Connor, Thomas. Dissenting opinions:* Souter, *Breyer, Ginsburg, Stevens;* Ginsburg.

CHIEF JUSTICE REHNQUIST delivered the opinion of the Court.

As this school desegregation litigation enters its 18th year, we are called upon again to review the decisions of the lower courts. In this case, the State of Missouri has challenged the District Court's order of salary increases for virtually all instructional and noninstructional staff within the Kansas City, Missouri, School District (KCMSD) and the District Court's order requiring the State to continue to fund remedial "quality education" programs because student achievement levels were still "at or below national norms at many grade levels."

First, the State has challenged the District Court's requirement that it fund salary increases for KCMSD instructional and noninstructional staff. The State claimed that funding for salaries was beyond the scope of the District Court's remedial authority. Second, the State has challenged the District Court's order requiring it to continue to fund the remedial quality education programs for the 1992–1993 school year. The State contended that under *Freeman* v. *Pitts*, 503 US. 467 (1992), it had achieved partial unitary status with respect to the quality education programs already in place. As a result, the State argued that the District Court should have relieved it of responsibility for funding those programs.

The District Court rejected the State's arguments. It first determined that the salary increases were warranted because "[h]igh quality personnel are necessary not only to implement specialized desegregation programs intended to 'improve educational opportunities and reduce racial isolation' . . . but also to 'ensure that there is no diminution in the quality of its regular academic program.'" Its "ruling [was] grounded in remedying the vestiges of segregation by improving the desegregative attractiveness of the KCMSD." The District Court did not address the State's *Freeman* arguments; nevertheless, it ordered the State to continue to fund the quality

education programs for the 1992–1993 school year. . . . The Court of Appeals for the Eighth Circuit affirmed. . . .

Because of the importance of the issues, we granted certiorari to consider the following: (1) whether the District Court exceeded its constitutional authority when it granted salary increases to virtually all instructional and noninstructional employees of the KCMSD, and (2) whether the District Court properly relied upon the fact that students achievement test scores had failed to rise to some unspecified level when it declined to find that the State had achieved partial unitary status as to the quality education programs. . . .

Proper analysis of the District Court's orders challenged here . . . must rest upon their serving as proper means to the end of restoring the victims of discriminatory conduct to the position they would have occupied in the absence of that conduct and their eventual restoration of "state and local authorities to the control of a school system that is operating in compliance with the Constitution." We turn to that analysis.

The State argues that the order approving salary increases is beyond the District Court's authority because it was crafted to serve an "interdistrict goal," in spite of the fact that the constitutional violation in this case is "intradistrict" in nature. . . . The proper response to an intradistrict violation is an intradistrict remedy that serves to eliminate the racial identity of the schools within the effected school district by eliminating, as far as practicable, the vestiges of *de jure* segregation in all facets of their operation.

Here, the District Court has found, and the Court of Appeals has affirmed, that this case involved no interdistrict constitutional violation that would support interdistrict relief. Thus, the proper response by the District Court should have been to eliminate to the extent practicable the the vestiges of prior *de jure* segregation within the KCMSD. . . . The District Court and

Court of Appeals, however, have felt that because the KCMSD's enrollment remained 68.3% black, a purely *intra*district remedy would be insufficient. But, as noted in *Milliken* v. *Bradley*, 418 U.S. 717 (1974), we have rejected the suggestion "that schools which have a majority of Negro students are not 'desegregated' whatever the racial makeup of the school district's population and however neutrally the district lines have been drawn and administered."

Instead of seeking to remove the racial identity of the various schools within the KCMSD, the District Court has set out on a program to create a school district that was equal to or superior to the surrounding [suburban school districts]. Its remedy has focused on "desegregative attractiveness," coupled with "suburban comparability." Examination of the District Court's reliance on "desegregative attractiveness" and "suburban comparabilty" is instructive for our ultimate resolution of the salary-order issue.

The purpose of desegregative attractiveness has been not only to remedy the system-wide reduction in student achievement, but also to attract nonminority students not presently enrolled in the KCMSD. This remedy has included an elaborate program of capital improvements, course enrichment, and extracurricular enhancement not simply in the formerly identifiable black schools, but in schools throughout the district. The District Court's remedial orders have converted every senior high school, every middle school, and one-half of the elementary schools in the KCMSD into "magnet"' schools. The District Court's remedial order has all but made the KCMSD itself into a magnet district.

We previously have approved of intradistrict desegregation remedies involving magnet schools. Magnet schools have the advantage of encouraging voluntary movement of students within a school district in a pattern that aids desegregation on a voluntary basis, without requiring extensive busing and redrawing of district boundary lines. As a component in an intradistrict remedy, magnet schools also are attractive because they promote desegregation while limiting the withdrawal of white student enrollment that may result from mandatory student reassignment.

The District Court's remedial plan in this case, however, is not designed solely to redistribute the students within the KCMSD in order to eliminate racially identifiable schools within the KCMSD. Instead, its purpose is to attract nonminority students from outside the KCMSD schools. But this *inter*district goal is beyond the scope of the *intra*district violation identified by the District Court. In effect, the District Court has devised a remedy to accomplish indirectly what it admittedly lacks the remedial authority to mandate directly: the interdistrict transfer of students. . . .

The District Court's pursuit of the goal of "desegregative attractiveness" results in so many imponderables and is so far removed from the task of eliminating the racial identifiability of the schools within the KCMSD that we believe it is beyond the admittedly broad discretion of the District Court. In this posture, we conclude that the District Court's order of salary increases, which was "grounded in remedying the vestiges of segregation by improving the desegregative attractiveness of the KCMSD," is simply too far removed from an acceptable implementation of a permissible means to remedy previous legally mandated segregation.

Similar considerations lead us to conclude that the District Court's order requiring the State to continue to fund the quality education programs because student achievement levels were still "at or below national norms at many grade levels" cannot be sustained. The State does not seek from this Court a declaration of partial unitary status with respect to the quality education programs. It challenges the requirement of indefinite funding of a quality education program until national norms are met, based on the assumption that while a mandate for significant educational improvement, both in teaching and in facilities, may have been justified originally, its indefinite extension is not.

Our review in this respect is needlessly complicated because the District Court made no findings in its order approving continued funding of the quality education programs. . . . The basic task of the District Court is to decide whether the reduction in achievement by minority students attributable to prior *de jure* segregation has been remedied to the extent practicable. Under our precedents, the State and the KCMSD are "entitled to a rather precise statement of [their] obligations under a desegregation decree. . . ." In reconsidering this order, the District Court should apply our three-part test from *Freeman* v. *Pitts*. The District Court should consider that the State's role with respect to the quality education programs has been limited to the funding, not the implementation, of those programs. As all the parties agree that improved achievement on test scores is not necessarily required for the State to achieve partial unitary status as to the quality education programs, the District Court should sharply limit, if not dispense with, its reliance on this factor. Just as demographic changes independent of *de jure* segregation will affect the racial composition of student assignments, so too will numerous external factors beyond the control of the KCMSD and the State affect minority student achievement. So long as these external factors are not the result of segregation, they do not figure in the remedial calculus. Insistence upon academic goals unrelated to the effects of legal segregation unwarrantably postpones the day when the KCMSD will be able to operate on its own. . . .

On remand, the District Court must bear in mind that its end purpose is not only "to remedy the violation" to the extent practicable, but also "to restore state and local authorities to the control of a school system that is operating in compliance with the Constitution." The judgment of the Court of Appeals is reversed.

JUSTICE THOMAS, concurring.

It never ceases to amaze me that the courts are so willing to assume that anything that is predominantly black must be inferior. Instead of focusing on remedying the harm done to those black schoolchildren injured by segregation, the District Court here sought to convert the Kansas City, Missouri, School District (KCMSD) into a "magnet district" that would reverse the "white flight" caused by *de*segregation. In this respect, I join the Court's decision concerning the two remedial issues presented for review. I write separately, however, to add a few thoughts with respect to the overall course of this litigation. In order to evaluate the scope of the remedy, we must understand the scope of the constitutional violation and the nature of the remedial powers of the federal courts.

Two threads in our jurisprudence have produced this unfortunate situation, in which a District Court has taken it upon itself to experiment with the education of the KCMSD's black youth. First, the court has read our cases to support the theory that black students suffer an unspecified psychological harm from segregation that retards their mental and educational development. This approach not only relies upon questionable social science research rather than constitutional principle, but it also rests on an assumption of black inferiority. Second, we have permitted the federal courts to exercise virtually unlimited equitable powers to remedy this alleged constitutional violation. The exercise of this authority has trampled upon principles of federalism and the separation of powers and has freed courts to pursue other agendas unrelated to the narrow purpose of precisely remedying a constitutional harm.

The mere fact that a school is black does not mean that it is the product of a constitutional violation. A "racial imbalance does not itself establish a violation of the Constitution." Instead, in order to find unconstitutional segregation, we require that plaintiffs "prove all of the essential elements of *de jure* segregation—that is, stated simply, a current condition of segregation resulting from *intentional state action directed specifically* to the [allegedly segregated] schools."

In the present case, the District Court inferred a continuing constitutional violation from two primary facts: the existence of *de jure* segregation in the KCMSD prior to 1954, and the existence of *de facto* segregation today. The District Court found that in 1954, the KCMSD operated 16 segregated schools for black students, and that in 1974 39 schools in the district were more than 90% black. Desegregation efforts reduced this figure somewhat, but the District Court stressed that 24 schools remained "racially isolated," that is, more than 90% black, in 1983–1984. For the District Court, it followed that the KCMSD had not dismantled the dual system entirely. The District Court also concluded that because of the KCMSD's failure to "become integrated on a system-wide basis," the dual system still exerted "lingering effects" upon KCMSD black students, whose "general attitude of inferiority" produced "low achievement . . . which ultimately limits employment opportunities and causes poverty."

Without more, the District Court's findings could not have supported a finding of liability against the state. It should by now be clear that the existence of one-race schools is not by itself an indication that the State is practicing segregation. The continuing "racial isolation" of schools after *de jure* segregation has ended may well reflect voluntary housing choices or other private decisions. Here, for instance, the demography of the entire KCMSD has changed considerably since 1954. Though blacks accounted for only 18.9% of KCMSD's enrollment in 1954, by 1983–1984 the school district was 67.7% black. That certain schools are overwhelmingly black in a district that is now more than two-thirds black is hardly a sure sign of intentional state action. . . .

When a district court holds the State liable for discrimination almost 30 years after the last official state action, it must do more than show that there are schools with high black populations or low test scores. Here, the district judge did not make clear how the high black enrollments in certain schools were fairly traceable to the State of Missouri's actions. I do not doubt that Missouri maintained the despicable system of segregation until 1954. But I question the District Court's conclusion that because the State had enforced segregation until 1954, its actions, or lack thereof, proximately caused the "racial isolation" of the predominantly black schools in 1984. In fact, where, as here, the finding of liability comes so late in the day, I would think it incumbent upon the District Court to explain how more recent social or demographic phenomena did not cause the "vestiges." This the District Court did not do.

Without a basis in any real finding of intentional government action, the District Court's imposition of liability upon the State of Missouri improperly rests upon a theory that racial imbalances are unconstitutional. That is, the court has "indulged the presumption, often irrebuttable in practice, that a presently observed [racial] imbalance has been proximately caused by intentional state action during the prior *de jure* era." In effect, the court found that racial imbalances constituted an ongoing constitutional violation that continued to inflict harm on black students. This position appears to rest upon the idea that any school that is black is inferior, and that blacks cannot succeed without the benefit of the company of whites.

The District Court's willingness to adopt such stereotypes stemmed from a misreading of our earliest desegregation case. In *Brown v. Board of Education*, 347 U.S. 483 (1954) *(Brown I)*, the Court noted several psychological and sociological studies purporting to show that *de jure* segregation harmed black students by generating "a feeling of inferiority" in them. Seizing upon this passage in *Brown I*, the District Court asserted that "forced segregation ruins attitudes and is inherently unequal." The District Court suggested that this inequality continues in full force even after the end of *de jure* segregation. . . . Thus, the District Court seemed to believe that black students in the KCMSD would continue to receive an "inferior education" despite the end of *de jure* segregation, as long as *de facto* segregation persisted. As the District Court later concluded, compensatory educational programs were necessary "as a means of remedying many of the educational problems which go hand in hand with racially isolated minority student populations." Such assumptions and any social science research upon which they rely certainly cannot form the basis upon which we decide matters of constitutional principle.

It is clear that the District Court misunderstood the meaning of *Brown I*. *Brown I* did not say that "racially isolated" schools were inherently inferior; the harm that it identified was tied purely to *de jure* segregation, not *de facto* segregation. Indeed, *Brown I* itself did not need to rely upon any psychological or social science research in order to announce the simple, yet fundamental truth that the Government cannot discriminate among its citizens on the basis of race. As the Court's unanimous opinion indicated: "[I]n the field of public education the doctrine of 'separate but equal' has no place. Separate educational facilities are inherently unequal." At the heart of this interpretation of the Equal Protection Clause lies the principle that the Government must treat citizens as individuals, and not as members of racial, ethnic or religious groups. It is for this reason that we must subject all racial classifications to the strictest of scrutiny, which (aside from two decisions rendered in the midst of wartime, see *Hirabayashi v. United States*, 320 U.S. 81 (1943); *Korematsu*

v. *United States*, 323 U.S. 214 (1944) has proven automatically fatal.

Segregation was not unconstitutional because it might have caused psychological feelings of inferiority. Public school systems that separated blacks and provided them with superior educational resources—making blacks "feel" superior to whites sent to lesser schools—would violate the Fourteenth Amendment, whether or not the white students felt stigmatized, just as do school systems in which the positions of the races are reversed. Psychological injury or benefit is irrelevant to the question whether state actors have engaged in intentional discrimination—the critical inquiry for ascertaining violations of the Equal Protection Clause. The judiciary is fully competent to make independent determinations concerning the existence of state action without the unnecessary and misleading assistance of the social sciences.

Regardless of the relative quality of the schools, segregation violated the Constitution because the State classified students based on their race. Of course, segregation additionally harmed black students by relegating them to schools with substandard facilities and resources. But neutral policies, such as local school assignments, do not offend the Constitution when individual private choices concerning work or residence produce schools with high black populations. The Constitution does not prevent individuals from choosing to live together, to work together, or to send their children to school together, so long as the State does not interfere with their choices on the basis of race.

Given that desegregation has not produced the predicted leaps forward in black educational achievement, there is no reason to think that black students cannot learn as well when surrounded by members of their own race as when they are in an integrated environment. Indeed, it may very well be that what has been true for historically black colleges is true for black middle and high schools. Despite their origins in "the shameful history of state-enforced segregation," these institutions can be "'both a source of pride to blacks who have attended them and a source of hope to black families who want the benefits of . . . learning for their children.'" Because of their "distinctive histories and traditions," black schools can function as the center and symbol of black communities, and provide examples of independent black leadership, success, and achievement.

Thus, even if the District Court had been on firmer ground in identifying a link between the KCMSD's pre-1954 *de jure* segregation and the present "racial isolation" of some of the district's schools, mere *de facto* segregation (unaccompanied by discriminatory inequalities in educational resources) does not constitute a continuing harm after the end of *de jure* segregation. "Racial isolation" itself is not a harm; only state-enforced segregation is. After all, if separation itself is a harm, and if integration therefore is the only way that blacks can receive a proper education, then there must be something inferior about blacks. Under this theory, segregation injures blacks because blacks, when left on their own, cannot achieve. To my way of thinking, that conclusion is the result of a jurisprudence based upon a theory of black inferiority.

This misconception has drawn the courts away from the important goal in desegregation. The point of the Equal Protection Clause is not to enforce strict race-mixing, but to ensure that blacks and whites are treated equally by the State without regard to their skin color. The lower courts should not be swayed by the easy answers of social science, nor should they accept the findings, and the assumptions, of sociology and psychology at the price of constitutional principle.

We have authorized the district courts to remedy past *de jure* segregation by reassigning students in order to eliminate or decrease observed racial imbalances, even if present methods of pupils assignment are facially neutral. The District Court here merely took this approach to its logical next step. If racial proportions are the goal, then schools must improve their facilities to attract white students until the district's racial balance is restored to the "right" proportions. Thus, fault for the problem we correct today lies not only with a twisted theory of racial injuries, but also with our approach to the remedies necessary to correct racial imbalances.

The District Court's unwarranted focus on the psychological harm to blacks and on racial imbalances has been only half of the tale. Not only did the court subscribe to a theory of injury that was predicted on black inferiority, it also married this concept of liability to our expansive approach to remedial powers. We have given the federal courts the freedom to use any measure necessary to reverse problems—such as racial isolation or low educational achievement—that has proven stubbornly resistant to government policies. We have not permitted constitutional principles such as federalism or the separation of powers to stand in the way of our drive to reform the schools. Thus, the District Court here ordered massive expenditures by local and state authorities, without congressional or executive authorization and without any indication that such measures would attract whites back to KCMSD or raise KCMSD test scores. The time has come for us to put the genie back in the bottle.

The Constitution extends "[t]he judicial Power of the United States" to "all Cases, in Law and Equity, arising under this Constitution, the Laws of the United States, and Treaties made . . . under their Authority." I assume for purposes of this case that the remedial authority of the federal courts is inherent in the "judicial Power," as there is no general equitable remedial power expressly granted by the Constitution or by statute. As with any inherent judicial power, however, we ought to be reluctant to approve its aggressive or extravagant use, and instead we should exercise it in a manner consistent with our history and traditions. . . .

Motivated by our worthy desire to eradicate segregation, however, we have disregarded this principle and given the courts unprecedented authority to shape a remedy in equity. . . . The judicial overreaching we see before us today perhaps is the price we now pay for our approval of such extraordinary remedies in the past. . . . Such extravagant uses of judicial power are at odds with the history and tradition of the equity power and the Framers' design. . . . Anticipating the growth of our modern doctrine, the Anti-Federalists criticized the Constitution because it might be read to grant broad equitable powers to the federal courts. In response, the defenders of the Constitution "sold" the new framework of government to the public by espousing a narrower interpretation of the equity power. When an attack on the Constitution is followed by an open Federalist effort to narrow the provision, the appropriate conclusion is that the drafters and ratifiers of the Constitution approved the more limited construction offered in response. . . . [G]iven the Federalists' public explanation during the ratification of the federal equity power, we should exercise the power to impose equitable remedies only sparingly, subject to clear rules guiding its use.

Two clear restraints on the use of the equity power—federalism and the separation of powers—derive from the very form of our Government. Federal courts should pause before using their inherent equitable powers to intrude into the proper sphere of the States. We have long recognized that education is primarily a concern of local authorities. "[L]ocal autonomy of school districts is a vital national tradition. . . ."

Federal courts do not possess the capabilities of state and local governments in addressing difficult educational problems. State and local school officials not only bear the responsibility for educational decisions, they also are better equipped than a single federal judge to make the day-to-day policy, curricular, and funding choices necessary to bring a school district into compliance with the Constitution. Federal courts simply cannot gather sufficient information to render an effective decree, have limited resources to induce compliance, and cannot seek political and public support for their remedies. When we presume to have the institutional ability to set effective educational, budgetary, or administrative policy, we transform the least dangerous branch into the most dangerous one.

The separation of powers imposes additional restraints on the judiciary's exercise of its remedial powers. To be sure, this is not a case of one branch of Government encroaching on the prerogatives of another, but rather of the power of the Federal Government over the States. Nonetheless, what the federal courts cannot do at the federal level they cannot do against the States; in either case, Article III courts are constrained by the inherent constitutional limitations on their powers. There simply are certain things that courts, in order to remain courts, cannot and should not do. There is no difference between courts running school systems or prisons and courts running executive branch agencies.

In this case, not only did the District Court exercise the legislative power to tax, it also engaged in budgeting, staffing, and educational decisions, in judgments about the location and aesthetic quality of the schools, and in administrative oversight and monitoring. These functions involve a legislative or executive, rather than a judicial, power. As Alexander Hamilton explained the limited authority of the federal courts: "The courts must declare the sense of the law; and if they should be disposed to exercise WILL instead of JUDGMENT, the consequence would equally be the substitution of their pleasure to that of the legislative body." Federal judges cannot make the fundamentally political decisions as to which priorities are to receive funds and staff, which educational goals are to be sought, and which values are to be taught. When federal judges undertake such local, day-to-day tasks, they detract from the independence and dignity of the federal courts and intrude into areas in which they have little expertise.

It is perhaps not surprising that broad equitable powers have crept into our jurisprudence, for they vest judges with the discretion to escape the constraints and dictates of the law and legal rules. But I believe that we must impose more precise standards and guidelines on the federal equitable power, not only to restore predictability to the law and reduce judicial discretion, but also to ensure that constitutional remedies are actually targeted toward those who have been injured. . . .

To ensure that district courts do not embark on such broad initiatives in the future, we should demand that remedial decrees be more precisely designed to benefit only those who have been victims of segregation. Race-conscious remedies for discrimination not only must serve a compelling governmental interest (which is met in desegregation cases), but also must be narrowly tailored to further that interest. In the absence of special circumstances, the remedy for *de jure* segregation ordinarily should not include educational programs for students who were not in school (or were even alive) during the period of segregation. Although I do not doubt that all KCMSD students benefit from many of the initiatives ordered by the court below, it is for the democratically accountable state and local officials to decide whether they are to be made available even to those who were never harmed by segregation.

This Court should never approve a State's efforts to deny students, because of their race, an equal opportunity for an education. But the federal courts also should avoid using racial equality as a pretext for solving social problems that do not violate the Constitution. It seems apparent to me that the District Court undertook the worthy task of providing a quality education to the children of KCMSD. As far as I can tell, however, the District Court sought to bring new funds and facilities into the KCMSD by finding a constitutional violation on the part of the State where there was none. Federal courts should not lightly assume that States have caused "racial isolation" in 1984 by maintaining a segregated school system in 1954. We must forever put aside the notion that simply because a school district today is black, it must be educationally inferior. . . .

JUSTICE SOUTER, with whom JUSTICE STEVENS, JUSTICE GINSBURG, and JUSTICE BREYER join, dissenting.

The Court's process of orderly adjudication has broken down in this case. The Court disposes of challenges to only two of the District Court's many discrete remedial orders by declaring that the District Court erroneously provided an interdistrict remedy for an intradistrict violation. In doing so, it resolves a foundational issue going to one element of the District Court's decree that we did not accept for review in this case, that we need not reach in order to answer the questions that we did accept for review, and that we specifically refused to consider when it was presented in a prior petition for certiorari. Since, under these circumstances, the respondent school district and pupils naturally came to this Court without expecting that a fundamental premise of a portion of the District Court's remedial order would become the focus of the case, the essence of the Court's misjudgment in reviewing and repudiating that central premise lies in its failure to have warned the respondents of what was really at stake. This failure lulled the respondents into addressing the case without sufficient attention to the foundational issue, and their lack of attention has now infected the Court's decision.

No one on the Court has had the benefit of briefing and argument informed by an appreciation of the potential breadth of the ruling. The deficiencies from which we suffer have led the Court effectively to overrule a unanimous constitutional precedent of 20 years standing, which was not even addressed in argument, was mentioned merely in passing by one of the parties, and discussed by another of them only in a misleading way.

The Court's departures from the practices that produce informed adjudication would call for dissent even in a simple case. But in this one, with a trial history of more than 10 years of litigation, the Court's failure to provide adequate notice of the issue to be decided (or to limit the decision to issues on which certiorari was clearly granted) rules out any confidence that today's result is sound, either in fact or in law.

United States v. *Fordice*
505 U.S. 717, 112 S. Ct. 2727, 120 L. Ed. 2d 575 (1992)

Prior to the Supreme Court's decision in *Brown* v. *Board of Education* (1954), the State of Mississippi operated five universities exclusively for whites (the University of Mississippi, Mississippi State University, Mississippi University for Women, the University of Southern Mississippi, and Delta State University) and three exclusively for blacks (Alcorn State University, Jackson State University, and Mississippi Valley State University). After *Brown*, Mississippi continued its policy of *de jure* segregation in its public university system, maintaining five almost completely white and three almost completely black institutions. Private petitioners initiated litigation in U.S. District Court in 1975, and the United States government intervened, charging that state officials had failed to satisfy their obligations under the Equal Protection Clause of the Fourteenth Amenment and Title VI of the Civil Rights Act of 1964 to dismantle the dual system.

In an attempt to resolve the suit without going to trial through "voluntary dismantlement," the State Board of Trustees in 1981 issued "Mission Statements" for the eight institutions which (a) classified three white institutions (the University of Mississippi, Mississippi State, and Southern Mississippi) as "comprehensive" universities having the most varied degree programs and offering doctoral degrees; (b) redesignated one of the black institutions (Jackson State) as an "urban" university with limited research and degree functions geared toward its urban setting; and (c) characterized the rest as "regional" institutions providing primarily undergraduate education.

Despite these efforts, by the mid-1980s, more than 99 percent of Mississippi's white students were still enrolled at the State's five historically white institutions. Moreover, the student bodies at these universities also remained predominantly white, averaging between 80 and 91 percent white students. Seventy-one percent of the State's black students continued to attend the three historically black institutions, where the racial composition ranged from 92 to 99 percent black. The suit proceeded to trial, where after voluminous evidence was presented on a full range of educational issues, the District Court entered extensive findings of fact on, among other things, admission requirements, institutional classification and mission assignments, duplication of programs, and funding. It concluded, based on its reading of *Bazemore* v. *Friday*, 478

U.S. 385 (1986), that the affirmative duty of a state to desegregate its institutions of higher education does not include the obligation to restrict student choice or to achieve racial balance. The District Court held only that state policies and practices must be racially neutral, be developed and implemented in good faith, and not contribute substantially to the racial identifiability of individual institutions. Employing this test, it concluded that Mississippi had demonstrated conclusively that it was fulfilling its affirmative duty to disestablish its formerly segregated system. The Court of Appeals for the Fifth Circuit affirmed, and the Supreme Court granted the writ of certiorari filed by the United States and the private petitioners. *Opinion of the Court: White, Blackmun, Kennedy, O'Connor, Rehnquist, Souter, Stevens, Thomas. Concurring opinions: O'Connor; Thomas. Concurring in the judgment and dissenting in part: Scalia.*

JUSTICE WHITE delivered the opinion of the Court.

In 1954, this Court held that the concept of "'separate but equal'" has no place in the field of public education. *Brown* v. *Board of Education (Brown I)*, 347 U.S. 483 (1954). The following year, the Court ordered an end to segregated public education "with all deliberate speed." *Brown* v. *Board of Education (Brown II)*, 349 U.S. 294 (1955). Since these decisions, the Court has had many occasions to evaluate whether a public school district has met its affirmative obligation to dismantle its prior *de jure* segregated system in elementary and secondary schools. In this case we decide what standards to apply in determining whether the State of Mississippi has met this obligation in the university context. . . .

The District Court, the Court of Appeals, and respondents recognize and acknowledge that the State of Mississippi had the constitutional duty to dismantle the dual school system that its laws once mandated. Nor is there any dispute that this obligation applies to its higher education system. If the State has not discharged this duty, it remains in violation of the Fourteenth Amendment. *Brown* v. *Board of Education* and its progeny clearly mandate this observation. Thus, the primary issue in this case is whether the State has met its affirmative duty to dismantle its prior dual university system.

Our decisions establish that a State does not discharge its constitutional obligations until it eradicates policies and practices traceable to its prior *de jure* dual system that continue to foster segregation.

The Court of Appeals concluded that the State had fulfilled its affirmative obligation to disestablish its prior *de jure* segregated system by adopting and implementing race-neutral policies governing its college and university system. Because students seeking higher education had "real freedom" to choose the institution of their choice, the State need do no more. Even though neutral policies and free choice were not enough to dismantle a dual system of primary or secondary schools, *Green* v. *New Kent County School Board*, the Court of Appeals thought that universities "differ in character fundamentally" from lower levels of schools sufficiently so that our decision in *Bazemore* v. *Friday* justified the conclusion that the State had dismantled its former dual system.

Like the United States, we do not disagree with the Court of Appeals' observation that a state university system is quite different in very relevant respects from primary and secondary schools. Unlike attendance at the lower level schools, a student's decision to seek higher education has been a matter of choice. The State historically has not assigned university students to a particular institution. Moreover, like public universities throughout the country, Mississippi's institutions of higher learning are not fungible—they have been designated to perform certain missions. Students who qualify for admission enjoy a range of choices of which institution to attend. Thus, as the Court of Appeals stated, "[i]t hardly needs mention that remedies common to public school desegregation, such as pupil assignments, busing, attendance quotas, and zoning, are unavailable when persons may freely choose whether to pursue an advanced education and, when the choice is made, which of several universities to attend."

We do not agree with the Court of Appeals or the District Court, however, that the adoption and implementation of race-neutral policies alone suffice to demonstrate that the State has completely abandoned its prior dual system. That college attendance is by choice and not by assignment does not mean that a race-neutral admissions policy cures the constitutional violation of a dual system. In a system based on choice, student attendance is determined not simply by admissions policies, but also by many other factors. Although some of these factors clearly cannot be attributed to State policies, many can be. Thus, even after a State dismantles its segregative *admissions* policy, there may still be state action that is traceable to the State's prior *de jure* segregation and that continues to foster segregation. The Equal Protection Clause is offended by "sophisticated as well as simple-minded modes of discrimination." If policies traceable to the *de jure* system are still in force and have discriminatory effects, those policies too must be reformed to the extent practicable and consistent with sound educational practices. We also disagree with respondents that the Court of Appeals and District Court properly relied on our decision in *Bazemore* v. *Friday*, 478 U.S. 385 (1986). *Bazemore* neither requires nor justifies the conclusions reached by the two courts below.

Bazemore raised the issue whether the financing and operational assistance provided by a state university's extension service to voluntary 4-H and Homemaker Clubs was inconsistent with the Equal Protection Clause because of the existence of numerous all-white and all-black clubs. Though prior to 1965 the clubs were supported on a segregated basis, the District Court had found that the policy of segregation had been completely abandoned and that no evidence existed of any lingering discrimination in either services or membership; any racial imbalance resulted from the wholly voluntary and unfettered choice of private individuals. In this context, we held inapplicable the *Green* Court's judgment that a voluntary choice program was insufficient to dismantle a *de jure* dual system in public pri-

mary and secondary schools, but only after satisfying ourselves that the State had not fostered segregation by playing a part in the decision of which club an individual chose to join.

Bazemore plainly does not excuse inquiry into whether Mississippi has left in place certain aspects of its prior dual system that perpetuate the racially segregated higher education system. If the State perpetuates policies and practices traceable to its prior system that continue to have segregative effects—whether by influencing student enrollment decisions or by fostering segregation in other facets of the university system—and such policies are without sound educational justification and can be practicably eliminated, the State has not satisfied its burden of proving that it has dismantled its prior system. Such policies run afoul of the Equal Protection Clause, even though the State has abolished the legal requirement that whites and blacks be educated separately and has established racially neutral policies not animated by a discriminatory purpose. Because the standard applied by the District Court did not make these inquiries, we hold that the Court of Appeals erred in affirming the District Court's ruling that the State had brought itself into compliance with the Equal Protection Clause in the operation of its higher education system.

Had the Court of Appeals applied the correct legal standard, it would have been apparent from the undisturbed factual findings of the District Court that there are several surviving aspects of Mississippi's prior dual system which are constitutionally suspect; for even though such policies may be race-neutral on their face, they substantially restrict a person's choice of which institution to enter and they contribute to the racial identifiability of the eight public universities. Mississippi must justify these policies or eliminate them. . . .

We deal first with the current admissions policies of Mississippi's public universities. As the District Court found, the three flagship historically white universities in the system—University of Mississippi, Mississippi State University, and University of Southern Mississippi—enacted policies in 1963 requiring all entrants to achieve a minimum composite score of 15 on the American College Testing Program (ACT). The court described the "discriminatory taint" of this policy, an obvious reference to the fact that, at that time, the average ACT score for white students was 18 and the average score for blacks was 7. The District Court concluded, and the en banc Court of Appeals agreed, that present admissions standards derived from policies enacted in the 1970's to redress the problem of student unpreparedness. Obviously, this mid-passage justification for perpetuating a policy enacted originally to discriminate against black students does not make the present admissions standards any less constitutionally suspect.

The present admission standards are not only traceable to the *de jure* system and were originally adopted for a discriminatory purpose, but they also have present discriminatory effects. Every Mississippi resident under 21 seeking admission to the university system must take the ACT. Any applicant who scores at least 15 qualifies for automatic admission to any of the five historically white institutions except Mississippi University for Women, which requires a score of 18 for automatic admission unless the student has a 3.0 high school grade average. Those scoring less than 15 but at least 13 automatically qualify to enter Jackson State University, Alcorn State University, and Mississippi Valley State University. Without doubt, these requirements restrict the range of choices of entering students as to which institution they may attend in a way that perpetuates segregation. Those scoring 13 or 14, with some exceptions, are excluded from the five historically white universities and if they want a higher education must go to one of the historically black institutions or attend junior college with the hope of transferring to a historically white institution. Proportionately more blacks than whites face this choice: in 1985, 72 percent of Mississippi's white high school seniors achieved an ACT composite score of 15 or better, while less than 30 percent of black high school seniors earned that score. App. 1524–1525. It is not surprising then that Mississippi's universities remain predominantly identifiable by race. . . .

Another constitutionally problematic aspect of the State's use of the ACT test scores is its policy of denying automatic admission if an applicant fails to earn the minimum ACT score specified for the particular institution, without also resorting to the applicant's high school grades as an additional factor in predicting college performance. The United States produced evidence that the American College Testing Program (ACTP), the administering organization of the ACT, discourages use of ACT scores as the sole admissions criterion on the ground that it gives an incomplete "picture" of the student applicant's ability to perform adequately in college. One ACTP report presented into evidence suggests that "it would be foolish" to substitute a 3- or 4-hour test in place of a student's high school grades as a means of predicting college performance.

The record also indicated that the disparity between black and white students' high school grade averages was much narrower than the gap between their average ACT scores, thereby suggesting that an admissions formula which included grades would increase the number of black students eligible for automatic admission to all of Mississippi's public universities.

A second aspect of the present system that necessitates further inquiry is the widespread duplication of programs. "Unnecessary" duplication refers, under the District Court's definition, "to those instances where two or more institutions offer the same nonessential or noncore program. Under this definition, all duplication at the bachelor's level of nonbasic liberal arts and sciences course work and all duplication at the master's level and above are considered to be unnecessary." The District Court found that 34.6 percent of the 29 undergraduate programs at historically black institutions are "unnecessarily duplicated" by the historically white universities, and that 90 percent of the graduate programs at the historically black institutions are unnecessarily duplicated at the historically white institutions. In its conclusions of law on this point, the District Court nevertheless determined that "there is no proof" that such duplication "is directly associated with the racial identifiability of institutions," and that "there is no proof that the elimination of unnecessary program duplication would be justifiable from an educational standpoint or that its elimination would have a substantial effect on student choice."

The District Court's treatment of this issue is problematic from several different perspectives. By stating that "there is no proof" that elimination of unnecessary duplication would decrease institutional racial identifiability, affect student choice, and promote educationally sound policies, the court did not make clear whether it had directed the parties to develop evidence on these points, and if so, what that evidence revealed. Finally, by treating this issue in isolation, the court failed to consider the combined effects of unnecessary program duplication with other policies, such as differential admissions standards, in evaluating whether the State had met its duty to dismantle its prior *de jure* segregated system.

We next address Mississippi's scheme of institutional mission classification, and whether it perpetuates the State's formerly *de jure* dual system.

The institutional mission designations adopted in 1981 have as their antecedents the policies enacted to perpetuate racial separation during the *de jure* segregated regime. We do not suggest that absent discriminatory purpose the assignment of different missions to various institutions in a State's higher education system would raise an equal protection issue where one or more of the institutions become or remain predominantly black or white. But here the issue is whether the State has sufficiently dismantled its prior dual system; and when combined with the differential admission practices and unnecessary program duplication, it is likely that the mission designations interfere with student choice and tend to perpetuate the segregated system. On remand, the court should inquire whether it would be practicable and consistent with sound educational practices to eliminate any such discriminatory effects of the State's present policy of mission assignments.

Fourth, the State attempted to bring itself into compliance with the Constitution by continuing to maintain and operate all eight higher educational institutions. The existence of eight instead of some lesser number was undoubtedly occasioned by State laws forbidding the mingling of the races. And as the District Court recognized, continuing to maintain all eight universities in Mississippi is wasteful and irrational. The District Court pointed especially to the facts that Delta State and Mississippi Valley are only 35 miles apart and that only 20 miles separate Mississippi State and Mississippi University for Women. It was evident to the District Court that "the defendants undertake to fund more institutions of higher learning than are justified by the

amount of financial resources available to the state," but the court concluded that such fiscal irresponsibility was a policy choice of the legislature rather than a feature of a system subject to constitutional scrutiny.

Unquestionably, a larger rather than a smaller number of institutions from which to choose in itself makes for different choices, particularly when examined in the light of other factors present in the operation of the system, such as admissions, program duplication, and institutional mission designations. Though certainly closure of one or more institutions would decrease the discriminatory effects of the present system, based on the present record we are unable to say whether such action is constitutionally required. Elimination of program duplication and revision of admissions criteria may make institutional closure unnecessary. However, on remand this issue should be carefully explored by inquiring and determining whether retention of all eight institutions itself affects student choice and perpetuates the segregated higher education system, whether maintenance of each of the universities is educationally justifiable, and whether one or more of them can be practicably closed or merged with other existing institutions.

Because the former *de jure* segregated system of public universities in Mississippi impeded the free choice of prospective students, the State in dismantling that system must take the necessary steps to ensure that this choice now is truly free. The full range of policies and practices must be examined with this duty in mind. That an institution is predominantly white or black does not in itself make out a constitutional violation. But surely the State may not leave in place policies rooted in its prior officially segregated system that serve to maintain the racial identifiability of its universities if those policies can practicably be eliminated without eroding sound educational policies.

If we understand private petitioners to press us to order the upgrading of Jackson State, Alcorn State, and Mississippi Valley *solely* so that they may be publicly financed, exclusively black enclaves by private choice, we reject that request. The State provides these facilities for *all* its citizens and it has not met its burden under *Brown* to take affirmative steps to dismantle its prior *de jure* system when it perpetuates a separate, but "more equal" one. Whether such an increase in funding is necessary to achieve a full dismantlement under the standards we have outlined, however, is a different question, and one that must be addressed on remand.

Because the District Court and the Court of Appeals failed to consider the State's duties in their proper light, the cases must be remanded. To the extent that the State has not met its affirmative obligation to dismantle its prior dual system, it shall be adjudged in violation of the Constitution and Title VI and remedial proceedings shall be conducted. The decision of the Court of Appeals is vacated, and the cases are remanded for further proceedings consistent with this opinion.

JUSTICE THOMAS, concurring.

> We must rally to the defense of our schools. We must repudiate this unbearable assumption of the right to kill institutions unless they conform to one narrow standard.— W.E.B. Du Bois, Schools, 13 The Crisis 111, 112 (1917).

I agree with the Court that a State does not satisfy its obligation to dismantle a dual system of higher education merely by adopting race-neutral policies for the future administration of that system. Today, we hold that "[i]f policies traceable to the *de jure* system are still in force and have discriminatory effects, those policies too must be reformed to the extent practicable and consistent with sound educational policies." I agree that this statement defines the appropriate standard to apply in the higher-education context. I write separately to emphasize that this standard is far different from the one adopted to govern the grade-school context in *Green* v. *New Kent County School Bd.* (1968) and its progeny. In particular, because it does not compel the elimination of all observed racial imbalance, it portends neither the destruction of historically black colleges nor the severing of those institutions from . . . their distinctive histories and traditions.

A challenged policy does not survive under the standard we announce today if it began during the prior *de jure* era, produces adverse impacts, and persists without sound educational justification.

We have no occasion to elaborate upon what constitutes an adequate justification. Nonetheless, I find most encouraging the Court's emphasis on "sound *educational* practices." From the beginning, we have recognized that desegregation remedies cannot be designed to ensure the elimination of any remnant at any price, but rather must display "a practical flexibility" and "a facility for adjusting and reconciling public and private needs." *Brown* v. *Board of Ed.*, 349 U.S. 294, 300 (1955). Quite obviously, one compelling need to be considered is the *educational* need of the present and future *students* in the Mississippi university system, for whose benefit the remedies will be crafted.

In particular, we do not foreclose the possibility that there exists "sound educational justification" for maintaining historically black colleges *as such*. Despite the shameful history of state-enforced segregation, these institutions have survived and flourished. Indeed, they have expanded as opportunities for blacks to enter historically white institutions have expanded. Between 1954 and 1980, for example, enrollment at historically black colleges increased from 70,000 to 200,000 students, while degrees awarded increased from 13,000 to 32,000. These accomplishments have not gone unnoticed:

> The colleges founded for Negroes are both a source of pride to blacks who have attended them and a source of hope to black families who want the benefits of higher learning for their children. They have exercised leadership in developing educational opportunities for young blacks at all levels of instruction, and, especially in the South, they are still regarded as key institutions for enhancing the general quality of the lives of black Americans. Carnegie Commission on Higher Education, From Isolation to Mainstream: Problems of the Colleges Founded for Negroes 11 (1971).

I think it undisputable that these institutions have succeeded in part because of their distinctive histories and traditions; for many, historically black colleges have become "a symbol of the highest attainments of black culture." Obviously, a State cannot maintain such traditions by closing particular institutions, historically white or historically black, to particular racial groups. Nonetheless, it hardly follows that a State cannot operate a diverse assortment of institutions—including historically black institutions—open to all on a race—neutral basis, but with established traditions and programs that might disproportionately appeal to one race or another. No one, I imagine, would argue that such institutional *diversity* is without "sound educational justification," or that it is even remotely akin to program *duplication,* which is designed to separate the races for the sake of separating the races. The Court at least hints at the importance of this value when it distinguishes *Green* in part on the ground that colleges and universities "are not fungible." Although I agree that a State is not constitutionally *required* to maintain its historically black institutions as such, I do not understand our opinion to hold that a State is *forbidden* from doing so. It would be ironic, to say the least, if the institutions that sustained blacks during segregation were themselves destroyed in an effort to combat its vestiges.

JUSTICE SCALIA, concurring in the judgment in part and dissenting in part.

With some of what the Court says today, I agree. I agree, of course, that the Constitution compels Mississippi to remove all discriminatory barriers to its state-funded universities. I agree that the Constitution does not compel Mississippi to remedy funding disparities between its historically black institutions (HBIs) and its historically white institutions (HWIs). And I agree that Mississippi's American College Testing Program (ACT) requirements need further review. I reject, however, the effectively unsustainable burden the Court imposes on Mississippi, and all States that formerly operated segregated universities, to demonstrate compliance with *Brown I.* That requirement, which resembles what we prescribed for primary and secondary schools in *Green* v. *New Kent County School Board* (1968), has no proper application in the context of higher education, provides no genuine guidance to States and lower courts, and is as likely to subvert as to promote the interests of

those citizens on whose behalf the present suit was brought. . . .

Whether one consults the Court's description of what it purports to be doing, or what the Court actually does, one must conclude that the Court is essentially applying to universities the amorphous standard adopted for primary and secondary schools in *Green* v. *New Kent County School Board* (1968). Like that case, today's decision places upon the State the ordinarily unsustainable burden of proving the negative proposition that *it* is not responsible for extant racial disparity in enrollment. *Green* requires school boards to prove that racially identifiable schools are *not* the consequence of past or present discriminatory state action; today's opinion requires state university administrators to prove that racially identifiable schools are *not* the consequence of any practice or practices (in such impromptu "aggregation" as might strike the fancy of a district judge) held over from the prior *de jure* regime. This will imperil virtually any practice or program plaintiffs decide to challenge—just as *Green* has—so long as racial imbalance remains. And just as under *Green,* so also under today's decision, the only practicable way of disproving that "existing racial identifiability is attributable to the State" *is to eliminate extant segregation, i.e., to assure racial proportionality in the schools.* Failing that, the State's only defense will be to establish an excuse for each challenged practice—either impracticability of elimination or sound educational value.

Application of the standard (or standards) announced today has no justification in precedent, and in fact runs contrary to a case decided six years ago, see *Bazemore* v. *Friday* (1986). An accurate description of *Bazemore* was set forth in *Richmond* v. *J.A. Croson Co.,* 488 U.S. 469 (1989): "mere existence of single-race clubs . . . cannot create a duty to integrate," we said *Bazemore* held, "in absence of *evidence of exclusion by race*"—not "in absence of evidence of state action playing a part in the decision of which club an individual chose to join."

Bazemore's standard for dismantling a dual system ought to control here: discontinuation of discriminatory practices and adoption of a neutral admissions policy.

It is my view that the requirement of compelled integration (whether by student assignment, as in *Green* itself, or by elimination of nonintegrated options, as the Court today effectively decrees) does not apply to higher education. Only one aspect of an historically segregated university system need be eliminated: discriminatory admissions standards. The burden is upon the formerly *de jure* system to show that that has been achieved. Once that has been done, however, it is not just unprecedented, but illogical as well, to establish that former *de jure* States continue to deny equal protection of the law to students whose choices among public university offerings are unimpeded by discriminatory barriers. Unless one takes the position that *Brown I* required States not only to provide equal access to their universities but also to correct lingering disparities between them, that is, to remedy institutional noncompliance with the "equal" requirement of *Plessy*, a State is in compliance with *Brown I* once it establishes that it has dismantled all discriminatory barriers to its public universities. Having done that, a State is free to govern its public institutions of higher learning as it will, unless it is convicted of discriminating anew—which requires both discriminatory intent and discriminatory causation.

That analysis brings me to agree with the judgment that the Court of Appeals must be reversed in part—for the reason (quite different from the Court's) that Mississippi has not borne the burden of demonstrating that intentionally discriminatory admissions standards have been eliminated. It has been established that Mississippi originally adopted ACT assessments as an admissions criterion because that was an effective means of excluding blacks from the HWIs. Given that finding, the District Court should have required Mississippi to prove that its continued use of ACT requirements does not have a racially exclusionary purpose and effect—a not insubstantial task. What the Court's test is designed to achieve is the elimination of predominantly black institutions. While that may be good social policy, the present petitioners, I suspect, would not agree; and there is much to be said for the Court of Appeals' perception that "if no [state] authority exists to deny [the student] the right to attend the institution of his choice, he is done a severe disservice by remedies which, in seeking to maximize integration, min-

imize diversity and vitiate his choices." But whether or not the Court's antagonism to unintegrated schooling is good policy, it is assuredly not good constitutional law. There is nothing unconstitutional about a "black" school in the sense, not of a school that blacks *must* attend and that whites *cannot*, but of a school that, as a consequence of private choice in residence or in school selection, contains, and has long contained, a large black majority. (The Court says this, but does not appear to mean it.) In a perverse way, in fact, the insistence, whether explicit or implicit, that such institutions not be permitted to endure perpetuates the very stigma of black inferiority that *Brown I* sought to destroy. Not only Mississippi but Congress itself seems out of step with the drum that the Court beats today, judging by its passage of an Act entitled "Strengthening Historically Black Colleges and Universities," which authorizes the Education Department to provide money grants to historically black colleges. The implementing regulations designate Alcorn State University, Jackson State University, and Mississippi Valley State University as eligible recipients.

I would not predict, however, that today's opinion will succeed in producing the same result as *Green*—viz., compelling the States to compel racial "balance" in their schools—because of several practical imperfections: because the Court deprives district judges of the most efficient (and perhaps the only effective) *Green* remedy, mandatory student assignment; because some contradictory elements of the opinion (its suggestion, for example, that Mississippi's mission designations foster, rather than deter, segregation) will prevent clarity of application; and because the virtually standardless discretion conferred upon district judges will permit them to do pretty much what they please. What I do predict is a number of years of litigation-driven confusion and destabilization in the university systems of all the formerly *de jure* States, that will benefit neither blacks nor whites, neither predominantly black institutions nor predominantly white ones. Nothing good will come of this judicially ordained turmoil, except the public recognition that any Court that would knowingly impose it must hate segregation. We must find some other way of making that point.

Shelley v. *Kraemer*

334 U.S. 1; 68 S. Ct. 836; 92 L. Ed. 1161 (1948)

J.D. Shelley, a black, purchased a house from Josephine Fitzgerald in a St. Louis neighborhood in which deeds held by three-fourths of the property owners contained a racially restrictive covenant—that is, an agreement by the property holders not to sell their property to "people of the Negro or Mongolian Race." The covenant had been in force since 1911, when the holders of the properties in question had entered into a fifty-year contract not to sell to "any person not of the Caucasian race." Neither Shelley nor Fitzgerald was aware of the restrictive covenant at the time of the sale. When Shelley refused to reconsider the purchase after learning of the racial exclusion, Louis Kraemer, a resident of the neighborhood whose deed contained a similar restriction, sued to enjoin Shelley from taking possession of the property. The Missouri Supreme Court ultimately granted Kraemer the relief he sought and directed the trial court to issue the injunction. Shelley appealed to the United States Supreme Court, where his case was heard in conjunction with a controversy from Michigan involving a similar restrictive covenant. *Opinion of the Court: Vinson, Black, Burton, Douglas, Frankfurter, Murphy. Not participating: Jackson, Reed, Rutledge.*

MR. CHIEF JUSTICE VINSON delivered the opinion of the Court.

These cases present for our consideration questions relating to the validity of court enforcement of private agreements, generally described as restrictive covenants, which have as their purpose the exclusion of persons of designated race or color from the ownership or occupancy of real property. Basic constitutional issues of obvious importance have been raised. . . .

It is well, at the outset, to scrutinize the terms of the restrictive agreements involved in these cases. In the Missouri case, the covenant declares that no part of the affected property shall be "occupied by any person not of the Caucasian race, it being intended hereby to restrict the use of said property . . . against the occupancy as owners or tenants of any portion of said property for resident or other purpose by people of the Negro or Mongolian Race." Not only does the restriction seek to proscribe use and occupancy of the affected properties by members of the excluded class, but as construed by the Missouri courts, the agreement requires that title of any person who uses his property in violation of the restriction shall be divested. The restriction of the covenant in the Michigan case seeks to bar occupancy by persons of the excluded class. It provides that "This property shall not be used or occupied by any person or persons except those of the Caucasian race." . . .

It cannot be doubted that among the civil rights intended to be protected from discriminatory state action by the Fourteenth Amendment are the rights to acquire, enjoy, own and dispose of property. Equality in the enjoyment of property rights was regarded by the framers of that Amendment as an essential pre-condition to the realization of other basic civil rights and liberties which the Amendment was intended to guarantee. . . .

It is likewise clear that restrictions on the right of occupancy of the sort sought to be created by the private agreements in these cases could not be squared with the requirements of the Fourteenth Amendment if imposed by state statute or local ordinance. We do not understand respondents to urge the contrary. . . .

But the present cases . . . do not involve action by state legislatures or city councils. Here the particular patterns of discrimination and the areas in which the restrictions are to operate, are determined, in the first instance, by the terms of agreements among private individuals. Participation of the State consists in the enforcement of the restrictions so defined. The crucial issue with which we are here confronted is whether this distinction removes these cases from the operation of the prohibitory provisions of the Fourteenth Amendment.

Since the decision of this Court in the *Civil Rights Cases*, . . . the principle has become firmly embedded in our constitutional law that the action inhibited by the first section of the Fourteenth Amendment is only such action as may fairly be said to be that of the States. That Amendment erects no shield against merely private conduct, however discriminatory or wrongful.

We conclude, therefore, that the restrictive agreements standing alone cannot be regarded as violative of any rights guaranteed to petitioners by the Fourteenth Amendment. So long as the purposes of those agreements are effectuated by voluntary adherence to their terms, it would appear clear that there has been no action by the State and the provisions of the Amendment have not been violated. . . .

But here there was more. These are cases in which the purposes of the agreements were secured only by judicial enforcement by state courts of the restrictive terms of the agreements.

We have no doubt that there has been state action in these cases in the full and complete sense of the phrase. The undisputed facts disclose that petitioners were willing purchasers of properties upon which they desired to establish homes. The owners of the properties were willing sellers; and contracts of sale were accordingly consummated. It is clear that but for the active intervention of the state courts, supported by the full panoply of state power, petitioners would have been free to occupy the properties in question without restraint.

These are not cases, as has been suggested, in which the States have merely abstained from action, leaving private individuals free to impose such discriminations as they see fit. Rather, these are cases in which the States have made available to such individuals the full coercive power of government to deny to petitioners, on the grounds of race or color, the enjoyment of property rights in premises which petitioners are willing and financially able to acquire and which the grantors are willing to sell. The difference between judicial enforcement and non-enforcement of the restrictive covenants is the differ-

ence to petitioners between being denied rights of property available to other members of the community and being accorded full enjoyment of those rights on an equal footing. . . .

. . . We have noted that previous decisions of this Court have established the proposition that judicial action is not immunized from the operation of the Fourteenth Amendment simply because it is taken pursuant to the state's common-law policy. Nor is the Amendment ineffective simply because the particular pattern of discrimination, which the State has enforced, was defined initially by the terms of a private agreement. State action, as that phrase is understood for the purposes of the Fourteenth Amendment, refers to exertions of state power in all forms. And when the effect of that action is to deny rights subject to the protection of the Fourteenth Amendment, it is the obligation of this Court to enforce the constitutional commands.

We hold that in granting judicial enforcement of the restrictive agreements in these cases, the States have denied petitioners the equal protection of the laws and that, therefore, the action of the state courts cannot stand. . . .

Respondents urge, however, that since the state courts stand ready to enforce restrictive covenants excluding white persons from the ownership or occupancy of property covered by such agreements, enforcement of covenants excluding colored persons may not be deemed a denial of equal protection of the laws to the colored persons who are thereby affected. This contention does not bear scrutiny. The parties have directed our attention to no case in which a court, state or federal, has been called upon to enforce a covenant excluding members of the white majority from ownership or occupancy of real property on grounds of race or color. But there are more fundamental considerations. The rights created by the first section of the Fourteenth Amendment are, by its terms, guaranteed to the individual. The rights established are personal rights. It is, therefore, no answer to these petitioners to say that the courts may also be induced to deny white persons rights of ownership and occupancy on grounds of race or color. Equal protection of the laws is not achieved through indiscriminate imposition of inequalities. . . .

The historical context in which the Fourteenth Amendment became a part of the Constitution should not be forgotten. Whatever else the framers sought to achieve, it is clear that the matter of primary concern was the establishment of equality in the enjoyment of basic civil and political rights and the preservation of those rights from discriminatory action on the part of the States based on considerations of race or color. Seventy-five years ago this Court announced that the provisions of the Amendment are to be construed with this fundamental pur-

pose in mind. Upon full consideration, we have concluded that in these cases the States have acted to deny petitioners the equal protection of the laws guaranteed by the Fourteenth Amendment. . . .

For the reasons stated, the judgment of the Supreme Court of Missouri and the judgment of the Supreme Court of Michigan must be reversed.

Reversed.

Moose Lodge No. 107 v. *Irvis*
407 U.S. 163; 92 S. Ct. 1965; 32 L. Ed. 627 (1972)

Leroy Irvis, a black guest at the Moose Lodge in Harrisburg, Pennsylvania, was refused service at its dining room and bar solely because of his race. Irvis sued in federal district court for injunctive relief, charging that the discrimination was state action and thus in violation of the Equal Protection Clause of the Fourteenth Amendment, because the Pennsylvania liquor board had issued a liquor license to the Moose Lodge, a private club. The district court agreed with Irvis that state action was present and declared the Moose Lodge's liquor license invalid as long as it continued its discriminatory practices. The Moose Lodge appealed to the Supreme Court. *Opinion of the Court:* Rehnquist, *Blackmun, Burger, Powell, Stewart, White. Dissenting opinions:* Brennan, *Marshall;* Douglas, *Marshall.*

MR. JUSTICE REHNQUIST delivered the opinion of the Court. . . .

Moose Lodge is a private club in the ordinary meaning of that term. It is a local chapter of a national fraternal organization having well defined requirements for membership. It conducts all of its activities in a building that is owned by it. It is not publicly funded. Only members and guests are permitted in any lodge of the order; one may become a guest only by invitation of a member or upon invitation of the house committee.

Appellee, while conceding the right of private clubs to choose members upon a discriminatory basis, asserts that the licensing of Moose Lodge to serve liquor by the Pennsylvania Liquor Control Board amounts to such State involvement with the club's activities as to make its discriminatory practices forbidden by the Equal Protection Clause of the Fourteenth Amendment. The relief sought and obtained by appellee in the District Court was an injunction forbidding the li-

censing by the liquor authority of Moose Lodge until it ceased its discriminatory practices. We conclude that Moose Lodge's refusal to serve food and beverages to a guest by reason of the fact that he was a Negro does not, under the circumstances here presented, violate the Fourteenth Amendment.

In 1883, this Court in *The Civil Rights Cases* . . . set forth the essential dichotomy between discriminatory action by the State, which is prohibited by the Equal Protection Clause, and private conduct, "however discriminatory or wrongful," against which that clause "erects no shield," *Shelley* v. *Kraemer* . . . 1948. . . .

While the principle is easily stated, the question of whether particular discriminatory conduct is private, on the one hand, or amounts to "State action," on the other hand, frequently admits of no easy answer. "Only by sifting facts and weighing circumstances can the nonobvious involvement of the State in private conduct be attributed its true significance." . . .

Our cases make clear that the impetus for the forbidden discrimination need not originate with the State if it is state action that enforces privately originated discrimination. . . . The Court held in *Burton* v. *Wilmington Parking Authority* 1962 . . . that a private restaurant owner who refused service because of a customer's race violated the Fourteenth Amendment, where the restaurant was located in a building owned by a state created parking authority and leased from the authority. The Court, after a comprehensive review of the relationship between the lessee and the parking authority concluded that the latter had "so far insinuated itself into a position of interdependence with Eagle [the restaurant owner] that it must be recognized as a joint participant in the challenged activity, which, on that account, cannot be considered to have been so 'purely private' as to fall without the scope of the Fourteenth Amendment." . . .

The Court has never held, of course, that discrimination by an otherwise private entity would be violative of the Equal Protection Clause if the private entity receives any sort of benefit or service at all from the State, or if it is subject to state regulation in any degree whatever. Since state-furnished services include such necessities of life as electricity, water, and police and fire protection, such a holding would utterly emasculate the distinction between private as distinguished from State conduct set forth in *The Civil Rights Cases* . . . and adhered to in subsequent decisions. Our holdings indicate that where the impetus for the discrimination is private, the State must have "significantly involved itself with invidious discriminations," . . . in order for the discriminatory action to fall within the ambit of the constitutional prohibition. . . .

Here there is nothing approaching the symbiotic relationship between lessor and lessee that was present in *Burton*, where the private lessee obtained the benefit of locating in a building owned by the State created parking authority, and the parking authority was enabled to carry out its primary public purpose of furnishing parking space by advantageously leasing portions of the building constructed for that purpose to commercial lessees such as the owner of the Eagle Restaurant. . . .

. . . The Pennsylvania Liquor Control Board plays absolutely no part in establishing or enforcing the membership or guest policies of the club which it licenses to serve liquor. There is no suggestion in this record that the Pennsylvania Act, either as written or as applied, discriminates against minority groups either in their right to apply for club licenses themselves or in their right to purchase and be served liquor in places of public accommodation. The only effect that the state licensing of Moose Lodge to serve liquor can be said to have on the right of any other Pennsylvanian to buy or be served liquor on premises other than those of Moose Lodge is that for some purposes club licenses are counted in the maximum number of licenses which may be issued in a given municipality. Basically each municipality has a quota of one retail license for each 1,500 inhabitants. Licenses issued to hotels, municipal golf courses and airport restaurants are not counted in this quota, nor are club licenses until the maximum number of retail licenses is reached. Beyond that point, neither additional retail licenses nor additional club licenses may be issued so long as the number of issued and outstanding retail licenses remains above the statutory maximum.

The District Court was at pains to point out in its opinion what it considered to be the "pervasive" nature of the regulation of private clubs by the Pennsylvania Liquor Control Board. As that court noted, an applicant for a club license must make such physical alterations in its premises as the board may require, must file a list of the names and addresses of its members and employees, and must keep extensive financial records. The board is granted the right to inspect the licensed premises at any time when patrons, guests or members are present.

However detailed this type of regulation may be in some particulars, it cannot be said to in any way foster or encourage racial discrimination. Nor can it be said to make the State in any realistic sense a partner or even a joint venturer in the club's enterprise. The limited effect of the prohibition against obtaining additional club licenses when the maximum number of retail licenses allotted to a municipality has been issued, when considered together with the availability of liquor from hotel, restaurant, and retail licensees falls far short of conferring upon club licensee monopoly in the dispensing of liquor given municipality or in the State as a therefore hold that, with the exception hereafter noted, the operation of the regulatory scheme enforced by the Pennsylvania Liquor Control Board does not sufficiently implicate the State in the discriminatory guest policies of Moose Lodge so as to make the latter "State action" within the ambit of the Equal Protection Clause of the Fourteenth Amendment. . . .

MR. JUSTICE DOUGLAS, with whom MR. JUSTICE MARSHALL joins, dissenting. . . .

. . . Liquor licenses in Pennsylvania, unlike driver's licenses, or marriage licenses, are not freely available to those who meet racially neutral qualifications. There is a complex quota system, which the majority accurately describes. . . . What the majority neglects to say is that the Harrisburg quota, where Moose Lodge No. 107 is located, has been full for many years. No more club licenses may be issued in that city.

This state-enforced scarcity of licenses restricts the ability of blacks to obtain liquor, for liquor is commercially available *only* at private clubs for a significant portion of each week. Access by blacks to places that serve liquor is further limited by the fact that the state quota is filled. A group desiring to form a nondiscriminatory club which would serve blacks must purchase a license held by an existing club, which can exact a monopoly price for the transfer. The availability of such a license is speculative at best, however, for, as Moose Lodge itself concedes, without a liquor license a fraternal organization would be hard-pressed to survive.

Thus, the State of Pennsylvania is putting the weight of its liquor license, concededly a valued and important adjunct to a private club, behind racial discrimination.

MR. JUSTICE BRENNAN, with whom MR. JUSTICE MARSHALL joins, dissenting.

When Moose Lodge obtained its liquor license, the State of Pennsylvania became an active participant in the operation of the Lodge bar. Liquor licensing laws are only incidentally revenue measures; they are primarily pervasive regulatory schemes under which the State dictates and continually supervises virtually every detail of the operation of the licensee's business. Very few, if any, other licensed businesses experience such complete state involvement. . . .

Plainly, the State of Pennsylvania's liquor regulations intertwine the State with the operation of the Lodge bar in a "significant way [and] lend [the State's] authority to the sordid business of racial discrimination." . . .

Palmore v. Sidoti
446 U.S. 429, 104 S. Ct. 1879; 80 L. Ed. 2d 632 (1984)

When the Sidotis, both Caucasians, were divorced in Florida, Linda Sidoti was awarded custody of their three-year-old daughter. The following year, Anthony Sidoti sought custody of the child by filing a petition to modify the prior judgment because of changed conditions. The change was that Linda Sidoti was then cohabitating with Clarence Palmore, a Negro, whom she married later. The Florida trial court awarded custody to the father, concluding that the child's best interests would be served thereby. Acknowledging that there was no evidence that Linda Sidoti was unfit to continue the custody of her child, the court nevertheless shifted custody to the father in order to avoid the damaging impact on the child that would otherwise result from remaining in a racially mixed household. As it declared: "This Court feels that despite the strides that have been made in bettering relations between the races in this country, it is inevitable that . . . [the child] will, if allowed to remain in her present situation and attain school age and thus [be] more vulnerable to peer pressures, suffer from the social stigmatization that is sure to come."

The Second District Court of Appeals affirmed without opinion, thereby denying the Florida Supreme Court jurisdiction to review the case. The U.S. Supreme Court granted certiorari. *Unanimous opinion of the Court:* Burger, *Blackmun, Brennan, Marshall, O'Connor, Powell, Rehnquist, Stevens, White.*

CHIEF JUSTICE BURGER delivered the opinion of the Court.

We granted certiorari to review a judgment of a state court divesting a natural mother of the custody of her infant child because of her remarriage to a person of a different race. . . .

The judgment of a state court determining or reviewing a child custody decision is not ordinarily a likely candidate for review by this Court. However, the court's opinion, after stating that the "father's evident resentment of the mother's choice of a black partner is not sufficient" to deprive her of custody, then turns to what it regarded as the damaging impact on the child from remaining in a racially-mixed household. . . . This raises important federal concerns arising from the Constitution's commitment to eradicating discrimination based on race.

The Florida court did not focus directly on the parental qualifications of the natural mother or her present husband, or indeed on the father's qualifications to have custody of the child. The court found that "there is no issue as to either party's devotion to the child, adequacy of housing facilities, or respect[a]bility of the new spouse of either parent." . . . This, taken with the absence of any negative finding as to the quality of the care provided by the mother, constitutes a rejection of any claim of petitioner's unfitness to continue the custody of her child.

The court correctly stated that the child's welfare was the controlling factor. But that court was entirely candid and made no effort to place its holding on any ground other than race. Taking the court's findings and rationale at face value, it is clear that the outcome would have been different had petitioner married a Caucasian male of similar respectability.

A core purpose of the Fourteenth Amendment was to do away with all governmentally-imposed discrimination based on race. . . . Classifying persons according to their race is more likely to reflect racial prejudice than legitimate public concerns; the race, not the person, dictates the category. . . . Such classifications are subject to the most exacting scrutiny; to pass constitutional muster, they must be justified by a compelling governmental interest and must be "necessary . . . to the accomplishment" of its legitimate purpose. . . .

The State, of course, has a duty of the highest order to protect the interests of minor children, particularly those of tender years. In common with most states, Florida law mandates that custody determinations be made in the best interests of the children involved. . . . The goal of granting custody based on the best interests of the child is indisputably a substantial governmental interest for purposes of the Equal Protection Clause.

It would ignore reality to suggest that racial and ethnic prejudices do not exist or that all manifestations of those prejudices have been eliminated. There is a risk that a child living with a step-parent of a different race may be subject to a variety of pressures and stresses not present if the child were living with parents of the same racial or ethnic origin.

The question, however, is whether the reality of private biases and the possible injury they might inflict are permissible considerations for removal of an infant child from the custody of its natural mother. We have little difficulty concluding that they are not. The Constitution cannot control such prejudices but neither can it tolerate them. Private biases may be outside the reach of the law, but the law cannot, directly or indirectly, give them effect. "Public officials sworn to uphold the Constitution may not avoid a constitutional duty by bowing to the hypothetical effects of private racial prejudice that they assume to be both widely and deeply held.". . .

This is by no means the first time that acknowledged racial prejudice has been invoked to justify racial classifications. In *Buchanan* v. *Warley* . . . (1917), for example, this Court invalidated a Kentucky law forbidding Negroes from buying homes in white neighborhoods.

"It is urged that this proposed segregation will promote the public peace by preventing race conflicts. Desirable as this is, and important as is the preservation of the public peace, this aim cannot be accomplished by laws or ordinances which deny rights created or protected by the Federal Constitution.". . .

Whatever problems racially-mixed households may pose for children in 1984 can no more support a denial of constitutional rights than could the stresses that residential integration was thought to entail in 1917. The effects of racial prejudice, however real, cannot justify a racial classification removing an infant child from the custody of its natural mother found to be an appropriate person to have such custody.

The judgment of the District Court of Appeal is reversed.

Georgia v. McCollum
505 U.S. 42; 112 S. Ct. 2348;120 L. Ed. 2d 33 (1992)

Thomas McCollum, William Joseph McCollum, and Ella Hampton McCollum, who were white, were charged with assaulting Jerry and Myra Collins, who were black. Before jury selection began, the trial judge denied the prosecutor's motion to prohibit the defendants from exercising their peremptory challenges to exclude all blacks from participating as jurors in the trial. The Georgia Supreme Court affirmed, distinguishing *Edmonson* v. *Leesville Concrete Co.* (1991), in which the U.S. Supreme Court had held that private litigants cannot exercise peremptory challenges in a racially discriminatory manner, on the grounds that *Edmonson* involved civil litigants rather than criminal defendants. The U.S. Supreme Court granted certiorari. *Opinion of the Court:* <u>Blackmun</u>, *Kennedy, Rehnquist, Stevens, Souter, White. Concurring opinion:* <u>Rehnquist</u>. *Concurring in the judgment:* <u>Thomas</u>. *Dissenting opinions:* <u>O'Connor</u>; <u>Scalia</u>.

JUSTICE BLACKMUN delivered the opinion of the Court.

For more than a century, this Court consistently and repeatedly has reaffirmed that racial discrimination by the State in jury selection offends the Equal Protection Clause. See, *e.g.*, *Strauder* v. *West Virginia*, 100 U.S. 303 (1880). Last Term this Court held that racial discrimination in a civil litigant's exercise of peremptory challenges also violates the Equal Protection Clause. See *Edmonson* v. *Leesville Concrete Co.*, 111 S. Ct. 2077 (1991). Today, we are asked to decide whether the Constitution prohibits a *criminal defendant* from engaging in purposeful racial discrimination in the exercise of peremptory challenges. . . .

Over the last century, in an almost unbroken chain of decisions, this Court gradually has abolished race as a consideration for jury service. In *Strauder* v. *West Virginia* (1880), the Court invalidated a state statute providing that only white men could serve as jurors. While stating that a defendant has no right to a "petit jury composed in whole or in part of persons of his own race," the Court held that a defendant does have the right to be tried by a jury whose members are selected by nondiscriminatory criteria.

In *Swain* v. *Alabama*, 380 U.S. 202 (1965), the Court was confronted with the question whether an African-American defendant was denied equal protection by the State's exercise of peremptory challenges to exclude members of his race from the petit jury. Although the Court rejected the defendant's attempt to establish an equal protection claim premised solely on the pattern of jury strikes in his own case, it acknowledged that proof of systematic exclusion of African-Americans through the use of peremptories over a period of time might establish such a violation.

In *Batson* v. *Kentucky*, 476 U.S. 79 (1986), the Court discarded *Swain's* evidentiary formulation. The *Batson* Court held that a defendant may establish a prima facie case of purposeful discrimination in selection of the petit jury based solely on the prosecutor's exercise of peremptory challenges at the defendant's trial. "Once the defendant makes a prima facie showing, the burden shifts to the State to come forward with a neutral explanation for challenging black jurors."

Last Term this Court applied the *Batson* framework in two other contexts. In *Powers* v. *Ohio*, 111 S. Ct. 1364 (1991), it held that in the trial of a white criminal defendant, a prosecutor is prohibited from excluding African-American jurors on the basis of race. In *Edmonson* v. *Leesville Concrete Co.*, 111 S. Ct. 2077 (1991), the Court decided that in a civil case, private litigants cannot exercise their peremptory strikes in a racially discriminatory manner.

In deciding whether the Constitution prohibits criminal defendants from exercising racially discriminatory peremptory challenges, we must answer four questions. First, whether a criminal defendant's exercise of peremptory challenges in a racially discriminatory manner inflicts the harms addressed by *Batson*. Second, whether the exercise of peremptory challenges by a criminal defendant constitutes state action. Third, whether prosecutors have standing to raise this constitutional challenge. And fourth, whether the constitutional rights of a criminal defendant nonetheless preclude the extension of our precedents to this case.

The majority in *Powers* recognized that "*Batson* 'was designed to serve multiple ends,'" only one of which was to protect individual defendants from discrimination in the selection of jurors. As in *Powers* and *Edmonson*, the extension of *Batson* in this context is designed to remedy the harm done to the "dignity of persons" and to the "integrity of the courts."

As long ago as *Strauder*, this Court recognized that denying a person participation in jury service on account of his race unconstitutionally discriminates against the excluded juror. While "[a]n individual juror does not have a right to sit on any particular petit jury, . . . he or she does possess the right not to be excluded from one on account of race." Regardless of who invokes the discriminatory challenge, there can be no doubt that the harm is the same—in all cases, the juror is subjected to open and public racial discrimination.

But "the harm from discriminatory jury selection extends beyond that inflicted on the defen-

dant and the excluded juror to touch the entire community." One of the goals of our jury system is "to impress upon the criminal defendant and the community as a whole that a verdict of conviction or acquittal is given in accordance with the law by persons who are fair." Selection procedures that purposefully exclude African-Americans from juries undermine that public confidence—as well they should.

The need for public confidence is especially high in cases involving race-related crimes. In such cases, emotions in the affected community will inevitably be heated and volatile. Public confidence in the integrity of the criminal justice system is essential for preserving community peace in trials involving race-related crimes.

Be it at the hands of the State or the defense, if a court allows jurors to be excluded because of group bias, it is a willing participant in a scheme that could only undermine the very foundation of our system of justice—our citizens' confidence in it. Just as public confidence in criminal justice is undermined by a conviction in a trial where racial discrimination has occurred in jury selection, so is public confidence undermined where a defendant, assisted by racially discriminatory peremptory strikes, obtains an acquittal.

The fact that a defendant's use of discriminatory peremptory challenges harms the jurors and the community does not end our equal protection inquiry. Racial discrimination, although repugnant in all contexts, violates the Constitution only when it is attributable to state action. Thus, the second question that must be answered is whether a criminal defendant's exercise of a peremptory challenge constitutes state action for purposes of the Equal Protection Clause.

Until *Edmonson*, the cases decided by this Court that presented the problem of racially discriminatory peremptory challenges involved assertions of discrimination by a prosecutor, a quintessential state actor. In *Edmonson*, by contrast, the contested peremptory challenges were exercised by a private defendant in a civil action. In order to determine whether state action was present in that setting, the Court in *Edmonson* used the analytical framework summarized in *Lugar* v. *Edmonson Oil Co.*, 457 U.S. 922 (1982).

The first inquiry is "whether the claimed [constitutional] deprivation has resulted from the exercise of a right or privilege having its source in state authority." "There can be no question" that peremptory challenges satisfy this first requirement, as they "are permitted only when the government, by statute or decisional law, deems it appropriate to allow parties to exclude a given number of persons who otherwise would satisfy the requirements for service on the petit jury."

The second inquiry is whether the private party charged with the deprivation can be described as a state actor. The Court in *Edmonson* found that peremptory challenges perform a traditional function of the government: "Their sole purpose is to permit litigants to assist the government in the selection of an impartial trier of fact." And, as the *Edmonson* Court recognized, the jury system in turn "performs the critical governmental functions of guarding the rights of litigants and 'insur[ing] continued acceptance of the laws by all of the people.'" These same conclusions apply with even greater force in the criminal context because the selection of a jury in a criminal case fulfills a unique and constitutionally compelled governmental function.

Respondents nonetheless contend that the adversarial relationship between the defendant and the prosecution negates the governmental character of the peremptory challenge. In exercising a peremptory challenge, a criminal defendant is wielding the power to choose a quintessential governmental body—indeed, the institution of government on which our judicial system depends. Thus, as we held in *Edmonson*, when "a government confers on a private body the power to choose the government's employees or officials, the private body will be bound by the constitutional mandate of race neutrality."

The fact that a defendant exercises a peremptory challenge to further his interest in acquittal does not conflict with a finding of state action. Whenever a private actor's conduct is deemed "fairly attributable" to the government, it is likely that private motives will have animated the actor's decision. Indeed, in *Edmonson*, the Court recognized that the private party's exercise of peremptory challenges constituted state action, even though the motive underlying the exercise of the peremptory challenge may be to protect a private interest.

Having held that a defendant's discriminatory exercise of a peremptory challenge is a violation of equal protection, we move to the question whether the State has standing to challenge a defendant's discriminatory use of peremptory challenges. In *Powers*, this Court held that a white criminal defendant has standing to raise the equal protection rights of black jurors wrongfully excluded from jury service. While third-party standing is a limited exception, the *Powers* Court recognized that a litigant may raise a claim on behalf of a third party if the litigant can demonstrate that he has suffered a concrete injury, that he has a close relation to the third party, and that there exists some hindrance to the third party's ability to protect its own interests. In *Edmonson*, the Court applied the same analysis in deciding that civil litigants had standing to raise the equal protection rights of jurors excluded on the basis of their race.

The State's relation to potential jurors in this case is closer than the relationships approved in *Powers* and *Edmonson*. As the representative of all its citizens, the State is the logical and proper party to assert the invasion of the constitutional rights of the excluded jurors in a criminal trial. Indeed, the Fourteenth Amendment forbids the State from denying persons within its jurisdiction the equal protection of the laws. . . . Accordingly, we hold that the State has standing to assert the excluded jurors' rights.

The final question is whether the interests served by *Batson* must give way to the rights of a criminal defendant. As a preliminary matter, it is important to recall that peremptory challenges are not constitutionally protected fundamental rights; rather, they are but one state-created means to the constitutional end of an impartial jury and a fair trial. This Court repeatedly has stated that the right to a peremptory challenge may be withheld altogether without impairing the constitutional guarantee of an impartial jury and a fair trial.

We do not believe that this decision will undermine the contribution of the peremptory challenge to the administration of justice. Nonetheless, "if race stereotypes are the price for acceptance of a jury panel as fair," we reaffirm today that such a "price is too high to meet the standard of the Constitution." It is an affront to justice to argue that a fair trial includes the right to discriminate against a group of citizens based upon their race. . . .

We hold that the Constitution prohibits a criminal defendant from engaging in purposeful discrimination on the ground of race in the exercise of peremptory challenges. Accordingly, if the State demonstrates a prima facie case of racial discrimination by the defendants, the defendants must articulate a racially neutral explanation for peremptory challenges. The judgment of the Supreme Court of Georgia is reversed and the case is remanded for further proceedings not inconsistent with this opinion.

CHIEF JUSTICE REHNQUIST, concurring.

I was in dissent in *Edmonson* v. *Leesville Concrete Co.* (1991), and continue to believe that case to have been wrongly decided. But so long as it remains the law, I believe that it controls the disposition of this case on the issue of "state action" under the Fourteenth Amendment. I therefore join the opinion of the Court.

JUSTICE THOMAS, concurring in the judgment.

As a matter of first impression, I think that I would have shared the view of the dissenting opinions: A criminal defendant's use of peremptory strikes cannot violate the Fourteenth Amendment because it does not involve state action. Yet, I agree with the Court and the Chief Justice that our decision last term in *Edmonson* v. *Leesville Concrete Co.* (1991) governs this case and requires the opposite conclusion. Because the respondents do not question *Edmonson*, I believe that we must accept its consequences. I therefore concur in the judgment reversing the Georgia Supreme Court.

I write separately to express my general dissatisfaction with our continuing attempts to use the Constitution to regulate peremptory challenges. In my view, by restricting a criminal defendant's use of such challenges, this case takes us further from the reasoning and the result of *Strauder* v. *West Virginia* (1880). I doubt that this departure will produce favorable consequences. On the contrary, I am certain that black criminal defendants will rue the day that this court ventured down this road that inexorably will lead to the elimination of peremptory strikes.

In *Strauder*, as the Court notes, we invalidated a state law that prohibited blacks from serving on juries. In the course of the decision, we observed that the racial composition of a jury may affect the outcome of a criminal case. We explained: "It is well known that prejudices often exist against particular classes in the community, which sway the judgment of jurors, and which, therefore, operate in some cases to deny to persons of those classes the full enjoyment of that protection which others enjoy." We thus recognized, over a century ago, the precise point that Justice O'Connor makes today. Simply stated, securing representation of the defendant's race on the jury may help to overcome racial bias and provide the defendant with a better chance of having a fair trial.

I do not think that this basic premise of *Strauder* has become obsolete. The public, in general, continues to believe that the makeup of juries can matter in certain instances. Consider, for example, how the press reports criminal trials. Major newspapers regularly note the number of whites and blacks that sit on juries in important cases. Their editors and readers apparently recognize that conscious and unconscious prejudice persists in our society and that it may influence some juries. Common experience and common sense confirm this understanding.

In *Batson*, however, this Court began to depart from Strauder by holding that, without some actual showing, suppositions about the possibility that jurors may harbor prejudice have no legitimacy. We said, in particular, that a prosecutor could not justify peremptory strikes "by stating merely that he challenged jurors of the defendant's race on the assumption— or his intuitive judgment—that they would be partial to the defendant because of their shared race." As noted, however, our decision in *Strauder* rested on precisely such an "assumption" or "intuition." We reasonably surmised, without direct evidence in any particular case, that all-white juries might judge black defendants unfairly.

Our departure from *Strauder* has two negative consequences. First, it produces a serious misordering of our priorities. In Strauder, we put the rights of defendants foremost. Today's decision, while protecting jurors, leaves defendants with less means of protecting themselves. Unless jurors actually admit prejudice during *voir dire*, defendants generally must allow them to sit and run the risk that racial animus will affect the verdict. In effect, we have exalted the right of citizens to sit on juries over the rights of the criminal defendant, even though it is the defendant, not the jurors, who faces imprisonment or even death. At a minimum, I think that this inversion of priorities should give us pause.

Second, our departure from *Strauder* has taken us down a slope of inquiry that had no clear stopping point. Today, we decide only that white defendants may not strike black veniremen on the basis of race. Eventually, we will have to decide whether black defendants may strike white veniremen. Next will come the question whether defendants may exercise peremptories on the basis of sex. The consequences for defendants of our decision and of these future cases remain to be seen. But whatever the benefits were that this Court perceived in a criminal defendant's having members of his class on the jury, they have evaporated.

JUSTICE O'CONNOR, dissenting.

The Court reaches the remarkable conclusion that criminal defendants being prosecuted by the State act on behalf of their adversary when they exercise peremptory challenges during jury selection. The Court purports merely to follow precedents, but our cases do not compel this perverse result. To the contrary, our decisions specifically establish that criminal defendants and their lawyers are not government actors when they perform traditional trial functions.

It is well and properly settled that the Constitution's equal protection guarantee forbids prosecutors from exercising peremptory challenges in a racially discriminatory fashion. The Constitution, however, affords no similar protection against private action. "Embedded in our Fourteenth Amendment jurisprudence is a dichotomy between state action, which is subject to scrutiny under the Amendmen[t] . . . , and private conduct, against which the Amendment affords no shield, no matter how unfair that conduct may be." *National Collegiate Athletic Assn.* v. *Tarkanian*, 488 U.S. 179 (1988). This distinction appears on the face of the Fourteenth Amendment, which provides that "*No State* shall . . . deny to any person within its jurisdiction the equal protection of the laws." The critical but straightforward question this case presents is whether criminal defendants and their lawyers,

when exercising peremptory challenges as part of a defense, are state actors. . . .

From arrest, to trial, to possible sentencing and punishment, the antagonistic relationship between government and the accused is clear for all to see. Rather than squarely facing this fact, the Court, as in *Edmonson*, rests its finding of governmental action on the points that defendants exercise peremptory challenges in a courtroom and judges alter the composition of the jury in response to defendants' choices. I found this approach wanting in the context of civil controversies between private litigants, for reasons that need not be repeated here. But even if I thought *Edmonson* was correctly decided, I could not accept today's simplistic extension of it. The unique relationship between criminal defendants and the State precludes attributing defendants' actions to the State, whatever is the case in civil trials.

That the Constitution does not give federal judges the reach to wipe all marks of racism from every courtroom in the land is frustrating, to be sure. But such limitations are the necessary and intended consequence of the Fourteenth Amendment's state action requirement. Because I cannot accept the Court's conclusion that government is responsible for decisions criminal defendants make while fighting state prosecution, I respectfully dissent.

JUSTICE SCALIA, dissenting.

I agree with the Court that its judgment follows logically from *Edmonson* v. *Leesville Concrete Co., Inc.* (1991). For the reasons given in the *Edmonson* dissents, however, I think that case was wrongly decided. Barely a year later, we witness its reduction to the terminally absurd: A criminal defendant, in the process of defending himself against the state, is held to be acting on behalf of the state. Justice O'Connor demonstrates the sheer inanity of this proposition (in case the mere statement of it does not suffice), and the contrived nature of the Court's justifications. I see no need to add to her discussion, and differ from her views only in that I do not consider *Edmonson* distinguishable in principle—except in the principle that a bad decision should not be followed logically to its illogical conclusion.

Today's decision gives the lie once again to the belief that an activist, "evolutionary" constitutional jurisprudence always evolves in the direction of greater individual rights. In the interest of promoting the supposedly greater good of race relations in the society as a whole (make no mistake that that is what underlies all of this), we use the Constitution to destroy the ages-old right of criminal defendants to exercise peremptory challenges as they wish, to secure a jury that they consider fair. I dissent.

Wards Cove Packing Co. v. *Atonio*

490 U.S. 642; 109 S. Ct. 2115; 104 L. Ed. 2d 733 (1989)

Jobs at the Alaskan canneries of Wards Cove Packing Co. were of two general types: unskilled "cannery" jobs on the cannery lines, filled predominantly by nonwhites, and higher-paying "noncannery" jobs, skilled posts filled predominantly by whites. Frank Atonio and other nonwhite cannery workers filed suit in U.S. District Court under Title VII of the Civil Rights Act of 1964, alleging that the petitioner's hiring and promotion practices were responsible for the racial stratification of the work force and denied them noncannery jobs on the basis of race. The District Court rejected the respondents' claims, but the U.S. Court of Appeals for the Ninth Court reversed, holding that the respondents had, on the basis of their statistics, made out a prima facie case of disparate impact in hiring for both skilled and unskilled jobs. The Supreme Court granted certiorari. *Opinion of the Court:* <u>White</u>, *Kennedy, O'Connor, Rehnquist, Scalia. Dissenting opinions:* <u>Blackmun</u>, *Brennan, Marshall;* <u>Stevens</u>, *Blackmun, Brennan, Marshall.*

JUSTICE WHITE delivered the opinion of the Court.

Title VII of the Civil Rights Act of 1964 . . . makes it an unfair employment practice for an employer to discriminate against any individual with respect to hiring or the terms and condition of employment because of such individual's race, color, religion, sex, or national origin; or to limit, segregate or classify his employees in ways that would adversely affect any employee because of the employee's race, color, religion, sex, or national origin. *Griggs* v. *Duke Power Co.* . . . (1971) construed Title VII to proscribe "not only overt discrimination but also practices that are fair in form but discriminatory in practice." Under this basis for liability, which is known as the "disparate impact" theory and which is involved in this case, a facially neutral employment practice may be deemed violative of Title VII without evidence of the employer's subjective intent to discriminate that is required in a "disparate treatment" case. . . .

In holding that respondents had made out a prima facie case of disparate impact, the court of appeals relied solely on respondents' statistics showing a high percentage of nonwhite workers in the cannery jobs and a low percentage of such workers in the noncannery positions. Although statistical proof can alone make out a prima facie case, . . . the Court of Appeals' ruling here misapprehends our precedents and the purposes of Title VII, and we therefore reverse. . . .

It is clear to us that the Court of Appeals' acceptance of the comparison between the racial composition of the cannery work force and that of the noncannery work force, as probative of a prima facie case of disparate impact in the selection of the latter group of workers, was flawed for several reasons. Most obviously, with respect to the skilled noncannery jobs at issue here, the cannery work force in no way reflected "the pool of *qualified* job applicants" or the "*qualified* population in the labor force." Measuring alleged discrimination in the selection of accountants, managers, boat captains, electricians, doctors, and engineers—and the long list of other "skilled" noncannery positions found to exist by the District Court . . . —by comparing the number of nonwhites occupying these jobs to the number of nonwhites filling cannery worker positions is nonsensical. If the absence of minorities holding such skilled positions is due to a dearth of qualified nonwhite applicants (for reasons that are not petitioners' fault), petitioners' selection methods or employment practices cannot be said to have had a "disparate impact" on nonwhites.

One example illustrates why this must be so. Respondents' own statistics concerning the noncannery work force at one of the canneries at issue here indicate that approximately 17% of the new hires for medical jobs, and 15% of the new hires for officer worker positions, were nonwhite. . . . If it were the case that less than 15–17% of the applicants for these jobs were nonwhite and that nonwhites made up a lower percentage of the relevant qualified labor market, it is hard to see how respondents . . . would have made out a prima facie case of disparate impact. Yet, under the Court of Appeals' theory, simply because nonwhites comprise 52% of the cannery workers at the cannery in question, . . . respondents would be successful in establishing a prima facie case of racial discrimination under Title VII.

Such a result cannot be squared with our cases or with the goals behind the statute. The Court of Appeals' theory, at the very least, would mean that any employer who had a segment of his work force that was—for some reason—racially imbalanced, could be haled into court and forced to engage in the expensive and time-consuming task of defending the "business necessity" of the methods used to select the other members of his work force. The only practicable option for many employers will be to adopt racial quotas, insuring that no portion of his work force deviates in racial composition from the other portions thereof; this is a result that Congress expressly rejected in drafting Title VII . . . The Court of Appeals' theory would "leave the employer little choice . . . but to engage in a subjective quota system of employment selection. This, of course, is far from the intent of Title VII."

The Court of Appeals also erred with respect to the unskilled noncannery positions. Racial imbalance in one segment of an employer's work force does not, without more, establish a prima facie case of disparate impact with respect to the selection of workers for the employer's other positions, even where workers for the different positions may have somewhat fungible skills (as is arguably the case for cannery and unskilled noncannery workers). As long as there are no barriers or practices deterring qualified nonwhites from applying for noncannery positions, if the percentage of selected applicants who are nonwhite is not significantly less than the percentage of qualified applicants who are nonwhite, the employer's selection mechanism probably does not operate with a disparate impact on minorities. Where this is the case, the percentage of nonwhite workers found in other positions in the employer's labor force is irrelevant to the question of a prima facie statistical case of disparate impact. As noted above, a contrary ruling on this point would almost inexorably lead to the use of numerical quotas in the workplace, a result that Congress and this Court have rejected repeatedly in the past.

Moreover, isolating the cannery workers as the potential "labor force" for unskilled noncannery positions is at once both too broad and too narrow in its focus. Too broad because the vast majority of these cannery workers did not seek jobs in unskilled noncannery positions; there is no showing that many of them would have done so even if none of the arguably "deterring" practices existed. Thus, the pool of cannery workers cannot be used as a surrogate for the class of qualified job applicants because it contains many persons who have not (and would not) be noncannery job applicants. Conversely, if respondents propose to use the cannery workers for comparison purposes because they represent the "qualified labor population" generally, the group is too narrow because there are obviously many qualified persons in the labor market for noncannery jobs who are not cannery workers. . . .

Consequently, we reverse the Court of Appeals' ruling that a comparison between the percentage of cannery workers who are nonwhite and the percentage of noncannery workers who are nonwhite makes out a prima facie case of disparate impact. Of course, this leaves unresolved whether the record made in the District Court will support a conclusion that a prima facie case of disparate impact has been established on some basis other than the racial disparity between cannery and noncannery workers. This is an issue that the Court of Appeals or the District Court should address in the first instance. . . . Because we remand for further proceedings, however, on whether a prima facie case of disparate impact has been made in defensible fashion in this case, we address two other challenges petitioners have made to the decision of the Court of Appeals. . . .

First is the question of causation in a disparate-impact case. . . .

Even if on remand respondents can show that nonwhites are underrepresented in the at-issue jobs . . . this alone *will not* suffice to make out a prima facie case of disparate impact. Respondents will also have to demonstrate that the disparity they complain of is the result of one or more of the employment practices that they are attacking here, specifically showing that each challenged practice has a significantly disparate impact on employment opportunities for whites and nonwhites. To hold otherwise would result in employers being potentially liable for "the myriad of innocent causes that may lead to statistical imbalances in the composition of their work forces." . . .

Some will complain that this specific causation requirement is unduly burdensome on Title VII plaintiffs. But liberal civil discovery rules give plaintiffs broad access to employers' records in an effort to document their claims. . . .

If, on remand, respondents meet the proof burdens outlined above, and establish a prima facie case of disparate impact with respect to any of petitioners' employment practices, the case will shift to any business justification petitioners offer for their use of these practices. . . .

In this phase, the employer carries the burden of producing evidence of a business justification for his employment practice. The burden of persuasion, however, remains with the disparate-impact plaintiff. . . . "[T]he ultimate burden of proving that discrimination against a protected group has been caused by a specific employment practice remains with the plaintiff *at all times.*" . . . This rule conforms with the usual method for allocating persuasion and production burdens in the federal courts, . . . and more specifically, it conforms to the rule in disparate treatment cases

that the plaintiff bears the burden of disproving an employer's assertion that the adverse employment action or practice was based solely on a legitimate neutral consideration. . . .

The persuasion burden here must remain with the plaintiff, for it is he who must prove that it was "because of such individual's race, color," etc., that he was denied a desired employment opportunity. . . .

For the reasons given above, the judgment of the Court of Appeals is reversed, and the case is remanded for further proceedings consistent with this opinion.

JUSTICE BLACKMUN, with whom JUSTICE BRENNAN and JUSTICE MARSHALL join, dissenting. . . .

This industry long has been characterized by a taste for discrimination of the old-fashioned sort: a preference for hiring nonwhites to fill its lowest-level positions, on the condition that they stay there. The majority's legal rulings essentially immunize these practices from attack under a Title VII disparate-impact analysis.

Sadly, this comes as no surprise. One wonders whether the majority still believes that race discrimination—or, more accurately, race discrimination against nonwhites—is a problem in our society, or even remembers that it ever was.

JUSTICE STEVENS, with whom JUSTICE BRENNAN, JUSTICE MARSHALL, and JUSTICE BLACKMUN join, dissenting.

Fully 18 years ago, this Court unanimously held that Title VII of the Civil Rights Act of 1964 prohibits employment practices that have discriminatory effects as well as those that are intended to discriminate. *Griggs* v. *Duke Power Co.* . . . Federal courts and agencies consistently have enforced that interpretation, thus promoting our national goal of eliminating barriers that define economic opportunity not by aptitude and ability but by race, color, national origin, and other traits that are easily identified but utterly irrelevant to one's qualification for a particular job. Regrettably, the Court retreats from these efforts in its review of an interlocutory judgment respecting the "peculiar facts" of this lawsuit. Turning a blind eye to the meaning and purpose of Title VII, the majority's opinion perfunctorily rejects a longstanding rule of law and underestimates the probative value of evidence of a racially stratified work force. I cannot join this latest sojourn into judicial activism. . . .

The majority's opinion begins with recognition of the settled rule that that "a facially neutral employment practice may be deemed violative of Title VII without evidence of the employer's subjective intent to discriminate that is required in a 'disparate treatment' case." It then departs from the body of law engendered by this disparate impact theory, reformulating the order of proof and the weight of the parties' burdens. Why the Court undertakes these unwise changes in elementary and eminently fair rules is a mystery to me.

I respectfully dissent.

The Civil Rights Act of 1991
P.L. 102–166

In *Wards Cove Packing Co.* v. *Atonio* (1989), a five-member Court majority implicitly overturned its earlier interpretation of Title VII of the 1964 Civil Rights Act in *Griggs* v. *Duke Power Co.* (1971) and held that the burden of proving that a defendant company's employment practice discriminates against a protected group always remains with the plaintiff and does not shift to the defendant. In this act, Congress rejects the Court's holding in *Wards Cove* and places the burden of proving that its employment practices do not discriminate squarely on the defendant.

SECTION 1. SHORT TITLE

This Act may be cited as the "Civil Rights Act of 1991."

SEC. 2. FINDINGS

The Congress finds that—

(1) additional remedies under Federal law are needed to deter unlawful harassment and intentional discrimination in the workplace;

(2) the decision of the Supreme Court in *Wards Cove Packing Co.* v. *Atonio*, 490 U.S. 642 (1989) has weakened the scope and effectiveness of Federal civil rights protections; and

(3) legislation is necessary to provide additional protections against unlawful discrimination in employment.

SEC. 3. PURPOSES

The purposes of this Act are—

(1) to provide appropriate remedies for intentional discrimination and unlawful harassment in the workplace;

(2) to codify the concepts of "business necessity" and "job related" enunciated by the Supreme Court in *Griggs* v. *Duke Power Co.*, 401 U.S. 424 (1971), and in the other Supreme Court decisions prior to *Wards Cove Packing Co.* v. *Atonio*, 490 U.S. 642 (1989);

(3) to confirm statutory authority and provide statutory guidelines for the adjudication of disparate impact suits under title VII of the Civil Rights Act of 1964 (42 U.S.C. 2000e et seq.); and

(4) to respond to recent decisions of the Supreme Court by expanding the scope of relevant civil rights statutes in order to provide adequate protection to victims of discrimination.

SEC. 104. DEFINITIONS

Section 701 of the Civil Rights Act of 1964 (42 U.S.C. 2000e) is amended by adding at the end the following new subsections:

"(l) The term 'complaining party' means the Commission, the Attorney General, or a person who may bring an action or proceeding under this title.

"(m) The term 'demonstrates' means meets the burdens of production and persuasion.

"(n) The term 'respondent' means an employer, employment agency, labor organization, joint labor-management committee controlling apprenticeship or other training or retraining program, including an on-the-job training program, or Federal entity subject to section 717."

SEC. 105. BURDEN OF PROOF IN DISPARATE IMPACT CASES

(a) Section 703 of the Civil Rights Act of 1964 (42 U.S.C. 2000e-2) is amended by adding at the end the following new subsection:

"(k)(1)(A) An unlawful employment practice based on disparate impact is established under this title only if—

"(i) a complaining party demonstrates that a respondent uses a particular employment practice that causes a disparate impact on the basis of race, color, religion, sex, or national origin and the respondent fails to demonstrate that the challenged practice is job related for the position in question and consistent with business necessity; or

"(ii) the complaining party makes the demonstration described in subparagraph (C) with respect to an alternative employment practice and the respondent refuses to adopt such alternative employment practice.

"(B)(i) With respect to demonstrating that a particular employment practice causes a disparate impact as described in subparagraph (A)(i), the complaining party shall demonstrate that each particular challenged employment practice causes a disparate impact, except that if the complaining party can demonstrate to the court that the elements of a respondent's decision-making process are not capable of separation for analysis, the decision-making process may be analyzed as one employment practice.

"(ii) If the respondent demonstrates that a specific employment practice does not cause the disparate impact, the respondent shall not be required to demonstrate that such practice is required by business necessity.

"(C) The demonstration referred to by subparagraph (A)(ii) shall be in accordance with the law as it existed on June 4, 1989 [the date of *Wards Cove*], with respect to the concept of 'alternative employment practice.'"

★

9

SUBSTANTIVE EQUAL PROTECTION

As Chapter 8 indicated, the Supreme Court initially viewed the Equal Protection Clause simply as a means for prohibiting racial discrimination. In keeping with this understanding, it customarily rejected invitations by counsel to employ the clause to strike down economic and social regulations that introduced distinctions among persons (i.e., that discriminated) on a nonracial basis. Even at the height of the *Lochner* era, when the justices were so willing to rely on the Due Process Clause to invalidate what were thought to be unduly restrictive (and hence, arbitrary and capricious) regulations, they flatly refused to consider using the Equal Protection Clause for matters unrelated to race. Clearly stating the Court's contempt for such equal protection claims, Justice Oliver Wendell Holmes described them in *Buck* v. *Bell* (1927) as "the usual last resort of constitutional arguments."

However, the wording of the Equal Protection Clause guarantees equal protection of the laws to *all persons,* not merely to black persons or ex-slaves. In this respect, it advances ends identical to those advanced by the original Constitution: namely, the empowerment and employment of a powerful national government capable of protecting individual rights and liberties from the tyrannical tendencies of the majority while, in the words of *The Federalist,* "preserving the spirit and form of popular government."[1] On its face, then, the Equal Protection Clause mandates equality under the law for all persons, regardless of race, gender, socioeconomic condition, nationality, age, place or duration of residence, etc. Judicial acknowledgment of this fact came under the Warren Court (1953–1969), which for the first time systematically installed the clause as governing in cases involving types of unequal treatment wholly unrelated to traditional forms of racial discrimination. As a result of its seminal decisions, the judiciary has been called on to determine whether the Equal Protection Clause has been violated by state laws and practices that, *inter alia*, discriminated in favor of (rather than against) blacks; imposed burdens on aliens and illegitimate children; treated the sexes differently; or impinged on the rights to interstate travel, welfare assistance, educational opportunity, and exercise of the franchise.

This increased receptivity to a wide range of equal protection challenges has posed new and difficult questions for the Court. So long as it understood the clause to prohibit only racial classifications, problems of interpretation remained manageable: the justices had only to look at the law or practice in question, determine whether it treated the races differently, and rule accordingly. Once the Court began employing the clause to evaluate other forms of unequal treatment, however, the problems grew in number and difficulty and became virtually identical to the problems the Court faced in the area of substantive due process. The primary question facing the Court then became, does equal protection of the laws prohibit all legal categories or classifications? In other words, must all people be treated identically with respect to all matters? Because virtually all laws and regulations create legal categories, the Court understandably refused to respond affirmatively to these questions; to do so would be to render government wholly inoperable. Instead, it sought to interpret the Equal Protection Clause in such a way as to permit what it considered to be legitimate classifications— which led inevitably to the question of what constitutes a legitimate classification.

As the justices grappled with these and other problems, they found it necessary to develop standards or criteria for interpreting the Equal Protection Clause and for determining whether the laws and practices in question passed constitutional muster. This chapter spells out these standards, examines how and where they have been employed, and identifies the many criticisms that have been leveled against them.

THE TWO-TIER APPROACH

As an aid in determining whether particular classifications are legitimate and hence permissible under the Equal Protection Clause, the Court gradually developed what has been commonly called the two-tier approach. The tiers represent the level of scrutiny that the Court will give to the classification under review. The relatively lenient standard imposed on the lower tier usually is called the rational basis test. The upper tier imposes a much more stringent standard, referred to as the compelling-state-interest test or the strict scrutiny standard.

Most statutory categorizations or classifications have been reviewed under the rational basis test, which is governed by the operation of four general principles:

1. The Equal Protection Clause not only does not prohibit the state from creating legal categories but also allows a great deal of discretion in this regard; such categories, therefore, should be invalidated only when they lack any reasonable basis and hence are purely arbitrary.
2. A classification having some reasonable basis does not offend against the Equal Protection Clause merely because it is not made with mathematical nicety or because in practice it results in some inequality.
3. When a classification in the law is called into question, it should not be set aside if any state of facts can be conceived to justify it, and the existence of that state of facts at the time the law was enacted must be assumed.
4. The party challenging the classification must carry the burden of showing that it does not rest on any reasonable basis.

Some kinds of classifications have had to satisfy much more stringent standards. Under the two-tier system, the Court has subjected to strict scrutiny all laws that created "suspect classifications" or that impinged upon "fundamental rights" and has upheld them only if the state was able to show that they advanced a compelling governmental interest.

Whenever suspect classifications or fundamental rights have been involved, the Court has reversed the normal presumption of constitutionality, in that it has demanded that the state establish a compelling need for these statutory discriminations. And even if such a need is demonstrated, the state must show that no less-restrictive alternatives exist.[2] This is a stringent standard indeed, and it has been applied both to the ends that the state is seeking and the means it employs to achieve those ends. Initially, this test was appropriately characterized by Professor Gerald Gunther as " 'strict' in theory and fatal in practice."[3] As Chief Justice Burger noted in his dissent in *Dunn* v. *Blumstein* (1972), "To challenge [state policies] by the 'compelling state interest' standard is to condemn them all. So far as I am aware, no state law has ever satisfied this seemingly insurmountable standard and I doubt that one ever will, for it demands nothing less than perfection." Over time, however, certain justices have come to argue that a state has a compelling interest in diversifying a student body—Justice Powell in *Regents of the University of California* v. *Bakke* (1978)—or in remedying "unlawful treatment of racial or ethnic groups subject to discrimination" provided the means chosen are narrowly tailored, i.e., "specifically and narrowly framed to accomplish that purpose"—*Wygant* v. *Jackson Board of Education* (1986). This relaxation of what strict scrutiny demands prompted Justice O'Connor in *Adarand Constructors, Inc.* v. *Pena* (1995) to declare: "[W]e wish to dispel the notion that strict scrutiny is 'strict in theory, but fatal in fact.' The unhappy persistence of both the practice and the lingering effects of racial discrimination against minority groups in this country is an unfortunate reality, and government is not disqualified from acting in response to it."

THE DEVELOPMENT OF AN INTERMEDIATE LEVEL OF REVIEW

The two-tier approach has caused the Court a number of problems. To begin with, under this approach, the Court has experienced great difficulty in determining which classifications to label suspect. There has been complete agreement that blacks constitute a suspect class; the clear intention of the framers of the Fourteenth Amendment was to have blacks considered as such. Until recently, there also was general agreement that racial classifications of any kind should be considered formally suspect and hence should be subject to scrutiny under the compelling-state-interest test. That agreement, however, largely broke up on the shoals of the controversy surrounding ameliorative racial preference. Similar controversies have also raged over whether other classifications are suspect, and if so, why. The Court attempted to provide a framework for analyzing these questions when it declared in *Johnson* v. *Robinson* (1974) that a classification was suspect if based on "an immutable characteristic determined solely by the accident of birth, or a class saddled with such disabilities, or subjected to such a history of purposeful unequal treatment, or relegated to such political powerlessness as to command extraordinary protection from the majoritarian political process." These words, however, have failed to bind the Court together, and it has split badly when it has addressed equal protection challenges to classifications based on alienage (the condition of being an alien), illegitimacy, age, gender, and indigency.

A second difficulty with the two-tier approach has been that it has provided the Court with very little guidance as to the definition of a fundamental right. Over time, the Court has come to recognize as fundamental the right of free speech, the right of freedom of religion, the right of freedom of association, the right of personal privacy, the right to vote, the right to procreate, the right to marry, and the right to travel from state to state. At the same time, it has refused to recognize as fundamental interests that many people would regard as equally important, including the rights to education, shelter, and food. The Court has defended its position by insisting that only those rights explicitly or implicitly guaranteed in the Constitution are fundamental, and that nothing in the Constitution guarantees that the government will provide individuals with an education, a house, or welfare benefits. But as Justice Thurgood Marshall mused in his dissent in *San Antonio* v. *Rodriguez*, "I would like to know where the Constitution guarantees the right to procreate, or the right to vote in state elections, or the right to appeal a criminal conviction. These are instances in which, due to the importance of the interests at stake, the Court has displayed a strong concern with the existence of discriminatory state treatment. But, the Court has never said or indicated that these are interests which independently enjoy full-blown constitutional protection." Marshall's critique could be underscored with other examples, but his point is well taken. In fact the Court's method of determining fundamental rights appears to be of greater utility in providing the Court with an explanation for why it has refused to bestow fundamental status on a particular right than in assisting it in ascertaining what rights are fundamental. This approach, in Justice William Rehnquist's words in *Rostker* v. *Goldberg* (1981), "all too readily [lends itself to] facile abstractions used to justify a result."

Of the several major problems involved in the two-tier approach, perhaps the most serious has been its rigid, all-or-nothing character. The lenient rational basis test almost never has resulted in the invalidation of legislation, whereas the stringent compelling-state-interest standard almost invariably has led to invalidation. Between these two widely varying levels of scrutiny, there is no room for rights and classes of intermediate importance. As Justice Thurgood Marshall complained in his dissent in *Massachusetts Board of Retirement* v. *Murgia* (1976), "All interests not fundamental and all classes not suspect are not the same; and it is time for the Court to drop the pretense that, for purposes of the Equal Protection Clause, they are." So long as the Court remained committed to the two-tier approach, however, that pretense could not be dropped, and the only critical decision facing the Court was, as Justice Marshall further remonstrated, "whether strict scrutiny should be invoked at all."

In place of this simplistic and rigid approach, Justice Marshall argued, in both *Murgia* and *San Antonio* v. *Rodriguez* (1973), for a "more sophisticated" approach in which "concentration is placed upon the character of the classification in question, the relative importance to the individuals in the class discriminated against of the governmental benefits they do not receive, and the asserted state interests in support of the classification." Following Justice Marshall's lead but rejecting his precise formulation, a majority of the Court has, over time, come to acknowledge as legitimate and to employ an intermediate level of scrutiny. Under this "middle-tier" approach, the Court has held that the classification in question must "serve important governmental objectives" and be "substantially related to the achievement of those objectives." This standard is intermediate with respect both to ends and means. As Professor Gunther has observed: "Where ends must be 'compelling' to survive strict scrutiny and merely 'legitimate' under the 'old' mode, 'important' objectives are required here, and where means must be 'necessary' under the 'new' equal protection, and merely 'rationally related' under the 'old' equal protection, they must be 'substantially related' to survive the 'intermediate' level of review."[4]

The exact meaning of this new intermediate level of review, however, remains very much in doubt. To begin with, the justices do not agree when the use of this "middle-tier" approach is justified. Some would limit it to classifications based on gender as in *United States* v. *Virginia* (1996) or illegitimacy as in *Clark* v. *Jeter* (1988); others (Justice Brennan in *Regents of the University of California* v. *Bakke* [1978], for instance) would extend it as well to cases involving ameliorative racial preference. This has prompted Justice Scalia to quip: "We have not established criterion for 'intermediate scrutiny' . . . , but essentially apply it when it seems like a good idea to load the dice." Additionally, some justices, through imprecision or an intentional desire to hold together fragile Court majorities, have all but obliterated the distinctions between the tiers. Justice Brennan's majority opinion in *Plyler* v. *Doe* (1982) is a case in point, as it totally blurred the distinctions between the lower and middle tiers. In this 5–4 decision, the Court invalidated on equal protection grounds a Texas statute that withheld state funds from local school districts for the education of children who were illegal aliens and that further authorized the local school districts to deny enrollment to such children. Mixing language associated with different levels of review, Justice Brennan declared that a state law or practice "can hardly be considered rational unless it furthers some substantial goal of the State." Justice Ginsburg's opinion in *United States* v. *Virginia* is another. By holding that the "proffered justification" must be "exceedingly persuasive," that it "must be genuine, not hypothesized or invented *post hoc* in response to litigation," and that it "must not rely on overbroad generalizations about the different talents, capacities, or preferences of males and females," Justice Ginsburg so redefined intermediate scrutiny that it became, as Justice Scalia complained in his dissent, "indistinguishable from strict scrutiny."

CLASSIFICATIONS WARRANTING HEIGHTENED SCRUTINY

Affirmative Action

Affirmative action raises two distinct and difficult questions that highlight the difficulties attending the Court's approach to equal protection analysis: (1) Should racial classifications that burden whites be viewed as suspect? (2) Should classifications employed for the asserted purpose of aiding a minority (typically blacks) be subjected to the strict scrutiny to which invidious classifications have been subjected? The judiciary has split badly on both of these questions.

Some justices reject the contention that discrimination against whites should be subjected to the same stringent review under the Fourteenth Amendment used in cases of discrimination against blacks. They argue that whites as a class have none of the "traditional indicia of suspectness." As a class, that is to say, whites have not been subjected to historical and pervasive discriminations and deprivations, have not been stigmatized and set apart, and have not been relegated to a position of political powerlessness. Relying on that portion of *Plessy* that *Brown* v. *Board of Education* (1954) did not repudiate, and on Chief Justice Warren's contention in *Brown* that the Equal Protection Clause merely proscribes classifications that "generate a feeling of inferiority" (i.e., that imply prejudice), advocates of this position have concluded that the clause offers whites no particular protections because discrimination in favor of blacks will not lead whites to assume that they are inferior. The most forceful defenders of this position have been Justice Thurgood Marshall in his dissent in *Croson* and Justice William Brennan in his opinions in *Bakke* and *Metro Broadcasting* v. *Federal Communications Commission* (1990). In *Metro Broadcasting*, Justice Brennan held in a 5–4 decision that benign race-conscious measures mandated by Congress, even though not remedial in the sense of being designed to compensate victims of past governmental or societal discrimination, are permissible under the equal protection component of the Fifth Amendment's Due Process Clause. He concluded, therefore, that the Federal Communication Commission's policy of giving preference to minority bids in competitive proceedings for new broadcast licenses and permitting limited categories of licenses to be transferred to minority-controlled firms in "distress sales" are mandated by Congress, serve an important government interest in promoting broadcasting diversity, are substantially related to the achievement of that objective, and do not violate the Fifth Amendment's equal protection component.

Other justices insist that discriminations against whites are as suspect as discriminations against blacks. This position is consistent with the First Justice Harlan's famous dictum, in his dissent in *Plessy* v. *Ferguson* (1896), that " 'the Constitution is color-blind and neither knows nor tolerates classes among citizens.' " That position was taken by the California Supreme Court in *Bakke* v. *Regents of the University of California* (1976), Justice Powell (although he also used "middle-tier" language) in *Regents of the University of California* v. *Bakke* (1978), and most recently by a majority of the Supreme Court in *Richmond* v. *Croson* (1989) and *Adarand Constructors, Inc.* v. *Pena* (1995).

In *Croson,* the Court struck down Richmond's minority set-aside program requiring that 30 percent of the total dollar amount of all city contracts go to minority business enterprises. Justice Sandra Day O'Connor declared that "the standard of review under the Equal Protection Clause is not dependent on the race of those burdened or benefited by a particular classification." For the *Croson* majority, "racial classifications are suspect," regardless of the race of those discriminated against or the reason for the discrimination. In fact, Justice Scalia went so far in his concurrence as to brand all racial classifications impermissible except for those undertaken in response to "a social emergency rising to the level of imminent danger to life or limb—for example, a prison race riot, requiring temporary segregation of inmates." For Scalia, any lesser justification, including the need to ameliorate the effects of past discrimination, is insufficient, for "the difficulty of overcoming the effects of past discrimination is as nothing compared with the difficulty of eradicating from our society the source of those effects, which is the tendency—fatal to a nation such as ours—to classify and judge men and women on the basis of their country of origin or the color of their skin. A solution to the first problem that aggravates the second is no solution at all."

In *Adarand,* the Court applied the same principles announced in *Croson* to the federal government. Justice O'Connor held for the majority that a federal subcontractor compensation clause designed to provide the prime contractor of a federal highway project with a financial incentive to hire disadvantaged business enterprises was suspect and could be sustained only if it passed the strict scrutiny test. In so, doing, she and her fellow colleagues in the majority expressly overturned *Metro Broadcasting* and its use of intermediate scrutiny as the standard of review for Congressionally mandated ameliorative racial preference.

Intimately related to the dispute over whites as a suspect class has been the question of whether classifications employed for the asserted purpose of aiding minorities should be subjected to the same strict-scrutiny standard as invidious classifications. Justices who have not viewed whites as a suspect class generally have refused to invoke the strict-scrutiny standard in reviewing ameliorative-racial-preference cases.[5] Justice Brennan's opinion in *Bakke* reflected this point of view. The use of the compelling-state-interest test, he argued, would result in a denial of the aid that the classification was intended to provide. On the other hand, "because of the significant risk that racial classifications established for ostensibly benign purposes can be misused, causing effects not unlike that created by invidious classifications" (e.g., reinforcement of racial stereotypes), he deemed it inappropriate to inquire only whether there was any conceivable basis on which to sustain such a classification. Instead, he argued, that such ameliorative racial preference be upheld if it could be shown that it served "an important and articulated purpose." Such a finding, he concluded, would require the same intermediate level of review appropriate in gender-based classifications—the classification in question "must serve important governmental objectives and be substantially related to the achievement of those objectives." Justice Brennan's opinion in *Metro Broadcasting* employed the same logic and relied on the same intermediate level of review.

By contrast, those justices who have viewed whites as a suspect class invariably have invoked the strict-scrutiny standard; and because classifications intended to aid blacks almost inevitably come at the expense of whites, they typically have invalidated the offending classification as failing to advance a compelling state interest.[6] One exception to this generalization is Justice Powell. In his opinion in *Bakke*, he sustained the use of race in admissions decisions on the ground that it served the state's compelling interest in achieving a diverse student body. Powell provided an interesting "swing vote" in that case. Four justices in *Bakke* held that both racial quotas and racial preferences in admissions violated the Civil Rights Act of 1964 (as a consequence, they never reached the constitutional question); four justices held that both racial quotas and racial preferences in admissions were sustainable under intermediate scrutiny and were permitted under the Civil Rights Act and the Fourteenth Amendment; and Justice Powell stood alone. Using the compelling-state-interest test, he condemned racial quotas for their "disregard of individual rights" but upheld racial preferences (at least in those admissions programs that treated race as "a plus"—as "simply one element to be weighed fairly against others elements") because "the attainment of a diverse student body clearly is a constitutionally permissible goal for an institution of higher education." Justice Powell rejected the reasoning of both camps, yet he agreed with some of each camp's conclusions; he therefore ended up writing the judgment of the Court, and for twenty years, his opinion has carried great weight. But, as Judge Jerry E. Smith of the Fifth Circuit Court of Appeals made clear in *Hopwood* v. *State of Texas* (1996), in which he held unconstitutional the use of racial preferences in admissions at the University of Texas Law School, those who would rely on Justice Powell's opinion in *Bakke* to defend the use of race or ethnicity to achieve a diverse student body must understand that "Justice Powell's view is not binding precedent on this issue." As Judge Smith noted, while Justice Powell "announced the judgment, no other Justice joined in that part of the opinion discussing the diversity rationale. In *Bakke,* the word 'diversity' is mentioned nowhere except in Justice Powell's single-Justice opinion. In fact, the four-Justice opinion, which would have upheld the special admissions program under intermediate scrutiny, implicitly rejected Justice Powell's position. ('We also agree with Mr. Justice Powell that a plan like the 'Harvard' plan . . . is constitutional under our approach, at least so long as the use of race to achieve an integrated student body is necessitated by the lingering effects of past discrimination.') Thus, only one Justice concluded that race could be used solely for the reason of obtaining a heterogenous student body." The Supreme Court declined the opportunity to disassociate itself from Judge Smith's comments when it refused to hear the University of Texas's appeal.

Alienage

The Court's responses to statutory classifications that deprive aliens of rights enjoyed by citizens have highlighted the problems confronting the justices in consistently applying strict-scrutiny standards to equal protection challenges. In *Graham* v. *Richardson* (1971) the Court held that aliens were a suspect class and that restrictions on aliens were to be treated by the Court with "heightened judicial solicitude." With *Graham* as precedent and employing the compelling-state-interest test, the justices subsequently voided a Connecticut law denying aliens the right to practice law, *In re Griffiths* (1973); a New York statute barring aliens from holding positions in the competitive class of the state civil service, *Sugarman* v. *Dougall* (1973); a regulation of the Civil Service Commission limiting employment in the U.S. competitive civil service to citizens of the United States, *Hampton* v. *Wong* (1976); and a New York law denying resident aliens financial aid for higher education unless they applied for U.S. citizenship, *Nyquist* v. *Mauclet* (1977). In *Foley* v. *Connelie* (1978), however, the Court sustained a New York law barring aliens from the state police force. And in *Ambach* v. *Norwick* (1979) it upheld a New York statute forbidding certification as a public school teacher to any person who was not a citizen, unless that person had manifested an intention to apply for citizenship. In both cases, the Court insisted that not all limitations on aliens were suspect and employed the rational basis test to sustain the challenged classifications.

The Court argued in *Foley* and *Ambach* that some state functions, such as serving as a state trooper and teaching in the public schools, are so bound up with the operation of the state as a governmental entity as to permit the exclusion of all persons who have not become part of the process of self-government. "A discussion of the police function is essentially a description of one of the basic functions of government, especially in a complex modern society where police presence is pervasive," Chief Justice Burger wrote in *Foley*. Justice Powell in *Ambach* saw the teachers as performing an equally important and central function: "Public education, like the police function, 'fulfills a most fundamental obligation of government to its constituency.' The importance of public schools in the preparation of individuals for participation as citizens, and in the preservation of the values on which our society rests, long has been recognized by our decisions."

In recognizing this rule for governmental functions as an exception to the strict-scrutiny standard generally applicable to classifications based on alienage, the Court followed important principles inherent in the Constitution. The distinction between citizens and aliens, though ordinarily irrelevant to private activity, is fundamental to the definition and government of a state, and the constitutional references to such a distinction indicate that the status of citizenship was meant to have significance in the structure of our government. Because of this special significance, the Court ruled in *Foley* and *Ambach*, governmental entities, when exercising the functions of government, must have wide latitude in limiting the participation of aliens. The *Foley* and *Ambach* rulings, however, are difficult to reconcile with the Court's earlier holdings, especially *In re Griffiths*. If a state may bar aliens from law enforcement or teaching because those tasks go to the heart of representative government, it is difficult to understand why a state may not also bar aliens from practicing law. Lawyers after all, serve as officers of the court and participate directly in the formulation, execution, and review of broad public policy. The Court, however, has never overturned *In re Griffiths* nor reconciled its apparently contradictory holdings on the exact status of alienage as a suspect classification.

Illegitimacy

The Court's course in reviewing classifications based on illegitimacy has been even more wavering than its course in reviewing classifications based on alienage. Although it has never labeled illegitimacy a suspect classification, the Court has exercised a degree of heightened scrutiny in most cases involving illegitimacy classifications, which have been struck down with some frequency. Nowhere in its rulings, however, has the Court explained precisely what degree of heightened scrutiny is warranted, and why.

The Court's first encounter with illegitimacy classifications under the two-tier approach came in *Levy* v. *Louisiana* (1968), in which it held that a law that denied unacknowledged illegitimate children the right to recover damages for the wrongful death of their mothers violated the Equal Protection Clause. The exact reason for the law's unconstitutionality, however, was left in doubt, as Justice Douglas's majority opinion hinted at both the rational basis test and the compelling-state-interest standard. Three years later, in *Labine* v. *Vin-*

cent (1971), the Court withdrew from the heightened scrutiny suggested in *Levy* and upheld an intestate succession provision that suboridinated the rights of acknowledged illegitimate children to those of the parent's other relatives. Employing the rational basis test, the *Labine* majority argued that absent an express constitutional guarantee, "it is for the legislature, not this Court, to select from among possible laws." Barely one year later, in *Weber* v. *Aetna Casualty and Surety Company* (1972), the Court abandoned what it had said in *Labine* and returned to its formulations in *Levy* by holding that the claims of dependent unacknowledged illegitimate children to death benefits under a workmen's compensation law could not be subordinated to the claims of legitimate children.

Such vacillation continued in *Mathews* v. *Lucas* (1976) and *Trimble* v. *Gordon* (1977). *Lucas* sustained death-benefits provisions of the Social Security Act that presumed legitimate children to have been dependent on their fathers but required proof of dependency on the part of illegitimate children. In *Trimble,* on the other hand, the Court struck down a provision of the Illinois law governing intestate succession that barred illegitimate children from inheriting from their fathers.

Lucas and *Trimble* illustrate the Court's uneasy search for an articulable and consistently applicable standard of review for illegitimacy classifications. Both cases rejected the strict-scrutiny standard while indicating that the rational basis test was only a minimum criterion and that sometimes the Court "requires more." Justice O'Connor's unanimous opinion in *Clark* v. Jeter (1988) identified that something more as the "intermediate" level of review, which the Court then used to conclude that Pennsylvania's six-year statute of limitations for support actions on behalf of illegitimate children "does not withstand heightened scrutiny."

Age

In reviewing classifications based on age, the Court consistently has adopted a deferential posture and employed the rational basis test. In *Massachusetts Board of Retirement* v. *Murgia* (1976) the Court upheld a state law mandating that state police officers retire at age fifty. Three years later, in *Vance* v. *Bradley* (1979), it rejected an equal protection challenge to a federal law requiring Foreign Service personnel to retire at age sixty. The Court has refused to recognize the aged as a suspect class, noting in *Murgia* that old age is a universal condition and that "even if the statute could be said to impose a penalty upon a class defined as the aged, it would not impose a distinction sufficiently akin to those classifications that we have found suspect to call for strict judicial scrutiny." Both *Murgia* and *Vance* elicited strongly worded dissents from Justice Marshall, who urged the adoption of a more flexible approach in which the Court would review the importance of the governmental benefits denied, the character of the class, and the asserted state interests.

Mental Retardation

In *City of Cleburne, Texas* v. *Cleburne Living Center* (1985), the Supreme Court in a 6–3 decision refused to apply a "heightened" level of scrutiny to legislation affecting the mentally retarded. Cleburne Living Center had sought to lease a building for the operation of a group home for the mentally retarded; when it was denied a special use permit to do so by the city (which classified the group home under its zoning ordinance as a "hospital for the feebleminded"), it brought suit alleging that the zoning ordinance in question was unconstitutional, both on its face and as applied. The federal district court rejected its contentions, but the Court of Appeals for the Fifth Circuit reversed, holding that mental retardation was a "quasi-suspect" classification and that under a "heightened scrutiny equal protection test," the ordinance was unconstitutional, for it did not substantially further an important governmental purpose. Justice White spoke for the Court when he held that where individuals in a group affected by a statute or ordinance have distinguishing characteristics relevant to interests a state has the authority to implement, the Equal Protection Clause requires only that the classification drawn by the statute or ordinance be rationally related to a legitimate government interest. That requirement was met in the case; since mentally retarded persons have a reduced ability to cope with and function in the everyday world, they are in fact different from other persons, and the state's interest in dealing with and providing for them is legitimate. The Court, nonetheless, struck down Cleburne's zoning ordinance. Justice White found that requiring a permit in this case rested on "an irrational prejudice against the mentally retarded." Justice Marshall concurred in the Court's judgment but objected to its refusal to bring a heightened level of scrutiny to bear on legislation affecting the rights of the mentally retarded.

Gender-Based Classifications

The problems encountered by the Court in reviewing gender-based classifications clearly exposed the deficiencies of the two-tier approach and were the impetus for the development of the intermediate level of scrutiny.

The Court's traditional stance toward sex discrimination claims was exhibited in *Goesaert* v. *Cleary* (1948) when it rejected an attack on a Michigan law that provided that no woman could obtain a bartender's license unless she was "the wife or daughter of the male owner" of a licensed liquor establishment. A radical break with that tradition occurred in 1971, when the Court in *Reed* v. *Reed* struck down a provision of Idaho's probate code that gave preference to men over women as administrators of estates. Employing the rational basis test, Chief Justice Burger declared for a unanimous Court in *Reed* that the question before it was "whether a difference in sex of competing applicants for letters of administration bears a rational relationship to a state objective that is sought to be advanced by the operation of [the Idaho law]." Finding no such relationship, he branded the mandatory preference given to men over women as "the very kind of arbitrary legislative choice" forbidden by the Equal Protection Clause.

This apparent consensus that classifications based on sex were to be reviewed under the rational basis test lasted a scant two years. In *Frontiero* v. *Richardson* (1973), four members of the Court argued that "classifications based upon sex, like classifications based on race, alienage, and national origin, are inherently suspect." Justices Douglas, White, and Marshall joined Justice Brennan in applying the compelling-state-interest test to find unconstitutional a federal statute under which married servicemen automatically qualified for increased housing allowances and medical and dental benefits for their wives, whereas married servicewomen qualified for those fringe benefits only if their husbands were dependent on them for at least one-half of their support. Four other justices concurred in Brennan's judgment that the statute was unconstitutional but rejected his claim that sex is a suspect classification in favor of *Reed*'s rational basis test. Justice Powell's concurrence in *Frontiero* was especially interesting in that one of his principal reasons for refusing to view sex as a suspect classification was that the Equal Rights Amendment (ERA) had been approved by the Congress and submitted to the states for ratification. If ratified, the amendment would have made sex-based classifications suspect, and Justice Powell saw no reason or need to "preempt by judicial action a major political decision" then in process of resolution.

Had a fifth member joined Justices Brennan, Douglas, White, and Marshall in either *Frontiero* or a subsequent case, a majority of the Court would have been on record as declaring that sex was a suspect classification. Ratification of the ERA would have had the same result. In the absence of either of these developments, sex-based classifications have failed to achieve suspect status, although movement toward what Justice Brennan sought in *Frontiero* has occurred. In *Craig* v. *Boren* (1976), Brennan was able to prevail on his judicial brethren to heighten somewhat the review given to sex-based classifications. Without formally acknowledging that the Court was about to embrace a new intermediate level of review, he announced that "classifications by gender must serve important governmental objectives and must be substantially related to achievement of those objectives." Using this middle-tier test, he invalidated sections of an Oklahoma statute that allowed females to purchase 3.2 percent beer at age eighteen but prohibited males from doing so until age twenty-one. He found unpersuasive the state's contention that such legislation was the proper way to deal with "the pervasiveness of youthful participation in motor vehicle accidents following the imbibing of alcohol." Then, in *Mississippi University for Women* v. *Hogan* (1982), Justice O'Connor applied an intermediate level of scrutiny to sustain an equal protection challenge to Mississippi's policy of excluding men from MUW's School of Nursing. Interestingly, O'Connor never even mentioned *Craig* and, in fact, offered a different formulation of the middle tier: A governmental classification based on gender will be upheld, she insisted, only if the government meets the burden of showing a "legitimate" and "exceedingly persuasive justification" for the classification and demonstrating "the requisite direct, substantial relationship" between the governmental objective and the means it employs to achieve the objective. This MUW had failed to do, and the result was the perpetuation of "the stereotyped view of nursing as an exclusively woman's job."

In *United States* v. *Virginia* (1996), the Court employed intermediate review to find unconstitutional Virginia's policy of excluding women from Virginia Military Institute (VMI), a school whose mission was to produce "citizen-soldiers"—men prepared for leadership in civilian life and in military service. Justice Ginsburg's formulation of the "middle-tier" test was as follows: "The burden of justification is demanding and it rests entirely on the State. The State must show 'at least that the [challenged] classification serves 'important governmental objectives and that the discriminatory means employed' are 'substantially related to the achievement of those objectives.' The justification must be genuine, not hypothesized or invented *post hoc* in response to litigation. And it must not rely on overbroad generalizations about the different talents, capacities, or preferences of males and females."

Employing this intermediate level of review, the Court has, however, upheld a number of "benevolent" classifications that accord women preferential treatment. In every ruling of this type, the Court has based its decision on the argument that such treatment is a compensation for past economic discrimination. In *Kahn* v. *Shevin* (1974), for example, the Court sustained a Florida statute granting a $500 property tax exemption to widows but not to widowers. Justice Douglas wrote for the Court:

> There can be no dispute that the financial difficulties confronting the lone woman . . . exceed those facing the man. Whether from overt discrimination or from the socialization process of a male dominated culture, the job market is inhospitable to the woman seeking any but the lowest paid jobs. There are, of course, efforts under way to remedy this situation. . . . But firmly entrenched practices are resistant to such pressures. . . . We deal here with a state tax law reasonably designed to further the state policy of cushioning the financial impact of spousal loss upon the sex for whom that loss imposes a disproportionately heavy burden.

Similarly, in *Schlesinger* v. *Ballard* (1975) the Court sustained a sex classification in a congressional enactment providing for mandatory discharge of naval officers who, after designated periods of service, have failed to gain promotion. The service period was set at nine years for men and thirteen years for women. Ballard, a male officer who failed to receive promotion after nine years, challenged the statute. In sustaining it, the Court pointed out that female officers "because of restriction on their participation in combat . . . do not have equal opportunities for professional service equal to those of male line officers."[7]

Finally, in *Heckler* v. *Mathews* (1984), the Court upheld a temporary pension offset provision, applicable to nondependent men but not to similarly situated nondependent women, that required a reduction of spousal benefits by the amount of federal or state government pensions received by Social Security applicants. This provision temporarily revived a gender-based classification that the Court had invalidated earlier in *Califano* v. *Goldfarb* (1977), but, Justice Brennan insisted, it was "directly and substantially related to the important governmental interest of protecting individuals who planned their retirements in reasonable reliance on the law" invalidated in *Goldfarb*.

The Court has not upheld all "benevolent" classifications, however. Attempts to justify sex-based classifications as compensation for past discrimination against women have been rejected when the classifications involved have penalized women. Thus, in *Weinberger* v. *Wiesenfeld* (1975) the Court held void a provision of the Social Security Act that provided survivor's benefits for the widow of a deceased husband but not for the widower of a deceased wife. And in *Califano* v. *Goldfarb* (1977) it set aside a gender-based distinction in the Federal Old-Age, Survivors, and Disability Insurance Benefits program, under which a widow automatically received survivors' benefits based on the earnings of a deceased husband but a widower received benefits on the same basis only if he had been receiving at least one-half of his support from his deceased wife. In both cases, the Court rejected the government's claim that the provisions at issue were benevolent because they sought to compensate women beneficiaries as a group for the economic difficulties confronting women who sought to support themselves and their families. Instead, it found that the provisions discriminated against women in that their Social Security taxes produced less protection for their spouses than was produced by the taxes paid by men. The Court's 1979 decision in *Orr* v. *Orr* reinforced this approach to gender-based distinctions. Here the Court again employed the intermediate-scrutiny standard, this time to strike down an Alabama law authorizing the payment of alimony to wives but not to husbands. In his opinion for the Court, Justice Brennan stressed that "statutes purportedly designed to compensate for and ameliorate the effects of past discrimination must be carefully tailored," as benevolent gender classifications "carry the inherent risk of reinforcing stereotypes about the 'proper place' of women and their need for special protection." Brennan argued that the state's purposes could as well have been served "by a gender-neutral classification as by one that genderclassifies and therefore carries with it the baggage of sexual stereotypes."

It could be argued that *Wiesenfeld, Goldfarb,* and *Orr* also presented instances of discrimination against men. Although it was not made in those cases, this argument has been employed to challenge the constitutionality of various classifications, and the Court has responded inconsistently. In *Craig,* for example, it held that the Equal Protection Clause can be used to strike down statutory classifications that discriminate against men, at least where no claim of compensation on behalf of women is made to justify them. As Justice Brennan observed in a footnote, "*Kahn* v. *Shevin* and *Schlesinger* v. *Ballard,* upholding the use of gender-based classifications, rested upon the Court's perception of the laudatory purposes of those laws as remedying disadvantageous conditions suffered by women in economic and military life. Needless to say, in this case Oklahoma does not suggest that the age-sex differential was enacted to insure the availability of 3.2 percent beer for women as compensation for previous deprivations." In *Michael M.* v. *Sonoma County Superior Court* (1981), however, the Court upheld a California statutory rape statute that made it a criminal offense to have sexual intercourse with a female under the age of eighteen. It rejected the petitioner's gender-discrimination challenge that the law was unconstitutional because it did not make it illegal to have sexual intercourse with a male under the age of eighteen. In his opinion announcing the judgment of the Court, Justice Rehnquist declared that the operative standard for reviewing the law in question was "the principle that a legislature may not make overbroad generalizations based on sex which are entirely unrelated to any differences between men and women or which demean the ability or social status of the affected class." Employing this standard, he declared that the statute passed constitutional muster:

> Because virtually all of the significant harmful and inescapably identifiable consequences of teenage pregnancy fall on the young female, a legislature acts well within its authority when it elects to punish only the participant who, by nature, suffers few of the consequences of his conduct. It is hardly unreasonable for a legislature acting to protect minor females to exclude them from punishment. Moreover, risk of pregnancy itself constitutes a substantial deterrence to young females. No similar natural sanctions deter males. A criminal sanction imposed solely on males thus serves to roughly "equalize" the deterrents on the sexes.

Justice Brennan strenuously dissented, insisting that California had not shown that its statutory rape statute "is any more effective than a gender-neutral law would be in deterring minor females from engaging in sexual intercourse. It has, therefore, not met its burden of proving that the statutory classification is substantially related to the achievement of its asserted goal."

A final case involving gender-based classifications, *Rostker* v. *Goldberg* (1981), must be dealt with separately, because, as the Court majority noted, it arose "in the context of Congress' authority over national defense and military affairs, and perhaps in no other area has the Court accorded Congress greater deference." In this case the Court concluded that Congress did not violate the equal protection component of the Fifth Amendment when it authorized the registration of men only under the Military Selective Service Act. In the majority opinion, Justice Rehnquist refused to clarify whether he was employing the rational relation test or some heightened level of scrutiny: "We do not think that the substantive guarantee of due process or certainty in the law will be advanced by any further 'refinement' in the applicable tests." Such refinement was unnecessary, as "this is not a case of Congress arbitrarily choosing to burden one of two similarly situated groups, such as would be the case with an all-black or all-white, or an all-Catholic or an all-Lutheran, or an all-Republican or an all-Democratic registration. Men and women, because of the combat restrictions on women, are simply not similarly situated for purposes of a draft or a registration for a draft." In his dissent, Justice Marshall accused the Court majority of focusing on the wrong question. What it should have asked, he maintained, was "whether the gender-based classification is itself substantially related to the achievement of the asserted governmental interest. Thus, the Government's task in this case is to demonstrate that excluding women from registration substantially furthers the goal of preparing a draft of combat troops. Or to put it another way, the government must show that drafting women would substantially impede its efforts to prepare for such a draft."

Indigency

In a variety of decisions, primarily in the realm of criminal justice, the Warren Court hinted that classifications based on indigency were suspect. In *Griffin* v. *Illinois* (1958), for example, it ruled that the state must provide indigent defendants with copies of trial transcripts necessary for filing a criminal appeal, and in *Douglas* v. *California* (1963) it declared that indigent defendants have a right of court-appointed counsel on appeal. The suspectness of indigency-based classifications seemed all the more clearly established when Justice Douglas declared for the Court in *Harper* v. *Virginia Board of Elections* (1966) that "lines drawn on the basis of wealth or property, like those of race, are traditionally disfavored," and when the Burger Court invalidated, in *Williams* v. *Illinois* (1970) and *Tate* v. *Short* (1971), the imprisonment of indigent defendants who lacked the means to avoid jail by paying fines.

These cases proved to be inconclusive, however. *Griffin* and *Douglas* came in a context involving the fundamental interest of access to the criminal process; *Williams* and *Tate* applied deferential review; and *Harper* involved the fundamental right of exercise of the franchise. In such subsequent decisions as *James* v. *Valtierra* (1971) and *San Antonio* v. *Rodriguez* (1973), moreover, the Court indicated that indigency-based classifications were far from being considered suspect. *Valtierra* involved an equal protection challenge to a California constitutional requirement that prohibited the state from developing low-rent housing projects "without prior approval in a local referendum." In upholding the requirement, Justice Black denied that lawmaking procedures which disadvantage the poor violate equal protection for that reason alone. Justice Powell argued along much the same lines in *Rodriguez*, holding that the Court had never held "that wealth discrimination alone provides an adequate basis for invoking strict scrutiny." Justice Marshall vigorously dissented in both cases. In his *Valtierra* opinion, in which Justices Brennan and Blackmun joined, he insisted that poverty-based classifications were suspect and thus demanded strict scrutiny. For him, "singling out the poor to bear a burden not placed on any other class of citizens tramples the values the Fourteenth Amendment was designed to protect." He resurrected this argument in *Rodriguez,* in which he contended that children living in impoverished school districts "constitute a sufficient class" to justify heightened review.

FUNDAMENTAL RIGHTS

The Court's efforts to identify and defend fundamental rights have sparked controversy but have not been characterized by the vacillation and indecision that have marked its endeavors to define suspect classifications and to determine the level of scrutiny with which those classifications should be reviewed. One of the first rights to be recognized as fundamental under the Warren Court's two-tier approach was the exercise of the franchise. Over time, this right came to embody three distinct principles: (1) each vote must count equally—i.e., the one-man, one-vote principle; (2) the franchise must be broadly available; and (3) for the vote to be meaningful, the ballot must reflect a sufficiently representative choice of parties and candidates. The franchise and the right to vote are addressed at length in Chapter 10.

Along with the franchise, the Warren Court also recognized as fundamental the right to travel from state to state. In *Shapiro* v. *Thompson* (1969), it found that this right of a citizen had been burdened for no compelling reason when Connecticut conditioned eligibility to receive public assistance on having satisfied a one-year residency requirement. Justice Harlan, alarmed by this elevation of the right to travel to "fundamental" status, voiced his fear that the Court in *Shapiro* had understood the justification for strict scrutiny to stem entirely from the Equal Protection Clause itself, and not from any independent source elsewhere in the Constitution. The implications of such an understanding disturbed him greatly. Noting that almost all state statutes affect important rights, he charged that if the Court were "to pick out particular human activities, characterize them as 'fundamental,' and give them added protection under an unusually stringent equal protection test," it would soon become a "super-legislature."

Justice Harlan's fears were allayed, however, when the Burger Court refused to build on *Shapiro.* In *Dandridge* v. *Williams* (1970) it rejected the contention that the right to welfare was fundamental, and in *Lindsey* v. *Normet* (1972) it rebuffed efforts to establish "decent housing" and "possession of one's home" as fundamental rights. "It is not the province of this Court to create substantive constitutional rights in the name of guaranteeing equal protection of the laws," it declared in *San Antonio Independent School District* v. *Rodriguez* (1973), a case in which it denied that education is a fundamental right.[8] For a right to be fundamental, the Court insisted, it must be "expressly or implicitly guaranteed by the Constitution."

Nordlinger v. *Hahn* (1992) is a recent example of the refusal by the Rehnquist Court as well to build on *Shapiro.* The petitioner claimed that the Supreme Court should strictly scrutinize California's Proposition 13, because it infringed on the constitutional right to travel. Proposition 13 capped real property taxes at 1 percent of the property's full cash value at the time this statewide ballot initiative was passed and, thereafter, at its appraised value on construction or change of ownership. As housing values in California continued to soar during the late 1970s and 1980s, owners of property purchased before the passage of Proposition 13 ended up paying much lower taxes than owners who built or purchased after its passage. The petitioner claimed that Proposition 13 was unconstitutional, for it impeded her and others from traveling to and settling in California. The Court, in an 8–1 decision, rejected this contention; it went on to apply the rational basis test to Proposition 13 and ascertained "at least two rational or reasonable considerations . . . that justify denying petitioner the benefits of her neighbors' lower assessments." Justice Stevens filed an impassioned dissent, condemning Proposition 13 for irrationally treating "similarly situated persons differently on the basis of the date they joined the class of property owners."

THE FUTURE OF EQUAL-PROTECTION ANALYSIS

As is apparent, the Court's approach to equal protection issues is fraught with difficulties, which have prompted members of the Court to propose, and on occasion to employ, alternative analytical frameworks for resolving these issues. One such alternative is the "irrebuttable presumptions" doctrine. For a brief time in the mid-1970s, the Court flirted with and even embraced this approach, which asked whether the challenged classification simply presumes something to be the case while at the same time preventing an individual so classified from proving otherwise. In *Vlandis* v. *Kline* (1973), for example, the Court struck down Connecticut's residency requirements for favorable tuition status at state universities on the ground that the requirements did not allow students who had recently arrived in the state a chance to prove that they had in fact become bona fide residents.

The Court's embrace of the irrebuttable-assumptions approach was short-lived, however. In *Weinberger* v. *Salfi* (1975), it overturned a lower court decision that had invalidated, on irrebuttable-presumption grounds, a Social Security duration-of-relationship eligibility requirement for surviving wives and stepchildren of deceased wage earners. In like manner, it refused to acknowledge in *Murgia*, the presence in Massachusetts's mandatory retirement law of an irrebuttable presumption that policemen over the age of fifty are unfit for duty.

Another approach to equal protection analysis was suggested by Justice Rehnquist in his dissent in *Trimble* v. *Gordon*. The problems involved in reviewing equal protection claims, he argued, stemmed "not from the Equal Protection Clause but from the Court's insistence on reading so much into it." To his mind, anything more intensive than the most deferential kind of judicial scrutiny was indefensible, on both theoretical and practical grounds, "except in the area of the law in which the Framers obviously meant it to apply—classifications based on race or on national origin, the first cousin of race." Rehnquist's proposal fell on the deaf ears of those who, with Justice Marshall in *James* v. *Valtierra* (1971), remained convinced that "it is far too late in the day to contend that the Fourteenth Amendment prohibits only racial discrimination."

In *United States* v. *Virginia* (1996), Justice Scalia offered still another proposal—not a new test but mooring the present tests in "those constant and unbroken national traditions that embody the people's understanding of ambiguous constitutional texts." He indicated that he had "no problem with a system of abstract tests such as rational-basis, intermediate, and strict scrutiny." He declared that such formulas "are essential to evaluating whether the new restrictions that a changing society constantly imposes upon private conduct comport with that 'equal protection' our society has always accorded in the past." But, he continued, "in my view the function of this Court is to preserve our society's values regarding (among other things) equal protection, not to revise them; to prevent backsliding from the degree of restriction the Constitution imposed upon democratic government, not to prescribe, on our own authority, progressively higher degrees." His deference to tradition, however, is not widely endorsed by his colleagues. And so the Court continues to search for a satisfactory and acceptable approach to the questions posed by substantive equal protection. The need for such an approach is great, for equal protection has gone from the "last resort of constitutional argument" to a prolific source of constitutional litigation. As Archibald Cox noted, "once loosed, the idea of Equality is not easily cabined."[9]

NOTES

1 *The Federalist*, No. 10, p. 61.
2 The need for strict scrutiny of classifications that are suspect or that burden fundamental rights may be found in Justice Harlan Stone's celebrated *Carolene Products* footnote (1938), which is reprinted in Chapter 4.
3 Gerald Gunther, "The Supreme Court, 1971 Term—Foreword: In Search of Evolving Doctrine on a Changing Court: A Model for a Newer Equal Protection." *Harvard Law Review* 86 (November 1972): 8.
4 Gerald Gunther, *Constitutional Law*, 11th ed. (Mineola, New York: Foundation Press, 1985), p. 591.
5 *Coalition for Economic Equity* v. *Wilson*, 122 F. 3d 692 (1997), is an interesting variant on this theme. When the voters of California in November of 1996 passed Proposition 209 (barring the state from discriminating against or granting preference to any individual or group on the basis of race, sex, color, ethnicity, or national origin), a federal judge quickly enjoined its implementation on the ground that it prohibited governmental entities at every level from taking voluntary action to remediate past and present discrimination through the use of constitutionally permissible race and gender-conscious affirmative action programs. The Ninth Circuit Court of Appeals lifted the injunction and rejected the district court's reasoning. Judge Diarmuid F. O'Scannlain declared: "The Constitution permits the people to grant a narrowly tailored racial preference only if they come forward with a compelling interest to back it up. '[I]n the context of a Fourteenth Amendment challenge, courts must bear in mind the difference between what the law permits, and what it requires.' To hold that a democratically enacted affirmative action program is

constitutionally permissible because the people have demonstrated a compelling state interest is hardly to hold that the program is constitutionally required. The Fourteenth Amendment, lest we lose sight of the forest for the trees, does not require what it barely permits."

6 See also *Martin* v. *Wilks* (1989), in which the Supreme Court held in a 5–4 decision that white employees who allege that they have been the victims of racial discrimination because of the employment practices which their employer has undertaken pursuant to a consent decree, cannot be precluded from challenging those practices or consent decree.

7 Although both *Kahn* and *Ballard* were decided before *Craig* v. *Boren* and the *de facto* employment of the middle-tier test, *Califano* v. *Webster* left no doubt that the Court considered these earlier cases to be fully consistent with *Craig*.

8 See, however, *Plyler* v. *Doe* (1982). Here Justice Brennan, although stating explicitly that education is not a fundamental right and that state denials of educational opportunity are not to be held to the compelling-state-interest test, appeared to argue that the right to education warrants some heightened level of review. The level of review he implicitly employed is the same middle-tier test that he used in *Boren* and *Bakke*.

9 Archibald Cox, "The Supreme Court, 1965 Term—Foreword: Constitutional Adjudication and the Promotion of Human Rights." *Harvard Law Review* 82 (November 1966): 91.

SELECTED READING

Ambach v. *Norwick*, 441 U.S. 68 (1979).

Coalition for Economic Equity v. *Wilson*, 122 F. 3d 692 (1997).

Fullilove v. *Klutznick*, 448 U.S. 448 (1980).

Hopwood v. *State of Texas*, 78 F. 3d 932 (1996).

James v. *Valtierra*, 402 U.S. 137 (1971).

Metro Broadcasting Co. v. *Federal Communications Commission*, 497 U.S. 547 (1990).

Mississippi University for Women v. *Hogan*, 458 U.S. 718 (1982).

Plyler v. *Doe*, 462 U.S. 725 (1982).

Sosna v. *Iowa*, 419 U.S. 393 (1975).

Weber v. *Aetna Casualty and Surety Company*, 406 U.S. 164 (1972).

Wengler v. *Druggists Mutual Insurance Company*, 446 U.S. 142 (1980).

Wygant v. *Jackson Board of Education*, 476 U.S. 267 (1986).

Ackerman, Bruce L. "The Conclusive Presumption Shuffle." *University of Pennsylvania Law Review* 125 (April 1977): 761–810.

Baer, Judith A. *The Chains of Protection: The Judicial Response to Women's Labor Legislation* (Westport, Conn.: Greenwood Press, 1978).

Baer, Judith A. *Equality Under the Constitution: Reclaiming the Fourteenth Amendment* (Ithaca, N.Y.: Cornell University Press, 1983).

Belz, Herman. *Equality Transformed: A Quarter-Century of Affirmative Action* (Bowling Green, Ohio: Transaction Publishers, 1991).

Carter, Stephen L. *Reflections of an Affirmative Action Baby* (New York: Basic Books, 1991).

Eastland, Terry, and William J. Bennett. *Counting by Race: Equality from the Founding Fathers to Bakke and Weber* (New York: Basic Books, 1979).

Ely, John Hart. *Democracy and Distrust: A Theory of Judicial Review* (Cambridge, Mass.: Harvard University Press, 1980).

Eule, Julian N. "Promoting Speaker Diversity: *Austin* and *Metro Broadcasting.*" *1990 Supreme Court Review*, edited by Gerhard Casper, Dennis J. Hutchinson, and David A. Strauss (Chicago: University of Chicago Press, 1991).

Gunther, Gerald. "The Supreme Court, 1971 Term—Foreword: In Search of Evolving Doctrine on a Changing Court: A Model for a Newer Equal Protection." *Harvard Law Review* 86 (November 1972): 1–48.

Jencks, Christopher. "Affirmative Action for Blacks." *American Behavioral Scientist* 28 (July/August 1985): 731–760.

Presser, Stephen B. *Recapturing the Constitution: Race, Religion, and Abortion Reconsidered* (Washington, D.C.: Regnery Publishing Co., 1994).

Rossum, Ralph A. *Reverse Discrimination: The Constitutional Debate* (New York: Marcel Dekker, 1980).

Sindler, Allan P. *Bakke, DeFunis, and Minority Admissions: The Quest for Equal Opportunity* (New York: Longman, 1978).

Sowell, Thomas. T*he Economics and Politics of Race: An International Perspective* (New York: Morrow, 1983).

West, Thomas G. *Vindicating the Founders: Race, Sex, Class, and Justice in the Origins of America* (Lanham, MD: Rowman & Littlefield Publishers, Inc., 1997).

Wilkinson, J. Harvie III. *From Brown to Bakke: The Supreme Court and School Integration* (New York: Oxford University Press, 1979).

Bakke v. *Regents of the University of California*
553 P. 2d 1152 (1976)

Allan Bakke earned a baccalaureate degree in engineering from the University of Minnesota in 1962, graduating with a 3.51 grade-point average. He was employed as an engineer for a space-agency laboratory when he applied for admission to the 1973 entering class (and subsequently the 1974 entering class) of the Medical School of the University of California at Davis.

In an effort to increase the number of minority students attending the medical school, UC Davis had established a two-track system for applicants: Of the one hundred places available each year, sixteen were set aside for minority students and were filled under a special admissions program. Bakke's grade-point average and Medical College Admission Test (MCAT) scores were highly competitive with those of the regular admittees and much higher than those of the special admittees, as the following table indicates.

Class Entering in 1974

				MCAT (Percentiles)		
	Science GPA	*Overall GPA*	*Verbal*	*Quanti- tative*	*Science*	*General Information*
Bakke	3.44	3.51	96	94	97	72
Average of regular admittees	3.36	3.29	69	67	82	72
Average of special admittees	2.42	2.62	34	30	37	18

Nonetheless, Bakke was denied admission both years. He thereupon filed suit in California Superior Court. The trial court judge held for Bakke, ruling, among other things, that Bakke was discriminated against because of his race in violation of the Equal Protection Clause of the Fourteenth Amendment. The judge also determined, however, that Bakke was *not* entitled to an order for admission to the university, because although he was qualified to be admitted both years in which he applied, he had not shown that he would have been selected even if there had been no special program for minorities. Both parties appealed to the California Supreme Court—Bakke from that portion of the judgment which denied him admission and the university from the determination that its special admissions program was unconstitutional. Because of the importance of the issues involved, the California Supreme Court took the case without intermediate appeal and ruled, 6–1 for Bakke.

MR. JUSTICE MOSK delivered the opinion of the Court. . . .

The issue to be determined . . . [is] whether a racial classification which is intended to assist minorities, but which also has the effect of de- priving those who are not so classified of benefits they would enjoy but for their race, violates the constitutional rights of the majority.

Two distinct inquiries emerge at this point; first, what test is to be used in determining whether the program violates the equal protection clause; and second, does the program meet the requirements of the applicable test.

The general rule is that classifications made by government regulations are valid "if any state of facts reasonably may be conceived" in their justification. But in some circumstances a more stringent standard is imposed. Classification by race is subject to strict scrutiny, at least where the classification results in detriment to a person because of his race. In the case of such a racial classification, not only must the purpose of the classification serve a "compelling state interest," but it must be demonstrated by rigid scrutiny that there are no reasonable ways to achieve the state's goals by means which impose a lesser limitation on the rights of the group disadvantaged by the classification. The burden in both respects is upon the government. . . .

The University asserts that the appropriate standard to be applied in determining the validity of the special admission program is the more lenient "rational basis" test. It contends that the "compelling interest" measure is applicable only to a classification which discriminates against a minority, reasoning that racial classifications are suspect only if they result in invidious discrimination; and that invidious discrimination occurs only if the classification excludes, disadvantages, isolates, or stigmatizes a minority or is designed to segregate the races. The argument is that white applicants denied admission are not stigmatized in the sense of having cast about them an aura of inferiority; therefore, it is sufficient if the special admission program has a rational relation to the University's goals.

We cannot agree with the proposition that deprivation based upon race is subject to a less demanding standard of review under the Fourteenth Amendment if the race discriminated against is the majority rather than a minority. We have found no case so holding, and we do not hesitate to reject the notion that racial discrimination may be more easily justified against one race than another, nor can we permit the validity of such discrimination to be determined by a mere census count of the races.

That whites suffer a grievous disadvantage by reason of their exclusion from the University on racial grounds is abundantly clear. The fact that they are not also invidiously discriminated against in the sense that a stigma is cast upon them because of their race, as is often the circumstance when the discriminatory conduct is directed against a minority, does not justify the conclusion that race is a suspect classification only if the consequences of the classification are detrimental to minorities.

Regardless of its historical origin, the equal protection clause by its literal terms applies to "any person," and its lofty purpose, to secure equality of treatment to all, is incompatible with the premise that some races may be afforded a higher degree of protection against unequal treatment than others.

We come, then, to the question whether the University has demonstrated that the special admission program is necessary to serve a compelling governmental interest and that the objectives of the program cannot reasonably be achieved by some means which would impose a lesser burden on the rights of the majority.

The University seeks to justify the program on the ground that the admission of minority students is necessary in order to integrate the medical school and the profession. The presence of a substantial number of minority students will not only provide diversity in the student body, it is said, but will influence the students and the remainder of the profession so that they will become aware of the medical needs of the minority community and be encouraged to assist in meeting those demands. Minority doctors will, moreover, provide role models for younger persons in the minority community, demonstrating to them that they can overcome the residual handicaps inherent from past discrimination.

Furthermore, the special admission program will assertedly increase the number of doctors willing to serve the minority community, which is desperately short of physicians. While the University concedes it cannot guarantee that all the applicants admitted under the special program will ultimately practice as doctors in disadvantaged communities, they have expressed an interest in serving those communities and there is a likelihood that many of them will thus fashion their careers.

Finally, it is urged, black physicians would have a greater rapport with patients of their own race and a greater interest in treating diseases which are especially prevalent among blacks, such as sickle cell anemia, hypertension, and certain skin ailments.

We reject the University's assertion that the special admission program may be justified as compelling on the ground that minorities would have more rapport with doctors of their own race and that black doctors would have a greater interest in treating diseases prevalent among blacks. The record contains no evidence to justify the parochialism implicit in the latter assertion; and as to the former, we cite as eloquent refutation to racial exclusivity the comment of Justice Douglas in his dissenting opinion in *DeFunis:* "The Equal Protection Clause commands the elimination of racial barriers, not their creation in order to satisfy our theory as to how society ought to be organized. The purpose of the University of Washington cannot be to produce black lawyers for blacks, Polish lawyers for Poles, Jewish lawyers for Jews, Irish lawyers for Irish. It should be to produce good lawyers for Americans. . . . " *DeFunis* v. *Odegaard* (1974).

We may assume *arguendo* that the remaining objectives which the University seeks to achieve by the special admission program meet the exacting standards required to uphold the validity of a racial classification insofar as they establish a compelling governmental interest. Nevertheless, we are not convinced that the University has met its burden of demonstrating that the basic goals of the program cannot be substantially achieved by means less detrimental to the rights of the majority.

The two major aims of the University are to integrate the student body and to improve medical care for minorities. In our view, the University has not established that a program which discriminates against white applicants because of their race is necessary to achieve either of these goals.

It is the University's claim that if special consideration is not afforded to disadvantaged minority applicants, almost none of them would gain admission because, no matter how large the pool of applicants, the grades and test scores of most minority applicants are lower than those of white applicants. . . .

While minority applicants may have lower grade point averages and test scores than others, we are aware of no rule of law which requires the University to afford determinative weight in admissions to these quantitative factors. In practice, colleges and universities generally consider matters other than strict numerical ranking in admission decisions. The University is entitled to consider, as it does with respect to applicants in the special program, that low grades and test scores may not accurately reflect the abilities of some disadvantaged students; and it may reasonably conclude that although their academic scores are lower, their potential for success in the school and the profession is equal to or greater than that of an applicant with higher grades who has not been similarly handicapped.

In addition, the University may properly as it in fact does, consider other factors in evaluating an applicant, such as the personal interview, recommendations, character, and matters relating to the needs of the profession and society, such as an applicant's professional goals. In short, the standards for admission employed by the University are not constitutionally infirm except to the extent that they are utilized in a racially discriminatory manner. Disadvantaged applicants of all races must be eligible for sympathetic consideration, and no applicant may be rejected because of his race, in favor of another who is less qualified, as measured by standards applied without regard to race. We reiterate, in view of the dissent's misinterpretation, that we do not compel the University to utilize only "the highest objective academic credentials" as the criterion for admission.

. . . The University has not shown that the second major objective of the program—the need for more doctors to serve the minority community—will be appreciably impaired. . . .

An applicant of whatever race who demonstrated his concern for disadvantaged minorities in the past and who declares that practice in such a community is his primary professional goal would be more likely to contribute to alleviation of the medical shortage than one who is chosen entirely on the basis of race and disadvantage. In short, there is no empirical data to demonstrate that any one race is more selflessly socially oriented or by contrast that another is more selfishly acquisitive.

Moreover, while it may be true that the influence exerted by minorities upon the student body and the profession will persuade some nonminority doctors to assist in meeting these community medical needs, it is at best a circuitous and uncertain means to accomplish the University's objective. It would appear that more directly effective methods can be devised, such as academic and clinical courses directed to the medical needs of minorities, and emphasis upon the training of general practitioners to serve the basic needs of the poor. . . .

While a program can be damned by semantics, it is difficult to avoid considering the University scheme as a form of an education quota system, benevolent in concept perhaps, but a revival of quotas nevertheless. No college admission policy in history has been so thoroughly discredited in contemporary times as the use of racial percentages. Originated as a means of exclusion of racial and religious minorities from higher education, a quota becomes no less offensive when it serves to exclude a racial majority. "No form of discrimination should be opposed more vigorously than the quota system."

To uphold the University would call for the sacrifice of principle for the sake of dubious expediency and would represent a retreat in the struggle to assure that each man and woman shall be judged on the basis of individual merit alone, a struggle which has only lately achieved success in removing legal barriers to racial equality. The safest course, the one most consistent with the fundamental interests of all races and with the design of the Constitution is to hold, as we do, that the special admission program is unconstitutional because it violates the rights guaranteed to the majority by the equal protection clause of the Fourteenth Amendment of the United States Constitution. . . .

Regents of the University of California v. Bakke
438 U.S. 265; 98 S. Ct. 2733; 57 L. Ed. 2d 750 (1978)

After the California Supreme Court held that the preferential admissions program of the Medical School of the University of California at Davis violated the Equal Protection Clause of the Fourteenth Amendment, the regents of the university successfully petitioned the United States Supreme Court for a writ of certiorari. *Judgment of the Court: Powell.* *Concurring in the judgment in part and dissenting: Brennan, Blackmun, Marshall, White. Concurring in the judgment in part and dissenting in part: Stevens, Burger, Rehnquist, Stewart.*

MR. JUSTICE POWELL announced the judgment of the Court. . . .

The guarantees of the Fourteenth Amendment extend to persons. Its language is explicit: "No state shall . . . deny to any person within its jurisdiction the equal protection of the laws." It is settled beyond question that the "rights created by the first section of the Fourteenth Amendment are, by its terms, guaranteed to the individual. They are personal rights," *Shelley* v. *Kraemer*. . . .The guarantee of equal protection cannot mean one thing when applied to one individual and something else when applied to a person of another color. If both are not accorded the same protection, then it is not equal.

Nevertheless, petitioner argues that the court below erred in applying strict scrutiny to the special admissions programs because white males, such as respondent, are not a "discrete and insular minority" requiring extraordinary protection from the majoritarian political process. *Carolene Products Co.* . . . This rationale, however, has never been invoked in our decisions as a prerequisite to subjecting racial or ethnic distinctions to strict scrutiny. Nor has this Court held that discreteness and insularity constitute necessary preconditions to a holding that a particular classification is invidious. These characteristics may be relevant in deciding whether or not to add new types of classifications to the list of "suspect" categories or whether a particular classification survives close examination. . . . Racial and ethnic classifications, however, are inherently suspect and thus call for the most exacting judicial examination.

This perception of racial and ethnic distinctions is rooted in our Nation's constitutional and demographic history. The Court's initial view of the Fourteenth Amendment was that its "one pervading purpose" was "the freedom of the slave race, the security and firm establishment of that freedom, and the protection of the newly-made freeman and citizen from the oppressions of those who had formerly exercised dominion over him." *Slaughterhouse Cases* . . . (1873).

Although many of the Framers of the Fourteenth Amendment conceived of its primary function as bridging the vast distance between members of the Negro race and the white "majority," *Slaughterhouse Cases,* . . . the Amendment itself was framed in universal terms, without reference to color, ethnic origin, or condition of prior servitude. . . .

Petitioner urges us to adopt for the first time a more restrictive view of the Equal Protection Clause and hold that discrimination against members of the white "majority" cannot be suspect if its purpose can be characterized as "benign." The clock of our liberties, however, cannot be turned back to 1868. It is far too late to argue that the guarantee of equal protection to *all* persons permits the recognition of special wards entitled to a degree of protection greater than that accorded others. "The Fourteenth Amendment is not directed solely against discrimination due to a 'two-class theory'—that is, based upon differences between 'white' and Negro."

Once the artificial line of a "two-class theory" of the Fourteenth Amendment is put aside, the difficulties entailed in varying the level of judicial review according to a perceived "preferred" status of a particular racial or ethnic minority are intractable. The concepts of "majority" and "minority" necessarily reflect temporary arrangements and political judgments. As observed above, the white "majority" itself is composed of various minority groups, most of which can lay claim to a history of prior discrimination at the hands of the state and private individuals. Not all of these groups can receive preferential treatment and corresponding judicial tolerance of distinctions drawn in terms of race and nationality, for then the only "majority" left would be a new minority of White Anglo-Saxon Protestants. There is no principled basis for deciding which groups would merit "heightened judicial solicitude" and which would not. Courts would be asked to evaluate the extent of the prejudice and consequent harm suffered by various minority groups. Those whose societal injury is thought to exceed some arbitrary level of tolerability then would be entitled to preferential classifications at the expense of individuals belonging to other groups. Those classifications would be free from exacting judicial scrutiny. As these preferences began to have their desired effect, and the consequences of past discrimination were undone,

new judicial rankings would be necessary. The kind of variable sociological and political analysis necessary to produce such rankings simply does not lie within the judicial competence—even if they otherwise were politically feasible and socially desirable.

Moreover, there are serious problems of justice connected with the idea of preference itself. First, it may not always be clear that a so-called preference is in fact benign. Courts may be asked to validate burdens imposed upon individual members of particular groups in order to advance the group's general interest. Nothing in the Constitution supports the notion that individuals may be asked to suffer otherwise impermissible burdens in order to enhance the societal standing of their ethnic groups. Second, preferential programs may only reinforce common stereotypes holding that certain groups are unable to achieve success without special protection based on a factor having no relationship to individual worth. Third, there is a measure of inequity in forcing innocent persons in respondent's position to bear the burdens of redressing grievances not of their making.

By hitching the meaning of the Equal Protection Clause to these transitory considerations, we would be holding, as a constitutional principle, that judicial scrutiny of classifications touching on racial and ethnic background may vary with the ebb and flow of political forces. Disparate constitutional tolerance of such classifications well may serve to exacerbate racial and ethnic antagonisms rather than alleviate them. Also, the mutability of a constitutional principle, based upon shifting political and social judgments, undermines the chances for consistent application of the Constitution from one generation to the next, a critical feature of its coherent interpretation. In expounding the Constitution, the Court's role is to discern "principles sufficiently absolute to give them roots throughout the community and continuity over significant periods of time and to lift them above the level of the pragmatic political judgments of a particular time and place." . . . The special admissions program purports to serve the purpose of obtaining the educational benefits that flow from an ethnically diverse student body. It is necessary to decide which, if any, of these purposes is substantial enough to support the use of a suspect classification.

The attainment of a diverse student body clearly is a constitutionally permissible goal for an institution of higher education. Academic freedom, though not a specifically enumerated constitutional right, long has been viewed as a special concern of the First Amendment. The freedom of a university to make its own judgments as to education includes the selection of its student body. Mr. Justice Frankfurter summarized the "four essential freedoms" that comprise academic freedom: "It is the business of a university to provide that atmosphere which is most conducive to speculation, experiment and creation. It is an atmosphere in which there prevail 'the four essential freedoms' of a university—to determine for itself on academic grounds who may teach, what may be taught, how it shall be taught, and who may be admitted to study" [*Sweezy* v. *New Hampshire* . . . (1957). . . .].

The atmosphere of "speculation, experiment and creation"—so essential to the quality of higher education—is widely believed to be promoted by a diverse student body. . . . It is not too much to say that the "nation's future depends upon leaders trained through wide exposure" to the ideas and mores of students as diverse as this Nation of many peoples.

Thus, in arguing that its universities must be accorded the right to select those students who will contribute the most to the "robust exchange of ideas," petitioner invokes a countervailing constitutional interest, that of the First Amendment. In this light, petitioner must be viewed as seeking to achieve a goal that is of paramount importance in the fulfillment of its mission.

Ethnic diversity, however, is only one element in a range of factors a university properly may consider in attaining the goal of a heterogeneous student body. Although a university must have wide discretion in making the sensitive judgments as to who should be admitted, constitutional limitations protecting individual rights may not be disregarded. Respondent urges—and the courts below have held—that petitioner's dual admissions program is a racial classification that impermissibly infringes his rights under the Fourteenth Amendment. As the interest of diversity is compelling in the context of a university's admissions program, the question remains whether the program's racial classification is necessary to promote this interest.

It may be assumed that the reservation of a specified number of seats in each class for individuals from the preferred ethnic groups would contribute to the attainment of considerable ethnic diversity in the student body. But petitioner's argument that this is the only effective means of serving the interest of diversity is seriously flawed. In a most fundamental sense the argument misconceives the nature of the state interest that would justify consideration of race or ethnic background. It is not an interest in simple ethnic diversity, in which a specified percentage of the student body is in effect guaranteed to be members of selected ethnic groups, with the remaining percentage an undifferentiated aggregation of students. The diversity that furthers a compelling state interest encompasses a far broader array of qualifications and characteristics of which racial or ethnic origin is but a single though important element. Petitioner's special admissions program, focused *solely* on ethnic diversity, would hinder rather than further attainment of genuine diversity.

The experience of other university admissions programs, which take race into account in achieving the educational diversity valued by the First Amendment, demonstrates that the assignment of a fixed number of places to a minority group is not a necessary means toward that end. An illuminating example is found in the Harvard College program.

In . . . [Harvard's] admissions program, race or ethnic background may be deemed a "plus" in a particular applicant's file, yet it does not insulate the individual from comparison with all other candidates for the available seats. The file of a particular black applicant may be examined for his potential contribution to diversity without the factor of race being decisive when compared, for example, with that of an applicant identified as an Italian-American if the latter is thought to exhibit qualities more likely to promote beneficial educational pluralism. Such qualities could include exceptional personal talents, unique work or service experience, leadership potential, maturity, demonstrated compassion, a history of overcoming disadvantage, ability to communicate with the poor, or other qualifications deemed important. In short, an admissions program operated in this way is flexible enough to consider all pertinent elements of diversity in light of the particular qualifications of each applicant, and to place them on the same footing for consideration, although not necessarily according them the same weight. Indeed, the weight attributed to a particular quality may vary from year to year depending upon the "mix" both of the student body and the applicants for the incoming class.

This kind of program treats each applicant as an individual in the admissions process. The applicant who loses out on the last available seat to another candidate receiving a "plus" on the basis of ethnic background will not have been foreclosed from all consideration for that seat simply because he was not the right color or had the wrong surname. It would mean only that his combined qualifications, which may have included similar nonobjective factors, did not outweigh those of the other applicant. His qualifications would have been weighed fairly and competitively, and he would have no basis to complain of unequal treatment under the Fourteenth Amendment.

It has been suggested that an admissions program which considers race only as one factor is simply a subtle and more sophisticated—but not less effective—means of according racial preference than the Davis program. A facial intent to discriminate, however, is evident in petitioner's preference program and not denied in this case. No such facial infirmity exists in an admissions program where race or ethnic background is simply one element—to be weighed fairly against other elements—in the selection process. "A boundary line," as Mr. Justice Frankfurter remarked in another connection, "is none the worse for being narrow." . . . And a Court would not assume that a university, professing to employ a facially nondiscriminatory admissions policy, would operate it as a cover for the functional equivalent of a quota system. In short, good faith would be presumed in the absence of a showing to the contrary in the manner permitted by our cases.

In summary, it is evident that the Davis special admission program involves the use of an explicit racial classification never before countenanced by this Court. It tells applicants who are not Negro, Asian, or "Chicano" that they are totally excluded from a specific percentage of the seats in an entering class. No matter how strong their qualifications, quantitative and extracurricular, including their own potential for contribution to educational diversity, they are never afforded the chance to compete with applicants from the preferred groups for the special admission seats. At the same time, the preferred applicants have the opportunity to compete for every seat in the class.

The fatal flaw in petitioner's preferential program is its disregard of individual rights as guaranteed by the Fourteenth Amendment. Such rights are not absolute. But when a State's distribution of benefits or imposition of burdens hinges on the color of a person's skin or ancestry, that individual is entitled to a demonstration that the challenged classification is necessary to promote a substantial state interest. Petitioner has failed to carry this burden. For this reason, that portion of the California court's judgment holding petitioner's special admissions program invalid under the Fourteenth Amendment must be affirmed.

In enjoining petitioner from ever considering the race of any applicant, however, the courts below failed to recognize that the State has a substantial interest that legitimately may be served by a properly devised admissions program involving the competitive consideration of race and ethnic origin. For this reason, so much of the California court's judgment as enjoins petitioner from any consideration of the race of any applicant must be reversed.

Mr. Justice Brennan, concurring in the judgment in part and dissenting.

Government may take race into account when it acts not to demean or insult any racial group, but to remedy disadvantages cast on minorities by past racial prejudice, at least when appropriate findings have been made by judicial, legislative, or administrative bodies with competence to act in this area. . . .

Against this background, claims that law must be "color-blind" or that the datum of race is no longer relevant to public policy must be seen as aspiration rather than as description of reality. This is not to denigrate aspiration; for reality rebukes us that race has too often been used by those who would stigmatize and oppress minorities. Yet we cannot—and as we shall demonstrate, need not under our Constitution or Title VI, which merely extends the constraints of the Fourteenth Amendment to private parties who receive federal funds—let color blindness become myopia which masks the reality that many "created equal" have been treated within our lifetimes as inferior both by the law and by their fellow citizens.

The assertion of human equality is closely associated with the proposition that differences in color or creed, birth or status, are neither significant nor relevant to the way in which persons should be treated. Nonetheless, the position that such factors must be "[c]onstitutionally an irrelevance," . . . summed up by the shorthand phrase "[o]ur Constitution is color-blind," . . . has never been adopted by this Court as the proper meaning of the Equal Protection Clause. Indeed, we have expressly rejected this proposition on a number of occasions.

Our cases have always implied that an "overriding statutory purpose" . . . could be found that would justify racial classifications. . . .

We conclude, therefore, that racial classifications are not *per se* invalid under the Fourteenth Amendment. Accordingly, we turn to the problem of articulating what our role should be in reviewing state action that expressly classifies by race. . . .

. . . We have held that a government practice or statute which restricts "fundamental rights" or which contains "suspect classifications" is to be subjected to "strict scrutiny" and can be justified only if it furthers a compelling government purpose and, even then, only if no less restrictive alternative is available. . . . But no fundamental right is involved here. Nor do whites as a class have any of the "traditional indicia of suspectness: the class is not saddled with such disabilities, or subjected to such a history of purposeful unequal treatment, or relegated to such a position of political powerlessness as to command extraordinary protection from the majoritarian political process."

On the other hand, the fact that this case does not fit neatly into our prior analytic framework for race cases does not mean that it should be analyzed by applying the very loose rational-basis standard of review that is the very least that is always applied in equal protection cases. "[T]he mere recitation of a benign, compensatory purpose is not an automatic shield which protects against any inquiry into the actual purposes underlying a statutory scheme." Instead, a number of considerations—developed in gender discrimination cases but which carry even more force when applied to racial classifications—lead us to conclude that racial classifications designed to further remedial purposes " 'must serve impor-

tant governmental objectives and must be substantially related to achievement of those objectives.' "

First, race, like, "gender-based classifications too often [has] been inexcusably utilized to stereotype and stigmatize politically powerless segments of society." While a carefully tailored statute designed to remedy past discrimination could avoid these vices, we nonetheless have recognized that the line between honest and thoughtful appraisal of the effects of past discrimination and paternalistic stereotyping is not so clear and that a statute based on the latter is patently capable of stigmatizing all women with a badge of inferiority. State programs designed ostensibly to ameliorate the effects of past racial discrimination obviously create the same hazard of stigma, since they may promote racial separatism and reinforce the views of those who believe that members of racial minorities are inherently incapable of succeeding on their own.

Second, race, like gender and illegitimacy, is an immutable characteristic which its possessors are powerless to escape or set aside. While a classification is not *per se* invalid because it divides classes on the basis of an immutable characteristic, it is nevertheless true that such divisions are contrary to our deep belief that "legal burdens should bear some relationship to individual responsibility or wrongdoing," and that advancement sanctioned, sponsored, or approved by the State should ideally be based on individual merit or achievement, or at the least on factors within the control of an individual.

In sum, because of the significant risk that racial classifications established for ostensibly benign purposes can be misused, causing effects not unlike those created by invidious classifications, it is inappropriate to inquire only whether there is any conceivable basis that might sustain such a classification. Instead, to justify such a classification an important and articulated purpose for its use must be shown. In addition, any statute must be striken that stigmatizes any group or that singles out those least well represented in the political process to bear the brunt of a benign program.

Properly construed, therefore, our prior cases unequivocally show that a state government may adopt race-conscious programs if the purpose of such programs is to remove the disparate racial impact its actions might otherwise have and if there is reason to believe that the disparate impact is itself the product of past discrimination, whether its own or that of society at large. There is no question that Davis' program is valid under this test.

Certainly, on the basis of the undisputed factual submissions before this Court, Davis had a sound basis for believing that the problem of underrepresentation of minorities was substantial and chronic and that the problem was attributable to handicaps imposed on minority applicants by past and present racial discrimination. Until at least 1973, the practice of medicine in this country was, in fact, if not in law, largely the prerogative of whites. In 1950, for example, while Negroes comprised 10% of the total population, Negro physicians constituted only 2.2% of the total number of physicians. The overwhelming majority of these, moreover, were educated in two predominantly Negro medical schools, Howard and Meharry. By 1970, the gap between the proportion of Negroes in medicine and their proportion in the population had widened: The number of Negroes employed in medicine remained frozen at 2.2% while the Negro population had increased to 11.1%. The number of Negro admittees to predominantly white medical schools, moreover, had declined in absolute numbers during the years 1955 to 1964.

Moreover, Davis had very good reason to believe that the national pattern of underrepresentation of minorities in medicine would be perpetuated if it retained a single admissions standard. For example, the entering classes in 1968 and 1969, the years in which such a standard was used, included only one Chicano and two Negroes out of 100 admittees. Nor is there any relief from this pattern of underrepresentation in the statistics for the regular admissions program in later years.

Davis clearly could conclude that the serious and persistent underrepresentation of minorities in medicine depicted by these statistics is the result of handicaps under which minority applicants labor as a consequence of a background of deliberate, purposeful discrimination against minorities in education and in society generally, as well as in the medical profession.

The second prong of our test—whether the Davis program stigmatizes any discrete group or individual and whether race is reasonably used in light of the program's objectives—is clearly satisfied by the Davis program.

It is not even claimed that Davis' program in any way operates to stigmatize or single out any discrete and insular, or even any identifiable nonminority group. Nor will harm comparable to that imposed upon racial minorities by exclusion or separation on grounds of race be the likely result of the program. It does not, for example, establish an exclusive preserve for minority students apart from and exclusive of whites. Rather, its purpose is to overcome the effects of segregation by bringing the races together. True, whites are excluded from participation in the special admissions program, but this fact only operates to reduce the number of whites to be admitted in the regular admissions program in order to permit admission of a reasonable percentage—less than their proportion of the California population—of otherwise underrepresented qualified minority applicants.

Nor was Bakke in any sense stamped as inferior by the Medical School's rejection of him. Indeed, it is conceded by all that he satisfied those criteria regarded by the School as generally relevant to academic performance better than most of the minority members who were admitted. Moreover, there is absolutely no basis for concluding that Bakke's rejection as a result of Davis' use of racial preference will affect him throughout his life in the same way as the segregation of the Negro school children in *Brown I* would have affected them. Unlike discrimination against racial minorities, the use of racial preferences for remedial purposes does not inflict a pervasive injury upon individual whites in the sense that wherever they go or whatever they do there is a significant likelihood that they will be treated as second-class citizens because of their color. This distinction does not mean that the exclusion of a white resulting from preferential use of race is not sufficiently serious to require justification; but it does mean that the injury inflicted by such a policy is not distinguishable from disadvantages caused by a wide range of government actions, none of which has ever been thought impermissible for that reason alone.

In addition, there is simply no evidence that the Davis program discriminates intentionally or unintentionally against any minority group which it purports to benefit. The program does not establish a quota in the invidious sense of a ceiling on the number of minority applicants to be admitted. Nor can the program reasonably be regarded as stigmatizing the program's beneficiaries of their race as inferior. The Davis program does not simply advance less qualified applicants; rather it compensates applicants, whom . . . it is uncontested are fully qualified to study medicine, for educational disadvantage which it was reasonable to conclude was a product of state-fostered discrimination. Once admitted, these students must satisfy the same degree requirements as regularly admitted students; they are taught by the same faculty in the same classes; and their performance is evaluated by the same standards by which regularly admitted students are judged. Under these circumstances, their performance and degrees must be regarded equally with the regularly admitted students with whom they compete for standing. Since minority graduates cannot justifiably be regarded as less well qualified than nonminority graduates by virtue of the special admissions program, there is no reasonable basis to conclude that minority graduates at schools using such programs would be stigmatized as inferior by the existence of such programs.

We disagree with the lower courts' conclusion that the Davis program's use of race was unreasonable in light of its objectives. First, as petitioner argues, there are no practical means by which it could achieve its ends in the foreseeable future without the use of race-conscious measures. With respect to any factor (such as poverty or family educational background) that may be used as a substitute for race as an indicator of past discrimination, whites greatly outnumber racial minorities simply because whites make up a far larger percentage of the total population and therefore far outnumber minorities in absolute terms at every socio-economic level. For example, of a class of recent medical school applicants from families with less than $10,000 income, at least 71% were white. Of all 1970 families headed by a person *not* a high school graduate which included related children under 18, 80 were white and 20% were racial minorities. Moreover, while race is positively correlated with differences in GPA and MCAT scores, economic disadvantage is not. Thus, it appears that economically disadvantaged whites do not score less well than economically advantaged whites, while economically advantaged blacks score less well than do disadvantaged whites. These statistics graphically illustrate that the University's purpose to integrate its classes by compensating for past discrimination

could not be achieved by a general preference for the economically disadvantaged or the children of parents of limited education unless such groups were to make up the entire class.

Second, the Davis admissions program does not simply equate minority status with disadvantage. Rather, Davis considers on an individual basis each applicant's personal history to determine whether he or she has likely been disadvantaged by racial discrimination. The record makes clear that only minority applicants likely to have been isolated from the mainstream of American life are considered in the special program; other minority applicants are eligible only through the regular admissions program. True, the procedure by which disadvantage is detected is informal, but we have never insisted that educators conduct their affairs through adjudicatory proceedings, and such insistence here is misplaced. A case-by-case inquiry into the extent to which each individual applicant has been affected, either directly or indirectly, by racial discrimination, would seem to be, as a practical matter, virtually impossible, despite the fact that there are excellent reasons for concluding that such effects generally exist. When individual measurement is impossible or extremely impractical, there is nothing to prevent a State from using categorical means to achieve its ends, at least where the category is closely related to the goal. And it is clear from our cases that specific proof that a person has been victimized by discrimination is not a necessary predicate to offering him relief where the probability of victimization is great.

Finally, Davis' special admissions program cannot be said to violate the Constitution simply because it has set aside a predetermined number of places for qualified minority applicants rather than using minority status as a positive factor to be considered in evaluating the applications of disadvantaged minority applicants. For purposes of constitutional adjudication, there is no difference between the two approaches.

The "Harvard" program, as those employing it readily concede, openly and successfully employs a racial criterion for the purpose of ensuring that some of the scarce places in institutions of higher education are allocated to disadvantaged minority students. That the Harvard approach does not also make public the extent of the preference and the precise workings of the system while the Davis program employs a specific, openly stated number, does not condemn the latter plan for purposes of Fourteenth Amendment adjudication. It may be that the Harvard plan is more acceptable to the public than is the Davis "quota." But there is no basis for preferring a particular preference program simply because in achieving the same goals that the Davis Medical School is pursuing, it proceeds in a manner that is not immediately apparent to the public.

Richmond v. *Croson Company*
488 U.S. 469; 109 S. Ct. 706; 102 L. Ed. 2d 854 (1989)

The City of Richmond, Virginia, adopted a Minority Business Utilization Plan requiring prime contractors awarded city construction contracts to subcontract at least 30 percent of the total dollar amount of each contract to one or more Minority Business Enterprises (MBEs), which the city defined to include a business from anywhere in the country at least 51 percent of which is owned and controlled by black, Spanish-speaking, Oriental, Indian, Eskimo, or Aleut citizens. Although Richmond declared that the plan was "remedial" in nature, the city adopted it after a public hearing at which no direct evidence was presented that the city had discriminated on the basis of race in letting contracts or that its prime contractors had discriminated against minority subcontractors. What was introduced was a statistical study indicating that, while the city's population was 50 percent black, only .67 percent of its prime construction contracts had been awarded to minority subcontractors in recent years; figures showing that local contractors' associations had virtually no MBE members; the conclusion of the city's counsel that the plan was constitutional under *Fullilove* v. *Klutznick*, 448 U.S. 448 (1980); and statements of plan proponents indicating that there had been widespread racial discrimination in the local, state, and national construction industries.

Pursuant to this plan, the city adopted rules requiring individualized consideration of each bid or request for a waiver of the 30 percent set-aside, and providing that a waiver could be granted only upon proof that sufficient qualified MBEs were unavailable or unwilling to participate. After J.A. Croson Co., the sole bidder on a city contract, was denied a waiver and lost its contract, it brought suit in Federal District Court for the Eastern District of Virginia, alleging that the city's plan was unconstitutional under the Fourteenth Amendment's Equal Protection Clause. The District Court upheld the plan in all respects, and the Court of Appeals for the Fourth Circuit affirmed, applying a test derived from the Supreme Court's principal opinion in *Fullilove*, which accorded great deference to Congress's findings of past societal discrimination in holding that a 10 percent minority set-aside for certain federal construction grants did not violate the equal protection component of the Fifth Amendment. When Croson petitioned the Supreme Court for a writ of certiorari, the Court vacated the judgment from below and remanded the case for further consideration in light of its intervening decision in *Wygant* v. *Jackson Board of Education*, 476 U.S. 267 (1986), in which a plurality of the Supreme Court applied a strict-scrutiny standard in holding that a race-based layoff program agreed to by a school district and the local teacher's union violated the Fourteenth Amendment's Equal Protection Clause. On remand, the Court of Appeals held that the city's plan violated both prongs of strict scrutiny in that it was not justified by a compelling governmental interest—the record revealed no prior discrimination by the city itself in awarding contracts—and the 30 percent set-aside was not narrowly tailored to accomplish a remedial purpose. The City appealed. *Opinion of the Court: O'Connor, Kennedy, Rehnquist, Stevens, White. Concurring in part and concurring in the judgment: Kennedy; Stevens. Concurring in the judgment: Scalia. Dissenting opinion: Marshall, Brennan, Blackmun; Blackmun, Brennan.*

JUSTICE O'CONNOR . . . delivered the opinion of the Court. . . .

In this case, we confront once again the tension between the Fourteenth Amendment's guarantee of equal treatment to all citizens, and the use of race-based measures to ameliorate the effects of past discrimination on the opportunities enjoyed by members of minority groups in our society. In *Fullilove* v. *Klutznick* . . . (1980), we held that a congressional program requiring that 10% of certain federal construction grants be awarded to minority contractors did not violate the equal protection principles embodied in the Due Process Clause of the Fifth Amendment. Relying largely on our decision in *Fullilove,* some lower federal courts have applied a similar standard of review in assessing the constitutionality of state and local minority set-aside provisions under the Equal Protection Clause of the Fourteenth Amendment. . . . Since our decision two Terms ago in *Wygant* v. *Jackson Board of Education* . . . (1986), the lower federal courts have attempted to apply its standards in evaluating the constitutionality of state and local programs which allocate a portion of public contracting opportunities exclusively to minority-owned businesses. . . . We noted probable jurisdiction in this case to consider the applicability of our decision in *Wygant* to a minority set-aside program adopted by the city of Richmond, Virginia . . .

The parties and their supporting *amici* fight an initial battle over the scope of the city's power to adopt legislation designed to address the effects of past discrimination. Relying on our decision in *Wygant,* appellee argues that the city must limit any race-based remedial efforts to eradicating the effects of its own prior discrimination. This is essentially the position taken by the Court of Appeals below. Appellant argues that our decision in *Fullilove* is controlling, and

that as a result the city of Richmond enjoys sweeping legislative power to define and attack the effects of prior discrimination in its local construction industry. We find that neither of these two rather stark alternatives can withstand analysis.

In *Fullilove,* we upheld the minority set-aside contained in § 103(f)(2) of the Public Works Employment Act of 1977, . . . against a challenge based on the equal protection component of the Due Process Clause . . .

The principal opinion in *Fullilove,* written by Chief Justice Burger, did not employ "strict scrutiny" or any other traditional standard of equal protection review. The Chief Justice noted at the outset that although racial classifications call for close examination, the Court was at the same time, "bound to approach [its] task with appropriate deference to the Congress, a co-equal branch charged by the Constitution with the power to "provide for the . . . general Welfare of the United States' and 'to enforce by appropriate legislation,' the equal protection guarantees of the Fourteenth Amendment." . . . The principal opinion asked two questions: first, were the objectives of the legislation within the power of Congress? Second, was the limited use of racial and ethnic criteria a permissible means for Congress to carry out its objectives within the constraints of the Due Process Clause?

On the issue of congressional power, the Chief Justice found that Congress' commerce power was sufficiently broad to allow it to reach the practices of prime contractors on federally funded local construction projects. . . . Congress could mandate state and local government compliance with the set-aside program under its § 5 power to enforce the Fourteenth Amendment . . .

The Chief Justice next turned to the constraints on Congress' power to employ race-conscious remedial relief. His opinion stressed two factors in upholding the MBE set-aside. First was the unique remedial powers of Congress under § 5 of the Fourteenth Amendment:

> Here we deal . . . not with the limited reme-dial powers of a federal court, for example, but with the broad remedial powers of Congress. It is fundamental that *in no organ of govern-ment, state or federal, does there repose a more comprehensive remedial power than in the Congress,* expressly charged by the Con-stitution with competence and authority to enforce equal protection guarantees. . . .

Because of these unique powers, the Chief Jus-tice concluded that "Congress not only may in-duce voluntary action to assure compliance with existing federal statutory or constitutional an-tidiscrimination provisions, but also, where Con-gress has authority to *declare certain conduct unlawful,* it may, as here, authorize and induce state action to avoid such conduct."

The second factor emphasized by the principal opinion in *Fullilove* was the flexible nature of the 10% set-aside. Two "congressional assump-tions" underlay the MBE program: first, that the effects of past discrimination had impaired the competitive position of minority businesses, and second, that "adjustment for the effects of past discrimination" would assure that at least 10% of the funds from the federal grant program would flow to minority businesses. The Chief Justice noted that both of these "assumptions" could be "rebutted" by a grantee seeking a waiver of the 10% requirement. . . . Thus a waiver could be sought where minority busi-nesses were not available to fill the 10% require-ment or, more importantly, where an MBE at-tempted "to exploit the remedial aspects of the program by charging an unreasonable price, *i.e.,* a price not attributable to the present effects of prior discrimination." . . . The Chief Justice indi-cated that without this fine tuning to remedial purpose, the statute would not have "pass[ed] muster." . . .

Appellant and its supporting *amici* rely heav-ily on *Fullilove* for the proposition that a city council, like Congress, need not make specific findings of discrimination to engage in race-con-scious relief. Thus, appellant argues "[i]t would be a perversion of federalism to hold that the fed-eral government has a compelling interest in remedying the effects of racial discrimination in its own public works program, but a city govern-ment does not."

What appellant ignores is that Congress, un-like any State or political subdivision, has a spe-cific constitutional mandate to enforce the dic-tates of the Fourteenth Amendment. The power to "enforce" may at times also include the power to define situations which *Congress* determines threaten principles of equality and to adopt pro-phylactic rules to deal with those situations. . . . The Civil War Amendments themselves worked a dramatic change in the balance between con-gressional and state power over matters of race. Speaking of the Thirteenth and Fourteenth Amendments in *Ex parte Virginia,* 100 U.S. 339, 345 (1880), the Court stated: "They were in-tended to be, what they really are, limitations of the powers of the States and enlargements of the power of Congress."

That Congress may identify and redress the ef-fects of society-wide discrimination does not mean that, *a fortiori,* the States and their politi-cal subdivisions are free to decide that such remedies are appropriate. Section 1 of the Four-teenth Amendment is an explicit *constraint* on state power, and the States must undertake any remedial efforts in accordance with that provi-sion. To hold otherwise would be to cede control over the content of the Equal Protection Clause to the 50 state legislatures and their myriad polit-ical subdivisions. The mere recitation of a benign or compensatory purpose for the use of a racial classification would essentially entitle the States to exercise the full power of Congress under § 5 of the Fourteenth Amendment and insulate any racial classification from judicial scrutiny under § 1. We believe that such a result would be con-trary to the intentions of the Framers of the Four-teenth Amendment, who desired to place clear limits on the States' use of race as a criterion for legislative action, and to have the federal courts enforce those limitations. . . .

It would seem equally clear, however, that a state or local subdivision (if delegated the author-ity from the State) has the authority to eradicate the effects of private discrimination within its own legislative jurisdiction. This authority must, of course, be exercised within the con-straints of § 1 of the Fourteenth Amendment. Our decision in *Wygant* is not to the contrary.

Wygant addressed the constitutionality of the use of racial quotas by local school authorities pursuant to an agreement reached with the local teachers' union. It was in the context of addressing the school board's power to adopt a race-based layoff program affecting its own work force that the *Wygant* plurality indicated that the Equal Protection Clause required "some showing of prior discrimination by the governmental unit involved." . . . As a matter of state law, the city of Richmond has legislative authority over its procurement policies, and can use its spending powers to remedy private discrimination, if it identifies that discrimination with the particularity required by the Fourteenth Amendment. . . .

The Equal Protection Clause of the Fourteenth Amendment provides that "[N]o State shall . . . deny to *any person* within its jurisdiction the equal protection of the laws" (emphasis added). As this Court has noted in the past, the "rights created by the first section of the Fourteenth Amendment are, by its terms, guaranteed to the individual. The rights established are personal rights." *Shelley* v. *Kraemer*, . . . (1948). The Richmond Plan denies certain citizens the opportunity to compete for a fixed percentage of public contracts based solely upon their race. To whatever racial group these citizens belong, their "personal rights" to be treated with equal dignity and respect are implicated by a rigid rule erecting race as the sole criterion in an aspect of public decision-making.

Absent searching judicial inquiry into the justification for such race-based measures, there is simply no way of determining what classifications are "benign" or "remedial" and what classifications are in fact motivated by illegitimate notions of racial inferiority or simple racial politics. Indeed, the purpose of strict scrutiny is to "smoke out" illegitimate uses of race by assuring that the legislative body is pursuing a goal important enough to warrant use of a highly suspect tool. The test also ensures that the means chosen "fit" this compelling goal so closely that there is little or no possibility that the motive for the classification was illegitimate racial prejudice or stereotype.

Classifications based on race carry a danger of stigmatic harm. Unless they are strictly reserved for remedial settings, they may in fact promote notions of racial inferiority and lead to a politics of racial hostility. . . . We thus reaffirm the view expressed by the plurality in *Wygant* that the standard of review under the Equal Protection Clause is not dependent on the race of those burdened or benefited by a particular classification. . . .

Under the standard proposed by Justice Marshall's dissent, "[r]ace-conscious classifications designed to further remedial goals," . . . are forthwith subject to a relaxed standard of review. How the dissent arrives at the legal conclusion that a racial classification is "designed to further remedial goals," without first engaging in an examination of the factual basis for its enactment and the nexus between its scope and that factual basis we are not told. However, once the "remedial" conclusion is reached, the dissent's standard is singularly deferential, and bears little resemblance to the close examination of legislative purpose we have engaged in when reviewing classifications based either on race or gender. . . . The dissent's watered-down version of equal protection review effectively assures that race will always be relevant in American life, and that the "ultimate goal" of "eliminat[ing] entirely from governmental decision-making such irrelevant factors as a human being's race," . . . will never be achieved.

Even were we to accept a reading of the guarantee of equal protection under which the level of scrutiny varies according to the ability of different groups to defend their interests in the representative process, heightened scrutiny would still be appropriate in the circumstances of this case. One of the central arguments for applying a less exacting standard to "benign" racial classifications is that such measures essentially involve a choice made by dominant racial groups to disadvantage themselves. If one aspect of the judiciary's role under the Equal Protection Clause is to protect "discrete and insular minorities" from majoritarian prejudice or indifference, . . . some maintain that these concerns are not implicated when the "white majority" places burdens upon itself.

In this case, blacks comprise approximately 50% of the population of the city of Richmond. Five of the nine seats on the City Council are held by blacks. The concern that a political majority will more easily act to the disadvantage of a minority based on unwarranted assumptions or incomplete facts would seem to militate for, not against, the application of heightened judicial scrutiny in this case. . . .

Appellant argues that it is attempting to remedy various forms of past discrimination that are alleged to be responsible for the small number of minority businesses in the local contracting industry. Among these the city cites the exclusion of blacks from skilled construction trade unions and training programs. This past discrimination has prevented them "from following the traditional path from laborer to entrepreneur." The city also lists a host of nonracial factors which would seem to face a member of any racial group attempting to establish a new business enterprise, such as deficiencies in working capital, inability to meet bonding requirements, unfamiliarity with bidding procedures, and disability caused by an inadequate track record. . . .

While there is no doubt that the sorry history of both private and public discrimination in this country has contributed to a lack of opportunities for black entrepreneurs, this observation, standing alone, cannot justify a rigid racial quota in the awarding of public contracts in Richmond, Virginia. Like the claim that discrimination in primary and secondary schooling justifies a rigid racial preference in medical school admissions, an amorphous claim that there has been past discrimination in a particular industry cannot justify the use of an unyielding racial quota.

It is sheer speculation how many minority firms there would be in Richmond absent past societal discrimination, just as it was sheer speculation how many minority medical students would have been admitted to the medical school at Davis absent past discrimination in educational opportunities. Defining these sorts of injuries as "identified discrimination" would give local governments license to create a patchwork of racial preferences based on statistical generalizations about any particular field of endeavor.

These defects are readily apparent in this case. The 30% quota cannot in any realistic sense be tied to any injury suffered by anyone. The District Court relied upon five predicate "facts" in reaching its conclusion that there was an adequate basis for the 30% quota: (1) the ordinance declares itself to be remedial; (2) several proponents of the measure stated their views that there had been past discrimination in the construction industry; (3) minority businesses received .67% of prime contracts from the city while minorities constituted 50% of the city's population; (4) there were very few minority contractors in local and state contractors' associations; and (5) in 1977, Congress made a determination that the effects of past discrimination had stifled minority participation in the construction industry nationally. . . .

None of these "findings," singly or together, provide the city of Richmond with a "strong basis in evidence for its conclusion that remedial action was necessary." . . . There is nothing approaching a prima facie case of a constitutional or statutory violation by anyone in the Richmond construction industry. . . .

The District Court accorded great weight to the fact that the city council designated the Plan as "remedial." But the mere recitation of a "benign" or legitimate purpose for a racial classification, is entitled to little or no weight. . . . Racial classifications are suspect, and that means that simple legislative assurances of good intention cannot suffice.

The District Court also relied on the highly conclusionary statement of a proponent of the Plan that there was racial discrimination in the construction industry "in this area, and the State, and around the nation." . . . It also noted that the city manager had related his view that racial discrimination still plagued the construction industry in his home city of Pittsburgh. . . . These statements are of little probative value in establishing identified discrimination in the Richmond construction industry. The factfinding process of legislative bodies is generally entitled to a presumption of regularity and deferential review by the judiciary. . . . But when a legislative body chooses to employ a suspect classification, it cannot rest upon a generalized assertion as to the classification's relevance to its goals. . . . A governmental actor cannot render race a legitimate proxy for a particular condition merely by declaring that the condition exists. . . . The history of racial classifications in this country suggests that blind judicial deference to legislative or executive pronouncements of necessity has no place in equal protection analysis. . . .

Reliance on the disparity between the number of prime contracts awarded to minority firms and the minority population of the city of Richmond is similarly misplaced. There is no doubt that "[w]here gross statistical disparities can be shown, they alone in a proper case may constitute prima facie proof of a pattern or practice of discrimination" under Title VII. . . . But it is equally clear that "[w]hen special qualifications are required to fill particular jobs, comparisons to the general population (rather than to the smaller group of individuals who possess the necessary qualifications) may have little probative value." . . .

In the employment context, we have recognized that for certain entry level positions or positions requiring minimal training, statistical comparisons of the racial composition of an employer's workforce to the racial composition of the relevant population may be probative of a pattern of discrimination. . . . But where special qualifications are necessary, the relevant statistical pool for purposes of demonstrating discriminatory exclusion must be the number of minorities qualified to undertake the particular task. . . .

In this case, the city does not even know how many MBEs in the relevant market are qualified to undertake prime or subcontracting work in public construction projects. . . . Nor does the city know what percentage of total city construction dollars minority firms now receive as subcontractors on prime contracts let by the city.

To a large extent, the set-aside of subcontracting dollars seems to rest on the unsupported assumption that white prime contractors simply will not hire minority firms. . . . Indeed, there is evidence in this record that overall minority participation in city contracts in Richmond is seven to eight percent, and that minority contractor participation in Community Block Development Grant *construction* projects is 17% to 22%. . . . Without any information on minority participation in subcontracting, it is quite simply impossible to evaluate overall minority representation in the city's construction expenditures.

The city and the District Court also relied on evidence that MBE membership in local contractors' associations was extremely low. Again, standing alone this evidence is not probative of any discrimination in the local construction industry. There are numerous explanations for this dearth of minority participation, including past societal discrimination in education and economic opportunities as well as both black and white career and entrepreneurial choices. Blacks may be disproportionately attracted to industries other than construction. . . . The mere fact that black membership in these trade organizations is low, standing alone, cannot establish a prima facie case of discrimination.

In sum, none of the evidence presented by the city points to any identified discrimination in the Richmond construction industry. We, therefore, hold that the city has failed to demonstrate a compelling interest in apportioning public contracting opportunities on the basis of race. To accept Richmond's claim that past societal discrimination alone can serve as the basis for rigid racial preferences would be to open the door to competing claims for "remedial relief" for every disadvantaged group. The dream of a Nation of equal citizens in a society where race is irrelevant to personal opportunity and achievement would be lost in a mosaic of shifting preferences based on inherently unmeasurable claims of past wrongs. . . .

The foregoing analysis applies only to the inclusion of blacks within the Richmond set-aside program. There is *absolutely no evidence* of past discrimination against Spanish-speaking, Oriental, Indian, Eskimo, or Aleut persons in any aspect of the Richmond construction industry. The District Court took judicial notice of the fact that the vast majority of "minority" persons in Richmond were black. . . . It may well be that Richmond has never had an Aleut or Eskimo citizen. The random inclusion of racial groups that, as a practical matter, may never have suffered from discrimination in the construction industry in Richmond, suggests that perhaps the city's purpose was not in fact to remedy past discrimination.

If a 30% set-aside was "narrowly tailored" to compensate black contractors for past discrimination, one may legitimately ask why they are forced to share this "remedial relief" with an Aleut citizen who moves to Richmond tomorrow? The gross overinclusiveness of Richmond's racial preference strongly impugns the city's claim of remedial motivation. . . .

As noted by the court below, it is almost impossible to assess whether the Richmond Plan is narrowly tailored to remedy prior discrimination since it is not linked to identified discrimination in any way. We limit ourselves to two observations in this regard.

First, there does not appear to have been any consideration of the use of race-neutral means to increase minority business participation in city contracting. . . .

Many of the barriers to minority participation in the construction industry relied upon by the city to justify a racial classification appear to be race neutral. If MBEs disproportionately lack capital or cannot meet bonding requirements, a race-neutral program of city financing for small firms would, *a fortiori*, lead to greater minority participation. . . . There is no evidence in this record that the Richmond City Council has considered any alternatives to a race-based quota.

Second, the 30% quota cannot be said to be narrowly tailored to any goal, except perhaps outright racial balancing. It rests upon the "completely unrealistic" assumption that minorities will choose a particular trade in lockstep proportion to their representation in the local population. . . .

Since the city must already consider bids and waivers on a case-by-case basis, it is difficult to see the need for a rigid numerical quota. As noted above, the congressional scheme upheld in *Fullilove* allowed for a waiver of the set-aside provision where an MBE's higher price was not attributable to the effect of past discrimination. Based upon proper findings, such programs are less problematic from an equal protection standpoint because they treat all candidates individually, rather than making the color of an applicant's skin the sole relevant consideration. Unlike the program upheld in *Fullilove*, the Richmond Plan's waiver system focuses solely on the availability of MBEs; there is no inquiry into whether or not the particular MBE seeking a racial preference has suffered from the effects of past discrimination by the city or prime contractors.

Given the existence of an individualized procedure, the city's only interest in maintaining a quota system rather than investigating the need for remedial action in particular cases would seem to be simple administrative convenience. But the interest in avoiding the bureaucratic effort necessary to tailor remedial relief to those who truly have suffered the effects of prior discrimination cannot justify a rigid line drawn on the basis of a suspect classification. . . . Under Richmond's scheme, a successful black, Hispanic, or Oriental entrepreneur from anywhere in the country enjoys an absolute preference over other citizens based solely on their race. We think it obvious that such a program is not narrowly tailored to remedy the effects of prior discrimination. . . .

Because the city of Richmond has failed to identify the need for remedial action in the awarding of its public construction contracts, its treatment of its citizens on a racial basis violates the dictates of the Equal Protection Clause. Accordingly, the judgment of the Court of Appeals for the Fourth Circuit is

Affirmed.

JUSTICE SCALIA, concurring in the judgment.

I agree with much of the Court's opinion, and, in particular, with its conclusion that strict scrutiny must be applied to all governmental classification by race, whether or not its asserted purpose is "remedial" or "benign." . . . I do not agree, however, with the Court's dicta suggesting that, despite the Fourteenth Amendment, state and local governments may in some circumstances discriminate on the basis of race in order (in a broad sense) "to ameliorate the effects of past discrimination." The difficulty of overcoming the effects of past discrimination is as nothing compared with the difficulty of eradicating from our society the source of those effects, which is the tendency—fatal to a nation such as ours—to classify and judge men and women on the basis of their country of origin or the color of their skin. A solution to the first problem that aggravates the second is no solution at all. I share the view expressed by Alexander Bickel that "[t]he lesson of the great decisions of the Supreme Court and the lesson of contemporary history have been the same for at least a generation: discrimination on the basis of race is illegal, immoral, unconstitutional, inherently wrong, and destructive of democratic society." A. Bickel, The Morality of Consent 133 (1975). At least where state or local action is at issue, only a social engineering rising to the level of imminent danger to life and limb—for example, a prison race riot, requiring temporary segregation of inmates . . . —can justify an exception to the principle embodied in the Fourteenth Amendment that "[o]ur Constitution is color-blind, and neither knows nor tolerates classes among citizens," . . .

We have in some contexts approved the use of racial classifications by the Federal Government to remedy the effects of past discrimination. I do not believe that we must or should extend these holdings to the States. . . .

A sound distinction between federal and state (or local) action based on race rests not only upon the substance of the Civil War Amendments, but upon social reality and governmental theory. It is a simple fact that what Justice Stewart described in *Fullilove* as "the dispassionate objectivity [and] the flexibility that are needed to mold a race-conscious remedy around the single objective of eliminating the effects of past or present discrimination" . . . are substantially less likely to exist at the state or local level. The struggle for racial justice has historically been a struggle by the national society against oppression in the individual States. . . . What the record shows, in other words, is that racial discrimination against any group finds a more ready expression at the state and local than at the federal level. To the children of the Founding Fathers, this should come as no surprise. An acute awareness of the heightened danger of oppression from political factions in small, rather than large, political units dates to the very beginning of our national history. . . . As James Madison observed in support of the proposed Constitution's enhancement of national powers:

> The smaller the society, the fewer probably will be the distinct parties and interests composing it; the fewer the distinct parties and interests, the more frequently will a majority be found of the same party; and the smaller the number of individuals composing a majority, and the smaller the compass within which they are placed, the more easily will they concert and execute their plan of oppression. Extend the sphere and you take in a greater variety of parties and interests; you make it less probable that a majority of the whole will have a common motive to invade the rights of other citizens; or if such a common motive exists, it will be more difficult for all who feel it to discover their own strength and to act in unison with each other. The Federalist No. 10. . . .

The prophesy of these words came to fruition in Richmond in the enactment of a set-aside clearly and directly beneficial to the dominant political group, which happens also to be the dominant racial group. The same thing has no doubt happened before in other cities (though the racial basis of the preference has rarely been made textually explicit)—and blacks have often been on the receiving end of the injustice. Where injustice is the game, however, turn-about is not fair play. . . .

In his final book, Professor Bickel wrote:

> [A] racial quota derogates the human dignity and individuality of all to whom it is applied; it is invidious in principle as well as in practice. Moreover, it can easily be turned against those it purports to help. The history of the racial quota is a history of subjugation, not beneficence. Its evil lies not in its name, but in its effects: a quota is a divider of society, a creator of castes, and it is all the worse for its racial base, especially in a society desperately striving for an equality that will make race irrelevant. Bickel, The Morality of Consent, at 133.

Those statements are true and increasingly prophetic. Apart from their societal effects, however, which are "in the aggregate disastrous," . . . it is important not to lose sight of the fact that even "benign" racial quotas have individual victims, whose very real injustice we ignore whenever we deny them enforcement of their right not to be disadvantaged on the basis of race. . . . As Justice Douglas observed: "A De-Funis who is white is entitled to no advantage by virtue of that fact; nor is he subject to any disability, no matter what his race or color. Whatever his race, he had a constitutional right to have his application considered on its individual merits in a racially neutral manner." De-Funis v. Odegaard . . . (1974). When we depart from this American principle we play with fire, and much more than an occasional DeFunis . . . or Croson burns.

It is plainly true that in our society blacks have suffered discrimination immeasurably greater than any directed at other racial groups. But those who believe that racial preferences can help to "even the score" display, and reinforce, a manner of thinking by race that was the source of the injustice and that will, if it endures within our society, be the source of more injustice still. The relevant proposition is not that it was blacks, or Jews, or Irish who were discriminated against, but that it was individual men and women, "created equal," who were discriminated against. And the relevant resolve is that that should never happen again. Racial preferences appear to "even the score" (in some small degree) only if one embraces the proposition that our society is appropriately viewed as divided into races, making it right that an injustice rendered in the past to a black man should be compensated for by discriminating against a white. Nothing is worth that embrace. Since blacks have been disproportionately disadvantaged by racial discrimination, any race-neutral remedial program aimed at the disadvantaged as such will have a disproportionately beneficial impact on blacks. Only such a program, and not one that operates on the basis of race, is in accord with the letter and the spirit of our Constitution.

Since I believe that the appellee here had a constitutional right to have its bid succeed or fail under a decisionmaking process uninfected with racial bias, I concur in the judgment of the Court.

JUSTICE STEVENS, concurring in part and concurring in the judgment. . . .

The ordinance is . . . vulnerable because of its failure to identify the characteristics of the disadvantaged class of white contractors that justify the disparate treatment. . . . The composition of the disadvantaged class of white contractors presumably includes some who have been guilty of unlawful discrimination, some who practiced discrimination before it was forbidden by law, and some who have never discriminated against anyone on the basis of race. Imposing a common burden on such a disparate class merely because each member of the class is of the same race stems from reliance on a stereotype rather than fact or reason.

There is a special irony in the stereotypical thinking that prompts legislation of this kind. Although it stigmatizes the disadvantaged class with the unproven charge of past racial discrimination, it actually imposes a greater stigma on its supposed beneficiaries. For, as I explained in my *Fullilove* opinion:

> [E]ven though it is not the actual predicate for this legislation, a statute of this kind inevitably is perceived by many as resting on an assumption that those who are granted this special preference are less qualified in some respect that is identified purely by their race. . . .
>
> The risk that habitual attitudes toward classes of persons, rather than analysis of the relevant characteristics of the class, will serve as a basis for a legislative classification is present when benefits are distributed as well as when burdens are imposed. In the past, traditional attitudes too often provided the only explanation for discrimination against women, aliens, illegitimates, and black citizens. Today there is a danger that awareness of past injustice will lead to automatic acceptance of new classifications that are not in fact justified by attributes characteristic of the class as a whole.

When [government] creates a special preference, or a special disability, for a class of persons, it should identify the characteristic that justifies the special treatment. When the classification is defined in racial terms, I believe that such particular identification is imperative.

In this case, only two conceivable bases for differentiating the preferred classes from society as a whole have occurred to me: (1) that they were the victims of unfair treatment in the past and (2) that they are less able to compete in the future. Although the first of these factors would justify an appropriate remedy for past wrongs, for reasons that I have already stated, this statute is not such a remedial measure. The second factor is simply not true. Nothing in the record of this case, the legislative history of the Act, or experience that we may notice judicially provides any support for such a proposition.

JUSTICE MARSHALL, with whom JUSTICE BRENNAN and JUSTICE BLACKMUN join, dissenting.

It is a welcome symbol of racial progress when the former capital of the Confederacy acts forthrightly to confront the effects of racial discrimination in its midst. In my view, nothing in the Constitution can be construed to prevent Richmond, Virginia, from allocating a portion of its contracting dollars for businesses owned or controlled by members of minority groups. Indeed, Richmond's set-aside program is indistinguishable in all meaningful respects from—and in fact was patterned upon—the federal set-aside plan which this Court upheld in *Fullilove* v. *Klutznick.* . . .

A majority of this Court holds today, however, that the Equal Protection Clause of the Fourteenth Amendment blocks Richmond's initiative. The essence of the majority's position is that Richmond has failed to catalogue adequate findings to prove that past discrimination has impeded minorities from joining or participating fully in Richmond's construction contracting industry. I find deep irony in second-guessing Richmond's judgment on this point. As much as any municipality in the United States, Richmond knows what racial discrimination is; a century of decisions by this and other federal courts has richly documented the city's disgraceful history of public and private racial discrimination. In any event, the Richmond City Council *has* supported its determination that minorities have been wrongly excluded from local construction contracting. Its proof includes statistics showing that minority-owned businesses have received virtually no city contracting dollars and rarely if ever belonged to area trade associations; testimony by municipal officials that discrimination has been widespread in the local construction industry; and the same exhaustive and widely publicized federal studies relied on in *Fullilove*, studies which showed that pervasive discrimination in the Nation's tight-knit construction industry had operated to exclude minorities from public contracting. These are precisely the types of statistical and testimonial evidence which, until today, this Court had credited in cases approving of race-conscious measures designed to remedy past discrimination.

More fundamentally, today's decision marks a deliberate and giant step backward in this Court's affirmative action jurisprudence. Cynical of one municipality's attempt to redress the effects of past racial discrimination in a particular industry, the majority launches a grapeshot attack on race-conscious remedies in general. The majority's unnecessary pronouncements will inevitably discourage or prevent governmental entities, particularly States and localities, from acting to rectify the scourge of past discrimination. This is the harsh reality of the majority's decision, but it is not the Constitution's command. . . . My view has long been that race-conscious classifications designed to further remedial goals "must serve important governmental objectives and must be substantially related to achievement of those objectives" in order to withstand constitutional scrutiny. . . . Analyzed in terms of this two-prong standard, Richmond's set-aside, like the federal program on which it was modeled, is "plainly constitutional." . . .

Turning first to the governmental interest inquiry, Richmond has two powerful interests in setting aside a portion of public contracting funds for minority-owned enterprises. The first is the city's interest in eradicating the effects of past racial discrimination. It is far too late in the day to doubt that remedying such discrimination is a compelling, let alone an important, interest. . . .

Richmond has a second compelling interest in setting aside, where possible, a portion of its contracting dollars. That interest is the prospective one of preventing the city's own spending decisions from reinforcing and perpetuating the exclusionary effects of past discrimination.

. . . When government channels all its contracting funds to a white-dominated community of established contractors whose racial homogeneity is the product of private discrimination, it does more than place its imprimatur on the practices which forged and which continue to define that community. It also provides a measurable boost to those economic entities that have thrived within it, while denying important economic benefits to those entities which, but for prior discrimination, might well be better qualified to receive valuable government contracts. In my view, the interest in ensuring that the government does not reflect and reinforce prior private discrimination in dispensing public contracts is every bit as strong as the interest in eliminating private discrimination—an interest which this Court has repeatedly deemed compelling. . . . The more government bestows its rewards on those persons or businesses that were positioned to thrive during a period of private racial discrimination, the tighter the deadhand grip of prior discrimination becomes on the present and future. Cities like Richmond may not be constitutionally required to adopt set-aside plans. . . . But there can be no doubt that when Richmond acted affirmatively to stem the perpetuation of patterns of discrimination through its own decisionmaking, it served an interest of the highest order. . . .

In my judgment, Richmond's set-aside plan also comports with the second prong of the equal protection inquiry, for it is substantially related to the interests it seeks to serve in remedying past discrimination and in ensuring that municipal contract procurement does not perpetuate that discrimination. The most striking aspect of the city's ordinance is the similarity it bears to the "appropriately limited" federal set-aside provision upheld in *Fullilove*. . . .

Today, for the first time, a majority of this Court has adopted strict scrutiny as its standard of Equal Protection Clause review of race-conscious remedial measures. . . . This is an unwelcome development. A profound difference separates governmental actions that themselves are racist, and governmental actions that seek to remedy the effects of prior racism or to prevent neutral governmental activity from perpetuating the effects of such racism. . . .

In concluding that remedial classifications warrant no different standard of review under the Constitution than the most brute and repugnant forms of state-sponsored racism, a majority of this Court signals that it regards racial discrimination as largely a phenomenon of the past, and that government bodies need no longer preoccupy themselves with rectifying racial injustice. . . .

I am also troubled by the majority's assertion that, even if it did not believe generally in strict scrutiny of race-based remedial measures, "the circumstances of this case" require this Court to look upon the Richmond City Council's measure with the strictest scrutiny. . . . The sole such circumstance which the majority cites, however, is the fact that blacks in Richmond are a "dominant racial grou[p]" in the city. . . . In support of this characterization of dominance, the majority observes that "blacks comprise approximately 50% of the population of the city of Richmond" and that "[f]ive of the nine seats on the City Council are held by blacks." . . .

While I agree that the numerical and political supremacy of a given racial group is a factor bearing upon the level of scrutiny to be applied, this Court has never held that numerical inferiority, standing alone, makes a racial group "suspect" and thus entitled to strict scrutiny review. . . .

In my view, the "circumstances of this case . . . underscore the importance of *not* subjecting to a strict scrutiny straitjacket the increasing number of cities which have recently come under minority leadership and are eager to rectify, or at least prevent the perpetuation of, past racial discrimination. In many cases, these cases will be the ones with the most in the way of prior discrimination to rectify. Richmond's leaders had just witnessed decades of publicly sanctioned racial discrimination in virtually all walks of life—discrimination amply documented in the decisions of the federal judiciary. . . . This history of "purposefully unequal treatment" forced upon minorities, not imposed by them, should raise an inference that minorities in Richmond had much to remedy—and that the 1983 set-aside was undertaken with sincere remedial goals in mind, not "simple racial politics." . . .

The majority today sounds a full-scale retreat from the Court's longstanding solicitude to race-conscious remedial efforts "directed toward deliverance of the century-old promise of equality of economic opportunity." . . . The new and restrictive tests it applies scuttle one city's effort to surmount its discriminatory past, and imperil those of dozens more localities. I, however, profoundly disagree with the cramped vision of the Equal Protection Clause which the majority offers today and with its application of that vision to Richmond, Virginia's, laudable set-aside plan. The battle against pernicious racial discrimination or its effects is nowhere near won. I must dissent.

Adarand Constructors, Inc. v. *Pena*
515 U.S. 200; 115 S. Ct. 2097; 132 L. Ed. 2d 158 (1995)

Adarand Constructors, which submitted the low bid on the guardrail portion of a federal highway project, was not awarded the subcontract because of a federal subcontractor compensation clause designed to provide the prime contractor with a financial incentive to hire disadvantaged business enterprises. Relying on the reasoning of *Richmond* v. *J.A. Croson Co.*, 448 U.S. 469 (1989), Adarand Constructors filed suit against Secretary of Transportation Frederico Pena and others, claiming a violation of the equal protection component of the Fifth Amendment. The U.S. District Court for the District of Colorado granted the respondents' summary judgment, and the Court of Appeals for the Tenth Circuit affirmed, basing its decision on *Fullilove* v. *Klutznick*, 448 (1980), and *Metro Broadcasting, Inc.* v. *F.C.C.*, 497 U.S. 547 (1990). The Supreme Court granted certiorari. *Opinion of the Court: O'Connor, Kennedy, Rehnquist, Scalia, Thomas. Concurring in part and concurring in the judgment: Scalia; Thomas. Dissenting opinions: Stevens, Ginsburg; Souter, Breyer, Ginsburg; Ginsburg, Breyer.*

JUSTICE O'CONNOR *delivered the opinion of the Court.*

Petitioner Adarand Constructors, Inc., claims that the Federal Government's practice of giving general contractors on government projects a financial incentive to hire subcontractors controlled by "socially and economically disadvantaged individuals," and in particular, the Government's use of race-based presumptions in identifying such individuals, violates the equal protection component of the Fifth Amendment's Due Process Clause. The Court of Appeals rejected Adarand's claim. We conclude, however, that courts should analyze cases of this kind under a different standard of review than the one the Court of Appeals applied. We therefore vacate the Court of Appeals' judgment and remand the case for further proceedings.

In 1989, the Central Federal Lands Highway Division (CFLHD), which is part of the United States Department of Transportation (DOT), awarded the prime contract for a highway construction project in Colorado to Mountain Gravel & Construction Company. Mountain Gravel then solicited bids from subcontractors for the guardrail portion of the contract. Adarand, a Colorado-based highway construction company specializing in guardrail work, submitted the low bid. Gonzales Construction Company also submitted a bid.

The prime contract's terms provide that Mountain Gravel would receive additional compensation if it hired subcontractors certified as small businesses controlled by "socially and economically disadvantaged individuals." Gonzales is certified as such a business; Adarand is not. Mountain Gravel awarded the subcontract to Gonzales, despite Adarand's low bid, and Mountain Gravel's Chief Estimator has submitted an affidavit stating that Mountain Gravel would have accepted Adarand's bid, had it not been for the additional payment it received by hiring Gonzales instead. Federal law requires that a subcontracting clause similar to the one used here must appear in most federal agency contracts, and it also requires the clause to state that "[t]he contractor shall presume that socially and economically disadvantaged individuals include Black Americans, Hispanic Americans, Native Americans, Asian Pacific Americans, and other minorities, or any other individual found to be disadvantaged by the [Small Business] Administration pursuant to section 8(a) of the Small Business Act." Adarand claims that the presumption set forth in that statute discriminates on the basis of race in violation of the Federal Government's Fifth Amendment obligation not to deny anyone equal protection of the laws. . . .

The Government urges that "[t]he Subcontracting Compensation Clause program is . . . a program based on *disadvantage,* not on race," and thus that it is subject only to "the most relaxed judicial scrutiny." To the extent that the statutes and regulations involved in this case are race neutral, we agree. The Government concedes, however, that "the race-based rebuttable presumption used in some certification determinations under the Subcontracting Compensation Clause" is subject to some heightened level of scrutiny. The parties disagree as to what that level should be.

Adarand's claim arises under the Fifth Amendment to the Constitution, which provides that "No person shall . . . be deprived of life, liberty, or property, without due process of law." Although this Court has always understood that Clause to provide some measure of protection against *arbitrary* treatment by the Federal Government, it is not as explicit a guarantee of *equal* treatment as the Fourteenth Amendment, which provides that "No *State* shall . . . deny to any person within its jurisdiction the equal protection of the laws." Our cases have accorded varying degrees of significance to the difference in the language of those two Clauses. We think it necessary to revisit the issue here. . . .

With *Richmond* v. *J.A. Croson Co.,* 488 U.S. 469 (1989), the Court . . . agreed that the Fourteenth Amendment requires strict scrutiny of all race-based action by state and local governments. But *Croson* of course had no occasion to declare what standard of review the Fifth Amendment requires for such action taken by the Federal Government. *Croson* observed simply that the Court's "treatment of an exercise of congressional power in *Fullilove* cannot be dispositive here," because *Croson's* facts did not implicate Congress' broad power under § 5 of the Fourteenth Amendment. . . .

Despite lingering uncertainty in the details, however, the Court's cases through *Croson* had established three general propositions with respect to governmental racial classifications. First, skepticism: " '[A]ny preference based on racial or ethnic criteria must necessarily receive a most searching examination.' " Second, consistency: "The standard of review under the Equal Protection Clause is not dependent on the race of those burdened or benefited by a particular classification." And third, congruence: "[E]qual protection analysis in the Fifth Amendment area is the same as that under the Fourteenth Amendment." Taken together, these three propositions lead to the conclusion that any person, of whatever race, has the right to demand that any governmental actor subject to the Constitution justify any racial classification subjecting that person to unequal treatment under the strictest judicial scrutiny. . . .

A year later, however, the Court took a surprising turn. *Metro Broadcasting, Inc.* v. *FCC,* 497 U.S. 547 (1990), involved a Fifth Amendment challenge to two race-based policies of the Federal Communications Commission. In *Metro Broadcasting,* the Court repudiated the long-held notion that "it would be unthinkable that the same Constitution would impose a lesser duty on the Federal Government" than it does on a State to afford equal protection of the laws. It did so by holding that "benign" federal racial classifications need only satisfy intermediate scrutiny, even though *Croson* had recently concluded that such classifications enacted by a State must satisfy strict scrutiny. "[B]enign" federal racial classifications, the Court said, "—even if those measures are not 'remedial' in the sense of being designed to compensate victims of past governmental or societal discrimination—are constitutionally permissible to the extent that they serve *important* governmental objectives within the power of Congress and are *substantially related* to achievement of those objectives." The Court did not explain how to tell whether a racial classification should be deemed "benign," other than to express "confiden[ce]" that an 'examination of the legislative scheme and its history' will separate benign measures from other types of racial classifications."

Applying this test, the Court first noted that the FCC policies at issue did not serve as a remedy for past discrimination. Proceeding on the assumption that the policies were nonetheless "benign," it concluded that they served the "important governmental objective" of "enhancing broadcast diversity," and that they were "substantially related" to that objective. It therefore upheld the policies.

By adopting intermediate scrutiny as the standard of review for congressionally mandated "benign" racial classifications, *Metro Broadcasting* departed from prior cases in two significant respects. First, it turned its back on *Croson's* explanation of why strict scrutiny of all governmental racial classifications is essential:

> Absent searching judicial inquiry into the justification for such race-based measures, there is simply no way of determining what classifications are "benign" or "remedial" and what classifications are in fact motivated by illegitimate notions of racial inferiority or simple racial politics. Indeed, the purpose of strict scrutiny is to "smoke out" illegitimate uses of race by assuring that the legislative body is pursuing a goal important enough to warrant use of a highly suspect tool. The test also ensures that the means chosen "fit" this compelling goal so closely that there is little or no possibility that the motive for the classification was illegitimate racial prejudice or stereotype. . . . We adhere to that view today, despite the surface appeal of holding "benign" racial classifications to a lower standard, because "it may not always be clear that a so-called preference is in fact benign."

Second, *Metro Broadcasting* squarely rejected one of the three propositions established by the Court's earlier equal protection cases, namely, congruence between the standards applicable to federal and state racial classifications, and in so doing also undermined the other two—skepticism of all racial classifications, and consistency of treatment irrespective of the race of the burdened or benefited group. Under *Metro Broadcasting,* certain racial classifications ("benign" ones enacted by the Federal Government) should be treated less skeptically than others; and the race of the benefited group is critical to the determination of which standard of review to apply. *Metro Broadcasting* was thus a significant departure from much of what had come before it.

The three propositions undermined by *Metro Broadcasting* all derive from the basic principle that the Fifth and Fourteenth Amendments to the Constitution protect *persons,* not *groups.* It follows from that principle that all governmental action based on race—a *group* classification long recognized as "in most circumstances irrelevant and therefore prohibited,"—should be subjected to detailed judicial inquiry to ensure that the *personal* right to equal protection of the laws has not been infringed. These ideas have long been central to this Court's understanding of equal protection, and holding "benign" state and federal racial classifications to different standards does not square with them. [A] free people whose institutions are founded upon the doctrine of equality," should tolerate no retreat from the principle that government may treat people differently because of their race only for the most compelling reasons. Accordingly, we hold today that all racial classifications, imposed by whatever federal, state, or local government actor, must be analyzed by a reviewing court under strict scrutiny. In other words, such classifications are constitutional only if they are narrowly tailored measures that further compelling governmental interests. To the extent that *Metro Broadcasting* is inconsistent with that holding, it is overruled.

In dissent, Justice Stevens criticizes us for "deliver[ing] a disconcerting lecture about the evils of governmental racial classifications." With respect, we believe his criticisms reflect a serious misunderstanding of our opinion. [He] chides us for our "supposed inability to differentiate between 'invidious' and 'benign' discrimination," because it is in his view sufficient that "people understand the difference between good intentions and bad." But, as we have just explained, the point of strict scrutiny is to "differentiate between" permissible and impermissible governmental use of race. And Justice Stevens himself has already explained in his dissent in *Fullilove* why "good intentions" alone are not enough to sustain a supposedly "benign" racial classification: "[E]ven though it is not the actual predicate for this legislation, a statute of this kind inevitably is perceived by many as resting on an assumption that those who are granted this special preference are less qualified in some respect that is identified purely by their race. Because that perception—*especially when fostered by the Congress of the United States*—can only exacerbate rather than reduce racial prejudice, it will delay the time when race will become a truly irrelevant, or at least insignificant, factor. *Unless Congress clearly articulates the need and basis for a racial classification, and also tailors the classification to its justification, the Court should not uphold this kind of statute. . . . "*

These passages make a persuasive case for requiring strict scrutiny of congressional racial classifications.

Perhaps it is not the standard of strict scrutiny itself, but our use of the concepts of "consistency" and "congruence" in conjunction with it, that leads Justice Stevens to dissent. According to Justice Stevens, our view of consistency "equate[s] remedial preferences with invidious discrimination," and ignores the difference between "an engine of oppression" and an effort "to foster equality in society," or, more colorfully, "between a 'No Trespassing' sign and a welcome mat." It does nothing of the kind. The principle of consistency simply means that whenever the government treats any person unequally because of his or her race, that person has suffered an injury that falls squarely within the language and spirit of the Constitution's guarantee of equal protection. It says nothing about the ultimate validity of any particular law; that determination is the job of the court applying strict scrutiny. The principle of consistency explains the circumstances in which the injury requiring strict scrutiny occurs. The application of strict scrutiny, in turn, determines whether a compelling governmental interest justifies the infliction of that injury.

Consistency *does* recognize that any individual suffers an injury when he or she is disadvantaged by the government because of his or her race, whatever that race may be. This Court clearly stated that principle in *Croson. . . .*

Justice Stevens also claims that we have ignored any difference between federal and state legislatures. But requiring that Congress, like the States, enact racial classifications only when doing so is necessary to further a "compelling interest" does not contravene any principle of appropriate respect for a co-equal Branch of the Government. . . .

Finally, we wish to dispel the notion that strict scrutiny is "strict in theory, but fatal in fact." The unhappy persistence of both the practice and the lingering effects of racial discrimination against minority groups in this country is an unfortunate reality, and government is not disqualified from acting in response to it. As recently as 1987, for example, every Justice of this Court agreed that the Alabama Department of Public Safety's "pervasive, systematic, and obstinate discriminatory conduct" justified a narrowly tailored race-based remedy. See *United*

States v. *Paradise*, 480 U.S. 149. When race-based action is necessary to further a compelling interest, such action is within constitutional constraints if it satisfies the "narrow tailoring" test this Court has set out in previous cases. . . .

The judgment of the Court of Appeals is vacated, and the case is remanded for further proceedings consistent with this opinion.

JUSTICE SCALIA, concurring in part and concurring in the judgment.

I join the opinion of the Court, . . . except insofar as it may be inconsistent with the following: In my view, government can never have a "compelling interest" in discriminating on the basis of race in order to "make up" for past racial discrimination in the opposite direction. Individuals who have been wronged by unlawful racial discrimination should be made whole; but under our Constitution there can be no such thing as either a creditor or a debtor race. That concept is alien to the Constitution's focus upon the individual, see Amdt. 14, § 1 ("[N]or shall any State . . . deny *to any person*" the equal protection of the laws) (emphasis added), and its rejection of dispositions based on race, see Amdt. 15, § 1 (prohibiting abridgment of the right to vote "on account of race") or based on blood, see Art. III, § 3 ("[N]o Attainder of Treason shall work Corruption of Blood"); Art. I, § 9 ("No Title of Nobility shall be granted by the United States"). To pursue the concept of racial entitlement—even for the most admirable and benign of purposes—is to reinforce and preserve for future mischief the way of thinking that produced race slavery, race privilege and race hatred. In the eyes of government, we are just one race here. It is American.

It is unlikely, if not impossible, that the challenged program would survive under this understanding of strict scrutiny, but I am content to leave that to be decided on remand.

JUSTICE THOMAS, concurring in part and concurring in the judgment.

I agree with the majority's conclusion that strict scrutiny applies to *all* government classifications based on race. I write separately, however, to express my disagreement with the premise . . . that there is a racial paternalism exception to the principle of equal protection. I believe that there is a "moral [and] constitutional equivalence" between laws designed to subjugate a race and those that distribute benefits on the basis of race in order to foster some current notion of equality. Government cannot make us equal; it can only recognize, respect, and protect us as equal before the law.

That these programs may have been motivated, in part, by good intentions cannot provide refuge from the principle that under our Constitution, the government may not make distinctions on the basis of race. As far as the Constitution is concerned, it is irrelevant whether a government's racial classifications are drawn by those who wish to oppress a race or by those who have a sincere desire to help those thought to be disadvantaged. There can be no doubt that the parternalism that appears to lie at the heart of this program is at war with the principle of inherent equality that underlies and infuses our Constitution. See Declaration of Independence ("We hold these truths to be self-evident, that all men are created equal, that they are endowed by their Creator with certain unalienable Rights, that among these are Life, Liberty, and the pursuit of Happiness").

These programs not only raise grave constitutional questions, they also undermine the moral basis of the equal protection principle. Purchased at the price of immeasurable human suffering, the equal protection principle reflects our Nation's understanding that such classifications ultimately have a destructive impact on the individual and our society. Unquestionably, "[i]nvidious [racial] discrimination is an engine of oppression." It is also true that "[r]emedial" racial preferences may reflect "a desire to foster equality in society." But there can be no doubt that racial paternalism and its unintended consequences can be as poisonous and pernicious as any other form of discrimination. So-called "benign" discrimination teaches many that because of chronic and apparently immutable handicaps, minorities cannot compete with them without their patronizing indulgence. Inevitably, such programs engender attitudes of superiority or, alternatively, provoke resentment among those who believe that they have been wronged by the government's use of race. These programs stamp minorities with a badge of inferiority and may cause them to develop dependencies or to adopt an attitude that they are "entitled" to preferences. . . .

In my mind, government-sponsored racial discrimination based on benign prejudice is just as noxious as discrimination inspired by malicious prejudice. In each instance, it is racial discrimination, plain and simple.

JUSTICE STEVENS, with whom JUSTICE GINSBURG joins, dissenting.

Instead of deciding this case in accordance with controlling precedent, the Court today delivers a disconcerting lecture about the evils of governmental racial classifications. . . .

The Court's concept of "consistency" assumes that there is no significant difference between a decision by the majority to impose a special burden on the members of a minority race and a decision by the majority to provide a benefit to certain members of that minority notwithstanding its incidental burden on some members of the majority. In my opinion that assumption is untenable. There is no moral or constitutional equivalence between a policy that is designed to perpetuate a caste system and one that seeks to eradicate racial subordination. Invidious discrimination is an engine of oppression, subjugating a disfavored group to enhance or maintain the power of the majority. Remedial race-based preferences reflect the opposite impulse: a desire to foster equality in society. No sensible conception of the Government's constitutional obligation to "govern impartially" should ignore this distinction. . . .

The consistency that the Court espouses would disregard the difference between a "No Trespassing" sign and a welcome mat. It would treat a Dixiecrat Senator's decision to vote against Thurgood Marshall's confirmation in order to keep African Americans off the Supreme Court as on a par with President Johnson's evaluation of his nominee's race as a positive factor. It would equate a law that made black citizens ineligible for military service with a program aimed at recruiting black soldiers. An attempt by the majority to exclude members of a minority race from a regulated market is fundamentally different from a subsidy that enables a relatively small group of newcomers to enter that market. An interest in "consistency" does not justify treating differences as though they were similarities.

The Court's explanation for treating dissimilar race-based decisions as though they were equally objectionable is a supposed inability to differentiate between "invidious" and "benign" discrimination. But the term "affirmative action" is common and well understood. Its presence in everyday parlance shows that people understand the difference between good intentions and bad. As with any legal concept, some cases may be difficult to classify, but our equal protection jurisprudence has identified a critical difference between state action that imposes burdens on a disfavored few and state action that benefits the few "in spite of" its adverse effects on the many. . . .

Moreover, the Court may find that its new "consistency" approach to race-based classifications is difficult to square with its insistence upon rigidly separate categories for discrimination against different classes of individuals. For example, as the law currently stands, the Court will apply "intermediate scrutiny" to cases of invidious gender discrimination and "strict scrutiny" to cases of invidious race discrimination, while applying the same standard for benign classifications as for invidious ones. If this remains the law, then today's lecture about "consistency" will produce the anomalous result that the Government can more easily enact affirmative-action programs to remedy discrimination against women than it can enact affirmative-action programs to remedy discrimination against African Americans—even though the primary purpose of the Equal Protection Clause was to end discrimination against the former slaves. When a court becomes preoccupied with abstract standards, it risks sacrificing common sense at the altar of formal consistency. . . .

The Court's concept of "congruence" assumes that there is no significant difference between a decision by the Congress of the United States to adopt an affirmative-action program and such a decision by a State or a municipality. In my opinion that assumption is untenable. It ignores important practical and legal differences between federal and state or local decisionmakers. . . . [A] reason for giving greater deference to the National Legislature than to a local law-making body is that federal affirmative-action programs represent the will of our entire Nation's elected representatives, whereas a state or local program may have an impact on nonresident entities who played no part in the decision to enact it. Thus, in the state or local context, individuals who were unable to vote for the local representatives who enacted a race-conscious program may nonetheless feel the effects of that program. . . .

Presumably, the majority is now satisfied that its theory of "congruence" between the substantive rights provided by the Fifth and Fourteenth Amendments disposes of the objection based upon divided constitutional powers. But it is one thing to say (as no one seems to dispute) that the Fifth Amendment encompasses a general guarantee of equal protection as broad as that contained within the Fourteenth Amendment. It is another thing entirely to say that Congress' institutional competence and constitutional authority entitles it to no greater deference when it enacts a program designed to foster equality than the deference due a State legislature. The latter is an extraordinary proposition; and, as the foregoing discussion demonstrates, our precedents have rejected it explicitly and repeatedly. . . .

The Court's holding in *Fullilove* surely governs the result in this case. The Public Works Employment Act of 1977 (1977 Act), which this Court upheld in *Fullilove,* is different in several critical respects from the portions of the Small Business Act and the Surface Transportation and Uniform Relocation Assistance Act of 1987 challenged in this case. Each of those differences makes the current program designed to provide assistance to disadvantaged business enterprises (DBE's) significantly less objectionable than the 1977 categorical grant of $400 million in exchange for a 10% set-aside in public contracts to "a class of investors defined solely by racial characteristics." In no meaningful respect is the current scheme more objectionable than the 1977 Act. Thus, if the 1977 Act was constitutional, then so must be the SBA and STURAA. Indeed,

even if my dissenting views in *Fullilove* had prevailed, this program would be valid. . . .

The majority's concept of "consistency" ignores a difference, fundamental to the idea of equal protection, between oppression and assistance. The majority's concept of "congruence" ignores a difference, fundamental to our constitutional system, between the Federal Government and the States. And the majority's concept of *stare decisis* ignores the force of binding precedent. I would affirm the judgment of the Court of Appeals.

JUSTICE SOUTER, with whom JUSTICE GINSBURG and JUSTICE BREYER join, dissenting. . . .

In assessing the degree to which today's holding portends a departure from past practice, it is also worth noting that nothing in today's opinion implies any view of Congress's § 5 power and the deference due its exercise that differs from the views expressed by the *Fullilove* plurality. The Court simply notes the observation in *Croson* "that the Court's 'treatment of an exercise of congressional power in *Fullilove* cannot be dispositive here,' because *Croson*'s facts did not implicate Congress' broad power under § 5 of the Fourteenth Amendment," and explains that there is disagreement among today's majority about the extent of the § 5 power. . . . Thus, today's decision should leave § 5 exactly where it is as the source of an interest of the national government sufficiently important to satisfy the corresponding requirement of the strict scrutiny test. . . .

Foley v. Connelie

435 U.S. 291; 98 S. Ct. 1067; 55 L. Ed. 2d 287 (1978)

Edmund Foley, a lawfully admitted resident alien, applied for appointment as a New York state trooper, a position filled on the basis of competitive examinations. State authorities refused to allow Foley to take the examination, on the basis of a New York statute that provided that "no person shall be appointed to the New York state police force unless he shall be a citizen of the United States." Foley thereupon brought a class action suit in federal district court against the superintendent of the New York state police, seeking a declaratory judgment that the statute in question violated the Equal Protection Clause of the Fourteenth Amendment. A three-judge district court held the statute to be constitutional, and Foley appealed. *Opinion of the Court: Burger, Powell, Rehnquist, Stewart, White. Concurring in result: Blackmun. Dissenting opinions: Marshall, Brennan, Stevens; Stevens, Brennan.*

MR. CHIEF JUSTICE BURGER delivered the opinion of the Court. . . .

Appellant claims that the relevant New York statute violates his rights under the Equal Protection Clause.

The decisions of this Court with regard to the rights of aliens living in our society have reflected fine, and often difficult, questions of values. As a Nation we exhibit extraordinary hospitality to those who come to our country, which is not surprising for we have often been described as "a nation of immigrants." Indeed, aliens lawfully residing in this society have many rights which are accorded to noncitizens by few other countries. Our cases generally reflect a close scrutiny of restraints imposed by States on aliens. But we have never suggested that such legislation is inherently invalid, nor have we held that all limitations on aliens are suspect . . . Rather, beginning with a case which involved the denial of welfare assistance essential to life itself, the Court has treated certain restrictions on aliens with "heightened judicial solicitude," *Graham* v. *Richardson* . . . (1971), a treatment deemed necessary since aliens—pending their eligibility for citizenship—have no direct voice in the political processes.

It would be inappropriate, however, to require every statutory exclusion of aliens to clear the high hurdle of "strict scrutiny," because to do so would "obliterate all the distinctions between citizens and aliens and thus depreciate the historic values of citizenship." . . . The act of becoming a citizen is more than a ritual with no content beyond the fanfare of ceremony. A new citizen has become a member of a Nation, part of a people distinct from others. . . . The individual, at that point, belongs to the polity and is entitled to participate in the processes of democratic decisionmaking. Accordingly, we have recognized "a State's historical power to exclude aliens from participation in its democratic political institutions" . . . as part of the sovereign's obligation " 'to preserve the basic conception of a political community.' " . . .

The practical consequence of this theory is that "our scrutiny will not be so demanding where we deal with matters firmly within a State's constitutional prerogatives." . . . The State need only justify its classification by a showing of some rational relationship between the interest sought to be protected and the limit-ing classification. This is not intended to denigrate the valuable contribution of aliens who benefit from our traditional hospitality. It is no more than recognition of the fact that a democratic society is ruled by its people. Thus, it is clear that a State may deny aliens the right to vote, or to run for elective office, for these lie at the heart of our political institutions. . . . Similar considerations support a legislative determination to exclude aliens from jury service. . . . Likewise, we have recognized that citizenship may be a relevant qualification for fulfilling those "important nonelective executive, legislative, and judicial positions," held by "officers who participate directly in the formulation, execution, or review of broad public policy." . . . This is not because our society seeks to reserve the better jobs to its members. Rather, it is because this country entrusts many of its most important policy responsibilities to these officers, the discretionary exercise of which can often more immediately affect the lives of citizens than even the ballot of a voter or the choice of a legislator. In sum, then, it represents the choice, and right, of the people to be governed by their citizen peers. To effectuate this result, we must necessarily examine each position in question to determine whether it involves discretionary decisionmaking, or execution of policy, which substantially affects members of the political community.

The essence of our holdings to date is that although we extend to aliens the right to education and public welfare, along with the ability to earn a livelihood and engage in licensed professions, the right to govern is reserved to citizens. . . .

A discussion of the police function is essentially a description of one of the basic functions of government, especially in a complex modern society where police presence is pervasive. The police function fulfills a most fundamental obligation of government to its constituency. Police officers in the ranks do not formulate policy, *per se*, but they are clothed with authority to exercise an almost infinite variety of discretionary powers. The execution of the broad powers vested in them affects members of the public significantly and often in the most sensitive areas of daily life. . . .

Clearly, the exercise of police authority calls for a very high degree of judgment and discretion, the abuse or misuse of which can have serious impact on individuals. . . . A policeman vested with the plenary discretionary powers we have described is not to be equated with a private person engaged in routine public employment or other "common occupations of the community" who exercises no broad power over people generally. Indeed, the rationale for the qualified immunity historically granted to the police rests on the difficult and delicate judgments these officers must often make. . . .

In short, it would be as anomalous to conclude that citizens may be subjected to the broad discretionary powers of noncitizen police officers as it would be to say that judicial officers and jurors with power to judge citizens can be aliens. It is not surprising, therefore, that most States expressly confine the employment of police officers to citizens, whom the State may reasonably presume to be more familiar with and sympathetic to American traditions. Police officers very clearly fall within the category of "important nonelective . . . officers who participate directly in the . . . *execution* . . . of broad public policy." . . . In the enforcement and execution of the laws the police function is one where citizenship bears a rational relationship to the special demands of the particular position. A State may, therefore, consonant with the Constitution, confine the performance of this important public responsibility to citizens of the United States.

Accordingly, the judgment of the District Court is

Affirmed.

MR. JUSTICE STEWART, concurring.

The dissenting opinions convincingly demonstrate that it is difficult if not impossible to reconcile the Court's judgment in this case with the full sweep of the reasoning and authority of some of our past decisions. It is only because I have become increasingly doubtful about the validity of those decisions (in at least some of which I concurred) that I join the opinion of the Court in this case.

MR. JUSTICE MARSHALL, with whom MR. JUSTICE BRENNAN and MR. JUSTICE STEVENS join, dissenting. . . .

Today the Court upholds a law excluding aliens from public employment as state troopers. It [argues] . . . that aliens may be barred from holding "state elective or important nonelective executive, legislative, and judicial positions," because persons in these positions "participate directly in the formulation, execution, or review of broad public policy." . . . I do not agree with the Court that state troopers perform functions placing them within this "narro[w] . . . exception" . . . to our usual rule that discrimination against aliens is presumptively unconstitutional. Accordingly I dissent. . . .

There is a vast difference between the formulation and execution of broad public policy and the application of that policy to specific factual settings. While the Court is correct that "the exercise of police authority calls for a very high degree of judgment and discretion," . . . the judgments required are factual in nature; the policy judgments that govern an officer's conduct are contained in the Federal and State Constitutions, statutes, and regulations. . . . It is . . . not a denigration of the important public role of the state trooper—who, as the Court notes, . . . operates "in the most sensitive areas of daily life"—to find that his law enforcement responsibilities do not "make him a formulator of governmental policy." . . . Since no other rational reason, let alone a compelling state interest, has been advanced in support of the statute here at issue, I would hold that the statute's exclusion of aliens from state trooper positions violates the Equal Protection Clause of the Fourteenth Amendment.

MR. JUSTICE STEVENS, with whom MR. JUSTICE BRENNAN joins, dissenting.

. . . What is the group characteristic that justifies the unfavorable treatment of an otherwise qualified individual simply because he is an alien?

No one suggests that aliens as a class lack the intelligence or the courage to serve the public as police officers. The disqualifying characteristic is apparently a foreign allegiance which raises a doubt concerning trustworthiness and loyalty so pervasive that a flat ban against the employment of any alien in any law enforcement position is thought to be justified. But if the integrity of all aliens is suspect, why may not a State deny aliens the right to practice law? Are untrustworthy or disloyal lawyers more tolerable than untrustworthy or disloyal policemen? Or is the legal profession better able to detect such characteristics on an individual basis than is the police department? Unless the Court repudiates its holding in *In re Griffiths* [1973], . . . it must reject any conclusive presumption that aliens, as a class, are disloyal or untrustworthy.

. . . The Court . . . should not uphold a statutory discrimination against aliens, as a class, without expressly identifying the group characteristic that justifies the discrimination. If the unarticulated characteristic is concern about possible disloyalty, it must equally disqualify aliens from the practice of law; yet the Court does not question the continuing vitality of its decision in *Griffiths*. Or if that characteristic is the fact that aliens do not participate in our democratic decisionmaking process, it is irrelevant to eligibility for this category of public service. If there is no group characteristic that explains the discrimination, one can only conclude that it is without any justification that has not already been rejected by the Court.

Trimble v. *Gordon*
430 U.S. 762; 97 S. Ct. 1459; 52 L. Ed. 2d 31 (1977)

According to Section 12 of the Illinois Probate Act, illegitimate children could inherit by intestate succession only from their mothers, whereas legitimate children could inherit by intestate succession from both their mothers and their fathers. When Sherman Gordon died intestate, an Illinois probate court, acting under the authority of Section 12, rejected the claim to heirship of Deta Trimble, Gordon's illegitimate daughter. After the Illinois Supreme Court dismissed her challenge to the constitutionality of Section 12, she appealed to the United States Supreme Court. *Opinion of the Court:* Powell, *Brennan, Marshall, Stevens, White. Dissenting opinions:* Burger, *Blackmun, Rehnquist, Stewart;* Rehnquist.

MR. JUSTICE POWELL delivered the opinion of the Court. . . .

. . . In weighing the constitutional sufficiency of these justifications, we are guided by our previous decisions involving equal protection challenges to laws discriminating on the basis of illegitimacy. "[T]his Court requires, at a minimum, that a statutory classification bear some rational relationship to a legitimate state purpose." *Webe*r v. *Aetna Casualty & Surety Co.* . . . (1972). In this context, the standard just stated is a minimum; the Court sometimes requires more. "Though the latitude given state economic and social regulation is necessarily broad, when state statutory classifications approach sensitive and fundamental personal rights, this Court exercises a stricter scrutiny . . . " *Ibid.*

Appellants urge us to hold that classifications based on illegitimacy are "suspect," so that any justifications must survive "strict scrutiny." We considered and rejected a similar argument last Term in *Mathews* v. *Lucas* . . . (1976). As we recognized in *Lucas*, illegitimacy is analogous in many respects to the personal characteristics that have been held to be suspect when used as the basis of statutory differentiations. . . . We nevertheless concluded that the analogy was not sufficient to require "our most exacting scrutiny." . . . Despite the conclusion that classifications based on illegitimacy fall in a "realm of less than strictest scrutiny," *Lucas* also establishes that the scrutiny "is not a toothless one," . . . a proposition clearly demonstrated by our previous decisions in this area. . . .

The Illinois Supreme Court relied in part on the State's purported interest in "the promotion of legitimate family relationships." . . .

In a case like this, the Equal Protection Clause requires more than the mere incantation of a proper state purpose. No one disputes the appropriateness of Illinois' concern with the family unit, perhaps the most fundamental social institution of our society. The flaw in the analysis lies elsewhere. As we said in *Lucas*, the constitutionality of this law "depends upon the character of the discrimination and its relation to legitimate legislative aims." . . . We have expressly considered and [reject] the argument that a State may attempt to influence the actions of men and women by imposing sanctions on the children born of their illegitimate relationships. . . .

The Illinois Supreme Court also noted that the decedents whose estates were involved in the consolidated appeals could have left substantial parts of their estates to their illegitimate children by writing a will. . . .

By focusing on the steps that an intestate might have taken to assure some inheritance for his illegitimate children, the analysis loses sight of the essential question: the constitutionality of discrimination against illegitimates in a state intestate succession law. If the decedent had written a will devising property to his illegitimate child, the case no longer would involve intestate succession law at all. . . .

Finally, appellees urge us to affirm the decision below on the theory that the Illinois Probate Act, including § 12, mirrors the presumed intentions of the citizens of the State regarding the disposition of their property at death. Individualizing this theory, appellees argue that we must assume that Sherman Gordon knew the disposition of his estate under the Illinois Probate Act and that his failure to make a will shows his approval of that disposition. We need not resolve the question whether presumed intent alone can ever justify discrimination against illegitimates, for we do not think that § 12 was enacted for this purpose. . . . We find in § 12 a primary purpose to provide a system of intestate succession more just to illegitimate children than the prior law, a purpose tempered by a secondary interest in protecting against spurious claims of paternity. In the absence of a more convincing demonstration, we will not hypothesize an additional state purpose that has been ignored by the Illinois Supreme Court. . . .

For the reasons stated above, we conclude that § 12 of the Illinois Probate Act cannot be squared with the command of the Equal Protection Clause of the Fourteenth Amendment. Accordingly, we reverse the judgment of the Illinois Supreme Court and remand the case for further proceedings not inconsistent with this opinion. . . .

MR. JUSTICE REHNQUIST, dissenting.

The Fourteenth Amendment's prohibition against "any State . . . denying to any person . . . the equal protection of the laws" is undoubtedly one of the majestic generalities of the Constitution. If, during the period of more than a century since its adoption, this Court had developed a consistent body of doctrine which could reasonably be said to expound the intent of those who drafted and adopted the Clause of the Amendment, there would be no cause for judicial complaint, however unwise or incapable of effective

administration one might find those intentions. If, on the other hand, recognizing that those who drafted and adopted this language had rather imprecise notions about what it meant, the Court had evolved a body of doctrine which both was consistent and served some arguable useful purpose, there would likewise be little cause for great dissatisfaction with the existing state of the law.

Unfortunately, more than a century of decisions under this Clause of the Fourteenth Amendment have produced neither of these results. They have instead produced a syndrome wherein this Court seems to regard the Equal Protection Clause as a cat-o'-nine-tails to be kept in the judicial closet as a threat to legislatures which may, in the view of the judiciary, get out of hand and pass "arbitrary," "illogical," or "unreasonable" laws. Except in the area of the law in which the Framers obviously meant it to apply—classifications based on race or on national origin, the first cousin of race—the Court's decisions can fairly be described as an endless tinkering with legislative judgments, a series of conclusions unsupported by any central guiding principle.

. . . In providing the Court with the duty of enforcing such generalities as the Equal Protection Clause, the Framers of the Civil War Amendments placed it in the position of Adam in the Garden of Eden. As members of a tripartite institution of government which is responsible to no constituency, and which is held back only by its own sense of self-restraint, . . . we are constantly subjected to the human temptation to hold that any law containing a number of imperfections denies equal protection simply because those who drafted it could have made it a fairer or a better law. The Court's opinion in the instant case is no better and no worse than the long series of cases in this line, a line which unfortunately proclaims that the Court has indeed succumbed to the temptation implicit in the Amendment.

The Equal Protection Clause is itself a classic paradox, and makes sense only in the context of a recently fought Civil War. It creates a requirement of equal treatment to be applied to the process of legislation—legislation whose very purpose is to draw lines in such a way that different people are treated differently. The problem presented is one of sorting the legislative distinctions which are acceptable from those which involve invidiously unequal treatment.

All constitutional provisions for protection of individuals involve difficult questions of line drawing. But most others have implicit within them an understandable value judgment that certain types of conduct have a favored place and are to be protected to a greater or lesser degree. Obvious examples are free speech, freedom from unreasonable search and seizure, and the right to a fair trial. The remaining judicial task in applying those guarantees is to determine whether, on given facts, the constitutional value judgment embodied in such a provision has been offended in a particular case.

In the case of equality and equal protection, the constitutional principle—the thing to be protected to a greater or lesser degree—is not even identifiable from within the four corners of the Constitution. For equal protection does not mean that all persons must be treated alike. Rather, its general principle is that persons similarly situated should be treated similarly. But that statement of the rule does little to determine whether or not a question of equality is even involved in a given case. For the crux of the problem is *whether persons are similarly situated* for the purposes of the state action in issue. Nothing in the words of the Fourteenth Amendment specifically addresses this question in any way.

The essential problem of the Equal Protection Clause is therefore the one of determining where the courts are to look for guidance in defining "equality" as that word is used in the Fourteenth Amendment. Since the Amendment grew out of the Civil War and the freeing of the slaves, the core prohibition was early held to be aimed at the protection of blacks. . . . If race was an invalid sorting tool where blacks were concerned, it followed logically that it should not be valid where other races were concerned either. . . . A logical, though not inexorable, next step, was the extension of the projection to prohibit classifications resting on national origin. . . .

The presumptive invalidity of all of these classifications has made decisions involving them, for the most part, relatively easy. But when the Court has been required to adjudicate equal protection claims not based on race or national origin, it has faced a much more difficult task. . . .

Illegitimacy, which is involved in this case, has never been held by the Court to be a "suspect classification." Nonetheless, in several opinions of the Court, statements are found which suggest that although illegitimates are not members of a "suspect class," laws which treat them differently from those born in wedlock will receive a more far-reaching scrutiny under the Equal Protection Clause than will other laws regulating economic and social conditions. . . . The Court's opinion today contains language to that effect. . . . In one sense this language is a source of consolation, since it suggests that parts of the Court's analysis used in this case will not be carried over to traditional "rational basis" or "minimum scrutiny" cases. At the same time, though, it is a source of confusion, since the unanswered question remains as to the precise sort of scrutiny to which classifications based on illegitimacy will be subject. . . .

The "difficulty" of the "judicial task" is, I suggest, a self-imposed one, stemming not from the Equal Protection Clause but from the Court's insistence on reading so much into it. I do not see how it can be doubted that the purpose (in the ordinary sense of that word) of the Illinois Legislature in enacting § 12 of the Illinois Probate Act was to make the language contained in that section a part of the Illinois law. I presume even the Court will concede that this purpose was accomplished. It was this particular language which the Illinois Legislature, by the required vote of both of its houses and the signature of the Governor, enacted into law. The use of the word "purpose" in today's opinion actually expands the normal meaning of the word into something more like motive. Indeed, the Court says that the law "must be considered in light of this motivating purpose." . . . The question of what "motivated" the various individual legislators to vote for this particular section of the Probate Act, and the Governor of Illinois to sign it, is an extremely complex and difficult one to answer even if it were relevant to the constitutional question. . . . This Court . . . takes it upon itself to inquire into whether the Act in question accomplished the "purpose" which the Court first determines the legislature had in mind. It should be apparent that litigants who wish to succeed in invalidating a law under the Equal Protection Clause must have a certain schizophrenia if they are to be successful in their advocacy: They must first convince this Court that the legislature had a particular purpose in mind in enacting the law, and then convince it that the law was not at all suited to the accomplishment of that purpose.

But a graver defect than this in the Court's analysis is that it also requires a conscious second-guessing of legislative judgment in an area where this Court has no special expertise whatever. Even assuming that a court has properly accomplished the difficult task of identifying the "purpose" which a statute seeks to serve, it then sits in judgment to consider the so-called "fit" between that "purpose" and the statutory means adopted to achieve it. In most cases, and all but invariably if the Court insists on singling out a unitary "purpose," the "fit" will involve a greater or lesser degree of imperfection. Then the Court asks itself: How much "imperfection" between means and ends is permissible? In making this judgment it must throw into the judicial hopper the whole range of factors which were first thrown into the legislative hopper. What alternatives were reasonably available? What reasons are there for the legislature to accomplish this "purpose" in the way it did? What obstacles stood in the way of other solutions?

The fundamental flaw, to me, in this approach is that there is absolutely nothing to be implied from the fact that we hold judicial commissions that would enable us to answer any one of these questions better than the legislators to whose initial decision they were committed. Without any antecedent constitutional mandate, we have created on the premises of the Equal Protection Clause a school for legislators, whereby opinions of this Court are written to instruct them in a better understanding of how to accomplish their ordinary legislative tasks.

Here the Illinois Legislature was dealing with a problem of intestate succession of illegitimates from their fathers, which as the Court concedes frequently presents difficult problems of proof. The provisions of Illinois Probate Act § 12, as most recently amended, alleviate some of the difficulties which previously stood in the way of such succession. The fact that the Act in question does not alleviate all of the difficulties, or that it might have gone further than it did, is to me wholly irrelevant under the Equal Protection Clause. The circumstances which justify the distinction between illegitimates and legitimates contained in § 12 are apparent with no great exercise of imagination; they are stated in the opinion of the Court, though they are there rejected as constitutionally insufficient. Since Illinois' distinction is not mindless and patently irrational, I would affirm the judgment of the Supreme Court of Illinois.

Massachusetts Board of Retirement v. *Murgia*
427 U.S. 307; 96 S. Ct. 2562; 49 L. Ed. 2d 520 (1976)

Robert Murgia, a uniformed officer in the Massachusetts State Police who was in excellent physical and mental health, was forced by state law to retire upon reaching his fiftieth birthday. He challenged the constitutionality of this law, arguing that such compulsory retirement discriminated on the basis of age in violation of the Equal Protection Clause. A three-judge federal district court agreed, holding that the statute lacked "a rational basis in furthering any substantial state interest." The Retirement Board appealed. *Per Curiam: Blackmun, Brennan, Burger, Powell, Rehnquist, Stewart, White. Dissenting opinion: Marshall. Not participating: Stevens.*

PER CURIAM. . . .

. . . Uniformed state officers [must] pass a comprehensive physical examination biennially until age 40. After that, until mandatory retirement at age 50, uniformed officers must pass annually a more rigorous examination, including an electrocardiogram and tests for gastro-intestinal bleeding. Appellee Murgia had passed such an examination four months before he was retired, and there is no dispute that, when he retired, his excellent physical and mental health still rendered him capable of performing the duties of a uniformed officer.

The record includes the testimony of three physicians . . . that clearly established that the risk of physical failure, particularly in the cardiovascular system, increases with age, and that the number of individuals in a given age group incapable of performing stress functions increases with the age of the group. . . .

In assessing appellee's equal protection claim, the District Court found it unnecessary to apply a strict-scrutiny test, . . . for it determined that the age classification established by the Massachusetts statutory scheme could not in any event withstand a test of rationality. . . . Since there had been no showing that reaching age 50 forecasts even "imminent change" in an officer's physical condition, the District Court held that compulsory retirement at age 50 was irrational under a scheme that assessed the capabilities of officers individually by means of comprehensive annual physical examinations. We agree that rationality is the proper standard by which to test whether compulsory retirement at age 50 violates equal protection. We disagree, however, with the District Court's determination that the age 50 classification is not rationally related to furthering a legitimate state interest.

. . . Equal protection analysis requires strict scrutiny of a legislative classification only when the classification impermissibly interferes with the exercise of a fundamental right or operates to the peculiar disadvantage of a suspect class. Mandatory retirement at age 50 under the Massachusetts statute involves neither situation.

This Court's decisions give no support to the proposition that a right of governmental employment *per se* is fundamental. . . . Accordingly, we have expressly stated that a standard less than strict scrutiny "has consistently been applied to state legislation restricting the availability of employment opportunities."

Nor does the class of uniformed state police officers over 50 constitute a suspect class for purposes of equal protection analysis. . . . A suspect class is one "saddled with such disabilities, or subjected to such a history of purposeful unequal treatment, or relegated to such a position of political powerlessness as to command extraordinary protection from the majoritarian political process." While the treatment of the aged in this Nation has not been wholly free of discrimination, such persons, unlike, say, those who have been discriminated against on the basis of race or national origin, have not experienced a "history of purposeful unequal treatment" or been subjected to unique disabilities on the basis of stereotyped characteristics not truly indicative of their abilities. The class subject to the compulsory retirement feature of the Massachusetts statute consists of uniformed state police officers over the age of 50. It cannot be said to discriminate only against the elderly. Rather, it draws the line at a certain age in middle life. But even old age does not define a "discrete and insular" group . . . in need of "extraordinary protection from the majoritarian political process." Instead, it marks a stage that each of us will reach if we live out our normal span. Even if the statute could be said to impose a penalty upon a class defined as the aged, it would not impose a distinction sufficiently akin to those classifications that we have found suspect to call for strict judicial scrutiny.

Under the circumstances, it is unnecessary to subject the State's resolution of competing interests in this case to the degree of critical examination that our cases under the Equal Protection Clause recently have characterized as "strict judicial scrutiny." . . .

We turn then to examine this state classification under the rational-basis standard. This inquiry employs a relatively relaxed standard reflecting the Court's awareness that the drawing of lines that create distinctions is peculiarly a legislative task and an unavoidable one. Perfection in making the necessary classifications is neither possible nor necessary. . . . Such action by a legislature is presumed to be valid.

In this case, the Massachusetts statute clearly meets the requirements of the Equal Protection Clause, for the State's classification rationally furthers the purpose identified by the State: Through mandatory retirement at age 50, the legislature seeks to protect the public by assuring physical preparedness of its uniformed police. Since physical ability generally declines with age, mandatory retirement at 50 serves to remove from police service those whose fitness for uniformed work presumptively has diminished with age. This clearly is rationally related to the State's objective. There is no indication that [the statute] has the effect of excluding from service so few officers who are in fact unqualified as to render age 50 a criterion wholly unrelated to the objective of the statute.

That the State chooses not to determine fitness more precisely through individualized testing after age 50 is not to say that the objective of assuring physical fitness is not rationally furthered by a maximum-age limitation. It is only to say that with regard to the interest of all concerned, the State perhaps has not chosen the best means to accomplish this purpose. But where rationality is the test, a State "does not violate the

Equal Protection Clause merely because the classifications made by its laws are imperfect." . . .

We do not make light of the substantial economic and psychological effects premature and compulsory retirement can have on an individual; nor do we denigrate the ability of elderly citizens to continue to contribute to society. The problems of retirement have been well documented and are beyond serious dispute. But "[we] do not decide today that the [Massachusetts statute] is wise, that it best fulfills the relevant social and economic objectives that [Massachusetts] might ideally espouse, or that a more just and humane system could not be devised." . . . We decide only that the system enacted by the Massachusetts legislature does not deny appellee equal protection of the laws. . . .

MR. JUSTICE MARSHALL, dissenting. . . .

Although there are signs that its grasp on the law is weakening, the rigid two-tier model still holds sway as the Court's articulated description of the equal protection test. Again, I must object to its perpetuation. The model's two fixed modes of analysis, strict scrutiny and mere rationality, simply do not describe the inquiry the Court has undertaken—or should undertake—in equal protection cases. Rather, the inquiry has been much more sophisticated and the Court should admit as much. It has focused upon the character of the classification in question, the relative importance to individuals in the class discriminated against of the governmental benefits that they do not receive, and the state interests asserted in support of the classification. . . .

Although the Court outwardly adheres to the two-tier model, it has apparently lost interest in recognizing further "fundamental" rights and "suspect" classes. . . . . In my view, this result is the natural consequence of the limitations of the Court's traditional equal protection analysis. If a statute invades a "fundamental" right or discriminates against a "suspect" class, it is subject to strict scrutiny. If a statute is subject to strict scrutiny, the statute always, or nearly always, . . . is struck down. Quite obviously, the only critical decision is whether strict scrutiny should be invoked at all. It should be no surprise, then, that the Court is hesitant to expand the number of categories of rights and classes subject to strict scrutiny, when each expansion involves the invalidation of virtually every classification bearing upon a newly covered category.

But however understandable the Court's hesitancy to invoke strict scrutiny, all remaining legislation should not drop into the bottom tier, and be measured by the mere rationality test. For that test, too, when applied as articulated, leaves little doubt about the outcome; the challenged legislation is always upheld. . . . It cannot be gainsaid that there remain rights, not now classified as "fundamental," that remain vital to the flourishing of a free society, and classes, not now classified as "suspect," that are unfairly burdened by invidious discrimination unrelated to the individual worth of their members. Whatever we call these rights and classes, we simply cannot forgo all judicial protection against discriminatory legislation bearing upon them, but for the rare instances when the legislative choice can be termed "wholly irrelevant" to the legislative goal. . . .

While the Court's traditional articulation of the rational-basis test does suggest just such an abdication, happily the Court's deeds have not matched its words. Time and again, met with cases touching upon the prized rights and burdened classes of our society, the Court has acted only after a reasonably probing look at the legislative goals and means, and at the significance of the personal rights and interests invaded. . . .

But there are problems with deciding cases based on factors not encompassed by the applicable standards. First, the approach is rudderless, affording no notice to interested parties of the standards governing particular cases and giving no firm guidance to judges who, as a consequence, must assess the constitutionality of legislation before them on an *ad hoc* basis. Second, and not unrelatedly, the approach is unpredictable and requires holding this Court to standards it has never publicly adopted. Thus, the approach presents the danger that, as I suggest has happened here, relevant factors will be misapplied or ignored. All interests not "fundamental" and all classes not "suspect" are not the same; and it is time for the Court to drop the pretense that, for purposes of the Equal Protection Clause, they are.

The danger of the Court's verbal adherence to the rigid two-tier test, despite its effective repudiation of that test in the cases, is demonstrated by its efforts here. There is simply no reason why a statute that tells able-bodied police officers, ready and willing to work, that they no longer have the right to earn a living in their chosen profession merely because they are 50 years old should be judged by the same minimal standards of rationality that we use to test economic legislation that discriminates against business interests. . . . Yet, the Court today not only invokes the minimal level of scrutiny, it wrongly adheres to it. Analysis of the three factors I have identified above—the importance of the governmental benefits denied, the character of the class, and the asserted state interests—demonstrates the Court's error.

Whether "fundamental" or not, " 'the right of the individual . . . to engage in any of the common occupations of life' " has been repeatedly recognized by this Court as falling within the concept of liberty guaranteed by the Fourteenth Amendment. . . .

While depriving any government employee of his job is a significant deprivation, it is particularly burdensome when the person deprived is an older citizen. Once terminated, the elderly cannot readily find alternative employment. The lack of work is not only economically damaging, but emotionally and physically draining. Deprived of his status in the community and of the opportunity for meaningful activity, fearful of becoming dependent on others for his support, and lonely in his new-found isolation, the involuntarily retired person is susceptible to physical and emotional ailments as a direct consequence of his enforced idleness. . . .

Not only are the elderly denied important benefits when they are terminated on the basis of age, but the classification of older workers is itself one that merits judicial attention. Whether older workers constitute a "suspect" class or not, it cannot be disputed that they constitute a class subject to repeated and arbitrary discrimination in employment. . . .

Of course, the Court is quite right in suggesting that distinctions exist between the elderly and traditional suspect classes such as Negroes, and between the elderly and "quasi-suspect" classes such as women or illegitimates. The elderly are protected not only by certain anti-discrimination legislation, but by legislation that provides them with positive benefits not enjoyed by the public at large. Moreover, the elderly are not isolated in society, and discrimination against them is not pervasive but is centered primarily in employment. The advantage of a flexible equal protection standard, however, is that it can readily accommodate such variables. The elderly are undoubtedly discriminated against, and when legislation denies them an important benefit—employment—I conclude that to sustain the legislation appellants must show a reasonably substantial interest and a scheme reasonably closely tailored to achieving that interest. . . .

. . . The Commonwealth's mandatory retirement law cannot stand when measured against the significant deprivation the Commonwealth's action works upon the terminated employees. I would affirm the judgment of the District Court.

Frontiero v. Richardson

411 U.S. 677; 93 S. Ct. 1764; 36 L. Ed. 2d 583 (1973)

Federal statutes provided that married servicemen would automatically qualify to receive increased quarters allowances and medical and dental benefits for their wives, but that female personnel in the armed services would not receive these fringe benefits unless their husbands were in fact dependent on them for over 50 percent of their support. Sharron Frontiero, a married Air Force officer, brought suit in federal district court against Secretary of Defense Elliott Richardson, challenging this sex-based differential treatment. She argued that it violated the equal protection component of the Due Process Clause of the Fifth Amendment, in that the statutes required a servicewoman to prove the actual dependency of her husband. A three-judge court denied relief, and she appealed. *Judgment of the Court: Brennan, Douglas, Marshall, White. Concurring in the judgment: Powell, Blackmun, Burger; Stewart. Dissenting opinion: Rehnquist.*

MR. JUSTICE BRENNAN announced the judgment of the Court. . . .

At the outset, appellants contend that classifications based upon sex, like classifications based upon race, alienage, and national origin, are inherently suspect and must therefore be subjected to close judicial scrutiny. We agree and, indeed, find at least implicit support for such an approach in our unanimous decision only last Term in *Reed* v. *Reed* . . . (1971). . . .

There can be no doubt that our Nation has had a long and unfortunate history of sex discrimination. Traditionally, such discrimination was rationalized by an attitude of "romantic paternalism" which, in practical effect, put women not on a pedestal, but in a cage. . . .

As a result . . . , our statute books gradually became laden with gross, stereotypical distinctions between the sexes and, indeed, throughout much of the 19th century the position of women in our society was, in many respects, comparable to that of blacks under the pre-Civil War slave codes. Neither slaves nor women could hold office, serve on juries, or bring suit in their own names, and married women traditionally were denied the legal capacity to hold or convey property or to serve as legal guardians of their own children. . . . And although blacks were guaranteed the right to vote in 1870, women were denied even that right—which is itself "preservative of other basic civil and political rights"—until adoption of the Nineteenth Amendment half a century later. It is true, of course, that the position of women in America has improved markedly in recent decades. Nevertheless, it can hardly be doubted that, in part because of the high visibility of the sex characteristic, women still face pervasive, although at times more subtle, discrimination in our educational institutions, on the job market and, perhaps most conspicuously, in the political arena. . . .

Moreover, since sex, like race and national origin, is an immutable characteristic determined solely by the accident of birth, the imposition of special disabilities upon the members of a particular sex because of their sex would seem to violate "the basic concept of our system that legal burdens should bear some relationship to individual responsibility. . . . " And what differentiates sex from such nonsuspect statutes as intelligence or physical disability, and aligns it with the recognized suspect criteria, is that the sex characteristic frequently bears no relation to ability to perform or contribute to society. As a result, statutory distinctions between the sexes often have the effect of invidiously relegating the entire class of females to inferior legal status without regard to the actual capabilities of its individual members. . . .

With these considerations in mind, we can only conclude that classifications based upon sex, like classifications based upon race, alienage, or national origin, are inherently suspect, and must therefore be subjected to strict judicial scrutiny. Applying the analysis mandated by that statutory standard of review, it is clear that the statutory scheme now before us is constitutionally invalid.

The sole basis of the classification established in the challenged statutes is the sex of the individuals involved. . . .

Moreover, the Government concedes that the differential treatment accorded men and women under these statutes serves no purpose other than mere "administrative convenience." In essence, the Government maintains that, as an empirical matter, wives in our society frequently are dependent upon their husbands, while husbands rarely are dependent upon their wives. Thus, the Government argues that Congress might reasonably have concluded that it would be both cheaper and easier simply conclusively to presume that wives of male members are financially dependent upon their husbands, while burdening female members with the task of establishing dependency in fact.

The Government offers no concrete evidence, however, tending to support its views that such differential treatment in fact saves the Government any money. In order to satisfy the demands of strict judicial scrutiny, the Government must demonstrate, for example, that it is actually cheaper to grant increased benefits with respect to *all* male members, than it is to determine which male members are in fact entitled to such benefits and to grant increased benefits only to those members whose wives actually meet the dependency requirement. Here, however, there is substantial evidence that, if put to the test, many of the wives of male members would fail to qualify for benefits. And in light of the fact that the dependency determination with respect to the husbands of female members is presently made solely on the basis of affidavits, rather than through the more costly hearing process, the

Government's explanation of the statutory scheme is, to say the least, questionnable.

In any case, our prior decisions make clear that, although efficacious administration of governmental programs is not without some importance, "the Constitution recognizes higher values than speed and efficiency." . . . And when we enter the realm of "strict judicial scrutiny," there can be no doubt that "administrative convenience" is not a shibboleth, the mere recitation of which dictates constitutionality. . . . On the contrary, any statutory scheme which draws a sharp line between the sexes, *solely* for the purpose of achieving administrative convenience, necessarily commands "dissimilar treatment for men and women who are . . . similarly situated," and therefore involves the "very kind of arbitrary legislative choice forbidden by the [Constitution]." . . . We therefore conclude that, by according differential treatment to male and female members of the uniformed services for the sole purpose of achieving administrative convenience, the challenged statutes violate the Due Process Clause of the Fifth Amendment insofar as they require a female member to prove the dependency of her husband.

Reversed.

MR. JUSTICE POWELL, with whom THE CHIEF JUSTICE and MR. JUSTICE BLACKMUN join, concurring.

I agree that the challenged statutes constitute an unconstitutional discrimination against service women in violation of the Due Process Clause of the Fifth Amendment, but I cannot join the opinion of MR. JUSTICE BRENNAN, which would hold that all classifications based upon sex, "like classifications based upon race, alienage, and national origin," are "inherently suspect and must therefore be subjected to close judicial scrutiny." . . . It is unnecessary for the Court in this case to characterize sex as a suspect classification, with all of the far-reaching implications of such a holding. *Reed* v. *Reed* . . . (1971), which abundantly supports our decision today, did not add sex to the narrowly limited group of classifications which are inherently suspect. In my view, we can and should decide this case on the authority of *Reed* and reserve for the future any expansion of its rationale.

There is another, and I find compelling, reason for deferring a general categorizing of sex classifications as invoking the strictest test of judicial scrutiny. The Equal Rights Amendment, which if adopted will resolve the substance of this precise question, has been approved by the Congress and submitted for ratification by the States. If this Amendment is duly adopted, it will represent the will of the people accomplished in the manner prescribed by the Constitution. By acting prematurely and unnecessarily, as I view it, the Court has assumed a decisional responsibility at the very time when state legislatures, functioning within the traditional democratic process, are debating the proposed Amendment. It seems to me that this reaching out to pre-empt by judicial action a major political decision which is currently in process of resolution does not reflect appropriate respect for duly prescribed legislature processes.

United States v. *Virginia*

518 U.S. 515; 116 S. Ct. 2264; 135 L. Ed. 2d 735 (1996)

Virginia Military Institute (VMI) was the sole single-sex school among Virginia's public institutions of higher learning; its mission was to produce "citizen-soldiers," men prepared for leadership in civilian life and in military service. Using an "adversative method" of training not available elsewhere in Virginia, VMI sought to instill physical and mental discipline in its cadets and impart to them a strong moral code. Reflecting the high value alumni placed on their VMI training, VMI had the largest per-student endowment of all undergraduate institutions in the Nation. The United States sued Virginia and VMI, alleging that VMI's exclusively male admission policy violated the Fourteenth Amendment's Equal Protection Clause. The District Court ruled in VMI's favor. The Court of Appeals for the Fourth Circuit reversed and ordered Virginia to remedy the constitutional violation. In response, Virginia proposed a parallel program for women: Virginia Women's Institute for Leadership (VWIL), located at Mary Baldwin College, a private liberal arts school for women. The District Court found that Virginia's proposal satisfied the Constitution's equal protection requirement, and the Fourth Circuit affirmed. Although the Court of Appeals acknowledged that the VWIL degree lacked the historical benefit and prestige of a VMI degree, the court nevertheless found the educational opportunities at the two schools sufficiently comparable. The United States petitioned the Supreme Court for a writ of certiorari. *Opinion of the Court:* Ginsburg, *Breyer, Kennedy, O'Connor, Souter, Stevens, Kennedy. Concurring in the judgment:* Rehnquist. *Dissenting opinion:* Scalia. *Not participating (because his son was a student at VMI): Thomas.*

JUSTICE GINSBURG delivered the opinion of the Court.

. . . [T]his case present[s] two ultimate issues. First, does Virginia's exclusion of women from the educational opportunities provided by VMI—extraordinary opportunities for military training and civilian leadership development—deny to women "capable of all of the individual activities required of VMI cadets" the equal protection of the laws guaranteed by the Fourteenth Amendment? Second, if VMI's 'unique' situation—as Virginia's sole single-sex public institution of higher education—offends the Constitution's equal protection principle, what is the remedial requirement?

We note, once again, the core instruction of this Court's pathmarking decisions in *J. E. B.* v. *Alabama ex rel. T.B.,* 511 U.S. 127 (1994), and *Mississippi University for Women* [v. *Hogan*], 458 U.S. 718 (1982): Parties who seek to defend gender-based government action must demonstrate an "exceedingly persuasive justification" for that action. . . .

To summarize the Court's current directions for cases of official classification based on gender: Focusing on the differential treatment or denial of opportunity for which relief is sought, the reviewing court must determine whether the proffered justification is "exceedingly persuasive." The burden of justification is demanding and it rests entirely on the State. The State must show "at least that the [challenged] classification serves 'important governmental objectives and that the discriminatory means employed' are 'substantially related to the achievement of those objectives.' " The justification must be genuine, not hypothesized or invented *post hoc* in response to litigation. And it must not rely on overbroad generalizations about the different talents, capacities, or preferences of males and females.

The heightened review standard our precedent establishes does not make sex a proscribed classification. Supposed "inherent differences" are no longer accepted as a ground for race or national origin classifications. Physical differences between men and women, however, are enduring: "[T]he two sexes are not fungible; a community made up exclusively of one [sex] is different from a community composed of both." *Ballard* v. *United States,* 329 U.S. 187, 193 (1946).

"Inherent differences" between men and women, we have come to appreciate, remain cause for celebration, but not for denigration of the members of either sex or for artificial constraints on an individual's opportunity. Sex classifications may be used to compensate women "for particular economic disabilities [they have] suffered," *Califano* v. *Webster,* 430 U.S. 313 (1977), to "promot[e] equal employment opportunity," see *California Federal Saving & Loan Association* v. *Guerra,* 479 U.S. 272 (1987), to advance full development of the talent and capacities of our Nation's people. But such classifications may not be used, as they once were to create or perpetuate the legal, social, and economic inferiority of women.

Measuring the record in this case against the review standard just described, we conclude that Virginia has shown no "exceedingly persuasive justification" for excluding all women from the citizen-soldier training afforded by VMI. We therefore affirm the Fourth Circuit's initial judgment, which held that Virginia had violated the Fourteenth Amendment's Equal Protection Clause. Because the remedy proffered by Virginia—the Mary Baldwin VWIL program—does not cure the constitutional violation, i.e., it does not provide equal opportunity, we reverse the Fourth Circuit's final judgment in this case.

The Fourth Circuit initially held that Virginia had advanced no state policy by which it could justify, under equal protection principles, its determination "to afford VMI's unique type of program to men and not to women." Virginia challenges that "liability" ruling and asserts two justifications in defense of VMI's exclusion of women. First, the Commonwealth contends, "single-sex education provides important educational benefits," and the option of single-sex education contributes to "diversity in educational approaches." Second, the Commonwealth argues, "the unique VMI method of character development and leadership training," the school's adversative approach, would have to be modified were VMI to admit women. We consider these two justifications in turn.

Single-sex education affords pedagogical benefits to at least some students, Virginia emphasizes, and that reality is uncontested in this litigation. Similarly, it is not disputed that diversity among public educational institutions can serve the public good. But Virginia has not shown that VMI was established, or has been maintained, with a view to diversifying, by its categorical exclusion of women, educational opportunities within the State. . . . A purpose genuinely to advance an array of educational options, as the Court of Appeals recognized, is not served by VMI's historic and constant plan—a plan to "afford[d] a unique educational benefit only to males." However "liberally" this plan serves the State's sons, it makes no provision whatever for her daughters. That is not equal protection.

Virginia next argues that VMI's adversative method of training provides educational benefits that cannot be made available, unmodified, to women. Alterations to accommodate women would necessarily be "radical," so "drastic," Virginia asserts, as to transform, indeed "destroy" VMI's program. Neither sex would be favored by the transformation, Virginia maintains: Men would be deprived of the unique opportunity currently available to them; women would not gain that opportunity because their participation would "eliminat[e] the very aspects of [the] program that distinguish [VMI] from . . . other institutions of higher education in Virginia." . . .

The United States does not challenge any expert witness estimation on average capacities or preferences of men and women. Instead, the United States emphasizes that time and again since this Court's turning point decision in *Reed v. Reed*, 404 U.S. 71 (1971), we have cautioned reviewing courts to take a "hard look" at generalizations or "tendencies" of the kind pressed by Virginia, and relied upon by the District Court. . . .

The notion that admission of women would downgrade VMI's stature, destroy the adversative system and, with it, even the school, is a judgment hardly proved, a prediction hardly different from other "self-fulfilling prophec[ies]" once routinely used to deny rights or opportunities. . . .

Women's successful entry into the federal military academies, and their participation in the Nation's military forces, indicate that Virginia's fears for the future of VMI may not be solidly grounded. The State's justification for excluding all women from "citizen-soldier" training for which some are qualified, in any event, cannot rank as "exceedingly persuasive," as we have explained and applied that standard. . . .

In the second phase of the litigation, Virginia presented its remedial plan—maintain VMI as a male-only college and create VWIL as a separate program for women. The plan met District Court approval. The Fourth Circuit, in turn, deferentially . . . concluded that Virginia had arranged for men and women opportunities "sufficiently comparable" to survive equal protection evaluation. The United States challenges this "remedial" ruling as pervasively misguided. . . .

Virginia chose not to eliminate, but to leave untouched, VMI's exclusionary policy. For women only, however, Virginia proposed a separate program, different in kind from VMI and unequal in tangible and intangible facilities. Having violated the Constitution's equal protection requirement, Virginia was obliged to show that its remedial proposal "directly address[ed] and related[d] to" the violation, the equal protection denied to women ready, willing, and able to benefit from educational opportunities of the kind VMI offers. . . .

VWIL affords women no opportunity to experience the rigorous military training for which VMI is famed. Instead, the VWIL program "deemphasize[s]" military education and uses a "cooperative method" of education "which reinforces self-esteem." VWIL students participate in ROTC and a "largely ceremonial" Virginia Corps of Cadets, but Virginia deliberately did not make VWIL a military institute. The VWIL House is not a military-style residence and VWIL students need not live together throughout the 4-year program, eat meals together, or wear uniforms during the school day. VWIL students thus do not experience the "barracks" life "crucial to the VMI experience," the spartan living arrangements designed to foster an "egalitarian ethic." "[T]he most important aspects of the VMI educational experience occur in the barracks," the District Court found, yet Virginia deemed that core experience nonessential, indeed inappropriate, for training its female citizen-soldiers.

VWIL students receive their "leadership training" in seminars, externships, and speaker series, episodes and encounters lacking the "[p]hysical rigor, mental stress, . . . minute regulation of behavior, and indoctrination in desirable values" made hallmarks of VMI's citizen-soldier training. Kept away from the pressures, hazards, and psychological bonding characteristic of VMI's adversative training, VWIL students will not know the "feeling of tremendous accomplishment" commonly experienced by VMI's successful cadets.

Virginia maintains that these methodological differences are "justified pedagogically," based on "important differences between men and women in learning and developmental needs," "psychological and sociological differences" Virginia describes as "real" and "not stereotypes." . . . In contrast to the generalizations about women on which Virginia rests, we note again these dispositive realities: VMI's "implementing methodology" is not "inherently unsuitable to women," "some women . . . do well under [the] adversative model," "some women, at least, would want to attend [VMI] if they had the opportunity," "some women are capable of all of the individual activities required of VMI cadets" and "can meet the physical standards [VMI] now impose[s] on men." It is on behalf of these women that the United States has instituted this suit, and it is for them that a remedy must be crafted, a remedy that will end their exclusion from a state-supplied educational opportunity for which they are fit, a decree that will "bar like discrimination in the future."

In myriad respects other than military training, VWIL does not qualify as VMI's equal. VWIL's student body, faculty, course offerings, and facilities hardly match VMI's. Nor can the VWIL graduate anticipate the benefits associated with VMI's 157-year history, the school's prestige, and its influential alumni network. . . .

Virginia's VWIL solution is reminiscent of the remedy Texas proposed 50 years ago, in response to a state trial court's 1946 ruling that, given the equal protection guarantee, African Americans could not be denied a legal education at a state facility. See *Sweatt* v. *Painter*, 339 U.S. 629 (1950). Reluctant to admit African Americans to its flagship University of Texas Law School, the State set up a separate school for Herman Sweatt and other black law students . . . This Court contrasted resources at the new school with those at the school from which Sweatt had been excluded. . . . [But, m]ore important than the tangible features, the Court emphasized, are "those qualities which are incapable of objective measurement but which make for greatness" in a school, including "reputation of the faculty, experience of the administration, position and influence of the alumni, standing in the community, traditions and prestige." Facing the marked differences reported in the *Sweatt* opinion, the Court unanimously ruled that Texas had not shown "substantial equality in the [separate] educational opportunities" the State offered. Accordingly, the Court held, the Equal Protection Clause required Texas to admit African Americans to the University of Texas Law School. In line with *Sweatt*, we rule here that Virginia has not shown substantial equality in the separate educational opportunities the State supports at VWIL and VMI.

When Virginia tendered its VWIL plan, the Fourth Circuit did not inquire whether the proposed remedy, approved by the District Court, placed women denied the VMI advantage in "the position they would have occupied in the absence of [discrimination]." Instead, the Court of Appeals considered whether the State could provide, with fidelity to the equal protection principle, separate and unequal educational programs for men and women. . . .

The Fourth Circuit plainly erred in exposing Virginia's VWIL plan to a deferential analysis, for "all gender-based classifications today" warrant "heightened scrutiny." Valuable as VWIL may prove for students who seek the program offered, Virginia's remedy affords no cure at all for the opportunities and advantages withheld from women who want a VMI education and can make the grade. In sum, Virginia's remedy does not match the constitutional violation; the State has shown no "exceedingly persuasive justification" for withholding from women qualified for the experience premier training of the kind VMI affords. . . .

For the reasons stated, the initial judgment of the Court of Appeals is affirmed, the final judgment of the Court of Appeals is reversed, and the case is remanded for further proceedings consistent with this opinion.

CHIEF JUSTICE REHNQUIST, concurring in judgment.

While I agree with [the Court's] conclusions, I disagree with the Court's analysis and so I write separately.

Two decades ago in *Craig* v. *Boren*, 429 U.S. 190 (1976), we announced that "[t]o withstand constitutional challenge, . . . classifications by gender must serve important governmental objectives and must be substantially related to achievement of those objectives." We have adhered to that standard of scrutiny ever since. . . .

While terms like "important governmental objective" and "substantially related" are hardly models of precision, they have more content and specificity than does the phrase "exceedingly persuasive justification." That phrase is best confined, as it was first used, as an observation on the difficulty of meeting the applicable test, not as a formulation of the test itself.

Our cases dealing with gender discrimination also require that the proffered purpose for the challenged law be the actual purpose. . . . Before this Court, Virginia has sought to justify VMI's single-sex admissions policy primarily on the basis that diversity in education is desirable, and that while most of the public institutions of higher learning in the State are coeducational, there should also be room for single-sex institutions. I agree with the Court that there is scant evidence in the record that this was the real reason that Virginia decided to maintain VMI as men only. But, unlike the majority, I would consider only evidence that postdates our decision in *Hogan*, and would draw no negative inferences from the State's actions before that time. I think that after *Hogan*, the State was entitled to reconsider its policy with respect to VMI, and to not have earlier justifications, or lack thereof, held against it. . . .

Virginia offers a second justification for the single-sex admissions policy: maintenance of the adversative method. I agree with the Court that this justification does not serve an important governmental objective. A State does not have substantial interest in the adversative methodology unless it is pedagogically beneficial. While considerable evidence shows that a single-sex education is pedagogically beneficial for some students and hence a State may have a valid interest in promoting that methodology, there is no similar evidence in the record that an adversative method is pedagogically beneficial or is any more likely to produce character traits than other methodologies. . . .

[I]t is not the "exclusion of women" that violates the Equal Protection Clause, but the maintenance of an all-men school without providing any—much less a comparable—institution for women. Accordingly, the remedy should not necessarily require either the admission of women to VMI, or the creation of a VMI clone for women. An adequate remedy in my opinion might be a demonstration by Virginia that its interest in educating men in a single-sex environment is matched by its interest in educating women in a single-sex institution. . . . If a state decides to create single-sex programs, the state would, I expect, consider the public's interest and demand in designing curricula. And rightfully so. But the state should avoid assuming demand based on stereotypes; it must not assume a priori, without evidence, that there would be no interest in a women's school of civil engineering, or in a men's school of nursing.

In the end, the women's institution Virginia proposes, VWIL, fails as a remedy, because it is distinctly inferior to the existing men's institution and will continue to be for the foreseeable future. VWIL simply is not, in any sense, the institution that VMI is. In particular, VWIL is a program appended to a private college, not a self-standing institution; and VWIL is substantially underfunded as compared to VMI. I therefore ultimately agree with the Court that Virginia has not provided an adequate remedy.

JUSTICE SCALIA, dissenting.

Today the Court shuts down an institution that has served the people of the Commonwealth of Virginia with pride and distinction for over a century and a half. To achieve that desired result, it rejects (contrary to our established practice) the factual findings of two courts below, sweeps aside the precedents of this Court, and ignores the history of our people. As to facts: it explicitly rejects the finding that there exist "gender-based developmental differences" supporting Virginia's restriction of the "adversative" method to only a men's institution, and the finding that the all-male composition of the Virginia Military Institute (VMI) is essential to that institution's character. As to precedent: it drastically revises our established standards for reviewing sex-based classifications. And as to history: it counts for nothing the long tradition, enduring down to the present, of men's military colleges supported by both States and the Federal Government.

Much of the Court's opinion is devoted to deprecating the closed-mindedness of our forebears with regard to women's education, and even with regard to the treatment of women in areas that have nothing to do with education. Closed-minded they were—as every age is, including our own, with regard to matters it cannot guess, because it simply does not consider them debatable. The virtue of a democratic system with a First Amendment is that it readily enables the people, over time, to be persuaded that what they took for granted is not so, and to change their laws accordingly. That system is destroyed if the smug assurances of each age are removed from the democratic process and written into the Constitution. So to counterbalance the Court's criticism of our ancestors, let me say a word in their praise: they left us free to change. The same cannot be said of this most illiberal Court, which has embarked on a course of inscribing one after another of the current preferences of the society (and in some cases only the counter-majoritarian preferences of the society's law-trained elite) into our Basic Law. Today it enshrines the notion that no substantial educational value is to be served by an all-men's military academy—so that the decision by the people of Virginia to maintain such an institution denies equal protection to women who cannot attend that institution but can attend others. Since it is entirely clear that the Constitution of the United States—the old one—takes no sides in this educational debate, I dissent.

[O]ur current equal-protection jurisprudence . . . regards this Court as free to evaluate everything under the sun by applying one of three tests: "rational basis" scrutiny, intermediate scrutiny, or strict scrutiny. These tests are no more scientific than their names suggest, and a further element of randomness is added by the fact that it is largely up to us which test will be applied in each case. Strict scrutiny, we have said, is reserved for state "classifications based on race or national origin and classifications affecting fundamental rights," *Clark* v. *Jeter*, 486 U.S. 456 (1988). It is my position that the term "fundamental rights" should be limited to "interest[s] traditionally protected by our society." *Michael H.* v. *Gerald D.*, 491 U.S. 110 (1989); but the Court has not accepted that view, so that strict scrutiny will be applied to the deprivation of whatever sort of right we consider "fundamental." We have no established criterion for "intermediate scrutiny" either, but essentially apply it when it seems like a good idea to load the dice. So far it has been applied to content-neutral restrictions that place an incidental burden on speech, to disabilities attendant to illegitimacy, and to discrimination on the basis of sex.

I have no problem with a system of abstract tests such as rational-basis, intermediate, and strict scrutiny (though I think we can do better than applying strict scrutiny and intermediate scrutiny whenever we feel like it). Such formulas are essential to evaluating whether the new restrictions that a changing society constantly imposes upon private conduct comport with that "equal protection" our society has always accorded in the past. But in my view the function of this Court is to preserve our society's values regarding (among other things) equal protection, not to revise them; to prevent backsliding from the degree of restriction the Constitution imposed upon democratic government, not to prescribe, on our own authority, progressively higher degrees. For that reason it is my view that, whatever abstract tests we may choose to devise, they cannot supersede—and indeed ought to be crafted so as to reflect—those constant and unbroken national traditions that embody the people's understanding of ambiguous constitutional texts. More specifically, it is my view that "when a practice not expressly prohibited by the text of the Bill of Rights bears the endorsement of a long tradition of open, widespread, and unchallenged use that dates back to the beginning of the Republic, we have no proper basis for striking it down." *Rutan* v. *Republican Party of Illinois*, 497 U.S. 62, 95 (1990). The same applies, *mutatis mutandis*, to a practice asserted to be in violation of the post-Civil War Fourteenth Amendment. . . .

Today, . . . change is forced upon Virginia, and reversion to single-sex education is prohibited nationwide, not by democratic processes but by order of this Court. Even while bemoaning the sorry, bygone days of "fixed notions" concerning women's education, the Court favors current notions so fixedly that it is willing to write them into the Constitution of the United States by application of custom-built "tests." This is not the interpretation of a Constitution, but the creation of one.

And the rationale of today's decision is sweeping: for sex based classifications, a redefinition of intermediate scrutiny that makes it indistinguishable from strict scrutiny. Indeed, the Court indicates that if any program restricted to one sex is "uniqu[e]," it must be opened to members of the opposite sex "who have the will and capacity" to participate in it. I suggest that the single-sex program that will not be capable of being characterized as "unique" is not only unique but nonexistent.

In any event, regardless of whether the Court's rationale leaves some small amount of room for lawyers to argue, it ensures that single-sex public education is functionally dead. The costs of liti-gating the constitutionality of a single-sex education program, and the risks of ultimately losing that litigation, are simply too high to be embraced by public officials. Any person with standing to challenge any sex based classification can haul the State into federal court and compel it to establish by evidence (presumably in the form of expert testimony) that there is an "exceedingly persuasive justification" for the classification. Should the courts happen to interpret that vacuous phrase as establishing a standard that is not utterly impossible of achievement, there is considerable risk that whether the standard has been met will not be determined on the basis of the record evidence—indeed, that will necessarily be the approach of any court that seeks to walk the path the Court has trod today. No state official in his right mind will buy such a high cost, high risk lawsuit by commencing a single-sex program. The enemies of single-sex education have won; by persuading only seven Justices (five would have been enough) that their view of the world is enshrined in the Constitution, they have effectively imposed that view on all 50 States.

Rostker v. *Goldberg*
453 U.S. 57; 101 S. Ct. 2646; 69 L. Ed. 2d 478 (1981)

The Military Selective Service Act (MSSA) authorizes the president to require the registration for possible military service of males, but not females, the purpose of registration being to facilitate any eventual conscription under the act. Registration for the draft was discontinued by a presidential proclamation in 1975, but President Jimmy Carter decided in 1980 that it was necessary to reactivate the registration process and requested Congress to allocate funds for that purpose. He also recommended that Congress amend the MSSA to permit the registration and conscription of women. Although Congress agreed to reactivate the registration process, it declined to amend the MSSA to permit the registration of women and allocated funds only to register males. Thereafter, the president ordered the registration of specified groups of young men. A lawsuit was brought against Bernard Rostker, director of Selective Service, by several men, challenging the act's constitutionality. A three-judge district court held that the act's gender-based discrimination violated the Due Process Clause of the Fifth Amendment and enjoined registration under the act, whereupon the United States government appealed to the Supreme Court. *Opinion of the Court: Rehnquist, Blackmun, Burger, Powell, Stevens, Stewart. Dissenting opinions: Marshall, Brennan; White, Brennan.*

MR. JUSTICE REHNQUIST delivered the opinion of the Court.

The question presented is whether the Military Selective Service Act . . . violates the Fifth Amendment to the United States Constitution in authorizing the President to require the registration of males and not females. . . .

Congress is given the power under the Constitution "To raise and support Armies," "To provide and maintain a Navy," and "To make Rules for the Government and Regulation of the land and naval Forces." . . . Pursuant to this grant of authority Congress has enacted the Military Selective Service Act . . . Section 3 of the Act . . . empowers the President, by proclamation, to require the registration of "every male citizen" and male resident aliens between the ages of 18 and 26. . . . The MSSA registration provision serves no other purpose beyond providing a pool for subsequent induction.

Registration for the draft under § 3 was discontinued in 1975. . . . In early 1980, President Carter determined that it was necessary to reactivate the draft registration process. The immediate impetus for this decision was the Soviet armed invasion of Afghanistan. . . . The resulting crisis in Southwestern Asia convinced the President that the "time has come" "to use his present authority to require registration . . . as a necessary step to preserving or enhancing our national security interests." . . . The Selective Service System had been inactive, however, and funds were needed before reactivating registration. The President therefore recommended that funds be transferred from the Department of Defense to the separate Selective Service System. . . . He also recommended that Congress take action to amend the MSSA to permit the registration and conscription of women as well as men. . . .

Congress agreed that it was necessary to reactivate the registration process, and allocated funds for that purpose in a joint resolution which passed the House on April 22 and the Senate on June 12. . . . The resolution did not allocate all the funds originally requested by the President, but only those necessary to register males. . . . Although Congress considered the question at great length, . . . it declined to amend the MSSA to permit the registration of women.

On July 2, 1980, the President, by proclamation, ordered the registration of specified groups of young men pursuant to the authority conferred by § 3 of the Act. . . .

Whenever called upon to judge the constitutionality of an Act of Congress—"the gravest and most delicate duty that this Court is called upon to perform" . . . the Court accords "great weight to the decisions of Congress." . . . The Congress is a coequal branch of government whose members take the same oath we do to uphold the Constitution of the United States. . . . The customary deference accorded the judgments of Congress is certainly appropriate when, as here, Congress specifically considered the question of the Act's constitutionality. . . .

This is not, however, merely a case involving the customary deference accorded congressional decisions. The case arises in the context of Congress' authority over national defense and military affairs, and perhaps in no other area has the Court accorded Congress greater deference. In rejecting the registration of women, Congress explicitly relied upon its constitutional powers under Art. I, § 8, cls. 12–14. . . . This Court has consistently recognized Congress' "broad constitutional power" to raise and regulate armies and navies, *Schlesinger* v. *Ballard* . . . (1975).

Not only is the scope of Congress' constitutional power in this area broad, but the lack of competence on the part of the courts is marked. In *Gilligan* v. *Morgan* . . . (1973), the Court noted: "It is difficult to conceive of an area of governmental activity in which the courts have less competence. The complex, subtle, and professional decisions as to the composition, training, equipping, and control of a military force are essentially professional military judgments, subject always to civilian control of the Legislative and Executive branches." . . .

None of this is to say that Congress is free to disregard the Constitution when it acts in the area of military affairs. In that area as any other Congress remains subject to the limitations of the Due Process Clause, . . . but the tests and limitations to be applied may differ because of the military context. We of course do not abdicate our ultimate responsibility to decide the constitutional question, but simply recognize that the Constitution itself requires such deference to congressional choice. . . . In deciding the question before us we must be particularly careful not to substitute our judgment of what is desirable for that of Congress, or our own evaluation of evidence for a reasonable evaluation by the Legislative Branch.

The District Court purported to recognize the appropriateness of deference to Congress when that body was exercising its constitutionally delegated authority over military affairs, . . . but it stressed that "we are not here concerned with military operations or day-to-day conduct of the military into which we have no desire to intrude." . . . Appellees also stress that this case involves civilians, not the military, and that "the impact of registration on the military is only indirect and attenuated." . . . We find these efforts to divorce registration from the military and national defense context, with all the deference called for in that context, singularly unpersuasive. . . . Registration is not an end in itself in the civilian world but rather the first step in the induction process into the military one, and Congress specifically linked its consideration of registration to induction. . . . Congressional judgments concerning registration and the draft are based on judgments concerning military operations and needs . . . and the deference unquestionably due the latter judgments is necessarily required in assessing the former as well.

The Solicitor General argues . . . that this Court should scrutinize the MSSA only to determine if the distinction drawn between men and women bears a rational relation to some legitimate government purpose, . . . and should not examine the Act under the heightened scrutiny with which we have approached gender-based discrimination. . . . We do not think that the substantive guarantee of due process or certainty in the law will be advanced by any further "refinement" in the applicable tests as suggested by the Government. Announced degrees of "deference" to legislative judgments, just as levels of "scrutiny" which this Court announces that it applies to particular classifications made by a legislative body, may all too readily become facile abstractions used to justify a result. In this case the courts are called upon to decide whether Congress, acting under an explicit constitutional grant of authority, has by that action transgressed an explicit guarantee of individual rights which limits the authority so conferred. Simply labelling the legislative decision "military" on the one hand or "gender-based" on the other does not automatically guide a court to the correct constitutional result.

No one could deny that under the test of *Craig v. Boren* [1976] . . . the Government's interest in raising and supporting armies is an "important governmental interest." Congress and its committees carefully considered and debated two alternative means of furthering that interest: the first was to register only males for potential conscription, and the other was to register both sexes. Congress chose the former alternative. When that decision is challenged on equal protection grounds, the question a court must decide is not which alternative it would have chosen, had it been the primary decision-maker, but whether that chosen by Congress denies equal protection of the laws. . . .

This case is quite different from several of the gender-based discrimination cases we have considered in that, despite appellees' assertions, Congress did not act "unthinkingly" or "reflexively and not for any considered reason." . . . The question of registering women for the draft not only received considerable national attention and was the subject of wide-ranging public debate, but also was extensively considered by Congress in hearings, floor debate, and in committee. Hearings held by both Houses of Congress in response to the President's request for authorization to register women adduced extensive testimony and evidence concerning the issue. . . . These hearings built on other hearings held the previous year addressed to the same question.

The House declined to provide for the registration of women when it passed the Joint Resolution allocating funds for the Selective Service System. . . . When the Senate considered the Joint resolution, it defeated, after extensive debate, an amendment which in effect would have authorized the registration of women. . . .

While proposals to register women were being rejected in the course of transferring funds to register males, committees in both Houses which had conducted hearings on the issue were also rejecting the registration of women. The House Subcommittee on Military Personnel of the House Armed Services Committee tabled a bill which would have amended the MSSA to authorize registration of women. . . . The Senate Armed Services Committee rejected a proposal to register women, . . . as it had one year before. . . .

The foregoing clearly establishes that the decision to exempt women from registration was not the "accidental byproduct of a traditional way of thinking about women." . . . The issue was considered at great length and Congress clearly expressed its purpose and intent. . . .

The MSSA established a plan for maintaining "adequate armed strength . . . to ensure the security of the nation." . . . Registration is the first step "in a united and continuous process designed to raise an army speedily and efficiently," . . . and Congress provided for the reactivation of registration in order to "provide the means for the early delivery of inductees in an emergency." . . . Congress rather clearly linked the need for renewed registration with its views on the character of a subsequent draft. Any assessment of the congressional purpose and its chosen means must therefore consider the registration scheme as a prelude to a draft in a time of national emergency. Any other approach would not be testing the Act in light of the purposes Congress sought to achieve.

Congress determined that any future draft, which would be facilitated by the registration scheme, would be characterized by a need for combat troops. The Senate Report explained, in a specific finding later adopted by both Houses, that "if mobilization were to be ordered in a wartime scenario, the primary manpower need would be for combat replacements." . . .

Women as a group, however, unlike men as a group, are not eligible for combat. The restrictions on the participation of women in combat in the Navy and Air Force are statutory. . . . The Army and Marine Corps preclude the use of women in combat as a matter of established policy. . . . Congress specifically recognized and endorsed the exclusion of women from combat in exempting women from registration. In the words of the Senate Report: "The principle that women should not intentionally and routinely engage in combat is fundamental, and enjoys wide support among our people." . . .

The existence of the combat restrictions clearly indicates the basis for Congress' decision to exempt women from registration. The purpose of registration was to prepare for a draft of combat troops. Since women are excluded from combat, Congress concluded that they would not be needed in the event of a draft, and therefore decided not to register them. . . .

The District Court stressed that the military need for women was irrelevant to the issue of their registration. As that court put it: "Congress could not constitutionally require registration under MSSA of only black citizens or only white citizens, or single out any political or religious group simply because those groups contained sufficient persons to fill the needs of the Selective Service System." . . . This reasoning is beside the point. The reason women are exempt from registration is not because military needs can be met by drafting men. This is not a case of Congress arbitrarily choosing to burden one of two similarly situated groups, such as would be the case with an all-black or all-white, or an all-Catholic or all-Lutheran, or an all-Republican or all-Democratic registration. Men and women, because of the combat restrictions on women, are simply not similarly situated for purposes of a draft or registration for a draft.

Congress' decision to authorize the registration of only men, therefore, does not violate the Due Process Clause. The exemption of women from registration is not only sufficiently but closely related to Congress' purpose in authorizing registration. . . . The fact that Congress and the Executive have decided that women should not serve in combat fully justifies Congress in not authorizing their registration, since the purpose of registration is to develop a pool of potential combat troops. As was the case in *Schlesinger* v. *Ballard, supra,* "the gender classification is not invidious, but rather realistically reflects the fact that the sexes are not similarly situated" in this case. . . . The Constitution requires that Congress treat similarly situated persons similarly, not that it engage in gestures of superficial equality.

In holding the MSSA constitutionally invalid the District Court relied heavily on the President's decision to seek authority to register women and the testimony of members of the Executive Branch and the military in support of that decision. . . . As stated by the Administration's witnesses before Congress, however, the President's decision to ask for authority to register women is based on equity." . . . This was also the basis for the testimony by military officials. . . . The Senate Report, evaluating the testimony before the Committee, recognized that "the argument for registration and induction of women . . . is not based on military necessity, but on considerations of equity." . . . Congress was certainly entitled, in the exercise of its constitutional powers to raise and regulate armies and navies, to focus on the question of military need rather than "equity." . . .

In light of the foregoing, we conclude that

Congress acted well within its constitutional authority when it authorized the registration of men, and not women, under the Military Selective Service Act. The decision of the District Court holding otherwise is accordingly

Reversed.

MR. JUSTICE MARSHALL, with whom MR. JUSTICE BRENNAN joins, dissenting.

The Court today places its imprimatur on one of the most potent remaining public expressions of "ancient canards about the proper role of women." . . . It upholds a statute that requires males but not females to register for the draft, and which thereby categorically excludes women from a fundamental civic obligation. Because I believe the Court's decision is inconsistent with the Constitution's guarantee of equal protection of the laws, I dissent.

By now it should be clear that statutes like the MSSA, which discriminate on the basis of gender, must be examined under the "heightened" scrutiny mandated by *Craig* v. *Boren* . . . (1976). Under this test, a gender-based classification cannot withstand constitutional challenge unless the classification is substantially related to the achievement of an important governmental objective. . . . This test applies whether the classification discriminates against males or females. . . . The party defending the challenged classification carries the burden of demonstrating both the importance of the governmental objective it serves and the substantial relationship between the discriminatory means and the asserted end. . . . Consequently, before we can sustain the MSSA, the Government must demonstrate that the gender-based classification it employs bears "a close and substantial relationship to [the achievement of] important governmental objectives." . . .

. . . I agree with the majority, . . . that "none could deny that . . . the Government's interest in raising and supporting armies is an 'important governmental interest.' " Consequently, the first part of the *Craig* v. *Boren* test is satisfied. But the question remains whether the discriminatory means employed itself substantially serves the statutory end. . . . When, as here, a federal law that classifies on the basis of gender is challenged as violating this constitutional guarantee, it is ultimately for this Court, not Congress, to decide whether there exists the constitutionally required "close and substantial relationship" between the discriminatory means employed and the asserted governmental objective. . . . In my judgment, there simply is no basis for concluding in this case that excluding women from registration is substantially related to the achievement of a concededly important governmental interest in maintaining an effective defense. . . .

In the first place, although the Court purports to apply the *Craig* v. *Boren* test, the "similarly situated" analysis the Court employs is in fact significantly different from the *Craig* v. *Boren* approach. . . . The Court essentially reasons that the gender classification employed by the MSSA is constitutionally permissible because nondiscrimination is not necessary to achieve the purpose of registration to prepare for a draft of combat troops. In other words, the majority concludes that women may be excluded from registration because they will not be needed in the event of a draft.

This analysis, however, focuses on the wrong question. The relevant inquiry under the *Craig* v. *Boren* test is not whether a *gender-neutral* classification would substantially advance important governmental interests. Rather, the question is whether the gender-based classification is itself substantially related to the achievement of the asserted governmental interest. Thus, the Government's task in this case is to demonstrate that excluding women from registration substantially furthers the goal of preparing for a draft of combat troops. Or to put it another way, the Government must show that registering women would substantially impede its efforts to prepare for such a draft. Under our precedents, the Government cannot meet this burden without showing that a gender neutral statute would be a less effective means of attaining this end. . . . In this case, the Government makes no claim that preparing for a draft of combat troops cannot be accomplished just as effectively by *registering* both men and women but *drafting* only men if only men turn out to be needed. Nor can the Government argue that this alternative entails the additional cost and administrative inconvenience of registering women. This Court has repeatedly stated that the administrative convenience of employing a gender classification is not an adequate constitutional justification under the *Craig* v. *Boren* test. . . .

The fact that registering women in no way obstructs the governmental interest in preparing for a draft of combat troops points up a second flaw in the Court's analysis. The Court essentially reduces the question of the constitutionality of male-only *registration* to the validity of a hypothetical program for *conscripting* only men. The Court posits a draft in which *all* conscripts are either assigned to those specific combat posts presently closed to women or must be available for rotation into such positions. . . . If it could indeed be guaranteed in advance that conscription would be reimposed by Congress only in circumstances where, and in a form under which, all conscripts would have to be trained for and assigned to combat or combat rotation positions from which women are categorically excluded, then it could be argued that registration of women would be pointless.

But of course, no such guarantee is possible. Certainly, nothing about the MSSA limits Congress to reinstituting the draft only in such circumstances. . . .

. . . The discussion and findings in the Senate Report do not enable the Government to carry its burden of demonstrating that *completely* excluding women from the draft by excluding them from registration substantially furthers important governmental objectives. . . . Congressional enactments in the area of military affairs must, like all other laws, be *judged* by the standards of the Constitution. For the Constitution is the supreme law of the land and *all* legislation must conform to the principles it lay down. . . .

Furthermore, "when it appears that an Act of Congress conflicts with [a constitutional] provision, we have no choice but to enforce the paramount commands of the Constitution. We are sworn to do no less. We cannot push back the limits of the Constitution merely to accommodate challenged legislation." . . . In some 106 instances since this court was established it has determined that congressional action exceeded the bounds of the Constitution. I believe the same is true of this statute. In an attempt to avoid its constitutional obligation, the Court today "pushes back the limits of the Constitution" to accommodate an Act of Congress.

I would affirm the judgment of the District Court.

Shapiro v. *Thompson*
394 U.S. 618; 89 S. Ct. 1322; 22 L. Ed. 2d 600 (1969)

Vivian Marie Thompson, a pregnant, nineteen-year-old unwed mother who already had one child, moved to Connecticut from Massachusetts in June 1966. Two months later, she applied for public assistance money under the Aid to Families with Dependent Children (AFDC) program. Her application was denied on the sole ground that she had not met the state's one-year residency requirement, which was a prerequisite for eligibility to receive aid. She thereupon brought suit against Bernard Shapiro, the Connecticut welfare commissioner, in federal district court. The three-judge court found the state residency requirement unconstitutional because of its "chilling effect on the right to travel." Shapiro appealed to the Supreme Court. The Court heard this case in conjunction with similar cases from Pennsylvania and the District of Columbia, both of which also involved the validity of one-year residency requirements. *Opinion of the Court: Brennan, Douglas, Fortas, Marshall, Stewart, White. Concurring opinion: Stewart. Dissenting opinions: Harlan; Warren, Black.*

JUSTICE BRENNAN delivered the opinion of the Court. . . .

There is no dispute that the effect of the waiting-period requirement in each case is to create two classes of needy resident families indistinguishable from each other except that one is composed of residents who have resided a year or more, and the second of residents who have resided less than a year, in the jurisdiction. On the basis of this sole difference the first class is granted and the second class is denied welfare aid upon which may depend the ability of the families to obtain the very means to subsist—food, shelter, and other necessities of life. In each case, the District Court found that appellees met the test for residence in their jurisdictions, as well as all other eligibility requirements except the requirement of residence for a full year prior to their applications. On reargument, appellees' central contention is that the statutory prohibition of benefits to residents of less than a year creates a classification which constitutes an invidious discrimination denying them equal protection of the laws. We agree. The interests which appellants assert are promoted by the classification either may not constitutionally be promoted by government or are not compelling governmental interests.

Primarily, appellants justify the waiting-period requirement as a protective device to preserve the fiscal integrity of state public assistance programs. It is asserted that people who require welfare assistance during their first year of residence in a State are likely to become continuing burdens on state welfare programs. Therefore, the argument runs, if such people can be deterred from entering the jurisdiction by denying them welfare benefits during the first year, state programs to assist long-time residents will not be impaired by a substantial influx of indigent newcomers.

There is weighty evidence that exclusion from the jurisdiction of the poor who need or may need relief was the specific objective of these provisions. In the Congress, sponsors of federal legislation to eliminate all residence requirements have been consistently opposed by representatives of state and local welfare agencies who have stressed the fears of the States that elimination of the requirements would result in a heavy influx of individuals into States providing the most generous benefits. . . .

We do not doubt that the one-year waiting-period device is well suited to discourage the influx of poor families in need of assistance. An indigent who desires to migrate, resettle, find a new job, and start a new life will doubtless hesitate if he knows that he must risk making the move without the possibility of falling back on state welfare assistance during his first year of residence when his need may be most acute. But the purpose of inhibiting migration by needy persons into the State is constitutionally impermissible.

This Court long ago recognized that the nature of our Federal Union and our constitutional concepts of personal liberty unite to require that all citizens be free to travel throughout the length and breadth of our land uninhibited by statutes, rules, or regulations which unreasonably burden or restrict this movement. . . .

We have no occasion to ascribe the source of this right to travel interstate to a particular constitutional provision. It suffices that, as Mr. Justice Stewart said for the Court in United *States* v. *Guest* . . . (1966): "The constitutional right to travel from one State to another . . . occupies a position fundamental to the concept of our Federal Union. It is a right that has been firmly established and repeatedly recognized. "

". . . [The] right finds no explicit mention in the Constitution. The reason, it has been suggested, is that a right so elementary was conceived from the beginning to be a necessary concomitant of the stronger Union the Constitution created. In any event, freedom to travel throughout the United States has long been recognized as a basic right under the Constitution." . . .

Alternatively, appellants argue that even if it is impermissible for a State to attempt to deter the entry of all indigents, the challenged classification may be justified as a permissible state attempt to discourage those indigents who would enter the State solely to obtain larger benefits. We observe first that none of the statutes before us is tailored to serve that objective. Rather, the class of barred newcomers is all-inclusive, lumping the great majority who come to the State for other purposes with those who come for the sole purpose of collecting higher benefits. In actual operation, therefore, the three statutes enact what in effect are nonrebuttable presumptions that every applicant for assistance in his first year of residence came to the jurisdiction solely to obtain higher benefits. Nothing whatever in any of these records supplies any basis in fact for such a presumption.

More fundamentally, a State may no more try to fence out those indigents who seek higher welfare benefits than it may try to fence out indigents generally. Implicit in any such distinction is the notion that indigents who enter a State with the hope of securing higher welfare benefits are somehow less deserving than indigents who do not take this consideration into account. But we do not perceive why a mother who is seeking to make a new life for herself and her children should be regarded as less deserving because she considers, among other factors, the level of a State's public assistance. Surely such a mother is no less deserving than a mother who moves into a particular State in order to take advantage of its better educational facilities. . . .

We recognize that a State has a valid interest in preserving the fiscal integrity of its programs. It may legitimately attempt to limit its expenditures, whether for public assistance, public education, or any other program. But a State may not accomplish such a purpose by invidious distinctions between classes of its citizens. It could not, for example, reduce expenditures for education by barring indigent children from its schools. Similarly, in the cases before us, appellants must do more than show that denying welfare benefits to new residents saves money. The saving of welfare costs cannot justify an otherwise invidious classification. . . .

Appellants next advance as justification certain administrative and related governmental objectives allegedly served by the waiting-period requirement. They argue that the requirement (1) facilitates the planning of the welfare budget; (2) provides an objective test of residency; (3) minimizes the opportunity for recipients fraudulently to receive payments from more than one jurisdiction; and (4) encourages early entry of new residents into the labor force.

. . . We reject appellants' argument that a mere showing of a rational relationship between the waiting period and these four admittedly permissible state objectives will suffice to justify the classification. . . . Any classification which serves to penalize the exercise of that right, unless shown to be necessary to promote a *compelling* governmental interest, is unconstitutional. . . .

MR. JUSTICE HARLAN, dissenting. . . .

In upholding the equal protection argument, the Court has applied an equal protection doctrine of relatively recent vintage: the rule that statutory classifications which either are based upon certain "suspect" criteria or affect "fundamental rights" will be held to deny equal protection unless justified by a "compelling" governmental interest.

I think that this branch of the "compelling interest" doctrine is sound when applied to racial classifications, for historically the Equal Protection Clause was largely a product of the desire to eradicate legal distinctions founded upon race.

However, I believe that the more recent extensions have been unwise. . . .

The second branch of the "compelling interest" principle is even more troublesome. For it has been held that a statutory classification is subject to the "compelling interest" test if the result of the classification may be to affect a "fundamental right," . . . I think the "compelling interest" doctrine particularly unfortunate and unnecessary. It is unfortunate because it creates an exception which threatens to swallow the standard equal protection rule. Virtually every state statute affects important rights. This Court has repeatedly held, for example, that the traditional equal protection standard is applicable to statutory classifications affecting such fundamental matters as the right to pursue a particular occupation, the right to receive greater or smaller wages or to work more or less hours, and the right to inherit property. Rights such as these are in principle indistinguishable from those involved here, and to extend the "compelling interest" rule to all cases in which such rights are affected would go far toward making this Court a "super-legislature." But when a statute affects only matters not mentioned in the Federal Constitution and is not arbitrary or irrational, I must reiterate that I know of nothing which entitles this Court to pick out particular human activities, characterize them as "fundamental," and give them added protection under an unusually stringent equal protection test. . . .

I do not consider that the factors which have been urged . . . are sufficient to render unconstitutional these state and federal enactments. It is said, first, that this Court . . . . has acknowledged that the right to travel interstate is a "fundamental" freedom. Second, it is contended that the governmental objectives mentioned above either are ephemeral or could be accomplished by means which do not impinge as heavily on the right to travel, and hence that the requirements are unconstitutional because they "sweep unnecessarily broadly and thereby invade the area of protected freedoms." . . .

Taking all of these competing considerations into account, I believe that the balance definitely favors constitutionality. In reaching that conclusion, I do not minimize the importance of the right to travel interstate. However, the impact of residence conditions upon that right is indirect and apparently quite insubstantial. On the other hand, the governmental purposes served by the requirements are legitimate and real, and the residence requirements are clearly suited to their accomplishment. To abolish residence requirements might well discourage highly worthwhile experimentation in the welfare field . . . Moreover, although the appellees assert that the same objectives could have been achieved by less restrictive means, this is an area in which the judiciary should be especially slow to fetter the judgment of Congress and of some 46 state legislatures in the choice of methods. Residence requirements have advantages, such as administrative simplicity and relative certainty, which are not shared by the alternative solutions proposed by the appellees. In these circumstances, I cannot find that the burden imposed by residence requirements upon ability to travel outweighs the governmental interests in their continued employment. Nor do I believe that the period of residence required in these cases—one year—is so excessively long as to justify a finding of unconstitutionality on that score.

I conclude with the following observations. Today's decision, it seems to me, reflects to an unusual degree the current notion that this Court possesses a peculiar wisdom all its own whose capacity to lead this Nation out of its present troubles is contained only by the limits of judicial ingenuity in contriving new constitutional principles to meet each problem as it arises. For anyone who, like myself, believes that it is an essential function of this Court to maintain the constitutional divisions between state and federal authority and among the three branches of the Federal Government, today's decision is a step in the wrong direction. This resurgence of the expansive view of "equal protection" carries the seeds of more judicial interference with the state and federal legislative process, much more indeed than does the judicial application of "due process" according to traditional concepts, . . . about which some members of this Court have expressed fears as to its potentialities for setting us judges "at large." I consider it particularly unfortunate that this judicial roadblock to the powers of Congress in this field should occur at the very threshold of the current discussions regarding the "federalizing" of these aspects of welfare relief.

San Antonio Independent School District v. *Rodriguez*
411 U.S. 1; 93 S. Ct. 1278; 36 L. Ed. 2d 16 (1973)

The financing of public elementary and secondary education in Texas is a product of state and local participation. Almost half of the revenues are derived from a largely state-funded program designed to provide basic minimum education in every school. Each district then supplements this state aid through an *ad valorem* tax on property within its jurisdiction. Demetrio Rodriguez and others brought a class action on behalf of schoolchildren who were members of poor families that resided in school districts with low property-tax bases, claiming that the Texas system's reliance on local property taxation favored the more affluent and that it violated equal protection requirements because of the substantial interdistrict disparities in per-pupil expenditures that resulted primarily from differences in the value of assessable property among the districts. A three-judge federal district court, finding that wealth is a "suspect" classification and that education is a "fundamental right," concluded that the system could be upheld only upon a showing (which appellants failed to make) that there was a compelling state interest for the system. The court further concluded that appellants failed even to demonstrate a rational basis for Texas's system. The state appealed. *Opinion of the Court: Powell, Blackmun, Burger, Rehnquist, Stewart. Concurring opinion: Stewart. Dissenting opinions: Brennan; Marshall, Douglas; White, Brennan, Douglas.*

MR. JUSTICE POWELL delivered the opinion of the Court....

... We must decide, first, whether the Texas system of financing public education operates to the disadvantage of some suspect class or impinges upon a fundamental right explicitly or implicitly protected by the Constitution, thereby requiring strict judicial scrutiny. If so, the judgment of the District Court should be affirmed. If not, the Texas scheme must still be examined to determine whether it rationally furthers some legitimate, articulated state purpose and therefore does not constitute an invidious discrimination in violation of the Equal Protection Clause of the Fourteenth Amendment....

We are unable to agree that this case, which in significant aspects is *sui generis*, may be so neatly fitted into the conventional mosaic of constitutional analysis under the Equal Protection Clause. Indeed, for the several reasons that follow, we find neither the suspect classification nor the fundamental interest analysis persuasive....

The precedents of this Court provide the proper starting point. The individuals or groups of individuals who constituted the class discriminated against in our prior cases shared two distinguishing characteristics: because of their impecunity they were completely unable to pay for some desired benefit, and as a consequence, they sustained an absolute deprivation of a meaningful opportunity to enjoy that benefit....

... Even a cursory examination, however, demonstrates that neither of the two distinguishing characteristics of wealth classifications can be found here. First, in support of their charge that the system discriminates against the "poor," appellees have made no effort to demonstrate that it operates to the peculiar disadvantage of any class fairly definable as indigent, or as composed of persons whose incomes are beneath any designated poverty level. Indeed, there is reason to believe that the poorest families are not necessarily clustered in the poorest property districts. A recent and exhaustive study of school districts in Connecticut concluded that "[i]t is clearly incorrect ... to contend that the "poor' live in "poor' districts. ... " Defining "poor" families as those below the Bureau of the Census "poverty level," the Connecticut study found, not surprisingly, that the poor were clustered around commercial and industrial areas—those same areas that provide the most attractive sources of property tax income for school districts. Whether a similar pattern would be discovered in Texas is not known, but there is no basis on the record in this case for assuming that the poorest people—defined by reference to any level of absolute impecunity—are concentrated in the poorest districts.

Second, neither appellees nor the District Court addressed the fact that, unlike each of the foregoing cases, lack of personal resources has not occasioned an absolute deprivation of the desired benefit. The argument here is not that the children in districts having relatively low assessable property values are receiving no public education; rather, it is that they are receiving a poorer quality education than that available to children in districts having more assessable wealth. Apart from the unsettled and disputed question whether the quality of education may be determined by the amount of money expended for it, a sufficient answer to appellees' argument is that at least where wealth is involved the Equal Protection Clause does not require absolute equality or precisely equal advantages. Nor, indeed, in view of the infinite variables affecting the educational process, can any system assure equal quality of education except in the most relative sense....

For these two reasons—the absence of any evidence that the financing system discriminates against any definable category of "poor" people or that it results in the absolute deprivation of education—the disadvantaged class is not susceptible to identification in traditional terms....

We thus conclude that the Texas system does not operate to the peculiar disadvantage of any suspect class. But in recognition of the fact that this Court has never heretofore held that wealth discrimination alone provides an adequate basis for invoking strict scrutiny, appellees have not relied solely on this contention. They also assert that the State's system impermissibly interferes with the exercise of a "fundamental" right and that accordingly the prior decisions of this Court require the application of the strict standard of judicial review. ... It is this question—whether education is a fundamental right, in the sense that it is among the rights and liberties protected by the Constitution—which has so consumed the attention of courts and commentators in recent years.

In *Brown* v. *Board of Education* . . . (1954), a unanimous Court recognized that "education is perhaps the most important function of state and local governments." . . . What was said there in the context of racial discrimination has lost none of its vitality with the passage of time: "Compulsory school attendance laws and the great expenditures for education both demonstrate our recognition of the importance of education to our democratic society. It is required in the performance of our most basic responsibilities, even service in the armed forces. It is the very foundation of good citizenship. Today it is a principal instrument in awakening the child to cultural values, in preparing him for later professional training, and in helping him to adjust normally to his environment. In these days, it is doubtful that any child may reasonably be expected to succeed in life if he is denied the opportunity of an education. Such an opportunity, where the state has undertaken to provide it, is a right which must be made available to all on equal terms." . . . This theme, expressing an abiding respect for the vital role of education in a free society, may be found in numerous opinions of Justices of this Court writing both before and after Brown was decided. . . .

Nothing this court holds today in any way detracts from our historic dedication to public education. We are in complete agreement with the conclusion of the three-judge panel below that "the grave significance of education both to the individual and to our society" cannot be doubted. But the importance of a service performed by the State does not determine whether it must be regarded as fundamental for purposes of examination under the Equal Protection Clause.

. . . It is not the province of this Court to create substantive constitutional rights in the name of guaranteeing equal protection of the laws. Thus the key to discovering whether education is "fundamental" is not to be found in comparisons of the relative societal significance of education as opposed to subsistence or housing. Nor is it to be found by weighing whether education is as important as the right to travel. Rather, the answer lies in assessing whether there is a right to education explicitly or implicitly guaranteed by the Constitution. . . .

Education, of course, is not among the rights afforded explicit protection under our Federal Constitution. Nor do we find any basis for saying it is implicitly so protected. As we have said, the undisputed importance of education will not alone cause this Court to depart from the usual standard for reviewing a State's social and economic legislation. It is appellees' contention, however, that education is distinguishable from other services and benefits provided by the State because it bears a peculiarly close relationship to other rights and liberties accorded protection under the Constitution. Specifically, they insist that education is itself a fundamental personal right because it is essential to the effective exercise of First Amendment freedoms and to intelligent utilization of the right to vote. In asserting a nexus between speech and education, appellees urge that the right to speak is meaningless unless the speaker is capable of articulating his thoughts intelligently and persuasively. The "marketplace of ideas" is an empty forum for those lacking basic communicative tools. Likewise, they argue that the corollary right to receive information becomes little more than a hollow privilege when the recipient has not been taught to read, assimilate, and utilize available knowledge.

A similar line of reasoning is pursued with respect to the right to vote. Exercise of the franchise, it is contended, cannot be divorced from the educational foundation of the voter. The electoral process, if reality is to conform to the democratic ideal, depends on an informed electorate: a voter cannot cast his ballot intelligently unless his reading skills and thought processes have been adequately developed.

We need not dispute any of these propositions. The Court has long afforded zealous protection against unjustifiable governmental interference with the individual's rights to speak and to vote. Yet we have never presumed to possess either the ability or the authority to guarantee to the citizenry the most *effective* speech or the most *informed* electoral choice. That these may be desirable goals of a system of freedom of expression and of a representative form of government is not to be doubted. These are indeed goals to be pursued by a people whose thoughts and beliefs are freed from governmental interference. But they are not values to be implemented by judicial intrusion into otherwise legitimate state activities.

Even if it were conceded that some identifiable quantum of education is a constitutionally protected prerequisite to the meaningful exercise of either right, we have no indication that the present levels of educational expenditure in

Texas provide an education that falls short. Whatever merit appellees' argument might have if a State's financing system occasioned an absolute denial of educational opportunities to any of its children, that argument provides no basis for finding an interference with fundamental rights where only relative differences in spending levels are involved and where—as is true in the present case—no charge fairly could be made that the system fails to provide each child with an opportunity to acquire the basic minimal skills necessary for the enjoyment of the rights of speech and of full participation in the political process. . . .

We have carefully considered each of the arguments supportive of the District Court's finding that education is a fundamental right or liberty and have found those arguments unpersuasive. In one further respect we find this a particularly inappropriate case in which to subject state action to strict judicial scrutiny. The present case, . . . involves the most persistent and difficult questions of educational policy, another area in which this Court's lack of specialized knowledge and experience counsels against premature interference with the informed judgments made at the state and local levels. . . . On even the most basic questions in this area the scholars and educational experts are divided. Indeed, one of the hottest sources of controversy concerns the extent to which there is a demonstrable correlation between educational expenditures and the quality of education—an assumed correlation underlying virtually every legal conclusion drawn by the District Court in this case. Related to the questioned relationship between cost and quality is the equally unsettled controversy as to the proper goals of a system of public education. And the question regarding the most effective relationship between state boards of education and local school boards, in terms of their respective responsibilities and degrees of control, is now undergoing searching re-examination. The ultimate wisdom as to these and related problems of education is not likely to be defined for all time even by the scholars who now so earnestly debate the issues. In such circumstances the judiciary is well advised to refrain from interposing on the States inflexible constitutional restraints that could circumscribe or handicap the continued research and experimentation so vital to finding even partial solutions to educational

problems and to keeping abreast of ever changing conditions. . . .

The foregoing considerations buttress our conclusion that Texas' system of public school finance is an inappropriate candidate for strict judicial scrutiny. These same considerations are relevant to the determination whether that system, with its conceded imperfections, nevertheless bears some rational relationship to a legitimate state purpose. It is to this question that we next turn our attention. . . .

. . . The Texas plan is not the result of hurried, ill-conceived legislation. It certainly is not the product of purposeful discrimination against any group or class. On the contrary, it is rooted in decades of experience in Texas and elsewhere, and in major part is the product of responsible studies by qualified people. In giving substance to the presumption of validity to which the Texas system is entitled . . . it is important to remember that at every stage of its development it has constituted a "rough accommodation" of interests in an effort to arrive at practical and workable solutions. . . . One also must remember that the system here challenged is not peculiar to Texas or to any other State. In its essential characteristics the Texas plan for financing public education reflects what many educators for a half century have thought was an enlightened approach to a problem for which there is no perfect solution. We are unwilling to assume for ourselves a level of wisdom superior to that of legislators, scholars, and educational authorities in 49 States, especially where the alternatives proposed are only recently conceived and nowhere yet tested. The constitutional standard under the Equal Protection Clause is whether the challenged state action rationally furthers a legitimate state purpose or interest. . . . We hold that the Texas plan abundantly satisfies this standard.

MR. JUSTICE WHITE, with whom MR. JUSTICE DOUGLAS and MR. JUSTICE BRENNAN join, dissenting. . . .

The Equal Protection Clause permits discriminations between classes but requires that the classification bear some rational relationship to a permissible object sought to be attained by the statute. It is not enough that the Texas system before us seeks to achieve the valid, rational purpose of maximizing local initiative; the means chosen by the State must also be rationally related to the end sought to be achieved. . . .

Neither Texas nor the majority heeds this rule. If the State aims at maximizing local initiative and local choice, by permitting school districts to resort to the real property tax if they choose to do so, it utterly fails in achieving its purpose in districts with property tax bases so low that there is little if any opportunity for interested parents, rich or poor, to augment school district revenues. Requiring the State to establish only that unequal treatment is in furtherance of a permissible goal, without also requiring the State to show that the means chosen to effectuate that goal are rationally related to its achievement, makes equal protection analysis no more than an empty gesture. In my view, the parents and children in Edgewood, and in like districts, suffer from an invidious discrimination violative of the Equal Protection Clause. . . .

MR. JUSTICE MARSHALL, with whom MR. JUSTICE DOUGLAS concurs, dissenting. . . .

This Court has repeatedly held that state discrimination which either adversely affects a "fundamental interest" . . . or is based on a distinction of a suspect character . . . must be carefully scrutinized to ensure that the scheme is necessary to promote a substantial, legitimate state interest. . . . The majority today concludes, however, that the Texas scheme is not subject to such a strict standard of review under the Equal Protection Clause. Instead, in its view, the Texas scheme must be tested by nothing more than that lenient standard of rationality which we have traditionally applied to discriminatory state action in the context of economic and commercial matters. . . . By so doing, the Court avoids the telling task of searching for a substantial state interest which the Texas financing scheme, with its variations in taxable district property wealth, is necessary to further. I cannot accept such an emasculation of the Equal Protection Clause in the context of this case. . . .

To begin, I must once more voice my disagreement with the Court's rigidified approach to equal protection analysis. . . .

I therefore cannot accept the majority's labored efforts to demonstrate that fundamental interests, which call for strict scrutiny of the challenged classification, encompass only established rights which we are somehow bound to recognize from the text of the Constitution itself. To be sure, some interests which the Court has deemed to be fundamental for purposes of equal protection analysis are themselves constitutionally protected rights. . . . But it will not do to suggest that the "answer" to whether an interest is fundamental for purposes of equal protection analysis is *always* determined by whether that interest "is a right . . . explicitly or implicitly guaranteed by the Constitution." . . .

I would like to know where the Constitution guarantees the right to procreate, *Skinner* v. *Oklahoma ex rel. Williamson* . . . (1942), or the right to vote in state elections, *e.g.*, *Reynolds* v. *Sims* . . . (1964), or the right to an appeal from a criminal conviction, *e.g.*, *Griffin* v. *Illinois* . . . (1956). These are instances in which, due to the importance of the interests at stake, the Court has displayed a strong concern with the existence of discriminatory state treatment. But the Court has never said or indicated that these are interests which independently enjoy full-blown constitutional protection.

The majority is, of course, correct when it suggests that the process of determining which interests are fundamental is a difficult one. But I do not think the problem is insurmountable. And I certainly do not accept the view that the process need necessarily degenerate into an unprincipled, subjective "picking-and-choosing" between various interests or that it must involve this Court in creating "substantive constitutional rights in the name of guaranteeing equal protection of the laws." . . . Although not all fundamental interests are constitutionally guaranteed, the determination of which interests are fundamental should be firmly rooted in the text of the Constitution. The task in every case should be to determine the extent to which constitutionally guaranteed rights are dependent on interests not mentioned in the Constitution. As the nexus between the specific constitutional guarantee and the nonconstitutional interest draws closer, the nonconstitutional interest becomes more fundamental and the degree of judicial scrutiny applied when the interest is infringed on a discriminatory basis must be adjusted accordingly. Thus, it cannot be denied that interests such as procreation, the exercise of the state franchise, and access to criminal appellate processes are not fully guaranteed to the citizen by our Constitution. But these interests have nonetheless been afforded special judicial consideration in the face of discrimination because they are, to some extent, interrelated with constitutional guarantees. Procreation is now understood to be important because of its interaction with the established constitutional right of privacy. The exercise of the state franchise is closely tied to basic civil and political rights inherent in the First Amendment. And access to criminal appellate processes enhances the integrity of the range of rights implicit in the Fourteenth Amendment guarantee of due process of law. Only if we closely protect the related interests from state discrimination do we ultimately ensure the integrity of the constitutional guarantee itself. This is the real lesson that must be taken from our previous decisions involving interests deemed to be fundamental. . . .

A similar process of analysis with respect to the invidiousness of the basis on which a particular classification is drawn has also influenced the Court as to the appropriate degree of scrutiny to be accorded any particular case. The highly suspect character of classifications based on race, nationality, or alienage is well established. The reasons why such classifications call for close judicial scrutiny are manifold. Certain racial and ethnic groups have frequently been recognized as "discrete and insular minorities" who are relatively powerless to protect their interests in the political process. . . . Moreover, race, nationality, or alienage is "'in most circumstances irrelevant' to any constitutionally acceptable legislative purpose. . . . Instead, lines drawn on such bases are frequently the reflection of historic prejudices rather than legislative rationality. It may be that all of these considerations, which make for particular judicial solicitude in the face of discrimination on the basis of race, nationality, or alienage, do not coalesce—or at least not to the same degree—in other forms of discrimination. Nevertheless, these considerations have undoubtedly influenced the care with which the Court has scrutinized other forms of discrimination. . . .

In summary, it seems to me inescapably clear that this Court has consistently adjusted the care with which it will review state discrimination in light of the constitutional significance of the interests affected and the invidiousness of the particular classification. In the context of economic interests, we find that discriminatory state action is almost always sustained for such

interests are generally far removed from constitutional guarantees. Moreover, "[t]he extremes to which the Court has gone in dreaming up rational bases for state regulation in that area may in many instances be ascribed to a healthy revulsion from the Court's earlier excesses in using the Constitution to protect interests that have more than enough power to protect themselves in the legislative halls." . . . But the situation differs markedly when discrimination against important individual interests with constitutional implications and against particularly disadvantaged or powerless classes is involved. The majority suggests, however, that a variable standard of review would give this Court the appearance of a "super-legislature." . . . I cannot agree. Such an approach seems to me a part of the guarantees of our Constitution and of the historic experiences with oppression of and discrimination against discrete, powerless minorities which underlie that Document. In truth, the Court itself will be open to the criticism raised by the majority so long as it continues on its present course of effectively selecting in private which cases will be afforded special consideration without acknowledging the true basis of its action. . . . Such obfuscated action may be appropriate to a political body such as a legislature, but it is not appropriate to this Court. Open debate of the bases for the Court's action is essential to the rationality and consistency of our decisionmaking process. Only in this way can we avoid the label of legislature and ensure the integrity of the judicial process.

Nevertheless, the majority today attempts to force this case into the same category for purposes of equal protection analysis as decisions involving discrimination affecting commercial interests. By so doing, the majority singles this case out for analytic treatment at odds with what seems to me to be the clear trend of recent decisions in this Court, and thereby ignores the constitutional importance of the interest at stake and the invidiousness of the particular classification, factors that call for far more than the lenient scrutiny of the Texas financing scheme which the majority pursues. Yet if the discrimination inherent in the Texas scheme is scrutinized with the care demanded by the interest and classification present in this case, the unconstitutionality of that scheme is unmistakable.

Nordlinger v. *Hahn*
505 U.S. 1; 112 S. Ct. 2326; 120 L. Ed. 2d 1 (1992)

In response to rapidly rising property taxes, California voters in 1978 approved a statewide ballot initiative called Proposition 13, which added Article XIIIA to the State Constitution. Proposition 13 capped real property taxes at 1 percent of the property's full cash value (defined as the assessed valuation as of the 1975–1976 tax year or, thereafter, as the appraised value of real property upon new construction or change of ownership). It also capped at 2 percent annual increases in assessed valuations. Exceptions for this "acquisition value" system of taxation were made for two types of transfers: exchanges of principal residences by persons over the age of 55 and transfers between parents and children. Over time, Proposition 13 created dramatic disparities in the taxes paid by persons owning similar pieces of property. Longer-term owners paid taxes reflecting historic property values, while newer owners paid higher taxes reflecting more recent values. Faced with this disparity, Stephanie Nordlinger, a Los Angeles apartment renter who had recently purchased a house in Los Angeles County, brought suit against the county and its tax assessor, claiming that Proposition 13's reassessment scheme violated the Equal Protection Clause of the Fourteenth Amendment. The Superior Court for Los Angeles County dismissed her suit, and the Court of Appeals of California for the Second Appellate District affirmed. The California Supreme Court denied review, and the U.S. Supreme Court granted certiorari. *Opinion of the Court:* <u>Blackmun</u>, *Kennedy, O'Connor, Rehnquist, Scalia, Souter, Thomas, White. Concurring in part and concurring in the judgment:* <u>Thomas</u>. *Dissenting opinion:* <u>Stevens</u>.

JUSTICE BLACKMUN delivered the opinion of the Court.

The Equal Protection Clause of the Fourteenth Amendment, § 1, commands that no State shall "deny to any person within its jurisdiction the equal protection of the laws." Of course, most laws differentiate in some fashion between classes of persons. The Equal Protection Clause does not forbid classifications. It simply keeps governmental decisionmakers from treating differently persons who are in all relevant respects alike.

As a general rule, "legislatures are presumed to have acted within their constitutional power despite the fact that, in practice, their laws result in some inequality." Accordingly, this Court's cases are clear that, unless a classification warrants some form of heightened review because it jeopardizes exercise of a fundamental right or categorizes on the basis of an inherently suspect characteristic, the Equal Protection Clause requires only that the classification rationally further a legitimate state interest. At the outset,

petitioner suggests that her challenge to Article XIIIA qualifies for heightened scrutiny because it infringes upon the constitutional right to travel. In particular, petitioner alleges that the exemptions to reassessment for transfers by owners over 55 and for transfers between parents and children run afoul of the right to travel, because they classify directly on the basis of California residency. But the complaint does not allege that petitioner herself has been impeded from traveling or from settling in California because, as has been noted, prior to purchasing her home, petitioner lived in an apartment in Los Angeles. This Court's prudential standing principles impose a "general prohibition on a litigant's raising another person's legal rights." Petitioner has not identified any obstacle preventing others who wish to travel or settle in California from asserting claims on their own behalf, nor has she shown any special relationship with those whose rights she seeks to assert, such that we might overlook this prudential limitation. Accordingly, petitioner may not assert the constitutional right to travel as a basis for heightened review. . . .

The appropriate standard of review is whether the difference in treatment between newer and older owners rationally furthers a legitimate state interest. In general, the Equal Protection Clause is satisfied so long as there is a plausible policy reason for the classification, the legislative facts on which the classification is apparently based rationally may have been considered to be true by the governmental decisionmaker, and the relationship of the classification to its goal is not so attenuated as to render the distinction arbitrary or irrational. This standard is especially deferential in the context of classifications made by complex tax laws.

As between newer and older owners, Article XIIIA does not discriminate with respect to either the tax rate or the annual rate of adjustment in assessments. Newer and older owners alike benefit in both the short and long run from the protections of a 1 percent tax rate ceiling and no more than a 2 percent increase in assessment value per year. New owners and old owners arc treated differently with respect to one factor only—the basis on which their property is initially assessed. Petitioner's true complaint is that the State has denied her—a new owner—the benefit of the same assessment value that her neighbors—older owners— enjoy.

We have no difficulty in ascertaining at least two rational or reasonable considerations of difference or policy that justify denying petitioner the benefits of her neighbors' lower assessments. First, the state has a legitimate interest in local neighborhood preservation, continuity, and stability.

The State therefore legitimately can decide to structure its tax system to discourage rapid turnover in ownership of homes and businesses, for example, in order to inhibit displacement of lower income families by the forces of gentrification or established, "mom-and-pop" businesses by newer chain operations. By permitting older owners to pay progressively less in taxes than new owners of comparable property, the Article XIIIA assessment scheme rationally furthers this interest.

Second, the State legitimately can conclude that a new owner at the time of acquiring his property does not have the same reliance interest warranting protection against higher taxes as does an existing owner. The State may deny a new owner at the point of purchase the right to "lock in" to the same assessed value as is enjoyed by an existing owner of comparable property, because an existing owner rationally may be thought to have vested expectations in his property or home that are more deserving of protection than the anticipatory expectations of a new owner at the point of purchase. A new owner has full information about the scope of future tax liability before acquiring the property, and if he thinks the future tax burden is too demanding, he can decide not to complete the purchase at all. By contrast, the existing owner, already saddled with his purchase, does not have the option of deciding not to buy his home if taxes become prohibitively high. To meet his tax obligations, he might be forced to sell his home or to divert his income away from the purchase of food, clothing, and other necessities. In short, the State may decide that it is worse to have owned and lost, than never to have owned at all. . . .

Petitioner contends that the unfairness of Article XIIIA is made worse by its exemptions from reassessment for two special classes of new owners: persons aged 55 and older, who exchange principal residences, and children who acquire property from their parents. . . .

The two exemptions at issue here rationally further legitimate purposes. The people of California reasonably could have concluded that older persons in general should not be discouraged from moving to a residence more suitable to their changing family size or income. Similarly, the people of California reasonably could have concluded that the interests of family and neighborhood continuity and stability are furthered by and warrant an exemption for transfers between parents and children. Petitioner has not demonstrated that no rational bases lie for either of these exemptions. . . .

Time and again, however, this Court has made clear in the rational-basis context that the "Constitution presumes that, absent some reason to infer antipathy, even improvident decisions will eventually be rectified by the democratic process and that judicial intervention is generally unwarranted no matter how unwisely we may think a political branch has acted." Certainly, California's grand experiment appears to vest benefits in a broad, powerful, and entrenched segment of society, and, as the Court of Appeal surmised, ordinary democratic processes may be unlikely to prompt its reconsideration or repeal. Yet many wise and well-intentioned laws suffer from the same malady. Article XIIIA is not palpably arbitrary, and we must decline petitioner's request to upset the will of the people of California.

The judgment of the Court of Appeals is affirmed.

JUSTICE STEVENS, dissenting.

During the two past decades, California property owners have enjoyed extraordinary prosperity. As the State's population has mushroomed, so has the value of its real estate. Between 1976 and 1986 alone, the total assessed value of California property subject to property taxation increased tenfold. Simply put, those who invested in California real estate in the 1970s are among the most fortunate capitalists in the world.

Proposition 13 has provided these successful investors with a tremendous windfall and, in doing so, has created severe inequities in California's property tax scheme. These property owners (hereinafter "the Squires") are guaranteed that, so long as they retain their property and do not improve it, their taxes will not increase more than 2 percent in any given year. As a direct result of this windfall for the Squires, later purchasers must pay far more than their fair share of property taxes.

The specific disparity that prompted petitioner to challenge the constitutionality of Proposition 13 is the fact that her annual property tax bill is almost 5 times as large as that of her neighbors who own comparable homes: While her neighbors' 1989 taxes averaged less than $400, petitioner was taxed $1,700. This disparity is not unusual under Proposition 13. Indeed, some homeowners pay 17 times as much in taxes as their neighbors with comparable property. For vacant land, the disparities may be as great as 500 to 1. Moreover, as Proposition 13 controls the taxation of commercial property as well as residential property, the regime greatly favors the commercial enterprises of the Squires, placing new businesses at a substantial disadvantage.

As a result of Proposition 13, the Squires, who own 44 percent of the owner-occupied residences, paid only 25 percent of the total taxes collected from homeowners in 1989. These disparities are aggravated by § 2 of Proposition 13, which exempts from reappraisal a property

owner's home and up to $1 million of other real property when that property is transferred to a child of the owner. This exemption can be invoked repeatedly and indefinitely, allowing the Proposition 13 windfall to be passed from generation to generation. . . .

Under contemporary equal protection doctrine, the test of whether a classification is arbitrary is "whether the difference in treatment between [earlier and later purchasers] rationally furthers a legitimate state interest." The adjectives and adverbs in this standard are more important than the nouns and verbs.

A *legitimate* state interest must encompass the interests of members of the disadvantaged class and the community at large as well as the direct interests of the members of the favored class. It must have a purpose or goal independent of the direct effect of the legislation and one " 'that we may reasonably presume to have motivated an impartial legislature.' "

A classification *rationally* furthers state interest when there is some fit between the disparate treatment and the legislative purpose. As noted above, in the review of tax statutes we have allowed such fit to be generous and approximate, recognizing that "rational distinctions may be made with substantially less than mathematical exactitude." Nonetheless, in some cases the underinclusiveness or the overinclusiveness of a classification will be so severe that it cannot be said that the legislative distinction "rationally furthers" the posited state interest.

The Court's cursory analysis of Proposition 13 pays little attention to either of these aspects of the controlling standard of review. The first state interest identified by the Court is California's "interest in local neighborhood preservation, continuity, and stability." Although I agree with the Court that "neighborhood preservation" is a legitimate state interest, I cannot agree that a tax windfall for all persons who purchased property before 1978 *rationally* furthers that interest. To my mind, Proposition 13 is too blunt a tool to accomplish such a specialized goal. The severe inequalities created by Proposition 13 cannot be justified by such an interest.

The second state interest identified by the Court is the "reliance interests" of the earlier purchasers. Here I find the Court's reasoning difficult to follow. In this case, those who purchased property before Proposition 13 was enacted received no assurances that assessments would only increase at a limited rate; indeed, to the contrary, many purchased property in the hope that property values (and assessments) would appreciate substantially and quickly. It cannot be said, therefore, that the earlier purchasers of property somehow have a reliance interest in limited tax increases.

In my opinion, it is irrational to treat similarly situated persons differently on the basis of the date they joined the class of property owners. Until today, I would have thought this proposition far from controversial.

★

EQUAL PROTECTION AND THE RIGHT TO VOTE

Wesberry v. Sanders (1964)
Reynolds v. Sims (1964)
Harper v. Virginia State Board of Elections (1966)
Dunn v. Blumstein (1972)

RACE AND REPRESENTATION: THE FIFTEENTH AMENDMENT AND THE VOTING RIGHTS ACT

Katzenbach v. Morgan (1966)
Thornburg v. Gingles (1986)
Shaw v. Reno (1993)

NOTES

SELECTED READING

CASES

★

10
VOTING AND REPRESENTATION

The right to vote is one of the most fundamental rights secured by the Constitution. Article I, Section 2 authorizes any person who is qualified to vote for the lower house of a state's legislature to vote for members of the House of Representatives. The Fourteenth Amendment specifies (in Section 2) that if the right to vote of a citizen is denied or "in any way abridged" by a state, the size of that state's congressional delegation shall be reduced proportionately to the percentage of citizens in that state whose right has been denied or abridged. (Interestingly, the Fourteenth Amendment's Equal Protection Clause was not initially understood as guaranteeing the right to vote; otherwise, Section 2 would have been unnecessary, as would subsequent amendments.) The Constitution also prohibits a state from denying a citizen the right to vote "on account of race, color, or previous condition of servitude" (Fifteenth Amendment); "on account of sex" (Nineteenth Amendment); "by reason of failure to pay any poll tax or other tax" (Twenty-Fourth Amendment); or, for those who are eighteen years of age or older, "on account of age" (Twenty-Sixth Amendment). Each of these amendments gives Congress the "power to enforce," by "appropriate legislation," the right it declares.

Over time, the two constitutional provisions that have figured most prominently in right-to-vote cases have been the Equal Protection Clause of the Fourteenth Amendment and the Fifteenth Amendment. This chapter focuses on how the Court has employed these two provisions not only to guarantee the right to vote but also to establish a right to representation that is as personal as the right to vote itself.

EQUAL PROTECTION AND THE RIGHT TO VOTE

As discussed in Chapter 9, one of the first rights to be recognized as fundamental under the Supreme Court's two-tier approach to equal protection analysis was the exercise of the franchise. Over time, this right has come to embody three distinct principles: (1) each vote must count equally—that is, the one-man, one-vote principle; (2) the franchise must be broadly available; and (3) for the vote to be meaningful, the ballot must reflect a sufficiently representative choice of parties and candidates.

The "One-Man, One-Vote" Decisions

Gray v. *Sanders* (1963), *Wesberry* v. *Sanders* (1964), and *Reynolds* v. *Sims* (1964) collectively introduced the principle of "one-man, one-vote." *Gray*, decided just one year after the Supreme Court concluded in *Baker* v. *Carr* that issues of apportionment were justiciable, held that Georgia's county-unit system of primary elections to statewide office violated the Equal Protection Clause. This system was somewhat analogous to the federal electoral college. Unit votes were allocated among the counties in such a manner that the eight largest counties had six unit votes each, the next 30 had four unit votes each, and the remaining 121 counties had two unit votes each. The candidate for nomination who received the most popular votes in a primary was awarded the unit votes for that county. The practical consequence of this system was that the vote of citizens counted less and less as the population of their county increased. In fact, a combination of the units from the counties with the smallest populations gave counties having only one-third of the total state population a clear majority of county votes. Justice Douglas wrote the opinion for the eight-member majority; he began by dismissing the analogy of the federal electoral college as not only inapposite but also unpersuasive. Moreover, he continued, the concept of "we the people" under the Constitution "visualizes no preferred class of voters but equality among those who meet the basic qualifications." "Every voter is equal to every other voter in his State." He declared that, "the conception of political equality from the Declaration of Independence, to Lincoln's Gettysburg Address, to the Fifteenth, Seventeenth, and Nineteenth Amendments, can mean only one thing—one person, one vote." Applying his conception to the factual setting in *Gray*, he concluded: "Once the geographical unit for which a representative is to be chosen is designated, all who participate in the election are to have an equal vote—whatever their race, whatever their sex, whatever their occupation, whatever their income, and wherever their home may be in that geographical unit. This is required by the Equal Protection Clause of the Fourteenth Amendment."

In *Wesberry* v. *Sanders*, the Court extended the one-person, one-vote principle to congressional elections. The Georgia district in which the City of Atlanta was located had a 1960 population of 823,680, as compared with the average of 394,312 for all ten Georgia districts. Justice Black held for the Court that such a disparity in the population of congressional districts was contrary to the constitutional requirement of Article I, Section 2, that representatives in Congress be chosen "by the people of the several States," which, Black continued, "means that as nearly as practicable one man's vote in a congressional election is to be worth as much as another's." Black reviewed the history of the adoption and ratification of the Constitution and concluded, among other things, that "it would defeat the principle solemnly embodied in the Great Compromise—equal representation in the House for equal numbers of people—for us to hold that, within the States, legislatures may draw the lines of congressional districts in such a way as to give some voters a greater voice in choosing a Congressman than others. The House of Representatives, the Convention agreed, was to represent the people as individuals, and on the basis of complete equality for each voter." In dissent, Justice Harlan accused Black of confusing two issues: "direct election of representatives within the states and the apportionment of representatives among the states." All of Black's historical evidence merely established the latter, which was not the issue, but left altogether unresolved the former, which was the very point of contention. As Harlan complained: "The Great Compromise concerned representation of the States in the Congress. In all the discussion surrounding the basis of representation of the House and all the discussion whether Representatives should be elected by the legislatures or by the people of the states, there is nothing which suggests even remotely that the delegates had in mind the problem of districting within a State."

In *Reynolds* v. *Sims*, the Court built on *Gray* and *Wesberry* and made "one man, one vote" the constitutional rule for apportioning both houses of a bicameral state legislature. Chief Justice Warren wrote the majority opinion, arguing that in a republican government, "legislators represent people, not trees or acres. Legislators are elected by voters, not farms or cities or economic interests." Representative government is "self-government through the medium of elected representatives." Moreover, "each and every citizen has an inalienable right to full and effective participation in the political processes of his State's legislative bodies." Since most citizens can achieve this participation only as qualified voters through the election of legislators to represent them, Chief Justice Warren went on to declare that "full and effective participation by all citizens in state government requires that each citizen have an equally effective voice in the election of members of his state legislature." Any "infringements" of this right must be "carefully and meticulously scrutinized." Employing the strict-scrutiny standard, the Chief Justice ruled that both houses of a state legislature had to be apportioned strictly according to population.[1]

In his *Reynolds* dissent, Justice Harlan noted that the Court was so busy reading between the lines of the Equal Protection Clause that it failed to read at all the words of Section 2 of the Fourteenth Amendment. "I am unable to understand the Court's utter disregard of the second section which expressly recognizes the States' power to deny 'or in any way' abridge the right of their inhabitants to vote for 'the members of their

[State] Legislature,' and its express provision of a remedy for such a denial or abridgement." What Harlan implied there, he explicitly argued in his dissent in *Wesberry:* namely, that the "one man, one vote" decisions do not involve the right to vote at all, but only the personal right to representation. Justice Frankfurter had made this argument first in his dissent in *Baker:*

> What, then, is this question of legislative apportionment? Appellants invoke the right to vote and to have their votes counted. But they are permitted to vote and their votes are counted. They go to the polls, they cast their ballots, they send their representatives to the state councils. Their complaint is simply that the representatives are not sufficiently numerous or powerful—in short, that Tennessee has adopted a basis of representation with which they are dissatisfied. Talk of "debasement" or "dilution" is circular talk. One cannot speak of "debasement" or "dilution" of the value of a vote until there is first defined a standard or reference as to what a vote should be worth. What is actually asked of the Court in this case is to choose among competing bases of representation—ultimately, really among competing theories of political philosophy—in order to establish an appropriate frame of government for the State of Tennessee and thereby for all the states of the Union.

The Court, in *Gray, Wesberry,* and *Reynolds* held that citizens have not only the right to vote but also the right to equal representation—a right as personal as the right to vote and which the Court is authorized under the Equal Protection Clause to secure.

The Court acknowledged in *Reynolds* that it would be almost impossible to arrange legislative districts so that each one had an identical number of "residents, or citizens, or voters," and that "mathematical exactness or precision is hardly a workable constitutional requirement." This concession notwithstanding, the Warren Court later struck down a Missouri reapportionment plan that contained no more than a 5.97 percent disparity between the largest and smallest congressional districts.[2] And the Burger Court, in the 1983 case of *Karcher* v. *Daggett*, invalidated an apportionment plan for congressional districts in New Jersey in which each of the 14 districts differed from the "ideal" population figure by 0.1384 percent and in which the largest district had a population of 527,472, and the smallest district had a population of 523,798, with a difference between them being only 0.6984 percent of the average district.

While these decisions were consistent with Chief Justice Warren's argument in *Reynolds* that "population" is not only "the starting point for consideration" but also "the controlling criterion for judgment in legislative apportionment controversies," they conflicted with other statements in *Reynolds*. After all, the Chief Justice declared that "legislators are elected by voters, not farms or cities or economic interests"—or, as he also should have added, by nonvoters, that is, by the entire population. Warren spoke of "residents, or citizens, or voters" interchangeably, as if apportionment on any one of these three bases would result in complete voter equality. However, this blurring of distinct meanings is acceptable only if the ratio of voters to the total population or citizen population or both is constant throughout the state. If no such uniform ratio exists, Warren's language also conflicts with Douglas's pronouncement in *Gray* that "all who participate in the election are to have an equal vote." Ample evidence was available to the Court to establish that widely varying ratios were, in fact, prevalent among the states, and that, as a consequence, the use of any population base broader than actual voters would simply magnify the electoral power of the voter who happens to live in a district where relatively large numbers of nonvoters reside. Thus, for example, in the 1962 congressional elections in Missouri, the actual number of voters per 100 adult inhabitants ranged from 7.75 in Pulaski County to 44.41 in Camden County—a ratio of over 5.7 to 1. Following the Court's directive in *Reynolds* and constructing districts in Missouri that were precisely equal in population, the result would be to give each vote cast in Pulaski County 5.7 times the weight of each vote cast in Camden County. This, of course, raises a serious question: if the Court is willing to allow nonvoters to affect the complete ballot equality of voters, why is it unwilling to allow other factors such as geography and historical subdivisions?

While the Warren Court never explained why it treated "residents, or citizens, or voters" interchangeably, or why it demanded in practice a "mathematical exactness" among congressional districts that it denied in theory, the Burger Court subsequently expanded considerably, at least at the state legislative level, the limits of constitutionally permissible population disparities. In *Mahan* v. *Howell* (1973), it held a 16.4 percent deviation in the lower house of the Virginia legislature to be justified by "the State's policy of maintaining the integrity of political subdivision lines." And, in *Brown* v. *Thomson* (1983), it upheld an apportionment plan of Wyoming's House of Representatives which allowed an average deviation from population equality of 16 percent and a maximum deviation of 89 percent, noting that "Wyoming's constitutional policy— followed since statehood—of using counties as representative districts and ensuring that each county has one representative is supported by substantial and legitimate state concerns."

One consequence of the Court's one-person, one-vote decisions has been to free those who draw district lines from the need to respect geographical, historical, or political boundaries or to draw districts that are contiguous and compact. This has unleashed a political gerrymandering revolution on the land. In California, for example, congressional district lines were drawn by the Democratic-controlled state legislature after the 1980 census in such a way that for the next decade Democratic candidates routinely won two-thirds of the seats from California in the U.S. House of Representatives, even though they received only one-half of the popular vote statewide. Partisan gerrymandering is, of course, a game that both parties play. In Indiana, the Republicans controlled reapportionment and drew lines to benefit themselves. The Indiana Democratic Party brought suit in federal court, alleging that the partisan gerrymander in their state constituted an equal protection violation. A badly divided Supreme Court gave them some modest encouragement. Justice White spoke for a four-member plurality in *Davis* v. *Bandemer* (1986), when he held that an equal protection challenge to a gerrymander is not barred by the political questions doctrine. However, he rejected their specific equal protection claims, declaring that "the mere fact that a particular apportionment scheme makes it more difficult for a particular group in a particular district to elect the representatives of its choice does not render that scheme constitutionally infirm." Justice White insisted that "an individual or a group of individuals who votes for a losing candidate is usually deemed to be adequately represented by the winning candidate and to have as much opportunity to influence that candidate as other voters in the district. We cannot presume in such a situation, without actual proof to the contrary, that the candidate elected will entirely ignore the interest of those voters." He concluded that "a group's electoral power is not unconstitutionally diminished by the simple fact of an apportionment scheme that makes winning elections more difficult." White and the plurality departed from earlier cases that had categorically dismissed claims of gerrymandering by holding that "unconstitutional discrimination" could indeed occur if "the electoral system is arranged in a manner that will consistently degrade a voter's or a group of voters' influence on the political process as a whole." Such a finding of unconstitutionality would, however, have to "be supported by evidence of continued frustration of the will of the majority of the voters or effective denial to a minority of voters of a fair chance to influence the political process."

Invalidating Restrictions on the Franchise

To advance its second principle of the right to vote, that the franchise be broadly available, the Supreme Court has invalidated, on strict scrutiny grounds, the payment of poll taxes, *Harper* v. *Virginia Board of Elections* (1966); military status, *Carrington* v. *Rush* (1965); property ownership, *Kramer* v. *Union Free School District* (1969); durational residency, *Dunn* v. *Blumstein* (1972); and prior party affiliation, *Kusper* v. *Pontikes* (1973) as conditions to exercise of the franchise. As Judge J. Harvie Wilkinson III has observed, the Court's decisions involving this principle have implicitly rejected the view that voting is not only a right but a duty and is to be engaged in only upon "some demonstration of civic responsibility—whether of interest in public affairs by paying a poll tax, of a stake in political life stemming from ownership of property, or of a familiarity with and commitment to state politics resulting from living within the state's boundaries a respectable period."[3] That view was rejected, Justice

Harlan complained in his dissent in *Harper*, because it was "not in accord with current egalitarian notions of how a modern democracy should be organized."

The rejection of this view began with *Harper* v. *Virginia Board of Elections*. In this case, the Court overruled *Breedlove* v. *Suttles* (1937) and invalidated Virginia's poll tax. Justice Douglas spoke for a six-member majority when he declared that "voter qualifications have no relation to wealth nor to paying or not paying this or any other tax." He waxed eloquent that "wealth like race, creed, or color, is not germane to one's ability to participate intelligently in the electoral process." Virginia had defended its poll tax on the grounds that it fostered responsible voting. It noted that the convention that had drafted Virginia's Constitution had declared that "the voter has to pay a poll tax, prepare his own application, and cast his own ballot. The plan virtually eliminates the incompetent from politics." Elaborating upon this theme, it stressed in its brief in *Harper* that "the tax . . . only requires an annual payment of $1.50 by December 4 in every year and this serves as a 'simple and objective test of certain minimal capacity for ordering one's own affairs and thus of qualification to participate in the ordering of the affairs of state.' " The Brief for the Appellant complained, however, that "many persons through inadvertence or lack of diligence let the deadline go by without paying their poll taxes, but when the election draws near and candidates and issues are known, find that they cannot vote because they did not pay their poll taxes on time." The *amicus curiae* brief of the United States made much the same argument: the voter must pay the tax well "in advance of the election—at a time, that is, when political activity is relatively quiescent and the actual election campaign has not begun." The Supreme Court held that this means of promoting responsible voting could not withstand strict scrutiny and voided Virginia's poll tax.

The Court's use of the "strict scrutiny" test to sever the nexus between voting and civic responsibility was also apparent in *Kramer* v. *Union Free School District* (1969) and *Hill* v. *Stone* (1975). In these cases, the Supreme Court held that the states of New York and Texas could not deny the franchise to nonproperty owners in municipal elections to approve the issuance of general obligation bonds, even when the general bonded indebtedness of the municipality effectively operated as a lien on all taxable property within its borders. The Union Free School District had defended its property qualification requirement as encouraging more knowledgeable and interested voters. In its brief, it stressed: "It is apodictic that those persons whose properties in the school district are assessed for payment through the local property tax of the cost of rendering services to pupils . . . of the district will have enough of an interest, through the burden on their pocketbooks, to acquire such information as they may need in order to try to evaluate the operation of the public school system and the reasonableness of expenditures." Texas had argued that the qualification protected those who would have a lien placed on their property for the payment of a tax from having that lien placed on them by others who would not. In the words of the Texas Supreme Court: "One who is willing to vote for and impose a tax on the property of another should be willing to assume his distributive share of the burden."[4] The Court rejected these justifications, however, and voided this property qualification, contending that it erected a classification that impermissibly discriminated on the basis of wealth and disenfranchised persons otherwise qualified to vote.

The Court's use of the strict-scrutiny test to free the right to vote from restrictions designed to promote responsible voting is also clear in its consideration of durational residency requirements in *Dunn* v. *Blumstein*. In a 6–1 decision, it invalidated a Tennessee requirement of residence in the state for one year and in the county for three months as a condition of voting. Tennessee had argued that it had a legitimate interest in securing knowledgeable voters with a genuine interest in the governance of the community and in educating citizens on the importance of casting informed, considered, and responsible votes, and that durational residency requirements contributed to both. Common Cause, in its *amicus curiae* brief for the appellee, disagreed; it insisted that all the knowledge and experience a voter needs to exercise the franchise could be gained in the thirty-day period before an election. "Advertising and news coverage reach and sustain a fever pitch only during the month before an election. Because this is so, a new resident can acquire all the knowledge he wants or needs during that period." Justice Marshall agreed: "Given modern communications, and given the clear indication that campaign spending and voter education occur largely during the month before the election, the state cannot seriously maintain that it is 'necessary' to reside for a year in the state and three months in the county in order to be knowledgeable about congressional, state, or even purely local elections."

Guaranteeing Access to the Ballot

The third principle recognized by the Court as implicit in the fundamental right to vote is that the exercise of the franchise must be meaningful as well as available. Among "our most precious freedoms," the Court declared in *Williams* v. *Rhodes* (1968), is "the right of qualified voters, regardless of their political persuasion, to cast their votes effectively." It therefore invalidated an Ohio election law that allowed the major parties to retain their positions on the ballot simply by obtaining 10 percent of the votes in the last gubernatorial election but required new parties seeking access to the presidential election ballot to file petitions signed by 15 percent of the number of ballots cast in the last gubernatorial election. In addition to greater ballot access for third-party and independent candidates such as George Wallace, John Anderson, and Ross Perot, this principle has required elimination of filing fees for indigent candidates. As the Court held in *Lubin* v. *Panish* (1974), "it is to be expected that a voter hopes to find on the ballot a candidate who comes near to reflecting his policy preferences on competing issues."[5]

RACE AND REPRESENTATION:
THE FIFTEENTH AMENDMENT AND THE VOTING RIGHTS ACT

The Fifteenth Amendment guarantees the right to vote irrespective of "race, color, or previous condition of servitude." Despite this guarantee, prior to 1965 southern states had effectively denied blacks the franchise through a variety of institutional mechanisms, including white primaries,[6] poll taxes,[7] racial gerrymandering of electoral districts,[8] literacy tests,[9] and grandfather clauses (effectively excepting whites from literacy tests).[10] In some cases, the Supreme Court was able to strike down barriers denying blacks the franchise; however, neither the Court nor the federal government could keep up with the ingenuity of states intent on keeping blacks from the polls. While the Civil Rights Acts of 1957, 1960, and 1964 were, in part, intended to redress voting rights violations, they did little to achieve this goal. As Chandler Davidson has pointed out: "The burden remained on black voters to seek relief in the courts case by case, a time-consuming and extremely inefficient process," especially given the makeup of the southern district courts.[11] Chief Justice Warren argued similarly in *South Carolina* v. *Katzenbach* (1966); he declared that these laws

> proved ineffective for a number of reasons. Voting suits are unusually onerous to prepare, sometimes requiring as many as 6,000 manhours spent combing through registration records in preparation for trial. Litigation has been exceedingly slow, in part because of the ample opportunities for delay afforded by voting officials and others involved in the proceedings. Even when favorable decisions have finally been obtained, some of the States affected have merely switched to discriminatory devices not covered by the federal decrees or have enacted difficult new tests designed to prolong the existing disparity between white and Negro registration. [Alternatively,] certain local officials have defied and evaded court orders or have simply closed their registration offices to freeze the voting rolls.

To overcome these barriers, to fulfill, as Abigail Thernstrom has put it, "the promise of the Fifteenth Amendment ninety-five years late,"[12] Congress passed the Voting Rights Act of 1965. The act originally applied to seven southern states (although through the years it has come to have national coverage). In Section 4, it proscribed electoral practices and procedures (and, in particular, literacy tests) that had historically been used to deny blacks the franchise; additionally in Section 5, it prohibited the replacement of old procedures for disenfranchisement with new ones by requiring that new voting procedures in states covered by its provisions would have to be pre-cleared by the federal government before they could be implemented.

The Voting Rights Act gave the federal government extraordinary power over the states. The Supreme Court nonetheless affirmed its constitutionality in *South Carolina* v. *Katzenbach*, holding that the act was a valid exercise of Congress's enforcement power under Section 2 of the Fifteenth Amendment. Chief Justice Warren spoke for the Court: "Congress may use any rational means to effectuate the constitutional prohibition of racial discrimination in voting. The basic test to be applied [with respect to Congress's power under Section 2] is the same as in all cases concerning the express powers of Congress with relation to the reserved powers of the States. *McCulloch* v. *Maryland.*" Justice Black strenuously dissented: "Section 5, by providing that some of the States cannot pass state laws or adopt state constitutional amendments without first being compelled to beg federal authorities to approve their policies, so distorts our constitutional structure of government as to render any distinction drawn in the Constitution between state and federal power almost meaningless." His objection, however, was unavailing. In fact, the Court not only held in *South Carolina* v. *Katzenbach* that Congress had power to pass the Voting Rights Act but subsequently in *Katzenbach* v. *Morgan* (1966) also held that Congress could engage in substantive constructions of the Fourteenth and Fifteenth Amendments and could ban state electoral practices that the Court was unable to void as unconstitutional.

The Voting Rights Act proved to be one of the most successful federal laws ever passed.[13] Reporting in 1975, the U.S. Commission on Civil Rights noted that "minority political participation has increased substantially in the 10 years since the enactment of the Voting Rights Act." It reported that "more than 1 million new black voters were registered in the seven covered Southern states between 1964 and 1972, increasing the percentage of eligible blacks registered from about 29 percent to over 56 percent." In addition, over the same period of time, "the gap between white and black registration rates" was "reduced from 44.1 percentage points to 11.2 percentage points." The number of blacks elected in the seven covered states grew from an amount estimated at "well under 100 black officials" prior to 1965 to 156 by February of 1968 and 963 by April of 1974.[14]

The very purpose of the Voting Rights Act was fundamentally altered, however, in 1969 when the Supreme Court handed down *Allen* v. *State Board of Elections.* At issue in *Allen* were proposed changes to state election laws in Mississippi and Virginia. None of the proposed changes related to access to registration or to the counting of ballots; rather, they concerned switching from single-member districts to at-large districts, changing a school superintendent office from being elective to being appointive, and changing the procedures by which independent candidates were to be nominated. Chief Justice Warren, writing for the Court, argued that the remedial powers of the Voting Rights Act were not limited to protecting voter registration and ballot access. The "Act was aimed at the subtle, as well as the obvious, state regulations that had the effect of denying citizens their right to vote because of their race." This meant that electoral practices or procedures that might adversely affect the political effectiveness of black voters were subject to pre-clearance, not just direct bars to registration and polling booths.

> The right to vote can be affected by a dilution of voting power as well as by an absolute prohibition on casting a ballot. . . . Voters who are members of a racial minority might be in the majority in one district, but in a decided minority in the county as a whole. This type of change could therefore nullify their ability to elect the candidate of their choice just as would prohibiting some of them from voting.

Justice Warren determined that the intent of the Voting Rights Act was "to reach any state enactment which altered the election law of a covered State in even a minor way." It was to ensure that electoral practices neither prevented blacks from voting nor interfered with their ability to elect candidates of their choice. Just as the one-man, one-vote decisions transformed the Constitution's guarantee of the right to vote into the right to representation, so, too, *Allen* transformed the right to vote guaranteed to black citizens by the Voting Rights Act into the right to black representation.

Allen further enlarged the federal power of supervision over state electoral practices. When the Court itself subsequently attempted to curtail somewhat this federal supervisory power in *Mobile* v. *Bolden* (1980) by holding that the Voting Rights Act applied only to purposeful or intentional discrimination against the voting rights of blacks, the Congress responded in 1982 by amending the Voting Rights Act to allow black plaintiffs to show discrimination solely on the effects of a voting plan. In *Thornburg* v. *Gingles* (1986), the Court accepted the amended act's "results test" and Congress's decision to invalidate districting plans that have the effect (even if not the intention) of diluting the black vote. Addressing the issue of whether multimember districts are ever permissible or whether they invariably disadvantage minorities, the *Gingles* majority spelled out the circumstances under which it would conclude that multimember districts "operate to impair minority voters' ability to elect representatives of their choice."[15]

The 1982 amendments to the Voting Rights Act ban state electoral schemes that have the effect of preventing minority voters from electing "representatives of their choice."[16] How are the courts and the federal government to determine if minority voters have been prevented from electing "'representatives of their choice"? The unspoken answer is, if they fail to elect a representative of their own race or ethnicity. While the 1982 amendments declare that nothing in the Voting Rights Act "establishes a right to have members of a protected class elected in numbers equal to their proportion in the population," any districting scheme that provides for less than proportional representation would seem to fail the "results test." As the states redrew their congressional and state legislative district lines after the 1990 decennial census, many sought to pass the "results test" by engaging in racial gerrymandering—creating districts that maximized the number of minority candidates who could be elected to office. In *Shaw* v. *Reno* (1993), however, the Court placed a major roadblock in the path of those who would employ this strategy by declaring that racial gerrymandering would have to survive strict scrutiny. As Justice O'Connor wrote for a five-member majority:

> Racial classifications of any sort pose the risk of lasting harm to our society. They reinforce the belief, held by too many for too much of our history, that individuals should be judged by the color of their skin. Racial classifications with respect to voting carry particular dangers. Racial gerrymandering, even for remedial purposes, may balkanize us into competing racial factions; it threatens to carry us further from the goal of a political system in which race no longer matters—a goal that the Fourteenth and Fifteenth Amendments embody, and to which the Nation continues to aspire. It is for these reasons that race-based districting by our state legislatures demands close judicial scrutiny.

In *Miller* v. *Johnson* (1995), the prospects that a racial gerrymander could survive strict scrutiny were dealt a serious blow when the Court rejected "the contention that the State has a compelling interest in complying with whatever preclearance mandates the Justice Department issues." Justice Kennedy spoke for the Court when he held:

> When a state governmental entity seeks to justify race based remedies to cure the effects of past discrimination, we do not accept the government's mere assertion that the remedial action is required. Rather, we insist on a strong basis in evidence of the harm being remedied. "The history of racial classifications in this country suggests that blind judicial deference to legislative or executive pronouncements of necessity has no place in equal protection analysis." Our presumptive skepticism of all racial classifications prohibits us as well from accepting on its face the Justice Department's conclusion that racial districting is necessary under the Voting Rights Act. Where a State relies on the Department's determination that race based districting is necessary to comply with the Voting Rights Act, the judiciary retains an independent obligation in adjudicating consequent equal protection challenges to ensure that the State's actions are narrowly tailored to achieve a compelling interest. Were we to accept the Justice Department's objection itself as a compelling interest adequate to insulate racial districting from constitutional review, we would be surrendering to the Executive Branch our role in enforcing the constitutional limits on race based official action. We may not do so.

What seemed certain in *Shaw* v. *Reno* and *Miller* v. *Johnson*, however, became murky in the Court's 1996 decisions in *Shaw* v. *Hunt* and *Bush* v. *Vera*. In *Shaw* v. *Hunt*, Chief Justice Rehnquist accepted "*arguendo*, for the purpose of resolving this case," that compliance with the "results test" mandated by the 1982 amendments to the Voting Rights Act "could be a compelling interest." He continued, however, that even with the benefit of this assumption, North Carolina's racial gerrymander did not survive strict scrutiny because it was not narrowly tailored to that asserted end. Then, in *Bush*, Justice O'Connor, the critical fifth vote in *Shaw* v. *Hunt*, concurred separately to state that "[in] my view, the States have a compelling interest in complying with the results test." Her language seems to contain the very terms of surrender the Court was unwilling to offer up in *Miller*.[17] While the Court in *Miller* refused to surrender "to the Executive Branch our role in enforcing the constitutional limits on race based official action," O'Connor and the four dissenting justices in *Shaw* v. *Reno* and the subsequent racial gerrymander cases were apparently willing to surrender to the Congress and its adoption of the "results test" that very same role. O'Connor insisted that "[a]lthough I agree with the dissenters about Section 2's role as part of our national commitment to racial equality, I differ from them in my belief that that commitment can and must be reconciled with the complementary commitment of our Fourteenth Amendment jurisprudence to eliminate the unjustified use of racial stereotypes." Her concurring opinion reveals how the Court continues to grapple with the difficult issue of squaring the "results test" insisted on by Congress with the dictates of the Equal Protection Clause.

NOTES

1 The Warren Court ultimately came to apply this same one-man, one-vote principle not only to state legislatures but also to local governments, *Avery* v. *Midland County* (1968), nominating petitions, *Moore* v. *Ogilvie* (1969), and elected junior-college trustees, *Hadley* v. *Junior College District of Metropolitan Kansas City* (1970). For a sustained criticism of these decisions, see Ralph A. Rossum, "Representation and Republican Government: Contemporary Court Variations on the Founders' Theme," *American Journal of Jurisprudence* 23 (1978): 88–109.

2 *Kirkpatrick* v. *Preisler* (1969).

3 J. Harvie Wilkinson III, "The Supreme Court, the Equal Protection Clause, and the Three Faces of Constitutional Equality." *Virginia Law Review* 61 (June 1975): 958.

4 *Montgomery Independent School District* v. *Martin* (Texas, 1971).

5 However, see *Clements* v. *Fashing* (1982).

6 See *Nixon* v. *Herndon* (1927); *Nixon* v. *Condon* (1932); *Grovey* v. *Townsend* (1935); *Smith* v. *Allwright* (1944); and *Terry* v. *Adams* (1953).

7 See *Breedlove* v. *Suttles* (1937) and *Harper* v. *Virginia Board of Elections* (1966).

8 See *Gomillion* v. *Lightfoot* (1960) and *Wright* v. *Rockefeller* (1964).

9 See *Schnell* v. *Davis* (1949), *Alabama* v. *United States* (1962), and *Louisiana* v. *United States* (1965).

10 *Guinn* v. *United States* (1915) and *Myers* v. *Anderson* (1915).

11 Chandler Davidson, "The Voting Rights Act: A Brief History," in *Controversies in Minority Voting*, edited by Bernard Grofman and Chandler Davidson (Washington, D.C.: Brookings Institution Press, 1992), p. 13.

12 Abigail Thernstrom, *Whose Votes Count: Affirmative Action and Minority Voting Rights* (Cambridge, Mass.: Harvard University Press, 1987), p. 1.

13 The following discussion relies heavily on Chapter 3 of Anthony A. Peacock, *The Despair of Equality: Voting Rights and the Problem of Representation* (unpublished Ph.D. dissertation, Claremont Graduate School, 1997).

14 U.S. Commission on Civil Rights, *The Voting Rights Act: Ten Years After* (Washington, D.C.: Government Printing Office, 1975), pp. 39–49.

15 See Justice Thomas's powerful critique of *Gingles* in his concurrence in *Holder* v. *Hall*, 507 U.S. 959 (1993).

16 In *Chisom* v. *Roemer*, 501 U.S. 380 (1991), the Supreme Court held that the 1982 amendments applied to judicial elections as well, despite (1) the fact that judges are typically not regarded as "representatives" and (2) the difficulty of determining whether minorities have had a chance to elect "representatives of their choice" in the absence of judicial districts of equal population—because the size of judicial districts is determined by the volume and nature of litigation arising in various parts of the state, the Supreme Court has never held that the one-man, one-vote principle must apply to judicial elections. See Ralph A. Rossom, "Applying the Voting Rights Act to Judicial Elections: The Supreme Court's Misconstruction of Section 2 and Misconception of the Judicial Role," in Anthony A. Peacock (ed.), *Affirmative Action and Representation:* Shaw v. Reno *and the Future of Voting Rights* (Durham, N.C.: Carolina Academic Press, 1997), pp. 317–341.

17 See Anthony A. Peacock, "The Supreme Court and the Future of Voting Rights," in Peacock, *Affirmative Action and Representation:* Shaw v. Reno *and the Future of Voting Rights*, p. 410.

SELECTED READING

The Federalist, Nos. 52–54, 57.

Allen v. *State Board of Elections*, 393 U.S. 544 (1969).
Avery v. *Midland County*, 390 U.S. 474 (1968).
Brown v. *Thomson*, 462 U.S. 835 (1983).
Bush v. *Vera*, 517 U.S. 952 (1996).
Chisom v. *Roemer*, 501 U.S. 380 (1991).
Davis v. *Bandemer*, 478 U.S. 109 (1986).
Foster v. *Love*, 118 S. Ct. 464 (1997).
Gray v. *Sanders*, 372 U.S. 368 (1963).
Karcher v. *Daggett*, 462 U.S. 725 (1983).
Kramer v. *Union Free School District No. 15*, 395 U.S. 621 (1969).
Lucas v. *Colorado General Assembly*, 377 U.S. 713 (1964).
Miller v. *Johnson*, 515 U.S. 900 (1995).
Mobile v. *Bolden*, 466 U.S. 55 (1980).
Shaw v. *Hunt*, 517 U.S. 899 (1996).
South Carolina v. *Katzenbach*, 383 U.S. 301 (1966).
United Jewish Organizations of Williamsburgh v. *Carey*, 430 U.S. 144 (1977).
Whitcomb v. *Chavis*, 403 U.S. 124 (1971).
White v. *Regester*, 412 U.S. 755 (1973).

Aleinikoff, T. Alexander, and Samuel Issacharoff. "Race and Redistricting: Drawing Constitutional Lines after *Shaw* v. *Reno*." *Michigan Law Review* 92 (December 1993): 588–651.

Alfange, Dean, Jr. "Gerrymandering and the Constitution: Into the Thorns of the Thicket at Last." *1986 Supreme Court Review,* edited by Philip B. Kurland, Gerhard Casper, and Dennis J. Hutchinson (Chicago: University of Chicago Press, 1987).

Elliott, Ward E. Y. *The Rise of Guardian Democracy: The Supreme Court's Role in Voting Rights Disputes, 1845–1969* (Cambridge, Mass.: Harvard University Press, 1974).

Grofman, Bernard, ed. *Political Gerrymandering and the Court* (New York: Agathon Press, 1990).

Grofman, Bernard, and Chandler Davidson, eds. *Controversies in Minority Voting: The Voting Rights Act in Perspective* (Washington, D.C.: Brookings Institution Press, 1992).

Guinier, Lani. *The Tyranny of the Majority: Fundamental Fairness in Representative Democracy* (New York: Free Press, 1994).

Issacharoff, Samuel. "Judging Politics: The Elusive Quest for Judicial Review of Political Fairness." *Texas Law Review* 71 (June 1993): 1643–1703.

O'Rourke, Timothy G. *The Impact of Reapportionment* (New Brunswick, N.J.: Transaction Books, 1980).

Peacock, Anthony A., ed. *Affirmative Action and Representation:* Shaw *v.* Reno *and the Future of Voting Rights* (Durham, N.C.: Carolina Academic Press, 1977).

Rush, Mark E. *Does Redistricting Make a Difference: Partisan Representation and Electoral Behavior* (Baltimore, Md.: Johns Hopkins University Press, 1993).

Swain, Carol M. *Black Faces, Black Interests: The Representation of African Americans* (Cambridge, Mass.: Harvard University Press, 1993).

Thernstrom, Abigail. *Whose Votes Count? Affirmative Action and Minority Voting Rights* (Cambridge, Mass.: Harvard University Press, 1987).

Wesberry v. Sanders

376 U.S. 1; 84 S. Ct. 526; 11 L. Ed. 2d 481 (1964)

Georgia had a long-established system of single-member districts for congressional elections, but since 1931 it had failed to realign the state's districts to equalize the population of each district. As a result, the Fifth Congressional District by 1960 had a population of 823,680, more than double the average population of other districts in the state. Several voters in the Fifth District filed a class-action suit in federal court, claiming that the population disparities deprived them and other voters in the district of a right to have their votes for members of Congress given the same weight as the votes of other Georgians. A three-judge District Court, while acknowledging that the population of the Fifth District was "grossly out of balance" with those of other districts, dismissed the complaint for "want of equity." The voters then appealed their case to the U.S. Supreme Court. *Opinion of the Court:* <u>Black</u>, *Warren, Douglas, Brennan,* <u>White</u>, *Goldberg. Concurring opinion:* <u>Clark</u>. *Dissenting opinion:* <u>Harlan</u>, *Stewart (in part).*

JUSTICE BLACK delivered the opinion of the Court.

Baker v. *Carr* considered a challenge to a 1901 Tennessee statute providing for apportionment of State Representatives and Senators under the State's constitution, which called for apportionment among counties or districts "according to the number of qualified voters in each." The complaint there charged that the State's constitutional command to apportion on the basis of the number of qualified voters had not been followed in the 1901 statute and that the districts were so discriminatorily disparate in number of qualified voters that the plaintiffs and persons similarly situated were, "by virtue of the debasement of their votes," denied the equal protection of the laws guaranteed them by the Fourteenth Amendment. The cause there of the alleged "debasement" of votes for state legislators—districts containing widely varying numbers of people—was precisely that which was alleged to debase votes for Congressmen in *Colegrove* v. *Green* and in the present case. The Court in *Baker* pointed out that the opinion of Justice Frankfurter in *Colegrove*, upon the reasoning of which the majority below leaned heavily in dismissing "for want of equity," was approved by only three of the seven Justices sitting. After full consideration of *Colegrove*, the Court in *Baker* held (1) that the District Court had jurisdiction of the subject matter; (2) that the qualified Tennessee voters there had standing to sue; and (3) that the

plaintiffs had stated a justiciable cause of action on which relief could be granted.

The reasons which led to these conclusions in *Baker* are equally persuasive here.

This brings us to the merits. We agree with the District Court that the 1931 Georgia apportionment grossly discriminates against voters in the Fifth Congressional District. A single Congressman represents from two to three times as many Fifth District voters as are represented by each of the Congressmen from the other Georgia congressional districts. The apportionment statute thus contracts the value of some votes and expands that of others. If the Federal Constitution intends that when qualified voters elect members of Congress each vote be given as much weight as any other vote, then this statute cannot stand.

We hold that, construed in its historical context, the command of Art. I, § 2, that Representatives be chosen "by the people of the several States" means that as nearly as is practicable one man's vote in a congressional election is to be worth as much as another's. This rule is followed automatically, of course, when Representatives are chosen as a group on a statewide basis, as was a widespread practice in the first 50 years of our Nation's history. It would be extraordinary to suggest that in such statewide elections the votes of inhabitants of some parts of a State, for example, Georgia's thinly populated Ninth District, could be weighed at two or three times the value of the votes of people living in more populous parts of the State, for example, the Fifth District around Atlanta. We do not believe that the Framers of the Constitution intended to permit the same vote-diluting discrimination to be accomplished through the device of districts containing widely varied numbers of inhabitants. To say that a vote is worth more in one district than in another would not only run counter to our fundamental ideas of democratic government, it would cast aside the principle of a House of Representatives elected "'by the People," a principle tenaciously fought for and established at the Constitutional Convention. The history of the Constitution, particularly that part of it relating to the adoption of Art. I, § 2, reveals that those who framed the Constitution meant that, no matter what the mechanics of an election, whether statewide or by districts, it was population which was to be the basis of the House of Representatives. . . .

No right is more precious in a free country than that of having a voice in the election of those who make the laws under which, as good citizens, we must live. Other rights, even the most basic, are illusory if the right to vote is undermined. Our constitution leaves no room for classification of people in a way that unnecessarily abridges this right. In urging the people to adopt the Constitution, Madison said in No. 57 of *The Federalist:*

> Who are to be the electors of the Federal Representatives? Not the rich more than the poor; not the learned more than the ignorant; not the haughty heirs of distinguished names, more than the humble sons of obscure and unpropitious fortune. The electors are to be the great body of the people of the United States. . . .

Readers surely could have fairly taken this to mean "one person, one vote."

While it may not be possible to draw congressional districts with mathematical precision, that is no excuse for ignoring our Constitution's plain objective of making equal representation for equal numbers of people the fundamental goal for the House of Representatives. That is the high standard of justice and common sense which the Founders set for us.

JUSTICE HARLAN, dissenting.

I had not expected to witness the day when the Supreme Court of the United States would render a decision which casts grave doubt on the constitutionality of the composition of the House of Representatives. It is not an exaggeration to say that such is the effect of today's decision. The Court's holding that the Constitution requires States to select Representatives either by elections at large or by elections in districts composed "as nearly as is practicable" of equal population places in jeopardy the seats of almost all the members of the present House of Representatives.

In the last congressional election, in 1962, Representatives from 42 States were elected from congressional districts. In all but five of those States, the difference between the populations of the largest and smallest districts exceeded 100,000 persons. A difference of this magnitude in the size of districts the average population of which in each state is less than 500,000 is presumably not equality among districts "as nearly as is practicable," although the Court does not reveal its definition of that phrase. Thus, today's decision impugns the validity of the election of 398 Representatives from 37 States, leaving a "constitutional" House of 37 members now sitting. . . .

The Court holds that the provision in Art. I, § 2, for election of Representatives "by the People" *means* that congressional districts are to be "as nearly as is practicable" equal in population. Stripped of rhetoric and a "historical context," which bears little resemblance to the evidence found in the pages of history, the Court's opinion supports its holding only with the bland assertion that "the principle of a House of Representatives elected 'by the People' " would be "cast aside" if "a vote is worth more in one district than in another," if congressional districts within a State, each electing a single Representative, are not equal in population. The fact is, however, that Georgia's 10 Representatives *are* elected "by the People" of Georgia, just as Representatives from other States are elected "by the People of the several States." This is all that the Constitution requires.

Although the Court finds necessity for its artificial construction of Article I in the undoubted importance of the right to vote, that right is not involved in this case. All of the appellants do vote. The Court's talk about "debasement" and "dilution" of the vote is a model of circular reasoning, in which the premises of the argument feed on the conclusion. Moreover, by focusing exclusively on numbers in disregard of the area and shape of a congressional district as well as party affiliations within the district, the Court deals in abstractions which will be recognized even by the politically unsophisticated to have little relevance to the realities of political life.

Far from supporting the Court, the apportionment of Representatives among the States shows how blindly the Court has marched to its decision. Representatives were to be apportioned among the States on the basis of free population plus three-fifths of the slave population. Since no slave voted, the inclusion of three-fifths of their number in the basis of apportionment gave the favored States representation far in excess of their voting population. If, then, slaves were intended to be without representation, Article I did exactly what the Court now says it prohibited: it "weighted" the vote of voters in the slave States. Alternatively, it might have been thought that Representatives elected by free men of a State would speak also for the slaves. But since the slaves added to the representation only of their own State, Representatives from the slave States could have been thought to speak only for the slaves of their own States, indicating both that the Convention believed it possible for a Representative elected by one group to speak for another nonvoting group and that Representatives were in large degree still thought of as speaking for the whole population *of a State*. . . .

Today's decision has portents for our society and the Court itself which should be recognized. This is not a case in which the Court vindicates the kind of individual rights that are assured by the Due Process Clause of the Fourteenth Amendment, whose "vague contours" of course leave much room for constitutional developments necessitated by changing conditions in a dynamic society. Nor is this a case in which an emergent set of facts requires the Court to frame new principles to protect recognized constitutional rights. The claim for judicial relief in this case strikes at one of the fundamental doctrines of our system of government, the separation of powers. In upholding that claim, the Court attempts to effect reforms in a field which the Constitution, as plainly as can be, has committed exclusively to the political process.

This Court, no less than all other branches of the Government, is bound by the Constitution. The Constitution does not confer on the Court blanket authority to step into every situation where the political branch may be thought to have fallen short. The stability of this institution ultimately depends not only upon its being alert to keep the other branches of government within constitutional bounds but equally upon recognition of the limitations on the Court's own functions in the constitutional system.

What is done today saps the political process. The promise of judicial intervention in matters of this sort cannot but encourage popular inertia in efforts for political reform through the political process, with the inevitable result that the process is itself weakened. By yielding to the demand for a judicial remedy in this instance, the Court in my view does a disservice both to itself and to the broader values of our system of government.

Believing that the complaint fails to disclose a constitutional claim, I would affirm the judgment below dismissing the complaint.

Reynolds v. *Sims*

377 U.S. 533; 84 S. Ct. 1362; 12 L. Ed. 2d 506 (1964)

M. O. Sims and other Alabama residents brought suit against B. A. Reynolds and other state election officials, challenging the apportionment of the state legislature. The Alabama Constitution provided that the legislature be reapportioned dicennially on the basis of population, but with the qualification that each county be allocated one representative and that no county be apportioned more than one senator. Since no reapportionment had taken place since 1901, however, a substantial degree of malapportionment existed: some highly populous senatorial districts had over forty-one times as many people as others, and some legislative districts had populations sixteen times larger than others. It was possible, under the existing scheme of apportionment, for 25 percent of the population to elect a majority in the state senate and for approximately the same percentage to elect a majority of the state's representatives. A federal district court held that Alabama's scheme of apportionment violated the Equal Protection Clause of the Fourteenth Amendment. In response to this decision, the Alabama legislature adopted two alternative reapportionment plans, neither of which apportioned the legislature solely on the basis of population. When the district court also invalidated those plans, the defendants appealed to the Supreme Court. *Opinion of the Court:* Warren, *Black, Brennan, Douglas, Goldberg, White. Concurring in judgment:* Clark; Stewart. *Dissenting opinion:* Harlan.

MR. CHIEF JUSTICE WARREN delivered the opinion of the Court. . . .

. . . Our problem is to ascertain . . . whether there are any constitutionally cognizable principles which would justify departures from the basic standard of equality among voters in the apportionment of seats in state legislatures.

A predominant consideration in determining whether a State's legislative apportionment scheme constitutes an invidious discrimination violative of rights asserted under the Equal Protection Clause is that the rights allegedly impaired are individual and personal in nature. . . . While the result of a court decision in a state legislative apportionment controversy may be to require the restructuring of the geographical distribution of seats in a state legislature, the judicial focus must be concentrated upon ascertaining whether there has been any discrimination against certain of the State's citizens which constitutes an impermissible impairment of their constitutionally protected right to vote. . . . Undoubtedly, the right of suffrage is a fundamental matter in a free and democratic society. Especially since the right to exercise the franchise in a free and unimpaired manner is preservative of other basic civil and political rights, any alleged infringement of the right of citizens to vote must be carefully and meticulously scrutinized.

Legislators represent people, not trees or acres. Legislators are elected by voters, not farms or cities or economic interests. As long as ours is a representative form of government, and our legislatures are those instruments of government elected directly by and directly representative of the people, the right to elect legislators in a free and unimpaired fashion is a bedrock of our political system. It could hardly be gainsaid that a constitutional claim had been asserted by an allegation that certain otherwise qualified voters had been entirely prohibited from voting for members of their state legislature. And, if a State should provide that the votes of citizens in one part of the State should be given two times, or five times, or 10 times the weight of votes of citizens in another part of the State, it could hardly be contended that the right to vote of those residing in the disfavored areas had not been effectively diluted. It would appear extraordinary to suggest that a State could be constitutionally permitted to enact a law providing that certain of the State's voters could vote two, five, or 10 times for their legislative representatives, while voters living elsewhere could vote only once. And it is inconceivable that a state law to the effect that, in counting votes for legislators, the votes of citizens in one part of the State would be multiplied by two, five, or 10, while the votes of persons in another area would be counted only at face value, could be constitutionally sustainable. Of course, the effect of state legislative districting schemes which give the same number of representatives to unequal numbers of constituents is identical. Overweighting and overvaluation of the votes of those living here has the certain effect of dilution and undervaluation of the votes of those living there. The resulting discrimination against those individual voters living in disfavored areas is easily demonstrable mathematically. Their right to vote is simply not the same right to vote as that of those living in a favored part of the State. Two, five, or 10 of them must vote before the effect of their voting is equivalent to that of their favored neighbor. Weighting the votes of citizens differently, by any method or means, merely because of where they happen to reside, hardly seems justifiable. One must be ever aware that the Constitution forbids "sophisticated as well as simple-minded modes of discrimination." . . .

. . . Representative government is in essence self-government through the medium of elected representatives of the people, and each and every citizen has an inalienable right to full and effective participation in the political processes of his State's legislative bodies. Most citizens can achieve this participation only as qualified voters through the election of legislators to represent them. Full and effective participation by all citizens in state government requires, therefore, that each citizen have an equally effective voice in the election of members of his state legislature. Modern and viable state government needs, and the Constitution demands, no less.

Logically, in a society ostensibly grounded on representative government, it would seem reasonable that a majority of the people of a State could elect a majority of that State's legislators. To conclude differently, and to sanction minority control of state legislative bodies, would appear to deny majority rights in a way that far surpasses any possible denial of minority rights that might otherwise be thought to result. Since legislatures are responsible for enacting laws by which all citizens are to be governed, they should be bodies which are collectively responsive to the popular will. And the concept of equal protection has been traditionally viewed as requiring the uniform treatment of persons standing in the same relation to the governmental action questioned or challenged. With respect to the allocation of legislative representation, all voters, as citizens of a State, stand in the same relation regardless of where they live. Any suggested criteria for the differentiation of citizens are insufficient to justify any discrimination, as to the weight of their votes, unless relevant to the permissible purposes of legislative apportionment. Since the achieving of fair and effective

representation for all citizens is concededly the basic aim of legislative apportionment, we conclude that the Equal Protection Clause guarantees the opportunity for equal participation by all voters in the election of state legislators. Diluting the weight of votes because of place of residence impairs basic constitutional rights under the Fourteenth Amendment just as much as invidious discriminations based upon factors such as race . . . or economic status. . . . Our constitutional system amply provides for the protection of minorities by means other than giving them majority control of state legislatures. . . .

We are told that the matter of apportioning representation in a state legislature is a complex and many-faceted one. We are advised that States can rationally consider factors other than population in apportioning legislative representation. We are admonished not to restrict the power of the States to impose differing views as to political philosophy on their citizens. We are cautioned about the dangers of entering into political thickets and mathematical quagmires. Our answer is this: a denial of constitutionally protected rights demands judicial protection; our oath and our office require no less of us. . . . To the extent that a citizen's right to vote is debased, he is that much less a citizen. The fact that an individual lives here or there is not a legitimate reason for overweighting or diluting the efficacy of his vote. . . .

. . . Population is, of necessity, the starting point for consideration and the controlling criterion for judgment in legislative apportionment controversies.

We hold that, as a basic constitutional standard, the Equal Protection Clause requires that the seats in both houses of a bicameral state legislature must be apportioned on a population basis. Simply stated, an individual's right to vote for state legislators is unconstitutionally impaired when its weight is in a substantial fashion diluted when compared with votes of citizens living in other parts of the State. . . .

Since neither of the houses of the Alabama Legislature, under any of the three plans considered by the District Court, was apportioned on a population basis, we would be justified in proceeding no further. However, one of the proposed plans . . . at least superficially resembles the scheme of legislative representation followed in the Federal Congress. Under this plan, each of Alabama's 67 counties is allotted one senator, and no counties are given more than one Senate seat. Arguably, this is analogous to the allocation of two Senate seats, in the Federal Congress, to each of the 50 States, regardless of population. . . .

After considering the matter, the court below concluded that no conceivable analogy could be drawn between the federal scheme and the apportionment of seats in the Alabama Legislature under the proposed constitutional amendment. We agree with the District Court, and find the federal analogy inapposite and irrelevant to state legislative districting schemes. Attempted reliance on the federal analogy appears often to be little more than an after-the-fact rationalization offered in defense of maladjusted state apportionment arrangements.

The system of representation in the two Houses of the Federal Congress is one ingrained in our Constitution, as part of the law of the land. It is one conceived out of compromise and concession indispensable to the establishment of our federal republic. Arising from unique historical circumstances, it is based on the consideration that in establishing our type of federalism a group of formerly independent States bound themselves together under one national government. . . .

Political subdivisions of States—counties, cities, or whatever—never were and never have been considered as sovereign entities. Rather, they have been traditionally regarded as subordinate governmental instrumentalities created by the State to assist in the carrying out of state governmental functions. . . .

Since we find the so-called federal analogy inapposite to a consideration of the constitutional validity of state legislative apportionment schemes, we necessarily hold that the Equal Protection Clause requires both houses of a state legislature to be apportioned on a population basis. The right of a citizen to equal representation and to have his vote weighted equally with those of all other citizens in the election of members of one house of a bicameral state legislature would amount to little if States could effectively submerge the equal-population principle in the apportionment of seats in the other house. . . .

MR. JUSTICE HARLAN, dissenting.

The Court's constitutional discussion . . . is remarkable . . . for its failure to address itself at all to the Fourteenth Amendment as a whole. . . .

The Court relies exclusively on that portion of § 1 of the Fourteenth Amendment which provides that no State shall "deny to any person within its jurisdiction the equal protection of the laws," and disregards entirely the significance of § 2, which reads: "Representatives shall be apportioned among the several States according to their respective numbers, counting the whole number of persons in each State, excluding Indians not taxed. *But when the right to vote at any election for* the choice of electors for President and Vice President of the United States, Representatives in Congress, *the Executive and Judicial officers of a State, or the members of the Legislature thereof, is denied* to any of the male inhabitants of such State, being twenty-one years of age, and citizens of the United States, *or in any way abridged,* except for participation in rebellion, or other crime, the basis of representation therein shall be reduced in the proportion which the number of such male citizens shall bear to the whole number of male citizens twenty-one years of age in such State." (Emphasis added.)

The Amendment is a single text. It was introduced and discussed as such in the Reconstruction Committee, which reported it to the Congress. It was discussed as a unit in Congress and proposed as a unit to the States, which ratified it as a unit. A proposal to split up the Amendment and submit each section to the States as a separate amendment was rejected by the Senate. Whatever one might take to be the application to these cases of the Equal Protection Clause if it stood alone, I am unable to understand the Court's utter disregard of the second section which expressly recognizes the States' power to deny "or in any way" abridge the right of their inhabitants to vote for "the members of the [State] Legislature," and its express provision of a remedy for such denial or abridgment. The comprehensive scope of the second section and its particular reference to the state legislatures preclude the suggestion that the first section was intended to have the result reached by the Court today. If indeed the words of the Fourteenth Amendment speak for themselves, as the majority's disregard of history seems to imply, they speak as clearly as may be against the construction which the majority puts on them. . . .

. . . Note should be taken of the Fifteenth and Nineteenth Amendments. The former prohibited the States from denying or abridging the right to vote "on account of race, color, or previous condition of servitude." The latter, certified as part of the Constitution in 1920, added sex to the prohibited classifications. . . .

. . . Unless one takes the highly implausible view that the Fourteenth Amendment controls methods of apportionment but leaves the right to vote itself unprotected, the conclusion is inescapable that the Court has, for purposes of these cases, relegated the Fifteenth and Nineteenth Amendments to the same limbo of constitutional anachronisms to which the second section of the Fourteenth Amendment has been assigned. . . .

Although the Court—necessarily, as I believe—provides only generalities in elaboration of its main thesis, its opinion nevertheless fully demonstrates how far removed these problems are from fields of judicial competence. Recognizing that "indiscriminate districting" is an invitation to "partisan gerrymandering," . . . the Court nevertheless excludes virtually every basis for the formation of electoral districts other than "indiscriminate districting." . . . So far as presently appears, the *only* factor which a State may consider, apart from numbers, is political subdivisions. But even "a clearly rational state policy" recognizing this factor is unconstitutional if "population is submerged as the controlling consideration." . . .

. . . These decisions give support to a current mistaken view of the Constitution and the constitutional function of this Court. This view, in a nutshell, is that every major social ill in this country can find its cure in some constitutional "principle," and that this Court should "take the lead" in promoting reform when other branches of government fail to act. The Constitution is not a panacea for every blot upon the public welfare, nor should this Court, ordained as a judicial body, be thought of as a general haven for reform movements. The Constitution is an instrument of government, fundamental to which is the premise that in a diffusion of governmental authority lies the greatest promise that this Nation will realize liberty for all its citizens. This Court, limited in function in accordance with that premise, does not serve its high purpose when it exceeds its authority, even to satisfy justified impatience with the slow workings of the political process. For when, in the name of constitutional interpretation, the Court *adds* something to the Constitution that was deliberately excluded from it, the Court in reality substitutes its view of what should be so for the amending process.

Harper v. Virginia State Board of Elections

383 U.S. 663; 86 S. Ct. 1079; 16 L. Ed. 2d 169 (1966)

The state of Virginia imposed an annual poll tax of $1.50 on all residents over the age of twenty-one; payment of the tax was a precondition for voting in state elections. Proceeds from the tax were used to support local government activities, including education. A suit by Harper and others to have the poll tax declared unconstitutional was dismissed by a three-judge federal district court on the basis of *Breedlove* v. *Suttles* (1937), in which the Court had unanimously rejected an equal-protection attack on Georgia's poll tax. Harper appealed to the United States Supreme Court. *Opinion of the Court: Douglas, Brennan, Clark, Fortas, Warren, White. Dissenting opinions: Black; Harlan, Stewart.*

MR. JUSTICE DOUGLAS delivered the opinion of the Court. . . .

We conclude that a State violates the Equal Protection Clause of the Fourteenth Amendment whenever it makes the affluence of the voter or payment of any fee an electoral standard. Voter qualifications have no relation to wealth nor to paying or not paying this or any other tax. Our cases demonstrate that the Equal Protection Clause of the Fourteenth Amendment restrains the States from fixing voter qualifications which invidiously discriminate. . . .

Long ago in *Yick Wo* v. *Hopkins* [1886] . . . the Court referred to "the political franchise of voting" as a "fundamental political right, because preservative of all rights." Recently in *Reynolds* v. *Sims*, . . . we said, "Undoubtedly, the right of suffrage is a fundamental matter in a free and democratic society. Especially since the right to exercise the franchise in a free and unimpaired manner is preservative of other basic civil and political rights, any alleged infringement of the right of citizens to vote must be carefully and meticulously scrutinized." There we were considering charges that voters in one part of the State had greater representation per person in the State Legislature than voters in another part of the State. We concluded: "A citizen, a qualified voter, is no more nor no less so because he lives in the city or on the farm."

We say the same whether the citizen, otherwise qualified to vote, has $1.50 in his pocket or nothing at all, pays the fee or fails to pay it. The principle that denies the State the right to dilute a citizen's vote on account of his economic status or other such factors by analogy bars a system which excludes those unable to pay a fee to vote or who fail to pay.

It is argued that a State may exact fees from citizens for many different kind of licenses; that if it can demand from all an equal fee for a driver's license, it can demand from all an equal poll tax for voting. But we must remember that the interest of the State, when it comes to voting, is limited to the power to fix qualifications. Wealth, like race, creed, or color, is not germane to one's ability to participate intelligently in the electoral process. Lines drawn on the basis of wealth or property, like those of race . . . are traditionally disfavored. . . . To introduce wealth or payment of a fee as a measure of a voter's qualifications is to introduce a capricious or irrelevant factor. The degree of the discrimination is irrelevant. In this context—that is, as a condition of obtaining a ballot—the requirement of fee paying causes an "invidious" discrimination . . . that runs afoul of the Equal Protection Clause. Levy "by the poll," as stated in *Breedlove* v. *Suttles* . . . is an old familiar form of taxation; and we say nothing to impair its validity so long as it is not made a condition to the exercise of the franchise.

Breedlove v. *Suttles* sanctioned its use as "a prerequisite of voting." . . . To that extent the Breedlove case is overruled. . . .

In a recent searching re-examination of the Equal Protection Clause, we held, as already noted, that "the opportunity for equal participation by all voters in the election of state legislators" is required. . . . We decline to qualify that principle by sustaining this poll tax. Our conclusion, like that in *Reynolds* v. *Sims*, is founded not on what we think governmental policy should be, but on what the Equal Protection Clause requires.

We have long been mindful that where fundamental rights and liberties are asserted under the Equal Protection Clause, classifications which might invade or restrain them must be closely scrutinized and carefully confined. . . .

Those principles apply here. For to repeat, wealth or fee paying has, in our view, no relation to voting qualifications; the right to vote is too precious, too fundamental to be so burdened or conditioned.

Reversed.

Mr. Justice Black, dissenting.

In *Breedlove* v. *Suttles* . . . decided December 6, 1937, a few weeks after I took my seat as a member of this Court, we unanimously upheld the right of the State of Georgia to make payment of its state poll tax a prerequisite to voting in state elections. We rejected at that time contentions that the state law violated the Equal Protection Clause of the Fourteenth Amendment because it put an unequal burden on different groups of people according to their age, sex, and ability to pay. . . . Later, May 28, 1951, I joined the Court's judgment in *Butler* v. *Thompson* . . . upholding, over the dissent of Mr. Justice Douglas, the Virginia state poll tax law challenged here against the same equal protection challenges. Since the *Breedlove* and *Butler* cases were decided the Federal Constitution has not been amended in the only way it could constitutionally have been, that is, as provided in Article V of the Constitution. I would adhere to the holding of those cases. The Court, however, overrules *Breedlove* in part, but its opinion reveals that it does so not by using its limited power to interpret the original meaning of the Equal Protection Clause, but by giving that clause a new meaning which it believes represents a better governmental policy. From this action I dissent.

It should be pointed out at once that the Court's decision is to no extent based on a finding that the Virginia law as written or as applied is being used as a device or mechanism to deny Negro citizens of Virginia the right to vote on account of their color. . . .

. . . In view of the purpose of the terms to restrain the courts from a wholesale invalidation of state laws under the Equal Protection Clause it would be difficult to say that the poll tax requirement is "irrational" or "arbitrary" or works "invidious discriminations." State poll tax legislation can "reasonably," "rationally" and without an "invidious" or evil purpose to injure anyone be found to rest on a number of state policies including (1) the State's desire to collect its revenue, and (2) its belief that voters who pay a poll tax will be interested in furthering the State's welfare when they vote. . . .

The Court's failure to give any reasons to show that these purposes of the poll tax are "irrational," "unreasonable," "arbitrary," or "invidious" is a pretty clear indication to me that none exist. I can only conclude that the primary, controlling, predominant, if not the exclusive reason for declaring the Virginia law unconstitutional is the Court's deep-seated hostility and antagonism, which I share, to making payment of a tax a prerequisite to voting. . . .

. . . For us to undertake in the guise of constitutional interpretation to decide the constitutional policy question of this case amounts, in my judgment, to a plain exercise of power which the Constitution has denied us but has specifically granted to Congress. I cannot join in holding that the Virginia state poll tax law violates the Equal Protection Clause.

MR. JUSTICE HARLAN, whom MR. JUSTICE STEWART joins, dissenting. . . .

. . . Is there a rational basis for Virginia's poll tax as a voting qualification? I think the answer to that question is undoubtedly "yes."

. . . It is certainly a rational argument that payment of some minimal poll tax promotes civic responsibility, weeding out those who do not care enough about public affairs to pay $1.50 or thereabouts a year for the exercise of the franchise. It is also arguable, indeed it was probably accepted as sound political theory by a large percentage of Americans through most of our history, that people with some property have a deeper stake in community affairs, and are consequently more responsible, more educated, more knowledgeable, more worthy of confidence, than those without means, and that the community and Nation would be better managed if the franchise were restricted to such citizens. Nondiscriminatory and fairly applied literacy tests . . . find justification on very similar grounds.

These viewpoints, to be sure, ring hollow on most contemporary ears. Their lack of acceptance today is evidenced by the fact that nearly all of the States, left to their own devices, have eliminated property or poll-tax qualifications; by the cognate fact that Congress and three-quarters of the States quickly ratified the Twenty-Fourth Amendment; and by the fact that rules such as the "pauper exclusion" in Virginia law . . . have never been enforced.

Property and poll-tax qualifications, very simply, are not in accord with current egalitarian notions of how a modern democracy should be organized. It is of course entirely fitting that legislatures should modify the law to reflect such changes in popular attitudes. However, it is all wrong, in my view, for the Court to adopt the political doctrines popularly accepted at a particular moment of our history and to declare all others to be irrational and invidious, barring them from the range of choice by reasonably minded people acting through the political process. It was not too long ago that Mr. Justice Holmes felt impelled to remind the Court that the Due Process Clause of the Fourteenth Amendment does not enact the *laissez-faire* theory of society. . . . The times have changed, and perhaps it is appropriate to observe that neither does the Equal Protection Clause of that Amendment rigidly impose upon America an ideology of unrestrained egalitarianism.

Dunn v. Blumstein

405 U.S. 330; 92 S. Ct. 995; 31 L. Ed. 2d 274 (1972)

Tennessee law required a one-year residence in the state and a three-month residence in the county as a condition of voting. James Blumstein, a newly appointed faculty member at Vanderbilt University Law School, brought an action in federal district court against Governor Winfield Dunn and various other Tennessee public officials, challenging the constitutionality of this durational residency requirement. A three-judge court, in finding for Blumstein, concluded that the Tennessee law impermissibly interfered with the right to vote and created a "suspect" classification, penalizing some Tennessee residences because of recent interstate travel. Tennessee appealed to the U.S. Supreme Court. *Opinion of the Court: Marshall, Brennan, Douglas, Stewart, White. Concurring in judgment: Blackmun. Dissenting opinion: Burger. Not participating: Powell, Rehnquist.*

MR. JUSTICE MARSHALL delivered the opinion of the Court. . . .

Durational residence laws penalize those persons who have traveled from one place to another to establish a new residence during the qualifying period. Such laws divide residents into two classes, old residents and new residents, and discriminate against the latter to the extent of totally denying them the opportunity to vote. The constitutional question presented is whether the Equal Protection Clause of the Fourteenth Amendment permits a State to discriminate in this way among its citizens.

To decide whether a law violates the Equal Protection Clause, we look, in essence, to three things: the character of the classification in question; the individual interests affected by the classification; and the governmental interests asserted in support of the classification. . . . In considering laws challenged under the Equal Protection Clause, this Court has evolved more than one test, depending upon the interests affected and the classification involved. First, then, we must determine what standard of review is appropriate. In the present case, whether we look to the benefit withheld by the classification (the opportunity to vote) or the basis for the classifications (recent interstate travel) we conclude that the State must show a substantial and compelling reason for imposing durational residence requirements.

Durational residence requirements completely bar from voting all residents not meeting the fixed durational standards. By denying some citizens the right to vote, such laws deprive them of "a fundamental political right, . . . preservative of all rights." . . . If a challenged statute grants the right to vote to some citizens and denies the franchise to others, "the Court must determine whether the exclusions are *necessary* to promote a *compelling* state interest." . . . This is the test we apply here.

This exacting test is appropriate for another reason: . . . Tennessee's durational residence laws classify bona fide residents on the basis of recent travel, penalizing those persons, and only those persons, who have gone from one jurisdiction to another during the qualifying period. Thus, the durational residence requirement directly impinges on the exercise of a second fundamental personal right, the right to travel.

. . . Durational residence laws must be measured by a strict equal protection test: they are unconstitutional unless the State can demonstrate that such laws are "*necessary* to promote a *compelling* governmental interest." . . .

It is not sufficient for the State to show that durational residence requirements further a very substantial state interest. In pursuing that important interest, the State cannot choose means which unnecessarily burden or restrict constitutionally protected activity. Statutes affecting constitutional rights must be drawn with "precision" . . . , and must be "tailored" to serve their legitimate objectives. . . . And if there are other, reasonable ways to achieve those goals with a lesser burden on constitutionally protected activity, a State may not choose the way of greater interference. If it acts at all, it must choose "less drastic means." . . .

We turn, then, to the question of whether the State has shown that durational residence requirements are needed to further a sufficiently substantial state interest. We emphasize again the difference between bona fide residence requirements and durational residence requirements. We have in the past noted approvingly that the States have the power to require that voters be bona fide residents of the relevant political subdivision. . . . An appropriately defined and uniformly applied requirement of bona fide residence may be necessary to preserve the basic conception of a political community, and therefore could withstand close constitutional scrutiny. But *durational* residence requirements, representing a separate voting qualification imposed on bona fide residents, must be separately tested by the stringent standard. . . .

Tennessee tenders "two basic purposes" served by its durational residence requirements: "(1) INSURE PURITY OF BALLOT BOX—Protection against fraud through colonization and inability to identify persons offering to vote, and (2) KNOWLEDGEABLE VOTER—Afford some surety that the voter has, in fact, become a member of the community and that as such, he has a common interest in all matters pertaining to its government and is, therefore, more likely to exercise his right more intelligently." . . .

Preservation of the "purity of the ballot box" is a formidable sounding state interest. The impurities feared, variously called "dual voting" and "colonization," all involve voting by nonresidents, either singly or in groups. The main concern is that nonresidents will temporarily invade the State or county, falsely swear that they are residents to become eligible to vote, and, by voting, allow a candidate to win by fraud. Surely the prevention of such fraud is a legitimate and compelling government goal. But it is impossible to view durational residence requirements as necessary to achieve that state interest.

Preventing fraud, the asserted evil which justifies state lawmaking, means keeping nonresidents from voting. But, by definition, a durational residence law bars *newly arrived* residents from the franchise along with nonresidents. . . .

Durational residence laws may once have been necessary to prevent a fraudulent evasion of state voter standards, but today in Tennessee, as in most other States, this purpose is served by a system of voter registration. . . .

Our conclusion that the waiting period is not the least restrictive means necessary for preventing fraud is bolstered by the recognition that Tennessee has at its disposal a variety of criminal laws which are more than adequate to detect and deter whatever fraud may be feared. . . .

The argument that durational residence requirements further the goal of having "knowledgeable voters" appears to involve three separate claims. The first is that such requirements "afford some surety that the voter has, in fact, become a member of the community." But here the State appears to confuse a bona fide residence requirement with a durational residence requirement. As already noted, a State does have an interest in limiting the franchise to bona fide members of the community. But this does not justify or explain the exclusion from the franchise of persons, not because their bona fide residence is questioned, but because they are recent rather than long-time residents.

The second branch of the "knowledgeable voters" justification is that durational residence requirements assure that the voter "has a common interest in all matters pertaining to the community's government. . . . " By this, presumably, the State means that it may require a period of residence sufficiently lengthy to impress upon its voters the local viewpoint. This is precisely the sort of argument this court has repeatedly rejected. . . .

. . . Tennessee's hopes for voters with a "common interest in all matters pertaining to [the community's] government" is impermissible. . . .

Finally, the State urges that a long-time resident is "more likely to exercise his right to vote more intelligently." To the extent that this is different from the previous argument, the State is apparently asserting an interest in limiting the franchise to voters who are minimally knowledgeable about the issues. In this case, Tennessee argues that people who have been in the State less than a year and the county less than three months are likely to be unaware of the issues involved in the congressional, state, and local elections, and therefore can be barred from the franchise. We note that the criterion of "intelligent" voting is an elusive one, and susceptible to abuse. But without deciding as a general matter the extent to which a State can bar less knowledgeable or intelligent citizens from the franchise, . . . we conclude that durational residence requirements cannot be justified on this basis.

The durational residence requirements in this case founder because of their crudeness as a device for achieving the articulated state goal of assuring the knowledgeable exercise of the franchise. The classifications created by durational residence requirements obviously permit any long-time resident to vote regardless of his knowledge of the issues—and obviously many long-time residents do not have any. On the other hand, the classifications bar from the franchise many other, admittedly new, residents who have become minimally, and often fully, informed about the issues. Indeed, recent migrants who take the time to register and vote shortly after moving are likely to be those citizens, such as appellee, who make it a point to be informed and knowledgeable about the issues. Given modern communications, and given the clear indication that campaign spending and voter education occur largely during the month before an election, the State cannot seriously maintain that it is "necessary" to reside for a year in the State and three months in the county in order to be minimally knowledgeable about congressional, state or even purely local elections. There is simply nothing in the record to support the conclusive presumption that residents who have lived in the State for less than a year and their county for less than three months are uninformed about elections. . . .

It is pertinent to note that Tennessee has never made an attempt to further its alleged interest in an informed electorate in a universally applicable way. Knowledge or competence has never been a criterion for participation in Tennessee's electoral process for long-time residents. Indeed, the State specifically provides for voting by various types of absentee persons. These provisions permit many long-time residents who leave the county or State to participate in a constituency in which they have only the slightest political interest, and from whose political debates they are likely to be cut off. That the State specifically permits such voting is not consistent with its claimed compelling interest in intelligent, informed use of the ballot. If the State seeks to assure intelligent use of the ballot, it may not try to serve this interest only with respect to new arrivals. . . .

We are aware that classifications are always imprecise. By requiring classifications to be tailored to their purpose, we do not secretly require the impossible. Here, there is simply too attenuated a relationship between the state interest in an informed electorate and the fixed requirement that voters must have been residents in the State for a year and the county for three months. Given the exacting standard of precision we require of statutes affecting constitutional rights, we cannot say that durational residence requirements are necessary to further a compelling state interest. . . .

MR. CHIEF JUSTICE BURGER, dissenting.

. . . It is no more a denial of Equal Protection for a State to require newcomers to be exposed to state and local problems for a reasonable period such as one year before voting, than it is to require children to wait 18 years before voting. . . . In both cases some informed and responsible persons are denied the vote, while others less informed and less responsible are permitted to vote. Some lines must be drawn. To challenge such lines by the "compelling state interest" standard is to condemn them all. So far as I am aware, no state law has ever satisfied this seemingly insurmountable standard, and I doubt one ever will, for it demands nothing less than perfection. . . .

Katzenbach v. Morgan
384 U.S. 641; 86 S. Ct. 1717; 16 L. Ed. 2d 828 (1966)

Voters of New York City entered U.S. District Court for the District of Columbia, seeking declaratory and injunctive relief restraining enforcement of § 4(e) of the Voting Rights Act of 1965. That section provided that no person who had successfully completed the sixth grade in an American-flag school in which the predominant language of instruction was other than English could be disqualified from voting under any literacy test. It was being applied to prohibit enforcement against Puerto Ricans living in New York City of a New York election law requiring the ability to read and write English as a condition of voting. The three-judge District Court granted relief, and an appeal was taken directly to the United States Supreme Court. *Opinion of the Court: Brennan, Black, Clark, Douglas, Fortas, Warren, White. Dissenting opinion: Harlan, Stewart.*

JUSTICE BRENNAN delivered the opinion of the Court.

We hold that, in the application challenged in these cases, § 4(e) is a proper exercise of the powers granted to Congress by § 5 of the Fourteenth Amendment and that by force of the Supremacy Clause, Article VI, the New York English literacy requirement cannot be enforced to the extent that it is inconsistent with § 4(e). . . .

The Attorney General of the State of New York argues that an exercise of congressional power under § 5 of the Fourteenth Amendment that prohibits the enforcement of a state law can only be sustained if the judicial branch determines that the state law is prohibited by the provisions of the Amendment that Congress sought to enforce. More specifically, he urges that § 4(e) cannot be sustained as appropriate legislation to enforce the Equal Protection Clause unless the judiciary decides—even with the guidance of a congressional judgment—that the application of the English literacy requirement prohibited by § 4(e) is forbidden by the Equal Protection Clause itself. We disagree. Neither the language nor history of § 5 supports such a construction. As was said with regard to § 5 in *Ex parte Com. of Virginia*, 100 U.S. 339: "It is the power of Congress which has been enlarged. Congress is authorized to *enforce* the prohibitions by appropriate legislation. Some legislation is contemplated to make the amendments fully effective." A construction of § 5 that would require a judicial determination that the enforcement of the state law precluded by Congress violated the Amendment, as a condition of sustaining the congressional enactment, would depreciate both congressional resourcefulness and congressional responsibility for implementing the Amendment. It would confine the legislative power in this context to the insignificant role of abrogating only those state laws that the judicial branch was prepared to adjudge unconstitutional, or of merely informing the judgment of the judiciary by particularizing the "majestic generalities" of § 1 of the Amendment.

Thus our task in this case is not to determine whether the New York English literacy requirement as applied to deny the right to vote to a person who successfully completed the sixth grade in a Puerto Rican school violates the Equal Pro-

tection Clause. Accordingly, our decision in *Lassiter* v. *Northampton County Bd. of Election*, 360 U.S. 45, sustaining the North Carolina English literacy requirement as not in all circumstances prohibited by the first sections of the Fourteenth and Fifteenth Amendments, is inapposite. *Lassiter* did not present the question before us here: Without regard to whether the judiciary would find that the Equal Protection Clause itself nullifies New York's English literacy requirement as so applied, could Congress prohibit the enforcement of the state law by legislating under § 5 of the Fourteenth Amendment? In answering this question, our task is limited to determining whether such legislation is, as required by § 5, appropriate legislation to enforce the Equal Protection Clause.

By including § 5 the draftsmen sought to grant to Congress, by a specific provision applicable to the Fourteenth Amendment, the same broad powers expressed in the Necessary and Proper Clause, Art. I, § 8, cl. 18.

Correctly viewed, § 5 is a positive grant of legislative power authorizing Congress to exercise its discretion in determining whether and what legislation is needed to secure the guarantees of the Fourteenth Amendment.

We therefore proceed to the consideration whether § 4(e) is "appropriate legislation" to enforce the Equal Protection Clause, that is, under the *McCulloch* v. *Maryland* standard, whether § 4(e) may be regarded as an enactment to enforce the Equal Protection Clause, whether it is "plainly adapted to that end" and whether it is not prohibited by but is consistent with "the letter and spirit of the constitution."*

There can be no doubt that § 4(e) may be regarded as an enactment to enforce the Equal Pro-

---

*Contrary to the suggestion of the dissent, § 5 does not grant Congress power to exercise discretion in the other direction and to enact "statutes so as in effect to dilute equal protection and due process decisions of this Court." We emphasize that Congress's power under § 5 is limited to adopting measures to enforce the guarantees of the Amendment; § 5 grants Congress no power to restrict, abrogate, or dilute these guarantees. Thus, for example, an enactment authorizing the States to establish racially segregated systems of education would not be—as required by § 5—a measure "to enforce" the Equal Protection Clause since that clause of its own force prohibits such state laws.

tection Clause. Congress explicitly declared that it enacted § 4(e) "to secure the rights under the fourteenth amendment of persons educated in American-flag schools in which the predominant classroom language was other than English." More specifically, § 4(e) may be viewed as a measure to secure for the Puerto Rican community residing in New York nondiscriminatory treatment by government—both in the imposition of voting qualifications and the provision or administration of governmental services, such as public schools, public housing, and law enforcement.

It was for Congress, as the branch that made this judgment, to assess and weigh the various conflicting considerations—the risk or pervasiveness of the discrimination in governmental services, the effectiveness of eliminating the state restriction on the right to vote as a means of dealing with the evil, the adequacy or availability of alternative remedies, and the nature and significance of the state interests that would be affected by the nullification of the English literacy requirement as applied to residents who have successfully completed the sixth grade in a Puerto Rican school. It is not for us to review the congressional resolution of these factors. It is enough that we be able to perceive a basis upon which the Congress might resolve the conflict as it did. There plainly was such a basis to support § 4(e) in the application in question in this case. Any contrary conclusion would require us to be blind to the realities familiar to the legislators.

Section 4(e) does not restrict or deny the franchise but in effect extends the franchise to persons who otherwise would be denied it by state law. Thus we need not decide whether a state literacy law conditioning the right to vote on achieving a certain level of education in an American-flag school (regardless of the language of instruction) discriminates invidiously against those educated in non-American-flag schools. We need only decide whether the challenged limitation on the relief effected in § 4(e) was permissible. In deciding that question, the principle that calls for the closest scrutiny of distinctions in laws *denying* fundamental rights is inapplicable; for the distinction challenged by appellees is presented only as a limitation on a reform measure aimed at eliminating an existing barrier to the exercise of the franchise. Rather, in deciding the constitutional propriety of the limitations in

such a reform measure we are guided by the familiar principles that a "statute is not invalid under the Constitution because it might have gone farther than it did," that a legislature need not "strike at all evils at the same time," and that "'reform may take one step at a time, addressing itself to the phase of the problem which seems most acute to the legislative mind."

Guided by these principles, we are satisfied that appellees' challenge to this limitation in § 4(e) is without merit.

We therefore conclude that § 4(e), in the application challenged in this case, is appropriate legislation to enforce the Equal Protection Clause and that the judgment of the District Court must be and hereby is reversed.

Reversed.

JUSTICE HARLAN, whom JUSTICE STEWART joins, dissenting.

Worthy as its purposes may be thought by many, I do not see how § 4(e) of the Voting Rights Act of 1965 can be sustained except at the sacrifice of fundamentals in the American constitutional system—the separation between the legislative and judicial function and the boundaries between federal and state political authority.

I believe the Court has confused the issue of how much enforcement power Congress possesses under § 5 with the distinct issue of what questions are appropriate for congressional determination and what questions are essentially judicial in nature.

When recognized state violations of federal constitutional standards have occurred, Congress is of course empowered by § 5 to take appropriate remedial measures to redress and prevent the wrongs. But it is a judicial question whether the condition with which Congress has thus sought to deal is in truth an infringement of the Constitution, something that is the necessary prerequisite to bringing the § 5 power into play at all.

The question here is not whether the statute is appropriate remedial legislation to cure an established violation of a constitutional command, but whether there has in fact been an infringement of that constitutional command, that is, whether a particular state practice or, as here, a statute is so arbitrary or irrational as to offend the command of the Equal Protection Clause of the Fourteenth Amendment. That question is one for the judicial branch ultimately to determine. Were the rule otherwise, Congress would be able to qualify this Court's constitutional decisions under the Fourteenth and Fifteenth Amendments let alone those under other provisions of the Constitution, by resorting to congressional power under the Necessary and Proper Clause. In view of this Court's holding in *Lassiter* that an English literacy test is a permissible exercise of state supervision over its franchise, I do not think it is open to Congress to limit the effect of that decision as it has undertaken to do by § 4(e). In effect the Court reads § 5 of the Fourteenth Amendment as giving Congress the power to define the *substantive* scope of the Amendment. If that indeed be the true reach of § 5, then I do not see why Congress should not be able as well to exercise its § 5 "discretion" by enacting statutes so as in effect to dilute equal protection and due process decisions of this Court. In all such cases there is room for reasonable men to differ as to whether or not a denial of equal protection or due process has occurred, and the final decision is one of judgment. Until today this judgment has always been one for the judiciary to resolve.

Thornburg v. *Gingles*
478 U.S. 30; 106 S. Ct. 2752; 92 L. Ed. 2d 25 (1986)

In 1982, black citizens in North Carolina brought suit in Federal District Court against a legislative redistricting plan for the state's Senate and House of Representatives, challenging one single-member district and six multimember districts on the grounds that they impaired the ability of black citizens to elect representatives of their choice in violation of § 2 of the Voting Rights Act of 1965. After they brought suit, but before the trial, Congress amended § 2, largely in response to the Supreme Court's decision in *Mobile* v. *Bolden*, 446 U.S. 55 (1980), to make clear that a violation of § 2 could be proved by showing discriminatory effect alone, rather than having to show a discriminatory purpose, and to establish as the relevant legal standard the "results test." The District Court, applying these amendments, held that the redistricting plan violated amended § 2 because it resulted in the dilution of black citizens' votes in all of the disputed districts. Lacy H. Thornburg, the Attorney-General of North Carolina, took a direct appeal to the U.S. Supreme Court. *Opinion of the Court: Brennan, Blackmun, Marshall, Stevens, White. Concurring opinion: White. Concurring in the judgment: O'Connor, Burger, Powell, Rehnquist. Concurring in part and dissenting in part: Stevens, Blackmun, Marshall.*

JUSTICE BRENNAN delivered the opinion of the Court.

The essence of a § 2 claim is that a certain electoral law, practice, or structure interacts with social and historical conditions to cause an inequality in the opportunities enjoyed by black and white voters to elect their preferred representatives. This Court has long recognized that multimember districts and at-large voting schemes may " 'operate to minimize or cancel out the voting strength of racial [minorities in] the voting population.' " The theoretical basis for this type of impairment is that where minority and majority voters consistently prefer different candidates, the majority, by virtue of its numerical superiority, will regularly defeat the choices of minority voters. Minority voters who contend that the multimember form of districting violates § 2 must prove that the use of a multimember electoral structure operates to minimize or cancel out their ability to elect their preferred candidates.

These circumstances are necessary preconditions for multimember districts to operate to impair minority voters' ability to elect representatives of their choice for the following reasons. First, the minority group must be able to demonstrate that it is sufficiently large and geographically compact to constitute a majority in a single-member district. If it is not, as would be the case in a substantially integrated district, the *multimember form* of the district cannot be responsible for minority voters' inability to elect its candidates. Second, the minority group must be able to show that it is politically cohesive. If the minority group is not politically cohesive, it cannot be said that the selection of a multimember electoral structure thwarts distinctive minority group interests. Third, the minority must be able to demonstrate that the white majority votes sufficiently as a bloc to enable it—in the absence of special circumstances, such as the minority candidate running unopposed—usually to defeat the minority's preferred candidate. In establishing this last circumstance, the minority group demonstrates that submergence in a white multimember district impedes its ability to elect its chosen representatives. . . .

The purpose of inquiring into the existence of racially polarized voting is twofold: to ascertain whether minority group members constitute a politically cohesive unit and to determine whether whites vote sufficiently as a bloc usually to defeat the minority's preferred candidates. Thus, the question whether a given district experiences legally significant racially polarized voting requires discrete inquiries into minority and white voting practices. A showing that a significant number of minority group members usually vote for the same candidates is one way of proving the political cohesiveness necessary to a vote dilution claim and, consequently, establishes minority bloc voting within the context of § 2. And, in general, a white bloc that normally will defeat the combined strength of minority support plus white "'crossover" votes rises to the level of legally significant white bloc voting.

Because loss of political power through vote dilution is distinct from the mere inability to win a particular election, *Whitcomb*, 403 U. S., at 153, a pattern of racial bloc voting that extends over a period of time is more probative of a claim that a district experiences legally significant polarization than are the results of a single election. Also for this reason, in a district where

elections are shown usually to be polarized, the fact that racially polarized voting is not present in one or a few individual elections does not necessarily negate the conclusion that the district experiences legally significant bloc voting. Furthermore, the success of a minority candidate in a particlular election does not necessarily prove that the district did not experience polarized voting in that election; special circumstances, such as the absence of an opponent, incumbency, or the utilization of bullet voting, may explain minority electoral success in a polarized contest.

As must be apparent, the degree of racial bloc voting that is cognizable as an element of a § 2 vote dilution claim will vary according to a variety of factual circumstances. Consequently, there is no simple doctrinal test for the existence of legally significant racial bloc voting. However, the foregoing general principles should provide courts with substantial guidance in determining whether evidence that black and white voters generally prefer different candidates rises to the level of legal significance under § 2. . . .

North Carolina and thc United States maintain that the District Court failed to accord the proper weight to the success of some black candidates in the challenged districts. Black residents of these districts, they point out, achieved improved representation in the 1982 General Assembly elections. They also note that blacks in House District 23 have enjoyed proportional representation consistently since 1973 and that blacks in the other districts have occasionally enjoyed nearly proportional representation. This electoral success demonstrates conclusively, appellants and the United States argue, that blacks in those districts do not have "less opportunity than other members of the electorate to participate in the political process and to elect representatives of their choice." Essentially, appellants and the United States contend that if a racial minority gains proportional or nearly proportional representation in a single election, that fact alone precludes, as a matter of law, finding a § 2 violation. . . .

Nothing in the statute or its legislative history prohibited the court from viewing with some caution black candidates' success in the 1982 election, and from deciding on the basis of all the relevant circumstances to accord greater weight to blacks' relative lack of success over the course of several recent elections. Consequently, we hold that the District Court did not err, as a matter of law, in refusing to treat the fact that some black candidates have succeeded as dispositive of appellees' § 2 claim. Where multimember districting generally works to dilute the minority vote, it cannot be defended on the ground that it sporadically and serendipitously benefits minority voters. . . .

The District Court in this case carefully considered the totality of the cicumstances and found that in each district racially polarized voting; the legacy of official discrimination in voting matters, education, housing, employment, and health services; and the persistence of campaign appeals to racial prejudice acted in concert with the multimember districting scheme to impair the ability of geographically insular and politically cohesive groups of black voters to participate equally in the political process and to elect candidates of their choice. It found that the success a few black candidates have enjoyed in these districts is too recent, too limited, and, with regard to the 1982 elections, perhaps too aberrational, to disprove its conclusion. We cannot say that the District Court, composed of local judges who are well acquainted with the political realities of the State, clearly erred in concluding that use of a multimember electoral structure has caused black voters in the districts other than House District 23 to have less opportunity than white voters to elect representatives of their choice. . . .

Shaw v. Reno
509 U.S. 630; 113 S. Ct. 2816; 125 L. Ed. 2d 511 (1993)

As a result of population growth during the 1980s, North Carolina's congressional delegation was increased from 11 to 12 after the 1990 census. The North Carolina legislature redrew the state's congressional district lines in such a way that it protected the state's 11 incumbent congressmen while simultaneously carving out a new, majority-black district, thereby assuring the election of the state's first black congressman since Reconstruction. The Attorney-General of the United States, enforcing the Voting Rights Act of 1965 as amended in 1982, rejected the state's plan, however, on the grounds that a second majority-black congressional district could also be created. The state revised its plan and created a second majority-black district. It came to be known as the Interstate 85 District—a district that stretched over 160 miles along I-85 and that for much of its length was no wider than the I-85 corridor. Five state residents filed suit against this plan, alleging that the state had created a racial gerrymander in violation of the Fourteenth Amendment. A three-judge District Court for the Eastern District of North Carolina dismissed the appellants' complaint, and an appeal was taken to the United States Supreme Court. *Opinion of the Court: O'Connor, Kennedy, Rehnquist, Scalia, Thomas. Dissenting opinions: White, Blackmun, Stevens; Blackmun; Stevens; Souter.*

JUSTICE O'CONNOR delivered the opinion of the Court.

This case involves two of the most complex and sensitive issues this Court has faced in recent years: the meaning of the constitutional "right" to vote, and the propriety of race-based state legislation designed to benefit members of historically disadvantaged racial minority groups. As a result of the 1990 census, North Carolina became entitled to a twelfth seat in the United States House of Representatives. The General Assembly enacted a reapportionment plan that included one majority-black congressional district. After the Attorney General of the United States objected to the plan pursuant to § 5 of the Voting Rights Act of 1965, the General

Assembly passed new legislation creating a second majority-black district. Appellants allege that the revised plan, which contains district boundary lines of dramatically irregular shape, constitutes an unconstitutional racial gerrymander. The question before us is whether appellants have stated a cognizable claim.

The voting age population of North Carolina is approximately 78% white, 20% black, and 1% Native American; the remaining 1% is predominantly Asian. The black population is relatively dispersed; blacks constitute a majority of the general population in only 5 of the State's 100 counties. Geographically, the State divides into three regions: the eastern Coastal Plain, the central Piedmont Plateau, and the western mountains. The largest concentrations of black citizens live in the Coastal Plain, primarily in the northern part. The General Assembly's first redistricting plan contained one majority-black district centered in that area of the State.

Forty of North Carolina's one hundred counties are covered by § 5 of the Voting Rights Act of 1965, which prohibits a jurisdiction subject to its provisions from implementing changes in a "standard, practice, or procedure with respect to voting" without federal authorization. The jurisdiction must obtain either a judgment from the United States District Court for the District of Columbia declaring that the proposed change "does not have the purpose and will not have the effect of denying or abridging the right to vote on account of race or color" or administrative pre-clearance from the Attorney General. Because the General Assembly's reapportionment plan affected the covered counties, the parties agree that § 5 applied. The State chose to submit its plan to the Attorney General for pre-clearance.

The Attorney General, acting through the Assistant Attorney General for the Civil Rights Division, interposed a formal objection to the General Assembly's plan. The Attorney General specifically objected to the configuration of boundary lines drawn in the south-central to southeastern region of the State. In the Attorney General's view, the General Assembly could have created a second majority-minority district "to give effect to black and Native American voting strength in this area" by using boundary lines "no more irregular than [those] found elsewhere in the proposed plan" but failed to do so for "pretextual reasons."

Under § 5, the State remained free to seek a declaratory judgment from the District Court for the District of Columbia notwithstanding the Attorney General's objection. It did not do so. Instead, the General Assembly enacted a revised redistricting plan that included a second majority-black district. The General Assembly located the second district not in the south-central to southeastern part of the State, but in the north-central region along Interstate 85.

The first of the two majority-black districts contained in the revised plan, District 1, is somewhat hook shaped. Centered in the northeast portion of the State, it moves southward until it tapers to a narrow band; then, with finger-like extensions, it reaches far into the southernmost part of the State near the South Carolina border. District I has been compared to a "Rorschach inkblot test," and a "bug splattered on a windshield."

The second majority-black district, District 12, is even more unusually shaped. It is approximately 160 miles long and, for much of its length, no wider than the I-85 corridor. It winds in snakelike fashion through tobacco country, financial centers, and manufacturing areas "until it gobbles in enough enclaves of black neighborhoods." Northbound and southbound drivers on I-85 sometimes find themselves in separate districts in one county, only to "trade" districts when they enter the next county. Of the 10 counties through which District 12 passes, five are cut into three different districts; even towns are divided. At one point the district remains contiguous only because it intersects at a single point with two other districts before crossing over them. One state legislator has remarked that "[i]f you drove down the interstate with both car doors open, you'd kill most of the people in the district." The district even has inspired poetry: "Ask not for whom the line is drawn; it is drawn to avoid thee."

The Attorney General did not object to the General Assembly's revised plan. But numerous North Carolinians did. Appellants instituted the present action in the United States District Court for the Eastern District of North Carolina. Appellants alleged not that the revised plan constituted a political gerrymander, nor that it violated the "one-person, one-vote" principle, but that the State had created an unconstitutional *racial* gerrymander. Appellants are five residents of Durham County, North Carolina, all registered to vote in that county. Under the General Assembly's plan, two will vote for congressional representatives in District 12 and three will vote in neighboring District 2.

Appellants contended that the General Assembly's revised reapportionment plan violated several provisions of the United States Constitution, including the Fourteenth Amendment. They alleged that the General Assembly deliberately "create[d] two Congressional Districts in which a majority of black voters was concentrated arbitrarily—without regard to any other considerations, such as compactness, contiguousness, geographical boundaries, or political subdivisions" with the purpose "to create Congressional Districts along racial lines" and to assure the election of two black representatives to Congress.

By a 2-to-1 vote, the District Court . . . dismissed the complaint against the state appellees. An understanding of the nature of appellants' claim is critical to our resolution of this case. In their complaint, appellants did not claim that the General Assembly's reapportionment plan unconstitutionally "diluted" white voting strength. They did not even claim to be white. Rather, appellants' complaint alleged that the deliberate segregation of voters into separate districts on the basis of race violated their constitutional right to participate in a "color-blind" electoral process.

Despite their invocation of the ideal of a "color-blind" Constitution, see *Plessy* v. *Ferguson* (1896) (Justice Harlan, dissenting), appellants appear to concede that race-conscious redistricting is not always unconstitutional. That concession is wise: This Court never has held that race-conscious state decisionmaking is impermissible in *all* circumstances. What appellants object to is redistricting legislation that is so extremely irregular on its face that it rationally can be viewed only as an effort to segregate the races for purposes of voting, without regard for traditional districting principles and without sufficiently compelling justification. For the reasons that follow, we conclude that appellants have stated a claim upon which relief can be granted under the Equal Protection Clause.

The Equal Protection Clause provides that "[n]o State shall . . . deny to any person within its jurisdiction the equal protection of the laws." Its central purpose is to prevent the States from purposefully discriminating between individuals on the basis of race. Laws that explicitly distinguish between individuals on racial grounds fall within the core of that prohibition.

Classifications of citizens solely on the basis of race "are by their very nature odious to a free people whose institutions are founded upon the doctrine of equality." They threaten to stigmatize individuals by reason of their membership in a racial group and to incite racial hostility. Accordingly, we have held that the Fourteenth Amendment requires state legislation that expressly distinguishes among citizens because of their race to be narrowly tailored to further a compelling governmental interest.

These principles apply not only to legislation that contains explicit racial distinctions, but also to those "rare" statutes that, although race-neutral, are, on their face, "unexplainable on grounds other than race."

Appellants contend that redistricting legislation that is so bizarre on its face that it is "unexplainable on grounds other than race," demands the same close scrutiny that we give other state laws that classify citizens by race. Our voting rights precedents support that conclusion. . . .

We believe that reapportionment is one area in which appearances do matter. A reapportionment plan that includes in one district individuals who belong to the same race, but who are otherwise widely separated by geographical and political boundaries, and who may have little in common with one another but the color of their skin, bears an uncomfortable resemblance to political apartheid. It reinforces the perception that members of the same racial group—regardless of their age, education, economic status, or the community in which they live—think alike, share the same political interests, and will prefer the same candidates at the polls. We have rejected such perceptions elsewhere as impermissible racial stereotypes. By perpetuating such notions, a racial gerrymander may exacerbate the very patterns of racial block voting that majority-minority districting is sometimes said to counteract.

The message that such districting sends to elected representatives is equally pernicious.

When a district obviously is created solely to effectuate the perceived common interests of one racial group, elected officials are more likely to believe that their primary obligation is to represent only the members of that group, rather than their constituency as a whole. This is altogether antithetical to our system of representative democracy.

For these reasons, we conclude that a plaintiff challenging a reapportionment statute under the Equal Protection Clause may state a claim by alleging that the legislation, though race-neutral on its face, rationally cannot be understood as anything other than an effort to separate voters into different districts on the basis of race, and that the separation lacks sufficient justification. We hold only that, on the facts of this case, plaintiffs have stated a claim sufficient to defeat the state appellees' motion to dismiss. . . .

Justice Souter apparently believes that racial gerrymandering is harmless unless it dilutes a racial group's voting strength. As we have explained, however, reapportionment legislation that cannot be understood as anything other than an effort to classify and separate voters by race injures voters in other ways. It reinforces racial stereotypes and threatens to undermine our system of representative democracy by signaling to elected officials that they represent a particular racial group rather than their constituency as a whole. Justice Souter does not adequately explain why these harms are not cognizable under the Fourteenth Amendment. . . .

The dissenters make two other arguments that cannot be reconciled with our precedents. First, they suggest that a racial gerrymander of the sort alleged here is functionally equivalent to gerrymanders for nonracial purposes, such as political gerrymanders. This Court has held political gerrymanders to be justiciable under the Equal Protection Clause. But nothing in our case law compels the conclusion that racial and political gerrymanders are subject to precisely the same constitutional scrutiny. In fact, our country's long and persistent history of racial discrimination in voting—as well as our Fourteenth Amendment jurisprudence, which always has reserved the strictest scrutiny for discrimination on the basis of race, would seem to compel opposite conclusions.

Second, Justice Stevens argues that racial gerrymandering poses no constitutional difficulties when district lines are drawn to favor the minority, rather than the majority. We have made clear, however, that equal protection analysis "is not dependent on the race of those burdened or benefitted by a particular classification." Indeed, racial classifications receive close scrutiny even when they may be said to burden or benefit the races equally.

Racial classifications of any sort pose the risk of lasting harm to our society. They reinforce the belief, held by too many for too much of our history, that individuals should be judged by the color of their skin. Racial classifications with respect to voting carry particular dangers. Racial gerrymandering, even for remedial purposes, may balkanize us into competing racial factions; it threatens to carry us further from the goal of a political system in which race no longer matters—a goal that the Fourteenth and Fifteenth Amendments embody, and to which the Nation continues to aspire. It is for these reasons that race-based districting by our state legislatures demands close judicial scrutiny.

In this case, the Attorney General suggested that North Carolina could have created a reasonably compact second majority-minority district in the south-central to southeastern part of the State. We express no view as to whether appellants successfully could have challenged such a district under the Fourteenth Amendment. We also do not decide whether appellants' complaint stated a claim under constitutional provisions other than the Fourteenth Amendment. Today we hold only that appellants have stated a claim under the Equal Protection Clause by alleging that the North Carolina General Assembly adopted a reapportionment scheme so irrational on its face that it can be understood only as an effort to segregate voters into separate voting districts because of their race, and that the separation lacks sufficient justification. If the allegation of racial gerrymandering remains uncontradicted, the District Court further must determine whether the North Carolina plan is narrowly tailored to further a compelling governmental interest. Accordingly, we reverse the judgment of the District Court and remand the case for further proceedings consistent with this opinion.

It is so ordered.

JUSTICE WHITE, with whom JUSTICE BLACKMUN and JUSTICE STEVENS join, dissenting.

The grounds for my disagreement with the majority are simply stated: Appellants have not presented a cognizable claim, because they have not alleged a cognizable injury. To date, we have held that only two types of state voting practices could give rise to a constitutional claim. The first involves direct and outright deprivation of the right to vote, for example by means of a poll tax or literacy test. Plainly, this variety is not implicated by appellants' allegations and need not detain us further. The second type of unconstitutional practice is that which "affects the political strength of various groups," *Mobile* v. *Bolden*, in violation of the Equal Protection Clause. As for this latter category, we have insisted that members of the political or racial group demonstrate that the challenged action have the intent and effect of unduly diminishing their influence on the political process.

It strains credulity to suggest that North Carolina's purpose in creating a second majority-minority district was to discriminate against members of the majority group by "impair[ing] or burden[ing their] opportunity . . . to participate in the political process." The State has made no mystery of its intent, which was to respond to the Attorney General's objections, by improving the minority group's prospects of electing a candidate of its choice. I doubt that this constitutes a discriminatory purpose as defined in the Court's equal protection case—*i.e.*, an intent to aggravate "the unequal distribution of electoral power." But even assuming that it does, there is no question that appellants have not alleged the requisite discriminatory effects. Whites constitute roughly 76 percent of the total population and 79 percent of the voting age population in North Carolina. Yet, under the State's plan, they still constitute a voting majority in 10 (or 83 percent) of the 12 congressional districts. Though they might be dissatisfied at the prospect of casting a vote for a losing candidate—a lot shared by many, including a disproportionate number of minority voters—surely they cannot complain of discriminatory treatment.

Part of the majority's explanation of its holding is related to its simultaneous discomfort and fascination with irregularly shaped districts. Lack of compactness or contiguity, like uncouth district lines, certainly is a helpful indicator that some form of gerrymandering (racial or other) might have taken place and that "something may be amiss." Disregard for geographic divisions and compactness often goes hand in hand with partisan gerrymandering.

But while district irregularities may provide strong indicia of a potential gerrymander, they do no more than that. In particular, they have no bearing on whether the plan ultimately is found to violate the Constitution. Given two districts drawn on similar, race-based grounds, the one does not become more injurious than the other simply by virtue of being snakelike, at least so far as the Constitution is concerned and absent any evidence of differential racial impact. The majority's contrary view is perplexing in light of its concession that "compactness or attractiveness has never been held to constitute an independent federal constitutional requirement for state legislative districts." It is shortsighted as well, for a regularly shaped district can just as effectively effectuate racially discriminatory gerrymandering as an odd-shaped one. By focusing on looks rather than impact, the majority "immediately casts attention in the wrong direction—toward superficialities of shape and size, rather than toward the political realities of district composition."

Limited by its own terms to cases involving unusually shaped districts, the Court's approach nonetheless will unnecessarily hinder to some extent a State's voluntary effort to ensure a modicum of minority representation. This will be true in areas where the minority population is geographically dispersed. It also will be true where the minority population is not scattered but, for reasons unrelated to race—for example incumbency protection—the State would rather not create the majority-minority district in its most "obvious" location. When, as is the case here, the creation of a majority-minority district does not unfairly minimize the voting power of any other group, the Constitution does not justify, much less mandate, such obstruction.

Although I disagree with the holding that appellants' claim is cognizable, the Court's discussion of the level of scrutiny it requires warrants a few comments. I have no doubt that a State's compliance with the Voting Rights Act clearly constitutes a compelling interest.

JUSTICE STEVENS, dissenting.

The duty to govern impartially is abused when a group with power over the electoral process defines electoral boundaries solely to enhance its own political strength at the expense of any weaker group. That duty, however, is not violated when the majority acts to facilitate the election of a member of a group that lacks such power because it remains underrepresented in the state legislature—whether that group is defined by political affiliation, by common economic interests, or by religious, ethnic, or racial characteristics. The difference between constitutional and unconstitutional gerrymanders has nothing to do with whether they are based on assumptions about the groups they affect, but whether their purpose is to enhance the power of the group in control of the districting process at the expense of any minority group, and thereby to strengthen the unequal distribution of electoral power. When an assumption that people in particular a minority group (whether they are defined by the political party, religion, ethnic group, or race to which they belong) will vote in a particular way is used to *benefit* that group, no constitutional violation occurs. Politicians have always relied on assumptions that people in particular groups are likely to vote in a particular way when they draw new district lines, and I cannot believe that anything in today's opinion will stop them from doing so in the future.

JUSTICE SOUTER, dissenting.

In districting, the mere placement of an individual in one district instead of another denies no one a right or benefit provided to others. All citizens may register, vote, and be represented. In whatever district, the individual voter has a right to vote in each election, and the election will result in the voter's representation. As we have held, one's constitutional rights are not violated merely because the candidate one supports loses the election or because a group (including a racial group) to which one belongs winds up with a representative from outside that group.

It may be that the terms for pleading this cause of action will be met so rarely that this case will wind up an aberration. The shape of the district at issue in this case is indeed so bizarre that few other examples are ever likely to carry the unequivocal implication of impermissible use of race that the Court finds here. It may therefore be that few electoral districting cases are ever likely to employ the strict scrutiny the Court holds to be applicable on remand if appellants' allegations are "not contradicted." I would not respond to the seeming egregiousness of the redistricting now before us by untethering the concept of racial gerrymander in such a case from the concept of harm exemplified by dilution. In the absence of an allegation of such harm, I would affirm the judgment of the District Court. I respectfully dissent.

★

THE CONSTITUTIONAL BASIS

WHAT THE RIGHT TO PRIVACY PROTECTS

Griswold v. Connecticut (1965)
Roe v. Wade (1973)
Planned Parenthood of Southeastern Pennsylvania v. Casey (1992)

QUALIFICATIONS ON THE RIGHT TO PRIVACY

Bowers v. Hardwick (1986)
Romer v. Evans (1996)

PRIVACY AND THE RIGHT TO DIE

Cruzan v. Director, Missouri Department of Health (1990)
Washington v. Glucksberg (1997)
Vacco v. Quill (1997)

NOTES

SELECTED READING

CASES

★

11
THE RIGHT
TO PRIVACY

Any consideration of the right to privacy must begin with Louis D. Brandeis. In a pioneering exposition, Brandeis, then a young legal scholar, asserted in the 1890 *Harvard Law Review* that the right to privacy means fundamentally "the right to be let alone."[1] The significance of this article, which he wrote with Samuel Warren, cannot be overstated; it generally is regarded as the most influential law review article ever published. Thirty-eight years later, as a justice of the Supreme Court, Brandeis expanded on the theme of the article in his dissent in *Olmstead* v. *United States* (1928): "The right to be let alone . . . is the most comprehensive of rights and the right most valued by civilized men. To protect that right, every unjustified intrusion of the government upon the privacy of the individual, whatever the means employed, must be deemed a constitutional violation." Another thirty-seven years would pass before Justice Brandeis's words were vindicated in *Griswold* v. *Connecticut* (1965), a landmark case in which the Court for the first time acknowledged the individual's constitutional right to privacy. Once vindicated, however, Brandeis's words, along with the right they declare, came to have a profound and troubling impact, for the right to privacy has figured prominently in some of the most controversial and divisive decisions the Court has ever rendered—those on abortion and the right to die. This chapter explores three principal issues arising out of this right to privacy:

1. Is there a constitutional right to privacy, and if so, what is its constitutional basis?

2. What exactly does this right protect? Does the privacy to be protected inhere in places, relationships, or people?
3. What qualifications, if any, limit this right?

THE CONSTITUTIONAL BASIS

In his *Olmstead* dissent, Justice Brandeis considered the right to privacy to be "the most comprehensive of rights," and so it may well be. That same comprehensive nature, however, has made it exceedingly difficult for the Court to ascertain precisely what provision (or provisions) of the Constitution protect this right. Various justices have identified and relied on different constitutional bases. Justice Brandeis in *Olmstead* (discussed in Chapter 7) based the right to privacy on the Fourth Amendment's protections against unreasonable searches and seizures and on the Fifth Amendment's guarantee against self-incrimination. But Justice John Marshall Harlan, in his concurrence in *Griswold,* and Justice Harry Blackmun, in his opinion for the Court in *Roe* v. *Wade* (1973), declared that privacy claims were protected by the Due Process Clause of the Fourteenth Amendment; Justice William Brennan, in both his opinion for the Court in *Eisenstadt* v. *Baird* (1972) and his dissent in *Harris* v. *McRae* (1980), based the right to privacy on the Equal Protection Clause of the Fourteenth Amendment; Justice Arthur Goldberg, in his *Griswold* concurrence, relied on the Ninth Amendment; and Justice William Douglas, in his majority opinion in *Griswold,* unable to identify any single constitutional provision but taking comfort in the fact that "specific guarantees in the Bill of Rights have penumbras, formed by emanations from those guarantees that help give them life and substance," argued that a penumbral right of privacy emanates from particular guarantees found in the First, Third, Fourth, Fifth, and Ninth amendments.

These differences of opinion over the constitutional basis of the right to privacy apparently reflect a reluctance on the part of the Court to rely on the Due Process Clause. To many justices, grounding the right to privacy on the Due Process Clause and then employing that provision to bar legislative regulation of an entire area of conduct—as exemplified in *Griswold*—has raised the specter of substantive due process and provided too many parallels to the Court's pre-1937 espousal of "liberty of contract" as a defense against business regulation (see Chapter 4). They have, therefore, pressed into service other constitutional provisions, including the Equal Protection Clause, the Ninth Amendment, and Justice Douglas's "penumbras." Reliance on these provisions has enabled the justices to provide the same level of protection for the right to privacy as would be provided by substantive due process. As Justice William Rehnquist has noted, these provisions—at least insofar as they have been employed by the Court in privacy cases—are "sisters under the skin" to substantive due process.[2] By invoking them, the justices apparently considered that they would escape the onus so often attached to substantive due process. Consider, for example, the following statement by Justice

Douglas in *Griswold*, in which substantive due process is repudiated publicly but embraced *sub silentio*.

> We are met with a wide range of questions that implicate the Due Process Clause of the Fourteenth Amendment. Overtones of some arguments suggest that *Lochner* v. *State of New York* . . . should be our guide. But we decline that invitation. . . . We do not sit as a super-legislature to determine the wisdom, need, and propriety of laws that touch economic problems, business affairs, or social conditions.

That substantive due process is not without its merits was made clear by the Warren Court's embrace of it in *Bolling* v. *Sharpe* (1954). (See Chapter 8 for a full discussion of this issue.) The contemporary Court, however, is for the most part reluctant to employ substantive due process formally and defend it publicly, preferring instead to rely on its "sisters under the skin." As a result, the right to privacy has emerged as an issue in its own right, rather than as a dependency of due process, equal protection, or any other specific constitutional guarantee.

WHAT THE RIGHT TO PRIVACY PROTECTS

A second major issue arising out of the right to privacy centers on the question of what exactly does this right protect. In its initial decisions regarding privacy, the Court tended to view the right to privacy as place oriented and property based, and hence as narrow in the range of its protections. This tendency was understandable in view of the fact that these decisions invariably concerned questions of criminal procedure and the meaning and reach of the Fourth Amendment's protections against unreasonable searches and seizures. In the landmark *Olmstead* decision, for example, the Court majority upheld the courtroom use of wiretap evidence that had been obtained without a search warrant, arguing that because there had been no "actual physical invasion" or trespass of the defendants' homes or offices, there had been no search involved, and hence no violation of the Fourth Amendment and the privacy it guarantees. Justice Brandeis, in dissent, argued that privacy inheres in the individual (i.e., the person) and involves nothing less than the "right to be let alone." Despite this eloquent plea, the majority opinion in *Olmstead* remained in force well into the 1960s. A long line of cases, stretching from *Olmstead* through *Goldman* v. *United States* (1942) to *Silverman* v. *United States* (1961), consistently presented privacy as place oriented and property based. (The frequent repetition by the courts of the aphorism "A man's home is his castle" underscored the judiciary's identification of privacy with property rights.) Anything less than physical trespass onto private premises, these cases held, fell outside the ambit of Fourth Amendment protection.

In the mid-1960s, however, this long-standing approach to privacy questions underwent drastic changes. In *Griswold*, the Court declared that privacy inheres in legally protected relationships (in this case, marriage). It went further in *Katz* v. *United States* (1967), declaring that the privacy component of the "Fourth Amendment protects people, not places"[3] and thus broadened considerably the scope of coverage of the right to privacy.

Griswold struck down a Connecticut statute that had made it a criminal offense either to use birth control devices or to give information or instruction on their use. In defending this decision, Justice Douglas observed that to enforce the law, the police would have to search the bedrooms of married couples for evidence of contraceptive use—an idea that struck him as "repulsive to the notions of privacy surrounding the marriage relationship." Justice Douglas placed heavy emphasis on the "intimate relation of husband and wife": the privacy he sought to protect inhered in neither places nor persons, but in a relationship. He waxed poetic concerning this relationship: "Marriage is a coming together for better or for worse, hopefully enduring, and intimate to the degree of being sacred." Ironically, his efforts to protect the privacy of the conjugal bed by stressing the sacred intimacy of marriage soon were rendered superfluous by *Eisenstadt* v. *Baird* (1972), in which the Court invalidated a Massachusetts law that had made it a felony to give anyone other than a married person contraceptive medicines or devices. Justice Brennan, speaking for the Court, argued that the right to privacy inheres in the person and is not limited to certain relationships:

> If under *Griswold* the distribution of contraceptives to married persons cannot be prohibited, a ban on distribution to unmarried persons would be equally impermissible. It is true that in *Griswold* the right of privacy in question inhered in the marital relationship. Yet the marital couple is not an independent entity with a mind and heart of its own, but an association of two individuals each with a separate intellectual and emotional make-up. If the right of privacy means anything, it is the right of the individual, married or single, to be free from unwarranted governmental intrusion into matters so fundamentally affecting a person as the decision whether to bear or beget a child.

The ground for the Court's claim in *Eisenstadt* that the right to privacy inheres in the person and not necessarily in the relationship had been prepared in the *Katz* ruling that the privacy component of the Fourth Amendment "protects people, not places." Writing for the *Katz* majority, Justice Stewart had abandoned the line of cases from *Olmstead* through *Silverman* that had limited the reach of the Fourth Amendment to "constitutionally protected areas" and declared that "what a person knowingly exposes to the public, even in his own home or office, is not a subject of Fourth Amendment protection. . . . But what he seeks to preserve as private, even in an area accessible to the public, may be constitutionally protected." Because it emerged in a Fourth Amendment case, this new, person-oriented right to privacy initially was limited to cases involving unreasonable searches and seizures. In subsequent cases, however, the Court used this expanded conception of privacy not only to regulate particular practices in law enforcement and criminal procedure but also (and more importantly) to invalidate substantive governmental regulation of entire areas of conduct. Thus, it employed a broad conception of the right to privacy in banning legislative restrictions of birth control in Eisenstadt and in invalidating antiabortion statutes in the highly controversial case of *Roe* v. *Wade* (1973).

By declaring that "the personal right of privacy includes the abortion decision," *Roe*, together with the companion case of *Doe* v. *Bolton* (1973), generated a firestorm of controversy that has enveloped the Court ever since. To begin with, critics have charged that *Roe* and *Doe* gave an entirely new meaning to the term *privacy*. As Justice Rehnquist noted in his dissent, "A transaction resulting in an operation such as this is not 'private' in the ordinary usage of the word." Professor Louis Henkin elaborated:

> What the Court has been talking about is not at all what most people mean by privacy. . . . Ms. Roe sought her abortion openly, "publicly." In a word, the Court has been vindicating not a right to freedom from official intrusion, but to freedom from official regulation. . . . [T]hey are, I think, different notions conceptually, with different philosophical, political and social (and, one might have thought, legal) assumptions and consequences; they may look different also if viewed as aspects of the confrontation of private right with public good.[4]

This point leads to a second criticism. If what was at stake in *Roe* v. *Wade* was "freedom from official regulation," the Court was guilty of "*Lochnering*"; that is, of superimposing its own views of wise social policy on those of the legislature. The remarkable similarities between *Roe* and *Lochner* v. *New York* (1905) have led critics to ask why the right to be let alone should give a woman control over her body with regard to an abortion but not, since the Court's repudiation of *Lochner*, control over her body concerning the sale of her labor (i.e., the wages she shall receive and the hours she shall work). *Roe* and *Doe* also have been attacked on the ground that in them, the Court paid insufficient attention to protecting the interests of the fetus—that in protecting the woman's right to be let alone, it unnecessarily jeopardized the fetus's "right to be." Justice Harry Blackmun's majority opinion attempted with little success to parry this criticism. Blackmun admitted that if a fetus is a person, its right to life is guaranteed by the Fourteenth Amendment.[5] But he then skirted the question of whether a fetus is a person (i.e., the question of when the life of a person begins): "We need not resolve the difficult question of when life begins. When those trained in the respective disciplines of medicine, philosophy, and theology are unable to arrive at any consensus, the judiciary, at this point in the development of man's knowledge, is not in a position to speculate as to the answer."[6]

Despite these criticisms, the Court supported *Roe* in subsequent decisions. *Planned Parenthood of Central Missouri* v. *Danforth* (1976), an especially important case in this respect, involved a Missouri abortion statute passed in response to *Roe*. Although the Court upheld the statute's flexible definition of viability, affirmed the state's right to require the informed, voluntary, and written consent of the woman, and sustained the reporting and record-keeping provisions of the law, it emasculated the statute by declaring unconstitutional the following crucial elements:

1. The requirement that written consent must also be obtained from the spouse in nontherapeutic abortions.
2. The requirement that written consent must be obtained from the woman's parents if she is under 18 and unmarried, except in a life-saving situation.
3. The blanket prohibition on the use of saline amniocentesis as a technique for inducing abortion.
4. The imposition of a criminal penalty on the attending physicians for any failure on their part to exercise due care and skill to preserve the life and health of the fetus, insofar as that is possible.

Here, as in *Roe* v. *Wade,* the Court's decision hinged on the priority it placed on guaranteeing to the pregnant woman the right to be let alone. As for spousal consent, Justice Blackmun noted that the majority could not hold that the state "has the constitutional authority to give the spouse unilaterally the ability to prohibit the wife from terminating her pregnancy, when the State itself lacks that right." The spouse, then, was viewed as having no more of an interest in the abortion decision than the state had. And as to the parental consent requirement, Blackmun observed that "any independent interest the parent may have in the termination of the minor daughter's pregnancy is no more weighty than the right of privacy of the competent minor mature enough to have become pregnant." The Court thereby held, for the first time, that minors have constitutional rights as against their parents.

In *Akron* v. *Akron Center for Reproductive Health* (1983), the Court dramatically reaffirmed *Roe* v. *Wade,* going so far as to announce that a woman has a "fundamental right" to have an abortion. The City of Akron had passed an ordinance that imposed a number of restrictions on the abortion process. Perhaps the most important was a requirement that any abortion performed after the first trimester of pregnancy had to be performed in a hospital. A six-member majority invalidated this requirement because it placed "a significant obstacle in the path of women seeking an abortion," a burden not justifiable as a reasonable health regulation. While hospitalization for abortions performed after the first trimester was recommended at the time of *Roe,* the safety of such abortions had "increased dramatically" since then because of improved technology and procedures, and there was no compelling reason why these abortions could not be performed on an outpatient basis in appropriate nonhospital settings. As Justice Powell declared for the majority: "[P]resent medical knowledge convincingly undercuts Akron's justification for requiring that all second-trimester abortions be performed in a hospital." Justice O'Connor dissented, observing that it was not until 1982, four years after Akron had passed its ordinance, that even the American College of Obstetricians and Gynecologists revised its standards and no longer recommended that all mid-trimester abortions be performed in a hospital. Her real objection, however, was with *Roe* itself. As she noted:

> The *Roe* framework . . . is clearly on a collision course with itself. As the medical risks of various abortion procedures decrease, the point at which the State may regulate for reasons of maternal health is moved further forward to actual childbirth. As medical science becomes better able to provide for the separate existence of the fetus, the point of viability is moved further back toward conception. Moreover, it is clear that the trimester approach violates the fundamental aspiration of judicial decision making through the application of neutral principles "sufficiently absolute to give them roots throughout the community and continuity over significant periods of time. . . . " The *Roe* framework is inherently tied to the state of medical technology that exists whenever particular litigation ensues. Although legislatures are better suited to make the necessary factual judgments in this area, the Court's framework forces legislatures, as a matter of constitutional law, to speculate about what constitutes "acceptable medical practice" at any given time. Without the necessary expertise or ability, courts must then pretend to act as science review boards and examine those legislative judgments.

Interestingly, when the opportunity for Justice O'Connor to help overturn *Roe* presented itself in *Webster* v. *Reproductive Health Services* (1989), she declined to do so on grounds of judicial self-restraint. The Missouri legislature had passed an abortion statute that, among other things, declared in its preamble that human life begins at conception and that "unborn children have protectable interests in life, health, and well-being." The law required medical tests to ascertain whether any fetus over 20 weeks old was viable and prohibited the use of public employees and facilities to perform abortions not necessary to save the life of the mother. Chief Justice Rehnquist wrote the judgment of the Court upholding all sections of the law. He favored overturning *Roe* but lacked the necessary fifth vote that Justice O'Connor could have supplied to do so. O'Connor concurred in the judgment, but did so because Missouri's statute did not, in her estimation, "conflict with any of the Court's past decisions concerning state regulation of abortion." Her actions left Justice Scalia furious; wishing the Court to overturn *Roe* completely and explicitly, he lamented that "the mansion of constitutionalized abortion-law, constructed overnight in *Roe* v. *Wade*, must be disassembled door-jamb by door-jamb, and never entirely brought down, no matter how wrong it may be."

By the time that the next major abortion case, *Planned Parenthood of Southern Pennsylvania* v. *Casey* (1992), was heard by the Court, the conventional wisdom was that Chief Justice Rehnquist and Justice Scalia would finally have their way and that *Roe* would be overturned. Two new justices had been added to the Court since *Webster*—David Souter and Clarence Thomas, both appointed by President Bush who had made no secret of his opposition to *Roe* and abortion. For Rehnquist and Scalia, however, *Casey* proved to be a major disappointment. In *Casey*, the Court considered five key provisions of the Pennsylvania Abortion Control Act of 1982; they required informed consent of, and imposed a 24-hour waiting period on, all women seeking an abortion; required the informed consent of one parent for a minor to obtain an abortion while also providing for a judicial bypass procedure; required that wives seeking abortions notify their husbands; provided that the previous requirements could be waived in a "medical emergency"; and imposed certain reporting requirements on facilities providing abortions. The Court ended up sustaining the constitutionality of all the act's provisions except for the one requiring spousal notification. While it abandoned *Roe*'s "rigid trimester framework," emphasized the "state's profound interest in potential life," and adopted a new "undue burden" test to evaluate restrictions on abortion, it nevertheless insisted that it was affirming the "central holding of *Roe* v. *Wade*" and remaining faithful to precedent.

Justice O'Connor, who refused to depart from precedent in *Webster*, refused to do so once again in *Casey*. She joined with Justices Kennedy and Souter in an unusual, jointly signed plurality opinion that concluded that even though *Roe* was probably wrongly decided, it should not be overturned. They argued that if the Court were to overturn *Roe* merely because newly appointed justices regarded it as a bad decision, it would create the impression that the justices yielded to political pressure and more generally that constitutional decisions are determined by politics.[7] That, they insisted, would result in "both profound and unnecessary damage to the Court's legitimacy, and to the Nation's commitment to the rule of law. It is therefore imperative to adhere to the essence of *Roe*'s original decision, and we do so today." Chief Justice Rehnquist objected: "Our constitutional watch does not cease merely because we have spoken before on an issue; when it becomes clear that a prior constitutional interpretation is unsound we are obliged to reexamine the question." Rehnquist's objection, however, was unavailing. To overturn the precedent that *Roe* had set would, the plurality insisted, jeopardize the very "character of a Nation of people who aspire to live according to the rule of law. Their belief in themselves as such a people is not readily separable from their understanding of the Court invested with the authority to decide their constitutional cases and speak before all others for their constitutional ideals. The Court's concern with legitimacy is not for the sake of the Court but for the sake of the Nation to which it is responsible."

In the name of precedent, therefore, Justices O'Connor, Kennedy, and Souter upheld *Roe*, even as they discarded the trimester framework that *Roe* had created and sustained a variety of restrictions on abortion contrary to the Court's original holding in *Roe*. Chief Justice Rehnquist complained in his dissent that, instead of adhering to precedent, the three justice's joint opinion revised it. "*Roe* continues to exist, but only in the way a storefront on a western movie set exists: a mere facade to give the illusion of reality." He also objected to the plurality's "undue burden" test, labeling it "a standard that is not built to last." Justice Scalia likewise filed an especially vigorous dissent. He responded to the joint opinion's argument that "to overrule under fire would subvert the Court's legitimacy" by thundering: "The Imperial Judiciary lives. It is instructive to compare this Nietzschean vision of us unelected, life-tenured judges—leading a Volk who will be 'tested by following,' and whose very 'belief in themselves' is mystically bound up in their 'understanding' of a Court that 'speak[s] before all others for their constitutional ideals'—with the somewhat more modest role envisioned for these lawyers by the Founders: 'The judiciary . . . has neither FORCE nor WILL but merely judgment.' *The Federalist*, No. 78."

As is made clear from Justice Blackmun's objections in *Casey* to the plurality's substitution of the "undue burden" test for the "strict scrutiny" test and to its abandonment of *Roe*'s trimester framework, the Court's commitment to guaranteeing a woman's right to an abortion has faltered somewhat. By contrast, however, the Court's refusal to hold that the government is compelled to fund abortions for women in financial need has been unwavering. In *Maher* v. *Roe* (1977), the Court held that Connecticut's decision not to pay for nontherapeutic abortions for indigent women, despite the fact that it did pay for childbirth, did not violate the Constitution. Justice Powell held for a six-member majority that the state's policy did not impinge on *Roe*'s recognition of a woman's fundamental right to protection "from unduly burdensome interference with her freedom to decide whether to terminate her pregnancy." That right, he declared, "implies no limitation on the authority of a State to make a value judgment favoring childbirth over abortion, and to implement that judgment by the allocation of public funds." He continued,

> The Connecticut regulation places no obstacles—absolute or otherwise—in the pregnant woman's path to an abortion. An indigent woman who desires an abortion suffers no disadvantage as a consequence of Connecticut's decision to fund childbirth; she continues as before to be dependent on private sources for the services she desires. The State may have made childbirth a more attractive alternative, thereby influencing the woman's decision, but it has imposed no restriction on access to abortions that was not already there. The indigency that may make it difficult—and in some cases, perhaps, impos-

sible—for some women to have abortions is neither created nor in any way affected by the Connecticut regulation.

Justice Brennan, in dissent, accused the majority of a "distressing insensitivity to the plight of impoverished pregnant women."

In its 5–4 decision in *Harris* v. *McRae* (1980), the Court not only reaffirmed *Maher*, but also carried Justice Powell's argument one step further. Whereas *Maher* dealt only with nontherapeutic abortions, *Harris* sustained the constitutionality of the Hyde Amendment, which drastically limited federal funding for most medically necessary abortions as well. Justice Stewart's majority opinion relied heavily on the analysis in *Maher*:

> Although the liberty protected by the Due Process Clause affords protection against unwarranted governmental interference with freedom of choice in the context of certain personal decisions, it does not confer an entitlement to such funds as may be necessary to realize all the advantages of that freedom. To hold otherwise would make a drastic change in our understanding of the Constitution.

Justice Brennan again dissented:

> Abortion and childbirth, when stripped of the sensitive moral arguments surrounding the abortion controversy, are simply two alternative medical methods of dealing with pregnancy. In every pregnancy, one of these two courses of treatment is medically necessary and the poverty-stricken woman depends on the Medicaid Act to pay for the expenses associated with that procedure. But under the Hyde Amendment, the Government will fund only those procedures incidental to childbirth. By thus injecting coercive financial incentives favoring childbirth into a decision that is constitutionally guaranteed to be free from governmental intrusion, the Hyde Amendment deprives the indigent woman of her freedom to choose abortion over maternity, thereby impinging on the due process liberty right recognized in *Roe* v. *Wade*.

QUALIFICATIONS ON THE RIGHT TO PRIVACY

Professor Paul Freund observed that privacy is a "greedy legal concept."[8] In light of *Roe*, this observation seems especially apt. The Court has come to understand the "right to be let alone" to protect not only against official intrusion but also against official regulation. This expansion of what privacy is understood to secure could well render government itself problematic, were privacy to be regarded as an absolute right.

The Court has demonstrated, however, that it is aware of this problem. In *Roe*, the decision that more than any other has expanded the right to privacy, the Court stressed that "this right is not unqualified and must be considered against important state interests in regulation." Consistent with this understanding, it went on to argue that a pregnant woman's right to be let alone and to elect whether or not to have an abortion can be subordinated to the state's interest in "protecting fetal life after viability . . . except when it is necessary to preserve the life or health of the mother." The Supreme Court has also recognized the qualified nature of the right to privacy in such cases as *Bowers* v. *Hardwick* (1986). In *Bowers*, the Supreme Court overturned a decision of the Eleventh Circuit Court of Appeals that had invalidated a Georgia statute that made consensual homosexual sodomy a criminal offense. Justice White spoke for a five-member majority when he rejected the claim that the federal Constitution confers a "fundamental right upon homosexuals to engage in sodomy." He insisted that there should be "great resistance to expand the substantive reach" of the Due Process Clause, "particularly if it requires redefining the category of rights deemed to be fundamental. Otherwise, the Judiciary necessarily takes to itself further authority to govern the country without express constitutional authority. The claimed right pressed on us today falls far short of overcoming this resistance." In his dissent, Justice Blackmun charged that while the Court "claims that its decision today merely refuses to recognize a fundamental right to engage in homosexual sodomy, what the Court really has refused to recognize is the fundamental interest all individuals have in controlling the nature of their intimate associations with others."

The status of *Bowers* was, however, called into question in *Romer* v. *Evans* (1996) in which the Court held, 6–3, that the Equal Protection Clause of the Fourteenth Amendment was violated when the people of Colorado in 1992 passed Amendment 2—a statewide referendum amending the Colorado Constitution and prohibiting all legislative, executive, or judicial action at any level of state or local government designed to protect the status of persons based on their "homosexual, lesbian or bisexual orientation, conduct, practices or relationships." Justice Kennedy spoke for the Court when he declared: "Amendment 2 classifies homosexuals not to further a proper legislative end but to make them unequal to everyone else. This Colorado cannot do. A State cannot so deem a class of persons a stranger to its laws." As Justice Scalia pointed out in his dissent, however: "The case most relevant to the issue before us today is not even mentioned in the Court's opinion: In *Bowers* v. *Hardwick*, we held that the Constitution does not prohibit what virtually all States had done from the founding of the Republic until very recent years—making homosexual conduct a crime." *Bowers*, he continued, "is a given in the present case: Respondents' briefs did not urge overruling *Bowers*, and at oral argument respondents' counsel expressly disavowed any intent to seek such overruling. If it is constitutionally permissible for a State to make homosexual conduct criminal, surely it is constitutionally permissible for a State to enact other laws merely disfavoring homosexual conduct."

To date, the Court's most expansive interpretations of the right to privacy have come in the area of sexual behavior. Claims to personal autonomy in other areas of life have met with a less favorable reception. *Kelley* v. *Johnson* and *Paul* v. *Davis*, both decided in 1976, are cases in point. In *Kelley*, decided 6–2, Justice Rehnquist held for the Court that a county regulation limiting the length of county policemen's hair did not violate any right guaranteed by the Fourteenth Amendment. In particular, he denied that the regulation impermissibly limited the right of privacy or the personal autonomy of the policemen, maintaining that the protections of this right were limited to "infringements on the individual's freedom of choice with respect to certain basic matters of procreation, marriage, and family life." Justice Marshall strenuously dissented: "To say that the liberty guarantee of the Fourteenth Amendment does not encompass matters of personal appearance would be fundamentally inconsistent with the values of privacy, self-identity, autonomy, and personal integrity that I have always assumed the Constitution was designed to protect." In *Paul*, Justice Rehnquist again spoke for the Court, this time to reject, among other things, a privacy claim made by a person who had been listed as an "active shoplifter" in a flyer made up by the Louisville police and distributed to city merchants. He had been arrested for shoplifting but never tried, and the charges against him ultimately had been dropped. Rehnquist held that because the police had not invaded any area traditionally regarded as private, such as "matters related to marriage, procreation, contraception, family relationships, and child rearing and education," there had been no constitutional violation of the right to privacy.

In *Whalen* v. *Roe* (1977), a related case, the Court unanimously sustained a New York statute requiring that the names of persons receiving dangerous prescription drugs be kept in a computer file. The statute had been challenged by an individual who claimed that such lists violated his right to privacy because of the risk that the information might become public. Justice Stevens noted for the Court that privacy cases involve, at minimum, two different types of interests: the individual interest in avoiding disclosure of a personal matter, of which the *Griswold* decision was representative; and the interest in securing independence in making certain kinds of important decisions, of which *Roe* v. *Wade* was illustrative. He concluded that "the New York program does not, on its face, pose a sufficiently grievous threat to either interest to establish a constitutional violation." With respect to a disclosure of personal matters, he emphasized the careful security provisions in the law and insisted that there was no justification for assuming that those provisions would be administered improperly. And with respect to an infringement of the interest in making important decisions independently, he dismissed the claim that patients would decline needed medication in order to keep their names out of the computerized file, insisting that the law did not significantly inhibit the patient-physician decision regarding needed medication.

PRIVACY AND THE RIGHT TO DIE

In his classic work *The Nature of the Judicial Process*, Benjamin Cardozo observed that there is a tendency for a legal principle "to expand to the limits of its logic." That this tendency is especially true of a "greedy concept" such as the "right to be let alone" is apparent in what have come to be called the "right to die" cases.[9]

In *The Matter of Karen Ann Quinlan* (1976), the New Jersey Supreme Court held that the "right to be let alone" extended to the right to die with dignity and that the State of New Jersey could not prevent Karen Ann Quinlan, existing in a "persistent vegetative state," on the request of her legal guardian, from being disconnected from her respirator. To date, the United States Supreme Court has taken a less expansive view. In *Cruzan* v. *Director, Missouri Department of Health* (1990), it held, in a 5–4 decision, that the State of Missouri could involve itself in the decision of whether or not to terminate the artificial nutrition and hydration procedures keeping incompetent patients alive by demanding the production of clear and convincing evidence of the incompetent's wishes as to the withdrawal of treatment. And, in *Washington* v. *Glucksberg* (1997) and *Vacco* v. *Quill* (1997), it overturned Court of Appeals decisions from the Ninth and Second Circuits that had declared unconstitutional laws banning physician-assisted suicide. In *Glucksberg,* it rejected the Ninth Circuit's reliance on *Planned Parenthood of Southeastern Pennsylvania* v. *Casey* and its contention that "[l]ike the decision of whether or not to have an abortion, the decision how and when to die is one of 'the most intimate and personal choices a person may make in a lifetime,' a choice 'central to personal dignity and autonomy.'" In *Vacco,* it rejected the Second Circuit's insistence that the Equal Protection Clause is violated when "some terminally ill people—those who are on life-support systems—are treated differently than those who are not, in that the former may 'hasten death' by ending treatment, but the latter may not 'hasten death' through physician-assisted suicide." As Justice Souter's concurring opinions in *Glucksberg* and *Vacco* make clear, however, he and several of his colleagues were unwilling to deny categorically the existence of a right to die with dignity or to concede anything more than that this is a question best left for now in the hands of state legislators rather than judges. As he wrote in *Glucksberg:* "While I do not decide for all time that respondents' claim should not be recognized, I acknowledge the legislative institutional competence as the better one to deal with that claim at this time."

NOTES

1 Samuel D. Warren and Louis D. Brandeis, "The Right to Privacy." *Harvard Law Review* 4, no. 5 (1890): 193.

2 William H. Rehnquist, "Is an Expanded Right to Privacy Consistent with Fair and Effective Law Enforcement? Or, Privacy, You've Come a Long Way, Baby." *Kansas Law Review* 23 (1974): 6.

3 It should be noted that these decisions, which conceptualized privacy as inhering in the relationship or in the person, supplemented but did not supplant the earlier view that privacy inheres in the place. In *Stanley* v. *Georgia* (1969), for example, the Court operated from the assumption that privacy inheres in the place when it declared that "whereas the States retain broad power to reg-

ulate obscenity, that power simply does not extend to mere possession by the individual in the privacy of his own home."

4 Louis Henkin, "Privacy and Autonomy." *Columbia Law Review* 74 (1974): 1410, 1424–1427.

5 Consider, however, Professor John Hart Ely's observations that a determination of whether a fetus is a "Fourteenth Amendment person" is irrelevant to the question of whether a fetus can be protected: "It has never been held or even asserted that the state interest needed to justify forcing a person to refrain from an activity, whether or not that activity is constitutionally protected, must implicate either the life or the constitutional rights of another person. Dogs are not "persons in the whole sense" nor have they constitutional rights, but that does not mean the state cannot prohibit killing them. It does not even mean the state cannot prohibit killing them in the exercise of the First Amendment right of political protest. Come to think of it, draft cards aren't persons either." John Hart Ely, "The Wages of Crying Wolf: A Comment on *Roe* v. *Wade*." *Yale Law Journal* 82 (1973): 929.

6 The Court's language here is of critical importance to the proponents of the Human Life Statute, which would declare that "the life of each human being begins at conception." They claim that the Court's refusal in *Roe* to treat the fetus as a person merely represented an admission that the judiciary was incapable of deciding the question of when human life begins. Further, they argue, under Section 5 of the Fourteenth Amendment, which empowers Congress to enforce by appropriate legislation the provisions of the amendment, Congress is the appropriate body to resolve that question and, if it finds life to begin at conception, to enforce the obligation of the States under the Fourteenth Amendment not to deprive persons (including unborn children) of life without due process of law. See Stephen H. Galebach, "A Human Life Statute." *The Human Life Review* 5 (1981):3.

7 As Justices O'Connor, Kennedy, and Souter readily acknowledged in their joint opinion, abortion has proved to be an especially "divisive" issue. Organizations opposed to the morality of abortion, such as Operation Rescue, have adopted the tactic of protesting in front of abortion clinics and illegally obstructing access to them in the hopes of thereby dissuading pregnant women seeking abortions from entering. This tactic was challenged by abortion clinics and supporting organizations in *Bray* v. *Alexandria Women's Health Clinic*, 113 S. Ct. 753 (1993). They sought a permanent injunction against Operation Rescue, enjoining them from trespassing on, impeding, or obstructing ingress to or egress from Washington, D.C. area abortion clinics. They claimed that Operation Rescue was conspiring to deprive women seeking abortions of their right to interstate travel and was therefore in violation of the first clause of 42 U.S.C. § 1985—the surviving version of § 2 of the Civil Rights Act of 1871 (otherwise known as the Ku Klux Klan Act of 1871)—which prohibited private conspiracies to deprive "any person or class of persons of the equal protection of the laws, or of equal privileges and immunities under the law." In a 5–4 decision, the Supreme Court rejected this challenge. As Justice Scalia noted for the majority in *Bray*, Operation Rescue's demonstrations were not directed toward any "class of persons." "Whatever one thinks of abortion, it cannot be denied that there are common and respectable reasons for opposing it, other than hatred of or condescension toward (or indeed any view at all concerning) women as a class—as is evident from the fact that men and women are on both sides of the issues, just as men and women

are on both sides of petitioners' unlawful demonstrations." However, in *National Organization of Women* v. *Scheidler*, 114 S. Ct. 798 (1994), the Court unanimously upheld a different kind of challenge to the obstructionist tactics of antiabortion groups; it held that abortion clinics had standing to bring an action against the Pro-Life Action Network and other antiabortion groups for allegedly conspiring to use force to dissuade pregnant women from receiving the clinics' abortion services and therefore to injure the clinics' business and property interests in violation of the Racketeer Influenced and Corrupt Organizations Act (RICO). The antiabortion groups argued that RICO did not apply to them, because they were engaged in "non-economic crimes committed in furtherance of non-economic motives." Chief Justice Rehnquist declared, however, that RICO does not require proof that either the racketeering enterprise or the acts of racketeering themselves have to be motivated by an economic interest. Because of *Scheidler*, antiabortion groups convicted of illegal acts under RICO are subject to treble damage judgments.

8 Paul Freund, "Privacy: One Concept or Many" in *Privacy*, edited by J. Roland Pennock and John W. Chapman (New York: Atherton Press, 1971), p. 192.

9 See also *American Motorcycle Association* v. *Davids*, 158 N.W. 2d 72 (1968), in which the Michigan Court of Appeals invalidated a state law requiring motorcyclists and riders to wear crash helmets by citing Brandeis in *Olmstead* and quoting his language: "The makers of our Constitution . . . conferred, as against the government, the right to be let alone—the most comprehensive of rights and the right most valued by civilized men."

SELECTED READING

Belloti v. *Baird*, 443 U.S. 622 (1979).
Bray v. *Alexandria Women's Health Clinic*, 113 S.Ct. 753 (1993).
Carey v. *Population Services International*, 431 U.S. 678 (1977).
Eisenstadt v. *Baird*, 405 U.S. 438 (1972).
Harris v. *McRae*, 448 U.S. 297 (1980).
Maher v. *Roe*, 432 U.S. 464 (1977).
The Matter of Karen Ann Quinlan, 355 A.2d 647 (1976).
National Organization of Women v. *Scheidler*, 114 S.Ct. 798 (1994).
Planned Parenthood of Central Missouri v. *Danforth*, 428 U.S. 52 (1976).
Time v. *Hill*, 385 U.S. 374 (1967).

Barnett, Randy, ed. *The Rights Retained by the People: The History and Meaning of the Ninth Amendment* (Fairfax, Va.: George Mason University Press, 1989).
Berger, Raoul. "The Ninth Amendment." *Cornell Law Review* 66 (1980): 1–26.
Bork, Robert H. *The Tempting of America: The Political Seduction of Law* (New York: Free Press, 1990), pp. 110–132.
Burgess, Susan R. *Contest for Constitutional Authority: The Abortion and War Powers Debates* (Lawrence: University Press of Kansas, 1992).
DeRosa, Marshall L. *The Ninth Amendment and the Politics of Creative Jurisprudence* (New Brunswick, N.J.: Transaction Publishers, 1996).
Dionisopoulos, P. Alan, and Craig R. Ducat. *The Right to Privacy: Essays and Cases* (St. Paul, Minn.: West, 1976).
Ely, John Hart. "The Wages of Crying Wolf: A Comment on *Roe* v. *Wade*." *Yale Law Journal* 82 (1973): 920–949.

Epstein, Lee. *The Supreme Court and Legal Change: Abortion and the Death Penalty* (Chapel Hill: University of North Carolina Press, 1992).

Galebach, Stephan H. "A Human Life Statute." *The Human Life Review* 5 (1981): 3–31.

Garrow, David. *Liberty and Sexuality* (New York: Macmillan, 1994).

Glendon, Mary Ann. *Abortion and Divorce in Western Law* (Cambridge, Mass: Harvard University Press, 1987).

Hixson, Richard F. *Privacy in a Public Society: Human Rights in Conflict* (New York: Oxford University Press, 1987).

Judges, Donald P. *Hard Choices, Lost Voices: How the Abortion Conflict Has Divided America, Distorted Constitutional Law, and Damaged the Courts* (Chicago: Ivan R. Dee, 1993).

McConnell, Michael W. "The Selective Funding Problem: Abortions and Religious Schools." *Harvard Law Review* 104 (1991): 989–1050.

McWhirter, Darien A. *Privacy as a Constitutional Right: Sex, Drugs, and the Right to Life* (New York: Quorum Books, 1992).

Pennock, J. Roland and John W. Chapman, eds. *Privacy* (New York: Atherton Press, 1971).

Posner, Richard A. *Sex and Reason* (Cambridge, Mass.: Harvard University Press, 1992).

Presser, Stephen B. *Recapturing the Constitution: Race, Religion, and Abortion Reconsidered* (Washington, D.C.: Regnery Publishing Co., 1994).

Rubin, Eva R. *Abortion, Politics, and the Courts:* Roe v. Wade *and Its Aftermath* (New York: Greenwood, 1987).

Seidman, Louis Michael. "Confusion at the Border: *Cruzan,* "The Right to Die," and the Public/Private Distinction." *1991 Supreme Court Review,* edited by Dennis J. Hutchinson, David A. Strauss, and Geoffrey R. Stone (Chicago: University of Chicago Press, 1992).

Uhlmann, Michael M. *Last Rights? Assisted Suicide and Euthanasia Debated* (Grand Rapids, Mich.: Eerdmans, 1998).

Warren, Samuel D. and Louis D. Brandeis. "The Right to Privacy." *Harvard Law Review* 4 (1890): 193.

Westin, Alan F. *Privacy and Freedom* (New York: Atheneum, 1967).

Who Cares?

Griswold v. Connecticut

381 U.S. 479; 85 S. Ct. 1678; 14 L. Ed. 2d 510 (1965)

A Connecticut statute proscribed the use of birth control devices and made it a criminal offense for anyone to give information or instruction on their use. Estelle Griswold, executive director of the Planned Parenthood League of Connecticut, and Dr. Buxton, its medical director and a professor at the Yale Medical School, were convicted of dispensing such information to married persons in violation of the law and were fined $100. After a state appellate court and the Connecticut Supreme Court of Errors affirmed the convictions, the defendants appealed to the United States Supreme Court. It should be noted that the same statute had previously been unsuccessfully challenged in *Tileston* v. *Ullman* (1943) and *Poe* v. *Ullman* (1961). *Opinion of the Court:* <u>Douglas</u>, Brennan, Clark, Goldberg, Warren. *Concurring opinion:* <u>Goldberg</u>, Brennan, Warren. *Concurring in result:* Harlan; White. *Dissenting opinions:* <u>Black</u>, Stewart; <u>Stewart</u>, Black.

MR. JUSTICE DOUGLAS delivered the opinion of the Court. . . .

. . . We are met with a wide range of questions that implicate the Due Process Clause of the Fourteenth Amendment. Overtones of some arguments suggest that *Lochner* v. *State of New York* [1905] . . . should be our guide. But we decline that invitation as we did in *West Coast Hotel Co.* v. *Parrish* [1937] . . . We do not sit as a superlegislature to determine the wisdom, need, and propriety of laws that touch economic problems, business affairs, or social conditions. This law, however, operates directly on an intimate relation of husband and wife and their physician's role in one aspect of that relation.

The association of people is not mentioned in the Constitution nor in the Bill of Rights. The right to educate a child in a school of the parents' choice—whether public or private or parochial—is also not mentioned. Nor is the right to study any particular subject or any foreign language. Yet the First Amendment has been construed to include certain of those rights. . . .

[Previous] cases suggest that specific guarantees in the Bill of Rights have penumbras, formed by emanations from those guarantees that help give them life and substance. . . . Various guarantees create zones of privacy. The right of association contained in the penumbra of the First Amendment is one. . . . The Third Amendment in its prohibition against the quartering of soldiers "in any house" in time of peace without the consent of the owner is another facet of that privacy. The Fourth Amendment explicitly affirms the "right of the people to be secure in their persons, houses, papers, and effects, against unreasonable searches and seizures." The Fifth Amendment in its Self-Incrimination Clause enables the citizen to create a zone of privacy which government may not force him to surrender to his detriment. The Ninth Amendment provides: "The enumeration in the Constitution, of certain rights, shall not be construed to deny or disparage others retained by the people. . . .

The Fourth and Fifth Amendments were described in *Boyd* v. *United States* [1886] . . . as protection against all governmental invasions "of the sanctity of a man's home and the privacies of life." We recently referred in *Mapp* v. *Ohio* [1961] . . . to the Fourth Amendment as creating a "right to privacy, no less important than any other right carefully and particularly reserved to the people." . . .

We have had many controversies over these penumbral rights of "privacy and repose." . . . These cases bear witness that the right of privacy which presses for recognition here is a legitimate one.

The present case, then, concerns a relationship lying within the zone of privacy created by several fundamental constitutional guarantees. And it concerns a law which, in forbidding the *use* of contraceptives rather than regulating their manufacture or sale, seeks to achieve its goals by means having a maximum destructive impact upon that relationship. Such a law cannot stand in light of the familiar principle, so often applied by this Court, that a "governmental purpose to control or prevent activities constitutionally subject to state regulation may not be achieved by means which sweep unnecessarily broadly and thereby invade the area of protected freedoms." . . . Would we allow the police to search the sacred precincts of marital bedrooms for telltale signs of the use of contraceptives? The very idea is repulsive to the notions of privacy surrounding the marriage relationship.

We deal with a right of privacy older than the Bill of Rights—older than our political parties, older than our school system. Marriage is a coming together for better or worse, hopefully enduring, and intimate to the degree of being sacred. It is an association that promotes a way of life, not causes; a harmony in living, not political faiths; a bilateral loyalty, not commercial or social projects. Yet it is an association for as noble a purpose as any involved in our prior decisions.

Reversed.

Mr. Justice Goldberg, whom The Chief Justice and Mr. Justice Brennan join, concurring.

I agree with the Court that Connecticut's birth-control law unconstitutionally intrudes upon the right of marital privacy, and I join in its opinion and judgment. Although I have not accepted the view that "due process" as used in the Fourteenth Amendment includes all of the first eight Amendments, . . . I do agree that the concept of liberty protects those personal rights that are fundamental, and is not confined to the specific terms of the Bill of Rights. My conclusion that the concept of liberty is not so restricted and that it embraces the right of marital privacy though that right is not mentioned explicitly in the Constitution is supported both by numerous decisions of this Court, referred to in the Court's opinion, and by the language and history of the Ninth Amendment. In reaching the conclusion that the right of marital privacy is protected, as being within the protected penumbra of specific guarantees of the Bill of Rights, the Court refers to the Ninth Amendment. . . . I add these words to emphasize the relevance of that Amendment to the Court's holding.

The Court stated many years ago that the Due Process Clause protects those liberties that are "so rooted in the traditions and conscience of our people as to be ranked as fundamental." . . . This Court, in a series of decisions, has held that the Fourteenth Amendment absorbs and applies to the States those specifics of the first eight amendments which express fundamental personal rights. The language and history of the Ninth Amendment reveal that the Framers of the Constitution believed that there are additional fundamental rights, protected from governmental infringement, which exist alongside those fundamental rights specifically mentioned in the first eight constitutional amendments.

. . . It was proffered to quiet expressed fears that a bill of specifically enumerated rights could not be sufficiently broad to cover all essential rights and that the specific mention of certain rights would be interpreted as a denial that others were protected. . . .

A dissenting opinion suggests that my interpretation of the Ninth Amendment somehow "broaden[s] the powers of this Court." . . . I do not mean to imply that the Ninth Amendment is applied against the States by the Fourteenth. Nor do I mean to state that the Ninth Amendment constitutes an independent source of rights protected from infringement by either the States or the Federal Government. Rather, the Ninth Amendment shows a belief of the Constitution's authors that fundamental rights exist that are not expressly enumerated in the first eight amendments and an intent that the list of rights included there not be deemed exhaustive. As any student of this Court's opinions knows, this Court has held, often unanimously, that the Fifth and Fourteenth Amendments protect certain fundamental personal liberties from abridgment by the Federal Government or the States. . . . The Ninth Amendment simply shows the intent of the Constitution's authors that other fundamental personal rights should not be denied such protection or disparaged in any other way simply because they are not specifically listed in the first eight constitutional amendments. I do not see how this broadens the authority of the Court; rather it serves to support what this Court has been doing in protecting fundamental rights.

Nor am I turning somersaults with history in arguing that the Ninth Amendment is relevant in a case dealing with a *State's* infringement of a fundamental right. While the Ninth Amendment—and indeed the entire Bill of Rights—originally concerned restrictions upon *federal* power, the subsequently enacted Fourteenth Amendment prohibits the States as well from abridging fundamental personal liberties. And, the Ninth Amendment, in indicating that not all such liberties are specifically mentioned in the first eight amendments, is surely relevant in showing the existence of other fundamental personal rights, now protected from state, as well as federal, infringement. In sum, the Ninth Amendment simply lends strong support to the view that the "liberty" protected by the Fifth and Fourteenth Amendments from infringement by the Federal Government or the States is not restricted to rights specifically mentioned in the first eight amendments. . . .

The entire fabric of the Constitution and the purposes that clearly underlie its specific guarantees demonstrate that the rights to marital privacy and to marry and raise a family are of similar order and magnitude as the fundamental rights specifically protected.

Although the Constitution does not speak in so many words of the right of privacy in marriage, I cannot believe that it offers these fundamental rights no protection. The fact that no particular provision of the Constitution explicitly forbids the State from disrupting the traditional relation of the family—a relation as old and as fundamental as our entire civilization—surely does not show that the Government was meant to have the power to do so. Rather, as the Ninth Amendment expressly recognizes, there are fundamental personal rights such as this one, which are protected from abridgment by the Government though not specifically mentioned in the Constitution. . . .

The logic of the dissents would sanction federal or state legislation that seems to me even more plainly unconstitutional than the statute before us. Surely the Government, absent a showing of a compelling subordinating state interest, could not decree that all husbands and wives must be sterilized after two children have been born to them. Yet by their reasoning such an invasion of marital privacy would not be subject to constitutional challenge because, while it might be "silly," no provision of the Constitution specifically prevents the Government from curtailing the marital right to bear children and raise a family. While it may shock some of my Brethren that the Court today holds that the

Constitution protects the right of marital privacy, in my view it is far more shocking to believe that the personal liberty guaranteed by the Constitution does not include protection against such totalitarian limitation of family size, which is at complete variance with our constitutional concepts. Yet, if upon a showing of a slender basis of rationality, a law outlawing voluntary birth control by married persons is valid, then, by the same reasoning, a law requiring compulsory birth control also would seem to be valid. In my view, however, both types of law would unjustifiably intrude upon rights of marital privacy which are constitutionally protected.

In sum, I believe that the right of privacy in the marital relation is fundamental and basic—a personal right "retained by the people" within the meaning of the Ninth Amendment. Connecticut cannot constitutionally abridge this fundamental right, which is protected by the Fourteenth Amendment from infringement by the States. I agree with the Court that petitioners' convictions must therefore be reversed.

MR. JUSTICE HARLAN, concurring.

I fully agree with the judgment of reversal, but find myself unable to join the Court's opinion. . . .

In my view, the proper constitutional inquiry in this case is whether this Connecticut statute infringes the Due Process Clause of the Fourteenth Amendment because the enactment violates basic values "implicit in the concept of ordered liberty," *Palko* v. *State of Connecticut.* [1937] . . . I believe that it does. While the relevant inquiry may be aided by resort to one or more of the provisions of the Bill of Rights, it is not dependent on them or any of their radiations. The Due Process Clause of the Fourteenth Amendment stands, in my opinion, on its own bottom. . . .

While I could not more heartily agree that judicial "self restraint" is an indispensable ingredient of sound constitutional adjudication, I do submit that the formula suggested for achieving it is more hollow than real. "Specific" provisions of the Constitution, no less than "due process," lend themselves as readily to "personal" interpretations by judges whose constitutional outlook is simply to keep the Constitution in supposed "tune with the times." . . .

Judicial self-restraint will not, I suggest, be brought about in the "due process" area by the historically unfounded incorporation formula long advanced by my Brother Black, and now in part espoused by my Brother Stewart. It will be achieved in this area, as in other constitutional areas, only by continual insistence upon respect for the teachings of history, solid recognition of the basic values that underlie our society, and wise appreciation of the great roles that the doctrines of federalism and separation of powers have played in establishing and preserving American freedoms. . . . Adherence to these principles will not, of course, obviate all constitutional differences of opinion among judges, nor should it. Their continued recognition will, however, go farther toward keeping most judges from roaming at large in the constitutional field than will the interpolation into the Constitution of an artificial and largely illusory restriction on the content of the Due Process Clause.

MR. JUSTICE BLACK, with whom MR. JUSTICE STEWART joins, dissenting.

I agree with my Brother Stewart's dissenting opinion. And like him I do not to any extent whatever base my view that this Connecticut law is constitutional on a belief that the law is wise or that its policy is a good one. In order that there may be no room at all to doubt why I vote as I do, I feel constrained to add that the law is every bit as [personally] offensive to me as it is my Brethren. . . .

. . . I get nowhere in this case by talk about a constitutional "right of privacy" as an emanation from one or more constitutional provisions. I like my privacy as well as the next one, but I am nevertheless compelled to admit that government has a right to invade it unless prohibited by some specific constitutional provision. For these reasons I cannot agree with the Court's judgment and the reasons it gives for holding this Connecticut law unconstitutional. . . .

I realize that many good and able men have eloquently spoken and written, sometimes in rhapsodical strains, about the duty of this Court to keep the Constitution in tune with the times. The idea is that the Constitution must be changed from time to time and that this Court is charged with a duty to make those changes. For myself, I must with all deference reject that philosophy. The Constitution makers knew the need for change and provided for it. Amendments suggested by the people's elected representatives can be submitted to the people or their selected agents for ratification. That method of change was good for our Fathers, and being somewhat old-fashioned I must add it is good enough for me. And so, I cannot rely on the Due Process Clause or the Ninth Amendment or any mysterious and uncertain natural law concept as a reason for striking down this state law. The Due Process Clause with an "arbitrary and capricious" or "shocking to the conscience" formula was liberally used by this Court to strike down economic legislation in the early decades of this century, threatening, many people thought, the tranquility and stability of the Nation. . . . That formula, based on subjective considerations of "natural justice," is no less dangerous when used to enforce this Court's views about personal rights than those about economic rights. I had thought that we had laid that formula, as a means for striking down state legislation to rest once and for all in cases like *West Coast Hotel Co.* v. *Parrish*. . . .

MR. JUSTICE STEWART, whom MR. JUSTICE BLACK joins, dissenting.

Since 1879 Connecticut has had on its books a law which forbids the use of contraceptives by anyone. I think this is an uncommonly silly law. As a practical matter, the law is obviously unenforceable, except in the oblique context of the present case. . . . But we are not asked in this case to say whether we think this law is unwise, or even asinine. We are asked to hold that it violates the United States Constitution. And that I cannot do.

In the course of its opinion the Court refers to no less than six Amendments to the Constitution: the First, the Third, the Fourth, the Fifth, the Ninth, and the Fourteenth. But the Court does not say which of these Amendments, if any, it thinks is infringed by this Connecticut law. . . .

The Court also quotes the Ninth Amendment, and my Brother Goldberg's concurring opinion relies heavily upon it. But to say that the Ninth Amendment has anything to do with this case is to turn somersaults with history. The Ninth Amendment, like its companion the Tenth, which this Court held "states but a truism that all is retained which has not been surrendered," *United States* v. *Darby* [1941], . . . was framed by James Madison and adopted by the States simply to make clear that the adoption of the Bill of Rights did not alter the plan that the *Federal* Government was to be a government of express and limited powers, and that all rights and powers not delegated to it were retained by the people and the individual States. Until today no member of this Court has ever suggested that the Ninth Amendment meant anything else, and the idea that a federal court could ever use the Ninth Amendment to annul a law passed by the elected representatives of the people of the State of Connecticut would have caused James Madison no little wonder.

What provision of the Constitution, then, does make this state law invalid? The Court says it is the right of privacy "created by several fundamental constitutional guarantees." With all deference, I can find no such general right of privacy in the Bill of Rights, in any other part of the Constitution, or in any case ever before decided by this Court. . . .

Roe v. *Wade*
410 U.S. 113; 93 S. Ct. 705; 35 L. Ed. 2d 147 (1973)

A Texas abortion statute made it a felony for anyone to destroy a fetus except on "medical advice for the purpose of saving the life of the mother." This law was typical of abortion statutes in effect in most states for approximately a century. Jane Roe (the pseudonym for an unmarried pregnant woman) brought suit against District Attorney Wade of Dallas County for declaratory and injunctive relief. She challenged the statute on grounds that it denied equal protection (in that it forced women who did not have the money to have a baby when those who had money could go elsewhere and procure a safe, legal abortion), due process (because the statute was vague as to what "saving the life of the mother" actually meant), and the mother's right of privacy guaranteed under the First, Fourth, Fifth, Ninth, and Fourteenth Amendments. A three-judge federal district court found the statute unconstitutional, and Texas appealed to the Supreme Court. The Court heard *Roe* in conjunction with *Doe* v. *Bolton* (1973), in which a modern "reform" abortion statute from Georgia was also challenged. *Opinion of the Court:* Blackmun, Brennan, Burger, Douglas, Marshall, Powell, Stewart. *Concurring opinions:* Burger, Douglas; Stewart. *Dissenting opinions:* White, Rehnquist; Rehnquist.

MR. JUSTICE BLACKMUN delivered the opinion of the Court. . . .

We forthwith acknowledge our awareness of the sensitive and emotional nature of the abortion controversy, of the vigorous opposing views, even among physicians, and of the deep and seemingly absolute convictions that the subject inspires. One's philosophy, one's experiences, one's exposure to the raw edges of human existence, one's religious training, one's attitudes toward life and family and their values, and the moral standards one establishes and seeks to observe, are all likely to influence and to color one's thinking and conclusions about abortion.

In addition, population growth, pollution, poverty, and racial overtones tend to complicate and not to simplify the problem.

Our task, of course, is to resolve the issue by constitutional measurement, free of emotion and of predilection. We seek earnestly to do this, and, because we do, we have inquired into, and in this opinion place some emphasis upon, medical and medical-legal history and what that history reveals about man's attitudes toward the abortion procedure over the centuries. We bear in mind, too, Mr. Justice Holmes' admonition in his now-vindicated dissent in *Lochner* v. *New York* . . . (1905): "[The Constitution] is made for people of fundamentally differing views, and the accident of our finding certain opinions natural and familiar or novel and even shocking ought not to conclude our judgment upon the question whether statutes embodying them conflict with the Constitution of the United States." . . .

The principal thrust of appellant's attack on the Texas statutes is that they improperly invade a right, said to be possessed by the pregnant woman, to choose to terminate her pregnancy. Appellant would discover this right in the concept of personal "liberty" embodied in the Fourteenth Amendment's Due Process Clause; or in personal, marital, familial, and sexual privacy said to be protected by the Bill of Rights or its penumbras, . . . or among those rights reserved to the people by the Ninth Amendment. . . . Before addressing this claim, we feel it desirable briefly to survey, in several aspects, the history of abortion, for such insight as that history may afford us, and then to examine the state purposes and interests behind the criminal abortion laws. . . .

It perhaps is not generally appreciated that the restrictive criminal abortion laws in effect in a majority of States today are of relatively recent vintage. Those laws, generally proscribing abortion or its attempt at any time during pregnancy except when necessary to preserve the pregnant woman's life, are not of ancient or even of common-law origin. Instead, they derive from statutory changes effected, for the most part, in the latter half of the 19th century. . . .

Three reasons have been advanced to explain historically the enactment of criminal abortion laws in the 19th century and to justify their continued existence.

It has been argued occasionally that these laws were the product of a Victorian social concern to discourage illicit sexual conduct. Texas, however, does not advance this justification in the present case, and it appears that no court or commentator has taken the argument seriously. . . .

A second reason is concerned with abortion as a medical procedure. When most criminal abortion laws were first enacted, the procedure was a hazardous one for the woman. . . . Thus, it has been argued that a State's real concern in enacting a criminal abortion law was to protect the pregnant woman, that is, to restrain her from submitting to a procedure that placed her life in serious jeopardy.

Modern medical techniques have altered this situation. . . .

The third reason is the State's interest—some phrase it in terms of duty—in protecting prenatal life. Some of the argument for this justification rests on the theory that a new human life is present from the moment of conception. The State's interest and general obligation to protect life then extends, it is argued, to prenatal life. Only when the life of the pregnant mother herself is at stake, balanced against the life she carries within her, should the interest of the embryo or fetus not prevail. Logically, of course, a legitimate state interest in this area need not stand or fall on acceptance of the belief that life begins at conception or at some other point prior to live birth. In assessing the State's interest, recognition may be given to the less rigid claim that as long as at least *potential* life is involved, the State may assert interests beyond the protection of the pregnant woman alone. . . .

It is with these interests, and the weight to be attached to them, that this case is concerned. . . .

The Constitution does not explicitly mention any right of privacy. In a line of decisions, however, going back perhaps as far as . . . 1891, the Court has recognized that a right of personal privacy, or a guarantee of certain areas or zones of privacy, does exist under the Constitution. In varying contexts, the Court or individual Justices have, indeed, found at least the roots of that right in the First Amendment, . . . in the Fourth and Fifth Amendments, . . . in the penumbras of the Bill of Rights, . . . in the Ninth Amendment, . . . or in the concept of liberty guaranteed by the first section of the Fourteenth Amendment. . . . These decisions make it clear that only personal rights that can be deemed "fundamental" or "implicit in the concept of ordered liberty" . . . are included in this guarantee of personal privacy. They also make it clear that the right has some extension to activities relating to marriage, . . . procreation, . . . contraception, . . . family relationships, . . . and child rearing and education. . . .

This right of privacy, whether it be founded in the Fourteenth Amendment's concept of personal liberty and restrictions upon state action, as we feel it is, or, as the District Court determined, in the Ninth Amendment's reservation of rights to the people, is broad enough to encompass a woman's decision whether or not to terminate her pregnancy. The detriment that the State would impose upon the pregnant woman by denying this choice altogether is apparent. Specific and direct harm medically diagnosable even in early pregnancy may be involved. Maternity, or additional offspring, may force upon the woman a distressful life and future. Psychological harm may be imminent. Mental and physical health may be taxed by child care. There is also the distress, for all concerned, associated with the unwanted child, and there is the problem of bringing a child into a family already unable, psychologically and otherwise, to care for it. In other cases, as in this one, the additional difficulties and continuing stigma of unwed motherhood may be involved. All these are factors the woman and her responsible physician necessarily will consider in consultation.

On the basis of elements such as these, appellant and some *amici* argue that the woman's right is absolute and that she is entitled to terminate her pregnancy at whatever time, in whatever way, and for whatever reason she alone chooses. With this we do not agree. Appellant's arguments that Texas either has no valid interest at all in regulating the abortion decision, or no interest strong enough to support any limitation upon the woman's sole determination, is unpersuasive. The Court's decisions recognizing a right of privacy also acknowledge that some state regulation in areas protected by that right is appropriate. As noted above, a State may properly assert important interests in safeguarding health, in maintaining medical standards, and in protecting potential life. At some point in pregnancy, these respective interests become sufficiently compelling to sustain regulation of the factors that govern the abortion decision. The privacy right involved, therefore, cannot be said to be absolute. In fact, it is not clear to us that the claim asserted by some *amici* that one has an unlimited right to do with one's body as one pleases bears a close relationship to the right of privacy previously articulated in the Court's decisions. The Court has refused to recognize an unlimited right of this kind in the past. . . .

We, therefore, conclude that the right of personal privacy includes the abortion decision, but that this right is not unqualified and must be considered against important state interests in regulation. . . .

Where certain "fundamental rights" are involved, the Court has held that a regulation limiting these rights may be justified only by a "compelling state interest" . . . and that legislative enactments must be narrowly drawn to express only the legitimate state interests at stake. . . .

The District Court held that the appellee failed to meet his burden of demonstrating that the Texas statute's infringement upon Roe's rights was necessary to support a compelling state interest, and that, although the appellee presented "several compelling justifications for state presence in the area of abortions," the statutes outstripped these justifications and swept "far beyond any areas of compelling state interest." . . . Appellant and appellee both contest that holding. Appellant, as has been indicated, claims an absolute right that bars any state imposition of criminal penalties in the area. Appellee argues that the State's determination to recognize and protect prenatal life from and after conception constitutes a compelling state interest. . . . We do not agree fully with either formulation.

A. The appellee and certain *amici* argue that the fetus is a "person" within the language and meaning of the Fourteenth Amendment. In support of this, they outline at length and in detail the well-known facts of fetal development. If this suggestion of personhood is established, the appellant's case, of course, collapses, for the fetus' right to life is then guaranteed specifically by the Amendment. The appellant conceded as much on reargument. On the other hand, the appellee conceded on reargument that no case could be cited that holds that a fetus is a person within the meaning of the Fourteenth Amendment.

The Constitution does not define "persons" in so many words. . . . [I]n nearly all . . . instances [in which the word *person* is used], the use of the word is such that it has application only postnatally. None indicates, with any assurance, that it has any possible pre-natal application.

All this, together with our observation . . . that throughout the major portion of the 19th century prevailing legal abortion practices were far freer than they are today, persuades us that the word "person," as used in the Fourteenth Amendment, does not include the unborn. . . .

This conclusion, however, does not of itself fully answer the contentions raised by Texas, and we pass on to other considerations.

B. The pregnant woman cannot be isolated in her privacy. She carries an embryo and, later, a fetus, if one accepts the medical definitions of the developing young in the human uterus. . . . The situation therefore is inherently different from marital intimacy, or bedroom possession of obscene material, or marriage, or procreation, or education. . . . As we have intimated above, it is reasonable and appropriate for a State to decide that at some point in time another interest, that of health of the mother or that of potential human life, becomes significantly involved. The woman's privacy is no longer sole and any right of privacy she possesses must be measured accordingly.

Texas urges that, apart from the Fourteenth Amendment, life begins at conception and is present throughout pregnancy, and that, therefore, the State has a compelling interest in protecting that life from and after conception. We need not resolve the difficult question of when life begins. When those trained in the respective disciplines of medicine, philosophy, and theology are unable to arrive at any consensus, the judiciary, at this point in the development of man's knowledge, is not in a position to speculate as to the answer. . . .

In view of . . . this, we do not agree that, by adopting one theory of life, Texas may override the rights of the pregnant woman that are at stake. We repeat, however, that the State does have an important and legitimate interest in preserving and protecting the health of the pregnant woman, whether she be a resident of the State or a nonresident who seeks medical consultation and treatment there, and that it has still *another* important and legitimate interest in protecting the potentiality of human life. These interests are separate and distinct. Each grows in substantiality as the woman approaches term and, at a point during pregnancy, each becomes "compelling."

With respect to the State's important and legitimate interest in the health of the mother, the "compelling" point, in the light of present medical knowledge, is at approximately the end of the first trimester. This is so because of the now-established medical fact . . . that until the end of the first trimester mortality in abortion may be less than mortality in normal childbirth. It follows that, from and after this point, a State may regulate the abortion procedure to the extent that the regulation reasonably relates to the preservation and protection of maternal health. Examples of permissible state regulation in this area are requirements as to the qualifications of the person who is to perform the abortion; as to the licensure of that person; as to the facility in which the procedure is to be performed, that is, whether it must be a hospital or may be a clinic or some other place of less-than-hospital status; as to the licensing of the facility; and the like.

This means, on the other hand, that, for the period of pregnancy prior to this "compelling" point, the attending physician, in consultation with his patient, is free to determine, without regulation by the State, that, in his medical judgment, the patient's pregnancy should be terminated. If that decision is reached, the judgment may be effectuated by an abortion free of interference by the State. With respect to the State's important and legitimate interest in potential life, the "compelling" point is at viability. This is so because the fetus then presumably has the capability of meaningful life outside the mother's womb. State regulation protective of fetal life after viability thus has both logical and biological justifications. If the State is interested in protecting fetal life after viability, it may go so far as to proscribe abortion during that period, except when it is necessary to preserve the life or health of the mother.

Measured against these standards, Art. 1196 of the Texas Penal Code, in restricting legal abortions to those "procured or attempted by medical advice for the purpose of saving the life of the mother," sweeps too broadly. The statute makes no distinction between abortions performed early in pregnancy and those performed later, and it limits to a single reason, "saving" the mother's life, the legal justification for the procedure. The statute, therefore, cannot survive the constitutional attack made upon it here. . . .

To summarize and to repeat:

1. A state criminal abortion statute of the current Texas type, that excepts from criminality only a *lifesaving* procedure on behalf of the mother, without regard to pregnancy stage and without recognition of the other interests involved, is violative of the Due Process Clause of the Fourteenth Amendment. (*a*) For the stage prior to approximately the end of the first trimester, the abortion decision and its effectuation must be left to the medical judgment of the pregnant woman's attending physician. (*b*) For the stage subsequent to approximately the end of the first trimester, the State, in promoting its interest in the health of the mother, may, if it chooses, regulate the abortion procedure in ways that are reasonably related to maternal health. (*c*) For the stage subsequent to viability, the State in promoting its interest in the potentiality of human life may, if it chooses, regulate, and even proscribe, abortion except where it is necessary, in appropriate medical judgment, for the preservation of the life or health of the mother. . . .

This holding, we feel, is consistent with the relative weights of the respective interests involved, with the lessons and examples of medical and legal history, with the lenity of the common law, and with the demands of the profound problems of the present day. . . .

MR. JUSTICE REHNQUIST, dissenting.

. . . I have difficulty in concluding, as the Court does, that the right of "privacy" is involved in this case. Texas, by the statute here challenged, bars the performance of a medical abortion by a licensed physician on a plaintiff such as Roe. A transaction resulting in an operation such as this is not "private" in the ordinary usage of that word. Nor is the "privacy" that the Court finds here even a distant relative of the freedom from searches and seizures protected by the Fourth Amendment to the Constitution, which the Court has referred to as embodying a right to privacy. . . .

If the Court means by the term "privacy" no more than that the claim of a person to be free from unwanted state regulation of consensual transactions may be a form of "liberty" protected by the Fourteenth Amendment, there is no doubt that similar claims have been upheld in our earlier decisions on the basis of that liberty. I agree with the statement of Mr. Justice Stewart in his concurring opinion that the "liberty," against deprivation of which without due process the Fourteenth Amendment protects, embraces more than the rights found in the Bill of Rights. But that liberty is not guaranteed absolutely against deprivation, only against deprivation without due process of law. The test traditionally applied in the area of social and economic legislation is whether or not a law such as that challenged has a rational relation to a valid state objective. . . . The Due Process Clause of the Fourteenth Amendment undoubtedly does place a limit, albeit a broad one, on legislative power to enact laws such as this. If the Texas statute were to prohibit an abortion even where the mother's life is in jeopardy, I have little doubt that such a statute would lack a rational relation to a valid state objective. . . . But the Court's sweeping invalidation of any restrictions on abortion during the first trimester is impossible to justify under that standard, and the conscious weighing of competing factors that the Court's opinion apparently substitutes for the established test is far more appropriate to a legislative judgment than to a judicial one.

The Court eschews the history of the Fourteenth Amendment in its reliance on the "compelling state interest" test. . . . But the Court adds a new wrinkle to this test by transposing it from the legal considerations associated with the Equal Protection Clause of the Fourteenth Amendment to this case arising under the Due Process Clause of the Fourteenth Amendment. Unless I misapprehend the consequences of this transplanting of the "compelling state interest test," the Court's opinion will accomplish the seemingly impossible feat of leaving this area of the law more confused than it found it.

While the Court's opinion quotes from the dissent of Mr. Justice Holmes in *Lochner* v. *New York*, . . . the result it reaches is more closely attuned to the majority opinion of Mr. Justice Peckham in that case. As in *Lochner* and similar cases applying substantive due process standards to economic and social welfare legislation, the adoption of the compelling state interest standard will inevitably require this Court to exam-

inc the legislative policies and pass on the wisdom of these policies in the very process of deciding whether a particular state interest put forward may or may not be "compelling." The
decision here to break pregnancy into three distinct terms and to outline the permissible restrictions the State may impose in each one, for
example, partakes more of judicial legislation
than it does of a determination of the intent of
the drafters of the Fourteenth Amendment.

Planned Parenthood of Southeastern Pennsylvania v. Casey
505 U.S. 833; 112 S. Ct. 2791; 120 L. Ed. 2d 674 (1992)

Central to this case were five provisions of the Pennsylvania Abortion
Control Act of 1982. One required that a woman seeking an abortion
give her informed consent prior to the procedure and specified that she
be provided with certain information at least twenty-four hours before
the abortion is performed; the second mandated the informed consent of
one parent for a minor to obtain an abortion, but provided for a judicial
bypass procedure; the third required, subject to certain exceptions, that a
married woman seeking an abortion must sign a statement indicating
that she has notified her husband; the fourth defined a "medical emergency" that will excuse compliance with the foregoing requirements;
and the fifth imposed certain reporting requirements on facilities providing abortion services.

Before any of these provisions took effect, five abortion clinics and a
physician, representing himself and a class of doctors who provided abortion services, brought suit in U.S. District Court for the Eastern District of
Pennsylvania, seeking a declaratory judgment that each of these provisions was unconstitutional, as well as injunctive relief. On the basis of
Roe v. *Wade* (1973), *Akron* v. *Akron Center for Reproductive Health*
(1983), and *Thornburgh* v. *American College of Obstetricians and Gynecologists* (1986), the district court held all of the provisions unconstitutional and permanently enjoined their enforcement. The Court of Appeals
for the Third Circuit reversed in part and affirmed in part, upholding all of
the act's provisions with the exception of spousal notification. The
Supreme Court granted certiorari. *Judgment of the Court and opinion of
the Court in part:* O'Connor, Kennedy, Souter. *Concurring in the opinion
in part and the judgment in part and dissenting in part:* Blackmun;
Stevens. *Concurring in the judgment in part and dissenting in part:* Rehnquist, *Scalia, Thomas, White;* Scalia, *Rehnquist, Thomas, White.*

JUSTICE O'CONNOR, JUSTICE KENNEDY, and JUSTICE
SOUTER announced the judgment of the Court
and delivered the opinion of the Court in part.

After considering the fundamental constitutional questions resolved by *Roe*, principles of institutional integrity, and the rule of *stare decisis*,
we are led to conclude this: the essential holding
of *Roe* v. *Wade* should be retained and once again
reaffirmed.

It must be stated at the outset and with clarity
that *Roe's* essential holding, the holding we reaffirm, has three parts. First is a recognition of the
right of the woman to choose to have an abortion
before viability and to obtain it without undue
interference from the State. Before viability, the
State's interests are not strong enough to support
a prohibition of abortion or the imposition of a
substantial obstacle to the woman's effective

right to elect the procedure. Second is a confirmation of the State's power to restrict abortions after fetal viability, if the law contains exceptions for pregnancies which endanger a woman's life or health. And third is the principle that the State has legitimate interests from the outset of the pregnancy in protecting the health of the woman and the life of the fetus that may become a child. These principles do not contradict one another; and we adhere to each. . . . .

The obligation to follow precedent begins with necessity, and a contrary necessity marks its outer limit. With Cardozo, we recognize that no judicial system could do society's work if it eyed each issue afresh in every case that raised it. Indeed, the very concept of the rule of law underlying our own Constitution requires such continuity over time that a respect for precedent is, by definition, indispensable. At the other extreme, a different necessity would make itself felt if a prior judicial ruling should come to be seen so clearly as error that its enforcement was for that very reason doomed. . . .

So in this case we may inquire whether Roe's central rule has been found unworkable; whether the rule's limitation on state power could be removed without serious inequity to those who have relied upon it or significant damage to the stability of the society governed by the rule in question; whether the law's growth in the intervening years has left Roe's central rule a doctrinal anachronism discounted by society; and whether Roe's premises of fact have so far changed in the ensuing two decades as to render its central holding somehow irrelevant or unjustifiable in dealing with the issue it addressed.

Although Roe has engendered opposition, it has in no sense proven "unworkable," representing as it does a simple limitation beyond which a state law is unenforceable. While Roe has, of course, required judicial assessment of state laws affecting the exercise of the choice guaranteed against government infringement, and although the need for such review will remain as a consequence of today's decision, the required determinations fall within judicial competence.

The inquiry into reliance counts the cost of a rule's repudiation as it would fall on those who have relied reasonably on the rule's continued application. . . . For two decades of economic and social developments, people have organized intimate relationships and made choices that define their views of themselves and their places in society, in reliance on the availability of abortion in the event that contraception should fail. The ability of women to participate equally in the economic and social life of the Nation has been facilitated by their ability to control their reproductive lives. The Constitution serves human values, and while the effect of reliance on Roe cannot be exactly measured, neither can the certain cost of overruling Roe for people who have ordered their thinking and living around that case be dismissed.

No evolution of legal principle has left Roe's doctrinal footings weaker than they were in 1973. No development of constitutional law since the case was decided has implicitly or explicitly left Roe behind as a mere survivor of obsolete constitutional thinking. . . .

We have seen how time has overtaken some of Roe's factual assumptions: advances in maternal health care allow for abortions safe to the mother later in pregnancy than was true in 1973, and advances in neonatal care have advanced viability to a point somewhat earlier. But these facts go only to the scheme of time limits on the realization of competing interests, and the divergences from the factual premises of 1973 have no bearing on the validity of Roe's central holding, that viability marks the earliest point at which the State's interest in fetal life is constitutionally adequate to justify a legislative ban on nontherapeutic abortions. The soundness or unsoundness of that constitutional judgment in no sense turns on whether viability occurs at approximately 28 weeks, as was usual at the time of Roe, at 23 to 24 weeks, as it sometimes does today. . . .

The sum of the precedential inquiry to this point shows Roe's underpinnings unweakened in any way affecting its central holding. While it has engendered disapproval, it has not been unworkable. An entire generation has come of age free to assume Roe's concept of liberty in defining the capacity of women to act in society, and to make reproductive decisions; no erosion of principle going to liberty or personal autonomy has left Roe's central holding a doctrinal remnant; Roe portends no developments at odds with other precedent for the analysis of personal liberty; and no changes of fact have rendered viability more or less appropriate as the point at which the balance of interests tips. Within the bounds of normal *stare decisis* analysis, then, and subject to the considerations on which it customarily turns, the stronger argument is for affirming *Roe*'s central holding, with whatever degree of personal reluctance any of us may have, not for overruling it. . . .

Our analysis would not be complete, however, without explaining why overruling *Roe*'s central holding would not only reach an unjustifiable result under principles of *stare decisis*, but would seriously weaken the Court's capacity to exercise the judicial power and to function as the Supreme Court of a Nation dedicated to the rule of law. To understand why this would be so it is necessary to understand the source of this Court's authority, the conditions necessary for its preservation, and its relationship to the country's understanding of itself as a constitutional Republic.

The root of American governmental power is revealed most clearly in the instance of the power conferred by the Constitution upon the Judiciary of the United States and specifically upon this Court. As Americans of each succeeding generation are rightly told, the Court cannot buy support for its decisions by spending money and, except to a minor degree, it cannot independently coerce obedience to its decrees. The Court's power lies, rather, in its legitimacy, a product of substance and perception that shows itself in the people's acceptance of the Judiciary as fit to determine what the Nation's law means and to declare what it demands. The Court must take care to speak and act in ways that allow people to accept its decisions on the terms the Court claims for them, as grounded truly in principle, not as compromises with social and political pressures having, as such, no bearing on the principled choices that the Court is obliged to make. Thus, the Court's legitimacy depends on making legally principled decisions under circumstances in which their principled character is sufficiently plausible to be accepted by the Nation.

The need for principled action to be perceived as such is implicated to some degree whenever this, or any other appellate court, overrules a prior case. This is not to say, of course, that this Court cannot give a perfectly satisfactory explanation in most cases. People understand that some of the Constitution's language is hard to

fathom and that the Court's Justices are sometimes able to perceive significant facts or to understand principles of law that eluded their predecessors and that justify departures from existing decisions. However upsetting it may be to those most directly affected when one judicially derived rule replaces another, the country can accept some correction of error without necessarily questioning the legitimacy of the Court.

In two circumstances, however, the Court would almost certainly fail to receive the benefit of the doubt in overruling prior cases. There is, first, a point beyond which frequent overruling would overtax the country's belief in the Court's good faith. Despite the variety of reasons that may inform and justify a decision to overrule, we cannot forget that such a decision is usually perceived (and perceived correctly) as, at the least, a statement that a prior decision was wrong. There is a limit to the amount of error that can plausibly be imputed to prior courts. If that limit should be exceeded, disturbance of prior rulings would be taken as evidence that justifiable reexamination of principle had given way to drives for particular results in the short term.

The legitimacy of the Court would fade with the frequency of its vacillation. That first circumstance can be described as hypothetical; the second is to the point here and now. Where, in the performance of its judicial duties, the Court decides a case in such a way as to resolve the sort of intensely divisive controversy reflected in *Roe* and those rare, comparable cases, its decision has a dimension that the resolution of the normal case does not carry. It is the dimension present whenever the Court's interpretation of the Constitution calls the contending sides of a national controversy to end their national division by accepting a common mandate rooted in the Constitution.

The Court is not asked to do this very often, having thus addressed the Nation only twice in our lifetime, in the decisions of *Brown* and *Roe*. But when the Court does act in this way, its decision requires an equally rare precedential force to counter the inevitable efforts to overturn it and to thwart its implementation. Some of those efforts may be mere unprincipled emotional reactions; others may proceed from principles worthy of profound respect. But whatever the premises of opposition may be, only the most convincing justification under accepted standards of precedent could suffice to demonstrate that a later decision overruling the first was anything but a surrender to political pressure, and an unjustified repudiation of the principle on which the Court staked its authority in the first instance. So to overrule under fire in the absence of the most compelling reason to reexamine a watershed decision would subvert the Court's legitimacy beyond any serious question.

It is true that diminished legitimacy may be restored, but only slowly. Unlike the political branches, a Court thus weakened could not seek to regain its position with a new mandate from the voters, and even if the Court could somehow go to the polls, the loss of its principled character could not be retrieved by the casting of so many votes. Like the character of an individual, the legitimacy of the Court must be earned over time. So, indeed, must be the character of a Nation of people who aspire to live according to the rule of law. Their belief in themselves as such a people is not readily separable from their understanding of the Court invested with the authority to decide their constitutional cases and speak before all others for their constitutional ideals. If the Court's legitimacy should be undermined, then, so would the country be in its very ability to see itself through its constitutional ideals. The Court's concern with legitimacy is not for the sake of the Court but for the sake of the Nation to which it is responsible.

The Court's duty in the present case is clear. In 1973, it confronted the already-divisive issue of governmental power to limit personal choice to undergo abortion, for which it provided a new resolution based on the due process guaranteed by the Fourteenth Amendment. Whether or not a new social consensus is developing on that issue, its divisiveness is no less today than in 1973, and pressure to overrule the decision, like pressure to retain it, has grown only more intense. A decision to overrule *Roe*'s essential holding under the existing circumstances would address error, if error there was, at the cost of both profound and unnecessary damage to the Court's legitimacy, and to the Nation's commitment to the rule of law. It is therefore imperative to adhere to the essence of *Roe*'s original decision, and we do so today.

From what we have said so far it follows that it is a constitutional liberty of the woman to have some freedom to terminate her pregnancy. We conclude that the basic decision in *Roe* was based on a constitutional analysis which we cannot now repudiate. The woman's liberty is not so unlimited, however, that from the outset the State cannot show its concern for the life of the unborn, and at a later point in fetal development the State's interest in life has sufficient force so that the right of the woman to terminate the pregnancy can be restricted.

That brings us, of course, to the point where much criticism has been directed at *Roe*, a criticism that always inheres when the Court draws a specific rule from what in the Constitution is but a general standard. We conclude, however, that the urgent claims of the woman to retain the ultimate control over her destiny and her body, claims implicit in the meaning of liberty, require us to perform that function. Liberty must not be extinguished for want of a line that is clear. And it falls to us to give some real substance to the woman's liberty to determine whether to carry her pregnancy to full term.

We conclude the line should be drawn at viability, so that before that time the woman has a right to choose to terminate her pregnancy. We adhere to this principle for two reasons. First, as we have said, is the doctrine of *stare decisis*. Any judicial act of line-drawing may seem somewhat arbitrary, but *Roe* was a reasoned statement, elaborated with great care. We have twice reaffirmed it in the face of great opposition.

The second reason is that the concept of viability, as we noted in *Roe*, is the time at which there is a realistic possibility of maintaining and nourishing a life outside the womb, so that the independent existence of the second life can in reason and all fairness be the object of state protection that now overrides the rights of the woman. Consistent with other constitutional norms, legislatures may draw lines which appear arbitrary without the necessity of offering a justification. But courts may not. We must justify the lines we draw. And there is no line other than viability which is more workable. To be sure, as we have said, there may be some medical developments that affect the precise point of viability, but this is an imprecision within tolerable limits given that the medical community and all those who must apply its discoveries will continue to explore the matter. The viability line also has, as a practical matter, an element of fairness. In some broad sense it might be said that a woman who fails to act before viability has consented to the State's intervention on behalf of the developing child.

The woman's right to terminate her pregnancy before viability is the most central principle of *Roe* v. *Wade*. It is a rule of law and a component of liberty we cannot renounce.

Yet it must be remembered that *Roe* v. *Wade* speaks with clarity in establishing not only the woman's liberty but also the State's "important and legitimate interest in potential life." That portion of the decision in *Roe* has been given too little acknowledgment and implementation by the Court in its subsequent cases. Those cases decided that any regulation touching upon the abortion decision must survive strict scrutiny, to be sustained only if drawn in narrow terms to further a compelling state interest. Not all of the cases decided under that formulation can be reconciled with the holding in *Roe* itself that the State has legitimate interests in the health of the woman and in protecting the potential life within her. In resolving this tension, we choose to rely upon *Roe,* as against the later cases.

Roe established a trimester framework to govern abortion regulations. Under this elaborate but rigid construct, almost no regulation at all is permitted during the first trimester of pregnancy; regulations designed to protect the woman's health, but not to further the State's interest in potential life, are permitted during the second trimester; and during the third trimester, when the fetus is viable, prohibitions are permitted provided the life or health of the mother is not at stake. Most of our cases since *Roe* have involved the application of rules derived from the trimester framework.

The trimester framework no doubt was erected to ensure that the woman's right to choose not become so subordinate to the State's interest in promoting fetal life that her choice exists in theory but not in fact. We do not agree, however, that the trimester approach is necessary to accomplish this objective. A framework of this rigidity was unnecessary and in its later interpretation sometimes contradicted the State's permissible exercise of its powers.

Though the woman has a right to choose to terminate or continue her pregnancy before viability, it does not at all follow that the State is prohibited from taking steps to ensure that this choice is thoughtful and informed. Even in the earliest stages of pregnancy, the State may enact rules and regulations designed to encourage her to know that there are philosophic and social arguments of great weight that can be brought to bear in favor of continuing the pregnancy to full term and that there are procedures and institutions to allow adoption of unwanted children as well as a certain degree of state assistance if the mother chooses to raise the child herself. " '[T]he Constitution does not forbid a State or city, pursuant to democratic processes, from expressing a preference for normal childbirth.' "

It follows that States are free to enact laws to provide a reasonable framework for a woman to make a decision that has such profound and lasting meaning. This, too, we find consistent with *Roe*'s central premises, and indeed the inevitable consequence of our holding that the State has an interest in protecting the life of the unborn.

We reject the trimester framework, which we do not consider to be part of the essential holding of *Roe*. Measures aimed at ensuring that a woman's choice contemplates the consequences for the fetus do not necessarily interfere with the right recognized in *Roe,* although those measures have been found to be inconsistent with the rigid trimester framework announced in that case. A logical reading of the central holding in *Roe* itself, and a necessary reconciliation of the liberty of the woman and the interest of the State in promoting prenatal life, require, in our view, that we abandon the trimester framework as a rigid prohibition on all previability regulation aimed at the protection of fetal life. The trimester framework suffers from these basic flaws: in its formulation it misconceives the nature of the pregnant woman's interest; and in practice it undervalues the State's interest in potential life, as recognized in *Roe*.

As our jurisprudence relating to all liberties save perhaps abortion has recognized, not every law which makes a right more difficult to exercise is, *ipso facto,* an infringement of that right. An example clarifies the point. We have held that not every ballot access limitation amounts to an infringement of the right to vote. Rather, the States are granted substantial flexibility in establishing the framework within which voters choose the candidates for whom they wish to vote.

The abortion right is similar. Numerous forms of state regulation might have the incidental effect of increasing the cost or decreasing the availability of medical care, whether for abortion or any other medical procedure. The fact that a law which serves a valid purpose, one not designed to strike at the right itself, has the incidental effect of making it more difficult or more expensive to procure an abortion cannot be enough to invalidate it. Only where state regulation imposes an undue burden on a woman's ability to make this decision does the power of the State reach into the heart of the liberty protected by the Due Process Clause.

The very notion that the State has a substantial interest in potential life leads to the conclusion that not all regulations must be deemed unwarranted. Not all burdens on the right to decide whether to terminate a pregnancy will be undue. In our view, the undue burden standard is the appropriate means of reconciling the State's interest with the woman's constitutionally protected liberty.

The concept of an undue burden has been utilized by the Court as well as individual members of the Court, including two of us, in ways that could be considered inconsistent. Because we set forth a standard of general application to which we intend to adhere, it is important to clarify what is meant by an undue burden.

A finding of an undue burden is a shorthand for the conclusion that a state regulation has the purpose or effect of placing a substantial obstacle in the path of a woman seeking an abortion of a nonviable fetus. A statute with this purpose is invalid because the means chosen by the State to further the interest in potential life must be calculated to inform the woman's free choice, not hinder it. And a statute which, while furthering the interest in potential life or some other valid state interest, has the effect of placing a substantial obstacle in the path of a woman's choice cannot be considered a permissible means of serving its legitimate ends. . . . In our considered judgment, an undue burden is an unconstitutional burden. Understood another way, we answer the question, left open in previous opinions discussing the undue burden formulation, whether a law designed to further the State's interest in fetal life which imposes an undue burden on the woman's decision before fetal viability could be constitutional. The answer is no.

Some guiding principles should emerge. What is at stake is the woman's right to make the ultimate decision, not a right to be insulated from all others in doing so. Regulations which do no more than create a structural mechanism by which the State, or the parent or guardian of a minor, may express profound respect for the life of the unborn are permitted, if they are not a substantial obstacle to the woman's exercise of the right to choose. Unless it has that effect on her right of choice, a state measure designed to persuade her to choose childbirth over abortion will be upheld if reasonably related to that goal. Regulations designed to foster the health of a woman seeking an abortion are valid if they do not constitute an undue burden.

Even when jurists reason from shared premises, some disagreement is inevitable. That is to be expected in the application of any legal standard which must accommodate life's complexity. We do not expect it to be otherwise with respect to the undue burden standard. We give this summary:

(a) To protect the central right recognized by *Roe* v. *Wade* while at the same time accommodating the State's profound interest in potential life, we will employ the undue burden analysis as explained in this opinion. An undue burden exists, and therefore a provision of law is invalid, if its purpose or effect is to place a substantial obstacle in the path of a woman seeking an abortion before the fetus attains viability.

(b) We reject the rigid trimester framework of *Roe* v. *Wade.* To promote the State's profound interest in potential life, throughout pregnancy, the State may take measures to ensure that the woman's choice is informed, and measures designed to advance this interest will not be invalidated as long as their purpose is to persuade the woman to choose childbirth over abortion. These measures must not be an undue burden on the right.

(c) As with any medical procedure, the State may enact regulations to further the health or safety of a woman seeking an abortion. Unnecessary health regulations that have the purpose or effect of presenting a substantial obstacle to a woman seeking an abortion impose an undue burden on the right.

(d) Our adoption of the undue burden analysis does not disturb the central holding of *Roe* v.

Wade, and we reaffirm that holding. Regardless of whether exceptions are made for particular circumstances, a State may not prohibit any woman from making the ultimate decision to terminate her pregnancy before viability.

(e) We also reaffirm *Roe*'s holding that "subsequent to viability, the State in promoting its interest in the potentiality of human life may, if it chooses, regulate, and even proscribe, abortion except where it is necessary, in appropriate medical judgment, for the preservation of the life or health of the mother."

These principles control our assessment of the Pennsylvania statute, and we now turn to the issue of the validity of its challenged provisions.

The Court of Appeals applied what it believed to be the undue burden standard and upheld each of the provisions except for the husband notification requirement. We agree generally with this conclusion, but refine the undue burden analysis in accordance with the principles articulated above. We now consider the separate statutory sections at issue.

Because it is central to the operation of various other requirements, we begin with the statute's definition of medical emergency. Under the statute, a medical emergency is

> [t]hat condition which, on the basis of the physician's good faith clinical judgment, so complicates the medical condition of a pregnant woman as to necessitate the immediate abortion of her pregnancy to avert her death or for which a delay will create serious risk of substantial and irreversible impairment of a major bodily function.

We adhere to that course today, and conclude that, as construed by the Court of Appeals, the medical emergency definition imposes no undue burden on a woman's abortion right.

We next consider the informed consent requirement. Except in a medical emergency, the statute requires that at least 24 hours before performing an abortion a physician inform the woman of the nature of the procedure, the health risks of the abortion and of childbirth, and the "probable gestational age of the unborn child." The physician or a qualified nonphysician must inform the woman of the availability of printed materials published by the State describing the fetus and providing information about medical

assistance for child-birth, information about child support from the father, and a list of agencies which provide adoption and other services as alternatives to abortion. An abortion may not be performed unless the woman certifies in writing that she has been informed of the availability of these printed materials and has been provided them if she chooses to view them.

We also see no reason why the State may not require doctors to inform a woman seeking an abortion of the availability of materials relating to the consequences to the fetus, even when those consequences have no direct relation to her health. . . . Requiring that the woman be informed of the availability of information relating to fetal development and the assistance available should she decide to carry the pregnancy to full term is a reasonable measure to insure an informed choice, one which might cause the woman to choose childbirth over abortion. This requirement cannot be considered a substantial obstacle to obtaining an abortion, and, it follows, there is no undue burden. . . .

All that is left of petitioners' argument is an asserted First Amendment right of a physician not to provide information about the risks of abortion, and childbirth, in a manner mandated by the State. To be sure, the physician's First Amendment rights not to speak are implicated, but only as part of the practice of medicine, subject to reasonable licensing and regulation by the State. We see no constitutional infirmity in the requirement that the physician provide the information mandated by the State here.

. . . Our analysis of Pennsylvania's 24-hour waiting period between the provision of the information deemed necessary to informed consent and the performance of an abortion under the undue burden standard requires us to reconsider the premise behind the decision in *Akron I* invalidating a parallel requirement. In *Akron I* we said: "Nor are we convinced that the State's legitimate concern that the woman's decision be informed is reasonably served by requiring a 24-hour delay as a matter of course." We consider that conclusion to be wrong. The idea that important decisions will be more informed and deliberate if they follow some period of reflection does not strike us as unreasonable, particularly where the statute directs that important information become part of the background of the decision. The statute, as construed by the Court of

Appeals, permits avoidance of the waiting period in the event of a medical emergency and the record evidence shows that in the vast majority of cases, a 24-hour delay does not create any appreciable health risk. In theory, at least, the waiting period is a reasonable measure to implement the State's interest in protecting the life of the unborn, a measure that does not amount to an undue burden.

Pennsylvania's abortion law provides, except in cases of medical emergency, that no physician shall perform an abortion on a married woman without receiving a signed statement from the woman that she has notified her spouse that she is about to undergo an abortion. The woman has the option of providing an alternative signed statement certifying that her husband is not the man who impregnated her; that her husband could not be located; that the pregnancy is the result of spousal sexual assault which she has reported; or that the woman believes that notifying her husband will cause him or someone else to inflict bodily injury upon her. A physician who performs an abortion on a married woman without receiving the appropriate signed statement will have his or her license revoked, and is liable to the husband for damages. . . . [T]here are millions of women in this country who are the victims of regular physical and psychological abuse at the hands of their husbands. Should these women become pregnant, they may have very good reasons for not wishing to inform their husbands of their decision to obtain an abortion.

The spousal notification requirement is thus likely to prevent a significant number of women from obtaining an abortion. It does not merely make abortions a little more difficult or expensive to obtain; for many women, it will impose a substantial obstacle. We must not blind ourselves to the fact that the significant number of women who fear for their safety and the safety of their children are likely to be deterred from procuring an abortion as surely as if the Commonwealth had outlawed abortion in all cases. . . .

The husband's interest in the life of the child his wife is carrying does not permit the State to empower him with . . . authority over his wife. The contrary view leads to consequences reminiscent of the common law. A husband has no enforceable right to require a wife to advise him before she exercises her personal choices. If a husband's interest in the potential life of the child outweighs a wife's liberty, the State could require a married woman to notify her husband before she uses a postfertilization contraceptive. Perhaps next in line would be a statute requiring pregnant married women to notify their husbands before engaging in conduct causing risk to the fetus. After all, if the husband's interest in the fetus's safety is a sufficient predicate for state regulation, the State could reasonably conclude that pregnant wives should notify their husbands before drinking alcohol or smoking. Perhaps married women should notify their husbands before using contraceptives or before undergoing any type of surgery that may have complications affecting the husband's interest in his wife's reproductive organs. A State may not give to a man the kind of dominion over his wife that parents exercise over their children.

[The act] embodies a view of marriage consonant with the common-law status of married women but repugnant to our present understanding of marriage and of the nature of the rights secured by the Constitution. Women do not lose their constitutionally protected liberty when they marry. The Constitution protects all individuals, male or female, married or unmarried, from the abuse of governmental power, even where that power is employed for the supposed benefit of a member of the individual's family. These considerations confirm our conclusion that the spousal notification provision is invalid.

We next consider the parental consent provision. Except in a medical emergency, an unemancipated young woman under 18 may not obtain an abortion unless she and one of her parents (or guardian) provides informed consent as defined above. If neither a parent nor a guardian provides consent, a court may authorize the performance of an abortion upon a determination that the young woman is mature and capable of giving informed consent and has in fact given her informed consent, or that an abortion would be in her best interests.

We have been over most of this ground before. Our cases establish, and we reaffirm today, that a State may require a minor seeking an abortion to obtain the consent of a parent or guardian, provided that there is an adequate judicial bypass procedure. Under these precedents, in our view, the one-parent consent requirement and judicial bypass procedure are constitutional.

Under the recordkeeping and reporting requirements of the statute, every facility which performs abortions is required to file a report stating its name and address as well as the name and address of any related entity, such as a controlling or subsidiary organization. In the case of state-funded institutions, the information becomes public. For each abortion performed, a report must be filed identifying: the physician (and the second physician where required); the facility; the referring physician or agency; the woman's age; the number of prior pregnancies and prior abortions she has had; gestational age; the type of abortion procedure; the date of the abortion; whether there were any pre-existing medical conditions which would complicate pregnancy; medical complications with the abortion; where applicable, the basis for the determination that the abortion was medically necessary; the weight of the aborted fetus; and whether the woman was married, and if so, whether notice was provided or the basis for the failure to give notice. Every abortion facility must also file quarterly reports showing the number of abortions performed broken down by trimester. In all events, the identity of each woman who has had an abortion remains confidential.

We think that all the provisions at issue here except that relating to spousal notice are constitutional. Although they do not relate to the State's interest in informing the woman's choice, they do relate to health. The collection of information with respect to actual patients is a vital element of medical research, and so it cannot be said that the requirements serve no purpose other than to make abortions more difficult. Nor do we find that the requirements impose a substantial obstacle to a woman's choice. At most they might increase the cost of some abortions by a slight amount. While at some point increased cost could become a substantial obstacle, there is no such showing on the record before us.

Our Constitution is a covenant running from the first generation of Americans to us and then to future generations. It is a coherent succession. Each generation must learn anew that the Constitution's written terms embody ideas and aspirations that must survive more ages than one. We accept our responsibility not to retreat from interpreting the full meaning of the covenant in light of all of our precedents. We invoke it once again to define the freedom guaranteed by the Constitution's own promise of liberty.

JUSTICE STEVENS, concurring in part and dissenting in part.

Serious questions arise when a State attempts to "persuade the woman to choose childbirth over abortion." Decisional autonomy must limit the State's power to inject into a woman's most personal deliberations its own views of what is best. The State may promote its preferences by funding childbirth, by creating and maintaining alternatives to abortion, and by espousing the virtues of family; but it must respect the individual's freedom to make such judgments.

The 24-hour waiting period required by . . . the Pennsylvania statute raises even more serious concerns. [E]ven in those cases in which the delay is not especially onerous, it is, in my opinion, "undue" because there is no evidence that such a delay serves a useful and legitimate purpose. [T]here is no legitimate reason to require a woman who has agonized over her decision to leave the clinic or hospital and return again another day. While a general requirement that a physician notify her patients about the risks of a proposed medical procedure is appropriate, a rigid requirement that all patients wait 24 hours or (what is true in practice) much longer to evaluate the significance of information that is either common knowledge or irrelevant is an irrational and, therefore, "undue" burden.

JUSTICE BLACKMUN, concurring in part, concurring in the judgment in part, and dissenting in part.

. . . Today, no less than yesterday, the Constitution and decisions of this Court require that a State's abortion restrictions be subjected to the strictest of judicial scrutiny. Our precedents and the joint opinion's principles require us to subject all non-de minimis abortion regulations to strict scrutiny. Under this standard, the Pennsylvania statute's provisions requiring content-based counseling, a 24-hour delay, informed parental consent, and reporting of abortion-related information must be invalidated.

. . . Strict scrutiny of state limitations on reproductive choice still offers the most secure protection of the woman's right to make her own reproductive decisions, free from state coercion. No majority of this Court has ever agreed upon an alternative approach. The factual premises of the trimester framework have not been undermined, and the *Roe* framework is far more administrable, and far less manipulable, than the "undue burden" standard adopted by the joint opinion. . . . *Roe*'s requirement of strict scrutiny as implemented through a trimester framework should not be disturbed. No other approach has gained a majority, and no other is more protective of the woman's fundamental right. Lastly, no other approach properly accommodates the woman's constitutional right with the State's legitimate interests. . . .

If there is much reason to applaud the advances made by the joint opinion today, there is far more to fear from the Chief Justice's opinion. The Chief Justice's criticism of *Roe* follows from his stunted conception of individual liberty. While recognizing that the Due Process Clause protects more than simple physical liberty, he then goes on to construe this Court's personal-liberty cases as establishing only a laundry list of particular rights, rather than a principled account of how these particular rights are grounded in a more general right of privacy. This constricted view is reinforced by the Chief Justice's exclusive reliance on tradition as a source of fundamental rights. . . .

In one sense, the Court's approach is worlds apart from that of the Chief Justice and Justice Scalia. And yet, in another sense, the distance between the two approaches is short—the distance is but a single vote.

I am 83 years old. I cannot remain on this Court forever, and when I do step down, the confirmation process for my successor well may focus on the issue before us today. That, I regret, may be exactly where the choice between the two worlds will be made.

CHIEF JUSTICE REHNQUIST, with whom JUSTICE WHITE, JUSTICE SCALIA, and JUSTICE THOMAS join, concurring in the judgment in part and dissenting in part.

The joint opinion, following its newly-minted variation on *stare decisis*, retains the outer shell of *Roe* v. *Wade* (1973), but beats a wholesale retreat from the substance of that case. We believe that *Roe* was wrongly decided, and that it can and should be overruled consistently with our traditional approach to *stare decisis* in constitu-

tional cases. We would adopt the approach of the plurality in *Webster* v. *Reproductive Health Services* (1989), and uphold the challenged provisions of the Pennsylvania statute in their entirety. . . .

The joint opinion of Justices O'Connor, Kennedy, and Souter cannot bring itself to say that *Roe* was correct as an original matter, but the authors are of the view that "the immediate question is not the soundness of *Roe*'s resolution of the issue, but the precedential force that must be accorded to its holding." Instead of claiming that *Roe* was correct as a matter of original constitutional interpretation, the opinion therefore contains an elaborate discussion of *stare decisis*. This discussion of the principle of stare decisis appears to be almost entirely dicta, because the joint opinion does not apply that principle in dealing with *Roe*. *Roe* decided that a woman had a fundamental right to an abortion. The joint opinion rejects that view. *Roe* decided that abortion regulations were to be subjected to "strict scrutiny" and could be justified only in the light of "compelling state interests." The joint opinion rejects that view. *Roe* analyzed abortion regulation under a rigid trimester framework, a framework which has guided this Court's decisionmaking for 19 years. The joint opinion rejects that framework. While purporting to adhere to precedent, the joint opinion instead revises it. Roe continues to exist, but only in the way a storefront on a western movie set exists: a mere facade to give the illusion of reality.

The joint opinion discusses several *stare decisis* factors which, it asserts, point toward retaining a portion of *Roe*. Two of these factors are that the main "factual underpinning" of *Roe* has remained the same, and that its doctrinal foundation is no weaker now than it was in 1973. Of course, what might be called the basic facts which give rise to *Roe* have remained the same— women become pregnant, there is a point somewhere, depending on medical technology, where a fetus becomes viable, and women give birth to children. But this is only to say that the same facts which gave rise to *Roe* will continue to give rise to similar cases. It is not a reason, in and of itself, why those cases must be decided in the same incorrect manner as was the first case to deal with the question. And surely there is no requirement, in considering whether to depart from *stare decisis* in a constitutional case, that a decision be more wrong now than it was at the time it was rendered. If that were true, the most outlandish constitutional decision could survive forever, based simply on the fact that it was no more outlandish later than it was when originally rendered.

Nor does the joint opinion faithfully follow this alleged requirement. The opinion frankly concludes that *Roe* and its progeny were wrong in failing to recognize that the State's interests in maternal health and in the protection of unborn human life exist throughout pregnancy. But there is no indication that these components of *Roe* are any more incorrect at this juncture than they were at its inception. . . .

In the end, having failed to put forth any evidence to prove any true reliance, the joint opinion's argument is based solely on generalized assertions about the national psyche, on a belief that the people of this country have grown accustomed to the *Roe* decision over the last 19 years and have "ordered their thinking and living around" it. As an initial matter, one might inquire how the joint opinion can view the "central holding" of *Roe* as so deeply rooted in our constitutional culture, when it so casually uproots and disposes of that same decision's trimester framework. Furthermore, at various points in the past, the same could have been said about this Court's erroneous decisions that the Constitution allowed "separate but equal" treatment of minorities, see *Plessy* v. *Ferguson* (1896), or that "liberty" under the Due Process Clause protected "freedom of contract." See *Adkins* v. *Children's Hospital* (1923).

Apparently realizing that conventional *stare decisis* principles do not support its position, the joint opinion advances a belief that retaining a portion of *Roe* is necessary to protect the "legitimacy" of this Court. Because the Court must take care to render decisions "grounded truly in principle," and not simply as political and social compromises, the joint opinion properly declares it to be this Court's duty to ignore the public criticism and protest that may arise as a result of a decision. Few would quarrel with this statement, although it may be doubted that Members of this Court, holding their tenure as they do during constitutional "good behavior," are at all likely to be intimidated by such public protests.

But the joint opinion goes on to state that when the Court "resolve[s] the sort of intensely divisive controversy reflected in *Roe* and those rare, comparable cases," its decision is exempt from reconsideration under established principles of *stare decisis* in constitutional cases. This is so, the joint opinion contends, because in those "intensely divisive" cases, the Court has "call[ed] the contending sides of a national controversy to end their national division by accepting a common mandate rooted in the Constitution," and must therefore take special care not to be perceived as "surrender[ing] to political pressure" and continued opposition. This is a truly novel principle, one which is contrary to both the Court's historical practice and to the Court's traditional willingness to tolerate criticism of its opinions. Under this principle, when the Court has ruled on a divisive issue, it is apparently prevented from overruling that decision for the sole reason that it was incorrect, unless opposition to the original decision has died away. . . .

There are other reasons why the joint opinion's discussion of legitimacy is unconvincing as well. In assuming that the Court is perceived as "surrender[ing] to political pressure" when it overrules a controversial decision, the joint opinion forgets that there are two sides to any controversy. The joint opinion asserts that, in order to protect its legitimacy, the Court must refrain from overruling a controversial decision lest it be viewed as favoring those who oppose the decision. But a decision to adhere to prior precedent is subject to the same criticism, for in such a case one can easily argue that the Court is responding to those who have demonstrated in favor of the original decision. The decision in *Roe* has engendered large demonstrations, including repeated marches on this Court and on Congress, both in opposition to and in support of that opinion. A decision either way on *Roe* can therefore be perceived as favoring one group or the other. But this perceived dilemma arises only if one assumes, as the joint opinion does, that the Court should make its decisions with a view toward speculative public perceptions. If one assumes instead, that the Court's legitimacy is enhanced by faithful interpretation of the Constitution irrespective of public opposition, such self-engendered difficulties may be put to one side.

Roe is not this Court's only decision to generate conflict. Our decisions in some recent capital cases, and in *Bowers* v. *Hardwick* (1986), have also engendered demonstrations in opposition. The joint opinion's message to such protesters appears to be that they must cease their activities in order to serve their cause, because their protests will only cement in place a decision which by normal standards of *stare decisis* should be reconsidered. Strong and often misguided criticism of a decision should not render the decision immune from reconsideration, lest a fetish for legitimacy penalize freedom of expression.

The end result of the joint opinion's paeans of praise for legitimacy is the enunciation of a brand new standard for evaluating state regulation of a woman's right to abortion—the "undue burden" standard. As indicated above, *Roe* v. *Wade* adopted a "fundamental right" standard under which state regulations could survive only if they met the requirement of "strict scrutiny." While we disagree with that standard, it at least had a recognized basis in constitutional law at the time *Roe* was decided. The same cannot be said for the "undue burden" standard, which is created largely out of whole cloth by the authors of the joint opinion. It is a standard which even today does not command the support of a majority of this Court. And it will not, we believe, result in the sort of "simple limitation," easily applied, which the joint opinion anticipates. In sum, it is a standard which is not built to last.

In evaluating abortion regulations under that standard, judges will have to decide whether they place a "substantial obstacle" in the path of a woman seeking an abortion. In that this standard is based even more on a judge's subjective determinations than was the trimester framework, the standard will do nothing to prevent "judges from roaming at large in the constitutional field" guided only by their personal views. Because the undue burden standard is plucked from nowhere, the question of what is a "substantial obstacle" to abortion will undoubtedly engender a variety of conflicting views. For example, in the very matter before us now, the authors of the joint opinion would uphold Pennsylvania's 24-hour waiting period, concluding that a "particular burden" on some women is not a substantial obstacle. But the authors would at the same time strike down Pennsylvania's spousal notice provision, after finding that in a "large fraction" of cases the provision will be a substantial obstacle. And, while the authors conclude that the informed consent provisions do not constitute an "undue burden," Justice Stevens would hold that they do.

Furthermore, while striking down the spousal notice regulation, the joint opinion would uphold a parental consent restriction that certainly places very substantial obstacles in the path of a minor's abortion choice. The joint opinion is forthright in admitting that it draws this distinction based on a policy judgment that parents will have the best interests of their children at heart, while the same is not necessarily true of husbands as to their wives. This may or may not be a correct judgment, but it is quintessentially a legislative one. The "undue burden" inquiry does not in any way supply the distinction between parental consent and spousal consent which the joint opinion adopts.

The sum of the joint opinion's labors in the name of *stare decisis* and "legitimacy" is this: *Roe* v. *Wade* stands as a sort of judicial Potemkin Village, which may be pointed out to passersby as a monument to the importance of adhering to precedent. But behind the facade, an entirely new method of analysis, without any roots in constitutional law, is imported to decide the constitutionality of state laws regulating abortion. Neither *stare decisis* nor "legitimacy" are truly served by such an effort.

We have stated above our belief that the Constitution does not subject state abortion regulations to heightened scrutiny. Accordingly, we think that the correct analysis is that a woman's interest in having an abortion is a form of liberty protected by the Due Process Clause, but States may regulate abortion procedures in ways rationally related to a legitimate state interest.

[With this rule in mind] . . . we therefore would hold that each of the challenged provisions of the Pennsylvania statute is consistent with the Constitution. It bears emphasis that our conclusion in this regard does not carry with it any necessary approval of these regulations. Our task is, as always, to decide only whether the challenged provisions of a law comport with the United States Constitution. If, as we believe, these do, their wisdom as a matter of public policy is for the people of Pennsylvania to decide.

JUSTICE SCALIA, with whom the CHIEF JUSTICE, JUS-
TICE WHITE, and JUSTICE THOMAS join, concurring
in the judgment in part and dissenting in part.

The States may, if they wish, permit abortion-
on-demand, but the Constitution does not require them to do so. The permissibility of abortion, and the limitations upon it, are to be
resolved like most important questions in our
democracy: by citizens trying to persuade one another and then voting. As the Court acknowledges, "where reasonable people disagree the
government can adopt one position or the other."
The Court is correct in adding the qualification
that this "assumes a state of affairs in which the
choice does not intrude upon a protected liberty"—but the crucial part of that qualification
is the penultimate word. A State's choice between two positions on which reasonable people
can disagree is constitutional even when (as is often the case) it intrudes upon a "liberty" in the
absolute sense. Laws against bigamy, for example—which entire societies of reasonable people
disagree with—intrude upon men and women's
liberty to marry and live with one another. But
bigamy happens not to be a liberty specially
"protected" by the Constitution.

That is, quite simply, the issue in this case:
not whether the power of a woman to abort her
unborn child is a "liberty" in the absolute sense;
or even whether it is a liberty of great importance to many women. Of course it is both. The
issue is whether it is a liberty protected by the
Constitution of the United States. I am sure it is
not. I reach that conclusion not because of anything so exalted as my views concerning the
"concept of existence, of meaning, of the universe, and of the mystery of human life." Rather,
I reach it for the same reason I reach the conclusion that bigamy is not constitutionally protected—because of two simple facts: (1) the Constitution says absolutely nothing about it, and (2)
the long-standing traditions of American society
have permitted it to be legally proscribed. . . .

I cannot agree with, indeed I am appalled by,
the Court's suggestion that the decision whether
to stand by an erroneous constitutional decision
must be strongly influenced—against overruling,
no less—by the substantial and continuing public opposition the decision has generated. The
Court's judgment that any other course would
"subvert the Court's legitimacy" must be an-

other consequence of reading the error-filled history book that described the deeply divided country brought together by *Roe.* In my history book,
the Court was covered with dishonor and deprived of legitimacy by *Dred Scott* v. *Sandford*
(1857), an erroneous (and widely opposed) opinion that it did not abandon, rather than by *West
Coast Hotel Co.* v. *Parrish* (1937), which produced the famous "switch in time" from the
Court's erroneous (and widely opposed) constitutional opposition to the social measures of
the New Deal. (Both *Dred Scott* and one line
of the cases resisting the New Deal rested upon
the concept of "substantive due process" that the
Court praises and employs today.)

In truth, I am as distressed as the Court is
about the "political pressure" directed to the
Court: the marches, the mail, the protests aimed
at inducing us to change our opinions. How upsetting it is, that so many of our citizens (good
people, not lawless ones, on both sides of this
abortion issue, and on various sides of other issues as well) think that we Justices should properly take into account their views, as though we
were engaged not in ascertaining an objective
law but in determining some kind of social consensus. The Court would profit, I think, from
giving less attention to the fact of this distressing
phenomenon, and more attention to the cause of
it. That cause permeates today's opinion: a new
mode of constitutional adjudication that relies
not upon text and traditional practice to determine the law, but upon what the Court calls
"reasoned judgment," which turns out to be
nothing but philosophical predilection and moral
intuition. All manner of "liberties," the Court
tells us, inhere in the Constitution and are enforceable by this Court—not just those mentioned in the text or established in the traditions
of our society.

What makes all this relevant to the bother-
some application of "political pressure" against
the Court are the twin facts that the American
people love democracy and the American people
are not fools. As long as this Court thought (and
the people thought) that we Justices were doing
essentially lawyers' work up here—reading text
and discerning our society's traditional understanding of that text—the public pretty much
left us alone. Texts and traditions are facts to
study, not convictions to demonstrate about. But

if in reality our process of constitutional adjudication consists primarily of making value judgments; if we can ignore a long and clear tradition clarifying an ambiguous text; . . . if, as I say, our pronouncement of constitutional law rests primarily on value judgments, then a free and intelligent people's attitude towards us can be expected to be (ought to be) quite different. The people know that their value judgments are quite as good as those taught in any law school—maybe better. If, indeed, the "liberties" protected by the Constitution are, as the Court says, undefined and unbounded, then the people should demonstrate, to protest that we do not implement their values instead of ours. Not only that, but confirmation hearings for new Justices should deteriorate into question-and-answer sessions in which Senators go through a list of their constituents' most favored and most disfavored alleged constitutional rights, and seek the nominee's commitment to support or oppose them. Value judgments, after all, should be voted on, not dictated; and if our Constitution has somehow accidentally committed them to the Supreme Court, at least we can have a sort of plebiscite each time a new nominee to that body is put forward. Justice Blackmun not only regards his prospect with equanimity, he solicits it.

Bowers v. *Hardwick*
478 U.S. 186; 106 S. Ct. 2841; 926 L. Ed. 2d 140 (1986)

After being charged with violating Section 16-6-2 of the Georgia Code Annotated, which criminalized sodomy, by committing that act with another adult male in the bedroom of his home, Michael Hardwick brought suit in federal district court challenging the constitutionality of Section 16-6-2 insofar as it criminalized consensual sodomy. He asserted that he was a practicing homosexual, that the Georgia sodomy statute, as administered by Michael Bowers, Attorney-General of Georgia, placed him in imminent danger of arrest, and that the statute for several reasons violated the federal Constitution. The district court granted Bowers's motion to dismiss for failure to state a claim, relying on *Doe* v. *Commonwealth's Attorney for the City of Richmond*, 403 F. Supp. 1199 (E.D. Va. 1975). A divided panel of the Court of Appeals for the Eleventh Circuit reversed. Relying on the Supreme Court's decisions in *Griswold* v. *Connecticut* (1965), *Eisenstadt* v. *Baird* (1972), *Stanley* v. *Georgia* (1969), and *Roe* v. *Wade* (1973), it held that the Georgia statute violated Hardwick's fundamental rights because his homosexual activity is a private and intimate association that is beyond the reach of state regulation by reason of the Ninth Amendment and the Due Process Clause of the Fourteenth Amendment. Bowers petitioned the Supreme Court for a writ of certiorari. *Opinion of the Court:* White, *Burger, O'Connor, Powell, Rehnquist.* *Concurring opinions:* Burger; Powell. *Dissenting opinions:* Blackmun, *Brennan, Marshall, Stevens;* Stevens, *Brennan, Marshall.*

JUSTICE WHITE delivered the opinion of the Court.

This case does not require a judgment on whether laws against sodomy between consenting adults in general, or between homosexuals in particular, are wise or desirable. It raises no question about the right or propriety of state legislative decisions to repeal their laws that criminalize homosexual sodomy, or of state-court decisions invalidating those laws on state constitutional grounds. The issue presented is whether the Federal Constitution confers a fundamental right upon homosexuals to engage in sodomy and hence invalidates the laws of the many States that still make such conduct illegal and have done so for a very long time. The case also calls for some judgment about the limits of the Court's role in carrying out its constitutional mandate.

We first register our disagreement with the Court of Appeals and with respondent that the Court's prior cases [*Griswold, Eisenstadt, Stanley,* and *Roe*] have construed the Constitution to confer a right of privacy that extends to homosexual sodomy and for all intents and purposes have decided this case. . . .

. . . We think it evident that none of the right announced in those cases bears any resemblance to that claimed constitutional right of homosexuals to engage in acts of sodomy that is asserted in this case. No connection between family, marriage, or procreation on the one hand and homosexual activity on the other has been demonstrated, either by the Court of Appeals or by respondent. Moreover, any claim that these cases nevertheless stand for the proposition that any kind of private sexual conduct between consenting adults is constitutionally insulated from state proscription is unsupportable. . . .

Precedent aside, however, respondent would have us announce, as the Court of Appeals did, a fundamental right to engage in homosexual sodomy. This we are quite unwilling to do. It is true that despite the language of the Due Process Clauses of the Fifth and Fourteenth Amendments, which appears to focus only on the processes by which life, liberty, or property is taken, the cases are legion in which those Clauses have been interpreted to have substantive content, subsuming rights that to a great extent are immune from federal or state regulation or proscription. Among such cases are those recognizing rights that have little or no textual support in the constitutional language. *Meyer, Prince,* and *Pierce* fall in this category, as do the privacy cases from *Griswold* to *Carey.*

Striving to assure itself and the public that announcing rights not readily identifiable in the Constitution's text involves much more than the imposition of the Justices' own choice of values on the States and the Federal Government, the Court has sought to identify the nature of the rights qualifying for heightened judicial protection. In *Palko* v. *Connecticut* . . . (1937), it was said that this category includes those fundamental liberties that are "implicit in the concept of ordered liberty," such that "neither liberty nor justice would exist if [they] were sacrificed." A different description of fundamental liberties appeared in *Moore* v. *East Cleveland,* 431 U.S. 494, 503 (1977) (opinion of Powell, J.), where they are characterized as those liberties that are "deeply rooted in this Nation's history and tradition." . . .

It is obvious to us that neither of these formulations would extend a fundamental right to homosexuals to engage in acts of consensual sodomy. Proscriptions against that conduct have ancient roots. . . . Sodomy was a criminal offense at common law and was forbidden by the laws of the original 13 States when they ratified the Bill of Rights. In 1868, when the Fourteenth Amendment was ratified, all but 5 of the 37 States in the Union had criminal sodomy laws. In fact, until 1961, all 50 States outlawed sodomy, and today, 25 States and the District of Columbia continue to provide criminal penalties for sodomy performed in private and between consenting adults. . . . Against this background, to claim that a right to engage in such conduct is "deeply rooted in this Nation's history and tradition" or "implicit in the concept of ordered liberty" is, at best, facetious.

Nor are we inclined to take a more expansive view of our authority to discover new fundamental rights imbedded in the Due Process Clause. The Court is most vulnerable and comes nearest to illegitimacy when it deals with judge-made constitutional law having little or no cognizable roots in the language or design of the Constitution. That this is so was painfully demonstrated by the face-off between the Executive and the Court in the 1930's, which resulted in the repudiation of much of the substantive gloss that the Court had placed on the Due Process Clauses of the Fifth and Fourteenth Amendments. There should be, therefore, great resistance to expand the substantive reach of those Clauses, particularly if it requires redefining the category of rights deemed to be fundamental. Otherwise, the Judiciary necessarily takes to itself further authority to govern the country without express constitutional authority. The claimed right pressed on us today falls far short of overcoming this resistance.

Respondent, however, asserts that the result should be different where the homosexual conduct occurs in the privacy of the home. He relies on *Stanley* v. *Georgia,* 394 U.S. 557 (1969), where the Court held that the First Amendment prevents conviction for possessing and reading obscene material in the privacy of one's home: "If the First Amendment means anything, it means that a State has no business telling a man, sitting alone in his house, what books he may read or what films he may watch."

Stanley did protect conduct that would not have been protected outside the home, and it partially prevented the enforcement of state obscenity laws; but the decision was firmly grounded in the First Amendment. The right pressed upon us here has no similar support in the text of the Constitution, and it does not qualify for recognition under the prevailing principles for construing the Fourteenth Amendment. Its limits are also difficult to discern. Plainly enough, otherwise illegal conduct is not always immunized whenever it occurs in the home. Victimless crimes, such as the possession and use of illegal drugs, do not escape the law where they are committed at home. *Stanley* itself recognized that its holding offered no protection for the possession in the home of drugs, firearms, or stolen goods. . . . And if respondent's submission is limited to the voluntary sexual conduct between consenting adults, it would be difficult, except by fiat, to limit the claimed right to homosexual conduct while leaving exposed to prosecution adultery, incest, and other sexual crimes even though they are committed in the home. We are unwilling to start down that road.

Even if the conduct at issue here is not a fundamental right, respondent asserts that there must be a rational basis for the law and that there is none in this case other than the presumed belief of a majority of the electorate in Georgia that homosexual sodomy is immoral and unacceptable. This is said to be an inadequate rationale to support the law. The law, however, is constantly based on notions of morality, and if all laws representing essentially moral choices are to be invalidated under the Due Process Clause, the courts will be very busy indeed. Even respondent makes no such claim, but insists that majority sentiments about the morality of homosexuality should be declared inadequate. We do not agree, and are unpersuaded that the sodomy laws of some 25 States should be invalidated on this basis.

Accordingly, the judgment of the Court of Appeals is

Reversed.

JUSTICE POWELL, concurring.

I join the opinion of the Court. I agree with the Court that there is no fundamental right— *i.e.,* no substantive right under the Due Process Clause—such as that claimed by respondent Hardwick, and found to exist by the Court of Appeals. This is not to suggest, however, that respondent may not be protected by the Eighth Amendment of the Constitution. The Georgia statute at issue in this case, . . . authorizes a court to imprison a person for up to 20 years for a single private, consensual act of sodomy. In my view, a prison sentence for such conduct—certainly a sentence of long duration—would create a serious Eighth Amendment issue. . . .

JUSTICE BLACKMUN, with whom JUSTICE BRENNAN, JUSTICE MARSHALL, and JUSTICE STEVENS join, dissenting.

This case is no more about "a fundamental right to engage in homosexual sodomy," as the Court purports to declare, . . . than *Stanley* v. *Georgia,* 394 U.S. 557 (1969), was about a fundamental right to watch obscene movies, or *Katz* v. *United States,* 389 U.S. 347 (1967), was about a fundamental right to place interstate bets from a telephone booth. Rather, this case is about "the most comprehensive of rights and the right most valued by civilized men," namely, "the right to be let alone." *Olmstead* v. *United States,* 277 U.S. 438, 478 (1928) (Brandeis, J., dissenting).

The statute at issue . . . denies individuals the right to decide for themselves whether to engage in particular forms of private, consensual sexual activity. The Court concludes that § 16-6-2 is valid essentially because "the laws of . . . many States . . . still make such conduct illegal and have done so for a very long time." . . . But the fact that the moral judgments expressed by statutes like § 16-6-2 may be "natural and familiar . . . ought not to conclude our judgment upon the question whether statutes embodying them conflict with the Constitution of the United States." . . . Like Justice Holmes, I believe that "[i]t is revolting to have no better reason for a rule of law than that so it was laid down in the time of Henry IV. It is still more revolting if the grounds upon which it was laid down have vanished long since, and the rule simply persists from blind imitation of the past." Holmes, The Path of the Law, 10 Harv. L. Rev. 457, 469 (1897). I believe we must analyze respondent Hardwick's claim in the light of the values that underlie the constitutional right to privacy . . .

The Court concludes today that none of our prior cases dealing with various decisions that individuals are entitled to make free of governmental interference "bears any resemblance to the claimed constitutional right of homosexuals to engage in acts of sodomy that is asserted in this case." . . .

Only the most willful blindness could obscure the fact that sexual intimacy is "a sensitive, key relationship of human existence, central to family life, community welfare, and the development of human personality." . . . The fact that individuals define themselves in a significant way through their intimate sexual relationships with others suggests, in a Nation as diverse as ours, that there may be many "right" ways of conducting those relationships, and that much of the richness of a relationship will come from the freedom an individual has to *choose* the form and nature of these intensely personal bonds. . . .

. . . The Court claims that its decision today merely refuses to recognize a fundamental right to engage in homosexual sodomy; what the Court really has refused to recognize is the fundamental interest all individuals have in controlling the nature of their intimate associations with others. . . .

The behavior for which Hardwick faces prosecution occurred in his own home, a place to which the Fourth Amendment attaches special significance. The Court's treatment of this aspect of the case is symptomatic of its overall refusal to consider the broad principles that have informed our treatment of privacy in specific cases . . .

The Court's interpretation of the pivotal case of *Stanley* v. *Georgia* . . . is entirely unconvincing. *Stanley* held that Georgia's undoubted power to punish the public distribution of constitutionally unprotected, obscene material did not permit the State to punish the private possession of such material. According to the majority here, *Stanley* relied entirely on the First Amendment, and thus, it is claimed, sheds no light on cases not involving printed materials . . . . But that is not what *Stanley* said. Rather, the *Stanley* Court anchored its holding in the Fourth Amendment's special protection for the individual in his home. . . .

. . . I see no justification for the Court's attempt to equate the private, consensual sexual activity at issue here with the "possession in the home of drugs, firearms, or stolen goods," . . . to which *Stanley* refused to extend its protection. . . . None of the behavior so mentioned in *Stanley* can properly be viewed as "[v]ictimless": . . . drugs and weapons are inherently dangerous, . . . and for property to be "stolen," someone must have been wrongfully deprived of it. Nothing in the record before the Court provides any justification for finding the activity forbidden by § 16-6-2 to be physically dangerous, either to the persons engaged in it or to others. . . .

The assertion that "traditional Judeo-Christian values proscribe" the conduct involved, . . . cannot provide an adequate justification for § 16-6-2. That certain, but by no means all, religious groups condemn the behavior at issue gives the State no license to impose their judgments on the entire citizenry. The legitimacy of secular legislation depends instead on whether the State can advance some justification for its law beyond its conformity to religious doctrine . . .

JUSTICE STEVENS, with whom JUSTICE BRENNAN and JUSTICE MARSHALL join, dissenting.

Like the statute that is challenged in this case, the rationale of the Court's opinion applies equally to the prohibited conduct regardless of whether the parties who engage in it are married or unmarried, or are of the same or different sexes. Sodomy was condemned as an odious and sinful type of behavior during the formative period of the common law. That condemnation was equally damning for heterosexual and homosexual sodomy. Moreover, it provided no special exemption for married couples. The license to cohabit and to produce legitimate offspring simply did not include any permission to engage in sexual conduct that was considered a "crime against nature."

The history of the Georgia statute before us clearly reveals this traditional prohibition of heterosexual, as well as homosexual, sodomy. . . .

Because the Georgia statute expresses the traditional view that sodomy is an immoral kind of conduct regardless of the identity of the persons who engage in it, I believe that a proper analysis of its constitutionality requires consideration of two questions: First, may a State totally prohibit the described conduct by means of a neutral law applying without exception to all persons subject to its jurisdiction? If not, may the State save the statute by announcing that it will only enforce the law against homosexuals? The two questions merit separate discussion. . . .

Our prior cases make two propositions abundantly clear. First, the fact that the governing majority in a State has traditionally viewed a particular practice as immoral is not a sufficient reason for upholding a law prohibiting the practice; neither history nor tradition could save a law prohibiting miscegenation from constitutional attack. Second, individual decisions by married persons, concerning the intimacies of their physical relationship, even when not intended to produce offspring, are a form of "liberty" protected by the Due Process Clause of the Fourteenth Amendment. *Griswold* v. *Connecticut*, 381 U.S. 479 (1965). Moreover, this protection extends to intimate choices by unmarried as well as married persons. *Carey* v. *Population Services International*, 431 U.S. 678 (1977); *Eisenstadt* v. *Baird*, 405 U.S. 438 (1972). . . .

Paradoxical as it may seem, our prior cases thus establish that a State may not prohibit sodomy within "the sacred precincts of marital bedrooms," . . . or, indeed, between unmarried heterosexual adults . . . In all events, it is perfectly clear that the State of Georgia may not totally prohibit the conduct proscribed by § 16-6-2 of the Georgia Criminal Code. . . .

If the Georgia statute cannot be enforced as it is written—if the conduct it seeks to prohibit is a protected form of liberty for the vast majority of Georgia's citizens—the State must assume the burden of justifying a selective application of its law. Either the persons to whom Georgia seeks to apply its statute do not have the same interest in "liberty" that others have, or there must be a reason why the State may be permitted to apply a generally applicable law to certain persons that it does not apply to others.

The first possibility is plainly unacceptable. Although the meaning of the principle that "all men are created equal" is not always clear, it surely must mean that every free citizen has the same interest in "liberty" that the members of the majority share. From the standpoint of the individual, the homosexual and the heterosexual have the same interest in deciding how he will live his own life, and, more narrowly, how he will conduct himself in his personal and voluntary associations with his companions. State intrusion into the private conduct of either is equally burdensome.

The second possibility is similarly unacceptable. A policy of selective application must be supported by a neutral and legitimate interest—something more substantial than a habitual dislike for, or ignorance about, the disfavored group. Neither the State nor the Court has identified any such interest in this case. The Court has posited as a justification for the Georgia statute "the presumed belief of a majority of the electorate in Georgia that homosexual sodomy is immoral and unacceptable." . . . But the Georgia electorate has expressed no such belief—instead, its representatives enacted a law that presumably reflects the belief that *all sodomy* is immoral and unacceptable. Unless the Court is prepared to conclude that such a law is constitutional, it may not rely on the work product of the Georgia Legislature to support its holding. For the Georgia statute does not single out homosexuals as a separate class meriting special disfavored treatment. . . .

I respectfully dissent.

Romer v. Evans

517 U.S. 620; 116 S. Ct. 1620; 134 L. Ed. 2d 855 (1996)

After various Colorado municipalities including Aspen, Boulder, and the City and County of Denver passed ordinances banning discrimination based on sexual orientation in housing, employment, education, public accommodations, health and welfare services, and other transactions and activities, Colorado voters in 1992 adopted by statewide referendum Amendment 2 to the Colorado Constitution, which precluded all legislative, executive, or judicial action at any level of state or local government designed to protect the status of persons based on their "homosexual, lesbian or bisexual orientation, conduct, practices or relationships." Respondents, who included aggrieved homosexuals and municipalities, brought suit in state court against Governor Roy Romer and the Colorado Attorney-General, in their official capacities, and against the State of Colorado seeking to declare Amendment 2 invalid and to enjoin its enforcement. The trial court granted a preliminary injunction, subsequently sustained by the Colorado Supreme Court on the grounds that Amendment 2 was subject to strict scrutiny under the Equal Protection Clause of the Fourteenth Amendment because it infringed the fundamental right of gays and lesbians to participate in the political process. On remand, the trial court found that the Amendment failed to satisfy strict scrutiny and permanently enjoined Amendment 2's enforcement. When the State Supreme Court affirmed, the United States Supreme Court granted certiorari. *Opinion of the Court: Kennedy, Breyer, Ginsburg, O'Connor, Souter, Stevens. Dissenting opinion: Scalia, Rehnquist, Thomas.*

JUSTICE KENNEDY delivered the opinion of the Court.

One century ago, the first Justice Harlan admonished this Court that the Constitution "neither knows nor tolerates classes among citizens." *Plessy* v. *Ferguson*, 163 U.S. 537, 559 (1896) (dissenting opinion). Unheeded then, those words now are understood to state a commitment to the law's neutrality where the rights of persons are at stake. The Equal Protection Clause enforces this principle and today requires us to hold invalid a provision of Colorado's Constitution. . . .

Amendment 2 . . . prohibits all legislative, executive or judicial action at any level of state or local government designed to protect the named class, a class we shall refer to as homosexual persons or gays and lesbians. The amendment reads: "No Protected Status Based on Homosexual, Lesbian, or Bisexual Orientation. Neither the State of Colorado, through any of its branches or departments, nor any of its agencies, political subdivisions, municipalities or school districts, shall enact, adopt or enforce any statute, regulation, ordinance or policy whereby homosexual, lesbian or bisexual orientation, conduct, practices or relationships shall constitute or otherwise be the basis of or entitle any person or class of per-

sons to have or claim any minority status, quota preferences, protected status or claim of discrimination. This Section of the Constitution shall be in all respects self-executing." . . .

The State's principal argument in defense of Amendment 2 is that it puts gays and lesbians in the same position as all other persons. So, the State says, the measure does no more than deny homosexuals special rights. This reading of the amendment's language is implausible. We rely not upon our own interpretation of the amendment but upon the authoritative construction of Colorado's Supreme Court. The state court, deeming it unnecessary to determine the full extent of the amendment's reach, found it invalid even on a modest reading of its implications. The critical discussion of the amendment, set out in [by the Colorado Supreme Court] is as follows: "The immediate objective of Amendment 2 is, at a minimum, to repeal existing statutes, regulations, ordinances, and policies of state and local entities that barred discrimination based on sexual orientation. . . . The 'ultimate effect' of Amendment 2 is to prohibit any governmental entity from adopting similar, or more protective statutes, regulations, ordinances, or policies in the future unless the state constitution is first amended to permit such measures."

Sweeping and comprehensive is the change in legal status effected by this law. So much is evident from the ordinances that the Colorado Supreme Court declared would be void by operation of Amendment 2. Homosexuals, by state decree, are put in a solitary class with respect to transactions and relations in both the private and governmental spheres. The amendment withdraws from homosexuals, but no others, specific legal protection from the injuries caused by discrimination, and it forbids reinstatement of these laws and policies.

The change that Amendment 2 works in the legal status of gays and lesbians in the private sphere is far-reaching, both on its own terms and when considered in light of the structure and operation of modern anti-discrimination laws. That structure is well illustrated by contemporary statutes and ordinances prohibiting discrimination by providers of public accommodations . . . [and] enumerating the groups or persons within their ambit of protection. Enumeration is the essential device used to make the duty not to discriminate concrete and to provide guidance for those who must comply. In following this approach, Colorado's state and local governments have not limited anti-discrimination laws to groups that have so far been given the protection of heightened equal protection scrutiny under our cases. Rather, they set forth an extensive catalogue of traits which cannot be the basis for discrimination, including age, military status, marital status, pregnancy, parenthood, custody of a minor child, political affiliation, physical or mental disability of an individual or of his or her associates—and, in recent times, sexual orientation.

Amendment 2 bars homosexuals from securing protection against the injuries that these public-accommodations laws address. That in itself is a severe consequence, but there is more. Amendment 2, in addition, nullifies specific legal protections for this targeted class in all transactions in housing, sale of real estate, insurance, health and welfare services, private education, and employment.

Not confined to the private sphere, Amendment 2 also operates to repeal and forbid all laws or policies providing specific protection for gays or lesbians from discrimination by every level of Colorado government. . . .

Amendment 2's reach may not be limited to specific laws passed for the benefit of gays and lesbians. It is a fair, if not necessary, inference from the broad language of the amendment that it deprives gays and lesbians even of the protection of general laws and policies that prohibit arbitrary discrimination in governmental and private settings. At some point in the systematic administration of these laws, an official must determine whether homosexuality is an arbitrary and thus forbidden basis for decision. Yet a decision to that effect would itself amount to a policy prohibiting discrimination on the basis of homosexuality, and so would appear to be no more valid under Amendment 2 than the specific prohibitions against discrimination the state court held invalid.

If this consequence follows from Amendment 2, as its broad language suggests, it would compound the constitutional difficulties the law creates. . . . In any event, even if, as we doubt, homosexuals could find some safe harbor in laws of general application, we cannot accept the view that Amendment 2's prohibition on specific legal protections does no more than deprive homosexuals of special rights. To the contrary, the amendment imposes a special disability upon those persons alone. Homosexuals are forbidden the safeguards that others enjoy or may seek without constraint. They can obtain specific protection against discrimination only by enlisting the citizenry of Colorado to amend the state constitution or perhaps, on the State's view, by trying to pass helpful laws of general applicability. This is so no matter how local or discrete the harm, no matter how public and widespread the injury. We find nothing special in the protections Amendment 2 withholds. These are protections taken for granted by most people either because they already have them or do not need them; these are protections against exclusion from an almost limitless number of transactions and endeavors that constitute ordinary civic life in a free society.

The Fourteenth Amendment's promise that no person shall be denied the equal protection of the laws must coexist with the practical necessity that most legislation classifies for one purpose or another, with resulting disadvantage to various groups or persons. We have attempted to reconcile the principle with the reality by stating that, if a law neither burdens a fundamental right nor targets a suspect class, we will uphold the legislative classification so long as it bears a rational relation to some legitimate end.

Amendment 2 fails, indeed defies, even this conventional inquiry. First, the amendment has the peculiar property of imposing a broad and undifferentiated disability on a single named group, an exceptional and, as we shall explain, invalid form of legislation. Second, its sheer breadth is so discontinuous with the reasons offered for it that the amendment seems inexplicable by anything but animus toward the class that it affects; it lacks a rational relationship to legitimate state interests.

Taking the first point, even in the ordinary equal protection case calling for the most deferential of standards, we insist on knowing the relation between the classification adopted and the object to be attained. The search for the link between classification and objective gives substance to the Equal Protection Clause; it provides guidance and discipline for the legislature, which is entitled to know what sorts of laws it can pass; and it marks the limits of our own authority. In the ordinary case, a law will be sustained if it can be said to advance a legitimate government interest, even if the law seems unwise or works to the disadvantage of a particular group, or if the rationale for it seems tenuous. . . . By requiring that the classification bear a rational relationship to an independent and legitimate legislative end, we ensure that classifications are not drawn for the purpose of disadvantaging the group burdened by the law.

Amendment 2 confounds this normal process of judicial review. It is at once too narrow and too broad. It identifies persons by a single trait and then denies them protection across the board. The resulting disqualification of a class of persons from the right to seek specific protection from the law is unprecedented in our jurisprudence. . . .

It is not within our constitutional tradition to enact laws of this sort. Central both to the idea of the rule of law and to our own Constitution's guarantee of equal protection is the principle that government and each of its parts remain open on impartial terms to all who seek its assistance. . . . Respect for this principle explains why laws singling out a certain class of citizens for

disfavored legal status or general hardships are rare. A law declaring that in general it shall be more difficult for one group of citizens than for all others to seek aid from the government is itself a denial of equal protection of the laws in the most literal sense. . . .

Even laws enacted for broad and ambitious purposes often can be explained by reference to legitimate public policies which justify the incidental disadvantages they impose on certain persons. Amendment 2, however, in making a general announcement that gays and lesbians shall not have any particular protections from the law, inflicts on them immediate, continuing, and real injuries that outrun and belie any legitimate justifications that may be claimed for it. We conclude that, in addition to the far-reaching deficiencies of Amendment 2 that we have noted, the principles it offends, in another sense, are conventional and venerable; a law must bear a rational relationship to a legitimate governmental purpose, and Amendment 2 does not.

The primary rationale the State offers for Amendment 2 is respect for other citizens' freedom of association, and in particular the liberties of landlords or employers who have personal or religious objections to homosexuality. Colorado also cites its interest in conserving resources to fight discrimination against other groups. The breadth of the Amendment is so far removed from these particular justifications that we find it impossible to credit them. We cannot say that Amendment 2 is directed to any identifiable legitimate purpose or discrete objective. It is a status-based enactment divorced from any factual context from which we could discern a relationship to legitimate state interests; it is a classification of persons undertaken for its own sake, something the Equal Protection Clause does not permit.

We must conclude that Amendment 2 classifies homosexuals not to further a proper legislative end but to make them unequal to everyone else. This Colorado cannot do. A State cannot so deem a class of persons a stranger to its laws. Amendment 2 violates the Equal Protection Clause, and the judgment of the Supreme Court of Colorado is affirmed.

JUSTICE SCALIA, with whom THE CHIEF JUSTICE and JUSTICE THOMAS join, dissenting.

The Court has mistaken a Kulturkampf for a fit of spite. The constitutional amendment before us here is not the manifestation of a "bare . . . desire to harm" homosexuals, but is rather a modest attempt by seemingly tolerant Coloradans to preserve traditional sexual mores against the efforts of a politically powerful minority to revise those mores through use of the laws. That objective, and the means chosen to achieve it, are not only unimpeachable under any constitutional doctrine hitherto pronounced (hence the opinion's heavy reliance upon principles of righteousness rather than judicial holdings); they have been specifically approved by the Congress of the United States and by this Court.

In holding that homosexuality cannot be singled out for disfavorable treatment, the Court contradicts a decision, unchallenged here, pronounced only 10 years ago, see *Bowers* v. *Hardwick*, 478 U.S. 186 (1986), and places the prestige of this institution behind the proposition that opposition to homosexuality is as reprehensible as racial or religious bias. Whether it is or not is precisely the cultural debate that gave rise to the Colorado constitutional amendment (and to the preferential laws against which the amendment was directed). Since the Constitution of the United States says nothing about this subject, it is left to be resolved by normal democratic means, including the democratic adoption of provisions in state constitutions. This Court has no business imposing upon all Americans the resolution favored by the elite class from which the Members of this institution are selected, pronouncing that "animosity" toward homosexuality is evil. I vigorously dissent.

Let me first discuss . . . the Court's . . . longest section, which is devoted to rejecting the State's arguments that Amendment 2 "puts gays and lesbians in the same position as all other persons," and "does no more than deny homosexuals special rights." The Court concludes that this reading of Amendment 2's language is "implausible" under the "authoritative construction" given Amendment 2 by the Supreme Court of Colorado.

In reaching this conclusion, the Court considers it unnecessary to decide the validity of the State's argument that Amendment 2 does not deprive homosexuals of the "protection [afforded by] general laws and policies that prohibit arbitrary discrimination in governmental and private

settings." I agree that we need not resolve that dispute, because the Supreme Court of Colorado has resolved it for us. In *Evans* v. *Romer*, 882 P. 2d 1335 (1994), the Colorado court stated . . . that "general laws and policies that prohibit arbitrary discrimination" would continue to prohibit discrimination on the basis of homosexual conduct as well. This analysis, which is fully in accord with (indeed, follows inescapably from) the text of the constitutional provision, lays to rest such horribles, raised in the course of oral argument, as the prospect that assaults upon homosexuals could not be prosecuted. The amendment prohibits special treatment of homosexuals, and nothing more. It would not affect, for example, a requirement of state law that pensions be paid to all retiring state employees with a certain length of service; homosexual employees, as well as others, would be entitled to that benefit. But it would prevent the State or any municipality from making death-benefit payments to the "life partner" of a homosexual when it does not make such payments to the long-time roommate of a nonhomosexual employee. Or again, it does not affect the requirement of the State's general insurance laws that customers be afforded coverage without discrimination unrelated to anticipated risk. Thus, homosexuals could not be denied coverage, or charged a greater premium, with respect to auto collision insurance; but neither the State nor any municipality could require that distinctive health insurance risks associated with homosexuality (if there are any) be ignored.

Despite all of its hand-wringing about the potential effect of Amendment 2 on general antidiscrimination laws, the Court's opinion ultimately does not dispute all this, but assumes it to be true. The only denial of equal treatment it contends homosexuals have suffered is this: They may not obtain preferential treatment without amending the state constitution. That is to say, the principle underlying the Court's opinion is that one who is accorded equal treatment under the laws, but cannot as readily as others obtain preferential treatment under the laws, has been denied equal protection of the laws. If merely stating this alleged equal protection violation does not suffice to refute it, our constitutional jurisprudence has achieved terminal silliness. . . .

I turn next to whether there was a legitimate rational basis for the substance of the constitutional amendment—for the prohibition of special protection for homosexuals. It is unsurprising that the Court avoids discussion of this question, since the answer is so obviously yes. The case most relevant to the issue before us today is not even mentioned in the Court's opinion: In *Bowers* v. *Hardwick*, we held that the Constitution does not prohibit what virtually all States had done from the founding of the Republic until very recent years—making homosexual conduct a crime. That holding is unassailable, except by those who think that the Constitution changes to suit current fashions. But in any event it is a given in the present case: Respondents' briefs did not urge overruling *Bowers*, and at oral argument respondents' counsel expressly disavowed any intent to seek such overruling. If it is constitutionally permissible for a State to make homosexual conduct criminal, surely it is constitutionally permissible for a State to enact other laws merely disfavoring homosexual conduct. (As the Court of Appeals for the District of Columbia Circuit has aptly put it: "If the Court [in *Bowers*] was unwilling to object to state laws that criminalize the behavior that defines the class, it is hardly open . . . to conclude that state sponsored discrimination against the class is invidious. After all, there can hardly be more palpable discrimination against a class than making the conduct that defines the class criminal." And a fortiori it is constitutionally permissible for a State to adopt a provision not even disfavoring homosexual conduct, but merely prohibiting all levels of state government from bestowing special protections upon homosexual conduct. Responents (who, unlike the Court, cannot afford the luxury of ignoring inconvenient precedent) counter *Bowers* with the argument that a greater-includes-the-lesser rationale cannot justify Amendment 2's application to individuals who do not engage in homosexual acts, but are merely of homosexual orientation. . . .

But assuming that, in Amendment 2, a person of homosexual "orientation" is someone who does not engage in homosexual conduct but merely has a tendency or desire to do so, *Bowers* still suffices to establish a rational basis for the provision. If it is rational to criminalize the conduct, surely it is rational to deny special favor and protection to those with a self-avowed tendency or desire to engage in the conduct.

Moreover, even if the provision regarding homosexual "orientation" were invalid, respondents' challenge to Amendment 2—which is a facial challenge—must fail. "A facial challenge to a legislative Act is, of course, the most difficult challenge to mount successfully, since the challenger must establish that no set of circumstances exists under which the Act would be valid." It would not be enough for respondents to establish (if they could) that Amendment 2 is unconstitutional as applied to those of homosexual "orientation"; since, under *Bowers*, Amendment 2 is unquestionably constitutional as applied to those who engage in homosexual conduct, the facial challenge cannot succeed. Some individuals of homosexual orientation who do not engage in homosexual acts might successfully bring an as-applied challenge to Amendment 2, but so far as the record indicates, none of the respondents is such a person.

The foregoing suffices to establish what the Court's failure to cite any case remotely in point would lead one to suspect: No principle set forth in the Constitution, nor even any imagined by this Court in the past 200 years, prohibits what Colorado has done here. But the case for Colorado is much stronger than that. What it has done is not only unprohibited, but eminently reasonable, with close, congressionally approved precedent in earlier constitutional practice.

First, as to its eminent reasonableness. The Court's opinion contains grim, disapproving hints that Coloradans have been guilty of "animus" or "animosity" toward homosexuality, as though that has been established as Unamerican. Of course it is our moral heritage that one should not hate any human being or class of human beings. But I had thought that one could consider certain conduct reprehensible—murder, for example, or polygamy, or cruelty to animals—and could exhibit even "animus" toward such conduct. Surely that is the only sort of "animus" at issue here: moral disapproval of homosexual conduct, the same sort of moral disapproval that produced the centuries-old criminal laws that we held constitutional in *Bowers*. The Colorado amendment does not, to speak entirely precisely, prohibit giving favored status to people who are homosexuals; they can be favored for many reasons—for example, because they are senior citizens or members of racial minorities. But it prohibits giving them favored status because of their homosexual conduct—that is, it prohibits favored status for homosexuality.

But though Coloradans are, as I say, entitled to be hostile toward homosexual conduct, the fact is that the degree of hostility reflected by Amendment 2 is the smallest conceivable. The Court's portrayal of Coloradans as a society fallen victim to pointless, hate-filled "gay-bashing" is so false as to be comical. Colorado not only is one of the 25 States that have repealed their antisodomy laws, but was among the first to do so. But the society that eliminates criminal punishment for homosexual acts does not necessarily abandon the view that homosexuality is morally wrong and socially harmful; often abolition simply reflects the view that enforcement of such criminal laws involves unseemly intrusion into the intimate lives of citizens.

There is a problem, however, which arises when criminal sanction of homosexuality is eliminated but moral and social disapprobation of homosexuality is meant to be retained. The Court cannot be unaware of that problem; it is evident in many cities of the country, and occasionally bubbles to the surface of the news, in heated political disputes over such matters as the introduction into local schools of books teaching that homosexuality is an optional and fully acceptable "alternate life style." The problem (a problem, that is, for those who wish to retain social disapprobation of homosexuality) is that, because those who engage in homosexual conduct tend to reside in disproportionate numbers in certain communities, have high disposable income, and of course care about homosexual-rights issues much more ardently than the public at large, they possess political power much greater than their numbers, both locally and statewide. Quite understandably, they devote this political power to achieving not merely a grudging social toleration, but full social acceptance, of homosexuality. See, e.g., Jacobs, The Rhetorical Construction of Rights: The Case of the Gay Rights Movement, 1969–1991, 72 Neb. L. Rev. 723, 724 (1993) ("[T]he task of gay rights proponents is to move the center of public discourse along a continuum from the rhetoric of disapprobation, to rhetoric of tolerance, and finally to affirmation.").

By the time Coloradans were asked to vote on Amendment 2, their exposure to homosexuals' quest for social endorsement was not limited to newspaper accounts of happenings in places such as New York, Los Angeles, San Francisco, and Key West. Three Colorado cities—Aspen, Boulder, and Denver—had enacted ordinances that listed "sexual orientation" as an impermissible ground for discrimination, equating the moral disapproval of homosexual conduct with racial and religious bigotry. . . . I do not mean to be critical of these legislative successes; homosexuals are as entitled to use the legal system for reinforcement of their moral sentiments as are the rest of society. But they are subject to being countered by lawful, democratic countermeasures as well.

That is where Amendment 2 came in. It sought to counter both the geographic concentration and the disproportionate political power of homosexuals by (1) resolving the controversy at the statewide level, and (2) making the election a single-issue contest for both sides. It put directly, to all the citizens of the State, the question: Should homosexuality be given special protection? They answered no. The Court today asserts that this most democratic of procedures is unconstitutional. Lacking any cases to establish that facially absurd proposition, it simply asserts that it must be unconstitutional, because it has never happened before. . . . What the Court says is . . . demonstrably false [even] at the constitutional level. The Eighteenth Amendment to the Federal Constitution, for example, deprived those who drank alcohol not only of the power to alter the policy of prohibition locally or through state legislation, but even of the power to alter it through state constitutional amendment or federal legislation. The Establishment Clause of the First Amendment prevents theocrats from having their way by converting their fellow citizens at the local, state, or federal statutory level; as does the Republican Form of Government Clause prevent monarchists.

But there is a much closer analogy, one that involves precisely the effort by the majority of citizens to preserve its view of sexual morality statewide, against the efforts of a geographically concentrated and politically powerful minority to undermine it. The constitutions of the States of Arizona, Idaho, New Mexico, Oklahoma, and Utah to this day contain provisions stating that polygamy is "forever prohibited." . . .

The United States Congress, by the way, required the inclusion of these antipolygamy provisions in the constitutions of Arizona, New Mexico, Oklahoma, and Utah, as a condition of their admission to statehood. . . . Thus, this "singling out" of the sexual practices of a single group for statewide, democratic vote—so utterly alien to our constitutional system, the Court would have us believe—has not only happened, but has received the explicit approval of the United States Congress. . . .

It remains to be explained how . . . [these state constitutional provisions are] not an "impermissible targeting" of polygamists, but (the much more mild) Amendment 2 is an "impermissible targeting" of homosexuals. Has the Court concluded that the perceived social harm of polygamy is a "legitimate concern of government," and the perceived social harm of homosexuality is not?

I strongly suspect that the answer to the last question is yes, which leads me to the last point I wish to make: . . . I think it no business of the courts (as opposed to the political branches) to take sides in this culture war. But the Court today has done so, not only by inventing a novel and extravagant constitutional doctrine to take the victory away from traditional forces, but even by verbally disparaging as bigotry adherence to traditional attitudes. . . .

When the Court takes sides in the culture wars, it tends to be with the knights rather than the villains—and more specifically with the Templars, reflecting the views and values of the lawyer class from which the Court's Members are drawn. How that class feels about homosexuality will be evident to anyone who wishes to interview job applicants at virtually any of the Nation's law schools. The interviewer may refuse to offer a job because the applicant is a Republican; because he is an adulterer; because he went to the wrong prep school or belongs to the wrong country club; because he eats snails; because he is a womanizer; because she wears real-animal fur; or even because he hates the Chicago Cubs. But if the interviewer should wish not to be an associate or partner of an applicant because he disapproves of the applicant's homosexuality, then he will have violated the pledge which the Association of American Law Schools requires all its member-schools to exact from job interviewers: "assurance of the employer's willingness" to hire homosexuals. This law-school view of what "prejudices" must be stamped out may be contrasted with the more plebeian attitudes that apparently still prevail in the United States Congress, which has been unresponsive to repeated attempts to extend to homosexuals the protections of federal civil rights laws and which took the pains to exclude them specifically from the Americans With Disabilities Act of 1900.

Today's opinion has no foundation in American constitutional law, and barely pretends to. The people of Colorado have adopted an entirely reasonable provision which does not even disfavor homosexuals in any substantive sense, but merely denies them preferential treatment. Amendment 2 is designed to prevent piecemeal deterioration of the sexual morality favored by a majority of Coloradans, and is not only an appropriate means to that legitimate end, but a means that Americans have employed before. Striking it down is an act, not of judicial judgment, but of political will. I dissent.

Cruzan v. Director, Missouri Department of Health
497 U.S. 261; 110 S. Ct. 2841; 111 L. Ed. 2d 224 (1990)

Nancy Cruzan was thrown from her car and sustained severe injuries in an automobile accident in 1983. Before paramedics arrived on the scene and restored her heartbeat and breathing, her brain had been deprived of oxygen for twelve to fourteen minutes. She remained in a coma for about three weeks and then fell into a persistent vegetative state, exhibiting motor reflexes but evincing no indications of significant cognitive function. When subsequent rehabilitative efforts proved unsuccessful, she was moved to a Missouri state hospital and cared for at state expense. As it became increasingly apparent that she had virtually no chance of regaining her mental faculties, her parents asked the state hospital employees to terminate the artificial nutrition and hydration procedures keeping her alive. They refused, without a court order, to honor the parents' request, since that would result in her death. A state court judge authorized the termination, finding that Cruzan had a fundamental right under the Fourteenth Amendment to direct or refuse the withdrawal of life-prolonging procedures and that Cruzan's expression to a former housemate that she would not wish to continue her life if sick or injured unless she could live "at least halfway normally" suggested that she would not wish to continue on with artificial nutrition and hydration. The Missouri Supreme Court reversed; it declined to read into either the Missouri or U.S. Constitutions a broad right to privacy that would support an unrestricted right to refuse treatment, and it rejected the argument that her parents were entitled to order the termination of her medical treatment, concluding that no person can assume that choice for an incompetent in the absence of a living will or clear and convincing evidence of the patient's wishes. The Supreme Court granted certiorari. *Opinion of the Court: Rehnquist, Kennedy, O'Connor, Scalia, White. Concurring opinions: O'Connor; Scalia. Dissenting opinions: Brennan, Blackmun, Marshall; Stevens.*

CHIEF JUSTICE REHNQUIST delivered the opinion of the Court.

. . . This is the first case in which we have been squarely presented with the issue of whether the United States Constitution grants what is in common parlance referred to as a "right to die." We follow the judicious counsel of our decision in *Twin City Bank* v. *Nebeker*, 167 U.S. 196, 202 (1897), where we said that in deciding "a question of such magnitude and importance . . . it is the [better] part of wisdom not to attempt, by any general statement, to cover every possible phase of the subject."

The Fourteenth Amendment provides that no State shall "deprive any person of life, liberty, or property, without due process of law." The principle that a competent person has a constitutionally protected liberty interest in refusing unwanted medical treatment may be inferred from our prior decisions. In *Jacobson* v. *Massachusetts*, 197 U.S. 11, 24-30 (1905), for instance, the Court balanced an individual's liberty interest in declining an unwanted smallpox vaccine against the State's interest in preventing disease. . . .

But determining that a person has a "liberty interest" under the Due Process Clause does not end the inquiry; "whether respondent's constitutional rights have been violated must be determined by balancing his liberty interests against the relevant state interests."

[F]or purposes of this case, we assume that the United States Constitution would grant a competent person a constitutionally protected right to refuse lifesaving hydration and nutrition.

Petitioners go on to assert that an incompetent person should possess the same right in this respect as is possessed by a competent person. . . .

The difficulty with petitioners' claim is that in a sense it begs the question: an incompetent person is not able to make an informed and voluntary choice to exercise a hypothetical right to refuse treatment or any other right. Such a "right" must be exercised for her, if at all, by some sort of surrogate. Here, Missouri has in effect recognized that under certain circumstances a surrogate may act for the patient in electing to have hydration and nutrition withdrawn in such a way as to cause death, but it has established a procedural safeguard to assure that the action of the surrogate conforms as best it may to the wishes expressed by the patient while competent. Missouri requires that evidence of the incompetent's wishes as to the withdrawal of treatment be proved by clear and convincing evidence. The question, then, is whether the United States Constitution forbids the establishment of this procedural requirement by the State. We hold that it does not.

Whether or not Missouri's clear and convincing evidence requirement comports with the

United States Constitution depends in part on what interests the State may properly seek to protect in this situation. Missouri relies on its interest in the protection and preservation of human life, and there can be no gainsaying this interest. As a general matter, the States—indeed, all civilized nations—demonstrate their commitment to life by treating homicide as serious crime. Moreover, the majority of States in this country have laws imposing criminal penalties on one who assists another to commit suicide. We do not think a State is required to remain neutral in the face of an informed and voluntary decision by a physically-able adult to starve to death.

But in the context presented here, a State has more particular interests at stake. The choice between life and death is a deeply personal decision of obvious and overwhelming finality. We believe Missouri may legitimately seek to safeguard the personal element of this choice through the imposition of heightened evidentiary requirements. It cannot be disputed that the Due Process Clause protects an interest in life as well as an interest in refusing life-sustaining medical treatment. Not all incompetent patients will have loved ones available to serve as surrogate decisionmakers.

In our view, Missouri has permissibly sought to advance these interests through the adoption of a "clear and convincing" standard of proof to govern such proceedings. "The function of a standard of proof, as that concept is embodied in the Due Process Clause and in the realm of factfinding, is to 'instruct the factfinder concerning the degree of confidence our society thinks he should have in the correctness of factual conclusions for a particular type of adjudication.' "

We think it self-evident that the interests at stake in the instant proceedings are more substantial, both on an individual and societal level, than those involved in a run-of-the-mill civil dispute. But not only does the standard of proof reflect the importance of a particular adjudication, it also serves as " a societal judgment about how the risk of error should be distributed between the litigants." The more stringent the burden of proof a party must bear, the more that party bears the risk of an erroneous decision. We believe that Missouri may permissibly place an increased risk of an erroneous decision on those seeking to terminate an incompetent individual's

life-sustaining treatment. An erroneous decision not to terminate results in a maintenance of the status quo; the possibility of subsequent developments such as advancements in medical science, the discovery of new evidence regarding the patient's intent, changes in the law, or simply the unexpected death of the patient despite the administration of life-sustaining treatment, at least create the potential that a wrong decision will eventually be corrected or its impact mitigated. An erroneous decision to withdraw life-sustaining treatment, however, is not susceptible of correction. . . .

In sum, we conclude that a State may apply a clear and convincing evidence standard in proceedings where a guardian seeks to discontinue nutrition and hydration of a person diagnosed to be in a persistent vegetative state. We note that many courts which have adopted some sort of substituted judgment procedure in situations like this, whether they limit consideration of evidence to the prior expressed wishes of the incompetent individual, or whether they allow more general proof of what the individual's decision would have been, require a clear and convincing standard of proof for such evidence. . . .

No doubt is engendered by anything in this record but that Nancy Cruzan's mother and father are loving and caring parents. If the State were required by the United States Constitution to repose a right of "substituted judgment" with anyone, the Cruzans would surely qualify. But we do not think the Due Process Clause requires the State to repose judgment on these matters with anyone but the patient herself. Close family members may have a strong feeling—a feeling not at all ignoble or unworthy, but not entirely disinterested, either—that they do not wish to witness the continuation of the life of a loved one which they regard as hopeless, meaningless, and even degrading. But there is no automatic assurance that the view of close family members will necessarily be the same as the patient's would have been had she been confronted with the prospect of her situation while competent. All of the reasons previously discussed for allowing Missouri to require clear and convincing evidence of the patient's wishes lead us to conclude that the State may choose to defer only to those wishes, rather than confide the decision to close family members.

The judgment of the Supreme Court of Missouri is

Affirmed.

JUSTICE O'CONNOR concurring.

I agree that a protected liberty interest in refusing unwanted medical treatment may be inferred from our prior decisions, and that the refusal of artificially delivered food and water is encompassed within that liberty interest. I write separately to clarify why I believe this to be so.

As the Court notes, the liberty interest in refusing medical treatment flows from decisions involving the State's invasions into the body. Because our notions of liberty are inextricably entwined with our idea of physical freedom and self-determination, the Court has often deemed state incursions into the body repugnant to the interests protected by the Due Process Clause....

Accordingly, the liberty guaranteed by the Due Process Clause must protect, if it protects anything, an individual's deeply personal decision to reject medical treatment, including the artificial delivery of food and water.

I also write separately to emphasize that the Court does not today decide the issue whether a State must also give effect to the decisions of a surrogate decisionmaker. In my view, such a duty may well be constitutionally required to protect the patient's liberty interest in refusing medical treatment. Few individuals provide explicit oral or written instructions regarding their intent to refuse medical treatment should they become incompetent. States which decline to consider any evidence other than such instructions may frequently fail to honor a patient's intent. Such failures might be avoided if the State considered an equally probative source of evidence: the patient's appointment of a proxy to make health care decisions on her behalf. Delegating the authority to make medical decisions to a family member or friend is becoming a common method of planning for the future....

Today's decision, holding only that the Constitution permits a State to require clear and convincing evidence of Nancy Cruzan's desire to have artificial hydration and nutrition withdrawn, does not preclude a future determination that the Constitution requires the States to implement the decisions of a patient's duly appointed surrogate. Nor does it prevent States from developing other approaches for protecting an incompetent individual's liberty interest in refusing medical treatment. As is evident from the Court's survey of state court decisions, no national consensus has yet emerged on the best solution for this difficult and sensitive problem. Today we decide only that one State's practice does not violate the Constitution; the more challenging task of crafting appropriate procedures for safeguarding incompetents' liberty interests is entrusted to the "laboratory" of the States in the first instance.

JUSTICE SCALIA, concurring.

The various opinions in this case portray quite clearly the difficult, indeed agonizing, questions that are presented by the constantly increasing power of science to keep the human body alive for longer than any reasonable person would want to inhabit it. The States have begun to grapple with these problems through legislation. I am concerned, from the tenor of today's opinions, that we are poised to confuse that enterprise as successfully as we have confused the enterprise of legislating concerning abortion—requiring it to be conducted against a background of federal constitutional imperatives that are unknown because they are being newly crafted from Term to Term. That would be a great misfortune.

While I agree with the Court's analysis today, and therefore join in its opinion, I would have preferred that we announce, clearly and promptly, that the federal courts have no business in this field; that American law has always accorded the State the power to prevent, by force if necessary, suicide—including suicide by refusing to take appropriate measures necessary to preserve one's life; that the point at which life becomes "worthless," and the point at which the means necessary to preserve it become "extraordinary" or "inappropriate," are neither set forth in the Constitution nor known to the nine Justices of this Court any better than they are known to nine people picked at random from the Kansas City telephone directory; and hence, that even when it *is* demonstrated by clear and convincing evidence that a patient no longer wishes certain measures to be taken to preserve her life, it is up to the citizens of Missouri to decide, through their elected representatives, whether that wish will be honored. It is quite impossible (because the Constitution says nothing about the matter) that those citizens will decide upon a line less lawful than the one we would choose; and it is unlikely (because we know no more about "life-and-death" than they do) that they will decide upon a line less reasonable.

The text of the Due Process Clause does not protect individuals against deprivations of liberty *simpliciter*. It protects them against deprivations of liberty "without due process of law." To determine that such a deprivation would not occur if Nancy Cruzan were forced to take nourishment against her will, it is unnecessary to reopen the historically recurrent debate over whether "due process" includes substantive restrictions. . . . It is at least true that no "substantive due process" claim can be maintained unless the claimant demonstrates that the State has deprived him of a right historically and traditionally protected against State interference. *Bowers* v. *Hardwick*, 478 U.S. 186 (1986). . . . That cannot possibly be established here. . . .

I assert only that the Constitution has nothing to say about [a "right to die"]. To raise up a constitutional right here we would have to create out of nothing (for it exists neither in text nor tradition) some constitutional principle whereby, although the State may insist that an individual come in out of the cold and eat food, it may not insist that he take medicine; and although it may pump his stomach empty of poison he has ingested, it may not fill his stomach with food he has failed to ingest. Are there, then, no reasonable and humane limits that ought not to be exceeded in requiring an individual to preserve his own life? There obviously are, but they are not set forth in the Due Process Clause. What assures us that those limits will not be exceeded is the same constitutional guarantee that is the source of most of our protection—what protects us, for example, from being assessed a tax of 100% of our income above the subsistence level, from being forbidden to drive cars, or from being required to send our children to school for 10 hours a day, none of which horribles is categorically prohibited by the Constitution. Our salvation is the Equal Protection Clause, which requires the democratic majority to accept for themselves and their loved ones what they impose on you and me. This Court need not, and has no authority to, inject itself into every field of human activity where irrationality and op-

pression may theoretically occur, and if it tries to do so it will destroy itself.

JUSTICE BRENNAN, with whom JUSTICE MARSHALL and JUSTICE BLACKMUN join, dissenting.

Because I believe that Nancy Cruzan has a fundamental right to be free of unwanted artificial nutrition and hydration, which right is not outweighed by any interests of the State, and because I find that the improperly biased procedural obstacles imposed by the Missouri Supreme Court impermissibly burden that right, I respectfully dissent. Nancy Cruzan is entitled to choose to die with dignity. . . .

The question before this Court is a relatively narrow one: whether the Due Process Clause allows Missouri to require a now-incompetent patient in an irreversible persistent vegetative state to remain on life-support absent rigorously clear and convincing evidence that avoiding the treatment represents the patient's prior, express choice. . . .

The starting point for our legal analysis must be whether a competent person has a constitutional right to avoid unwanted medical care. Earlier this Term, this Court held that the Due Process Clause of the Fourteenth Amendment confers a significant liberty interest in avoiding unwanted medical treatment. Today, the Court concedes that our prior decisions "support the recognition of a general liberty interest in refusing medical treatment." . . .

But if a competent person has a liberty interest to be free of unwanted medical treatment, as both the majority and Justice O'Connor concede, it must be fundamental. "We are dealing here with [a decision] which involves one of the basic civil rights of man."

The right to be free from medical attention without consent, to determine what shall be done with one's own body, *is* deeply rooted in this Nation's traditions, as the majority acknowledges. This right has long been "firmly entrenched in American tort law" and is securely grounded in the earliest common law.

That there may be serious consequences involved in refusal of the medical treatment at issue here does not vitiate the right under our common law tradition of medical self-determination. . . .

The right to be free from unwanted medical attention is a right to evaluate the potential benefit of treatment and its possible consequences according to one's own values and to make a personal decision whether to subject oneself to the intrusion. For a patient like Nancy Cruzan, the sole benefit of medical treatment is being kept metabolically alive. Neither artificial nutrition nor any other form of medical treatment available today can cure or in any way ameliorate her condition. Irreversibly vegetative patients are devoid of thought, emotion and sensation; they are permanently and completely unconscious. . . .

There are also affirmative reasons why someone like Nancy might choose to forgo artificial nutrition and hydration under these circumstances. Dying is personal. And it is profound. For many, the thought of an ignoble end, steeped in decay, is abhorrent. A quiet, proud death, bodily integrity intact, is a matter of extreme consequence. . . .

Although the right to be free of unwanted medical intervention, like other constitutionally protected interests, may not be absolute, no State interest could outweigh the rights of an individual in Nancy Cruzan's position. Whatever a State's possible interests in mandating life-support treatment under other circumstances, there is no good to be obtained here by Missouri's insistence that Nancy Cruzan remain on life-support systems if it is indeed her wish not to do so. Missouri does not claim, nor could it, that society as a whole will be benefited by Nancy's receiving medical treatment. No third party's situation will be improved and no harm to others will be averted.

The only state interest asserted here is a general interest in the preservation of life. But the State has no legitimate general interest in someone's life, completely abstracted from the interest of the person living that life, that could outweigh the person's choice to avoid medical treatment. . . . Thus, the State's general interest in life must accede to Nancy Cruzan's particularized and intense interest in self-determination in her choice of medical treatment. There is simply nothing legitimately within the State's purview to be gained by superseding her decision. . . .

This is not to say that the State has no legitimate interests to assert here. As the majority recognizes, Missouri has a *parens patriae* interest in providing Nancy Cruzan, now incompetent, with as accurate as possible a determination of how she would exercise her rights under these circum-

stances. Second, if and when it is determined that Nancy Cruzan would want to continue treatment, the State may legitimately assert an interest in providing that treatment. But *until* Nancy's wishes have been determined, the only state interest that may be asserted is an interest in safeguarding the accuracy of that determination.

Accuracy, therefore, must be our touchstone. Missouri may constitutionally impose only those procedural requirements that serve to enhance the accuracy of a determination of Nancy Cruzan's wishes or are at least consistent with an accurate determination. The Missouri "safeguard" that the Court upholds today does not meet that standard. The determination needed in this context is whether the incompetent person would choose to live in a persistent vegetative state on life-support or to avoid this medical treatment. Missouri's rule of decision imposes a markedly asymmetrical evidentiary burden. Only evidence of specific statements of treatment choice made by the patient when competent is admissible to support a finding that the patient, now in a persistent vegetative state, would wish to avoid further medical treatment. Moreover, this evidence must be clear and convincing. No proof is required to support a finding that the incompetent person would wish to continue treatment. . . .

The majority offers several justifications for Missouri's heightened evidentiary standard. First, the majority explains that the State may constitutionally adopt this rule to govern determinations of an incompetent's wishes in order to advance the State's substantive interests, including its unqualified interest in the preservation of human life. Missouri's evidentiary standard, however, cannot rest on the State's own interest in a particular substantive result. To be sure, courts have long erected clear and convincing evidence standards to place the greater risk of erroneous decisions on those bringing disfavored claims. In such cases, however, the choice to discourage certain claims was a legitimate, constitutional policy choice. In contrast, Missouri has no such power to disfavor a choice by Nancy Cruzan to avoid medical treatment, because Missouri has no legitimate interest in providing Nancy with treatment until it is established that this represents her choice. Just as a State may not override Nancy's choice directly, it may not do so indirectly through the imposition of a procedural rule.

The majority claims that the allocation of the risk of error is justified because it is more important not to terminate life-support for someone who would wish it continued than to honor the wishes of someone who would not. An erroneous decision to terminate life-support is irrevocable, says the majority, while an erroneous decision not to terminate "results in a maintenance of the status quo." But, from the point of view of the patient, an erroneous decision in either direction is irrevocable. An erroneous decision to terminate artificial nutrition and hydration, to be sure, will lead to failure of that last remnant of physiological life, the brain stem, and result in complete brain death. An erroneous decision not to terminate life-support, however, robs a patient of the very qualities protected by the right to avoid unwanted medical treatment. His own degraded existence is perpetuated; his family's suffering is protracted; the memory he leaves behind becomes more and more distorted. . . .

Even more than its heightened evidentiary standard, the Missouri court's categorical exclusion of relevant evidence dispenses with any semblance of accurate factfinding. The court adverted to no evidence supporting its decision, but held that no clear and convincing, inherently reliable evidence had been presented to show that Nancy would want to avoid further treatment. In doing so, the court failed to consider statements Nancy had made to family members and a close friend. The court also failed to consider testimony from Nancy's mother and sister that they were certain that Nancy would want to discontinue artificial nutrition and hydration, even after the court found that Nancy's family was loving and without malignant motive. The court also failed to consider the conclusions of the guardian ad litem, appointed by the trial court, that there was clear and convincing evidence that Nancy would want to discontinue medical treatment and that this was in her best interests. The court did not specifically define what kind of evidence it would consider clear and convincing, but its general discussion suggests that only a living will or equivalently formal directive from the patient when competent would meet this standard. . . .

Too few people execute living wills or equivalently formal directives for such an evidentiary rule to ensure adequately that the wishes of incompetent persons will be honored. While it might be a wise social policy to encourage people to furnish such instructions, no general conclusion about a patient's choice can be drawn from the absence of formalities. The probability of becoming irreversibly vegetative is so low that many people may not feel an urgency to marshal formal evidence of their preferences. Some may not wish to dwell on their own physical deterioration and mortality. Even someone with a resolute determination to avoid life-support under circumstances such as Nancy's would still need to know that such things as living wills exist and how to execute one. Often legal help would be necessary, especially given the majority's apparent willingness to permit States to insist that a person's wishes are not truly known unless the particular medical treatment is specified. . . .

I do not suggest that States must sit by helplessly if the choices of incompetent patients are in danger of being ignored. Even if the Court had ruled that Missouri's rule of decision is unconstitutional, as I believe it should have, States would nevertheless remain free to fashion procedural protections to safeguard the interests of incompetents under these circumstances. The Constitution provides merely a framework here: protections must be genuinely aimed at ensuring decisions commensurate with the will of the patient, and must be reliable as instruments to that end. Of the many States which have instituted such protections, Missouri is virtually the only one to have fashioned a rule that lessens the likelihood of accurate determinations. In contrast, nothing in the Constitution prevents States from reviewing the advisability of a family decision, by requiring a court proceeding or by appointing an impartial guardian ad litem. . . .

Finally, I cannot agree with the majority that where it is not possible to determine what choice an incompetent patient would make, a State's role as *parens patriae* permits the State automatically to make that choice itself. . . .

The majority justifies its position by arguing that, while close family members may have a strong feeling about the question, "there is no automatic assurance that the view of close family members will necessarily be the same as the patient's would have been had she been confronted with the prospect of her situation while competent." I cannot quarrel with this observation. But it leads only to another question: Is there any reason to suppose that a State is *more* likely to make the choice that the patient would have made than someone who knew the patient intimately? To ask this is to answer it. As the New Jersey Supreme Court observed: "Family members are best qualified to make substituted judgments for incompetent patients not only because of their peculiar grasp of the patient's approach to life, but also because of their special bonds with him or her. . . . It is . . . they who treat the patient as a person, rather than a symbol of a cause." The State, in contrast, is a stranger to the patient.

I respectfully dissent.

JUSTICE STEVENS, dissenting.

Nancy Cruzan's interest in life, no less than that of any other person, includes an interest in how she will be thought of after her death by those whose opinions mattered to her. There can be no doubt that her life made her dear to her family, and to others. How she dies will affect how that life is remembered. The trial court's order authorizing Nancy's parents to cease their daughter's treatment would have permitted the family that cares for Nancy to bring to a close her tragedy and her death. Missouri's objection to that order subordinates Nancy's body, her family, and the lasting significance of her life to the State's own interests. The decision we review thereby interferes with constitutional interests of the highest order.

To be constitutionally permissible, Missouri's intrusion upon these fundamental liberties must, at a minimum, bear a reasonable relationship to a legitimate state end. Missouri asserts that its policy is related to a state interest in the protection of life. In my view, however, it is an effort to define life, rather than to protect it, that is the heart of Missouri's policy. Missouri insists, without regard to Nancy Cruzan's own interests, upon equating her life with the biological persistence of her bodily functions. Nancy Cruzan, it must be remembered, is not now simply incompetent. She is in a persistent vegetative state, and has been so for seven years. The trial court found, and no party contested, that Nancy has no possibility of recovery and no consciousness.

It seems to me that the Court errs insofar as it characterizes this case as involving "judgments about the 'quality' of life that a particular individual may enjoy." Nancy Cruzan is obviously "*alive*" in a physiological sense. But for patients like Nancy Cruzan, who have no consciousness and no chance of recovery, there is a serious question as to whether the mere persistence of their bodies is "*life*" as that word is commonly understood, or as it is used in both the Constitution and the Declaration of Independence. The State's unflagging determination to perpetuate Nancy Cruzan's physical existence is comprehensible only as an effort to define life's meaning, not as an attempt to preserve its sanctity.

This much should be clear from the oddity of Missouri's definition alone. Life, particularly human life, is not commonly thought of as a merely physiological condition or function. Its sanctity is often thought to derive from the impossibility of any such reduction. When people speak of life, they often mean to describe the experiences that comprise a person's history, as when it is said that somebody "led a good life." They may also mean to refer to the practical manifestation of the human spirit, a meaning captured by the familiar observation that somebody "added life" to an assembly. If there is a shared thread among the various opinions on this subject, it may be that life is an activity which is at once the matrix for and an integration of a person's interests. In any event, absent some theological abstraction, the idea of life is not conceived separately from the idea of a living person. Yet, it is by precisely such a separation that Missouri asserts an interest in Nancy Cruzan's life in opposition to Nancy Cruzan's own interests. The resulting definition is uncommon indeed.

Washington v. *Glucksberg*

117 S. Ct. 2258; 138 L. Ed. 2d 772 (1997)

Since its first territorial legislature outlawed "assisting another in the commission of self-murder" in 1854, it has always been a crime to assist a suicide in the State of Washington. The State's present law makes "[p]romoting a suicide attempt" a felony, and provides: "A person is guilty of [that crime] when he knowingly causes or aids another person to attempt suicide." Dr. Harold Glucksberg and three other Washington physicians who occasionally treated terminally ill, suffering patients, declared that they would assist these patients in ending their lives were it not for the State's assisted-suicide ban. They, along with three gravely ill plaintiffs who subsequently died and a nonprofit organization that counsels people considering physician-assisted suicide, filed suit in U.S. District Court against petitioners, the State and its Attorney-General, seeking a declaration that the ban is, on its face, unconstitutional. They asserted a liberty interest protected by the Fourteenth Amendment's Due Process Clause which extends to a personal choice by a mentally competent, terminally ill adult to commit physician-assisted suicide. Relying primarily on *Planned Parenthood of Southeastern Pennsylvania v. Casey*, 505 U.S. 833, and *Cruzan* v. *Director, Missouri Department of Health*, 497 U.S. 261, the federal district court agreed, concluding that Washington's assisted-suicide ban was unconstitutional because it places an undue burden on the exercise of that constitutionally protected liberty interest. A panel of the Court of Appeals for the Ninth Circuit reversed, emphasizing that "[i]n the two hundred and five years of our existence no constitutional right to aid in killing oneself has ever been asserted and upheld by a court of final jurisdiction." The Ninth Circuit reheard the case *en banc*, reversed the panel's decision, and affirmed the district court. Like the district court, the *en banc* court of appeals emphasized the *Casey* and *Cruzan* decisions. The U.S. Supreme Court granted certiorari and heard it in conjunction with *Vacco* v. *Quill* (which follows next), a case in which the Second Circuit invalidated New York's ban on assisted suicide on equal protection grounds. Except for Chief Justice Rehnquist's separate majority opinions in the two cases, and Justice Souter's separate concurrences, all of the other justices who wrote opinions in these cases wrote combined concurrences which are found here. *Opinion of the Court: Rehnquist, Kennedy, O'Connor, Scalia, Thomas. Concurring opinion: O'Connor, Breyer, Ginsburg. Concurring in the judgment: Breyer, Ginsburg, Souter, Stevens.*

CHIEF JUSTICE REHNQUIST delivered the opinion of the Court.

The question presented in this case is whether Washington's prohibition against "caus[ing]" or "aid[ing]" a suicide offends the Fourteenth Amendment to the United States Constitution. We hold that it does not. . . .

We begin, as we do in all due-process cases, by examining our Nation's history, legal traditions, and practices. In almost every State—indeed, in almost every western democracy—it is a crime to assist a suicide. The States' assisted-suicide bans are not innovations. Rather, they are long-standing expressions of the States' commitment to the protection and preservation of all human life. Indeed, opposition to and condemnation of suicide—and, therefore, of assisting suicide—are consistent and enduring themes of our philosophical, legal, and cultural heritages.

More specifically, for over 700 years, the Anglo-American common-law tradition has punished or otherwise disapproved of both suicide and assisting suicide. . . . Though deeply rooted, the States' assisted-suicide bans have in recent years been reexamined and, generally, reaffirmed. Because of advances in medicine and technology, Americans today are increasingly likely to die in institutions, from chronic illnesses. Public concern and democratic action are therefore sharply focused on how best to protect dignity and independence at the end of life, with the result that there have been many significant changes in state laws and in the attitudes these reflect. Many States, for example, now permit "living wills," surrogate health-care decision-making, and the withdrawal or refusal of life-sustaining medical treatment. At the same time, however, voters and legislators continue for the most part to reaffirm their States' prohibitions on assisting suicide.

The Washington statute at issue in this case was enacted in 1975 as part of a revision of that State's criminal code. Four years later, Washington passed its Natural Death Act, which specifically stated that the "withholding or withdrawal of life-sustaining treatment . . . shall not, for any purpose, constitute a suicide" and that "[n]othing in this chapter shall be construed to condone, authorize, or approve every mercy killing. . . ." In 1991, Washington voters rejected a ballot initiative which, had it passed, would have permitted a form of physician-assisted suicide. Washington then added a provision to the Natural Death Act expressly excluding physician-assisted suicide.

California voters rejected an assisted-suicide initiative similar to Washington's in 1993. On the other hand, in 1994, voters in Oregon enacted, also through ballot initiative, that State's "Death With Dignity Act," which legalized physician-assisted suicide for competent, terminally ill adults. Since the Oregon vote, many proposals to legalize assisted-suicide have been and continue to be introduced in the States' legislatures, but none has been enacted. And just last year, Iowa and Rhode Island joined the overwhelming majority of States explicitly prohibiting assisted suicide. Also, on April 30, 1997, President Clinton signed the Federal Assisted Suicide Funding Restriction Act of 1997, which prohibits the use of federal funds in support of physician-assisted suicide.

Thus, the States are currently engaged in serious, thoughtful examinations of physician-assisted suicide and other similar issues. . . .

Attitudes toward suicide itself have changed [over the centuries], but our laws have consistently condemned, and continue to prohibit, assisting suicide. Despite changes in medical technology and notwithstanding an increased emphasis on the importance of end-of-life decisionmaking, we have not retreated from this prohibition. Against this backdrop of history, tradition, and practice, we now turn to respondents' constitutional claim.

The Due Process Clause guarantees more than fair process, and the "liberty" it protects includes more than the absence of physical restraint. The Clause also provides heightened protection against government interference with certain fundamental rights and liberty interests. In a long line of cases, we have held that, in addition to the specific freedoms protected by the Bill of Rights, the "liberty" specially protected by the Due Process Clause includes the rights to marry, *Loving* v. *Virginia*, 388 U.S. 1 (1967); to have children, *Skinner* v. *Oklahoma ex rel. Williamson*, 316 U.S. 535 (1942); to direct the education and upbringing of one's children, *Meyer* v. *Nebraska*, 262 U.S. 390 (1923); *Pierce* v. *Society of Sisters*, 268 U.S. 510 (1925); to marital privacy, *Griswold* v. *Connecticut*, 381 U.S. 479 (1965); to use contraception, *ibid; Eisenstadt* v. *Baird*, 405 U.S. 438 (1972); to bodily integrity, *Rochin* v. *California*, 342 U.S. 165 (1952); and to abortion, *Casey*. We have also assumed, and strongly suggested, that the Due Process Clause protects the traditional right to refuse unwanted lifesaving medical treatment.

But we "ha[ve] always been reluctant to expand the concept of substantive due process because guideposts for responsible decisionmaking in this unchartered area are scarce and open-ended." By extending constitutional protection to an asserted right or liberty interest, we, to a great extent, place the matter outside the arena of public debate and legislative action. We must therefore "exercise the utmost care whenever we are asked to break new ground in this field," lest the liberty protected by the Due Process Clause be subtly transformed into the policy preferences of the members of this Court.

Our established method of substantive-due-process analysis has two primary features: First, we have regularly observed that the Due Process Clause specially protects those fundamental rights and liberties which are, objectively, "deeply rooted in this Nation's history and tradition." Second, we have required in substantive-due-process cases a "careful description" of the asserted fundamental liberty interest. . . . This approach tends to rein in the subjective elements that are necessarily present in due-process judicial review. In addition, by establishing a threshold requirement—that a challenged state action implicate a fundamental right—before requiring more than a reasonable relation to a legitimate state interest to justify the action, it avoids the need for complex balancing of competing interests in every case.

Turning to the claim at issue here, the Court of Appeals stated that "[p]roperly analyzed, the first issue to be resolved is whether there is a liberty interest in determining the time and manner of one's death," or, in other words, "[i]s there a right to die?" Similarly, respondents assert a "liberty to choose how to die" and a right to "control of one's final days" and describe the asserted liberty as "the right to choose a humane, dignified death" and "the liberty to shape death." . . .

We now inquire whether this asserted right has any place in our Nation's traditions. Here, as discussed above, we are confronted with a consistent and almost universal tradition that has long rejected the asserted right, and continues explicitly to reject it today, even for terminally ill, mentally competent adults. To hold for respondents, we would have to reverse centuries of legal doctrine and practice, and strike down the considered policy choice of almost every State.

Respondents contend, however, that the liberty interest they assert *is* consistent with this Court's substantive-due-process line of cases, if not with this Nation's history and practice. Pointing to *Casey* and *Cruzan,* respondents read our jurisprudence in this area as reflecting a general tradition of "self-sovereignty" and as teaching that the "liberty" protected by the Due Process Clause includes "basic and intimate exercises of personal autonomy." . . . The question presented in this case, however, is whether the protections of the Due Process Clause include a right to commit suicide with another's assistance. With this "careful description" of respondents' claim in mind, we turn to *Casey* and *Cruzan.*

In *Cruzan,* we considered whether Nancy Beth Cruzan, who had been severely injured in an automobile accident and was in a persistive vegetative state, "ha[d] a right under the United States Constitution which would require the hospital to withdraw life-sustaining treatment"

at her parents' request. . . . "[F]or purposes of [that] case, we assume[d] that the United States Constitution would grant a competent person a constitutionally protected right to refuse lifesaving hydration and nutrition." We concluded that, notwithstanding this right, the Constitution permitted Missouri to require clear and convincing evidence of an incompetent patient's wishes concerning the withdrawal of life-sustaining treatment. . . . In *Cruzan* itself, we recognized that most States outlawed assisted suicide—and even more do today—and we certainly gave no intimation that the right to refuse unwanted medical treatment could be somehow transmuted into a right to assistance in committing suicide.

Respondents also rely on *Casey.* There, the Court's opinion . . . discussed in some detail this Court's substantive-due-process tradition of interpreting the Due Process Clause to protect certain fundamental rights and "personal decisions relating to marriage, procreation, contraception, family relationships, child rearing, and education," and noted that many of those rights and liberties "involv[e] the most intimate and personal choices a person may make in a lifetime."

The Court of Appeals, like the District Court, found *Casey* "'highly instructive'" and "'almost prescriptive'" for determining "'what liberty interest may inhere in a terminally ill person's choice to commit suicide'":

> Like the decision of whether or not to have an abortion, the decision how and when to die is one of "the most intimate and personal choices a person may make in a lifetime," a choice "central to personal dignity and autonomy."

Similarly, respondents emphasize the statement in *Casey* that:

> At the heart of liberty is the right to define one's own concept of existence, of meaning, of the universe, and of the mystery of human life. Beliefs about these matters could not define the attributes of personhood were they formed under compulsion of the State.

. . . That many of the rights and liberties protected by the Due Process Clause [are grounded] in personal autonomy does not warrant the sweeping conclusion that any and all important, intimate, and personal decisions are so protected, and *Casey* did not suggest otherwise.

The history of the law's treatment of assisted suicide in this country has been and continues to be one of the rejection of nearly all efforts to permit it. That being the case, our decisions lead us to conclude that the asserted "right" to assistance in committing suicide is not a fundamental liberty interest protected by the Due Process Clause. The Constitution also requires, however, that Washington's assisted-suicide ban be rationally related to legitimate government interests. This requirement is unquestionably met here. . . .

First, Washington has an "unqualified interest in the preservation of human life." The State's prohibition on assisted suicide, like all homicide laws, both reflects and advances its commitment to this interest. . . .

The State also has an interest in protecting the integrity and ethics of the medical profession. In contrast to the Court of Appeals' conclusion that "the integrity of the medical profession would [not] be threatened in any way by [physician-assisted suicide]," the American Medical Association, like many other medical and physicians' groups, has concluded that "[p]hysician-assisted suicide is fundamentally incompatible with the physician's role as healer." . . .

Next, the State has an interest in protecting vulnerable groups—including the poor, the elderly, and disabled persons—from abuse, neglect, and mistakes. The Court of Appeals dismissed the State's concern that disadvantaged persons might be pressured into physician-assisted suicide as "ludicrous on its face." We have recognized, however, the real risk of subtle coercion and undue influence in end-of-life situations. . . .

The State's interest here goes beyond protecting the vulnerable from coercion; it extends to protecting disabled and terminally ill people from prejudice, negative and inaccurate stereotypes, and "societal indifference." The State's assisted-suicide ban reflects and reinforces its policy that the lives of terminally ill, disabled, and elderly people must be no less valued than the lives of the young and healthy, and that a seriously disabled person's suicidal impulses should be interpreted and treated the same way as anyone else's. . . .

Finally, the State may fear that permitting assisted suicide will start it down the path to voluntary and perhaps even involuntary euthanasia. The Court of Appeals struck down Washington's assisted-suicide ban only "as applied to competent, terminally ill adults who wish to hasten their deaths by obtaining medication prescribed by their doctors." Washington insists, however, that the impact of the court's decision will not and cannot be so limited. If suicide is protected as a matter of constitutional right, it is argued, "every man and woman in the United States must enjoy it." The Court of Appeals' decision, and its expansive reasoning, provide ample support for the State's concerns. . . .

This concern is further supported by evidence about the practice of euthanasia in the Netherlands. The Dutch government's own study revealed that in 1990, there were 2,300 cases of voluntary euthanasia (defined as "the deliberate termination of another's life at his request"), 400 cases of assisted suicide, and more than 1,000 cases of euthanasia without an explicit request. In addition to these latter 1,000 cases, the study found an additional 4,941 cases where physicians administered lethal morphine overdoses without the patients' explicit consent. This study suggests that, despite the existence of various reporting procedures, euthanasia in the Netherlands has not been limited to competent, terminally ill adults who are enduring physical suffering, and that regulation of the practice may not have prevented abuses in cases involving vulnerable persons, including severely disabled neonates and elderly persons suffering from dementia. . . .

Throughout the Nation, Americans are engaged in an earnest and profound debate about the morality, legality, and practicality of physician-assisted suicide. Our holding permits this debate to continue, as it should in a democratic society. The decision of the *en banc* Court of Appeals is reversed, and the case is remanded for further proceedings consistent with this opinion.

JUSTICE O'CONNOR, concurring.

. . . Every one of us at some point may be affected by our own or a family member's terminal illness. There is no reason to think the democratic process will not strike the proper balance between the interests of terminally ill, mentally competent individuals who would seek to end their suffering and the State's interests in protecting those who might seek to end life mistakenly or under pressure. As the Court recognizes, States are presently undertaking extensive and serious evaluation of physician-assisted suicide and other related issues. In such circumstances, "the . . . challenging task of crafting appropriate procedures for safeguarding . . . liberty interests is entrusted to the 'laboratory' of the States . . . in the first instance."

JUSTICE BREYER, concurring in the judgments.

. . . I do not agree . . . with the Court's formulation of that claimed "liberty" interest. The Court describes it as a "right to commit suicide with another's assistance." But I would not reject the respondents' claim without considering a different formulation, for which our legal tradition may provide greater support. That formulation would use words roughly like a "right to die with dignity." But irrespective of the exact words used, at its core would lie personal control over the manner of death, professional medical assistance, and the avoidance of unnecessary and severe physical suffering—combined. . . .

I do not believe, however, that this Court need or now should decide whether or not such a right is "fundamental." That is because, in my view, the avoidance of severe physical pain (connected with death) would have to comprise an essential part of any successful claim and because the laws before us do not *force* a dying person to undergo that kind of pain. Rather, the laws of New York and of Washington do not prohibit doctors from providing patients with drugs sufficient to control pain despite the risk that those drugs themselves will kill. And under these circumstances the laws of New York and Washington would overcome any remaining significant interests and would be justified, regardless.

JUSTICE STEVENS, concurring in the judgments.

The Court ends its opinion with the important observation that our holding today is fully consistent with a continuation of the vigorous debate about the "morality, legality, and practicality of physician-assisted suicide" in a democratic society. I write separately to make it clear that there is also room for further debate about the limits that the Constitution places on the power of the States to punish the practice. . . .

[J]ust as our conclusion that capital punishment is not always unconstitutional did not preclude later decisions holding that it is sometimes impermissibly cruel, so is it equally clear that a decision upholding a general statutory prohibition of assisted suicide does not mean that every possible application of the statute would be valid. A State, like Washington, that has authorized the death penalty and thereby has concluded that the sanctity of human life does not require that it always be preserved, must acknowledge that there are situations in which an interest in hastening death is legitimate. Indeed, not only is that interest sometimes legitimate, I am also convinced that there are times when it is entitled to constitutional protection. . . .

In New York, a doctor must respect a competent person's decision to refuse or to discontinue medical treatment even though death will thereby ensue, but the same doctor would be guilty of a felony if she provided her patient assistance in committing suicide. Today we hold that the Equal Protection Clause is not violated by the resulting disparate treatment of two classes of terminally ill people who may have the same interest in hastening death. I agree that the distinction between permitting death to ensue from an underlying fatal disease and causing it to occur by the administration of medication or other means provides a constitutionally sufficient basis for the State's classification. Unlike the Court, however, see *Vacco,* I am not persuaded that in all cases there will in fact be a significant difference between the intent of the physicians, the patients or the families in the two situations.

There may be little distinction between the intent of a terminally-ill patient who decides to remove her life-support and one who seeks the assistance of a doctor in ending her life; in both situations, the patient is seeking to hasten a certain, impending death. The doctor's intent might also be the same in prescribing lethal medication as it is in terminating life-support. . . .

There remains room for vigorous debate about the outcome of particular cases that are not necessarily resolved by the opinions announced today. How such cases may be decided will depend on their specific facts. In my judgment, however, it is clear that the so-called "unqualified interest in the preservation of human life" is not itself sufficient to outweigh the interest in liberty that may justify the only possible means of preserving a dying patient's dignity and alleviating her intolerable suffering.

JUSTICE SOUTER, concurring in the judgment.

. . . The argument supporting respondents' position . . . progresses through three steps of increasing forcefulness. First, it emphasizes the decriminalization of suicide. Reliance on this fact is sanctioned under the standard that looks not only to the tradition retained, but to society's occasional choices to reject traditions of the legal past. . . . The second step in the argument is to emphasize that the State's own act of decriminalization gives a freedom of choice much like the individual's option in recognized instances of bodily autonomy. One of these, abortion, is a legal right to choose in spite of the interest a State may legitimately invoke in discouraging the practice, just as suicide is now subject to choice, despite a state interest in discouraging it. The third step is to emphasize that respondents claim a right to assistance not on the basis of some broad principle that would be subject to exceptions if that continuing interest of the State's in discouraging suicide were to be recognized at all. Respondents base their claim on the traditional right to medical care and counsel, subject to the limiting conditions of informed, responsible choice when death is imminent, conditions that support a strong analogy to rights of care in other situations in which medical counsel and assistance have been available as a matter of course. There can be no stronger claim to a physician's assistance than at the time when death is imminent, a moral judgment implied by the State's own recognition of the legitimacy of medical procedures necessarily hastening the moment of impending death.

In my judgment, the importance of the individual interest here, as within that class of "certain interests" demanding careful scrutiny of the State's contrary claim, cannot be gainsaid. Whether that interest might in some circumstances, or at some time, be seen as "fundamental" to the degree entitled to prevail is not, however, a conclusion that I need draw here, for I am satisfied that the State's interests described in the following section are sufficiently serious to defeat the present claim that its law is arbitrary or purposeless. . . .

I take it that the basic concept of judicial review with its possible displacement of legislative judgment bars any finding that a legislature has acted arbitrarily when the following conditions are met: there is a serious factual controversy over the feasibility of recognizing the claimed right without at the same time making it impossible for the State to engage in an undoubtedly legitimate exercise of power; facts necessary to resolve the controversy are not readily ascertainable through the judicial process; but they are more readily subject to discovery through legislative factfinding and experimentation. It is assumed in this case, and must be, that a State's interest in protecting those unable to make responsible decisions and those who make no decisions at all entitles the State to bar aid to any but a knowing and responsible person intending suicide, and to prohibit euthanasia. How, and how far, a State should act in that interest are judgments for the State, but the legitimacy of its action to deny a physician the option to aid any but the knowing and responsible is beyond question. . . .

Now it is enough to say that our examination of legislative reasonableness should consider the fact that the Legislature of the State of Washington is no more obviously at fault than this Court is in being uncertain about what would happen if respondents prevailed today. We therefore have a clear question about which institution, a legislature or a court, is relatively more competent to deal with an emerging issue as to which facts currently unknown could be dispositive. The answer has to be, for the reasons already stated, that the legislative process is to be preferred. There is a closely related further reason as well. . . . The experimentation that should be out of the question in constitutional adjudication displacing legislative judgments is entirely proper, as well as highly desirable, when the legislative power addresses an emerging issue like assisted suicide. The Court should accordingly stay its hand to allow reasonable legislative consideration. While I do not decide for all time that respondents' claim should not be recognized, I acknowledge the legislative institutional competence as the better one to deal with that claim at this time.

Vacco v. Quill

117 S. Ct. 2293; 138 L. Ed. 2d 834 (1997)

New York State made it a crime to aid another to commit or attempt suicide; however, it allowed competent patients to refuse "medical treatment, even if the withdrawal of such treatment will result in death." Dr. Timothy Quill and two other New York physicians asserted that, although it would be consistent with the standards of their medical practices to prescribe lethal medication for mentally competent, terminally ill patients who are suffering great pain and desire a doctor's help in taking their own lives, they were deterred from doing so by New York's assisted-suicide ban. They and three gravely ill patients who subsequently died entered New York District Court for the Southern District of New York and sued Dennis C. Vacco, the State's Attorney-General, claiming that the ban violated the Fourteenth Amendment's Equal Protection Clause. The federal district court disagreed, but the Second Circuit reversed. It held that New York accorded different treatment to those competent, terminally ill persons who wished to hasten their deaths by self-administering prescribed drugs than it did to those who wished to do so by directing the removal of life-support systems. This unequal treatment, it held, was not rationally related to any legitimate state interests. The United States Supreme Court granted certiorari and heard it in conjunction with *Washington* v. *Glucksberg* (which precedes this case), a case in which the Ninth Circuit invalidated Washington State's ban on assisted suicide on due process grounds. Except for Chief Justice Rehnquist's majority opinions in the two cases, and Justice Souter's separate concurrences, all of the other justices who wrote opinions in these cases wrote combined concurrences, which can be found with the *Glucksberg* decision. *Opinion of the Court: Rehnquist, Kennedy, O'Connor, Scalia, Thomas, Concurrent opinion: O'Connor, Breyer, Ginsburg. Concurring in the judgment: Breyer, Ginsburg, Souter, Stevens.*

CHIEF JUSTICE REHNQUIST delivered the opinion of the Court.

In New York, as in most States, it is a crime to aid another to commit or attempt suicide, but patients may refuse even lifesaving medical treatment. The question presented by this case is whether New York's prohibition on assisting suicide therefore violates the Equal Protection Clause. . . .

The Equal Protection Clause commands that no State shall "deny to any person within its jurisdiction the equal protection of the laws." This provision creates no substantive rights. Instead, it embodies a general rule that States must treat like cases alike but may treat unlike cases accordingly. If a legislative classification or distinc-

tion "neither burdens a fundamental right nor targets a suspect class, we will uphold [it] so long as it bears a rational relation to some legitimate end."

New York's statutes outlawing assisting suicide affect and address matters of profound significance to all New Yorkers alike. They neither infringe fundamental rights nor involve suspect classifications. . . . On their faces, neither New York's ban on assisting suicide nor its statutes permitting patients to refuse medical treatment treat anyone differently than anyone else or draw any distinctions between persons. *Everyone*, regardless of physical condition, is entitled, if competent, to refuse unwanted lifesaving medical treatment; *no one* is permitted to assist a suicide.

Generally speaking, laws that apply evenhandedly to all "unquestionably comply" with the Equal Protection Clause.

The Court of Appeals, however, concluded that some terminally ill people—those who are on life-support systems—are treated differently than those who are not, in that the former may "hasten death" by ending treatment, but the latter may not "hasten death" through physician-assisted suicide. This conclusion depends on the submission that ending or refusing lifesaving medical treatment "is nothing more nor less than assisted suicide." Unlike the Court of Appeals, we think the distinction between assisting suicide and withdrawing life-sustaining treatment, a distinction widely recognized and endorsed in the medical profession and in our legal traditions, is both important and logical; it is certainly rational.

The distinction comports with fundamental legal principles of causation and intent. First, when a patient refuses life-sustaining medical treatment, he dies from an underlying fatal disease or pathology; but if a patient ingests lethal medication prescribed by a physician, he is killed by that medication. . . . Furthermore, a physician who withdraws, or honors a patient's refusal to begin, life-sustaining medical treatment purposefully intends, or may so intend, only to respect his patient's wishes and "to cease doing useless and futile or degrading things to the patient when [the patient] no longer stands to benefit from them." The same is true when a doctor provides aggressive palliative care; in some cases, painkilling drugs may hasten a patient's death, but the physician's purpose and intent is, or may be, only to ease his patient's pain. A doctor who assists a suicide, however, "must, necessarily and indubitably, intend primarily that the patient be made dead." . . .

Given these general principles, it is not surprising that many courts, including New York courts, have carefully distinguished refusing life-sustaining treatment from suicide. . . . Similarly, the overwhelming majority of state legislature have drawn a clear line between assisting suicide and withdrawing or permitting the refusal of unwanted lifesaving medical treatment by prohibiting the former and permitting the latter. . . .

This Court has also recognized, at least implicitly, the distinction between letting a patient die and making that patient die. . . . For all these reasons, we disagree with respondents' claim that the distinction between refusing lifesaving medical treatment and assisted suicide is "arbitrary" and "irrational." . . . By permitting everyone to refuse unwanted medical treatment while prohibiting anyone from assisting a suicide, New York law follows a longstanding and rational distinction.

New York's reasons for recognizing and acting on this distinction—including prohibiting intentional killing and preserving life; preventing suicide; maintaining physicians' role as their patients' healers; protecting vulnerable people from indifference, prejudice, and psychological and financial pressure to end their lives; and avoiding a possible slide towards euthanasia—are discussed in greater detail in our opinion in *Glucksberg*. These valid and important public interests easily satisfy the constitutional requirement that a legislative classification bear a rational relation to some legitimate end.

The judgment of the Court of Appeals is reversed.

JUSTICE SOUTER, concurring in the judgment.

Even though I do not conclude that assisted suicide is a fundamental right entitled to recognition at this time, I accord the claims raised by the patients and physicians in this case and *Washington* v. *Glucksberg* a high degree of importance, requiring a commensurate justification. The reasons that lead me to conclude in *Glucksberg* that the prohibition on assisted suicide is not arbitrary under the due process standard also support the distinction between assistance to suicide, which is banned, and practices such as termination of artificial life support and death-hastening pain medication, which permitted. I accordingly concur in the judgment of the Court.

THE CONSTITUTION OF THE UNITED STATES OF AMERICA

We the People of the United States, in Order to form a more perfect Union, establish Justice, insure domestic Tranquility, provide for the common defence, promote the general Welfare, and secure the Blessings of Liberty to ourselves and our Posterity, do ordain and establish this CONSTITUTION for the United States of America.

ARTICLE I

SECTION 1. All legislative Powers herein granted shall be vested in a Congress of the United States, which shall consist of a Senate and House of Representatives.

SECTION 2. [1] The House of Representatives shall be composed of Members chosen every second Year by the People of the several States, and the Electors in each State shall have the Qualifications requisite for Electors of the most numerous Branch of the State Legislature.

[2] No person shall be a Representative who shall not have attained to the Age of twenty-five Years, and been seven Years a Citizen of the United States, and who shall not, when elected, be an Inhabitant of that State in which he shall be chosen.

[3] Representatives and direct Taxes shall be apportioned among the several States which may be included within this Union, according to their respective Numbers, which shall be determined by adding to the whole Number of free Persons, including those bound to Service for a Term of Years, and excluding Indians not taxed, three fifths of all other Persons. The actual Enumeration shall be made within three Years after the first Meeting of the Congress of the United States, and within every subsequent Term of ten Years, in such Manner as they shall by Law direct. The Number of Representatives shall not exceed one for every thirty Thousand, but each State shall have at Least one Representative; and until such enumeration shall be made, the State of New Hampshire shall be entitled to chuse three, Massachusetts eight, Rhode-Island and Providence Plantations

one, Connecticut five, New York six, New Jersey four, Pennsylvania eight, Delaware one, Maryland six, Virginia ten, North Carolina five, South Carolina five, and Georgia three.

[4] When vacancies happen in the Representation from any State, the Executive Authority thereof shall issue Writs of Election to fill such Vacancies.

[5] The House of Representatives shall chuse their Speaker and other Officers; and shall have the sole Power of Impeachment.

SECTION 3. [1] The Senate of the United States shall be composed of two Senators from each State, chosen by the Legislature thereof, for six Years; and each Senator shall have one Vote.

[2] Immediately after they shall be assembled in Consequence of the first Election, they shall be divided as equally as may be into three Classes. The Seats of the Senators of the first Class shall be vacated at the Expiration of the Second Year, of the second Class at the Expiration of the fourth Year, and of the third Class at the Expiration of the sixth Year, so that one-third may be chosen every second Year; and if Vacancies happen by Resignation, or otherwise, during the Recess of the Legislature of any State, the Executive thereof may make temporary Appointments until the next Meeting of the Legislature, which shall then fill such Vacancies.

[3] No person shall be a Senator who shall not have attained to the Age of thirty Years, and been nine Years a Citizen of the United States, and who shall not, when elected, be an Inhabitant of that State for which he shall be chosen.

[4] The Vice President of the United States shall be President of the Senate, but shall have no Vote, unless they be equally divided.

[5] The Senate shall chuse their Officers, and also a President pro tempore, in the absence of the Vice President, or when he shall exercise the Office of the President of the United States.

[6] The Senate shall have the sole Power to try all Impeachments. When sitting for that Purpose, they shall be on Oath or Affirmation. When the President of the United States is tried, the Chief Justice shall preside: And no Person shall be convicted without the Concurrence of two-thirds of the Members present.

[7] Judgment in Cases of Impeachment shall not extend further than to removal from Office, and disqualification to hold and enjoy any Office of honor, Trust, or Profit under the United States: but the Party convicted shall nevertheless be liable and subject to Indictment, Trial, Judgment and Punishment, according to Law.

SECTION 4. [1] The Times, Places and Manner of holding Elections for Senators and Representatives, shall be prescribed in each State by the Legislature thereof; but the Congress may at any time by Law make or alter such Regulations, except as to the Places of chusing Senators.

[2] The Congress shall assemble at least one in every Year, and such Meeting shall be on the first Monday in December, unless they shall by Law appoint a different Day.

SECTION 5. [1] Each House shall be the Judge of the Elections, Returns, and Qualifications of its own Members, and a Majority of each shall constitute a Quorum to do Business, but a smaller Number may adjourn for day to day, and may be authorized to compel the Attendance of absent Members, in such Manner, and under such Penalties as each House may provide.

[2] Each House may determine the Rules of its Proceedings, punish its Members for disorderly Behavior, and with the Concurrence of two thirds, expel a Member.

[3] Each House shall keep a Journal of its Proceedings, and from time to time publish the same, excepting such Parts as may in their Judgment require Secrecy; and the Yeas and Nays of the Members of either House or any question shall, at the Desire of one fifth of those Present, be entered on the Journal.

[4] Neither House, during the Session of Congress, shall, without the Consent of the other, adjourn for more than three days, nor to any other Place than that in which the two Houses shall be sitting.

SECTION 6. [1] The Senators and Representatives shall receive a Compensation for their Services, to be ascertained by Law, and paid out of the treasury of the United States. They shall in all Cases, except Treason, Felony and Breach of the Peace, be privileged from Arrest during their Attendance at the Session of their respective Houses, and in going to and returning from the same; and for any Speech or Debate in either House, they shall not be questioned in any other Place.

[2] No Senator or Representative shall, during the Time for which he was elected, be appointed to any civil Office under the Authority of the United States, which shall have been created, or the Emoluments whereof shall have been encreased during such time; and no Person holding any Office under the United States, shall be a Member of either House during his Continuance in Office.

SECTION 7. [1] All Bills for raising Revenue shall originate in the House of Representatives; but the Senate may propose or concur with Amendments as on other Bills.

[2] Every Bill shall have passed the House of Representatives and the Senate, shall, before it become a Law, be presented to the President of the United States; if he approve he shall sign it, but if not he shall return it, with his Objections to that House in which it shall have originated, who shall enter the Objections at large on their Journal, and proceed to reconsider it. If after such Reconsideration two thirds of that House shall agree to pass the Bill, it shall be sent, together with the Objections, to the other House, by which it shall likewise be reconsidered, and if approved by two thirds of that House, it shall become a Law. But in all such Cases, the Votes of both Houses shall be determined by Yeas and Nays, and the Names of the Persons voting for and against the Bill shall be entered on the Journal of each House respectively. If any Bill shall not be returned by the President within ten Days (Sundays excepted) after it shall have been presented to him, the Same shall be a Law, in like Manner as if he had signed it, unless the Congress by their Adjournment prevent its Return, in which Case it shall not be a Law.

[3] Every Order, Resolution, or Vote to which the Concurrence of the Senate and House of Representatives may be necessary (except on a question of Adjournment) shall be presented to the President of the United States; and before the Same shall take Effect, shall be approved by him, or being disapproved by him, shall be repassed by two thirds of the Senate and House of Representatives, according to the Rules and Limitations prescribed in the Case of a Bill.

SECTION 8. The Congress shall have Power

[1] To lay and collect Taxes, Duties, Imposts and Excises, to pay the Debts and provide for the common Defence and general Welfare of the United States, but all Duties, Imposts and Excises shall be uniform throughout the United States;

[2] To borrow money on the credit of the United States;

[3] To regulate Commerce with foreign Nations, and among the several States, and with the Indian Tribes;

[4] To establish an uniform Rule of Naturalization, and uniform Laws on the subject of Bankruptcies throughout the United States;

[5] To coin Money, regulate the Value thereof, and of foreign Coin, and fix the Standard of Weights and Measures;

[6] To provide for the Punishment of counterfeiting the Securities and current Coin of the United States;

[7] To Establish Post Offices and post Roads;

[8] To promote the Progress of Science and useful Arts, by securing for limited Times to Authors and Inventors the exclusive Right to their respective Writings and Discoveries;

[9] To constitute Tribunals inferior to the Supreme Court;

[10] To define and punish Piracies and Felonies committed on the high Seas, and Offenses against the Law of Nations;

[11] To declare War, grant Letters of Marque and Reprisal, and make Rules concerning Captures on Land and Water;

[12] To raise and support Armies, but no Appropriation of Money to that Use shall be for a longer Term than two Years;

[13] To provide and maintain a Navy;

[14] To make Rules for the Government and Regulation of the land and naval Forces;

[15] To provide for calling forth the Militia to execute the Laws of the Union, suppress Insurrections and repel Invasions;

[16] To provide for organizing, arming, and disciplining the Militia, and for Governing such Part of them as may be employed in the Service of the United States, reserving to the States respectively, the Appointment of the Officers, and the Authority of training the Militia according to the discipline prescribed by Congress;

[17] To exercise exclusive Legislation in all Cases whatsoever, over such District (not exceeding ten Miles square) as may, by Cession of particular States, and the acceptance of Con-

gress, become the Seat of the Government of the United States, and to exercise like Authority over all Places purchased by the Consent of the Legislature of the State in which the Same shall be, for the Erection of Forts, Magazines, Arsenals, dock-Yards, and other needful Buildings;—And

[18] To make all Laws which shall be necessary and proper for carrying into Execution the foregoing Powers, and all other Powers vested by this Constitution in the Government of the United States, or in any Department or Officer thereof.

SECTION 9. [1] The Migration or Importation of Such Persons as any of the States now existing shall think proper to admit, shall not be prohibited by the Congress prior to the Year one thousand eight hundred and eight, but a tax or duty may be imposed on such Importation, not exceeding ten dollars for each Person.

[2] The privilege of the Writ of Habeas Corpus shall not be suspended, unless when in Cases of Rebellion or Invasion the public Safety may require it.

[3] No Bill of Attainder or ex post facto Law shall be passed.

[4] No capitation, or other direct, Tax shall be laid, unless in Proportion to the Census or Enumeration herein before directed to be taken.

[5] No Tax or Duty shall be laid on Articles exported from any State.

[6] No preference shall be given by any Regulation of Commerce or Revenue to the Ports of one State over those of another; nor shall Vessels bound to, or from, one State be obliged to enter, clear, or pay Duties in another.

[7] No money shall be drawn from the Treasury, but in Consequence of Appropriations made by Law; and a regular Statement and Account of the Receipts and Expenditures of all public Money shall be published from time to time.

[8] No Title of Nobility shall be granted by the United States: And no Person holding any Office of Profit or Trust under them, shall, without the Consent of the Congress, accept of any present, Emolument, Office, or Title, of any kind whatever, from any King, Prince, or foreign State.

SECTION 10. [1] No State shall enter into any Treaty, Alliance, or Confederation; grant Letters of Marque and Reprisal; coin Money; emit Bills of Credit; make any Thing but gold and silver Coin a Tender in Payment of Debts; pass any Bill of Attainder, ex post facto Law, or Law impairing the Obligation of Contracts, or grant any Title of Nobility.

[2] No State shall, without the Consent of the Congress, lay any Imposts or Duties on Imports or Exports, except what may be absolutely necessary for executing its inspection Laws: and the net Produce of all Duties and Imposts, laid by any State on Imports or Exports, shall be for the Use of the Treasury of the United States; and all such Laws shall be subject to the Revision and Control of the Congress.

[3] No State shall, without the Consent of Congress, lay any duty of Tonnage, keep Troops, or Ships of War in time of Peace, enter into any Agreement or Compact with another State, or with a foreign Power, or engage in War, unless actually invaded, or in such imminent Danger as will not admit of delay.

ARTICLE II

SECTION 1. [1] The executive Power shall be vested in a President of the United States of America. He shall hold his Office during the Term of four Years, and together with the Vice President, chosen for the same Term, be elected, as follows:

[2] Each State shall appoint, in such Manner as the Legislature thereof may direct, a Number of Senators and Representatives to which the State may be entitled in the Congress: but no Senator or Representative, or Person holding an Office of Trust or Profit under the United States, shall be appointed an Elector.

[3] The Electors shall meet in their respective States, and vote by Ballot for two persons, of whom one at least shall not be an Inhabitant of the same State with themselves. And they shall make a List of all the Persons voted for, and of the Number of Votes for each; which List they shall sign and certify, and transmit sealed to the Seat of the Government of the United States, directed to the President of the Senate. The President of the Senate shall, in the Presence of the Senate and House of Representatives, open all the Certificates, and the Votes shall then be counted. The Person having the greatest Number of Votes shall be the President, if such Number

be a Majority of the whole Number of Electors appointed; and if there be more than one who have such Majority, and have an equal Number of Votes, then the House of Representatives shall immediately chuse by Ballot one of them for President; and if no Person have a Majority, then from the five highest on the List the said House shall in like Manner chuse the President. But in chusing the President, the Votes shall be taken by States, the Representation from each State having one Vote; A quorum for this Purpose shall consist of a Member or Members from two-thirds of the States, and a Majority of all the States shall be necessary to a Choice. In every Case, after the Choice of the President, the Person having the greatest Number of Votes of the Electors shall be the Vice President. But if there shall remain two or more who have equal Votes, the Senate shall chuse from them by Ballot the Vice President.

[4] The Congress may determine the Time of chusing the Electors, and the Day on which they shall give their Votes; which Day shall be the same throughout the United States.

[5] No person except a natural born Citizen, or a Citizen of the United States, at the time of the Adoption of this Constitution, shall be eligible to the Office of President; neither shall any Person be eligible to that Office who shall not have attained to the Age of thirty-five Years, and been fourteen Years a Resident within the United States.

[6] In case of the removal of the President from Office, or of his Death, Resignation, or Inability to discharge the Powers and Duties of the said Office, the same shall devolve on the Vice President, and the Congress may by Law provide for the Case of Removal, Death, Resignation or Inability, both of the President and Vice President, declaring what Officer shall then act as President, and such Officer shall act accordingly, until the Disability be removed, or a President shall be elected.

[7] The President shall, at stated Times, receive for his Services, a Compensation, which shall neither be encreased nor diminished during the Period for which he shall have been elected, and he shall not receive within that Period any other Emolument from the United States, or any of them.

[8] Before he enter on the Execution of his Office, he shall take the following Oath or Affirmation:—"I do solemnly swear [or affirm] that I will faithfully execute the Office of President of the United States, and will to the best of my Ability, preserve, protect and defend the Constitution of the United States."

SECTION 2. [1] The President shall be Commander in Chief of the Army and Navy of the United States, and of the Militia of the several States, when called into the actual Service of the United States; he may require the Opinion, in writing, of the Principal Officer in each of the executive Departments, upon any subject relating to the Duties of their respective Offices, and he shall have Power to grant Reprieves and pardons for Offenses against the United States, except in Cases of Impeachment.

[2] He shall have Power, by and with the Advice and Consent of the Senate, to make Treaties, provided two-thirds of the Senators present concur; and he shall nominate, and by and with the Advice and Consent of the Senate, shall appoint Ambassadors, other public Ministers and Consuls, Judges of the Supreme Court, and all other Officers of the United States, whose Appointments are not herein otherwise provided for, and shall be established by Law, but the Congress may by Law vest the Appointment of such inferior Officers, as they think proper, in the President alone, in the Courts of Law, or in the Heads of Departments.

[3] The President shall have Power to fill up all Vacancies that may happen during the Recess of the Senate, by granting Commissions which shall expire at the End of their next Session.

SECTION 3. He shall from time to time give to the Congress Information of the State of the Union, and recommend to their Consideration such Measures as he shall judge necessary and expedient; he may, on extraordinary Occasions, convene both Houses, or either of them, and in Case of Disagreement between them, with Respect to the Time of Adjournment, he may adjourn them to such Time as he shall think proper; he shall receive Ambassadors and other public Ministers; he shall take Care that the Laws be faithfully executed, and shall Commission all the Officers of the United States.

SECTION 4. The President, Vice President and all civil Officers of the United States, shall be removed from Office on Impeachment for, and Conviction of, Treason, Bribery, or other high Crimes and Misdemeanors.

ARTICLE III

SECTION 1. The judicial Power of the United States, shall be vested in one supreme Court, and in such inferior Courts as the Congress may from time to time ordain and establish. The Judges, both of the supreme and inferior Courts, shall hold their Offices during good Behaviour, and shall, at stated Times, receive for their Services a Compensation which shall not be diminished during their Continuance in Office.

SECTION 2. [1] The judicial Power shall extend to all Cases, in Law and Equity, arising under this Constitution, the Laws of the United States, and Treaties made, or which shall be made under their Authority;—to all Cases affecting Ambassadors, other public Ministers and Consuls;—to all Cases of admiralty and maritime Jurisdiction;—to Controversies to which the United States shall be a Party;—to Controversies between two or more States;—between a State and Citizens of another State;—between Citizens of different States;—between Citizens of the same State claiming Lands under Grants of different States, and between a State, or the Citizens thereof, and foreign States, Citizens or Subjects.

[2] In all Cases affecting Ambassadors, other public Ministers and Consuls, and those in which a State shall be Party, the supreme Court shall have original Jurisdiction. In all the other Cases before mentioned, the supreme Court shall have appellate Jurisdiction, both as to Law and Fact, with such Exceptions, and under such Regulations as the Congress shall make.

[3] The trial of all Crimes, except in Case of Impeachment, shall be by Jury; and such Trial shall be held in the State where the said Crimes shall have been committed, but when not committed within any State, the Trial shall be at such Place or Places as the Congress may by Law have directed.

SECTION 3. [1] Treason against the United States, shall consist only in levying War against them, or, in adhering to their Enemies, giving them Aid and Comfort. No Person shall be convicted of Treason unless on the Testimony of two Witnesses to the same overt Act, or on Confession in open Court.

[2] The Congress shall have power to declare the Punishment of Treason, but no Attainder of Treason shall work Corruption of Blood, or Forfeiture except during the Life of the Person attained.

ARTICLE IV

SECTION 1. Full Faith and Credit shall be given in each State to the public Acts, Records, and judicial Proceedings of every other State. And the Congress may by general Laws prescribe the Manner in which such Acts, Records and Proceedings shall be proved, and the Effect thereof.

SECTION 2. [1] The Citizens of each State shall be entitled to all Privileges and Immunities of Citizens in the several States.

[2] A Person charged in any State with Treason, Felony, or other Crime, who shall flee from Justice, and be found in another State, shall on demand of the executive Authority of the State from which he fled, be delivered up, to be removed to the State having Jurisdiction of the Crime.

[3] No Person held to Service or Labour in one State, under the Laws thereof, escaping into another, shall, in Consequence of any Law or Regulation therein, be discharged from such Service or Labour, but shall be delivered up on Claim of the Party to whom such Service or Labour may be due.

SECTION 3. [1] New States may be admitted by the Congress into this Union; but no new State shall be formed or erected within the Jurisdiction of any other State; nor any State be formed by the Junction of two or more States, or parts of States, without the Consent of the Legislature of the States concerned as well as of the Congress.

[2] The Congress shall have Power to dispose of and make all needful Rules and Regulations respecting the Territory or other Property belonging to the United States; and nothing in this Constitution shall be so construed as to Prejudice any Claims of the United States, or of any particular State.

SECTION 4. The United States shall guarantee to every State in this Union a Republican Form of Government, and shall protect each of them against Invasion; and on Application of the Legislature, or of the Executive (when the Legislature cannot be convened) against domestic Violence.

ARTICLE V

The Congress, whenever two-thirds of both Houses shall deem it necessary, shall propose Amendments to this Constitution, or, on the Application of the Legislatures of two-thirds of the several States, shall call a Convention for proposing Amendments, which, in either Case, shall be valid to all Intents and Purposes, as part of this Constitution, when ratified by the Legislatures of three-fourths of the several States, or by Conventions in three-fourths thereof, as the one or the other Mode of Ratification may be proposed by the Congress; Provided that no Amendment which may be made prior to the Year One thousand eight hundred and eight shall in any Manner affect the first and fourth Clauses in the Ninth Section of the first Article; and that no State, without its Consent, shall be deprived of its equal Suffrage in the Senate.

ARTICLE VI

[1] All Debts contracted and Engagements entered into, before the Adoption of this Constitution shall be valid against the United States under this Constitution, as under the Confederation.

[2] This Constitution, and the Laws of the United States which shall be made in Pursuance thereof; and all Treaties made, or which shall be made, under the Authority of the United States, shall be the supreme Law of the Land; and the Judges in every State shall be bound thereby, any Thing in the Constitution or Laws of any State to the Contrary notwithstanding.

[3] The Senators and Representatives before mentioned, and the Members of the several State Legislatures, and all executive and judicial Officers, both of the United States and of the several States, shall be bound by Oath or Affirmation, to support this Constitution; but no religious Test shall ever be required as a Qualification to any Office or public Trust under the United States.

ARTICLE VII

The Ratification of the Conventions of nine States shall be sufficient for the Establishment of this Constitution between the States so ratifying the Same.

Done in Convention by the Unanimous Consent of the States present the Seventeenth Day of September in the Year of our Lord one thousand seven hundred and Eighty seven and of the Independence of the United States of America the Twelfth. In witness whereof We have hereunto subscribed our Names,

Go WASHINGTON—Presid^t
and deputy from Virginia

New Hampshire	{ JOHN LANGDON NICHOLAS GILMAN
Massachusetts	{ NATHANIEL GORHAM RUFUS KING
Connecticut	{ W^M SAM^L JOHNSON ROGER SHERMAN
New York	{ ALEXANDER HAMILTON
New Jersey	{ WIL: LIVINGSTON DAVID BREARLEY W^M PATERSON JONA: DAYTON
Pennsylvania	{ B FRANKLIN THOMAS MIFFLIN ROB^T MORRIS GEO. CLYMER THO^S FITZSIMONS JARED INGERSOLL JAMES WILSON GOUV MORRIS
Delaware	{ GEO: READ GUNNING BEDFORD JUN JOHN DICKINSON RICHARD BASSETT JACO: BROOM
Maryland	{ JAMES M^{C}HENRY DAN OF S^T THO^S JENIFER DAN^L CARROLL
Virginia	{ JOHN BLAIR— JAMES MADISON JR.

North Carolina	{	Wᴹ Blount Richᴰ Dobbs Spaight Hu Williamson
South Carolina	{	J. Rutledge Charles Cotesworth Pinckney Charles Pinckney Pierce Butler
Georgia	{	William Few Abr Baldwin

ARTICLES IN ADDITION TO, AND AMENDMENT OF, THE CONSTITUTION OF THE UNITED STATES OF AMERICA, PROPOSED BY CONGRESS, AND RATIFIED BY THE LEGISLATURES OF THE SEVERAL STATES, PURSUANT TO THE FIFTH ARTICLE OF THE ORIGINAL CONSTITUTION

AMENDMENT I [1791]

Congress shall make no law respecting an establishment of religion, or prohibiting the free exercise thereof; or abridging the freedom of speech, or of the press; or the right of the people peaceably to assemble and to petition the Government for a redress of grievances.

AMENDMENT II [1791]

A well regulated Militia, being necessary to the security of a free State, the right of the people to keep and bear Arms, shall not be infringed.

AMENDMENT III [1791]

No Soldier shall, in time of peace be quartered in any house, without the consent of the Owner, nor in time of war, but in a manner to be prescribed by Law.

AMENDMENT IV [1791]

The right of the people to be secure in their persons, houses, papers, and effects, against unreasonable searches nd seizures, shall not be violated, and no Warrants shall issue, but upon probable cause, supported by Oath or affirmation, and particularly describing the place to be searched, and the persons or things to be seized.

AMENDMENT V [1791]

No person shall be held to answer for a capital, or otherwise infamous crime, unless on a presentment or indictment of a Grand Jury, except in cases arising in the land or naval forces, or in the Militia, when in actual service in time of War or public danger; nor shall any person be subject for the same offence to be twice put in jeopardy of life or limb; nor shall be compelled in any criminal case to be a witness against himself, nor be deprived of life, liberty, or property, without due process of law; nor shall private property be taken for public use, without just compensation.

AMENDMENT VI [1791]

In all criminal prosecutions, the accused shall enjoy the right to a speedy and public trial, by an impartial jury of the State and district wherein the crime shall have been committed, which district shall have been previously ascertained by law, and to be informed of the nature and cause of the accusation; to be confronted with the witnesses against him; to have compulsory process for obtaining witnesses in his favor, and to have the Assistance of Counsel for his defence.

AMENDMENT VII [1791]

In suits at common law, where the value in controversy shall exceed twenty dollars, the right of trial by jury shall be preserved, and no fact tried by jury, shall be otherwise reexamined in any Court of the United States, than according to the rules of the common law.

AMENDMENT VIII [1791]

Excessive bail shall not be required, nor excessive fines imposed, nor cruel and unusual punishments inflicted.

AMENDMENT IX [1791]

The enumeration in the Constitution, of certain rights, shall not be construed to deny or disparage others retained by the people.

AMENDMENT X [1791]

The powers not delegated to the United States by the Constitution, nor prohibited by it to the States, are reserved to the States respectively, or to the people.

AMENDMENT IX [1798]

The Judicial power of the United States shall not be construed to extend to any suit in law or equity, commenced or prosecuted against one of the United States by Citizens of another State, or by Citizens or Subjects of any Foreign State.

AMENDMENT XII [1804]

The electors shall meet in their respective states and vote by ballot for President and Vice-President, one of whom, at least, shall not be an inhabitant of the same state with themselves; they shall name in their ballots the person voted for as President, and in distinct ballots the person voted for as Vice-President, and they shall make distinct lists of all persons voted for as President, and of all persons voted for as Vice-President, and of the number of votes for each, which lists they shall sign and certify, and transmit sealed to the seat of the government of the United States, directed to the President of the Senate;—The President of the Senate shall, in presence of the Senate and House of Representatives, open all the certificates and the votes shall then be counted;— The person having the greatest number of votes for President, shall be the President, if such number be a majority of the whole number of Electors appointed; and if no person have such majority, then from the persons having the highest numbers not exceeding three on the list of those voted for as President, the House of Representatives shall choose immediately, by ballot, the President. But in choosing the President, the votes shall be taken by states, the representation from each state have one vote; a quorum for this purpose shall consist of a member or members from two-thirds of the states, and a majority of all the states shall be necessary to a choice. And if the House of Representatives shall not choose a President whenever the right of choice shall devolve upon them, before the fourth day of March next following, then the Vice-President shall act as President, as in the case of the death or other constitutional disability of the President.—The person having the greatest number of votes as Vice-President, shall be the Vice-President, if such number be a majority of the whole number of Electors appointed, and if no person have a majority, then from the two highest numbers on the list, the Senate shall choose the Vice-President; a quorum for the purpose shall consist of two-thirds of the whole number of Senators, and a majority of the whole number shall be necessary to a choice. But no person constitutionally ineligible to the office of President shall be eligible to that of Vice-President of the United States.

AMENDMENT XIII [1865]

SECTION 1. Neither slavery nor involuntary servitude, except as a punishment for crime whereof the party shall have been duly convicted, shall exist within the United States, or any place subject to their jurisdiction.

SECTION 2. Congress shall have power to enforce this article by appropriate legislation.

AMENDMENT XIV [1868]

SECTION 1. All persons born or naturalized in the United States, and subject to the jurisdiction thereof, are citizens of the United States and of the State wherein they reside. No State shall make or enforce any law which shall abridge the privileges or immunities of citizens of the United States; nor shall any State deprive any person of life, liberty, or property, without due process of law; nor deny to any person within its jurisdiction the equal protection of the laws.

SECTION 2. Representatives shall be apportioned among the several States according to their respective numbers, counting the whole number of persons in each State, excluding Indians not taxed. But when the right to vote at any election for the choice of electors for President and Vice-President of the United States, Representatives in Congress, the Executive and Judicial officers of a State, or the members of the Legislature thereof, is denied to any of the male inhabitants of such State, being twenty-one years of age, and citizens of the United

States, or in any way abridged, except for participation in rebellion, or other crime, the basis of representation therein shall be reduced in the proportions which the number of such male citizens shall bear to the whole number of male citizens twenty-one years of age in such State.

SECTION 3. No person shall be a Senator or Representative in Congress, or elector of President and Vice-President, or hold any office, civil or military, under the United States, or under any State, who, having previously taken an oath, as a member of Congress, or as an officer of the United States, or as a member of any State legislature, or as an executive or judicial officer of any State, to support the Constitution of the United States, shall have engaged in insurrection or rebellion against the same, or given aid or comfort to the enemies thereof. But congress may by a vote of two-thirds of each House, remove such disability.

SECTION 4. The validity of the public debt of the United States, authorized by law, including debts incurred for payment of pensions and bounties for services in suppressing insurrection or rebellion, shall not be questioned. But neither the United States nor any State shall assume or pay any debt or obligation incurred in aid of insurrection or rebellion against the United States, or any claim for the loss or emancipation of any slave; but all such debts, obligations and claims shall be held illegal and void.

SECTION 5. The Congress shall have power to enforce, by appropriate legislation, the provisions of this article.

AMENDMENT XV [1870]

SECTION 1. The right of citizens of the United States to vote shall not be denied or abridged by the United States or by any State on account of race, color, or previous condition of servitude.

SECTION 2. The Congress shall have power to enforce this article by appropriate legislation.

AMENDMENT XVI [1913]

The Congress shall have power to lay and collect taxes on incomes, from whatever source derived, without apportionment among the several States, and without regard to any census or enumeration.

AMENDMENT XVII [1913]

The Senate of the United States shall be composed of two Senators from each State, elected by the people thereof, for six years, and each Senator shall have one vote. The electors in each State shall have the qualifications requisite for electors of the most numerous branch of the State legislatures.

When vacancies happen in the representation of any State in the Senate, the executive authority of such State shall issue writs of election to fill such vacancies: *Provided*, That the legislature of any State may empower the executive thereof to make temporary appointments until the people fill the vacancies by election as the legislature may direct.

This amendment shall not be so construed as to affect the election or term of any Senator chosen before it becomes valid as part of the Constitution.

AMENDMENT XVIII [1919]

SECTION 1. After one year from the ratification of this article the manufacture, sale, or transportation of intoxicating liquors within, the importation thereof into, or the exportation thereof from the United States and all territory subject to the jurisdiction thereof for beverage purposes is hereby prohibited.

SECTION 2. The Congress and the several States shall have concurrent power to enforce this article by appropriate legislation.

SECTION 3. This article shall be inoperative unless it shall have been ratified as an amendment to the Constitution by the legislatures of the several States, as provided in the Constitution, within seven years from the date of the submission hereof to the States by the Congress.

AMENDMENT XIX [1920]

The right of citizens of the United States to vote shall not be denied or abridged by the United States or by any State on account of sex.

Congress shall have the power to enforce this article by appropriate legislation.

AMENDMENT XX [1933]

SECTION 1. The terms of the President and Vice President shall end at noon on the 20th day of January, and the terms of Senators and Representatives at noon on the 3rd day of January, of the years in which such terms would have ended if this article had not been ratified; and the terms of their successors shall then begin.

SECTION 2. The Congress shall assemble at least once in every year, and such meeting shall begin at noon on the 3rd day of January, unless they shall by law appoint a different day.

SECTION 3. If, at the time fixed for the beginning of the term of the President, the President elect shall have died, the Vice President elect shall become President. If a President shall not have been chosen before the time fixed for the beginning of his term, or if the President elect shall have failed to qualify, then the Vice President elect shall act as President until a President shall have qualified; and the Congress may by law provide for the case wherein neither a President elect nor a Vice President elect shall have qualified, declaring who shall then act as President, or the manner in which one who is to act shall be selected, and such person shall act accordingly until a President or vice President shall have qualified.

SECTION 4. The Congress may by law provide for the case of the death of any of the persons from whom the House of Representatives may choose a President whenever the right of choice shall have devolved upon them, and for the case of the death of any of the persons from whom the Senate may choose a Vice President whenever the right of choice shall have devolved upon them.

SECTION 5. Sections 1 and 2 shall take effect on the 15th day of October following the ratification of this article.

SECTION 6. This article shall be inoperative unless it shall have been ratified as an amendment to the Constitution by the legislatures of three-fourths of the several States within seven years from the date of its submission.

AMENDMENT XXI [1933]

SECTION 1. The eighteenth article of amendment to the Constitution of the United States is hereby repealed.

SECTION 2. The transportation or importation into any State, Territory, or possession of the United States for delivery of use therein of intoxicating liquors, in violation of the laws thereof, is hereby prohibited.

SECTION 3. This article shall be inoperative unless it shall have been ratified as an amendment to the Constitution by conventions in the several States, as provided in the Constitution, within seven years from the date of the submission hereof to the States by the Congress.

AMENDMENT XXII [1951]

SECTION 1. No person shall be elected to the office of the President more than twice, and no person who has held the office of President, or acted as President, for more than two years of a term to which some other person was elected President shall be elected to the office of the President more than once. But this Article shall not apply to any person holding the office of President when this Article was proposed by the Congress, and shall not prevent any person who may be holding the office of President, or acting as President, during the term within which the Article becomes operative from holding the office of President or acting as President during the remainder of such term.

SECTION 2. This article shall be inoperative unless it shall have been ratified as an amendment to the Constitution by the legislatures of three-fourths of the several States within seven years from the date of its submission to the States by the Congress.

AMENDMENT XXIII [1961]

SECTION 1. The District constituting the seat of Government of the United States shall appoint in such manner as the Congress may direct:

A number of electors of President and Vice President equal to the whole number of Senators and Representatives in Congress to which the District would be entitled if it were a State, but in no event more than the least populous State; they shall be in addition to those appointed by the States, but they shall be considered, for the purposes of the election of President and Vice President, to be electors appointed by a State; and they shall meet in the District and perform such duties as provided by the twelfth article of amendment.

SECTION 2. The Congress shall have power to enforce this article by appropriate legislation.

AMENDMENT XXIV [1964]

SECTION 1. The right of citizens of the United States to vote in any primary or other election for President or Vice President, for electors for President or Vice President, or for Senator or Representative in Congress, shall not be denied or abridged by the United States or any State by reason of failure to pay any poll tax or other tax.

SECTION 2. The Congress shall have power to enforce this article by appropriate legislation.

AMENDMENT XXV [1967]

SECTION 1. In case of the removal of the President from office or his death or resignation, the Vice President shall become President.

SECTION 2. Whenever there is a vacancy in the office of the Vice President, the President shall nominate a Vice President who shall take the Office upon confirmation by a majority vote of both houses of Congress.

SECTION 3. Whenever the President transmits to the President pro tempore of the Senate and the Speaker of the House of Representatives his written declaration that he is unable to discharge the powers and duties of his office, and until he transmits to them a written declaration to the contrary, such powers and duties shall be discharged by the Vice President as Acting President.

SECTION 4. Whenever the Vice President and a majority of either the principal officers of the executive departments, or of such other body as Congress may by law provide, transmit to the President pro tempore of the Senate and the Speaker of the House of Representatives their written declaration that the President is unable to discharge the powers and duties of his office, the Vice President shall immediately assume the powers and duties of the office as Acting President.

Thereafter, when the President transmits to the President pro tempore of the Senate and the Speaker of the House of Representatives his written declaration that no inability exists, he shall resume the powers and the duties of his office unless the Vice President and a majority of either the principal officers of the executive department, or of such other body as Congress may by law provide, transmit within four days to the President pro tempore of the Senate and the Speaker of the House of Representatives their written declaration that the President is unable to discharge the powers and duties of his office. Thereupon Congress shall decide the issue, assembling within 48 hours for that purpose if not in session. If the Congress, within 21 days after receipt of the latter written declaration, or, if Congress is not in session, within 21 days after Congress is required to assemble, determines by two-thirds vote of both houses that the President is unable to discharge the powers and duties of his office, the Vice President shall continue to discharge the same as Acting President; otherwise, the President shall resume the powers and duties of his office.

AMENDMENT XXVI [1971]

SECTION 1. The right of citizens of the United States, who are eighteen years of age, or older, to vote shall not be denied or abridged by the United States or by any state on account of age.

SECTION 2. The Congress shall have the power to enforce this article by appropriate legislation.

AMENDMENT XXVII [1992]

No law varying the compensation for the services of the Senators and Representatives shall take effect until an election of Representatives shall have intervened. *

---

*Adopted in 1992, 203 years after it was first proposed by James Madison and approved by the First Congress. Six states ratified the amendment in 1792, a seventh in 1873, an eighth in 1978, and 32 more in recent years, with Illinois becoming the thirty-eighth state to ratify it on May 12, 1992.

JUSTICES
OF THE
SUPREME COURT

	Term	Appointed by	Replaced
*John Jay**	1789–1795	Washington	
John Rutledge	1789–1791	Washington	
William Cushing	1789–1810	Washington	
James Wilson	1789–1798	Washington	
John Blair	1789–1796	Washington	
James Iredell	1790–1799	Washington	
Thomas Johnson	1791–1793	Washington	Rutledge
William Paterson	1793–1806	Washington	Johnson
John Rutledge	1795	Washington	Jay
Samuel Chase	1796–1811	Washington	Blair
Oliver Ellsworth	1796–1800	Washington	Rutledge
Bushrod Washington	1798–1829	J. Adams	Wilson
Alfred Moore	1799–1804	J. Adams	Iredell
John Marshall	1801–1835	J. Adams	Ellsworth
William Johnson	1804–1834	Jefferson	Moore
Brockholst Livingston	1806–1823	Jefferson	Paterson
Thomas Todd	1807–1826	Jefferson	(new seat)
Gabriel Duval	1811–1835	Madison	Chase
Joseph Story	1811–1845	Madison	Cushing
Smith Thompson	1823–1843	Monroe	Livingston
Robert Trimble	1826–1828	J.Q. Adams	Todd
John McLean	1829–1861	Jackson	Trimble
Henry Baldwin	1830–1844	Jackson	Washington
James Wayne	1835–1867	Jackson	Johnson

*The names of the Chief Justices are italicized.

	Term	Appointed by	Replaced
Roger Taney	1836–1864	Jackson	Marshall
Philip Barbour	1836–1841	Jackson	Duval
John Catron	1837–1865	Van Buren	(new seat)
John McKinley	1837–1852	Van Buren	(new seat)
Peter Daniel	1841–1860	Van Buren	Barbour
Samuel Nelson	1845–1872	Tyler	Thompson
Levi Woodbury	1845–1851	Polk	Story
Robert Grier	1846–1870	Polk	Baldwin
Benjamin Curtis	1851–1857	Fillmore	Woodbury
John Campbell	1853–1861	Pierce	McKinley
Nathan Clifford	1858–1881	Buchanan	Curtis
Noah Swayne	1862–1881	Lincoln	McLean
Samuel Miller	1862–1890	Lincoln	Daniel
David Davis	1862–1877	Lincoln	Campbell
Stephen Field	1863–1897	Lincoln	(new seat)
Salmon Chase	1864–1873	Lincoln	Taney
William Strong	1870–1880	Grant	Grier
Joseph Bradley	1870–1892	Grant	Wayne
Ward Hunt	1872–1882	Grant	Nelson
Morrison Waite	1874–1888	Grant	Chase
John Marshall Harlan	1877–1911	Hayes	Davis
William Woods	1880–1887	Hayes	Strong
Stanley Matthews	1881–1889	Garfield	Swayne
Horace Gray	1881–1902	Arthur	Clifford
Samuel Blatchford	1882–1893	Arthur	Hunt
Lucius Lamar	1888–1893	Cleveland	Woods
Melville Fuller	1888–1910	Cleveland	Waite
David Brewer	1889–1910	Harrison	Matthews
Henry Brown	1890–1906	Harrison	Miller
George Shiras	1892–1903	Harrison	Bradley
Howell Jackson	1893–1895	Harrison	Lamar
Edward White	1894–1910	Cleveland	Blatchford
Rufus Peckham	1895–1909	Cleveland	Jackson
Joseph McKenna	1898–1925	McKinley	Field
Oliver Wendell Holmes	1902–1932	T. Roosevelt	Gray
William Day	1903–1922	T. Roosevelt	Shiras
William Moody	1906–1910	T. Roosevelt	Brown
Horace Lurton	1909–1914	Taft	Peckham
Charles Evans Hughes	1910–1916	Taft	Brewer
Edward White	1910–1921	Taft	Fuller
Willis Van Devanter	1910–1937	Taft	White
Joseph Lamar	1910–1916	Taft	Moody
Mahlon Pitney	1912–1922	Taft	Harlan
James McReynolds	1914–1941	Wilson	Lurton
Louis Brandeis	1916–1939	Wilson	Lamar
John Clarke	1916–1922	Wilson	Hughes
William Taft	1921–1930	Harding	White
George Sutherland	1922–1938	Harding	Clarke
Pierce Butler	1922–1939	Harding	Day
Edward Sanford	1923–1930	Harding	Pitney
Harlan Stone	1925–1941	Coolidge	McKenna
Charles Evans Hughes	1930–1941	Hoover	Taft
Owen Roberts	1932–1945	Hoover	Sanford
Benjamin Cardozo	1932–1938	Hoover	Holmes

	Term	Appointed by	Replaced
Hugo Black	1937–1971	F. Roosevelt	Van Devanter
Stanley Reed	1938–1957	F. Roosevelt	Sutherland
Felix Frankfurter	1939–1962	F. Roosevelt	Cardozo
William Douglas	1939–1975	F. Roosevelt	Brandeis
Frank Murphy	1940–1949	F. Roosevelt	Butler
James Byrnes	1941–1942	F. Roosevelt	McReynolds
Harlan Stone	1941–1946	F. Roosevelt	Hughes
Robert Jackson	1941–1954	F. Roosevelt	Stone
Wiley Rutledge	1943–1949	F. Roosevelt	Byrnes
Harold Burton	1945–1958	Truman	Roberts
Fred Vinson	1946–1953	Truman	Stone
Tom Clark	1949–1967	Truman	Murphy
Sherman Minton	1949–1956	Truman	Rutledge
Earl Warren	1953–1969	Eisenhower	Vinson
John Harlan	1955–1971	Eisenhower	Jackson
William Brennan	1956–1990	Eisenhower	Minton
Charles Whittaker	1957–1962	Eisenhower	Reed
Potter Stewart	1958–1981	Eisenhower	Burton
Arthur Goldberg	1962–1965	Kennedy	Frankfurter
Byron White	1962–1993	Kennedy	Whittaker
Abe Fortas	1965–1969	Johnson	Goldberg
Thurgood Marshall	1967–1991	Johnson	Clark
Warren Burger	1969–1986	Nixon	Warren
Harry Blackmun	1970–1994	Nixon	Fortas
Lewis Powell	1972–1987	Nixon	Black
William Rehnquist	1972–1986	Nixon	Harlan
John Stevens	1975–	Ford	Douglas
Sandra Day O'Connor	1981–	Reagan	Stewart
William Rehnquist	1986–	Reagan	Burger
Antonin Scalia	1986–	Reagan	Rehnquist
Anthony Kennedy	1988–	Reagan	Powell
David Souter	1990–	Bush	Brennan
Clarence Thomas	1991–	Bush	Marshall
Ruth Bader Ginsburg	1993–	Clinton	White
Stephen Breyer	1994–	Clinton	Blackmun

*The names of the Chief Justices are italicized.

GLOSSARY
OF
COMMON LEGAL
TERMS

Abstention   The doctrine under which the U.S. Supreme Court and other federal courts choose not to rule on state cases, even when empowered to do so, so as to allow the issue to be decided on the basis of state law.

Advisory Opinion   A legal opinion rendered at the request of the government or another party indicating how the court would rule if the issue arose in an adversary context.

Amicus Curiae   "Friend of the court." A person or group not directly involved in a particular case that volunteers or is requested by the court to supply its views on the case (usually through the submission of a brief).

Appeal   The procedure whereby a case is brought from an inferior to a superior court. In the Supreme Court, certain cases are designated as appeals under federal law and must be heard formally by the court.

Appellant   The party who appeals a decision from a lower to a higher court.

Appellate Jurisdiction   The authority of a court to hear, determine, and render judgment in an action on appeal from an inferior court.

Appellee   The party against whom an appeal to a superior court is taken and who has an interest in upholding the lower court's decision.

Arraignment   The formal process of charging a person with a crime, reading the charge, and asking for and entering his plea.

Bail   The security (cash or a bail bond) given as a guarantee that a released prisoner will appear at trial.

Bill of Attainder   A legislative act declaring a person guilty of a crime and passing sentence without benefit of trial.

Brief   A document prepared by counsel as the basis for an argument in court. It sets forth the facts of the case and the legal arguments in support of the party's position.

Case Law   The law as defined by previously decided cases.

Certification   A method of appeal whereby a lower court requests a higher court to rule on certain legal questions so that the lower court can make the correct decision in light of the answer given.

Certiorari, Writ of   An order from a superior court to an inferior court to forward the entire record of a case to the superior court for review. The U.S. Supreme Court may issue such writs at its discretion.

Civil Action   A lawsuit, usually brought by a private party, seeking redress for a noncriminal act (e.g., a suit in negligence, contract, or defamation).

Class Action   A lawsuit brought by one person or by a group on behalf of all persons similarly situated.

Comity   Courtesy and respect. In the legal sense, the respect federal courts give to the decisions of state courts.

Common Law   Principles and rules of action, particularly from unwritten English law, whose authority stems from long-standing usage and custom or from judicial recognition and enforcement of those customs.

Concurrent Powers   Powers which may be exercised by both the national government and state governments.

Concurring Opinion   An opinion submitted by a member of a court who agrees with the result by the court in a case but either disagrees with the court's reasons for the decision or wishes to address matters not touched in the opinion of the court.

Declaratory Judgment   A judicial pronouncement declaring the legal rights of the parties involved in an actual case or controversy but not ordering a specific action.

De Facto   "In fact." The existence of something in fact or reality, as opposed to *de jure* (by right).

Defendant   The person against whom a civil or criminal charge is brought.

De Jure   "By right." Lawful, rightful, legitimate; as a result of official action.

Dissenting Opinion   An opinion submitted by a member of a court who disagrees with the result reached by the court.

Distinguish   To point out why a previous decision is not applicable.

Diversity Jurisdiction   The authority of federal courts to hear cases involving citizens of different states.

Dual Federalism   The view that national powers should be interpreted so as not to invade traditional spheres of state activity.

Equity   The administration of justice based upon principles of fairness rather than upon strictly applied rules found in the law.

Error, Writ of   A writ issued by a superior court directing a lower court to send it the record of a case in which the lower court has entered a final judgment, for the purpose of reviewing alleged errors made by the lower court.

Exclusionary Rule   The rule that evidence obtained by illegal means, such as unreasonable searches and seizures, cannot be introduced by the prosecution in a criminal trial.

Ex parte   "From (or on) one side." A hearing in the presence of only one of the parties to a case, such as a hearing to review a petition for a writ of habeas corpus.

Ex Post Facto   "After the fact." A law which makes an action for a crime after it has already been committed.

Ex Rel   "By (or on) the information of." The designation of suit instituted by a state but at the instigation of a private individual interested in the matter.

Federal Question   A case that contains a major issue involving the U.S. Constitution, or U.S. laws or treaties. (The jurisdiction of the federal courts is limited to federal questions and diversity suits.)

Habeas Corpus   "You have the body." A writ inquiring of an official who has custody of a person whether that person is imprisoned or detained lawfully.

In Camera   "In chambers." The hearing of a case or part of a case in private (without spectators).

Incorporation   The process by which provisions of the Bill of Rights were applied as limitations on state governments through the Due Process Clause of the Fourteenth Amendment.

In Forma Pauperis   "In the manner of a pauper." Permission for indigents to bring legal action without payment of the required fees.

Injunction   A writ prohibiting the person to whom it is directed from performing some specified act.

In Re   "In the matter of; concerning." The designation of judicial proceedings in which there are no adversaries.

Judgment of the Court   The ruling of the court (independent of the reasons for the court's ruling).

Judicial Review   The power of a court to review legislation or other governmental action in order to determine its validity with respect to the U.S. constitution or state constitutions.

Juris Belli   "Under the law of war." That part of the law of nations which defines the rights of belligerent and neutral nations during wartime.

Jurisdiction   The authority of a court to hear, determine, and render final judgment in an action, and to enforce its judgments by legal process.

Justiciability   The question of whether a matter is appropriate for judicial decision. A justiciable issue is one that appropriately can be decided by a court.

Litigant An active participant in a lawsuit.

Mandamus "We command." A court order directing an individual or organization to perform a particular act.

Moot Unsettled, undecided. A moot question is one in which either the result sought by the lawsuit has occurred or the conditions have so changed as to render it impossible for the court to grant the relief sought.

Obiter Dicta (Also called *dictum* or *dicta*.) That part of the reasoning in a judicial opinion which is not necessary to resolve the case. Dicta are not necessarily binding in future cases.

Opinion of the Court The opinion which announces the court's decision and is adhered to by a majority of the participating judges.

Original Jurisdiction The authority of a court to hear, determine, and render judgment in an action as a trial court.

Per Curiam "By the court." an unsigned opinion by the court, or a collectively authored opinion.

Petitioner The party who files a petition with a court seeking action.

Plaintiff The party who brings a civil action or sues to obtain a remedy for an injury to his or her rights.

Plea Bargain Negotiations between the prosecution and defense aimed at exchanging a plea of guilty for concessions by the prosecution.

Police Power The power of the states to protect the health, safety, welfare, and morals of their citizens.

Political Question An issue that the court believes should be decided by a nonjudicial unit of government.

Precedent A prior case relied upon in deciding a present dispute.

Preemption The doctrine under which issues previously subject to state control are brought, through congressional action, within the primary or exclusive jurisdiction of the national government.

Prima Facie "At first sight." Evidence that, unless contradicted, is sufficient to establish a claim without investigation or evaluation.

Pro Bono "For the good." Legal services rendered without charge.

Ratio Decidendi "Reason for the decision." The principle of the case.

Remand To send back. In remanding a decision, a higher court sends it, for further action, back to the court from which it came.

Respondent The party against whom a legal action is taken.

Special Master A person designated by a court to hear evidence and submit findings and recommendations based on that evidence. The Supreme Court typically uses special masters in original jurisdiction cases.

Standing The qualifications needed to bring or participate in a case. To have standing to sue, plaintiffs must demonstrate the existence of a controversy in which they personally have suffered or are about to suffer an injury or infringement of a legally protected right.

Stare Decisis "Let the decision stand." The doctrine that a point settled in a previous case is a precedent that should be followed in subsequent cases with similar facts.

State Action   Action by the state or by a private entity closely associated with it ("under color of state law"). The basis for redress under the Due Process and Equal Protection Clauses of the Fourteenth Amendments.

Stay   To halt or suspend further judicial proceedings.

Subpoena   An order to present oneself and to testify before a court, grand jury, or legislative hearing.

Subpoena Duces Tecum   An order by a court or other authorized body that specified documents or papers be produced.

Tort   Willful or negligent injury to the person, property, or reputation of another.

Ultra Vires   "Beyond power." An action beyond the legal authority of the person or body performing it.

Vacate   To make void, annul, or rescind.

Venue   The jurisdiction in which a case is to be heard.

Vested Rights   Long established rights which government should recognize and protect and which a person cannot be deprived of without injustice.

Writ   A written court order commanding the recipient to perform or refrain from performing acts specified in the order.

TABLE
OF
CASES

Case titles in capital letters are reprinted in this volume; the bold italic page numbers indicate where the case is reprinted in this volume.